graphic JAVA

Mastering the JFC

VOLUME II
SWING

THE SUN MICROSYSTEMS PRESS
JAVA SERIES

graphic JAVA™ 2
Mastering the JFC

VOLUME II
SWING

DAVID M. GEARY

Sun Microsystems Press
A Prentice Hall Title

The publisher offers discounts on this book when ordered in bulk quantities. For more information, contact: Corporate Sales Department, Phone: 800-382-3419; Fax: 201-236-7141; E-mail: corpsales@prenhall.com; or write: Prentice Hall PTR, Corp. Sales Dept., One Lake Street, Upper Saddle River, NJ 07458.

Editorial/production supervision: *Patti Guerrieri*
Cover design director: *Jerry Votta*
Cover designer: *Scott Weiss*
Cover illustration: *Karen Strelecki*
Manufacturing manager: *Alexis R. Heydt*
Marketing Manager: *Kaylie Smith*
Acquisitions editor: *Gregory G. Doench*
Sun Microsystems Press publisher: *Rachel Borden*

10 9 8 7 6 5 4

ISBN 0-13- 079667-0

Sun Microsystems Press
A Prentice Hall Title

For Winkster B.

Contents

Foreword

by James Gosling

I hate to admit how long I've been using and building computer user interfaces. How many of you have ever taken apart and rebuilt an actual teletype? Or even remember when teletype had a capitol 'T' because it was the name of a corporation and its product? Fortunately, those days are dust and I get to reuse all those old neurons. It's no longer the case that every CPU cycle gets dedicated to the task at hand, so that user interfaces had to be simple and the users had to be sophisticated. In many modern applications, the application's computational requirements are challenged or exceeded by the computational requirements of the user interface. This is only going to get more skewed as interfaces based on speech and artificial intelligence start to emerge.

In today's world, if you look at all the different programming interfaces that a developer needs to use, the facilities for interacting with us humans are easily the most important and most widely used. User interfaces are no longer something slapped onto the side of an application: they are now often the center from which the application grows. In this world we built Swing to be a full-blown industrial-strength system for constructing sophisticated user interfaces.

I had a hand in the early days of Swing. I had a lot of fun building pieces (most long gone!) and working with the team; and I've had a lot of fun since then as a user of Swing. I hope you have as much fun with it as I've had.

Don't be intimidated by the mass of this book. The Swing user interface toolkit is a very sophisticated one, with a large array of bells and whistles. This was a difficult trade-off in the design of Swing: on the one hand, there was a lot of demand for expansive industrial-strength capabilities, while on the other hand, one of the most admired aspects of Java has been its ease of programming. A key to coping with this as a developer is understanding the distinctions between simple and easy: The Swing toolkit is not simple—the requirements list was too long for that to ever be possible. But it can be easy to use, since there are many shortcut methods (for example, take a look at the `JOptionPane` class), and since the vast majority of features can be ignored by the general developer.

Cruise over the treetops of this book. It has the breadth you need to understand all the components of Swing. Then dive in and let it lead you deeply into the places where you need all of the sophistication.

James Gosling

VP and Fellow,
Java Software, Sun Microsystems

Preface

This book has been my full-time passion for more than a year. After Sun closed its office in Colorado Springs in August of 1997, I decided to forego traditional employment to give the Graphic Java series my complete attention. I was determined that the Swing volume would be the definitive guide to Swing, which meant that it had to be the most comprehensive, accurate and insightful Swing book available. I believe that to be the case, but of course, you will be the final judge.

Before I began writing, I spent a considerable amount of effort designing a book that would be beneficial to Swing novices in addition to developers with some Swing experience. As a software developer who has used numerous object oriented GUI frameworks, I realized that the fastest way to climb a framework's learning curve is to study code examples that illustrate specific concepts. As a result, code examples are the foundation upon which this book is built; nearly 300 code examples are discussed in detail—an average of approximately one code example every 5 pages.

However, code examples in and of themselves, cannot suffice as a reference for developers who have advanced along the Swing learning curve. As a result, every Swing component discussion is accompanied by a component summary that includes class diagrams, an examination of the component's properties and events and a class summary that discusses the `public` and `protected` methods implemented by the component.

The first part of this book explores fundamental aspects of Swing including:

- Swing applets and applications
- Swing and multithreading
- Swing's Model-View-Controller architecture
- Pluggable Look And Feel
- The `JComponent` class
- Borders, icons and actions
- Miscellaneous features including timers and Swing utilities

The second part of the book examines Swing's components in detail. Numerous code examples are discussed for every Swing component, from labels and buttons to tables, trees and the text package. For example, more than 150 pages containing 25 code examples are dedicated to the table component, and 120 pages and 20 code examples illustrate how to get the most out of the tree component.

Audience

This book assumes that the reader has a good grasp of the Java language including recent additions to the language such as inner classes. This book also assumes a rudimentary understanding of the AWT; specifically, the delegation event model and the `Component` and `Container` classes upon which all Swing components are based. See "Graphic Java 2 Mastering the JFC Volume I: AWT" for a thorough investigation of AWT infrastructure and components.

How To Use This Book

Before diving into the Swing components, it is useful to have an understanding of fundamental concepts such as Swing's Model-View-Controller (MVC) design and pluggable look and feel. The former is discussed in "Swing Component Architecture" on page 71 and the latter is covered in "Pluggable Look and Feel" on page 317. It is also important to understand the services provided by the `JComponent` class, which is the ultimate superclass of all lightweight Swing components. The `JComponent` class is examined in "The JComponent Class" on page 123.

Component Summaries

Each Swing component is introduced with numerous code examples that illustrate various component features. Code examples are followed by component summaries, such as the `JScrollPane` component summary that is partially listed below.

Component summaries begin with a listing of the component's model, UI delegate, renderer and editor, in addition to the events fired by the component. If a component is a replacement for an AWT component, the AWT component is also listed.

Component Summary 13-1   JScrollPane

Model(s)	——
UI Delegate(s)	javax.swing.plaf.basic.BasicScrollPaneUI
Renderer(s)	——
Editor(s)	——
Events Fired	PropertyChangeEvent
Replacement For	java.awt.ScrollPane

Class Diagrams

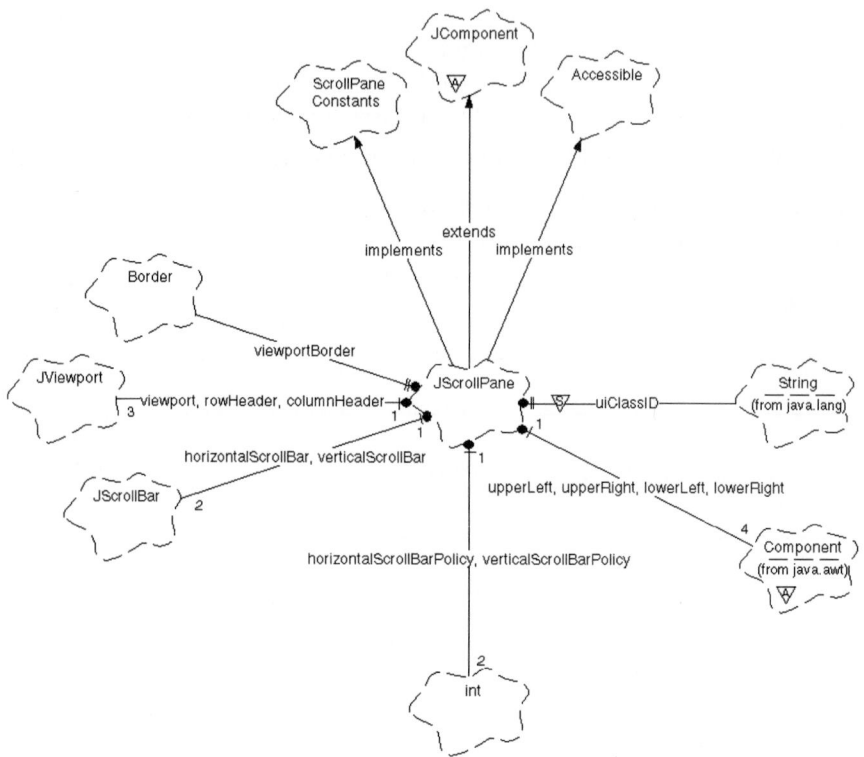

The static relationships that a component maintains with other objects are illustrated with a class diagram, such as the class diagram for the JScrollPane class shown above. Class diagrams are introduced in Appendix A, *Class Diagrams*.

Properties

Property tables, such as the property table for the JScrollPane class shown below, are used to communicate a component's properties. Property tables include property names, the property's data type and whether a property is boolean, bound (a property change event is fired when the property is changed), simple (no events are fired when the property is changed), constrained (changes to the property can be vetoed), or indexed (a parameter, usually an integer, is used to access the property).

Some properties can be specified when a component is instantiated, and a component may provide setter and getter methods for a property. The manner in which a property can be specified is listed in the Access column of a property table.

Property tables also include a column for property default values.

Property tables are followed by a short description of each of the properties listed in the table.

Table 13-2   JScrollPane Properties

Property Name	Data Type	Property Type[1]	Access[2]	Default[5]
columnHeader	JViewport	B	SG	null
columnHeaderView	Component	B	S[3]	null
corner	Component	IB	SG	null
horizontalScrollbar	JScrollBar	B	SG	——
horizontalScrollbarPolicy	int	B	CSG	As needed[6]
rowHeader	JViewport	B	SG	null
rowHeaderView	Component	B	S[4]	null
verticalScrollbar	JScrollBar	B	SG	——
verticalScrollbarPolicy	int	B	CSG	As needed[7]
viewport	JViewport	B	SG	JViewport
viewportBorder	Border	B	SG	null
viewportView	Component	B	CSG	null

1. b = boolean / B = bound (fires PropertyChangeEvent) / C = constrained/ I = indexed /
   S = simple / Ch = fires ChangeEvent
2. C = settable at construction time / G = getter method / S = setter method
3. getColumnHeader.getView() returns the column header view
4. getRowHeader.getView() returns the row header view
5. L&F = look and feel dependent
6. JScrollPane.HORIZONTAL_SCROLLBAR_AS_NEEDED
7. JScrollPane.VERTICAL_SCROLLBAR_AS_NEEDED

columnHeader — An instance of JViewport for the column header.

columnHeaderView — An instance of Component used as the column header viewport's view.

`corner` — A component that is displayed in one of the scrollpane's corners. The corner is specified by one of the following strings:

- `ScrollPaneConstants.UPPER_LEFT_CORNER`
- `ScrollPaneConstants.LOWER_LEFT_CORNER`
- `ScrollPaneConstants.UPPER_RIGHT_CORNER`
- `ScrollPaneConstants.LOWER_RIGHT_CORNER`

`horizontalScrollbar` — The horizontal scrollbar used by the scrollpane. The scrollbar is an instance of `JScrollPane.ScrollBar`, an extension of `JScrollBar` that takes into account whether the view contained in the scrollpane implements the `Scrollable` interface.

The remaining property descriptions for the `JScrollPane` *class are omitted.*

Events

Code examples are presented that illustrate event handling for a component. For example, the Tree chapter provides five code examples that illustrate handling of tree mouse, editing, selection, and expansion events.

Class Summaries

Each component summary concludes with a class summary that provides descriptions of the component's constructors and methods, such as the class summary for the `JScrollPane` class listed below.

Class Summary 13-2   JScrollPane

Extends: JComponent
Implements: ScrollPaneConstants, javax.accessibility.Accessible

Constructors

---

public JScrollPane()

public JScrollPane(int vsbPolicy, int hsbPolicy)
public JScrollPane(Component view)
public JScrollPane(Component view, int vsbPolicy, int hsbPolicy)

JScrollPane provides four constructors. The integer values passed to JScrollPane constructors represent the vertical and horizontal scrollbar display policies, in that order. The component passed to the constructors is used as the viewport's view, meaning it is the component that is scrolled by the scrollpane.

The no-argument constructor constructs a scrollpane with a null component for the viewport's view, and scrollbar display policies that display both the horizontal and vertical scrollbars as needed.

Methods

Creation Methods

---

public JScrollBar createHorizontalScrollBar()
public JScrollBar createVerticalScrollBar()
protected JViewport createViewport()

Like most Swing components, JScrollPane provides create... methods that create its subcomponents. Unlike most Swing components however, JScrollPane implements the methods that create its scrollbars as public instead of protected because the methods are invoked from the scrollpane's UI delegate.

The createHorizontalScrollBar and createVerticalScrollBar methods both return instances of JScrollPane.ScrollBar, which is an extension of JScrollBar that takes into account whether the scrollpane's view implements the Scrollable interface. See Interface Summary 13-2 on page 779 for more information on the Scrollable interface.

The `createViewport` method returns an instance of `JViewport` that is used as the scrollpane's default viewport.

As with all Swing components that implement `create...` methods, the methods can be overridden in extension classes to replace the default sub-components with custom versions.

The remaining method descriptions for the `JScrollPane` class are omitted.

Swing Bugs

Swing has come a long way in terms of quality. The early beta releases contained numerous bugs, many of which have subsequently been fixed. However, like any software, Swing still has its share of bugs. Throughout this book, I have tried to point out as many bugs as possible so that developers can avoid the frustration of debugging code only to discover that a problem is due to a Swing bug.

It is also important to keep in mind that this book is based on Swing 1.1 FCS. As we went to press, a 1.1.1 version of Swing was released that was mostly a bug fix release. Therefore, it is a certainty that some of the bugs cited in this book will have been fixed by the time this book is on the shelves.

Using the CD-ROM

The CD in the back of the book contains the following:

- 1.1.7 JDK and Swing 1.1.1
- 1.2 JDK and Swing 1.1 FCS
- Code examples from this book

Swing and the JDK

As mentioned previously, Swing 1.1.1 is mostly a bug fix release. Swing 1.1.1 does not work with the 1.2 JDK, and therefore the 1.1.7 JDK is included on the CD. Swing 1.1 FCS works with both the 1.1.7 and 1.2 versions of the JDK.

Code Examples from the Book

All of the code examples in this book that are accompanied by a CD-ROM icon[1] are included on the CD in the back of the book. Figure P-1 shows the directory structure for the code examples. A directory exists for every chapter in the book,[2] and subdirectories are included for each example, which should make it trivial to locate examples. For instance, Example 3-1 on page 91 can be found in the chapters/3/1 directory.

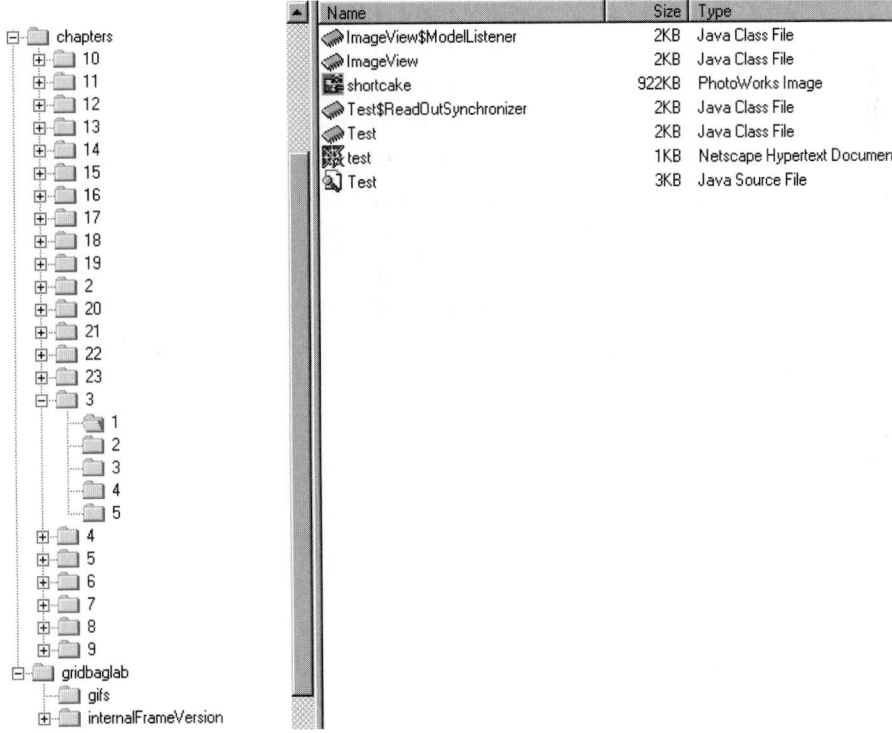

Name	Size	Type
ImageView$ModelListener	2KB	Java Class File
ImageView	2KB	Java Class File
shortcake	922KB	PhotoWorks Image
Test$ReadOutSynchronizer	2KB	Java Class File
Test	2KB	Java Class File
test	1KB	Netscape Hypertext Documen
Test	3KB	Java Source File

Figure P-1 Code Examples Directory Structure

1. See Table P-2.
2. Except for chapter 1, which does not contain any code examples.

Every example is compiled and ready to run. Some of the directories representing code examples contain a README.txt file if the examples exhibit bugs or have been modified from their listing in the book.

The CD also contains two versions of the GridBagLab application that comes with "Graphic Java 2 Mastering the JFC Volume I: AWT." One version uses external windows and another uses Swing internal frames. The application provides an example of a fairly complete Swing application and illustrates the use of Swing internal frames. Additionally, the application can be used to explore the intricacies of the `GridBagLayout` layout manager.

Applets Vs. Applications

Most of the code examples discussed in this book are applets, but a fair percentage of examples are applications. Applications are typically implemented instead of applets either because files are manipulated or dialogs are shown—applets have restricted access to files, and under JDK 1.2 dialogs displayed from an applet contain a warning string. Sometimes applications are implemented instead of applets simply for the sake of variety. Nearly all of the applications discussed in this book that do not manipulate files can easily be rewritten as applets.

Conventions Used in This Book

Table P-1 shows the coding conventions used in this book.

Table P-1 Coding Conventions

Convention	Example
Class names have initial capital letters.	`public class ClassName`
Method names have initial lower case and the rest of the words have an initial capital letter.	`getLength()`
Variable names have initial lower case and the rest of the words have an initial capital letter.	`private int length` `private int bufferLength`

Note that, for the most part, methods are referred to without their arguments; however, arguments are included when the discussion warrants them.

Table P-2 shows the typographic conventions used in this book.

Table P-2 Typographic Conventions

Typeface or Symbol	Description
	Indicates that the accompanying code, command, or file is available on the CD that accompanies this book.
`courier`	Indicates a command, file name, class name, method, argument, Java keyword, HTML tag, file content, or code excerpt.
`bold courier`	Indicates a sample command-line entry.
italics	Indicates definitions, emphasis, a book title, or a variable that should be replaced with a valid value.

Acknowledgments

First, I would like to thank members of the Swing team that have patiently endured my multitude—and I do mean *multitude*—of questions and bug reports. The following Swing team members, in no particular order, have been especially helpful: Rick Levenson, Amy Fowler, Hans Muller, Philip Milne, Georges Saab, Jeff Dinkins, Jeff Shapiro, Scott Violet, Tom Ball, Tom Santos, Willie Walker, Timothy Prinzing, Steve Wilson and Nancy Schorr. Additionally, Monica Gaines and Sue Palmer from JavaSoft have provided insightful review comments. Also, I am grateful to James Gosling, who was gracious enough to write the foreword. Everyone listed above has significantly contributed to the overall quality of this book.

Rachel Borden of Sun Microsystems Press, along with Greg Doench, Patti Guerrieri, Lisa Iarkowski and Mary Treacy from Prentice Hall, have all bent over backwards to get this volume on the shelves. Mary Lou Nohr, my editor, is worthy of the highest praise because she gives me fish and at the same time, teaches me to fish for myself.

I am also indebted to Keith Ohlfs of Pixelsite for granting permission to use his cool images. Rational, Inc. was also kind enough to provide me with a copy of Rational Rose which was used to create the class and sequence diagrams in the book.

Finally, I would like to thank Lesa and Ashley Anna Geary. Without their patience and understanding, I would never have been able to get this behemoth out the door. A final tip of the hat to Mariko and Blazey who have been my constant companions while writing this book.

Swing Fundamentals

CHAPTER

1

Introduction

The Java Foundation Classes, or JFC, is a collection of APIs for developing graphical user interfaces. The Java Foundation Classes include the following APIs:

- Abstract Window Toolkit (versions 1.1 and beyond)
- 2D API
- Swing Components
- Accessibility API

The Abstract Window Toolkit, or AWT, is Java's original toolkit for developing user interfaces. The AWT provides the foundation upon which the rest of the JFC is built and is discussed at length in the first volume of *Graphic Java*.

The 2D API provides additional graphical capabilities that are lacking in the AWT. For example, the AWT provides only a single pen size for graphical operations—a one-pixel-sized square. In addition to providing a variable-sized pen, the 2D API offers a wealth of other two-dimensional rendering capabilities. The 2D API is discussed at length in the 2D API volume of *Graphic Java*.

Swing is a set of mostly lightweight components built on top of the AWT.[1] Swing provides lightweight replacements for the AWT's heavyweight components, in

---

1. See "Lightweight Vs. Heavyweight Components" on page 5 for a discussion of lightweight vs. heavyweight components.

addition to a multitude of additional components that the AWT lacks. Swing also contains an impressive infrastructure for implementing graphical user interfaces that includes features such as pluggable look and feel; thus, Swing components can take on the look and feel of components on different platforms—double buffering, debug graphics, and a text editing package, just to mention a few.

The `Accessibility` API consists of a set of classes that enable Swing components to interact with assistive technologies for users with disabilities. The JFC also includes a number of accessibility tools that work in conjunction with the `Accessibility` API.

Swing History

In order to understand Swing, it is first necessary to understand the infrastructure upon which it is based, the Abstract Window Toolkit, or AWT.

Java took off faster than anyone could have imagined, and the most visible of the Java APIs—the AWT—was suddenly thrust into the limelight. Unfortunately, the original AWT was ill prepared for such a fate.

The original AWT was not designed to be anything akin to a high-powered user interface (UI) toolkit to be used by more than a half million developers—instead, it was aimed at supporting the development of simple user interfaces for simple applets. For example, the original AWT lacked a great many features that one would expect in an object-oriented UI toolkit—clipboards, printing support, and keyboard navigation, for example, were all conspicuously absent from the AWT. The original AWT did not even include such basic amenities as popup menus or scroll panes, two staples of modern user interface development.

In addition, the AWT's infrastructure was badly flawed. The AWT was fitted with an inheritance-based event model that scaled horribly and, even worse, a peer-based architecture that was destined to become the AWT's Achilles' heel.

The lure of quick time to market and the promise of retaining native look and feel resulted in a peer-based architecture that was doomed to failure. Peers are native user interface components delegated to by wafer-thin AWT objects. Peers take care of all the grunt work—painting themselves and reacting to events, for example—leaving the AWT components with little to do other than interact with their peers when the time is right. Since the AWT classes were mere shells around somewhat complex native peers, the AWT's original designers were able to crank out components in record time.[2] For example, the `java.awt.Panel` class contains a mere twelve lines of code.

The peer design, however, is not without serious drawbacks. First, on most platforms, each peer is rendered in a native window. A ratio of one native window per component is not exactly a formula for high performance, and applets that contained a large number of AWT components paid a steep performance penalty as a result.

Shoehorning native peers from diverse platforms into a Java framework is one thing. Doing it in a manner that results in AWT components that behave consistently across platforms is flat-out impossible. As a result, instead of implementing badly needed new components, development time was squandered on fixing peer bugs and incompatibility problems.

As if that weren't bad enough, the AWT had a high incidence of bugs. Third parties started to offer their own toolkits that provided more solid infrastructures and offered more functionality than the AWT. One of those toolkits was Netscape's Internet Foundation Classes (IFC), a set of lightweight classes based on concepts from NEXTSTEP's user interface toolkits. The IFC components were peerless and outshined the AWT's components in many respects. The IFC also began to attract more than its share of developers.

Realizing that the Java community was likely to split over a standard user interface toolkit, JavaSoft struck a deal with Netscape to implement the Java Foundation Classes (Apple and IBM have also participated in the development of the JFC). Netscape developers have worked with Swing engineers to embed much of the IFC's functionality into Swing components.

Originally, Swing was meant to closely resemble Netscape's IFC. Over time, however, Swing diverged considerably from its original intent as features, such as pluggable look and feel, were added and designs were modified. With the advent of its 1.0 release, Swing's outward similarities to IFC had, for the most part, vanished, although a great deal of IFC technology remains embedded within Swing. Today, Swing provides the best of both the AWT and IFC in a comprehensive user interface toolkit.

Lightweight Vs. Heavyweight Components

Lightweight components debuted in the 1.1 release of the AWT. Originally, the AWT included only heavyweight components that were associated with a native peer component and were rendered in their own native, opaque window.

---

2.   The original AWT was developed in a scant *six weeks*.

Lightweight components, on the other hand, do not have a native peer and are rendered in their heavyweight container's window.

Since lightweight components are not rendered in a native, opaque window, they can have transparent backgrounds. A transparent background enables lightweight components to appear to be nonrectangular, even though all components, heavyweight or lightweight, have a rectangular bounding box.

Nearly all Swing components are lightweight. The only exceptions are Swing's top-level containers: frames, applets, windows, and dialogs. Because lightweight components are rendered in their container's window instead of a window of their own, lightweights must ultimately be contained in a heavyweight container. As a result, Swing frames, applets, and dialogs must be heavyweight to provide a window into which lightweight Swing components can draw.

Swing Components

Swing contains over 250 classes, representing a mix of components and support classes. Swing provides more than 40 components—four times the number of components provided by the AWT. In addition to providing lightweight replacements for the AWT's heavyweights, Swing also provides a wealth of additional components to facilitate the development of graphical user interfaces.

AWT Replacement Components

Figure 1-2 shows Swing lightweight components that can be used to replace the AWT's heavyweight components. Many of the components pictured in Figure 1-2 are nearly source-code compatible with their AWT counterparts, which makes replacing AWT components in existing code a fairly simple matter.

In addition to mimicking functionality that was provided with the AWT components, nearly all of the Swing replacement components have extra features. For instance, Swing buttons and labels can display icons and text, whereas AWT buttons and labels could only display text.

All of the components pictured in Figure 1-2 are shown with the Windows look and feel.

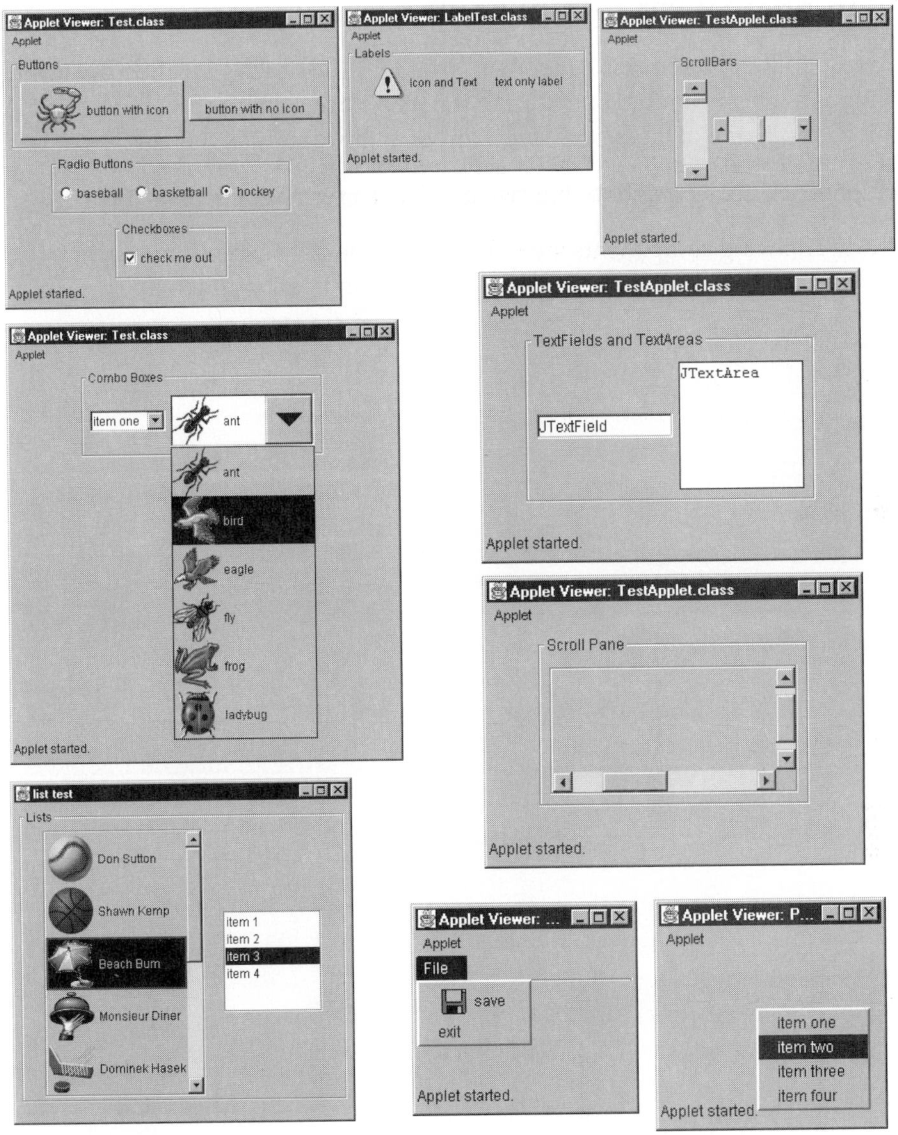

Figure 1-2 Swing AWT Replacement Components
From top-left, clockwise: buttons, radio buttons, and checkboxes; labels; scrollbars; text fields and text areas; scroll pane; popup menus and menubar menus; lists; combo boxes.

Additional Swing Components

In addition to replacement components for the AWT's heavyweight components, Swing provides a number of extra components, such as tables, trees, custom dialogs, etc. Some of the new Swing components are shown in Figure 1-3.

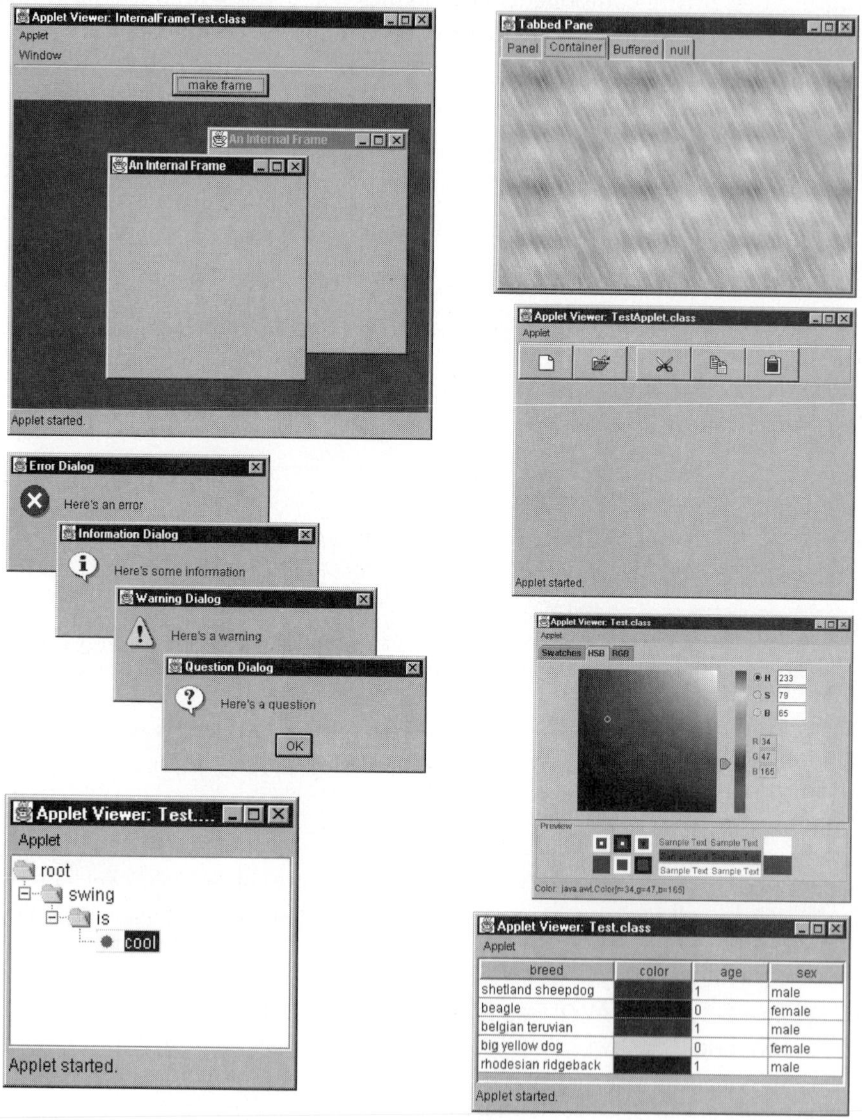

Figure 1-3 Some Additional Swing Components
From top-left, clockwise: internal frames; tabbed pane; toolbar; color chooser; table; tree; dialog boxes.

J Components

As mentioned previously, Swing contains more than 250 classes; some are UI components and others are support classes. To distinguish UI components from support classes, Swing components have names that begin with the letter **J**. Table 1-1 lists the **J** components that Swing provides.; italicized components are replacements for AWT components.

Table 1-1   Swing UI Components[1]

Component Class	Description
JApplet	An extension of the `java.applet.Applet` class that contains an instance of `JRootPane`
JButton	A button that can display text and graphics and that replaces the AWT's button component
JCheckBox	A checkbox that can display text and graphics and that replaces the AWT's choice component
JCheckBoxMenuItem	A checkbox menu item that replaces the AWT's checkbox menu item component
JComboBox	A textfield with a drop-down list that replaces the AWT's choice component
JComponent	The base class for all lightweight J components
JDesktopPane	A container for internal frames
JDialog	Base class for Swing dialogs—extends the AWT `Dialog` class
JEditorPane	A text pane for editing text
JFrame	An external frame that extends `java.awt.Frame`
JInternalFrame	An internal frame that resides in a `JDesktopPane`
JLabel	A label that can display text and graphics and that replaces the AWT's label component
JLayeredPane	A container that can display components on different layers
JList	A component that displays a list of items and that replaces the AWT's list component
JMenu	A menu displayed in a menubar that replaces the AWT's menu component
JMenuBar	A menubar for displaying menus that replaces the AWT's menubar component
JMenuItem	A menu item that replaces the AWT's menu item component
JOptionPane	Displays standard dialogs, such as message and question dialogs

Table 1-1   Swing UI Components[1] (Continued)

Component Class	Description
JPanel	A generic container that replaces both the AWT's panel and canvas components
JPasswordField	An extension of JTextField that obscures the characters entered
JPopupMenu	A popup menu that replaces the AWT's popup menu component
JProgressBar	A progress indicator
JRadioButton	A radio button that replaces the AWT's checkbox component
JRootPane	A top-level container that contains a glass pane, layered pane, content pane and optional menubar
JScrollBar	A scrollbar that replaces the AWT's scrollbar component
JScrollPane	A scroll pane that replaces the AWT's scroll pane component
JSeparator	A horizontal or vertical separator
JSlider	A slider
JSplitPane	A container with two separate areas—arranged vertically or horizontally—that can be resized dynamically
JTabbedPane	A tabbed pane
JTable	A table
JTableHeader	A header for a table
JTextArea	A textarea for entering multiple lines of text that replaces the AWT's textarea component
JTextComponent	The base class for text components that replaces the AWT's TextComponent class
JTextField	A single line text field that replaces the AWT's textfield component
JTextPane	A simple text editor
JToggleButton	A two-state button that is the base class for the JCheckBox and JRadioButton components
JToolBar	A toolbar
JToolTip	A one-liner displayed above a component when the cursor rests over the component
JTree	An outline control for hierarchical data
JViewport	A viewport for viewing scrollable components
JWindow	An external window that's an extension of java.awt.Window

1. AWT replacement components are italicized.

Pluggable Look and Feel

Swing supports the concept of a pluggable look and feel that is based on a
variation of the Model-View-Controller architecture. Figure 1-4 illustrates an
applet running under different look and feel variations.

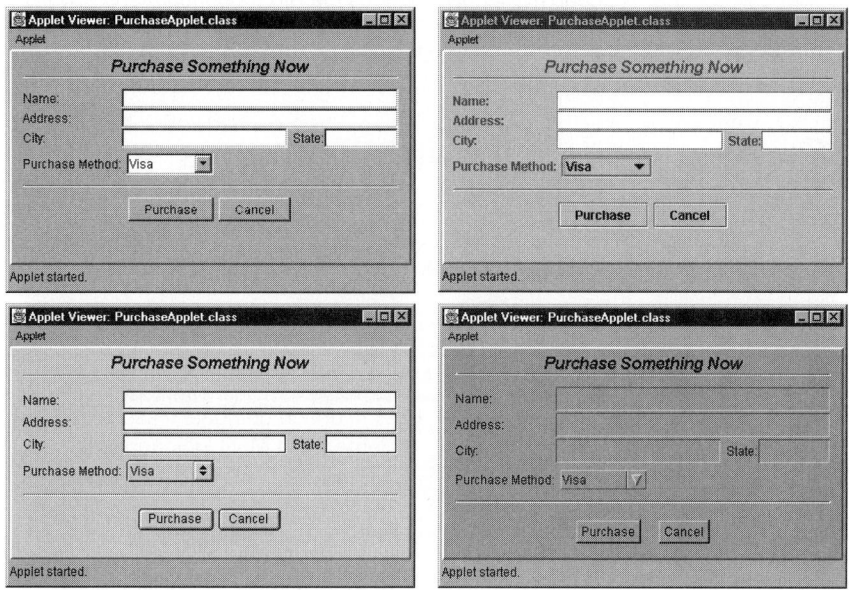

Figure 1-4 Pluggable Look and Feel
Look and feels, clockwise from upper left: Windows, Metal (a.k.a. the Java
Look & Feel), Motif, and Macintosh.

Modifying the look and feel of an applet or application requires no code
changes—the default look and feel is settable at runtime by setting the
`swing.defaultlaf` property to the desired look-and-feel class in the
`swing.properties` file in the `$JDK_HOME/lib` directory. Here's an example of
a `swing.properties` file that sets the default look and feel, specified by the
`defaultlaf` property:

```
# swing.properties example file. Lines that begin with '#' are
# comments.
# The Mac look and feel is specified as the default look and
# feel below. If no look and feel is specified, then the default
# look and feel (metal) is used.
```

```
# the next line specifies which look and feels are installed.
swing.installedlafts=metal,motif,windows,mac

# default set to Mac look and feel
swing.defaultlaf=javax.swing.plaf.mac.MacLookAndFeel
#swing.defaultlaf=javax.swing.plaf.windows.WindowsLookAndFeel

#swing.defaultlaf=javax.swing.plaf.motif.MotifLookAndFeel
```

Swing's implementation of pluggable look and feel is discussed in the "Pluggable Look and Feel" chapter beginning on page 317.

An Overview of the Swing Packages

Swing consists of several packages, listed in Table 1-2.

Table 1-2   Swing Packages

Packages	Description
`com.sun.java.swing.plaf.motif`	User interface delegate classes that implement the Motif look and feel.
`com.sun.java.swing.plaf.windows`	User interface delegate classes that implement the Windows look and feel.
`javax.swing`	Swing components and utilities
`javax.swing.border`	Borders for lightweight Swing components
`javax.swing.colorchooser`	Support classes/interfaces for JColorChooser
`javax.swing.event`	Event and listener classes
`javax.swing.filechooser`	Support classes/interfaces for JFileChooser
`javax.swing.pending`	Swing components that are pending
`javax.swing.plaf`	Abstract classes that define the behavior of UI delegates
`javax.swing.plaf.basic`	Base classes that implement common functionality among all standard look and feels
`javax.swing.plaf.metal`	User interface delegate classes that implement the metal look and feel
`javax.swing.table`	Support classes for the `JTable` component
`javax.swing.text`	Support for document display and editing

Table 1-2 Swing Packages (Continued)

Packages	Description
`javax.swing.text.html`	Support for displaying and editing HTML files
`javax.swing.text.html.parser`	Parser classes for html files
`javax.swing.text.rtf`	Support for displaying and editing RTF files
`javax.swing.tree`	Support classes for the `JTree` component
`javax.swing.undo`	Support for undoing operations

The `swing` package is the largest package Swing provides, containing nearly 100 classes and 25 interfaces. Almost all of the Swing components reside in the `swing` package—`JTableHeader` and `JTextComponent` are the only exceptions and can be found in the `swing.table` and `swing.text` packages, respectively.

The `swing.border` package contains several classes that draw borders in the margins of lightweight Swing components. A `Border` interface, an `AbstractBorder` class, and a number of concrete extensions of `AbstractBorder` make up the `border` package.

Event and event listener classes are defined in the `swing.event` package, which is analogous to the AWT's `event` package. Both the `awt.event` and `swing.event` packages contain event classes and listener interfaces that are used to react to events fired by AWT and Swing components, respectively. For example, Swing's `TreeExpansionListener` interface is implemented when notification of node expansion (or collapse) is desired in a tree component. The methods defined in the `TreeExpansionListener` interface are passed instances of `TreeExpansionEvent`. Both `TreeExpansionListener` and `TreeExpansionEvent` are defined in the `swing.event` package.

The `swing.pending` package contains Swing components that are not yet fully implemented. As of Swing 1.1 FCS, the pending package contained choosers, (date and money choosers), a calculator, a popup button, and more. Components that are in the pending package will eventually make their way into the `swing` package.

Although Swing's table component—`JTable`—resides in the `swing` package, its support classes can be found in the `swing.table` package. The table's model, cell renderers, and editors all reside in the `swing.table` package.

Like the JTable class, Swing's tree class—JTree, an outline component for hierarchical data—resides in the swing package, but its support classes are in the swing.tree package. The swing.tree package provides support classes that include the tree model, tree nodes, tree cell editors, and renderers.

Swing contains four packages for displaying and editing documents: swing.text, swing.text.html, swing.text.html.parser, and swing.text.rtf. The swing.text package provides all the necessary infrastructure for Swing's document model, including classes and interfaces for documents, elements, carets, highlighters, editor kits, etc. The swing.text.html and swing.text.rtf packages are Swing's smallest packages; both provide editor kits for implementing HTML (Hypertext Markup Language) and rtf (Rich Text Format) document editors, respectively. The swing.text.html.parser package contains support classes for parsing html files.

The swing.undo package provides support for implementing undoable operations.

Classes in the swing.plaf package form the foundation for the UI delegate portion of Swing's pluggable look and feel. UI delegates implement the look and feel for their associated component.

Most of the classes in the swing.plaf package either define UI resources or extend the swing.ComponentUI class, which defines behavior common among all UI delegates. The UI delegate classes—classes whose names end in "UI"—in the swing.plaf package typically define additional abstract methods for specific components. For example, the swing.plaf.ButtonUI class extends the swing.ComponentUI class and adds a single abstract method: getDefaultMargin(), which returns the margin between the button's border and the contents of the button.

The swing.plaf.basic package extends classes defined in the swing.plaf package and implements functionality that is shared among all of the standard Swing look and feels. For example, the swing.plaf.basic.BasicButtonUI class provides default implementations of the methods defined by the swing.ComponentUI class and the swing.plaf.ButtonUI class. The BasicButtonUI class provides meaningful implementations for methods such as the paint method, which paints the button's text and icon. BasicButtonUI implements other look-and-feel-specific methods, such as paintButtonPressed(), as no-ops, which are overridden by look-and-feel-specific extensions.

The `metal` and `motif` packages implement UI delegate classes for their specific look and feels. Typically, the UI delegate classes extend classes in the `swing.plaf.basic` package and implement look-and-feel-specific behavior. For example, the `metal.ButtonUI` class overrides the no-op implementation of the `paintButtonPressed` method from the `swing.plaf.basic.ButtonUI` class.

The `swing.plaf.multi` package supports multiplexing look and feels. Multiplexing look and feels allow more than one UI delegate to be associated with a single component. For example, a button UI delegate may have both a visual and an audio UI delegate associated with it that causes the button to play a sound when it is activated in addition to the usual visual feedback for activation. Multiplexing UIs are mainly useful for augmenting the behavior of a component for accessibility purposes.

Swing also provides two other look-and-feel implementations, the Macintosh and Organic look and feels, which are available in a separate download.

Swing and the AWT

A common misconception about Swing is that it is designed to replace the AWT. In actuality, Swing is built on top of the AWT, as shown in Figure 1-5.

Swing Heavyweight Components	Swing Lightweight Components
AWT Frame, Window, Dialog	
Component, Container, Graphics, Color, Font, Toolkit, Layout Managers, etc.	

Figure 1-5 Swing's Relationship to the AWT

Swing takes advantage of the AWT's infrastructure, including graphics, colors, fonts, toolkit and layout managers; however, Swing does not use the AWT's components. The only AWT components that have any relevance for Swing are the `Frame`, `Window`, and `Dialog` classes, that are extended by Swing's heavyweight components: `JFrame`, `JWindow`, and `JDialog`, respectively. In essence, Swing uses the best of the AWT to build a new set of mostly lightweight components, while leaving the AWT's problem child—heavyweight components—behind.

Swing is designed to replace the AWT's heavyweight components, but not the AWT itself. To get the most out of Swing, it is essential to have a basic knowledge of the AWT's infrastructure.

In addition to using AWT functionality such as graphics, fonts, and layout managers, all Swing lightweight components are ultimately derived from the AWT's `Container` class, which in turn extends the AWT's `Component` class. In other words, not only does Swing take advantage of the infrastructure provided by the AWT, but all Swing components are actually AWT containers. It should be noted that the AWT `Container` class is itself lightweight—meaning it has no peer[3]—and is painted in its container's window.

Peers Vs. Pluggable Look and Feel

Both Swing and AWT components delegate to other objects that perform much of the work associated with displaying the component and dealing with its events. For AWT components, the delegate is a native peer, whereas for Swing components, the delegate is an extension of the `ComponentUI` class. Although both Swing and AWT components employ delegation, the results of delegating responsibilities to another object are markedly different between the two toolkits.

Since AWT components delegate to a native peer, their behavior can be difficult to extend. For example, it is not possible to add an image to an AWT button because the rendering of the button is performed by a native peer that is probably written in C++ and whose behavior cannot be extended. Likewise, the manner in which a text area highlights its text cannot be modified because the text area's peer is responsible for highlighting text. The point is that any behavior implemented by a native peer cannot be modified or extended.

---

3.   Actually, `java.awt.Container` has a do-nothing peer that is a placeholder.

On the other hand, a Swing component's delegate—its `ComponentUI`—is a Java class from the Swing toolkit that can be extended to modify the component's behavior. Swing's pluggable look-and-feel design employs a modified Model-View-Controller architecture where the component's UI delegate represents the View-Controller, which is responsible for displaying the component and handling input events. When a Swing component is outfitted with a modified component UI, aspects of the component's visual representation or event handling can be modified.

Getting Started

Swing can be used with either the 1.1 or 1.2 releases of the JDK. Swing is included in the 1.2 release of the JDK, but not in the 1.1 release. To use Swing with the 1.1 release, you must download Swing from JFC web site, at http://java.sun.com/products/jfc/index.html.

Using Swing With Internet Browsers

Swing applets will work in both Netscape Navigator and Internet Explorer; however, you must have the appropriate versions of each browser and make sure that support is included for the 1.1 JDK.

Netscape Navigator

For Netscape Navigator, you must have version 4.04 or later, and you must have the 1.1 JDK patch installed. To download Netscape Navigator and the 1.1 JDK patch, point your web browser to:

```
http://developer.netscape.com/software/jdk/download.html
```

Figure 1-6 shows a simple Swing applet running in Netscape Navigator.

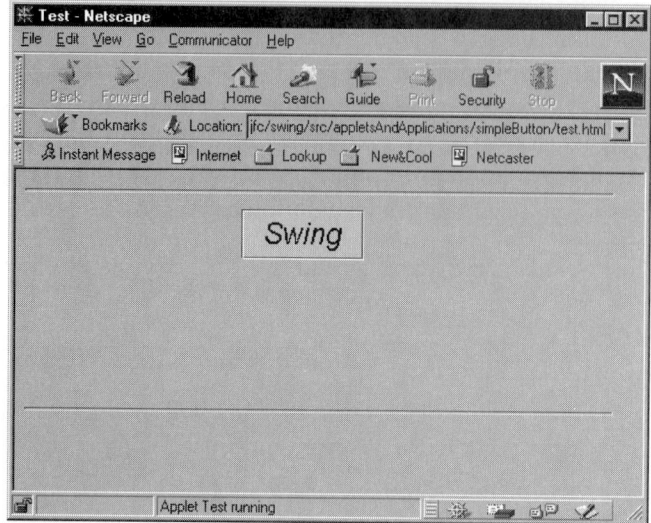

Figure 1-6 A Swing Applet Running in Netscape Navigator

Once you have downloaded an appropriate version of Netscape Navigator and the
1.1 JDK patch, you must make the Swing jar files available to Netscape. There are
two ways to do this: either copy the Swing jar files to a well-known Netscape
directory or modify the system CLASSPATH variable. The first option is discussed
in this section, and since the second option is the same for both Internet Explorer
and Netscape navigator, it is discussed in the "Internet Explorer" section.

Swing jar files can be copied to Netscape's `Java\Classes` directory. For
example, if you have Netscape installed on your `C:\` drive and Swing installed in
a directory named `C:\swing`, copy all of the Swing jar files from `C:\swing` to
`C:\ProgramFiles\Netscape\Communicator\Program\Java\Classes`.
Once you have the latest release of Netscape Navigator, the 1.1 JDK patch
installed, and have made the Swing jar files available to Netscape, you are ready
to run Swing applets in Netscape Navigator.

Internet Explorer

Versions 4.0 and later of Internet Explorer support the 1.1 JDK. As long as you
have the appropriate version of Internet Explorer and have set your system
CLASSPATH variable so that Internet Explorer can find the Swing jar files, you
should be able to run Swing applets inside of Internet Explorer. Here's how to set
your system CLASSPATH variable.

Windows NT: For Windows NT, bring up the Windows control panel and double-
click the System icon. In the System Properties window, click the Environment
tab. Add a CLASSPATH variable to the lower list titled "User Variables for
Administrator:" as shown in Figure 1-7.

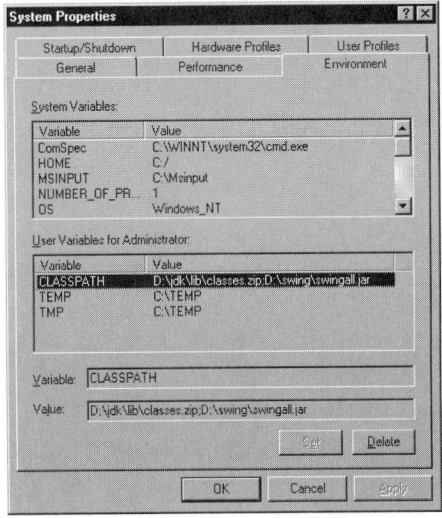

Figure 1-7 Configuring CLASSPATH with Windows NT

The CLASSPATH variable should include the classes.zip file for the JDK, and
the swingall.jar file. For example, Figure 1-7 shows the CLASSPATH variable
set for the JDK and Swing both installed on the D:\ drive. Once you have added
(or modified) the CLASSPATH variable, click the OK button to close the System
Properties window. At this point, you will need to reboot your system and when
it comes back up, you will be ready to run Swing applets in Internet Explorer.

Windows 95: With Windows 95, you must manually edit the autoexec.bat file that resides on the C:\ drive. Simply add an entry in the file that looks like the following:

```
SET CLASSPATH=C:\jdk\lib\classes.zip;C:\swing\swingall.jar
```

Once again, after adding (or modifying) the `CLASSPATH` variable in the `autoexec.bat` file, you must reboot your system.

Figure 1-8 shows a Swing applet running in Internet Explorer.

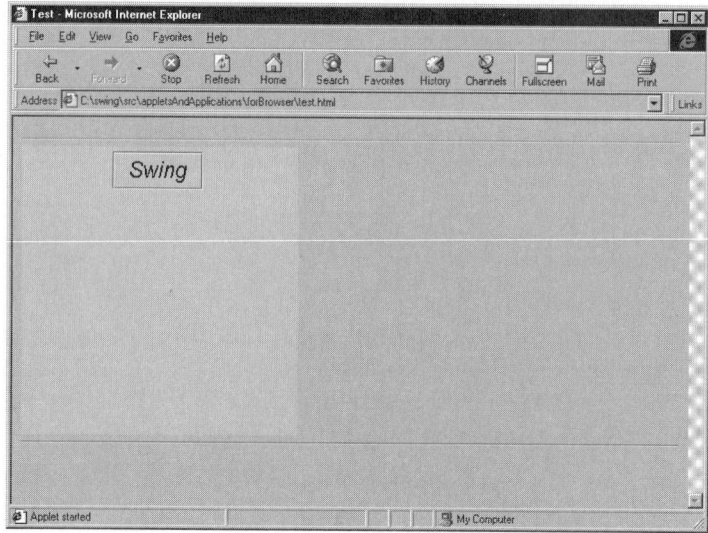

Figure 1-8 A Swing Applet Running in Internet Explorer

Java Plug-in

After setting up Netscape Navigator or Internet Explorer, you will undoubtedly discover numerous bugs when you try to run Swing applets. This problem may have nothing to do with Swing per se; it may be a manifestation of one of the major drawbacks to developing Java applets for use on the Internet.

One of the most difficult tasks an applet developer faces is trying to get applets to behave in a consistent matter from one browser to the next. In addition, browser vendors have historically been slow to update their browsers to work with the

latest version of the JDK. Fortunately, Sun has come up with a nifty solution to this problem with its Java Plug-in product (formerly known as Activator).

Java Plug-in works by inserting a plug-in into Netscape's Navigator and running an ActiveX control in Internet Explorer. Effectively, the plug-in or ActiveX control installs Sun's latest version of the JDK into the browser. Using Java Plug-in ensures that applets will behave in a consistent matter from one browser to the next.

The only drawback to Java Plug-in is that it requires some changes to HTML files; however, Sun provides a utility that will make the required changes for you. To learn more about the freely available Java Plug-in product, point your browser to the following web site:

```
http://java.sun.com/features/1998/04/plugin.html
```

Swing Resources

In addition to this book, numerous resources are available for learning Swing. Typically, you'll want to turn to other resources when you need answers to specific questions that are not covered in this book.

One of the best places to start is with the example code that comes with Swing itself. The examples provide a number of small but complete applets and applications that exercise a wide array of Swing features. The Swing examples can be found in the `examples` directory under the Swing main directory; so, for example, if you have Swing installed in the `C:\swing` directory, you will find the Swing examples in `C:\swing\examples`.

There are also a number of Internet resources, including mailing lists and newsgroups. The newsgroups listed below are good places to go with Swing questions:

```
comp.lang.java.programmer
comp.lang.java.gui
```

In addition, there are a couple of mailing lists for beginners and advanced users of Swing alike. For information on the mailing lists, go to the following web site:

```
http://www.eos.dk/
```

The Swing Connection is the official Swing site, maintained by Sun. It can be found at:

```
http://java.sun.com/products/jfc/tsc/
```

Parting Shots

Java burst onto the scene in 1995 and took off so rapidly that its success came as a surprise even to the developers of the language. Java existed in a previous incarnation as Oak—a research language at Sun meant to be a gentler and kinder variant of C++—for more than five years before it was retargeted for the Internet and renamed Java.

Whereas Java the language was in development for a number of years and was used internally at Sun, the language had little in the way of a user interface toolkit. When Java's success started to become evident, it was apparent that the language had to have a user interface toolkit and that it had to be developed in short order. The quickest way to develop a user interface toolkit was to rely on native components, referred to as peers, to do most of the work, and layer a thin veneer of Java classes on top of the native components. Thus, the AWT was implemented by a small team of developers in a scant six weeks.

The peer architecture was not scalable and resulted in many inconsistencies from one platform to the next. In addition, the AWT did not have a solid object-oriented base; for example, the original event model required a switch statement that switched off event types in order to invoke code that was dependent upon the type of event. Such switch statements are an object-oriented blasphemy; switch statements that switch off the type of an object should instead be handled through polymorphism.[4]

The shortcomings of the original AWT did not go unnoticed by Java developers, Sun, or Sun's competitors. It wasn't long before a number of alternative toolkits that were meant to be replacements for the AWT began to appear on the scene. In the meantime, Sun had released the 1.1 version of the AWT, which offered many improvements, including a new event model and support for lightweight (peerless) components. However, the improvements offered by the 1.1 version of the AWT were not enough to stop developers from moving to other user interface toolkits.

4.   Switch statements are sometimes valid in an object-oriented design, but the AWT's event model was not such a case.

JavaSoft realized that the Java community was about to split over the use of user interface toolkits and collaborated with Netscape to implement the Swing set of components. Swing has been in development for approximately a year and a half by Netscape and Sun engineers and is a huge improvement over the AWT.

Although some Swing components are meant to be replacements for the AWT's heavyweight components, Swing itself is not a replacement for the AWT. On the contrary, Swing is an extension of the AWT and uses much of the AWT's infrastructure, including support for graphics, fonts, and layout management. To get the most out of Swing, it is imperative to have a basic understanding of the infrastructure provided by the AWT.[5]

Swing, like all software, is not perfect. To date, Swing contains its share of bugs and, in some places, exhibits design flaws, but it is a solid user interface toolkit that is a vast improvement over the original AWT.

5.   See Volume I of *Graphic Java*.

CHAPTER

2

Swing Basics

This chapter discusses fundamental Swing concepts involved in developing Swing applets and applications.

Although Swing is an extension of the AWT, there are a number of fundamental differences between the two. To begin with, Swing applets and applications are implemented in a slightly different manner than their AWT counterparts. Also, there are a number of issues concerning mixing lightweight and heavyweight components that developers need to be aware of if they intend to develop applets or applications that use both AWT and Swing components.

Swing is not thread safe, which means that Swing components, for the most part, can only be accessed from the event dispatch thread. The reasons for, and the ramifications of, this approach are discussed in this chapter, in addition to mechanisms Swing provides that enable other threads to execute code from the event dispatch thread.

Applets and Applications

Applets and applications that use Swing components should extend Swing's `JApplet` (an extension of `java.applet.Applet`) and `JFrame` (an extension of `java.awt.Frame`), respectively. Both `JApplet` and `JFrame` provide Swing

support in addition to the functionality provided by their superclasses. Although the `Applet` and `Frame` classes can be used for Swing applets and applications respectively, event handling and repainting problems will likely occur. As a result, `JApplet` and `JFrame` should always be used for implementing Swing applets and applications.

Both `JApplet` and `JFrame` are containers that contain a single component—an instance of `JRootPane`, which is discussed in "JRootPane" on page 636. For now, it is sufficient to understand that `JRootPane` contains a container known as the content pane. The content pane is meant to contain all of the *content* associated with a particular applet or application, where content refers to the components contained in the applet or application. In practice, this means that applets and applications must add components to the content pane instead of adding them directly to the applet or application (or the root pane itself). Additionally, layout managers should not be set directly for either Swing applets or applications. Since components are added to the content pane, layout managers should be set for the content pane instead of the applet or application.

Swing containers that contain an instance of `JRootPane` override methods for adding components and setting layout managers. The methods throw exceptions that serve as a reminder that components should not be added directly to, and layout managers should not be set for, Swing containers that contain an instance of `JRootPane`.

Applets

The applet shown in Figure 2-1 contains an instance of JLabel that has an icon and some text. The applet extends JApplet and obtains a reference to its content pane by invoking JApplet.getContentPane(). The label is subsequently instantiated and added to the content pane.

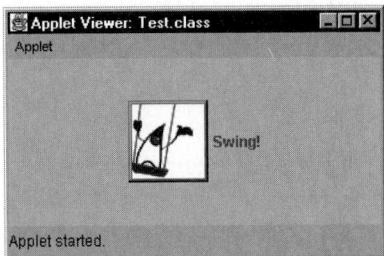

Figure 2-1 A Swing Applet

The applet shown in Figure 2-1 is listed in Example 2-1.

Example 2-1 A Swing Applet

```
import javax.swing.*;
import java.awt.*;
import java.awt.event.*;

public class Test extends JApplet {
    public void init() {
        Container contentPane = getContentPane();

        Icon icon = new ImageIcon("swing.gif",
                    "An animated GIF of Duke on a swing");

        JLabel label = new JLabel("Swing!", icon,
                                        JLabel.CENTER);

        contentPane.add(label, BorderLayout.CENTER);
    }
}
```

The JApplet class uses an instance of BorderLayout as the layout manager for its content pane. In order to stress this fact, the applet listed in Example 2-1 specifies a layout constraint of BorderLayout.CENTER, which centers the label in the content pane. The default constraint for a component laid out by BorderLayout is BorderLayout.CENTER, so the specification of the constraint in the applet is not strictly necessary.

Note: *The use of* BorderConstraints.CENTER *in the applet listed in Example 2-1 is necessary with Internet Explorer.*

The fact that the content pane for JApplet lays out components with an instance of BorderLayout is significant because by contrast, java.applet.Applet uses an instance of FlowLayout to lay out its components.

The JApplet Class

Swing's JApplet class extends java.applet.Applet and implements the Accessibility and RootPaneContainer interfaces. The Accessibility interface is part of the accessibility package, and the RootPaneContainer interface, as its name suggests, is a container that contains the root pane. The RootPaneContainer interface is implemented by all Swing containers that contain an instance of JRootPane.

JApplet provides the public and protected methods listed in Class Summary 2-1.

Class Summary 2-1   JApplet

Extends: java.applet.Applet

Implements: javax.accessibility.Accessible, RootPaneContainer

Constructors

---

public <u>JApplet</u>()

`JApplet` provides a lone no-argument constructor. Because applets are instantiated by a browser (or applet viewer), under normal circumstances it should not be necessary to directly instantiate an instance of `JApplet`. See "Applet/Application Combinations" on page 38 for a situation that calls for direct instantiation of an instance of `JApplet`.

Methods

Methods Overridden from java.awt.Container

---

protected void <u>addImpl</u>(Component, Object, int)
public void <u>setLayout</u>(LayoutManager)
public void <u>addNotify</u>()
public void <u>removeNotify</u>()

The four methods listed above are all overridden from the `java.awt.Container` class.

`addImpl()` is the method that ultimately adds components to a container. `JApplet.addImpl()` will throw an exception if components are added directly to the applet. The message associated with the exception is customized for each applet;[1] for instance, if the label in the applet in Example 2-1 on page 27 is added directly to the applet, the message associated with the exception is as follows:

```
java.lang.Error: Do not use Test.add() use Test.getContent-
Pane().add() instead
        at javax.swing.JApplet.createRootPaneException(JAp-
plet.java:198)
        at javax.swing.JApplet.addImpl(JApplet.java:220)
        at java.awt.Container.add(Container.java:179)
        at Test.init(Test.java:11)
```

---

1.   The message is customized by referring to the name of the `JApplet` extension.

```
        at sun.applet.AppletPanel.run(AppletPanel.java:287)
        at java.lang.Thread.run(Thread.java:474)
```

`JApplet` overrides `setLayout()` for the same reason it overrides `addImpl()`.
If an applet's layout manager is set, `setLayout()` will throw an exception. If the
applet listed in Example 2-1 on page 27 is modified so that it tries to set its layout
manager, an exception will be thrown with the following error message:

```
java.lang.Error: Do not use Test.setLayout() use Test.getContent-
Pane().setLayout() instead
        at javax.swing.JApplet.createRootPaneException(JAp-
plet.java:198)
        at javax.swing.JApplet.setLayout(JApplet.java:244)
        at Test.init(Test.java:10)
        at sun.applet.AppletPanel.run(AppletPanel.java:287)
        at java.lang.Thread.run(Thread.java:474)
```

`addNotify()` is invoked when a component's peer is instantiated. `JApplet`
overrides `addNotify()` to enable key events and to set the visibility of the
applet to `true`.

Root Pane / Content Pane / Glass Pane

---

protected JRootPane <u>createRootPane</u>()
protected boolean <u>isRootPaneCheckingEnabled</u>()
protected void <u>setRootPaneCheckingEnabled</u>(boolean)

public Container <u>getContentPane</u>()
public Component <u>getGlassPane</u>()
public JLayeredPane <u>getLayeredPane</u>()
public JRootPane <u>getRootPane</u>()
public void <u>setContentPane</u>(Container)
public void <u>setGlassPane</u>(Component)
public void <u>setLayeredPane</u>(JLayeredPane)
public void <u>setRootPane</u>(JRootPane)

Swing applets create their root pane by invoking the `protected`
`JApplet.createRootPane` method, which subsequently invokes
`setRootPane()`. The `createRootPane` method can be overridden by

extensions of `JApplet` to substitute an extension of the `JRootPane` class for the root pane of the applet.

Recall that adding a component directly to an instance of `JApplet` or explicitly setting its layout manager may result in an exception being thrown. However, at some time, an instance of `JRootPane` must be added to the applet without an exception being thrown. As a result, exceptions are only thrown when *root pane checking* is enabled. A flag that tracks whether root pane checking is enabled is set by invoking `setRootPaneCheckingEnabled()` with a `boolean` value; a `true` value indicates that root pane checking is enabled, whereas a `false` value indicates that root pane checking is disabled. `isRootPaneCheckingEnabled()` returns the last `boolean` value passed to `setRootPaneCheckingEnabled()`.

Notice that both `setRootPaneCheckingEnabled()` and `isRootPaneCheckingEnabled()` are `protected` methods. Although it is not possible to add components directly to an instance of `JApplet` or to explicitly set its layout manager, it is possible to implement extensions of `JApplet` that can control whether root pane checking is enabled. This capability enables extensions of `JApplet` to directly add components or set the applet's layout manager if needed.

In practice, `JApplet.createRootPane()` will rarely be overridden, and extensions of `JApplet` will rarely use `setRootPaneCheckingEnabled()` to allow the direct addition of components or the setting of the applet's layout manager.

The second group of methods listed above are defined by the `RootPaneContainer` interface. The methods provide the ability to get and set the containers contained in an instance of `JRootPane`. `JRootPane` and `RootPaneContainer` are discussed in "JRootPane" on page 636.

Accessible Context / Menu Bar / Key Events / Updating

---

public AccessibleContext getAccessibleContext()
public JMenuBar getJMenuBar()
public void setJMenuBar(JMenuBar)
protected void processKeyEvent(KeyEvent)
public void update(Graphics)

`getAccessibleContext()` returns an instance of `AccessibleContext` that provides accessibility information about an applet to accessibility tools.

Instances of `JApplet` can have a menu bar, which is specified by the `setJMenuBar` method. Note that Swing applets can have a menu bar whereas AWT applets cannot. Figure 2-1 shows a Swing applet equipped with a menu bar running in the Netscape browser.

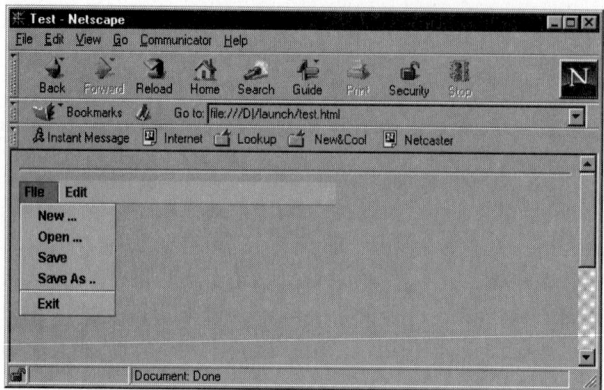

Figure 2-2 A Swing Applet with a Menu Bar

There are actually two ways to add a menu bar to a Swing applet. One way, of course, is to invoke `JApplet.setJMenuBar`, and the other is to obtain a reference to the applet's root pane and add the menu bar directly to the root pane.

`processKeyEvent()` is overridden to process key bindings. See "Keystroke Handling" on page 180 for more information on keystroke handling within Swing components.

The `JApplet.update` method is overridden to invoke `paint()` directly. By default, AWT components implement their update method to clear the background and then invoke `paint()`. This technique can result in considerable flickering when a component is updated repeatedly. As a result, the `JApplet` class dispenses with the erasing of the background, which eliminates the flickering. See the first volume of *Graphic Java* for more about painting and updating AWT components.

Content Panes for JApplet and JFrame Use an Instance of BorderLayout

If you have developed applets and applications with the AWT, you are no doubt familiar with the fact that java.applet.Applet uses an instance of FlowLayout as its layout manager, whereas java.awt.Frame uses an instance of BorderLayout as its layout manager.

The fact that AWT applets and applications use different layout managers can be confusing when you are migrating applets to applications, or vice versa—not to mention implementing an applet/application combination. Swing, on the other hand, uses the same type of layout manager—an instance of BorderLayout—for the content pane contained in both applets and applications.

Applications

The application shown in Example 2-2 is functionally identical to the applet shown in Example 2-1 on page 27. Both the applet and application add an instance of JLabel to their root pane's content pane.

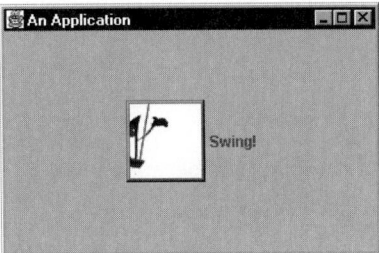

Figure 2-3 A Swing Application

The application shown in Figure 2-3 is listed in Example 2-2.

Example 2-2 A Swing Application

```
import javax.swing.*;
import java.awt.*;
import java.awt.event.*;

public class Test extends JFrame {
    public Test() {
        super("An Application");

        Container contentPane = getContentPane();

        Icon icon = new ImageIcon("swing.gif",
                    "An animated GIF of Duke on a swing");

        JLabel label = new JLabel("Swing!", icon,
                    SwingConstants.CENTER);

        contentPane.add(label, BorderLayout.CENTER);
    }
    public static void main(String args[]) {
        JFrame f = new Test();

        f.setBounds(100,100,300,250);
        f.setVisible(true);
        f.setDefaultCloseOperation(DISPOSE_ON_CLOSE);

        f.addWindowListener(new WindowAdapter() {
            public void windowClosed(WindowEvent e) {
                System.exit(0);
            }
        });
    }
}
```

Applications are somewhat more complicated than applets because they do not run inside a browser that starts them up and sets their size. Applications must provide a `main` method and must instantiate a frame that is subsequently sized[2] and made visible.

The application listed in Example 2-2 also sets the frame's default close operation and adds a window listener that exits the application after the frame has been closed. See "The JFrame Class" for more information on default close operations for Swing frames.

---

2. `JFrame.pack()` could be used in lieu of explicit sizing.

Swing applets and applications have much in common. Both contain a single instance of JRootPane, and both must add components to the root pane's content pane. Additionally, layout managers may not be explicitly set for either Swing applets or applications.

The JFrame Class

The JFrame class extends java.awt.Frame and, like JApplet, implements the Accessible and RootPaneContainer interfaces. JFrame also implements the Swing.WindowConstants interface that defines constants for default close operations. See "Swing Constants" on page 271, for more on Swing constants in general.

JFrame implements many of the same methods found in JApplet. Like JApplet, JFrame overrides the setLayout and addImpl methods in order to disallow explicitly setting its layout manager or adding components directly to the frame. JFrame implements all of the methods defined in the RootPaneContainer interface, in addition to methods for enabling and disabling root pane checking and for determining whether root pane checking is currently enabled.

The JFrame class is summarized in Class Summary 2-2.

Class Summary 2-2   JFrame

Extends: java.applet.Frame

Implements: javax.accessibility.Accessible, RootPaneContainer

Constructors

---

public <u>JFrame</u>()
public <u>JFrame</u>(String title)

JFrame comes with two constructors, one that takes no arguments and another that takes a string, which represents the title of the frame.

Whereas constructors for Swing applets are invoked by either a browser or applet viewer and are therefore typically not invoked by developer code, applications are responsible for constructing and sizing a frame. The constructor of choice for an instance of JFrame is typically the one that takes a string; the constructor that takes no arguments results in a frame with no title.

Methods that Overlap With JApplet

```
protected void addImpl(Component, Object, int)
protected JRootPane createRootPane()
public AccessibleContext getAccessibleContext()
public Container getContentPane()
public Component getGlassPane()
public JMenuBar getJMenuBar()
public JLayeredPane getLayeredPane()
public JRootPane getRootPane()
protected boolean isRootPaneCheckingEnabled()
protected void processKeyEvent(KeyEvent)
public void setContentPane(Container)
public void setGlassPane(Component)
public void setJMenuBar(JMenuBar)
public void setLayeredPane(JLayeredPane)
public void setLayout(LayoutManager)
protected void setRootPane(JRootPane)
protected void setRootPaneCheckingEnabled(boolean)
public void update(Graphics)
```

The JFrame methods listed above overlap with the methods defined in JApplet. For the most part, they are implemented in exactly the same manner as the corresponding methods in JApplet. For example, JFrame.setLayout and JFrame.addImpl will both throw an exception if root pane checking is enabled.

Refer to the JApplet Class Summary 2-1 on page 28 for more information on the methods listed above.

Frame Initialization / Default Close Operation / Window Events

---

protected void <u>frameInit</u>()
public int <u>getDefaultCloseOperation</u>()
public void <u>setDefaultCloseOperation</u>(int)
protected void <u>processWindowEvent</u>(WindowEvent)

The `frameInit` method is called by `JFrame`'s constructors to initialize the frame. The `JFrame` implementation of `frameInit()` enables key and window events for the frame, sets the frame's root pane and background color, and enables root pane checking. Extensions of `JFrame` are free to override the `frameInit` method if the default behavior is unsatisfactory.

With AWT frames, the developer is responsible for handling window close events. Typically, this entails overriding event handler methods and either simply hiding the window or hiding the window and disposing of its native resources. Swing makes window closing events easier to handle by associating a default close operation with each instance of `JFrame`. The default close operation can be set with the `setDefaultCloseOperation` method and can be retrieved with `getDefaultCloseOperation()`. The valid `integer` values that can be passed to `setDefaultCloseOperation()` are defined in the `WindowConstants` class and are enumerated in Table 2-1.

Table 2-1   WindowConstants Public Constants

Method Name	Implemenation
DO_NOTHING_ON_CLOSE	Does nothing when window is closed
HIDE_ON_CLOSE	Hides the window when it is closed
DISPOSE_ON_CLOSE	Hides the window and disposes of its native resources when the window is closed

If the default close operation for a `JFrame` is not explicitly set, then it defaults to DO_NOTHING_ON_CLOSE.

DISPOSE_ON_CLOSE hides the frame and disposes of the system resources associated with the frame. If the frame is an application frame, *the application will continue to run after the frame is disposed of.* For example, the application listed in Example 2-2 on page 34 sets the default close operation for the application frame to DISPOSE_ON_CLOSE, but the application is still responsible for handling the frame closed event. By the time the application is notified that the frame has been closed (when the `windowClosed` method is invoked) the frame has been hidden and disposed of, but the application is still running; as a result, the application invokes `System.exit()` in the `windowClosed` method.

Applet/Application Combinations

It is sometimes desirable to implement one source file that can be run either as an application or applet. One of the ways to implement a combination applet/application is shown in Example 2-3.

Example 2-3 Swing Applet/Application Combination

```
import javax.swing.*;
import java.awt.*;
import java.awt.event.*;

public class Test extends JApplet {
    public void init() {
        Container contentPane = getContentPane();

        Icon icon = new ImageIcon("swing.gif",
                    "An animated GIF of Duke on a swing");

        JLabel label = new JLabel("Swing!", icon,
                    SwingConstants.CENTER);

        contentPane.add(label);
    }
    public static void main(String args[]) {
        // f is final because it is accessed from
        // the inner class below
        final JFrame f = new JFrame();
        JApplet applet = new Test();

        applet.init();

        f.setContentPane(applet.getContentPane());
        f.setBounds(100,100,308,199);
        f.setTitle("An Application");
        f.setVisible(true);

        f.setDefaultCloseOperation(
            WindowConstants.DISPOSE_ON_CLOSE);

        f.addWindowListener(new WindowAdapter() {
            public void windowClosed(WindowEvent e) {
                System.exit(0);
```

```
            }
        });
    }
}
```

The idea is to implement an applet that contains a `main` method. The `main` method instantiates an instance of `JFrame` and also creates an instance of the applet. After invoking the applet's `init` method, the frame replaces its content pane with the content pane of the applet. The frame subsequently sets its bounds and title and sets its visibility to `true`.

Essentially, this technique results in an application and an applet that both share a content pane. After the code in Example 2-3 is compiled, it can be run as either an applet or an application.

It should be noted that applications implemented as an application/applet combination must be careful how they use the applet instance created in the `main` method. Because the applet is not instantiated by a browser or applet viewer, it is not complete (technically, it has no applet context). As a result, the applet cannot be used, for instance, to obtain an image with the `Applet.getImage` method. In practice, this is not much of a limitation because applications should not need to use an applet other than to borrow its content pane. Applications, for example, generally use the AWT toolkit to obtain an image and therefore have no need of the `Applet.getImage` method.

Swing Tip ...

Don't Add Components Directly to a Swing Applet or Application, and Don't Explicitly Set Its Layout Manager

Swing applets and applications both contain an instance of JRootPane, which in turn contains a container known as the content pane. The content—meaning the components—of an applet or application must be added to the content pane. If an attempt is made to add components directly to an instance of JApplet or JFrame, an exception will be thrown indicating that components can only be added to the content pane.

Swing applets and applications both use a BorderLayout layout manager to lay out their instance of JRootPane and disallow explicit setting of their layout manager. If an attempt is made to explicitly set the layout manager for a JApplet or JFrame, an exception is thrown indicating that the layout manager may not be explicitly set.

GJApp

The applications discussed in this book are implemented with the help of a class—GJApp—that provides a status area and the ability to read resources from a property file. The application shown in Figure 2-4 is an extension of JFrame that uses the GJApp class to access a status area that displays a string obtained from a GJApp.properties file.

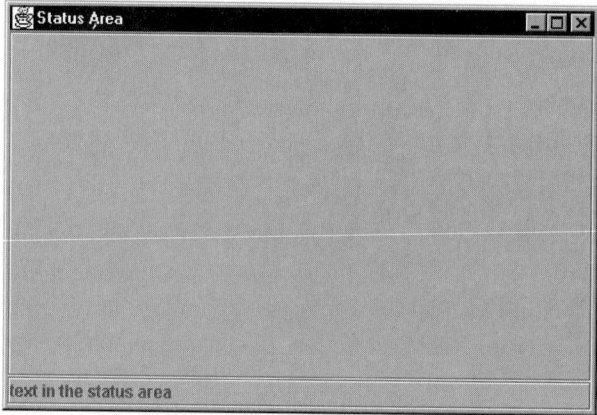

Figure 2-4 GJApp: Status Area and Resources

The GJApp.properties file defines one property:

```
# Simple properties file

statusAreaText=text in the status area
```

The application shown in Figure 2-4 is listed in Example 2-4.

Example 2-4 Using the GJApp Class

```
import javax.swing.*;
import java.awt.*;
import java.awt.event.*;
import java.util.*;

public class Test extends JFrame {
    public Test() {
        Container contentPane = getContentPane();
        JPanel panel = new JPanel();

        panel.setBorder(BorderFactory.createEtchedBorder());

        contentPane.add(panel,BorderLayout.CENTER);

        // Add GJApp's status area to contentPane
        contentPane.add(GJApp.getStatusArea(),BorderLayout.SOUTH);

        // Update GJApp's status area with resource string
        GJApp.showStatus(GJApp.getResource("statusAreaText"));
    }
    public static void main(String args[]) {
        // launch application
        GJApp.launch(new Test(),"Status Area",300,300,450,300);
    }
}
```

The application creates an instance of JPanel that is specified as the content pane's center component. The panel is (only) used to highlight the space above the status area, and to that end the panel is fitted with an etched border.

The application obtains a reference to the GJApp's status area by invoking the static GJApp.getStatusArea method. The status area is specified as the content pane's south component.

The static GJApp.showStatus method initializes the status area with the string associated with a statusAreaText resource. The resource's string is obtained with the static GJApp.getResource method.

The GJApp class handles three responsibilities:

- Initialize and display the frame passed to the static launch method
- Provide access to a panel that can be used like an applet's status area
- Look up resource strings from a GJApp.properties file

The GJApp class is listed in Example 2-5.

Example 2-5 The GJApp Class

```
class GJApp {
    static private JPanel statusArea = new JPanel();
    static private JLabel status = new JLabel("");
    static private ResourceBundle resources;
    private GJApp() {}  // defeat instantiation

    static {
        resources = ResourceBundle.getBundle(
                            "GJApp", Locale.getDefault());
    };

    public static void launch(final JFrame f, String title,
                        final int x, final int y,
                        final int w, int h) {
        f.setTitle(title);
        f.setBounds(x,y,w,h);
        f.setVisible(true);

        statusArea.setBorder(BorderFactory.createEtchedBorder());
        statusArea.setLayout(new FlowLayout(FlowLayout.LEFT,0,0));
        statusArea.add(status);
        status.setHorizontalAlignment(JLabel.LEFT);

        f.setDefaultCloseOperation(
                        WindowConstants.DISPOSE_ON_CLOSE);

        f.addWindowListener(new WindowAdapter() {
            public void windowClosed(WindowEvent e) {
                System.exit(0);
            }
        });
    }
    static public JPanel getStatusArea() {
        return statusArea;
    }
    static public void showStatus(String s) {
        status.setText(s);
    }
    static String getResource(String key) {
        return (resources == null) ? null :
                                resources.getString(key);
    }
}
```

The GJApp class is strictly a helper class that implements exclusively static methods. Instances of GJApp should not be instantiated; this restraint is enforced by the GJApp private constructor.

A `static` block of code (that is executed before `main()`) tries to obtain a reference to a resource bundle for the `GJApp.properties` file. The resource bundle is used in the `GJApp.getResource` method to obtain a string, given a resource key.

The `GJApp.launch` method sets the bounds and title for the frame it is passed and sets the frame's visibility to `true`, opening the frame. The launch method also configures the status area and sets the frame's default close operation to `WindowConstants.DISPOSE_ON_CLOSE`. Added to the frame is a window listener that exits the application when the window is closed.

The `GJApp` class provides access to its status area panel with the `getStatusArea` method. Like applets, the `GJApp` class provides a `showStatus` method that updates the status area.

Note: *Subsequent applications discussed in this book are all implemented with the help of the* `GJApp` *class; however, for the sake of brevity, Example 2-5 is the only place in the book where the* `GJApp` *class is listed.*

Mixing Swing and AWT Components

Originally the AWT was designed for heavyweight components only; lightweight components were not introduced until the 1.1 version of the AWT. As a result, the AWT had to be refactored to accommodate lightweight components.

As any software developer can attest to, refactoring a complex system to incorporate a previously unforeseen design is no simple task, and incorporating lightweight components into the AWT is no exception. To this day, mixing lightweight and heavyweight components in the same applet or application can be problematic, especially embedding heavyweight components inside lightweight containers.

Zorder

The zorder of a component represents the depth at which the component is shown in relation to other components in the same container.

If a container is homogeneous—meaning it contains all lightweight or all heavyweight components—zorder is determined by the order in which components are added to the container. The first component added to a container has the highest zorder, meaning it is displayed above all other components in the same container. The last component added to a container has the lowest zorder, meaning it is displayed underneath all other components in the same container.

If a container is heterogeneous—meaning it contains a mixture of lightweight and heavyweight components—then things are slightly more complicated. Recall from "Lightweight Vs. Heavyweight Components" on page 5 that lightweight components are not displayed in a window of their own but instead are displayed in their heavyweight container's window. As a result, lightweight components have the same zorder as the heavyweight container in which they reside. If more than one lightweight component is added to a container, the zorder among the lightweights is determined by order in which the components are added to the container.

If all that sounds confusing, the following two applets should clear things up. The applet shown in Figure 2-5 contains seven buttons, four of which are heavyweight AWT buttons and three that are lightweight Swing buttons. All of the heavyweight buttons are displayed on top of the lightweight buttons because the lightweight buttons have the same zorder as their container.

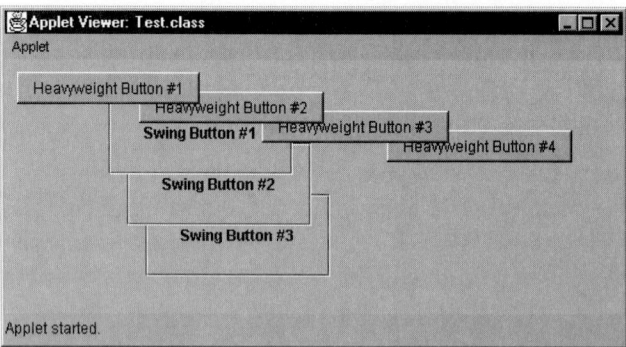

Figure 2-5 Mixing Lightweight and Heavyweight Components

The applet shown in Figure 2-5 is listed in Example 2-6.

Example 2-6 Mixing Heavyweight and Lightweight Components

```java
import javax.swing.*;
import java.awt.*;
import java.awt.event.*;

public class Test extends JApplet {
    Button b1, b2, b3, b4;
    JButton jb1, jb2, jb3;

    public void init() {
        Container contentPane = getContentPane();
        contentPane.setLayout(null);

        // create heavyweight AWT buttons
        b1 = new Button("Heavyweight Button #1");
        b2 = new Button("Heavyweight Button #2");
        b3 = new Button("Heavyweight Button #3");
        b4 = new Button("Heavyweight Button #4");

        // create lightweight Swing buttons
        jb1 = new JButton("Swing Button #1");
        jb2 = new JButton("Swing Button #2");
        jb3 = new JButton("Swing Button #3");

        // set bounds for heavyweight buttons
        b1.setBounds(10, 10, 150, 25);
        b2.setBounds(110, 25, 150, 25);
        b3.setBounds(210, 40, 150, 25);
        b4.setBounds(310, 55, 150, 25);

        // set bounds for lightweight buttons
        jb1.setBounds(85, 25, 150, 65);
        jb2.setBounds(100, 65, 150, 65);
        jb3.setBounds(115, 105, 150, 65);

        // add lightweight buttons
        contentPane.add(jb1);
        contentPane.add(jb2);
        contentPane.add(jb3);

        // add heavyweight buttons
        contentPane.add(b1);
        contentPane.add(b2);
        contentPane.add(b3);
        contentPane.add(b4);
    }
}
```

The applet sets the layout manager of the content pane to `null` so that the buttons can be explicitly positioned and sized to overlap one another. The applet then creates the buttons, sets their bounds, and adds each one to the content pane.

Even though the lightweight buttons are added to the content pane before the heavyweight buttons, the lightweights are displayed beneath the heavyweight buttons. Because lightweight components take on the zorder of the heavyweight container in which they reside, the lightweight buttons have the same zorder as their container, which is the applet's content pane.

Notice that the first lightweight button added to the content pane is displayed on top of the other lightweight buttons. Likewise, the first heavyweight button added to the content pane is displayed above all the other heavyweight buttons.

The applet shown in Figure 2-6 emphasizes the fact that lightweight components take on the zorder of their heavyweight container. The applet is almost identical to the one shown in Figure 2-5; however, the applet shown in Figure 2-6 places the three lightweight Swing buttons in a heavyweight panel. The panel is then added to the content pane after the second heavyweight button and before the third heavyweight button. As a result, the lightweight buttons take on the zorder of the panel in which they reside and are displayed below the second heavyweight button and above the third heavyweight button.

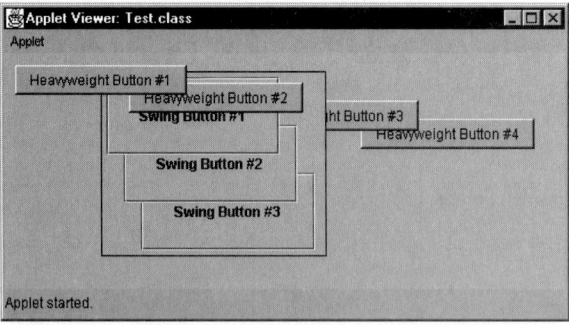

Figure 2-6 Lightweights Take on the Zorder of Their Heavyweight Container

The applet shown in Figure 2-6 is listed in Example 2-7.

Example 2-7 Controlling the Zorder of Lightweights

```java
import javax.swing.*;
import java.awt.*;
import java.awt.event.*;

public class Test extends JApplet {
    Button b1, b2, b3, b4;
    JButton jb1, jb2, jb3;

    public void init() {
        Container contentPane = getContentPane();
        Panel p = new BorderedPanel();

        // set layout managers for content pane and panel
        // to null so their components can be explicitly
        // positioned and sized
        contentPane.setLayout(null);
        p.setLayout(null);

        // create heavyweight AWT buttons
        b1 = new Button("Heavyweight Button #1");
        b2 = new Button("Heavyweight Button #2");
        b3 = new Button("Heavyweight Button #3");
        b4 = new Button("Heavyweight Button #4");

        // create lightweight Swing buttons
        jb1 = new JButton("Swing Button #1");
        jb2 = new JButton("Swing Button #2");
        jb3 = new JButton("Swing Button #3");

        // set bounds for heavyweights
        b1.setBounds(10, 10, 150, 25);
        b2.setBounds(110, 25, 150, 25);
        b3.setBounds(210, 40, 150, 25);
        b4.setBounds(310, 55, 150, 25);

        // set bounds for lightweights
        jb1.setBounds(5, 5, 150, 65);
        jb2.setBounds(20, 45, 150, 65);
        jb3.setBounds(35, 85, 150, 65);

        // set bounds for panel and add lightweights
        p.setBounds(85, 15, 195, 155);
        p.add(jb1);
        p.add(jb2);
        p.add(jb3);

        // add AWT buttons and panel to content pane
        contentPane.add(b1);
        contentPane.add(b2);
        contentPane.add(p);
```

```
            contentPane.add(b3);
            contentPane.add(b4);
        }
    }
    class BorderedPanel extends Panel {
        public void paint(Graphics g) {
            Dimension size = getSize();

            g.setColor(Color.black);
            g.drawRect(0,0,size.width-1,size.height-1);
            super.paint(g);   // paint lightweights
        }
    }
```

The applet listed in Example 2-7 implements an extension of the
java.awt.Panel class—BorderedPanel—that draws a black border around
the outside of the panel so the panel can be seen.

As an aside, notice that the BorderedPanel class invokes super.paint().
Whenever a container is extended and its paint method overridden, it must
explicitly invoke super.paint() in order for any lightweight components
contained in the container to be drawn.[3] If the call to super.paint() is omitted,
the lightweight Swing buttons will not be drawn in the panel.

---

3. See the first volume of *Graphic Java* for more information on lightweight compo-
    nents.

Swing Popup Menus

By default, Swing popup menus are lightweight.[4] If a lightweight popup menu overlaps a heavyweight component, the popup will be shown underneath the heavyweight component, as the applet shown in Figure 2-7 illustrates.

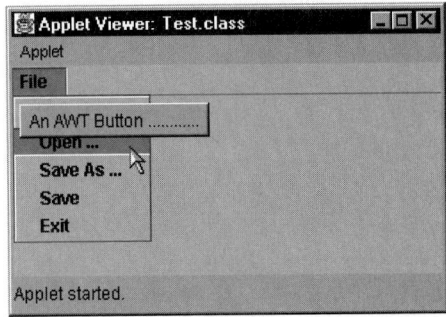

Figure 2-7 Lightweight Popups Pop Up Underneath Heavyweight Components

Popup menus are used by a few Swing components. One of the components that uses popup menus is the Swing menu component, which displays a popup menu when a menu is activated. By default, if a popup menu associated with a menu completely fits within the window in which the popup resides, a lightweight component is used for the popup menu. The popup menu associated with the File menu in the applet shown in Figure 2-7 is a lightweight component and therefore is shown beneath the heavyweight AWT button.

The applet shown in Figure 2-7 is listed in Example 2-8.

Example 2-8 A Lightweight Popup Displayed Beneath a Heavyweight Component

```
import javax.swing.*;
import java.awt.*;
import java.awt.event.*;

public class Test extends JApplet {
    public void init() {
        Container contentPane = getContentPane();
        JMenuBar menubar = new JMenuBar();
```

4. This is a simplification, but it will do for this discussion—see "JPopupMenu" on page 525 for a complete explanation.

```
JMenu menu = new JMenu("File");

menu.add("New ...");
menu.add("Open ...");
menu.add("Save As ...");
menu.add("Save");
menu.add("Exit");

contentPane.setLayout(new FlowLayout(FlowLayout.LEFT));
contentPane.add(new Button("An AWT Button ............"));

menubar.add(menu);
setJMenuBar(menubar);
    }
}
```

The applet creates a menu bar, an AWT button, and a menu. Items are added to the menu, the menu is added to the menu bar, and the button is added to the applet's content pane. Finally, `JApplet.setJMenuBar()` is invoked to attach the menu bar to the applet.

Fortunately, Swing provides a mechanism to force popup menus to be heavyweight so that they do not pop up under heavyweight components. The `JPopupMenu` class provides a `static` method that forces popup menus to be either heavyweight or lightweight.[5]

`JPopupMenu.setDefaultLightWeightPopupEnabled()` is passed a `boolean` value indicating whether popup menus are instantiated as lightweights or heavyweights; a `true` value forces popup menus created after the call to `setDefaultLightWeightPopupEnabled()` to be lightweight, whereas a `false` value forces them to be heavyweight.[6]

The applet shown in Figure 2-8 is identical to the applet shown in Figure 2-7, except that `JPopupMenu.setDefaultLightWeightPopupEnabled(false)` is called before the menu bar is instantiated.

---

5.   Individual popup menus may also be specified as lightweight or heavyweight.
6.   Again, this is a simplification, but it will do for this discussion.

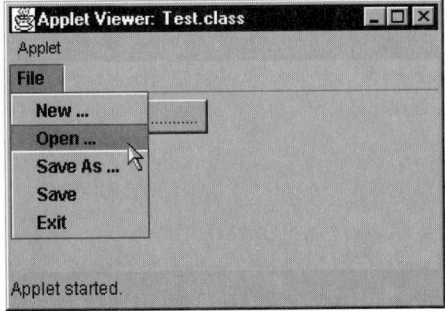

Figure 2-8 Heavyweight Popups Pop Up Over Heavyweight Components

The applet shown in Figure 2-8 is listed in Example 2-9.

Example 2-9 Using Heavyweight Popup Menus

```
import javax.swing.*;
import java.awt.*;
import java.awt.event.*;

public class Test extends JApplet {
    public void init() {
        JPopupMenu.setDefaultLightWeightPopupEnabled(false);

        Container contentPane = getContentPane();
        JMenuBar menubar = new JMenuBar();
        JMenu menu = new JMenu("File");

        menu.add("New ...");
        menu.add("Open ...");
        menu.add("Save As ...");
        menu.add("Save");
        menu.add("Exit");

        contentPane.setLayout(new FlowLayout(FlowLayout.LEFT));
        contentPane.add(new Button("An AWT Button ............"));

        menubar.add(menu);
        setJMenuBar(menubar);
    }
}
```

Scrolling

Another area of concern when it comes to mixing heavyweight and lightweight components has to do with scrolling.

Swing provides a lightweight alternative to the AWT's heavyweight scroll pane—the JScrollPane component. Because JScrollPane is lightweight, any heavyweight components that are added to an instance of JScrollPane will be displayed above the scroll pane itself. As a result, heavyweight components are not clipped properly when they are scrolled outside the bounds of an instance of JScrollPane.

The applet shown in Figure 2-9 illustrates the effect of adding a heavyweight component to an instance of JScrollPane and scrolling the heavyweight outside the bounds of the scroll pane.

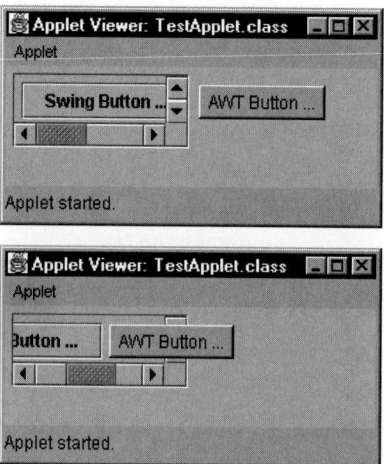

Figure 2-9 JScrollPane Cannot Properly Clip AWT Components

The top picture in Figure 2-9 shows the applet just after it is started, and the bottom picture shows the applet after the scroll pane has been scrolled. Notice that in both cases the AWT button is not properly clipped.

The applet shown in Figure 2-9 is listed in Example 2-10.

Example 2-10 Scrolling Heavyweights with JScrollPane

```java
import javax.swing.*;
import java.awt.*;
import java.awt.event.*;

public class Test extends JApplet {
    public Test() {
        JPanel panel = new JPanel();

        panel.add(new JButton("Swing Button ..."));
        panel.add(new Button("AWT Button ..."));

        Container contentPane = getContentPane();
        JScrollPane scrollPane = new JScrollPane(panel);

        scrollPane.setPreferredSize(new Dimension(125,50));
        contentPane.setLayout(new FlowLayout(FlowLayout.LEFT));
        contentPane.add(scrollPane);
    }
}
```

The applet shown in Figure 2-9 adds a Swing button and an AWT button to a panel that is specified as the component to be scrolled. The preferred size of the scroll pane is set, and the scroll pane is added to the applet's content pane.

It is highly probable that the clipping effect shown in Figure 2-9 is undesirable. Unfortunately, JScrollPane does not have an option to be instantiated as a heavyweight component as is the case for popup menus. Fortunately however, the AWT's ScrollPane component is a heavyweight scroll pane that is almost identical to Swing's JScrollPane.

Figure 2-10 shows the same applet as the one shown in Figure 2-9, but a heavyweight AWT ScrollPane is used instead of Swing's lightweight JScrollPane. Since AWT scroll panes are heavyweight, they have no difficulty scrolling both lightweight and heavyweight components.

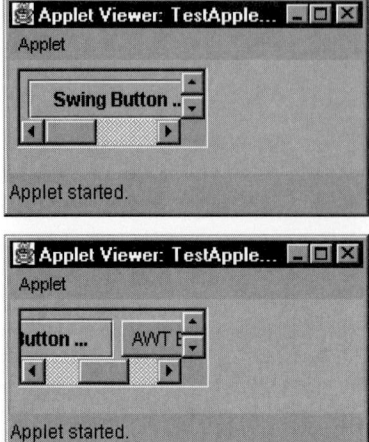

Figure 2-10 java.awt.ScrollPane Scrolls Both AWT and Swing Components

For completeness, the applet shown in Figure 2-10 is listed below in Example 2-11.

Example 2-11 Using the AWT's ScrollPane to Scroll Heavyweight Components

```java
import javax.swing.*;
import java.awt.*;
import java.awt.event.*;

public class Test extends JApplet {
    public Test() {
        JPanel panel = new JPanel();

        panel.add(new JButton("Swing Button ..."));
        panel.add(new Button("AWT Button ..."));

        Container contentPane = getContentPane();
        SizedScrollPane scrollPane = new SizedScrollPane();

        scrollPane.add(panel);

        contentPane.setLayout(new FlowLayout(FlowLayout.LEFT));
        contentPane.add(scrollPane);
    }
}
class SizedScrollPane extends ScrollPane {
    public Dimension getPreferredSize() {
        return new Dimension(125,50);
    }
}
```

Notice that an extension of `java.awt.ScrollPane` is implemented in the applet listed in Example 2-11 in order to set the preferred size of the scroll pane. See "Minimum, Maximum, and Preferred Sizes" on page 133 for more on the differences involved in setting preferred sizes for Swing components vs. AWT components.

Internal Frames

Swing's internal frames—frames that are contained in a desktop pane, see "Internal Frames and Desktop Panes" on page 873—are lightweight components, and it is possible to run into difficulties if heavyweight components are added to an internal frame.

The applet shown in Figure 2-11 contains two instances of `JInternalFrame`, both of which contain a heavyweight AWT canvas. If one internal frame overlaps another, the heavyweight canvas of the bottom-most internal frame will obscure portions of the topmost internal frame because the heavyweight canvas has a higher zorder then the lightweight internal frame.

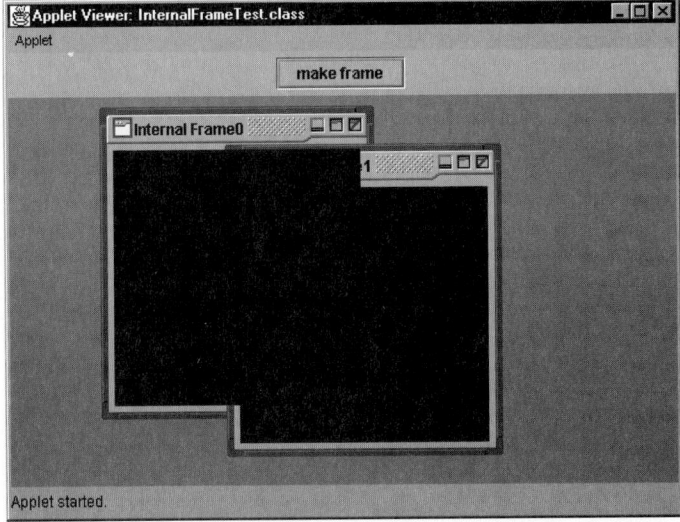

Figure 2-11 Internal Frames with Heavyweight Components

The applet shown in Figure 2-11 is listed in Example 2-12.

Example 2-12 Adding Heavyweight Components to Swing Internal Frames

```java
import java.awt.*;
import java.awt.event.*;
import javax.swing.*;

public class InternalFrameTest extends JApplet {
    JDesktopPane dtp = new JDesktopPane();

    public void init() {
        JPanel  controlPanel = new ControlPanel(dtp);
        Container contentPane = getContentPane();
        JPanel centerPanel = new JPanel();

        contentPane.setLayout(new BorderLayout());
        contentPane.add(controlPanel, BorderLayout.NORTH);
        contentPane.add(dtp, BorderLayout.CENTER);
    }
}
class ControlPanel extends JPanel {
    private static int cnt=0;

    public ControlPanel(final JDesktopPane dtp) {
        JButton b = new JButton("make frame");

        add(b);

        b.addActionListener(new ActionListener() {
            public void actionPerformed(ActionEvent event) {
                JInternalFrame jif = new JInternalFrame();
                Container contentPane = jif.getContentPane();

                jif.setLocation(10,50);
                jif.setTitle("Internal Frame" + cnt++);
                jif.setResizable(true);
                jif.setMaximizable(true);
                jif.setClosable(true);
                jif.setVisible(true);
                jif.setIconifiable(true);

                contentPane.setLayout(new FlowLayout());
                contentPane.add(new ColoredCanvas(), "Center");
                jif.pack();

                dtp.add(jif, 2);  // add at layer 2
            }
        });
    }
}
```

```
class ColoredCanvas extends Canvas {
    public void paint(Graphics g) {
        Dimension sz = getSize();
        g.setColor(Color.blue);
        g.fillRect(0,0,sz.width,sz.height);
    }
    public Dimension getPreferredSize() {
        return new Dimension(200,200);
    }
}
```

Swing Tip ...

Guidelines for Mixing AWT and Swing Components

In general, it is not advisable to mix lightweight Swing components with heavy-weight AWT components. For the most part, this should not be a problem since Swing provides lightweight replacement components for all AWT components. For existing applets or applications that use AWT components, the best approach is to replace the AWT components with their Swing counterparts. If that is not possible, then the following guidelines should be followed:

1. Do not mix lightweight and heavyweight components in a container if the lightweight component must be displayed on top of the heavyweight.

2. If a popup menu intersects a heavyweight component, force the popup menu to be heavyweight.

3. Don't add heavyweight components to an instance of JScrollPane. Instead, use an instance above java.awt.ScrollPane.

4. Don't add heavyweight components to Swing internal frames.

Swing and Threads

For the most part, Swing is not thread safe, meaning that Swing components can only be accessed from a single thread. First, we'll discuss why Swing is not thread safe, and then we'll discuss the ramifications a single-threaded design has for developers using Swing.

Let's face it, developing multithreaded applications, even in Java, is not easy. Designing a thread-safe toolkit is no simple matter; for example, determining how to synchronize access to a class can be a complex undertaking.[7] Likewise, extending thread-safe classes is somewhat of an art of its own and can be fraught with peril when undertaken by developers who are not experts at threads programming, which includes most developers. One of the main reasons that Swing is not thread safe is to simplify the task of extending its components.

Another reason that Swing is not thread safe is due to the overhead involved in obtaining and releasing locks and restoring state. All applications that use a thread-safe GUI toolkit, whether they are multithreaded or not, must pay the same performance penalty.

The use of threads increases the difficulty associated with debugging, testing, maintenance, and extensibility. For example, testing and maintenance, which are normally arduous tasks, become even more difficult—and sometimes nearly impossible—for most multithreaded applications.

Some Swing component methods do support multithreaded access. For example, the `JComponent` methods `repaint`, `revalidate`, and `invalidate` all queue requests that are placed on the event dispatch thread, and therefore the methods can be called from any thread. Also, event listener lists—see "Event Listener Lists" on page 258—can have listeners added to and removed from the lists from multiple threads. Finally, some component methods are synchronized; for example, the `JCheckBoxMenuItem.setState()` is synchronized and therefore may be invoked from multiple threads.

Ramifications of Swing's Single-Threaded Design

The main consequence of Swing's single-threaded design is as follows: *Swing components, for the most part, can only be accessed from the event dispatch thread once a component is available for painting onscreen.*

The event dispatch thread is the thread that invokes callback methods such as `paint` and `update` in addition to event handler methods defined in event listener interfaces. For example, implementors of the `ActionListener` and `PropertyListener` interfaces have their `actionPerformed` and `propertyChange` methods invoked on the event dispatch thread.

---

7. See Lea, Doug. *Concurrent Programming in Java*. Addison-Wesley, 1997.

Technically, Swing components can be accessed from multiple threads before the component's peer has been created[8]—meaning that the component is available for painting onscreen. This means, for instance, that components can be constructed and manipulated in an applet's `init` method as long as the components are not made visible before they are manipulated.

SwingUtilities invokeLater and invokeAndWait Methods

Since the AWT—and therefore Swing—are event-driven toolkits, it is natural to implement the updating of a visible GUI in callback methods. For example, if a list of items needs to be updated when a button is activated, the updating of the list is typically implemented in the `actionPerformed` method of an event listener attached to the button.

Sometimes, however, it may be necessary to update Swing components from a thread other than the event dispatch thread. For instance, if the list of items mentioned above is populated with data obtained from a database or over the Internet, there may be a perceptible delay from the time the button is activated until the list is updated. If the information retrieval is implemented within the `actionPerformed` method, the button will remain painted in its pressed state until the call to `actionPerformed` returns. Not only will it take awhile for the button to pop up, but in general, lengthy operations should not be performed in event handler methods because other events cannot be dispatched until the event handler method in question returns.

At times, it may be better to perform time-consuming operations on a separate thread, which allows the user interface to update immediately and frees the event dispatch thread to dispatch other events. Fortunately, Swing offers two mechanisms that support such a scenario.

The `SwingUtilities` class provides two methods: `invokeLater` and `invokeAndWait` that queue a runnable object on the event dispatch thread. When the runnable object makes its way to the front of the event dispatch queue, its run method is invoked. In effect, this allows an arbitrary block of code from another thread to be invoked from the event dispatch thread.

8. Peers are created by the `addNotify` method.

SwingUtilities.invokeLater

Before illustrating the `invokeLater` and `invokeAndWait` methods, let's first look at an applet that misbehaves by updating a Swing component on a thread other than the event dispatch thread. The applet shown in Figure 2-12 contains a button and a progress bar. When the button is activated, some lengthy operation to retrieve information is simulated. Once the information (an `integer` value) is retrieved, it is used to update the applet's progress bar.

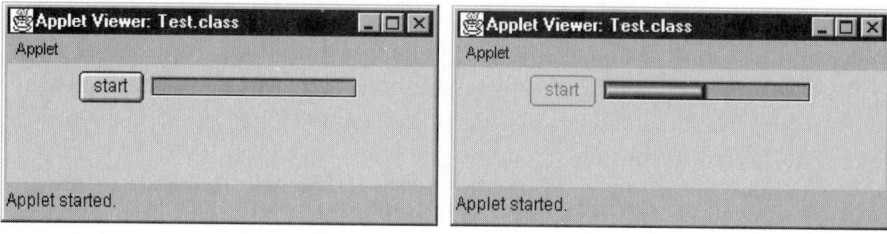

Figure 2-12 Updating Swing Components from Multiple Threads (shown with the Mac look and feel)

The picture on the left in Figure 2-12 shows the applet in its initial state. The picture on the right shows the applet after the start button has been activated, information has been retrieved, and the progress bar has been updated.

The applet adds an action listener to the button, and the listener creates a new thread that continuously retrieves information and updates the progress bar. The information retrieval is simulated by sleeping for half a second, and the thread obtains a reference to the progress bar from the applet itself.

```
public class Test extends JApplet {
    ...
    public void init() {
        ...
        startButton.addActionListener(new ActionListener() {
            public void actionPerformed(ActionEvent e) {
                GetInfoThread t = new GetInfoThread(Test.this);
                t.start();

                // this is ok, because actionPerformed
                // is called on the event dispatch thread
                startButton.setEnabled(false);
            }
        });
    }
```

```
    ...
}
class GetInfoThread extends Thread {
    Test applet;

    public GetInfoThread(Test applet) {
        this.applet = applet;
    }
    public void run() {
        while(true) {
            try {
                // simulate "lengthy" information retrieval
                Thread.currentThread().sleep(500);

                // this is not ok, because it is not called
                // on the event dispatch thread
                applet.getProgressBar.setValue(Math.random()*100);
            }
            catch(InterruptedException e) {
                e.printStackTrace();
            }
        }
    }
}
```

After the button's listener starts the thread, it sets the enabled state of the button to false. This is a valid operation because the actionPerformed method is invoked on the event dispatch thread. However, setting the value of the progress bar in the GetInfoThread is a risky proposition because the progress bar is being updated from a thread other than the event dispatch thread.

The applet shown in Figure 2-12 is listed in its entirety in Example 2-13.

Example 2-13 The Wrong Way to Update Components from Another Thread

```
import javax.swing.*;
import java.awt.*;
import java.awt.event.*;

public class Test extends JApplet {
    JProgressBar pb = new JProgressBar();

    public void init() {
        Container contentPane = getContentPane();
        final JButton startButton = new JButton("start");

        contentPane.setLayout(new FlowLayout());
        contentPane.add(startButton);
        contentPane.add(pb);
```

```
            startButton.addActionListener(new ActionListener() {
                public void actionPerformed(ActionEvent e) {
                    GetInfoThread t = new GetInfoThread(Test.this);
                    t.start();

                    // this is ok, because actionPerformed
                    // is called on the event dispatch thread
                    startButton.setEnabled(false);
                }
            });
        }
        public JProgressBar getProgressBar() {
            return pb;
        }
    }
    class GetInfoThread extends Thread {
        Test applet;

        public GetInfoThread(Test applet) {
            this.applet = applet;
        }
        public void run() {
            while(true) {
                try {
                    // simulate "lengthy" information retrieval
                    Thread.currentThread().sleep(500);

                    // this is not ok, because it is not called
                    // on the event dispatch thread
                    applet.getProgressBar.setValue(Math.random()*100);
                }
                catch(InterruptedException e) {
                    e.printStackTrace();
                }
            }
        }
    }
}
```

The correct way to update the progress bar in the applet shown in Example 2-13 is to use SwingUtilities.invokeLater() (or alternatively, invokeAndWait()). The constructor for the GetInfoThread class listed below is modified to instantiate a runnable object that obtains a reference to the progress bar from the applet and updates its value. The run method of the GetInfoThread class invokes SwingUtilities.invokeLater and passes a reference to the runnable object.

```java
class GetInfoThread extends Thread {
    Runnable runnable;
    int value;

    public GetInfoThread(final Test applet) {
        runnable = new Runnable() {
            public void run() {
                JProgressBar pb = applet.getProgressBar();
                pb.setValue(value);
            }
        };
    }
    public void run() {
        while(true) {
            try {
                Thread.currentThread().sleep(500);

                // This is okay because the runnable's run()
                // will be invoked on the event dispatch thread
                value = (int)(Math.random() * 100);
                SwingUtilities.invokeLater(runnable);
            }
            catch(InterruptedException e) {
                e.printStackTrace();
            }
        }
    }
}
```

A revised version of the applet shown in Example 2-13 is listed in its entirety in Example 2-14.

Example 2-14 The Right Way to Update Components from Another Thread

```java
import javax.swing.*;
import java.awt.*;
import java.awt.event.*;

public class Test extends JApplet {
    private JProgressBar pb = new JProgressBar();

    public void init() {
        Container contentPane = getContentPane();
        final JButton startButton = new JButton("start");

        contentPane.setLayout(new FlowLayout());
        contentPane.add(startButton);
        contentPane.add(pb);

        startButton.addActionListener(new ActionListener() {
```

```
            public void actionPerformed(ActionEvent e) {
                GetInfoThread t = new GetInfoThread(Test.this);
                t.start();

                // this is okay because actionPerformed
                // is called on the event dispatch thread
                startButton.setEnabled(false);
            }
        });
    }
    public JProgressBar getProgressBar() {
        return pb;
    }
}
class GetInfoThread extends Thread {
    Runnable runnable;
    int value;

    public GetInfoThread(final Test applet) {
        runnable = new Runnable() {
            public void run() {
                JProgressBar pb = applet.getProgressBar();
                pb.setValue(value);
            }
        };
    }
    public void run() {
        while(true) {
            try {
                Thread.currentThread().sleep(500);

                // This is okay because the runnable's run()
                // is invoked on the event dispatch thread
                value = (int)(Math.random() * 100);
                SwingUtilities.invokeLater(runnable);
            }
            catch(InterruptedException e) {
                e.printStackTrace();
            }
        }
    }
}
```

SwingUtilities.invokeAndWait

SwingUtilities.invokeAndWait(), like invokeLater(), queues a runnable object on the event dispatch thread. However, whereas invokeLater() returns immediately after it has queued the runnable object, invokeAndWait() waits until the run method of the runnable object has been

started before returning. The `invokeAndWait` method is useful when information must be retrieved from a component before another operation can be carried out on another thread.

For example, the applet listed in Example 2-14 updates the value of the progress bar regardless of whether the new value is the same as the current value of the progress bar. It would be ever-so-slightly more efficient if the progress bar's value were only updated when the new value differs from the current value of the progress bar. Modifying the applet to do so will afford us the opportunity to investigate the `invokeAndWait` method.

First, the `GetInfoThread` class is modified to create two runnable objects—one that gets the current value of the progress bar, and another that sets the value of the progress bar.

```
class GetInfoThread extends Thread {
    Runnable getValue, setValue;
    int value, currentValue;

    public GetInfoThread(final Test applet) {
        getValue = new Runnable() {
            public void run() {
                JProgressBar pb = applet.getProgressBar();
                currentValue = pb.getValue();
            }
        };
        setValue = new Runnable() {
            public void run() {
                JProgressBar pb = applet.getProgressBar();
                pb.setValue(value);
            }
        };
    }
    ...
```

Next, the run method of the `GetInfoThread` class is modified to obtain the current value of the progress bar by using `invokeAndWait()`.

```
public void run() {
    while(true) {
        try {
            // simulate "lengthy" information retrieval
            Thread.currentThread().sleep(500);

            value = (int)(Math.random() * 100);
```

```
            try {
                SwingUtilities.invokeAndWait(getValue);
            }
            catch(InvocationTargetException ite) {
                ite.printStackTrace();
            }
            catch(InterruptedException ie) {
                ie.printStackTrace();
            }

            if(currentValue != value) {
                SwingUtilities.invokeLater(setValue);
            }
        }
        catch(InterruptedException e) {
            e.printStackTrace();
        }
    }
}
```

SwingUtilities.invokeAndWait() obtains the current value of the progress bar, and invokeLater() sets the value of the progress bar. The call to InvokeAndWait will not return until the run method of the getValue runnable object returns.

SwingUtilities.invokeAndWait() may throw one of two exceptions: either an InterruptedException or an InvocationTargetException. The exceptions must be caught whenever invokeAndWait() is used, or the method in which the call is made must have a throws clause.

The complete revised applet is listed in Example 2-15.

Example 2-15 Using SwingUtilities.invokeAndWait()

```
import javax.swing.*;
import java.awt.*;
import java.awt.event.*;
import java.lang.reflect.*;   // for InvocationTargetException

public class Test extends JApplet {
    private JProgressBar pb = new JProgressBar();

    public void init() {
        Container contentPane = getContentPane();
        final JButton startButton = new JButton("start");

        contentPane.setLayout(new FlowLayout());
        contentPane.add(startButton);
        contentPane.add(pb);
```

```
        startButton.addActionListener(new ActionListener() {
            public void actionPerformed(ActionEvent e) {
                GetInfoThread t = new GetInfoThread(Test.this);
                t.start();

                // this is okay because actionPerformed
                // is called on the event dispatch thread
                startButton.setEnabled(false);
            }
        });
    }
    public JProgressBar getProgressBar() {
        return pb;
    }
}
class GetInfoThread extends Thread {
    Runnable getValue, setValue;
    int value, currentValue;

    public GetInfoThread(final Test applet) {
        getValue = new Runnable() {
            public void run() {
                JProgressBar pb = applet.getProgressBar();
                currentValue = pb.getValue();
            }
        };
        setValue = new Runnable() {
            public void run() {
                JProgressBar pb = applet.getProgressBar();
                pb.setValue(value);
            }
        };
    }
    public void run() {
        while(true) {
            try {
                Thread.currentThread().sleep(500);

                // This is okay because the getValue's run()
                // is invoked on the event dispatch thread
                value = (int)(Math.random() * 100);

                try {
                    SwingUtilities.invokeAndWait(getValue);
                }
                catch(InvocationTargetException ite) {
                    ite.printStackTrace();
                }
                catch(InterruptedException ie) {
                    ie.printStackTrace();
                }
```

```
            if(currentValue != value) {
                SwingUtilities.invokeLater(setValue);
            }
        }
        catch(InterruptedException e) {
            e.printStackTrace();
        }
    }
}
}
```

One important distinction between invokeLater() and invokeAndWait() is that invokeLater() can be called from the event dispatch thread, whereas invokeAndWait() cannot. The problem with calling invokeAndWait() from the event dispatch thread is that invokeAndWait() blocks the thread that it is called from until the runnable object is dispatched from the event dispatch thread and its run method invoked. If invokeAndWait() is called from the event dispatch thread, thread deadlock will occur because invokeAndWait() is waiting for events to be dispatched, but since it is called from the event dispatch thread, events cannot be dispatched until invokeAndWait() returns.

Swing Tip ...

Use SwingUtilities.invokeLater() and SwingUtilities.invokeAndWait() For Accessing Components from a Thread Other Than the Event Dispatch Thread

Because Swing is not thread safe, it is not safe to access Swing components from a thread other than the event dispatch thread. The SwingUtilities class provides two methods that can be used to execute code on the event dispatch thread: invokeLater and invokeAndWait.

Note that SwingUtilities.invokeLater can be called from the event dispatch thread, but the same is not true for SwingUtilities.invokeAndWait. If invokeAndWait is called from the event dispatch thread, thread deadlock will occur because invokeAndWait is waiting for a runnable object to be dispatched from the event dispatch thread, but events cannot be dispatched until the call to invokeAndWait returns.

Parting Shots

One of the design goals for Swing was to leave the conventions for implementing applets and applications intact. For the most part, this goal was achieved; however, Swing applets and applications contain an instance of JRootPane, which means that components cannot be added directly to, or layout managers explicitly set for, instances of JApplet or JFrame. Instead, components are added to the root pane's content pane, and, likewise, layout managers must be set for the content pane and not for the applet or application itself. Fortunately, JApplet and JFrame will both throw exceptions with understandable error messages whenever a component is an added directly to, or a layout manager is explicitly set for, an applet or frame.

There is bound to be some backlash concerning the decision to implement Swing as thread unsafe. After all, Java has multithreading built into the language, and therefore there are those who will argue that Swing should have been implemented in a thread-safe manner.

However, just because Java has built-in support for threading does not mean that it is a simple matter to implement bulletproof multithreaded applets or applications—not to mention toolkits—in Java. In fact, the contrary is true; it can be quite difficult to implement nontrivial applets and applications in a thread-safe manner. Additionally, most developers are not well versed in the intricacies of developing multithreaded code. One of the more difficult areas that one encounters when multiple threads are introduced into an object-oriented language is exactly how to extend thread-safe classes. In this respect, the single-threaded approach taken by the Swing developers results in classes that are much easier to extend.

All in all, the decision to disallow access to Swing components from threads other than the event dispatch thread was the correct one; it resulted in a simpler toolkit that is easier to extend. Additionally, it is possible for threads other than event dispatch thread to schedule runnable objects to be implemented on the event dispatch thread.

Swing is a solid, industrial-strength user interface toolkit that is a vast improvement over the AWT. However, as with any nontrivial software, Swing has its share of bugs and a fairly steep learning curve.

CHAPTER

3

Swing Component Architecture

Lightweight Swing components delegate their look and feel to a *UI delegate* that is responsible for painting the component (look) and handling its events (feel). UI delegates can be plugged into a component when components are constructed or anytime thereafter: thus the term pluggable look and feel that was introduced in "Pluggable Look and Feel" on page 11.

Swing's pluggable look and feel comprises a component architecture based on Smalltalk's Model-View-Controller (MVC) design and an infrastructure for managing look and feels. The former is the focus of this chapter, which begins with an overview of classic MVC, followed by a discussion of Swing's MVC implementation. The latter is discussed in "Pluggable Look and Feel" on page 317.

Classic Model-View-Controller Architecture

The MVC architecture is designed for applications that need to provide multiple views of the same data. MVC separates applications into three types of objects:

- **Models:** Maintain data and provide data accessor methods
- **Views:** Paint a visual representation of some or all of a model's data
- **Controllers:** Handle events

Models are responsible for maintaining data; for example, a notepad application would store the current document's text in a model. Models typically provide methods to access and modify their data. Models also fire events to registered views when a model is changed, and the views respond by updating themselves based on the model change.

Views are responsible for providing a visual representation of some portion of a model's data. For example, a notepad application would provide a view of the current document by displaying some or all of the text stored in the model.

Controllers handle events for views. AWT and Swing listeners such as mouse and action listeners are, for all intents and purposes, MVC controllers. The notepad application mentioned previously would have mouse and key listeners that made changes to the model or view(s) as appropriate.

MVC is a powerful design for a number of reasons. First, multiple views and controllers can be plugged into a single model, which is the basis for Swing's pluggable look and feel.

Second, a model's views are automatically notified when the model is changed; changing a model property in one view results in subsequent updates of the model's other views.

Third, because models are not dependent upon views, models do not have to be modified to accommodate new types of views or controllers.

Pluggable Views and Controllers

Swing (and AWT) containers delegate sizing and positioning of the components they contain to a layout manager, which encapsulates a strategy for laying out components. For example, the `FlowLayout` layout manager's strategy is to size components according to their preferred sizes and to position them from left to right and top to bottom.

Encapsulating strategies makes them pluggable; for example, layout managers can be plugged into containers both at compile and runtime.

The MVC architecture provides pluggable views and controllers by encapsulating strategies for visually representing data in views and by encapsulating event handling strategies in controllers. Just as layout managers can be plugged into AWT and Swing components, views and controllers can be plugged into models.

View Updates

Swing (and AWT) events are handled by event listeners that register with an event source. For example, activation of a button is handled by an object that implements the `ActionListener` interface and that has registered with the button by invoking the button's `addActionListener` method. When the button is activated, it fires an action event, and the listener's `actionPerformed` method is invoked.[1]

Event sources and listeners are an example of the `Observer` pattern, which allows a single object to notify many observers when the observed object is modified.[2] The `Observer` pattern requires very little surface area (the amount of knowledge one object needs to know about another) between an observed object and its observers. For example, the action listener described above can be any type of object as long as it implements the `ActionListener` interface. Furthermore, the button knows nothing about its observers, other than how and when to notify them.

The MVC architecture employs the `Observer` pattern to notify views when a model changes. Models can have many views, all of which are typically synchronized as a result of notifications from the model. Also, any type of view can observe a model without any changes whatsoever to the model itself.

Figure 3-1 shows the flow of information for a typical MVC implementation and illustrates how views are updated when changes are made to a model.

1. See "JButton Events" on page 397 for examples of handling button action events.
2. See Gamma, Helm, Johnson, Vlissides. *Design Patterns*, Addison-Wesley 1994.

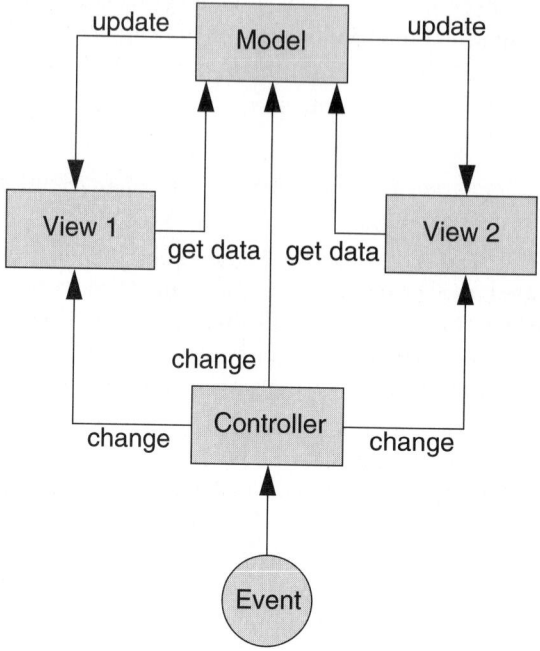

Figure 3-1 Classic MVC Communication

Events are handled by controllers that typically make changes to the model or one or more views, depending upon the type of event.

Models maintain a list of views that have registered with the model for change notification. When a change is made to a model, the model notifies each view that has registered with the model. Views typically obtain information from the model to further clarify the event and subsequently update themselves accordingly.

Swing Tip ...

The Benefits of MVC

The MVC architecture has long been the foundation upon which Smalltalk applications are built, and for good reason.

The most fundamental aspect of object-oriented development is identifying abstractions and encapsulating them in classes. For example, a payroll application would identify abstractions such as employees, salaries, etc. Encapsulating abstractions in classes allows for loose coupling between objects, which reduces dependencies and increases flexibility and reuse.

MVC encapsulates three general abstractions that are present in most graphical applications: models, views, and controllers. By encapsulating what other architectures intertwine, MVC applications are much more flexible and reusable than their traditional counterparts.

Swing MVC

Swing MVC is a specialized version of classic MVC meant to support pluggable look and feel instead of applications in general. Swing lightweight components comprise the following objects:

- A *model* that maintains a component's data
- A *UI delegate* that is a view with listeners for handling events
- A *component* that extends `JComponent`[3]

Swing models translate directly to classic MVC models; both maintain data and provide data accessor methods, and both notify listeners when they are changed.

Swing components delegate their look and feel to a *UI delegate*. UI delegates correspond to a view/controller(s) combination in classic MVC. Controllers are referred to as *listeners* from here on.

---

3. See "The JComponent Class" chapter on page 123.

Swing listeners are typically implemented as inner classes of UI delegates. For example, a slider's UI delegate implements a change listener that reacts to model changes. The change listener is implemented as an inner class of BasicSliderUI:

```
// From javax.swing.plaf.basic.BasicSliderUI.java:

public class BasicSliderUI extends SliderUI {
    ...
    // installUI is called when a UI is being installed
    // for a component

    public void installUI(JComponent c)   {
        ...
        changeListener = createChangeListener( slider );
        ...
        installListeners( slider );
    }
    ...
    protected ChangeListener
                    createChangeListener( JSlider slider ) {
        return new ChangeHandler();
    }
    ...
    protected void installListeners( JSlider slider ) {
        ...
        slider.getModel().addChangeListener(changeListener);
        ...
    }
    ...
    public class ChangeHandler implements ChangeListener {
        public void stateChanged(ChangeEvent e) {
            if ( !isDragging ) {
                calculateThumbLocation();
                slider.repaint();
            }
        }
    }
    ...
}
```

BasicSliderUI creates an instance of ChangeHandler that calculates the location of the slider's thumb (a.k.a. grip) and repaints the slider.

Component delegates, depending upon the complexity of the component they represent, can have a number of inner class listeners that handle events. For example, the BasicSliderUI class implements six inner class listeners, as can be seen from Figure 3-2 on page 79.

Swing Components

Components provide an API for developers to manipulate the collection of objects that constitute a Swing component. Components indirectly create their UI delegates and delegate to them when the time is right. See "Installing a UI Delegate" on page 104 for a discussion of UI delegate creation, and see "UI Delegate Painting" on page 103 for discussion of components delegating painting to their UI delegates.

Components also make their models transparent to developers by providing pass-through methods and by forwarding model events.

Model Pass-Through Methods

Swing components provide pass-through methods for their models so that developers do not have to access models directly to modify or query state. For example, the methods listed below from the `JSlider` class show how sliders pass through their model's minimum value.

```
// From JSlider.java, pass-through model methods:

public int getMinimum() {
    return getModel().getMinimum();
}
public void setMinimum(int minimum) {
    int oldMin = getModel().getMinimum();

    getModel().setMinimum(minimum);

    firePropertyChange("minimum",
        new Integer( oldMin ), new Integer( minimum ) );
}
```

`JSlider.setMinimum()` fires a property change event after setting the minimum value. All component model properties, such as the minimum and maximum values for a slider, should fire property change events.

Model Event Forwarding

Swing components also forward model events to listeners that are registered with a component. For example, a slider registers as a change listener with its model. When the slider's model fires a change event, the slider in turn fires a change event to its own change listeners. The `JSlider` class implements a change listener that simply fires a state-changed event to the slider's change listeners. Like component UIs, component classes such as `JSlider` often encapsulate event handling within inner classes.

The severely abbreviated `JSlider` listing below illustrates the manner in which sliders—in a manner similar to other Swing component classes—fire state changes to their listeners in response to model state changes.

```
// From JSlider.java:

public class JSlider extends JComponent
                     implements SwingConstants, Accessible {
    ...
    protected ChangeListener changeListener =
                             createChangeListener();
    ...
    public JSlider(int orientation, int min,
                                int max, int value) {
        ...
        sliderModel.addChangeListener(changeListener);
        ...
    }
    ...
    public void addChangeListener(ChangeListener l) {
        listenerList.add(ChangeListener.class, l);
    }
    public void removeChangeListener(ChangeListener l) {
        listenerList.remove(ChangeListener.class, l);
    }
    ...
    protected ChangeListener createChangeListener() {
        return new ModelListener();
    }
    ...
    private class ModelListener
                implements ChangeListener, Serializable {
        public void stateChanged(ChangeEvent e) {
            // fire event to change listener registered
            // with addChangeListener() listed above
            fireStateChanged();
        }
    }
}
```

The `JSlider` constructor adds an instance of `JSlider.ModelListener` to the slider's model. `JSlider.ModelListener` reacts to model changes by invoking `JSlider.fireStateChanged()`, which fires a change event to the slider's listeners.

A Static Perspective

Lightweight Swing components are implemented in a similar fashion as far as the objects that make up their MVC structure. For example, Swing buttons consist of, among other things, the `JButton` and `ButtonUI` classes. Other lightweight Swing components follow suit by implementing similarly named classes with similar roles: `JLabel` and `LabelUI`, `JCheckBox` and `CheckBoxUI`, `JTree` and `TreeUI`, etc.

Because of the consistent MVC implementation of lightweight Swing components, a class diagram of the classes that comprise Swing sliders—shown in Figure 3-2—provides some insights into Swing MVC in general.

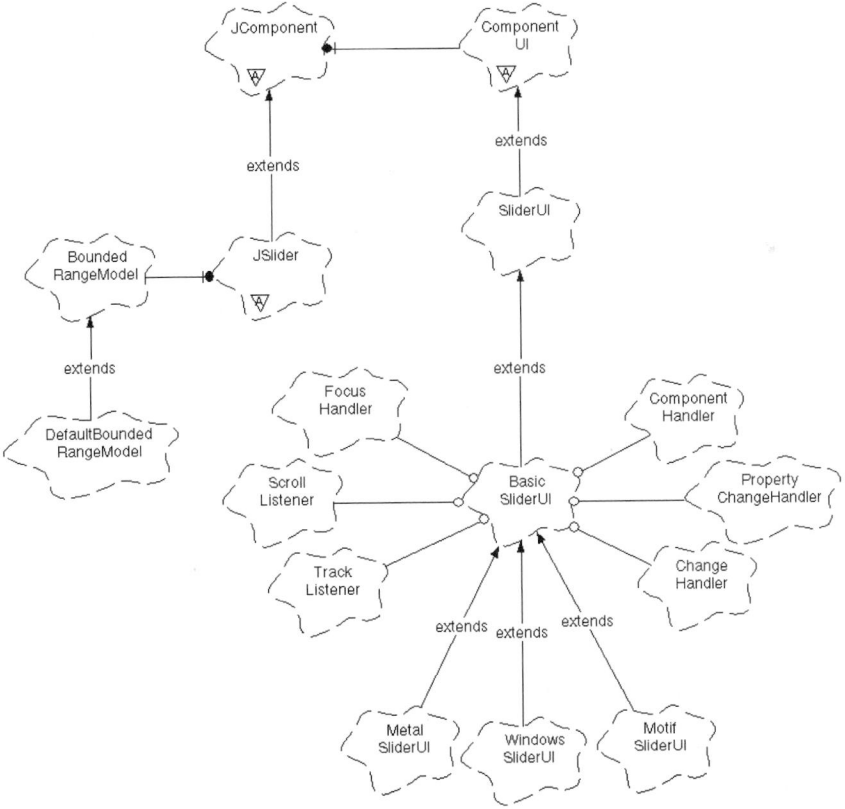

Figure 3-2 Slider Component Classes

Like most lightweight Swing components, `JSlider` maintains a reference to its model. Swing models are defined by interfaces, and a slider's model implements the `BoundedRangeModel` interface. Bounded range models keep track of minimum, maximum, and current values.[4]

Swing provides default model implementations that are used when component models are not explicitly specified. For example, if a slider's model is not explicitly specified—which is normally the case—sliders are fitted with an instance of `DefaultBoundedRangeModel`.

All Swing lightweight components extend the `JComponent` class, which maintains a reference to a component UI. The `ComponentUI` class is an abstract class from the `javax.swing.plaf` package that defines the fundamental responsibilities of UI delegates.

The `BasicSliderUI` class resides in the `javax.swing.plaf.basic` package and encapsulates basic button functionality. Slider UI classes for the standard Swing look and feels extend the `BasicSliderUI` class and customize the default functionality.

The `BasicSliderUI` class implements six inner class listeners, five of which listen to the `JSlider` component; the `BasicSliderUI.ChangeHandler` is added to the slider's model.

A Dynamic Perspective

The preceding section provided a static view of the relationships between objects that make up lightweight Swing components. This section provides a dynamic perspective of the interaction among a component's constituents.

Figure 3-3 shows a diagram, similar in intent to Figure 3-1 on page 74, that illustrates the flow of information for Swing's MVC implementation.

The Component shown in Figure 3-3 represents a lightweight Swing component class such as `JButton`, `JLabel`, `JSlider`, etc.

Because a UI delegate's listeners are nearly always implemented as inner classes, listeners are shown contained in the UI delegate in Figure 3-3.

The Model in Figure 3-3 represents the component's model; for example, a button's model is an implementation of the `ButtonModel` interface.

---

4.   See "JSlider" on page 595 for more information sliders and their models.

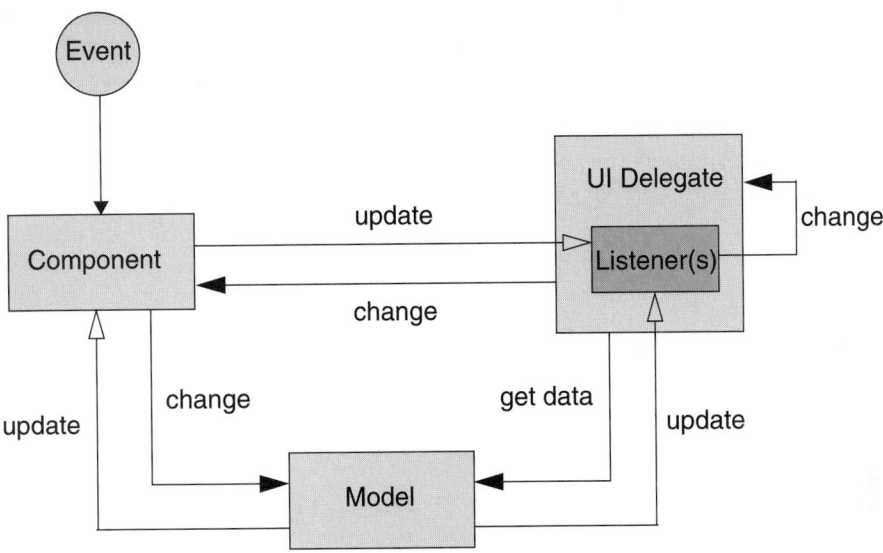

Figure 3-3 Swing MVC Communication

Recall from "Swing MVC" on page 75 that components provide pass-through methods for their models, so model values can be manipulated without directly accessing a component's model. Hence, Figure 3-3 shows that components make changes to their models.

Also recall that components, such as JButton, JLabel, JSlider, etc., listen to their models for the purpose of forwarding model events to the component's own listeners. Figure 3-3 therefore depicts the model as updating the component when the model changes.

UI delegate listeners typically listen to the component or the component's model, so Figure 3-3 shows listeners being updated by both the component and the model. Listeners typically respond to events by optionally obtaining information from the model and changing the component or the UI delegate.

Scenarios

Figure 3-3 illustrates communication between objects that constitute a lightweight Swing component in general. This section discusses two specific interactions to further clarify lightweight Swing component communication.

Figure 3-4 shows the sequence of events that occurs when a slider property is modified programmatically. The `paintTicks JSlider` property is a property of the slider's UI delegate and is not a model property.

Swing sliders maintain a `boolean` property that determines whether a slider paints tick marks, and Figure 3-4 shows the sequence of events that occurs when `JSlider.setPaintTicks()` is invoked.

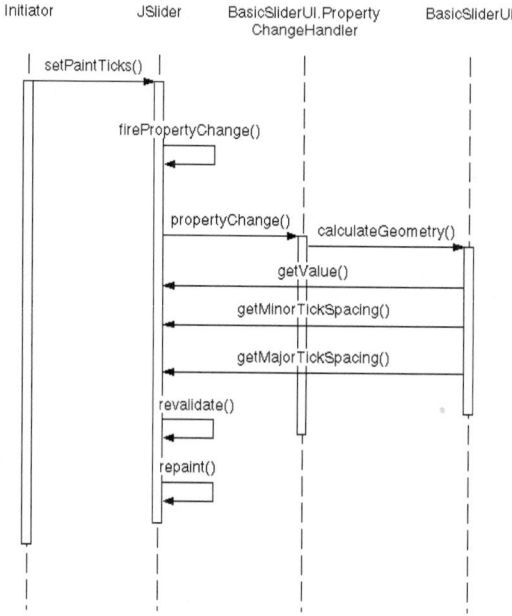

Figure 3-4 Programmatically Setting Model Values

After setting the `paintTicks` property, `JSlider.setPaintTicks()` invokes `firePropertyChange()`, which fires a property change event to the slider's property change listeners. One of the slider's property change listeners is an instance of `BasicSliderUI.PropertyChangeHandler`, which responds to the event by forcing the slider's UI delegate to update its geometry.

After notifying listeners of the change, `JSlider.setPaintTicks()` revalidates and repaints the slider.

Figure 3-5 is similar to the diagram shown in Figure 3-3 on page 81, except that Figure 3-5 is customized for the sequence of events shown in Figure 3-4. When `JSlider.setPaintTicks()` is invoked, the slider updates one of the UI delegate's listeners. The listener subsequently modifies the UI delegate, and the UI delegate obtains information from the component itself.

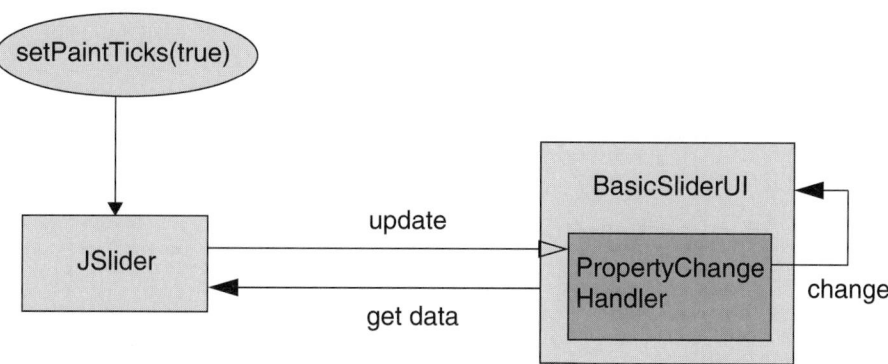

Figure 3-5 Modifying a JSlider Property

Figure 3-6 shows the sequence of events that occurs for a mouse pressed event in a slider's track. The event is dispatched to the slider, which responds by firing an event to its listeners, one of which is an instance of `BasicSliderUI`'s `TrackListener`.

The listener manipulates the slider's UI delegate by invoking `BasicSliderUI.scrollDueToClickInTrack()`. The UI delegate subsequently sets the slider's value with a call to `JSlider.setValue()`, which is a pass-through to `DefaultBoundedRangeModel.setValue()`. See "Swing Components" on page 77 for a discussion of component pass-through methods for model properties.

When the model's value is set, the model fires a state-changed event, which is handled by an instance of `BasicSliderUI.ChangeHandler`. The change listener handles the event by calculating the slider's thumb location and subsequently repainting the component.

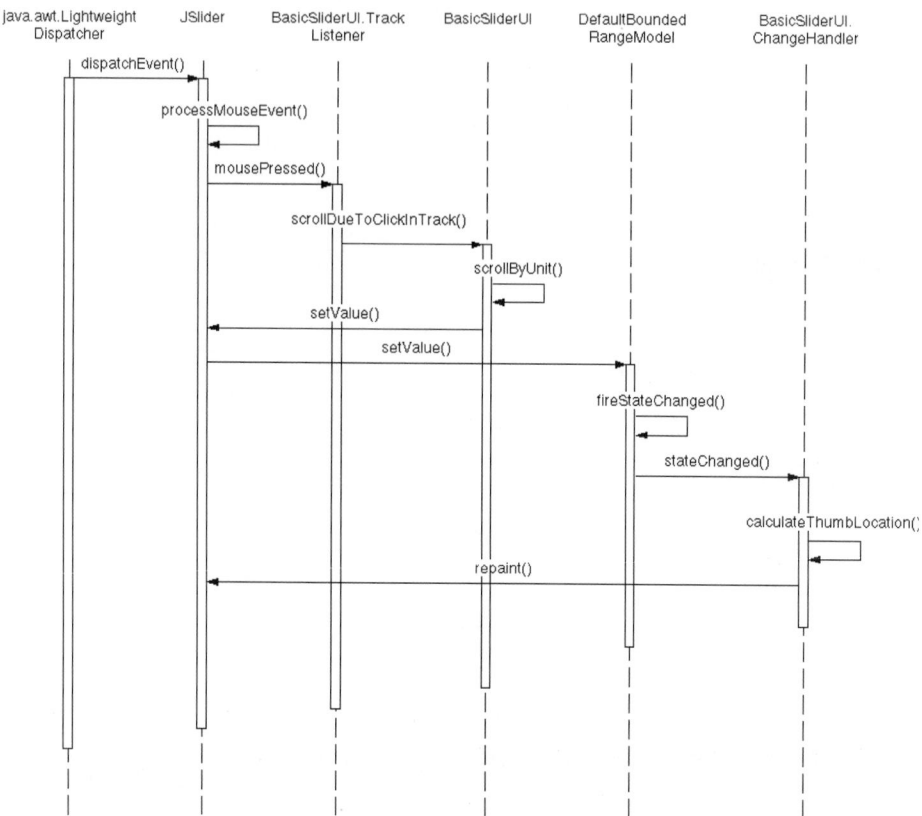

Figure 3-6 Scenario Diagram for Mouse Press in Slider Track

Figure 3-7 diagrams the component communication for the sequence of events illustrated in Figure 3-6. The slider fires an event that is handled by a track listener. The listener modifies the UI delegate, which updates the slider, which in turn updates the model. The model fires a state changed event that is handled by a change listener by repainting the component.

Models

Most lightweight Swing components have a model that maintains state information and fires events when the information changes.[5] For example, a button's model keeps track of, among other things, a button's mnemonic and

5.   Some components, for example, `JSeparator`, do not have models.

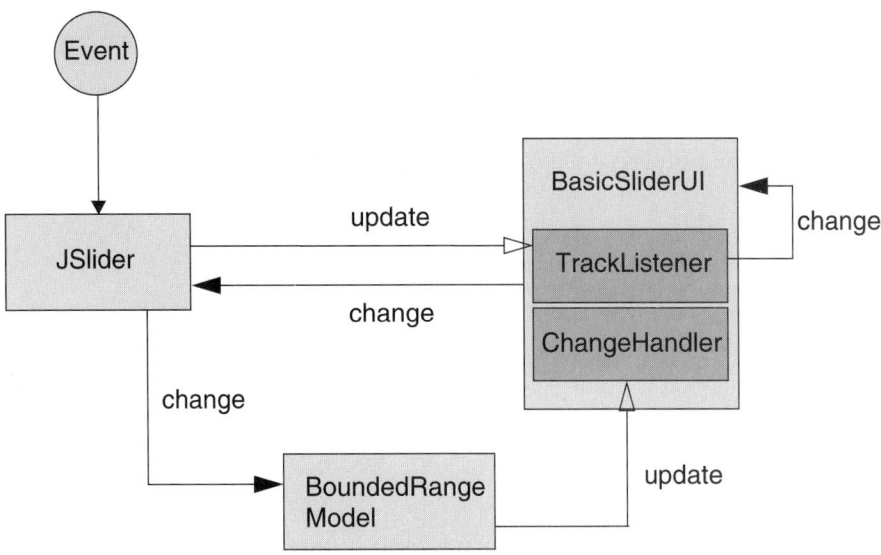

Figure 3-7 Mouse Press in a Slider's Track

Swing Tip ...

Who's Listening?

Swing components are composed of a number of objects; for example, a slider is made up of at least nine objects—see "Slider Component Classes" on page 79. Keeping track of what the objects do and how they interact can be facilitated by remembering who listens to whom.

Components listen to their models, mostly for the purpose of forwarding events to listeners that are registered with the component. Components also provide pass-through methods for model properties. Forwarding model events and providing model property pass-through methods lessens the need to directly access a component's model.

UI delegate listeners listen primarily to a component and on occasion listen directly to a component's model. UI delegates typically react to component and model changes by updating their appearance, which usually involves accessing the component or model for more information about the change.

whether the button is armed, pressed, or selected. Button models fire change events when their model is changed and fire item events when the model's selected status changes.

Models are implemented as JavaBeans bound properties. A property is bound if its modification results in the firing of a property change event, and accessor methods for the property follow the naming convention shown below:

```
public void setModel(<ModelInterface> model)
public <ModelInterface> getModel()
```

<ModelInterface> represents the name of an interface that defines the model type.

Model Events

Models have the potential to fire an enormous number of events. For example, when a slider's thumb (a.k.a. grip) is dragged, the slider's model fires a steady stream of events indicating that the slider's value is changing. Therefore, from a performance perspective, it is not always practical for models to create an event for every event that is fired.

To drastically reduce the number of event objects created by a model, models fire a special type of event defined by the `javax.swing.event.ChangeEvent` class. Change events differ from most other events because they do not contain any information about the event other than the event's source; as a result, *each model can reuse a single change event for all of its change notifications.*

Firing change events is referred to as a *lightweight notification* because so little information is associated with the event. Firing other events, such as action events fired by buttons, for example, is referred to as *stateful notification* because the event contains more state information than just the event source.

Lightweight notifications are used for model properties that are prone to frequent modification. Listeners that listen for lightweight notifications, meaning listeners that implement the `ChangeListener` interface, query the event source obtained from the change event for more information concerning the nature of the change.

Stateful notifications are used for model properties that vary infrequently. For example, removing an element from a list model results in a stateful notification that includes the index of the removed row.

Swing Models

Table 3-1 lists Swing model interfaces and the components associated with the model. The table also indicates whether a model provides lightweight or stateful notification and whether Swing provides an abstract implementation of the model interface.

Table 3-1   Swing Models

Model Interface	Used by ...	Notification[2]	Abstract Class
BoundedRangeModel	JProgressBar, JScrollBar, JSlider	LW	
ButtonModel	JButton, JCheckBox, JCheckBoxMenuItem, JMenu, JMenuItem, JRadioButton, JRadioButtonMenuItem, JToggleButton	LW/ST	
ComboBoxModel	JComboBox	ST	
Document[1]	JEditorPane, JPasswordField, JTextArea, JTextField, JTextPane	ST	•
ListModel	JList	ST	•
ListSelectionModel	JList, JTable	ST	
SingleSelectionModel	JMenuBar, JPopupMenu, JTabbedPane	LW	
TableModel	JTable	ST	•
TableColumnModel	JTable	ST	
TreeModel	JTree	ST	
TreeSelectionModel	JTree	ST	

1. The Document interface resides in the javax.swing.text package
2. LW = lightweight notification, ST = stateful notification

Swing models are all defined by interfaces from the javax.swing package, and all have a default implementation. For example, the ButtonModel interface is implemented by the DefaultButtonModel class, ListModel is implemented by DefaultListModel, and so forth. The default implementations are used when models are not explicitly set for components.

Some models, namely, ListModel, TableModel, and the Document interface from the text package, have abstract implementations provided for developers to extend. Abstract model implementations provide, at the very least, registration

methods for listeners and event firing methods, making them attractive for subclassing. Models that provide abstract implementations represent the more complex Swing models.

Multiple Views for a Single Model

One of the benefits of the MVC architecture is that multiple views can be attached to a single model. Furthermore, because models broadcast changes to their views, all of a model's views are easily kept in sync.

The applet shown in Figure 3-8 contains two components—a slider and a scrollpane—that share a single instance of `DefaultBoundedRangeModel`. The slider uses the model to position its grip, and the scrollpane uses the model to scale the picture it displays.

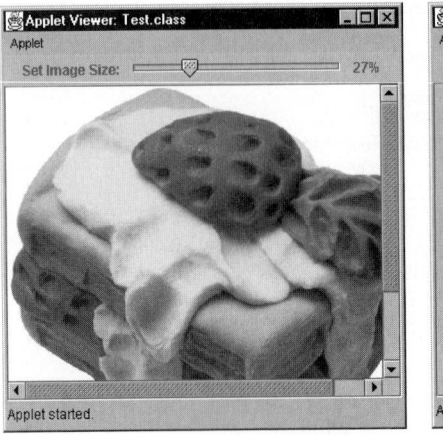 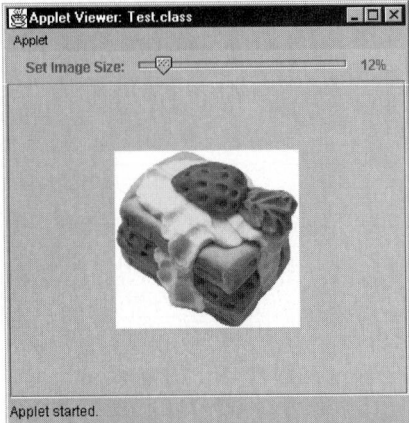

Figure 3-8 A Single Model with Multiple Views

The slider and the scrollpane (`ImageView` instance) share a single instance of `DefaultBoundedRangeModel`. Changing the model's value by adjusting the slider results in a model change notification. The scrollpane responds to the model's notification by scaling the image it displays according to the model's value.

The applet creates the model, slider, and scrollpane. The model is passed to the `JSlider` and `ImageView` constructors, and a change listener is added to the model.

```
public class Test extends JApplet {
    DefaultBoundedRangeModel model =
            new DefaultBoundedRangeModel(100,0,0,100);

    JSlider slider = new JSlider(model);
    JLabel readOut = new JLabel("100%");

    ImageIcon image = new ImageIcon("shortcake.jpg");
    ImageView imageView = new ImageView(image, model);

    public void init() {
        Container contentPane = getContentPane();
        JPanel panel = new JPanel();

        panel.add(new JLabel("Set Image Size:"));
        panel.add(slider);
        panel.add(readOut);

        contentPane.add(panel, BorderLayout.NORTH);
        contentPane.add(imageView, BorderLayout.CENTER);

        model.addChangeListener(new ReadOutSynchronizer());
    }
    ...
```

The applet's change listener reacts to model changes by updating the readOut label that displays the image's scale. The label's revalidate method is invoked so that the label is subsequently laid out and repainted. See "Validate, Invalidate, and Revalidate Methods" on page 144 for more information concerning the revalidate method.

```
    ...
    class ReadOutSynchronizer implements ChangeListener {
        public void stateChanged(ChangeEvent e) {
            String s = Integer.toString(model.getValue());
            readOut.setText(s + "%");
            readOut.revalidate();
        }
    }
}
```

The ImageView class extends JScrollPane and must be constructed with an image icon and a bounded range model. See "Borders, Icons, and Actions" on page 203 for more information concerning icons, and see "JScrollPane" on page 739 for scrollpanes.

The `ImageView` constructor adds a change listener to the model. The change listener is implemented as an `ImageView` inner class that creates a scaled instance of the original image depending upon the model's value. The scaled instance of the original image is subsequently displayed in the scrollpane.

```
class ImageView extends JScrollPane {
   ...
   public ImageView(ImageIcon icon, BoundedRangeModel model) {
      ...
      model.addChangeListener(new ModelListener());
      ...
   }
   class ModelListener implements ChangeListener {
      public void stateChanged(ChangeEvent e) {
         BoundedRangeModel model =
                        (BoundedRangeModel)e.getSource();

         if( ! model.getValueIsAdjusting()) {
            int min = model.getMinimum(),
                max = model.getMaximum(),
                span = max - min,
                value = model.getValue();

            double multiplier = (double)value / (double)span;

            multiplier = multiplier == 0.0 ?
                        0.01 : multiplier;

            Image scaled = originalImage.getScaledInstance(
                (int)(originalSize.width * multiplier),
                (int)(originalSize.height * multiplier),
                Image.SCALE_FAST);

            icon.setImage(scaled);
            ...
         }
      }
   }
}
```

The applet shown in Figure 3-8 is listed in its entirety in Example 3-1.

Example 3-1 A Single Model with Multiple Views

```
import javax.swing.*;
import javax.swing.event.*;
import java.awt.*;
import java.awt.event.*;
import java.util.*;
```

```
public class Test extends JApplet {
    DefaultBoundedRangeModel model =
            new DefaultBoundedRangeModel(100,0,0,100);

    JSlider slider = new JSlider(model);
    JLabel readOut = new JLabel("100%");

    ImageIcon image = new ImageIcon("shortcake.jpg");
    ImageView imageView = new ImageView(image, model);

    public void init() {
        Container contentPane = getContentPane();
        JPanel panel = new JPanel();

        panel.add(new JLabel("Set Image Size:"));
        panel.add(slider);
        panel.add(readOut);

        contentPane.add(panel, BorderLayout.NORTH);
        contentPane.add(imageView, BorderLayout.CENTER);

        model.addChangeListener(new ReadOutSynchronizer());
    }
    class ReadOutSynchronizer implements ChangeListener {
        public void stateChanged(ChangeEvent e) {
            if( ! model.getValueIsAdjusting()) {
                String s = Integer.toString(model.getValue());
                readOut.setText(s + "%");
                readOut.revalidate();
            }
        }
    }
}
class ImageView extends JScrollPane {
    JPanel panel = new JPanel();
    Dimension originalSize = new Dimension();
    Image originalImage;
    ImageIcon icon;

    public ImageView(ImageIcon icon, BoundedRangeModel model) {
        panel.setLayout(new BorderLayout());
        panel.add(new JLabel(icon));

        this.icon = icon;
        this.originalImage = icon.getImage();

        setViewportView(panel);
        model.addChangeListener(new ModelListener());

        originalSize.width = icon.getIconWidth();
        originalSize.height = icon.getIconHeight();
```

```
        }
        class ModelListener implements ChangeListener {
            public void stateChanged(ChangeEvent e) {
                BoundedRangeModel model =
                                (BoundedRangeModel)e.getSource();

                if( ! model.getValueIsAdjusting()) {
                    int min = model.getMinimum(),
                        max = model.getMaximum(),
                        span = max - min,
                        value = model.getValue();

                    double multiplier = (double)value / (double)span;

                    multiplier = multiplier == 0.0 ?
                                    0.01 : multiplier;

                    Image scaled = originalImage.getScaledInstance(
                        (int)(originalSize.width * multiplier),
                        (int)(originalSize.height * multiplier),
                        Image.SCALE_FAST);

                    icon.setImage(scaled);
                    panel.revalidate();
                }
            }
        }
    }
```

Lightweight Event Notification

Recall from "Models" on page 86 that models provide both lightweight and stateful notifications, where the former uses a ChangeEvent that knows only the event source and the latter uses events that provide more information about the change at hand.

Change events are handled by objects whose class implements the ChangeListener interface, which is summarized in Interface Summary 3-1.

Interface Summary 3-1   ChangeListener

public abstract void <u>stateChanged</u>(ChangeEvent)

Like most listeners, the ChangeListener interface defines a single method. The stateChanged method is passed an instance of ChangeEvent, which is summarized in Class Summary 3-1.

Class Summary 3-1   ChangeEvent

Extends: java.util.EventObject

Constructors

public <u>ChangeEvent</u>(Object source)

The ChangeEvent class provides a single constructor and no methods. The ChangeEvent constructor is passed the source of the event.

Although it may appear from Class Summary 3-1 that there is no way to manipulate a change event, the ChangeEvent class inherits a getSource method from java.util.EventObject.

The applet shown in Figure 3-9 illustrates lightweight notification by monitoring the value of a slider. A change listener is added to the applet's slider to obtain the slider's value and update the applet's status area.

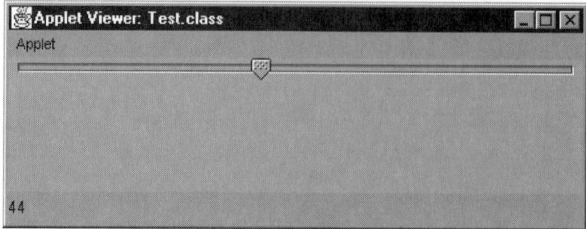

Figure 3-9 Lightweight Notification

The applet shown in Figure 3-9 is listed in Example 3-2.

Example 3-2 Lightweight Notification from a Slider

```
import java.awt.*;
import javax.swing.*;
import javax.swing.event.*;

public class Test extends JApplet {
    public void init() {
        JSlider slider = new JSlider(0,100,50);

        getContentPane().add(slider, BorderLayout.CENTER);

        slider.addChangeListener(new ChangeListener() {
            public void stateChanged(ChangeEvent e) {
                JSlider s = (JSlider)e.getSource();
                showStatus(Integer.toString(s.getValue()));
            }
        });
    }
}
```

Stateful Event Notification

For model properties that change infrequently, models use stateful notification. Stateful notifications fire all types of events and provide more information than just the event source, as is the case for lightweight event notification. For example, a button model fires an item event when a radio button is selected or deselected.

Property Change Notification

Models make stateful notifications—in the form of a
java.beans.PropertyChangeEvent—when their bound properties[6] are
modified. Property change notifications are handled by objects whose class
implements the java.beans.PropertyChangeListener interface, which is
summarized in Interface Summary 3-2.

Interface Summary 3-2   PropertyChangeListener

---

public void propertyChange(PropertyChangeEvent)

The PropertyChangeListener defines a single method that is passed an
instance of PropertyChangeEvent. The PropertyChangeEvent class is
summarized in Class Summary 3-2.

Class Summary 3-2   PropertyChangeEvent

Extends: java.util.EventObject

Constructors

---

public PropertyChangeEvent(Object source, String propertyName,
                    Object oldValue, Object newValue)

---

6.   A property is bound by definition, when its modification results in the firing of a
     property change event.

Property change events are constructed with the event source, the property's name, and the property's old and new values.

Methods

---

public String <u>getPropertyName</u>()

public Object <u>getNewValue</u>()
public Object <u>getOldValue</u>()

public void <u>setPropagationId</u>(Object propagationId)
public Object <u>getPropagationId</u>()

Property change listeners are almost always interested in the name of the property that changed because most listeners are selective about the properties they handle. Likewise, nearly all property change listeners are interested in the property's new value. Property change listeners are typically implemented in the following fashion:

```
// code fragment ...

SomePropertyChangeListener implements PropertyChangeListener {
    public void propertyChange(PropertyChangeEvent e) {
        String name = e.getName();

        // if property is one this listener is interested in ...
        if(name.equals("PropertyImInterestedIn")) {
            SomeType newValue = (SomeType)e.getNewValue();

            // act upon new value ...
        }
    }
}
```

The application shown in Figure 3-10 illustrates handling model property change events with a simple tree and a check box for setting the tree's rootVisible property. If the property is true, the tree's root node is visible; otherwise, it is hidden.

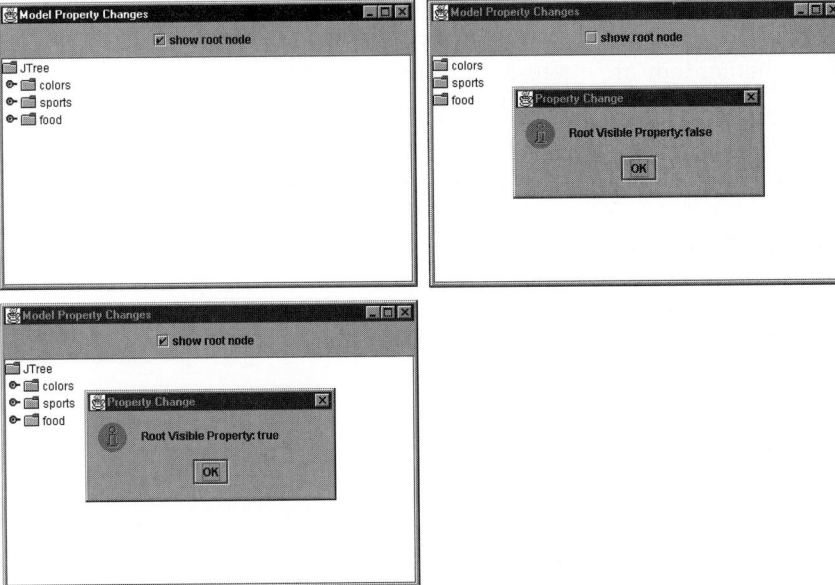

Figure 3-10 Model Property Change Notification

The application implements a property change listener that displays a message dialog whenever the tree's rootVisible property is modified.

```
class PropertyListener implements PropertyChangeListener {
    public void propertyChange(PropertyChangeEvent e) {
        String name = e.getPropertyName();

        if(name.equals(JTree.ROOT_VISIBLE_PROPERTY)) {
            String msg = "Root Visible Property: " +
                            e.getNewValue().toString();

            JOptionPane.showMessageDialog(
                    Test.this,           // parent comp
                    msg,                 // message
                    "Property Change",   // title
                    JOptionPane.INFORMATION_MESSAGE);
        }
    }
}
```

Most property change listeners are interested only in a subset of bound properties for a particular type of event source. Property change listeners typically determine whether they are interested in handling a property change by obtaining the name of the property that was changed and comparing it to a public constant. This is the case for the property change listener listed above.

The application shown in Figure 3-10 is listed in its entirety in Example 3-3.

Example 3-3 Handling Model Property Change Notification

```java
import javax.swing.*;
import java.awt.*;
import java.awt.event.*;
import java.util.*;
import java.beans.*;

public class Test extends JFrame {
    JTree tree = new JTree();

    public Test() {
        Container contentPane = getContentPane();
        JScrollPane scrollPane = new JScrollPane(tree);

        contentPane.add(new ControlPanel(), BorderLayout.NORTH);
        contentPane.add(scrollPane, BorderLayout.CENTER);

        tree.addPropertyChangeListener(new PropertyListener());
    }
    class ControlPanel extends JPanel {
        JCheckBox showRoot = new JCheckBox("show root node");

        public ControlPanel() {
            showRoot.setSelected(tree.isRootVisible());

            setLayout(new FlowLayout());
            add(showRoot);

            showRoot.addActionListener(new ActionListener() {
                public void actionPerformed(ActionEvent e) {
                    tree.setRootVisible(showRoot.isSelected());
                }
            });
        }
    }
    class PropertyListener implements PropertyChangeListener {
        public void propertyChange(PropertyChangeEvent e) {
            String name = e.getPropertyName();
```

```
        if(name.equals(JTree.ROOT_VISIBLE_PROPERTY)) {
            String msg = "Root Visible Property: " +
                        e.getNewValue().toString();

            JOptionPane.showMessageDialog(
                Test.this,          // parent comp
                msg,                        // message
                "Property Change", // title
                JOptionPane.INFORMATION_MESSAGE);
            }
        }
    }
    public static void main(String args[]) {
        GJApp.launch(new Test(),
                "Model Property Changes",300,300,450,300);
    }
}
```

Swing Tip ...

Multiple Views for a Model

The fact that Swing's models can have multiple views is often met with a yawn. At first glance it may seem that multiple views are somewhat frivolous; for example, what value is there in having a progress bar and scrollbar share a model?

The applet shown in Figure 3-8 on page 88 offers a subtle example of a single model represented by multiple views. The applet's slider and scrollpane share a model so that changes to the slider are reflected in the image displayed in the scrollpane.

There are many other circumstances in which a model can be represented by more than one view. For example, a table model could be shared between a JTable instance and a custom component that painted a graph of the data contained in the table model. Separating models from their views makes Swing components more flexible and reusable.

UI Delegates

Components *delegate* the implementation of their user interface (UI) to a UI delegate, which is where UI delegates get their name.

UI delegates are instantiated in their component's constructor and are accessible through the component as a bound property. For example, the code from `JSlider.java` listed below illustrates how a slider creates its UI delegate and how a slider's UI delegate is accessed.

```java
// From JSlider.java:
// Note: the ui object below is a protected member of JComponent

class JSlider extends JComponent
                        implements SwingConstants, Accessible {
    ...
    public JSlider(int orientation, int min, int max, int value) {
        ...
        updateUI();
    }
    ...
    public void updateUI() {
        ...
        setUI((SliderUI)UIManager.getUI(this));
    }
    ...
    public SliderUI getUI() {
        return (SliderUI)ui;
    }
    ...
}
```

`JSlider`, like all other lightweight Swing components, obtains a UI delegate from the `UIManager`. "Installing a UI Delegate" on page 104 discusses the manner in which `UIManager.getUI()` instantiates a UI delegate; for this discussion, it is enough to understand that `UIManager.getUI()` returns a UI delegate.

Table 3-2 shows the methods defined in the `JComponent` class that involve a component's UI delegate.[7]

---

7. The `JComponent` class is the superclass of all lightweight Swing components—see "The JComponent Class" chapter on page 123.

Table 3-2   JComponent UI Delegate Methods

Method[1]	Description
<UI> getUI()	Returns a reference to a component's UI delegate
void setUI(<UI>)	Sets a component's UI delegate
void updateUI()	Updates a component's UI delegate for the current look and feel
String getUIClassID()	Returns a string that identifies the class name of the UI delegate

1. <UI> = UI delegate class name; for example, ButtonUI, LabelUI, etc.

All lightweight Swing components inherit the methods listed in Table 3-2 for setting and getting their UI delegate, in addition to updateUI(), which updates the UI delegate to match the current look and feel. The getUIClassID method returns a string identifying the class of a component's UI delegate and is used to instantiate UI delegates; see "Installing a UI Delegate" on page 104 for a discussion of creating UI delegates.

The <UI> in Table 3-2 represents the class name of a component's UI delegate. For example, JButton defines the first two methods listed in Table 3-2 like this:

```
ButtonUI getUI()
void setUI(ButtonUI ui)
```

Class names for UI delegates can be obtained by removing the "J" from the component's class name and adding a "UI". For example, the UI delegate class name for JButton is ButtonUI; for JSlider, it is SliderUI.

The UI delegate class names represent abstract classes from the javax.swing.plaf package; for example, the fully qualified class name for a button's UI delegate is the abstract javax.swing.plaf.ButtonUI.

The javax.swing.plaf package also contains the abstract ComponentUI class, which defines fundamental behavior for all UI delegates; see "The ComponentUI Class" on page 106. The ComponentUI class is the superclass of the abstract UI delegate classes in javax.swing.plaf; for example, ButtonUI and SliderUI—in addition to all other javax.swing.plaf UI classes—extend javax.swing.plaf.ComponentUI.

The `javax.swing.plaf.basic` package provides classes that implement aspects of look and feels that are common across the standard Swing look and feels. UI delegate classes from the `javax.swing.plaf.basic` package provide default painting and event handling behavior that can be overridden by look-and-feel specific classes if necessary.

Figure 3-11 shows a class diagram for the `BasicSliderUI` class.

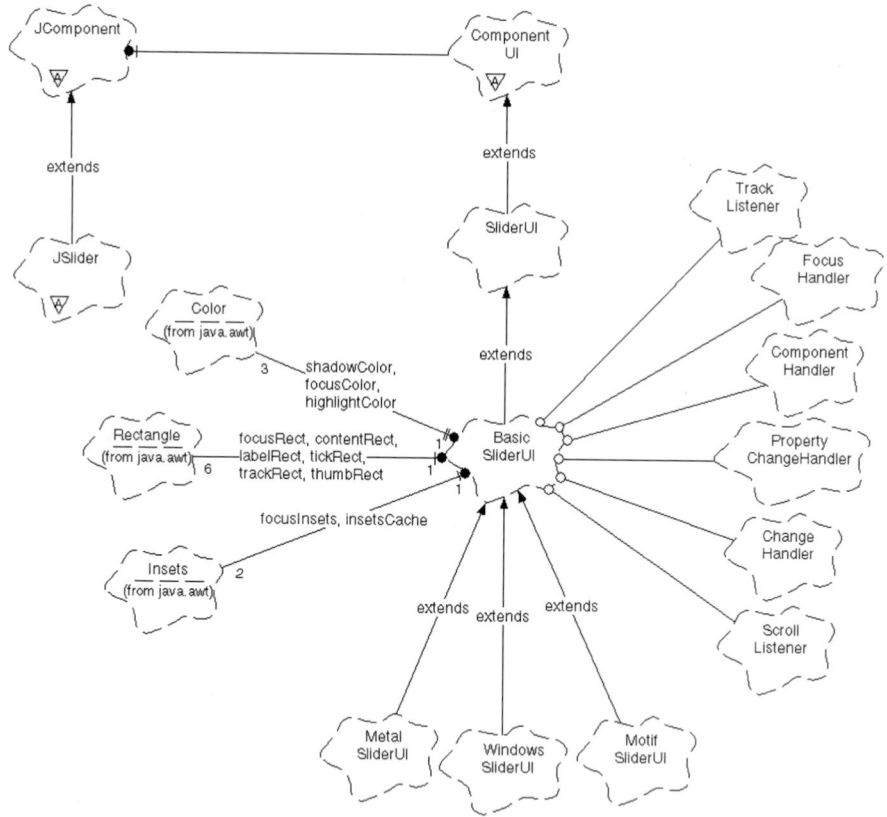

Figure 3-11 BasicSliderUI Class Diagram

A slider's UI delegate keeps track of properties for the visual representation of a slider. Slider UI delegates also use a number of listeners for default event handling behavior.

The `BasicSliderUI` class is extended by look-and-feel-specific slider UI classes, such as `MetalSliderUI`, `WindowsSliderUI`, and `MotifSiderUI`.

As with the model discussion in "Models" on page 86, the UI delegate discussion shifts from a static to dynamic perspective with an examination of UI delegate scenarios.

Component UI Scenarios

To understand how UI delegates work with their components, it is important to understand two key scenarios: when a UI delegate paints and when it is installed in a component.

UI Delegate Painting

The diagram shown in Figure 3-12 shows the sequence of events that occurs when Swing buttons are painted.[8] The sequence shown in Figure 3-12 is similar for all lightweight Swing components.

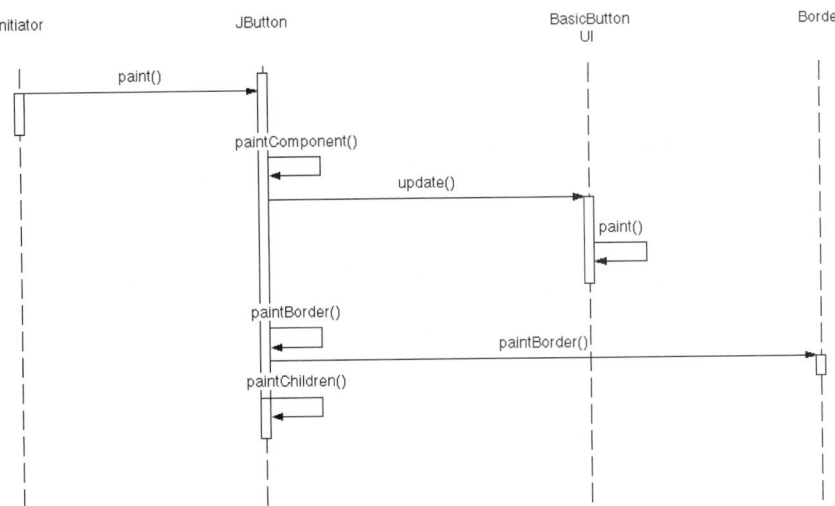

Figure 3-12 Swing Lightweight Component Painting

8. See "Rendering JComponents" on page 137 for a more detailed look at painting Swing lightweight components.

`JButton.paintComponent()` invokes the `update` method for the button's UI delegate. `BasicButtonUI.paint()` paints the component, and the button subsequently paints the button's border and the component's children.

As Figure 3-12 illustrates, component classes such as `JLabel`, `JButton`, etc., share painting duties with their UI delegates. UI delegates are responsible for painting the component itself, and the component class takes care of painting the component's border and the component's children.[9]

Installing a UI Delegate

Figure 3-13 illustrates the sequence of events that take place when a UI delegate is plugged into a component.

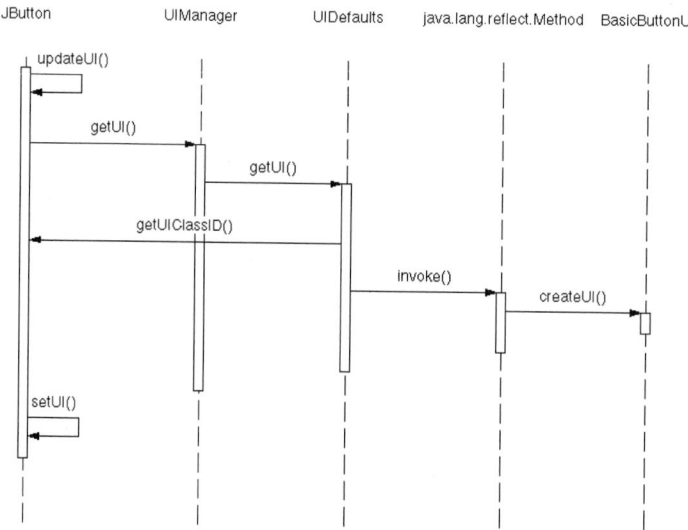

Figure 3-13 Installing a UI Delegate

`JButton.updateUI()` is invoked from `JButton` constructors. `JButton.updateUI()`, like the `updateUI` methods for other lightweight Swing components, obtains its UI delegate from the UI manager. The button passes a reference to itself to `UIManager.getUI()`:

9. Most components do not have children.

```
// From JButton.java:

public void updateUI() {
    setUI((ButtonUI)UIManager.getUI(this));
}
```

UIManager.getUI() uses an instance of UIDefaults to create the UI delegate by invoking UIDefaults.getUI().

```
// From UIManager.java:

public static ComponentUI getUI(JComponent target) {
    ...
    ComponentUI ui = null;
    ...
    if (ui == null) {
        ui = getDefaults().getUI(target);
    }
    return ui;
}
```

UIDefaults.getUI() is where all the action takes place as far as instantiating UI delegates. The UIDefaults.getUI method is listed below.

```
// From UIDefaults.java:

public ComponentUI getUI(JComponent target) {
    ClassLoader uiClassLoader =
                target.getClass().getClassLoader();

    Class uiClass = getUIClass(target.getUIClassID(),
                              uiClassLoader);
    Object uiObject = null;

    if (uiClass == null) {
        getUIError("no ComponentUI class for: " + target);
    }
    else {
        try {
            Method m = (Method)get(uiClass);

            if (m == null) {
                Class acClass = javax.swing.JComponent.class;
                m = uiClass.getMethod("createUI",
                                     new Class[]{acClass});
                put(uiClass, m);
            }
```

```
        uiObject = m.invoke(null, new Object[]{target});
    }
    catch (NoSuchMethodException e) {
        getUIError("static createUI() method not " +
                    "found in " + uiClass);
    }
    catch (Exception e) {
        getUIError("createUI() failed for " + target +
                    " " + e);
    }
}
return (ComponentUI)uiObject;
}
```

UIDefaults.getUI() must be able to instantiate any type of UI delegate. For example, MetalSliderUI instances must be instantiated for sliders if the current look and feel is the Java look and feel, and WindowsSliderUI instances for the Windows look and feel, etc. Additionally, UIDefaults.getUI() must be able to instantiate UI delegate instances that will be developed in the future. Obviously, instantiating UI delegates with a new statement is not a viable option.

To instantiate UI delegates of any type, UIDefaults.getUI() uses Java reflection. UIDefaults.getUI() is passed a reference to the component for which the UI delegate is being created. The component is used to obtain a reference to the UI delegate's class.

With the UI delegate's class in hand, reflection is used to obtain a reference to the UI delegate's static createUI method, and the method is subsequently invoked—with the component as an argument—with Method.invoke(). All UI delegates implement a static createUI method that returns a reference to a UI delegate. See "The ComponentUI Class" for more information concerning the createUI method.

The ComponentUI Class

The ComponentUI class from the swing.plaf package is the abstract base class for all Swing UI delegates. UI delegates do not maintain a reference to a component; instead, ComponentUI methods are passed a reference to a JComponent. As a result, one UI delegate can be shared among any number of Swing components. Sharing objects that operate on JComponents is a central theme in Swing—borders and icons, for instance, are designed to be shared in a similar manner.[10]

The ComponentUI class resides in the swing.plaf package and implements the following responsibilities:

- Installs and uninstalls itself for a component
- Paints and updates a component
- Reports preferred, minimum, and maximum sizes for a component
- Reports whether a point is contained inside a component
- Returns an instance of the UI that can be shared among components

Class Summary 3-3 lists the public methods implemented by the ComponentUI class.

Class Summary 3-3   javax.swing.plaf.ComponentUI

Extends: java.lang.Object

Constructors

---

public ComponentUI()

The lone constructor is generated by the compiler (and therefore has an empty implementation) because ComponentUI does not explicitly implement any constructors.

Instances of ComponentUI cannot be instantiated because the class is abstract. Therefore, the constructor for swing.plaf.ComponentUI is only invoked from the constructor of an extension class.

Extensions of ComponentUI are typically instantiated through the static createUI method.

10. See the "Borders, Icons, and Actions" chapter beginning on page 203.

Methods

UI Creation

---

public static ComponentUI <u>createUI</u>(JComponent)

In order to promote sharing and enable the use of reflection to instantiate UI delegates, UI delegates are never directly instantiated outside of their class. Instead, the `static createUI` method is invoked to obtain a UI for a given component, in a manner similar to the `MotifButtonUI`'s approach:

```
// from swing.plaf.motif.MotifButtonUI:

private final static MotifButtonUI motifButtonUI =
                                new MotifButtonUI();
...
public static ComponentUI createUI(JComponent c) {
   return motifButtonUI;
}
```

If a single UI delegate can be shared among all instances of a particular component, `createUI` is overridden to return a reference to a single UI instance. For instance, all Swing buttons that have a `Motif` look and feel share a single instance of `MotifButtonUI`. As a result, `MotifButtonUI.createUI()` returns a reference to a `static` instance of `MotifButtonUI`.

`swing.plaf.ComponentUI.createUI()` throws an error indicating that the method must be implemented by extensions of the `ComponentUI` class. The message associated with the error states: "`ComponentUI.createUI` not implemented."

Installing / Uninstalling

---

public void <u>installUI</u>(JComponent)
public void <u>uninstallUI</u>(JComponent)

UI delegates are often required to perform one or more actions when they are installed or uninstalled on a component. Typically, such actions include adding or removing listeners or setting keyboard actions. UI delegates are careful to ensure

that actions taken at the time of installation are undone when the UI delegate is uninstalled, in order to leave the component in the same state it was in before the UI delegate was installed.

Both the `installUI` and `uninstallUI` methods in the `swing.plaf.ComponentUI` class are implemented as no-ops.

Painting / Updating / Hit Detection

public void <u>paint</u>(Graphics, JComponent)

public void <u>update</u>(Graphics, JComponent)

public boolean <u>contains</u>(JComponent, int, int)

UI delegates are also responsible for painting and updating components. It is up to extensions of the `ComponentUI` class to implement the `paint` method—the `ComponentUI` version of `paint()` does nothing. `ComponentUI.update()` clears the background of the component only if the component is opaque. After taking care of the background, `update()` invokes `paint()`. See "Sequence Diagram for JComponent.paint()" on page 137 for an overall look at the painting sequence for Swing components.

The `contains` method returns a `boolean` value indicating whether a point lies within the bounds of a particular component. By default, the `contains` method returns the value of `JComponent.contains(int x, int y)` for the component in question. For components that are to appear nonrectangular, `ComponentUI.contains` can be overridden to take into account the component's shape.

Component Size

public Dimension <u>getMaximumSize</u>(JComponent)
public Dimension <u>getMinimumSize</u>(JComponent)

public Dimension <u>getPreferredSize</u>(JComponent)

Calculating preferred, minimum, and maximum sizes for a component is also a responsibility of a component UI. `ComponentUI.getPreferredSize()` returns a `null` dimension, so obviously it must be overridden by extensions. By default, the minimum and maximum sizes are the same as the preferred size; both `ComponentUI.getMaximumSize()` and `ComponetUI.getMinimumSize()` return the value returned by `ComponentUI.getPreferredSize()`. Extensions of `ComponentUI` typically override either `getMinimumSize()` or `getMaximumSize()`.

Swing Tip ...

Multiple Components for a UI Delegate

Just as a model can have multiple views, UI delegates can—and often do—have multiple components. Every public method defined in the ComponentUI class is passed a reference to a JComponent, which means that extensions of ComponentUI can be used with multiple components.

ComponentUI extensions must override the static ComponentUI.createUI method to return a reference to a UI delegate. For UI delegates that can be used with multiple components, the createUI method often returns the same UI delegate reference every time it is called.

Custom UI Delegates

It is a fairly simple matter to implement custom UI delegates that can be used with specific components or with all components of a given type.

The applet show in Figure 3-14 implements a custom UI delegate—`PopOutButton`—that is specified as the UI delegate for the applet's button. The UI delegate uses a larger version of the button's icon as a rollover icon and as the icon when the button is armed.

The top-left picture in Figure 3-14 shows the applet just before the cursor enters the button, and the top-right picture shows the applet just after cursor has entered the button. The bottom-left picture shows the applet while the button is armed—meaning the mouse is being held down over the button—and the bottom-right picture shows the applet after the button has been activated. The button appears to pop out when the mouse enters the button or the button is activated.

Figure 3-14 A Custom Look and Feel

The applet creates a button and sets its UI delegate to an instance of
PopOutButtonUI. The button is subsequently added to the applet's content pane.

```
public class Test extends JApplet {
    private String s = new String();

    public void init() {
        Container contentPane = getContentPane();
        JButton button = new JButton(new ImageIcon("punch.gif"));

        button.setUI(new PopOutButtonUI());
        contentPane.setLayout(new FlowLayout());
        contentPane.add(button);
    }
}
```

The PopOutButtonUI class extends BasicButtonUI and overrides the
following ComponentUI methods:

public void <u>installUI</u>(JComponent)
public void <u>uninstall</u>(JComponent)
public Dimension <u>getPreferredSize</u>()
public boolean <u>contains</u>(JComponent, int x, int y)
public void <u>paint</u>(Graphics, JComponent)

The installUI method obtains the button's border and saves it as a client property of the component; see "Client Properties" on page 186 for a discussion of components and client properties. The border is stored with the button as a client property because the installUI method sets the button's border to null, and therefore the border must be retrieved in the uninstallUI method and restored.

The installUI method also creates a version of the button's icon that is 30 percent larger than the original image. The large image is specified as the button's rollover icon.

```
class PopOutButtonUI extends BasicButtonUI {
    public void installUI(JComponent c) {
        AbstractButton button = (AbstractButton)c;
        Border border = button.getBorder();

        ImageIcon icon = (ImageIcon)button.getIcon();
        int iconW = icon.getIconWidth();
        int iconH = icon.getIconHeight();

        Image scaled = icon.getImage().getScaledInstance(
                            iconW + (iconW/3),
                            iconH + (iconH/3),
                            Image.SCALE_SMOOTH);

        c.putClientProperty("oldBorder", border);
        c.setBorder(null);

        button.setRolloverIcon(new ImageIcon(scaled));
        installListeners(button);
    }
    public void uninstallUI(JComponent c) {
        Border border = (Border)c.getClientProperty("oldBorder");

        c.putClientProperty("oldBorder", null);
        c.setBorder(border);
        uninstallListeners((AbstractButton)c);
    }
    . . .
```

Notice that the installUI and uninstallUI methods invoke installListeners and uninstallListeners, respectively, to ensure that the listeners implemented by the superclass (BasicButtonUI) are installed and uninstalled.

UI delegates are responsible for providing a preferred size for a component. `PopOutButtonUI` reports a preferred size that is 30 percent larger than the preferred size calculated by `PopOutButtonUI`'s superclass. The increase in preferred size is necessary to accommodate the large icon.

```
...
public Dimension getPreferredSize(JComponent c) {
    Dimension ps = super.getPreferredSize(c);

    ps.width += ps.width/3;
    ps.height += ps.height/3;

    return ps;
}
...
```

The `contains` method is used for hit detection in a component. `PopOutButtonUI` overrides `contains()` so that only points within the bounds of the icon currently displayed are defined as contained by the button.

```
...
public boolean contains(JComponent c, int x, int y) {
    AbstractButton button = (AbstractButton)c;
    ButtonModel model = button.getModel();
    Icon icon = getIcon(button, model);

    Rectangle iconBounds = new Rectangle(
            0,0,icon.getIconWidth(),icon.getIconHeight());

    return iconBounds.contains(x,y);
}
...
```

The `paint` method is overridden to simply paint the appropriate icon. The icon is obtained from a `private getIcon` method that returns the button's rollover icon if the button's state is rollover or pressed; otherwise, the button's original icon is returned.

```
    . . .
    public void paint(Graphics g, JComponent c) {
        AbstractButton button = (AbstractButton)c;
        ButtonModel model = button.getModel();

        Icon icon = getIcon(button, model);
        Insets insets = c.getInsets();

        icon.paintIcon(c,g,insets.left,insets.top);
    }
    private Icon getIcon(AbstractButton b, ButtonModel m) {
        return (m.isRollover() && ! m.isPressed()) ?
                b.getRolloverIcon() : b.getIcon();
    }
}
```

The applet shown in Figure 3-14 is listed in its entirety in Example 3-4.

Example 3-4   A Custom UI Delegate

```
import javax.swing.*;
import javax.swing.border.*;
import javax.swing.plaf.basic.*;
import java.awt.*;
import java.awt.event.*;

public class Test extends JApplet {
    private String s = new String();

    public void init() {
        Container contentPane = getContentPane();
        JButton button = new JButton(new ImageIcon("punch.gif"));

        button.setUI(new PopOutButtonUI());
        contentPane.setLayout(new FlowLayout());
        contentPane.add(button);

        button.addActionListener(new ActionListener() {
            public void actionPerformed(ActionEvent e) {
                showStatus(s += '+');
            }
        });
    }
}
class PopOutButtonUI extends BasicButtonUI {
    static protected BasicButtonListener listener;

    public void installUI(JComponent c) {
        AbstractButton button = (AbstractButton)c;
        Border border = button.getBorder();

        ImageIcon icon = (ImageIcon)button.getIcon();
        int iconW = icon.getIconWidth();
        int iconH = icon.getIconHeight();
```

```
        Image scaled = icon.getImage().getScaledInstance(
                         iconW + (iconW/3),
                         iconH + (iconH/3),
                         Image.SCALE_SMOOTH);

        c.putClientProperty("oldBorder", border);
        c.setBorder(null);

        button.setRolloverIcon(new ImageIcon(scaled));
        installListeners(button);
    }
    public void uninstallUI(JComponent c) {
        Border border = (Border)c.getClientProperty("oldBorder");

        c.putClientProperty("oldBorder", null);
        c.setBorder(border);
        uninstallListeners((AbstractButton)c);
    }
    public Dimension getPreferredSize(JComponent c) {
        Dimension ps = super.getPreferredSize(c);

        ps.width += ps.width/3;
        ps.height += ps.height/3;

        return ps;
    }
    public boolean contains(JComponent c, int x, int y) {
        AbstractButton button = (AbstractButton)c;
        ButtonModel model = button.getModel();
        Icon icon = getIcon(button, model);

        Rectangle iconBounds = new Rectangle(
                0,0,icon.getIconWidth(),icon.getIconHeight());

        return iconBounds.contains(x,y);
    }
    public void paint(Graphics g, JComponent c) {
        AbstractButton button = (AbstractButton)c;
        ButtonModel model = button.getModel();

        Icon icon = getIcon(button, model);
        Insets insets = c.getInsets();

        icon.paintIcon(c,g,insets.left,insets.top);
    }
    private Icon getIcon(AbstractButton b, ButtonModel m) {
        return (m.isRollover() && ! m.isPressed()) ?
                b.getRolloverIcon() : b.getIcon();
    }
}
```

Listeners

If a lightweight Swing component reacts to events—as nearly all of them do—it has one or more listeners that are implemented as inner classes of the component's UI delegate.[11]

UI delegates typically implement `protected installListeners` and `uninstallListeners` methods that are invoked from `installUI` and `uninstallUI`, respectively, as illustrated in "Custom UI Delegates" on page 110. For example, `BasicSliderUI.installListeners()` and BasicSliderUI.`uninstallListeners()` are listed below:

```
// From javax.swing.plaf.basic.BasicSliderUI:

protected void installListeners( JSlider slider ) {
    slider.addMouseListener(trackListener);
    slider.addMouseMotionListener(trackListener);
    slider.addFocusListener(focusListener);
    slider.addComponentListener(componentListener);
    slider.addPropertyChangeListener( propertyChangeListener );
    slider.getModel().addChangeListener(changeListener);
}
...
protected void uninstallListeners( JSlider slider ) {
    slider.removeMouseListener(trackListener);
    slider.removeMouseMotionListener(trackListener);
    slider.removeFocusListener(focusListener);
    slider.removeComponentListener(componentListener);
    slider.removePropertyChangeListener(
                                    propertyChangeListener );
    slider.getModel().removeChangeListener(changeListener);
}
```

By default, every slider has six listeners listening for various types of events. All but one of the listeners listens to the slider; the change listener listens directly to the slider's model.

---

11. Buttons, which have a `public` BasicButtonListener class, are the exception to the rule.

Custom Listeners

Because lightweight Swing components have pluggable UI delegates, a component's event handling is also pluggable.

Most UI delegates that extend classes from the `javax.swing.plaf.basic` package implement listeners as inner classes. Event listeners that are implemented as inner classes of a UI delegate class should only be instantiated in the UI delegate class or its extensions.[12] As a result, implementing a custom listener means implementing a custom UI delegate.

The applet shown in Figure 3-15 contains a slider with a custom UI delegate—an instance of `AnnotatedSliderUI`.

The UI delegate annotates sliders with a readout of the slider's value if the slider has a client property named `AnnotatedSliderUI.annotate` with a `true` value. If a slider does not have an annotate client property or the property's value is `false`, the UI delegate does not annotate the slider. The applet shown in Figure 3-15 provides a check box for setting the slider's annotate client property.[13]

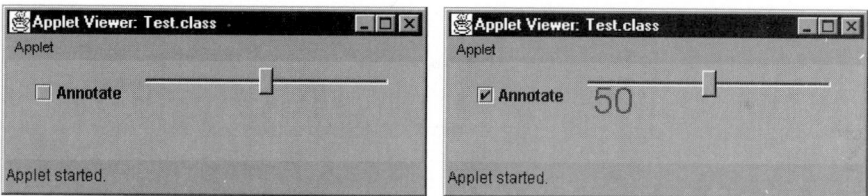

Figure 3-15 Custom Event Handling

The applet creates a slider and check box and sets the slider's UI delegate to an instance of `AnnotatedSliderUI`.

An action listener is added to the check box to set the slider's `annotate` property depending upon the selected status of check box. After updating the slider's `annotate` property, the check box action listener repaints the slider to reflect the change.

---

12. A compiler bug forces classes to be `public`, but they should be `protected`.
13. See "Client Properties" on page 186 for a discussion of components and client properties.

```
public class Test extends JApplet {
    public void init() {
        Container contentPane = getContentPane();
        final JSlider slider = new JSlider();
        final JCheckBox checkBox = new JCheckBox("Annotate");

        slider.setUI(new AnnotatedSliderUI(slider));

        contentPane.setLayout(new FlowLayout());
        contentPane.add(checkBox);
        contentPane.add(slider);

        checkBox.addActionListener(new ActionListener() {
            public void actionPerformed(ActionEvent e) {
                boolean selected = checkBox.isSelected();

                slider.putClientProperty(
                        AnnotatedSliderUI.ANNOTATE_PROPERTY,
                        selected ? Boolean.TRUE : Boolean.FALSE);

                slider.repaint();
            }
        });
    }
}
```

The `AnnotatedSliderUI` class extends `BasicSliderUI` and provides a public `static` string for the key of a slider's `annotate` property. The string is used by the check box's action listener to set the `annotate` property.

`AnnotatedSliderUI` overrides `BasicSliderUI`'s `createPropertyListener` method to return an instance of `AnnotatePropertyListener`. By overriding `createPropertyListener()`, `AnnotatedSliderUI` is replacing `BasicSliderUI`'s property change listener with its own.

```
class AnnotatedSliderUI extends BasicSliderUI {
    public static String ANNOTATE_PROPERTY =
                             "AnnotatedSliderUI.annotate";
    JSlider s;
    boolean annotate = false;
    ...
    protected PropertyChangeListener
            createPropertyChangeListener(JSlider slider) {
        return new AnnotatePropertyListener();
    }
    ...
```

`AnnotatedSliderUI.propertyChange()` invokes the `propertyChange` method of its superclass—`BasicSliderUI.PropertyChangeHandler`—to ensure that changes to other slider bound properties are handled in the default manner.

See "Property Change Notification" on page 95 for more information concerning handling property change events in general.

```
...
public class AnnotatePropertyListener
              extends BasicSliderUI.PropertyChangeHandler {
    public void propertyChange(PropertyChangeEvent e) {
        super.propertyChange(e);

        String name = e.getPropertyName();

        if(name.equals(ANNOTATE_PROPERTY)) {
            if(e.getNewValue() != null) {
                annotate =
                    ((Boolean)e.getNewValue()).booleanValue();
            }
        }
    }
}
...
```

`AnnotatedSliderUI` overrides `getPreferredSize()` to accommodate the annotation.

The `paint` method paints the annotation if the `annotate boolean` member variable is `true` and then invokes `super.paint()` to draw the rest of the slider.

```
...
public Dimension getPreferredSize(JComponent c) {
    Dimension d = super.getPreferredSize(c);
    return new Dimension(d.width,d.height+20);
}
public void paint(Graphics g, JComponent c) {
    if(annotate) {
        JSlider slider = (JSlider)c;
        int v = slider.getValue();

        g.setColor(UIManager.getColor("Label.foreground"));
        g.setFont(new Font("Dialog", Font.PLAIN, 28));
        g.drawString((new Integer(v)).toString(),10,33);
    }
    super.paint(g,c);
}
...
```

Notice that the `paint` and `getPreferredSize` methods, for simplicity, use constant values that are known to produce the desired effect. Use of hardcoded constant values is normally not recommended.

The applet shown in Figure 3-15 is listed in its entirety in Example 3-5.

Example 3-5 Implementing a Custom Listener

```java
import javax.swing.*;
import javax.swing.event.*;
import javax.swing.plaf.basic.*;
import java.awt.*;
import java.awt.event.*;
import java.beans.*;

public class Test extends JApplet {
    public void init() {
        Container contentPane = getContentPane();
        final JSlider slider = new JSlider();
        final JCheckBox checkBox = new JCheckBox("Annotate");

        slider.setUI(new AnnotatedSliderUI(slider));

        contentPane.setLayout(new FlowLayout());
        contentPane.add(checkBox);
        contentPane.add(slider);

        checkBox.addActionListener(new ActionListener() {
            public void actionPerformed(ActionEvent e) {
                boolean selected = checkBox.isSelected();

                slider.putClientProperty(
                        AnnotatedSliderUI.ANNOTATE_PROPERTY,
                        selected ? Boolean.TRUE : Boolean.FALSE);

                slider.repaint();
            }
        });
    }
}
class AnnotatedSliderUI extends BasicSliderUI {
    public static String ANNOTATE_PROPERTY =
                            "AnnotatedSliderUI.annotate";
    boolean annotate = false;

    public AnnotatedSliderUI(JSlider slider) {
        super(slider);
    }
    public Dimension getPreferredSize(JComponent c) {
        Dimension d = super.getPreferredSize(c);
        return new Dimension(d.width,d.height+20);
```

```
    }
    public void paint(Graphics g, JComponent c) {
        if(annotate) {
            JSlider slider = (JSlider)c;
            int v = slider.getValue();

            g.setColor(UIManager.getColor("Label.foreground"));
            g.setFont(new Font("Dialog", Font.PLAIN, 28));
            g.drawString((new Integer(v)).toString(),10,33);
        }
        super.paint(g,c);
    }
    protected PropertyChangeListener
            createPropertyChangeListener(JSlider slider) {
        return new AnnotatePropertyListener();
    }
    protected class AnnotatePropertyListener
                extends BasicSliderUI.PropertyChangeHandler {
        public void propertyChange(PropertyChangeEvent e) {
            super.propertyChange(e);

            String name = e.getPropertyName();

            if(name.equals(ANNOTATE_PROPERTY)) {
                if(e.getNewValue() != null) {
                    annotate =
                        ((Boolean)e.getNewValue()).booleanValue();
                }
            }
        }
    }
}
```

Parting Shots

Swing is based on a modified Model-View-Controller (MVC) architecture. The MVC architecture is a proven design that constitutes the foundation upon which Smalltalk applications are built. MVC encapsulates models, views and controllers as separate objects that communicate through a specific protocol. By encapsulating what other applications intertwine, MVC applications—and Swing components—are much more flexible end reusable than their traditional counterparts.

CHAPTER

4

The JComponent Class

The JComponent class is the base class for all Swing lightweight components, which entitles it to a chapter of its own. JComponent is to Swing what java.awt.Component is to the AWT; both serve as the base class for their respective framework's components.

As the ancestor of all Swing lightweight components, JComponent provides functionality that is essential and substantial. To get the most out of Swing, it is imperative to have a solid grasp of what the JComponent class has to offer and how to take advantage of it.

An Overview of the JComponent Class

JComponent extends java.awt.Container, which in turn extends java.awt.Component—therefore, all Swing components are AWT containers. The Component and Container classes provide a great deal of functionality themselves, so JComponent inherits an impressive array of capabilities. This chapter, and indeed this book, assume that you have a basic understanding of AWT components and containers, which are covered at length in the first volume of *Graphic Java*.

Because JComponent provides the infrastructure for nearly all Swing components, it is a large class containing over 100 public methods. The JComponent class provides the following facilities for its extensions:

- Borders
- Accessibility
- Double buffering
- Debug graphics
- Autoscrolling
- Tooltips
- Keystroke handling
- Client properties

Borders

Any extension of JComponent can be fitted with a border. Swing provides a number of different border styles, such as bevel, titled, etched. Although a component can have only one border, borders can be compound, so in effect a single component can have multiple borders. Figure 4-1 shows a compound border, a titled border, and a custom border.

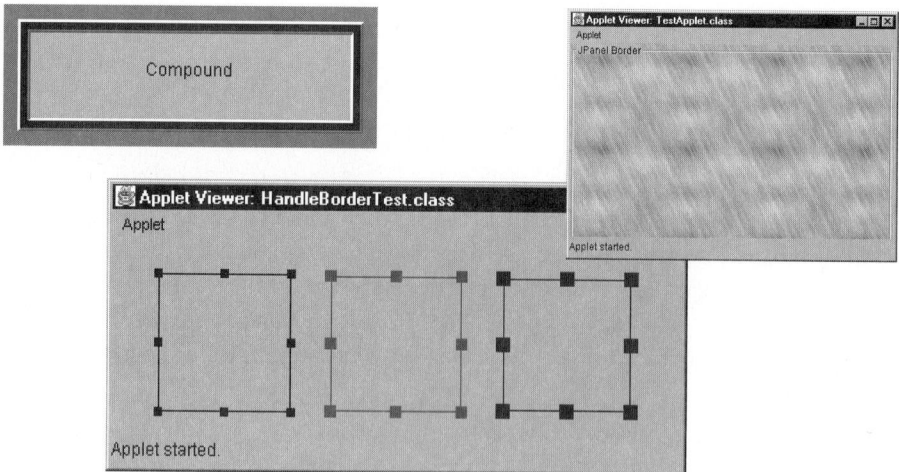

Figure 4-1 Borders
Clockwise, from upper left are a compound border, a titled border, and a custom border.

Borders are most commonly used to group a set of components, but they are also useful in a variety of other situations. For example, the compound border shown in Figure 4-1 might serve as a picture frame for a graphics program that shows thumbnails of artwork. *Handle* borders are commonly used by drawing programs for moving and resizing objects and are easily implemented as a Swing custom border.

Borders are not discussed in this chapter, see the "Borders, Icons, and Actions" chapter beginning on page 203.

Accessibility Support

The goal for accessibility support is to make software accessible to everyone. For example, accessibility may involve magnifying fonts for sight-impaired users, or displaying captions associated with sounds for hearing-impaired users.

Swing's pluggable look-and-feel architecture supports accessibility by allowing alternative look and feels to be assigned to a group of components. Figure 4-2 shows the SwingSet example application using a custom look and feel that is a high-contrast look with large fonts, increasing readability for sight-impaired users.

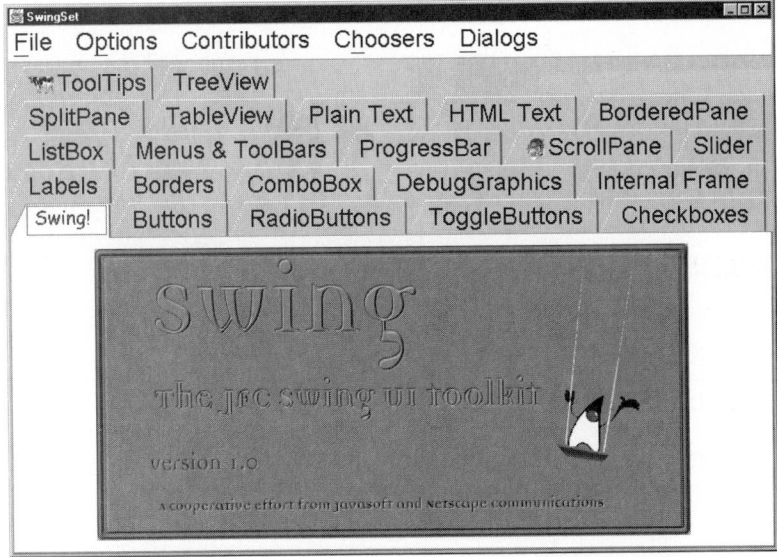

Figure 4-2 Accessibility with Custom Look and Feels

In addition to Swing's pluggable look and feel, accessibility is also supported by an accessibility API and a set of accessibility tools. Accessibility is discussed in "Accessibility" on page 196.

Double Buffering

When components are updated—erased and then repainted—onscreen, a perceptible flickering can result. Double buffering eliminates flickering by updating components in an offscreen buffer and subsequently copying the appropriate portion of the offscreen buffer to the component's onscreen representation.

All Swing lightweight components come with the inherent ability to double-buffer their displays. A single offscreen buffer—maintained by Swing's `RepaintManager`—is used to double-buffer `JComponent` extensions.

Figure 4-3 shows a simple animation that animates an image of a baseball, in addition to an application containing draggable lightweight components.

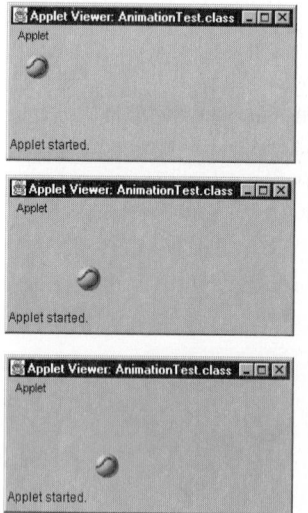 

Figure 4-3 Double Buffering Used for Draggable Icons and Animations

In addition to using the offscreen buffer for double buffering lightweight components, developers can access the buffer for other purposes, such as dragging lightweight components or implementing animations.

Debug Graphics

One call to JComponent.setDebugGraphicsOptions(int) can transform a component into a slow-motion painter that flashes before each graphics call and perhaps maintains a log of graphics calls.

Debug graphics allows developers to quickly understand exactly how components are drawn, which is especially handy when implementing a custom component that undertakes a fair amount of rendering. Figure 4-4 shows a slider that has the debug graphics flash option enabled. The slider paints in slow motion, flashing each graphical operation in red prior to the operation itself.

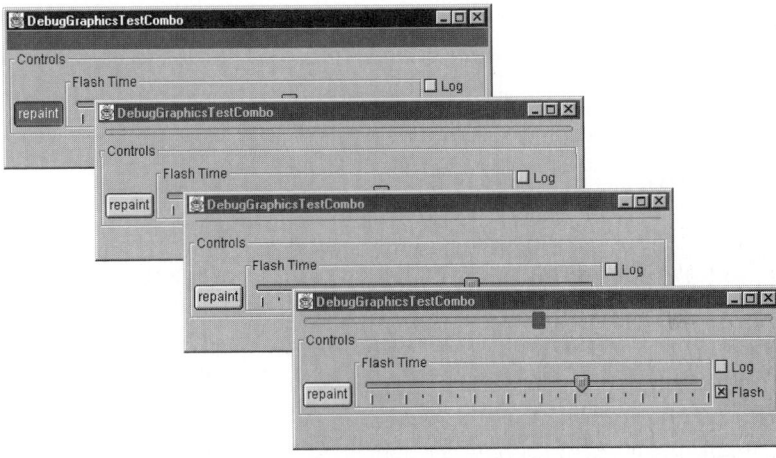

Figure 4-4 Debug Graphics—Slow-Motion Rendering

A portion of the graphics log associated with the graphical operations depicted in Figure 4-4 is shown below:

```
Graphics(0-3) Enabling debug

Graphics(0-3) Setting color:
javax.swing.plaf.ColorUIResource[r=153,g=153,b=204]

Graphics(0-3) Setting font:
javax.swing.plaf.FontUIResource[family=Dialog,name=Dia-
log,style=plain,size=12]
```

```
Graphics(1-3) Setting color:
javax.swing.plaf.ColorUIResource[r=204,g=204,b=204]

Graphics(1-3) Filling rect:
java.awt.Rectangle[x=0,y=0,width=300,height=21]

Graphics(1-3) Translating by: java.awt.Point[x=0,y=0]
Graphics(1-3) Setting color:
javax.swing.plaf.ColorUIResource[r=153,g=153,b=153]

Graphics(1-3) Drawing line: from (7, 8) to (292, 8)
Graphics(1-3) Drawing line: from (293, 8) to (293, 14)
Graphics(1-3) Drawing line: from (293, 15) to (8, 15)
Graphics(1-3) Drawing line: from (7, 15) to (7, 9)
Graphics(1-3) Translating by: java.awt.Point[x=0,y=0]
Graphics(1-3) Translating by: java.awt.Point[x=143,y=5]
Graphics(1-3) Translating by: java.awt.Point[x=0,y=0]
...
```

Many aspects of debug graphics are settable, including the flash color, flash timing, log stream, etc.

AutoScrolling

Swing lightweight components can scroll their contents when the cursor is dragged outside their bounds—a feature known as autoscrolling. All JComponent extensions inherit the ability to autoscroll. Autoscrolling can be enabled and disabled on a per-component basis. By default, JList and JTable have autoscrolling enabled.

Autoscrolling can also be implemented in custom components for some interesting effects. For example, Figure 4-5 shows a custom viewport that autoscrolls.

The image displayed in the viewport in Figure 4-5 can be scrolled by dragging the image itself. If the cursor is dragged outside the bounds of the viewport when dragging, the image is autoscrolled in the direction of the cursor.

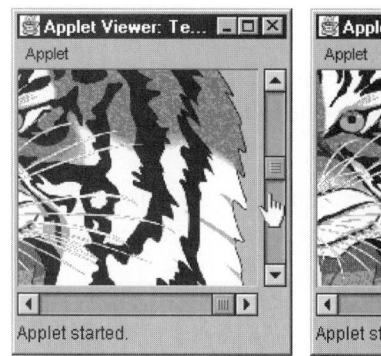  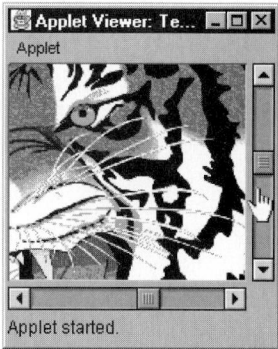

Figure 4-5 Autoscrolling in a Custom Component

Tooltips

Tooltips are strings that are displayed in a small window when the cursor rests over a tooltip-equipped extension of `JComponent`. Tooltips are most commonly used in toolbar buttons for describing the functionality associated with a particular button. Figure 4-6 shows tooltips being used under different circumstances.

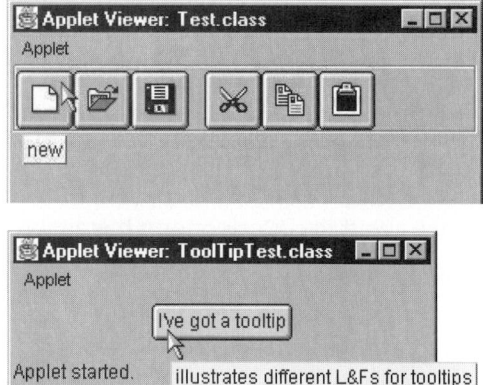 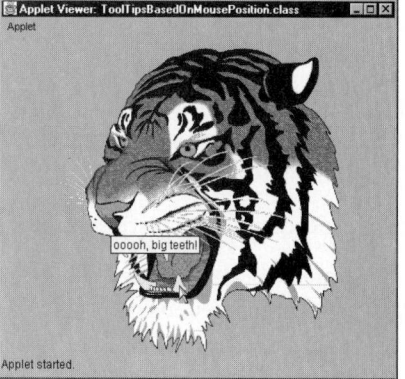

Figure 4-6 Tooltips

Tooltips are quite flexible; for instance, the text associated with a tooltip can change depending upon the position of the cursor as it rests over the component. Image maps that pop up short explanations of what's currently under the cursor are prime candidates for such a feature. VH1's popup video for example, could be done with tooltips.

Timing characteristics—such as the initial delay between the cursor coming to rest and showing the tooltip—are settable through the `ToolTipManager` class.

Keystroke Handling and Client Properties

The `JComponent` class provides support for handling nested keystrokes. Instead of requiring developers to filter all keystrokes and act upon the interesting ones, `JComponents` can be instructed to fire action events to a specific target when a keystroke is pressed or released under certain conditions.

Every `JComponent` maintains a dictionary known as client properties. Dictionaries maintain a set of key/value pairs that can be any type of object. Client properties enable any `JComponent` to be associated with another object without the need to extend the `JComponent` class.

The JComponent Class

Figure 4-7 shows an inheritance diagram of the `JComponent` class and its extensions.

All of Swing's **J** classes—lightweight components whose names begin with J—are ultimately derived from `swing.JComponent`. All of the classes shown in Figure 4-7 reside in the `swing` package, with exceptions noted.

There are a couple interesting points to make about the `JComponent` hierarchy.

First, something that is not evident from Figure 4-7: Every one of the 29 `JComponent` extensions inherits 277 `public` methods from its `Component`/`Container`/`JComponent` superclass chain designed to support the `JComponent`'s life as a lightweight Swing component. As a result, all extensions of `JComponent` step up to the plate with considerable skills.

Second, inheritance has been used sparingly in the JComponent hierarchy. The only substantial branches under JComponent are anchored by the JTextComponent and AbstractButton classes. Most extensions of JComponent are concrete components that do not need to be extended in order to be useful. Composition is heavily favored over inheritance in the JComponent hierarchy, which results in a more flexible framework[1].

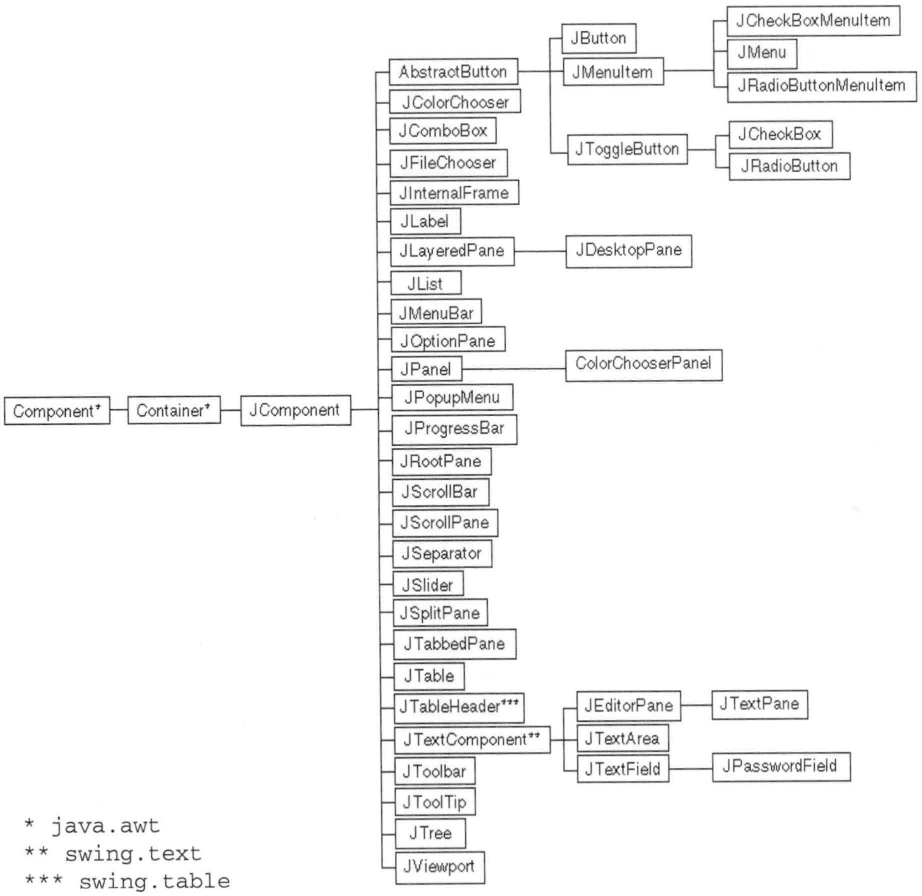

```
                                                              ┌─ JCheckBoxMenuItem
                                          ┌─ JButton          ├─ JMenu
                          ┌─ AbstractButton ─ JMenuItem ──────┴─ JRadioButtonMenuItem
                          ├─ JColorChooser
                          ├─ JComboBox                        ┌─ JCheckBox
                          ├─ JFileChooser   ┌─ JToggleButton ─┴─ JRadioButton
                          ├─ JInternalFrame
                          ├─ JLabel
                          ├─ JLayeredPane ─── JDesktopPane
                          ├─ JList
                          ├─ JMenuBar
                          ├─ JOptionPane
                          ├─ JPanel ───────── ColorChooserPanel
Component* ─ Container* ─ JComponent ─ JPopupMenu
                          ├─ JProgressBar
                          ├─ JRootPane
                          ├─ JScrollBar
                          ├─ JScrollPane
                          ├─ JSeparator
                          ├─ JSlider
                          ├─ JSplitPane
                          ├─ JTabbedPane
                          ├─ JTable
                          ├─ JTableHeader*** ┌─ JEditorPane ─── JTextPane
                          ├─ JTextComponent** ─ JTextArea
                          ├─ JToolbar        └─ JTextField ──── JPasswordField
                          ├─ JToolTip
   *   java.awt          ├─ JTree
   **  swing.text        └─ JViewport
   *** swing.table
```

Figure 4-7 The JComponent Inheritance Hierarchy

---

1. See Gamma/Helm/Johnson/Vlissides. *Design Patterns*, p. 18. Addison-Wesley, 1995.

Swing Components Are AWT Containers

Because JComponent extends java.awt.Container, every extension of JComponent can contain both AWT and Swing components. Figure 4-8 shows an applet that contains a Swing button which in turn contains an AWT button and another Swing button. The applet is listed in Example 4-1.

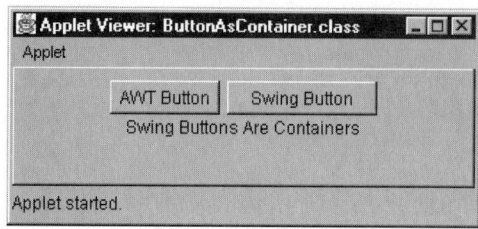

Figure 4-8 All JComponents Are AWT Containers

Disclaimer: Don't try this at work.

Example 4-1 A Swing Button Used as a Container

```java
import javax.swing.*;
import java.awt.*;

public class ButtonAsContainer extends JApplet {
    public void init() {
        JButton b = new JButton("Swing Buttons Are Containers");

        b.setLayout(new FlowLayout());
        b.add(new Button("AWT Button"));
        b.add(new JButton("Swing Button"));

        getContentPane().add(b);
    }
}
```

Although a design that embeds buttons within one another may be subject to question, the fact that JComponent extends java.awt.Container greatly facilitates the implementation of compound components.

Minimum, Maximum, and Preferred Sizes

Swing components, like AWT components, have minimum, maximum, and preferred sizes that are typically used by layout managers to size components.

Take note of the carefully worded previous sentence. Just because a component has a minimum, maximum, or preferred size guarantees nothing about its actual size. Typically, a layout manager sets the size of a component, and layout managers are given free reign as to whether they pay any attention to a component's minimum, maximum, or preferred size. In actuality, minimum, maximum, and preferred sizes are size *requests* that may or may not be taken into account when a component's size is determined.

Unlike AWT components, which must be extended in order to modify minimum, maximum, and preferred sizes, Swing components come with setter methods, as listed in Table 4-1.

Table 4-1   JComponent Methods Dealing with Component Sizes

Method Name	Implemenation
void setMaximumSize(Dimension)	Sets the component's maximum size
void setMinimumSize(Dimension)	Sets the component's minimum size
void setPreferredSize(Dimension)	Sets the component's preferred size
Dimension getMaximumSize()	Returns the component's maximum size
Dimension getMinimumSize()	Returns the component's minimum size
Dimension getPreferredSize()	Returns the component's preferred size

The getter methods listed in Table 4-1 use the following algorithm for calculating their respective sizes:

```
public Dimension getXXXSize() {
    if(size has been explicitly set via call to setXXXSize())
        return size explicitly set via call to setXXXSize()

    if(UI delegate is non-null)
        return size calculated by UI delegate

    if(UI delegate is null && size has not been explicitly set)
        return superclass implementation of getXXXSize()
}
```

If a size has been explicitly set, then it is returned from the getter method.

If the size has not been explicitly set and the component has a UI delegate, then the delegate is called upon to calculate the size in question.

If the size has not been explicitly set and the component does not have a UI delegate, then the superclass calculates the size. Since JComponent extensions are AWT containers, java.awt.Container calculates the preferred size by delegating to the component's layout manager.

Figure 4-9 shows an applet that allows the preferred size for an instance of JList to be set on-the-fly. If the preferred size is set to null, the UI delegate for the list calculates the list's preferred size. If the preferred size is set to (100,100), then that dimension is returned from the getPreferredSize method.

list's preferred size is null, so UI delegate calculates preferred size

list's preferred size is explicitly set to 100x100 pixels

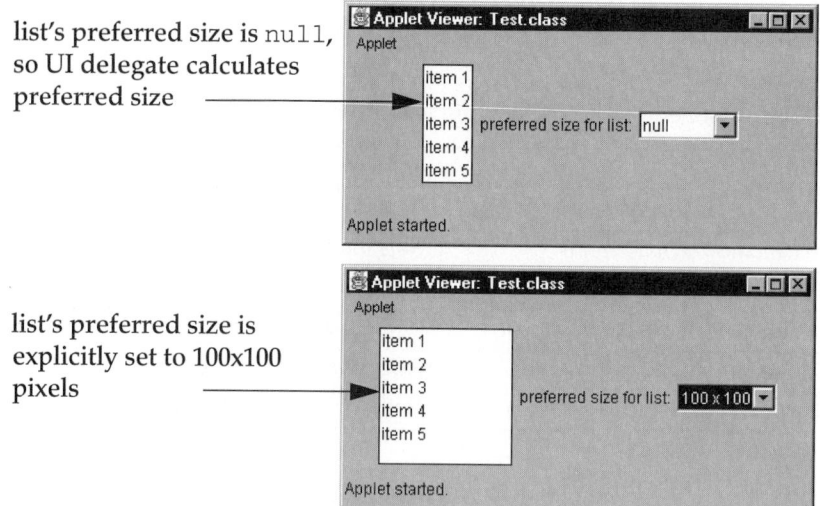

Figure 4-9 Setting Preferred Sizes for Extensions of JComponent

The layout manager for the applet's content pane is set to an instance of FlowLayout, which sizes components according to their preferred size.

If the list's preferred size is null, then the size is calculated by the list's UI delegate, as illustrated by the top picture in Figure 4-9. The list's UI delegate is obviously a master at sizing lists; the list is sized just large enough to contain the items in the list.

If the preferred size of the list is explicitly set to a 100-pixel square, then the UI delegate is out of the picture and the list is sized to a dimension of (100,100).

The applet shown in Figure 4-9 is listed in Example 4-2.

Example 4-2 Explicitly Setting Preferred Size for a JComponent

```
import javax.swing.*;
import java.awt.*;
import java.awt.event.*;

public class Test extends JApplet {
   JComboBox sizeCombo = new JComboBox(new Object[] {
                           "null",
                           "100 x 100"
                     });
   JList list = new JList(new Object[] {
                           "item 1",
                           "item 2",
                           "item 3",
                           "item 4",
                           "item 5",
                     });
   public void init() {
      final Container contentPane = getContentPane();

      list.setBorder(
         BorderFactory.createLineBorder(Color.black));

      sizeCombo.setSelectedIndex(0);

      contentPane.setLayout(new FlowLayout());
      contentPane.add(list);
      contentPane.add(new JLabel("preferred size for list:"));
      contentPane.add(sizeCombo);

      sizeCombo.addActionListener(new ActionListener() {
         public void actionPerformed(ActionEvent e) {
            int index = sizeCombo.getSelectedIndex();

            if(index == 0)
               list.setPreferredSize(null);
            else
               list.setPreferredSize(
                     new Dimension(100, 100));

            // force the content pane to update
            list.revalidate();
         }
      });
   }
}
```

When a choice is made from the combo box, the list's preferred size is set accordingly, and the list is revalidated, resulting in the list being resized and repainted. See "Validate, Invalidate, and Revalidate Methods" on page 144 for more information concerning the `revalidate` method.

Swing Tip ...

Swing's JComponent Makes Size Properties More User Friendly

The java.awt.Component class provides getter methods, but no corresponding setter methods, for minimum, maximum, and preferred sizes. For instance, there is a getPreferredSize method, but no corresponding setPreferredSize. This means that the min/max/preferred sizes are only settable on a per-class basis, by overriding a getter method in an extension class. For example, setting the preferred size for an AWT canvas would be done something like this:

```
// SomeCanvas has preferred size of 100x100 pixels ...

SomeCanvas canvas = new SomeCanvasExtension();

...

class SomeCanvasExtension extends Canvas {
  public Dimension getPreferredSize() {
    return new Dimension(100,100);
  }
}
```

The JComponent class provides setter methods so that min/max/preferred sizes can be set on a per-instance basis instead of a per-class basis. The preferred size for a JPanel, for instance, can be set as follows:

```
JPanel panel = new JPanel();

...

panel.setPreferredSize(new Dimension(100,100));
```

Thanks to JComponent, the use of inheritance is no longer required to modify a component's minimum, maximum, and preferred sizes.

Rendering JComponents

The rendering of Swing lightweight components is a collaborative effort between the component and the component's UI delegate. In general, developers do not need to be involved with the rendering process; lightweight components are simply instantiated and added to a container. At the appropriate time, the container lays out the components it contains and draws them. However, there are times when it is important to understand the process by which lightweight components are rendered. For instance, updating a component's visual representation or extending the JPanel class to draw custom graphics requires an understanding of the rendering process.

Lightweight Swing components are rendered by the JComponent.paint method, which is passed a Graphics in which to draw. JComponent.paint takes into account the fact that components can be double buffered, can have a border, and can contain other components. Figure 4-10 outlines the sequence of method calls triggered by JComponent.paint.

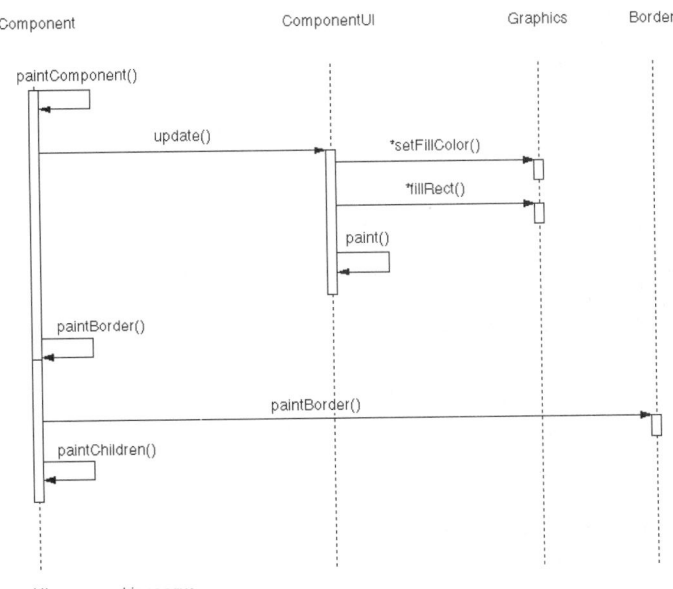

Figure 4-10 Sequence Diagram for JComponent.paint()

JComponent.paint paints the component, the component's border, and the component's children—in that order. The sequence of calls makes sure that the component, border, and child components are all visible.

If the component has a UI delegate, JComponent.paintComponent invokes the delegate's update method, which clears the background for opaque components and subsequently paints the component.

Both the UI delegate and the component's border are passed a copy of the actual graphics used to paint the component. As a result, the paintBorder and paintChildren methods can make changes to the graphics they are passed without affecting subsequent graphic operations. For more information on copying Graphics and setting their parameters, refer to the *Graphics* chapter from the first volume of *Graphic Java*.

Custom Painting in Swing Components

If you have any significant experience with the AWT, you are probably accustomed to overriding java.awt.Component.paint for the purpose of painting into a custom component.

Custom painting for Swing lightweight components is a little more complicated because Swing components are containers that may have child components and a border, not to mention a UI delegate. To illustrate the differences between custom painting in AWT components vs. custom painting in Swing components, this section discusses the implementation of a simple ImageCanvas class, first using the AWT and then using Swing.

Note: The image canvas classes implemented in the following sections are for illustrative purposes only. Swing, unlike the AWT, provides a component that can display an image— the JLabel class.

Overriding Paint Methods in AWT Components

Custom AWT components are commonly implemented by extending either java.awt.Canvas or java.awt.Panel and overriding paint(). For example, Figure 4-11 shows an applet that contains an instance of ImageCanvas, an extension of java.awt.Canvas.

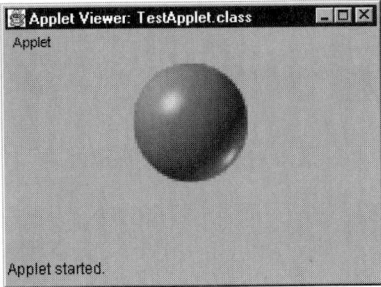

Figure 4-11 An ImageCanvas Class That Extends java.awt.Canvas

The `ImageCanvas` class fulfills three responsibilities: loading the image it will display, overriding the `paint` method to draw the image, and overriding `getPreferredSize` so that the preferred size of the canvas is the same size as the image. The applet shown in Figure 4-11 and the `ImageCanvas` class are listed in Example 4-3.

Example 4-3 Overriding paint() for Custom AWT Components

```
import java.applet.Applet;
import java.awt.*;

public class TestApplet extends Applet {
    public void init() {
        ImageCanvas imageCanvas = new ImageCanvas("sphere.gif");
        add(imageCanvas);
    }
}
class ImageCanvas extends Canvas {
    Image image;

    public ImageCanvas(String imageName) {
        image = Toolkit.getDefaultToolkit().getImage(imageName);

        MediaTracker mt = new MediaTracker(this);
        try {
            mt.addImage(image, 0);
            mt.waitForID(0);
        }
        catch(InterruptedException ex) {
            ex.printStackTrace();
        }
    }
    public void paint(Graphics g) {
        g.drawImage(image, 0, 0, null);
```

```
      }
  public Dimension getPreferredSize() {
      return new Dimension(image.getWidth(null),
                           image.getHeight(null));
      }
  }
```

The `ImageCanvas` constructor is passed a string representing the name of the file containing the image. An instance of `MediaTracker` is employed to ensure that the image is fully loaded before the constructor returns.

The `paint` method is overridden to simply draw the image in the upper-left corner of the canvas. `Graphics.drawImage()`, `Image.getWidth()` and `Image.getHeight()` are all passed a `null` reference for an image observer because the image is fully loaded before `paint()` is invoked.

`ImageCanvas` overrides `getPreferredSize()` to return the size of the image. The default layout manager for AWT applets is `FlowLayout`, which sizes components according to their preferred size.[2] Thus, the size of the image canvas is set to the size of the image it displays.

Overriding Paint Methods in Swing Components

Figure 4-12 shows an applet similar to the one in Figure 4-11.

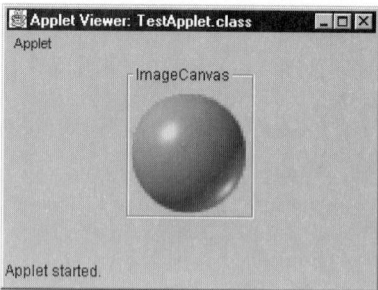

Figure 4-12 An ImageCanvas Class That Extends JPanel

---

2.   See the first volume of *Graphic Java* for more on layout managers and loading/displaying images.

The applet shown in Figure 4-12 creates an instance of `ImageCanvas` that is derived from the `swing.JPanel` class. The applet creates a titled border—with some help from Swing's border factory—and sets the border for the image canvas. The image canvas is then added to the applet's content pane. The applet is listed in Example 4-4.

Example 4-4 An Applet with an Image Canvas Derived from JComponent

```
public class TestApplet extends JApplet {
    public void init() {
        Container contentPane = getContentPane();
        ImageCanvas imagePanel = new ImageCanvas("sphere.gif");

        imagePanel.setBorder(
            BorderFactory.createTitledBorder("ImageCanvas"));

        contentPane.setLayout(new FlowLayout());
        contentPane.add(imagePanel);
    }
}
```

The applet also sets the layout manager for its content pane to an instance of `FlowLayout`, so the image canvas will be sized according to its preferred size. `JApplet`, unlike `java.awt.Applet`, uses a `BorderLayout` by default.

The `ImageCanvas` class is listed in Example 4-5.

Example 4-5 Overriding paintComponent() for Custom Swing Components

```
class ImageCanvas extends JPanel {
    ImageIcon icon;

    public ImageCanvas(String imageName) {
        icon = new ImageIcon(imageName);
    }
    public void paintComponent(Graphics g) {
        super.paintComponent(g);

        Insets insets = getInsets();
        icon.paintIcon(this, g, insets.left, insets.top);
    }
    public Dimension getPreferredSize() {
        Insets insets = getInsets();
        return new Dimension(
            icon.getIconWidth() + insets.left + insets.right,
            icon.getIconHeight() + insets.top + insets.bottom);
    }
}
```

Like the `ImageCanvas` listed in Example 4-3 on page 139, the `ImageCanvas` class listed in Example 4-4 derived from `swing.JPanel` has three responsibilities: loading the image, painting the image, and specifying the preferred size for the canvas.

Loading the image is accomplished by employing an instance of `ImageIcon`. Image icons fully load their image when the image is specified, so the `ImageCanvas` class is absolved of that responsibility. See "Icons" on page 222 for more information on icons.

Instead of overriding `paint()`, the `ImageCanvas` class overrides `paintComponent()`. Recall from "Sequence Diagram for JComponent.paint()" on page 137 that `JComponent.paint` orchestrates the painting of the component, the component's border, and the component's children. Additionally, for double-buffered components, `JComponent.paint` takes care of painting the component into an offscreen buffer and subsequently copying the offscreen buffer into the component's onscreen representation. Because of this behavior, it is rarely advisable to override `paint()` for Swing components. If you need to redefine how a component is painted, override `paintComponent()` instead of `paint()`.

`ImageCanvas.paintComponent()` invokes `super.paintComponent()`. This is a necessity for opaque components because the background is cleared either by the component's UI delegate or the superclass' `paintComponent` method.[3] Also, if the component has a UI delegate, the delegate will not be given a chance to do its part in rendering the component if `super.paintComponent()` is not invoked—see "Sequence Diagram for JComponent.paint()" on page 137.

`ImageCanvas.paintComponent()` does not paint the image in the upper-left corner of the panel, as was the case for the version of `ImageCanvas` listed in Example 4-3 on page 139. Instead, the icon is painted at a location of `(insets.left, insets.top)`, where `insets` refers to the insets of the panel. As a general guideline, since all Swing lightweight components are actually AWT containers, care should be taken to avoid painting into a component's insets region. For instance, in Example 4-5, if the icon had been painted at `(0,0)`, the border would have been painted over the outer edge of the image.

---

3.   Not all Swing components have a UI delegate. In the absence of a UI delegate, the component handles clearing the background itself.

The overridden `getPreferredSize` method is also careful to factor in the insets of the panel when calculating the panel's preferred size. The preferred size for the version of the AWT `ImageCanvas` listed in Example 4-3 on page 139 was simply the size of the image. Extensions of `JPanel`, on the other hand, must make sure that their preferred size takes into account the region defined by its insets.

Swing Tip ...

Display Images as JLabels

Images are not components—thus the need for the ImageCanvas class discussed in the previous pages. That's the AWT way of doing things; with Swing one typically displays images with an instance of the JLabel class. JLabel, like all Swing components is also an AWT component, and therefore is easily embedded in Swing and AWT containers.

Paint, Repaint, and Update Methods

The `update` method for AWT and Swing components is invoked as the result of calls to `repaint()`. For AWT components, `update()` erases the background of the component and subsequently invokes `paint()`. Sometimes erasing the background is undesirable. For, example, consider a bar graph that continuously updates its display as new data becomes available. Repeated erasing and repainting of the graph will result in a perceptible flicker. In such cases, it is common for extensions of AWT components to override `update()` to invoke `paint()` directly, thus avoiding the erasure of the component's background and the resultant flicker associated with it.

For Swing components, it is not necessary to override `update()` to invoke `paint()` directly in order to eliminate flicker. For one thing, the `JComponent` class overrides `update()` to invoke `paint()` directly. This does not mean however, that Swing components do not erase their backgrounds when they are repainted. The responsibility for erasing the background of a Swing component when it is repainted lies with the component's UI delegate if the component has one.

Fortunately, it is not necessary to subclass a component's UI delegate in order to eliminate flicker because, by default, Swing components are double buffered, meaning they are erased and then repainted in an offscreen buffer. After the

component has been updated in its offscreen buffer, it is copied to the screen. Double buffering eliminates flicker, and therefore it is not necessary to override the update method for Swing components. If a Swing component flickers, the solution is to make sure that the component is double buffered instead of overriding update().

Validate, Invalidate, and Revalidate Methods

Swing and AWT *components* are normally positioned and sized (laid out) by their container's layout manager. At any given time, a component is either valid or invalid; invalid components need to be laid out, whereas valid components do not. For example, if a button's text is set after construction, it is likely that the button will need to be resized to accommodate the new text. Therefore, setting a button's text results in the button being invalidated—by invoking invalidate() for the button—indicating that the button needs to be laid out.

Swing and AWT *containers* provide a validate method that lays out all of the components contained in the container. For example, if validate() is invoked for a container that contains a button whose text has been changed (and is therefore invalid), the container will lay out the button along with the other components that reside in the container.

Calls to invalidate() and validate() propagate up and down the containment hierarchy respectively, so that invalidating a component invalidates all of the containers in the component's containment hierarchy. Likewise, calls to validate() recursively validate all of the components in the container's hierarchy.

The JComponent class provides a revalidate method that invalidates the component and schedules a call to validate() on the event dispatch thread for the first container in the component's containment hierarchy whose isValidateRoot property is set to true; Swing's scrollpane and root pane set their isValidateRoot property to true. Because all Swing components that are contained in instances of JApplet or JFrame reside in a root pane, invoking revalidate() for a Swing component in a Swing applet or application will result in the component being laid out. After the component(s) are laid out, regions of the component(s) that have changed are repainted.

Three things should be noted about JComponent.revalidate().

First, calls to `revalidate()`, like calls to `repaint()`, are coalesced. Therefore, if `revalidate()` is called in succession for more than one component contained in the same container, the `revalidate()` calls will be coalesced, meaning only one call to `revalidate()` will result.

Second, any Swing component that is modified so that its position or size is changed should be revalidated by the component itself, resulting in the component being laid out and repainted. Unfortunately, as of Swing 1.1 FCS / 1.2 JDK, the revalidation is not always carried out. If a component is not laid out and repainted after a change to its position or size, it is a Swing bug.

Third, even though a call to `JComponent.revalidate()` should result in a repaint of regions of the component that have changed, the repainting does not always take place. As a result, it is sometimes necessary to call `repaint()` after invoking `revalidate()`.

Swing Tip ...

Custom Painting in Swing Components

Custom painting in Swing components is more complicated than painting in AWT components because Swing components are lightweight AWT containers that can have a border. Here are some general rules to remember about painting Swing components:

1. Override `JComponent.paintComponent()` if you need to control how the component itself is rendered but want default behavior for rendering the component's border and children.

2. Override `JComponent.paint()` if you need total control over how the component, its border, and its children are rendered.

3. Invoke `super.paintComponent()` in overridden `paintComponent` methods to ensure that the UI delegate gets a chance to clear the background for opaque components and paint.

4. Don't paint into the insets region in overridden `paintComponent` methods.

5. Account for insets when calculating minimum, maximum, or preferred sizes.

6. If a Swing component flickers when updated, make sure the component is double buffered instead of overriding its update method.

Opaque vs. Transparent Components

Swing lightweight components can be either opaque or partially transparent. For example, the applet shown in Figure 4-13 contains two instances of a `ColoredPanel` class. The panel on the left is opaque, whereas the panel on the right is partially transparent.

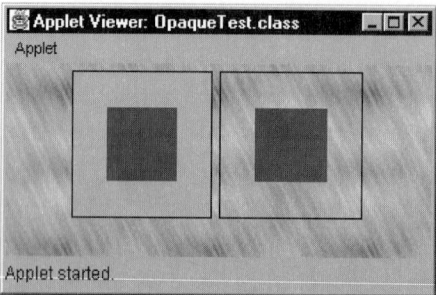

Figure 4-13 An Opaque Component and a Partially Transparent Component

The applet shown in Figure 4-13 instantiates an instance of `RainPanel`, which in turn contains two instances of `ColoredPanel`. `RainPanel` tiles an image over its background, and `ColoredPanel` paints a black border and a filled rectangle centered in the component. Both `RainPanel` and `ColoredPanel` extend `JPanel`. The applet is listed in Example 4-6.

Example 4-6 OpaqueTest Applet

```
public class OpaqueTest extends JApplet {
    public void init() {
        Container contentPane = getContentPane();
        RainPanel rainPanel = new RainPanel();

        ColoredPanel opaque = new ColoredPanel(),
                     transparent = new ColoredPanel();

        // JComponents are opaque by default, so the opaque
        // property only needs to be set for transparent
        transparent.setOpaque(false);

        rainPanel.add(opaque);
```

```
        rainPanel.add(transparent);

        contentPane.add(rainPanel, BorderLayout.CENTER);
    }
}
```

Swing components are opaque by default, so there is no need to set the opaque property for the opaque panel. The applet invokes setOpaque(false) for the transparent panel, which allows the background of the rain panel to show through. As illustrated in "Sequence Diagram for JComponent.paint()" on page 137, the background of an opaque component is filled with the component's background color, whereas transparent components have transparent backgrounds.

The applet shown in Figure 4-13 is listed in its entirety in Example 4-7.

Example 4-7 Opaque Swing Components

```
import javax.swing.*;
import java.awt.*;

public class OpaqueTest extends JApplet {
    public void init() {
        Container contentPane = getContentPane();
        RainPanel rainPanel = new RainPanel();

        ColoredPanel opaque = new ColoredPanel(),
                    transparent = new ColoredPanel();

        // JComponents are opaque by default, so the opaque
        // property only needs to be set for transparent
        transparent.setOpaque(false);

        rainPanel.add(opaque);
        rainPanel.add(transparent);

        contentPane.add(rainPanel, BorderLayout.CENTER);
    }
}
class RainPanel extends JPanel {
    ImageIcon rain = new ImageIcon("rain.gif");
    private int rainw = rain.getIconWidth();
    private int rainh = rain.getIconHeight();

    public void paintComponent(Graphics g) {
        Dimension size = getSize();

        for(int row=0; row < size.height; row += rainh)
            for(int col=0; col < size.width; col += rainw)
                rain.paintIcon(this,g,col,row);
    }
```

```
    }
    class ColoredPanel extends JPanel {
        public void paintComponent(Graphics g) {
            super.paintComponent(g);

            Dimension size = getSize();

            g.setColor(Color.black);
            g.drawRect(0,0,size.width-1,size.height-1);

            g.setColor(Color.red);
            g.fillRect(size.width/2-25,size.height/2-25,50,50);
        }
        public Dimension getPreferredSize() {
            return new Dimension(100,100);
        }
    }
```

Recall that one of the guidelines presented in the "Custom Painting in Swing Components" Swing Tip on page 145 recommends that overridden `paintComponent` methods call `super.paintComponent()` to clear the component's background. The code presented in Example 4-7 contains a class that adheres to the guideline, and another that does not. The `ColoredPanel` class must ensure that its background is filled in when it is painted so that opaque instances will actually appear to be opaque. `RainPanel`, on the other hand, tiles its background with an icon, and therefore clearing the background does not make sense. As a result, `ColoredPanel.paintComponent()` invokes `super.paintComponent()`, whereas `RainPanel` does not.

Immediate Painting of Swing Components

Invoking `repaint()` for a component results in a paint event being created that is placed upon the AWT's event queue. As a result, if `repaint()` is invoked from an event handler method, the repainting will not occur until after the event handler has returned.

The `JComponent` class provides a method that paints components immediately— `paintImmediately()`—which is suitable for use in event handler methods that need to update the appearance of a component immediately.[4] `paintImmediately()` should be used judiciously because in most cases it's more efficient to call `repaint()`, which collapses redundant paint requests.

4. The `paintImmediately` method may be migrated to `java.awt.Component` by the time you read this.

Figure 4-14 shows an applet that contains a button and an instance of
`ColoredPanel`. When the button is activated, its action listener sleeps for five
seconds to simulate some time-consuming action.

Before going any further, it should be stressed that time-consuming actions are
strongly discouraged in event handler methods. Since events are dispatched on a
single event dispatch thread, event handler methods are expected to take care of
business as quickly as possible, and time-consuming actions that are not GUI
related should normally be scheduled on a separate thread. However, there are
times when event handlers need to update the appearance of a component
immediately, and the delay induced in the applet shown in Figure 4-14 serves to
illustrate the benefits of the `paintImmediately` method.

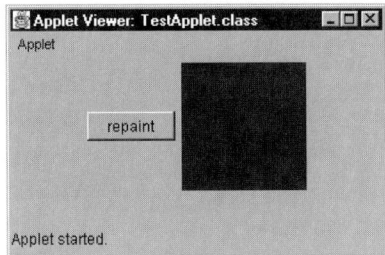 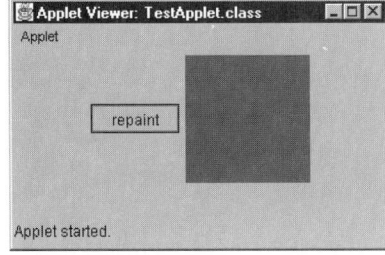

Figure 4-14 Immediate Painting of Swing Components

The applet starts out with a blue-colored panel. Clicking on the repaint button
results in the colored panel being repainted in red before the event handler
method returns. The applet is listed in Example 4-8.

Example 4-8 Using paintImmediately() in an Event Handler Method

```java
import javax.swing.*;
import java.awt.*;
import java.awt.event.*;

public class TestApplet extends JApplet {
    public void init() {
        Container contentPane = getContentPane();
        final JPanel panel = new JPanel();
        JButton button = new JButton("repaint");

        panel.setBackground(Color.blue);
        panel.setPreferredSize(new Dimension(100,100));
```

```
contentPane.setLayout(new FlowLayout());
contentPane.add(button);
contentPane.add(panel);

button.addActionListener(new ActionListener() {
    public void actionPerformed(ActionEvent e) {
        Color c = panel.getBackground();
        Dimension sz = panel.getSize();

        panel.setBackground(
            c == Color.blue ? Color.red : Color.blue);

        panel.paintImmediately(
                        0,0,sz.width,sz.height);

        // for illustrative purposes only
        try {
            Thread.currentThread().sleep(5000);
        }
        catch(InterruptedException ex) {
            ex.printStackTrace();
        }
    }
});
    }
}
```

paintImmediately() takes four integer arguments specifying the bounds of the component that are to be repainted (alternatively, an overloaded version of paintImmediately() takes a Rectangle as an argument). The applet in Example 4-8 specifies the bounds of the component as the rectangle to paint.

Double Buffering

Lightweight components are drawn entirely in Java code, as opposed to heavyweight components, which are drawn by native peers. As a result, it is imperative to double buffer lightweight components to avoid flickering resulting from the erasure of all or part of a component when components are repainted. For instance, if the thumb of a scrollbar is dragged and the scrollbar is not double buffered, the thumb will constantly be erased and redrawn onscreen, resulting in considerable—and presumably unacceptable—flickering.

Double buffering eliminates flickering by painting into an offscreen buffer that is subsequently copied onscreen. Double buffering is discussed at length in the *Double Buffering* chapter from the first volume of *Graphic Java*.

Although all Swing lightweight components can double-buffer their displays, only two are double buffered by default: JRootPane and JPanel. This may seem rather strange in light of the first paragraph of this section, but the rationale for not double-buffering the rest of the Swing lightweight components will become apparent once it's clear how Swing implements double buffering. Here's how Swing's double buffering works:

Swing includes a RepaintManager class that maintains a single offscreen buffer. The buffer is large enough to accommodate the size of the screen and is used to double-buffer all Swing lightweight components. If a JComponent—*or one of its ancestors in the component's containment hierarchy*—is double buffered, the component is drawn into the repaint manager's offscreen buffer and subsequently copied to the component's onscreen representation. Since components are automatically double buffered if they reside in a double-buffered container, it is only necessary for Swing's lightweight containers, namely, JRootPane and JPanel, to be double-buffered by default.

There are two ways to control whether or not a component is double buffered. First, the JComponent class provides a setDoubleBuffered method that is passed a boolean value indicating whether the component should be double buffered. Second, the RepaintManager class provides a setDoubleBufferingEnabled method, which is also passed a boolean, that enables or disables double buffering for all Swing lightweight components in one shot.[5]

The applet shown in Figure 4-15 contains a slider whose double-buffering status is controlled by a check box.

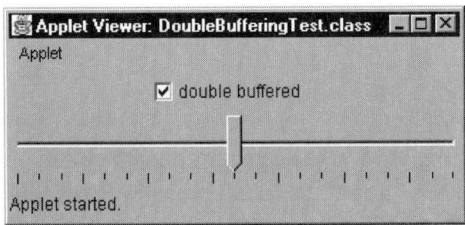

Figure 4-15 Enabling/Disabling Double Buffering for a JSlider

The applet shown in Figure 4-15 is listed in Example 4-9.

---

5. Actually, the method affects all components that belong to the same thread group. There is one repaint manager per thread group.

Example 4-9   DoubleBufferingTest Applet

```
import javax.swing.*;
import java.awt.*;
import java.awt.event.*;

public class DoubleBufferingTest extends JApplet {
    public void init() {
        final JSlider slider =
                    new JSlider(JSlider.HORIZONTAL,0,100,50);

        final Container contentPane = getContentPane();
        JCheckBox dbcheckBox = new JCheckBox("double buffered");
        JPanel controlPanel = new JPanel();

        dbcheckBox.setSelected(true);
        controlPanel.add(dbcheckBox);

        slider.setPaintTicks(true);
        slider.setMinorTickSpacing(5);
        slider.setMajorTickSpacing(15);

        contentPane.add(controlPanel, "North");
        contentPane.add(slider, "Center");

        dbcheckBox.addItemListener(new ItemListener() {
            public void itemStateChanged(ItemEvent event) {

                if(event.getStateChange() == ItemEvent.SELECTED) {
                    slider.setDoubleBuffered(true);
                }
                else {
                    slider.setDoubleBuffered(false);
                }
            }
        });
    }
}
```

If you run the applet listed in Example 4-9 from the CD, you may be surprised to find that toggling double buffering for the slider has no effect on how the slider is displayed. Regardless of whether double buffering is enabled for the slider, it repaints without flickering when its thumb is moved.

Although double buffering is indeed being enabled and disabled for the slider when the check box is checked and unchecked, respectively, it is inconsequential because the slider is displayed in a double-buffered container. Recall that instances of JApplet contain an instance of JRootPane, which in turn contains an instance of JPanel—the content pane to which the slider is added. As noted previously, JRootPane and JPanel are double buffered by default, and since

components that reside in a double-buffered container are unconditionally double buffered, setting the double-buffering status for the slider has no effect on how the slider is drawn.

To force the slider to be drawn directly onscreen, disable double buffering for both the applet's root pane and content pane, as is the case for the applet listed in Example 4-10.

Example 4-10 Disabling Double Buffering for a Component's Containers

```java
import javax.swing.*;
import java.awt.*;
import java.awt.event.*;

public class DoubleBufferingTest extends JApplet {
    public void init() {
        final Container contentPane = getContentPane();

        JSlider slider = new JSlider(JSlider.HORIZONTAL,0,100,50);
        JCheckBox dbcheckBox = new JCheckBox("double buffered");
        JPanel controlPanel = new JPanel();

        dbcheckBox.setSelected(true);
        controlPanel.add(dbcheckBox);

        slider.setPaintTicks(true);
        slider.setMinorTickSpacing(5);
        slider.setMajorTickSpacing(15);

        contentPane.add(controlPanel, "North");
        contentPane.add(slider, "Center");

        dbcheckBox.addItemListener(new ItemListener() {
            public void itemStateChanged(ItemEvent event) {
                JComponent cp = (JComponent)getContentPane();
                JComponent rp = (JComponent)getRootPane();

                if(event.getStateChange() == ItemEvent.SELECTED) {
                    rp.setDoubleBuffered(true);
                    cp.setDoubleBuffered(true);
                }
                else {
                    rp.setDoubleBuffered(false);
                    cp.setDoubleBuffered(false);
                }
            }
        });
    }
}
```

The applet listed in Example 4-10 never directly sets the double-buffered status of the slider itself. Enabling and disabling the double-buffered status of the containers in which the slider resides will determine whether the slider is double buffered. If you run the applet listed in Example 4-10, you'll notice that the slider's thumb flickers noticeably when double buffering is disabled and the thumb is dragged.

Another approach to controlling double buffering is to enable or disable double buffering for all components at once. The applet listed in Example 4-11 takes this approach by invoking `setDoubleBufferingEnabled` for the repaint manager associated with the applet.

Example 4-11 Invoking RepaintManager.setDoubleBufferingEnabled()

```
import javax.swing.*;
import java.awt.*;
import java.awt.event.*;

public class DoubleBufferingTest extends JApplet {
    public void init() {
        Container contentPane = getContentPane();
        JCheckBox dbcheckBox = new JCheckBox("double buffered");
        JPanel controlPanel = new JPanel();
        final JSlider slider =
                    new JSlider(JSlider.HORIZONTAL,0,100,50);

        dbcheckBox.setSelected(true);
        controlPanel.add(dbcheckBox);

        slider.setPaintTicks(true);
        slider.setMinorTickSpacing(5);
        slider.setMajorTickSpacing(15);

        contentPane.add(controlPanel, "North");
        contentPane.add(slider, "Center");

        dbcheckBox.addItemListener(new ItemListener() {
            public void itemStateChanged(ItemEvent event) {
                RepaintManager rm =
                    RepaintManager.currentManager(slider);

                if(event.getStateChange() == ItemEvent.SELECTED) {
                    rm.setDoubleBufferingEnabled(true);
                }
                else {
                    rm.setDoubleBufferingEnabled(false);
                }
            }
        });
    }
}
```

After all the preceding discussion concerning the pitfalls of enabling and disabling double buffering for a single component, doing so in practice will be quite rare. Swing's implementation of double buffering ensures that lightweight components will be double buffered by default.

Double Buffering in Custom Components

As luck would have it, Swing's repaint manager provides access to the aforementioned offscreen buffer used to double buffer Swing components. The offscreen buffer can be used for a variety of purposes. For example, the applet shown in Figure 4-16 uses the offscreen buffer to implement a simple, flicker-free animation.

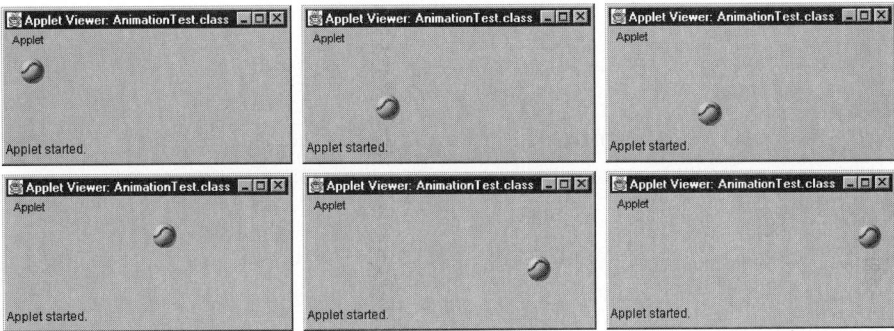

Figure 4-16 A Simple Animation That Uses Swing's Double Buffering

The applet instantiates an instance of `AnimationPane` and adds it to the applet's content pane. The `AnimationPane` class animates an image of a baseball, using the offscreen buffer maintained by Swing's `RepaintManager`. A timer is also instantiated and associated with the animation pane. See "Timers" on page 249 for more information on Swing timers.

The applet shown in Figure 4-16 is listed in Example 4-12.

Example 4-12 AnimationTest Applet

```
import javax.swing.*;
import java.awt.event.*;

public class AnimationTest extends JApplet {
    AnimationPane p = new AnimationPane();
    Timer      timer = new Timer(5, p);

    public void init() {
        getContentPane().add(p, "Center");

        timer.start();

        addMouseListener(new MouseAdapter() {
            public void mousePressed(MouseEvent event) {
                if(timer.isRunning()) timer.stop();
                else                  timer.start();
            }
        });
    }
}
```

All of the action, as far as performing the animation, takes place in the
AnimationPane class, which extends JPanel and implements
ActionListener.

AnimationPane instantiates an ImageIcon that is subsequently animated and
invokes setOpaque(false) so that its background is not cleared when it is
repainted.

```
public class AnimationPane extends JPanel
                        implements ActionListener {
    Icon    ball    = new ImageIcon("baseball.gif");
    Point   ulhc    = new Point(0,0);
    Point   moveVector = new Point(1,1);
    Dimension imsz = new Dimension(ball.getIconWidth(),
                               ball.getIconHeight());

    public AnimationPane() {
        setOpaque(false);  // don't clear bg when repainting
    }
    ...
```

AnimationPane.actionPerformed is invoked by the applet's timer every 5
milliseconds. The actionPerformed method obtains a reference to the current
repaint manager by invoking RepaintManager.currentManager(). A

reference to the offscreen buffer maintained by the repaint manager is obtained by invoking `RepaintManager.getOffscreenBuffer()`, which is passed a reference to the animation pane and the desired width and height of the buffer.

```
    ...
    public void actionPerformed(ActionEvent e) {
        Dimension size = getSize();
        RepaintManager rm = RepaintManager.currentManager(this);
        Image off = rm.getOffscreenBuffer(this,
                                          size.width,
                                          size.height);
        Graphics og = off.getGraphics();

        Graphics g  = getGraphics();

        ...
```

The location of the image icon is maintained by the animation pane and is used to clear a rectangle in the offscreen buffer where the icon previously resided.

```
    if(og != null && g != null) {
        try {
            Rectangle oldr =
                    new Rectangle(ulhc.x,ulhc.y,
                                  imsz.width,imsz.height);
            og.setColor(getBackground());
            og.fillRect(ulhc.x, ulhc.y,
                    imsz.width, imsz.height);
            ...
```

A check is then made for edge collisions. If the icon is about to hit one of the four sides of the animation pane, the move vector associated with the icon is modified so that the icon will bounce off the sides of the animation pane. A new location for the icon is subsequently calculated by adding the move vector to the current upper-left corner. The icon is then painted into the offscreen buffer at its new location.

```
            ...
            checkForEdgeCollision(size);
            ulhc.x += moveVector.x;
            ulhc.y += moveVector.y;
            ball.paintIcon(this, og, ulhc.x, ulhc.y);
            ...
```

Until now, all of the painting has taken place in the offscreen buffer. Finally, the union of the previous and current rectangles occupied by the icon are copied from the offscreen buffer to the onscreen buffer associated with the animation pane.

```
            . . .
            Rectangle union,
                       newr = new Rectangle(ulhc.x,ulhc.y,
                                    imsz.width,imsz.height);

            union = oldr.union(newr);

            g.setClip(union.x,union.y,
                        union.width,union.height);
            g.drawImage(off,0,0,this);
        }
        finally {
            og.dispose();
            g.dispose();
        }
    }
} // end of ActionPerformed method
```

After the appropriate region is copied to the onscreen buffer, both of the Graphics representing the offscreen and onscreen buffers are disposed of, which is a necessity anytime a reference to a Graphics is obtained by invoking getGraphics().

The AnimationPane class is listed in its entirety in Example 4-13.

Example 4-13 AnimationPane Class Listing

```
import javax.swing.*;
import java.awt.*;
import java.awt.event.*;

public class AnimationPane extends JPanel
                           implements ActionListener {
    Icon    ball      = new ImageIcon("baseball.gif");
    Point   ulhc      = new Point(0,0);
    Point   moveVector = new Point(1,1);
    Dimension imsz = new Dimension(ball.getIconWidth(),
                                ball.getIconHeight());

    public AnimationPane() {
        setOpaque(false);  // don't clear bg when repainting
    }
    public void actionPerformed(ActionEvent e) {
        Dimension size = getSize();
```

```
RepaintManager rm = RepaintManager.currentManager(this);
Image     off = rm.getOffscreenBuffer(this,
                                       size.width,
                                       size.height);

Graphics og = off.getGraphics();
Graphics g  = getGraphics();

if(og != null) {
    try {
        Rectangle oldr =
                new Rectangle(ulhc.x,ulhc.y,
                              imsz.width,imsz.height);
        og.setColor(getBackground());
        og.fillRect(ulhc.x, ulhc.y,
                imsz.width, imsz.height);

        checkForEdgeCollision(size);
        ulhc.x += moveVector.x;
        ulhc.y += moveVector.y;

        ball.paintIcon(this, og, ulhc.x, ulhc.y);

        Rectangle union,
                newr = new Rectangle(ulhc.x,ulhc.y,
                              imsz.width,imsz.height);

        union = oldr.union(newr);
        og.setColor(getBackground());

        g.setClip(union.x,union.y,
                union.width,union.height);
        g.drawImage(off,0,0,this);
    }
    finally {
        og.dispose();
        g.dispose();
    }
  }
}
private void checkForEdgeCollision(Dimension size) {
    if(ulhc.x + imsz.width + moveVector.x > size.width ||
                 ulhc.x + moveVector.x < 0)
        moveVector.x -= moveVector.x*2;
    if(ulhc.y + imsz.height + moveVector.y > size.height ||
                 ulhc.y + moveVector.y < 0)
        moveVector.y -= moveVector.y*2;
    }
}
```

Swing double-buffers its lightweight components by an efficient mechanism that maintains a single offscreen buffer. If a lightweight component resides in a double-buffered container or explicitly enables double buffering on its own, it

will be drawn into the offscreen buffer and subsequently copied to its onscreen representation. Swing also makes the offscreen buffer it uses for double buffering available through `RepaintManager.getOffscreenBuffer()`. This enables developers to use the offscreen buffer for their own purposes, such as the animation applet shown in Figure 4-16 on page 155.

Swing Tip ...

Swing and Double Buffering

Here are some things to keep in mind concerning Swing and double buffering:

1. Components in a double-buffered container are automatically double buffered.

2. `JComponent.setDoubleBuffered(boolean)`: Enables/disables double buffering for a single component; however, see item #1.

3. `RepaintManager.setDoubleBufferingEnabled(boolean)`: Enables/disables double buffering for all components.

4. `RepaintManager.getOffscreenBuffer(JComponent, int width, int height)`: Returns a reference to the offscreen buffer.

Debug Graphics

All graphical operations that take place in AWT components, and therefore Swing components, are performed through an instance of `Graphics`. A reference to a `Graphics` is passed to methods that need to perform graphical operations such as `paint(Graphics)` and `update(Graphics)`. The first volume of *Graphic Java* explores the `Graphics` class in detail.

Swing provides an extension of the `java.awt.Graphics` class— `swing.DebugGraphics`—that slows the rate of graphical operations and flashes prior to each operation. Additionally, the `DebugGraphics` class can print a log of the graphics calls that it performs. The rate at which operations are performed, the number of flashes per operation, the color of the flash, and the stream that the log is printed to are all settable via `static public` methods in the `DebugGraphics` class.

You already know more than you need to in order to take advantage of debug graphics. Like most Swing features, the complexity of debug graphics is neatly tucked away out of sight; for instance, it's not necessary to know that there's a `DebugGraphics` class that extends `java.awt.Graphics`. To use debug graphics, simply invoke the `JComponent` method `setDebugGraphicsOptions(int)`. The `integer` argument represents the following debugging options:

- `DebugGraphics.LOG_OPTION`
- `DebugGraphics.FLASH_OPTION`
- `DebugGraphics.BUFFERED_OPTION`
- `DebugGraphics.NONE_OPTION`

Setting the debug graphics options for a Swing component to anything other than `DebugGraphics.NONE_OPTION` causes the component to use an instance of `DebugGraphics` when it is painted.

The `BUFFERED_OPTION` is for double-buffered components and causes an external window to pop up and display the component's offscreen buffer. Deciphering the meaning of the other options is left as an exercise to the reader.

Note: *The* `BUFFERED_OPTION` *is not implemented for Swing 1.1 FCS.*

The applet shown in Figure 4-17 controls the debug graphics parameters for the disabled slider at the top of the applet. The slider is disabled to emphasize that its only function is to illustrate debug graphics.

Figure 4-17 Debug Graphics Flashes and Logs Graphical Operations

The applet's `init` method invokes `setDoubleBufferingEnabled(false)` for the repaint manager in order to disable double buffering for all the components contained in the applet. Double buffering is disabled because the effect of the `FLASH_OPTION` cannot be seen for double-buffered components since they are drawn in an offscreen buffer.

```
public class DebugGraphicsTest extends JApplet {
    private JSlider slider = new JSlider();
    boolean logIsOn = false, flashIsOn = false;

    public void init() {
        ...
        RepaintManager rm =
                    RepaintManager.currentManager(slider);

        rm.setDoubleBufferingEnabled(false);
        ...
        slider.setEnabled(false);
    }
    ...
```

The "Controls" panel contains the "repaint" button, "Flash Time" slider, and the "Log" and "Flash" check boxes. Each component in the "Controls" panel is fitted with a listener. The "Flash Time" slider has a change listener that sets the flash time by invoking the `static DebugGraphics.setFlashTime` method.

```
flashTimeSlider.addChangeListener(new ChangeListener() {
    public void stateChanged(ChangeEvent e) {
        DebugGraphics.setFlashTime(
                        flashTimeSlider.getValue());
    }
});
```

When activated, the "Log" and "Flash" check boxes set internal flags maintained by the applet.

```
flashCheckBox.addItemListener(new ItemListener() {
    public void itemStateChanged(ItemEvent e) {
        AbstractButton b = (AbstractButton)e.getSource();

        if(b.isSelected()) flashIsOn = true;
        else               flashIsOn = false;
    }
});
```

```
logCheckBox.addItemListener(new ItemListener() {
    public void itemStateChanged(ItemEvent e) {
        AbstractButton b = (AbstractButton)e.getSource();

        if(b.isSelected()) logIsOn = true;
        else               logIsOn = false;
    }
});
```

The "repaint" button's action listener sets the debug options for the disabled slider, depending upon the flags that have been set through activation of the check boxes, and repaints the applet.

```
repaintButton.addActionListener(new ActionListener() {
    public void actionPerformed(ActionEvent e) {
        int opts = 0;

        if(logIsOn) opts  |= DebugGraphics.LOG_OPTION;
        if(flashIsOn)opts |= DebugGraphics.FLASH_OPTION;

        slider.setDebugGraphicsOptions(opts);
        repaint();
    }
});
```

The applet shown in Figure 4-17 is listed in its entirety in Example 4-14.

Example 4-14 Using the Log and Flash Options for Debug Graphics

```
import javax.swing.*;
import javax.swing.event.*;
import java.awt.*;
import java.awt.event.*;
import java.io.*;

public class DebugGraphicsTest extends JApplet {
    private JSlider slider = new JSlider();
    boolean logIsOn = false, flashIsOn = false;

    public void init() {
        Container cp = getContentPane();
        RepaintManager rm =
                    RepaintManager.currentManager(slider);

        rm.setDoubleBufferingEnabled(false);

        cp.setLayout(new BoxLayout(cp, BoxLayout.Y_AXIS));
```

```
       cp.add(slider);
       cp.add(makeControlPanel());

       slider.setEnabled(false);
   }
   private JPanel makeControlPanel() {
       JPanel controls = new JPanel(),
               checkBoxes = new JPanel();
       JCheckBox logCheckBox = new JCheckBox("Log"),
               flashCheckBox = new JCheckBox("Flash");
       JButton repaintButton = new JButton("repaint");

       final JSlider flashTimeSlider =
                   new JSlider(JSlider.HORIZONTAL,0,250,100);

       flashTimeSlider.setPaintTicks(true);
       flashTimeSlider.setMajorTickSpacing(10);
       flashTimeSlider.setMinorTickSpacing(5);

       controls.setLayout(new BoxLayout(controls,
                   BoxLayout.X_AXIS));
       checkBoxes.setLayout(new BoxLayout(checkBoxes,
                   BoxLayout.Y_AXIS));

       flashTimeSlider.setBorder(
           BorderFactory.createTitledBorder("Flash Time"));
       controls.setBorder(
           BorderFactory.createTitledBorder("Controls"));

       checkBoxes.add(logCheckBox);
       checkBoxes.add(flashCheckBox);

       controls.add(repaintButton);
       controls.add(flashTimeSlider);
       controls.add(checkBoxes);

       repaintButton.addActionListener(new ActionListener() {
           public void actionPerformed(ActionEvent e) {
               int opts = 0;

               if(logIsOn) opts |= DebugGraphics.LOG_OPTION;
               if(flashIsOn)opts |= DebugGraphics.FLASH_OPTION;

               slider.setDebugGraphicsOptions(opts);
               repaint();
           }
       });

       flashTimeSlider.addChangeListener(new ChangeListener() {
           public void stateChanged(ChangeEvent e) {
               DebugGraphics.setFlashTime(
                       flashTimeSlider.getValue());
```

```
            }
        });

        flashCheckBox.addItemListener(new ItemListener() {
            public void itemStateChanged(ItemEvent e) {
                AbstractButton b = (AbstractButton)e.getSource();

                if(b.isSelected()) flashIsOn = true;
                else               flashIsOn = false;
            }
        });
        logCheckBox.addItemListener(new ItemListener() {
            public void itemStateChanged(ItemEvent e) {
                AbstractButton b = (AbstractButton)e.getSource();

                if(b.isSelected()) logIsOn = true;
                else               logIsOn = false;
            }
        });

        return controls;
    }
}
```

Autoscrolling

JComponents come with the ability to autoscroll. Autoscrolling enables a component to continue scrolling when the mouse is dragged outside its bounds.

Autoscrolling is activated and deactivated by invocation of the JComponent method setAutoScrolls(boolean). JComponent also provides a getAutoscrolls method that returns a boolean value indicating whether autoscrolling is enabled for the component. By default, autoscrolling is enabled only for lists and tables.

Figure 4-18 shows a list caught in the act of autoscrolling. An item in the list is selected initially, and the mouse is dragged down and outside the bounds of the list. As a result, the list continues scrolling until the last item in the list is displayed.

Example 4-15 lists the applet. The list is primed with six items, and JList.setVisibleRowCount() is invoked to set the number of visible rows to 3. Since JList automatically enables autoscrolling, it is not necessary to invoke setAutoscrolls(true) for the list. The list is wrapped in a scrollpane, and the scrollpane is added to the applet.

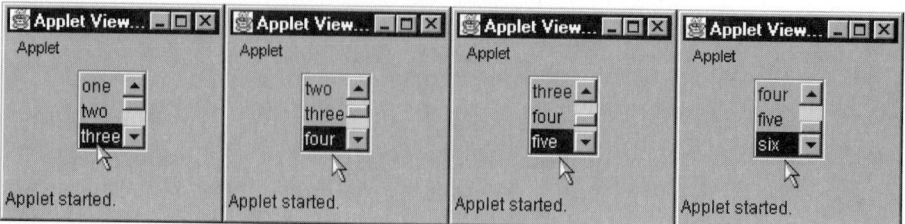

Figure 4-18 Autoscrolling with a JList

Example 4-15 A List Wrapped in a Scrollpane

```java
import javax.swing.*;
import java.awt.*;

public class TestApplet extends JApplet {
    public void init() {
        String[] items = { "one", "two", "three",
                           "four", "five", "six" };

        Container contentPane = getContentPane();
        JList list = new JList(items);

        list.setVisibleRowCount(3);

        contentPane.setLayout(new FlowLayout());
        contentPane.add(new JScrollPane(list));
    }
}
```

Autoscrolling in Custom Components

To implement autoscrolling in a custom component, you must understand how
autoscrolling works beneath the covers. When the mouse is dragged outside a
component that has autoscrolling enabled, the component is repeatedly sent a
mouse dragged event every 100 milliseconds, regardless of whether the mouse is
moving. Components such as JList handle the mouse dragged event by
automatically scrolling their contents. As soon as the mouse re-enters the
component or a mouse released event occurs, the onslaught of mouse dragged
events ceases.

Implementing autoscrolling in a custom component requires the component—or its UI delegate—to handle mouse dragged events that occur outside the bounds of the component. For example, the applet shown in Figure 4-19 contains an instance of `AutoscrollViewport`,[6] which is an extension of `JViewport`. Mouse dragged events that occur within the viewport result in the viewport's view being dragged in accordance with the movement of the mouse. Dragging the cursor outside of the viewport causes the view to scroll toward the cursor.

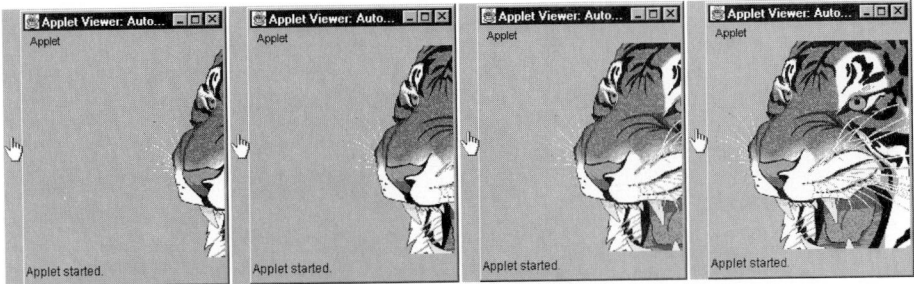

Figure 4-19 Autoscrolling in a Custom Component

Note: The `JViewport` class contains a single component referred to as the viewport's view. `JViewport` provides support for setting the position of its view, which is convenient for illustrating autoscrolling. The `JViewport` component is discussed in more detail in "JViewport" on page 718.

The applet shown in Figure 4-19 is listed in Example 4-16.

Example 4-16 AutoscrollTest Applet

```java
import javax.swing.*;

public class AutoscrollTest extends JApplet {
    public AutoscrollTest() {
        JLabel label = new JLabel(new ImageIcon("pic.gif"));
        JViewport vp = new AutoscrollViewport(label, 3);

        getContentPane().add(vp, "Center");
    }
}
```

6. `AutoscrollViewport` is not part of the Swing release.

The constructor for the `AutoscrollViewport` class is passed a component—an instance of `JLabel` that displays the image of the tiger—and an `integer` value that is used as a scrolling increment in pixels. The constructor specifies the component as the viewport's view, enables autoscrolling, and sets its cursor to the predefined hand cursor.

```
class AutoscrollViewport extends JViewport {
    Point scrollTo = new Point(), last = new Point();
    boolean manualDragUnderway = false;
    final int increment;

    public AutoscrollViewport(Component component, int inc) {
        this.increment = inc;

        setView(component);
        setAutoscrolls(true);
        setCursor(Cursor.getPredefinedCursor(Cursor.HAND_CURSOR));
        ...
```

Handling of mouse events is implemented by two inner classes. When a mouse pressed event occurs, the location of the mouse press is recorded and a flag is set indicating that manual dragging is underway.

```
        ...
        addMouseListener(new MouseAdapter() {
            public void mousePressed(MouseEvent e) {
                last.x = e.getPoint().x;
                last.y = e.getPoint().y;
                manualDragUnderway = true;
            }
        });
        ...
```

Mouse dragged events are generated in one of two scenarios. Either the event occurred within the viewport's bounds, or it occurred outside of the viewport.

Dragging the mouse inside the viewport drags the viewport's view—here's how it works: An offset is calculated between the location of the mouse dragged event and the position of the previous mouse event. The offset is subtracted from the current view position, and the result is used to reset the position of the viewport's view.

```
    . . .
addMouseMotionListener(new MouseMotionAdapter() {
    public void mouseDragged(MouseEvent e) {
        Point drag = e.getPoint();
        Point viewPos = getViewPosition();
        Point offset = new Point(drag.x - last.x,
                                    drag.y - last.y);

        last.x = drag.x;
        last.y = drag.y;

        if(contains(drag)) {
            if(manualDragUnderway) {
                scrollTo.x = viewPos.x - offset.x;
                scrollTo.y = viewPos.y - offset.y;
                setViewPosition(scrollTo);
            }
        }
    }
    . . .
```

If the mouse dragged event did not occur within the viewport's bounds, the viewport implements autoscrolling by incrementally moving the view toward the mouse cursor.

The viewport resets the position of its view—the label—depending upon whether the cursor is above, below, to the left, or to the right of the viewport. The view position is adjusted, either horizontally or vertically, by the increment that was passed to the AutoscrollViewport constructor.

```
        . . .
    else {  // autoscrolling ...
        Rectangle bounds = getBounds();
        . . .

        if(drag.x > bounds.x + bounds.width) {
            // scroll right
            viewPos.x -= increment;
            setViewPosition(viewPos);
        }
        if(drag.x < 0) {
            // scroll left
            viewPos.x += increment;
            setViewPosition(viewPos);
        }
        if(drag.y > bounds.y + bounds.height) {
            // scroll down
            viewPos.y -= increment;
            setViewPosition(viewPos);
        }
```

```
                    if(drag.y < 0) {
                        // scroll up
                        viewPos.y += increment;
                        setViewPosition(viewPos);
                    }
                }
            }
        });
    }
}
```

As long as the cursor is outside the viewport and the mouse button is pressed, the view will scroll toward the cursor. The simple-minded autoscrolling implementation shown above was chosen for simplicity; an industrial-strength version would stop autoscrolling when the view was just about to scroll out of sight.

The `AutoscrollViewport` is listed in its entirety in Example 4-17.

Example 4-17 AutoscrollViewport Listing

```
import javax.swing.*;
import java.awt.*;
import java.awt.event.*;

class AutoscrollViewport extends JViewport {
    Point scrollTo = new Point(), last = new Point();
    boolean manualDragUnderway = false;
    final int increment;

    public AutoscrollViewport(Component component, int inc) {
        this.increment = inc;

        setView(component);

        setAutoscrolls(true);
        setCursor(Cursor.getPredefinedCursor(Cursor.HAND_CURSOR));

        addMouseListener(new MouseAdapter() {
            public void mousePressed(MouseEvent e) {
                last.x = e.getPoint().x;
                last.y = e.getPoint().y;
                manualDragUnderway = true;
            }
        });
        addMouseMotionListener(new MouseMotionAdapter() {
            public void mouseDragged(MouseEvent e) {
                Point drag = e.getPoint();
                Point viewPos = getViewPosition();
```

```
            Point offset = new Point(drag.x - last.x,
                                      drag.y - last.y);
            last.x = drag.x;
            last.y = drag.y;

            if(contains(drag)) {
                if(manualDragUnderway) {
                    scrollTo.x = viewPos.x - offset.x;
                    scrollTo.y = viewPos.y - offset.y;
                    setViewPosition(scrollTo);
                }
            }
            else {  // autoscrolling ...
                Rectangle bounds = getBounds();

                manualDragUnderway = false;

                if(drag.x > bounds.x + bounds.width) {
                    // scroll right
                    viewPos.x -= increment;
                    setViewPosition(viewPos);
                }
                if(drag.x < 0) {
                    // scroll left
                    viewPos.x += increment;
                    setViewPosition(viewPos);
                }
                if(drag.y > bounds.y + bounds.height) {
                    // scroll down
                    viewPos.y -= increment;
                    setViewPosition(viewPos);
                }
                if(drag.y < 0) {
                    // scroll up
                    viewPos.y += increment;
                    setViewPosition(viewPos);
                }
            }
        }
    });
}
```

Tooltips

Tooltips are one-liners that are displayed in a window when the cursor rests over a component for a specific period of time. Associating a tooltip with a Swing component is accomplished by invoking JComponent.setToolTipText(), which is passed a string that will be displayed in the tooltip window. Passing a null string to setToolTipText() will nullify any previous tooltips set for the component.

Figure 4-20 shows a tooltip that's associated with an instance of JButton.

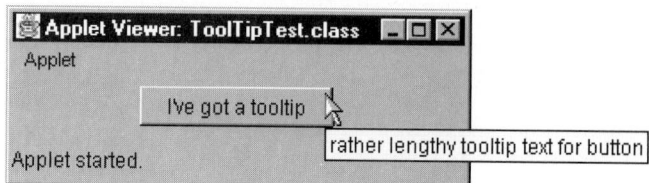

Figure 4-20 Tooltips Are Displayed in a Separate Window

The tooltip text for the button is set to a rather lengthy string to illustrate that tooltips are displayed in a window of their own (the tooltip's window extends past the border of the applet window). However, good GUI design dictates that tooltip text should be short and to the point; typically no more than a few words are appropriate for a tooltip. For that reason, multiple lines of text are not supported by tooltips. The applet shown in Figure 4-20 is listed in Example 4-18.

Example 4-18 Setting Tooltip Text for a Button

```
import javax.swing.*;
import java.awt.*;

public class ToolTipTest extends JApplet {
    public void init() {
        Container contentPane = getContentPane();
        JButton button = new JButton("I've got a tooltip");

        button.setToolTipText(
            "rather lengthy tooltip text for button");

        contentPane.setLayout(new FlowLayout());
        contentPane.add(button);
    }
}
```

The applet instantiates an instance of JButton, sets the tooltip text for the button, and adds the button to the applet's content pane. When the cursor rests over the button for a period of time, the tooltip is displayed. The initial delay for showing the tooltip is settable and is discussed in "Customizing Tooltip Behavior" on page 177.

The JComponent class provides a number of options for setting tooltips and customizing their behavior, such as setting tooltip text based on mouse position. JComponent public methods dealing with tooltips are listed in Table 4-2.

Table 4-2 JComponent Public Methods Dealing with Tooltips

Method Name	Implemenation
setToolTipText	Passed a string to be used as the tooltip text
getToolTipText	No arguments—returns the string passed to getToolTipText()
getToolTipText	Passed a MouseEvent—returns the string set by setToolTipText(). Extensions can override for tooltips dependent upon mouse position.
getToolTipLocation	Returns a Point representing the preferred location for tooltip text, based on mouse position
createToolTip	Returns a JTooltip used by the component. Can be overridden for components that require custom tooltips.

The setToolTipText method has already been discussed; the other methods listed in Table 4-2 are discussed in the following sections.

Tooltips Based on Mouse Position

As with most Swing features, there is a considerable amount of complexity behind the scenes associated with tooltips. However, as illustrated by the applet listed in Example 4-18 on page 172, the complexity is neatly tucked away such that most developers will never have to deal with it. If all you need to do is display a tooltip for a component, you can just invoke the component's setToolTipText method and be done with it. However, if you'd like to display different tooltips in a single component based on mouse position—for instance, displaying information over an image map—then you need to peel back the top layer of the tooltip complexity onion.

Three classes play a role in the implementation of tooltips.

First, the JComponent class, as described previously, provides a setToolTipText method that activates tooltips for the component and sets the text associated with the tooltip.

Second, there's the `JToolTip` class, which, thanks to Swing's pluggable look-and-feel implementation, does little more than maintain the tooltip text and a reference to the component with which the tooltip is associated. The code that actually displays the tooltip text is encapsulated in the tooltip's look and feel, which resides in an extension of the `swing.plaf.ToolTipUI` class.

Third, Swing's `ToolTipManager` class is responsible for providing a window in which to display tooltips and for prodding instances of `JToolTip` into displaying their wares in said window. The `ToolTipManager` also controls timing issues, such as the delay between the time the cursor comes to a stop over the component, and when the tooltip is displayed.

`JComponent` provides two versions of `getToolTipText()`: a no-argument version that simply returns the string passed to `setToolTipText()`, and another that is passed a `MouseEvent` argument.

When a tooltip is displayed, Swing's `ToolTipManager` invokes `JComponent.getToolTipText(MouseEvent)` to obtain the tooltip text. `JComponent.getToolTipText(MouseEvent)` ignores the `MouseEvent` and simply returns the string returned by `JComponent.getToolTipText()`. As a result, the text set by the call to `setToolTipText()` is always returned, regardless of the position of the cursor.

Obviously, `JComponent.getToolTipText(MouseEvent)` exists for the sole purpose of being overridden by `JComponent` extensions. Custom components can override `getToolTipText(MouseEvent)` to return text that is dependent upon the position of the cursor, as shown in Figure 4-21.

Figure 4-21 Tooltips Based on Mouse Location

The applet shown in Figure 4-21 is listed in Example 4-19.

Example 4-19   Showing Different ToolTips Depending upon Mouse Position

```
import javax.swing.*;
import java.awt.*;
import java.awt.event.*;

public class ToolTipsBasedOnMousePosition extends JApplet {
    public void init() {
        Container contentPane = getContentPane();
        ImageMap map = new ImageMap("tiger.gif");
        contentPane.setLayout(new FlowLayout());
        contentPane.add(map);
    }
}
class ImageMap extends JLabel {
    private Rectangle teeth= new Rectangle(62,203,80,55),
                      nose = new Rectangle(37,164,130,30),
                      ear = new Rectangle(228,10,65,55),
                      rEye = new Rectangle(137,103,20,17),
                      lEye = new Rectangle(65,97,16,15);

    public ImageMap(String imageName) {
        super(new ImageIcon(imageName));
        setToolTipText("tiger!");
    }
    public String getToolTipText(MouseEvent e) {
        Point p = e.getPoint();
        Strings = null;

        if(teeth.contains(p)) s = "ooooh, big teeth!";
        else if(nose.contains(p))s = "keen sense of smell";
        else if(ear.contains(p))s = "acute hearing";
        else if(rEye.contains(p) || lEye.contains(p))
            s = "excellent vision";

        return s == null ? getToolTipText() : s;
    }
}
```

The ImageMap class extends JLabel and overrides getToolTipText() in order to return text appropriate for the cursor position. If the cursor is not in a strategic location, the method mimics the implementation of JComponent.getToolTipText(MouseEvent) by invoking JComponent.getToolTipText().

`JComponent.setToolTipText()` registers the component with the `ToolTipManager` in addition to setting the tooltip text. As a result, even though the `ImageMap` class overrides `getToolTipText(MouseEvent)`, the call to `setToolTipText()` in the `ImageMap` constructor must be made in order for the tooltips to be displayed.

Preferred Locations for Tooltips

Preferred locations for tooltips can be set by overriding the `JComponent.getToolTipLocation` method. The `getToolTipLocation` method is passed a `MouseEvent` and returns a `Point` where the tooltip will be displayed. By default, `JComponent.getToolTipLocation()` returns `null`, indicating that tooltips should be displayed directly underneath the mouse. Extensions of `JComponent` can override `getToolTipLocation()` to specify the exact location at which the tooltip will be displayed.

For example, the applet listed in Example 4-19 can specify the locations at which the image map's tooltips will be displayed by overriding `getToolTipLocation`.

```
class ImageMap extends JLabel {
    private Rectangle teeth= new Rectangle(62,203,80,55),
                      nose = new Rectangle(37,164,130,30),
                      ear = new Rectangle(228,10,65,55),
                      rEye = new Rectangle(137,103,20,17),
                      lEye = new Rectangle(65,97,16,15);
    ...
    public Point getToolTipLocation(MouseEvent e) {
        if(teeth.contains(new Point(e.getX(),e.getY())))
            return new Point(teeth.x, teeth.y);
    }
}
```

If the cursor rests over the tiger's teeth, the upper-left corner of the tiger's mouth is specified as the location for the tooltip. Instead of the tooltip being displayed underneath the cursor, as in the left-hand picture in Figure 4-21, the tooltip is displayed as shown in Figure 4-22. Notice the position of the cursor relative to the position of the tooltip.

Another example of overriding `getToolTipLocation` can be found at "JToolBar" on page 560.

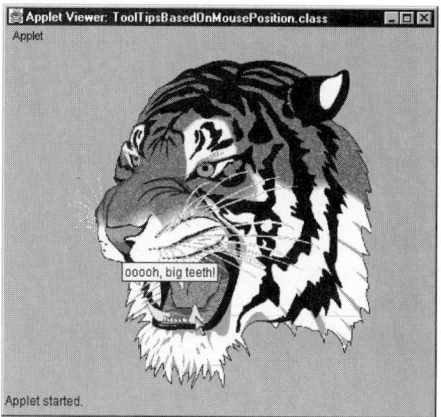

Figure 4-22 Tooltips Displayed at a Specific Location

Customizing Tooltip Behavior

As mentioned previously, tooltips are shown when the cursor rests over a component for a period of time, which is referred to as the *initial delay*. By default the initial delay is set to 750 milliseconds.

Tooltips are subsequently dismissed by one of three events:

- the cursor exits the component
- the mouse is pressed
- the dismiss delay expires

The *dismiss delay* is the amount of time conscientious tooltip readers are allotted to read the tooltip: 4 seconds, provided the cursor stays within the bounds of the component and the mouse is not pressed.

If the cursor exits a component whose tooltip is displayed and subsequently enters another component equipped with a tooltip, the second component's tooltip may be shown immediately. If the amount of time that expired between exiting the first component and entering the second is less than the *reshow delay*, the tooltip for the second component will be shown immediately. The reshow delay, by default, is 500 milliseconds. Tooltip delays are summarized in Table 4-3.

Graphic Java Mastering the JFC Volume II: Swing

Table 4-3   Tooltip Delays

Delay	Default Value	Meaning
Initial	750 milliseconds	Delay from the time the cursor rests over a component until the tooltip is displayed.
Dismiss	4 seconds	Delay from the time the tooltip is displayed until it is dismissed.
Reshow	500 milliseconds	If the cursor exits a component displaying a tooltip and enters another component equipped with a tooltip before the reshow delay expires, the second component's tooltip will be displayed immediately.

Tooltip delays are controlled by the `ToolTipManager` class, which comes with methods for setting the delays listed in Table 4-3. The `public` methods provided by the `ToolTipManager` class that are of interest to developers are listed in Table 4-4. All of the methods for setting and getting delays deal in integers.

Table 4-4   ToolTipManager Public Methods

Method Name	Implemention
setInitialDelay	Sets the initial delay in milliseconds
getInitialDelay	Returns the initial delay in milliseconds
setDismissDelay	Sets the dismiss delay in milliseconds
getDismissDelay	Returns the dismiss delay in milliseconds
setReshowDelay	Sets the reshow delay in milliseconds
getReshowDelay	Returns the reshow delay in milliseconds
setEnabled	Enables/disables all tooltips
isEnabled	Returns enabled state of all tooltips

Tooltips can be enabled or disabled for all components by invocation of the `ToolTipManager` method `setEnabled()`, which is passed a `boolean` value. If the method is passed `true`, tooltips will be enabled for all components that have registered tooltip text. If the method is passed `false`, tooltips will be disabled for all components.

 **Swing Tip ...**

How Tooltips Work

When the cursor comes to rest over a component equipped with a tooltip, a timer is started; it runs for 750 milliseconds by default. If the cursor does not move or the mouse button is not pressed while the timer ticks down, the tooltip is shown at the end of the delay. The delay is known as the *initial* delay.

When the tooltip is shown, a second timer that (by default) runs for 4 seconds is started. If the mouse does not move out of the component and the mouse button is not pressed, the tooltip will be shown until the 4 seconds is up. The delay is known as the *dismiss* delay.

When the cursor exits a component showing a tooltip, another timer is started; it runs for 0.5 seconds by default. If the cursor enters a second component equipped with a tooltip before the timer runs out, the second component's tooltip is shown immediately. The delay is known as the *reshow* delay.

All three delays are settable via ToolTipManager static methods.

Customizing Tooltip Look and Feel

Like most Swing components, tooltips have a UI delegate that determines the look and feel of the tooltip. For example, Figure 4-23 shows two buttons with different look and feels that both display a tooltip—the applet on the left is fitted with a Macintosh look and feel, and the applet on the right is fitted with an organic look and feel.

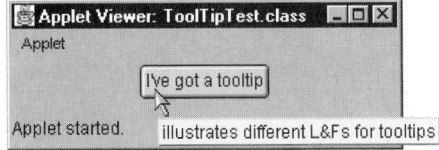 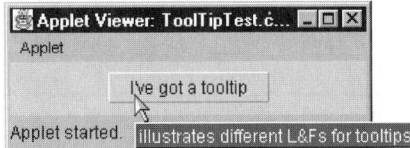

Figure 4-23 Tooltips with Different Look and Feels

The `JComponent` class is in charge of creating its own tooltip. Tooltip displaying is left to tooltips and the tooltip manager, but creation of tooltips is the component's responsibility.

`JComponent.createTooltip()` instantiates an instance of `JToolTip` and returns it. The `createToolTip` method can be overridden in the rare case that a specialized type of tooltip is required for a custom component. For instance, if multiple lines of text are desired in a tooltip, the `JToolTip` class could be extended to provide that functionality. Subsequently, components that require multiline tooltips could override their `createToolTip` method to return an instance of the multiline `JToolTip` extension. In practice, however, `JComponent.createToolTip` will rarely be overridden.

Keystroke Handling

The `JComponent` class provides a facility for handling keystrokes in nested components. Table 4-5 lists the `JComponent` methods that are concerned with keystrokes.

Table 4-5 JComponent Keystroke Handling Methods

Method Name	Implementation
registerKeyboardAction	Passed an `ActionListener`, `KeyStroke` and an integer condition—registers the keystroke with the component
unregisterKeyboardAction	Passed a keystroke to unregister
getActionForKeyStroke	Returns the Action associated with a `KeyStroke`
getConditionForKeyStroke	Returns the integer representing conditions for a specified `KeyStroke`
getRegisteredKeyStrokes	Returns an array of registered keystrokes
resetKeyboardActions	Wipes out all keyboard actions for the component

`JComponent.registerKeyboardAction(ActionListener, KeyStroke, int)` registers a keystroke; when the keystroke is typed, the specified `ActionListener`'s `actionPerformed` method is invoked if the conditions specified by the `integer` argument passed to `registerKeyboardAction()` are satisfied.

Keystrokes can be unregistered by invoking `unregisterKeyboardAction()`, and the `ActionListener` and conditions associated with a registered keystroke can be obtained by `getActionForKeyStroke()` and `getConditionForKeyStroke()`, respectively.

All of the keystrokes associated with a component are returned by the `getRegisteredKeyStrokes` method, and a component's keyboard actions can be erased with a single call to `resetKeyboardActions()`.

Keystrokes are specified by an instance of `KeyStroke`, which encapsulates a key, modifiers such as CRTL, ALT, or SHIFT, and whether or not the keystroke is associated with a key press or release.

The conditions under which keystrokes are handled are specified by `integer` constants that are passed to `registerKeyboardAction()`. The constants are listed in Table 4-6.

Table 4-6   JComponent Constants for Keystroke Handling

Constant	Meaning
WHEN_FOCUSED	Handle keystroke when the registered component has focus
WHEN_ANCESTOR_OF_FOCUSED _COMPONENT	Handle keystroke when the registered component has focus or the registered component is an ancestor of the component with focus
WHEN_IN_FOCUSED_WINDOW	Handle keystroke when the registered component has focus or any component in the same window as the registered component has focus

Keystrokes are registered with a particular component, which from here on out is referred to as the *registered* component. When a keystroke is *handled*, it means that the `ActionListener` associated with the keystroke has its `actionPerformed` method invoked.

Keystrokes that are qualified with the WHEN_FOCUSED condition are handled when the registered component has focus.

Keystrokes qualified by WHEN_ANCESTOR_OF_FOCUSED_COMPONENT are handled when either the registered component has focus or the registered component contains the component that currently has focus. For keystroke

handling, the term ancestor refers to the containment—not the inheritance—hierarchy. Ancestor in this sense is synonymous with container.

WHEN_IN_FOCUSED_WINDOW keystrokes are handled when any component that resides in the same window as the registered component has focus.

Figure 4-24 shows an applet that contains two components laid out by an instance of BorderLayout: a panel as the center component and a button as the south component. The panel in turn contains a button and a check box.

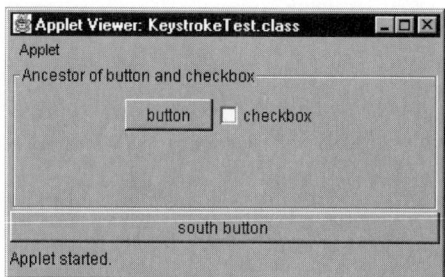

Figure 4-24 Keystroke Handling in Nested Components

After the components contained in the applet are created, keystrokes are registered with the panel, check box, and south button.

First, a keystroke is registered with the check box. KeyStrokes are unique and immutable—the only way to obtain a reference to a KeyStroke is through the static KeyStroke.getKeyStroke method, which returns a KeyStroke from a cache.

The keystroke associated with the check box is represented by an 'f'—for "focus"— key press with no modifiers. The keystroke is handled when the registered component—in this case, the check box—has focus. The keystroke is obtained by a call to KeyStroke.getKeyStroke() that takes three arguments: a constant from the java.awt.event.KeyEvent class representing the key (KeyEvent.VK_F), the modifiers associated with the key press (0), and whether the keystroke represents a key press (false) or release (true).

```
public class KeystrokeTest extends JApplet {
    ...
    public void init() {
        ...
        Listener listener = new Listener();
        ...
        checkbox.registerKeyboardAction(
                listener,
                KeyStroke.getKeyStroke(KeyEvent.VK_F,0,false),
                JComponent.WHEN_FOCUSED);
        ...
```

All of the keystrokes in the applet specify an instance of `Listener` as the
`ActionListener` whose `actionPerformed` method is invoked when the
keystrokes are handled. `Listener.actionPerformed()` determines the
component registered with the keystroke and prints an appropriate message.

```
class Listener implements ActionListener {
    public void actionPerformed(ActionEvent e) {
        Object src = e.getSource();
        String cname = src.getClass().getName();

        if(src instanceof JCheckBox) {
            System.out.print("'f' key PRESSED when checkbox");
            System.out.println(" had focus");
        }
        else if(src instanceof JPanel) {
            System.out.print("'ALT-a' key PRESSED when a");
            System.out.println(" component contained in the");
            System.out.println(" titled panel had focus");
        }
        else if(src instanceof JButton) {
            System.out.print("'w' key RELEASED when any");
            System.out.println(" component in window had focus");
        }
        System.out.println("Source:   " + cname);
        System.out.println();
    }
}
```

As a result, when the checkbox has focus, pressing the 'f' key results in the
following output:

```
'f' key PRESSED when checkbox had focus
Source:  javax.swing.JCheckBox
```

Next, a keystroke is registered with the panel. The keystroke represents an 'a'—for "ancestor"—key press with an ALT modifier.

```
...
panel.registerKeyboardAction(
        listener,
        KeyStroke.getKeyStroke(KeyEvent.VK_A,
        InputEvent.ALT_MASK, false),
        JComponent.WHEN_ANCESTOR_OF_FOCUSED_COMPONENT);
...
```

The keystroke is handled when the panel is an ancestor of the component with focus, meaning the keystroke will be handled when either the button or the check box contained in the panel has focus. Keystrokes qualified by the WHEN_ANCESTOR_OF_FOCUSED_COMPONENT condition are also handled when the registered component—in this case, the panel—has focus but the JPanel class does not accept keyboard focus.

If either the button or check box in the panel has focus, pressing ALT-a results in the following output:

```
'ALT-a' key PRESSED when a component contained in the titled
panel had focus Source:  javax.swing.JPanel
```

Finally, a keystroke is registered with the button that is added directly to the applet's content pane. The keystroke is represented by a 'w' key *release* with no modifiers. The keystroke is handled when either the registered component or any component in the same window as the button has focus.

```
...
southButton.registerKeyboardAction(
        listener,
        KeyStroke.getKeyStroke(KeyEvent.VK_W, 0, true),
        JComponent.WHEN_IN_FOCUSED_WINDOW);
...
```

The output when any component in the window has focus and the 'w' key is released is as follows:

```
'w' key RELEASED when any component in window had focus
Source:  javax.swing.JButton
```

To recap, here's how keystrokes are handled in the applet shown in Figure 4-24 on page 182. If the button contained in the panel has focus, both ALT-a key press and 'w' key release are handled. If the check box contained in the panel has focus, all three keystrokes are handled when the appropriate key is pressed or released. If the south button has focus, only the 'w' keystroke is handled when the 'w' key is released.

Note: The applet will not work as advertised with the Macintosh look and feel because Macintosh buttons cannot accept focus.

The applet is listed in its entirety in Example 4-20.

Example 4-20 Handling Nested Keystrokes

```
import java.applet.Applet;
import javax.swing.*;
import java.awt.*;
import java.awt.event.*;

public class KeystrokeTest extends JApplet {
    private JButton button = new JButton("button");

    public void init() {
        Container contentPane = getContentPane();
        JPanel panel  = new JPanel();
        JCheckBox checkbox = new JCheckBox("checkbox");
        JButton southButton = new JButton("south button");
        Listener listener = new Listener();

        panel.setBorder(
            BorderFactory.createTitledBorder(
                ("Ancestor of button and checkbox")));

        checkbox.registerKeyboardAction(
                listener,
                KeyStroke.getKeyStroke(KeyEvent.VK_F,0,false),
                JComponent.WHEN_FOCUSED);

        panel.registerKeyboardAction(
                listener,
                KeyStroke.getKeyStroke(KeyEvent.VK_A,
                InputEvent.ALT_MASK),
                JComponent.WHEN_ANCESTOR_OF_FOCUSED_COMPONENT);

        southButton.registerKeyboardAction(
                listener,
```

```
                    KeyStroke.getKeyStroke(KeyEvent.VK_W, 0, true),
                    JComponent.WHEN_IN_FOCUSED_WINDOW);

            panel.add(button);
            panel.add(checkbox);

            contentPane.add(panel, "Center");
            contentPane.add(southButton, "South");
        }
    }
    class Listener implements ActionListener {
        public void actionPerformed(ActionEvent e) {
            Object src = e.getSource();
            String cname = src.getClass().getName();

            if(src instanceof JCheckBox) {
                System.out.print("'f' key PRESSED when checkbox");
                System.out.println(" had focus");
            }
            else if(src instanceof JPanel) {
                System.out.print("'ALT-a' key PRESSED when a");
                System.out.println(" component contained in the");
                System.out.println(" titled panel had focus");
            }
            else if(src instanceof JButton) {
                System.out.print("'w' key RELEASED when any");
                System.out.println(" component in window had focus");
            }
            System.out.println("Source:   " + cname);
            System.out.println();
        }
    }
```

Client Properties

Every instance of JComponent maintains a dictionary of properties referred to as
client properties. A dictionary consists of a set of key/value pairs, where the keys
and values may be any type of object. Client properties are used by the Swing
classes themselves; for example, components maintain their tooltip text as a client
property, and the JLayeredPane[7] class maintains the layer for each of its
components as a client property.

---

7.   JLayeredPane is a container that can display its components on separate layers.

Client properties are bound properties, which means property change events are fired to the component's property change listeners whenever a client property is modified. Table 4-7 lists the JComponent methods dealing with client properties.

Table 4-7   JComponent Public Methods for Client Properties

Method Name	Implemenation
putClientProperty	Passed a key and value, both of type Object. Associates the value with an existing client property or creates a new client property with the specified key/value pair.
getClientProperty	Returns the value (an Object) associated with the specified client property key (also an Object)

The actual dictionary that maintains client properties is a private member of the JComponent class, and no public—or protected—accessor is provided for it. Consequently, it is not possible to peruse all of the client properties that have been set for a given component, for example. Only individual properties can be accessed by the methods listed in Table 4-7.

The putClientProperty method allows a key/value pair to be registered as a client property. If a null value is passed to putClientProperty() and a client property with the specified key exists, the property is removed from the dictionary of client properties.

The getClientProperty method returns the value associated with a client property identified by the specified key. If there is no such client property, then a null value is returned.

The applet shown in Figure 4-25 contains a button that maintains a dynamic target; when the button is activated, it toggles the background color of the component specified as its "target" client property.

The button's target is one of the three panels displayed in the applet and is set by a choice made from the combo box.

The applet creates the button, combo box, and three panels.

```
public class Test extends JApplet {
    JButton button = new JButton("toggle target color");
    JComboBox targetCombo = new JComboBox();
    JPanel[] targets = { new JPanel(),
                         new JPanel(),
                         new JPanel() };
    . . .
```

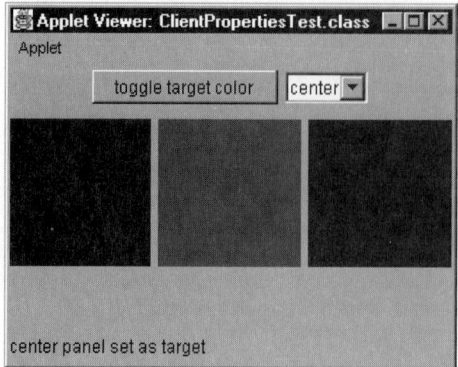

Figure 4-25 A Button with a Dynamic Target

The targets are instances of JPanel that have their preferred size set to a dimension 100 pixels wide and 100 pixels high.

When the combo box is activated, the button's target is set to the selected item.

```
targetCombo.addActionListener(new ActionListener() {
    public void actionPerformed(ActionEvent e) {
        button.putClientProperty(
                "target",
                targets[targetCombo.getSelectedIndex()]);
    }
});
```

The button's action listener obtains a reference to the component stashed away as the "target" client property. The target's background is set, and the target is subsequently repainted.

```
button.addActionListener(new ActionListener() {
    public void actionPerformed(ActionEvent e) {
        Component c =
                (Component)button.getClientProperty("target");

        if(c != null) {
            Color bg = c.getBackground();

            c.setBackground(bg == Color.blue ?
                                Color.red : Color.blue);
            c.repaint();
        }
    }
});
```

The applet adds a property change listener to the button. When the "target" client property is modified, the listener updates the applet's status bar accordingly.

```
button.addPropertyChangeListener(
                         new PropertyChangeListener() {
    public void propertyChange(PropertyChangeEvent e) {
        if(e.getPropertyName().equals("target")) {
            showStatus(
                (String)targetCombo.getSelectedItem() +
                " panel set as target");
        }
    }
});
```

The applet shown in Figure 4-25 is listed in its entirety in Example 4-21.

Example 4-21 Assigning a Dynamic Target to a Button, Using Client Properties

```
import javax.swing.*;
import java.util.*;
import java.awt.*;
import java.awt.event.*;
import java.beans.*;

public class ClientPropertiesTest extends JApplet {
    JButton button = new JButton("toggle target color");
    JComboBox targetCombo = new JComboBox();
    JPanel[] targets = { new JPanel(),
                         new JPanel(),
                         new JPanel() };
    public void init() {
        Container contentPane = getContentPane();
        Dimension targetPreferredSize = new Dimension(100,100);
        JPanel targetPanel = new JPanel();

        for(int i=0; i < targets.length; ++i) {
            targets[i].setBackground(Color.blue);
            targets[i].setPreferredSize(targetPreferredSize);
            targetPanel.add(targets[i]);

        }
        targetCombo.addItem("left");
        targetCombo.addItem("center");
        targetCombo.addItem("right");

        contentPane.setLayout(new FlowLayout());
        contentPane.add(button);
        contentPane.add(targetCombo);
        contentPane.add(targetPanel);

        button.putClientProperty("target", targets[0]);
```

```
button.addActionListener(new ActionListener() {
    public void actionPerformed(ActionEvent e) {
        Component c =
            (Component)button.getClientProperty("target");

        if(c != null) {
            Color bg = c.getBackground();

            c.setBackground(bg == Color.blue ?
                        Color.red : Color.blue);

            c.repaint();
        }
    }
});
targetCombo.addActionListener(new ActionListener() {
    public void actionPerformed(ActionEvent e) {
        button.putClientProperty(
            "target",
            targets[targetCombo.getSelectedIndex()]);
    }
});
button.addPropertyChangeListener(
                        new PropertyChangeListener() {
    public void propertyChange(PropertyChangeEvent e) {
        if(e.getPropertyName().equals("target")) {
            showStatus(
                (String)targetCombo.getSelectedItem() +
                " panel set as target");
        }
    }
});
    }
}
```

Swing Tip ...

Client Properties vs. Inheritance

Client properties lend a degree of extensibility to the JComponent class that would otherwise be available only through subclassing. For instance, instead of subclassing a component and maintaining a reference to an object in the subclass, a client property can be added to the original component. This possibility allows for greater flexibility and reduces the need to use inheritance when customizing component behavior.

Focus Management

By default, pressing the TAB key in a Swing container moves focus to the next focusable component, and SHIFT-TAB moves focus to the previous focusable component. The default behavior can be modified with JComponent focus properties or replacement of the default focus manager.

JComponent Focus Properties

All lightweight Swing components maintain the five properties pertaining to focus management that are listed in Table 4-8. The Setter Method column indicates whether the JComponent class provides methods to set the property. Setter methods are not provided for focusCycleRoot, focusTraversable, and managingFocus. Therefore, to modify the default behavior, the JComponent methods isFocusCycleRoot(), isFocusTraversable(), and isManagingFocus() must be overridden in an extension of JComponent.

Table 4-8   JComponent Focus Properties

Property Name	Data Type	Setter Method	Default[1]
focusCycleRoot	boolean		false
focusTraversable	boolean		true
managingFocus	boolean		false
requestFocusEnabled	boolean	•	true
nextFocusableComponent	Component	•	null

1. As defined by the JComponent class; some JComponent extensions may override the default behavior.

focusCycleRoot — Determines whether a container contains components that form their own focus cycle. If the property is set to true, pressing the TAB key will move focus into the container and among the container's components, but not out of the container itself.

focusTraversable — Determines whether the focus manager will transfer focus to a component. A component that specifies false for its focusTraversable property will still accept focus when requestFocus() is invoked. For example, if a button's focusTraversable property is set to false (by overriding isFocusTraversable() in an extension of JButton), clicking

in the button results in a call to `requestFocus()`, and the button will accept focus. On the other hand, if TAB or SHIFT-TAB is pressed, the button will not accept focus.

managingFocus — Determines whether keys pressed to shift focus to or from a component are passed onto the component itself; by default they are not.

requestFocusEnabled — Is essentially the inverse of the `focusTraversable` property; if the property is set to `false`, a component will not accept focus when `requestFocus()` is invoked, but the focus manager will transfer focus to the component as a result of a key press.

nextFocusableComponent — Specifies the next component to receive focus when a TAB key is pressed. Notice that there is no provision to set the previous focusable component.

The applet shown in Figure 4-26 illustrates setting the properties listed in Table 4-8.

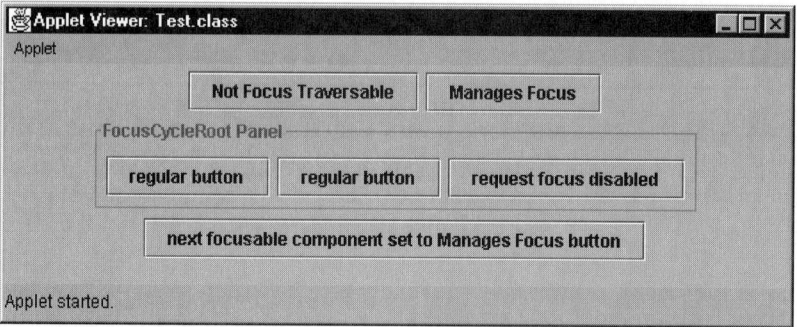

Figure 4-26 Specifying Focus Properties for Swing Components

The top-left button is an extension of `JButton` that overrides `isFocusTraversable` to return `false`. If the button is activated, it will receive focus; however, the component will not receive focus as the result of a TAB or SHIFT-TAB. The top-right button is also an extension of `JButton` that overrides `isManagingFocus` to return `false`. When the button receives focus as a result of a TAB or SHIFT-TAB key, the key press is passed to the component's `processComponentKeyEvent` method.

The "FocusCycleRoot Panel" is an extension of `JPanel` that overrides `isFocusCycleRoot()` to return `true`. Once the focus is given to one of the buttons in the panel, pressing TAB or SHIFT-TAB will not move focus out of the panel but will instead *cycle* through the buttons contained in the panel.

The "request focus disabled" button has `setRequestFocusEnabled(false)` invoked on its behalf. The button will not accept focus when `requestFocus()` is called (for example, when the button is activated) but will receive focus as a result of the TAB or SHIFT-TAB key press.

The bottom component specifies the next focusable component to be the "Manages Focus" button. Pressing TAB when the button has focus transfers focus to the "Manages Focus" button.

The applet shown in Figure 4-26 is listed in Example 4-22.

Example 4-22 Specifying Focus Properties for Swing Components

```java
import javax.swing.*;
import java.awt.*;
import java.awt.event.*;

public class Test extends JApplet {
    private JButton button_1 = new NotFocusTraversableButton(),
        button_2 = new ButtonThatManagesFocus(),
        button_3 = new JButton("regular button"),
        button_4 = new JButton("regular button"),
        button_5 = new JButton("request focus disabled"),
        button_6 = new JButton(
        "next focusable component set to Manages Focus button");

    public void init() {
        Container contentPane = getContentPane();
        FocusCycleRootPanel panel = new FocusCycleRootPanel();

        button_5.setRequestFocusEnabled(false);
        button_6.setNextFocusableComponent(button_2);

        panel.add(button_3);
        panel.add(button_4);
        panel.add(button_5);

        contentPane.setLayout(new FlowLayout());
        contentPane.add(button_1);
        contentPane.add(button_2);
        contentPane.add(panel);
        contentPane.add(button_6);
    }
}
```

```
class ButtonThatManagesFocus extends JButton {
    public ButtonThatManagesFocus() {
        super("Manages Focus");
    }
    public boolean isManagingFocus() {
        return true;
    }
    public void processComponentKeyEvent(KeyEvent e) {
        System.out.println(e);
    }
}
class NotFocusTraversableButton extends JButton {
    public NotFocusTraversableButton() {
        super("Not Focus Traversable");
    }
    public boolean isFocusTraversable() {
        return false;
    }
}
class FocusCycleRootPanel extends JPanel {
    public FocusCycleRootPanel() {
        setBorder(BorderFactory.createTitledBorder(
                "FocusCycleRoot Panel"));
    }
    public boolean isFocusCycleRoot() {
        return true;
    }
}
```

Focus Manager

Swing's focus manager is responsible for transferring focus from one component
to another. Swing provides an abstract FocusManager class and a
DefaultFocusManager extension. The DefaultFocusManager class
transfers focus from left to right and top to bottom, which corresponds to the
order in which words are read on a page.[8]

The default focus manager is responsible for determining which keys move focus.
By default, TAB and CTRL-TAB move focus forward, and SHIFT-TAB and CTRL-
SHIFT-TAB move focus backward. The DefaultFocusManager can be
extended and its processKeyEvent method overridden to modify the default
behavior.

8.   For Western languages.

The default focus manager determines which component will next receive focus
with the aid of the `compareTabOrder` method, provided that the component
that currently has focus has not overridden `getNextFocusedComponent()` to
return a non-`null` component. `DefaultFocusManager.compareTabOrder` is
passed two components and returns a `boolean` value that indicates whether the
first component it is passed comes before the second component in the tab order.

The applet shown in Figure 4-27 implements a focus manager with a tab order
that is the opposite of the default focus manager's tab order. The tab order for the
applet's focus manager is from right to left and bottom to top.

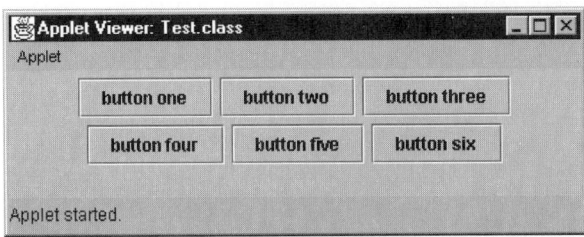

Figure 4-27 Implementing a Custom Focus Manager

The applet shown in Figure 4-27 is listed in Example 4-23.

Example 4-23 Implementing a Custom Focus Manager

```
import javax.swing.*;
import java.awt.*;
import java.awt.event.*;

public class Test extends JApplet {
    private JButton button_1 = new JButton("button one"),
                button_2 = new JButton("button two"),
                button_3 = new JButton("button three"),
                button_4 = new JButton("button four"),
                button_5 = new JButton("button five"),
                button_6 = new JButton("button six");

    public void init() {
        Container contentPane = getContentPane();

        javax.swing.FocusManager.setCurrentManager(
                        new CustomFocusManager());
```

```
        contentPane.setLayout(new FlowLayout());
        contentPane.add(button_1);
        contentPane.add(button_2);
        contentPane.add(button_3);
        contentPane.add(button_4);
        contentPane.add(button_5);
        contentPane.add(button_6);
    }
}
class CustomFocusManager extends DefaultFocusManager {
    public boolean compareTabOrder(Component a, Component b) {
        Point location_a = a.getLocation(),
              location_b = b.getLocation();

        int ax = location_a.x, ay = location_a.y;
        int bx = location_b.x, by = location_b.y;

        if(Math.abs(ay - by) < 10) {
            return (bx < ax);
        }
        return (ay > by);
    }
}
```

The applet sets the focus manager with a call to
FocusManager.setCurrentManager(). The applet uses the fully qualified
name of the FocusManager class because the AWT also has a focus manager
with the same name.

The CustomFocusManager class extends DefaultFocusManager and
overrides the compareTabOrder method. The x and y coordinates for each
component are obtained with a call to getLocation(), and a true value is
returned if the second component is to the left of or above the first component.

Accessibility

Historically, computer technology advancements have failed to account for users
with disabilities. For example, when windowing technology replaced textual
displays, it took years before screen readers became available to assist blind users
in navigating their displays. With Swing, assistive technology is built into
components from the ground up.

Accessibility is defined as technology that makes computers accessible to all users. This includes not only users with disabilities, but also users of nomadic systems. For instance, although a visual display may be included in an automobile's navigational system, it must also be accessible to drivers without requiring them to take their eyes off the road. This can be accomplished by interpreting the visual display and issuing audible commands for navigation.

The Java Foundation Classes support accessibility in three ways:

- Pluggable Look and Feel
- Java Accessibility API
- Java Accessibility Utilities

The pluggable look-and-feel design of the Swing classes enables developers to implement alternative look and feels for user interface components. For example, instead of a visual look and feel, components could be fitted with an audio look and feel for sight-impaired users. On the other hand, user interface components that have an audio aspect could be fitted with a look and feel that displays captions whenever an audio clip is played, for hearing-impaired users. The pluggable look-and-feel architecture also includes support for multiplexing UIs, so that auxiliary UIs can may be added to a component. For example, a multiplexing UI could be implemented to drive a Braille terminal in addition to the usual visual representation of the component. See "Auxiliary UIs" on page 354 for more information concerning Swing's multiplexing look and feel.

The Java Accessibility API enables user interface components to provide information to an assistive technology. The `AccessibleContext` class defines the basic set of information that components should provide. For example, an assistive technology should be able to recognize user interface components and (perhaps audibly) identify them to a user. The `AccessibleContext` class provides a `getAccessibleRole()` that identifies the role of a user interface component, which typically identifies the type of component. `AccessibleContext.getAccessibleName()` and `AccessibleContext.getAccessibleDescription()` provide more information specific to a particular component instance. A scrollbar's `AccessibleContext`, for example, would identify the component's role as `AccessibleRole.SCROLL_BAR`, whereas the name and description would identify the functionality embodied by a specific scrollbar instance.

`JComponent` provides built-in support for providing accessibility information. All of the Swing components take advantage of the capabilities built into `JComponent` to provide accessible information about themselves. For example,

the applet shown in Figure 4-28 prints the accessible roles for a text field when the "show accessible information" button is activated. The output for the applet is as follows:

```
Accessible Role: text
Accessible Description: Enter your first name
Accessible Name: First Name
```

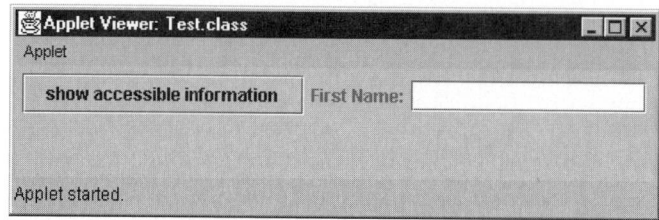

Figure 4-28 Accessing Accessibility Information

The applet shown in Figure 4-28 is listed Example 4-24.

Example 4-24 Accessing Accessibility Information

```java
import javax.swing.*;
import javax.accessibility.*;
import java.awt.*;
import java.awt.event.*;

public class Test extends JApplet {
    public void init() {
        Container contentPane = getContentPane();
        JLabel label  = new JLabel("First Name:");
        JButton showButton = new JButton(
                            "show accessible information");

        final JTextField field = new JTextField(15);

        AccessibleContext fieldContext =
                    field.getAccessibleContext();

        fieldContext.setAccessibleName("First Name");
        fieldContext.setAccessibleDescription(
                        "Enter your first name");

        contentPane.setLayout(new FlowLayout());
```

```
        contentPane.add(showButton);
        contentPane.add(label);
        contentPane.add(field);

        showButton.addActionListener(new ActionListener() {
            public void actionPerformed(ActionEvent e) {
                AccessibleContext context;
                AccessibleRole role;

                context = field.getAccessibleContext();
                role = context.getAccessibleRole();

                System.out.print("Accessible Role: ");
                System.out.println(
                        context.getAccessibleRole());

                System.out.print("Accessible Description: ");
                System.out.println(
                        context.getAccessibleDescription());

                System.out.print("Accessible Name: ");
                System.out.println(
                        context.getAccessibleName());

            }
        });

    }
}
```

The applet creates a text field and sets the field's accessible name and description. An action listener is added to the "show accessible information" button that obtains the field's accessible context, which is used to obtain the field's accessible role, description, and name.

Parting Shots

The JComponent class is the base class for all Swing lightweight components. JComponent extends the java.awt.Container class, which in turn extends java.awt.Component. As a result, each Swing lightweight component stands atop a veritable mountain of functionality.

In addition to inheriting functionality from its AWT superclasses, the JComponent class itself provides a substantial amount of infrastructure. More than 100 JComponent methods provide support for opaque and transparent components, double buffering, debug graphics, auto scrolling, tooltips, etc.

The JComponent class also remedies some design flaws inherited from its AWT superclasses. For instance, the AWT's Component class commits a cardinal object-oriented sin by requiring the use of inheritance to modify the minimum, maximum, and preferred sizes of its instances. In general, inheritance should not be required to modify characteristics that vary widely among instances of a class because it can result in an explosion of subclasses. The JComponent class provides the setter methods that are lacking in the Component class, and therefore sizes for Swing lightweight components are settable without the use of inheritance.

Although Swing components are built upon the infrastructure of the AWT, it is important to keep in mind that all JComponent extensions are actually AWT containers. In addition, Swing lightweight components can be equipped with a border and a UI delegate. This feature is significant, for instance, when overriding the rendering behavior of a Swing lightweight component. Instead of the paint method being overridden, as is common for AWT components, the paintComponent method is typically overridden for JComponent extensions. Also, care must be taken to account for the insets region of Swing lightweight components when minimum, maximum, and preferred sizes are calculated.

The JComponent class builds upon the functionality provided by its AWT superclasses and at the same time patches some of the object-oriented potholes it inherits. As a result, JComponent provides a solid base upon which all Swing lightweight components are based.

CHAPTER
5

Borders, Icons, and Actions

This chapter discusses three Swing utilities: borders, icons, and actions.

Borders are drawn around the edges of a component and come in a number of different varieties: line borders, bevel borders, matte borders, etc. Borders themselves are not components; instead, they draw into the insets of a specified component.

Icons are graphical objects, typically a small image. Like borders, icons draw into a specified component at a specific location.

Actions encapsulate a logical operation for a graphical user interface and also simplify the construction of user interface elements. Actions are typically composed of one or more icons or text strings. Actions can be added to certain containers that create an appropriate component from the action. For example, actions can be added to a menu by means of the `JMenu.add(Action)` method. When an action is added to a menu, the menu creates a menu item, using the text and icon associated with the action, and adds the menu item to itself.

Borders, icons, and actions are significant because each can be associated with any number of components. Because borders and icons are not components but instead draw into a component, they can be shared among any number of components that support their use. Actions are also meant to be shared among components and are used as a central point of control for maintaining the enabled state of the action's associated components.

Borders

All extensions of JComponent, with the exception of JViewport, can be fitted with a border by constructing the desired type of border and subsequently passing it to JComponent.setBorder(Border). Although each component can have only one border associated with it, Swing supports compound borders, so in practice a single component can have several borders nested to an arbitrary depth.

Borders are simple to use; for example, Figure 5-1 shows an instance of JPanel fitted with a titled border.

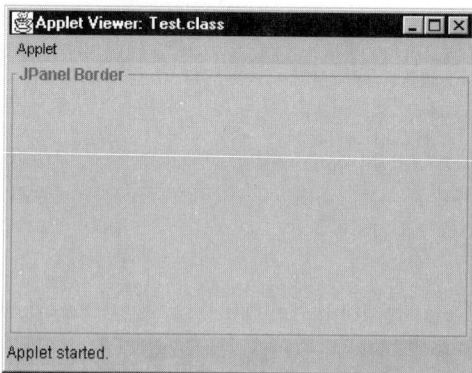

Figure 5-1 A JPanel with a Titled Border

The applet shown in Figure 5-1 is listed in Example 5-1.

Example 5-1 An Applet with a Bordered JPanel

```
import java.awt.BorderLayout;
import javax.swing.*;
import javax.swing.border.*;

public class Test extends JApplet {
    public void init() {
        JPanel panel = new JPanel();

        panel.setBorder(new TitledBorder("JPanel Border"));
        getContentPane().add(panel, BorderLayout.CENTER);
    }
}
```

The applet creates a titled border that is passed to the panel's `setBorder` method.

Borders and Insets

AWT containers have an `insets` property that defines padding around the outside of the container. Layout managers are careful to lay out a container's components so that the components do not encroach upon the container's insets region. The `insets` property for containers is a read-only property; the only way to modify an AWT container's insets is to subclass a container and override the `getInsets` method.

Other than `JViewport`, which does not allow itself to be fitted with a border, Swing components do not override `getInsets()` to define an insets region. Instead, Swing components are fitted with an empty border if they are to have empty space around their edges. When asked for their insets, Swing components return the insets of their border. If a Swing component does not have a border, only then will it return the `insets` property maintained by its superclass: `java.awt.Container`.

Custom components built using Swing should follow suit and not override `getInsets()`. Instead, custom components should use an empty border if padding around their edges is desired.

Using empty borders to specify insets effectively makes the `insets` property settable on a per-instance basis. Whereas AWT containers can modify their insets only by subclassing and overriding `getInsets()`, Swing components can modify their insets by setting their border to an instance of `EmptyBorder`.

Swing Border Types

Swing provides a number of different border types, as listed in Table 5-1.

Table 5-1   Swing Border Types

Border Type	Description	Opaque	Associated Constants
Bevel	A 3D border	Yes	RAISED, LOWERED
Compound	Contains an inner and outer border	Varies	n/a

Table 5-1 Swing Border Types (Continued)

Border Type	Description	Opaque	Associated Constants
Empty	A transparent border that does no drawing	No	n/a
Etched	An etched border	Yes	RAISED, LOWERED
Line	A single, colored line border with settable thickness	Yes	n/a
Matte	A border that paints a solid color or tiles an image in the border margin	Yes	n/a
SoftBevel	A bevel border with softened corners	No	RAISED, LOWERED
Titled	A border with a title. The title's position is settable.	No	DEFAULT_POSITION, ABOVE_TOP, TOP, BELOW_TOP, ABOVE_BOTTOM, BOTTOM, BELOW_BOTTOM, DEFAULT_JUSTIFICATION, LEFT, CENTER, RIGHT

Each of the border types listed in Table 5-1 corresponds to a class in the `swing.border` package. The bevel, soft bevel, and etched borders can be specified as either raised or lowered, and the title of a titled border can be placed in a number of different positions within the border. The difference between bevel and soft bevel is almost impossible to discern by the untrained, naked eye, but soft bevel rounds the corners of the bevel border somewhat.

Opaque borders paint every pixel in their insets region. Compound borders are opaque if both their inner and outer borders are opaque, hence the *Varies* designation for the compound border's opaque property in Table 5-1.

Oddly enough, the notion of a border being opaque has no meaning throughout the rest of Swing. In other words, there is no code in Swing itself that varies its behavior depending upon whether a border is opaque or not. In fact, if you search through the Swing source code, you'll find that the `Border.isBorderOpaque` method is never invoked.

The concept of a border being opaque is a remnant of an initial border design that never saw the light of day. Regardless, if you never need to optimize the drawing of a border depending upon whether the border is opaque or not, you've got a head start with the `Border.isBorderOpaque` method.

Figure 5-2 shows an applet that displays each type of Swing border.

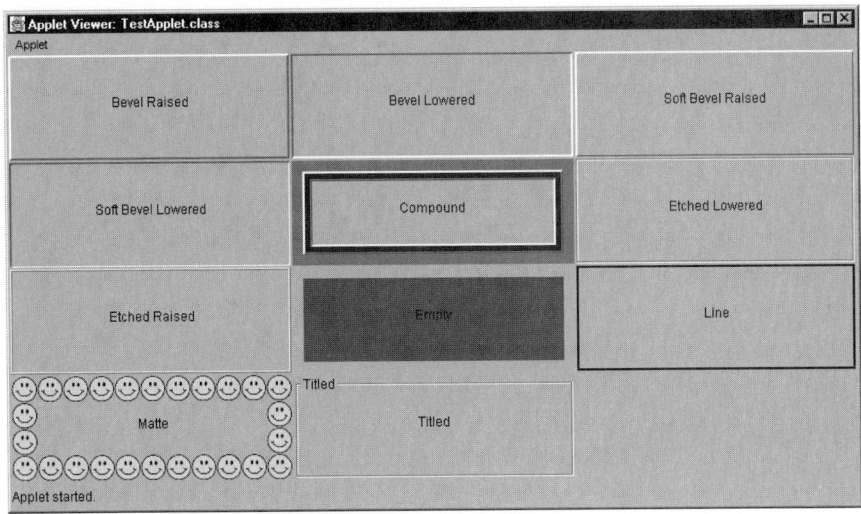

Figure 5-2 Swing Border Types

The applet shown in Figure 5-2 contains a single extension of JPanel—an
AllBordersPanel—that in turn contains eleven panels. Each of the eleven
panels is an instance of PanelWithTitle, another JPanel extension whose
overridden paint method paints a centered title.

All of the eleven panels are instantiated and fitted with a border.

```
class AllBordersPanel extends JPanel {
    public AllBordersPanel() {
        JPanel bl = new PanelWithTitle("Bevel Lowered"),
               br = new PanelWithTitle("Bevel Raised"),
               c = new PanelWithTitle("Compound"),
               l = new PanelWithTitle("Line"),
               m = new PanelWithTitle("Matte"),
               e = new PanelWithEmptyBorder("Empty"),
               t = new PanelWithTitle("Titled"),
               sbr = new PanelWithTitle("Soft Bevel Raised"),
               sbl = new PanelWithTitle("Soft Bevel Lowered"),
               el = new PanelWithTitle("Etched Lowered"),
               er = new PanelWithTitle("Etched Raised");
        ...

        bl.setBorder(BorderFactory.createLoweredBevelBorder());
        br.setBorder(BorderFactory.createRaisedBevelBorder());
        sbr.setBorder(new SoftBevelBorder(BevelBorder.RAISED));
```

```
    sbl.setBorder(new SoftBevelBorder(BevelBorder.LOWERED));
    t.setBorder(BorderFactory.createTitledBorder("Titled"));
    l.setBorder(
        BorderFactory.createLineBorder(Color.black,2));

    c.setBorder(
        BorderFactory.createCompoundBorder(
        // outer border
            BorderFactory.createCompoundBorder(
                BorderFactory.createLineBorder(Color.gray,10),
                BorderFactory.createRaisedBevelBorder()),
        // inner border
            BorderFactory.createCompoundBorder(
                BorderFactory.createLineBorder(Color.blue,5),
                BorderFactory.createLoweredBevelBorder())));

    el.setBorder(BorderFactory.createEtchedBorder(
                getBackground().brighter(),
                getBackground().darker()));

    er.setBorder(BorderFactory.createEtchedBorder(
                getBackground().darker(),
                getBackground().brighter()));

    m.setBorder(BorderFactory.createMatteBorder(
                iconsz.height, iconsz.width,
                iconsz.height, iconsz.width,
                icon));
    ...
    }
    ...
} // end of AllBordersPanel class
```

The borders are all obtained through the border factory—instead of being directly instantiated—with the exception of the soft bevel borders. The BorderFactory class in the 1.1 Swing release does not include methods for creating soft bevel borders. The border factory is discussed in "The Border Factory—Sharing Borders" on page 216.

Another annoyance with the border factory is the fact that its methods are not symmetric. For example, BorderFactory has methods for creating raised and lowered etched borders—createRaisedBevelBorder and createLoweredBevelBorder, respectively. However, BorderFactory does not have analogous methods for etched borders. To explicitly create raised or lowered etched borders, you must use the createEtchedBorder method, where two colors must be supplied, one for the highlight and one for the shadow.[1]

1. BorderFactory.createEtchedBorder() creates a raised etched border.

The matte border is created by specifying an `ImageIcon` that is tiled in the insets of the border. The panel with an empty border fills its interior with a solid color in order to highlight its border.

The compound border contains two borders, both of which are compound borders themselves. Therefore, the panel with the compound border actually has four nested borders. The first border passed to the `CompoundBorder` constructor is the outer border, and the second represents the inner border.

The applet is listed in its entirety in Example 5-2.

Example 5-2 An Applet That Displays All Swing Border Types

```java
import java.awt.*;
import javax.swing.*;
import javax.swing.border.*;

public class Test extends JApplet {
    public void init() {
        JPanel jpanel = new AllBordersPanel();
        getContentPane().add(jpanel, BorderLayout.CENTER);
    }
}
class AllBordersPanel extends JPanel {
    public AllBordersPanel() {
        JPanel bl = new PanelWithTitle("Bevel Lowered"),
                br = new PanelWithTitle("Bevel Raised"),
                c = new PanelWithTitle("Compound"),
                l = new PanelWithTitle("Line"),
                m = new PanelWithTitle("Matte"),
                e = new PanelWithEmptyBorder("Empty"),
                t = new PanelWithTitle("Titled"),
                sbr = new PanelWithTitle("Soft Bevel Raised"),
                sbl = new PanelWithTitle("Soft Bevel Lowered"),
                el = new PanelWithTitle("Etched Lowered"),
                er = new PanelWithTitle("Etched Raised");

        setLayout(new GridLayout(4,3,2,2));

        ImageIcon icon = new ImageIcon("smiley.gif");

        Dimension iconsz = new Dimension(icon.getIconWidth(),
                                    icon.getIconHeight());

        bl.setBorder(BorderFactory.createLoweredBevelBorder());
        br.setBorder(BorderFactory.createRaisedBevelBorder());
        sbr.setBorder(new SoftBevelBorder(BevelBorder.RAISED));
        sbl.setBorder(new SoftBevelBorder(BevelBorder.LOWERED));
        t.setBorder(BorderFactory.createTitledBorder("Titled"));
        l.setBorder(
            BorderFactory.createLineBorder(Color.black,2));
```

```
            c.setBorder(
                BorderFactory.createCompoundBorder(
                    BorderFactory.createCompoundBorder(
                        BorderFactory.createLineBorder(Color.gray,10),
                        BorderFactory.createRaisedBevelBorder()),
                    BorderFactory.createCompoundBorder(
                        BorderFactory.createLineBorder(Color.blue,5),
                        BorderFactory.createLoweredBevelBorder())));

            el.setBorder(BorderFactory.createEtchedBorder(
                        getBackground().brighter(),
                        getBackground().darker()));

            er.setBorder(BorderFactory.createEtchedBorder(
                        getBackground().darker(),
                        getBackground().brighter()));

            m.setBorder(BorderFactory.createMatteBorder(
                            iconsz.height, iconsz.width,
                            iconsz.height, iconsz.width,
                            icon));

            add(br); add(bl); add(sbr);
            add(sbl); add(c); add(el);
            add(er); add(e); add(l);
            add(m); add(t);
        }
    }
    class PanelWithTitle extends JPanel {
        private String title;

        public PanelWithTitle(String title) {
            this.title = title;
        }
        public void paintComponent(Graphics g) {
            FontMetrics fm = g.getFontMetrics();
            Dimension size = getSize();
            int titleW = fm.stringWidth(title);

            g.setColor(Color.black);
            g.drawString(title, size.width/2 - titleW/2,
                        size.height/2);
        }
    }
    class PanelWithEmptyBorder extends PanelWithTitle {
        public PanelWithEmptyBorder(String title) {
            super(title);
            setBorder(BorderFactory.createEmptyBorder(10,10,10,10));
        }
        public void paintComponent(Graphics g) {
            Dimension size = getSize();
            Insets insets = getInsets();
```

```
g.setColor(Color.red);
g.fillRect(insets.left,insets.top,
           size.width-2*insets.left,
           size.height-2*insets.top);

super.paintComponent(g);
    }
}
```

Swing Tip ...

Borders Are Not Components

Swing's border classes draw into components, but borders themselves are not components. The component that a border draws into is passed to the Border.paintBorder method. As a result, a single border may be shared among any number of components; when each component draws its border, it passes itself to Border.paintBorder() as the component to draw into.

Opaque vs. Transparent Borders

Borders, like Swing lightweight components, are designated as being either opaque or partially transparent. A border is opaque only if it paints every pixel; if a border fails to paint even one of its pixels, then it is not opaque.

Figure 5-3 shows an applet containing a JPanel extension that is fitted with a titled border. Titled borders are not opaque.

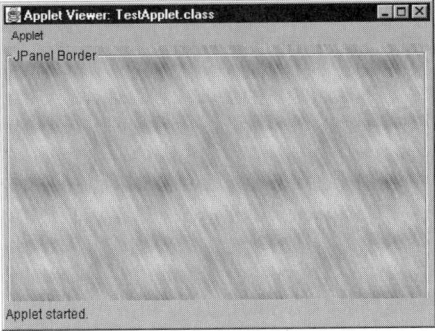

Figure 5-3 A JPanel with a Titled Border

The panel tiles an image icon over its background. The applet shown in Figure 5-3 is listed in Example 5-3.

Example 5-3 An Example of a Partially Transparent Border

```java
import javax.swing.*;
import javax.swing.border.*;
import java.awt.*;

public class Test extends JApplet {
    JPanel panel = new RainPanel();
    TitledBorder border = new TitledBorder("JPanel Border");

    public void init() {
        panel.setBorder(border);
        getContentPane().add(panel, BorderLayout.CENTER);

        System.out.println("opaque = " + border.isBorderOpaque());
        System.out.println(
                "insets = " + border.getBorderInsets(panel));
    }
}
class RainPanel extends JPanel {
    public void paintComponent(Graphics g) {
        Icon icon = new ImageIcon("rain.gif");
        Dimension size = getSize();

        int patchW = icon.getIconWidth(),
        patchH = icon.getIconHeight();

        for(int r=0; r < size.width; r += patchW) {
            for(int c=0; c < size.height; c += patchH)
                icon.paintIcon(this, g, r, c);
        }
    }
}
```

The applet prints whether the titled border is opaque and lists the insets occupied by the border:

```
opaque = false
insets = java.awt.Insets[top=21,left=6,bottom=6,right=6]
```

Although the border occupies the insets shown above, the background of the panel shows through the border because the border is not opaque.

Note that `RainPanel` is doing something that is normally considered bad design—painting into its insets area. Because components derived from `JComponent` are containers, they should be careful not to paint into their insets

region—see "Overriding Paint Methods in Swing Components" on page 140. In this case, painting into the insets region produces the desired effect to illustrate a semitransparent border.

The Border Package

All classes relevant to Swing borders, with the exception of the BorderFactory class, reside in the swing.border package. The package contains a Border interface, an AbstractBorder class, and a number of concrete border classes corresponding to the border types listed in Table 5-1 on page 205.

A class diagram of the border package is shown in Figure 5-4.

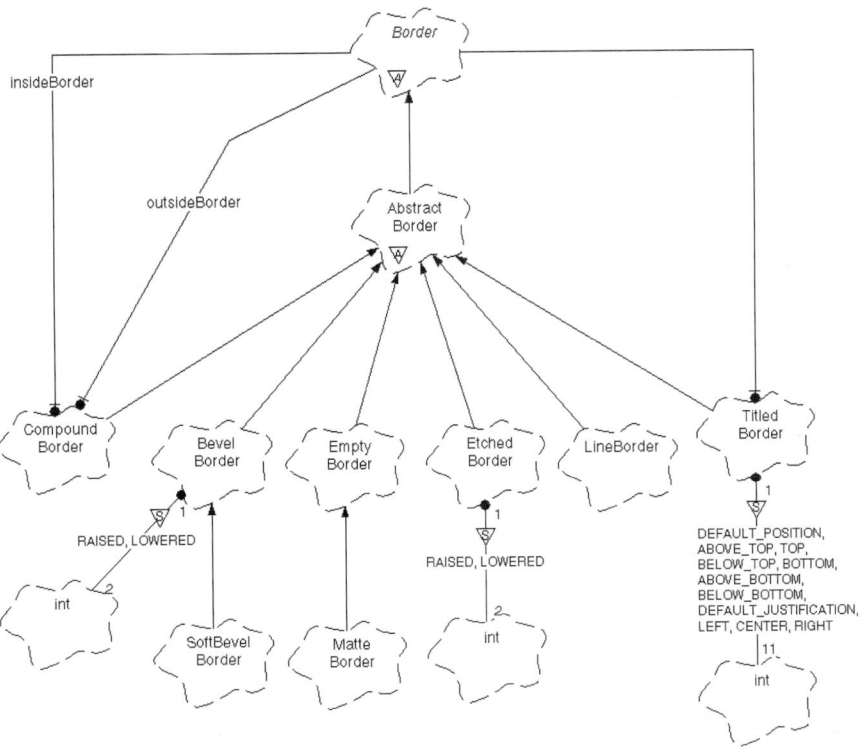

Figure 5-4 Swing Border Package Overview

The Border Interface

All borders implement the `Border` interface, whose methods are listed in Interface Summary 5-1.

Interface Summary 5-1   swing.border.Border

---

public abstract void <u>paintBorder</u>(Component, Graphics, int x, int y, int w, int h)
public abstract Insets <u>getBorderInsets</u>(Component)
public abstract boolean <u>isBorderOpaque</u>()

Borders are painted by invoking
`paintBorder(Component,Graphics,int,int,int,int)`. Notice the intentional difference in names between `Border.paintBorder()` and `JComponent.paint()`, accentuating the fact that borders are not components. The four `integer` arguments to `paintBorder` specify the border's location, width, and height.

The `Graphics` passed to `paintBorder()` is typically the `Graphics` associated with the component or with an offscreen buffer if the component is double buffered. The `Component` argument can be used to extract information about the component, such as the component's background and foreground colors, as needed. The `integer` arguments passed to `paintBorder()` specify the upper left-hand corner of the border and the border's width and height.

The AbstractBorder Class

All Swing borders extend the `AbstractBorder` class, which implements the `Border` interface. `AbstractBorder` implements default functionality for painting the border, returning insets, and specifying whether a border is opaque. The methods implemented by the `AbstractBorder` class are listed in Class Summary 5-1.

Class Summary 5-1   swing.border.AbstractBorder

Constructors

---

public <u>AbstractBorder</u>()

The `AbstractBorder` no-argument constructor is compiler generated.

Methods

---

public static Rectangle <u>getInteriorRectangle</u>(Component, Border, int x, int y, int w, int h)

public Rectangle <u>getInteriorRectangle</u>(Component, int x, int y, int w, int h)

public Insets <u>getBorderInsets</u>(Component)
public Insets <u>getBorderInsets</u>(Component, Insets)

public boolean <u>isBorderOpaque</u>()
public void <u>paintBorder</u>(Component, Graphics, int x, int y, int w, int h)

`AbstractBorder` provides a handy `static` method for determining a border's interior rectangle. An instance method that invokes the `static` method is also provided.

The first `getBorderInsets` method listed above returns an insets of (0,0,0,0), and the second `getBorderInsets` method sets the insets value it is passed to (0,0,0,0). Both methods must be overridden by `AbstractBorder` extensions.

`AbstractBorder` implements the `isBorderOpaque` method to return `false`, and the `paintBorder` method has an empty implementation that must be overridden by `AbstractBorder` extensions.

The Border Factory—Sharing Borders

Since a border is passed the component into which it draws, a single border can be used to decorate multiple components. In fact, the Swing package provides a BorderFactory class that constructs shared border instances. For example, the applet listed in Example 5-4 obtains two raised bevel borders from the border factory.

Example 5-4   Obtaining Borders from the Border Factory

```java
import java.awt.*;
import javax.swing.*;
import javax.swing.border.*;

public class Test extends JApplet {
    public void init() {
        Container contentPane = getContentPane();
        JPanel panel = new JPanel();
        JPanel panel2 = new JPanel();

        Border border = BorderFactory.createRaisedBevelBorder();
        Border border2 = BorderFactory.createRaisedBevelBorder();

        panel.setBorder(border);
        panel2.setBorder(border2);

        contentPane.add(panel, BorderLayout.NORTH);
        contentPane.add(panel2, BorderLayout.SOUTH);

        if(border == border2)
            System.out.println("bevel borders are shared");
        else
            System.out.println("bevel borders are NOT shared");
    }
}
```

The two borders obtained from the border factory are one and the same, as verified by the output of the applet:

```
bevel borders are shared
```

The BorderFactory class provides static methods that return instances of all the Swing border types—excluding soft bevel borders—in various configurations. For the Swing 1.1 FCS release, the only shared instances returned by the border factory are bevel and etched borders. For other border types, such as titled borders and matte borders, the border factory returns unique instances.

The fact that the border factory does not return shared instances of all border types begs a question: Why should you use the border factory for unshared borders, and why aren't all borders from the border factory shared instances? The answer, like the question, is twofold.

First, using the border factory does not require importing the Swing border package, as long as a reference to the returned border is not maintained. So, regardless of whether the border factory returns shared border instances, you may be able to bypass having to import swing.border. A small concession to be sure, but nonetheless a consideration.

Second, returning shared instances of simple borders such as etched borders and bevel borders is easy to implement. Borders with properties, such as a title, make it more difficult to return shared instances. Because of time constraints, the Swing team chose to return shared instances of simple border types only for the 1.1 FCS release of Swing.

Future Swing releases could very well return shared instances of other types of borders, so it is in your best interest to use the border factory whenever possible.

Swing Tip ...

Use the Border Factory

The next time you reach for a border to decorate your Swing component with, keep the border factory in mind. Using the border factory can eliminate the need to import the swing.border package and can also be more efficient, since the factory returns shared instances of some border types.

Replacing Built-in Borders

Some Swing components, by default, are fitted with built-in borders that paint differently depending upon the state of the component. Replacing borders for such components can have detrimental effects on the component's look and feel.

For example, the applet shown in Figure 5-5 contains two buttons. The top button has a custom border, and the bottom button has a standard Windows look-and-feel border.

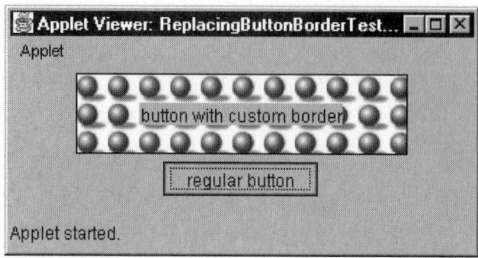

Figure 5-5 Replacing Built-in Borders

The picture in Figure 5-5 shows both buttons in their pressed state. It's easy to see that the regular button is pressed, but it's almost impossible to tell that the button with the custom border is also pressed. Explicitly fitting the top button with a border effectively eradicated the button's look and feel. As a result, care should be taken when replacing built-in borders.

Since built-in borders vary from one look and feel to another, there is no all-encompassing list of components that have them. If you specify a border for a component, it's a good idea to test the border out on a number of different look and feels to ensure that the border does not destroy the look-and-feel characteristics of the component.

Implementing Custom Borders

Even though Swing borders represent the most common border styles, you might find yourself pining for a custom border. For example, drawing programs often draw handles around objects; the handles can be used to either move or resize the selected object.

Handles are a perfect candidate for a Swing custom border. Custom borders, like the default Swing borders, should extend the `AbstractBorder` class and selectively override its methods. Typically, that means overriding `paintBorder` and `getBorderInsets`, since `AbstractBorder` does no painting and returns an insets of (0,0,0,0). Additionally, custom borders should override

isOpaque() to return true if the border paints every one of its pixels. By default, AbstractBorder is not opaque. Figure 5-6 shows an applet that displays three instances of a HandleBorder custom border class.

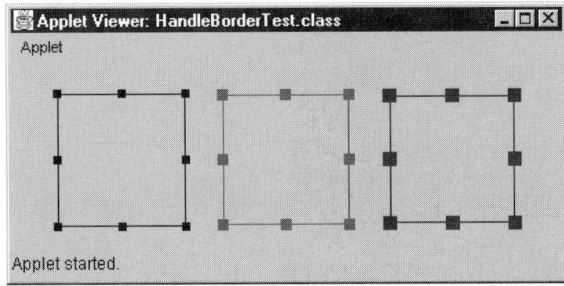

Figure 5-6 A Custom Border

The handle borders shown in Figure 5-6 are not opaque, so the HandleBorder class does not override isOpaque(); however, it does override paintBorder() and getBorderInsets().

The HandleBorder class is listed in Example 5-5.

Example 5-5 HandleBorder Class Listing

```java
import java.awt.*;
import javax.swing.*;
import javax.swing.border.*;

public class HandleBorder extends AbstractBorder {
    protected Color lineColor;
    protected int thick;

    public HandleBorder() {
        this(Color.black, 6);
    }
    public HandleBorder(Color lineColor, int thick) {
        this.lineColor = lineColor;
        this.thick = thick;
    }
    public void paintBorder(Component c, Graphics g, int x,
                       int y, int w, int h) {
        Graphics copy = g.create();
        if(copy != null) {
            try {
                copy.translate(x,y);
```

```
                            paintRectangle(c,copy,w,h);
                            paintHandles(c,copy,w,h);
                    }
                    finally {
                        copy.dispose();
                    }
                }
            }
            public Insets getBorderInsets() {
                return new Insets(thick,thick,thick,thick);
            }
            protected void paintRectangle(Component c, Graphics g,
                                    int w, int h) {
                g.setColor(lineColor);
                g.drawRect(thick/2,thick/2,w-thick-1,h-thick-1);
            }
            protected void paintHandles(Component c, Graphics g,
                                    int w, int h) {
                g.setColor(lineColor);

                g.fillRect(0,0,thick,thick); // upper-left
                g.fillRect(w-thick,0,thick,thick); // upper-right
                g.fillRect(0,h-thick,thick,thick); // lower-left
                g.fillRect(w-thick,h-thick,thick,thick); // lower-right
                g.fillRect(w/2-thick/2,0,thick,thick); // mid-top
                g.fillRect(0,h/2-thick/2,thick,thick); // mid-left
                g.fillRect(w/2-thick/2,h-thick,thick,thick); // mid-bottom
                g.fillRect(w-thick,h/2-thick/2,thick,thick); // mid-right
            }
        }
```

HandleBorder is designed to be used as a base class in addition to being useful in its own right. The paintBorder method invokes protected paintRectangle and paintHandles methods that can be overridden to suit the taste of extensions.

Since borders are passed the actual Graphics used to paint the component, a copy of the Graphics is used for painting the handle border. The copy of the Graphics is translated for the convenience of the paintRectangle and paintHandles methods. The Graphics copy is subsequently disposed of, as is required for all Graphics obtained by one of the several getGraphics methods provided by the AWT.

Custom borders are used in exactly the same manner as the borders that Swing provides. Example 5-6 lists the applet shown in Figure 5-6 on page 219.

Example 5-6 Using Custom Borders

```
import javax.swing.*;
import javax.swing.border.*;
import java.awt.*;
import java.awt.event.*;

public class Test extends JApplet {
    public void init() {
        Container contentPane = getContentPane();

        JPanel[] panels = { new JPanel(),
                        new JPanel(), new JPanel() };

        Border[] borders = { new HandleBorder(),
                        new HandleBorder(Color.red, 8),
                        new HandleBorder(Color.blue, 10) };

        contentPane.setLayout(
                new FlowLayout(FlowLayout.CENTER,20,20));

        for(int i=0; i < panels.length; ++i) {
            panels[i].setPreferredSize(new Dimension(100,100));
            panels[i].setBorder(borders[i]);
            contentPane.add(panels[i]);
        }
    }
}
```

Icons

Icons are conceptually very similar to borders; both icons and borders paint into a `Graphics` that is typically associated with a component. Interface Summary 5-2 lists the methods defined by the `Icon` interface.

Interface Summary 5-2   Icon

public abstract int <u>getIconHeight</u>()
public abstract int <u>getIconWidth</u>()
public abstract void <u>paintIcon</u>(Component, Graphics, int, int)

Icons can report their width and height, in addition to painting themselves into a component.

Swing provides a lone implementation of the `Icon` interface—the `ImageIcon` class, which paints an image. However, icons need not be restricted to painting images. For example, Figure 5-7 shows an applet that contains three instances of `ColorIcon`—a class that implements the `Icon` interface.

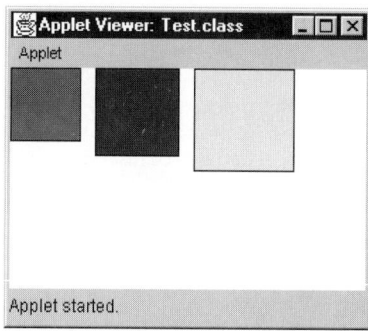

Figure 5-7 Three Instances of an Icon Extension

The applet shown in Figure 5-7 is listed in Example 5-7. The three `ColorIcons` are painted in the applet's `paint` method.

Example 5-7 An Applet That Paints Icons

```
import java.awt.*;
import javax.swing.*;

public class IconTest extends JApplet {
    ColorIcon redIcon = new ColorIcon(Color.red, 50, 50),
            blueIcon = new ColorIcon(Color.blue, 60, 60),
            yellowIcon = new ColorIcon(Color.yellow, 70, 70);

    public void paint(Graphics g) {
        redIcon.paintIcon(this, g, 0, 0);

        blueIcon.paintIcon(this, g,
                    redIcon.getIconWidth() + 10, 0);

        yellowIcon.paintIcon(this, g,
                    redIcon.getIconWidth() + 10 +
                    blueIcon.getIconWidth() + 10, 0);
    }
}
```

The `ColorIcon` class is listed in Example 5-8. `ColorIcon` is a simple class, but it will do for illustrating icons that are not image-based.

Example 5-8 `ColorIcon` Class Listing

```
import java.awt.*;
import javax.swing.*;

class ColorIcon implements Icon {
    private Color fillColor;
    private int w, h;

    public ColorIcon(Color fillColor, int w, int h) {
        this.fillColor = fillColor;
        this.w = w;
        this.h = h;
    }
    public void paintIcon(Component c, Graphics g, int x, int y) {
        // draw black border ...

        g.setColor(Color.black);
        g.drawRect(x, y, w-1, h-1);

        // fill icon ...

        g.setColor(fillColor);
        g.fillRect(x+1, y+1, w-2, h-2);
    }
    public int getIconWidth() {
        return w;
    }
    public int getIconHeight() {
        return h;
    }
}
```

A `ColorIcon` is instantiated with a fill color, width, and height. Its `paintIcon` method simply draws a black rectangle around the outside of its edges and fills the interior with the fill color specified at the time of construction.

Associating an Icon with a Component

In actuality, the use of icons in Example 5-7 is nothing more than a roundabout way of drawing into the applet. The real value of icons comes from associating them with a component. Figure 5-8 shows an applet with a menu bar. The lone menu in the menu bar contains three menu items that have been fitted with instances of `ColorIcon`.

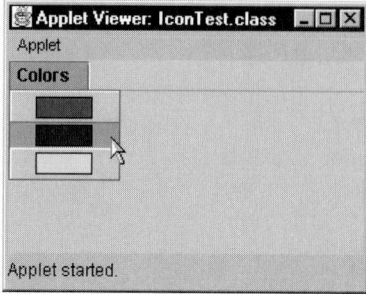

Figure 5-8 Icons Displayed in Menu Items

The applet shown in Figure 5-8 is listed in Example 5-9.

Example 5-9 Icons in Menu Items

```java
import java.awt.*;
import javax.swing.*;

public class Test extends JApplet {
    ColorIcon redIcon = new ColorIcon(Color.red, 40, 15),
              blueIcon = new ColorIcon(Color.blue, 40, 15),
              yellowIcon = new ColorIcon(Color.yellow, 40, 15);

    public void init() {
        JMenuBar mb = new JMenuBar();
        JMenu colors = new JMenu("Colors");

        colors.add(new JMenuItem(redIcon));
        colors.add(new JMenuItem(blueIcon));
        colors.add(new JMenuItem(yellowIcon));

        mb.add(colors);
        setJMenuBar(mb);
    }
}
```

The menu items are constructed with an icon. When the menu items are painted, each item's icon paints into the area occupied by the menu item. A number of Swing components, listed below, can display icons:

- `JButton`
- `JCheckBox`
- `JCheckBoxMenuItem`

- JFileChooser
- JLabel
- JList
- JMenuItem
- JOptionPane
- JPopupMenu
- JRadioButton
- JTabbedPane
- JTable
- JToolBar

Sharing Icons Among Components

Icons can be shared among any number of components that support displaying them. For example, the applet shown in Figure 5-9 contains a button with an icon representing a color. When the button is activated, a popup menu is displayed for color selection. After a color is selected from the popup menu, the icon displayed in the button is updated to reflect the selected color.

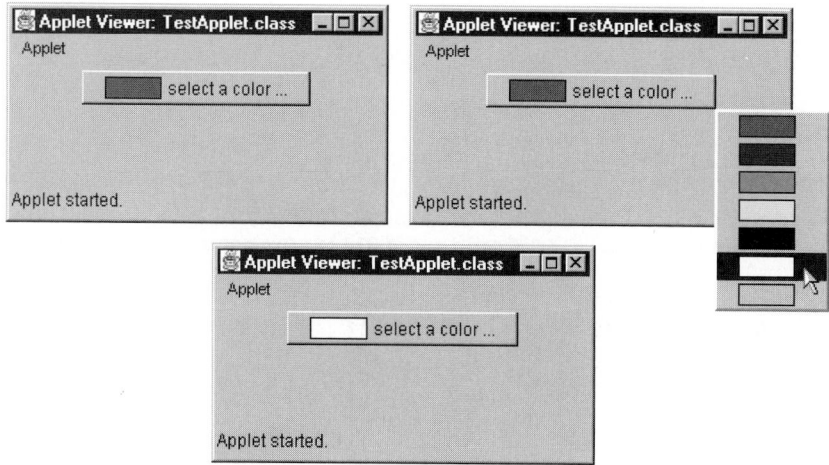

Figure 5-9 Sharing Icons

The most interesting aspect of the applet shown in Figure 5-9 is the fact that it contains exactly one `ColorIcon` instance that is shared among the button and menu items.

For instances of `ColorIcon` to be shared in the applet shown in Figure 5-9, a change must be made to the original `ColorIcon` class listed in Example 5-8 on page 223, which was passed a fill color at construction time. If the icon is shared among components representing different colors, the fill color needs to be a more dynamic property.

The version of `ColorIcon` listed in Example 5-10 expects Swing components passed to its `paintIcon` method to maintain a *fill color* property. When the icon is painted, it extracts the component's fill color property and sets its fill color accordingly—see "Client Properties" on page 186 for an introduction to client properties.

Example 5-10   Modified ColorIcon Listing

```java
import java.awt.*;
import javax.swing.*;

public class ColorIcon implements Icon {
    private int w, h;

    public ColorIcon(int w, int h) {
        this.w = w;
        this.h = h;
    }
    public void paintIcon(Component c, Graphics g, int x, int y) {
        Color fillColor = Color.lightGray;

        g.setColor(Color.black);
        g.drawRect(x, y, w-1, h-1);

        if(c instanceof JComponent) {
            JComponent jc = (JComponent)c;
            fillColor = (Color)jc.getClientProperty("fill color");
        }
        g.setColor(fillColor);
        g.fillRect(x+1, y+1, w-2, h-2);
    }
    public int getIconWidth() {
        return w;
    }
    public int getIconHeight() {
        return h;
    }
}
```

The applet shown in Figure 5-9 constructs a color icon, a popup menu, and a button. Passing the icon to the button's constructor causes the icon to be displayed inside the button.

```
public class TestApplet extends JApplet {
    private ColorIcon colorIcon = new ColorIcon(40, 15);
    private JPopupMenu popup = new JPopupMenu();
    private JButton button = new JButton("select a color ...",
                                         colorIcon);
    ...
```

Menu items for the popup menu are subsequently instantiated and passed a reference to the lone color icon. Appropriate fill color properties and an action listener are set for each menu item.

```
    ...
    private void addPopupMenuItems() {
        JMenuItem redItem = new JMenuItem(colorIcon),
                  blueItem = new JMenuItem(colorIcon),
                  grayItem = new JMenuItem(colorIcon),
                  yellowItem = new JMenuItem(colorIcon),
                  blackItem = new JMenuItem(colorIcon),
                  whiteItem = new JMenuItem(colorIcon),
                  orangeItem = new JMenuItem(colorIcon);

        MenuItemListener listener = new MenuItemListener();

        redItem.putClientProperty("fill color", Color.red);
        redItem.addActionListener(listener);
        popup.add(redItem);

        blueItem.putClientProperty("fill color", Color.blue);
        blueItem.addActionListener(listener);
        popup.add(blueItem);

        // add color propety and action listeners for the
        // the rest of the menu items ...
    }
```

When a menu item is activated, the `listener` extracts the fill color property from the menu item. The button's fill color is set to match the fill color of the menu item and the button is redrawn.

```
class MenuItemListener implements ActionListener {
    public void actionPerformed(ActionEvent e) {
        JComponent jc = (JComponent)e.getSource();
```

```
                  button.putClientProperty("fill color",
                              jc.getClientProperty("fill color"));
                  button.repaint();
            }
      }
}
```

When the button is repainted, it invokes the color icon's `paintIcon` method and passes itself as the component to draw into. The color icon extracts the fill property from the button and paints itself accordingly.

Example 5-11 lists the applet in its entirety.

Example 5-11 An Applet That Shares a Single Icon Among Many Components

```java
import java.awt.*;
import java.awt.event.*;
import javax.swing.*;

public class Test extends JApplet {
    private ColorIcon colorIcon = new ColorIcon(40, 15);
    private JPopupMenu popup = new JPopupMenu();
    private JButton button = new JButton("select a color ...",
                                colorIcon);
    public void init() {
        addPopupMenuItems();

        button.putClientProperty("fill color", Color.red);

        Container cp = getContentPane();
        cp.setLayout(new FlowLayout());
        cp.add(button);

        button.addActionListener(new ActionListener() {
            public void actionPerformed(ActionEvent e) {
                Dimension buttonsz = button.getSize();
                popup.show(button,buttonsz.width,
                              buttonsz.height);
            }
        });
    }
    private void addPopupMenuItems() {
        JMenuItem redItem = new JMenuItem(colorIcon),
                  blueItem = new JMenuItem(colorIcon),
                  grayItem = new JMenuItem(colorIcon),
                  yellowItem = new JMenuItem(colorIcon),
                  blackItem = new JMenuItem(colorIcon),
                  whiteItem = new JMenuItem(colorIcon),
                  orangeItem = new JMenuItem(colorIcon);
```

```
        MenuItemListener listener = new MenuItemListener();

        redItem.putClientProperty("fill color", Color.red);
        redItem.addActionListener(listener);
        popup.add(redItem);

        blueItem.putClientProperty("fill color", Color.blue);
        blueItem.addActionListener(listener);
        popup.add(blueItem);

        grayItem.putClientProperty("fill color", Color.gray);
        grayItem.addActionListener(listener);
        popup.add(grayItem);

        yellowItem.putClientProperty("fill color", Color.yellow);
        yellowItem.addActionListener(listener);
        popup.add(yellowItem);

        blackItem.putClientProperty("fill color", Color.black);
        blackItem.addActionListener(listener);
        popup.add(blackItem);

        whiteItem.putClientProperty("fill color", Color.white);
        whiteItem.addActionListener(listener);
        popup.add(whiteItem);

        orangeItem.putClientProperty("fill color", Color.orange);
        orangeItem.addActionListener(listener);
        popup.add(orangeItem);
    }
    class MenuItemListener implements ActionListener {
        public void actionPerformed(ActionEvent e) {
            JComponent jc = (JComponent)e.getSource();

            button.putClientProperty("fill color",
                        jc.getClientProperty("fill color"));

            button.repaint();
        }
    }
}
```

Image Icons

As mentioned previously, Swing provides one implementation of the Icon
interface—the ImageIcon class, which is summarized in Class Summary 5-2.

Class Summary 5-2   ImageIcon

Extends: Object
Implements: Icon, Serializable

Constructors

---

public <u>ImageIcon</u>()

public <u>ImageIcon</u>(byte[])
public <u>ImageIcon</u>(byte[], String description)
public <u>ImageIcon</u>(Image)
public <u>ImageIcon</u>(Image, String description)
public <u>ImageIcon</u>(String filename)
public <u>ImageIcon</u>(String filename, String description)
public <u>ImageIcon</u>(URL)
public <u>ImageIcon</u>(URL, String description)

The `ImageIcon` class provides a wealth of constructors. The image can be specified with a byte array, string representing the image's filename, or a URL. An optional description that is used for accessibility can also be provided.

The `ImageIcon` no-argument constructor instantiates an image icon with no image or description. It is assumed that the image or description will be set after construction.

Methods

Icon Interface Methods

---

public int <u>getIconHeight</u>()
public int <u>getIconWidth</u>()
public synchronized void <u>paintIcon</u>(Component, Graphics, int x, int y)

The methods listed above are defined in the `Icon` interface. The `getIconHeight` and `getIconWidth` methods return the height and width of the icon, respectively. The `paintIcon` method invokes `Graphics.drawImage()` and specifies the component passed to the method as the image observer if an image observer has not been explicitly specified. As a result, animated GIF images will animate when displayed as an image icon.

Description / Image

---

public String <u>getDescription</u>()
public void <u>setDescription</u>(String)

public Image <u>getImage</u>()
public void <u>setImage</u>(Image)

public int <u>getImageLoadStatus</u>()
protected void <u>loadImage</u>(Image)

public ImageObserver <u>getImageObserver</u>()
public void <u>setImageObserver</u>(ImageObserver)

In addition to implementing the methods defined in the `Icon` interface, `ImageIcon` also includes methods for maintaining a read-write description property. The description is meant to be used for accessibility; for instance, the description might be presented audibly to a sight-impaired user. `ImageIcon` also provides methods for setting and getting the image it displays.

Loading images with the AWT was always somewhat painful because images are loaded asynchronously. Typically, either an instance of `MediaTracker` was employed to ensure that an image was fully loaded before it was drawn, or an implementation of `ImageObserver` tracked the loading process. `ImageIcon` takes the former approach—when an image is specified, either at construction time or anytime thereafter, an instance of `MediaTracker` is called upon to fully load the image. Image loading is encapsulated in the `protected` `ImageIcon.loadImage` method, so extensions of `ImageIcon` are free to modify the default image loading policy if desired. Since `ImageIcon` loads images synchronously, it is recommended for use with small images.

If an error occurs during the loading process, the image maintained by the image icon is set to `null`; subsequent calls to `paintIcon()` will result in a no-op, and calls to `getIconWidth()` and `getIconHeight()` will return –1. The status of image loading can be obtained by invoking `getImageLoadStatus()`, which returns a `MediaTracker` constant.

`ImageIcon` also provides methods for setting and getting the image observer associated with the image. If no observer is explicitly set, then the component passed to `paintIcon` is specified as the image observer when the image is drawn. In practice, the image observer is rarely a concern for developers, especially considering that the image is fully loaded by an instance of `MediaTracker`.

Figure 5-10 shows an applet that displays an image icon.

Figure 5-10 An ImageIcon

The applet, listed in Example 5-12, simply instantiates an instance of ImageIcon and paints the icon in an overridden paint method.

Example 5-12 An Applet with an ImageIcon

```java
import java.awt.*;
import javax.swing.*;

public class Test extends JApplet {
    ImageIcon icon = new ImageIcon("coffeeCup.jpg");

    public void paint(Graphics g) {
        icon.paintIcon(this, g, 20, 15);
    }
}
```

Animated Image Icons

Although image icons are fully loaded by an instance of MediaTracker, multiframe images require an image observer in order to display successive frames of the image. For more information on the role of image observers with respect to multiframe images, see the *Loading and Displaying Images* chapter from *Graphic Java* Volume I: The AWT.

If an image observer has not been explicitly set for an image icon by invoking ImageIcon.setImageObserver(), the component passed to the icon's paintIcon method will be used as an image observer. Since java.awt.Component is an image observer capable of rendering multiframe images, animated images are handled automatically by the ImageIcon class.

Figure 5-11 shows an applet that displays an animated GIF image. In the interest of space, some of the frames of the animation are not displayed, but the frames shown should be enough to give you the general idea.

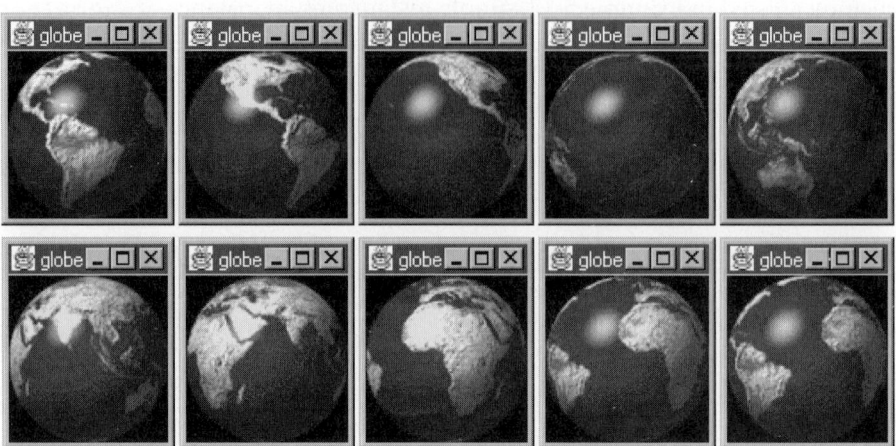

Figure 5-11 An Animated ImageIcon

The applet shown in Figure 5-11 is listed in Example 5-13.

Example 5-13 An Applet with an Animated Icon

```java
import java.awt.*;
import javax.swing.*;

public class Test extends JApplet {
    public void init() {
        JPanel panel = new MyJPanel();
        getContentPane().add(panel, "Center");
    }
}
class MyJPanel extends JPanel {
    ImageIcon animatedIcon =
            new ImageIcon("globe.gif");

    public void paintComponent(Graphics g) {
        super.paintComponent(g);
        animatedIcon.paintIcon(this, g, 20, 20);
    }
}
```

The icon is not painted directly into the applet because the `JApplet` class is not derived from `JComponent` and, therefore, cannot double-buffer its display; if double buffering is not used, the animation will flicker. `JPanel`, on the other hand, is derived from `JComponent` and by default double-buffers its display, so the icon is displayed in an instance of `JPanel` that is centered in the applet.

It's interesting to note that because `JPanel` is double buffered, the `Graphics` passed to the icon's `paintIcon` method is not the onscreen `Graphics` for the component. Instead, the `Graphics` passed to `MyJPanel.paint`, and subsequently passed to the icon's `paintIcon` method, is an offscreen buffer.

Actions

Actions encapsulate a fundamental operation associated with an applet or application. Actions maintain an enabled state, in addition to one or more values, which are typically icons and/or strings. The basic functionality of an action is defined by the `swing.Action` interface. The methods defined by the `Action` interface, which extends the `java.awt.event.ActionListener` interface, are listed in Interface Summary 5-3.

Interface Summary 5-3   Action

Constants

---

public static final String <u>DEFAULT</u>

public static final String <u>LONG_DESCRIPTION</u>
public static final String <u>NAME</u>
public static final String <u>SHORT_DESCRIPTION</u>
public static final String <u>SMALL_ICON</u>

The constants defined by the `Action` interface are discussed in "Action Constants" on page 243.

Methods

---

public abstract void <u>addPropertyChangeListener</u>(PropertyChangeListener)

public abstract void <u>removePropertyChangeListener</u>(PropertyChangeListener)

public abstract void <u>putValue</u>(String, Object)
public abstract Object <u>getValue</u>(String)

public abstract boolean <u>isEnabled</u>()
public abstract void <u>setEnabled</u>(boolean)

Actions fire property change events when their properties are modified. As a result, the `Action` interface defines methods for registering property change listeners. Actions maintain string/object pairs, which can be manipulated with the `putValue` and `getValue` methods. Actions also maintain an enabled state and therefore provide `setEnabled` and `isEnabled` methods.

The `swing` package also provides an `AbstractAction` class that implements the `Action` interface and provides default functionality for all of the methods listed in Interface Summary 5-3. The `AbstractAction` class is abstract because it does not implement the lone method defined by the `ActionListener` interface—`actionPerformed()`. The `actionPerformed` method is left for extensions to implement.

To understand how actions are used, consider the applet listed in Example 5-14.

Example 5-14 An Applet with a Menu Bar

```
import java.awt.*;
import java.awt.event.*;
import javax.swing.*;

public class Test extends JApplet {
    public void init() {
        JMenuBar mb = new JMenuBar();
        JMenu fileMenu = new JMenu("File");
        JMenuItem exitItem = new JMenuItem("exit");
```

```
        exitItem.addActionListener(new ExitListener());

        fileMenu.add(exitItem);
        mb.add(fileMenu);
        setJMenuBar(mb);
    }
}
class ExitListener implements ActionListener {
    public void actionPerformed(ActionEvent e) {
        System.exit(0);
    }
}
```

The applet in Example 5-14 creates a menu item and adds it to the file menu. An extension of `ActionListener` is implemented and added to the menu item. When the exit menu item is activated, `ExitListener.actionPerformed()` is invoked, resulting in the termination of the applet.

Now consider the same applet, listed in Example 5-15, implemented with an action.

Example 5-15 A Menu Item Is Created with an Action

```
import java.awt.*;
import java.awt.event.*;
import javax.swing.*;

public class Test extends JApplet {
    public void init() {
        JMenuBar mb = new JMenuBar();
        JMenu fileMenu = new JMenu("File");

        fileMenu.add(new ExitAction());
        mb.add(fileMenu);
        setJMenuBar(mb);
    }
}
class ExitAction extends AbstractAction {
    public ExitAction() {
        super("exit");
    }
    public void actionPerformed(ActionEvent e) {
        System.exit(0);
    }
}
```

The applet in Example 5-15 is functionally identical to the applet listed in Example 5-14. However, instead of creating a menu item and adding it to the file menu, an extension of `AbstractAction` is implemented and added to the file menu. The file menu extracts the string associated with the action—"exit"—and creates a menu item that it adds to itself. Additionally, the file menu adds the action to the list of `ActionListeners` maintained by the menu item. As a result, when the menu item is activated, `ExitAction.actionPerformed` is invoked and the applet is terminated.

Actions as a Central Point of Control

Just as icons might have been perceived to be nothing more than a roundabout way to paint into an applet in Example 5-7 on page 222, it might also appear that actions are nothing more than a roundabout way to create menu items. However, the real value of actions, like icons, stems from their ability to be associated with more than one component.

Recall that actions maintain an enabled state and can fire property change events. Additionally, a single action can be associated with more than one Swing component. When an action is enabled or disabled, it fires a property change event to all the components it's associated with. The components, in turn, set their enabled state to match the state of the action. Thus, actions can be used as a single point of control for a logical operation such as exiting an applet, opening a new document, cutting and pasting, etc.

The applet shown in Figure 5-12 implements a save operation. The operation is represented by a menu item and a toolbar button. The menu item and toolbar button are both constructed with a single instance of `SaveAction`. When the "action enabled" check box is activated, the state of the action is set accordingly. This causes the action to fire a property change event to the toolbar button and menu item. The property change event causes the menu item and toolbar button to update their enabled state to match that of the action. The left-hand pictures in Figure 5-12 show the action enabled, and the right-hand pictures show the action disabled.

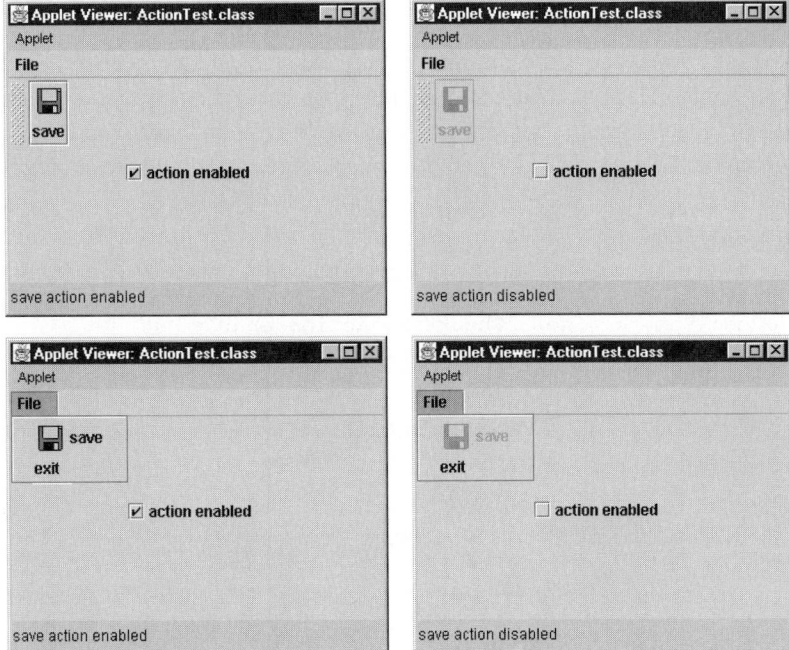

Figure 5-12 Actions: A Central Point of Control

The SaveAction class extends AbstractAction and passes the "save" string and the save icon to the AbstractAction constructor. SaveAction also implements the required actionPerformed method, which prints the identity of the component that triggered the save operation.

```
class SaveAction extends AbstractAction {
    public SaveAction() {
        super("save", new ImageIcon("save.gif"));
        setEnabled(false);
    }
    public void actionPerformed(ActionEvent event) {
        String s = new String();
        Object o = event.getSource();

        if(o instanceof JButton) s += "ToolBar:   ";
        else if(o instanceof JMenuItem) s += "MenuBar:   ";

        System.out.println(s + " save");
    }
}
```

The applet constructs the menu bar, file menu, toolbar, and check box. The save action is added to the file menu, and the file menu creates a menu item with the string and icon it extracts from the save action. The save action is also added to the toolbar, which also extracts the string and icon from the action and creates a toolbar button. The applet adds itself as a property change listener of the save action so that it will be notified when the save action's enabled state changes.

```
public class Test extends JApplet
                  implements PropertyChangeListener {
   ...
   JCheckBox jc = new JCheckBox("action enabled");
   JMenuBar mb = new JMenuBar();
   JToolBar tb = new JToolBar();

   Action saveAction = new SaveAction();
   Action exitAction = new ExitAction();

   public void init() {
      JMenu fileMenu = new JMenu("File");

      fileMenu.add(saveAction);
      fileMenu.add(exitAction);
      tb.add(saveAction);

      mb.add(fileMenu);

      saveAction.addPropertyChangeListener(this);
      ...
   }
   ...
}
```

When the check box is activated, the state of the save action's enabled property is toggled.

```
jc.addItemListener(new ItemListener() {
   public void itemStateChanged(ItemEvent event) {
      saveAction.setEnabled(!saveAction.isEnabled());
   }
});
```

When the `itemStateChanged` method invokes `setEnabled()`, a property change event is fired to the menu item, the toolbar button, and the applet. The menu item and toolbar button update their enabled state, and the applet prints out the component that triggered the save operation.

The applet shown in Figure 5-12 is listed in its entirety in Example 5-16.

Example 5-16 An Action Associated with a Toolbar Button and a Menu Item

```
import java.awt.*;
import java.awt.event.*;
import java.beans.*;
import javax.swing.*;

public class Test extends JApplet
                  implements PropertyChangeListener {
    JPanel jp = new JPanel();
    JPanel cp = new JPanel();  // cp = checkbox panel

    JCheckBox jc = new JCheckBox("action enabled");
    JMenuBar mb = new JMenuBar();
    JToolBar tb = new JToolBar();

    Action saveAction = new SaveAction();
    Action exitAction = new ExitAction();

    public void init() {
        JMenu fileMenu = new JMenu("File");

        fileMenu.add(saveAction);
        fileMenu.add(exitAction);
        tb.add(saveAction);

        JCheckBoxMenuItem checkBoxItem =
                    new JCheckBoxMenuItem("saved");

        associateActionAndCheckBoxItem(saveAction, checkBoxItem);
        fileMenu.add(checkBoxItem);

        mb.add(fileMenu);

        saveAction.addPropertyChangeListener(this);

        jp.setLayout(new BorderLayout(2,2));
        jp.add(tb, "North");  // toolbar
        jp.add(cp, "Center"); // checkbox panel

        cp.setLayout(new FlowLayout());
        cp.add(jc);

        Container contentPane = getContentPane();

        contentPane.setLayout(new BorderLayout());
        getRootPane().setJMenuBar(mb);
        contentPane.add(jp, "Center");

        jc.setSelected(saveAction.isEnabled());
```

```
        jc.addItemListener(new ItemListener() {
            public void itemStateChanged(ItemEvent event) {
                saveAction.setEnabled(!saveAction.isEnabled());
            }
        });
    }
    public void propertyChange(PropertyChangeEvent e) {
        boolean b = ((Boolean)e.getNewValue()).booleanValue();
        showStatus("save action " + (b ? "enabled" : "disabled"));
    }
    private void associateActionAndCheckBoxItem(
                        final Action action,
                        final JCheckBoxMenuItem item) {
        item.setHorizontalTextPosition(JButton.LEFT);
        item.setVerticalTextPosition(JButton.CENTER);
        item.setEnabled(action.isEnabled());
        item.addActionListener(action);
        action.addPropertyChangeListener(
                            new PropertyChangeListener() {
            public void propertyChange(PropertyChangeEvent e) {
                String name = e.getPropertyName();

                if(name.equals(Action.NAME)) {
                    item.setText((String)e.getNewValue());
                    item.revalidate();
                }
                else if(name.equals("enabled")) {
                    item.setEnabled(
                        ((Boolean)e.getNewValue()).booleanValue());
                    item.repaint();
                }
                else if(name.equals(Action.SMALL_ICON)) {
                    item.setIcon((Icon)e.getNewValue());
                    item.revalidate();
                }
            }
        });
    }
}
class SaveAction extends AbstractAction {
    public SaveAction() {
        super("save", new ImageIcon("save.gif"));
        setEnabled(false);
    }
    public void actionPerformed(ActionEvent event) {
        String s = new String();
        Object o = event.getSource();

        if(o instanceof JButton) s += "ToolBar:  ";
        else if(o instanceof JMenuItem) s += "MenuBar:  ";
```

```
            System.out.println(s + " save");
        }
    }
    class ExitAction extends AbstractAction {
        public ExitAction() {
            super("exit");
        }
        public void actionPerformed(ActionEvent event) {
            System.exit(0);
        }
    }
```

Action Constants

The `Action` interface also defines the constants listed in Table 5-2.

Table 5-2   Action Constants

Method	Meaning	Expected Type For Object
NAME	A string displayed in Swing components	String
SMALL_ICON	An icon displayed in Swing components	Icon
DEFAULT	Implementation defined	Implementation defined
LONG_DESCRIPTION	Implementation defined	String
SHORT_DESCRIPTION	Implementation defined	String

The constants are all defined within the `Action` class as `public static` strings. The `Action.putValue(String, Object)` method adds a value to an action. For example, the `AbstractAction` constructor that is passed a string and an icon assigns the string to `NAME` and the icon to `SMALL_ICON`:

```
// From swing.AbstractAction ...

public AbstractAction(String name, Icon icon) {
    this(name);
    putValue(Action.SMALL_ICON, icon);
}
public AbstractAction(String name) {
    putValue(Action.NAME, name);
}
```

When a Swing component has an action added to it, the constants are used to extract the string and icon. For instance, the `JMenu.add(Action)` extracts the text and icon like this:

```
// From swing.JMenu ...

public JMenuItem add(Action a) {
   JMenuItem mi =
      new JMenuItem((String)a.getValue(Action.NAME),
                     (Icon)a.getValue(Action.SMALL_ICON));
   ...
}
```

The DEFAULT, LONG_DESCRIPTION, and SHORT_DESCRIPTION constants are not used within Swing; their meaning is implementation defined. For example, the applet shown in Figure 5-13 contains an extension of `JButton` that can be constructed with an action. The SHORT_DESCRIPTION value is used to set the tooltip for the button.

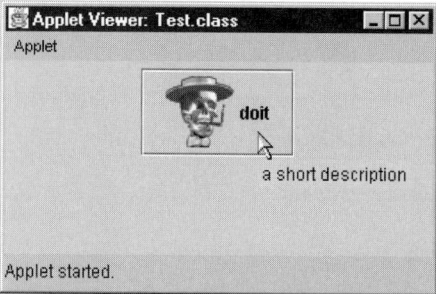

Figure 5-13 Using Actions with Custom Components

The `CustomButton` constructor is passed an action. The constructor extracts the NAME and SMALL_ICON properties and uses them to set the text and icon for the button by passing them to the `JButton` constructor.

The SHORT_DESCRIPTION property is also extracted from the action and is used to set the button's tooltip text.

Finally, the constructor adds the action as an action listener for the button.

```
...
    public CustomButton(Action action) {
        super((String)action.getValue(Action.NAME),
              (Icon)action.getValue(Action.SMALL_ICON));

        String shortDescription = (String)action.getValue(
                            Action.SHORT_DESCRIPTION);
        setToolTipText(shortDescription);

        addActionListener(action);
    }
...
```

The applet shown in Figure 5-13 is listed in Example 5-17.

Example 5-17 Using Action.SHORT_DESCRIPTION in a Custom Component

```
import java.awt.*;
import java.awt.event.*;
import javax.swing.*;

public class Test extends JApplet {
    public void init() {
        Container contentPane = getContentPane();
        CustomAction action = new CustomAction();
        CustomButton button = new CustomButton(action);

        contentPane.setLayout(new FlowLayout());
        contentPane.add(button);
    }
}
class CustomButton extends JButton {
    public CustomButton(Action action) {
        super((String)action.getValue(Action.NAME),
              (Icon)action.getValue(Action.SMALL_ICON));

        String shortDescription = (String)action.getValue(
                            Action.SHORT_DESCRIPTION);

        setToolTipText(shortDescription);
        addActionListener(action);
    }
}
class CustomAction extends AbstractAction {
    public CustomAction() {
        super("doit", new ImageIcon("skelly.gif"));
        putValue(Action.SHORT_DESCRIPTION, "a short description");
    }
    public void actionPerformed(ActionEvent e) {
        System.out.println("Custom action performed");
    }
}
```

Parting Shots

Borders, icons, and actions all share two things in common. First, they are not components, and second, they can be shared among any number of components that support using them. The ability to be shared among components is not only an efficiency issue but also provides uniformity, and for actions, a central point of control for GUI applets and applications.

Borders remedy a nuisance that existed with AWT containers—the fact that insets could only be specified on a per-class basis. `java.awt.Container` does not provide a `setInsets` method, so setting insets for AWT containers meant subclassing, often for the sole purpose of overriding `getInsets`. Forcing the use of inheritance to set a property that varies between different instances of the same type is not regarded as exemplary object-oriented design because it can lead to a proliferation of subclasses.

Swing components, on the other hand, use empty borders to specify their insets. The `JComponent` class implements a `setBorder` method, effectively elevating the read-only `insets` property to read-write, and does away with the need for subclassing. `JComponent` overrides `getInsets()` to return the insets of its border if it has one. If the component does not have a border, it returns the insets of its superclass. Thus, borders are seamlessly integrated with the `insets` property of the `java.awt.Container` class. Don't let all this good design fall by the wayside by overriding `getInsets()` for custom components you build on top of Swing. Instead, fit your custom components with an empty border.

Many look-and-feel classes maintain a single border that is shared among all components of a given type. For example, all buttons with a Windows look and feel share a single bevel border. The sharing of the border would not be possible if borders were implemented as components. Also, icons can be shared among components when they are associated with an action.

Another nifty feature of icons and borders is that they do not necessarily draw directly into a component. Instead, they draw into a `Graphics` that is passed to their `paintIcon` and `paintBorder` methods, respectively. The `paint` methods use the component they are passed to obtain information about the component, but they paint into the `Graphics`. This allows the caller of the `paint` methods to perform some sleight of hand by specifying a `Graphics` other than the `Graphics` directly associated with the component. For instance, if a Swing component is double buffered, the component's border inadvertently paints into an offscreen buffer. The offscreen buffer is subsequently copied to the

component's onscreen representation when the time is right. This eliminates the flicker involved with painting lightweight components and would not be possible if the border's `paint` method were only passed a component. See Double Buffering on page 150 for more on Swing's double buffering.

Actions provide a central point of control for logical operations and also simplify the construction of user interface components, such as menu items and toolbar buttons. Actions allow the enabled state of components to be controlled from a central location and therefore can be used to substantially simplify user interface code.

CHAPTER

6

Utilities

Swing includes a number of utilities that are discussed in this chapter. Some of the utilities, such as timers and the `static` methods provided by the `SwingUtilities` class, are used internally by Swing, whereas others, such as progress monitors and progress monitor streams, are not. All of the utilities discussed in this chapter are available for use by developers using Swing.

Timers

Timers are useful in many situations when some action must be performed periodically or at a specific time. For example, animations can use timers for updating the next frame of the animation and for controlling the rate at which animated objects move and change their appearance. See the first volume of *Graphic Java* for a complete animation system that uses timers in exactly the manner described above.[1] In fact, Swing itself uses timers for autoscrolling and tooltips.

---

1.   The timers used in the first volume of *Graphic Java* are not Swing timers.

Swing provides a `Timer` class whose instances can have one or more action listeners associated with them. When a timer "rings"—meaning, it fires an action event—each `ActionListener` associated with the timer has its `actionPerformed` method invoked.

Timers can ring once, or they can ring repeatedly at a periodic interval. Each timer can have two delays, specified in milliseconds, associated with it. An *initial delay* specifies the amount of time that elapses before the timer rings for the first time. A *periodic delay* specifies the amount of time that elapses between rings for a repeating timer. By default, all timers repeat.

The application listed in Example 6-1 creates three timers. The `oneSecondTimer` repeatedly rings at one-second intervals and has one `ActionListener`—the application—associated with it. When the `oneSecondTimer` rings, it invokes the application's `actionPerformed` method, which prints the number of seconds that have elapsed.

The application creates a second timer that rings repeatedly at two-second intervals and has an initial delay of five seconds. The action listener associated with the second timer is an instance of `TimerWithDelayListener`, which prints a message that the timer with delay is ringing.

A third timer does not repeat and has an initial delay of 10 seconds. The `ActionListener` associated with the third timer is an instance of `OneTimeListener`, which prints a notification that the "one time" timer is ringing. Note that the timer examples that follow do not display a window and must be killed with a CTRL-C.

Example 6-1 Using Swing Timers

```java
import java.awt.*;
import java.awt.event.*;
import javax.swing.*;

public class Test implements ActionListener {
    private int seconds=1;

    public Test() {
        Timer oneSecondTimer = new Timer(1000, this);
        Timer timerWithInitialDelay = new Timer(2000,
                            new TimerWithDelayListener());
        Timer oneTimeTimer = new Timer(10000,
                            new OneTimeListener());

        timerWithInitialDelay.setInitialDelay(5000);
        oneTimeTimer.setRepeats(false);

        oneSecondTimer.start();
```

```
            timerWithInitialDelay.start();
            oneTimeTimer.start();
    }
    public void actionPerformed(ActionEvent e) {
        if(seconds == 0)
            System.out.println("Time:   " + seconds + " second");
        else
            System.out.println("Time:   " + seconds + " seconds");

        seconds++;
    }
    public static void main(String args[]) {
        new Test();
        while(true);
    }
}
class TimerWithDelayListener implements ActionListener {
    public void actionPerformed(ActionEvent e) {
        System.out.println("Timer with Delay Ringing");
    }
}
class OneTimeListener implements ActionListener {
    public void actionPerformed(ActionEvent e) {
        System.out.println("One Time Timer Ringing");
    }
}
```

All three timers are instantiated with the only constructor that the Timer class provides. The constructor is passed two arguments; the first specifies the delay associated with the timer, and the second specifies a listener that is to be notified when the timer rings.

After the three timers are constructed, the timer with an initial delay has its initial delay specified by the Timer.setInitialDelay method. Because timers repeat by default, the "one time" timer invokes Timer.setRepeats(false) to specify that the timer does not repeat. Subsequently, all three timers are started with the Timer.start method.

The output of the application listed in Example 6-1 is as follows:

```
Time:   1 seconds
Time:   2 seconds
Time:   3 seconds
Time:   4 seconds
Timer with Delay Ringing
Time:   5 seconds
Time:   6 seconds
Timer with Delay Ringing
```

```
Time:   7 seconds
Time:   8 seconds
Timer with Delay Ringing
Time:   9 seconds
One Time Timer Ringing
Time:   10 seconds
Timer with Delay Ringing
Time:   11 seconds
Time:   12 seconds
...
```

The Timer Class

A summary of the `Timer` class methods is provided in Class Summary 6-1.

Class Summary 6-1   Timer

Constructors

---

public <u>Timer</u>(int delay, ActionListener)

The `Timer` class provides only one constructor. Timers must have a delay and at least one action listener, both of which must be supplied at construction time.

The `integer` value passed to the constructor specifies the delay associated with the timer. If the timer repeats, the delay specified in the call to the constructor represents both the initial delay and the delay between subsequent rings of the timer. If the timer does not repeat, the delay specified in the call to the constructor represents only the initial delay. If the initial delay is specified for a nonrepeating timer after construction with the `setInitialDelay` method or if the periodic display is specified for a repeating timer with the `setDelay` method, the delay passed to the constructor is superseded.

For example, the application listed in Example 6-2 constructs a timer with a delay of one second. After construction, the initial delay of the timer is set to 10 seconds, and `setRepeats(false)` is called so that the timer does not repeat. Since the

initial delay is specified after construction and the timer does not repeat, the delay of one second specified when the timer is constructed is irrelevant—the timer will ring once ten seconds after it is started and will not ring again.

Example 6-2 Overriding the Delay Specified at the Time of Construction

```
import java.awt.*;
import java.awt.event.*;
import javax.swing.*;

public class Test implements ActionListener {
    public Test() {
        Timer oneSecondTimer = new Timer(1000, this);

        oneSecondTimer.setInitialDelay(10000);
        oneSecondTimer.setRepeats(false);
        oneSecondTimer.start();
    }
    public void actionPerformed(ActionEvent e) {
        System.out.println("ring ...");
    }
    public static void main(String args[]) {
        new Test();
        while(true);
    }
}
```

Methods

Log Timers

---

public static boolean <u>getLogTimers</u>()
public static void <u>setLogTimers</u>(boolean)

Timers can be logged, meaning that a message is printed to the `System.out` stream whenever a timer rings. Logging can only be set for all timers at once by invoking the static `setLogTimers` method; there is no option to turn logging on for an individual timer.

By default, log messages print the string "`Timer ringing:` " followed by the return value of the timer's `toString` method. For example, the application listed in Example 6-3 invokes `Timer.setLogTimers()` to turn logging on.

Example 6-3   Timer Logging

```
import java.awt.*;
import java.awt.event.*;
import javax.swing.*;

public class Test implements ActionListener {
    public Test() {
        Timer.setLogTimers(true);

        Timer oneSecondTimer = new MyTimer(1000, this);
        oneSecondTimer.start();
    }
    public void actionPerformed(ActionEvent e) {
        System.out.println("ring ...");
    }
    public static void main(String args[]) {
        new Test();
        while(true);
    }
}
class MyTimer extends Timer {
    public MyTimer(int delay, ActionListener listener) {
        super(delay, listener);
    }
    public String toString() {
        return "MyTimer";
    }
}
```

The Timer class does not implement a toString method, so by default, Timer logging prints the value returned by Object.toString, which represents the location of the timer in memory. If timer logging is used, it makes sense to extend the timer class and implement a meaningful toString method, as is the case for the application listed in Example 6-3.

The output of the application listed in Example 6-3 is as follows:

```
Timer ringing: MyTimer
ring ...
Timer ringing: MyTimer
ring ...
...
```

Start / Stop / Restart

---

public void <u>start</u>()
public void <u>stop</u>()
public void <u>restart</u>()

Timers can be started, stopped, and restarted. If a timer is stopped and then restarted, the timer will go through its entire initial delay before ringing for the first time after being restarted.

---

public void <u>addActionListener</u>(ActionListener)
public void <u>removeActionListener</u>(ActionListener)
protected void <u>fireActionPerformed</u>(ActionEvent)

More than one action listener can be associated with a single timer, and action listeners can be removed from the timer's list of listeners after the timer is constructed.

The `fireActionPerformed` method invokes `actionPerformed` for each listener registered with the timer. For example, the application listed in Example 6-4 associates three action listeners with a single timer.

Example 6-4 Multiple Action Listeners Associated with a Single Timer

```java
import java.awt.*;
import java.awt.event.*;
import javax.swing.*;

public class Test implements ActionListener {
    private int seconds=1;

    public Test() {
        Timer oneSecondTimer = new Timer(1000, this);

        oneSecondTimer.addActionListener(new SecondListener());
        oneSecondTimer.addActionListener(new ThirdListener());
        oneSecondTimer.start();
    }
    public void actionPerformed(ActionEvent e) {
        if(seconds == 0)
            System.out.println("Time:   " + seconds + " second");
        else
            System.out.println("Time:   " + seconds + " seconds");
        seconds++;
    }
    public static void main(String args[]) {
        new Test();
        while(true);
    }
}
class SecondListener implements ActionListener {
    public void actionPerformed(ActionEvent e) {
```

```
        System.out.println("Second Listener");
    }
}
class ThirdListener implements ActionListener {
    public void actionPerformed(ActionEvent e) {
        System.out.println("Third Listener");
    }
}
```

The output of the application listed in Example 6-4 is as follows:

```
Third Listener
Second Listener
Time:   1 second
Third Listener
Second Listener
Time:   2 seconds
Third Listener
Second Listener
Time:   3 seconds
```

Notice that the `fireActionPerformed` method is `protected` and therefore can be overridden by extensions that wish to alter the order in which listeners are notified.

The source of the `ActionEvent` passed to the action listener's `actionPerformed` method is the timer that is ringing.

Delays

---

public int <u>getDelay</u>()
public int <u>getInitialDelay</u>()

public void <u>setDelay</u>(int milliseconds)
public void <u>setInitialDelay</u>(int milliseconds)

Both the initial delay and the repeat delay associated with a timer are settable after construction. Additionally, the `Timer` class provides methods for obtaining the delay associated with a timer.

Coalesce / Repeating / Running

---

public void <u>setCoalesce</u>(boolean)
public void <u>setRepeats</u>(boolean)

public boolean <u>isCoalesce</u>()
public boolean <u>isRepeats</u>()
public boolean <u>isRunning</u>()

The `Timer` class provides methods for finding out whether a timer repeats or is currently running. A method is also provided to set whether the timer repeats.

By default, timers coalesce events. If an applet or application is busy and cannot keep up with events generated by a timer, the timer will collapse pending events into a single notification. For example, the application listed in Example 6-5 explicitly turns coalescing off and therefore will receive 10 notifications, one right after the other, after it is done sleeping. If the call to `setCoalesce(false)` is commented out, the application receives only one event after it awakes.

Example 6-5 Coalescing Timer Events

```
import java.awt.*;
import java.awt.event.*;
import javax.swing.*;

public class Test implements ActionListener {
    private boolean firstRing = true;
    private int ring = 1;

    public Test() {
        Timer.setLogTimers(true);

        Timer oneSecondTimer = new Timer(1000, this);

        // comment out the following line for colaescing
        oneSecondTimer.setCoalesce(false);

        System.out.println("Timer is coalescing: " +
                    oneSecondTimer.isCoalesce());

        oneSecondTimer.start();
    }
    public void actionPerformed(ActionEvent e) {
        System.out.println("ring #" + ring++);
```

```
        if(firstRing) {
            // simulate a time consuming operation by sleeping
            // for 10 seconds ...
            try {
                Thread.currentThread().sleep(10000);
            }
            catch(InterruptedException ex) {
                ex.printStackTrace();
            }
            firstRing = false;
        }
    }
    public static void main(String args[]) {
        new Test();
        while(true);
    }
}
```

Event Listener Lists

The `swing.event` package includes an `EventListenerList` class that can be used to maintain a list of event listeners of different types. In effect, Swing's `EventListenerList` replaces the AWT's `AWTEventMulticaster` class; instances of `EventListenerList` are used by all Swing components that fire events. Instances of `EventListenerList` can be used for event listeners of any type, whereas the `AWTEventMulticaster` is limited to the set of event listeners types supported by the AWT.

Developers are encouraged to use the `EventListenerList` class for maintaining lists of event listeners for custom components (or any other class) that fire events. Using the `EventListenerList` class entails the following three steps: (where XXX represents the type of event)

1. Implement an `addXXXListener` method that adds listeners to the list.
2. Implement a `removeXXXListener` method that removes listeners from the list.
3. Implement a `fireXXXPerformed` method that iterates over the list and fires events to listeners.

Swing's timers use an instance of `EventListenerList` to maintain a list of `ActionListeners`. The code listed below is from the `swing.Timer` class:

```
// From swing.Timer ...

public void addActionListener(ActionListener listener) {
    listenerList.add(ActionListener.class, listener);
}
public void removeActionListener(ActionListener listener) {
    listenerList.remove(ActionListener.class, listener);
}
protected void fireActionPerformed(ActionEvent e) {
    // Guaranteed to return a non-null array
    Object[] listeners = listenerList.getListenerList();

    // Process the listeners last to first, notifying
    // those that are interested in this event
    for (int i = listeners.length-2; i>=0; i-=2) {
        if (listeners[i]==ActionListener.class) {
            ((ActionListener)listeners[i+1]).actionPerformed(e);
        }
    }
}
```

The addActionListener and removeActionListener methods for the Timer class simply delegate to the EventListenerList add and remove methods, which is typical. Both the add and remove methods of EventListenerList class take two arguments: the first argument is the class of the listener, and the second argument is a reference to the listener to be added or removed.

The EventListenerList class maintains an Object array that contains an alternating sequence of [Class, EventListener], enabling it to maintain listeners of different types on the same list. That is the reason that the Timer fireActionPerformed method iterates over the list of listeners by advancing two slots in the array every time through the for loop.

Notice that neither Timer.addActionListener nor Timer.removeActionListener is synchronized. Because the EventListenerList class is thread safe, its add and remove methods are synchronized, and therefore the Timer methods do not need to be synchronized.

As is almost always the case, the fireActionPerformed is protected. Firing action events is an implementation detail of the Timer class; other objects should not be allowed to invoke a timer's fireActionPerformed method, and therefore the method is not public. The method is protected so that extensions of the Timer class can modify the manner in which action events are fired. Also, as with all Swing components that fire events, the list of listeners is traversed from the last listener added to the list to the first.

There's nothing about the `EventListenerList` class that forces the list of listeners to be traversed from back to front. In fact, it is a simple matter to extend the `Timer` class and override the `fireActionPerformed` method so that traversal of the list is from front to back:

```
// An extension of Timer that reverses the traversal of the
// listener list when action events are fired.

class ReverseTimer extends Timer {
    public ReverseTimer(int delay, ActionListener listener) {
        super(delay, listener);
    }
    protected void fireActionPerformed(ActionEvent e) {
        Object[] list = listenerList.getListenerList();

        // Process the listeners first to last ...

        for (int i = 0; i <= list.length-2; i+=2) {
            if (list[i]==ActionListener.class) {
                ((ActionListener)list[i+1]).actionPerformed(e);
            }
        }
    }
}
```

The EventListenerList Class

Class Summary 6-2 lists the `public` methods implemented by the `EventListenerList` class.

Class Summary 6-2   swing.EventListenerList

Extends: java.lang.Object
Implements: java.io.Serializable

Constructors

---

public EventListenerList()

The no-argument constructor is compiler generated and therefore does nothing.

Methods

Add/Remove Listeners

---

public synchronized void add(Class, EventListener)
public synchronized void remove(Class, EventListener)

The add and remove methods are both passed the class of the listener and the listener to be added or removed. It is up to users of the EventListenerList class to ensure that the class passed to the methods matches the class of the listener.

Listener Count

---

public int getListenerCount()
public int getListenerCount(Class)

getListenerCount() returns the number of listeners that are currently on the list. getListenerCount(Class) returns the number of listeners of type Class that are currently on the list.

Listener List / String Representation

---

public Object[] getListenerList()
public String toString()

`getListenerList()` returns the actual `Object` array that holds the classes of the listeners and the listeners themselves. The array returned by `getListenerList()` is guaranteed to be non-`null`; if no listeners are currently on the list, the length of the array will be 0. For efficiency, the array returned is not a copy and therefore *should not be modified by the caller in any manner whatsoever.*

`EventListenerList.toString()` prints the number of listeners currently on the list, in addition to the type of each listener and its string representation.

Swing Utilities

The `swing` package includes a `SwingUtilities` class that contains more than 30 `static` utility methods. The methods are grouped into the following functional areas:

- *Computational methods* that compute intersections, unions, and differences of rectangles in addition to the width of a string with specific font metrics
- *Conversion methods* that convert events, points, and rectangles from one component's coordinate system to another
- *Accessibility methods* that return accessibility information for a given component
- *Retrieval methods* that retrieve objects associated with a given component, such as focus owners, ancestors, and the root pane in which a component resides
- *Methods for executing code from a thread* other than the event dispatch thread
- *Boolean methods* that can be used to determine relationships, for example, if one component is an ancestor of another, if the current thread is the event dispatch thread, and which mouse button has been pressed given a particular mouse event.
- *Layout, painting, and UI updating methods* for a given component

The methods provided by the `SwingUtilities` class are heavily used throughout Swing. For example, `SwingUtilities.layoutCompoundLabel` is used by both `JButton` and `JLabel` for laying out the text and icon associated with a button or label, respectively. The methods are also useful for developers using Swing and are therefore given `public` access.

The `public` methods implemented by the `SwingUtilities` class are listed in Class Summary 6-3.

Class Summary 6-3   SwingUtilities

Extends: java.lang.Object
Implements: SwingConstants

Constructors

---

public SwingUtilities()

The no-argument constructor is compiler generated. Because all of the methods implemented by the `SwingUtilities` class are `static`, there should never be any reason to instantiate an instance of `SwingUtilities`. In fact, it probably would have been a good idea to implement a `private` no-argument constructor so that instances of `SwingUtilities` could not be instantiated.

Methods

Computational Methods

---

public static Rectangle[] computeDifference(Rectangle, Rectangle)
public static Rectangle computeIntersection(int x, int y, int w, int h, Rectangle)
public static Rectangle computeUnion(int x, int y, int w, int h, Rectangle)
public static final boolean isRectangleContainingRectangle(Rectangle, Rectangle)
public static int computeStringWidth(FontMetrics, String)

The methods listed above compute the union, intersection, and difference between two rectangles, in addition to determining whether one rectangle completely contains another.

The applet shown in Figure 6-1 illustrates the use of the `computeDifference`, `computeIntersection`, and `computeUnion` methods.

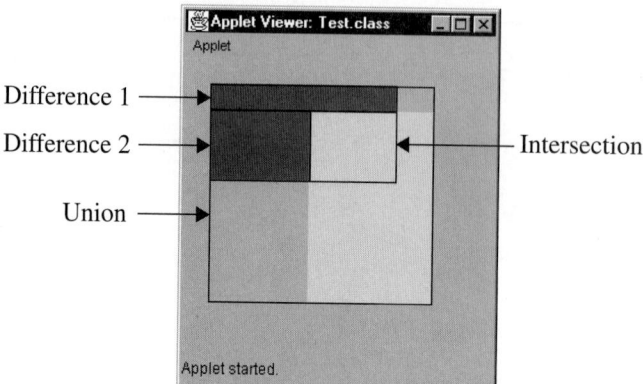

Difference 1

Difference 2 ———————▶ ◀——————— Intersection

Union

Figure 6-1 Computing Differences, Intersection, and Union of Two Rectangles

The `computeIntersection` and `computeUnion` methods both override the values of the rectangle they are passed so that a new `Rectangle` does not have to be instantiated. When the methods return, the rectangle passed to the method represents the intersection or union of the two rectangular regions.

The `computeDifference` method returns an array of rectangles representing the regions within the first rectangle that do not overlap with the second rectangle.

The applet shown in Figure 6-1 is listed in Example 6-6.

Example 6-6 Computing Differences, Intersection, and Union of Two Rectangles

```
import java.awt.*;
import java.awt.event.*;
import javax.swing.*;

public class Test extends JApplet {
    Rectangle r1 = new Rectangle(20,20,150,75);
    Rectangle r2 = new Rectangle(100,40,100,150);
    Rectangle destination;

    public Test() {
        destination = new Rectangle(r2);

        // print out the intersection of r1 and r2 ...
```

```
    // computeUnion stores the union of r1 and
    // destination in destination

    System.out.println("Intersection:   " +
        SwingUtilities.computeIntersection(r1.x,r1.y,
                        r1.width,r1.height,destination));
    System.out.println();

    // print out the union of r1 and r2 ...
    // computeUnion stores the union of r1 and
    // destination in destination

    System.out.println("Union:   " +
        SwingUtilities.computeUnion(r1.x,r1.y,
                        r1.width,r1.height,destination));
    System.out.println();

    // print out the difference of r1 and r2 ...
    // computeDifference does not stuff return values
    // in an input argument

    Rectangle[] difference =
                SwingUtilities.computeDifference(r1, r2);

    System.out.println("Difference:");

    for(int i=0; i < difference.length; ++i) {
        System.out.println(difference[i]);
    }
  }
  public void paint(Graphics g) {
      g.setColor(Color.red);
      g.fillRect(r1.x, r1.y, r1.width, r1.height);

      g.setColor(Color.yellow);
      g.fillRect(r2.x, r2.y, r2.width, r2.height);
  }
}
```

The output of the applet shown in Figure 6-1 is listed below.

```
Intersection:   java.awt.Rectangle[x=100,y=40,width=70,height=55]

Union:   java.awt.Rectangle[x=20,y=20,width=150,height=75]

Difference:
java.awt.Rectangle[x=20,y=20,width=150,height=20]
java.awt.Rectangle[x=20,y=40,width=80,height=55]
```

Conversion Methods

---

public static MouseEvent convertMouseEvent(Component, MouseEvent, Component)
public static Point convertPoint(Component, int x, int y, Component)
public static Point convertPoint(Component, Point, Component)
public static Rectangle convertRectangle(Component, Rectangle, Component)

public static void convertPointFromScreen(Point, Component)
public static void convertPointToScreen(Point, Component)

The methods listed above convert either a point, rectangle, or mouse event from one component's coordinate system to another's. The first group of methods listed above are all passed references to two components—a source and a destination. The source represents the component from which the location or event originated, and the destination is the component to which the location or event is translated.

The last two methods provide a convenient way to translate from a component's coordinate systems to screen coordinates, and vice versa.

The applet shown in Figure 6-2 contains three nested panels, all of which paint their backgrounds with a specific color and display mouse coordinates relative to their coordinate systems.

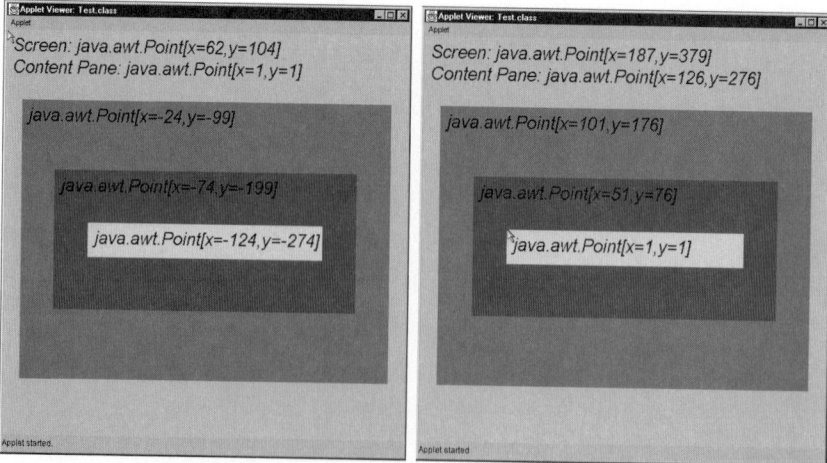

Figure 6-2 Converting Coordinates

A mouse motion listener added to the applet's content pane translates the location of mouse moved events from the content pane's coordinate system to that of the other panels and the screen. The string displayed in each panel is updated, and the applet repaints.

```
...
contentPane.addMouseMotionListener(
                    new MouseMotionAdapter() {
    public void mouseMoved(MouseEvent e) {
        Point pt = e.getPoint();

        outer.setString(SwingUtilities.convertPoint(
        contentPane, pt, outer).toString());

        inner.setString(SwingUtilities.convertPoint(
        contentPane, pt, inner).toString());

        innermost.setString(SwingUtilities.convertPoint(
        contentPane, pt, innermost).toString());

        SwingUtilities.convertPointToScreen(
                    pt, contentPane);

        lastScreenPt = pt;
        repaint();
    }
});
...
```

The applet shown in Figure 6-2 is listed in Example 6-7.

Example 6-7 Converting Mouse Coordinates

```java
import java.awt.*;
import java.awt.event.*;
import javax.swing.*;

public class Test extends JApplet {
    private Point lastScreenPt = null;
    private final Container contentPane = getContentPane();
    private PanelWithString
            outer = new PanelWithString(Color.orange),
            inner = new PanelWithString(Color.red),
            innermost = new PanelWithString(Color.yellow);

    public Test() {
        Font font = new Font("Times-Roman", Font.ITALIC, 26);

        contentPane.setLayout(new OverlayLayout(contentPane));
```

```
            contentPane.add(innermost);
            contentPane.add(inner);
            contentPane.add(outer);

            innermost.setMaximumSize(new Dimension(350,50));
            inner.setMaximumSize(new Dimension(450,200));
            outer.setMaximumSize(new Dimension(550,400));

            setFont(font);
            innermost.setFont(font);
            inner.setFont(font);
            outer.setFont(font);

            contentPane.addMouseMotionListener(
                                new MouseMotionAdapter() {
                public void mouseMoved(MouseEvent e) {
                    Point pt = e.getPoint();

                    outer.setString(SwingUtilities.convertPoint(
                    contentPane, pt, outer).toString());

                    inner.setString(SwingUtilities.convertPoint(
                    contentPane, pt, inner).toString());

                    innermost.setString(SwingUtilities.convertPoint(
                    contentPane, pt, innermost).toString());

                    SwingUtilities.convertPointToScreen(
                                    pt, contentPane);

                    lastScreenPt = pt;
                    repaint();
                }
            });
        }
        public void paint(Graphics g) {
            super.paint(g);

            if(lastScreenPt != null) {
                String s = new String("Screen: " + lastScreenPt);

                g.setColor(getForeground());
                g.drawString(s,10,g.getFontMetrics().getHeight());

                SwingUtilities.convertPointFromScreen(lastScreenPt,
                                    contentPane);

                s = "Content Pane: " + lastScreenPt;

                g.drawString(s,10,g.getFontMetrics().getHeight()*2);
            }
            else {
                g.setColor(getForeground());
                g.drawString("MOVE THE MOUSE IN HERE",10,
                            g.getFontMetrics().getHeight());
```

```
        }
      }
  }
  class PanelWithString extends JPanel {
      String s;
      Color color;

      public PanelWithString(Color color) {
          this.color = color;
      }
      public void setString(String s) {
          this.s = s;
      }
      public void paintComponent(Graphics g) {
          super.paintComponent(g);

          Dimension size = getSize();

          g.setColor(color);
          g.fillRect(0,0,size.width,size.height);

          if(s != null) {
              g.setColor(getForeground());
              g.drawString(s,10,g.getFontMetrics().getHeight());
          }
      }
  }
```

Accessibility Methods

---

public static Accessible <u>getAccessibleAt</u>(Component, Point)
public static Accessible <u>getAccessibleChild</u>(Component, int)
public static int <u>getAccessibleChildrenCount</u>(Component)
public static int <u>getAccessibleIndexInParent</u>(Component)
public static AccessibleStateSet <u>getAccessibleStateSet</u>(Component)

The methods listed above are used to obtain accessibility information from a given component.

Focus Owners / Ancestors / Root Pane / Window

---

public static Component <u>findFocusOwner</u>(Component)
public static Container <u>getAncestorNamed</u>(String, Component)
public static Container <u>getAncestorOfClass</u>(Class, Component)
public static Component <u>getDeepestComponentAt</u>(Component, int, int)

public static Rectangle getLocalBounds(Component)
public static JRootPane getRoot(Component)
public static JRootPane getRootPane(Component)
public static Window windowForComponent(Component)

The methods listed above return information associated with a particular component. Focus owners, named ancestors, root panes, windows, etc., can all be obtained, given a component.

Invoking Runnable Objects

---

public static void invokeAndWait(Runnable)
                              throws InterruptedException, InvocationTargetException;
public static void invokeLater(Runnable)

The invokeAndWait and invokeLater methods are used to execute code from a thread other than the event dispatch thread. Both methods are discussed in "Swing and Threads" on page 57 and therefore are not covered here.

Descendants / Event Dispatch Thread

---

public static boolean isDescendingFrom(Component allegedDescendent,
                              Component allegedAncestor)
public static boolean isEventDispatchThread()

The two methods listed above can be used to determine whether a component is a descendant of another and whether the current thread is the event dispatched thread.

Mouse Buttons

---

public static boolean isLeftMouseButton(MouseEvent)
public static boolean isMiddleMouseButton(MouseEvent)
public static boolean isRightMouseButton(MouseEvent)

With the AWT, determining which mouse button was pressed, given a mouse event, involved examining the modifiers of the event and ANDing them with a bit mask, a process that was nonintuitive and difficult to remember. Swing remedies this shortcoming of the AWT by providing three convenience methods for determining which mouse button was pressed for a given mouse event.

Compound Labels / Painting / Updating Component Tree UI

---

public static String layoutCompoundLabel(FontMetrics, String, Icon, int, int, int, int, Rectangle, Rectangle, Rectangle, int)
static String layoutCompoundLabel(JComponent, FontMetrics, String, Icon, int, int, int, int, Rectangle, Rectangle, Rectangle, int)

public static void paintComponent(Graphics, Component, Container, int, int, int, int)
public static void paintComponent(Graphics, Component, Container, Rectangle)

public static void updateComponentTreeUI(Component)

The `layoutCompoundLabel` methods are used by Swing buttons and labels to lay out their text and icon. The `paintComponent` methods are used to paint a component in an arbitrary graphics, and the `updateComponentTreeUI` method is used to update the UI delegates associated with a component's descendants.

Swing Constants

Swing provides three interfaces in the `swing` package that define constants. The `SwingConstants` class defines positional constants, in addition to `ScrollPaneConstants` and `WindowConstants` classes that define constants for their respective components.

Interface Summary 6-1 lists the constants defined by the `SwingConstants` interface.

Interface Summary 6-1   SwingConstants

Constants

---

public static final int <u>BOTTOM</u>
public static final int <u>CENTER</u>
public static final int <u>EAST</u>
public static final int <u>HORIZONTAL</u>
public static final int <u>LEFT</u>
public static final int <u>NORTH</u>
public static final int <u>NORTH_EAST</u>
public static final int <u>NORTH_WEST</u>
public static final int <u>RIGHT</u>
public static final int <u>SOUTH</u>
public static final int <u>SOUTH_EAST</u>
public static final int <u>SOUTH_WEST</u>
public static final int <u>TOP</u>
public static final int <u>VERTICAL</u>
public static final int <u>WEST</u>

A number of Swing classes implement the `SwingConstants` interface: `JCheckBoxMenuItem`, `JLabel`, `JProgressBar`, `JSlider`, and `JTextField`. Implementing the `SwingConstants` interface allows the constants defined by the `SwingConstants` interface to be accessed as though they were declared in the implementing class.

BoxLayout and the Box Class

Swing provides a layout manager—`BoxLayout`—for laying out components horizontally or vertically, and a container—`Box`—that utilizes a `BoxLayout`.

BoxLayout

BoxLayout lays out components in a horizontal or vertical line. An axis—either BoxLayout.X_AXIS or BoxLayout.Y_AXIS—is specified at the time of construction and determines the orientation of the components.

Components laid out along the x axis are laid out horizontally, and components laid out along the y axis are laid out vertically. Components are laid out top to bottom or left to right in the order in which they are added to their container.

BoxLayout sizes components laid out horizontally or vertically at their preferred widths or preferred heights, respectively. For a horizontal layout, if all of components are not the same height, BoxLayout attempts to set the height of each component to the height of the tallest component in the container. If a component's height cannot be set to the height of the tallest component, the component is placed vertically according to its vertical alignment. For vertical layouts, the component's width is adjusted in the same manner as component height for horizontal layout. This section provides a simple example of the use of the BoxLayout layout manager. See "JToolBar" on page 560 for an example that is somewhat more complicated and takes component alignment into account.

Figure 6-3 shows an applet that contains two containers, each of which contains buttons. Both containers have a BoxLayout as their layout manager; the container on the left lays out components along the X_AXIS, and the container on the right lays out components along the Y_AXIS.

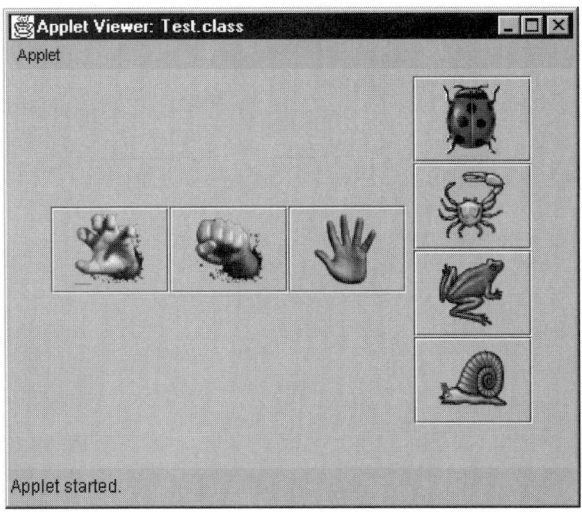

Figure 6-3 Two Containers Using BoxLayout

The applet shown in Figure 6-3 implements an extension of the `JPanel` class that is fitted with an instance of `BoxLayout` for its layout manager:

```
class ContainerWithBoxLayout extends JPanel {
    public ContainerWithBoxLayout(int orientation) {
        setLayout(new BoxLayout(this, orientation));
    }
}
```

The applet instantiates two instances of `ContainerWithBoxLayout`: one with an orientation of `BoxLayout.X_AXIS`, and the other with an orientation of `BoxLayout.Y_AXIS`:

```
public class Test extends JApplet {
    public Test() {
        ...
        ContainerWithBoxLayout yaxis =
                new ContainerWithBoxLayout(BoxLayout.Y_AXIS);

        ContainerWithBoxLayout xaxis =
                new ContainerWithBoxLayout(BoxLayout.X_AXIS);
```

Buttons are subsequently added to the two containers, and the containers are added to the applet's content pane.

```
        ...
        xaxis.add(new JButton(new ImageIcon("reach.gif")));
        xaxis.add(new JButton(new ImageIcon("punch.gif")));
        xaxis.add(new JButton(new ImageIcon("open_hand.gif")));

        yaxis.add(new JButton(new ImageIcon("ladybug.gif")));
        yaxis.add(new JButton(new ImageIcon("crab.gif")));
        yaxis.add(new JButton(new ImageIcon("frog.gif")));
        yaxis.add(new JButton(new ImageIcon("snail.gif")));

        contentPane.setLayout(new FlowLayout());
        contentPane.add(xaxis);
        contentPane.add(yaxis);
    }
}
```

The applet is listed in its entirety in Example 6-8.

Example 6-8 Using BoxLayout

```
import java.awt.*;
import java.awt.event.*;
import javax.swing.*;

public class Test extends JApplet {
    public Test() {
        Container contentPane = getContentPane();
        ContainerWithBoxLayout yaxis =
                new ContainerWithBoxLayout(BoxLayout.Y_AXIS);

        ContainerWithBoxLayout xaxis =
                new ContainerWithBoxLayout(BoxLayout.X_AXIS);

        contentPane.setLayout(new FlowLayout());

        xaxis.add(new JButton(new ImageIcon("reach.gif")));
        xaxis.add(new JButton(new ImageIcon("punch.gif")));
        xaxis.add(new JButton(new ImageIcon("open_hand.gif")));

        yaxis.add(new JButton(new ImageIcon("ladybug.gif")));
        yaxis.add(new JButton(new ImageIcon("crab.gif")));
        yaxis.add(new JButton(new ImageIcon("frog.gif")));
        yaxis.add(new JButton(new ImageIcon("snail.gif")));

        contentPane.add(xaxis);
        contentPane.add(yaxis);
    }
}
class ContainerWithBoxLayout extends JPanel {
    public ContainerWithBoxLayout(int orientation) {
        setLayout(new BoxLayout(this, orientation));
    }
}
```

BoxLayout is a simple layout manager. Unlike most of the AWT layout managers, there is no provision to set the gaps between components, or the gap between components and the edge of the container.

The Box Class

The best thing about BoxLayout is the Box class, an extension of java.awt.Container that lays out components with an instance of BoxLayout. The Box class doesn't really make using BoxLayout any easier; in fact, Box does little more than the ContainerWithBoxLayout class listed in Example 6-8 as far as reducing the complexities of dealing with BoxLayout. Where the Box class really shines is in the static methods it provides that return one of three substances: *glue*, *struts*, and *rigid areas*.

Glue components can be thought of as gooey substances that expand to fill the region defined by their neighboring components. Glue is somewhat of a misnomer because the "glue" never sets, and its use never results in the immobility of components that it borders. Perhaps a better analogy would be "slime balls," a gooey gel that is available in most toy stores.

Struts are fixed in a dimension of your choice, and they fill the other dimension. For example, the BoxLayout.createVerticalStrut method is passed a height, and the component—a.k.a. strut—maintains the height it was created with and expands its width as wide as it can get away with.

Rigid areas are constructed with a Dimension and, as you might guess, do not deviate from it. For example, if a rigid area is created with a dimension of (100,100), the size of the rigid area will always be (100,100).

Glue, struts, and rigid areas are useful in a number of different contexts, for example, designing input forms. Figure 6-4 shows before and after photos of a panel with some labels and combo boxes. The before picture (top) is straight GridBagLayout, whereas the after picture (bottom) uses horizontal and vertical struts to space things in a more aesthetically pleasing manner.

Example 6-9 lists a portion of the code for the panel shown in Figure 6-4. The panel uses an instance of GridBagLayout as its layout manager, in conjunction with horizontal and vertical struts.

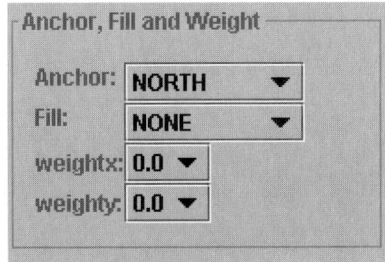

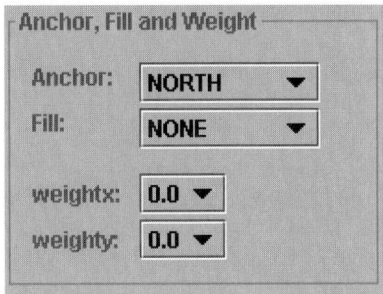

Figure 6-4 Using Struts: before (top) and after (bottom)

Example 6-9 Using Horizontal and Vertical Struts

```
class AnchorFillWeightPanel extends JPanel {
    ...
    public AnchorFillWeightPanel() {
        ...
        GridBagLayout gbl = new GridBagLayout();
        GridBagConstraints gbc = new GridBagConstraints();

        setLayout(gbl);

        gbc.anchor = GridBagConstraints.NORTHWEST;
        add(anchorLabel, gbc);
        add(Box.createHorizontalStrut(10), gbc);

        gbc.gridwidth = GridBagConstraints.REMAINDER;
        gbc.weightx = 1.0;
        add(anchorCombo, gbc);

        gbc.weightx = 0;
        add(Box.createVerticalStrut(3), gbc);

        gbc.gridwidth = 1;
```

```
        add(fillLabel, gbc);
        add(Box.createHorizontalStrut(10), gbc);

        gbc.gridwidth = GridBagConstraints.REMAINDER;
        gbc.weightx = 1.0;
        add(fillCombo, gbc);

        gbc.weightx = 0;
        add(Box.createVerticalStrut(13), gbc);

        gbc.gridwidth = 1;
        gbc.anchor = GridBagConstraints.WEST;
        add(weightxLabel, gbc);
        add(Box.createHorizontalStrut(10), gbc);

        gbc.gridwidth = GridBagConstraints.REMAINDER;
        gbc.weightx = 1.0;
        add(weightxCombo, gbc);

        gbc.weightx = 0;
        add(Box.createVerticalStrut(3), gbc);

        gbc.gridwidth = 1;
        add(weightyLabel, gbc);
        add(Box.createHorizontalStrut(10), gbc);

        gbc.gridwidth = GridBagConstraints.REMAINDER;
        gbc.weightx = 1.0;
        add(weightyCombo, gbc);
        ...
    }
    ...
}
```

Although GridBagLayout can be somewhat intimidating, it is actually easy to use for forms such as the one depicted in Figure 6-4. A simple pattern of rotating the grid width between GridBagConstraints.REMAINDER and 1 puts things in their respective columns. See "Using GridBagLayout to Lay Out Text Fields" on page 1468 for a more complicated example of using GridBagLayout to layout forms.

The Box class is summarized in Class Summary 6-4.

Class Summary 6-4   Box

Extends: java.awt.Container
Implements: Javax.accessibility.Accessible

Constructors

---

public <u>Box</u>(int axis)

All boxes are constructed with an `integer` value representing the axis upon which components will be laid out. Valid values are:

- `BoxLayout.X_AXIS`
- `BoxLayout.Y_AXIS`

Methods

Boxes and Box Substances

---

public static Box <u>createHorizontalBox</u>()
public static Box <u>createVerticalBox</u>()

public static Component <u>createGlue</u>()
public static Component <u>createHorizontalGlue</u>()
public static Component <u>createVerticalGlue</u>()

public static Component <u>createHorizontalStrut</u>(int width)
public static Component <u>createVerticalStrut</u>(int height)
public static Component <u>createRigidArea</u>(Dimension)

Boxes can be created with the `createHorizontalBox` and `createVerticalBox` convenience methods, which are equivalent to the following two lines of code, respectively:

```
Box hb = new Box(Box.X_AXIS);
Box vb = new Box(Box.Y_AXIS);
```

Glue, struts, and rigid areas are implemented by controlling their minimum, preferred, and maximum sizes. Table 6-1 shows the size requirements for each type of substance that can be created with `Box static` methods.

Table 6-1 Min/Pref/Max Sizes for Box Substances

Substance	Minimum Size	Preferred Size	Maximum Size
Glue	`0, 0`	`0, 0`	`Short.MAX_VALUE,` `Short.MAX_VALUE`
Horizontal Glue	`0, 0`	`0, 0`	`Short.MAX_VALUE, 0`
Vertical Glue	`0, 0`	`0, 0`	`0, Short.MAX_VALUE`
Horizontal Strut	`width, 0`	`width, 0`	`width, Short.MAX_VALUE`
Vertical Strut	`0, height`	`0, height`	`Short.MAX_VALUE,` `height`
Rigid Area	`dimension`[1]	`dimension`	`dimension`

1. Rigid areas are constructed with three dimensions.

It should be stressed that the substances returned by `static Box` methods may not behave like glue, struts, and rigid areas if they are added to a container that does not have a `BoxLayout` as its layout manager. Other layout managers are free to ignore the size requests for minimum, preferred, and maximum sizes.

Layout Manager / Accessible Context

public void <u>setLayout</u>(LayoutManager)
public AccessibleContext <u>getAccessibleContext</u>()

Each box uses an instance of `BoxLayout` as its layout manager, which it accomplishes by overriding the `setLayout` method.

Like all Swing components, the `Box` class implements `getAccessibleContext()`, which returns an instance of `AccessibleContext` for accessibility purposes.

Progress Monitoring

Operations that take a long time to complete should provide some visual indication of the percentage of the task that is completed. Typically, such visual indications involve a progress bar that is usually displayed in a dialog that allows the task to be canceled.

Swing includes a progress bar component—`JProgressBar`—that is used to communicate the percentage of a task that has been completed. In fact, "Progress Bars, Sliders, and Separators" on page 579 discusses an applet that monitors a time-consuming task with a progress bar.

Swing also provides two classes for monitoring progress that create and display a progress bar in a dialog: `ProgressMonitor` and `ProgressMonitorInputStream`. The former provides methods for setting progress, which updates the progress bar created by the monitor. The latter is an extension of `java.io.FilterInputStream` that is used like any other input stream, except that it displays a dialog containing a progress bar if reading the stream is time consuming.

ProgressMonitor

The `ProgressMonitor` class is used to monitor the progress of a time-consuming task by showing a progress dialog. Progress monitors decide whether an operation takes long enough to justify a progress dialog, with the help of two properties: `millisToDecideToPopup` and `millisToPopup`, which by default are 500 and 2000 milliseconds (0.5 and 2 seconds), respectively. Both properties are settable.

After `millisToDecideToPopup` milliseconds have expired since the creation of a progress monitor, the progress monitor calculates the total time required to complete the operation, depending on the percentage of the task that has been completed thus far. If the total time required is greater than `millisToPopup`, a progress dialog is displayed.

Using a progress monitor involves the following steps:

1.   Instantiate an instance of `ProgressMonitor`.

2.   Invoke `ProgressMonitor.setProgress(int)` periodically (and, optionally, `ProgressMonitor.setNote(String)`).

3.   Invoke `ProgressMonitor.close()` when the operation is complete.

The application shown in Figure 6-5 contains a button that initiates reading of a file. The application uses a progress monitor to show the progress being made while the file is read.

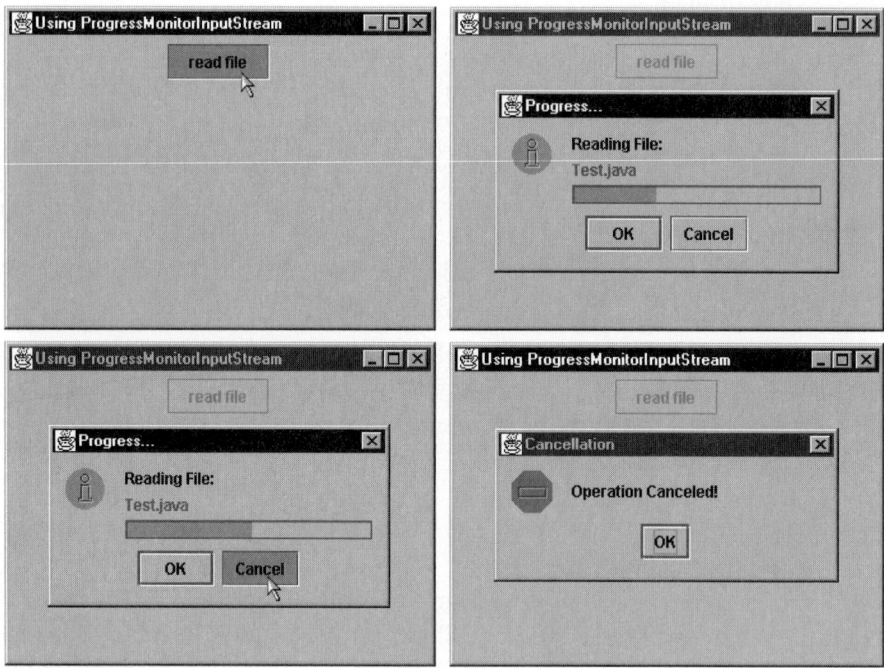

Figure 6-5 Using a ProgressMonitor

The upper-left picture shows the button being activated, thus initiating the reading of the file. The upper-right picture shows the progress monitor's dialog displayed as the file is being read. The lower-left picture shows the dialog (and the task) being canceled, handled by showing a message dialog.

The application adds an action listener to the button that creates a buffered input stream and a progress monitor. The listener subsequently creates an instance of ReadThread, which reads the file and updates the progress monitor.

Progress monitors are created with a parent component that is used to parent the monitor's progress dialog. The ProgressMonitor constructor is also passed a message that is displayed in the dialog, along with a note. The note can be updated while the dialog is displayed; for example, a progress monitor could be created with a "Reading Files" message, and the monitor's note could be updated for the particular file being read. Progress monitors are also created with minimum and maximum values representing the task at hand.

The application shown in Figure 6-5 creates a ProgressMonitor specifying the application's content pane as the parent component, with "Reading File" as the message and the name of the file as the note. The minimum value is specified as 0, and the maximum value is set to the number of bytes in the file.

```
public class Test extends JFrame {
    private JButton readButton = new JButton("read file");
    private BufferedInputStream in;
    private ProgressMonitor pm;
    private String fileName = "Test.java";

    public Test() {
        ...
        readButton.addActionListener(new ActionListener() {
            public void actionPerformed(ActionEvent e) {
                try {
                    in = new BufferedInputStream(
                        new FileInputStream(fileName));

                    pm = new ProgressMonitor(contentPane,
                            "Reading File:",
                            fileName,
                            0, in.available());
                }
                catch(FileNotFoundException fnfx) {
                    fnfx.printStackTrace();
                }
                catch(IOException iox) {
                    iox.printStackTrace();
                }
```

```
                 ReadThread t = new ReadThread();
                 t.start();
            }
        });
    }
    ...
```

The run method of the ReadThread class sets the button's enabled state to false. As long as the progress monitor has not been canceled, bytes are read from the file and the progress monitor is updated by invoking ProgressMonitor.setProgress(). If the progress monitor is canceled, a message dialog is displayed. Note that the thread sleeps for 25 milliseconds after every read and prints the character read to the standard out stream to slow the reading of the file.

After the file has been read or the progress monitor has been canceled, the progress monitor's dialog is closed by invoking ProgressMonitor.close() and the application's button is enabled.

```
    ...
class ReadThread extends Thread {
    public void run() {
        try {
            readButton.setEnabled(false);

            while(!pm.isCanceled() && (i = in.read()) != -1) {
                try {
                    Thread.currentThread().sleep(25);
                }
                catch(InterruptedException ex) {
                    ex.printStackTrace();
                }
                System.out.print((char)i);

                SwingUtilities.invokeLater(new Runnable(){
                    public void run() {
                        pm.setProgress(++cnt);
                    }
                });
            }
            if(pm.isCanceled()) {
                JOptionPane.showMessageDialog(
                        Test.this,
                        "Operation Canceled!",
                        "Cancellation",
                        JOptionPane.ERROR_MESSAGE);
            }
```

```
            pm.close();
        }
        catch(IOException ex) {
            ex.printStackTrace();
        }
        readButton.setEnabled(true);
    }
```

The application shown in Figure 6-5 is listed in its entirety in Example 6-10.

Example 6-10 Using a ProgressMonitor

```
import javax.swing.*;
import java.awt.*;
import java.awt.event.*;
import java.util.*;
import java.io.*;

public class Test extends JFrame {
    private JButton readButton = new JButton("read file");
    private BufferedInputStream in;
    private ProgressMonitor pm;
    private String fileName = "Test.java";

    public Test() {
        final Container contentPane = getContentPane();

        contentPane.setLayout(new FlowLayout());
        contentPane.add(readButton);

        readButton.addActionListener(new ActionListener() {
            public void actionPerformed(ActionEvent e) {
                try {
                    in = new BufferedInputStream(
                            new FileInputStream(fileName));

                    pm = new ProgressMonitor(contentPane,
                                "Reading File:",
                                fileName,
                                0, in.available());
                }
                catch(FileNotFoundException fnfx) {
                    fnfx.printStackTrace();
                }
                catch(IOException iox) {
                    iox.printStackTrace();
                }

                ReadThread t = new ReadThread();
                t.start();
```

```
                }
            });
        }
        class ReadThread extends Thread {
            int i, cnt=0;
            String s;

            public void run() {
                try {
                    readButton.setEnabled(false);

                    while(!pm.isCanceled() && (i = in.read()) != -1) {
                        try {
                            Thread.currentThread().sleep(25);
                        }
                        catch(InterruptedException ex) {
                            ex.printStackTrace();
                        }
                        System.out.print((char)i);

                        SwingUtilities.invokeLater(new Runnable(){
                            public void run() {
                                pm.setProgress(++cnt);
                            }
                        });
                    }
                    if(pm.isCanceled())
                        JOptionPane.showMessageDialog(
                                Test.this,
                                "Operation Canceled!",
                                "Cancellation",
                                JOptionPane.ERROR_MESSAGE);
                    pm.close();
                }
                catch(IOException ex) {
                    ex.printStackTrace();
                }
                readButton.setEnabled(true);
            }
        }
    }
    public static void main(String args[]) {
        GJApp.launch(new Test(),
                "Using Progress Monitors",300,300,450,300);
    }
}
```

The ProgressMonitor class is summarized in Class Summary 6-5.

Class Summary 6-5   ProgressMonitor

Extends: java.lang.Object

Constructors

public ProgressMonitor(Component parentComponent, Object message, String note,
                    int minimum, int maximum)

As noted previously, instances of ProgressMonitor are created with a parent
component, message, note, and minimum and maximum values.

Methods

public void close()

public int getMaximum()
public int getMillisToDecideToPopup()
public int getMillisToPopup()
public int getMinimum()
public String getNote()

public boolean isCanceled()

public void setMaximum(int)
public void setMillisToDecideToPopup(int)
public void setMillisToPopup(int)
public void setMinimum(int)
public void setNote(String)
public void setProgress(int)

`ProgressMonitor` provides a `close` method that closes the monitor's progress dialog. If a progress monitor has its `setProgress` method invoked with a value that is greater than the monitor's maximum value, the `close` method is called by the monitor itself.

The `ProgressMonitor` class also provides getter and setter methods for the `minimum`, `maximum`, `note`, `millisToPopup`, and `millisToDecideToPopup` properties.

ProgressMonitorInputStream

The `ProgressMonitorInputStream`, an extension of `java.io.FilterInputStream`, creates a progress monitor to monitor the reading of a stream. Instances of `ProgressMonitorInputStream` are used like any other input stream.

This section discusses an application that is functionally identical to the application shown in Figure 6-5 on page 282, except that a `ProgressMonitorInputStream` is used to read from a file. Because of the similarity, the application discussed in this section is not shown.

Like the application shown in Figure 6-5 on page 282, the application contains a button that initiates reading of a file. The application adds an action listener to its button that creates an instance of `ProgressMonitorInputStream` in addition to an instance of `ReadThread` that reads the file.

```
public class Test extends JFrame {
    private ProgressMonitorInputStream in;
    private JButton readButton = new JButton("read file");

    public Test() {
        ...
        readButton.addActionListener(new ActionListener() {
            public void actionPerformed(ActionEvent e) {
                try {
                    in = new ProgressMonitorInputStream(
                        contentPane,
                        "Reading " + fileName,
                        new FileInputStream(fileName));
                }
                catch(FileNotFoundException ex) {
                    ex.printStackTrace();
                }
```

```
            ReadThread t = new ReadThread();
            readButton.setEnabled(false);
            t.start();
        }
    });
}
...
```

The `ReadThread` method simply reads the file with a 10 milliseconds sleep
between reads to slow down the reading of the file. If the progress dialog shown
by the progress monitor input stream is canceled, the stream will throw an
`IOException`, which is handled by the application by displaying a message
dialog.

```
...
class ReadThread extends Thread {
    public void run() {
        int i;

        try {
            while((i = in.read()) != -1) {
                System.out.print((char)i);
                try {
                    Thread.currentThread().sleep(10);
                }
                catch(Exception ex) {
                    ex.printStackTrace();
                }
            }
            in.close();
        }
        catch(IOException ex) {
            JOptionPane.showMessageDialog(
                    Test.this,
                    "Operation Canceled!",
                    "Cancellation",
                    JOptionPane.ERROR_MESSAGE);
        }
        readButton.setEnabled(true);
    }
}
...
}
```

The application discussed above is listed in its entirety in Example 6-11.

Example 6-11 Using ProgressMonitorInputStream

```java
import javax.swing.*;
import java.awt.*;
import java.awt.event.*;
import java.util.*;
import java.io.*;

public class Test extends JFrame {
    private ProgressMonitorInputStream in;
    private JButton readButton = new JButton("read file");

    public Test() {
        final Container contentPane = getContentPane();
        final String fileName = "Test.java";

        contentPane.setLayout(new FlowLayout());
        contentPane.add(readButton);

        readButton.addActionListener(new ActionListener() {
            public void actionPerformed(ActionEvent e) {
                try {
                    in = new ProgressMonitorInputStream(
                        contentPane,
                        "Reading " + fileName,
                        new FileInputStream(fileName));
                }
                catch(FileNotFoundException ex) {
                    ex.printStackTrace();
                }

                ReadThread t = new ReadThread();
                readButton.setEnabled(false);
                t.start();
            }
        });
    }
    class ReadThread extends Thread {
        public void run() {
            int i;

            try {
                while((i = in.read()) != -1) {
                    System.out.print((char)i);
                    try {
                        Thread.currentThread().sleep(10);
                    }
                    catch(Exception ex) {
                        ex.printStackTrace();
                    }
                }
                in.close();
            }
```

```
        catch(IOException ex) {
            JOptionPane.showMessageDialog(
                    Test.this,
                    "Operation Canceled!",
                    "Cancellation",
                    JOptionPane.ERROR_MESSAGE);
        }
        readButton.setEnabled(true);
    }
}
public static void main(String args[]) {
    GJApp.launch(new Test(),
            "Using ProgressMonitorInputStream",
            300,300,450,300);
}
}
```

The `ProgressMonitorInputStream` is summarized in Class Summary 6-6.

Class Summary 6-6   ProgressMonitorInputStream

Extends: java.io.FilterInputStream

Constructors

---

public <u>ProgressMonitorInputStream</u>(Component parentComponent, Object message,
                                        InputStream)

Instances of `ProgressMonitorInputStream` are created with a parent
component, a message, and an input stream. Like the message specified for
instances of `ProgressMonitor`, the message passed to the
`ProgressMonitorInputStream` constructor is an `Object` reference. The
message specified for a `ProgressMonitorInputStream` is handled in the same
manner as messages for option panes; see "JOptionPane" on page 815 for more
information concerning option panes and messages.

Methods

---

public ProgressMonitor <u>getProgressMonitor</u>()

public void <u>close</u>() throws IOException

public int <u>read</u>() throws IOException
public int <u>read</u>(byte[]) throws IOException
public int <u>read</u>(byte[], int, int) throws IOException

public synchronized void <u>reset</u>() throws IOException

public long <u>skip</u>(long) throws IOException

The `ProgressMonitorInputStream` provides methods for obtaining a reference to the stream's progress monitor. The rest of the methods implemented by the `ProgressMonitorInputStream` class are overridden from the `java.io.FilterInputStream` class to manipulate the stream's progress monitor.

Undo/Redo

Swing provides support for undoing and redoing operations with classes and interfaces defined in the `javax.swing.undo` package, which represents a general undo/redo facility. A class diagram of the `javax.swing.undo` package is shown in Figure 6-6.

Undoable operations (a.k.a. edits) are represented by the `UndoableEdit` interface. The `javax.swing.undo` package provides four classes that implement the `UndoableEdit` interface: `AbstractUndoableEdit` (which, despite its name is not an abstract class), `CompoundEdit`, `UndoManager`, and `StateEdit`. An `UndoableEditSupport` class is also provided to assist with notifying listeners of undoable edits.

The `UndoableEdit` interface is summarized in Interface Summary 6-2.

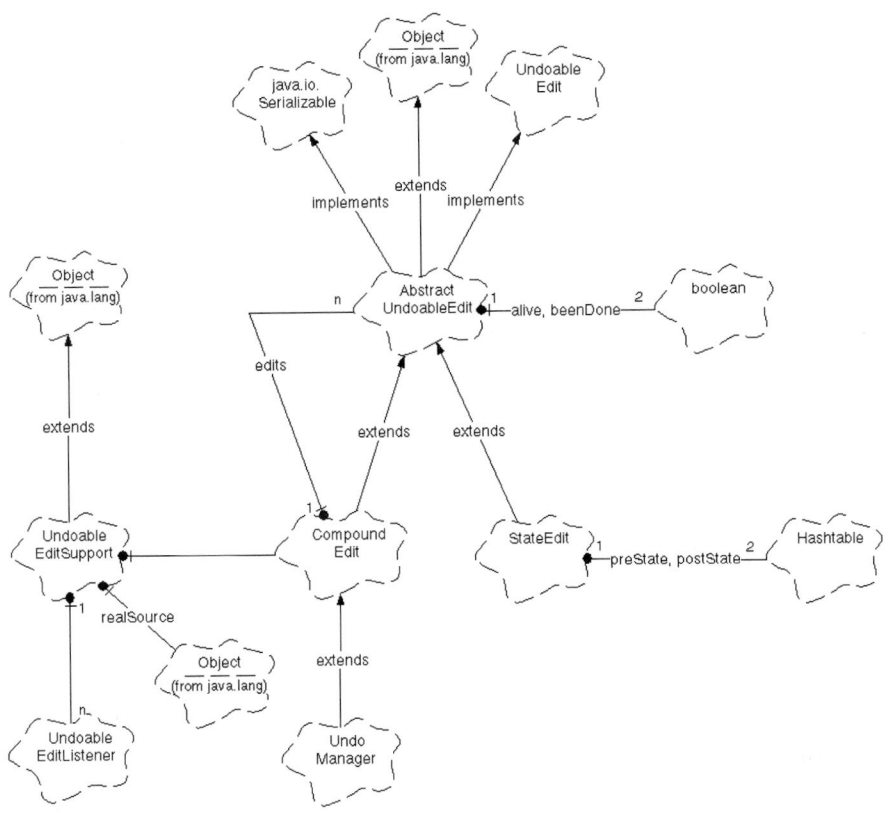

Figure 6-6 The javax.swing.undo Package

Interface Summary 6-2   UndoableEdit

Undo / Redo

---

public abstract boolean <u>canRedo</u>()
public abstract boolean <u>canUndo</u>()

public abstract void <u>redo</u>() throws CannotRedoException
public abstract void <u>undo</u>() throws CannotUndoException

public abstract void <u>die</u>()

Undoable edits must be able to report whether they can undo or redo an operation by implementing the `canRedo` and `canUndo` methods defined by the `UndoableEdit` interface.

The undo and `redo` methods perform the undo and redo operations, respectively. Notice that both the undo and `redo` methods may throw exceptions if they are called when an operation cannot be undone or redone, respectively.

The `die` method is called for edits that can no longer be undone or redone. Undoable edits typically use the `die` method to release resources associated with an operation.

Presentation Names

---

public abstract String <u>getPresentationName</u>()
public abstract String <u>getRedoPresentationName</u>()
public abstract String <u>getUndoPresentationName</u>()

Every edit must be able to report a presentation name, an undo presentation name, and a redo presentation name. An edit's presentation name should provide a localized human readable name that represents the edit. The undo presentation name represents a description of the undoable form of the edit, and the redo presentation name represents a description of the redoable form of the edit. All three names are typically presented to users in some fashion; for example, as the text displayed in a menu item.

Coalescing Edits

---

public abstract boolean <u>addEdit</u>(UndoableEdit)
public abstract boolean <u>replaceEdit</u>(UndoableEdit)

Undoable edits can be coalesced by having one edit absorb another. The `addEdit` method is passed an edit that is absorbed by the edit on whose behalf the method is invoked. The `replaceEdit` method is the inverse of the `addEdit` method and is called when the edit on whose behalf the method is invoked is absorbed by the edit passed to the method.

Significance

---

public abstract boolean <u>isSignificant</u>()

Edits can be specified as significant or insignificant. Insignificant edits are typically side effects of a significant edit; for example, when text is selected and subsequently deleted, the selection of the text would most likely be an insignificant edit.

The significance of an edit is typically used to determine which edits to present to users and is also used by the `UndoManager`, as outlined in "UndoManager" on page 308.

A Simple Undo/Redo Example

The applet shown in Figure 6-7 represents a simple example of undoing and redoing an operation. The applet provides a menu containing a menu item that allows the background color of a panel contained in the applet to be modified. The menu also provides a menu item that allows the background color change to be undone and redone.

The applet implements an extension of the `AbstractUndoableEdit` class— `BackgroundColorEdit`—and an instance of `BackgroundColorEdit` is used to undo and redo the background color change. The applet also keeps track of the previous (old) background color.

```
public class Test extends JApplet {
    private JPanel colorPanel = new JPanel();
    private BackgroundColorEdit edit = new BackgroundColorEdit();
    private Color oldColor;
    . . .
```

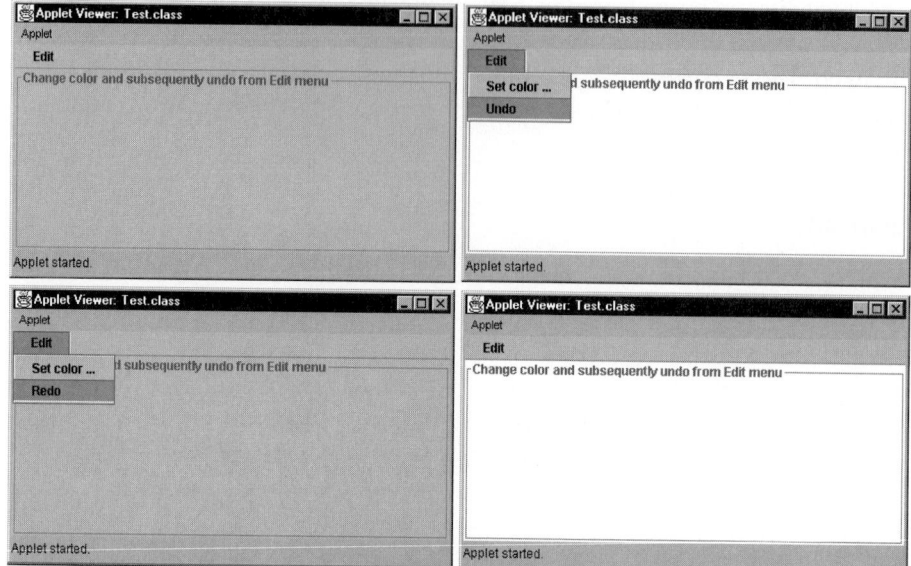

Figure 6-7 Simple Undo/Redo Example

The applet also implements two inner class extensions of the `AbstractAction` class for setting the background color and undoing/redoing the operation: `SetColorAction` and `UndoAction`, respectively. See "Actions" on page 235 for more information concerning actions in general and the `AbstractAction` class. An instance of `SetColorAction` is associated with the "Set color ..." menu item, and an instance of `UndoAction` is associated with the Undo/Redo menu item.

The `SetColorAction.actionPerformed` method—which is invoked when the Set color ... menu item is activated—displays a color chooser for selection of the new background color. If a color was selected from the color chooser, the current background color is saved and the panel's background color is set.

```
    ...
    class SetColorAction extends AbstractAction {
        public SetColorAction() {
            super("Set color ...");
        }
        public void actionPerformed(ActionEvent e) {
            Color color = JColorChooser.showDialog(
                        Test.this, // parent component
```

```
            "Pick A Color", // dialog title
            null); // initial color

    if(color != null) {
        oldColor = colorPanel.getBackground();
        colorPanel.setBackground(color);
    }
  }
}
...
```

The `UndoAction.actionPerformed` method—which is invoked when the Undo/Redo menu item is activated—obtains the text from the menu item (with the `Action.getValue` method). If the item's text is the same as the edit's undo presentation name, the `undo` method is called for the edit; otherwise, the `redo` method is invoked. The name of the action is subsequently updated, and the update is reflected by a change to the text displayed in the menu item.

```
...
class UndoAction extends AbstractAction {
    public UndoAction() {
        putValue(Action.NAME, edit.getUndoPresentationName());
    }
    public void actionPerformed(ActionEvent e) {
        String name = (String)getValue(Action.NAME);
        boolean isUndo = name.equals(
                        edit.getUndoPresentationName());

        if(isUndo) {
            edit.undo();
            putValue(Action.NAME,
                edit.getRedoPresentationName());
        }
        else {
            edit.redo();
            putValue(Action.NAME,
                edit.getUndoPresentationName());
        }
    }
}
...
```

The `BackgroundColorEdit` class extends `AbstractUndoableEdit`. Both the `undo` and `redo` methods simply restore the previous background color. Notice that both of the methods invoke their superclass' method of the same name to ensure that the action's state is kept in sync.

```
...
class BackgroundColorEdit extends AbstractUndoableEdit {
    public void undo() throws CannotUndoException {
        super.undo();
        toggleColor();
    }
    public void redo() throws CannotRedoException {
        super.redo();
        toggleColor();
    }
    public String getUndoPresentationName() {
        return "Undo";
    }
    public String getRedoPresentationName() {
        return "Redo";
    }
    private void toggleColor() {
        Color color = colorPanel.getBackground();
        colorPanel.setBackground(oldColor);
        oldColor = color;
    }
}
}
```

The applet shown in Figure 6-7 is listed in its entirety in Example 6-12.

Example 6-12 A Simple Undo/Redo Example

```
import javax.swing.*;
import javax.swing.undo.*;
import java.awt.*;
import java.awt.event.*;

public class Test extends JApplet {
    private JPanel colorPanel = new JPanel();
    private BackgroundColorEdit undo = new BackgroundColorEdit();
    private Color oldColor;

    public void init() {
        colorPanel.setBorder(
            BorderFactory.createTitledBorder(
                "Change color and subsequently undo " +
                "from the Edit menu"));

        makeMenuBar();
        getContentPane().add(colorPanel, BorderLayout.CENTER);
    }
    private void makeMenuBar() {
        JMenuBar menuBar = new JMenuBar();
        JMenu editMenu = new JMenu("Edit");
```

```java
        editMenu.add(new SetColorAction());
        editMenu.add(new UndoAction());

        menuBar.add(editMenu);
        setJMenuBar(menuBar);
    }
    class SetColorAction extends AbstractAction {
        public SetColorAction() {
            super("Set color ...");
        }
        public void actionPerformed(ActionEvent e) {
            Color color = JColorChooser.showDialog(
                            Test.this, // parent component
                            "Pick A Color", // dialog title
                            null); // initial color

            if(color != null) {
                oldColor = colorPanel.getBackground();
                colorPanel.setBackground(color);
            }
        }
    }
    class UndoAction extends AbstractAction {
        public UndoAction() {
            putValue(Action.NAME, undo.getUndoPresentationName());
        }
        public void actionPerformed(ActionEvent e) {
            String name = (String)getValue(Action.NAME);
            boolean isUndo = name.equals(
                            undo.getUndoPresentationName());

            if(isUndo) {
                undo.undo();
                putValue(Action.NAME,
                        undo.getRedoPresentationName());
            }
            else {
                undo.redo();
                putValue(Action.NAME,
                        undo.getUndoPresentationName());
            }
        }
    }
    class BackgroundColorEdit extends AbstractUndoableEdit {
        public void undo() throws CannotUndoException {
            super.undo();
            toggleColor();
        }
        public void redo() throws CannotRedoException {
            super.redo();
            toggleColor();
        }
        public String getUndoPresentationName() {
```

```
            return "Undo";
        }
        public String getRedoPresentationName() {
            return "Redo";
        }
        private void toggleColor() {
            Color color = colorPanel.getBackground();
            colorPanel.setBackground(oldColor);
            oldColor = color;
        }
    }
}
```

UndoableEditSupport

The example shown in Figure 6-7 on page 296 is a simple illustration of
implementing undo/redo; however, it is not very realistic. Typically, support for
undoing/redoing operations is built into a component. When an undoable edit is
performed on a component, the component fires an undoable edit to registered
undoable edit listeners. For example, the applet shown in Figure 6-7 on page 296
and listed in Example 6-12 is rewritten in Example 6-13 so that undoable edits are
created and fired to listeners by the ColorPanel class.

Example 6-13 Using UndoableEditSupport

```
import javax.swing.*;
import javax.swing.event.*;
import javax.swing.undo.*;
import java.awt.*;
import java.awt.event.*;

public class Test extends JApplet {
    private ColorPanel colorPanel = new ColorPanel();
    private UndoAction undoAction = new UndoAction();

    public void init() {
        colorPanel.setBorder(
            BorderFactory.createTitledBorder(
                "Change color and subsequently undo " +
                "from the Edit menu"));

        makeMenuBar();
        colorPanel.addUndoableEditListener(undoAction);
        getContentPane().add(colorPanel, BorderLayout.CENTER);
    }
    private void makeMenuBar() {
        JMenuBar menuBar = new JMenuBar();
        JMenu editMenu = new JMenu("Edit");
```

```
        editMenu.add(new SetColorAction());
        editMenu.add(undoAction);

        menuBar.add(editMenu);
        setJMenuBar(menuBar);
}
class UndoAction extends AbstractAction
                implements UndoableEditListener {
        UndoableEdit lastEdit;

        public UndoAction() {
            putValue(Action.NAME, "Undo");
            setEnabled(false);
        }
        public void actionPerformed(ActionEvent e) {
            String name = (String)getValue(Action.NAME);
            boolean isUndo = name.equals(
                        lastEdit.getUndoPresentationName());
            if(isUndo) {
                lastEdit.undo();
                putValue(Action.NAME,
                    lastEdit.getRedoPresentationName());
            }
            else {
                lastEdit.redo();
                putValue(Action.NAME,
                    lastEdit.getUndoPresentationName());
            }
        }
        public void undoableEditHappened(UndoableEditEvent e) {
            lastEdit = e.getEdit();

            putValue(Action.NAME,
                    lastEdit.getUndoPresentationName());

            if(lastEdit.canUndo())
                setEnabled(true);
        }
}
class SetColorAction extends AbstractAction {
        public SetColorAction() {
            super("Set color ...");
        }
        public void actionPerformed(ActionEvent e) {
            Color color = JColorChooser.showDialog(
                        Test.this, // parent component
                        "Pick A Color", // dialog title
                        null); // initial color

            if(color != null) {
                colorPanel.setBackground(color);
            }
        }
```

```
        }
    }
    class ColorPanel extends JPanel {
        UndoableEditSupport support;
        BackgroundColorEdit edit = new BackgroundColorEdit();
        Color oldColor;

        public void addUndoableEditListener(
                                    UndoableEditListener l) {
            support.addUndoableEditListener(l);
        }
        public void removeUndoableEditListener(
                                    UndoableEditListener l) {
            support.removeUndoableEditListener(l);
        }
        public void setBackground(Color color) {
            oldColor = getBackground();
            super.setBackground(color);

            if(support == null)
                support = new UndoableEditSupport();

            support.postEdit(edit);
        }
        class BackgroundColorEdit extends AbstractUndoableEdit {
            public void undo() throws CannotUndoException {
                super.undo();
                toggleColor();
            }
            public void redo() throws CannotRedoException {
                super.redo();
                toggleColor();
            }
            public String getUndoPresentationName() {
                return "Undo Background Color Change";
            }
            public String getRedoPresentationName() {
                return "Redo Background Color Change";
            }
            private void toggleColor() {
                Color color = getBackground();
                setBackground(oldColor);
                oldColor = color;
            }
        }
    }
```

The applet listed in Example 6-13 implements the BackgroundColorEdit class
as an inner class of the ColorPanel class, and the ColorPanel class fires
undoable edit events when its background color is modified.

The UndoAction class implements the UndoableEditListener interface by implementing the undoableEditHappened method, which retains a reference to the edit and sets the enabled status of the action depending upon whether the edit can be undone.

The ColorPanel class fires undoable edit events with the help of the UndoableEditSupport class, which provides methods for adding and removing undoable edit listeners and for firing events to the listeners.

Compound Edits

It is often the case that multiple undoable edits must be stored and undone all at once. The CompoundEdit class, which extends AbstractUndoableEdit, provides that capability.

Here's how compound edits work: A compound edit is instantiated, and undoable edits are added to the compound edit. While edits are being added to a compound edit, the compound edit is in an *in progress* state and cannot be undone until CompoundEdit.end() is invoked. Once CompoundEdit.end() is called, a call to CompoundEdit.undo() undoes all of the edits, from the last edit to the first, that were added to the compound edit while it was in progress.

The applet shown in Figure 6-8 illustrates the use of compound edits. The applet contains an extension of JList that provides an undoableAdd method that adds an object to the list and subsequently fires an undoable edit to the list's undoable edit listeners. The applet also maintains a compound edit that is used to undo additions to the list.

The top-left picture shows the applet after six items have been added to the list by six activations of the Add Item button. The top-right picture shows the applet after the End button has been activated, causing CompoundEdit.end() to be invoked for the compound edit maintained by the applet. The bottom-left picture shows the applet after the Undo button has been activated, thus invoking CompoundEdit.undo(), which causes the additions to be undone. The bottom-right picture shows the applet after CompoundEdit.redo() has been invoked by activating the Redo button.

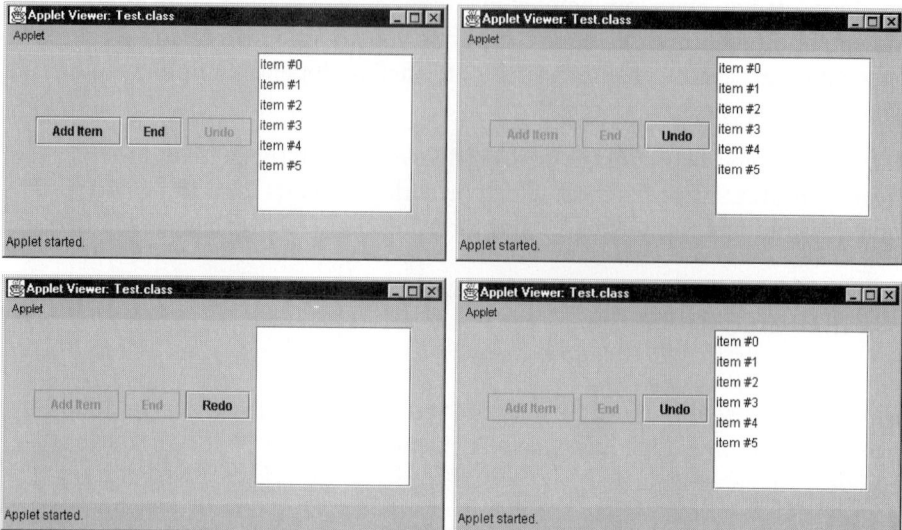

Figure 6-8 Using Compound Edits

The list contained in the applet shown in Figure 6-8 is an instance of UndoableList, which supports undoing additions to the list. The UndoableList class provides an undoableAdd method that adds an object to the list and fires an instance of UndoableList.AddItemEdit. Listener registration and event firing is performed with the aid of an instance of UndoableEditSupport.

The AddItemEdit class extends AbstractUndoableEdit and implements undo() by removing the last item added to the list. AddItemEdit.redo() adds the item that was removed by the undo method.

```
class UndoableList extends JList {
    UndoableEditSupport support = new UndoableEditSupport();
    DefaultListModel model;

    public UndoableList() {
        setModel(model = new DefaultListModel());
    }
    public void addUndoableEditListener(UndoableEditListener l) {
        support.addUndoableEditListener(l);
    }
    public void removeUndoableEditListener(
                                UndoableEditListener l) {
        support.removeUndoableEditListener(l);
```

```
    }
    public void undoableAdd(Object s) {
        model.addElement(s);
        support.postEdit(new AddItemEdit());
    }
    class AddItemEdit extends AbstractUndoableEdit {
        Object lastItemAdded;

        public void undo() throws CannotUndoException {
            super.undo();
            lastItemAdded = model.getElementAt(model.getSize()-1);
            model.removeElement(lastItemAdded);
        }
        public void redo() throws CannotRedoException {
            super.redo();
            model.addElement(lastItemAdded);
        }
    }
}
```

The applet creates an instance of UndoableList, wrapped in a scrollpane, that is added to the applet's content pane. The applet also creates an instance of UndoAction and an instance of CompoundEdit, in addition to the Add, End, and Undo buttons.

An action listener added to the End button invokes CompoundEdit.end(), and an action listener added to the Add button adds a string to the list. Both listeners invoke the applet's updateButtonsEnabledState, which sets the enabled state for the three buttons depending on the state of the compound edit.

```
public class Test extends JApplet {
    private UndoableList list = new UndoableList();
    private JScrollPane scrollPane = new JScrollPane(list);

    private JButton addButton = new JButton("Add Item"),
                    endButton = new JButton("End"),
                    undoButton = new JButton("Undo");

    private UndoAction undoAction = new UndoAction();
    private CompoundEdit compoundEdit = new CompoundEdit();
    private int cnt=0;

    public void init() {
        // add buttons and scrollpane to content pane ...

        endButton.addActionListener(new ActionListener() {
            public void actionPerformed(ActionEvent e) {
                compoundEdit.end();
                updateButtonsEnabledState();
```

```
        }
    });
    addButton.addActionListener(new ActionListener() {
        public void actionPerformed(ActionEvent e) {
            list.undoableAdd("item #" + cnt++);
            updateButtonsEnabledState();
        }
    });
    undoButton.addActionListener(undoAction);

    endButton.setEnabled(false);
    undoButton.setEnabled(false);
}
private void updateButtonsEnabledState() {
    boolean inProgress = compoundEdit.isInProgress();

    endButton.setEnabled(inProgress);
    addButton.setEnabled(inProgress);

    if(undoButton.getText().equals("Undo"))
        undoButton.setEnabled(compoundEdit.canUndo());
    else
        undoButton.setEnabled(compoundEdit.canRedo());
}
```

The applet shown in Figure 6-8 is listed in its entirety in Example 6-14.

Example 6-14 Using Compound Edits

```
import javax.swing.*;
import javax.swing.event.*;
import javax.swing.undo.*;
import java.awt.*;
import java.awt.event.*;

public class Test extends JApplet {
    private UndoableList list = new UndoableList();
    private JScrollPane scrollPane = new JScrollPane(list);

    private JButton addButton = new JButton("Add Item"),
                    endButton = new JButton("End"),
                    undoButton = new JButton("Undo");

    private UndoAction undoAction = new UndoAction();
    private CompoundEdit compoundEdit = new CompoundEdit();
    private int cnt=0;

    public void init() {
        Container contentPane = getContentPane();
```

```
        contentPane.setLayout(new FlowLayout());
        contentPane.add(addButton);
        contentPane.add(endButton);
        contentPane.add(undoButton);
        contentPane.add(scrollPane);

        scrollPane.setPreferredSize(new Dimension(150,150));
        list.addUndoableEditListener(undoAction);

        endButton.addActionListener(new ActionListener() {
            public void actionPerformed(ActionEvent e) {
                compoundEdit.end();
                updateButtonsEnabledState();
            }
        });
        addButton.addActionListener(new ActionListener() {
            public void actionPerformed(ActionEvent e) {
                list.undoableAdd("item #" + cnt++);
                updateButtonsEnabledState();
            }
        });
        undoButton.addActionListener(undoAction);

        endButton.setEnabled(false);
        undoButton.setEnabled(false);
    }
    private void updateButtonsEnabledState() {
        boolean inProgress = compoundEdit.isInProgress();

        endButton.setEnabled(inProgress);
        addButton.setEnabled(inProgress);

        if(undoButton.getText().equals("Undo"))
            undoButton.setEnabled(compoundEdit.canUndo());
        else
            undoButton.setEnabled(compoundEdit.canRedo());
    }
    class UndoAction extends AbstractAction
                  implements UndoableEditListener {

        public UndoAction() {
            putValue(Action.NAME, "Undo");
        }
        public void actionPerformed(ActionEvent e) {
            String name = undoButton.getText();
            boolean isUndo = name.equals("Undo");

            if(isUndo) compoundEdit.undo();
            else    compoundEdit.redo();

            undoButton.setText(isUndo ? "Redo" : "Undo");
```

```
            }
            public void undoableEditHappened(UndoableEditEvent e) {
                UndoableEdit edit = e.getEdit();
                compoundEdit.addEdit(edit);
                endButton.setEnabled(true);
            }
        }
    }
    class UndoableList extends JList {
        UndoableEditSupport support = new UndoableEditSupport();
        DefaultListModel model;

        public UndoableList() {
            setModel(model = new DefaultListModel());
        }
        public void addUndoableEditListener(UndoableEditListener l) {
            support.addUndoableEditListener(l);
        }
        public void removeUndoableEditListener(
                                    UndoableEditListener l) {
            support.removeUndoableEditListener(l);
        }
        public void undoableAdd(Object s) {
            model.addElement(s);
            support.postEdit(new AddItemEdit());
        }
        class AddItemEdit extends AbstractUndoableEdit {
            Object lastItemAdded;

            public void undo() throws CannotUndoException {
                super.undo();
                lastItemAdded = model.getElementAt(model.getSize()-1);
                model.removeElement(lastItemAdded);
            }
            public void redo() throws CannotRedoException {
                super.redo();
                model.addElement(lastItemAdded);
            }
        }
    }
}
```

UndoManager

The `javax.swing.undo` provides an `UndoManager` class that extends
`CompoundEdit`. `UndoManager` differs from its superclass in two ways. First, the
`UndoManager` class implements the `UndoableEditListener` interface by
adding edits it is passed to itself. This approach allows the undo manager to
manage undoable events from more than one source.

Second, the undo manager can undo while it is in progress, unlike the
CompoundEdit class, which can only undo after CompoundEdit.end() is
invoked. After end() is called for an instance of UndoManager, the undo
manager effectively transforms edits into a compound edit. This feature is useful
for situations where minor edits need to be available for undoing until they are
committed but afterward should be treated as a single edit.

The applet shown in Figure 6-9 is identical to the applet listed in Example 6-14,
except that the compound edit is replaced with an instance of UndoManager. The
applet shown in Figure 6-9 is not listed but is available on the CD in the back of
the book.

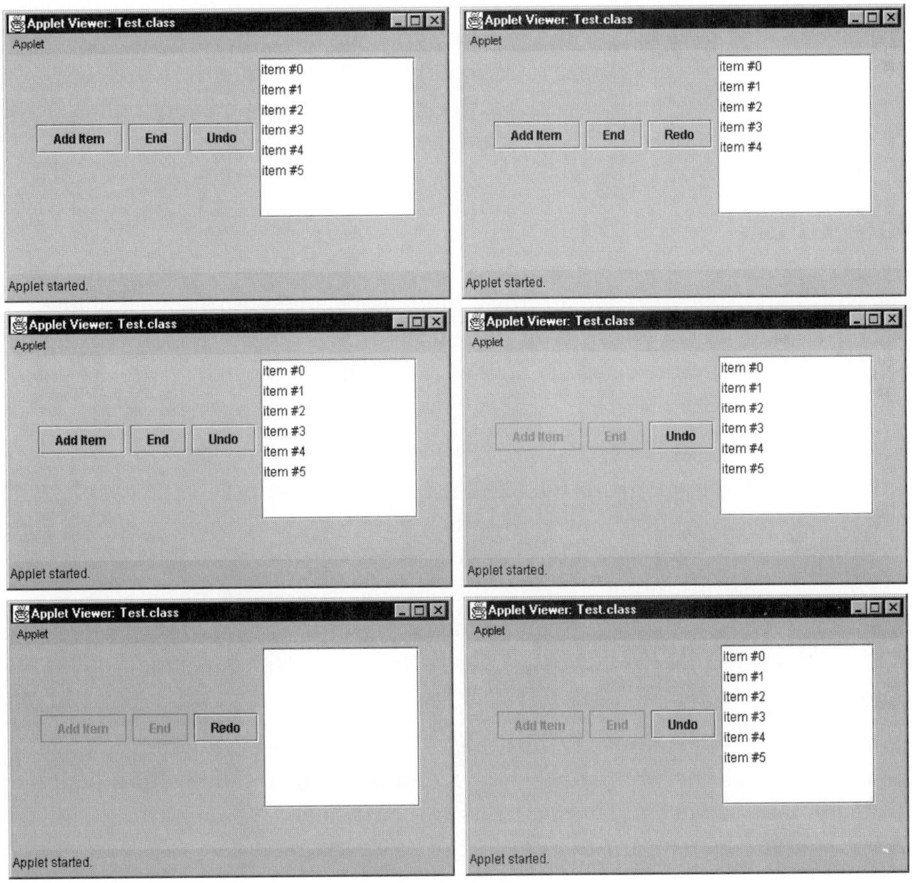

Figure 6-9 Using the Undo Manager

The top-left picture in Figure 6-9, like the top-left picture in Figure 6-8 on page 304, shows the applet after six items have been added to the list. Notice that the Undo button is enabled in the top-left picture in Figure 6-9, as opposed to the top-left picture in Figure 6-8, because undo can be invoked for instances of UndoManager before the manager's end method is invoked. The top-right picture in Figure 6-9 shows the applet after the Undo button has been activated, which undoes the addition of item #5.

The middle left picture in Figure 6-9 shows the applet after the Redo button has subsequently been activated, which undoes the deletion of item #5. The middle-right picture shows the applet after the End button has been activated.

The bottom-left picture shows the applet after the Undo button has subsequently been activated. Because the end method has been invoked for the undo manager, the manager now behaves like a compound edit, meaning that a call to UndoManager.undo calls undo on each of the edits added to the manager. Finally, the bottom-right picture shows the applet after the Redo button has been activated, which restores the items originally added to the list.

State Edits

State edits toggle between two arbitrary states associated with a state editable object that is associated with a state edit. State editable objects implement the StateEditable interface, which defines two methods: void storeState(Hashtable) and void restoreState(Hashtable).

State edits are represented by the StateEdit class, which must be constructed with an object that implements the StateEditable interface. Instances of StateEdit invoke storeState() for the StateEditable object passed to the StateEdit constructor when the state edit is constructed and when StateEdit.end() is invoked. Thus, the pre- and post-states for the state editable object are defined. Subsequent calls to undo and redo for the state edit result in calls to StateEditable.restoreState(), which is passed an appropriate hash table.

The applet shown in Figure 6-10 illustrates the use of state edits. The applet contains three buttons for starting, ending, and undoing or redoing an edit and a panel with four text fields. The text fields are contained in a panel that extends JPanel and implements the StateEditable interface.

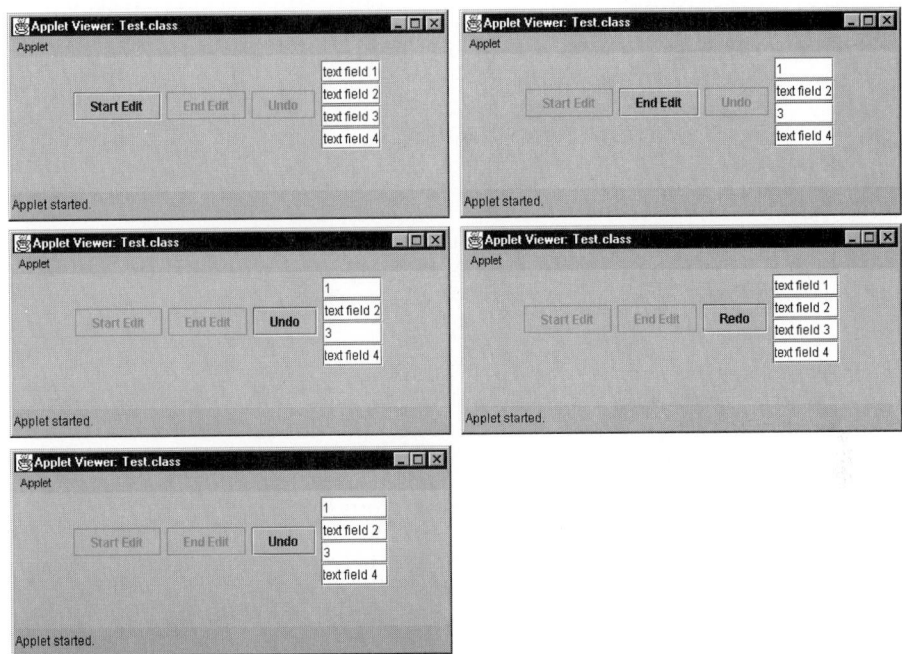

Figure 6-10 Using State Edits

The top-left picture shows the applet as it appears initially. The top-right picture shows the applet after the Start Edit button has been activated and the contents of two of the text fields have been changed. The middle-left picture shows the applet after the End Edit button has been activated, and the middle-right picture shows the applet after the Undo button has been activated. Finally, the bottom picture shows the applet after the Redo button has been activated.

The panel contained in the applet is an instance of `TextFieldPanel`, which contains four text fields that are laid out by an instance of `BoxLayout`. See "BoxLayout and the Box Class" on page 272 for more information concerning the `BoxLayout` layout manager.

The `TextFieldPanel.storeState` method puts a reference to each text field in the hash table it is passed as key/value pairs. The `TextFieldPanel.restoreState` method iterates over the key/value pairs in the hash table it is passed and sets the text for each of the text fields stored in the hash table as keys. It should be noted that hash tables passed to `StateEditable.restoreState()` contain only entries that have changed.

```
class TextFieldPanel extends JPanel implements StateEditable {
    JTextField[] fields = new JTextField[] {
        new JTextField("text field 1"),
        new JTextField("text field 2"),
        new JTextField("text field 3"),
        new JTextField("text field 4"),
    };

    public TextFieldPanel() {
        setLayout(new BoxLayout(this, BoxLayout.Y_AXIS));

        for(int i=0; i < fields.length; ++i)
            add(fields[i]);
    }
    public void storeState(Hashtable hashtable) {
        for(int i=0; i < fields.length; ++i)
            hashtable.put(fields[i], fields[i].getText());
    }
    public void restoreState(Hashtable hashtable) {
        Enumeration keys = hashtable.keys();

        while(keys.hasMoreElements()) {
            JTextField field = (JTextField)keys.nextElement();
            field.setText((String)hashtable.get(field));
        }
    }
}
```

The applet creates an instance of `TextFieldPanel` and the three buttons, all of which are subsequently added to the applet's content pane. Each of the buttons is fitted with an action listener.

The action listener associated with the Start button creates an instance of `StateEdit`, passing a reference to the `TextFieldPanel`. The listener also sets the enabled state of the End button to `true` and disables the Start button.

The action listener associated with the End button invokes `end()` for the state edit and enables the Undo button and disables the End button.

The action listener associated with the Undo button invokes either `undo()` or `redo()` for the state edit and updates the Undo button's text.

```
public class Test extends JApplet {
    private TextFieldPanel panel = new TextFieldPanel();
    private StateEdit stateEdit;

    private JButton startButton = new JButton("Start Edit"),
                    endButton = new JButton("End Edit"),
                    undoButton = new JButton("Undo");
```

```java
public void init() {
    // add buttons and panel to content pane ...

    endButton.setEnabled(false);
    undoButton.setEnabled(false);

    startButton.addActionListener(new ActionListener() {
        public void actionPerformed(ActionEvent e) {
            stateEdit = new StateEdit(panel);
            endButton.setEnabled(true);
            startButton.setEnabled(false);
        }
    });
    endButton.addActionListener(new ActionListener() {
        public void actionPerformed(ActionEvent e) {
            stateEdit.end();
            undoButton.setEnabled(true);
            endButton.setEnabled(false);
        }
    });
    undoButton.addActionListener(new ActionListener() {
        public void actionPerformed(ActionEvent e) {
            String name = undoButton.getText();
            boolean isUndo = name.equals("Undo");

            if(isUndo) stateEdit.undo();
            else       stateEdit.redo();

            undoButton.setText(isUndo ? "Redo" : "Undo");
        }
    });
}
```

The applet shown in Figure 6-10 is listed in its entirety in Example 6-15.

Example 6-15 Using State Edits

```java
import javax.swing.*;
import javax.swing.event.*;
import javax.swing.undo.*;
import java.awt.*;
import java.awt.event.*;
import java.util.*;

public class Test extends JApplet {
    private TextFieldPanel panel = new TextFieldPanel();
    private StateEdit stateEdit;

    private JButton startButton = new JButton("Start Edit"),
                    endButton = new JButton("End Edit"),
```

```
                    undoButton = new JButton("Undo");

    public void init() {
        Container contentPane = getContentPane();

        contentPane.setLayout(new FlowLayout());
        contentPane.add(startButton);
        contentPane.add(endButton);
        contentPane.add(undoButton);
        contentPane.add(panel);

        endButton.setEnabled(false);
        undoButton.setEnabled(false);

        startButton.addActionListener(new ActionListener() {
            public void actionPerformed(ActionEvent e) {
                stateEdit = new StateEdit(panel);
                endButton.setEnabled(true);
                startButton.setEnabled(false);
            }
        });
        endButton.addActionListener(new ActionListener() {
            public void actionPerformed(ActionEvent e) {
                stateEdit.end();
                undoButton.setEnabled(true);
                endButton.setEnabled(false);
            }
        });
        undoButton.addActionListener(new ActionListener() {
            public void actionPerformed(ActionEvent e) {
                String name = undoButton.getText();
                boolean isUndo = name.equals("Undo");

                if(isUndo) stateEdit.undo();
                else    stateEdit.redo();

                undoButton.setText(isUndo ? "Redo" : "Undo");
            }
        });
    }
}
class TextFieldPanel extends JPanel implements StateEditable {
    JTextField[] fields = new JTextField[] {
        new JTextField("text field 1"),
        new JTextField("text field 2"),
        new JTextField("text field 3"),
        new JTextField("text field 4"),
    };

    public TextFieldPanel() {
        setLayout(new BoxLayout(this, BoxLayout.Y_AXIS));

        for(int i=0; i < fields.length; ++i)
```

```
            add(fields[i]);
    }
    public void storeState(Hashtable hashtable) {
        for(int i=0; i < fields.length; ++i)
            hashtable.put(fields[i], fields[i].getText());
    }
    public void restoreState(Hashtable hashtable) {
        Enumeration keys = hashtable.keys();

        while(keys.hasMoreElements()) {
            JTextField field = (JTextField)keys.nextElement();
            field.setText((String)hashtable.get(field));
        }
    }
}
```

Parting Shots

Swing provides a number of utilities that are used internally within Swing, but can also be used by developers. The `Box` and `BoxLayout` classes provide the ability to layout components in a horizontal or vertical line—something that the AWT lacked. The `SwingUtilities` class provides a wide range of methods encompassing functionality that had been written in some form or another many times over by developers in the past.

Progress monitors and undo/redo support are fundamental features of most user interfaces and are relatively simple to use.

CHAPTER

7

Pluggable Look and Feel

Pluggable look and feel is based on the component architecture discussed in the "Swing Component Architecture" chapter on page 71; that is, a component's look and feel is set by plugging a particular UI delegate into the component.

Swing also provides an API for managing look and feels, including the following aspects: defining look and feels, specifying the current look and feel, adding auxiliary look and feels to the current look and feel, among other things. For example, Figure 7-1 shows a single applet running under different look and feels (clockwise, from upper left: Metal, Windows, Motif and Macintosh look and feels). The applet provides a combo box that allows the look and feel to be selected for all of the applet's components. The applet installs look and feels based upon selections made from the combo box, with the aid of Swing's `UIManager` class.[1]

---

1. The applet shown in Figure 7-1 is not listed; see Example 7-3 on page 337 for an example of changing look and feel.

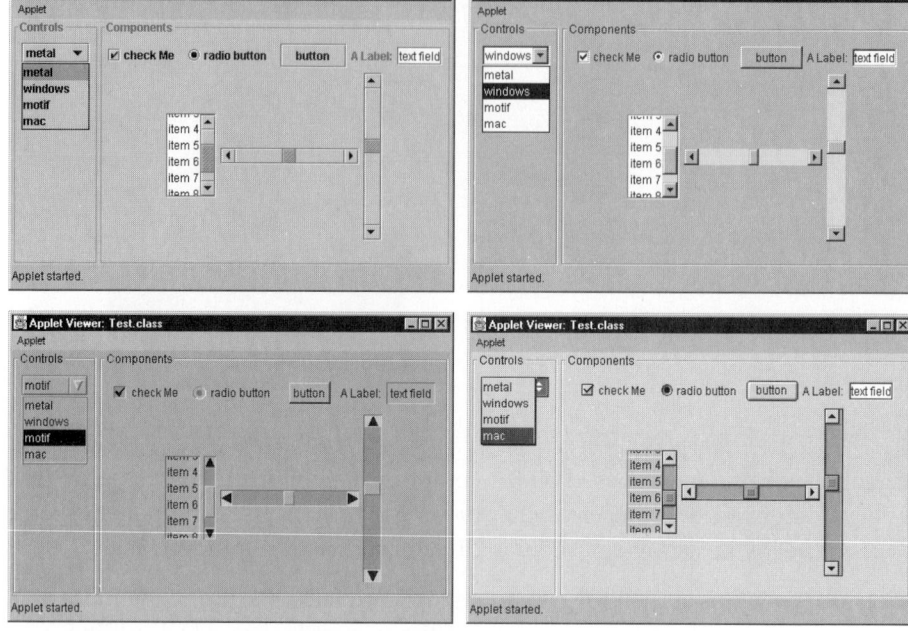

Figure 7-1 Switching Look and Feel for a Set of Components

Look-and-Feel Architecture

Three classes in the `javax.swing` package provide management of Swing look and feels: `LookAndFeel`, `UIDefaults`, and `UIManager`.

The `LookAndFeel`, `UIDefaults`, and `UIManager` classes are illustrated in Figure 7-2.

The `LookAndFeel` class is an abstract class that is extended to provide a characterization of a particular look and feel. The `LookAndFeel` class provides a handful of `static` convenience methods and defines abstract methods for specifying the following look-and-feel properties:

- name
- ID
- description
- native
- supported

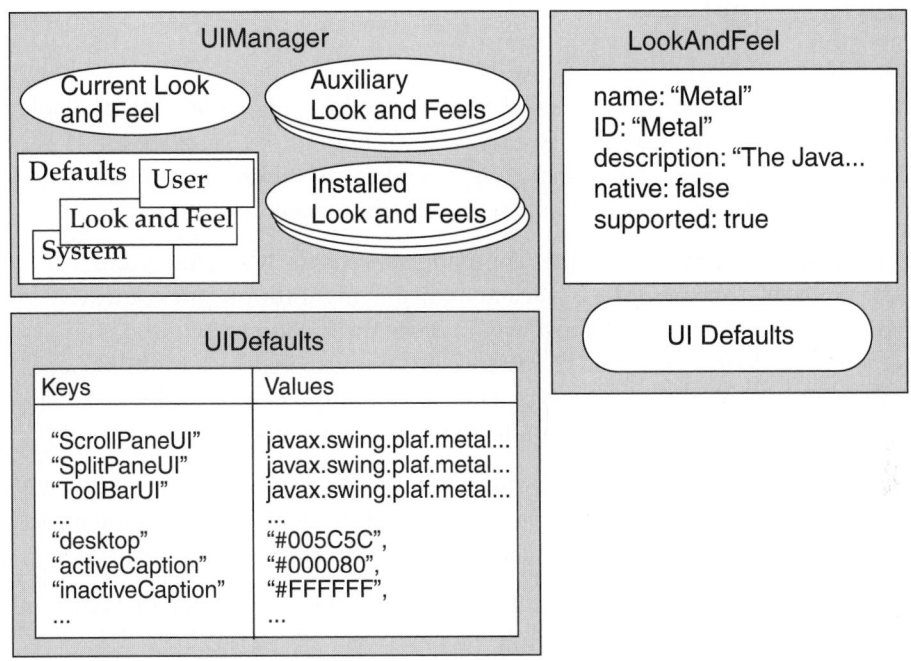

Figure 7-2 Look-and-Feel Architecture

The look-and-feel properties listed above are discussed in "The LookAndFeel Class" on page 323.

`UIDefaults` is a direct extension of `java.util.Hashtable` that maintains default values for look and feels. Developers should not directly manipulate `UIDefaults` instances; instead, they can access default values through the `UIManager` class.

The `UIManager` class is a directory service that provides `static` accessor methods for the following:

- Installed look and feels
- The current look and feel
- Default values for the current look and feel
- Auxiliary look and feels
- Class names for the system and cross-platform look and feels

All of the methods implemented by the `UIManager` class are `static`.

Look and Feels

A Swing frequently asked question is whether Swing supports labels that display multiple lines of text, and the answer is both yes and no. Swing labels are instances of the JLabel class, and JLabel makes no provision for displaying multiple lines of text; therefore, in that respect, the answer is no.

On the other hand, Swing includes components, such as JTextArea and JEditorPane, that are quite proficient at displaying multiple lines of text. It seems as though there should be a way to reuse the functionality provided by a text component—for example, an instance of JTextArea—for a multiline label component. The problem with using a text area to implement a multiline label is that a text area looks and feels like a text area and not a label.

Swing's pluggable look-and-feel architecture allows a component to be fitted with default properties, such as border, colors, and fonts from another component. As a result, a text area can be made to look and feel like a label—here's how.

Look and feels define a set of default properties with well-known names that are stored in a UIDefaults instance (a hash table). See "Pluggable Look & Feel Constants" on page 1569 for a complete list of well-known property names and their corresponding object types.

The LookAndFeel class provides convenience methods for installing default properties on a JComponent instance:

public static void <u>installBorder</u>(JComponent, String border)
public static void <u>installColors</u>(JComponent, String foreground, String background)
public static void <u>installColorsAndFont</u>(JComponent,
                        String foreground, String background, String font)

The installBorder method, for example, sets the border for a component based upon the string it is passed, which is expected to be a well-known property name. For example, a button's default border would be installed like this:

```
// code fragment: installing a button's default border
// "Button.border" is a well-known name for default button border

JButton button = new JButton("a button");
LookAndFeel.installBorder(button, "Button.border");
```

Therefore, a text area could be fitted with a look and feel's default border for buttons, like this:

```
// code fragment
JTextArea textArea = new JTextArea();
LookAndFeel.installBorder(textArea, "Label.border");
```

The applet shown in Figure 7-3 contains a label as the North component in the applet's content pane and an instance of MultilineLabel as the center component. Figure 7-3 shows the applet after being resized, to illustrate the capabilities of the multiline label.

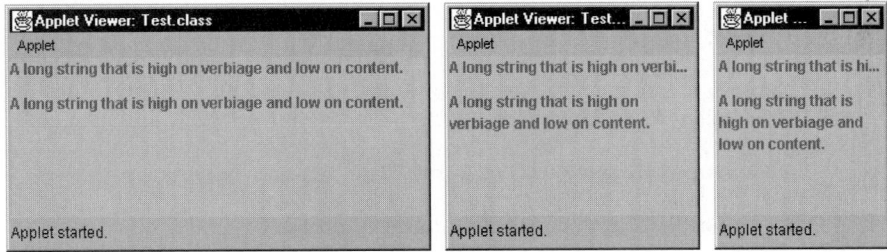

Figure 7-3 A Multiline Label

The applet shown in Figure 7-3 is listed in Example 7-1.

Example 7-1 A Multiline Label

```
import javax.swing.*;
import javax.swing.plaf.BorderUIResource;
import java.awt.*;
import java.awt.event.*;
import java.util.*;

public class Test extends JApplet {
    public void init() {
        Container contentPane = getContentPane();
        JLabel label = new JLabel(
                "A long string that is high on verbiage and " +
                "low on content.");

        MultilineLabel multilineLabel = new MultilineLabel(
                "A long string that is high on verbiage and " +
                "low on content.");
```

```
            contentPane.setLayout(new BorderLayout(2,10));

            contentPane.add(label, BorderLayout.NORTH);
            contentPane.add(multilineLabel, BorderLayout.CENTER);
        }
    }
    class MultilineLabel extends JTextArea {
        public MultilineLabel(String s) {
            super(s);
        }
        public void updateUI() {
            super.updateUI();

            // turn on wrapping and disable editing and highlighting

            setLineWrap(true);
            setWrapStyleWord(true);
            setHighlighter(null);
            setEditable(false);

            // Set the text area's border, colors and font to
            // that of a label

            LookAndFeel.installBorder(this, "Label.border");

            LookAndFeel.installColorsAndFont(this,
                            "Label.background",
                            "Label.foreground",
                            "Label.font");
        }
    }
```

The applet's init method creates an instance of JLabel and an instance of
MultilineLabel, which are added to the applet's content pane.

The MultilineLabel class extends JTextArea and overrides the updateUI
method to disguise the text area as a label. Recall that a component's updateUI
method updates the component's UI delegate according to the current look and
feel. Extending updateUI ensures that the disguising of the text area is carried
out every time the look and feel changes.

The text area's lineWrap property is set to true, as is the wrapStyleWord
property. The text area's highlighter is set to null, and the text area's editable
property is set to false because labels cannot be highlighted or edited.

The text area is fitted with border, colors, and font by invoking
LookAndFeel.installBorder() and
LookAndFeel.installColorsAndFont(). The border, colors, and font are
specified with well-known property names for the JLabel class.

The LookAndFeel Class

The LookAndFeel class provides static convenience methods, two of which—
installBorder() and installColorsAndFont()—were introduced in
"Look and Feels" on page 320. The LookAndFeel class also defines a handful of
abstract methods that characterize a look and feel.

public abstract String getName()
public abstract String getDescription()
public abstract String getID()

public abstract boolean isNativeLookAndFeel()
public abstract boolean isSupportedLookAndFeel()

A look and feel's name should be a short name such as `"Windows"` or `"Metal"`.
The string returned from the getName() method is typically used to identify
look and feels in menus, lists, etc.

The getDescription method should return a short description of the look and
feel. Descriptions are typically one or two sentences that provide more
information than the name; for example, a description may include a copyright.

The getID method returns a string used to identify a look and feel. Swing does
not use the getID method, nor does it is specify how a look and feel's ID should
be used. However, in general, the string returned from the getID method should
return a unique string that identifies the look and feel.

A look and feel is native if it emulates the look and feel of the platform upon
which an applet or application is running. If a look and feel does not emulate a
platform-specific look and feel, isNativeLookAndFeel should return false.
To determine whether a look and feel emulates the native platform, obtain the
operating system name from system properties. For example, the Windows look
and feel implements isNativeLookAndFeel like this:

```
// From javax.swing.plaf.Windows

public boolean isNativeLookAndFeel() {
    String osName = System.getProperty("os.name")
    return (osName != null) && (osName.indexOf("Windows") != -1);
}
```

If the name of the operating system contains `"Windows"`,
WindowsLookAndFeel.isNativeLookAndFeel() returns true; otherwise,
the method returns false.

A look and feel is supported if `isSupportedLookAndFeel()` returns `true`. There may be legal or competitive reasons to inhibit the use of a particular look and feel on certain platforms. For example, the Windows look and feel is supported only on Windows. The `WindowsLookAndFeel` class implements `isSupportedLookAndFeel()` like this:

```
// From javax.swing.plaf.Windows

public boolean isSupportedLookAndFeel() {
    return isNativeLookAndFeel();
}
```

Every look and feel implements a class that ultimately extends `javax.swing.LookAndFeel`. Figure 7-4 shows Swing's hierarchy of look-and-feel classes.

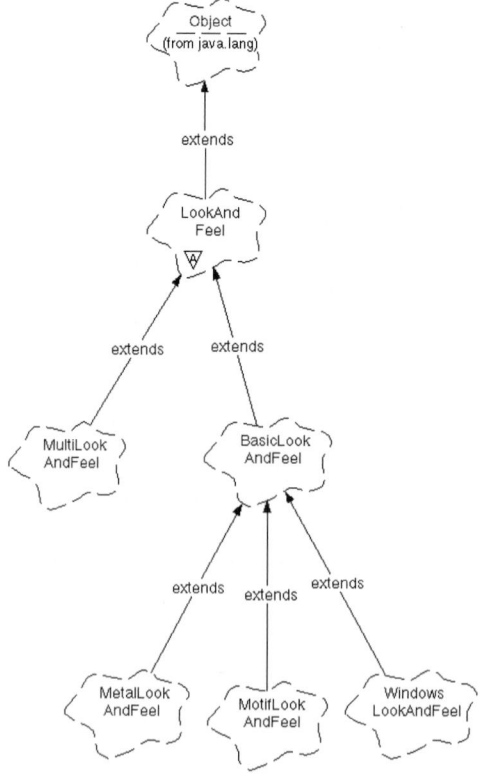

Figure 7-4 LookAndFeel Class Hierarchy

The LookAndFeel class is extended by BasicLookAndFeel and MultiLookAndFeel.[2] The BasicLookAndFeel class defines default properties that are common among most look and feels; for instance, BasicLookAndFeel defines a defaults table that includes the following button properties:

```
// From BasicLookAndFeel.java

Object[] defaults = {
    // *** Label
    "Label.font", dialogPlain12,
    "Label.background", table.get("control"),
    "Label.foreground", table.get("controlText"),
    "Label.disabledForeground", white,
    "Label.border", null,


    // Default properties for other components follow
}
```

The properties are stored in a hash table and can be modified by extensions of BasicLookAndFeel.

The LookAndFeel class is summarized in Class Summary 7-1.

Class Summary 7-1   LookAndFeel

Extends: java.lang.Object

Constructors

public LookAndFeel()

The LookAndFeel no-argument constructor is compiler generated because the LookAndFeel class does not implement a constructor of its own.

2. See "Auxiliary UIs" on page 354 for more information concerning the Multi-LookAndFeel class.

Methods

Initialization / toString()

---

public void <u>initialize</u>()
public void <u>uninitialize</u>()
public String <u>toString</u>()

The `initialize` and `uninitialize` methods are invoked when an applet or application's original look and feel is installed and when the look and feel is about to be replaced, respectively. The `LookAndFeel` class gives the methods empty implementations.

The `LookAndFeel` class overrides `toString()` to return a string that contains the look and feel's description followed by its class name.

Installing Borders, Colors and Fonts

---

public static void <u>installBorder</u>(JComponent, String defaultBorderName)
public static void <u>installColors</u>(JComponent, String defaultBackgroundName,
                    String defaultForegroundName)
public static void <u>installColorsAndFont</u>(JComponent, String defaultBackgroundName,
                    String defaultForegroundName, String defaultFontName)
public static void <u>uninstallBorder</u>(JComponent)

The component passed to the install methods listed above is fitted with default properties identified by well-known names. "Look and Feels" on page 320 illustrates the use of two of the methods (`installBorder()` and `installColorsAndFont()`) listed above.

Each of the three methods obtains an appropriate default from the `UIManager`, and the default is set for the component. For example, `LookAndFeel.installBorder()` is implemented like this:

```
// From LookAndFeel.java:

public static void installBorder(JComponent c,
```

```
                              String defaultBorderName) {
    Border b = c.getBorder();

    if (b == null || b instanceof UIResource) {
        c.setBorder(UIManager.getBorder(defaultBorderName));
    }
}
```

The property is set only if the current property is `null` or a UI resource. Swing differentiates between application and UI resources and resets only values that are marked as UI resources. See "UI Resources" on page 342 for more information concerning UI resources.

Defaults

---

public UIDefaults getDefaults()

The `getDefaults` method is called once for a given look and feel and returns a `UIDefaults` instance that contains the look and feel's default properties. See "The UIDefaults Class" on page 331 for more information concerning the `UIDefaults` class.

Descriptive Properties

---

public abstract String getDescription()
public abstract String getID()
public abstract String getName()

public abstract boolean isNativeLookAndFeel()
public abstract boolean isSupportedLookAndFeel()

The methods listed above are all abstract methods that characterize a look and feel. Extensions of `LookAndFeel` are required to provide implementations of the methods.

The abstract methods listed above are discussed further in "Look and Feels" on page 320.

Static Convenience Methods

---

public static Object <u>makeIcon</u>(Class, String)
public static JTextComponent.KeyBinding[] <u>makeKeyBindings</u>(Object[])

The methods listed above are convenience methods for extensions of the
LookAndFeel class. The makeIcon method returns a lazy value that creates an
image on demand. See "Active and Lazy Values" on page 334 for more
information concerning lazy values. The makeKeyBindings method creates key
bindings for Swing text components.

Look-and-Feel Defaults

All look and feels maintain a hash table of default component properties; for
example, BasicLookAndFeel defines defaults for button borders, background,
foreground colors, icon, etc.

```
// From javax.swing.plaf.basic.BasicLookAndFeel

Object[] defaults = {
        // *** Buttons
        "Button.font", dialogPlain12,
        "Button.background", table.get("control"),
        "Button.foreground", table.get("controlText"),
        "Button.border", buttonBorder,
        "Button.margin", new InsetsUIResource(2, 14, 2, 14),
        "Button.textIconGap", new Integer(4),
        "Button.textShiftOffset", new Integer(0),

        "ToggleButton.font", dialogPlain12,
        "ToggleButton.background", table.get("control"),
        "ToggleButton.foreground", table.get("controlText"),
        "ToggleButton.border", buttonToggleBorder,
        "ToggleButton.margin", new InsetsUIResource(2, 14, 2, 14),
        "ToggleButton.textIconGap", new Integer(4),
        "ToggleButton.textShiftOffset", new Integer(0),

        // many more defaults follow ...
    };
```

The defaults array listed above defines default values identified by well-known names such as "Button.background" and "Button.foreground". The array listed above is severely truncated; if the entire array were listed in the book, the listing would cover more than 9 pages.

Look-and-feel defaults are maintained in an instance of UIDefaults; however, developers should not access the defaults directly. Access to the default values for the current look and feel is provided by the UIManager class. See "UI Manager" on page 334 for more information concerning the UIManager class.

Look-and-feel defaults are used by UI delegates to set properties for a component. For example, the BasicButtonUI class installs default values for a button in the BasicButtonUI.installDefaults method.

```
// From javax.swing.plaf.basic.BasicButtonUI:

private final static String propertyPrefix = "Button" + ".";
...
protected String getPropertyPrefix() {
    return propertyPrefix;
}
...
protected void installDefaults(AbstractButton b) {
    String pp = getPropertyPrefix();

    if(!defaults_initialized) {
        defaultTextIconGap =
          ((Integer)UIManager.get(pp + "textIconGap")).intValue();

        defaultTextShiftOffset =
          ((Integer)UIManager.get(pp +
                              "textShiftOffset")).intValue();

        defaults_initialized = true;
    }
    ...
    if(b.getMargin() == null ||
                    (b.getMargin() instanceof UIResource)) {
        b.setMargin(UIManager.getInsets(pp + "margin"));
    }

    LookAndFeel.installColorsAndFont(b, pp +
                "background", pp + "foreground", pp + "font");

    LookAndFeel.installBorder(b, pp + "border");
}
```

UIManager static methods are used by BasicButtonUI.installDefaults to obtain default values for buttons under the current look and feel. LookAndFeel static methods are used to install the default button border, colors, and fonts. See "A Multiline Label" on page 321 for an alternative use of the LookAndFeel methods.

Two nearly identical applets are shown in Figure 7-5. Each applet creates a tree with the JTree no-argument constructor and adds the tree to the applet's content pane. The tree displayed by the left-hand applet is a default Java look & feel tree, whereas the tree displayed by the right-hand applet is the result of modifying a few well-known default values for trees.

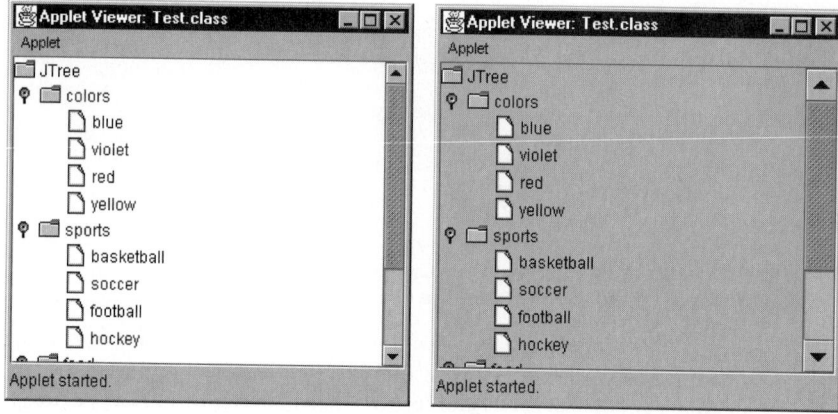

Figure 7-5 Manipulating UI Default Values

The applet shown in Figure 7-5 is listed in Example 7-2.

Example 7-2 Manipulating UI Default Values

```java
import java.awt.Color;
import javax.swing.*;

public class Test extends JApplet {
    public void init() {
        UIManager.put("Tree.background", Color.lightGray);
        UIManager.put("Tree.textBackground", Color.lightGray);
```

```
        //ScrollBar.width is peculiar to Metal L&F
        UIManager.put("ScrollBar.width", new Integer(25));

        getContentPane().add(new JScrollPane(new JTree()));
    }
}
```

The applet simply uses the `UIManager.put` method to modify the default tree background and text background colors to light gray, and to set the default scrollbar width to 25 pixels.

The scrollbar's width is modified by changing a scrollbar default, not a tree default. Therefore, all vertical scrollbars used by lightweight Swing components will be 25 pixels wide.

The UIDefaults Class

`UIDefaults` is a hash table that maintains default values for a look and feel and fires property change events when the defaults are modified. The `UIDefaults` class also provides convenience methods to eliminate casting of values—which are stored in the hash table as `Objects`—retrieved from the hash table.

The `UIDefaults` class is summarized in Class Summary 7-2.

Class Summary 7-2   UIDefaults

Extends: Java.util.Hashtable

Constructors

---

public <u>UIDefaults</u>()
public <u>UIDefaults</u>(Object[] keyValueArray)

UIDefaults can be constructed with a key-value array of objects. The array contains keys and objects that alternate. For example, the array passed to the UIDefaults constructor might have objects that look something like this:

```
..."Label.background", Color.Red, "Label.foreground",
Color.Blue,...
```

Methods

Property Change Events

---

public synchronized void addPropertyChangeListener(PropertyChangeListener)
public synchronized void removePropertyChangeListener(PropertyChangeListener)

protected void firePropertyChange(String propertyName,
                            Object oldValue,
                            Object newValue)

One of the ways in which instances of UIDefaults are different from their Hashtable superclass is that UIDefaults instances fire property change events when default values are modified. The UIDefaults class provides public registration methods for property change listeners and a private method that fires a property change.

Property Insertion Methods

---

public Object put(Object key, Object value)
public Object get(Object)
public void putDefaults(Object[])

The put method from Hashtable is overridden to fire a property change event if the key is a string. The put method returns the old value. The get method is overridden to take into account objects stored in the hash table that are lazy or active values. See "Active and Lazy Values" on page 334 for more information concerning active and lazy values.

The `putDefaults` method puts into the hash table all of the keys and values contained in the `Object` array it is passed.

Property Accessor Methods

```
public Border getBorder(Object key)
public Color getColor(Object key)
public Dimension getDimension(Object key)
public Font getFont(Object key)
public Icon getIcon(Object key)
public Insets getInsets(Object key)
public int getInt(Object key)
public String getString(Object key)

public ComponentUI getUI(JComponent)
public Class getUIClass(String)
public Class getUIClass(String, ClassLoader)
protected void getUIError(String)
```

The first group of methods listed above are accessors for specific types of properties that act to eliminate casting. For example, a border property with a key of "Label.border" could be obtained from a `UIDefaults` instance like this:

```
// code fragment

UIDefaults uiDefaults = ...
Border b = (Border)uiDefaults.get("Label.border");
```

The `LookAndFeel.getBorder` method allows the border to be obtained without a cast:

```
// code fragment

UIDefaults uiDefaults = ...
Border b = uiDefaults.getBorder("Label.border");
```

The second group of methods create a UI delegate, given a component. See "Installing a UI Delegate" on page 104 for more information on the manner in which UI delegates are created.

Active and Lazy Values

Some default properties, such as internal frame borders or checkbox menu item icons, are rarely, or infrequently accessed. In such cases, it is beneficial to delay the creation of the default value until the value is accessed for the first time.

Look and feels typically store infrequently accessed values in the defaults table as lazy values.[3] A lazy value is an object that implements the `UIDefaults.LazyValue` interface, which defines a single method:

Object <u>createValue</u>(UIDefaults table)

The `UIDefaults.get` method, before returning a value, checks to see if the value is an instance of `UIDefaults.LazyValue`; if so, the real value is obtained by invoking the lazy value's `createValue` method. After the real value is in hand, the `UIDefaults.get` method replaces the lazy value with the real value in the defaults table, and the real value is returned.

The `UIDefaults` class defines another interface— `UIDefaults.ActiveValue`—for values that must be created every time they are accessed. `UIDefaults.get()` treats active values just like lazy values, except that the active value is not replaced in the defaults table with the real value, and therefore active values are created every time they are accessed.

UI Manager

As its name suggests, the `UIManager` class manages information, namely, look-and-feel state for Swing applets and applications. The `UIManager` class provides access to the following information and services, in the form of `static` methods:

- Set a Swing applet or application's look and feel
- Provide access to the current look and feel's default values
- Provide access to look-and-feel state information
- Notification of look-and-feel changes
- Load Swing properties from the Swing properties file

3. Default values that are expensive to create are good lazy value candidates.

The ability to set the look and feel for a Swing applet or application is the
UIManager's most recognizable feature and is discussed in "Setting the Look
and Feel" on page 336.

The look-and-feel state information provided by UIManager includes the current
look and feel, installed look and feels, auxiliary look and feels, etc. UIManager
also manages three sets of default values: user, look and feel, and system—see "UI
Defaults Access" on page 335.

UIManager provides static methods for registering property change listeners
that are notified after a look and feel has been installed. Finally, the UIManager
class loads Swing properties from the Swing properties file when the UIManager
is initialized—typically, when the first UI delegate is created via
UIManager.getUI().

UI Defaults Access

The UIManager manages access to UIDefaults with static put(Object
key, Object value) and get(Object key) methods. Behind the scenes, the
UIManager class maintains user, look-and-feel, and system default values.

A call to UIManager.put(Object key, Object value) puts the key/value
pair in the user defaults, whereas a call to UIManager.get(Object key)
searches through the user, look-and-feel, and system defaults, in that order. The
value returned is the first one found, which means that user defaults have
precedence over look-and-feel defaults, which in turn have precedence over
system defaults.

Look-and-Feel Access

The UIManager class also provides static methods for accessing the following
look-and-feel information:

- The current look and feel
- The current look and feel's defaults
- Installed look and feels
- Auxiliary look and feels

Auxiliary look and feels are discussed in Auxiliary UIs on page 354.

Setting the Look and Feel

Figure 7-6 shows an applet that provides radio buttons for modifying its look and feel. The look and feel is set by the `UIManager.setLookAndFeel` method.

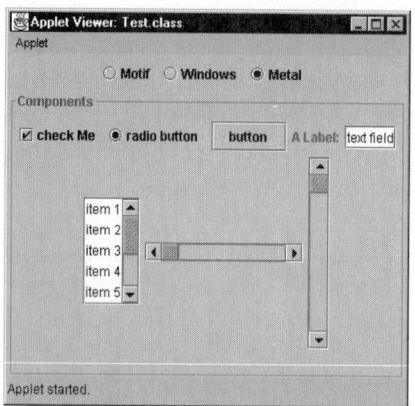
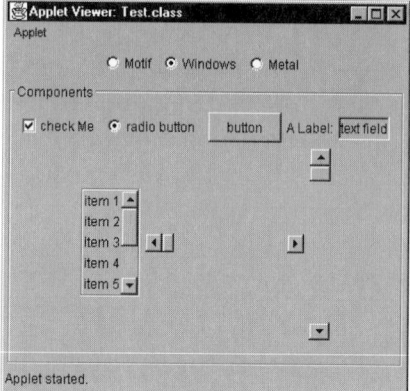
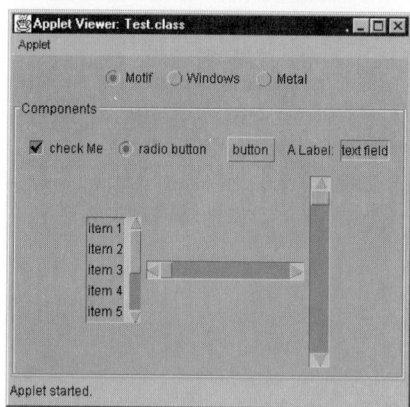

Figure 7-6 Switching Look and Feel for a Set of Components

Activation of the radio buttons is handled by an action listener, listed below, that sets the look and feel based upon which radio button was selected.

`UIManager.setLookAndFeel()` sets the current look and feel, but does not update the UI delegates of any existing components. The `SwingUtilities.updateComponentTreeUI()` updates UI delegates

recursively for all of the components contained in the container passed to the method.

```
class RadioHandler implements ActionListener {
    public void actionPerformed(ActionEvent e) {
        JRadioButton src = (JRadioButton)e.getSource();

        try {
            if(src == motifButton)
                UIManager.setLookAndFeel(
                        "javax.swing.plaf." +
                        "motif.MotifLookAndFeel");

            else if(src == windowsButton)
                UIManager.setLookAndFeel(
                    "javax.swing.plaf." +
                    "windows.WindowsLookAndFeel");

            else if(src == metalButton)
                UIManager.setLookAndFeel(
                    "javax.swing.plaf.metal." +
                    "MetalLookAndFeel");
        }
        catch(Exception ex) {
            ex.printStackTrace();
        }
        SwingUtilities.updateComponentTreeUI(
                                getContentPane());
    }
}
```

The applet shown in Figure 7-6 is listed in its entirety in Example 7-3.

Example 7-3 Switching Look and Feel for a Component Tree

```
import javax.swing.*;
import java.awt.*;
import java.awt.event.*;
import java.util.*;

import javax.swing.plaf.motif.MotifLookAndFeel;
import javax.swing.plaf.windows.WindowsLookAndFeel;
import javax.swing.plaf.metal.MetalLookAndFeel;

import javax.swing.plaf.ColorUIResource;

public class Test extends JApplet {
    public void init() {
        Container contentPane = getContentPane();
```

```
        contentPane.add(new ControlPanel(), BorderLayout.NORTH);
        contentPane.add(new ComponentPanel(),
                        BorderLayout.CENTER);
    }
class ComponentPanel extends JPanel {
    public ComponentPanel() {
        JList list;
        JScrollBar sb;

        setBorder(
            BorderFactory.createTitledBorder("Components"));

        add(new JCheckBox("check Me"));
        add(new JRadioButton("radio button"));
        add(new JButton("button"));
        add(new JLabel("A Label:"));
        add(new JTextField("text field"));
        add(new JScrollPane(list = new JList(new Object[] {
                        "item 1", "item 2", "item 3",
                        "item 4", "item 5", "item 6",
                        "item 7", "item 8", "item 9",
                        })));
        add(sb = new JScrollBar(SwingConstants.HORIZONTAL));
        sb.setPreferredSize(new Dimension(150,17));

        add(sb = new JScrollBar(SwingConstants.VERTICAL));
        sb.setPreferredSize(new Dimension(20,175));

        list.setVisibleRowCount(5);
    }
}
class ControlPanel extends JPanel {
    JCheckBox checkBox = new JCheckBox("UIResource");
    JRadioButton motifButton = new JRadioButton("Motif"),
                 windowsButton = new JRadioButton("Windows"),
                 metalButton = new JRadioButton("Metal");

    public ControlPanel() {
        ActionListener listener = new RadioHandler();
        ButtonGroup group = new ButtonGroup();

        group.add(motifButton);
        group.add(windowsButton);
        group.add(metalButton);

        motifButton.addActionListener(listener);
        windowsButton.addActionListener(listener);
        metalButton.addActionListener(listener);
```

```
            add(motifButton);
            add(windowsButton);
            add(metalButton);
        }
        class RadioHandler implements ActionListener {
            public void actionPerformed(ActionEvent e) {
                JRadioButton src = (JRadioButton)e.getSource();

                try {
                    if(src == motifButton)
                        UIManager.setLookAndFeel(
                            "javax.swing.plaf." +
                            "motif.MotifLookAndFeel");

                    else if(src == windowsButton)
                        UIManager.setLookAndFeel(
                            "javax.swing.plaf." +
                            "windows.WindowsLookAndFeel");

                    else if(src == metalButton)
                        UIManager.setLookAndFeel(
                            "javax.swing.plaf.metal." +
                            "MetalLookAndFeel");
                }
                catch(Exception ex) {
                    ex.printStackTrace();
                }
                SwingUtilities.updateComponentTreeUI(
                                        getContentPane());
            }
        }
    }
}
```

The UIManager class is summarized in Class Summary 7-3.

Class Summary 7-3   UIManager

Extends: java.lang.Object
Implements: java.io.Serializable

Constructors

public <u>UIManager</u>()

The `UIManager` constructor is compiler generated.

Methods

Property Change Listeners

public static synchronized void <u>addPropertyChangeListener</u>(PropertyChangeListener)
public static synchronized void <u>removePropertyChangeListener</u>(PropertyChangeListener)

The `UIManager.setLookAndFeel` fires a property change event to all property change listeners that have registered with the `addPropertyChangeListener` method listed above. Listeners can be removed by calling the `removePropertyChangeListener` method.

Notice that the methods listed above are `static`. Normally, listeners are registered with an object, but the `static` methods listed above essentially register listeners with the `UIManager` class.

Defaults

public static Object <u>put</u>(Object key, Object value)
public static Object <u>get</u>(Object key)

public static Border <u>getBorder</u>(Object)
public static Color <u>getColor</u>(Object)
public static UIDefaults <u>getDefaults</u>()
public static Dimension <u>getDimension</u>(Object)
public static Font <u>getFont</u>(Object)
public static Icon <u>getIcon</u>(Object)
public static Insets <u>getInsets</u>(Object)
public static int <u>getInt</u>(Object)
public static String <u>getString</u>(Object)

public static ComponentUI getUI(JComponent)

The methods listed above are all pass-through methods for the current look and feel's default values. For example, UIManager.put() obtains a reference to the user defaults and invokes UIDefaults.put().

UIManager.get() is a also pass-through to UIDefaults.get(); however, the value returned is from the user defaults, look-and-feel defaults, or system defaults. See "UI Manager" on page 334 for more information on how UIManager returns defaults.

Look and Feels

---

public static UIManager.LookAndFeelInfo[] getInstalledLookAndFeels()
public static void setInstalledLookAndFeels(UIManager.LookAndFeelInfo[]) throws
                                            SecurityException

public static void addAuxiliaryLookAndFeel(LookAndFeel)
public static LookAndFeel[] getAuxiliaryLookAndFeels()
public static boolean removeAuxiliaryLookAndFeel(LookAndFeel)

public static String getCrossPlatformLookAndFeelClassName()
public static String getSystemLookAndFeelClassName()

public static LookAndFeel getLookAndFeel()
public static UIDefaults getLookAndFeelDefaults()

public static void installLookAndFeel(String, String)
public static void installLookAndFeel(UIManager.LookAndFeelInfo)

public static void setLookAndFeel(String) throws ClassNotFoundException,
                InstantiationException, IllegalAccessException,
                UnsupportedLookAndFeelException
public static void setLookAndFeel(LookAndFeel) throws
                UnsupportedLookAndFeelException

The methods listed above all deal with look and feels. Swing keeps track of the installed look and feels, the current look and feel, and auxiliary look and feels. The static UIManager methods listed above are accessors for Swing's look and feels in addition to methods that return the system and cross-platform look-and-feel names.

UI Resources

If a button's foreground color is explicitly set and the button's UI delegate is subsequently changed,[4] does the button's foreground color change to the new look and feel's default button foreground color? The answer depends upon whether the color was specified as a UI resource (yes) or a color (no).

The javax.swing.plaf.UIResource interface is a *tagging interface* that marks objects as UI resources. The javax.swing.plaf package provides classes, such as ColorUIResource and FontUIResource, that extend a resource class and implement the UIResource interface. For example, ColorUIResource extends Color and implements UIResource. Therefore, instances of ColorUIResource are colors that are tagged with the UIResource interface.

Getting back to the original question, Swing will only replace UI resources, meaning resources that are instances of UIResource.

The applet shown in Figure 7-7 contains a button whose foreground color can be set as a Color instance (if the UIResource check box is not checked) or as a UI resource (if the UIResource check box is checked). The applet also provides radio buttons for selecting Motif or Java Look & Feel.

The left-hand pictures in Figure 7-7 show the effect of changing look and feel when the button's foreground color is specified as a color; for the right-hand pictures, the button's foreground color is specified as an instance of ColorUIResource.

---

4.   UI delegates are typically changed by changing look and feel.

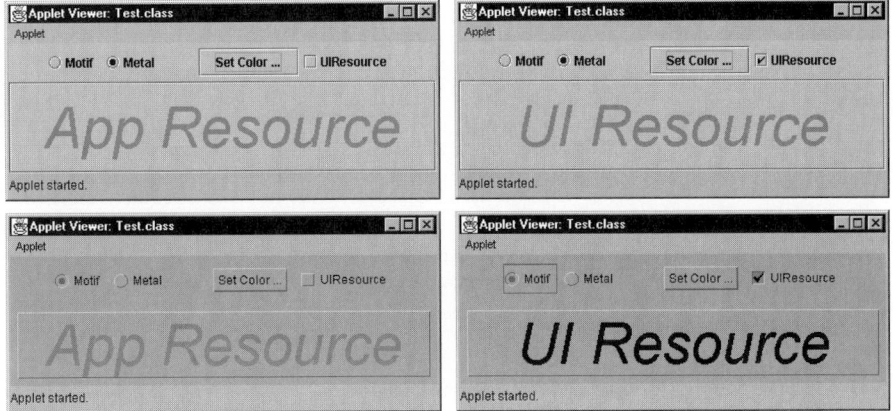

Figure 7-7 UIResources

The applet adds action listeners to the Set Color ... button and the UIResource check box. Both listeners invoke the applet's updateButtonColor method, which sets the button's color depending upon the color selected from a color chooser. The color is specified as a Color or a UI resource depending upon whether the check box is selected.

```java
public class Test extends JApplet {
    private JButton button = new JButton("App Resource");
    ...
    class ControlPanel extends JPanel {
        boolean resource = false;
        JButton colorSetButton = new JButton("Set Color ...");
        JCheckBox checkBox = new JCheckBox("UIResource");
        ...
        public ControlPanel() {
            ...
            colorSetButton.addActionListener(new ActionListener(){
                public void actionPerformed(ActionEvent e) {
                    updateButtonColor();
                }
            });
            checkBox.addActionListener(new ActionListener() {
                public void actionPerformed(ActionEvent e) {
                    resource = checkBox.isSelected();
                    updateButtonColor();
                }
            });
        }
        private void updateButtonColor() {
```

```
          Color c = JColorChooser.showDialog(
                getContentPane(), // parent component
                "Choose a Color", // title
                getBackground()); // initial color

          if(resource) {
             button.setText("UI Resource");
             button.setForeground(new ColorUIResource(c));
          }
          else {
             button.setText("App Resource");
             button.setForeground(c);
          }
       }
       ...
    }
 }
```

The applet shown in Figure 7-7 is listed in its entirety in Example 7-4.

Example 7-4   UI Resources

```
import javax.swing.*;
import java.awt.*;
import java.awt.event.*;
import java.util.*;

import javax.swing.plaf.motif.MotifLookAndFeel;
import javax.swing.plaf.metal.MetalLookAndFeel;

import javax.swing.plaf.ColorUIResource;

public class Test extends JApplet {
   private JButton button = new JButton("App Resource");

   public void init() {
      Container contentPane = getContentPane();

      contentPane.add(new ControlPanel(), BorderLayout.NORTH);
      contentPane.add(button, BorderLayout.CENTER);
   }
   class ControlPanel extends JPanel {
      boolean resource = false;
      JButton colorSetButton = new JButton("Set Color ...");
      JCheckBox checkBox = new JCheckBox("UIResource");
      JRadioButton motifButton = new JRadioButton("Motif"),
              metalButton = new JRadioButton("Metal");

      public ControlPanel() {
         ActionListener listener = new RadioHandler();
         ButtonGroup group = new ButtonGroup();

         group.add(motifButton);
```

```
        group.add(metalButton);

        motifButton.addActionListener(listener);
        metalButton.addActionListener(listener);

        metalButton.setSelected(true);

        add(motifButton);
        add(metalButton);
        add(Box.createHorizontalStrut(25));
        add(colorSetButton);
        add(checkBox);

        Font buttonFont = button.getFont();
        button.setFont(new Font(buttonFont.getFamily(),
                    Font.ITALIC, 56));

        colorSetButton.addActionListener(new ActionListener(){
            public void actionPerformed(ActionEvent e) {
                updateButtonColor();
            }
        });
        checkBox.addActionListener(new ActionListener() {
            public void actionPerformed(ActionEvent e) {
                resource = checkBox.isSelected();
                updateButtonColor();
            }
        });
    }
    private void updateButtonColor() {
        Color c = JColorChooser.showDialog(
                getContentPane(), // parent component
                "Choose a Color", // title
                getBackground()); // initial color

        if(resource) {
            button.setText("UI Resource");
            button.setForeground(new ColorUIResource(c));
        }
        else {
            button.setText("App Resource");
            button.setForeground(c);
        }
    }
    class RadioHandler implements ActionListener {
        public void actionPerformed(ActionEvent e) {
            JRadioButton src = (JRadioButton)e.getSource();

            try {
                if(src == motifButton)
                    UIManager.setLookAndFeel(
                        "javax.swing.plaf." +
                        "motif.MotifLookAndFeel");
```

```
            else if(src == metalButton)
                UIManager.setLookAndFeel(
                    "javax.swing.plaf.metal." +
                    "MetalLookAndFeel");
        }
        catch(Exception ex) {
            ex.printStackTrace();
        }
        SwingUtilities.updateComponentTreeUI(
                                getContentPane());
    }
}
}
}
```

The Java Look & Feel

The Java Look & Feel, which was code-named Metal, is the default cross-platform look and feel for Swing applets and applications. The Java Look & Feel offers two features that are not found in the other Swing standard look and feels: client properties and themes.

For some components, client properties can be set that affect the look and feel of the component under the Java Look & Feel. Themes allow the Java Look & Feel's appearance to be customized by defining colors and fonts used throughout the look and feel.

Client Properties

Client properties are key/value pairs that can be added to a lightweight Swing component at runtime; see "Client Properties" on page 186 for more information concerning client properties.

The Java Look & Feel is sensitive to specific client properties that can be set for a handful of components. The properties and their data types and default values are listed in Table 7-1.

Table 7-1 Java Look & Feel Client Properties

Client Property	Data Type	Default Values
JInternalFrame.isPalette	boolean	FALSE
JScrollBar.isFreeStanding	boolean	TRUE
JSlider.isFilled	boolean	FALSE
JToolBar.isRollover	boolean	FALSE
JTree.lineStyle	String	"Horizontal"

JInternalFrame.isPalette — Determines the type of border used for the internal frame. The palette border, which is used when JInternalFrame.isPalette is true, is thinner than the regular internal frame border.[5]

JScrollBar.isFreeStanding — If a scrollbar is freestanding, it has an etched border on all sides. If a scrollbar is not freestanding, its border is painted only for the top and left sides of the scrollbar. The effect of the freestanding property can be seen in Figure 7-8.

JSlider.isFilled — Filled horizontal sliders fill their track with a color to the left of the slider's grip. Vertical slider tracks are filled underneath the grip.

JToolBar.isRollover — Affects how toolbar button borders are drawn. If the property is true, button borders are painted when the cursor enters a button and are erased when the cursor exits. The effect is similar to the toolbar buttons found in Netscape Navigator.

JTree.lineStyle — Affects how connecting lines are drawn between nodes in a tree.

The applet shown in Figure 7-8 allows client properties to be set for the applet's components.

The top picture in Figure 7-8 shows the components with the boolean client properties all set to false, and the tree's lineStyle property set to "None". The bottom picture in Figure 7-8 shows the boolean client properties set to true, with the tree's lineStyle property set to "Angled".

---

5. Note: Due to a bug, the palette property has no effect with Swing 1.1 FCS.

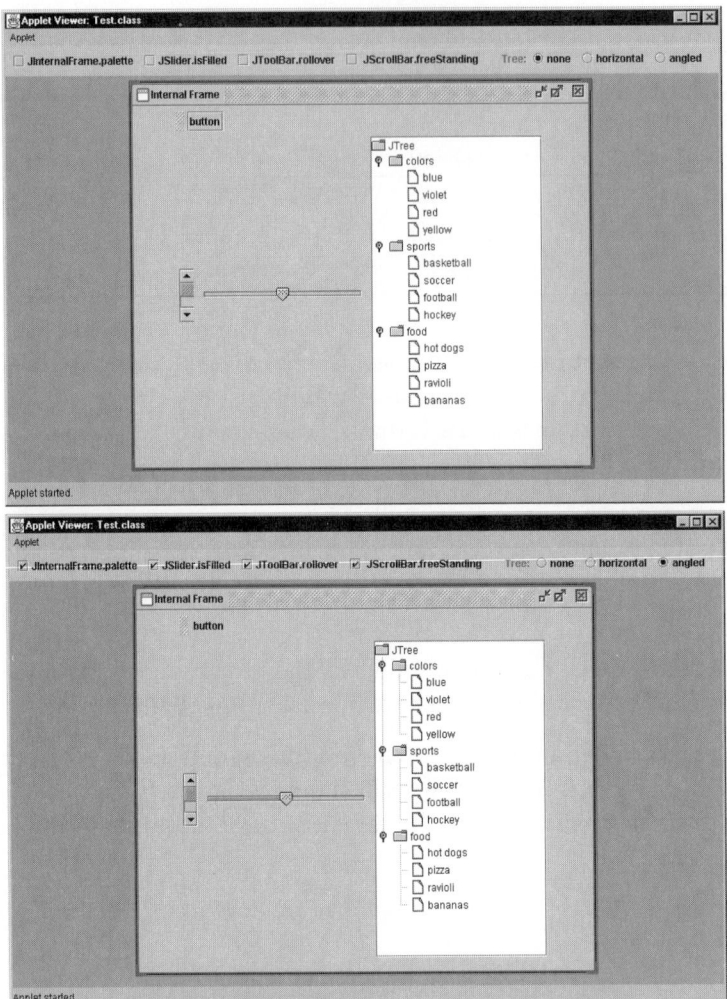

Figure 7-8 Metal Client Properties

The applet adds action listeners to the radio buttons and check boxes contained in the applet. The listeners set client properties according to the check box or radio button that is selected. Notice that `repaint()` (or `revalidate()`) must be invoked after a client property is specified, because components do not automatically update their appearance after a client property has been set.

```
...
class RadioButtonListener implements ActionListener {
    public void actionPerformed(ActionEvent e) {
        JRadioButton rb = (JRadioButton)e.getSource();

        if(rb == none) {
            tree.putClientProperty(
                "JTree.lineStyle", "None");
        }
        if(rb == horizontal) {
            tree.putClientProperty(
                "JTree.lineStyle", "Horizontal");
        }
        if(rb == angled) {
            tree.putClientProperty(
                "JTree.lineStyle", "Angled");
        }
        tree.repaint();
    }
}
class CheckBoxListener implements ActionListener {
    public void actionPerformed(ActionEvent e) {
        JCheckBox cb = (JCheckBox)e.getSource();

        if(cb == palette) {
            palette.putClientProperty(
                "JInternalFrame.isPalette",
                new Boolean(cb.isSelected()));

            jif.revalidate();
        }
        else if(cb == filled) {
            slider.putClientProperty(
                "JSlider.isFilled",
                new Boolean(cb.isSelected()));

            slider.repaint();
        }
        else if(cb == rollover) {
            toolbar.putClientProperty(
                "JToolBar.isRollover",
                new Boolean(cb.isSelected()));

            toolbar.repaint();
        }
        else if(cb == freeStanding) {
            scrollbar.putClientProperty(
                "JScrollBar.isFreeStanding",
                new Boolean(cb.isSelected()));

            scrollbar.repaint();
        }
    }
}
```

The applet shown in Figure 7-8 is listed in its entirety in Example 7-5.

Example 7-5   Metal Client Properties

```java
import javax.swing.*;
import java.awt.*;
import java.awt.event.*;
import java.util.*;

public class Test extends JApplet {
    JDesktopPane desktopPane = new JDesktopPane();

    JInternalFrame jif = new JInternalFrame(
                "Internal Frame ", // title
                true,  // resizable
                true,  // closable
                true,  // maximizable
                true); // iconifiable

    JScrollBar scrollbar = new JScrollBar();
    JSlider slider = new JSlider();
    JToolBar toolbar = new JToolBar();
    JTree tree = new JTree();

    public void init() {
        Container contentPane = getContentPane();

        jif.setPreferredSize(new Dimension(550, 450));
        jif.getContentPane().setLayout(new FlowLayout());
        jif.getContentPane().add(new ComponentPanel());

        desktopPane.setLayout(new FlowLayout());
        desktopPane.add(jif);

        contentPane.add(new ControlPanel(), BorderLayout.NORTH);
        contentPane.add(desktopPane, BorderLayout.CENTER);
    }
    class ComponentPanel extends JPanel {
        public ComponentPanel() {
            JPanel panel = new JPanel();

            setLayout(new BorderLayout());
            add(toolbar, BorderLayout.NORTH);
            add(panel, BorderLayout.CENTER);

            panel.add(scrollbar);
            panel.add(slider);
            panel.add(new JScrollPane(tree));

            tree.setPreferredSize(new Dimension(200,100));

            toolbar.add(new JButton("button"));
```

```
        }
}
class ControlPanel extends JPanel {
    JCheckBox rollover = new JCheckBox(
                        "JToolBar.rollover");
    JCheckBox palette = new JCheckBox(
                        "JInternalFrame.palette");
    JCheckBox filled = new JCheckBox(
                        "JSlider.isFilled");
    JCheckBox freeStanding = new JCheckBox(
                        " JScrollBar.freeStanding");

    JRadioButton none = new JRadioButton("none");
    JRadioButton horizontal = new JRadioButton("horizontal");
    JRadioButton angled = new JRadioButton("angled");

    public ControlPanel() {
        ActionListener checkBoxListener =
                            new CheckBoxListener();
        ActionListener radioButtonListener =
                            new RadioButtonListener();

        palette.addActionListener(checkBoxListener);
        filled.addActionListener(checkBoxListener);
        rollover.addActionListener(checkBoxListener);
        freeStanding.addActionListener(checkBoxListener);

        none.addActionListener(radioButtonListener);
        horizontal.addActionListener(radioButtonListener);
        angled.addActionListener(radioButtonListener);

        ButtonGroup group = new ButtonGroup();
        group.add(none);
        group.add(horizontal);
        group.add(filled);

        none.setSelected(true);
        freeStanding.setSelected(true);

        add(palette);
        add(filled);
        add(rollover);
        add(freeStanding);
        add(Box.createHorizontalStrut(10));
        add(new JLabel("Tree: "));
        add(none);
        add(horizontal);
        add(angled);
    }
    class RadioButtonListener implements ActionListener {
        public void actionPerformed(ActionEvent e) {
            JRadioButton rb = (JRadioButton)e.getSource();
```

```
            if(rb == none) {
                tree.putClientProperty(
                        "JTree.lineStyle", "None");
            }
            if(rb == horizontal) {
                tree.putClientProperty(
                        "JTree.lineStyle", "Horizontal");
            }
            if(rb == angled) {
                tree.putClientProperty(
                        "JTree.lineStyle", "Angled");
            }
            tree.repaint();
        }
    }
    class CheckBoxListener implements ActionListener {
        public void actionPerformed(ActionEvent e) {
            JCheckBox cb = (JCheckBox)e.getSource();

            if(cb == palette) {
                palette.putClientProperty(
                        "JInternalFrame.isPalette",
                        new Boolean(cb.isSelected()));

                jif.revalidate();
            }
            else if(cb == filled) {
                slider.putClientProperty(
                        "JSlider.isFilled",
                        new Boolean(cb.isSelected()));

                slider.repaint();
            }
            else if(cb == rollover) {
                toolbar.putClientProperty(
                        "JToolBar.isRollover",
                        new Boolean(cb.isSelected()));

                toolbar.repaint();
            }
            else if(cb == freeStanding) {
                scrollbar.putClientProperty(
                        "JScrollBar.isFreeStanding",
                        new Boolean(cb.isSelected()));

                scrollbar.repaint();
            }
        }
    }
  }
}
```

Themes

The Java Look & Feel defines themes, which are color and font definitions that are used throughout the Java Look & Feel. Themes are implemented by extending the abstract `javax.swing.plaf.metal.MetalTheme` class, which defines methods that return colors, such as `getControlColor()`, and methods that return fonts, such as `getControlTextFont()`.

The applet shown in Figure 7-9 implements a custom theme that simply sets the font for text used to draw components.

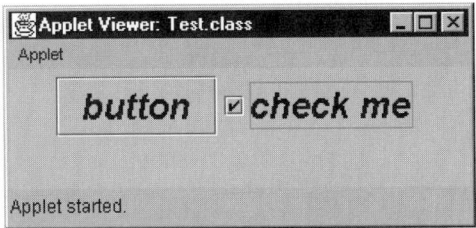

Figure 7-9 A Simple Custom Theme

The applet shown in Figure 7-9 is listed in Figure 7-6.

Example 7-6 A Simple Custom Theme

```
import java.awt.*;
import javax.swing.*;
import javax.swing.plaf.*;
import javax.swing.plaf.metal.*;
import javax.swing.plaf.*;

public class Test extends JApplet {
    public void init() {
        Container contentPane = getContentPane();

        contentPane.setLayout(new FlowLayout());

        setMetalTheme(new ExperimentalTheme());

        contentPane.add(new JButton("button"));
        contentPane.add(new JCheckBox("check me"));
    }
    private void setMetalTheme(MetalTheme theme) {
        MetalLookAndFeel.setCurrentTheme(new ExperimentalTheme());
```

```
            // Metal Look and Feel must be (re)loaded for the
            // new theme to take effect ...

            try {
                UIManager.setLookAndFeel(
                    "javax.swing.plaf.metal.MetalLookAndFeel");
            }
            catch(IllegalAccessException e1) {}
            catch(UnsupportedLookAndFeelException e2) {}
            catch(InstantiationException e3) {}
            catch(ClassNotFoundException e4) {}
        }
    }
    class ExperimentalTheme extends DefaultMetalTheme {
        public FontUIResource getControlTextFont() {
            return new FontUIResource("SanSerif",
                            Font.BOLD + Font.ITALIC, 24);
        }
    }
```

The `ExperimentalTheme` class extends the `DefaultMetalTheme` class, which is an extension of `MetalTheme` that defines the default metal theme. `ExperimentalTheme` overrides the `getControlTextFont` method to specify the font used to draw controls.

Notice that the theme is set with the `MetalLookAndFeel.setCurrentTheme` method, which must be followed by installation of the Java Look & Feel for the theme to take effect.

Auxiliary UIs

Instead of replacing an entire look and feel, sometimes it is desirable to add capabilities to the current look and feel. For example, adding sounds to components when they are activated, such as buttons that plop when activated or sliders that whir when dragged, is a tedious task if it requires an entirely new look and feel to be implemented and installed.

Swing provides a multiplexing look and feel that is actually a combination of look and feels that allows auxiliary capabilities to be added to the current look and feel. A component's UI delegate obtained through a call to `UIManager.getUI()` is actually a multiplexing UI delegate, such as `MultiButtonUI` or `MultiLabelUI`, from the `javax.swing.multi` package. Here's how multiplexing UI delegates work.

The multiplexing UI delegate is actually a combination of the UI delegate for the current look and feel and UI delegates for auxiliary look and feels that have been defined. When the multiplexing UI delegate is asked for something graphical in nature, for example, its maximum size, it returns the value from the current look and feel's UI delegate. When the multiplexing UI delegate is asked to perform something nongraphical, such as being installed or uninstalled for a component, the operation is performed for the current look and feel's UI delegate in addition to the auxiliary look and feel's UI delegates.

The applet shown in Figure 7-10 illustrates an auxiliary look and feel that simply prints a statement when the cursor enters a button.

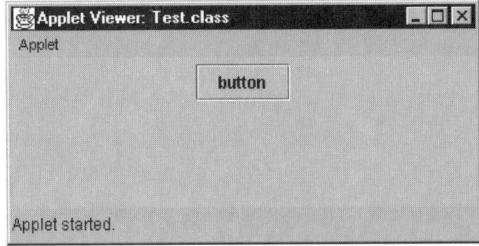

Figure 7-10 An Auxiliary UI for Buttons

The applet shown in Figure 7-10 is listed in Example 7-7.

Example 7-7 Installing an Auxiliary Look and Feel

```java
import javax.swing.*;
import java.awt.*;

public class Test extends JApplet {
    public void init() {
        UIManager.addAuxiliaryLookAndFeel(
                    new ExampleAuxiliaryLookAndFeel());

        Container contentPane = getContentPane();
        JButton button = new JButton("button");

        contentPane.setLayout(new FlowLayout());
        contentPane.add(button);
    }
}
```

The applet installs an instance of `ExampleAuxiliaryLookAndFeel` as an auxiliary look and feel with the `UIManager.addAuxiliaryLookAndFeel` method. The `ExampleAuxiliaryLookAndFeel` class is listed in Example 7-8.

Example 7-8 Example Auxiliary Look and Feel

```
import java.awt.*;
import javax.swing.*;

public class ExampleAuxiliaryLookAndFeel extends LookAndFeel {
    public String getDescription(){
        return "example auxiliary look and feel";
    }
    public String getID() {
        return "example";
    }
    public String getName() {
        return "example auxiliary";
    }
    public boolean isNativeLookAndFeel() {
        return false;
    }
    public boolean isSupportedLookAndFeel() {
        return true;
    }
    public UIDefaults getDefaults() {
        UIDefaults table = new UIDefaults();

        Object[] uiDefaults = {
            "ButtonUI", "AuxiliaryButtonUI"
        };

        table.putDefaults(uiDefaults);
        return table;
    }
}
```

The `ExampleAuxiliaryLookAndFeel` class extends `LookAndFeel` and implements the abstract classes defined by its superclass. See "The LookAndFeel Class" on page 323 or more information concerning the `LookAndFeel` class. The `ExampleAuxiliaryLookAndFeel` is supported on all platforms and is native to none.

The `AuxiliaryButtonUI` class is specified by the `ExampleAuxiliaryLookAndFeel` class as the UI delegate to be used with buttons. See "Look-and-Feel Defaults" on page 328 for more information on specifying defaults for look and feels.

The `AuxiliaryButtonUI` class implements the `createUI` method to return a shared instance of `AuxiliaryButtonUI`; the same `AuxiliaryButtonUI` instance is used for all buttons.

The `installUI` and `uninstallUI` methods are implemented to add and remove, respectively, a mouse listener to the button. The `update` method is overridden with an empty implementation, because the superclass' implementation of update clears the background and the auxiliary button UI should not affect the visual appearance of its component.

Example 7-9 An Auxiliary UI

```
import java.awt.*;
import java.awt.event.*;
import javax.accessibility.*;
import javax.swing.*;
import javax.swing.plaf.*;

public class AuxiliaryButtonUI extends ComponentUI {
    private static ComponentUI cui = new AuxiliaryButtonUI();
    private static AuxiliaryButtonMouseListener ml =
                   new AuxiliaryButtonMouseListener();

    // must be implemented
    public static ComponentUI createUI(JComponent c) {
        return cui;
    }
    public void installUI(JComponent c) {
        c.addMouseListener(ml);
    }
    public void uninstallUI(JComponent c) {
        c.removeMouseListener(ml);
    }
    public void update(Graphics g, JComponent c) {
        // don't want ComponentUI default behavior, which is
        // to clear the background
    }
}
class AuxiliaryButtonMouseListener extends MouseAdapter {
    public void mouseEntered(MouseEvent e) {
        JComponent c = (JComponent)e.getSource();
        AccessibleContext ac = c.getAccessibleContext();
        String role = ac.getAccessibleRole().toString();
        String name = ac.getAccessibleName();

        System.out.println("mouse entered component of type " +
                          role + " named " + name);
    }
}
```

The mouse listener handles mouse enter events by obtaining accessibility information from the button and printing it to the console.

Parting Shots

Pluggable look and feel, which allows Swing applications to look and feel like native applications, is perhaps Swing's most distinctive feature. Other than setting the look and feel for an applet or application, most developers will not access look and feel functionality directly. Nonetheless, it is important to have a basic understanding of the pluggable look and feel architecture; for example, as "Look and Feels" on page 320 illustrates, pluggable look and feel can be used for more than setting look and feel for a set of components.

Swing Components

CHAPTER

8

Labels and Buttons

Swing labels and buttons—represented by the JLabel and JButton classes, respectively—are simple components that are capable of displaying text or an icon.

Labels by default do not have a border and display a string, an icon, or both. Besides being useful for rather mundane purposes such as adorning text fields, Swing labels also fulfill the role of image canvas (a component that displays an image). Because AWT images are not components, they cannot be added to a container. As a result, many different variations of an image canvas class have been implemented by developers using the AWT; however, with Swing the JLabel class can be used as an image canvas.[1]

Buttons are perhaps the most ubiquitous of user interface components. Buttons typically have a border of some kind and can be activated either by a mouse click or keyboard accelerator. Swing buttons are considerably more complex than Swing labels, not only because they can be activated to perform some function, but also because a number of other Swing components are extensions of the AbstractButton class, which is the base class for Swing buttons.

---

1. See "Custom Painting in Swing Components" on page 138 for more information concerning image canvases.

JLabel and JButton

JLabel and JButton are not related through inheritance, but they have a number of methods—listed in Table 8-1—with the exact same signatures. As a result, even though a button can be manipulated in much the same fashion as a label, buttons and labels do not share a common base class and therefore cannot be manipulated in *exactly* the same fashion. For example, the gap between the text and icon displayed by a label is settable, but that is not the case for buttons. Conversely, although both buttons and labels can have a disabled icon, only buttons can have a "rollover" icon that is displayed when the cursor enters the button.

Table 8-1   JLabel and JButton Overlapping Methods

Method Signature
protected int checkHorizontalKey(int, String)
protected int checkVerticalKey(int, String)
public AccessibleContext getAccessibleContext()
public Icon getDisabledIcon()
public int getHorizontalAlignment()
public int getHorizontalTextPosition()
public Icon getIcon()
public String getText()
public LabelUI getUI()
public String getUIClassID()
public int getVerticalAlignment()
public int getVerticalTextPosition()
public void setDisabledIcon(Icon)
public void setFont(Font)
public void setHorizontalAlignment(int)
public void setHorizontalTextPosition(int)
public void setIcon(Icon)
public void setText(String)
public void setVerticalAlignment(int)
public void setVerticalTextPosition(int)
public void updateUI()

The text and/or icon displayed by a button or label are collectively referred to as the component's content. Both JLabel and JButton provide methods to control the alignment of their content, as illustrated in Figure 8-1.

Figure 8-1 Content Alignment for Buttons and Labels

Additionally, the position of the text relative to the icon can be specified for both buttons and labels, as illustrated in Figure 8-2.

There are 81 possible combinations of alignment and text position for Swing buttons and labels.

Figure 8-2 Text Position for Buttons and Labels

Swing Labels and Buttons Are Not Related Through Inheritance

Although Swing buttons and labels have a great deal of common functionality as far as displaying their text and icon, the JLabel and AbstractButton classes do not extend a base class that encapsulates their common functionality. As a result, although labels and buttons can be manipulated in a similar fashion, they cannot be manipulated in *exactly* the same manner.

JLabel

Swing labels can be used for many purposes. For example, in addition to serving as a component that can display an icon, labels are also typically used as cell renderers for Swing tables.

The left-hand applet shown in Figure 8-3 contains two labels—one that has an icon and text and another that is contained inside a Swing scroll pane. The applet on the right contains a Swing table that uses custom cell renderers. The cell renderers are extensions of the JLabel class.

Figure 8-3 Swing Labels Are Versatile

The left-hand applet shown in Figure 8-3 is listed in Example 8-1.

Example 8-1 JLabels in Action

```
import java.awt.*;
import java.awt.event.*;
import javax.swing.*;

public class Test extends JApplet {
    public Test() {
        Container contentPane = getContentPane();
        JLabel imageOnly = new JLabel(new ImageIcon("dogs.gif"));
        JLabel textAndImage = new JLabel("Vote!",
                    new ImageIcon("ballot_box.gif"),
                    JLabel.RIGHT);

        JScrollPane scrollPane = new JScrollPane(imageOnly);
        scrollPane.setPreferredSize(new Dimension(270,200));

        contentPane.setLayout(
            new FlowLayout(FlowLayout.CENTER, 25, 25));

        contentPane.add(textAndImage);
        contentPane.add(scrollPane);
    }
}
```

The applet creates two instances of JLabel and specifies one as the viewport for an instance of JScrollPane (by passing a reference to the label to the scroll pane's constructor).

The layout manager for the applet's content pane is set to an instance of
FlowLayout, and the textAndImage label and the scroll pane are added to the
applet's content pane.

Content Alignment

The applet shown in Figure 8-4 allows the horizontal and vertical alignment
properties of the label it displays to be set.

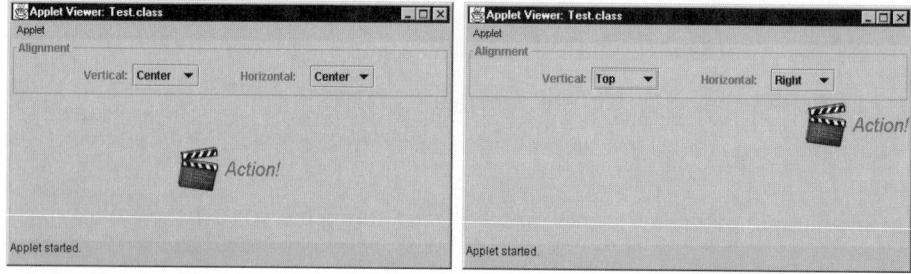

Figure 8-4 Label Alignment

The applet creates a label, a panel that will contain the two combo boxes, and the
two combo boxes themselves.[2] The combo boxes are added to the control panel,
and the label and control panel are added to the applet's content pane.

Because the icon displayed in the label is instantiated after the label, the label is
constructed with text only; subsequently, the label's icon and font are set.

The applet starts off with the label's contents centered both vertically and
horizontally. Because default values for horizontal and vertical alignment are
SwingConstants.LEFT and SwingConstants.CENTER, respectively, the
applet sets the horizontal alignment for the label to SwingConstants.CENTER.

```
public class Test extends JApplet implements SwingConstants {
    JLabel label = new JLabel("Action!");
    JPanel controlPanel = new JPanel();
    JComboBox alignmentHorizontal = new JComboBox();
    JComboBox alignmentVertical = new JComboBox();
```

---

2.   Combo boxes are discussed in "Combo Boxes" on page 1073.

```
public void init() {
    Container contentPane = getContentPane();
    ImageIcon icon = new ImageIcon("slate.gif");

    label.setIcon(icon);
    label.setHorizontalAlignment(CENTER);
    label.setFont(new Font("Times-Roman", Font.ITALIC, 20));

    setupComboBoxes();
    setupControlPanel();

    contentPane.setLayout(new BorderLayout());
    contentPane.add(controlPanel, "North");
    contentPane.add(label, "Center");
    ...
```

Each of the combo boxes has a listener that sets the appropriate alignment for the label. The selected string in each of the combo boxes is transformed into a corresponding SwingConstants value by the applet's getSwingConstantByName method. The label's alignment is then set by passing the constant to either JLabel.setVerticalAlignment() or JLabel.setHorizontalAlignment().

```
    ...
    alignmentVertical.addItemListener(new ItemListener() {
        public void itemStateChanged(ItemEvent event) {
            JComboBox b = (JComboBox)event.getSource();
            String   s = (String)b.getSelectedItem();
            int      c = getSwingConstantByName(s);

            label.setVerticalAlignment(c);
        }
    });
    alignmentHorizontal.addItemListener(new ItemListener() {
        public void itemStateChanged(ItemEvent event) {
            JComboBox b = (JComboBox)event.getSource();
            String   s = (String)b.getSelectedItem();
            int      c = getSwingConstantByName(s);

            label.setHorizontalAlignment(c);
        }
    });
} // end of init method
...
}
```

Notice that the label does not need to be repainted after its alignment property is set because the alignment property, like nearly all of JLabel's properties, results in a repaint of the label.[3]

The applet shown in Figure 8-4 is listed in Example 8-2.

Example 8-2 Setting Alignment Properties for a Swing Label

```java
import java.net.URL;
import java.awt.*;
import java.awt.event.*;
import javax.swing.*;
import javax.swing.border.*;

public class Test extends JApplet implements SwingConstants {
    JLabel label = new JLabel("Action!");
    JPanel controlPanel = new JPanel();
    JComboBox alignmentHorizontal = new JComboBox();
    JComboBoxalignmentVertical = new JComboBox();

    public void init() {
        Container contentPane = getContentPane();
        ImageIcon icon = new ImageIcon("slate.gif");

        label.setIcon(icon);
        label.setHorizontalAlignment(CENTER);
        label.setFont(new Font("Times-Roman", Font.ITALIC, 20));

        label.setMaximumSize(new Dimension(0, 150));

        setupComboBoxes();
        setupControlPanel();

        contentPane.setLayout(new BorderLayout());
        contentPane.add(controlPanel, "North");
        contentPane.add(label, "Center");

        alignmentVertical.addItemListener(new ItemListener() {
            public void itemStateChanged(ItemEvent event) {
                JComboBox b = (JComboBox)event.getSource();
                String   s = (String)b.getSelectedItem();
                int      c = getSwingConstantByName(s);

                label.setVerticalAlignment(c);
            }
        });
        alignmentHorizontal.addItemListener(new ItemListener() {
```

3. All modifications to properties that affect a component's visual representation should result in a repaint.

```
        public void itemStateChanged(ItemEvent event) {
            JComboBox b = (JComboBox)event.getSource();
            String   s = (String)b.getSelectedItem();
            int      c = getSwingConstantByName(s);

            label.setHorizontalAlignment(c);
        }
    });
}
void setupComboBoxes() {
    alignmentVertical.addItem("Top");
    alignmentVertical.addItem("Center");
    alignmentVertical.addItem("Bottom");

    alignmentHorizontal.addItem("Left");
    alignmentHorizontal.addItem("Center");
    alignmentHorizontal.addItem("Right");

    alignmentVertical.setSelectedItem(
        getSwingConstantName(
            label.getVerticalAlignment()));

    alignmentHorizontal.setSelectedItem(
        getSwingConstantName(
            label.getHorizontalAlignment()));
}
void setupControlPanel() {
    controlPanel.setBorder(
        BorderFactory.createTitledBorder("Alignment"));

    controlPanel.add(new JLabel("Vertical:"));
    controlPanel.add(alignmentVertical);
    controlPanel.add(Box.createHorizontalStrut(5));

    controlPanel.add(Box.createHorizontalStrut(25));

    controlPanel.add(new JLabel("Horizontal:"));
    controlPanel.add(Box.createHorizontalStrut(5));

    controlPanel.add(alignmentHorizontal);
}
int getSwingConstantByName(String s) {
    if(s.equalsIgnoreCase("left"))        return LEFT;
    else if(s.equalsIgnoreCase("center")) return CENTER;
    else if(s.equalsIgnoreCase("right"))  return RIGHT;
    else if(s.equalsIgnoreCase("top"))    return TOP;
    else if(s.equalsIgnoreCase("bottom")) return BOTTOM;

    return -1;
}
String getSwingConstantName(int c) {
    if(c == LEFT) return "Left";
```

```
        else if(c == CENTER)return "Center";
        else if(c == RIGHT) return "Right";
        else if(c == TOP) return "Top";
        else if(c == BOTTOM) return "Bottom";

        return "undefined";
    }
}
```

Text Position

The applet shown in Figure 8-5 allows the position of a label's text to be set relative to the position of the icon.

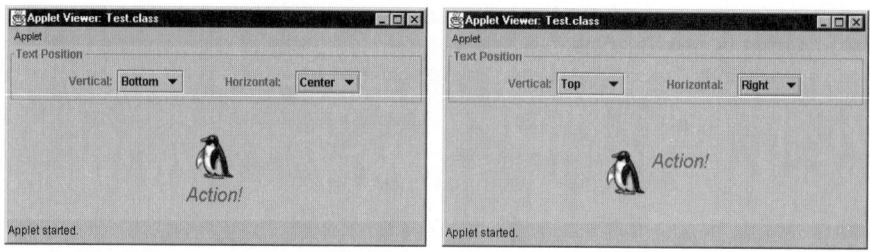

Figure 8-5 Setting Text Position Relative to Image Position

Because the applet shown in Figure 8-5 is nearly identical to the one shown in Figure 8-4 on page 366, except that the label's horizontal and vertical text position properties are set instead of alignment, the applet, listed in Example 8-3, is not discussed.

Example 8-3 Setting Text Position for Labels

```
import java.net.URL;
import java.awt.*;
import java.awt.event.*;
import javax.swing.*;
import javax.swing.border.*;

public class Test extends JApplet implements SwingConstants {
    JLabel label = new JLabel("Action!");
    JPanel controlPanel = new JPanel();
    JComboBox alignmentHorizontal = new JComboBox();
    JComboBox alignmentVertical = new JComboBox();
```

```
public void init() {
    Container contentPane = getContentPane();
    ImageIcon icon = new ImageIcon("penguin.gif");

    label.setIcon(icon);
    label.setHorizontalTextPosition(CENTER);
    label.setFont(new Font("Times-Roman", Font.ITALIC, 20));

    setupComboBoxes();
    setupControlPanel();

    label.setHorizontalAlignment(JLabel.CENTER);
    label.setVerticalAlignment(JLabel.CENTER);

    contentPane.setLayout(new BorderLayout());
    contentPane.add(controlPanel, "North");
    contentPane.add(label, "Center");

    alignmentVertical.addItemListener(new ItemListener() {
        public void itemStateChanged(ItemEvent event) {
            JComboBox b = (JComboBox)event.getSource();
            String    s = (String)b.getSelectedItem();
            int       c = getSwingConstantByName(s);

            label.setVerticalTextPosition(c);
        }
    });
    alignmentHorizontal.addItemListener(new ItemListener() {
        public void itemStateChanged(ItemEvent event) {
            JComboBox b = (JComboBox)event.getSource();
            String    s = (String)b.getSelectedItem();
            int       c = getSwingConstantByName(s);

            label.setHorizontalTextPosition(c);
        }
    });
}
void setupComboBoxes() {
    alignmentVertical.addItem("Top");
    alignmentVertical.addItem("Center");
    alignmentVertical.addItem("Bottom");

    alignmentHorizontal.addItem("Left");
    alignmentHorizontal.addItem("Center");
    alignmentHorizontal.addItem("Right");

    alignmentVertical.setSelectedItem(
        getSwingConstantName(
            label.getVerticalTextPosition()));

    alignmentHorizontal.setSelectedItem(
        getSwingConstantName(
```

```
                        label.getHorizontalTextPosition()));
        }
        void setupControlPanel() {
            controlPanel.setBorder(
                BorderFactory.createTitledBorder("Text Position"));

            controlPanel.add(new JLabel( "Vertical:"));
            controlPanel.add(alignmentVertical);
            controlPanel.add(Box.createHorizontalStrut(5));

            controlPanel.add(Box.createHorizontalStrut(25));

            controlPanel.add(new JLabel("Horizontal:"));
            controlPanel.add(Box.createHorizontalStrut(5));

            controlPanel.add(alignmentHorizontal);
        }
        int getSwingConstantByName(String s) {
            if(s.equalsIgnoreCase("left"))           return LEFT;
            else if(s.equalsIgnoreCase("center")) return CENTER;
            else if(s.equalsIgnoreCase("right"))  return RIGHT;
            else if(s.equalsIgnoreCase("top"))       return TOP;
            else if(s.equalsIgnoreCase("bottom")) return BOTTOM;

            return -1;
        }
        String getSwingConstantName(int c) {
            if(c == LEFT) return "Left";
            else if(c == CENTER)return "Center";
            else if(c == RIGHT) return "Right";
            else if(c == TOP) return "Top";
            else if(c == BOTTOM) return "Bottom";

            return "undefined";
        }
    }
```

Icon/Text Gap

The applet shown in Figure 8-6 allows the icon/text gap to be set for the label displayed in the applet.

The applet sets the label's icon/text gap in response to selections in the combo box. The item listener for the combo box extracts the selected string from the combo box and uses `Integer.parseInt()` to turn the string into an `integer` value. The `integer` value is then passed to the label's `setIconTextGap` method.

Figure 8-6 Icon/Text Gap for Labels

The applet shown in Figure 8-6 is listed in Example 8-4.

Example 8-4 Setting a Label's Icon/Text Gap

```java
import java.net.URL;
import java.awt.*;
import java.awt.event.*;
import javax.swing.*;
import javax.swing.border.*;

public class Test extends JApplet implements SwingConstants {
    public void init() {
        Container contentPane = getContentPane();
        JComboBox iconTextGap = new JComboBox();
        JPanel controlPanel = new JPanel();
        ImageIcon icon = new ImageIcon("ladybug.gif");

        final JLabel label = new JLabel("Lady Bug", icon, CENTER);

        label.setFont(new Font("Times-Roman", Font.ITALIC, 20));

        iconTextGap.addItem("4");
        iconTextGap.addItem("10");
        iconTextGap.addItem("15");
        iconTextGap.addItem("20");
        iconTextGap.addItem("25");

        controlPanel.add(new JLabel("Icon/Text Gap:"));
        controlPanel.add(iconTextGap);

        contentPane.setLayout(new BorderLayout());
        contentPane.add(controlPanel, "North");
        contentPane.add(label, "Center");
```

```
iconTextGap.addItemListener(new ItemListener() {
    public void itemStateChanged(ItemEvent event) {
        JComboBox b = (JComboBox)event.getSource();
        String   s = (String)b.getSelectedItem();
        int      gap = Integer.parseInt(s);

        label.setIconTextGap(gap);
    }
});
    }
}
```

Notice that the item listener for the combo box does not explicitly update the appearance of the label. Setting the icon/text property for labels results in the label being invalidated and subsequently validated and repainted.

Enabled State

Figure 8-7 shows an applet that allows the enabled state of a label to be set.

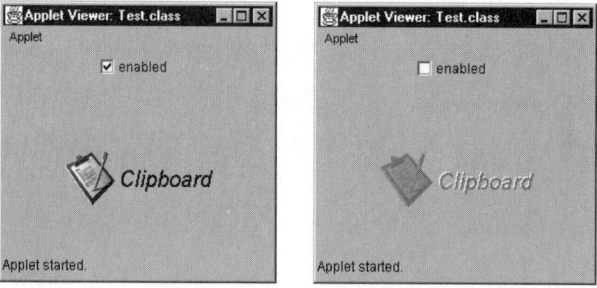

Figure 8-7 Enabling/Disabling a Label

The item listener for the `enabledDisabled` check box sets the enabled state of the label according to the selected state of the check box.

The applet shown in Figure 8-7 is listed in Example 8-5.

Example 8-5 Setting a Label's Enabled State

```
import java.net.URL;
import java.awt.*;
import java.awt.event.*;
import javax.swing.*;
import javax.swing.border.*;

public class Test extends JApplet implements SwingConstants {
    public void init() {
        final Container contentPane = getContentPane();
        JCheckBox enabledDisabled = new JCheckBox("enabled");
        JPanel controlPanel = new JPanel();
        ImageIcon icon = new ImageIcon("clipboard.gif");

        final JLabel label =
                        new JLabel("Clipboard", icon, CENTER);

        label.setFont(new Font("Times-Roman", Font.ITALIC, 20));

        controlPanel.add(enabledDisabled);
        enabledDisabled.setSelected(true);

        contentPane.setLayout(new BorderLayout());
        contentPane.add(controlPanel, "North");
        contentPane.add(label, "Center");

        enabledDisabled.addItemListener(new ItemListener() {
            public void itemStateChanged(ItemEvent event) {
                JCheckBox b = (JCheckBox)event.getSource();
                label.setEnabled(b.isSelected());
            }
        });
    }
}
```

By default, disabled icons, for Swing components that support them, are a version of the component's icon that is run through Swing's GrayFilter class. The effect of running an icon through an instance of GrayFilter can be seen in Figure 8-7.

Some Swing components support a custom disabled icon. If the applet listed in Example 8-5 is modified to set the label's disabled icon, the disabled icon is used instead of the default grayed-out icon, as shown in Figure 8-8.

 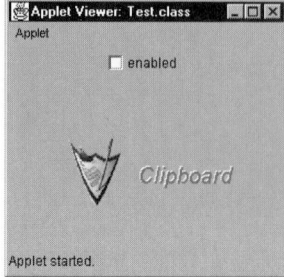

Figure 8-8 A Custom Disabled Image

The JLabel class is summarized in Component Summary 8-1.

Component Summary 8-1   JLabel

Model(s)	——
UI Delegate(s)	swing.plaf.basic.LabelUI
Renderer(s)	——
Editor(s)	——
Events Fired	PropertyChangeEvent
Replacement For	java.awt.Label

Class Diagrams

Figure 8-9 shows the class diagram for the JLabel class. JLabel extends the JComponent class, and is therefore a lightweight Swing component.

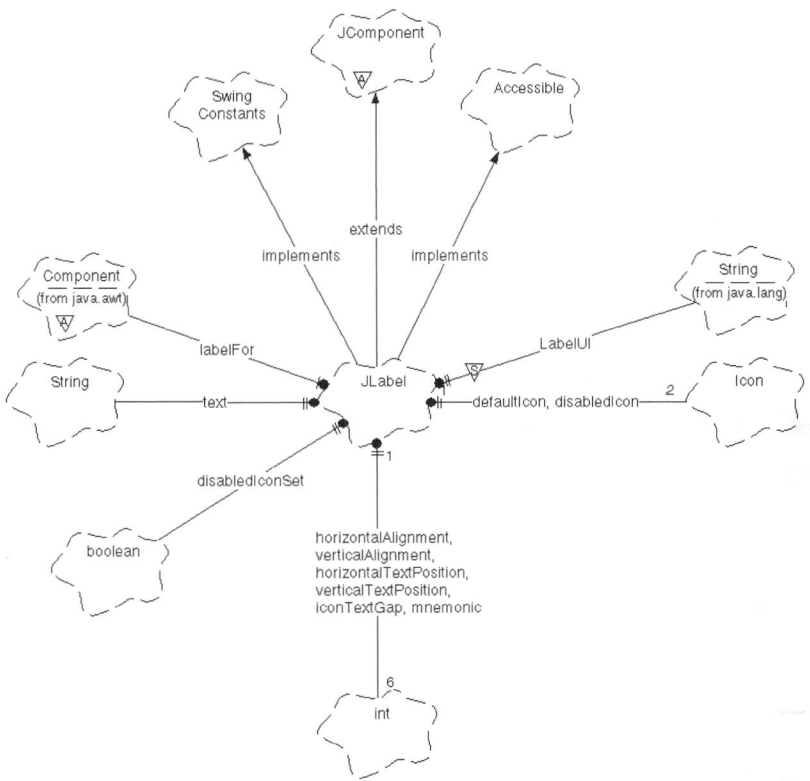

Figure 8-9 JLabel Class Diagram

Like all Swing components, JLabel implements the Accessible interface so that it can offer information to accessibility tools by way of an AccessibleContext object.

JLabel is also one of a number of Swing components that implements the SwingConstants interface. SwingConstants is implemented so that JLabel can specify constants defined in the SwingConstants interface without using a SwingConstants prefix. See "Swing Constants" on page 271 for more information on the SwingConstants class and its use.

JLabel maintains references to the text and icon it displays, in addition to an icon that is displayed when the label is disabled. JLabel also maintains six values for keeping track of a number of properties, which are discussed in "JLabel Properties".

Instances of JLabel also maintain a Component reference that is used for a label's labelFor property. See "JLabel Properties"" for more information concerning the labelFor property. Labels also keep track of the name of their UI delegate class and whether the disabled icon has been set.

Swing Tip ...

Swing Labels Are Versatile

Swing labels can be used for many purposes. In addition to simply displaying text, labels serve as an image canvas, and the JLabel class is often extended to provide custom cell renderers for Swing components such as JTable and JTree.

JLabel Properties

The properties maintained by instances of JLabel are listed in Table 8-2.

Table 8-2 JLabel Properties

Property Name	Data Type	Access[1]	Type[2]	Default[3]
disabledIcon	Icon	SG	B	gray filtered icon
displayedMnemonic	int	SG	B	—
horizontalAlignment	int	CSG	B	LEFT
horizontalTextPosition	int	SG	B	RIGHT
icon	Icon	CSG	B	null
iconTextGap	int	SG	B	4 pixels
labelFor	Component	SG	B	null
text	String	CSG	B	""
verticalAlignment	int	SG	B	CENTER
verticalTextPosition	int	SG	B	CENTER

1. C = settable at construction time / G = getter method / S = setter method
2. B = bound / Bool = boolean / C = constrained/ I = indexed / S = simple
3. L&F = look-and-feel dependent

disabledIcon — The icon displayed when a label is disabled. By default, disabled icons are a washed-out version of the label's icon, which is obtained by use of a `GrayFilter`. A different icon can be specified as the label's disabled icon.

displayedMnemonic — The mnemonic displayed when the `labelFor` property is set.

horizontalAlignment — The horizontal alignment for a label's content (meaning its text and icon). Possible values are `JLabel.LEFT`, `JLabel.RIGHT` and `JLabel.CENTER`.

horizontalTextPosition — Horizontal position of the text relative to the icon; valid values are the same as for horizontal alignment.

icon — The icon displayed by a label when the label is enabled.

iconTextGap — The gap, in pixels, between a label's text and its icon.

labelFor — A component that receives focus when the label's displayed mnemonic is typed.

text — The text displayed by a label.

verticalAlignment — The vertical alignment for a label's content. Possible values are `JLabel.TOP`, `JLabel.CENTER` and `JLabel.BOTTOM`.

verticalTextPosition — The vertical position of the text relative to the icon; valid values are the same as for vertical alignment.

All of the properties maintained by the `JLabel` class have both setter and getter methods and are bound properties, meaning that property change events are fired whenever the properties are modified. Only text, icon, and horizontal alignment properties can be specified at the time of construction.

The `displayedMnemonic` and `labelFor` properties work hand in hand. If `displayedMnemonic` is set, the label will underline the character representing the mnemonic. Subsequently, if the `labelFor` component has been set and the mnemonic is typed while any component that is in the same window as the label has focus, the `labelFor` component will receive focus. This feature comes in handy when a component such as a text field needs a keyboard mnemonic but is not capable of displaying it.

JLabel Events

JLabel is essentially a display-only component; the only events fired by the JLabel class are property change events that are fired when one of the properties listed in Table 8-2 is modified.

Although the JLabel *class* fires only property change events, Swing labels still fire a multitude of events, from ancestor to mouse events—behavior that is inherited from the JComponent class.

By default, instances of JLabel do not fire key events and as a result do not accept keyboard focus.

JLabel Class Summaries

The public and protected variables and methods for JLabel are listed in Class Summary 8-1.

Class Summary 8-1   JLabel

Extends: JComponent

Implements: SwingConstants, javax.accessibility.Accessible

Constructors

---

public JLabel()
public JLabel(Icon)
public JLabel(Icon, int horizontalAlignment)
public JLabel(String)
public JLabel(String, Icon, int horizontalAlignment)
public JLabel(String, int horizontalAlignment)

The `JLabel` class provides six constructors for instantiating labels of various configurations. The `integer` values passed to the constructors specify the horizontal alignment of the label's content.

Notice that the constructor that takes both a string and an icon must also be passed an `integer` value representing the horizontal alignment of the string and icon. It would be nice if `JLabel`—like `JButton`—provided a constructor that was passed only a string and an icon, where the horizontal alignment defaults to a particular value. As it stands now, if an instance of `JLabel` is constructed with a string and an icon, the horizontal alignment must be explicitly specified.

Figure 8-10 shows an applet that creates four `JLabel` instances.

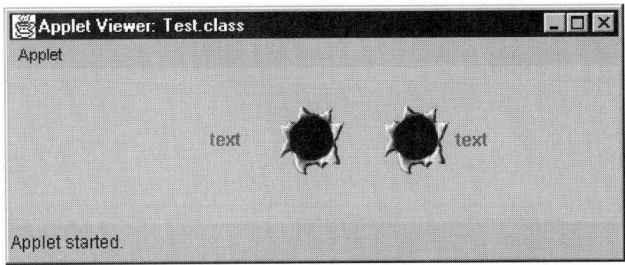

Figure 8-10 Instantiating Instances of `JLabel`

The applet creates the (invisible) label on the left with the no-argument constructor, which means that the label has no text or icon and therefore cannot be seen in the applet. The applet also creates a text-only label, an icon-only label, and a fourth label with both text and an icon.

The applet shown in Figure 8-10 is listed in Example 8-6.

Example 8-6 Instantiating Instances of JLabel

```
import java.awt.*;
import java.awt.event.*;
import javax.swing.*;

public class Test extends JApplet {
    Icon icon = new ImageIcon("icon.gif");

    JLabel defaultLabel = new JLabel(),
           textLabel = new JLabel("text"),
           textIconLabel = new JLabel("text", icon,
                                 SwingConstants.CENTER),
```

```
        iconLabel = new JLabel(icon);

    public Test() {
        Container contentPane = getContentPane();

        contentPane.setLayout(
            new FlowLayout(FlowLayout.CENTER, 25, 25));

        contentPane.add(defaultLabel);
        contentPane.add(textLabel);
        contentPane.add(iconLabel);
        contentPane.add(textIconLabel);
    }
}
```

Methods

Verification

---

protected int checkHorizontalKey(int, String)
protected int checkVerticalKey(int, String)

The two methods listed above ensure that the `integer` values they are passed are valid for specifying the horizontal and vertical alignment of the label's content and the text position relative to the icon—see Table 8-2 on page 378 for a list of valid values. If the values are invalid, both methods throw an `IllegalArgumentException` and the string passed to the methods is used as the message for the exception. If the values are valid, the methods quietly return.

The methods are `protected` so that they can be overridden by extensions of `JLabel`; however, the methods will rarely be overridden in practice.

Alignment and Text Position

---

public int getHorizontalAlignment()
public int getVerticalAlignment()

public int getHorizontalTextPosition()
public int getVerticalTextPosition()

public void <u>setHorizontalAlignment</u>(int)
public void <u>setHorizontalTextPosition</u>(int)

public void <u>setVerticalAlignment</u>(int)
public void <u>setVerticalTextPosition</u>(int)

The methods listed above are accessors for horizontal and vertical alignment and text position.

Property Accessors

---

public Icon <u>getDisabledIcon</u>()
public int <u>getDisplayedMnemonic</u>()
public Icon <u>getIcon</u>()
public int <u>getIconTextGap</u>()
public Component <u>getLabelFor</u>()
public String <u>getText</u>()

public void <u>setDisabledIcon</u>(Icon)
public void <u>setDisplayedMnemonic</u>(char)
public void <u>setDisplayedMnemonic</u>(int)
public void <u>setFont</u>(Font)
public void <u>setIcon</u>(Icon)
public void <u>setIconTextGap</u>(int)
public void <u>setLabelFor</u>(Component)
public void <u>setText</u>(String)

protected String <u>paramString</u>()

The first two groups of methods listed above are accessor methods for `JLabel` properties, which are listed in Table 8-2 on page 378 and discussed in "JLabel Properties" on page 378.

`JLabel` is not source compatible with its AWT counterpart, `java.awt.Label`. The only methods from `java.awt.Label` that are present in `JLabel` are the accessors for the label's text: `getText()` and `setText()`.

`java.awt.Label` has an alignment property that aligns the text displayed by the label. By contrast, `JLabel` provides two properties that effectively supersede the AWT label's alignment property: horizontal alignment and vertical alignment.

As a result, `java.awt.Label` provides a single pair of methods for setting and getting the label's alignment property, whereas `JLabel` provides setter and getter methods for both the horizontal and vertical alignment properties.

The `paramString` method returns a string representation of a label.

Accessibility / Pluggable Look and Feel

public LabelUI <u>getUI</u>()
public void <u>setUI</u>(LabelUI)
public AccessibleContext <u>getAccessibleContext</u>()
public String <u>getUIClassID</u>()
public void <u>updateUI</u>()

The methods listed above can be found in most extensions of `JComponent`. Swing lightweight components can return an accessibility context that contains accessibility information for the component, and the class name of their UI delegate. The `updateUI` method is invoked when the component is fitted with a UI delegate.

Buttons

Buttons are the Clark Kent of Swing; on one hand, they are simple push buttons, but on the other hand, they are one of Swing's most important building blocks.

The `JButton` class implements the push button abstraction, but it inherits nearly all of its functionality from the `AbstractButton` class. `JButton` is one of eight Swing components that are extensions of the `AbstractButton` class. They are:

- `JButton`
- `JToggleButton`
- `JCheckBox`
- `JRadioButton`
- `JMenuItem`
- `JMenu`
- `JRadioButtonMenuItem`
- `JCheckBoxMenuItem`

Additionally, JButton is the superclass of a handful of classes used by UI delegates to construct elements of the UI. For example, Motif scrollbar buttons and Metal combo box buttons are extensions of the JButton class.

The applet shown in Figure 8-11 contains at least one instance of each of the classes listed above.

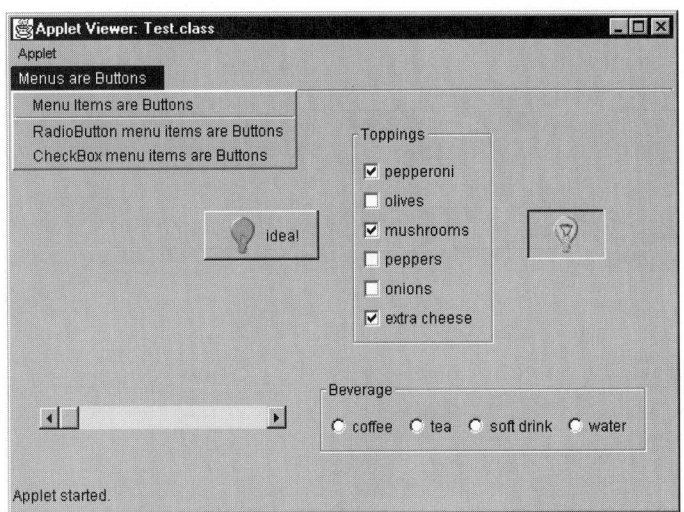

Figure 8-11 Swing's Buttons

Notice the inclusion of menus and menu items in the list of AbstractButton extensions. AWT menus and menu items are not extensions of the Component class and therefore cannot be manipulated in the same fashion as other types of components. For example, it is not possible to set the background color for an AWT menu or menu item. Swing menus and menu items on the other hand, are not only extensions of the Component[4] class but are also full-fledged buttons. As a result, anything that can be done to a button can be done to a menu or menu item.

An instance of JScrollBar is included in the applet shown in Figure 8-11,[5] not because scrollbars are buttons, but because the two arrow buttons for scrollbars with the Windows look and feel are extensions of JButton.

---

4.   JButton —> AbstractButton —> JComponent —> Container —> Component
5.   The applet in Figure 8-11 is not listed but is on the CD.

Button Class Hierarchy

A class diagram for Swing buttons is shown in Figure 8-12.

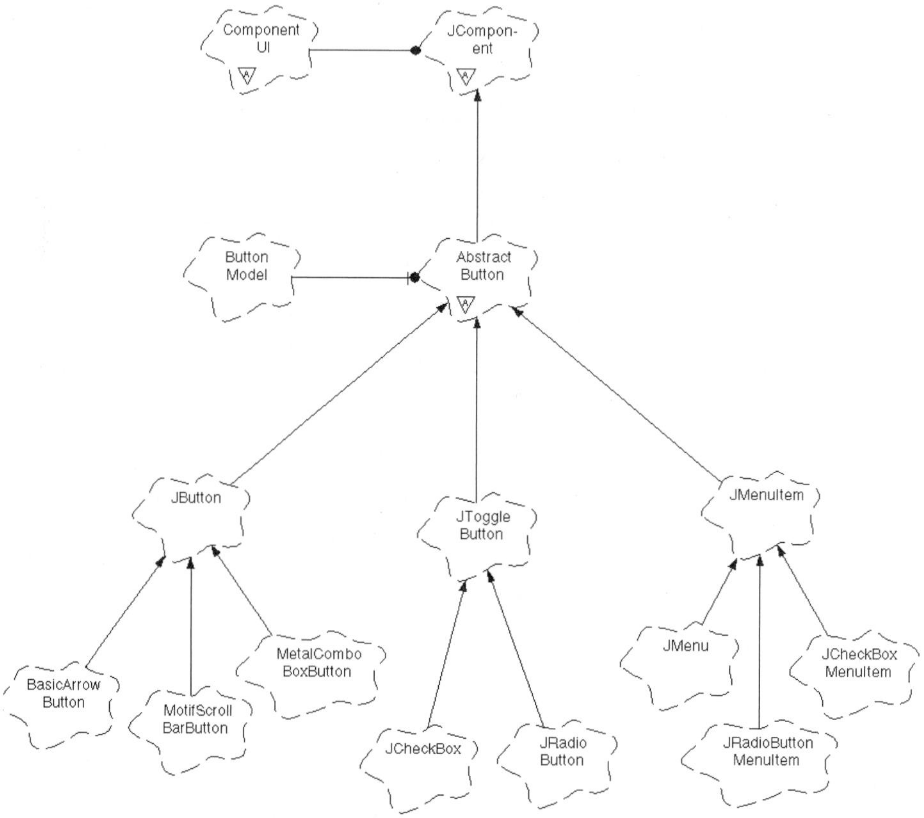

Figure 8-12 Swing Button Class Hierarchy

The UI delegate for buttons—just like all other lightweight Swing components—is stored as a reference to a ComponentUI in the JComponent class. The actual type of a button's UI delegate depends on the type of the button; for example, an instance of JToggleButton has a UI delegate of type ToggleButtonUI.

A button's model is stored as a reference to a `ButtonModel` in the `AbstractButton` class. As with a button's UI delegate, the type of a button's model depends upon the type of the button.

All Swing buttons are extensions of the `AbstractButton` class, which contributes the lion's share of button functionality for simple, toggle, checkbox and radio buttons in addition to menus and menu items. Extensions of `AbstractButton`—with the exception of `JMenu`—typically provide only a handful of constructors and a few methods.

AbstractButton Encapsulates Common Button Functionality

Nearly all of the functionality provided by Swing buttons—including menus and menu items—is encapsulated in the AbstractButton class. Encapsulating common functionality in a base class is one of the tenets of object-oriented development. Because common functionality is implemented in the AbstractButton class, extensions of AbstractButton have simple implementations and, more importantly, can be manipulated in a uniform fashion.

JButton

`JButton` is a push button that is a replacement for `java.awt.Button`. Instances of `JButton`, like Swing labels, can display text, an icon, or both.

Like AWT buttons, Swing buttons fire action events when they are activated. An action listener can register with a button, and the listener's `actionPerformed` method will be invoked whenever the button is activated. Figure 8-13 illustrates listening to an instance of `JButton` for action events.

The button's action listener prints the number of times that the button has been activated in the applet's status area. The string returned from `getActionCommand()` is used to identify the button; by default, `getActionCommand()` returns the button's text.

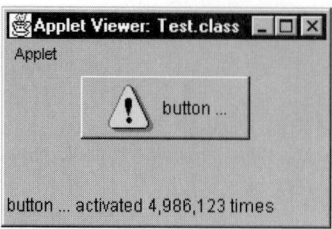

Figure 8-13 Listening to a Button's Action Events

The applet shown in Figure 8-13 is listed in Example 8-7.

Example 8-7 A Simple Button Example

```java
import javax.swing.*;
import java.awt.*;
import java.awt.event.*;

public class Test extends JApplet {
    JButton button = new JButton("button ...",
                            new ImageIcon("exclaim.gif"));
    int actCnt = 0;

    public void init() {
        Container contentPane = getContentPane();

        contentPane.setLayout(new FlowLayout());
        contentPane.add(button);

        button.addActionListener(new ActionListener() {
            public void actionPerformed(ActionEvent event) {
                showStatus(event.getActionCommand() +
                        " activated " + actCnt + " times");
                actCnt++;
            }
        });
    }
}
```

"JButton Events" on page 396 discusses button events in more detail. The JButton class is discussed further in Component Summary 8-2.

Component Summary 8-2   JButton

Model(s)	ButtonModel
UI Delegate(s)	swing.plaf.basic.ButtonUI
Renderer(s)	——
Editor(s)	——
Events Fired	ActionEvent/ChangeEvent/ItemEvent
Replacement For	java.awt.Button

Class Diagrams

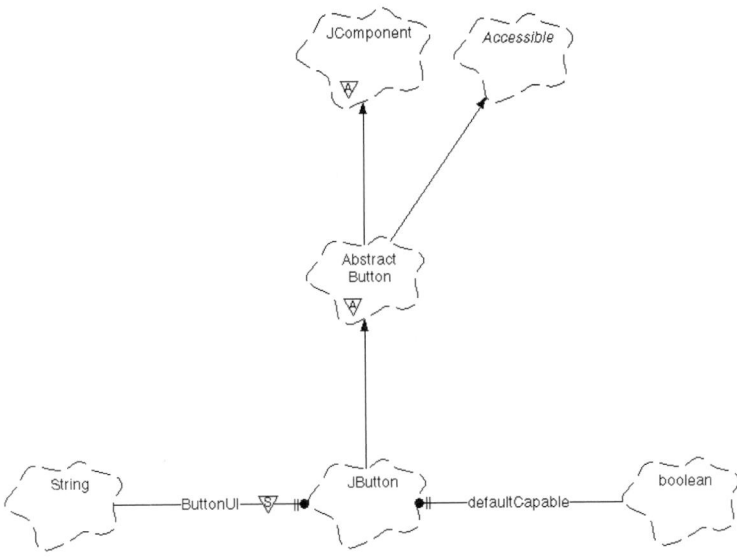

Figure 8-14 JButton Class Diagram

Figure 8-14 shows the class diagram for the JButton class. JButton extends the JComponent class, and is therefore a lightweight Swing component.

Like all Swing components, JButton implements the Accessible interface so that it can offer information to accessibility tools by way of an AccessibleContext object—see "Accessibility" on page 196 for more information on accessibility in general.

JButton has almost no implementation of its own—it is nothing more than a few constructors and support for accessibility. An instance of JButton keeps track of whether or not it is the default button in a root pane[6] but for the most part, JButton is a very thin veneer layered on top of the AbstractButton class. Since AbstractButton is where all the action occurs, Figure 8-15 shows the class diagram for the AbstractButton class.

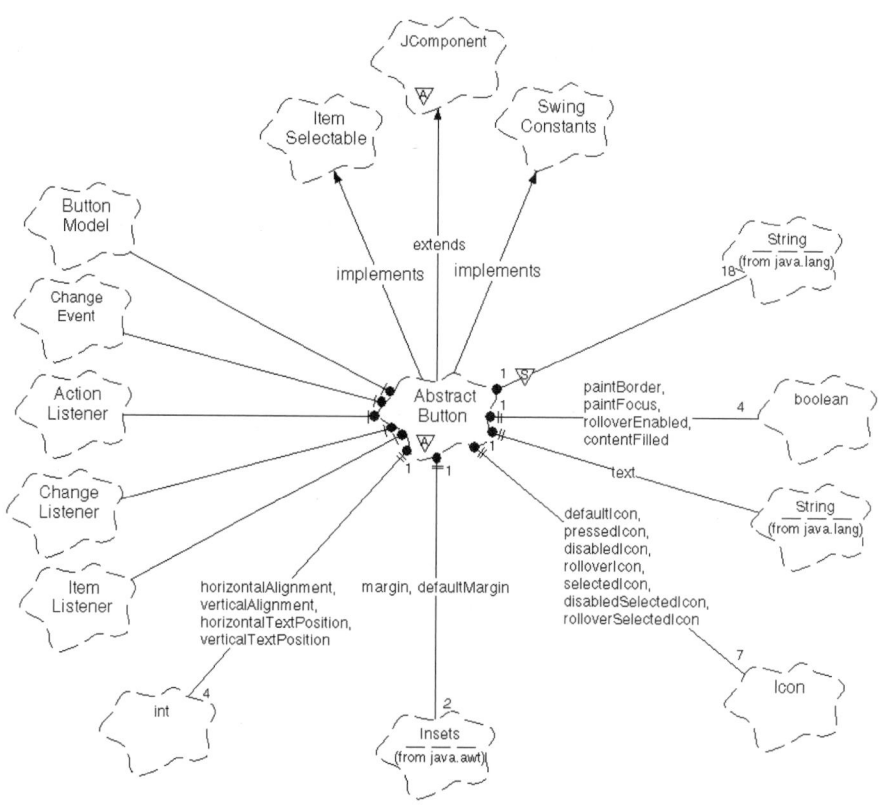

Figure 8-15 AbstractButton Class Diagram

6.   See "Designating a Button as the Default Button" on page 403.

AbstractButton extends JComponent and implements the SwingConstants interface for its own benefit.[7] AbstractButton also implements java.awt.ItemSelectable, which is an AWT interface designed for components that have zero or more selectable items.

AbstractButton maintains a protected reference to its model—an object that implements the ButtonModel interface. AbstractButton also maintains protected references to three listeners: an ActionListener, a ChangeListener, and an ItemListener. Each of the listeners is added to the button's model, for the purpose of forwarding model events to the button's own listeners. For example, the button's item listener is added to the model, and the listener is notified by the model whenever the model fires an item event. When notified, the listener forwards the event to the button's item listeners.

Change events have no state associated with them other than the source of the event. As a result, each instance of JButton needs only one instance of ChangeEvent that gets reused whenever the button fires a change event.

AbstractButton also maintains a number of private references to integers, booleans, and icons, which represent the properties associated with Swing buttons. AbstractButton properties are discussed in the next section.

JButton Properties

The properties maintained by instances of JButton are listed in Table 8-3.

Table 8-3 JButton Properties[1]

Property Name	Data Type	Access[2]	Type[3]	Default[4]
actionCommand	String	SG	S	button text
borderPainted	boolean	SG	B	true
defaultButton	boolean	G	S	false
defaultCapable	boolean	SG	B	true
disabledIcon	icon	SG	B	gray filtered icon
disabledSelected-Icon	icon	SG	B	gray filtered icon
focusPainted	boolean	SG	B	true

7. The benefit is that AbstractButton can use SwingConstants constants directly.

Table 8-3   JButton Properties[1] (Continued)

Property Name	Data Type	Access[2]	Type[3]	Default[4]
horizontal-Alignment	int	SG	B	CENTER
horizontalText-Position	int	SG	B	RIGHT
icon	icon	CSG	B	null
~~label~~	~~String~~	~~CSG~~	~~B~~	~~""~~
margin	Insets	SG	B	null
mnemonic	int	SG	B	0
model	ButtonModel	SG	B	DefaultButtonModel
pressedIcon	Icon	SG	B	null
rolloverIcon	Icon	SG	B	null
rolloverSelected-Icon	Icon	SG	B	null
selected	boolean	SG	B	false
text	String	CSG	B	""
verticalAlignment	int	SG	B	CENTER
verticalText-Position	int	SG	B	CENTER

1. ~~Strikethrough~~ indicates deprecated property
2. C = settable at construction time / G = getter method / S = setter method
3. B = bound / bool = boolean / C = constrained/ I = indexed / S = simple
4. L&F = look-and-feel dependent

actionCommand — A string that identifies the command associated with a button. By default, a button's action command is set to the button text.

borderPainted — Determines whether or not a button's border is painted.

defaultButton — Indicates whether a button is the default button for a root pane.

defaultCapable — Indicates whether a button is capable of being the default button for a root pane.

disabledIcon — The icon displayed when a button is disabled. By default, the icon is a grayed out version of the button's icon; however, the disabled button can be explicitly set.

disabledSelectedIcon — The `disabledSelectedIcon` property is not used as of Swing 1.1 FCS.

focusPainted — Determines whether a focus indicator is painted when a button has focus.

horizontalAlignment — The horizontal alignment for a button's content (meaning its text and icon). Possible values are `JButton.LEFT`, `JButton.RIGHT`, and `JButton.CENTER`.

horizontalTextPosition — Horizontal position of the text relative to the icon; valid values are the same as for horizontal alignment.

icon — The icon displayed by a label when the label is enabled.

label — The text displayed in a button. The `label` property has been deprecated; use the `text` property instead.

margin — A margin between a button's border and its content.

mnemonic — A key used to activate a button.

model — A button's model. By default, a button's model is an instance of `DefaultButtonModel`.

pressedIcon — An icon that is displayed when a button is pressed.

rolloverIcon — An icon displayed when the mouse cursor enters a button.

rolloverSelectedIcon — The `rolloverSelectedIcon` property is not currently used as of Swing 1.1 FCS.

selected — The `selected` property is inherited from `AbstractAction` and has no meaning for instances of `JButton`. Other extensions of `AbstractButton` are selectable; for example, a check box is selected when it is checked, and a menu is selected when it is activated.

text — The text displayed in a button. The `text` property should be used instead of the deprecated `label` property.

verticalAlignment — The vertical alignment for a button's content (meaning its text and icon). Possible values are `JButton.TOP`, `JButton.CENTER`, and `JButton.BOTTOM`.

verticalTextPosition — The vertical position of the text relative to the icon; valid values are the same as for vertical alignment.

The properties listed in Table 8-3 belong to `JButton` by way of inheritance from `AbstractButton`. The only properties that originate in the `JButton` class are the `defaultButton` property (which is actually maintained in the button's root pane) and the `defaultCapable` property.

Although they are not related by inheritance, `JButton` and `JLabel` have a number of identical properties: icon, text, disabled icon, mnemonic, horizontal alignment, horizontal text position, vertical alignment, and vertical text position. As a result, `JButton` and `JLabel` have a number of (nearly) identical accessor methods for the properties listed above. The only accessors that do not have identical signatures are those for the `mnemonic` property, which is accessed through `getDisplayedMnemonic()` for labels, but `getMnemonic()` for buttons.

The action command is a string that is typically used to identify the button that fired an action event. If a button's action command is not explicitly set, it defaults to the button's text. The action command's real value comes from the fact that the `java.awt.event.ActionEvent` class comes with a `getActionCommand` method that returns the action command associated with the event source. So, instead of doing this—

```
// the hard way ...

public void actionPerformed(ActionEvent e) {
    AbstractButton b = (AbstractButton)e.getSource();

    if(b.getActionCommand().equals("cut")) {
        // do cut action
    }
    else {
        // do something else
    }
    ...
}
```

—you can access the action command without accessing the button:

```
// the easy way ...

public void actionPerformed(ActionEvent e) {
    if(e.getActionCommand().equals("cut")) {
        // do cut action
    }
    else {
        // do something else
    }
    ...
}
```

`AbstractButton` maintains references to no less than seven icons, which is enough to warrant Table 8-4—a listing of the icons and their uses.

Table 8-4   Icons Maintained by AbstractButton

Icon	Use
icon	Displayed when button is enabled and unselected
pressed icon	Displayed when the button is armed
disabled icon	Displayed when the button is disabled
selected icon[1]	Displayed when the button is selected
rollover icon	Displayed when the mouse enters (rolls over) the button
disabled selected icon	Not used
rollover selected icon	Not used

1. Pertains to toggle buttons and menu items only

The rollover selected icon and disabled selected icon properties are not used anywhere throughout Swing.

Swing Tip ...

Use Action Commands to Identify Buttons

Every instance of AbstractButton maintains a string identifier known as the action command. By default, a button's action command is set to the text displayed in the button; however, AbstractButton provides a method to explicitly set the action command string.

The action command string can be used by action listeners to identify which button fired an action event because the ActionEvent class provides a method that returns the action command associated with the event. As a result, when a button fires an action event, it is not necessary to extract the source of the event to identify the button that fired the event.

JButton Events

Instances of `JButton` fire action events when they are activated, property change events when their bound properties are modified, and change events when their state changes. Button states are summarized in Table 8-5.

Table 8-5   Button States

State	Meaning
armed	Mouse button is pressed while the cursor is in the button. If mouse button is released inside the button, the button is activated, otherwise it is disarmed.
enabled	Button can change state.
pressed	Button has been pressed.
rollover	Cursor has entered button.
selected	Button has been selected.

Property change events and change events are discussed in "Property Change Notification" on page 95. The `ActionListener` interface and `ActionEvent` class reside in the `java.awt.event` package. The `ActionListener` interface is summarized in Interface Summary 8-1.

Interface Summary 8-1   ActionListener

public abstract void <u>actionPerformed</u>(ActionEvent)

The `actionPerformed` method is passed an instance of `ActionEvent`. The `ActionEvent` class is summarized in Class Summary 8-2.

Class Summary 8-2   ActionEvent

Extends: java.awt.AWTEvent

Constants

public static final int <u>ACTION_FIRST</u>
public static final int <u>ACTION_LAST</u>
public static final int <u>ACTION_PERFORMED</u>

public static final int <u>ALT_MASK</u>
public static final int <u>CTRL_MASK</u>
public static final int <u>META_MASK</u>
public static final int <u>SHIFT_MASK</u>

The first group of constants listed above represent valid event IDs for action events. See the first volume of *Graphic Java* for more information concerning event IDs. The second group of constants listed above represent modifier keys that may have been pressed when the action event occurred.

Constructors

public <u>ActionEvent</u>(Object source, int id, String command)
public <u>ActionEvent</u>(Object source, int id, String command, int modifiers)

Action events are constructed with the source of the event, the event ID, and the action command. An `integer` may also be specified, representing modifier keys that were held down during the event.

Methods

public String <u>getActionCommand</u>()
public int <u>getModifiers</u>()
public String <u>paramString</u>()

The `ActionEvent` class defines methods to obtain the action command string and modifiers and also provides a `paramString` method that is used to construct the string returned from the `toString` method.

All event firing for JButton is inherited from the AbstractButton class—
JButton fires no events of its own volition. It should also be noted that
AbstractButton comes equipped to fire item events. Item events are fired for
other extensions of AbstractButton that can be selected, such as check boxes
and radio buttons.

The applet shown in Figure 8-16 contains a button fitted with a change listener
and an action listener. When the button fires change or action events, the listeners
print information about the event.

Figure 8-16 Handling JButton Events

The applet shown in Figure 8-16 is listed in Example 8-8.

Example 8-8 Handling JButton Events

```
import java.awt.*;
import java.awt.event.*;
import javax.swing.*;
import javax.swing.event.*;

public class Test extends JApplet {
    Icon icon = new ImageIcon("icon.gif");
    JButton button = new JButton("button");

    public Test() {
        Container contentPane = getContentPane();

        button.setRolloverIcon(new ImageIcon("punch.gif"));
        button.setIcon(new ImageIcon("open_hand.gif"));

        contentPane.setLayout(new FlowLayout());
        contentPane.add(button);
```

```
    button.addActionListener(new ActionListener() {
        public void actionPerformed(ActionEvent e) {
            System.out.println("action!");
        }
    });
    button.addChangeListener(new ChangeListener() {
        public void stateChanged(ChangeEvent e) {
            System.out.println(getButtonState());
        }
    });
}
private String getButtonState() {
    ButtonModel model = button.getModel();
    String state = "Button State: ";

    state += model.isSelected() ? "selected" : "deselected";
    state += model.isPressed() ? ", pressed" :
                                ", not pressed";
    state += model.isArmed() ? ", armed" : ", disarmed";
    state += model.isRollover() ? ", rollover" :
                                ", not rollover";

    return state;
}
}
```

The applet's action listener simply prints the string "action!", whereas the change listener prints the button's state, which is obtained from the button's model.

When the cursor enters the button, as depicted by the second picture from the left in Figure 8-16, the rollover image is displayed, the button fires a change event, and the change listener prints the following:

```
Button State: not selected, not pressed, not armed, rollover
```

If the mouse is subsequently pressed while the cursor is in the button, as depicted by the third picture from the left in Figure 8-16, the following output is printed by the listeners:

```
Button State: not selected, not pressed, armed, rollover
Button State: not selected, pressed, armed, rollover
```

If the mouse is subsequently released while the cursor is in the button, the listeners print the following output:

```
action!
Button State: not selected, not pressed, armed, rollover
Button State: not selected, not pressed, not armed, rollover
```

Note: *There is a bug in Swing 1.1 FCS that causes the states printed above to include "rollover." The button state should include "not rollover" for all but the first printout above.*

When the cursor leaves the button, the change listener prints the following:

```
Button State: not selected, not pressed, not armed, not rollover
```

JButton Class Summaries

The `public` and `protected` variables and methods for `JButton` are listed in Class Summary 8-3.

`JButton` essentially bolts on a handful of constructors to the feature-laden `AbstractButton` class.

Class Summary 8-3   JButton

Extends: AbstractButton

Implements: javax.accessibility.Accessible

Constructors

---

public JButton()
public JButton(Icon)
public JButton(String)
public JButton(String, Icon)

The applet shown in Figure 8-17 creates four instances of JButton—one for each of JButton's constructors.

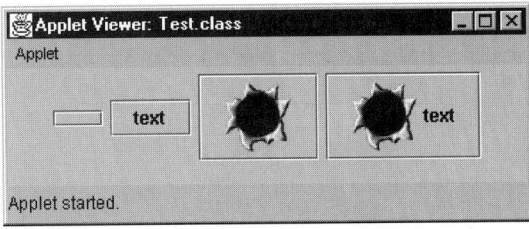

Figure 8-17 Instantiating JButtons

Unlike the label created with JLabel's no-argument constructor in the applet shown in Figure 8-10 on page 381, the button created with JButton's no-argument constructor in Figure 8-17 is visible because the button's border is painted.

The applet shown in Figure 8-17 is listed in Example 8-9.

Example 8-9 Instantiating Instances of JButton

```
import java.awt.*;
import java.awt.event.*;
import javax.swing.*;

public class Test extends JApplet {
    Icon icon = new ImageIcon("icon.gif");

    JButton noargButton = new JButton(),
            textButton = new JButton("text"),
            textIconButton = new JButton("text", icon),
            iconButton = new JButton(icon);

    public Test() {
        Container contentPane = getContentPane();

        contentPane.setLayout(new FlowLayout());
        contentPane.add(noargButton);
        contentPane.add(textButton);
        contentPane.add(iconButton);
        contentPane.add(textIconButton);
    }
}
```

Methods

Accessibility / Pluggable Look and Feel

---

public AccessibleContext getAccessibleContext()
public String getUIClassID()
public void updateUI()

protected String paramString()

The first groups of methods listed above can be found in any extension of JComponent. Swing lightweight components can return an accessibility context that contains accessibility information for the component, and the class name of the component's UI delegate. The updateUI method is invoked when the component is fitted with a UI delegate.

The paramString method returns a string representation of a button.

Default Button

---

public boolean isDefaultButton()
public void setDefaultCapable()
public boolean isDefaultCapable()

Buttons that are default capable can be specified as the default button for a root pane. Default buttons are typically drawn in such a manner that they stand out from regular buttons and can be activated with the keyboard shortcut. The exact prescription for how default buttons look and behave is up to the button's look and feel.

The applet shown in Figure 8-18 contains two buttons, one of which is designated as the default button.

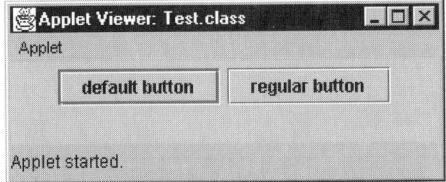

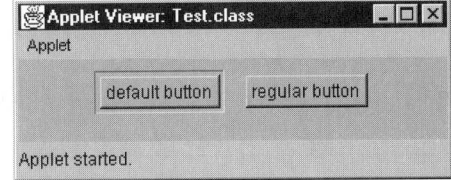

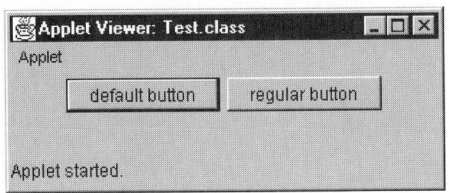

Figure 8-18 Default Buttons for Different Look and Feels
Look and feels from top left, clockwise: Metal, Motif, and Windows.

The applet shown in Figure 8-18 is listed in Example 8-10.

Example 8-10 Designating a Button as the Default Button

```java
import java.awt.*;
import java.awt.event.*;
import javax.swing.*;

public class Test extends JApplet {
    public Test() {
        Container contentPane = getContentPane();
        JRootPane rootPane = getRootPane();
        JButton def = new JButton("default button");
        JButton reg = new JButton("regular button");

        rootPane.setDefaultButton(def);

        contentPane.setLayout(new FlowLayout());
        contentPane.add(def);
        contentPane.add(reg);
    }
}
```

AbstractButton provides nearly all the functionality to be found in JButton and forms the basis for toggle and radio buttons, check boxes, menus, and menu items. The AbstractButton class is summarized in Class Summary 8-4.

Class Summary 8-4   AbstractButton

Extends: JComponent

Implements: SwingConstants, java.awt.ItemSelectable

Constructors

---

public AbstractButton()

The no-argument constructor for `AbstractButton` is compiler generated because `AbstractButton` does not explicitly implement a constructor. Since `AbstractButton` is an abstract class, its no-argument constructor will only be called from a constructor of an extension class.

Methods

Verification

---

protected int checkHorizontalKey(int, String)
protected int checkVerticalKey(int, String)

The two methods listed above ensure that the `integer` values they are passed are valid for specifying the horizontal and vertical alignment of the button's content and the text position relative to the icon—see Table 8-2 on page 378 for a list of valid values. If the values are invalid, both methods throw an `IllegalArgumentException` and the string passed to the methods is used as the message for the exception. If the values are valid, the methods quietly return.

The methods are `protected` so that they can be overridden by extensions of `JButton`; however, the methods will rarely be overridden in practice.

Action and Item Listeners

---

public void <u>addActionListener</u>(ActionListener)
public void <u>addChangeListener</u>(ChangeListener)

public void <u>removeActionListener</u>(ActionListener)
public void <u>removeChangeListener</u>(ChangeListener)

protected ActionListener <u>createActionListener</u>()
protected ChangeListener <u>createChangeListener</u>()
protected ItemListener <u>createItemListener</u>()

protected void <u>fireActionPerformed</u>(ActionEvent)
protected void <u>fireItemStateChanged</u>(ItemEvent)
protected void <u>fireStateChanged</u>()

public Object[] <u>getSelectedObjects</u>()
public void <u>addItemListener</u>(ItemListener)
public void <u>removeItemListener</u>(ItemListener)

The first two groups of `public` methods listed above are provided so that action and change listeners can be added and removed from Swing buttons.

The `protected` methods listed above perform two functions. The listeners returned from the `create...` methods are added to the button's model. By default, the `create...` methods are implemented so that the listeners they return simply forward model events to the button's listeners. In the unlikely event that model events need to be handled differently, the methods can be overridden and custom listeners can be returned.

The `fire...` methods fire events to the appropriate types of listeners that are registered with the button. Once again, the methods can be overridden by extensions of `AbstractButton` if the default behavior is not acceptable.

The `getSelectedObjects` method is part of the `ItemSelectable` interface, (along with the `addItemListener` and `removeItemListener` methods) and is intended to return an `Object` array containing references to the button's selected objects. Not all extensions of `AbstractButton` have selectable items, and therefore `AbstractButton` implements the `getSelectedObjects` method to return a `null` reference.

Initialization / Border

---

protected void <u>init</u>(String, Icon)
protected void <u>paintBorder</u>(Graphics)

The init method sets the layout manager, sets the text and icon, and updates the UI (by invoking updateUI()). It also adds a focus listener that fires property change events for accessibility purposes when focus is gained or lost and when the alignment of the button is set. Although AbstractButton.init() is a protected method, developers should ensure that buttons are initialized properly if the init method is overridden by extension classes.

paintBorder() is overridden so that the superclass (JComponent) implementation of the method is invoked only if the button's border painted property is true.

Programmatic Activation

---

public void <u>doClick</u>()
public void <u>doClick</u>(int)

Instances of AbstractButton can be clicked programmatically with the methods listed above. The integer value passed to doClick() represents the time, in milliseconds, that the button stays pressed. The no-argument version of doClick() calls doclick(68), so by calling doClick(), the button stays pressed for 68 milliseconds.

The applet shown in Figure 8-19 contains two buttons—when the button on the left is activated, it invokes doClick(int) for the button on the right. The integer value passed to doClick() is the current value displayed in the applet's combo box.

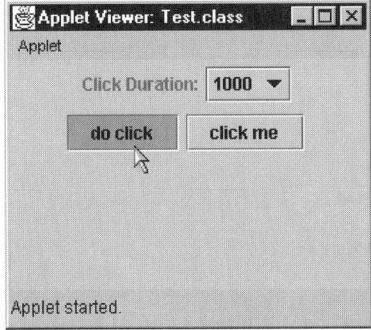 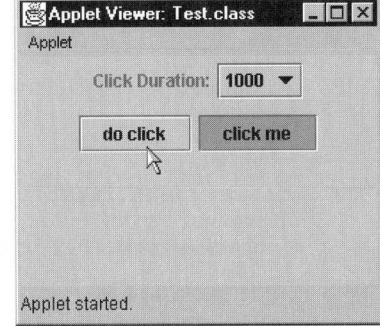

Figure 8-19 Programmatically Clicking a Button

The applet's content pane contains two panels—a control panel that contains the label and combo box, and a panel that holds the two buttons. The action listener for the `doClick` button simply invokes `doClick()` for the "click me" button, and the item listener for the combo box sets the `clickDuration` value.

The applet shown in Figure 8-19 is listed in Example 8-11.

Example 8-11 Programmatically Clicking a Button

```
import java.awt.*;
import java.awt.event.*;
import javax.swing.*;

public class Test extends JApplet {
    int clickDuration = 68;

    public Test() {
        Container contentPane = getContentPane();
        JPanel controlPanel = new JPanel();
        JPanel buttonPanel = new JPanel();

        JButton doClick = new JButton("do click");
        final JButton clickMe = new JButton("click me");

        final JComboBox comboBox = new JComboBox(new Object[] {
            "68", "250", "500", "750", "1000"
        });

        controlPanel.add(new JLabel("Click Duration:"));
        controlPanel.add(comboBox);
```

```
                    buttonPanel.add(doClick);
                    buttonPanel.add(clickMe);

                    contentPane.add(controlPanel, BorderLayout.NORTH);
                    contentPane.add(buttonPanel, BorderLayout.CENTER);

                    getRootPane().setDefaultButton(doClick);

                    doClick.addActionListener(new ActionListener() {
                        public void actionPerformed(ActionEvent e) {
                            clickMe.doClick(clickDuration);
                        }
                    });

                    comboBox.addItemListener(new ItemListener() {
                        public void itemStateChanged(ItemEvent e) {
                            if(e.getStateChange() == ItemEvent.SELECTED) {
                                clickDuration = Integer.parseInt((String)
                                            comboBox.getSelectedItem());
                            }
                        }
                    });
                }
            }
```

Icons

---

public Icon getIcon()
public Icon getDisabledIcon()
public Icon getDisabledSelectedIcon()
public Icon getPressedIcon()
public Icon getRolloverIcon()
public Icon getRolloverSelectedIcon()
public Icon getSelectedIcon()

public void setIcon(Icon)
public void setDisabledIcon(Icon)
public void setDisabledSelectedIcon(Icon)
public void setPressedIcon(Icon)
public void setRolloverIcon(Icon)
public void setRolloverSelectedIcon(Icon)
public void setSelectedIcon(Icon)

`AbstractButton` provides getter and setter methods for all of the icons it supports. Icons supported by `AbstractButton` and their uses are listed in Table 8-4 on page 395. `JButton` only uses four of the seven icons: default, rollover, pressed and disabled. `JButton` does not use the selected icon because instances of `JButton` cannot be selected. The rollover selected icon and disabled selected icon are not used anywhere within Swing.[8]

The applet shown in Figure 8-20 contains an instance of `JButton` that has icons assigned for each of the seven icons supported by the `AbstractButton` class.

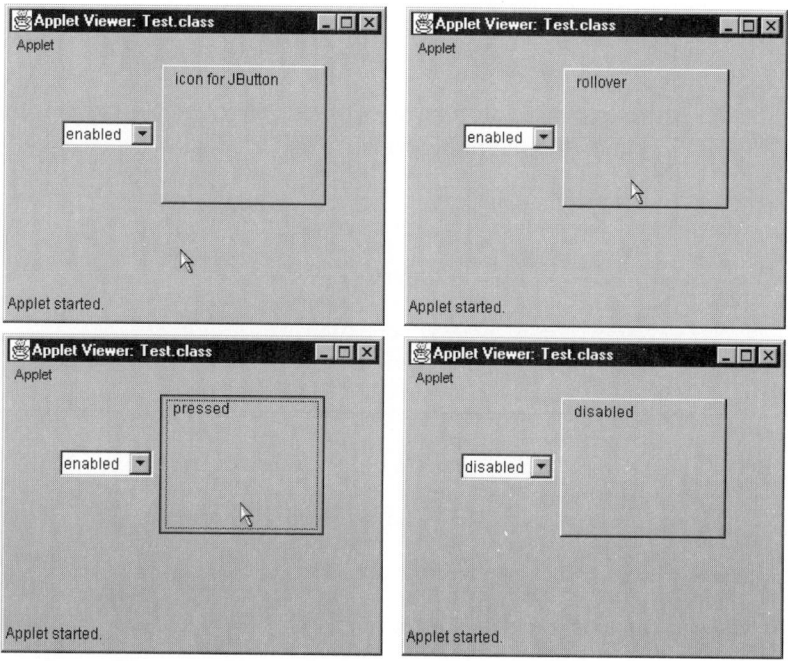

Figure 8-20 JButton Icons

The icons displayed in Figure 8-20 are instances of a `StringIcon` class that displays a string it is passed at construction time. The `StringIcon` class implements the `Icon` interface:

8. As of Swing 1.1 FCS

```
class StringIcon implements Icon {
    private String s;

    public StringIcon(String s) {
        this.s = s;
    }
    public int getIconWidth() { return 100; }
    public int getIconHeight() { return 100; }

    public void paintIcon(Component c, Graphics g, int x, int y) {
        FontMetrics fm = g.getFontMetrics();
        g.setColor(c.getForeground());
        g.drawString(s, 10, fm.getHeight());
    }
}
```

The applet creates seven instances of `StringIcon` and invokes the appropriate `AbstractButton` methods to assign the icons.

```
public class Test extends JApplet {
    public void init() {
        Container contentPane = getContentPane();
        Icon icon = new StringIcon("icon for JButton"),
            rolloverIcon = new StringIcon("rollover"),
            pressedIcon = new StringIcon("pressed"),
            disabledIcon = new StringIcon("disabled"),
            selectedIcon = new StringIcon("selected"),
            rolloverSelectedIcon =
                new StringIcon("rollover selected"),
            disabledSelectedIcon =
                new StringIcon("disabled selected");

        final JButton button = new JButton();

        button.setRolloverEnabled(true);

        button.setIcon(icon);
        button.setRolloverIcon(rolloverIcon);
        button.setRolloverSelectedIcon(rolloverSelectedIcon);
        button.setSelectedIcon(selectedIcon);
        button.setPressedIcon(pressedIcon);
        button.setDisabledIcon(disabledIcon);
        button.setDisabledSelectedIcon(disabledSelectedIcon);
        ...
    }
    ...
}
```

The applet shown in Figure 8-20 is listed in Example 8-12.

Example 8-12   JButton Icons

```
import javax.swing.*;
import javax.swing.border.*;
import javax.swing.plaf.basic.*;
import java.awt.*;
import java.awt.event.*;

public class Test extends JApplet {
    public void init() {
        Container contentPane = getContentPane();
        Icon icon = new StringIcon("icon for JButton"),
            rolloverIcon = new StringIcon("rollover"),
            pressedIcon = new StringIcon("pressed"),
            disabledIcon = new StringIcon("disabled"),
            selectedIcon = new StringIcon("selected"),
            rolloverSelectedIcon =
                    new StringIcon("rollover selected"),
            disabledSelectedIcon =
                    new StringIcon("disabled selected");

        final JButton button = new JButton();

        button.setRolloverEnabled(true);

        button.setIcon(icon);
        button.setRolloverIcon(rolloverIcon);
        button.setRolloverSelectedIcon(rolloverSelectedIcon);
        button.setSelectedIcon(selectedIcon);
        button.setPressedIcon(pressedIcon);
        button.setDisabledIcon(disabledIcon);
        button.setDisabledSelectedIcon(disabledSelectedIcon);

        JComboBox cb = new JComboBox();
        cb.addItem("enabled");
        cb.addItem("disabled");

        cb.addItemListener(new ItemListener() {
            public void itemStateChanged(ItemEvent e) {
                if(e.getStateChange() == ItemEvent.SELECTED) {
                    String item = (String)e.getItem();

                    if(item.equals("enabled")) {
                        button.setEnabled(true);
                    }
                    else {
                        button.setEnabled(false);
                    }
                }
```

```
                }
            });
            contentPane.setLayout(new FlowLayout());
            contentPane.add(cb);
            contentPane.add(button);
        }
    }
    class StringIcon implements Icon {
        private String s;

        public StringIcon(String s) {
            this.s = s;
        }
        public int getIconWidth() { return 100; }
        public int getIconHeight() { return 100; }

        public void paintIcon(Component c, Graphics g, int x, int y) {
            FontMetrics fm = g.getFontMetrics();
            g.setColor(c.getForeground());
            g.drawString(s, 10, fm.getHeight());
        }
    }
```

Boolean Property Accessors

---

public boolean isBorderPainted()
public boolean isContentAreaFilled()
public boolean isFocusPainted()
public boolean isRolloverEnabled()
public boolean isSelected()

public void setBorderPainted(boolean)
public void setContentAreaFilled(boolean)
public void setFocusPainted(boolean)
public void setRolloverEnabled(boolean)
public void setSelected(boolean)

The accessor methods listed above for AbstractButton's boolean properties control whether the button paints its border, paints a focus indicator, displays the rollover icon, and is currently selected.

The setContentAreaFilled method should be used instead of the setOpaque method for transparent buttons. Whether a button follows the repaint manager's concept of opacity is look-and-feel dependent, and therefore the setContentAreaFilled method should be used instead of setOpaque().

Property Accessors

---

public String getActionCommand()
public int getHorizontalAlignment()
public int getHorizontalTextPosition()
public int getMnemonic()
public ButtonModel getModel()
public Insets getMargin()
public String getText()
public ButtonUI getUI()
public int getVerticalAlignment()
public int getVerticalTextPosition()

public void setActionCommand()
public void setEnabled(boolean)
public void setHorizontalAlignment(int)
public void setHorizontalTextPosition(int)
public void setMargin(Insets)
public void setMnemonic(char)
public void setMnemonic(int)
public void setModel(ButtonModel)
public void setText(String)
public void setUI(ButtonUI)
public void setVerticalAlignment(int)
public void setVerticalTextPosition(int)

protected String paramString()

The methods listed above are accessors for AbstractButton properties. Accessors for text, icon, alignment and text position have the exact same signatures as the corresponding accessors in the JLabel class. The paramString method returns a string representation of an abstract button.

Content Alignment and Text Position

The two applets shown in Figure 8-21 are nearly identical to the applets shown in Figure 8-4 on page 366 and Figure 8-5 on page 370, except that the applets in Figure 8-21 manipulate alignment and text position properties for instances of JButton instead of JLabel. Because the AbstractButton and JLabel APIs for accessing common properties are nearly identical, the only difference between the JLabel and JButton versions of the applets involves the type of component being instantiated. Hence, the JButton versions of the applets are not listed; however, they are included on the CD in the back of the book.

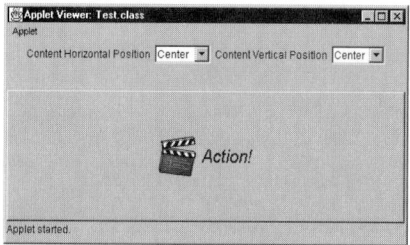 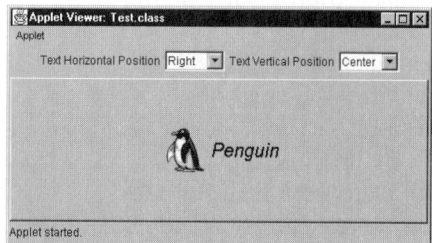

Figure 8-21 Content Alignment and Text Position for Swing Buttons

Button Margins

AbstractButton maintains a margin property, which specifies the distance from the inside edge of the button's border to the outer edge of the button's content.

The applet shown in Figure 8-22 sets the margin for the button to a value of Insets(50,25,10,5).[9]

9. Arguments to the Insets constructor are: top, left, bottom, and right margins.

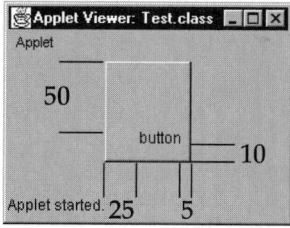

Figure 8-22 Button Margins

The applet shown in Figure 8-22 is listed in Figure 8-13.

Example 8-13 Setting Button Margins

```java
import java.awt.*;
import java.awt.event.*;
import javax.swing.*;

public class Test extends JApplet {
    public Test() {
        Container contentPane = getContentPane();
        JButton button = new JButton("button");

        button.setMargin(new Insets(50,25,10,5));
        contentPane.setLayout(new FlowLayout());
        contentPane.add(button);
    }
}
```

Button Mnemonics

The applet shown in Figure 8-23 sets a mnemonic for the button it displays. The visual indicator for a button mnemonic can change from one look and feel to another; however, the mnemonic character is typically drawn underlined and the button can be activated by typing the Meta character simultaneously with the mnemonic character.[10] Typing the mnemonic when the button has focus activates the button.

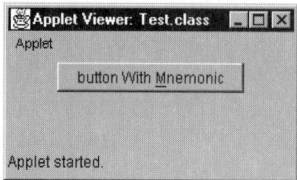

Figure 8-23 Button Mnemonics

The applet shown in Figure 8-23 is listed in Example 8-14.

Example 8-14 Button Mnemonics

```
import java.awt.*;
import java.awt.event.*;
import javax.swing.*;

public class Test extends JApplet {
    public Test() {
        Container contentPane = getContentPane();
        JButton button = new JButton("button With Mnemonic");

        button.setMnemonic('M');

        contentPane.setLayout(new FlowLayout());
        contentPane.add(button);
    }
}
```

10. The Meta character is platform dependent; for example, the Meta character for Windows is the ALT key.

AWT Compatibility

JButton is source compatible with its AWT counterpart—java.awt.Button. All of public methods of the java.awt.Button class can be found in Swing's AbstractButton class. The methods common to both classes are listed in Table 8-6.

Table 8-6   Methods Common to java.awt.Button and AbstractButton

```
public void addActionListener(ActionListener);

public void removeActionListener(ActionListener);

public String getLabel();

public String getActionCommand();

public void setActionCommand(String);

public void setLabel(String);
```

Parting Shots

Swing labels and buttons—represented by the JLabel and JButton classes, respectively—are strange bedfellows. Labels and buttons are both capable of displaying text or an icon. As a result, twenty of the methods found in the JLabel class have exact counterparts in the JButton class; however, JLabel and JButton are not related by inheritance.

Unfortunately, when two classes have a great deal of identical functionality but are not related through inheritance, the only thing that ensures that they can be manipulated in *exactly* the same manner is programmer discipline. In other words, accessor methods for properties common to JLabel and JButton should have getter and setter methods with the exact same signatures, and since the methods are not inherited, it is up to the developer(s)—not the compiler—to ensure uniformity. JLabel and JButton have uniform accessors for common properties with the exception of the mnemonic property, which is accessed through getDisplayedMnemonic() for labels but getMnemonic() for buttons.

The fact that `JLabel` and `AbstractButton` do not extend a base class that encapsulates their common functionality results in other mismatches between the two classes. For example, the gap between the text and icon displayed by a label is settable, but that is not the case for buttons. Additionally, although both buttons and labels can have a disabled icon, only buttons can have a "rollover" icon that is displayed when the cursor enters the button.

On the other hand, nearly all of the functionality for Swing buttons is encapsulated in the `AbstractButton` class. As a result, all extensions of the `AbstractButton` class—including menus and menu items—can be manipulated in a uniform manner. This is a huge improvement over the AWT, which does not provide a common base class for buttons and does not implement menus and menu items as extensions of the button class (or even as extensions of the AWT component class).

CHAPTER
9

Toggle Buttons, Check Boxes, and Radio Buttons

This chapter discusses three types of Swing buttons: toggle buttons, check boxes, and radio buttons, represented by the JToggleButton, JCheckBox, and JRadioButton classes, respectively.

All three buttons are ultimately extensions of the AbstractButton class, which implements nearly all of the functionality provided by the three classes listed above. See the "Labels and Buttons" chapter beginning on page 361 for more information concerning the AbstractButton class.

JToggleButton

Toggle buttons are buttons that have two states—selected and deselected. The JToggleButton class is the superclass for Swing check boxes and Swing radio buttons.

In addition to its role as the base class for check boxes and radio buttons, the JToggleButton component is useful in its own right. Figure 9-1 shows an applet with a single instance of JToggleButton. The left-hand picture shows the button in its deselected state, and the right-hand picture shows the button after it has been selected.

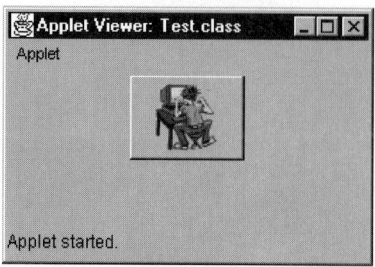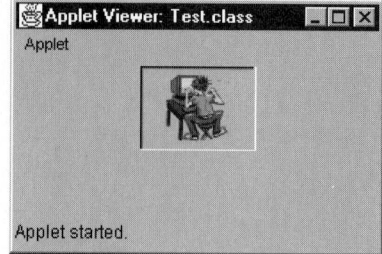

Figure 9-1 Toggle Button

The applet shown in Figure 9-1 is listed in Example 9-1.

Example 9-1   A Simple JToggleButton Example

```
import java.awt.*;
import java.awt.event.*;
import javax.swing.*;

public class Test extends JApplet {
    public Test() {
        Container contentPane = getContentPane();
        ImageIcon icon = new ImageIcon("togglebuttonImage.gif");
        JToggleButton button = new JToggleButton(icon);

        contentPane.setLayout(new FlowLayout());
        contentPane.add(button);
    }
}
```

The applet creates an image icon and an instance of JToggleButton. The layout manager for the applet's content pane is set to an instance of FlowLayout, and the button is added to the applet's content pane.

The JToggleButton class is summarized in Component Summary 9-1.

Component Summary 9-1 JToggleButton

Model(s)	JToggleButton.ToggleButtonModel
UI Delegate(s)	javax.swing.plaf.basic.BasicToggleButtonUI
Renderer(s)	——
Editor(s)	——
Events Fired	ActionEvent/ChangeEvent/ItemEvent
Replacement For	——
Class Diagrams	See Figure 8-12 on page 386

JToggleButton Properties

The `JToggleButton` class has no properties of its own—all properties are inherited from the `AbstractButton` class. See "JButton Events" on page 396 for information concerning `AbstractButton` properties.

JToggleButton Events

Like all Swing buttons, toggle buttons fire action events when activated, property change events when their bound properties are modified, and change events when their state changes. See "JButton Events" on page 396 for more information concerning action events and change events fired by buttons in general, and "Property Change Notification" on page 95 for more information concerning property change events. Additionally, toggle buttons fire item events when they are selected or deselected.

The `ItemListener` interface and `ItemEvent` class reside in the `java.awt.event` package. The `ItemListener` interface is summarized in Interface Summary 9-1.

Interface Summary 9-1   ItemListener

---

public abstract void <u>itemStateChanged</u>(ItemEvent)

`ItemListener.itemStateChanged()` is passed an instance of `ItemEvent`.
The `ItemEvent` class is summarized in Class Summary 9-1.

Class Summary 9-1   ItemEvent

Extends: java.awt.AWTEvent

Constants

---

public static final int <u>ITEM_FIRST</u>
public static final int <u>ITEM_LAST</u>
public static final int <u>ITEM_STATE_CHANGED</u>

public static final int <u>SELECTED</u>
public static final int <u>DESELECTED</u>

The first group of constants listed above represent valid event IDs for action
events. See the first volume of *Graphic Java* for more information concerning event
IDs. The `SELECTED` and `DESELECTED` constants represent whether the item event
represents the selection or deselection of an item.

Constructors

---

public <u>ItemEvent</u>(ItemSelectable source, int id, Object item, int stateChange)

Item events are constructed with the source of the event, the event ID, the item and the state change. The state change is always either `ItemEvent.SELECTED` or `ItemEvent.DESELECTED`.

Methods

---

public Object <u>getItem</u>()
public ItemSelectable <u>getItemSelectable</u>()
public int <u>getStateChange</u>()
public String <u>paramString</u>()

The `ItemEvent` class provides methods for obtaining a reference to the item, the source of the event, and the state change that the event represents. A `paramString` method that is also provided constructs the string returned from `ItemEvent.toString()`.

The applet shown in Figure 9-2 contains a toggle button that is fitted with an item listener that responds to selection and deselection of the button by updating the applet's status area accordingly.

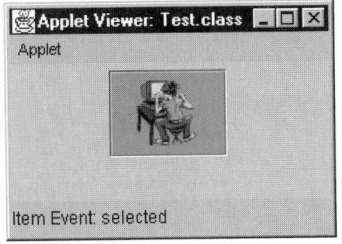 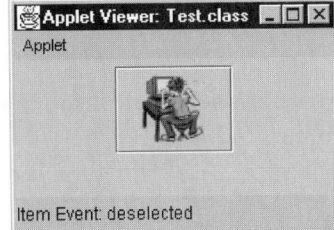

Figure 9-2 Handling JToggleButton Selection and Deselection

The applet shown in Figure 9-2 is listed in Example 9-2.

Example 9-2 Using an Item Listener to Handle Toggle Button Selection

```
import java.awt.*;
import java.awt.event.*;
import javax.swing.*;
import javax.swing.event.*;

public class Test extends JApplet {
    public Test() {
        Container contentPane = getContentPane();
        ImageIcon icon = new ImageIcon("togglebuttonImage.gif");
        final JToggleButton button = new JToggleButton(icon);

        contentPane.setLayout(new FlowLayout());
        contentPane.add(button);

        button.addItemListener(new ItemListener() {
            public void itemStateChanged(ItemEvent e) {
                int state = e.getStateChange();
                String s;

                if(state == ItemEvent.SELECTED) s = "selected";
                else s = "deselected";

                showStatus("Item Event: " + s);
            }
        });
    }
}
```

The item listener determines whether a selection or deselection occurred and
updates the applet's status area.

JToggleButton Class Summaries

The `public` and `protected` variables and methods for `JToggleButton` are
listed in Class Summary 9-2.

Class Summary 9-2   JToggleButton

Extends: JComponent
Implements: javax.accessibility.Accessible

Constructors

---

public <u>JToggleButton</u>()
public <u>JToggleButton</u>(Icon)
public <u>JToggleButton</u>(Icon, boolean selected)
public <u>JToggleButton</u>(String)
public <u>JToggleButton</u>(String, boolean selected)
public <u>JToggleButton</u>(String, Icon)
public <u>JToggleButton</u>(String, Icon, boolean selected)

The JToggleButton class provides seven constructors for instantiating toggle buttons of various configurations. The boolean values passed to the constructors specify whether the button is initially selected—a true value selects the button.

Figure 9-3 shows an applet that creates seven JToggleButton instances.

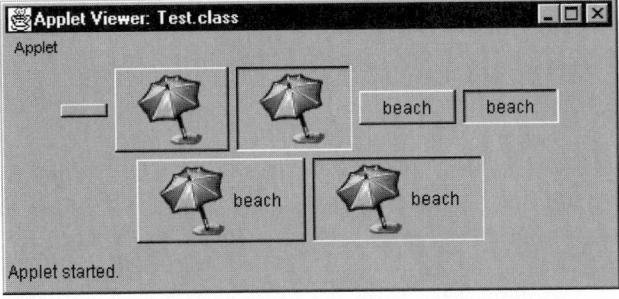

Figure 9-3 Instantiating Instances of JToggleButton

The applet creates the buttons with the `JToggleButton` constructors listed above. Constructors that take a `boolean` argument are invoked with a `true` value, meaning the buttons are initially selected.

The applet shown in Figure 9-3 is listed in Example 9-3.

Example 9-3 Instantiating Toggle Buttons

```
import java.awt.*;
import java.awt.event.*;
import javax.swing.*;

public class Test extends JApplet {
    public Test() {
        Container contentPane = getContentPane();
        Icon icon = new ImageIcon("beach_umbrella.gif");
        JToggleButton button_1 = new JToggleButton(),
                    button_2 = new JToggleButton(icon),
                    button_3 = new JToggleButton(icon, true),
                    button_4 = new  JToggleButton("beach"),
                    button_5 = new  JToggleButton("beach",true),
                    button_6 = new  JToggleButton("beach",icon),
                    button_7 = new  JToggleButton("beach",icon,
                                              true);
        contentPane.setLayout(new FlowLayout());
        contentPane.add(button_1);
        contentPane.add(button_2);
        contentPane.add(button_3);
        contentPane.add(button_4);
        contentPane.add(button_5);
        contentPane.add(button_6);
        contentPane.add(button_7);
    }
}
```

Methods

---

public String <u>paramString</u>()
public AccessibleContext <u>getAccessibleContext</u>()
public String <u>getUIClassID</u>()
public void <u>updateUI</u>()

The `paramString` method is overridden from the `AbstractButton` class and constructs a string that provides information about the toggle button.

The last three methods listed above can be found in most extensions of `JComponent`. Swing lightweight components can return an accessibility context that contains accessibility information for the component, and the class name of their UI delegate. The `updateUI` method is invoked when the component is fitted with a UI delegate.

AWT Compatibility

The `JToggleButton` class is not compatible with an AWT component because the AWT does not provide an analogous component.

Swing Toggle Buttons Are Useful in Their Own Right

Although the main role of the JToggleButton class is as the base class for JCheckBox and JRadioButton, Swing toggle buttons are useful in their own right. The JToggleButton class is a concrete (not abstract) class, and therefore Swing toggle buttons can be instantiated and added to a container, just like any other Swing button.

One use for Swing toggle buttons is depicted in Figure 9-4 on page 430. Toggle buttons can be used in a manner similar to radio buttons by providing a set of mutually exclusive buttons.

Button Groups

Swing allows for mutually exclusive selection behavior within a group of buttons with the `ButtonGroup` class. Buttons are created and added to a button group. Subsequently, selecting a button in the group deselects the previously selected button.

The applet shown in Figure 9-4 illustrates a fairly common user interface technique—a column of buttons that can be selected in a mutually exclusive manner.

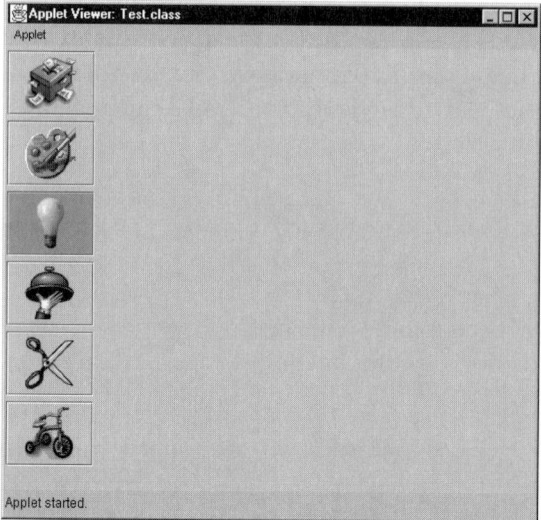

Figure 9-4 Toggle Buttons in a Button Group

The applet uses a container that is an instance of the Box class to lay out the buttons in a column. As the buttons are added to the box, they are also added to a button group.

The applet shown in Figure 9-4 is listed in Example 9-4.

Example 9-4 Using a ButtonGroup for Mutually Exclusive Selection Behavior

```java
import java.awt.*;
import java.awt.event.*;
import javax.swing.*;

public class Test extends JApplet {
    public Test() {
        Container contentPane = getContentPane();
        ButtonGroup group = new ButtonGroup();

        JToggleButton[] buttons = new JToggleButton[] {
            new JToggleButton(new ImageIcon("ballot_box.gif")),
            new JToggleButton(new ImageIcon("palette.gif")),
            new JToggleButton(new ImageIcon("light_bulb1.gif")),
            new JToggleButton(new ImageIcon("dining.gif")),
            new JToggleButton(new ImageIcon("scissors.gif")),
            new JToggleButton(new ImageIcon("tricycle.gif")),
```

```
    };
    Box box = Box.createVerticalBox();

    for(int i=0; i < buttons.length; ++i) {
        group.add(buttons[i]);
        box.add(Box.createVerticalStrut(5));
        box.add(buttons[i]);
    }
    box.add(Box.createVerticalStrut(5));
    contentPane.add(box);
    }
}
```

Notice that the button group is not added to the box container because instances of ButtonGroup are not components.

The public and protected methods for the ButtonGroup class are listed in Class Summary 9-3.

Class Summary 9-3   ButtonGroup

Extends: java.lang.Object
Implements: java.io.Serializable

Constructors

public ButtonGroup()

The no-argument constructor is the only constructor provided by the ButtonGroup class.

Methods

___

public void <u>add</u>(AbstractButton)
public void <u>remove</u>(AbstractButton)
public Enumeration <u>getElements</u>()

public ButtonModel <u>getSelection</u>()
public void <u>setSelected</u>(ButtonModel, boolean)
public boolean <u>isSelected</u>(ButtonModel)

The first group of methods listed above are used for adding and removing buttons from the button group and for obtaining an enumeration of the buttons that are currently in the group.

The getSelection method returns the selected button model. Initially, the getSelection method returns null until one of the buttons in the group is selected. The setSelected method can be used to select or deselect, depending upon the boolean argument, one of the buttons in the group. The isSelected method can be used to determine if a button in the group is selected.

Check Boxes

Check boxes are also two-state buttons that typically display text and have a visual indicator as to whether the check box is currently selected or deselected. Check boxes are usually displayed in groups but normally do not exhibit mutually exclusive selection behavior.

Figure 9-5 shows an applet that contains a set of four check boxes that could be used to select printing options. Whenever a check box is selected or deselected, the applet updates its status bar with the current status of each check box.

Figure 9-5 Check Boxes

The applet creates an instance of PrintOptionsPanel that is added to the applet's content pane.

```
public class Test extends JApplet {
    public void init() {
        Container contentPane = getContentPane();
        contentPane.add(new PrintOptionsPanel(this),
                        BorderLayout.CENTER);
    }
}
```

The PrintOptionsPanel is an extension of JPanel that contains the check boxes. The constructor for PrintOptionsPanel is passed a reference to the applet so that it can update the applet's status bar. The constructor creates the check boxes and adds them to the panel.

```
class PrintOptionsPanel extends JPanel {
    JCheckBox oddPages, evenPages, collate, lastFirst;
    Listener  listener = new Listener();
    JApplet   applet;

    public PrintOptionsPanel(JApplet applet) {
        this.applet = applet;
        oddPages  = new JCheckBox("Odd Pages");
        evenPages = new JCheckBox("Even Pages");
        collate   = new JCheckBox("Collate");
        lastFirst = new JCheckBox("Last Page First");

        oddPages.addItemListener (listener);
        evenPages.addItemListener(listener);
        collate.addItemListener   (listener);
        lastFirst.addItemListener(listener);
```

```
            add(oddPages);
            add(evenPages);
            add(collate);
            add(lastFirst);
        }
        ...
```

Instances of JCheckBox fire item events whenever they are selected or deselected. The PrintOptionsClass implements an item listener that updates the applet's status bar.

```
        ...
        class Listener implements ItemListener {
            public void itemStateChanged(ItemEvent event) {
                applet.showStatus(
                    "Odd Pages: "  + oddPages.isSelected()  + ",   " +
                    "Even Pages: " + evenPages.isSelected() + ",   " +
                    "Collate: "    + collate.isSelected()   + ",   " +
                    "Last Page First: " + lastFirst.isSelected());
            }
        }
        ...
    }
```

The applet shown in Figure 9-5 is listed in its entirety in Example 9-5.

Example 9-5   Swing Check Boxes in Action

```
    import javax.swing.*;
    import java.awt.*;
    import java.awt.event.*;

    public class Test extends JApplet {
        public void init() {
            Container contentPane = getContentPane();
            contentPane.add(new PrintOptionsPanel(this),
                            BorderLayout.CENTER);
        }
    }
    class PrintOptionsPanel extends JPanel {
        JCheckBox oddPages, evenPages, collate, lastFirst;
        Listener  listener = new Listener();
        JApplet   applet;

        public PrintOptionsPanel(JApplet applet) {
            this.applet = applet;
            oddPages  = new JCheckBox("Odd Pages");
```

```
        evenPages = new JCheckBox("Even Pages");
        collate   = new JCheckBox("Collate");
        lastFirst = new JCheckBox("Last Page First");

        oddPages.addItemListener (listener);
        evenPages.addItemListener(listener);
        collate.addItemListener  (listener);
        lastFirst.addItemListener(listener);

        add(oddPages);
        add(evenPages);
        add(collate);
        add(lastFirst);
    }
    class Listener implements ItemListener {
        public void itemStateChanged(ItemEvent event) {
            applet.showStatus(
                "Odd Pages: "  + oddPages.isSelected()  + ",  " +
                "Even Pages: " + evenPages.isSelected() + ",  " +
                "Collate: "    + collate.isSelected()   + ",  " +
                "Last Page First: " + lastFirst.isSelected());
        }
    }
}
```

The JCheckBox class is summarized in Component Summary 9-2.

Component Summary 9-2   JCheckBox

Model(s)	JToggleButton.ToggleButtonModel
UI Delegate(s)	javax.swing.plaf.basic.BasicCheckBoxUI
Renderer(s)	——
Editor(s)	——
Events Fired	ActionEvent/ChangeEvent/ItemEvent
Replacement For	java.awt.CheckBox
Class Diagrams	See Figure 8-12 on page 386

JCheckBox Properties

The JCheckBox class has no properties of its own—all properties are inherited from the AbstractButton class.

JCheckBox Events

Like all Swing buttons, check boxes fire action events when activated, property change events when their bound properties are modified, and change events when their state changes. See "JButton Events" on page 396 for more information concerning action events and change events fired by buttons in general, and "Property Change Notification" on page 95 for more information concerning property change events. Additionally, check boxes fire item events when they are selected or deselected. See Example 9-5 on page 434 for an example of handling checkbox selection and deselection with an item listener.

JCheckBox Class Summaries

The JCheckBox class is summarized in Class Summary 9-4.

Class Summary 9-4   JCheckBox

Extends: JToggleButton
Implements: javax.accessibility.Accessible

Constructors

---

public JCheckBox()
public JCheckBox(Icon)
public JCheckBox(Icon, boolean selected)

public <u>JCheckBox</u>(String)
public <u>JCheckBox</u>(String, boolean selected)
public <u>JCheckBox</u>(String, Icon)
public <u>JCheckBox</u>(String, Icon, boolean selected)

`JCheckBox` provides a set of constructors that are identical to those found in the `JToggleButton` and `JRadioButton` classes; instances of `JCheckBox` can be constructed with any combination of text and icon. Additionally, the selected state of the check box can be specified at construction time.

Figure 9-6 shows an applet that creates seven check boxes of various configurations.

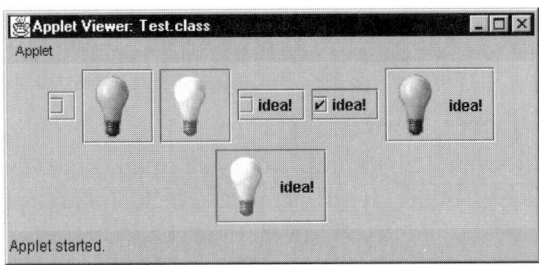

Figure 9-6 Instantiating Check Boxes

The applet shown in Figure 9-6 is listed in Example 9-6.

Example 9-6 Instantiating Check Boxes

```
import java.awt.*;
import java.awt.event.*;
import javax.swing.*;

public class Test extends JApplet {
    public Test() {
        Container contentPane = getContentPane();
        Icon icon = new ImageIcon("bulb.gif");

        JCheckBox[] checkboxes = new JCheckBox[] {
                new JCheckBox(),
                new JCheckBox(icon),
                new JCheckBox(icon, true),
                new JCheckBox("idea!"),
                new JCheckBox("idea!",true),
```

```
            new JCheckBox("idea!",icon),
            new JCheckBox("idea!",icon, true)
    };
    contentPane.setLayout(new FlowLayout());

    for(int i=0; i < checkboxes.length; ++i) {
        checkboxes[i].setBorderPainted(true);
        contentPane.add(checkboxes[i]);

        if(checkboxes[i].getIcon() != null) {
            checkboxes[i].setSelectedIcon(
                new ImageIcon("bulb_bright.gif"));
        }
    }
}
}
```

By default, check boxes do not paint their border. The applet listed above explicitly enables border painting for each of the check boxes so that it is apparent where one check box ends and the next begins.

If an instance of JCheckBox is instantiated without an icon, a small control is added to the check box to indicate whether the check box is selected. If an image is specified for instance of JCheckBox, it is assumed that the check box will be fitted with a selected image to indicate the selected state of the check box, and no control is added to check box.[1] As a result, the applet sets the selected image for each check box that has a null image.

Methods

---

public String paramString()
public AccessibleContext getAccessibleContext()
public String getUIClassID()
public void updateUI()

The paramString method is overridden from the AbstractButton class and constructs a string that provides information about the check box.

---

1. This behavior is common among all the standard look and feels.

The last three methods listed above can be found in most extensions of `JComponent`. Swing lightweight components can return an accessibility context that contains accessibility information for the component, and the class name of their UI delegate. The `updateUI` method is invoked when the component is fitted with a UI delegate.

Swing Tip ...

Explicitly Set Selected Icons for Check Boxes That Have an Image

If a Swing check box has an image, the check box will be drawn without a control to specify whether or not check box is selected. Therefore, if a check box with an image is selected, there is no visual indicator for selection. As result, it is best to explicitly set a selected icon for check boxes that have an image.

The same advice also applies for Swing radio buttons.

AWT Compatibility

`JCheckBox` is nearly source code compatible with `java.awt.Checkbox`. `JCheckBox` provides `getLabel` and `setLabel` methods for the sole purpose of maintaining compatibility with `java.awt.Checkbox`. Both `JCheckBox` and `java.awt.Checkbox` fire item events when they are selected or deselected.

`JCheckBox` deviates from the `java.awt.Checkbox` API in two areas. First, only AWT check boxes can be added to an instance of `java.awt.CheckboxGroup`, whereas any Swing button can be added to an instance of `swing.ButtonGroup`. Second, AWT check boxes are selected by invoking a `setState` method, which is passed a `boolean` value. Swing check boxes, on the other hand, are selected by invoking the `AbstractButton.setSelected` method. Notice that the Swing implementation is deliberately more general than that of the AWT.

Radio Buttons

Radio buttons and checkbox boxes are nearly identical, except for the control they display to depict their selection status. Additionally, radio buttons are almost always used to present an array of mutually exclusive options, meaning they are typically placed in a button group, whereas check boxes are typically used for choices that are not mutually exclusive.

Figure 9-7 shows an applet that contains two radio buttons that could be used to select a range of pages to be printed. The two radio buttons contained in the applet are mutually exclusive; when one of the radio buttons is selected, the other is deselected. When the "Print All" button is selected, the labels and text fields are disabled; selecting the "Print Range" button enables the labels and text fields so that a range of pages can be specified.

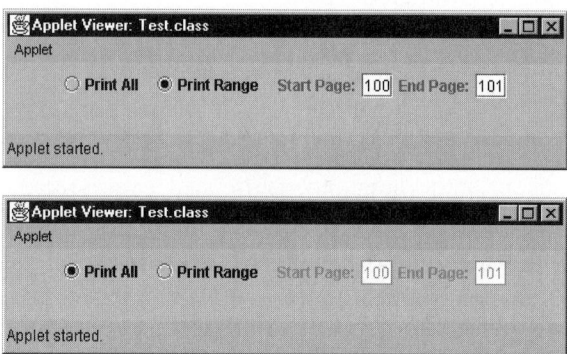

Figure 9-7 Radio Buttons

The applet contains an instance of `PrintRangePanel`, which is passed the start and end pages for the range of pages to be printed.

```
public class Test extends JApplet {
    public void init() {
        Container contentPane = getContentPane();
        contentPane.add(new PrintRangePanel(100, 101));
    }
}
```

The `PrintRangePanel` is an extension of `JPanel` that contains the radio
buttons, labels, and text fields. The `PrintRangePanel` constructor instantiates
the components and also creates an instance of `ButtonGroup`, to which the radio
buttons are subsequently added.

```
class PrintRangePanel extends JPanel {
    JRadioButton printAll, printRange;
    JLabel startPage, endPage;
    JTextField startField, endField;

    public PrintRangePanel(int start, int end) {
        ButtonGroup group = new ButtonGroup();

        printAll   = new JRadioButton("Print All");
        printRange = new JRadioButton("Print Range");

        . . .

        add(printAll)   add(printRange);
        add(startPage)  add(startField);
        add(endPage)    add(endField);

        printRange.setSelected(true);

        group.add(printAll);
        group.add(printRange);

        . . .
```

Item listeners are added to both radio buttons to enable and disable the labels and
text fields.

```
        . . .
        printRange.addItemListener(new ItemListener() {
            public void itemStateChanged(ItemEvent event) {
                if(printRange.isSelected()) {
                    startField.setEnabled(true);
                    endField.setEnabled  (true);
                    startPage.setEnabled (true);
                    endPage.setEnabled   (true);

                    startPage.repaint();
                    endPage.repaint();

                    startField.requestFocus();
                }
            }
        })
        printAll.addItemListener(new ItemListener() {
            public void itemStateChanged(ItemEvent event) {
```

```
                     if(printAll.isSelected()) {
                         startField.setEnabled(false);
                         endField.setEnabled   (false);
                         startPage.setEnabled  (false);
                         endPage.setEnabled     (false);

                         startPage.repaint();
                         endPage.repaint();
                     }
                 }
             })
         }
```

Note: *Due to a bug in Swing 1.1 FCS, labels must be repainted after they are enabled or disabled.*

The applet shown in Figure 9-7 is listed in Example 9-7.

Example 9-7 Radio Buttons in Action

```java
import java.awt.*;
import java.awt.event.*;
import javax.swing.*;

public class Test extends JApplet {
    public void init() {
        Container contentPane = getContentPane();
        contentPane.add(new PrintRangePanel(100, 101));
    }
}
class PrintRangePanel extends JPanel {
    JRadioButton printAll, printRange;
    JLabel startPage, endPage;
    JTextField OnstartField, endField;

    public PrintRangePanel(int start, int end) {
        ButtonGroup group= new ButtonGroup();

        printAll   = new JRadioButton("Print All");
        printRange = new JRadioButton("Print Range");

        startPage = new JLabel("Start Page:");
        endPage   = new JLabel("End Page:");

        startField = new JTextField(Integer.toString(start));
        endField   = new JTextField(Integer.toString(end));
```

```
            add(printAll)    add(printRange);
            add(startPage)  add(startField);
            add(endPage)     add(endField);

            printRange.setSelected(true);

            group.add(printAll);
            group.add(printRange);

            printRange.addItemListener(new ItemListener() {
                public void itemStateChanged(ItemEvent event) {
                    if(printRange.isSelected()) {
                        startField.setEnabled(true);
                        endField.setEnabled  (true);
                        startPage.setEnabled (true);
                        endPage.setEnabled   (true);

                        startPage.repaint();
                        endPage.repaint();

                        startField.requestFocus();
                    }
                }
            })
            printAll.addItemListener(new ItemListener() {
                public void itemStateChanged(ItemEvent event) {
                    if(printAll.isSelected()) {
                        startField.setEnabled(false);
                        endField.setEnabled  (false);
                        startPage.setEnabled (false);
                        endPage.setEnabled   (false);

                        startPage.repaint();
                        endPage.repaint();
                    }
                }
            })
        }
    }
```

The JRadioButton class is summarized in Component Summary 9-3.

Component Summary 9-3   JRadioButton

Model(s)	JToggleButton.ToggleButtonModel
UI Delegate(s)	javax.swing.plaf.basic.BasicRadioButtonUI
Renderer(s)	——
Editor(s)	——
Events Fired	ActionEvent/ChangeEvent/ItemEvent
Replacement For	java.awt.CheckBox
Class Diagrams	See Figure 8-12 on page 386

JRadioButton Properties

The JRadioButton class has no properties of its own—all properties are inherited from the AbstractButton class.

JRadioButton Events

Like all Swing buttons, radio buttons fire action events when activated, property change events when their bound properties are modified, and change events when their state changes. See "JButton Events" on page 396 for more information concerning action events and change events fired by buttons in general, and "Property Change Notification" on page 95 for more information concerning property change events. Additionally, radio buttons fire item events when they are selected or deselected. See Example 9-7 on page 442 for an example of handling radio button selection and deselection with an item listener.

JRadioButton Class Summaries

The JRadioButton class is summarized in Class Summary 9-5.

Class Summary 9-5   JRadioButton

Extends: JToggleButton

Implements: javax.accessiblity.Accessible

Constructors

---

public JRadioButton()
public JRadioButton(Icon)
public JRadioButton(Icon, boolean selected)
public JRadioButton(String)
public JRadioButton(String, boolean selected)
public JRadioButton(String, Icon)
public JRadioButton(String, Icon, boolean selected)

Like JToggleButton and JCheckBox, the constructors for JRadioButton allow radio buttons to be constructed with any combination of text and icon and selected state. The applet shown in Figure 9-8 is nearly identical to the one shown in Figure 9-6 on page 437, except that radio buttons are used instead of check boxes.

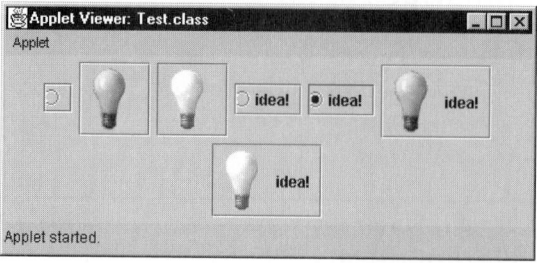

Figure 9-8 Instantiating Radio Buttons

The applet shown in Figure 9-8 is listed in Example 9-8.

Example 9-8 Instantiating Radio Buttons

```
import java.awt.*;
import java.awt.event.*;
import javax.swing.*;

public class Test extends JApplet {
    public Test() {
        Container contentPane = getContentPane();
        Icon icon = new ImageIcon("bulb.gif");
        JRadioButton[] radioButtons = new JRadioButton[] {
                new JRadioButton(),
                new JRadioButton(icon),
                new JRadioButton(icon, true),
                new JRadioButton("idea!"),
                new JRadioButton("idea!",true),
                new JRadioButton("idea!",icon),
                new JRadioButton("idea!",icon, true)
        };
        contentPane.setLayout(new FlowLayout());

        for(int i=0; i < radioButtons.length; ++i) {
            radioButtons[i].setBorderPainted(true);
            contentPane.add(radioButtons[i]);

            if(radioButtons[i].getIcon() != null) {
                radioButtons[i].setSelectedIcon(
                    new ImageIcon("bulb_bright.gif"));
            }
        }
    }
}
```

As is the case for checkbox boxes, radio buttons that have a non-null icon do not display a control for selecting and deselecting the radio button. As a result, a selected icon is set for the radio buttons that have a non-null icon.

Methods

---

public String <u>paramString</u>()
public AccessibleContext <u>getAccessibleContext</u>()
public String <u>getUIClassID</u>()
public void <u>updateUI</u>()

The `paramString` method is overridden from the `AbstractButton` class and constructs a string that provides information about the radio button.

The last three methods listed above can be found in most extensions of `JComponent`. Swing lightweight components can return an accessibility context that contains accessibility information for the component, and the class name of their UI delegate. The `updateUI` method is invoked when the component is fitted with a UI delegate.

AWT Compatibility

The AWT does not provide a radio button component—the AWT's checkbox component pulls double duty as both a check box and radio button. If AWT check boxes are added to a checkbox group, they become radio buttons.

Since Swing radio buttons are nearly identical to Swing check boxes except for the selection control, AWT compatibility issues for check boxes and radio buttons are the same—see "AWT Compatibility" on page 439 for checkbox AWT compatibility issues.

Parting Shots

Swing toggle buttons, check boxes, and radio buttons are all thin veneers layered on top of the `AbstractButton` class. `JToggleButton`, `JCheckBox`, and `JRadioButton` are nothing more than a handful of constructors and methods that return information about component's UI delegate.

Swing implementations of toggle buttons, check boxes, and radio buttons are considerably more robust than the AWT's `CheckBox` class, which serves as a check box/radio button combination. Swing buttons can display both text and/or an image, whereas AWT buttons can only display text. Swing's `ButtonGroup` class is similar in spirit to the AWT's `CheckboxGroup` class—both provide mutually exclusive selection behavior; however, the AWT's `CheckBoxGroup` only works with AWT check boxes, whereas Swing's `ButtonGroup` works with all types of Swing buttons.

CHAPTER
10

Menus and Toolbars

Menus and toolbars are staples of modern user interfaces, and Swing provides full support for both. Swing includes components for menus—both menus that reside in menu bars and popup menus—in addition to components for menu items including checkbox and radio button menu items.

Swing also provides a toolbar component that contains a row or column of buttons, depending upon the toolbar's orientation. Toolbars are typically used to provide easy access to common features. It is not uncommon for menu bars and toolbars to provide access to the same set of features, in addition to keyboard shortcuts that provide access to the same functionality. Toolbars can also float, which allows them to be dragged within a window or into a window of their own.

Swing menus and menu items are buttons by virtue of the fact that `JMenuItem` extends `AbstractButton`, and `JMenu` extends `JMenuItem`, as shown in Figure 10-1. Therefore, Swing menus and menu items inherit the ability to contain text and/or an icon, display rollover icons and mnemonics, etc.

Figure 10-1 shows the ancestry of `JMenuItem` and `JMenu` all the way back to `java.awt.Container` to emphasize that menus and menu items are also perfectly capable containers. Any type of component, from a label that contains an animated GIF to an instance of `JTree`, can be added to a menu or menu item.

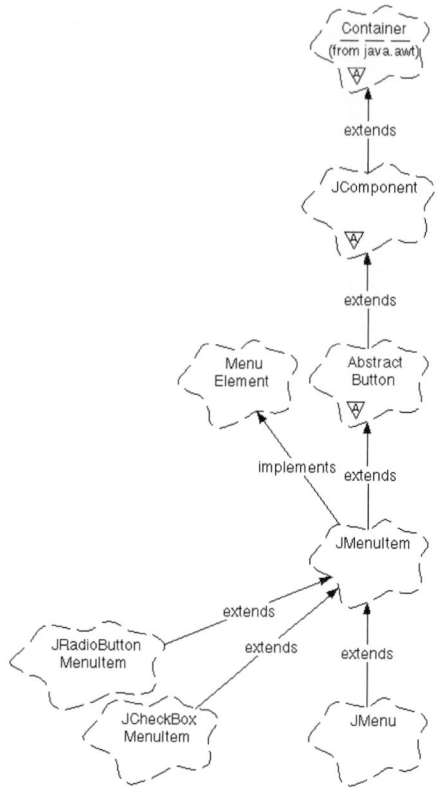

Figure 10-1 Menu Class Hierarchy

Menus and menu items also implement the `MenuElement` interface, for participation in menu event handling. The `MenuElement` interface is discussed in "Menu Elements" on page 518.

Toolbars and popup menus both extend the `JComponent` class, which means that arbitrary components can be added to a toolbar or popup menus.

The following components are discussed in this chapter:

- `JMenuItem`
- `JCheckBoxMenuItem`
- `JRadioButtonMenuItem`
- `JMenu`
- `JPopupMenu`
- `JMenuBar`
- `JToolBar`

Menus, Menu Bars, and Toolbars

Menus and toolbars are closely related because they both typically provide access to much of the same functionality. As a result, one or more actions can be shared by multiple menu bars and toolbars. See "Actions" on page 235 for a general discussion of actions and "Actions as a Central Point of Control" on page 238 for an example of sharing actions among components.

Additionally, because menus, menu bars, and toolbars are all extensions of the `JComponent` class, they are all lightweight containers. As a result, any type of component can be added to a Swing menu, menu bar, or toolbar.

The applet shown in Figure 10-2 illustrates sharing actions between a toolbar and a menu bar. The applet also adds arbitrary components, in the form of Swing radio buttons, to a toolbar, menu bar, and menu.

The upper-left picture in Figure 10-2 shows a radio button contained in a menu bar displaying a rollover image. The upper-right picture shows another radio button in the toolbar displaying its rollover image. The bottom pictures show the `File` menu and illustrates the fact that a radio button can be added to menus as well as to menu bars and toolbars.

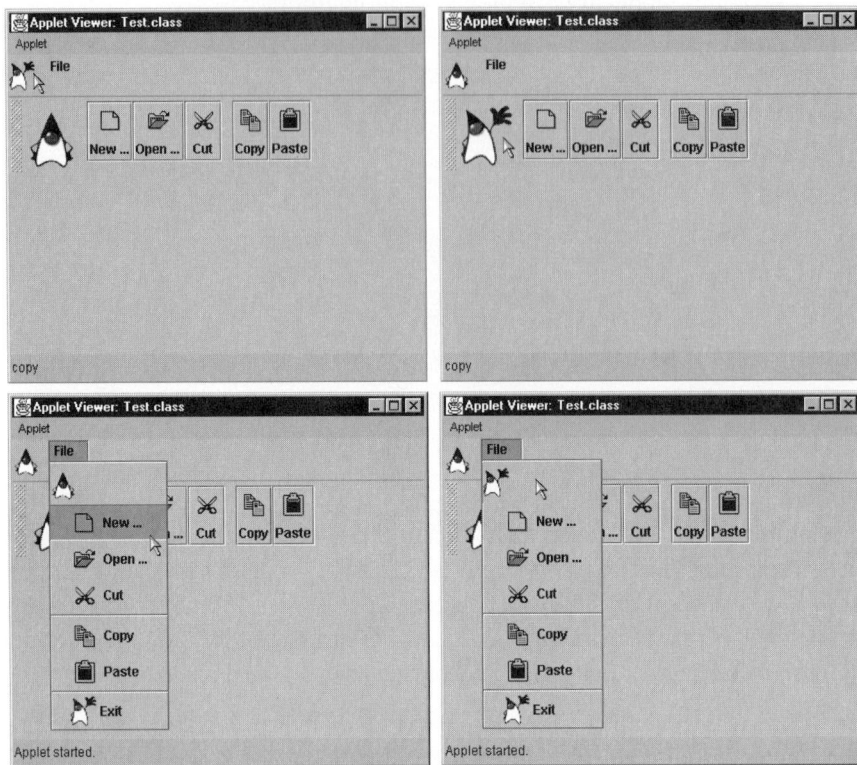

Figure 10-2 Menus and Toolbars

The applet creates a set of actions that are shared by the toolbar and File menu, and adds the actions to both the menu and toolbar. The exit action is added only to the menu bar, as it is considered questionable design to include a button that exits an application in a toolbar. Before the actions are added to the toolbar and File menu, radio buttons are added to the menu bar, toolbar, and File menu. Each radio button is fitted with a rollover icon.

```java
public class Test extends JApplet {
    ...
    public void init() {
        Container contentPane = getContentPane();
        Action[] actions = {
                    new NewAction(),
                    new OpenAction(),
                    new CutAction(),
                    new CopyAction(),
```

```
                    new PasteAction(),
                    new ExitAction()
          };
          JToolBar toolbar = new JToolBar();
          JMenuBar menubar = new JMenuBar();
          JMenu fileMenu = new JMenu("File");

          JRadioButton
              menubarDuke = new JRadioButton(dukeStandingSmall),
              menuDuke = new JRadioButton(dukeStandingSmall),
              toolbarDuke = new JRadioButton(dukeStanding);

          menuDuke.setRolloverIcon(dukeWavingSmall);
          menubarDuke.setRolloverIcon(dukeWavingSmall);
          toolbarDuke.setRolloverIcon(dukeWaving);

          menubar.add(menubarDuke);
          toolbar.add(toolbarDuke);
          fileMenu.add(menuDuke);

          . . .

          for(int i=0; i < actions.length; ++i) {
              fileMenu.add(actions[i]);

              if(i != actions.length-1) // all but exit action
                  toolbar.add(actions[i]);

              if(i == 2 || i == actions.length-2){
                  toolbar.addSeparator();
                  fileMenu.addSeparator();
              }
          }
          menubar.add(fileMenu);

          contentPane.add(toolbar, BorderLayout.NORTH);
          getRootPane().setMenuBar(menubar);
      }
      . . .
}
```

The applet shown in Figure 10-2 is listed in its entirety in Example 10-1.

Example 10-1 A Menu Bar and a Toolbar in a JRootPane

```
import javax.swing.*;
import java.awt.*;
import java.awt.event.*;

public class Test extends JApplet {
```

```
Icon
    dukeStanding = new ImageIcon("duke_standing.gif"),
    dukeWaving = new ImageIcon("duke_waving.gif"),
    dukeStandingSmall =
            new ImageIcon("duke_standing_small.gif"),
    dukeWavingSmall = new ImageIcon("duke_waving_small.gif");

public void init() {
    Container contentPane = getContentPane();
    Action[] actions = {
                    new NewAction(),
                    new OpenAction(),
                    new CutAction(),
                    new CopyAction(),
                    new PasteAction(),
                    new ExitAction()
    };
    JToolBar toolbar = new JToolBar();
    JMenuBar menubar = new JMenuBar();
    JMenu fileMenu = new JMenu("File");

    JRadioButton
        menubarDuke = new JRadioButton(dukeStandingSmall),
        menuDuke = new JRadioButton(dukeStandingSmall),
        toolbarDuke = new JRadioButton(dukeStanding);

    menuDuke.setRolloverIcon(dukeWavingSmall);
    menubarDuke.setRolloverIcon(dukeWavingSmall);
    toolbarDuke.setRolloverIcon(dukeWaving);

    menubar.add(menubarDuke);
    toolbar.add(toolbarDuke);
    fileMenu.add(menuDuke);

    for(int i=0; i < actions.length; ++i) {
        fileMenu.add(actions[i]);

        if(i != actions.length-1)
            toolbar.add(actions[i]);

        if(i == 2 || i == actions.length-2){
            toolbar.addSeparator();
            fileMenu.addSeparator();
        }
    }
    menubar.add(fileMenu);

    contentPane.add(toolbar, BorderLayout.NORTH);
    getRootPane().setMenuBar(menubar);
}
class NewAction extends AbstractAction {
    public NewAction() {
```

```java
            super("New ...", new ImageIcon("new.gif"));
        }
        public void actionPerformed(ActionEvent event) {
            showStatus("new");
        }
    }
    class OpenAction extends AbstractAction {
        public OpenAction() {
            super("Open ...", new ImageIcon("open.gif"));
        }
        public void actionPerformed(ActionEvent event) {
            showStatus("open");
        }
    }
    class CutAction extends AbstractAction {
        public CutAction() {
            super("Cut", new ImageIcon("cut.gif"));
        }
        public void actionPerformed(ActionEvent event) {
            showStatus("cut");
        }
    }
    class CopyAction extends AbstractAction {
        public CopyAction() {
            super("Copy", new ImageIcon("copy.gif"));
        }
        public void actionPerformed(ActionEvent event) {
            showStatus("copy");
        }
    }
    class PasteAction extends AbstractAction {
        public PasteAction() {
            super("Paste", new ImageIcon("paste.gif"));
        }
        public void actionPerformed(ActionEvent event) {
            showStatus("paste");
        }
    }
    class ExitAction extends AbstractAction {
        public ExitAction() {
            super("Exit");
            putValue(Action.SMALL_ICON, dukeWavingSmall);
        }
        public void actionPerformed(ActionEvent event) {
            System.exit(0);
        }
    }
}
```

Menus and Popup Menus

Swing menus are buttons that display a popup menu when they are activated. If a menu resides in a menu bar, it is referred to as a top-level menu, whereas menus that are contained in a menu are referred to as pull-right menus. (Pull-right menus are also referred to as cascading menus; for more on pull-right menus see "Pull-right Menus" on page 501)

The applet shown in Figure 10-3 contains a menu bar with two menus—a top-level menu and a pull-right menu. When the File menu is activated, a popup menu is displayed that contains menu items for the File menu. When the pull-right menu item is activated, another popup menu that contains check box menu items is displayed.

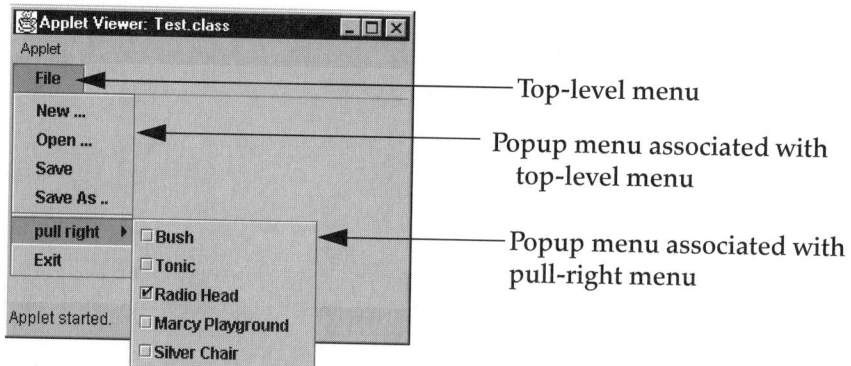

Figure 10-3 A File Menu

The applet shown in Figure 10-3 is listed in Example 10-2.

Example 10-2 A Simple Menu Example

```
import javax.swing.*;
import java.awt.*;
import java.awt.event.*;

public class Test extends JApplet {
    public void init() {
        JMenuBar mb = new JMenuBar();
```

```
JMenu fileMenu = new JMenu("File");
JMenu pullRightMenu = new JMenu("pull right");

fileMenu.add("New ...");
fileMenu.add("Open ...");
fileMenu.add("Save");
fileMenu.add("Save As ..");
fileMenu.addSeparator();
fileMenu.add(pullRightMenu);
fileMenu.add("Exit");

pullRightMenu.add(new JCheckBoxMenuItem("Bush"));
pullRightMenu.add(new JCheckBoxMenuItem("Tonic"));
pullRightMenu.add(new JCheckBoxMenuItem("Radio Head"));
pullRightMenu.add(new JCheckBoxMenuItem(
                              "Marcy Playground"));
pullRightMenu.add(new JRadioButtonMenuItem(
                              "Silver Chair"));
mb.add(fileMenu);
setJMenuBar(mb);
    }
}
```

The applet creates an instance of JMenuBar and two instances of JMenu. Items are added to menus by invocation of JMenu.add(String). The File menu is subsequently added to the menu bar, and the menu bar is attached to the applet by a call to JApplet.setJMenuBar(JMenuBar).

Notice that the applet shown in Figure 10-3 does not handle menu events; for example, activating the "Exit" menu item will not exit the applet. Handling menu events is discussed throughout the rest of this chapter. (To exit the applet listed in Figure 10-3, click the close button in the applet's window.)

JMenuItem

Menu items are buttons by virtue of the fact that JMenuItem extends AbstractButton, and therefore menu items can display text and an icon. Menu items also inherit the ability to fire action events when they are activated. Because AbstractButton ultimately extends java.awt.Container, menu items can also contain arbitrary types of AWT and Swing components.

Figure 10-4 shows an applet that creates five menu items.

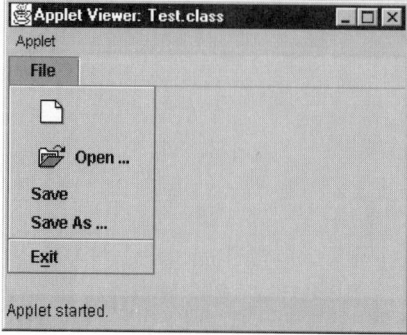

Figure 10-4 Instantiating Instances of JMenuItem

The applet instantiates two icons, a menu bar, and a File menu with five menu items. After the menu items are created, they are added to the File menu.

```
public class Test extends JApplet {
    public void init() {
        Icon newIcon = new ImageIcon("new.gif",
                                "Create a new document");
        Icon openIcon = new ImageIcon("open.gif",
                                "Open an existing document");

        JMenuBar mb = new JMenuBar();
        JMenu fileMenu = new JMenu("File");

        JMenuItem newItem = new JMenuItem(newIcon);
        JMenuItem openItem = new JMenuItem("Open ...", openIcon);
        JMenuItem saveItem = new JMenuItem("Save");
        JMenuItem saveAsItem = new JMenuItem("Save As ...");
        JMenuItem exitItem = new JMenuItem("Exit", 'x');

        fileMenu.add(newItem);
        fileMenu.add(openItem);
        fileMenu.add(saveItem);
        fileMenu.add(saveAsItem);
        fileMenu.addSeparator();
        fileMenu.add(exitItem);
        ...
```

The applet responds to activation of menu items by displaying a string that identifies the menu item that was activated. Each menu item is fitted with an instance of `MenuItemListener`, the menu is subsequently added to the menu bar, and the menu bar is attached to the applet.

```
...
MenuItemListener listener = new MenuItemListener(this);

newItem.addActionListener(listener);
openItem.addActionListener(listener);
saveItem.addActionListener(listener);
saveAsItem.addActionListener(listener);
...

mb.add(fileMenu);
setJMenuBar(mb);
    }
}
```

The `MenuItemListener` class implements the `ActionListener` interface by implementing the `actionPerformed` method to obtain a reference to the source of the event, which is an instance of `JMenuItem`, and a reference to the item's icon. If the menu item that was activated has a non-`null` icon, the icon's description is shown in the applet's status area. If the menu item does not have an icon, the item's text is shown in the applet's status area.

```
class MenuItemListener implements ActionListener {
    public void actionPerformed(ActionEvent e) {
        JMenuItem item = (JMenuItem)e.getSource();
        ImageIcon icon = (ImageIcon)item.getIcon();

        if(icon != null)
            System.out.println(icon.getDescription());
        else
            System.out.println(item.getText());
    }
}
```

The applet shown in Figure 10-4 is listed in its entirety in Example 10-3.

Example 10-3 Instantiating Menu Items

```
import javax.swing.*;
import java.awt.*;
import java.awt.event.*;

public class Test extends JApplet {
    public void init() {
        Icon newIcon = new ImageIcon("new.gif",
                                "Create a new document");
        Icon openIcon = new ImageIcon("open.gif",
                                "Open a existing document");

        JMenuBar mb = new JMenuBar();
        JMenu fileMenu = new JMenu("File");
```

```
            JMenuItem newItem = new JMenuItem(newIcon);
            JMenuItem openItem = new JMenuItem("Open ...", openIcon);
            JMenuItem saveItem = new JMenuItem("Save");
            JMenuItem saveAsItem = new JMenuItem("Save As ...");
            JMenuItem exitItem = new JMenuItem("Exit", 'x');

            fileMenu.add(newItem);
            fileMenu.add(openItem);
            fileMenu.add(saveItem);
            fileMenu.add(saveAsItem);
            fileMenu.addSeparator();
            fileMenu.add(exitItem);

            MenuItemListener listener = new MenuItemListener(this);

            newItem.addActionListener(listener);
            openItem.addActionListener(listener);
            saveItem.addActionListener(listener);
            saveAsItem.addActionListener(listener);

            exitItem.addActionListener(new ActionListener() {
                public void actionPerformed(ActionEvent e) {
                    System.exit(0);
                }
            });

            mb.add(fileMenu);

            setJMenuBar(mb);
        }
    }
    class MenuItemListener implements ActionListener {
        public void actionPerformed(ActionEvent e) {
            JMenuItem item = (JMenuItem)e.getSource();
            ImageIcon icon = (ImageIcon)item.getIcon();

            if(icon != null)
                System.out.println(icon.getDescription());
            else
                System.out.println(item.getText());
        }
    }
```

Menu Item Accelerators and Mnemonics

An accelerator, represented by an instance of `KeyStroke`, can be specified for menu items. Accelerators are similar to mnemonics in that both represent a keyboard shortcut that can be used to invoke an action associated with a menu item. However, a mnemonic is a key that is pressed in conjunction with a `Meta` key defined by a component's look and feel. For example, the applet shown in

Figure 10-4 on page 460 specifies a mnemonic of 'x' for the "Exit" menu item. With the Windows look and feel, the mnemonic must be pressed in conjunction with the ALT key in order to activate the menu item. On the other hand, accelerators are specified by an instance of KeyStroke, which specifies the exact combination of keys that must be pressed to activate the menu item.

To further clarify the use of accelerators and mnemonics for menu items, the application[1] shown in Figure 10-5 specifies mnemonics for the File menu and the Exit menu item and an accelerator for the Exit menu item.

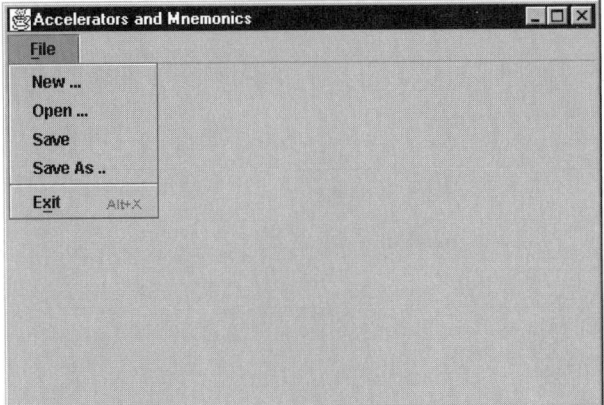

Figure 10-5 Menu Item Mnemonics and Accelerators

Users can exit the application by pressing Meta-F, which activates the File menu, followed by Meta-X, which activates the Exit menu item. Recall that the Meta key is look-and-feel dependent; for example, the Meta key for the Metal look and feel is the ALT key. Exiting the application by pressing Meta-F/Meta-X is a use of mnemonics, which traverses the menus.

Exiting the application can also be accomplished by means of the accelerator associated with the Exit menu item, that is, by pressing ALT-X. Notice that using an accelerator does not traverse menus; instead, an accelerator directly invokes the action associated with a menu item.

The accelerator is specified by obtaining a reference to an instance of KeyStroke from the static KeyStroke.getKeyStroke method, and the keystroke is passed to the JMenuItem.setAccelerator method. The key stroke specifies that the 'x' key must be pressed in conjunction with the ALT key.

---

1. Due to an AWT focus bug, the application shown in Figure 10-5 will not work properly as an applet.

The mnemonics are specified by use of the `AbstractButton.setMnemonics` method. For illustration, the mnemonic for the File menu is specified with a character by invoking `AbstractButton.setMnemonic(char)`, whereas the mnemonic for the `Exit` menu item is specified with `AbstractButton.setMnemonic(int)`. In general, specifying mnemonics with an `integer` value from the `KeyEvent` class is preferable to specifying a character value because using a constant from the `KeyEvent` class ensures that the mnemonic will work properly for internationalized applets and applications.

```
public class Test extends JFrame {
    public Test() {
        Container contentPane = getContentPane();

        JMenuBar mb = new JMenuBar();
        JMenu fileMenu = new JMenu("File");
        JMenuItem exitItem = new JMenuItem("Exit");

        fileMenu.add("New ...");
        fileMenu.add("Open ...");
        fileMenu.add("Save");
        fileMenu.add("Save As ..");
        fileMenu.addSeparator();
        fileMenu.add(exitItem);

        exitItem.addActionListener(new ActionListener() {
            public void actionPerformed(ActionEvent e) {
                System.exit(0);
            }
        });

        KeyStroke ks = KeyStroke.getKeyStroke(KeyEvent.VK_X,
                                  Event.ALT_MASK);
        exitItem.setAccelerator(ks);

        fileMenu.setMnemonic('F');
        exitItem.setMnemonic(KeyEvent.VK_X);

        mb.add(fileMenu);
        setJMenuBar(mb);
    }
```

The application shown in Figure 10-5 is listed in Example 10-4.

Example 10-4 Menu Items with Mnemonics and Accelerators

```
import javax.swing.*;
import java.awt.*;
import java.awt.event.*;

public class Test extends JFrame {
```

```
public Test() {
    Container contentPane = getContentPane();

    JMenuBar mb = new JMenuBar();
    JMenu fileMenu = new JMenu("File");
    JMenuItem exitItem = new JMenuItem("Exit");

    fileMenu.add("New ...");
    fileMenu.add("Open ...");
    fileMenu.add("Save");
    fileMenu.add("Save As ..");
    fileMenu.addSeparator();
    fileMenu.add(exitItem);

    exitItem.addActionListener(new ActionListener() {
        public void actionPerformed(ActionEvent e) {
            System.exit(0);
        }
    });

    KeyStroke ks = KeyStroke.getKeyStroke(KeyEvent.VK_X,
                                Event.ALT_MASK);
    exitItem.setAccelerator(ks);

    fileMenu.setMnemonic('F');
    exitItem.setMnemonic(KeyEvent.VK_X);

    mb.add(fileMenu);
    setJMenuBar(mb);
}
public static void main(String args[]) {
    GJApp.launch(new Test(),
            "Accelerators and Mnemonics",300,300,450,300);
}
}
```

Swing menu items are represented by the JMenuItem class, which is summarized in Component Summary 10-1.

Component Summary 10-1   JMenuItem

Model(s)	ButtonModel
UI Delegate(s)	swing.plaf.basic.BasicMenuItemUI
Renderer(s)	——

Editor(s)	——
Events Fired	ActionEvent/ChangeEvent/PropertyChangeEvent/ MenuDragMouseEvent
Replacement For	java.awt.MenuItem

Class Diagrams

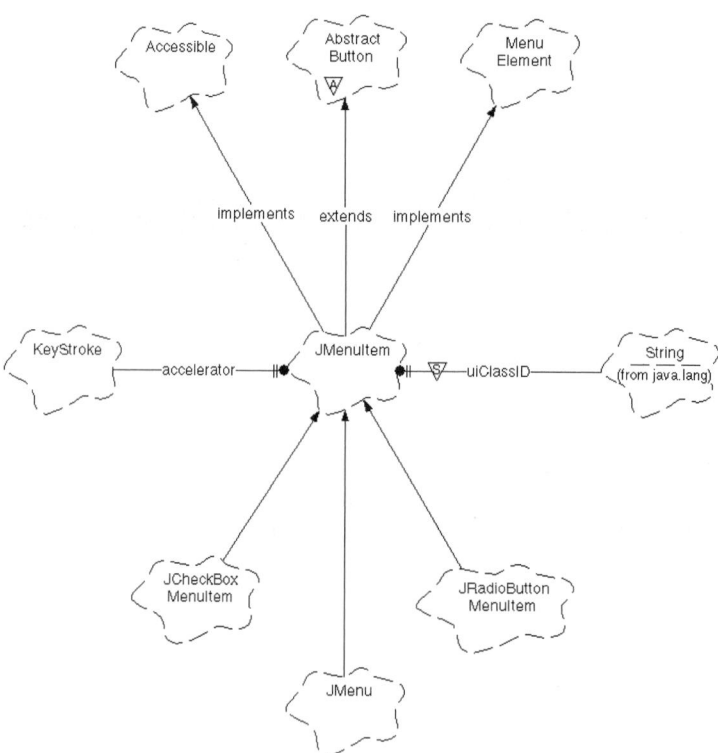

Figure 10-6 JMenuItem Class Diagram

JMenuItem extends AbstractButton and implements the Accessible and MenuElement interfaces. JMenuItem is the superclass for JCheckBoxMenuItem, JRadioButtonMenuItem, and JMenu. The fact that JMenu extends JMenuItem allows menus to be specified as menu items, resulting in pull-right menus.

Because JMenuItem extends AbstractButton, menu items (and menus) can be manipulated in exactly the same fashion as a button. See "JButton" on page 387 for more on the manner in which instances of AbstractButton can be manipulated.

Each instance of JMenuItem can be fitted with an accelerator. Accelerators are keyboard shortcuts that can be used to activate a menu item. Accelerators are represented by an instance of KeyStroke, which allows developers to specify the exact combination of keys that will activate a menu item. For more on key strokes and their use, see "Keystroke Handling" on page 180.

The MenuElement interface and the JMenuItem class are discussed in Class Summary 10-2 on page 473.

Swing Menus and Menu Items Are Buttons

It is important to keep in mind that Swing menus and menu items ultimately extend the AbstractButton class. This means that all of the properties, methods, and events discussed for the AbstractButton class—see "JButton" on page 387—apply to menus and menu items as well. For example, by default the horizontal text position for Swing menus is set to SwingConstants.LEFT, as can be seen from Figure 10-4 on page 460. Because the JMenu class extends AbstractButton, the default horizontal text position for a menu may be changed with AbstractButton.setVerticalTextPosition().

JMenuItem Properties

Aside from inherited properties, the JMenuItem class has a single property of its own—the accelerator property, which is used in Example 10-4 on page 464. For a listing of the properties JMenuItem inherits from AbstractButton, see Table 8-3 on page 391.

JMenuItem Events

Like all Swing buttons, menu items fire action events when activated, property change events when their bound properties are modified, and change events when their state changes. See "JButton Events" on page 396 for more information concerning action events and change events fired by buttons in general, and "Property Change Notification" on page 95 for more information concerning property change events. Additionally, menu items fire item events when they are selected or deselected. For more information on handling item events, see "JToggleButton Events" on page 423.

Menu items also fire `MenuDragMouseEvents` when the mouse is dragged over a menu item, and `MenuKeyEvents` when a key is pressed/released/typed while a menu item is armed.

Menu Change Events

The applet shown in Figure 10-7 listens for action events fired by the "Exit" menu item and responds by exiting the applet. The applet also listens to each menu item for change events and prints the action command associated with a menu item when the item is armed. A menu item is armed when it is selected but not activated; for example, the "Open ..." menu item shown in Figure 10-7 is armed.

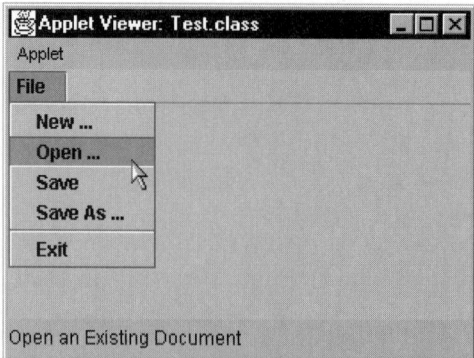

Figure 10-7 Menu Item Change Events

The applet shown in Figure 10-7 is listed in Example 10-5.

Example 10-5 Listening for Menu Item Action and Change Events

```
import javax.swing.*;
import javax.swing.event.*;
import java.awt.*;
import java.awt.event.*;

public class Test extends JApplet {
    public void init() {
        JMenuBar mb = new JMenuBar();
        JMenu fileMenu = new JMenu("File");
        JMenuItem newItem = new JMenuItem("New ..."),
                  openItem = new JMenuItem("Open ..."),
                  saveItem = new JMenuItem("Save"),
                  saveAsItem = new JMenuItem("Save As ..."),
                  exitItem = new JMenuItem("Exit");

        Listener listener = new Listener(this);

        fileMenu.add(newItem);
        fileMenu.add(openItem);
        fileMenu.add(saveItem);
        fileMenu.add(saveAsItem);
        fileMenu.addSeparator();
        fileMenu.add(exitItem);

        newItem.setActionCommand("Create a New Document");
        openItem.setActionCommand("Open an Existing Document");
        saveItem.setActionCommand("Save Document");
        saveAsItem.setActionCommand("Save Document As ...");
        exitItem.setActionCommand("Exit the applet");

        newItem.addChangeListener(listener);
        openItem.addChangeListener(listener);
        saveItem.addChangeListener(listener);
        saveAsItem.addChangeListener(listener);
        exitItem.addChangeListener(listener);

        mb.add(fileMenu);
        setJMenuBar(mb);

        exitItem.addActionListener(new ActionListener() {
            public void actionPerformed(ActionEvent e) {
                System.exit(0);
            }
        });
    }
}
class Listener implements ChangeListener {
    private JApplet applet;
```

```
public Listener(JApplet applet) {
    this.applet = applet;
}
public void stateChanged(ChangeEvent e) {
    JMenuItem b = (JMenuItem)e.getSource();

    if(b.isArmed())
        applet.showStatus(b.getActionCommand());
}
}
```

The applet creates a menu bar, the File menu, and its menu items. The menu items are subsequently added to the File menu, and the action command for each menu item is set. The applet then creates an instance of Listener—an event listener that implements the ChangeListener interface—and the listener is added to each menu item. The exitItem has an action listener added to it that exits the applet when the exitItem fires an ActionEvent.

The Listener class listens for menu item change events and responds by obtaining a reference to the menu item that fired the event. If the menu item is armed, its action command is retrieved and displayed in the applet's status area.

Menu Drag-Mouse Events

When the mouse cursor is dragged over a menu element, instances of MenuDragMouseEvents are fired to MenuDragMouseListeners registered with the menu item in question. The MenuDragMouseListener interface is summarized in Interface Summary 10-1.

Interface Summary 10-1   MenuDragMouseListener

---

public abstract void menuDragMouseDragged(MenuDragMouseEvent)
public abstract void menuDragMouseEntered(MenuDragMouseEvent)
public abstract void menuDragMouseExited(MenuDragMouseEvent)

public abstract void menuDragMouseReleased(MenuDragMouseEvent)

The methods in the first group listed above are invoked when the mouse cursor is dragged over, into, or out of a menu element, respectively. The last method is invoked when the mouse button is released over a menu element.

All of the methods listed above are passed an instance of `MenuDragMouseEvent`, which is summarized in Class Summary 10-1.

Class Summary 10-1   MenuDragMouseEvent

Extends: java.awt.event.MouseEvent

Constructors

---

public MenuDragMouseEvent(Component source, int id, long when, int modifiers, int x,
                int y, int clickCount, boolean popupTrigger, MenuElement[]
                path, MenuSelectionManager mgr)

The `MenuDragMouseEvent` class provides a single constructor that is passed a great deal of information concerning the event, including the modifier keys and click count associated with the event. Developers will rarely, if ever, instantiate instances of `MenuDragMouseEvent`.

Methods

---

public MenuSelectionManager getMenuSelectionManager()
public MenuElement[] getPath()

The `MenuDragMouseEvent` class provides the two methods listed above, which return references to the menu selection manager and an array of menu elements specifying a path to the menu element for which the event occurred.

The menu selection manager is an implementation detail of menu selection, and the getMenuSelectionManager method will rarely be used in practice. The last menu element in the array returned from the getPath method represents the menu element in which the event occurred.

The applet listed in Example 10-5 on page 469 could be rewritten with a menu drag-mouse listener instead of a change listener. The applet would be unchanged except for the Listener class, which could be implemented as follows:

```
class Listener implements MenuDragMouseListener {
    private JApplet applet;
    public Listener(JApplet applet) {
        this.applet = applet;
    }
    public void menuDragMouseEntered(MenuDragMouseEvent e) {
    }
    public void menuDragMouseDragged(MenuDragMouseEvent e) {
        MenuElement[] path = e.getPath();
        MenuElement lastPathElement = path[path.length-1];
        JMenuItem menuItem =
                (JMenuItem)lastPathElement.getComponent();

        applet.showStatus(menuItem.getActionCommand());
    }
    public void menuDragMouseExited(MenuDragMouseEvent e) {
    }
    public void menuDragMouseReleased(MenuDragMouseEvent e) {
    }
}
```

The menuDragMouseDragged method obtains the path to the menu element for which the event occurred with the MenuDragMouseEvent.getPath method and then proceeds to obtain a reference to the menu item. As with the applet listed in Example 10-5 on page 469, the menu item's action command is displayed in the applet's status area.

Note: *As of Swing 1.1 FCS, the* menuDragMouseEntered, menuDragMouseExited, *and* menuDragMouseReleased *methods are never invoked.*

JMenuItem Class Summaries

The `public` and `protected` variables and methods for `JMenuItem` are listed in Class Summary 10-2.

Class Summary 10-2 JMenuItem

Extends: AbstractButton
Implements: javax.accessibility.Accessible, MenuElement

Constructors

---

public JMenuItem()
public JMenuItem(Icon)
public JMenuItem(String)
public JMenuItem(String, Icon)
public JMenuItem(String, int mnemonic)

`JMenuItem` provides five constructors for instantiating menu items with various configurations of strings and icons. The last constructor listed above is passed an `integer` value that specifies a mnemonic for the menu item. Notice that menu items constructed with both a string and an icon cannot specify a mnemonic at the time of construction; however, a mnemonic may be specified after construction by invocation of either `AbstractButton.setMnemonic(int)` or `AbstractButton.setMnemonic(char)`.

The no-argument constructor creates a menu item that has no string or icon. The no-argument constructor is supplied mainly for JavaBeans builder tools.

Methods

Initialization

---

protected void <u>init</u>(String, Icon)

As is typically the case for Swing components, `JMenuItem` implements a
`protected init` method that initializes the component. `JMenuItem.init()`
sets the layout manager for the menu item, sets the text and icon for the item, and
adds a focus listener to the menu item. Extensions of `JMenuItem` are free to
override the `init` method if desired, but in practice the method will rarely be
overridden.

The MenuElement Interface

---

public Component <u>getComponent</u>()
public MenuElement[] <u>getSubElements</u>()
public void <u>menuSelectionChanged</u>(boolean)
public void <u>processKeyEvent</u>(KeyEvent, MenuElement[], MenuSelectionManager)
public void <u>processMouseEvent</u>(MouseEvent, MenuElement[], MenuSelectionManager)

`JMenuItem` implements the `MenuElement` interface, which is defined by the five
methods listed above. The `JMenuItem.processMouseEvent` method fires
`MenuDragMouseEvents` to registered `MenuDragMouseListeners`. See "Menu
Drag-Mouse Events" on page 470 for more information concerning menu drag
mouse events. The `processKeyEvent` method fires `MenuKeyEvents` to register
`MenuKeyListeners`.

`JMenuItem.menuSelectionChanged()` is the only other interesting
`MenuElement` method implemented by `JMenuItem`.
`JMenuItem.menuSelectionChanged()` arms the menu item if the menu item
is included in the selection.

See "Implementing the MenuElement Interface" on page 519 for a discussion of
implementing the `MenuElement` interface.

Accelerators / Arming / Enabling

public KeyStroke getAccelerator()
public void setAccelerator(KeyStroke)

public void setArmed(boolean)
public boolean isArmed()

public void setEnabled(boolean)

The methods listed above can be used to set and get an accelerator for a menu item and to set a menu item's enabled state. Menu items can also be programmatically armed with the `setArmed` method, and the `isArmed` method can be used to determine whether a menu item is armed.

Listeners / Event Firing

public void addMenuDragMouseListener(MenuDragMouseListener)
public void addMenuKeyListener(MenuKeyListener)

public void removeMenuDragMouseListener(MenuDragMouseListener)
public void removeMenuKeyListener(MenuKeyListener)

public void processMenuDragMouseEvent(MenuDragMouseEvent)

protected void fireMenuDragMouseDragged(MenuDragMouseEvent)
protected void fireMenuDragMouseEntered(MenuDragMouseEvent)
protected void fireMenuDragMouseExited(MenuDragMouseEvent)
protected void fireMenuDragMouseReleased(MenuDragMouseEvent)
protected void fireMenuKeyPressed(MenuKeyEvent)
protected void fireMenuKeyReleased(MenuKeyEvent)
protected void fireMenuKeyTyped(MenuKeyEvent)

The methods listed above add and remove menu drag-mouse listeners and menu key listeners, in addition to a number of `protected` methods that fire events to menu drag-mouse and menu key listeners.

Accessibility / Pluggable Look And Feel

---

public AccessibleContext <u>getAccessibleContext</u>()
public String <u>getUIClassID</u>()
public void <u>updateUI</u>()
public void <u>setUI</u>(MenuItemUI)

The methods listed above can be found in most extensions of `JComponent`. Swing lightweight components can return an accessibility context that contains accessibility information for the component and the class name of their UI delegate. The `updateUI` method is invoked when the component is fitted with a UI delegate.

The Difference Between Accelerators and Mnemonics

Accelerators and mnemonics both represent keyboard shortcuts, so it is useful to point out the difference between an accelerator and a mnemonic.

A mnemonic is a keyboard shortcut that is used in conjunction with a look-and-feel-specific "Meta" key. Mnemonics are specified by a single character, such as 'x', but the 'x' must be pressed in conjunction with the "Meta" key. For example, for the Windows look and feel, the "Meta" key is the ALT key, so a mnemonic specified by the character 'x' requires an ALT-X to be activated.

An accelerator is also a keyboard shortcut; however, there is no look-and-feel-specific "Meta" key associated with an accelerator. Whereas mnemonics are qualified by a character or integer, accelerators are specified by an instance of KeyStroke, which fully specifies the combination of keys that must be pressed to activate the associated component.

Finally, mnemonics are used to traverse menus, whereas accelerators do not activate menus; accelerators simply invoke the action associated with a menu item without displaying menus.

AWT Compatibility

The `public` methods implemented by `java.awt.MenuItem` and their `JMenuItem` equivalents are listed in Table 10-1.

Table 10-1 java.awt.MenuItem Methods and JMenuItem Equivalents[1]

java.awt.MenuItem Method	JMenuItem Equivalent
void addActionListener(ActionListener)	void addActionListener(ActionListener)
void disableEvents(long)	void disableEvents(long)
void deleteShortcut()	**void setAccelerator(null)**
void enableEvents(long)	void enableEvents(long)
String getActionCommand()	String getActionCommand()
String getLabel()	String getLabel()
MenuShortcut getShortcut()	KeyStroke getAccelerator()
boolean isEnabled()	boolean isEnabled()
String paramString()	String paramString()
void removeActionListener()	void removeActionListener()
void setActionCommand(String)	void setActionCommand(String)
void setEnabled(boolean)	void setEnabled(boolean)
void setLabel(String)	void setLabel(String)
void setShortcut(MenuShortcut)	**void setAccelerator(KeyStroke)**

1. Differing signatures are highlighted in bold.

Swing menu items are nearly source compatible with AWT menu items. The major difference between the two is that AWT menu items specify accelerators with an instance of `java.awt.MenuShortcut`, whereas Swing menu items specify accelerators with an instance of `KeyStroke`. When converting code that uses AWT menu items to Swing, specify accelerators as follows:

```
// AWT Menu Items:

menuItem.setShortcut(new MenuShortcut('x'));

//true means that SHIFT-x activates the menu item
menuItem.setShortcut(new MenuShortcut('x', true);

// Swing Equivalent:
```

```
menuItem.setAccelerator(KeyStroke.getKeyStroke(KeyEvent.VK_X));
menuItem.setAccelerator(KeyStroke.getKeyStroke(KeyEvent.VK_X,
                                         Event.SHIFT_MASK));
```

The second shortcut above is instantiated with a `MenuShortcut` constructor that takes two arguments—the first is the key that will activate the menu item, and the second (`boolean`) argument specifies whether a SHIFT modifier must be used to activate the menu item. The Swing equivalent obtains a reference to an instance of `KeyStroke`, specifying the `Event.SHIFT_MASK` as the modifier that must be pressed in conjunction with the 'x' key.

JCheckBoxMenuItem

`JCheckBoxMenuItem` is a simple extension of `JMenuItem` that draws a checkbox control on the left-hand side[2] (by default) of the text drawn in menu item.

Figure 10-8 shows an applet that creates three check box menu items.

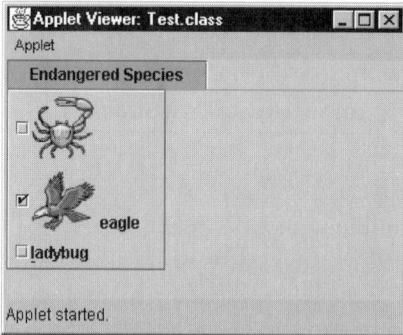

Figure 10-8 Instantiating Instances of JCheckBoxMenuItem

The eagle checkbox menu item is specified as selected at the time of construction, and the ladybug checkbox menu item has a mnemonic set after construction.

The applet shown in Figure 10-8 is listed in Example 10-6.

---

2.   All Swing look and feels draw the control on left-hand side.

Example 10-6 Instantiating Checkbox Menu Items

```
import javax.swing.*;
import java.awt.*;
import java.awt.event.*;

public class Test extends JApplet {
    public void init() {
        Container contentPane = getContentPane();

        JMenuBar mb = new JMenuBar();
        JMenu checkBoxMenu = new JMenu("Endangered Species");

        ImageIcon crabIcon = new ImageIcon("crab.gif");
        ImageIcon eagleIcon = new ImageIcon("eagle.gif");

        JMenuItem
            crabItem = new JCheckBoxMenuItem(crabIcon),
            eagleItem = new JCheckBoxMenuItem("eagle",
                                        eagleIcon, true),
            ladybugItem = new JCheckBoxMenuItem("ladybug");

        checkBoxMenu.add(crabItem);
        checkBoxMenu.add(eagleItem);
        checkBoxMenu.add(ladybugItem);

        ladybugItem.setMnemonic('l');

        mb.add(checkBoxMenu);
        setJMenuBar(mb);
    }
}
```

The `JCheckBoxMenuItem` class is summarized in Component Summary 10-2.

Component Summary 10-2   JCheckBoxMenuItem

Model(s)	JToggleButton.ToggleButtonModel
UI Delegate(s)	swing.plaf.basic.BasicCheckBoxMenuItemUI
Renderer(s)	——

Editor(s)	——
Events Fired	ActionEvent / ChangeEvent / ItemEvent
Replacement For	java.awt.CheckboxMenuItem
Class Diagrams	See Figure 10-6 on page 466.

JCheckBoxMenuItem Properties

The only property that originates in JCheckBoxMenuItem is the state property, which indicates whether or not a checkbox menu item is selected. Both setter and getter methods are provided for the state property. Determining the selected state of an instance of JCheckBoxMenuItem is illustrated by the applet listed in Example 10-7.

JCheckBoxMenuItem Events

Like all Swing buttons, checkbox menu items fire action events when activated, property change events when their bound properties are modified, and change events when their state changes. See "JButton Events" on page 396 for more information concerning action events and change events fired by buttons in general, and "Property Change Notification" on page 95 for more information concerning property change events. Additionally, checkbox menu items fire item events when they are selected or deselected. For more information on handling item events, see "JToggleButton Events" on page 423.

The applet shown in Figure 10-9 illustrates accessing checkbox menu item states. The applet instantiates three instances of JCheckBoxMenuItem and adds an action listener to each menu item. When one of the menu items is activated, the listener prints the state of each menu item in the applet's status area.

Figure 10-9 JCheckBoxMenuItem States

The applet shown in Figure 10-9 is listed in Example 10-7.

Example 10-7 Accessing JCheckBoxMenuItem States

```java
import javax.swing.*;
import javax.swing.event.*;
import java.awt.*;
import java.awt.event.*;

public class Test extends JApplet {
    private ImageIcon crabIcon = new ImageIcon("crab.gif");
    private ImageIcon eagleIcon = new ImageIcon("eagle.gif");

    private JCheckBoxMenuItem
        crabItem = new JCheckBoxMenuItem(crabIcon),
        eagleItem = new JCheckBoxMenuItem("eagle", eagleIcon),
        ladybugItem = new JCheckBoxMenuItem("ladybug");

    public void init() {
        JMenuBar mb = new JMenuBar();
        JMenu checkBoxMenu = new JMenu("Endangered Species");
        Listener listener = new Listener();

        checkBoxMenu.add(crabItem);
        checkBoxMenu.add(eagleItem);
        checkBoxMenu.add(ladybugItem);

        crabItem.addActionListener(listener);
        eagleItem.addActionListener(listener);
        ladybugItem.addActionListener(listener);

        mb.add(checkBoxMenu);
        setJMenuBar(mb);
```

```
            }
       class Listener implements ActionListener {
          public void actionPerformed(ActionEvent e) {
             showStatus("crab:   " + crabItem.getState() + ", " +
                        "eagle:   " + eagleItem.getState() + ", " +
                        "ladybug:   " + ladybugItem.getState());
          }
       }
    }
```

JCheckBoxMenuItem Class Summaries

The `public` and `protected` variables and methods for `JCheckBoxMenuItem` are listed in Class Summary 10-3.

Class Summary 10-3   JCheckBoxMenuItem

Extends: JMenuItem

Implements: javax.accessibility.Accessible, SwingConstants

Constructors

---

public <u>JCheckBoxMenuItem</u>()
public <u>JCheckBoxMenuItem</u>(Icon)
public <u>JCheckBoxMenuItem</u>(String)
public <u>JCheckBoxMenuItem</u>(String, boolean selected)
public <u>JCheckBoxMenuItem</u>(String, Icon)
public <u>JCheckBoxMenuItem</u>(String, Icon, boolean selected)

Constructors for `JCheckBoxMenuItem` are similar to those for `JMenuItem`, except that instances of `JCheckBoxMenuItem` can be constructed either selected or deselected—thus the `boolean` argument passed to the fourth and sixth constructors listed above.

Another discrepancy between the constructors for JCheckBoxMenuItem and JMenuItem is the fact that instances of JCheckBoxMenuItem cannot be constructed with a mnemonic. However, since JCheckBoxMenuItem is ultimately derived from AbstractButton, mnemonics can be set for checkbox menu items after they are constructed, as illustrated in Figure 10-8 on page 478.

Initialization and State

---

protected void init(String, Icon)

public synchronized Object[] getSelectedObjects()

public boolean getState()
public synchronized void setState(boolean)

The init method for JCheckBoxMenuItem is nearly identical to the init method for JMenuItem, except that the vertical text position for a checkbox menu item equipped with an icon is set to SwingConstants.BOTTOM. Extensions of JCheckBoxMenuItem can override the init method if the default behavior is unsatisfactory.

The getSelectedObjects method returns an Object array that contains exactly one item. If the checkbox menu item is selected, the item in the array is the text of the menu item; otherwise, if the menu item is not selected, the item in the array is null.

Because checkbox menu items can be selected, the JCheckBoxMenuItem API provides accessor methods for setting and getting the selected state of the menu item.

Accessibility / Pluggable Look And Feel

---

public AccessibleContext getAccessibleContext()
public String getUIClassID()
public void updateUI()
public void setUI(CheckBoxMenuItemUI)

The methods listed above can be found in most extensions of JComponent. Swing lightweight components can return an accessibility context that contains accessibility information for the component and the class name of their UI delegate. The updateUI method is invoked when the component is fitted with a UI delegate.

AWT Compatibility

The public methods implemented by java.awt.CheckboxMenuItem and their JCheckBoxMenuItem equivalents are listed in Table 10-2.

Table 10-2   java.awt.CheckboxMenuItem Methods and JCheckBoxMenuItem Equivalents

java.awt.CheckboxMenuItem Methods	JCheckBoxMenuItem Equivalents
void addItemListener(ItemListener)	void addItemListener(ItemListener)
Object[] getSelectedObjects()	Object[] getSelectedObjects()
boolean getState()	boolean getState()
String paramString()	String paramString()
void removeItemListener(ItemListener)	void removeItemListener(ItemListener)
void setState(boolean)	void setState(boolean)

JCheckBoxMenuItem is fully source code compatible with java.awt.CheckboxMenuItem. The JCheckBoxMenuItem API provides setState, getState, and getSelectedObjects methods to maintain compatibility with AWT checkbox menu items.

JRadioButtonMenuItem

Swing radio button menu items are similar to checkbox menu items—both JCheckBoxMenuItem and JRadioButtonMenuItem are simple extensions of JMenuItem.

There are two main difference between Swing checkbox menu items and radio button items.

First, even though radio button menu items can be selected and deselected, the `JRadioButtonMenuItem` class does not offer methods to get and set the selected state of the menu item. In other words, `JRadioButtonMenuItem` does not provide `setState` and `getState` methods as does `JCheckBoxMenuItem`. The `setState` and `getState` methods are implemented by `JCheckBoxMenuItem` to maintain compatibility with the AWT's `CheckboxMenuItem` class. Since the AWT does not provide a component analogous to Swing's `JRadioButtonMenuItem`, the methods are not necessary to maintain AWT compatibility. To determine the selected state of a Swing radio button menu item, call the inherited (from `AbstractButton`) `isSelected` method.

Second, the `getSelectedObjects` method is not overridden by the `JRadioButtonMenuItem` class, as is the case for `JCheckBoxMenuItem`. As a result, calls to `getSelectedObjects` for instances of `JRadioButtonMenuItem` result in the call to `AbstractButton.getSelectedObjects()`, which returns `null`.

Figure 10-10 shows an applet that creates three instances of `JRadioButtonMenuItem`.

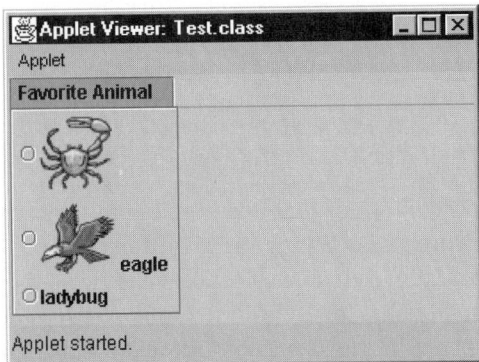

Figure 10-10 Using Radio Button Menu Items

The applet shown in Figure 10-10 is listed in Example 10-8.

Example 10-8 Instantiating Radio Button Menu Items

```
import javax.swing.*;
import javax.swing.event.*;
import java.awt.*;
import java.awt.event.*;

public class Test extends JApplet {
    public void init() {
        Container contentPane = getContentPane();

        JMenuBar mb = new JMenuBar();
        JMenu radioMenu = new JMenu("Favorite Animal");

        ImageIcon crabIcon = new ImageIcon("crab.gif");
        ImageIcon eagleIcon = new ImageIcon("eagle.gif");

        final JMenuItem
            crabItem = new JRadioButtonMenuItem(crabIcon),
            eagleItem = new JRadioButtonMenuItem("eagle",
                                        eagleIcon),
            ladybugItem = new JRadioButtonMenuItem("ladybug");

        radioMenu.add(crabItem);
        radioMenu.add(eagleItem);
        radioMenu.add(ladybugItem);

        mb.add(radioMenu);
        setJMenuBar(mb);
    }
}
```

If you run the applet listed above, you will notice that it is possible to select more than one radio button menu item at a time. Like Swing radio buttons, radio button menu items do not exhibit mutually exclusive selection behavior—they must be added to a button group if such behavior is desired. Unlike Swing radio buttons, radio button menu items that are instantiated without text are drawn with a selection control (See "Radio Buttons" on page 440).

The JRadioButtonMenuItem class is summarized in Component Summary 10-3.

Component Summary 10-3   JRadioButtonMenuItem

Model(s)	JToggleButton.ToggleButtonModel
UI Delegate(s)	swing.plaf.basic.BasicRadioButtonMenuItemUI
Renderer(s)	——
Editor(s)	——
Events Fired	ActionEvent / ChangeEvent / ItemEvent
Replacement For	——
Class Diagrams	See Figure 10-6 on page 466.

JRadioButtonMenuItemProperties

`JRadioButtonMenuItem` does not add any new properties of its own accord—all properties are inherited.

JRadioButtonMenuItem Events

Like all Swing buttons, radio button menu items fire action events when activated, property change events when their bound properties are modified, and change events when their state changes. See "JButton Events" on page 396 for more information concerning action events and change events fired by buttons in general, and "Property Change Notification" on page 95 for more information concerning property change events. Additionally, radio button menu items fire item events when they are selected or deselected. For more information on handling item events, see "JToggleButton Events" on page 423.

Figure 10-11 shows an applet that monitors events fired by instances of `JRadioButtonMenuItem`.

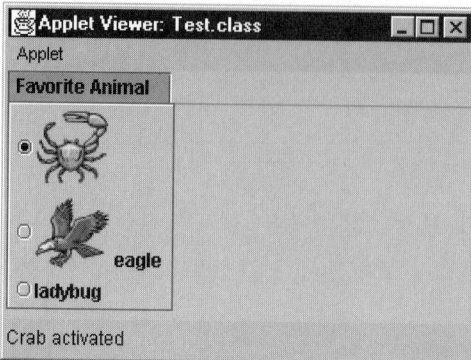

Figure 10-11 Handling Events for Instances of JRadioButtonMenuItem

The applet creates three instances of `JRadioButtonMenuItem` and adds them to the menu. Additionally, each menu item is added to a button group to ensure mutually exclusive selection behavior between the items.

Each menu item is fitted with three listeners: an `ItemListener`, a `ChangeListener`, and an `ActionListener`.

```
public class Test extends JApplet {
    private ImageIcon crabIcon = new ImageIcon("crab.gif",
                                        "Crab");
    private ImageIcon eagleIcon = new ImageIcon("eagle.gif",
                                          "Eagle");
    private JMenuItem
           crabItem = new JRadioButtonMenuItem(crabIcon),
           eagleItem = new JRadioButtonMenuItem("eagle",
                                        eagleIcon),
           ladybugItem = new JRadioButtonMenuItem("ladybug");

    public void init() {
        ...
        AnItemListener itemListener = new AnItemListener();
        AnActionListener actionListener = new AnActionListener();
        AChangeListener changeListener = new AChangeListener();

        radioMenu.add(crabItem);
        radioMenu.add(eagleItem);
        radioMenu.add(ladybugItem);

        ButtonGroup group = new ButtonGroup();
        group.add(crabItem);
        group.add(eagleItem);
```

```
        group.add(ladybugItem);

        ...
        crabItem.addItemListener(itemListener);
        eagleItem.addItemListener(itemListener);
        ladybugItem.addItemListener(itemListener);

        crabItem.addActionListener(actionListener);
        eagleItem.addActionListener(actionListener);
        ladybugItem.addActionListener(actionListener);

        crabItem.addChangeListener(changeListener);
        eagleItem.addChangeListener(changeListener);
        ladybugItem.addChangeListener(changeListener);
    }
    ...
```

The listeners are implemented as inner classes of the applet so that they can update the applet's status area. The action and item listeners both display information about events in the applet's status area.

```
    ...
    class AnActionListener implements ActionListener {
        public void actionPerformed(ActionEvent e) {
            JRadioButtonMenuItem item = (JRadioButtonMenuItem)
                                        e.getSource();
            String s = getItemDescription(item);
            showStatus(s + " activated");
        }
    };
    class AnItemListener implements ItemListener {
        public void itemStateChanged(ItemEvent e) {
            JRadioButtonMenuItem item = (JRadioButtonMenuItem)
                                        e.getSource();
            String s = getItemDescription(item);

            if(e.getStateChange() == ItemEvent.SELECTED)
                s += " selected";
            else
                s += " deselected";

            showStatus(s);
        }
    };
    ...
```

The listeners obtain a description of the menu item that fired the event by invoking the applet's getItemDescription method, which returns either the text of the item or a description of the item's icon if the item is so equipped.

To illustrate the fact that `getSelectedObjects()` always returns `null` for instances of `JRadioButtonMenuItem`, a change listener invokes `getSelectedObjects()` and prints the result. Additionally, the change listener prints a message to the applet's status area when the item that fired the event is armed.

```
    ...
    class AChangeListener implements ChangeListener {
        public void stateChanged(ChangeEvent e) {
            Object[] selectedObjs =
                        ladybugItem.getSelectedObjects();

            if(selectedObjs == null)
                System.out.println("selected objs is null");
            else
                System.out.println(selectedObjs[0] + "selected");

            JRadioButtonMenuItem item =
                    (JRadioButtonMenuItem)e.getSource();

            if(item.isArmed()) {
                String s = getItemDescription(item);
                showStatus(s + " armed");
            }
        }
    };
    ...
}
```

The applet shown in Figure 10-11 is listed in its entirety in Example 10-9.

Example 10-9 Monitoring Events for Instances of JRadioButton

```
import javax.swing.*;
import javax.swing.event.*;
import java.awt.*;
import java.awt.event.*;

public class Test extends JApplet {
    private ImageIcon crabIcon = new ImageIcon("crab.gif",
                                          "Crab");
    private ImageIcon eagleIcon = new ImageIcon("eagle.gif",
                                           "Eagle");
    private JMenuItem
            crabItem = new JRadioButtonMenuItem(crabIcon),
            eagleItem = new JRadioButtonMenuItem("eagle",
                                        eagleIcon),
            ladybugItem = new JRadioButtonMenuItem("ladybug");

    public void init() {
```

```
    JMenuBar mb = new JMenuBar();
    JMenu radioMenu = new JMenu("Favorite Animal");

    AnItemListener itemListener = new AnItemListener();
    AnActionListener actionListener = new AnActionListener();
    AChangeListener changeListener = new AChangeListener();

    radioMenu.add(crabItem);
    radioMenu.add(eagleItem);
    radioMenu.add(ladybugItem);

    ButtonGroup group = new ButtonGroup();
    group.add(crabItem);
    group.add(eagleItem);
    group.add(ladybugItem);

    mb.add(radioMenu);
    setJMenuBar(mb);

    crabItem.addItemListener(itemListener);
    eagleItem.addItemListener(itemListener);
    ladybugItem.addItemListener(itemListener);

    crabItem.addActionListener(actionListener);
    eagleItem.addActionListener(actionListener);
    ladybugItem.addActionListener(actionListener);

    crabItem.addChangeListener(changeListener);
    eagleItem.addChangeListener(changeListener);
    ladybugItem.addChangeListener(changeListener);
}
private String getItemDescription(
                            JRadioButtonMenuItem item) {
    String s;
    ImageIcon icon = (ImageIcon)item.getIcon();

    if(icon != null) return icon.getDescription();
    else        return item.getText();
}

// Inner class event handlers follow ...

class AnActionListener implements ActionListener {
    public void actionPerformed(ActionEvent e) {
        JRadioButtonMenuItem item = (JRadioButtonMenuItem)
                                     e.getSource();
        String s = getItemDescription(item);
        showStatus(s + " activated");
    }
};
class AChangeListener implements ChangeListener {
    public void stateChanged(ChangeEvent e) {
```

```
        Object[] selectedObjs =
                ladybugItem.getSelectedObjects();

        if(selectedObjs == null)
            System.out.println("selected objs is null");
        else
            System.out.println(selectedObjs[0] + "selected");

        JRadioButtonMenuItem item =
                (JRadioButtonMenuItem)e.getSource();

        if(item.isArmed()) {
            String s = getItemDescription(item);
            showStatus(s + " armed");
        }
    }
};
class AnItemListener implements ItemListener {
    public void itemStateChanged(ItemEvent e) {
        JRadioButtonMenuItem item = (JRadioButtonMenuItem)
                                    e.getSource();
        String s = getItemDescription(item);

        if(e.getStateChange() == ItemEvent.SELECTED)
            s += " selected";
        else
            s += " deselected";

        showStatus(s);
    }
};
}
```

JRadioButtonMenuItemClass Summaries

The public and protected variables and methods for
JRadioButtonMenuItem are listed in Class Summary 10-4.

Class Summary 10-4   JRadioButtonMenuItem

Extends: JMenuItem
Implements: javax.accessibility.Accessible

Constructors

public <u>JRadioButtonMenuItem</u>()
public <u>JRadioButtonMenuItem</u>(String)
public <u>JRadioButtonMenuItem</u>(String, boolean selected)
public <u>JRadioButtonMenuItem</u>(String, Icon)
public <u>JRadioButtonMenuItem</u>(String, Icon, boolean selected)
public <u>JRadioButtonMenuItem</u>(Icon)
public <u>JRadioButtonMenuItem</u>(Icon, boolean selected)

The string and icon displayed in the menu item, in addition to the selected state, can all be specified with the constructors listed above.

Methods

Initialization / Request Focus

protected void <u>init</u>(String, Icon)
public void <u>requestFocus</u>()

The `JRadioButtonMenuItem.init` method is identical to the `init` method for `JCheckBoxMenuItem`. Extensions are free to override the `init` method if so desired.

Like `JCheckBoxMenuItem`, instances of `JRadioButtonMenuItem` do not grab focus, which is ensured by overriding `requestFocus()` with an empty implementation.

Accessibility / Pluggable Look And Feel

public AccessibleContext <u>getAccessibleContext</u>()
public String <u>getUIClassID</u>()
public void <u>updateUI</u>()
public void <u>setUI</u>(RadioButtonMenuItemUI)

The methods listed above can be found in most extensions of `JComponent`. Swing lightweight components can return an accessibility context that contains accessibility information for the component and the class name of their UI delegate. The `updateUI` method is invoked when the component is fitted with a UI delegate.

AWT Compatibility

The AWT does not provide a component analagous to Swing's `JRadioButtonMenuItem`.

JCheckBoxMenuItem API Versus JRadioButtonMenuItem API

At first glance, it may seem that the APIs for JCheckBoxMenuItem and JRadioButtonMenuItem should be nearly identical. After all, the only perceptible difference between checkbox menu items and radio button menu items is the control that is drawn to indicate selection.

The API for JCheckBoxMenuItem differs from the API for JRadioButtonMenuItem because JCheckBoxMenuItem maintains compatibility with the API for AWT checkbox menu items. For example, JCheckBoxMenuItem provides setState and getState methods to maintain compatibility with java.awt.CheckboxMenuItem. JRadioButtonMenuItem, on the other hand, has no analogous AWT component and therefore does not include methods in its API for maintaining compatibility with an AWT class.

JMenu

As mentioned previously, Swing menus are essentially buttons that have a popup menu associated with them. When a menu is activated, its popup menu is displayed beneath the menu.

Figure 10-12 shows an applet with a File menu. The File menu is fitted with an icon, and a button is added to the menu. Components added to menus can be manipulated, as evidenced by the right-hand picture in Figure 10-12, which shows the button in the menu being activated.

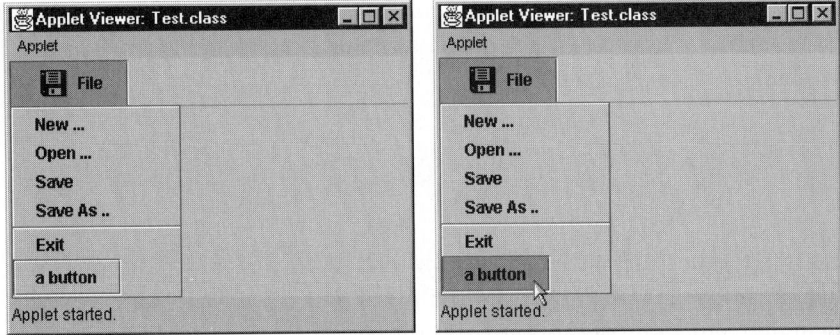

Figure 10-12 A Menu with an Icon and a Component

The applet shown in Figure 10-12 is listed in Example 10-10.

Example 10-10 A Simple JMenu Example

```java
import javax.swing.*;
import java.awt.*;
import java.awt.event.*;

public class Test extends JApplet {
    public void init() {
        JMenuBar mb = new JMenuBar();
        JMenu fileMenu = new JMenu("File");

        fileMenu.add("New ...");
        fileMenu.add("Open ...");
        fileMenu.add("Save");
        fileMenu.add("Save As ..");
        fileMenu.addSeparator();
        fileMenu.add("Exit");

        fileMenu.add(new JButton("a button"));
        fileMenu.setIcon(new ImageIcon("disk.gif"));

        mb.add(fileMenu);
        setJMenuBar(mb);
    }
}
```

Because Swing menus are buttons, an icon can be set for an instance of `JMenu`, which is exactly what the applet listed in Example 10-10 does. Swing menus can also have an arbitrary component added to them, as illustrated by the instance of `JButton` that is added to the File menu shown in Figure 10-12.

Note: *Swing menus, as of Swing 1.1 FCS, do not properly repaint when a component contained inside of a menu is manipulated such that the size of the component changes. For example, if a tree is added to a menu, the menu will not resize properly if the tree's folders are expanded or collapsed.*

Dynamically Modifying Menus

`JMenu` offers a number of ways to add/insert/remove items to/into/from menus. Methods that add or insert actions or menu items return a reference to the menu item that is ultimately added or inserted. Methods that add or insert a string do not return a reference to menu item; however, adding a string to a menu does result in the creation of menu item that is added to the menu.

In addition to menu items being added to menus, components and separators can also be added to instances of `JMenu`. Adding a component or separator to a menu does not result in the creation of a menu item—the component or separator is simply inserted into the menu's popup menu.

Menu listeners can be added and removed from any instance of `JMenu`. See "JMenu Events" on page 506 for more on menu listeners.

The applet shown in Figure 10-13 illustrates adding and removing menu items from a menu in addition to enabling and disabling items. The applet also illustrates setting the font of a menu item.

The applet implements an extension of `JMenu`—`SelfModifyingMenu`—that contains the menu items shown in Figure 10-13. The `SelfModifyingMenu` class adds the menu items and separators and attaches an action listener to the items.

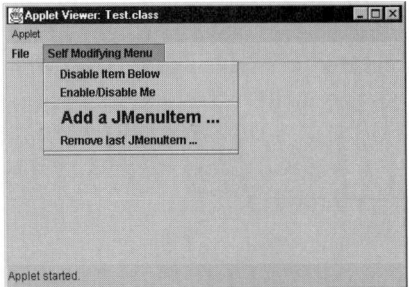 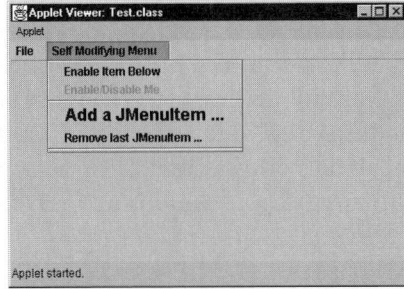

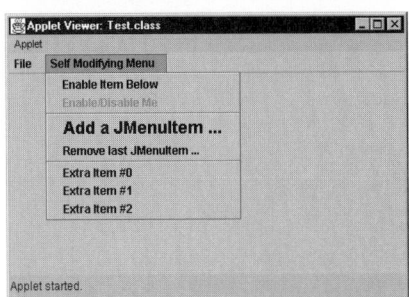 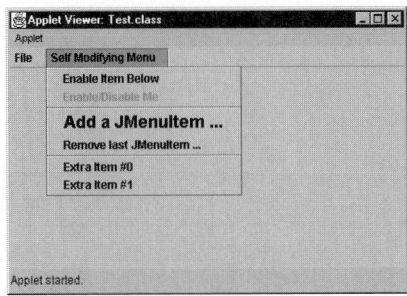

Figure 10-13 Dynamically Modifying Menu Items

```java
class SelfModifyingMenu extends JMenu {
    private Vector    newItems = new Vector();
    private Listener menuItemListener = new Listener();
    private JMenuItem toggleItem, enablerItem,
                      addItem, removeItem;

    public SelfModifyingMenu() {
        super("Self Modifying Menu"); // set menu title

        add(enablerItem = new JMenuItem("Disable Item Below"));
        add(toggleItem  = new JMenuItem("Enable/Disable Me"));
        addSeparator();

        add(addItem     = new JMenuItem("Add a JMenuItem ..."));
        add(removeItem = new JMenuItem(
                            "Remove last JMenuItem ..."));
        addItem.setFont(new Font("Helvetica", Font.BOLD, 18));
        addSeparator();

        enablerItem.addActionListener(menuItemListener);
        toggleItem.addActionListener(menuItemListener);
        addItem.addActionListener(menuItemListener);
        removeItem.addActionListener(menuItemListener);
    }
    ...
```

When a menu item is selected, the action listener determines which menu item was the source of the event and acts accordingly. If the menu item activated was the `enablerItem`, the applet's `toggleItem` method, which simply toggles the enabled state of the `toggleItem`, is invoked, and the text of the `enablerItem` is updated. If the activated menu item was the `addItem`, then the applet's `addItem` method, which adds a menu item to the menu, is called. If the menu item was the `removeItem`, then the applet's `removeItem` method, which removes the last item added to the menu, is called.

```
...
public void addItem() {
    JMenuItem newItem =
            new JMenuItem("Extra Item #" + newItems.size());

    add(newItem);
    newItems.addElement(newItem);
}
public void removeLastItem() {
    if(newItems.size() == 0)
        System.out.println("Nothing to remove!");
    else {
        JMenuItem removeMe =
                    (JMenuItem)newItems.lastElement();

        remove(removeMe);
        newItems.removeElement(removeMe);
    }
}
public void toggleItem() {
    if(toggleItem.isEnabled()) toggleItem.setEnabled(false);
    else                       toggleItem.setEnabled(true);
}
class Listener implements ActionListener {
    public void actionPerformed(ActionEvent event) {
        JMenuItem item = (JMenuItem)event.getSource();

        if(item == enablerItem) {
            toggleItem();

            if(toggleItem.isEnabled())
                enablerItem.setText("Disable Item Below");
            else
                enablerItem.setText("Enable Item Below");
        }
        else if(item == addItem)    addItem();
        else if(item == removeItem) removeLastItem();
    }
}
}
```

The applet shown in Figure 10-13 is listed in its entirety in Example 10-11.

Example 10-11 A Self-Modifying Menu

```java
import javax.swing.*;
import java.awt.*;
import java.awt.event.*;
import java.util.Vector;

public class Test extends JApplet {
    private SelfModifyingMenu selfModifyingMenu;

    public void init() {
        JMenuBar menuBar = To();
        createMenus(menuBar);
        setJMenuBar(menuBar);
    }
    public void createMenus(JMenuBar mbar) {
        mbar.add(createFileMenu());
        mbar.add(selfModifyingMenu = new SelfModifyingMenu());
    }
    private JMenu createFileMenu() {
        JMenu fileMenu = new JMenu("File");
        JMenuItem quitItem = new JMenuItem("Quit");

        fileMenu.add(quitItem);

        quitItem.addActionListener(new ActionListener() {
            public void actionPerformed(ActionEvent event) {
                System.exit(0);
            }
        });
        return fileMenu;
    }
}
class SelfModifyingMenu extends JMenu {
    private Vector    newItems = new Vector();
    private Listener menuItemListener = new Listener();
    private JMenuItem toggleItem, enablerItem,
                      addItem, removeItem;

    public SelfModifyingMenu() {
        super("Self Modifying Menu");

        add(enablerItem = new JMenuItem("Disable Item Below"));
        add(toggleItem  = new JMenuItem("Enable/Disable Me"));
        addSeparator();

        add(addItem    = new JMenuItem("Add a JMenuItem ..."));
        add(removeItem = new JMenuItem(
                            Remove last JMenuItem ...));
        addItem.setFont(new Font("Helvetica", Font.BOLD, 18));
```

```
            addSeparator();

            enablerItem.addActionListener(menuItemListener);
            toggleItem.addActionListener(menuItemListener);
            addItem.addActionListener(menuItemListener);
            removeItem.addActionListener(menuItemListener);
        }
        public void addItem() {
            JMenuItem newItem =
                    new JMenuItem("Extra Item #" + newItems.size());

            add(newItem);
            newItems.addElement(newItem);
        }
        public void removeLastItem() {
            if(newItems.size() == 0)
                System.out.println("Nothing to remove!");
            else {
                JMenuItem removeMe =
                            (JMenuItem)newItems.lastElement();

                remove(removeMe);
                newItems.removeElement(removeMe);
            }
        }
        public void toggleItem() {
            if(toggleItem.isEnabled()) toggleItem.setEnabled(false);
            else                       toggleItem.setEnabled(true);
        }
        class Listener implements ActionListener {
            public void actionPerformed(ActionEvent event) {
                JMenuItem item = (JMenuItem)event.getSource();

                if(item == enablerItem) {
                    toggleItem();

                    if(toggleItem.isEnabled())
                        enablerItem.setText("Disable Item Below");
                    else
                        enablerItem.setText("Enable Item Below");
                }
                else if(item == addItem)    addItem();
                else if(item == removeItem) removeLastItem();
            }
        }
    }
```

Pull-right Menus

JMenu extends JMenuItem, and therefore pull-right menus are easy to implement with Swing. The applet shown in Figure 10-14 creates a cascading menu three levels deep.

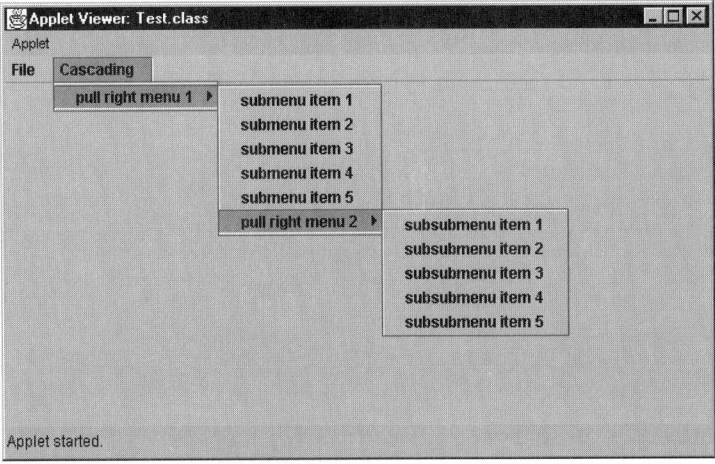

Figure 10-14 Pull-right Menus

The applet shown in Figure 10-14 is listed in Example 10-12.

Example 10-12 Pull-right Menus

```
import javax.swing.*;
import java.awt.*;
import java.awt.event.*;

public class Test extends JApplet {

    public void init() {
        JMenuBar menuBar = new JMenuBar();
        createMenus(menuBar);
        setJMenuBar(menuBar);
    }
```

```
public void createMenus(JMenuBar mbar) {
    mbar.add(createFileMenu());
    mbar.add(createCascadingMenu());
}
private JMenu createFileMenu() {
    JMenu fileMenu = new JMenu("File");
    JMenuItem quitItem = new JMenuItem("Quit");

    fileMenu.add(quitItem);

    quitItem.addActionListener(new ActionListener() {
        public void actionPerformed(ActionEvent event) {
            System.exit(0);
        }
    });
    return fileMenu;
}
private JMenu createCascadingMenu() {
    JMenu cascading  = new JMenu("Cascading");
    JMenu submenu    = new JMenu("pull right menu 1");
    JMenu subsubmenu = new JMenu("pull right menu 2");

    submenu.add("submenu item 1");
    submenu.add("submenu item 2");
    submenu.add("submenu item 3");
    submenu.add("submenu item 4");
    submenu.add("submenu item 5");

    subsubmenu.add("subsubmenu item 1");
    subsubmenu.add("subsubmenu item 2");
    subsubmenu.add("subsubmenu item 3");
    subsubmenu.add("subsubmenu item 4");
    subsubmenu.add("subsubmenu item 5");

    cascading.add(submenu);
    submenu.add(subsubmenu);

    return cascading;
}
}
```

The significant code in the applet listed above is formatted in bold. The cascading menu adds the submenu to itself, and the submenu adds the subsubmenu to itself.

The JMenu class is summarized in Component Summary 10-4.

Component Summary 10-4   JMenu

Model(s)	ButtonModel
UI Delegate(s)	javax.swing.plaf.basic.BasicMenuUI
Renderer(s)	——
Editor(s)	——
Events Fired	MenuEvent
Replacement For	java.awt.Menu

Class Diagrams

Figure 10-15 JMenu Class Diagram

JMenu extends JMenuItem and implements the Accessible and MenuElement interfaces. Because JMenu extends JMenuItem, instances of JMenu can be added to menus, resulting in the ability to create cascading menus. Also, because JMenu extends JMenuItem, and JMenuItem in turn extends AbstractButton, menus are buttons and can be manipulated accordingly.

Each instance of JMenu maintains a private reference to an instance of JPopupMenu—a popup menu that is displayed when the menu is activated. Menus also maintain a private hash table that is used to clean up references to the listeners when listeners are removed so that the listeners can be garbage collected.

Private references are also maintained to instances of MenuEvent and ChangeListener. The menu event is passed to menu listeners when a menu event occurs, and the change listener listens for changes to the menu's model.

Finally, menus maintain an integer value that represents the delay in milliseconds that occurs between the time that the menu is selected and its associated popup menu is displayed. By default, the delay is 0 milliseconds—see Table 10-3 for more on JMenu properties and their default values.

JMenu Properties

The properties associated with instances of JMenu are listed in Table 10-3.

Table 10-3   JMenu Properties

Property Name	Data Type	Access[2]	Type[3]	Default[4]
delay	int	SG	S	0
item	JMenuItem	G	I	—
itemCount	int	G	S	—
menuComponent	Component	G	I	—
menuComponentCount	int	G	S	—
menuComponents	int	G	S	—
menuLocation	Point	S	S	L&F
model	ButtonModel	SG	B	ButtonModel
popupMenu	JPopupMenu	G	S	JPopupMenu

Table 10-3 JMenu Properties (Continued)

Property Name	Data Type	Access[2]	Type[3]	Default[4]
popupMenuVisible	boolean	SG	S	false
tearOff[1]	boolean	CG	S	false
topLevelMenu	boolean	G	S	—

1. Not implemented as of Swing1.1 FCS
2. C = settable at construction time / G = getter method / S = setter method
3. B = bound / bool = boolean / C = constrained/ I = indexed / S = simple
4. L&F = look-and-feel dependent

`delay` — A delay, in milliseconds, between selecting the menu and displaying its popup menu. The `delay` property is provided for a menu's UI delegate; menu components themselves do not do anything with the property. As of Swing 1.1 FCS, none of the look and feels provided with Swing use the `delay` property.

`item` — An indexed property that provides access to a menu's menu items. An `integer` value representing the index for a menu item is passed to the `JMenu.getItem` method. If there is no menu item at the specified index, the `getItem` method returns a reference to the menu itself. Note that the `getItem` method provides access only to the menu items contained in a menu. If a menu contains other types of components, they can be accessed through the `menuComponent` property.

`itemCount` — The number of components contained in a menu. The `itemCount` property is provided for backward compatibility with `java.awt.Menu`. Unless compatibility with AWT menus is a necessity, use the `menuComponentCount` property, which is equivalent to the `itemCount` property.

`menuComponent` — An indexed property that provides access to the components—including menu items—contained in a menu's popup menu. Whereas the indexed `item` property provides access only to menu items, the `menuComponent` property provides access to all of the components contained in a menu's popup menu.

`menuComponentCount` — Represents the number of components contained in a menu's popup menu.

menuComponents — An array of the components contained in a menu's popup menu.

menuLocation — A write-only property representing the upper-left corner of a menu's popup menu.

model — Menu models are of type `ButtonModel`, and `JMenu` provides setter and getter methods for access to its model.

popupMenu — The popup menu associated with an instance of `JMenu`. The `popupMenu` property is read-only.

popupMenuVisible — The visibility of a popup menu associated with an instance of `JMenu`. The `popupMenuVisible` property is read-only.

tearOff — Indicates whether a menu can be "torn off" and placed in a separate window. As of Swing 1.1 FCS, the `tearOff` property is not supported.

topLevelMenu — A `boolean` property that indicates whether a menu is a top-level menu. Top-level menus are discussed in "Menus and Popup Menus" on page 458.

Note: *The following* `JMenu` *properties are not functional as of Swing 1.1 FCS:*

- delay[3]
- menu location
- popup size
- tear off

JMenu Events

Instances of `JMenu` fire menu events when they are selected, deselected, or canceled. A menu can be canceled by clicking outside of the menu's popup menu. A listener interface is defined in the `swing.event` package for menu selection events. The interface is summarized in Interface Summary 10-2.

3.   Is up to look and feels to set the delay; none of the default look and feels use the property.

Interface Summary 10-2   MenuListener

public abstract void menuCanceled(MenuEvent)
public abstract void menuDeselected(MenuEvent)
public abstract void menuSelected(MenuEvent)

As of Swing 1.1 FCS, menu canceled events are never fired by the JMenu class. In other words, menu listeners associated with an instance of JMenu will never have their menuCanceled method invoked.

The applet listed in Example 10-13 adds a menu listener to an instance of JMenu and prints a message whenever a method in the MenuListener interface is called.

Example 10-13 Listening for Menu Events

```
import javax.swing.*;
import javax.swing.event.*;
import java.awt.*;
import java.awt.event.*;

public class Test extends JApplet {
    public void init() {
        JMenuBar mb = new JMenuBar();
        JMenu fileMenu = new JMenu("File");

        fileMenu.add("New ...");
        fileMenu.add("Open ...");
        fileMenu.add("Save");
        fileMenu.add("Save As ..");
        fileMenu.addSeparator();
        fileMenu.add("Exit");

        mb.add(fileMenu);
        setJMenuBar(mb);

        fileMenu.addMenuListener(new MenuListener() {
            public void menuCanceled(MenuEvent e) {
                System.out.println("menu canceled");
            }
            public void menuSelected(MenuEvent e) {
                System.out.println("menu selected");
            }
```

```
        public void menuDeselected(MenuEvent e) {
            System.out.println("menu deselected");
        }
    });
}
}
```

Note that the MenuEvent class—which extends the java.util.EventObject class—provides no methods of its own. The only information that can be obtained from an instance of MenuEvent is the source of the event.

JMenu Class Summaries

The public and protected variables and methods for JMenu are listed in Class Summary 10-5.

Class Summary 10-5   JMenu

Extends: JMenuItem
Implements: MenuElement, javax.accessibility.Accessible

Constructors

---

public JMenu()
public JMenu(String)
public JMenu(String, boolean isTearOff)

JMenu provides a no-argument constructor that creates a menu with no text. The no-argument constructor can be used to construct menus where the title of the menu is determined after the menu is instantiated.

JMenu provides two variations of constructors that take a string argument. The string argument is the text that will be displayed in menu, and the `boolean` value specified in the third constructor listed above determines whether the menu is a tear-off menu. As of Swing 1.1 FCS, tear-off menus are not implemented.

Methods

Listeners

---

public void <u>addMenuListener</u>(MenuListener)
public void <u>removeMenuListener</u>(MenuListener)

The JMenu class provides methods for adding and removing menu listeners. See "JMenu Events" on page 506 for more information concerning the MenuListener class.

Populating

---

public JMenuItem <u>add</u>(Action)
public JMenuItem <u>add</u>(JMenuItem)
public JMenuItem <u>add</u>(String)
public Component <u>add</u>(Component)

public void <u>addSeparator</u>()

public JMenuItem <u>insert</u>(Action, int index)
public JMenuItem <u>insert</u>(JMenuItem, int index)
public void <u>insert</u>(String, int index)
public void <u>insertSeparator</u>(int index)

public void <u>remove</u>(JMenuItem)
public void <u>remove</u>(int index)
public void <u>removeAll</u>()

Populating menus is a straightforward proposition because JMenu provides the methods listed above for adding, inserting, and removing objects. Menu items, strings, components, actions, and separators can all be added to or removed from a menu. Because menus are in fact buttons that display a popup menu when activated, the methods listed above populate a menu's popup and not the menu itself.

All of the add... methods listed above append a menu item to the end of a menu. When actions or strings are added to a menu, the menu creates a menu item that is returned from add(Action) and add(String), respectively. The add(JMenuItem) method returns a reference to the item it is passed.

Adding a component to a menu does not result in the creation of a menu item; in other words, add(Component) does not create a menu item. Because menus are containers, components are added directly to a menu.

Menu items are not created for separators either. The addSeparator method adds a separator—an extension of JSeparator—to a menu's popup menu.

When actions are added to a menu, the menu item representing an action sets its text and icon according to information obtained from the action. See "Actions" on page 235 for a discussion of how menu items are constructed from an action.

Popup Menu Components

---

public Component <u>getMenuComponent</u>(int index)
public int <u>getMenuComponentCount</u>()
public Component[] <u>getMenuComponents</u>()

The methods listed above pertain to the menu's popup menu; for example, getMenuComponentCount() returns the number of components contained in the menu's popup menu.

Property Accessors

---

public int <u>getDelay</u>()
public JMenuItem <u>getItem</u>(int index)
public int <u>getItemCount</u>()

public JPopupMenu getPopupMenu()

public void setAccelerator(KeyStroke)
public void setDelay(int)
public void setMenuLocation(int x, int y)
public void setModel(ButtonModel)
public void setPopupMenuVisible(boolean)
public void setSelected(boolean)

public boolean isMenuComponent(Component)
public boolean isPopupMenuVisible()
public boolean isSelected()
public boolean isTearOff()
public boolean isTopLevelMenu()

The methods listed above are accessors for JMenu properties. See "JMenu Properties" on page 504 for description of the properties.

The applet shown in Figure 10-16 uses the getItemCount and getItem methods to print information about the menu items in the applet's menus when the button is activated.

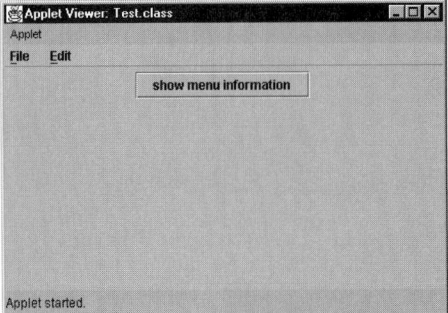

Figure 10-16 Accessing Information About Menus in a Menu Bar

The applet implements a class—MenuBarPrinter—that can print information about the menus and menu items contained in any Swing menu bar. MenuBarPrinter implements a static print method that uses JMenuBar.getMenuCount() and JMenuBar.getMenu() to iterate through the menus in the menu bar and to iterate through the items for each menu.

```
class MenuBarPrinter {
    static public void print(JMenuBar menubar) {
        int   numMenus = menubar.getMenuCount();
        JMenu nextMenu;

        JMenuItem nextItem;

        System.out.println();
        System.out.println("MenuBar has "          +
                           menubar.getMenuCount() +
                           " menus");
        System.out.println();

        for(int i=0; i < numMenus; ++i) {
           nextMenu = menubar.getMenu(i);

           System.out.println(nextMenu.getText() + " menu ...");
           System.out.println(nextMenu);

           int numItems = nextMenu.getItemCount();

           for(int j=0; j < numItems; ++j) {
              nextItem = nextMenu.getItem(j);
              System.out.println(nextItem);
           }
           System.out.println();
        }
    }
}
```

The output produced when the applet is run is listed below:

```
File menu ...
javax.swing.JMenu[,0,1,39x19,layout=javax.swing.OverlayLayout,
JMenu]
javax.swing.JMenuItem[,0,0,0x0,invalid,layout=javax.swing.Over-
layLayout]
javax.swing.JMenuItem[,0,0,0x0,invalid,layout=javax.swing.Over-
layLayout]
javax.swing.JMenuItem[,0,0,0x0,invalid,layout=javax.swing.Over-
layLayout]
javax.swing.JMenuItem[,0,0,0x0,invalid,layout=javax.swing.Over-
layLayout]
javax.swing.JMenu[,0,1,39x19,layout=javax.swing.OverlayLayout,
JMenu]
javax.swing.JMenuItem[,0,0,0x0,invalid,layout=javax.swing.Over-
layLayout]

Edit menu ...
```

```
javax.swing.JMenu[,39,1,41x19,layout=javax.swing.OverlayLayout,
JMenu]
javax.swing.JMenuItem[,0,0,0x0,invalid,layout=javax.swing.Over-
layLayout]
javax.swing.JMenuItem[,0,0,0x0,invalid,layout=javax.swing.Over-
layLayout]
javax.swing.JMenuItem[,0,0,0x0,invalid,layout=javax.swing.Over-
layLayout]
```

The applet shown in Figure 10-16 is listed in its entirety in Example 10-14.

Example 10-14 Printing Information About Menus in a Menu Bar

```
import javax.swing.*;
import java.awt.*;
import java.awt.event.*;

public class Test extends JApplet {
    public void init() {
        Container contentPane = getContentPane();

        final JMenuBar mb = new JMenuBar();
        final MenuBarPrinter printer = new MenuBarPrinter();

        JMenu fileMenu = new JMenu("File");
        JMenu editMenu = new JMenu("Edit");
        JMenuItem exitItem = new JMenuItem("Exit");

        fileMenu.setMnemonic('F');
        editMenu.setMnemonic('E');

        fileMenu.add("New ...");
        fileMenu.add("Open ...");
        fileMenu.add("Save");
        fileMenu.add("Save As ..");
        fileMenu.addSeparator();
        fileMenu.add(exitItem);

        editMenu.add("Cut");
        editMenu.add("Copy");
        editMenu.add("Paste");

        mb.add(fileMenu);
        mb.add(editMenu);
        setJMenuBar(mb);

        JButton button = new JButton("show menu information");
        contentPane.setLayout(new FlowLayout());
        contentPane.add(button);
```

```
            button.addActionListener(new ActionListener() {
                public void actionPerformed(ActionEvent e) {
                    printer.print(mb);
                }
            });

            exitItem.addActionListener(new ActionListener() {
                public void actionPerformed(ActionEvent e) {
                    System.exit(0);
                }
            });
        }
    }
    class MenuBarPrinter {
        static public void print(JMenuBar menubar) {
            int  numMenus = menubar.getMenuCount();
            JMenu nextMenu;

            JMenuItem nextItem;

            System.out.println();
            System.out.println("MenuBar has "        +
                                menubar.getMenuCount() +
                                " menus");
            System.out.println();

            for(int i=0; i < numMenus; ++i) {
               nextMenu = menubar.getMenu(i);
               System.out.println(nextMenu.getText() + " menu ...");
               System.out.println(nextMenu);

               int numItems = nextMenu.getItemCount();

               for(int j=0; j < numItems; ++j) {
                   nextItem = nextMenu.getItem(j);
                   System.out.println(nextItem);
               }
               System.out.println();
            }
        }
    }
```

The applet sets mnemonics for both the File and Edit menus. JMenu overrides setAccelerator to throw an exception indicating that accelerators cannot be used for menus and to use mnemonics instead.

Swing Menus Do Not Support Accelerators—Use Mnemonics Instead

Accelerators can be set for menu items but not for menus; JMenu.setAccelerator is overridden to throw an exception. Recall from "Menu Item Accelerators and Mnemonics" on page 462 that the use of mnemonics results in menus being traversed and displayed. Accelerators, on the other hand, are used to invoke the action associated with a menu item—accelerators do not display menus. Because there is no action associated with a menu other than to display the menu's popup menu, accelerators cannot be set for menus. Typing a mnemonic associated with a menu causes the menu's popup menu to be displayed.

Associating a keyboard shortcut with a menu is accomplished by using a mnemonic. Mnemonics are set by invoking the setMnemonic method that JMenu inherits from AbstractButton by way of JMenuItem.

MenuElement Interface

---

public Component getComponent()
public MenuElement[] getSubElements()
public void menuSelectionChanged(boolean)
public void processKeyEvent(KeyEvent, MenuElement[], MenuSelectionManager)
public void processMouseEvent(MouseEvent, MenuElement[], MenuSelectionManager)

The methods listed above are defined in the MenuElement interface. See "MenuElement" on page 518 for more on the MenuElement interface.

Listeners / Event Firing

---

protected PropertyChangeListener createActionChangeListener(JMenuItem)
protected JMenu.WinListener createWinListener(JPopupMenu)
protected void fireMenuCanceled()
protected void fireMenuDeselected()
protected void fireMenuSelected()
protected void processKeyEvent(KeyEvent)

The `protected` methods listed above implement fundamental `JMenu` behavior and can be overridden by extensions if the behavior is not satisfactory. As is typically the case for such `protected` methods, in practice it will rarely be necessary to override the methods listed above.

The `createActionChangeListener` method creates an instance of a class that implements the `PropertyChangeListener` interface to respond to property changes for instances of `Action` that have been added to a menu. By default, the property change listener reacts to changes in the action's name, small icon, and enabled state properties. Extensions of `JMenu` can override the `createActionChangeListener` method and install their own property change listener for responding to property changes for actions that are added to menus. See "Actions" on page 235 for more information on actions.

The `createWinListener` method creates an instance of a class that implements the `WindowListener` interface. By default, the window listener that is created by the method simply deselects the menu when the popup menu associated with the menu is about to close. Extensions of `JMenu` are free to override `createWinListener` and install their own window listener if different behavior is desired.

The `fireMenuSelected` and `fireMenuDeselected` methods fire menu events to listeners when the menu is selected and deselected, respectively. The `processKeyEvent` method is overridden to ignore consumed keystrokes.

Accessibility / Pluggable Look And Feel

---

public AccessibleContext getAccessibleContext()
public String getUIClassID()
public void updateUI()
public void setUI(MenuUI)

The methods listed above can be found in most extensions of `JComponent`. Swing lightweight components can return an accessibility context that contains accessibility information for the component and the class name of their UI delegate. The `updateUI` method is invoked when the component is fitted with a UI delegate.

AWT Compatibility

Swing's menus are markedly different from AWT menus. Swing menus (and menu items) are buttons by virtue of the fact that they extend the `AbstractButton` class and therefore can be manipulated in the same fashion as any button. Additionally, because `AbstractButton` extends `JComponent`, which in turn extends `java.awt.Container`, Swing menus (and menu items) are also capable containers.

Because Swing menus are buttons, they inherit methods for specifying text and an icon, and because Swing menus are also containers, any type of component can be added to a menu. AWT menus, on the other hand, are limited to text only.

AWT menu bars can be attached only to a frame, which means that AWT menus can reside only in a Java application. Swing menu bars, on the other hand, can be attached to both Java applets and applications.

The `public` methods implemented by `java.awt.Menu` and their `JMenu` equivalents are listed in Table 10-4.

Table 10-4   java.awt.Menu Methods and JMenu Equivalents[1]

`java.awt.Menu` Methods	JMenu Equivalents
void add(MenuItem)	**void add(JMenuItem)**
void add(String)	void add(String)
void addSeparator()	void addSeparator()
MenuItem getItem(int)	**JMenuItem getItem(int)**
int getItemCount()	int getItemCount()
void insert(MenuItem, int)	**JMenuItem insert(JMenuItem, int)**
void insert(String, int)	void insert(String, int)
void insertSeparator(int)	void insertSeparator(int)
boolean isTearOff()	boolean isTearOff()
String paramString()	String paramString()
void remove(int)	void remove(int)
void remove(MenuComponent)	**void remove(JMenuItem)**
void removeAll()	void removeAll()

1. Differing signatures are highlighted in bold.

JMenu maintains a fair degree of compatibility with its AWT counterpart—
java.awt.Menu. Both components can add/insert menu items (although AWT
menus add AWT menu items, and Swing menus add Swing menu items) and
separators. Also, both components provide access to a count of their menu items
and the menu items themselves.

Both Swing and AWT menus fire action events when one of their menu items is
activated. Swing menus also fire menu events when their items are selected or
deselected.

The JMenu and java.awt.Menu APIs both include provisions for tear-off
menus, but as of Swing 1.1, tear-off menus were not implemented for Swing
menus.

Menu Elements

JMenuItem, JMenu, JPopupMenu and JMenuBar implement the MenuElement
interface for the purpose of participating in menu event handling. Although
menus and menu items implement the MenuElement interface, it is not
necessary to understand the interface or how its methods are implemented by
JMenuItem and JMenu for everyday use of Swing menus and menu items.

This section focuses on using the MenuElement interface to implement a custom
menu element.

The MenuElement interface is listed in the Interface Summary 10-3.

Interface Summary 10-3   MenuElement

---

public abstract Component getComponent()
public abstract MenuElement[] getSubElements()
public abstract void menuSelectionChanged(boolean)
public abstract void processKeyEvent(KeyEvent, MenuElement[],
                                     MenuSelectionManager)
public abstract void processMouseEvent(MouseEvent, MenuElement[],
                                     MenuSelectionManager)

All of the methods defined by the MenuElement interface are invoked by an instance of MenuSelectionManager and should not be invoked directly. The MenuElement interface exists to ensure that menus and menu items are participants in menu event handling.

Implementing the MenuElement Interface

Components that are added directly to a menu do not behave like menu items; for example, dragging the cursor over a component in a menu does not cause the component to be highlighted. However, a component that implements the MenuElement interface can participate in menu event handling and can even define custom behavior.

The applet shown in Example 10-17 illustrates implementing custom menu elements with an element that underlines its text to indicate that the element is armed.

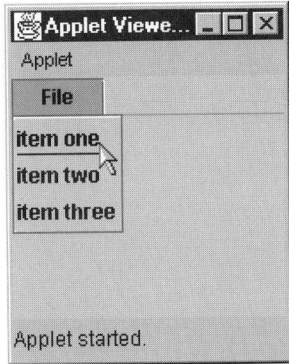

Figure 10-17 Implementing Custom Menu Elements

The UnderlineElement class extends JButton and implements the MenuElement interface. The constructor passes the element's text to the JButton constructor and sets its border to an empty border.

The getComponent method returns the component associated with a menu element, which in the case of UnderlineElement is the element itself. The getSubElements method returns an MenuElement array with zero items, indicating that UnderlineElement does not contain any elements.

```
class UnderlineElement extends JButton implements MenuElement {
    private boolean drawUnderline = false;

    public UnderlineElement(String s) {
        super(s);
        setBorder(BorderFactory.createEmptyBorder(2,2,2,2));
    }
    public Component getComponent() {
        return this;
    }
    public MenuElement[] getSubElements() {
        return new MenuElement[0];
    }
    ...
```

The menuSelectionChanged method is called when menu selection is
changed. The boolean variable passed to menuSelectionChanged represents
whether the element is selected.

The UnderlineElement.menuSelectionChanged method sets its
drawUnderline member variable and invokes repaint.

UnderlineElement also overrides paintComponent to underline the
element's text as needed.

```
    ...
    public void menuSelectionChanged(boolean b) {
        drawUnderline = b;
        repaint();
    }
    public void paintComponent(Graphics g) {
        super.paintComponent(g);

        Insets insets = getInsets();

        if(drawUnderline) {
            FontMetrics fm = g.getFontMetrics();
            g.drawLine(insets.left, insets.top + fm.getHeight(),
                    fm.stringWidth(getText()),
                    insets.top + fm.getHeight());
        }
    }
    ...
```

The `UnderlineElement` class is not interested in processing key events, so the `processKeyEvent` method is implemented with an empty body.

```
...
public void processKeyEvent(KeyEvent me,
                    MenuElement[] element,
                    MenuSelectionManager msm) {
}
...
```

`UnderlineElement` overrides the `processMouseEvent` method to invoke `super.processMouseEvent()` to ensure that the element's button state is updated and then calls `MenuSelectionManager.processMouseEvent()`. The menu selection manager determines the intended recipients of the event, detects enter/exit events while dragging, and dispatches appropriate events.

All of above is necessary because menu items fire `MenuDragMouseEvents` when the mouse is dragged over an item, and `MenuKeyEvents` when keys are pressed, released, or typed while a menu item is armed. See "JMenuItem Events" on page 468 for more information concerning `MenuDragMouseEvents`. *The important thing to remember is that menu elements must override* `processMouseEvent(MouseEvent)` *to invoke* `MenuSelectionManager.processMouseEvent()`.

```
...
public void processMouseEvent(MouseEvent me) {
    super.processMouseEvent(me);
    MenuSelectionManager.defaultManager().processMouseEvent(
                                    me);
}
...
```

`UnderlineElement` implements the `processMouseEvent` method defined by the `MenuElement` interface by setting the selected path for the menu selection manager, depending upon the type of event.

If the event is a mouse click or released, the path is set to `null` and `doClick()` is invoked, activating the button; see page 406 for more information concerning the `doClick` method.

If the event is any other type of mouse event, mouse enter or exit, for example, a path is constructed with the element in the path. The path must include the element itself in order for the element to receive subsequent events from the menu selection manager.

```
...
public void processMouseEvent(MouseEvent me,
                    MenuElement[] element,
                    MenuSelectionManager msm) {
    if(me.getID() == MouseEvent.MOUSE_CLICKED ||
       me.getID() == MouseEvent.MOUSE_RELEASED) {

        msm.setSelectedPath(null);
        doClick();
    }
    else
        msm.setSelectedPath(getPath());
}
public MenuElement[] getPath() {
    MenuSelectionManager defaultManager =
                    MenuSelectionManager.defaultManager();
    MenuElement oldPath[] = defaultManager.getSelectedPath();
    MenuElement newPath[];
    int len = oldPath.length;

    if(len > 0) {
        MenuElement lastElement = oldPath[len-1];
        Component parent = getParent();

        if (lastElement == parent) {
            newPath = new MenuElement[len+1];

            System.arraycopy(oldPath, 0, newPath, 0, len);
            newPath[len] = this;
        }
        else {
            int j;

            for (j = len-1; j >= 0; j--) {
                if (oldPath[j].getComponent() == parent)
                    break;
            }
            newPath = new MenuElement[j+2];
            System.arraycopy(oldPath, 0, newPath, 0, j+1);
            newPath[j+1] = this;
        }
    }
    else
        return new MenuElement[0];

    return newPath;
}
}
```

Implementing custom menu elements can appear to be rather intimidating, but the process really boils down to two things.

First, menu elements must override processMenuEvent(MenuEvent) to invoke MenuSelectionManager.processMouseEvent() so that the menu selection manager can perform appropriate housekeeping and event firing.

Second, menu elements should override processMouseEvent(MouseEvent, MenuElement[],MenuSelectionManager) to actually process the event. If the menu element wants to receive subsequent events from the menu selection manager, it must add itself to the path of menu elements it is passed.

The applet shown in Example 10-17 is listed in its entirety in Example 10-15.

Example 10-15 Implementing Custom Menu Elements

```java
import javax.swing.*;
import java.awt.*;
import java.awt.event.*;
import java.util.*;

public class Test extends JApplet {
    public void init() {
        Container contentPane = getContentPane();
        JMenuBar menuBar = new JMenuBar();
        JMenu fileMenu = new JMenu("File");

        fileMenu.add(new UnderlineElement("item one"));
        fileMenu.add(new UnderlineElement("item two"));
        fileMenu.add(new UnderlineElement("item three"));

        menuBar.add(fileMenu);
        setJMenuBar(menuBar);
    }
}
class UnderlineElement extends JButton implements MenuElement {
    private boolean drawUnderline = false;

    public UnderlineElement(String s) {
        super(s);
        setBorder(BorderFactory.createEmptyBorder(2,2,2,2));
    }
    public Component getComponent() {
        return this;
    }
    public MenuElement[] getSubElements() {
        return new MenuElement[0];
    }
    public void menuSelectionChanged(boolean b) {
        drawUnderline = b;
        repaint();
    }
    public void paintComponent(Graphics g) {
```

```java
        super.paintComponent(g);

        Insets insets = getInsets();

        if(drawUnderline) {
            FontMetrics fm = g.getFontMetrics();
            g.drawLine(insets.left, insets.top + fm.getHeight(),
                    fm.stringWidth(getText()),
                    insets.top + fm.getHeight());
        }
    }
    public void processKeyEvent(KeyEvent me,
                            MenuElement[] element,
                            MenuSelectionManager msm) {
    }
    public void processMouseEvent(MouseEvent me) {
        super.processMouseEvent(me);
        MenuSelectionManager.defaultManager().processMouseEvent(
                                                    me);
    }
    public void processMouseEvent(MouseEvent me,
                            MenuElement[] element,
                            MenuSelectionManager msm) {
        if(me.getID() == MouseEvent.MOUSE_CLICKED ||
           me.getID() == MouseEvent.MOUSE_RELEASED) {

            msm.setSelectedPath(null);
            doClick();
        }
        else
            msm.setSelectedPath(getPath());
    }
    public MenuElement[] getPath() {
        MenuSelectionManager defaultManager =
                        MenuSelectionManager.defaultManager();
        MenuElement oldPath[] = defaultManager.getSelectedPath();
        MenuElement newPath[];
        int len = oldPath.length;

        if(len > 0) {
            MenuElement lastElement = oldPath[len-1];
            Component parent = getParent();

            if (lastElement == parent) {
                newPath = new MenuElement[len+1];

                System.arraycopy(oldPath, 0, newPath, 0, len);
                newPath[len] = this;
            }
            else {
                int j;
```

```
        for (j = len-1; j >= 0; j--) {
            if (oldPath[j].getComponent() == parent)
                break;
        }
        newPath = new MenuElement[j+2];
        System.arraycopy(oldPath, 0, newPath, 0, j+1);
        newPath[j+1] = this;
    }
}
else
    return new MenuElement[0];

return newPath;
    }
}
```

JPopupMenu

Recall that menus are buttons that display a popup menu when armed. Popup menus—represented by the JPopupMenu class—can also be used outside the context of a menu; a popup menu can be displayed anywhere within a component or relative to the screen.

Actions, menu items, components, and separators can all be added to a Swing popup menu. When an action is added to a popup menu, the popup menu creates a menu item that is added to the popup menu. See "Actions" on page 235 for more information on adding actions to Swing components.

The applet shown in Figure 10-18 displays a popup menu that contains two menu items, a separator, and a component.

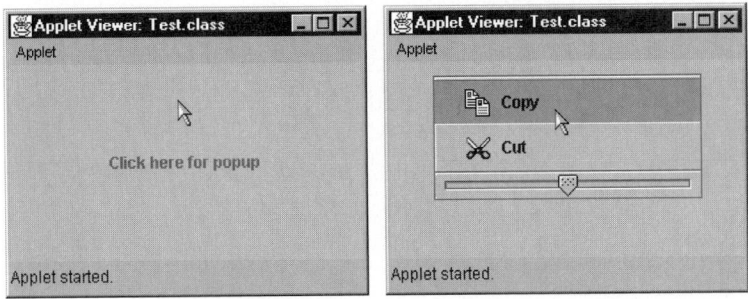

Figure 10-18 A Popup Menu with two Menu Items, Separator, and Component

The applet shown in Figure 10-18 is listed in Example 10-16.

Example 10-16 Using Popup Menus

```java
import javax.swing.*;
import javax.swing.event.*;
import java.awt.*;
import java.awt.event.*;

public class Test extends JApplet {
    public void init() {
        Container contentPane = getContentPane();
        final JLabel label = new JLabel("Click here for popup");
        final JPopupMenu popup = new JPopupMenu();
        final JSlider slider = new JSlider();

        popup.add(new JMenuItem("Copy",
                                new ImageIcon("copy.gif")));
        popup.add(new CutAction());
        popup.addSeparator();
        popup.add(slider);

        label.addMouseListener(new MouseAdapter() {
            public void mousePressed (MouseEvent e) {
                popup.show(label, e.getX(), e.getY());
            }
        });
        slider.addChangeListener(new ChangeListener() {
            public void stateChanged(ChangeEvent e) {
                if( ! slider.getValueIsAdjusting())
                    popup.setVisible(false);
            }
        });

        label.setHorizontalAlignment(JLabel.CENTER);
        contentPane.add(label, BorderLayout.CENTER);
    }
    class CutAction extends AbstractAction {
        public CutAction() {
            super("Cut", new ImageIcon("cut.gif"));
        }
        public void actionPerformed(ActionEvent e) {
            System.out.println("cut");
        }
    }
}
```

The applet creates an instance of JPopupMenu that is populated with menu items, a separator, and a slider. The applet's content pane contains a label that is fitted with a mouse listener that shows the popup menu underneath the mouse by invoking JPopupMenu.show().

The JPopupMenu.show method is passed a component representing the popup menu's *invoker* and coordinates, relative to the invoker, at which the popup's upper-left corner will be displayed. See "Popup Menu Invokers" on page 531 for more information concerning popup menu invokers.

A change listener is added to the slider that hides the popup menu after the slider's value has been adjusted. See the "Progress Bars, Sliders, and Separators" chapter on page 579 for more information on sliders.

The cut and copy menu items both display an icon and a string. The cut item is created by adding an action to the popup, whereas the copy item is created by instantiating an instance of JMenuItem. The dual approaches to creating nearly identical menu items is done to illustrate that both menu items and actions can be added to a popup menu.

Popup Trigger

Although it may sometimes be desirable to show a popup menu in response to a mouse pressed event, as was the case for the applet listed in Example 10-16, popups are typically shown in response to a sequence of events known as the *popup trigger*. Popup triggers are windowing system dependent; for example, the popup triggers for Motif and Windows are described below.

- **Motif Popup Trigger:** On a mouse button 3 down, the popup is displayed and stays up if the button is held down or released within a short period of time. A subsequent mouse down, either outside of the popup or in one of the popup's items, brings the popup down.

- **Windows Popup Trigger:** The popup is displayed on a mouse button 2 up. A subsequent mouse button 1 or mouse button 2 down either over an item in the popup or outside of the popup menu brings the popup down.

The applet listed in Example 10-17 displays a popup menu in response to the popup trigger.

Example 10-17 Showing a Popup Menu in Response to the Popup Trigger

```
import javax.swing.*;
import java.awt.*;
import java.awt.event.*;

public class Test extends JApplet {
    private JPopupMenu popup = new JPopupMenu();

    public void init() {
        Container contentPane = getContentPane();

        popup.add(new JMenuItem("item one"));
        popup.add(new JMenuItem("item two"));
        popup.add(new JMenuItem("item three"));
        popup.add(new JMenuItem("item four"));

        contentPane.addMouseListener(new MouseAdapter() {
            public void mousePressed(MouseEvent e) {
                showPopup(e);
            }
            public void mouseClicked(MouseEvent e) {
                showPopup(e);
            }
            public void mouseReleased(MouseEvent e) {
                showPopup(e);
            }
        });
    }
    void showPopup(MouseEvent e) {
        if(e.isPopupTrigger())
            popup.show(this, e.getX(), e.getY());
    }
}
```

The applet implements a mouse listener that handles mouse pressed, clicked, and released events. Each event is handled by invoking the applet's showPopup method, which in turn invokes the MouseEvent.isPopupTrigger method to detect the popup trigger. If the trigger has been "pulled," the popup is shown.

All three methods defined by java.awt.event.MouseListener that deal with mouse presses and clicks are overridden to check for the popup trigger. Overriding all three methods is necessary because the popup trigger could be associated with different mouse events on different platforms.

Note that this is a somewhat awkward way to have to detect the popup trigger. A better solution might have been to implement a popup trigger event. That way, a popup trigger listener could be registered with a component, and generic mouse events would not have to be handled. Not only would this be more convenient, but it would be much more in line with the delegation-based event model.

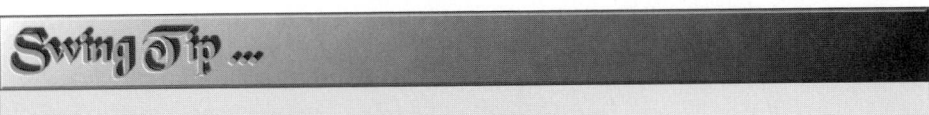

Use the Popup Trigger to Show Popups

Windowing systems define a popup trigger—a sequence of events that causes a popup to be displayed. Although it is not necessary to detect the popup trigger when showing a popup menu, it is typically expected that popup menus will only be shown in response to the popup trigger. As a result, good GUI design dictates that popup menus (other than the popups shown by menus) should only be shown in response to the popup trigger.

Light/Medium/HeavyWeight Popup Menus

The popup menu shown in Figure 10-18 was strategically located so that the popup was completely contained within the applet's window. If the popup is positioned so that its bounds exceeds the bounds of its window, the popup will be contained in a window of its own, as illustrated in Figure 10-19.

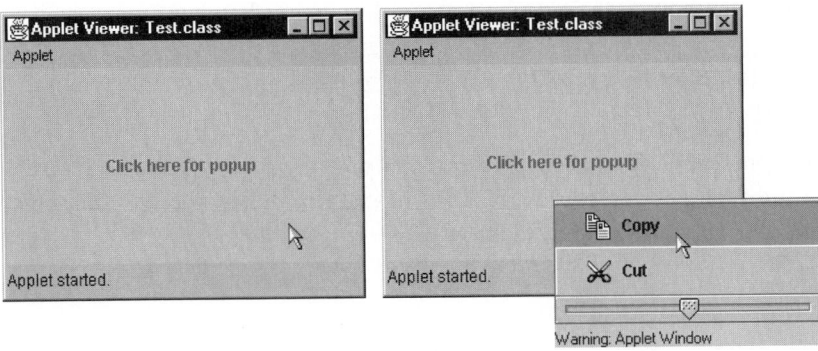

Figure 10-19 A Heavyweight Popup Menu

Swing popup menus are represented by a single class—JPopupMenu—but actually come in three distinct flavors, as listed in Table 10-5.

Table 10-5   Swing Popup Menu Types

Popup Type	Popup Menu Is Displayed in …
Light weight	a lightweight container
Medium weight	a heavyweight AWT panel
Heavy weight	an instance of JWindow

The reasons for the different types of Swing popup menus are as follows.

First, if the real estate of a lightweight Swing popup menu intersects with the real estate of a heavyweight AWT component, the lightweight popup menu will be displayed underneath the AWT component. The reason for this behavior has to do with the zorder—meaning the depth assigned to a component—of heavyweight components versus the zorder for lightweight components. To display the popup above the heavyweight component, the container in which the popup menu is displayed must be a heavyweight AWT container. See "Mixing Swing and AWT Components" on page 43 for a more in-depth explanation of zorder and the pitfalls of mixing lightweight and heavyweight components.

If a popup menu is not contained entirely within its top-level window, lightweight and medium weight popups would be clipped to the boundaries of the window. As a result, popups that do not reside entirely within their windows are displayed in a native window of their own.

As a result, when a Swing popup menu is displayed, the following algorithm determines the type of container in which the popup menu will be displayed:

If the popup menu does not fit entirely within its top-level window, a heavyweight popup menu is used, meaning the popup will be displayed in its own window to ensure that the entire popup menu will be visible when it is displayed.

If the popup menu fits entirely within its top-level window, either a lightweight or medium weight popup menu is used, depending upon the popup menu's lightweight popup enabled property.

Popup Menu Invokers

Popup menus have an associated component known as the popup menu's invoker. Popup menus are typically displayed relative to their invoker components, and invokers are used internally by JPopupMenu for a number of other things; for example, invokers are used to locate the window in which a popup menu resides to determine if the popup needs to be contained in a window of its own.

The applet shown in Figure 10-20 displays a popup menu when a selection is made from the combo box. The popup is shown relative to the canvas selected in combo box.

Figure 10-20 Showing a Popup Menu Relative to Its Invoker

The colored "canvases" are extensions of JPanel that fill their interior with a 3D rectangle.

```
class ColoredCanvas extends JPanel {
    private Color color;

    public ColoredCanvas(Color color) {
        this.color = color;
    }
    public void paintComponent(Graphics g) {
        super.paintComponent(g);

        Dimension size = getSize();
        g.setColor   (color);
        g.fill3DRect(0,0,size.width-1,size.height-1,true);
    }
    public Dimension getPreferredSize() {
        return new Dimension(100,100);
    }
}
```

An item listener is added to the combo box that shows the popup relative to the canvas selected from the combo box.

```
combobox.addItemListener(new ItemListener() {
    public void itemStateChanged(ItemEvent event) {
        JComboBox c = (JComboBox)event.getSource();
        String label = (String)c.getSelectedItem();

        if(label.equals("Blue Canvas"))
            popupRelativeToMe = blueCanvas;
        else if(label.equals("Red Canvas"))
            popupRelativeToMe = redCanvas;
        else if(label.equals("Yellow Canvas"))
            popupRelativeToMe = yellowCanvas;

        popup.show(popupRelativeToMe, 5, 5);
    }
});
```

The applet shown in Figure 10-20 is listed in its entirety in Example 10-18.

Example 10-18 Showing a Popup Menu Relative to Its Invoker

```
import javax.swing.*;
import java.awt.*;
import java.awt.event.*;

public class Test extends JApplet {
    JComboBox combobox = new JComboBox();
    JPopupMenu popup   = new JPopupMenu();
    ColoredCanvas popupRelativeToMe;
    ColoredCanvas blueCanvas, redCanvas, yellowCanvas;

    public void init() {
        Container contentPane = getContentPane();
        blueCanvas        = new ColoredCanvas(Color.blue);
        redCanvas         = new ColoredCanvas(Color.red);
        yellowCanvas      = new ColoredCanvas(Color.yellow);
        popupRelativeToMe = blueCanvas;

        popup.add(new JMenuItem("item one"));
        popup.add(new JMenuItem("item two"));
        popup.add(new JMenuItem("item three"));
        popup.add(new JMenuItem("item four"));

        contentPane.setLayout(new FlowLayout());
        contentPane.add(new JLabel("Popup Over:"));
        contentPane.add(combobox);
        contentPane.add(blueCanvas);
```

```
        contentPane.add(redCanvas);
        contentPane.add(yellowCanvas);

        combobox.addItem("Blue Canvas");
        combobox.addItem("Yellow Canvas");
        combobox.addItem("Red Canvas");

        combobox.addItemListener(new ItemListener() {
            public void itemStateChanged(ItemEvent event) {
                if(event.getStateChange() == ItemEvent.SELECTED) {
                    JComboBox c = (JComboBox)event.getSource();
                    String label = (String)c.getSelectedItem();

                    if(label.equals("Blue Canvas"))
                        popupRelativeToMe = blueCanvas;
                    else if(label.equals("Red Canvas"))
                        popupRelativeToMe = redCanvas;
                    else if(label.equals("Yellow Canvas"))
                        popupRelativeToMe = yellowCanvas;

                    popup.show(popupRelativeToMe, 5, 5);
                }
            }
        });
    }
}
class ColoredCanvas extends JPanel {
    private Color color;

    public ColoredCanvas(Color color) {
        this.color = color;
    }
    public void paintComponent(Graphics g) {
        super.paintComponent(g);

        Dimension size = getSize();
        g.setColor  (color);
        g.fill3DRect(0,0,size.width-1,size.height-1,true);
    }
    public Dimension getPreferredSize() {
        return new Dimension(100,100);
    }
}
```

The JPopupMenu class is summarized in Component Summary 10-5.

Component Summary 10-5   JPopupMenu

Model(s)	SingleSelectionModel
UI Delegate(s)	javax.swing.plaf.basic.BasicPopupMenuUI
Renderer(s)	——
Editor(s)	——
Events Fired	PropertyChangeEvent / PopupMenuEvent
Replacement For	java.awt.PopupMenu

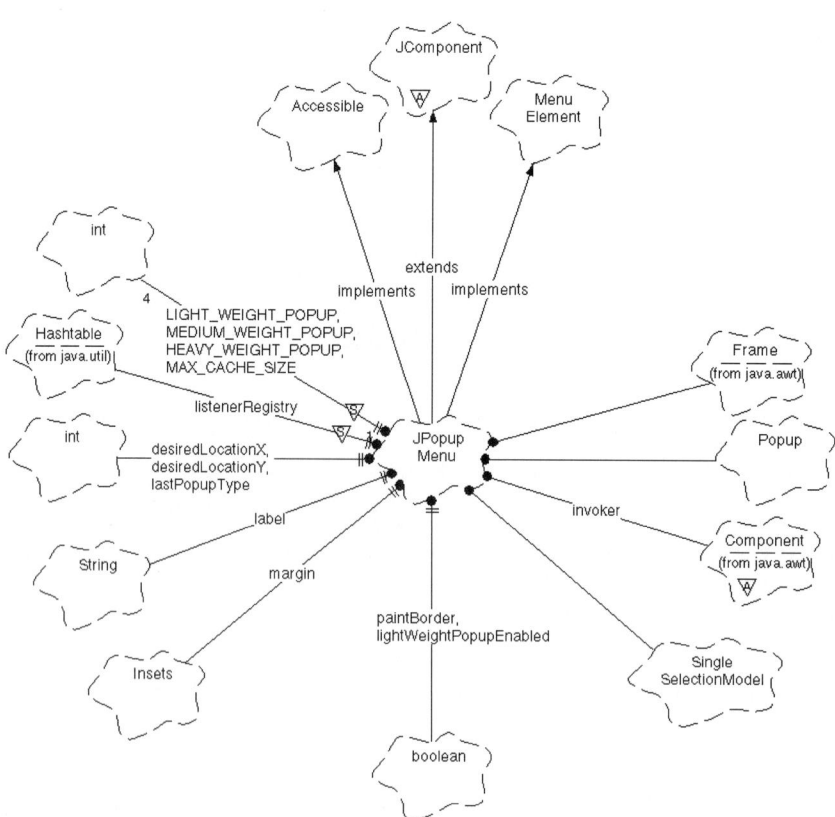

Figure 10-21 JPopupMenu Class Diagram

JPopupMenu extends JComponent and implements the Accessible and MenuElement interfaces. JPopupMenu maintains a private reference to an instance of Insets, which represents the margin between the popup menu's border and the items it displays.

JPopupMenu also maintains a private reference to a string that is used as the popup menu's title and private references to boolean properties that determine whether JPopupMenu paints its border and whether the popup is displayed in a lightweight container. Whether a popup menu's title is used is up to the popup menu's look and feel. As of Swing 1.1 FCS, none of the standard Swing look and feels display a title.

JPopupMenu keeps track of its *invoker*, the component that the popup menu is displayed within, and the frame of its invoker. By default, a popup's invoker is null (meaning the popup is not contained in a component) but a popup menu's invoker can be explicitly set as in Example 10-18 on page 532. The model for instances of JPopupMenu is a SingleSelectionModel that keeps track of which item is currently selected.

JPopupMenu also maintains a reference to a Popup, which is a private interface defined within the JPopupMenu class. The Popup interface is used so that JPopupMenu can manipulate the actual popup, whether it is heavyweight, medium weight, or lightweight, in a uniform manner. Because the Popup interface is private to the JPopupMenu class, it is not discussed here.

JPopupMenu Properties

The properties maintained by the JPopupMenu class are listed in Table 10-6.

Table 10-6 JPopupMenu Properties

Property Name	Data Type	Access[1]	Type[2]	Default[3]
borderPainted	boolean	SG	S	true
componentAtIndex	Component	G	S	—
componentIndex	int	G	I	—
invoker	Component	SG	S	null
label	String	CSG	B	null
lightWeightPopupEnabled	boolean	SG	S	true
margin	Insets	G	S	(0,0,0,0)

Table 10-6   JPopupMenu Properties (Continued)

Property Name	Data Type	Access[1]	Type[2]	Default[3]
popupSize	Dimension	S	S	L&F
rootPopupMenu	JPopupMenu	G	S	—
selectionModel	SingleSelectionModel	SG	S	DefaultSingle-SelectionModel

1. C = settable at construction time / G = getter method / S = setter method
2. B = bound / bool = boolean / C = constrained/ I = indexed / S = simple
3. L&F = look-and-feel dependent

borderPainted — Determines whether a popup menu's border is painted.

componentAtIndex, componentIndex — Popup menus can provide a component given an index, and vice versa by the componentAtIndex and componentIndex properties, respectively. Both setter methods use JPopupMenu's inherited (from java.awt.Container) getComponents method to obtain the array of components contained in the popup menu.

If componentAtIndex is passed an invalid index, a null reference is returned from the method. If getComponentIndex is passed a component that is not contained in the popup menu, the method returns −1.

invoker — Popup menus are typically displayed relative to their invoker component by the use of the JPopupMenu.show(Component invoker, int x, int y), which displays the popup in the invoker's coordinate system.

Popup menus can also be positioned relative to the screen with the JPopupMenu.setLocation(int x, int y) method, which is passed screen coordinates. Popup menus positioned relative to the screen can be displayed by invocation of JPopupMenu.setVisible() instead of by use of JPopupMenu.show(). However, all popup menus must have a non-null invoker, and therefore popups positioned with setLocation() and displayed with setVisible() must explicitly specify an invoker with the JPopupMenu.setInvoker method.

label — A popup menu's label is used as the menu's title. It is the responsibility of a popup menu's look and feel to display a popup menu's title. As of Swing 1.2 FCS, none of the look and feels display popup menu titles.

lightWeightPopupEnabled — Popup menus that are fully contained in a window can be displayed in either a lightweight or heavyweight container. If a popup menu's lightWeightPopupEnabled property is true, a lightweight container is used; if the property is false, the popup will be contained in an AWT panel.

margin — The margin property represents an insets between the inside of a popup menu's order and the outside of the bounding box containing the popup's components.

popupSize — The JPopupMenu class provides a setter method for the size of the popup, but no getter method.

rootPopupMenu — The rootPopupMenu property is a computed property that returns the topmost JPopupMenu ancestor.

selectionModel— Selection models for the JPopupMenu class are of type SingleSelectionModel. By default, popup menus are fitted with an instance of DefaultSingleSelectionModel.

Because popup menus are transient, meaning they do not occupy permanent real estate within a container, setting the majority of properties maintained by JPopupMenu does not result in an update of the popup's display. For example, setting the selected property does not result in a repaint of the popup menu. This is not the case for other Swing components that are selectable; setting the selection state for selectable Swing components typically results in update of the component's display.

JPopupMenu Events

Instances of JPopupMenu fire two types of events: PropertyChangeEvents and PopupMenuEvents. PropertyChangeEvents are fired whenever bound properties associated with a popup menu are modified (as is the case for all Swing components); for example, when a popup's visibility is modified, the popup menu fires a property change event.

PopupMenuEvents are fired when the popup menu will become visible or invisible and when the popup menu is canceled. A popup menu is canceled when it is made visible and subsequently made invisible by clicking outside of the menu (meaning no items from the popup were selected).

The `swing.event` package defines a `PopupMenuListener` interface. The methods defined by the `PopupMenuListener` interface are listed in Interface Summary 10-4.

Interface Summary 10-4   PopupMenuListener

Extends: java.util.EventListener

---

public abstract void <u>popupMenuCanceled</u>(PopupMenuEvent)
public abstract void <u>popupMenuWillBecomeInvisible</u>(PopupMenuEvent)
public abstract void <u>popupMenuWillBecomeVisible</u>(PopupMenuEvent)

The methods defined by the `PopupMenuListener` class are invoked when popup menus have been canceled or are about to become visible or invisible.

The applet shown in Figure 10-22 adds a popup menu listener to an instance of `JPopupMenu`. The listener prints a message whenever the popup menu is made visible or invisible or is canceled. The left picture in Figure 10-22 shows the applet just after the popup menu has been made visible; the right hand picture shows the applet just after the popup menu has been made invisible.

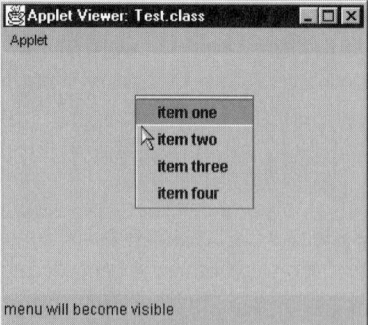 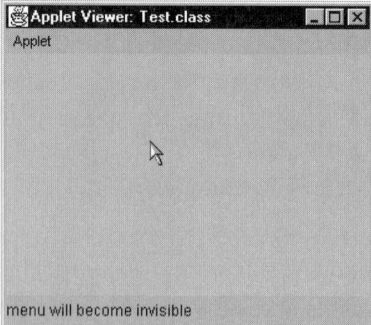

Figure 10-22 Popup Menu Events

The applet shown in Figure 10-22 is listed in Example 10-19.

Example 10-19 Listening for Popup Menu Events

```java
import javax.swing.*;
import javax.swing.event.*;
import java.awt.*;
import java.awt.event.*;
import java.beans.*;

public class Test extends JApplet {
    public void init() {
        final Container contentPane = getContentPane();
        final JPopupMenu popup = new JPopupMenu();

        popup.add(new JMenuItem("item one"));
        popup.add(new JMenuItem("item two"));
        popup.add(new JMenuItem("item three"));
        popup.add(new JMenuItem("item four"));

        popup.addPopupMenuListener(new PopupMenuListener() {
            public void popupMenuCanceled(PopupMenuEvent e) {
                System.out.println("menu canceled");
            }
            public void popupMenuWillBecomeVisible(
                                    PopupMenuEvent e) {
                System.out.println("menu will become visible");
            }
            public void popupMenuWillBecomeInvisible(
                                    PopupMenuEvent e) {
                System.out.println("menu will become invisible");
            }
        });
        addMouseListener(new MouseAdapter() {
            public void mousePressed (MouseEvent e) {
                popup.show(contentPane, e.getX(), e.getY());
            }
        });
    }
}
```

Like the MenuEvent class, PopupMenuEvent—which extends the java.util.EventObject class—provides no methods of its own. The only information that can be obtained from an instance of PopupMenuEvent is the source of the event.

JPopupMenu Class Summaries

The public and protected variables and methods for JPopupMenu are listed in Class Summary 10-6.

Class Summary 10-6   JPopupMenu

Extends: JComponent
Implements: MenuElement, javax.accessibility.Accessible

Constructors

---

public JPopupMenu()
public JPopupMenu(String)

The JPopupMenu class provides two constructors, a no-argument version and another that takes a string representing the menu's title. Whether or not the string specified as the popup menu's title is actually used depends upon the look and feel associated with the popup. As of Swing 1.1 FCS, none of the standard look and feels display a popup menu's title.

Methods

Lightweight Popups

---

public static boolean getDefaultLightWeightPopupEnabled()
public static void setDefaultLightWeightPopupEnabled(boolean)

public void setLightWeightPopupEnabled(boolean)

The methods listed above control the type of container in which popup menus are displayed. The static setDefaultLightWeightPopupEnabled method sets the type of container for all popup menus that are created after the call. If the method is passed true, popup menus subsequently created will be of the lightweight variety if the menu fits entirely within its top-level window. If the method is passed false, popup menus subsequently created that fit entirely within their top-level window will be contained in an AWT heavyweight panel.

The setLightWeightPopupEnabled method can be used on a per-popup menu basis to override the default behavior set by setDefaultLightWeightPopupEnabled, if desired. For example, after a call to JPopupMenu.setDefaultLightWeightPopupEnabled(true), all popup menus subsequently created will be of the lightweight variety; however, if setLightWeightPopupEnabled(false) is invoked for a particular popup menu instance, that popup menu will be contained in an AWT heavyweight panel (or in an instance of JFrame if the popup menu does not fit entirely within its top-level window).

For a more succinct description of the algorithm used to determine the type of container that a popup menu is displayed in, see "JPopupMenu" on page 525.

Adding and Inserting Objects

---

public JMenuItem <u>add</u>(Action)
public JMenuItem <u>add</u>(JMenuItem)
public Component <u>add</u>(Component)
public void <u>addSeparator</u>()

public void <u>insert</u>(Action, int index)
public void <u>insert</u>(Component, int index)

The methods listed above are used to add and insert objects in a popup menu. Actions, menu items, components and separators can be added to a popup menu, and actions and components can be inserted at a specified index.

When an action is added to a popup menu, the action's name and icon are used to create a menu item which is subsequently added to the popup menu.

Menu Bar Menus and Components

The JMenuBar API provides methods to access the menus and components contained in a menu bar.

Some of the JMenuBar accessors to print information about the components and menus contained in the menu bar.

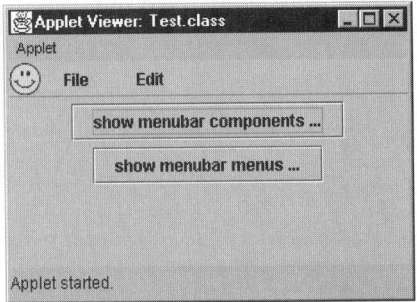

Figure 10-25 Accessing Menu Bar Components and Menus

The pertinent code in the application shown in Figure 10-25 consists of the action listeners associated with the two buttons.

```
    . . .
    menuButton.addActionListener(new ActionListener() {
        public void actionPerformed(ActionEvent e) {
            Component c;
            int cnt = mb.getMenuCount();

            for(int i=0; i < cnt; ++i) {
                c = mb.getMenu(i);
                System.out.println(c);
                System.out.println();
            }
        }
    });
    compButton.addActionListener(new ActionListener() {
        public void actionPerformed(ActionEvent e) {
            Component c;
            int cnt = mb.getComponentCount();

            for(int i=0; i < cnt; ++i) {
                c = mb.getComponentAtIndex(i);
```

```
                        System.out.println(c);
                        System.out.println();
                  }
             }
         });
      }
   }
```

The first action listener listed above prints information about the menus contained in the menu bar. The `actionPerformed` method of the listener invokes `JMenuBar.getMenuCount()` to obtain a count of the number of menus contained the menu bar. A reference to each menu is obtained by invocation of `JMenuBar.getMenu()`.

The output printed by the applet when the `menuButton` is activated is listed below.

```
javax.swing.JMenu[,24,1,55x24,alignmentX=null,alignmentY=null,bo
rder=javax.swing.plaf.metal.MetalBorders$MenuItemBorder@13642de,
flags=33,maximumSize=,minimumSize=,preferredSize=,defaultIcon=,d
isabledIcon=,disabledSelectedIcon=,margin=javax.swing.plaf.Inset
sUIResource[top=2,left=2,bottom=2,right=2],paintBorder=true,pain
tFocus=false,pressedIcon=,rolloverEnabled=false,rolloverI-
con=,rolloverSelectedIcon=,selectedIcon=,text=File]

javax.swing.JMenu[,79,1,57x24,alignmentX=null,alignmentY=null,bo
rder=javax.swing.plaf.metal.MetalBorders$MenuItemBorder@13642de,
flags=33,maximumSize=,minimumSize=,preferredSize=,defaultIcon=,d
isabledIcon=,disabledSelectedIcon=,margin=javax.swing.plaf.Inset
sUIResource[top=2,left=2,bottom=2,right=2],paintBorder=true,pain
tFocus=false,pressedIcon=,rolloverEnabled=false,rolloverI-
con=,rolloverSelectedIcon=,selectedIcon=,text=Edit]
```

The second action listener listed above prints information about the components contained in the menu bar by invoking `getComponentCount()` from the `java.awt.Container` class and `JMenuBar.getComponentAtIndex()`.

The output printed by the applet when the `compButton` is activated is listed below.

```
javax.swing.JLabel[,0,1,24x24,alignmentX=0.0,alignmentY=null,bor
der=,flags=0,maximumSize=,minimumSize=,preferredSize=,defaultIco
n=javax.swing.ImageIcon@9bc242de,disabledIcon=,horizontalAlignme
nt=CENTER,horizontalTextPosition=RIGHT,iconTextGap=4,label-
For=,text=,verticalAlignment=CENTER,verticalTextPosition=CENTER]

javax.swing.JMenu[,24,1,55x24,alignmentX=null,alignmentY=null,bo
rder=javax.swing.plaf.metal.MetalBorders$MenuItemBorder@13642de,
flags=33,maximumSize=,minimumSize=,preferredSize=,defaultIcon=,d
isabledIcon=,disabledSelectedIcon=,margin=javax.swing.plaf.Inset
sUIResource[top=2,left=2,bottom=2,right=2],paintBorder=true,pain
tFocus=false,pressedIcon=,rolloverEnabled=false,rolloverI-
con=,rolloverSelectedIcon=,selectedIcon=,text=File]

javax.swing.JMenu[,79,1,57x24,alignmentX=null,alignmentY=null,bo
rder=javax.swing.plaf.metal.MetalBorders$MenuItemBorder@13642de,
flags=33,maximumSize=,minimumSize=,preferredSize=,defaultIcon=,d
isabledIcon=,disabledSelectedIcon=,margin=javax.swing.plaf.Inset
sUIResource[top=2,left=2,bottom=2,right=2],paintBorder=true,pain
tFocus=false,pressedIcon=,rolloverEnabled=false,rolloverI-
con=,rolloverSelectedIcon=,selectedIcon=,text=Edit]
```

The applet shown in Figure 10-25 is listed in Example 10-22.

Example 10-22 Menus and Components in Menu Bars

```
import javax.swing.*;
import java.awt.*;
import java.awt.event.*;

public class Test extends JApplet {
    public void init() {
        Container contentPane = getContentPane();

        final JMenuBar mb = new JMenuBar();
        JMenu fileMenu = new JMenu("File");
        JMenu editMenu = new JMenu("Edit");
        JMenuItem exitItem = new JMenuItem("Exit");
        JButton compButton = new JButton(
                        "show menubar components ...");
        JButton menuButton = new JButton(
                        "show menubar menus ...");
```

```
fileMenu.add("New ...");
fileMenu.add("Open ...");
fileMenu.add("Save");
fileMenu.add("Save As ..");
fileMenu.addSeparator();
fileMenu.add(exitItem);

editMenu.add("Undo");
editMenu.addSeparator();
editMenu.add("Cut");
editMenu.add("Copy");
editMenu.add("Paste");

mb.setMargin(new Insets(30,20,10,5));
mb.add(new JLabel(new ImageIcon("smiley.gif")));
mb.add(fileMenu);
mb.add(editMenu);

setJMenuBar(mb);
contentPane.setLayout(new FlowLayout());
contentPane.add(compButton);
contentPane.add(menuButton);

exitItem.addActionListener(new ActionListener() {
    public void actionPerformed(ActionEvent e) {
        System.exit(0);
    }
});
menuButton.addActionListener(new ActionListener() {
    public void actionPerformed(ActionEvent e) {
        Component c;
        int cnt = mb.getMenuCount();

        for(int i=0; i < cnt; ++i) {
            c = mb.getMenu(i);
            System.out.println(c);
            System.out.println();
        }
    }
});
compButton.addActionListener(new ActionListener() {
    public void actionPerformed(ActionEvent e) {
        Component c;
        int cnt = mb.getComponentCount();
```

```
        for(int i=0; i < cnt; ++i) {
            c = mb.getComponentAtIndex(i);
            System.out.println(c);
            System.out.println();
        }
    }
});
    }
}
```

Notice that the applet listed in Figure 10-23 sets the margin for the menu bar, but the margin is ignored by the menu bar's look and feel, as can be seen from Figure 10-25.

The JMenuBar class is summarized in Component Summary 10-6.

Component Summary 10-6   JMenuBar

Model(s)	SingleSelectionModel
UI Delegate(s)	javax.swing.plaf.basic.BasicMenuBarUI
Renderer(s)	——
Editor(s)	——
Events Fired	——
Replacement For	java.awt.MenuBar

Class Diagrams

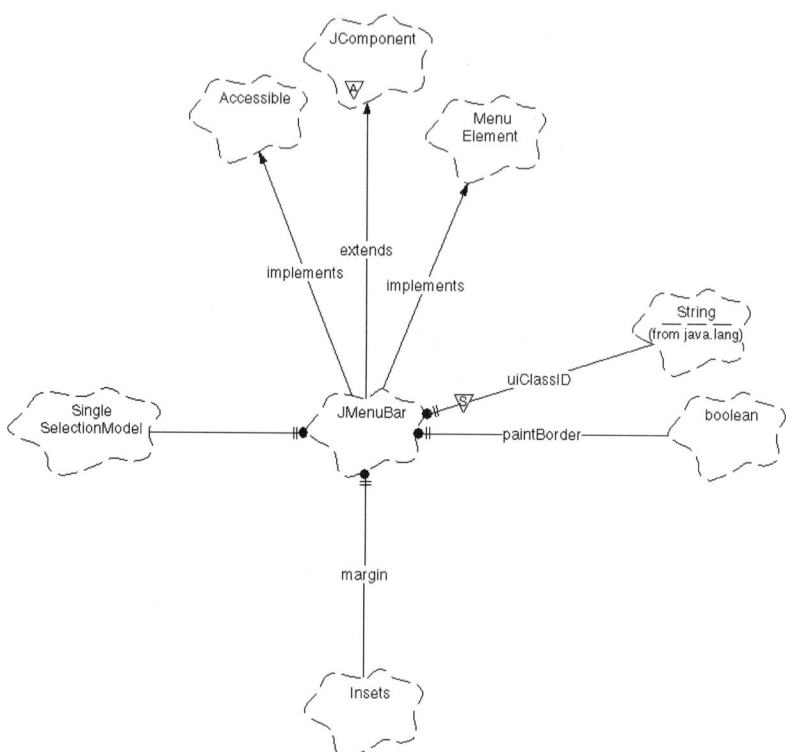

Figure 10-26   JMenuBar Class Diagram

JMenuBar extends JComponent and implements the `Accessible` and `MenuElement` interfaces. Instances of JMenuBar maintain a `private` reference to a `boolean` that tracks whether or not the menu bar draws a border. Additionally, JMenuBar maintains a `private` reference to an instance of `Insets` that represents the margin between the menu bar's border and the menus it contains. JMenuBar also maintains a `private` reference to a `SingleSelectionModel`, which is used to track the currently selected menu.

JMenuBar Properties

The properties maintained by instances of JMenuBar are listed in Table 10-7.

Table 10-7 JMenuBar Properties

Property Name	Data Type	Access[2]	Type[3]	Default[4]
borderPainted	boolean	SG	S	true
componentAtIndex	Component	G	I	—
componentIndex	int	G	S	—
helpMenu[1]	JMenu	SG	S	—
margin	int	SG	S	L&F
menuCount	int	G	S	—
selectionModel	SingleSelectionModel	SG	S	DefaultSingle-SelectionModel

1. As of Swing 1.1, help menus were not implemented
2. C = settable at construction time / G = getter method / S = setter method
3. B = bound / bool = boolean / C = constrained/ I = indexed / S = simple / RO = read only
4. L&F = look-and-feel dependent

borderPainted — Determines whether a menu bar's border is painted; by default, borders are painted. The borderPainted property may be ignored by some look and feels.

componentAtIndex — A computed property that returns a component at a given index. The index is zero based, starting with the first component added to the menu bar and ending with the last component at index (getComponentCount() − 1).

Recall that any type of component can be added to a menu bar because Swing lightweight components are all AWT containers. Therefore, it should not be assumed that a component returned from getComponentAtIndex() will be a menu.

componentIndex — Returns the index associated with a given component contained in a menu bar. The index is zero based, starting with the first component added to the menu bar and ending with the last component at index (getComponentCount() - 1).

helpMenu — A help menu whose representation within a menu bar is look-and-feel dependent. As of Swing 1.1 FCS, help menus are not implemented; in other words, setting the helpMenu property has no effect under Swing 1.1 FCS.

menuCount — The `menuCount` property does not necessarily represent the number of menus in a menu bar, as might be expected. Instead, the property represents the number of components contained in a menu bar.

selectionModel — By default, menu bars have a `DefaultSingleSelectionModel` that maintains the currently selected menu element in a menu bar.

JMenuBar Events

Other than property change events that are fired when bound properties are modified, `JMenuBar` does not fire events of its own accord.

JMenuBar Class Summaries

The `public` and `protected` variables and methods for `JMenuBar` are listed in Class Summary 10-7.

Class Summary 10-7   JMenuBar

Extends: JComponent

Implements: MenuElement, javax.accessibility.Accessible

Constructors

---

public <u>JMenuBar</u>()

There is only one way to construct an instance of `JMenuBar`—by invoking the no-argument constructor listed above. Menus and components can be added to Swing menu bars after construction by the methods listed below.

Methods

Menus

---

public JMenu <u>add</u>(JMenu)

public JMenu <u>getMenu</u>(int index)
public int <u>getMenuCount</u>()

public JMenu <u>getHelpMenu</u>()
public void <u>setHelpMenu</u>(JMenu)

Menus can be added to a menu bar with the `JMenuBar.add` method; however, the `JMenuBar` class does not provide a corresponding method to remove a menu from a menu bar. To remove a menu from `JMenuBar`, use the `remove(int index)` method that `JMenuBar` inherits from `java.awt.Container`.

As of Swing 1.1 FCS, the `getMenuCount` method returns the number of components—not the number of menus—contained in a menu bar. The `getMenu` method is passed a component index; for example, if a menu bar contains a component and two menus (added to the menu bar in that order), `getMenu(1)` is invoked to obtain a reference to the first menu.

As of Swing 1.1 FCS, setting the help menu has no effect, and the last two methods listed above will throw an error indicating the methods are not yet implemented.

Components

---

public Component <u>getComponentAtIndex</u>(int index)
public int <u>getComponentIndex</u>(Component)

public void <u>setSelected</u>(Component)
public boolean <u>isSelected</u>()

Components contained in a menu bar and their indexes can be determined from the methods listed above. The `getComponentAtIndex` method returns a reference to a component contained in a menu bar given a valid index. If the index

is invalid, a `null` reference is returned. The `getComponentIndex` returns an index given a component and returns –1 for components that are not contained in the menu bar.

The `setSelected` method selects the specified component by delegating to the menu bar's selection model.

Margin / Selection Model / Border Painting / Managing Focus

---

public Insets <u>getMargin</u>()
public void <u>setMargin</u>(Insets)

public SingleSelectionModel <u>getSelectionModel</u>()
public void <u>setSelectionModel</u>(SingleSelectionModel)

public boolean <u>isBorderPainted</u>()
public void <u>setBorderPainted</u>(boolean)
protected void <u>paintBorder</u>(Graphics)

public boolean <u>isManagingFocus</u>()

A menu bar's margin is defined as the space between the menu bar's components and the menu bar's border. For some look and feels, including the Metal look and feel, a menu bar's margin is ignored.

Accessors are provided for a menu bar's selection model, which is an instance of `SingleSelectionModel`. The `borderPainted` property can be specified; however, like the `margin` property, the `borderPainted` property may be ignored by certain look and feels.

MenuElement Interface

---

public abstract Component getComponent()
public abstract MenuElement[] getSubElements()

public abstract void menuSelectionChanged(boolean)
public abstract void processKeyEvent(KeyEvent, MenuElement[],
                                               MenuSelectionManager)
public abstract void processMouseEvent(MouseEvent, MenuElement[],
                                               MenuSelectionManager)

The methods listed above are defined in the `MenuElement` interface. See "MenuElement" on page 518 for more on the `MenuElement` interface.

The `getComponent` method returns a reference to the menu bar itself, and the `getSubElements` method returns an array of menu elements contained in the menu bar. Note that the array of `MenuElements` returned from `getSubElements()` may have `null` values because `getSubElements()` uses `JMenuBar.getMenu()`, which returns `null` references for menu bar component that are not menus.

Accessibility / Pluggable Look And Feel

---

public AccessibleContext getAccessibleContext()
public String getUIClassID()
public void updateUI()
public MenuBarUI getUI()
public void setUI(MenuBarUI)

The methods listed above can be found in most extensions of `JComponent`. Swing lightweight components can return an accessibility context that contains accessibility information for the component and the class name of their UI delegate. The `updateUI` method is invoked when the component is fitted with a UI delegate.

AWT Compatibility

The `public` methods implemented by `java.awt.MenuBar` and their `JMenuBar` equivalents are listed in Table 10-8.

Table 10-8   java.awt.MenuBar Methods and JMenuBar Equivalents[1]

`java.awt.MenuBar` Methods	`JMenuBar` Equivalents
add(Menu)	**add(JMenu)**
deleteShortcut(MenuShortcut)	—
getHelpMenu()	getHelpMenu()
getMenu(int)	getMenu(int)
getMenuCount()	getMenuCount()
getShortcutMenuItem(MenuShorcut)	—
remove(int)	remove(int)
remove(MenuComponent)	—
setHelpMenu(Menu)	**setHelpMenu(JMenu)**
shortcuts()	—

1. Differing signatures are highlighted in bold.

AWT menu shortcuts can be assigned to menu items through the AWT's `MenuBar` class. Assigning shortcuts to Swing menu items is not handled through the `JMenuBar` class—instead, shortcuts, in the form of accelerators, must be assigned directly to menu items.

JToolBar

Rarely does one come across a user interface nowadays that does not have a toolbar. With Swing, toolbars are finally available as part of the JDK.

Swing toolbars are represented by the `JToolBar` class, which is essentially a container that can be oriented horizontally or vertically. Swing toolbars can float, meaning they can be dragged to either the north, south, east, or west sides of a container or into a window of their own. Any type of component can be added to a toolbar, in addition to actions and separators by way of the `JToolBar` `add(Action)` and `addSeparator` methods. Unlike menu bars, there are no specific methods in Swing top-level containers (such as `JApplet` and

JRootPane) for adding toolbars. Toolbars are added to containers in the same manner as any Swing component, except that toolbars should be added to a container with an instance of BorderLayout as either the north, south, or west component in the container.

The applet shown in Figure 10-27 adds five buttons and two checkboxes to a toolbar. The applet subsequently adds the toolbar to the applet's content pane as the north component.

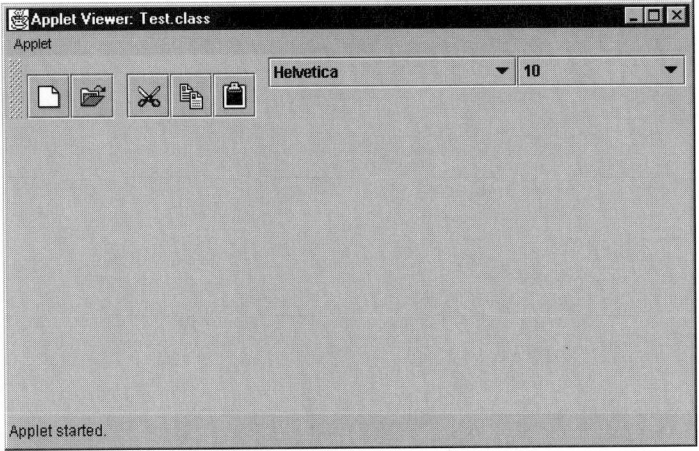

Figure 10-27 Adding Components to a Toolbar

The source code for the applet shown in Figure 10-27 is straightforward and is listed in its entirety in Figure 10-23.

Example 10-23 Adding Components to a Toolbar

```
import java.awt.*;
import java.awt.event.*;
import javax.swing.*;

public class Test extends JApplet {
    public Test() {
        Container contentPane = getContentPane();
        JToolBar tb = new JToolBar();
        JComboBox fontCombo = new JComboBox(),
                  fontSizeCombo = new JComboBox();

        JButton newButton = new JButton(new ImageIcon("new.gif")),
            openButton = new JButton(new ImageIcon("open.gif")),
```

```
                cutButton = new JButton(new ImageIcon("cut.gif")),
                copyButton = new JButton(new ImageIcon("copy.gif")),
                pasteButton = new JButton(new ImageIcon("paste.gif")));

        fontCombo.addItem("Helvetica");
        fontCombo.addItem("Palatino");
        fontCombo.addItem("Courier");
        fontCombo.addItem("Times");
        fontCombo.addItem("Times-Roman");

        fontSizeCombo.addItem("10");
        fontSizeCombo.addItem("12");
        fontSizeCombo.addItem("14");
        fontSizeCombo.addItem("16");
        fontSizeCombo.addItem("18");

        tb.add(newButton);
        tb.add(openButton);

        tb.addSeparator();

        tb.add(cutButton);
        tb.add(copyButton);
        tb.add(pasteButton);

        tb.addSeparator();

        tb.add(fontCombo);
        tb.add(fontSizeCombo);

        contentPane.setLayout(new BorderLayout());
        contentPane.add(tb, BorderLayout.NORTH);
    }
}
```

Notice that the layout manager for the applet's content pane is set to an instance of BorderLayout because, by default, the layout manager for an applet's content pane is an instance of FlowLayout.

Also notice that the toolbar lays out the buttons and combo boxes in the applet shown in Figure 10-27 in a rather aesthetically unpleasant manner; the vertical center of the buttons and combo boxes are not aligned, and the combo boxes are much wider than they need to be. The reasons for this are twofold.

First, instances of JToolBar use an instance of BoxLayout to lay out the components they contain. With no restrictions on the maximum size of the combo boxes, the combo boxes are stretched to fill the remaining available space in the toolbar.

Second, `BoxLayout` aligns components according to their X and Y alignments—see "BoxLayout" on page 273 for more information on `BoxLayout`. When laying out components horizontally, `BoxLayout` aligns the vertical centers of the components according to the component's Y alignment. By default, combo boxes have a Y alignment of 0.5, but buttons have a Y alignment of 0.0.

Figure 10-28 shows another version of the applet shown in Figure 10-27 with the components in the toolbar aligned and with more practical sizes for the combo boxes.

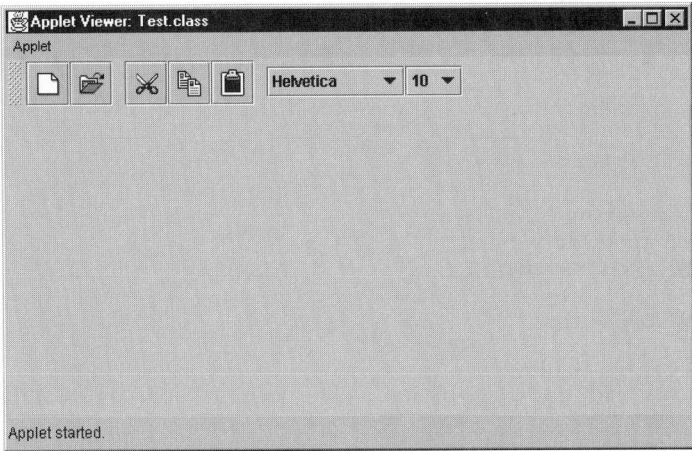

Figure 10-28 Adding Components to a Toolbar, Take II

The applet shown in Figure 10-28 is listed in Figure 10-24.

Example 10-24 Adding Components to a Toolbar, Take II

```
import java.awt.*;
import java.awt.event.*;
import javax.swing.*;

public class Test extends JApplet {
    public Test() {
        Container contentPane = getContentPane();
        JToolBar tb = new JToolBar();
        JComboBox fontCombo = new JComboBox(),
                  fontSizeCombo = new JComboBox();

        JButton newButton = new JButton(new ImageIcon("new.gif")),
            openButton = new JButton(new ImageIcon("open.gif")),
```

```
      cutButton = new JButton(new ImageIcon("cut.gif")),
      copyButton = new JButton(new ImageIcon("copy.gif")),
      pasteButton = new JButton(new ImageIcon("paste.gif")));

  fontCombo.addItem("Helvetica");
  fontCombo.addItem("Palatino");
  fontCombo.addItem("Courier");
  fontCombo.addItem("Times");
  fontCombo.addItem("Times-Roman");

  fontSizeCombo.addItem("10");
  fontSizeCombo.addItem("12");
  fontSizeCombo.addItem("14");
  fontSizeCombo.addItem("16");
  fontSizeCombo.addItem("18");

  tb.add(newButton);
  tb.add(openButton);

  tb.addSeparator();

  tb.add(cutButton);
  tb.add(copyButton);
  tb.add(pasteButton);

  tb.addSeparator();

  tb.add(fontCombo);
  tb.add(fontSizeCombo);

  newButton.setAlignmentY(0.5f);
  openButton.setAlignmentY(0.5f);
  cutButton.setAlignmentY(0.5f);
  copyButton.setAlignmentY(0.5f);
  pasteButton.setAlignmentY(0.5f);

  newButton.setAlignmentX(0.5f);
  openButton.setAlignmentX(0.5f);
  cutButton.setAlignmentX(0.5f);
  copyButton.setAlignmentX(0.5f);
  pasteButton.setAlignmentX(0.5f);


  fontCombo.setMaximumSize(fontCombo.getPreferredSize());
  fontSizeCombo.setMaximumSize(
              fontSizeCombo.getPreferredSize());

  contentPane.setLayout(new BorderLayout());
  contentPane.add(tb, BorderLayout.NORTH);
  }
}
```

The alignment for the buttons are set to match the alignment for the combo boxes, and the maximum size of the combo boxes is set to their preferred sizes.

As a result, the buttons and combo boxes are aligned according to their vertical centers, and the combo boxes are not sized wider than their preferred widths. Notice that both the X and Y alignments of the buttons are set to match that of the combo boxes, so that if the toolbar is dragged such that its orientation is vertical, the buttons and combo boxes will be aligned according to their horizontal centers.

Rollover Toolbars

Some look and feels are sensitive to an `isRollover` toolbar client property. Setting the property to `true` for a toolbar may result in toolbar button borders being displayed only when the cursor is over the button. The rollover effect is shown in Figure 10-29.

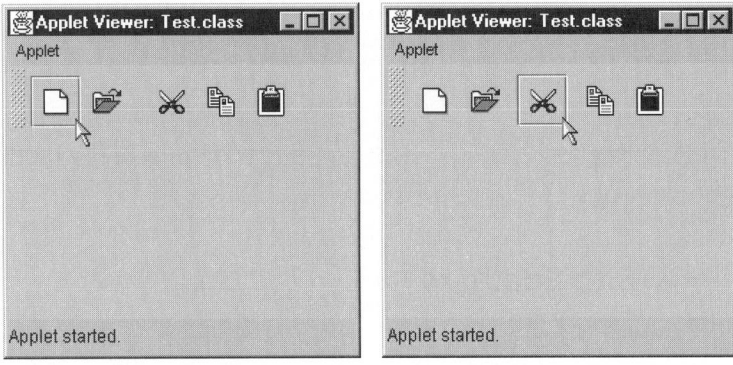

Figure 10-29 Specifying the JToolBar.isRollover Client Property

The applet shown in Figure 10-29 is listed in Example 10-25.

Example 10-25   JToolBar.isRollover Property

```
import javax.swing.*;
import java.awt.*;
import java.awt.event.*;

public class Test extends JApplet {
    public void init() {
        Container contentPane = getContentPane();
        JToolBar toolbar = new JToolBar();

        toolbar.add(new NewAction());
        toolbar.add(new OpenAction());
        toolbar.addSeparator();
        toolbar.add(new CutAction());
        toolbar.add(new CopyAction());
        toolbar.add(new PasteAction());

        toolbar.putClientProperty("JToolBar.isRollover",
                            Boolean.TRUE);

        contentPane.add(toolbar, BorderLayout.NORTH);
    }
    // Action class listings omitted:
    // see "A Menu Bar and a Toolbar in a JRootPane" on page 455
}
```

As of Swing 1.1 FCS, the `isRollover` client property takes effect only for the Java Look and Feel.

Using Actions with Toolbars

Like menus, actions can be added to toolbars. The `JToolBar.add(Action)` method extracts the icon and text associated with the action and creates an appropriate button.

The applet shown in Figure 10-30 contains another aesthetically unpleasant toolbar that mixes image-only toolbar buttons with buttons that contain both text and an image.

The applet shown in Figure 10-30 is listed in Example 10-26.

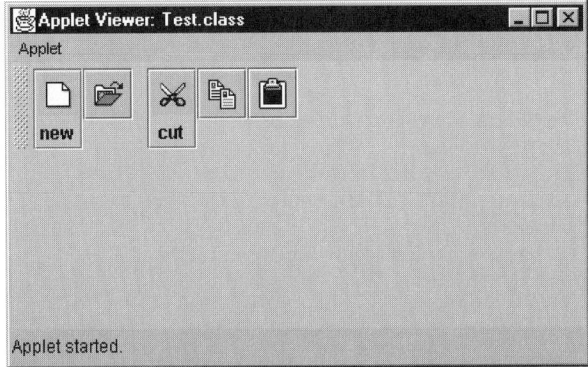

Figure 10-30 Adding Actions to a Toolbar

Example 10-26 Adding Actions to a Toolbar

```java
import javax.swing.*;
import java.awt.*;
import java.awt.event.*;

public class Test extends JApplet {
    public void init() {
        Container contentPane = getContentPane();
        JToolBar toolbar = new JToolBar();

        toolbar.add(new NewAction());
        toolbar.add(new OpenAction());
        toolbar.addSeparator();
        toolbar.add(new CutAction());
        toolbar.add(new CopyAction());
        toolbar.add(new PasteAction());

        contentPane.add(toolbar, BorderLayout.NORTH);
    }
    class NewAction extends AbstractAction {
        public NewAction() {
            super("new", new ImageIcon("new.gif"));
        }
        public void actionPerformed(ActionEvent event) {
            showStatus("new");
        }
    }
    class OpenAction extends AbstractAction {
        public OpenAction() {
            putValue(Action.SMALL_ICON,
                    new ImageIcon("open.gif"));
```

```
        }
        public void actionPerformed(ActionEvent event) {
            showStatus("open");
        }
    }
    class CutAction extends AbstractAction {
        public CutAction() {
            super("cut", new ImageIcon("cut.gif"));
            putValue(Action.SMALL_ICON, new ImageIcon("cut.gif"));
        }
        public void actionPerformed(ActionEvent event) {
            showStatus("cut");
        }
    }
    class CopyAction extends AbstractAction {
        public CopyAction() {
            putValue(Action.SMALL_ICON,
                        new ImageIcon("copy.gif"));
        }
        public void actionPerformed(ActionEvent event) {
            showStatus("copy");
        }
    }
    class PasteAction extends AbstractAction {
        public PasteAction() {
            putValue(Action.SMALL_ICON,
                        new ImageIcon("paste.gif"));
        }
        public void actionPerformed(ActionEvent event) {
            showStatus("paste");
        }
    }
}
```

The applet is rather long-winded, but most of it is taken up with the
implementation of actions for the toolbar buttons. As of Swing 1.1 FCS, there is no
way to repress the display of the text associated with an action that is added to a
toolbar.[4] This is unfortunate, because toolbar buttons do not typically display text,
and the benefit of using actions is that they can be shared among more than one
component; for example, actions are commonly shared between a menu and a
toolbar. Because menus typically display text, sharing actions between menus and
toolbars means that the text associated with the actions must be displayed in the
toolbar buttons.

4. The text can be repressed if toolbar button are created manually—see Example
    22-11 on page 1519.

Floating Toolbars

As previously mentioned, Swing toolbars can float, as illustrated by Figure 10-31. The applet shown in Figure 10-31 is the same applet listed in Figure 10-26, so it will not be listed again.

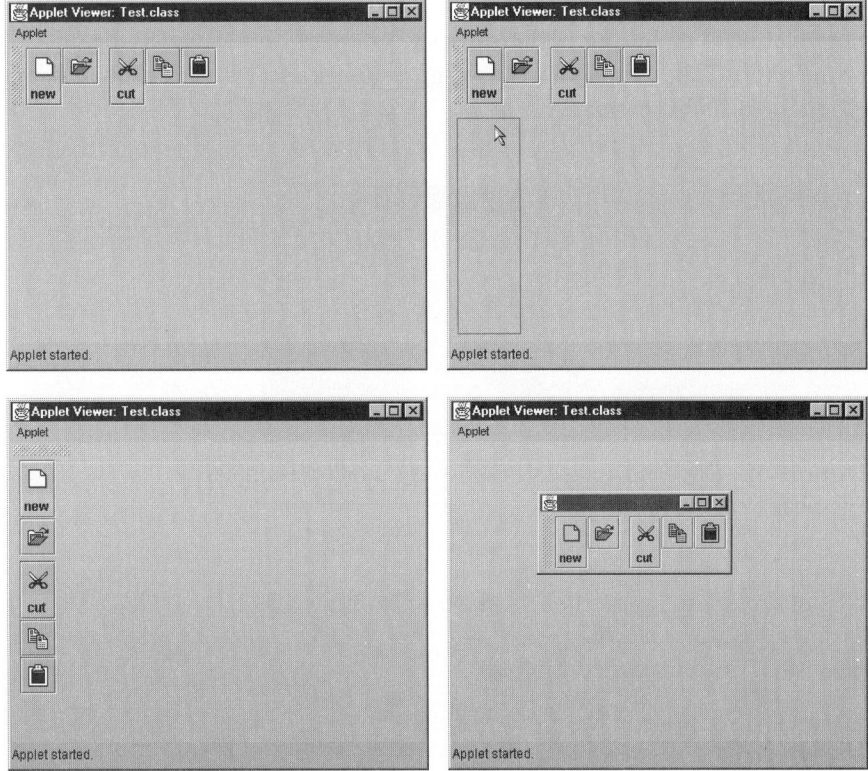

Figure 10-31 A Floating Toolbar

The upper-left picture in Figure 10-31 shows the applet in its initial state. The upper-right picture shows the toolbar as it is being dragged. The lower-left picture shows the toolbar after it has docked in the west region of the applet's content pane. The lower-right corner shows the toolbar after it has been dragged completely out of the window. When a toolbar is dragged out of the window in which it was originally contained, it is placed in a window of its own.

By default, toolbars are floatable—see Table 10-9 on page 573. The
`JToolBar.setFloatable` method can be invoked with a `false` argument to
prevent toolbars from floating.

Toolbar Buttons with Fixed-Location Tooltips

Tooltips associated with toolbar buttons are commonly displayed at a fixed
location relative to their button; typically such tooltips are displayed directly
below the button. The applet shown in Figure 10-32 contains buttons that display
their tooltips in such a manner.

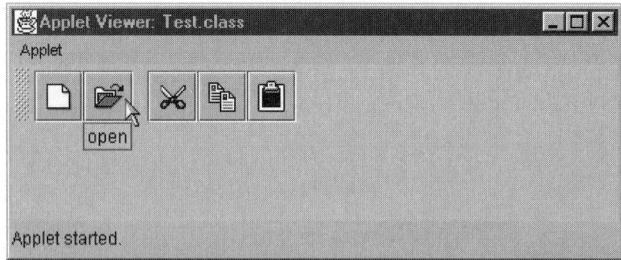

Figure 10-32 Showing Tooltips at a Fixed Location Relative
to Toolbar Buttons

The applet shown in Figure 10-32 is listed in Example 10-27.

Example 10-27 Fixed Location Tooltips

```
import java.awt.*;
import java.awt.event.*;
import javax.swing.*;

public class Test extends JApplet {
    public Test() {
        Container contentPane = getContentPane();
        JToolBar toolbar = new JToolBar();

        String[] tooltipTexts = { "new", "open", "cut", "copy",
                                  "paste"
        };

        ImageIcon[] icons = {
                new ImageIcon("new.gif"),
```

```
                new ImageIcon("open.gif"),
                new ImageIcon("cut.gif"),
                new ImageIcon("copy.gif"),
                new ImageIcon("paste.gif")
        };

        JButton[] buttons = {
            new ButtonWithFixedTooltip(icons[0],tooltipTexts[0]),
            new ButtonWithFixedTooltip(icons[1],tooltipTexts[1]),
            new ButtonWithFixedTooltip(icons[2],tooltipTexts[2]),
            new ButtonWithFixedTooltip(icons[3],tooltipTexts[3]),
            new ButtonWithFixedTooltip(icons[4],tooltipTexts[4])
        };

        for(int i=0; i < buttons.length; ++i) {
            toolbar.add(buttons[i]);

            if(tooltipTexts[i].equals("open"))
                toolbar.addSeparator();
        }
        contentPane.add(toolbar, BorderLayout.NORTH);
    }
}
class ButtonWithFixedTooltip extends JButton {
    public ButtonWithFixedTooltip(Icon icon,
                                  String tooltipText) {
        super(icon);
        setToolTipText(tooltipText);
    }
    public Point getToolTipLocation(MouseEvent e) {
        Dimension size = getSize();
        return new Point(0, size.height);
    }
}
```

The applet creates a toolbar and an array of ButtonWithFixedTooltips, and subsequently adds the buttons to the toolbar. The ButtonWithFixedTooltip class is a simple extension of JButton that overrides that getToolTipLocation method to return a location directly below the button. Specifying locations for tooltips is discussed in more detail in "Tooltips Based on Mouse Position" on page 173.

The JToolBar class is summarized in Component Summary 10-7.

Component Summary 10-7   JToolBar

Model(s)   ——

UI Delegate(s)   javax.swing.plaf.basic.BasicToolBarUI

Renderer(s)   ——

Editor(s)   ——

Events Fired   PropertyChangeEvent

Replacement For   ——

Class Diagrams

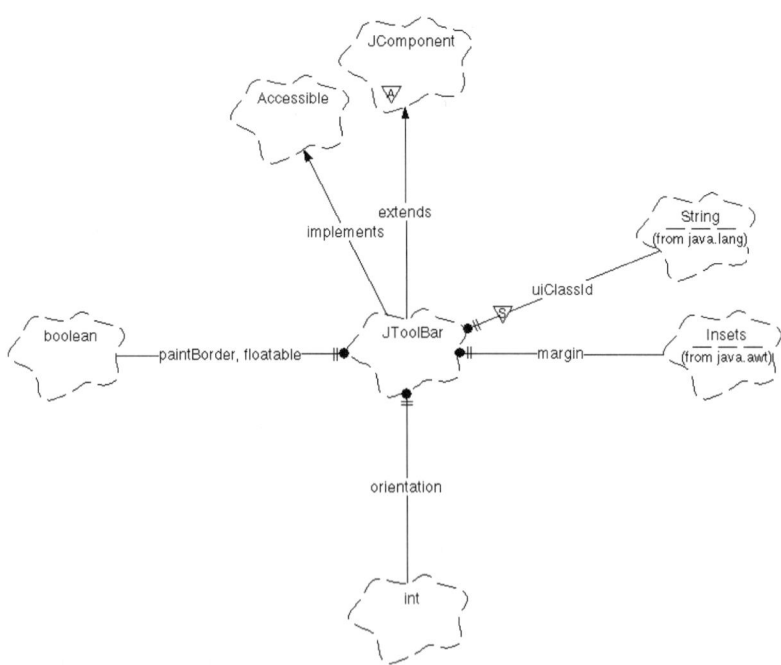

Figure 10-33 JToolBar Class Diagram

JToolBar is a simple extension of JComponent that is essentially a container that displays a row or column of buttons.

JToolBar maintains references to boolean values to help it keep track of whether to paint the border and whether the toolbar is floatable—toolbars can float, meaning they can be dragged to specific locations within their container or into a separate window. Toolbars also maintain a reference to an instance of Insets that represents the margin between the toolbar's border and its buttons.

JToolBar Properties

The properties maintained by the JToolBar class are listed in Table 10-9.

Table 10-9 JToolBar Properties

Property Name	Data Type	Access[1]	Type[2]	Default[3]
borderPainted	boolean	SG	B	true
componentIndex	int	G	S	—
componentAtIndex	Component	G	I	—
floatable	boolean	SG	B	true
orientation	int	SG	B	HORIZONTAL
margin	int	SG	B	(0,0,0,0)

1. C = settable at construction time / G = getter method / S = setter method
2. B = bound / bool = boolean / C = constrained/ I = indexed / S = simple /
3. L&F = look-and-feel dependent

borderPainted — Determines whether a toolbar's border is painted.

componentIndex — Represents the index of a specified component that resides in a toolbar. If the component is not contained in the toolbar, –1 is returned from the getComponentIndex method.

componentAtIndex — Represents a component contained in a toolbar at a specified location. If the index passed to the getComponentAtIndex method is invalid, the method returns a null index.

Separators must be accounted for when determining the index to pass to the getComponentAtIndex method. For example, to obtain a reference to the second component in a toolbar where the toolbar contains a component followed by a separator and another component, the index would be 2.

floatable — Represents whether a toolbar can be dragged to a new location in a window or into a window of its own.

orientation — Toolbars can be oriented horizontally or vertically, and the orientation property is always either JToolBar.HORIZONTAL or JToolBar.VERTICAL. The JToolBar.setOrientation method will throw an illegal argument exception if passed anything other than the two constants.

margin — Represents the space between the inside of a toolbar's border and the outside of the toolbar's components. If the margin is set to null, which is the default, the toolbar uses a default margin of (0,0,0,0).

If the margin is set to a non-null insets, the toolbar's default border uses the margin value to produce the space between the toolbar's border and its components. If a border is explicitly set for a toolbar, the border is responsible for taking the toolbar's margin into account.

JToolbar Events

Except for firing property change events when its bound properties are modified, the JToolBar class does not fire events of its own accord.

JToolBar Class Summaries

The public and protected variables and methods for JToolBar are listed in Class Summary 10-8.

Class Summary 10-8   JToolBar

Extends: JComponent
Implements: SwingConstants, javax.accessibility.Accessible

Constructors

---

public JToolBar()

`JToolBar` provides a lone, no-argument constructor. Buttons are added to toolbars after construction by invoking either the `add` or `add(Action)` methods.

Methods

Orientation

---

public int getOrientation()
public void setOrientation(int orientation)

The methods listed above are accessors for a toolbar's orientation property. Valid values for the `setOrientation` method are `JToolBar.HORIZONTAL` and `JToolBar.VERTICAL`. If `setOrientation` is passed an invalid `integer` value, an exception will be thrown.

Action Change Listener

---

protected PropertyChangeListener createActionChangeListener(JButton)

The `createActionChangeListener` method creates an action listener associated with a button that has been created from an action. By default, the listener is an instance of `ActionChangedListener`, which is a class that is private to the `JToolBar` class. The listener responds to changes made to the action from which the button was created. If the name or the small icon associated with the action is modified, the button is updated.

Extensions of `JToolBar` can override the `createActionChangeListener` method if the default behavior provided by the `ActionChangedListener` class is not sufficient, but in practice the method will rarely be overridden.

Add / Remove

---

public JButton add(Action)
public void addSeparator()
public void addSeparator(Dimension size)

public void remove(Component)

The methods listed above add a button and a separator, respectively, to a toolbar. Note that the separator is not the same as the separator that is added to a menu. Separators added to a menu draw an etched line, whereas separators added to toolbars just provide blank space between toolbar components.

Property Accessors

---

public Component getComponentAtIndex(int)
public int getComponentIndex(Component)
public Insets getMargin()

public void setBorderPainted(boolean)
public void setFloatable(boolean)
public void setMargin(Insets)

public boolean isBorderPainted()
public boolean isFloatable()
protected void paintBorder(Graphics)

The methods listed above are accessors for the properties listed in Table 10-9 on page 573.

Accessibility / Pluggable Look And Feel

---

public AccessibleContext getAccessibleContext()
public ToolBarUI getUI()
public String getUIClassID()
public void setUI(ToolBarUI)
public void updateUI()

The methods listed above can be found in most extensions of JComponent. Swing lightweight components can return an accessibility context that contains accessibility information for the component and the class name of their UI delegate. The updateUI method is invoked when the component is fitted with a UI delegate.

AWT Compatibility

The AWT does not provide a toolbar component.

Parting Shots

Swing's menu system is a vast improvement over AWT menus. Swing menu and menu items are both buttons and containers by virtue of their AbstractButton and java.awt.Container superclasses, respectively. Menus and menu items can be fitted with text and/or an icon and can also contain arbitrary components. See "The JComponent Class" on page 130 for more information concerning Swing components ability to contain components.

Swing popup menus are unique because they can be shown in three different types of containers: light, medium, and heavyweight. The terminology for the three types of popups can be somewhat confusing because medium weight actually means that the popup will be displayed in a heavyweight AWT panel; heavyweight popups, on the other hand, are displayed in a native window. Nonetheless, it is essential to have control over the type of container in which popup menus are displayed.

Toolbars, like popup menus, are fundamental user interface components that were conspicuously absent from the AWT. Swing toolbars, like menus and menu items, are ultimately an extension of java.awt.Container, so arbitrary components can be added to a toolbar.

CHAPTER 11

Progress Bars, Sliders, and Separators

Three Swing components are discussed in this chapter: JProgressBar, JSlider, and JSeparator.

Progress bars are frequently used to communicate the percentage of a time-consuming task that has been completed, and in fact, this chapter provides just such an example. However, providing feedback concerning the progress of a task is typically much easier to accomplish with the ProgressMonitor and ProgressMonitorInputStream utilities, which are discussed in "Progress Monitoring" on page 281.

JProgressBar and JSlider, like JScrollBar, depict a value that lies between a minimum and maximum integer value. As a result, the model associated with JProgressBar and JSlider is an implementation of the BoundedRangeModel interface.

JSeparator is a component that draws an etched line that can be oriented horizontally or vertically for separating components or groups of logically related components.

JProgressBar

`JProgressBar` is a simple component that is essentially a rectangle that can be either partially or entirely filled with a color. By default, progress bars are fitted with a lowered bevel border and are oriented horizontally.

Progress bars can also display an optional string that is displayed in the center of the progress bar's rectangle. The string defaults to the percentage of the time-consuming task that has been completed. The string can be customized with the `JProgressBar.setString` method.

The applet shown in Figure 11-1 creates four progress bars of various configurations.

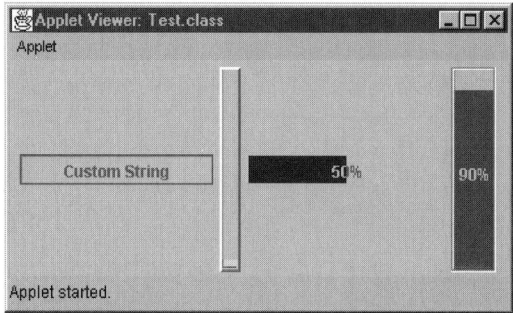

Figure 11-1 Progress Bars of Various Configurations

The applet shown in Figure 11-1 is listed in Example 11-1.

Example 11-1 Progress Bars of Various Configurations

```
import javax.swing.*;
import java.awt.*;
import java.awt.event.*;

public class Test extends JApplet {
    private JProgressBar[] progressBars = {
            new JProgressBar(),
            new JProgressBar(),
            new JProgressBar(),
            new JProgressBar()
```

```
    };

public void init() {
    Container contentPane = getContentPane();

    contentPane.setLayout(new FlowLayout());

    for(int i=0; i < progressBars.length; ++i) {
        JProgressBar pb = progressBars[i];

        if(i == 0) {
            pb.setStringPainted(true);
            pb.setString("Custom String");
        }
        if(i == 1) {
            pb.setOrientation(JProgressBar.VERTICAL);
            pb.setForeground(Color.yellow);
            pb.setMaximum(1000);
            pb.setValue(50);
            pb.setBorder(
                BorderFactory.createRaisedBevelBorder());
        }
        if(i == 2) {
            pb.setForeground(Color.blue);
            pb.setBorderPainted(false);
            pb.setValue(50);
            pb.setStringPainted(true);
        }
        if(i == 3) {
            pb.setOrientation(JProgressBar.VERTICAL);
            pb.setForeground(Color.red);
            pb.setValue(90);
            pb.setStringPainted(true);
            pb.setBorder(
                BorderFactory.createEtchedBorder());
        }

        contentPane.add(pb);
    }
  }
}
```

The applet creates an array of progress bars and sets various properties for each progress bar that results in the configurations shown in Figure 11-1.

Progress Bars and Threads

Progress bars are primarily used to communicate the percentage of time that has been completed, or remains, for a time-consuming task. However, time-consuming tasks should not be undertaken from the event dispatch thread, whereas Swing components should only be updated from the event dispatch thread. How, then, does one update a progress bar based on a separate thread? As discussed in "Swing and Threads" on page 57, this dilemma is solved by having the separate thread update a progress bar with the `SwingUtilities.invokeLater` method.

The applet shown in Figure 11-2 increments the value associated with a progress bar once every second, from the minimum value for the progress bar to its maximum value. Activating the button contained in the applet begins the sequence. The left picture shown in Figure 11-2 shows the applet just after the start button has been activated. The right picture shows the applet while the progress bar's value is being updated.

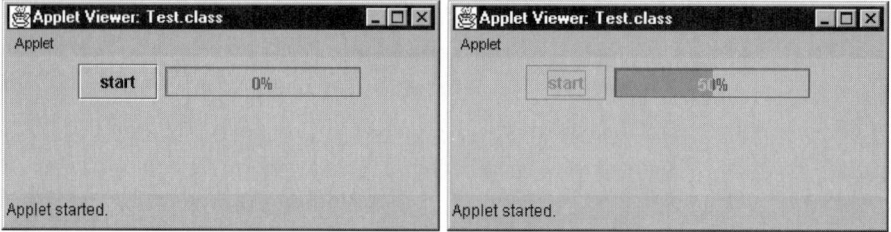

Figure 11-2 Progress Bar for a Time-Consuming Task

The applet creates an instance of `JProgressBar` and an instance of `JButton`, which are added to the applet's content pane. An action listener is added to the button that creates an instance of `UpdateThread` that is subsequently started.

```
public class Test extends JApplet {
    private JProgressBar progressBar = new JProgressBar();
    private JButton startButton = new JButton("start");

    public void init() {
        Container contentPane = getContentPane();
```

```
        contentPane.setLayout(new FlowLayout());
        contentPane.add(startButton);
        contentPane.add(progressBar);

        progressBar.setStringPainted(true);

        startButton.addActionListener(new ActionListener() {
            public void actionPerformed(ActionEvent e) {
                (new UpdateThread()).start();
            }
        });
    }
    ...
```

The UpdateThread class is an inner class of the applet that extends
java.lang.Thread. The UpdateThread constructor creates two Runnable
instances, one that increments the value associated with the progress bar—
update—and another that resets the progress bar's value to its minimum—
finish.

```
    ...
    class UpdateThread extends Thread {
        Runnable update, finish;
        int value, min, max, increment;

        public UpdateThread() {
            max = progressBar.getMaximum();
            min = progressBar.getMinimum();

            update = new Runnable() {
                public void run() {
                    value = progressBar.getValue() + increment;
                    updateProgressBar(value);
                }
            };
            finish = new Runnable() {
                public void run() {
                    updateProgressBar(min);
                }
            };
        }
        ...
```

The run method for the UpdateThread class simulates a time-consuming
activity by sleeping for a second. The simulateTimeConsumingActivity
method sets the increment for the slider's value and then calls
SwingUtilities.invokeLater(), passing the update Runnable. When the

maximum value of the progress bar is reached,
`SwingUtilities.invokeLater()` is once again invoked and is passed the
`finish` Runnable. Notice that it is not necessary to repaint the progress bar
when its value is updated because invoking `JProgressBar.setValue()`
results in a repaint of the progress bar.

```
   ...
   public void run() {
      startButton.setEnabled(false);

      while(value + increment <= max) {
         simulateTimeConsumingActivity();
         SwingUtilities.invokeLater(update);
      }
      SwingUtilities.invokeLater(finish);
      startButton.setEnabled(true);
   }
   ...
}
...
```

The applet shown in Figure 11-2 is listed in its entirety in Example 11-2.

Example 11-2 Using JProgressBar

```
import javax.swing.*;
import java.awt.*;
import java.awt.event.*;

public class Test extends JApplet {
   private JProgressBar progressBar = new JProgressBar();
   private JButton startButton = new JButton("start");

   public void init() {
      Container contentPane = getContentPane();

      contentPane.setLayout(new FlowLayout());
      contentPane.add(startButton);
      contentPane.add(progressBar);

      progressBar.setStringPainted(true);

      startButton.addActionListener(new ActionListener() {
         public void actionPerformed(ActionEvent e) {
            (new UpdateThread()).start();
         }
      });
   }
```

```
class UpdateThread extends Thread {
   Runnable update, finish;
   int value, min, max, increment;

   public UpdateThread() {
       max = progressBar.getMaximum();
       min = progressBar.getMinimum();

       update = new Runnable() {
          public void run() {
              value = progressBar.getValue() + increment;
              updateProgressBar(value);
          }
       };
       finish = new Runnable() {
          public void run() {
              updateProgressBar(min);
          }
       };
   }
   public void run() {
       startButton.setEnabled(false);

       while(value + increment <= max) {
          simulateTimeConsumingActivity();
          SwingUtilities.invokeLater(update);
       }
       SwingUtilities.invokeLater(finish);
       startButton.setEnabled(true);
   }
   private void updateProgressBar(int value) {
       progressBar.setValue(value);
   }
   private void simulateTimeConsumingActivity() {
       try {
          Thread.currentThread().sleep(1000);
          increment = (max - min) / 10;
       }
       catch(InterruptedException e) {
          e.printStackTrace();
       }
   }
}
```

Update Progress Bars in a Separate Thread

Because Swing is not thread safe, Swing components must be updated from the event dispatch thread. On the other hand, time-consuming activities should not be carried out from the event dispatch thread because events will not be processed until the time-consuming activity is completed.

Swing progress bars are typically used to communicate the percentage of a time-consuming activity that has been completed. If progress bars must be updated from the event dispatch thread, and progress bars are updated during a time-consuming activity that is performed on a thread other than the event dispatch thread, how can progress bars be used in a thread-safe manner?

The answer is to update progress bars from a separate thread, using the SwingUtilities.invokeLater method, which places a Runnable object on the event queue. The Runnable object is subsequently removed from the event queue and processed, on the event dispatch thread, by invoking its run method.

The JProgressBar component is summarized in Component Summary 11-1.

Component Summary 11-1   JProgressBar

Model(s)	BoundedRangeModel
UI Delegate(s)	javax.swing.plaf.basic.BasicProgressBarUI
Renderer(s)	——
Editor(s)	——
Events Fired	ChangeEvent
Replacement For	——

Class Diagrams

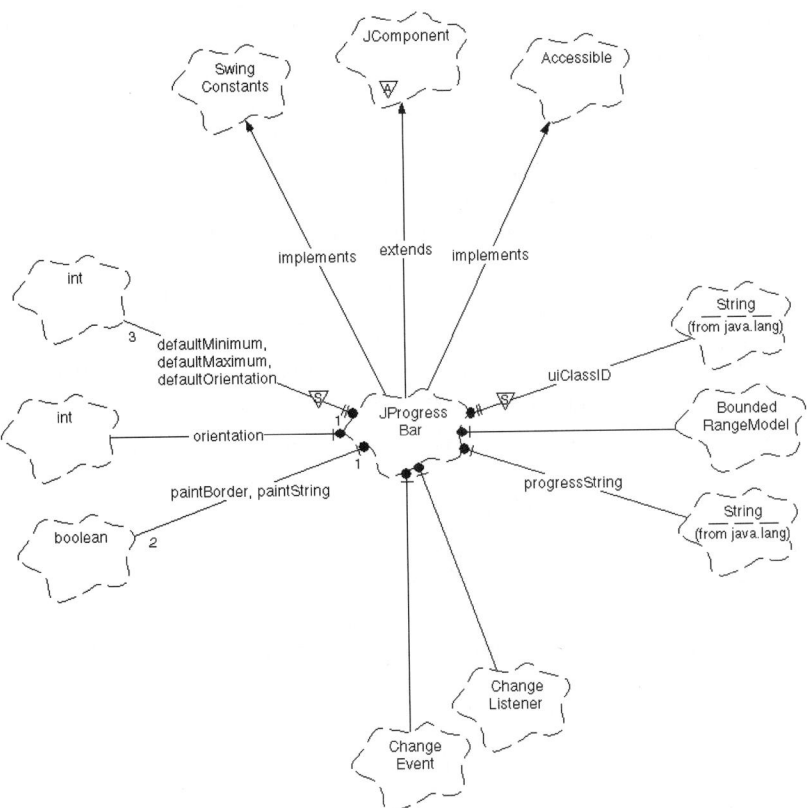

Figure 11-3 JProgressBar Class Diagram

JProgressBar extends JComponent, implements the SwingConstants and Accessible interfaces, and maintains protected references to its model—an instance of BoundedRangeModel. JProgressBar also maintains references to integer and boolean variables that track the orientation of the progress bar and whether or not a border or progress string is painted, respectively.

Like all Swing components that fire change events, the JProgressBar class uses a single ChangeEvent instance to fire change events to its change listeners because the only state associated with a change event is the event source. See "Lightweight Event Notification" on page 92 for more information concerning change events.

JProgressBar Properties

The properties maintained by the `JProgressBar` class are listed in Table 11-1.

Table 11-1   JProgressBar Properties

Property Name	Data Type	Property Type[1]	Access[2]	Default[3]
borderPainted	boolean	B	SG	true[4]
maximum	int	Ch	CSG	100
minimum	int	Ch	CSG	0
model	Bounded RangeModel	Ch	SG	DefaultBounded RangeModel
orientation	int	B	CSG	HORIZONTAL
percentComplete	double	S	G	—
string	String	B	SG	false
stringPainted	boolean	B	SG	false
value	int	Ch	SG	0

1. B = bound (fires PropertyChangeEvent) / C = constrained/ I = indexed / S = simple / Ch = ChangeEvent fired
2. C = settable at construction time / G = getter method / S = setter method
3. L&F = look-and-feel dependent
4. The default border is a lowered bevel border.

borderPainted — If `true`, a border is painted around the outside of the progress bar.

maximum — The maximum value the progress bar represents.

minimum — The minimum value the progress bar represents.

model — An implementation of the `BoundedRangeModel` interface; by default, a progress bar's model is an instance of `DefaultBoundedRangeModel`.

orientation — `JProgressBar.HORIZONTAL` or `JProgressBar.VERTICAL`.

percentCompleted — A progress bar's model maintains minimum, maximum, and current values. The `percentCompleted` property is calculated as follows:

```
(value - minimum) / (maximum - minimum)
```

string — The string displayed by the progress bar. By default, the string returned from JProgressBar.getString() is the percent completed followed by a % sign. The string can be explicitly set; in such cases, the string is typically constructed with the percentCompleted property.

stringPainted — A boolean property that determines whether a progress bar's string is displayed. By default, the stringPainted property is false.

value — The value represented by the progress bar's slider.

Modifications to any JProgressBar property results in a repaint of the progress bar. Also, modifications to JProgress properties result in the firing of either change events or property change events.

JProgressBar Events

Changes to the value, minimum, maximum, and model properties for instances of JProgressBar result in change events being fired. The applet shown in Figure 11-4 is identical to the applet shown in Figure 11-2 on page 582, except that it adds a change listener to its progress bar. When the progress bar fires a change event, its minimum, maximum, and current values are displayed in the applet's status area.

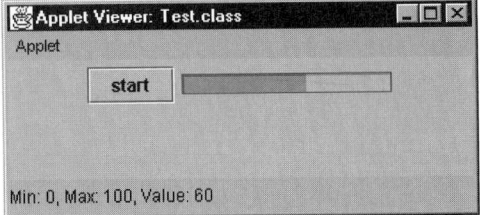

Figure 11-4 Monitoring the Values Associated with a Progress Bar

The change listener obtains the minimum, maximum, and current values for the progress bar from the component itself because change events record only the event source.

```
public class Test extends JApplet {
    private JProgressBar pb = new JProgressBar();

    public void init() {
        ...
        pb.addChangeListener(new ChangeListener() {
            public void stateChanged(ChangeEvent e) {
                int min = pb.getMinimum(), max = pb.getMaximum();
                int value = pb.getValue();

                showStatus("Min: " + min + ", Max: " + max +
                        ", Value: " + value);
            }
        });
    }
}
```

The applet shown in Figure 11-4 is listed in Example 11-3.

Example 11-3   Monitoring the Values of a Progress Bar

```
import javax.swing.*;
import javax.swing.event.*;
import java.awt.*;
import java.awt.event.*;

public class Test extends JApplet {
    private JProgressBar pb = new JProgressBar();

    public void init() {
        Container contentPane = getContentPane();
        final JButton startButton = new JButton("start");

        contentPane.setLayout(new FlowLayout());
        contentPane.add(startButton);
        contentPane.add(pb);

        startButton.addActionListener(new ActionListener() {
            public void actionPerformed(ActionEvent e) {
                (new UpdateThread(pb)).start();
            }
        });
        pb.addChangeListener(new ChangeListener() {
            public void stateChanged(ChangeEvent e) {
                int min = pb.getMinimum(), max = pb.getMaximum();
                int value = pb.getValue();

                showStatus("Min: " + min + ", Max: " + max +
                        ", Value: " + value);
            }
```

```
        });
    }
}
class UpdateThread extends Thread {
    Runnable update, finish;
    JProgressBar pb;
    int value, min, max, increment;

    public UpdateThread(JProgressBar progressBar) {
        pb = progressBar;

        max = pb.getMaximum();
        min = pb.getMinimum();

        update = new Runnable() {
            public void run() {
                value = pb.getValue() + increment;
                pb.setValue(value);
            }
        };
        finish = new Runnable() {
            public void run() {
                value = min;
                pb.setValue(value);
            }
        };
    }
    public void run() {
        while(value + increment <= max) {
            simulateTimeConsumingActivity();
            SwingUtilities.invokeLater(update);
        }
        SwingUtilities.invokeLater(finish);
    }
    private void simulateTimeConsumingActivity() {
        try {
            Thread.currentThread().sleep(1000);
            increment = (max - min) / 10;
        }
        catch(InterruptedException e) {
            e.printStackTrace();
        }
    }
}
```

JProgressBar Class Summaries

The `public` and `protected` variables and methods for `JProgressBar` are
listed in Class Summary 11-1.

Class Summary 11-1   JProgressBar

Constructors

---

public <u>JProgressBar</u>()
public <u>JProgressBar</u>(int orientation)
public <u>JProgressBar</u>(int minimum, int maximum)
public <u>JProgressBar</u>(int orientation, int minimum, int maximum)
public <u>JProgressBar</u>(BoundedRangeModel)

The `JProgressBar` no-argument constructor constructs a progress bar with the default property values listed in Table 11-1 on page 588. Orientation, minimum and maximum values, and a progress bar's model all can be specified at construction time.

Methods

State Changes

---

public void <u>addChangeListener</u>(ChangeListener)
public void <u>removeChangeListener</u>(ChangeListener)

protected ChangeListener <u>createChangeListener</u>()
protected void <u>fireStateChanged</u>()

Like most Swing components, `JProgressBar` fires change events when properties associated with its model are modified. `JProgressBar` provides `public` methods for adding and removing change listeners from its instances.

The `createChangeListener` method creates an instance of `JProgressBar.ModelListener` that handles change events fired by the progress bar's model and forwards them to the component's change listeners. The `fireStateChanged` method fires change events to the progress bar's change listeners.

Progress Bar String

---

public String <u>getString</u>()
public void <u>setString</u>()

public boolean <u>isStringPainted</u>(boolean)
public void <u>setStringPainted</u>(boolean)

The methods listed above are accessors for the `string` and `stringPainted` properties. See Table 11-1 on page 588 for more information concerning the properties.

Updating

---

public void <u>update</u>(Graphics)
protected void <u>paintBorder</u>(Graphics)

Normally, Swing and AWT components clear their background and repaint when their `update` method is called. `JProgressBar` overrides `update()` to forego clearing its background by invoking `paint` directly.

The `paintBorder` method is overridden from `JComponent` to paint the border only if the `isBorderPainted` property is `true`.

Miscellaneous Properties

---

public double <u>getPercentComplete</u>()
public int <u>getMaximum</u>()

public int <u>getMinimum</u>()
public BoundedRangeModel <u>getModel</u>()
public int <u>getOrientation</u>()
public int <u>getValue</u>()

public void <u>setBorderPainted</u>(boolean)
public void <u>setMaximum</u>(int)
public void <u>setMinimum</u>(int)
public void <u>setModel</u>(BoundedRangeModel)
public void <u>setOrientation</u>(int)
public void <u>setString</u>(String)
public void <u>setStringPainted</u>(boolean)
public void <u>setValue</u>(int)

public boolean <u>isBorderPainted</u>()

The methods listed above are accessors for `JProgressBar` properties. Because `JProgressBar` provides only a no-argument constructor, it provides both setter and getter methods for all of its properties.

Accessibility / Pluggable Look And Feel

---

public AccessibleContext <u>getAccessibleContext</u>()
public ProgressBarUI <u>getUI</u>()
public String <u>getUIClassID</u>()
public void <u>setUI</u>(ProgressBarUI)
public void <u>updateUI</u>()

The methods listed above can be found in most extensions of `JComponent`. Swing lightweight components can return the class name of their UI delegate and an accessibility context that contains accessibility information for the component. The `updateUI` method is invoked when the component is fitted with a UI delegate.

AWT Compatibility

The AWT does not provide a component analogous to `JProgressBar`.

JSlider

JSlider, like JProgressBar, displays a value that lies between minimum and maximum values. Whereas progress bars display values that can only be manipulated programmatically, the value associated with a slider can be directly manipulated by dragging the slider's knob or clicking in the slider's trough. Swing sliders contain a draggable knob with optional major and minor tick marks and labels.

The applet shown in Figure 11-5 contains an instance of JSlider, shown with the Metal look and feel.

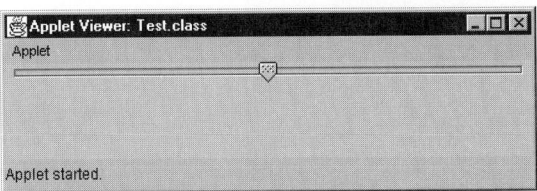

Figure 11-5 A Simple JSlider Example

The applet shown in Figure 11-5 is listed in Example 11-4.

Example 11-4 A Simple JSlider Example

```
import java.awt.*;
import java.awt.event.*;
import javax.swing.*;

public class Test extends JApplet {
    public Test() {
        Container contentPane = getContentPane();
        JSlider slider = new JSlider();

        contentPane.add(slider, BorderLayout.NORTH);
    }
}
```

The applet creates an instance of `JSlider` with a no-argument constructor that creates the slider with minimum, maximum, and initial values of 0, 100, and 50, respectively. After the slider is created, it is added to the applet's content pane as the north component.

Filled Sliders

If a slider's look and feel is the Java Look & Feel, the slider can be filled as illustrated in Figure 11-6 by the setting of a client property— `"JSlider.isFilled"`—for the slider.

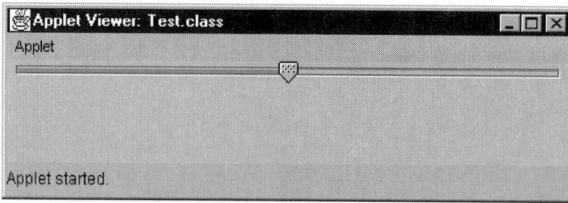

Figure 11-6 A Filled Slider

The applet shown in Figure 11-6 is listed in Example 11-5.

Example 11-5 A Filled Slider

```
import java.awt.*;
import java.awt.event.*;
import javax.swing.*;

public class Test extends JApplet {
    public Test() {
        Container contentPane = getContentPane();
        JSlider slider = new JSlider();

        slider.putClientProperty("JSlider.isFilled",Boolean.TRUE);

        contentPane.add(slider, BorderLayout.NORTH);
    }
}
```

The property `"JSlider.isFilled"` is specified as a client property with a `true` value, and therefore the trough to the left of the slider's grip is filled. If the value specified for the property is `false` or the property is not specified at all, the trough will not be filled.

Slider Tick Marks

Sliders can paint tick marks that delineate specific values associated with a slider. Tick marks are differentiated by major and minor tick marks. Major tick marks represent specific values, and minor tick marks represent values that lie between major tick marks. The visual representation of major and minor tick marks is left up to the slider's look and feel, but typically, major tick marks are larger than their minor counterparts.

Three methods are involved in painting a slider's tick marks: `setPaintTicks()`, `setMinorTickSpacing()`, and `setMajorTickSpacing()`. `setPaintTicks()` is passed a `boolean` variable indicating whether or not tick marks should be painted. `setMinorTickSpacing()` and `setMajorTickSpacing()` are passed `integer` values representing the number of units that lie between minor and major tick marks, respectively. Two things should be noted about the methods:

First, invoking `setPaintTicks()` with a `true` value will cause tick marks to be painted only if the spacing between major or minor tick marks has been set. In other words, if `setMinorTickSpacing()` or `setMajorTickSpacing()` is not invoked with a value greater than 0, calling `setPaintTicks(true)` will not result in tick marks being painted.

Second, the `integer` values passed to `setMinorTickSpacing()` and `setMajorTickSpacing()` do not directly represent the number of *pixels* between tick marks. Rather, the `integer` values represent the number of *units* between tick marks. For example, invoking `setMajorTickSpacing(25)` specifies that major tick marks should be drawn 25 units apart. If the minimum and maximum values associated with a slider are 0 and 100, respectively, specifying a major tick spacing of 25 will result in 5 major tick marks—at 0, 25, 50, 75, and 100—being drawn. If the slider is resized, 5 major tick marks will still be drawn.

The applet shown in Figure 11-7 contains an instance of `JSlider` and a check box and two combo boxes for setting the paint ticks property and the spacing between major and minor tick marks. The applet is shown with the Windows look and feel because the tick marks are easier to distinguish than with the Metal look and feel.

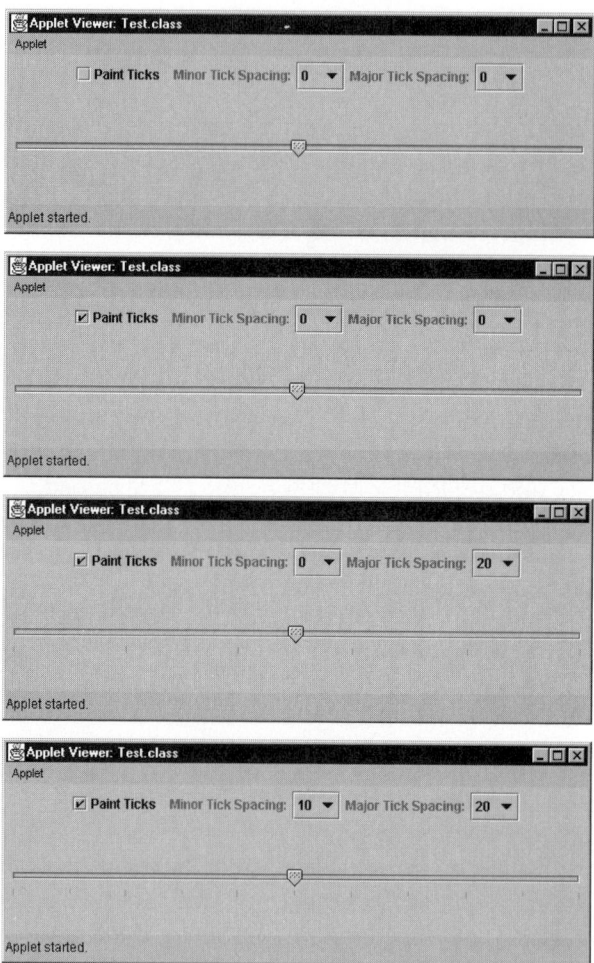

Figure 11-7 Slider Tick Marks

The top picture in Figure 11-7 shows the applet as it appears initially.

The second picture from the top shows the applet after the Paint Ticks check box has been selected. Notice that no tick marks are displayed because the spacing between major or minor tick marks has not been set.

The third picture from the top shows the applet after the spacing between major tick marks has been set, resulting in the major tick marks being displayed.

The bottom picture shows the applet after minor tick mark spacing has subsequently been set, resulting in both major and minor tick marks being displayed.

The applet creates an instance of `JSlider` with the `JSlider` no-argument constructor. The applet also creates an instance of `ControlPanel` which is an extension of `JPanel` that houses the check box and combo boxes. The control panel is added to the applet's content pane as the north component, and the slider is specified as the content pane's center component.

```
public class Test extends JApplet {
    public Test() {
        Container contentPane = getContentPane();
        JSlider slider = new JSlider();
        JPanel controlPanel = new ControlPanel(slider);

        contentPane.add(controlPanel, BorderLayout.NORTH);
        contentPane.add(slider, BorderLayout.CENTER);
    }
}
```

Listeners are added to the check box and combo boxes that manipulate the slider. When the Paint Ticks check box is activated, `JSlider.setPaintTicks()` is invoked with a `boolean` value representing the selected state of the check box. When a selection is made from the combo boxes, `setMinorTickSpacing()` or `setMajorTickSpacing()` is invoked with the value selected from the combo box.

As can be seen from Table 11-2 on page 611, none of the properties manipulated by the check box or combo boxes results in an automatic update of the slider's visual representation. As a result, `revalidate()` is invoked for the slider, and the slider is laid out and repainted. See "Validate, Invalidate, and Revalidate Methods" on page 144 for more information on the `revalidate` method.

```
class ControlPanel extends JPanel {
    public ControlPanel(final JSlider slider) {
        JCheckBox paintTicks = new JCheckBox("Paint Ticks");
        JComboBox minorSpacing = new JComboBox(),
                  majorSpacing = new JComboBox();

        ...

        paintTicks.addActionListener(new ActionListener() {
            public void actionPerformed(ActionEvent e) {
                JCheckBox cb = (JCheckBox)e.getSource();
                slider.setPaintTicks(cb.isSelected());
                slider.revalidate();
            }
        });
        minorSpacing.addItemListener(new ItemListener() {
            public void itemStateChanged(ItemEvent e) {
                JComboBox cb = (JComboBox)e.getSource();
                int spacing = Integer.parseInt(
                                (String)cb.getSelectedItem());

                slider.setMinorTickSpacing(spacing);
                slider.revalidate();
            }
        });
        majorSpacing.addItemListener(new ItemListener() {
            public void itemStateChanged(ItemEvent e) {
                JComboBox cb = (JComboBox)e.getSource();
                int spacing = Integer.parseInt(
                                (String)cb.getSelectedItem());

                slider.setMajorTickSpacing(spacing);
                slider.revalidate();
            }
        });
    }
}
```

The applet shown in Figure 11-7 is listed in its entirety in Example 11-6.

Example 11-6 Displaying Slider Tick Marks

```
import java.awt.*;
import java.awt.event.*;
import javax.swing.*;

public class Test extends JApplet {
    public Test() {
        Container contentPane = getContentPane();
        JSlider slider = new JSlider();
        JPanel controlPanel = new ControlPanel(slider);
```

```java
            contentPane.add(controlPanel, BorderLayout.NORTH);
            contentPane.add(slider, BorderLayout.CENTER);
        }
    }
    class ControlPanel extends JPanel {
        public ControlPanel(final JSlider slider) {
            JCheckBox paintTicks = new JCheckBox("Paint Ticks");
            JComboBox minorSpacing = new JComboBox(),
                      majorSpacing = new JComboBox();

            minorSpacing.addItem("0");
            minorSpacing.addItem("3");
            minorSpacing.addItem("5");
            minorSpacing.addItem("10");
            minorSpacing.addItem("20");

            majorSpacing.addItem("0");
            majorSpacing.addItem("3");
            majorSpacing.addItem("5");
            majorSpacing.addItem("10");
            majorSpacing.addItem("20");

            add(paintTicks);
            add(new JLabel("Minor Tick Spacing:"));
            add(minorSpacing);
            add(new JLabel("Major Tick Spacing:"));
            add(majorSpacing);

            paintTicks.addActionListener(new ActionListener() {
                public void actionPerformed(ActionEvent e) {
                    JCheckBox cb = (JCheckBox)e.getSource();
                    slider.setPaintTicks(cb.isSelected());
                    slider.repaint();
                }
            });
            minorSpacing.addItemListener(new ItemListener() {
                public void itemStateChanged(ItemEvent e) {
                    JComboBox cb = (JComboBox)e.getSource();
                    int spacing = Integer.parseInt(
                                    (String)cb.getSelectedItem());

                    slider.setMinorTickSpacing(spacing);
                    slider.revalidate();
                }
            });
            majorSpacing.addItemListener(new ItemListener() {
                public void itemStateChanged(ItemEvent e) {
                    JComboBox cb = (JComboBox)e.getSource();
                    int spacing = Integer.parseInt(
                                    (String)cb.getSelectedItem());
```

```
                    slider.setMajorTickSpacing(spacing);
                    slider.revalidate();
            }
        });
    }
}
```

Slider Labels

In addition to displaying tick marks, instances of `JSlider` can also display labels, which are painted at major tick mark locations. `JSlider` can generate numerical labels on its own, or custom labels can be specified by supplying a `Hashtable` containing `Integer`/`JLabel` pairs representing values and their associated labels.

The applet shown in Figure 11-8 contains an instance of `JSlider` that displays standard (meaning generated by the `JSlider` class) labels.

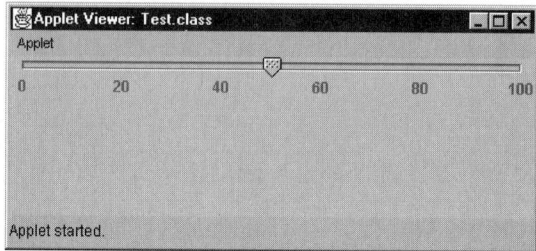

Figure 11-8 Default JSlider Labels

The applet shown in Figure 11-8 is listed in Example 11-7.

Example 11-7 Displaying Default JSlider Labels

```
import java.awt.*;
import java.awt.event.*;
import javax.swing.*;

public class Test extends JApplet {
    public Test() {
        Container contentPane = getContentPane();
        JSlider slider = new JSlider();
```

```
            slider.setPaintLabels(true);
            slider.setMajorTickSpacing(20);
            contentPane.add(slider, BorderLayout.NORTH);
        }
    }
```

The applet invokes `JSlider.setPaintLabels(true)`, which indicates that labels should be painted for the slider. However, invoking `setPaintLabels()` is not enough to cause the labels to be painted. Until spacing has been set for major ticks, the `JSlider` class cannot determine where the labels should be painted. As a result, `setMajorTickSpacing()` must be invoked for the labels to appear.

Swing Tip ...

Tick Marks and Labels Are Painted Only If Tick Spacing Is Specified

The JSlider class provides methods for setting the visibility of labels and tick marks: setPaintLabels() and setPaintTicks(), respectively. The methods are passed a boolean value—passing true makes labels and tick marks visible, and passing false makes them invisible. However, invoking setPaintTicks(true) or setPaintLabels(true) does not necessarily make labels and tick marks visible.

Automatically generated labels and tick marks cannot be drawn unless the spacing between tick marks is explicitly set because, unlike most properties for Swing components, tick spacing does not default to a reasonable value. As a result, spacing between tick marks must be explicitly set before automatically generated labels and tick marks can be drawn.[1]

1. Custom labels are drawn without explicitly setting tick mark spacing.

Custom Slider Labels

In addition to standard labels, custom labels can be specified for instances of `JSlider`. The applet shown in Figure 11-9 displays custom labels that contain text and an icon.

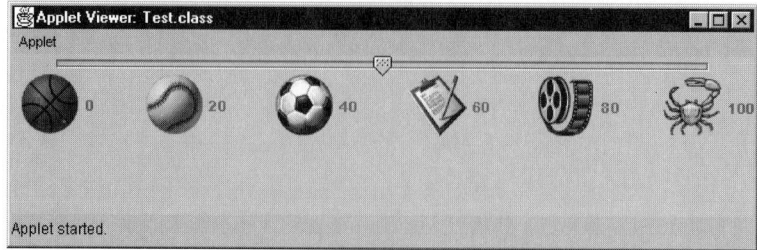

Figure 11-9 Custom Slider Labels

The applet shown in Figure 11-9 is listed in Example 11-8.

Example 11-8 Custom Slider Labels

```java
import java.util.*;
import java.awt.*;
import java.awt.event.*;
import javax.swing.*;

public class Test extends JApplet {
    public Test() {
        Container contentPane = getContentPane();
        JSlider slider = new JSlider();

        Icon[] icons = {
            new ImageIcon("basketball.gif"),
            new ImageIcon("baseball.gif"),
            new ImageIcon("soccer.gif"),
            new ImageIcon("clipboard.gif"),
            new ImageIcon("filmstrip.gif"),
            new ImageIcon("crab.gif"),
        };

        Hashtable table = new Hashtable();

        for(int i=0, loc=0; i < icons.length; i++, loc += 20) {
            table.put(new Integer(loc),
                    new JLabel(Integer.toString(loc),
                               icons[i],
                               JLabel.LEFT));
        }

        slider.setLabelTable(table);
        slider.setPaintLabels(true);
        slider.setMajorTickSpacing(20);

        contentPane.add(slider, BorderLayout.NORTH);
    }
}
```

The applet invokes `JSlider.setLabelTable()` which is passed a
`Hashtable` containing `Integer/Component` pairs, where the components are
labels. Each instance of `JLabel` is created with an icon and text representing a
value. The `JSlider` UI delegate uses the hash table to draw the labels and their
associated text.

Subsequently, `setPaintLabels()` and `setMajorTickSpacing()` are
invoked, both of which are required to cause the labels to be painted.

Inverting Slider Values

All sliders maintain an `inverted` property that determines the direction in
which a slider's values increase. By default, the `inverted` property is `false`,
and slider values increase from left to right for horizontal sliders and from bottom
to top for vertical sliders. When the `inverted` property is `true`, slider values for
horizontal sliders increase from right to left and slider values for vertical sliders
increase from top to bottom.

The effect of setting the `inverted` property can be seen from the applet shown in
Figure 11-10. The left-hand picture in Figure 11-10 shows the default orientation
of the slider's labels, and the right-hand picture shows the labels inverted.

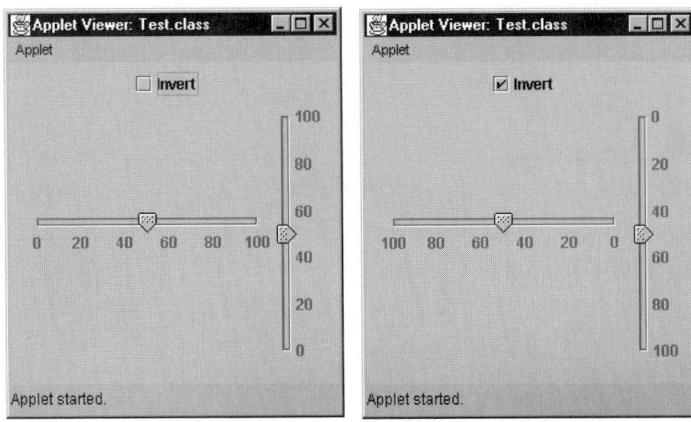

Figure 11-10 Inverting Sliders

The applet shown in Figure 11-10 is listed in Example 11-9.

Example 11-9 Inverting Sliders

```java
import java.awt.*;
import java.awt.event.*;
import javax.swing.*;

public class Test extends JApplet {
    private JCheckBox checkBox = new JCheckBox("Invert");
    private JSlider[] sliders = { new JSlider(),
                                  new JSlider(JSlider.VERTICAL) };

    public Test() {
        Container contentPane = getContentPane();

        contentPane.setLayout(new FlowLayout());
        contentPane.add(checkBox);

        for(int i=0; i < sliders.length; ++i) {
            sliders[i].setPaintLabels(true);
            sliders[i].setMajorTickSpacing(20);
            contentPane.add(sliders[i]);
        }

        checkBox.addActionListener(new ActionListener() {
            public void actionPerformed(ActionEvent e) {
                for(int i=0; i < sliders.length; ++i)
                    sliders[i].setInverted(checkBox.isSelected());
            }
        });
    }
}
```

Both sliders have their `paintLabels` and `majorTickSpacing` properties set to `true` and 20, respectively, and both sliders are added to the applet's content pane.

When the check box is activated, both sliders have their inverted properties set according to whether the check box is selected.

Slider Extent

A slider's extent determines the upper range of the slider's values. For example, if a slider has a maximum value of 100 and an extent of 20, the slider's value will never increase past (maximum − extent), meaning 80 in this case.

The applet shown in Figure 11-11 contains a slider and a combo box for selecting an extent. The top picture shows the applet as it appears initially, and the middle and bottom pictures show the applet after the slider's extent has been set to 10 and 20, respectively. Although a slider's value is restrained by its extent, the slider's grip can still be moved past the location presenting the maximum – extent value.[1]

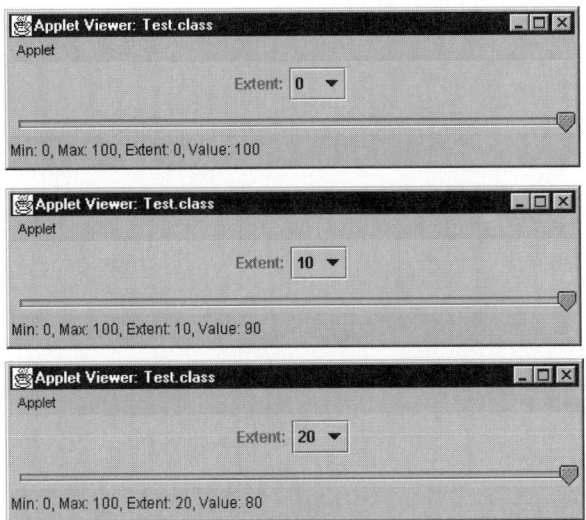

Figure 11-11 Slider Extent

The applet creates an instance of JSlider and a panel that contains the combo box. An item listener is added to the combo box that sets the slider's extent, based on the selection made from the combo box.

```
class ControlPanel extends JPanel {
    public ControlPanel(final JSlider slider) {
        JComboBox extent = new JComboBox();

        extent.addItem("0");
        extent.addItem("10");
        extent.addItem("20");
        extent.addItem("30");
```

1. Early versions of Swing moved the grip to (max – extent) if the grip was dragged passed the value.

```
            extent.addItem("40");

            add(new JLabel("Extent:"));
            add(extent);

            extent.addItemListener(new ItemListener() {
                public void itemStateChanged(ItemEvent e) {
                    JComboBox cb = (JComboBox)e.getSource();
                    int ext = Integer.parseInt(
                                   (String)cb.getSelectedItem());

                    slider.setExtent(ext);
                }
            });
        }
    }
```

The applet shown in Figure 11-11 is listed in its entirety in Example 11-10.

Example 11-10 Setting a Slider's Extent

```
import java.awt.*;
import java.awt.event.*;
import javax.swing.*;
import javax.swing.event.*;

public class Test extends JApplet {
    public Test() {
        Container contentPane = getContentPane();
        JSlider slider = new JSlider();
        JPanel controlPanel = new ControlPanel(slider);

        contentPane.add(controlPanel, BorderLayout.NORTH);
        contentPane.add(slider, BorderLayout.CENTER);

        slider.addChangeListener(new ChangeListener() {
            public void stateChanged(ChangeEvent e) {
                JSlider s = (JSlider)e.getSource();
                showStatus("Min: " + s.getMinimum() +
                        ", Max: " + s.getMaximum() +
                        ", Extent: " + s.getExtent() +
                        ", Value: " + s.getValue());
            }
        });
    }
}
class ControlPanel extends JPanel {
    public ControlPanel(final JSlider slider) {
        JComboBox extent = new JComboBox();
```

```
        extent.addItem("0");
        extent.addItem("10");
        extent.addItem("20");
        extent.addItem("30");
        extent.addItem("40");

        add(new JLabel("Extent:"));
        add(extent);

        extent.addItemListener(new ItemListener() {
            public void itemStateChanged(ItemEvent e) {
                JComboBox cb = (JComboBox)e.getSource();
                int ext = Integer.parseInt(
                                (String)cb.getSelectedItem());

                slider.setExtent(ext);
            }
        });
    }
}
```

The JSlider component is summarized in Component Summary 11-2.

Component Summary 11-2   JSlider

Model(s)	BoundedRangeModel
UI Delegate(s)	javax.swing.plaf.basic.BasicSliderUI
Renderer(s)	——
Editor(s)	——
Events Fired	——
Replacement For	——

Class Diagrams

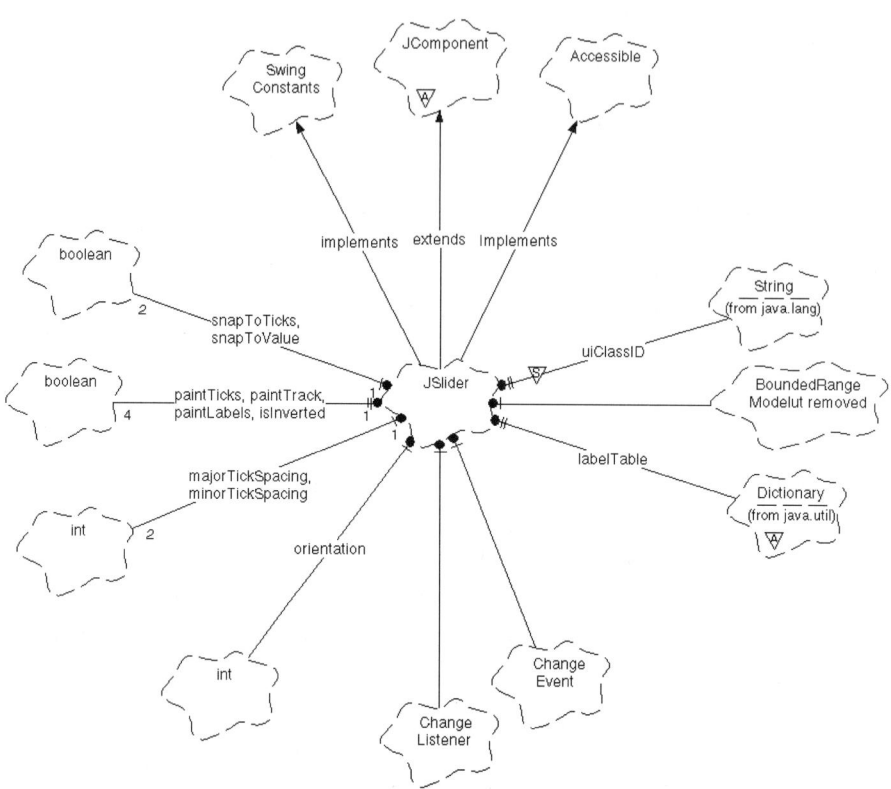

Figure 11-12 JSlider Class Diagram

JSlider's model is an instance of BoundedRangeModel, and the JSlider class maintains a protected reference to its model. JSlider also maintains a reference to a Dictionary that contains Integer/Component pairs representing slider values and an associated component that is displayed at the value.

JSlider maintains six protected boolean references for properties affecting the visibility of tick marks, the slider's track, and labels. The snapToTicks and snapToValue boolean variables determine whether the slider's grip snaps to a tick mark or to a value.

Like all Swing components that fire change events, the `JSlider` class uses a single `ChangeEvent` instance to fire change events to its change listeners because the only state associated with a change event is the event source. See "Lightweight Event Notification" on page 92 for more information concerning change events.

A slider's model, which is an instance of `BoundedRangeModel`, fires change events when the model's value is modified. Instances of `JSlider` register a change listener with their model and forward change events to their own change listeners; thus the `protected` references to instances of `ChangeEvent` and `ChangeListener` maintained by the `JSlider` class.

JSlider Properties

The properties maintained by the `JSlider` class are listed in Table 11-2.

Table 11-2   JSlider Properties

Property Name	Data Type	Property Type[1]	Access[2]	Default[3]
extent	int	Ch	SG	0
inverted	boolean	B	SG	false
labelTable	Dictionary	B	SG	——
majorTickSpacing	int	B	SG	——
maximum	int	Ch	CSG	100
minimum	int	Ch	CSG	0
minorTickSpacing	int	B	SG	——
model	Bounded RangeModel	B	CSG	Default BoundedRangeModel
orientation	int	B	CSG	HORIZONTAL
paintLabels	boolean	B	SG	false
paintTicks	boolean	B	SG	false
snapToTicks	boolean	Ch	SG	true
value	int	Ch	CSG	50
valueIsAdjusting	boolean	Ch	SG	false

1. B = bound (fires PropertyChangeEvent) / C = constrained/ I = indexed /
   S = simple / Ch = fires ChangeEvent
2. C = settable at construction time / G = getter method / S = setter method
3. L&F = look-and-feel dependent

extent — Defines the upper end of the range of values associated with a slider.

inverted — If `true`, values increase from right to left or bottom to top. If `false`, values increase from left to right or top to bottom.

labelTable — A `Dictionary` of label/value pairs.

majorTickSpacing — The number of *units* between major ticks.

maximum — The maximum value the slider represents.

minimum — The minimum value the slider represents.

minorTickSpacing — The number of units between minor ticks.

model — The model for instances of `JSlider`—an implementation of the `BoundedRangeModel` interface.

orientation — The orientation of the slider—either `JSlider.HORIZONTAL` or `JSlider.VERTICAL`.

paintLabels — If `true`, labels are painted at tick marks, but only if major or minor tick spacing has been set.

paintTicks — If `true`, tick marks are painted, but only if major or minor tick spacing has been set.

snapToTicks — If `true`, knob snaps to tick marks.

value — The current value represented by knob position.

valueIsAdjusting — `true` when knob is being dragged.

JSlider Events

Like most Swing components, instances of `JSlider` fire change events when their model properties are modified, as can be seen from Table 11-2.

The applet shown in Figure 11-13 reacts to slider change events by adding a change listener to the slider it contains, and displays the slider's minimum, maximum, and current values in the applet's status area.

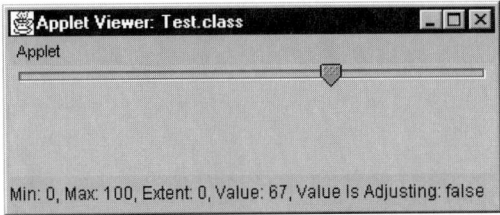

Figure 11-13 Monitoring a Slider's Value

The applet shown in Figure 11-13 is listed in Example 11-11.

Example 11-11 Monitoring a Slider's Value

```
import java.awt.*;
import java.awt.event.*;
import javax.swing.*;
import javax.swing.event.*;

public class Test extends JApplet {
    public Test() {
        Container contentPane = getContentPane();
        JSlider slider = new JSlider();

        contentPane.add(slider, BorderLayout.NORTH);

        slider.addChangeListener(new ChangeListener() {
            public void stateChanged(ChangeEvent e) {
                JSlider s = (JSlider)e.getSource();
                showStatus("Min: " + s.getMinimum() +
                        ", Max: " + s.getMaximum() +
                        ", Extent: " + s.getExtent() +
                        ", Value: " + s.getValue() +
                        ", Value Is Adjusting: " +
                        s.getValueIsAdjusting());
            }
        });
    }
}
```

The applet also displays the slider's valueIsAdjusting property, which is true when the slider's knob is being dragged. In some situations, it is desirable to react to slider events only when the knob has come to rest instead of continuously reacting to the knob being dragged.

JSlider Class Summaries

The `public` and `protected` variables and methods for `JSlider` are listed in Class Summary 11-2.

Class Summary 11-2   JSlider

Extends: JComponent

Implements: SwingConstants, javax.accessibility.Accessible

Constructors

---

public <u>JSlider</u>()
public <u>JSlider</u>(int orientation)
public <u>JSlider</u>(int minimum, int maximum)
public <u>JSlider</u>(int minimum, int maximum, int value)
public <u>JSlider</u>(int orientation, int minimum, int maximum, int value)

As can be seen from Table 11-2 on page 611, a slider's orientation, value, and minimum/maximum values can all be specified when a slider is constructed. The no-argument constructor creates a horizontal slider with minimum, maximum, and initial values of 0, 100, and 50, respectively.

Methods

Change listeners / Firing Change Events

---

public void <u>addChangeListener</u>(ChangeListener)
public void <u>removeChangeListener</u>(ChangeListener)

protected ChangeListener <u>createChangeListener</u>()
protected void <u>fireStateChanged</u>()

Change listeners are registered with instances of `JSlider` with the `public` `addChangeListener` and `removeChangeListener` methods listed above.

Like most Swing components, `JSlider` implements a `private` listener class— `JSlider.ModelListener`—that listens for change events fired by the slider's model. The `createChangeListener` method creates an instance of `JSlider.ModelListener` that is registered with the slider's model. Events fired by the model are subsequently forwarded to the slider's change listeners by invocation of the `fireStateChanged` method. In the rare event that this default behavior is not appropriate, extensions of `JSlider` are free to override both methods.

Standard Labels

public Hashtable <u>createStandardLabels</u>(int increment)
public Hashtable <u>createStandardLabels</u>(int increment, int start)

The two methods listed above generate standard labels for instances of `JSlider`. The first method listed above is passed an `integer` value representing the increment between labels. For example, if `createStandardLabels(int)` is passed a value of 5 for a slider that has a minimum value of 0 and a maximum value of 20, labels will be created for values at 0, 5, 10, 15, and 20.

The second method listed above is also passed an increment value and a starting value, in that order. For example, a call of `createStandardLabels(5,3)` for a slider with a minimum value of 0 and a maximum value of 20, will result in labels being created for values at 3, 8, 13, and 18.

Property Accessors

public int <u>getExtent</u>()
public boolean <u>getInverted</u>()
public Dictionary <u>getLabelTable</u>()
public int <u>getMajorTickSpacing</u>()

```
public int getMaximum()
public int getMinimum()
public int getMinorTickSpacing()
public BoundedRangeModel getModel()
public int getOrientation()
public boolean getPaintLabels()
public boolean getPaintTicks()
public boolean getSnapToTicks()
public int getValue()
public boolean getValueIsAdjusting()
```

```
public void setExtent(int)
public void setInverted(boolean)
public void setLabelTable(Dictionary)
public void setMajorTickSpacing(int)
public void setMaximum(int)
public void setMinimum(int)
public void setMinorTickSpacing(int)
public void setModel(BoundedRangeModel)
public void setOrientation(int)
public void setPaintLabels(boolean)
public void setPaintTicks(boolean)
public void setSnapToTicks(boolean)
public void setValue(int)
public void setValueIsAdjusting(boolean)
```

The methods listed above are accessors for `JSlider` properties. See Table 11-2 on page 611 for a summary of `JSlider` properties.

Convenience Methods

```
public String toString()
protected void updateLabelUIs()
```

The `toString` method returns a string that summarizes `JSlider` properties and their values. The `updateLabelUIs` method is invoked when the look and feel is modified to update the UI delegates for instances of `JLabel` used as a slider's labels. The `updateLabelUIs` method will rarely be overridden by extensions of `JSlider`.

Accessibility / Pluggable Look And Feel

public AccessibleContext getAccessibleContext()
public SliderUI getUI()
public String getUIClassID()
public void setUI(SliderUI)
public void updateUI()

The methods listed above can be found in most extensions of JComponent. Swing lightweight components can return the class name of their UI delegate and an accessibility context that contains accessibility information for the component. The updateUI method is invoked when the component is fitted with a UI delegate.

AWT Compatibility

The AWT does not provide a component analogous to JSlider.

JSeparator

Separators are typically used to separate—or group, depending upon your perspective—components or sets of components. Although separators are arguably Swing's simplest component,[2] they can be frustrating to use without a good understanding of layout managers and component minimum, maximum, and preferred sizes. For example, consider the applet, shown in Figure 11-14, that contains two buttons separated by an instance of JSeparator.

---

2. JPanel also makes a compelling argument.

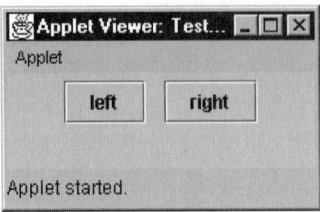

Figure 11-14 An Invisible Separator

The applet shown in Figure 11-14 is listed in Example 11-12.

Example 11-12 An Invisible Separator

```
import java.awt.*;
import javax.swing.*;

public class Test extends JApplet {
    public void init() {
        Container contentPane = getContentPane();

        contentPane.setLayout(new FlowLayout());

        contentPane.add(new JButton("left"));
        contentPane.add(new JSeparator(JSeparator.VERTICAL));
        contentPane.add(new JButton("right"));
    }
}
```

The applet sets the layout manager for its content pane to an instance of `FlowLayout` and adds a button followed by a separator and another button to the content pane.

Obviously, something is amiss because the separator is not visible in Figure 11-14. The separator is there, but it cannot be seen because its height is 0; here's why:

By default, a separator's UI delegate defines the preferred size for vertical separators as `new Dimension(2,0)`. It is assumed that separators will either be sized by a layout manager or explicitly sized when contained in a container that has a `null` layout manager. Because the layout manager for the applet's content pane is an instance of `FlowLayout`, the separator is sized according to its preferred size, and therefore its height is set to 0.

The solution to making the separator visible is simply to modify its preferred size, as is the case for the applet shown in Figure 11-15.

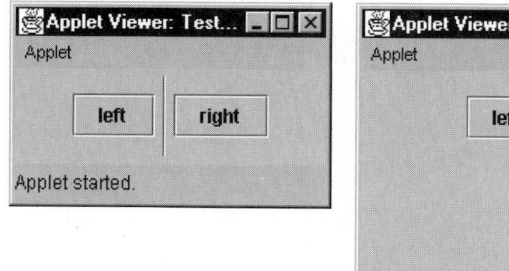

Figure 11-15 Controlling Separator Size

The applet shown in Figure 11-15 is listed in Example 11-13.

Example 11-13 Controlling Separator Size

```
import java.awt.*;
import javax.swing.*;

public class Test extends JApplet {
    public void init() {
        Container contentPane = getContentPane();
        JSeparator s = new JSeparator(JSeparator.VERTICAL);
        Dimension ps = s.getPreferredSize();

        contentPane.setLayout(new FlowLayout());

        contentPane.add(new JButton("left"));
        contentPane.add(s);
        contentPane.add(new JButton("right"));

        s.setPreferredSize(new Dimension(ps.width, 50));
    }
}
```

The applet does not change the separator's preferred width; however, the preferred height for the separator is specified as 50 pixels.

Notice from the right-hand picture in Figure 11-15 that the height of the separator is fixed. Often it is desirable to have separators grow with the container in which they reside, as is the case for the applet shown in Figure 11-16.

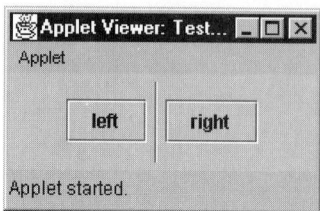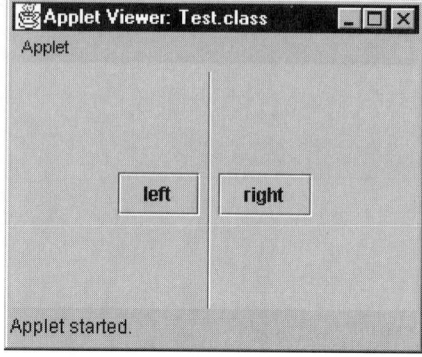

Figure 11-16 Monitoring Separator Size

The applet shown in Figure 11-16 is listed in Example 11-14.

Example 11-14 Monitoring Separator Size

```
import java.awt.*;
import java.awt.event.*;
import javax.swing.*;

public class Test extends JApplet {

    public void init() {
        Container contentPane = getContentPane();
        final JSeparator s =
                    new JSeparator(JSeparator.VERTICAL);
        final Dimension ps = s.getPreferredSize();

        contentPane.setLayout(new FlowLayout());

        contentPane.add(new JButton("left"));
        contentPane.add(s);
        contentPane.add(new JButton("right"));

        addComponentListener(new ComponentAdapter() {
            public void componentShown(ComponentEvent e) {
                adjustSeparatorPreferredSize();
            }
            public void componentResized(ComponentEvent e) {
```

```
System.out.println("resized");
    adjustSeparatorPreferredSize();
}
private void adjustSeparatorPreferredSize() {
    s.setPreferredSize(new Dimension(ps.width,
                            getSize().height));
    s.revalidate();
}
    });
}
}
```

The applet shown in Figure 11-16 adds a component listener to the applet that adjusts the preferred size of the separator whenever the content pane is shown or resized. After the separator's preferred size is set, `revalidate()` is invoked for the separator to force it to be laid out. See "Validate, Invalidate, and Revalidate Methods" on page 144 for more information concerning the `revalidate` method.

Separators and Boxes

Separators are well suited to Swing box containers—instances of the Box class—because boxes arrange components either horizontally or vertically. Typically, vertical separators are placed in horizontal boxes, and horizontal separators are placed in vertical boxes. The Box class is discussed in "The Box Class" on page 276.

The applet shown in Figure 11-17 illustrates the placement of separators in nested boxes. The applet's content pane contains a horizontal box containing a panel (the Left panel), a horizontal strut that is 10 pixels wide, a vertical separator followed by another strut, and another box.

Figure 11-17 Separators and Boxes

The second box is oriented vertically and contains a panel (the `Right Top` panel), a 10 pixel-high vertical strut, a horizontal separator followed by another strut, and another panel (the `Right Button` panel).

The maximum width of the vertical separator is set to the separator's preferred width, which by default is 2 pixels. The maximum height of the vertical separator is set to `Integer.MAX_VALUE` so that the separator is allowed to grow in the vertical direction.

```
public class Test extends JApplet {
    ...
    private JSeparator vs, hs;   // vs = vertical separator
                                 // hs = horizontal separator

    ...
    public void init() {
        ...
        setSeparatorPreferredSizes();
        ...
    }
    private void setSeparatorPreferredSizes() {
        vs.setMaximumSize(
            new Dimension(vs.getPreferredSize().width,
                    Integer.MAX_VALUE));
        ...
```

The maximum height of the horizontal separator is set to the separator's preferred height, which by default is also 2 pixels. The maximum width of the horizontal separator is set to `Integer.MAX_VALUE` so that the separator is allowed to grow in the horizontal direction.

```
      ...
      hs.setMaximumSize(
          new Dimension(Integer.MAX_VALUE,
                          hs.getPreferredSize().height));
      }
      ...
}
```

The applet shown in Figure 11-17 is listed in its entirety in Example 11-15.

Example 11-15 Separators and Boxes

```java
import java.awt.*;
import java.awt.event.*;
import javax.swing.*;

public class Test extends JApplet {
    private JPanel left, rightTop, rightBottom;

    private Box box = new Box(BoxLayout.X_AXIS),
                rightBox = new Box(BoxLayout.Y_AXIS);

    private JSeparator vs, hs;   // vs = vertical separator
                                 // hs = horizontal separator
    public void init() {
        createBoxes();
        setPanelBorders();
        setSeparatorPreferredSizes();

        left.setPreferredSize(new Dimension(150,0));

        getContentPane().add(box, BorderLayout.CENTER);
    }
    private void createBoxes() {

        Component vStrut = box.createVerticalStrut(10),
                  hStrut = box.createHorizontalStrut(10);

        rightBox.add(rightTop = new JPanel());
        rightBox.add(box.createVerticalStrut(10));
        rightBox.add(hs = new JSeparator());
        rightBox.add(box.createVerticalStrut(10));
        rightBox.add(rightBottom = new JPanel());
```

```
        box.add(left = new JPanel());
        box.add(box.createHorizontalStrut(10));
        box.add(vs = new JSeparator(JSeparator.VERTICAL));
        box.add(box.createHorizontalStrut(10));
        box.add(rightBox);
    }
    private void setSeparatorPreferredSizes() {
        vs.setMaximumSize(
            new Dimension(vs.getPreferredSize().width,
                          Integer.MAX_VALUE));

        hs.setMaximumSize(
            new Dimension(Integer.MAX_VALUE,
                          hs.getPreferredSize().height));
    }
    private void setPanelBorders() {
        left.setBorder(
            BorderFactory.createTitledBorder("Left"));
        rightTop.setBorder(
            BorderFactory.createTitledBorder("Right Top"));
        rightBottom.setBorder(
            BorderFactory.createTitledBorder("Right Bottom"));
    }
}
```

The JSeparator class is summarized in Component Summary 11-3.

Component Summary 11-3   JSeparator

Model(s)	—
UI Delegate(s)	javax.swing.plaf.basic.BasicSeparatorUI
Renderer(s)	—
Editor(s)	—
Events Fired	—
Replacement For	—

Class Diagrams

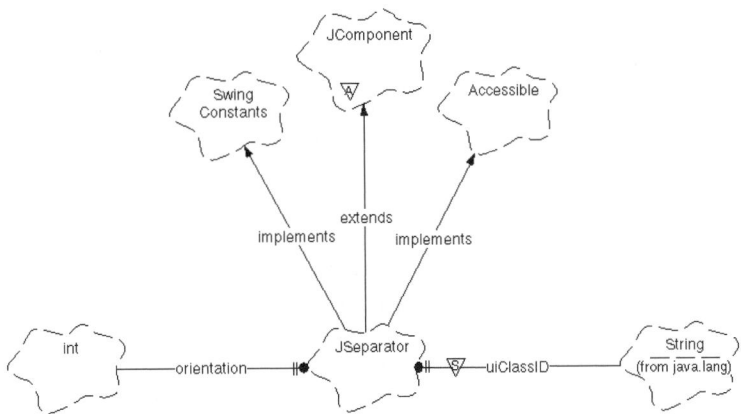

Figure 11-18 JSeparator Class Diagram

The JSeparator class extends JComponent and implements the
SwingConstants and Accessible interfaces. JSeparator maintains
private references to an integer value representing the separator's
orientation, and a string representing the class ID of the separator's UI delegate.

JSeparator Properties

Orientation is the only property maintained by the JSeparator class. The
orientation property is a bound property, and the JSeparator class provides
both setter and getter methods for it.[3] When a separator's orientation is modified,
revalidate() is invoked for the separator, causing the separator to be laid out
and repainted. See "Validate, Invalidate, and Revalidate Methods" on page 144
for more information concerning the revalidate method.

---

3. Orientation can also be specified at construction time.

JSeparator Events

The `JSeparator` class does not fire any events of its own accord; all event firing is inherited from the `JComponent` class.

The `JSeparator` class is summarized in Class Summary 11-3.

Class Summary 11-3   JSeparator

Extends: JComponent

Implements: SwingConstants, javax.accessibility.Accessible

Constructors

---

public JSeparator()
public JSeparator(int orientation)

Instances of `JSeparator` can be constructed with a specific orientation, or separators can be constructed with the default `JSeparator` constructor, which creates a horizontal separator.

Orientation / Focus Traversable / Param String

---

public int getOrientation()
public void setOrientation(int orientation)

public boolean isFocusTraversable()
protected String paramString()

JSeparator provides setter and getter methods for the orientation property. In addition, JSeparator overrides isFocusTraversable() to return false, indicating that separators are not interested in receiving focus. The paramString method returns a string representing a separator.

Accessibility / Pluggable Look And Feel

---

public AccessibleContext getAccessibleContext()
public SeparatorUI getUI()
public String getUIClassID()
public void setUI(SeparatorUI)
public void updateUI()

The methods listed above can be found in most extensions of JComponent. Swing lightweight components can return the class name of their UI delegate and an accessibility context that contains accessibility information for the component. The updateUI method is invoked when the component is fitted with a UI delegate.

AWT Compatibility

The AWT does not provide a component analogous to JSeparator.

Parting Shots

Progress bars, sliders, and separators are welcome additions to the Swing set of components that were conspicuously absent from the AWT. Whereas progress bars and sliders could be considered specialized components that are not part of a basic user interface toolkit, separators are one of the most basic user interface components. Nonetheless, Swing provides robust versions of each of the three components, which will find their way into many Java applets and applications.

CHAPTER

12

Lightweight Containers

This chapter discusses the Swing lightweight containers listed below:

- JPanel
- JRootPane
- JLayeredPane
- JTabbedPane
- JSplitPane

JPanel is the successor to the AWT's Canvas and Panel classes. Both text and graphics can be rendered in instances JPanel, and instances of JPanel can be used as a generic container.

JRootPane is a container that is contained in all of Swing's top-level containers, such as frames, dialogs, windows, internal frames, and Swing applets.

JLayeredPane allows components it contains to be placed on separate layers which control the depth at which the components are displayed.

JTabbedPane is a container that can contain multiple components, only one of which is displayed at a time. Instances of JTabbedPane contain tabs that can be used to select the component that is currently displayed.

JSplitPane contains two components separated by a divider. The divider can be dragged to change the amount of real estate that each component occupies.

JPanel

JPanel is one of Swing's simplest components; however, it is also one of the most heavily used. Swing uses instances of JPanel in a number of other Swing components; for example, by default the JRootPane container instantiates instances of JPanel for its content pane and glass pane, as can be seen from Table 12-1 on page 637.

The JPanel class doubles as a simple container and as a canvas for displaying graphics. Figure 12-1 shows an applet that instantiates three instances of JPanel: A control panel that contains the "Name:" label and text field, a panel that is used exclusively as a canvas for displaying text and graphics, and a third panel that contains the control panel and canvas.

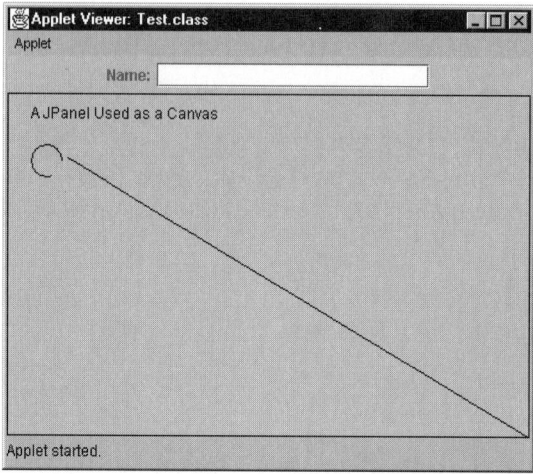

Figure 12-1 Panels as Containers and Canvases

The applet shown in Figure 12-1 is listed in Example 12-1.

Example 12-1 An Applet That Uses Three Instances of JPanel

```
import java.awt.*;
import java.awt.event.*;
import javax.swing.*;

public class Test extends JApplet {
    public Test() {
        Container contentPane = getContentPane();
        JPanel panel = new JPanel(new BorderLayout());
        JPanel controlPanel = new JPanel();
        JPanel canvas = new Canvas();

        canvas.setBorder(
            BorderFactory.createLineBorder(Color.black));

        controlPanel.add(new JLabel("Name:"));
        controlPanel.add(new JTextField(20));

        panel.add(controlPanel, BorderLayout.NORTH);
        panel.add(canvas, BorderLayout.CENTER);

        contentPane.add(panel);
    }
}
class Canvas extends JPanel {
    public void paintComponent(Graphics g) {
        super.paintComponent(g);

        Dimension size = getSize();
        g.setColor(Color.black);
        g.drawLine(50,50,size.width,size.height);
        g.drawArc(20,40,25,25,0,290);
        g.drawString("A JPanel Used as a Canvas", 20, 20);
    }
}
```

The panel instance contains the controlPanel and canvas panels, and is added to the applet's content pane. The layout manager for the panel is set to an instance of BorderLayout when the panel is constructed; the controlPanel is added to the panel as the NORTH component, and the canvas instance is added as the CENTER component.

The `canvas` is an instance of the `Canvas` class, which is an extension of `JPanel`. The `Canvas` class overrides `paintComponent` for the purpose of drawing its text and graphics.

Notice that the `Canvas` class invokes `super.paintComponent()` to ensure that its background is painted. In this simple example, it makes no difference whether `super.paintComponent()` is invoked or not, but the call is included as a reminder to invoke the superclass method when overriding `paintComponent()` for opaque panels. See "Custom Painting in Swing Components" on page 138 for more information on custom painting in Swing components.

The `JPanel` class is summarized in Component Summary 12-1.

Component Summary 12-1   JPanel

Model(s)	——
UI Delegate(s)	javax.swing.plaf.basic.BasicPanelUI
Renderer(s)	——
Editor(s)	——
Events Fired	——
Replacement For	java.awt.Canvas, java.awt.Panel

Class Diagrams

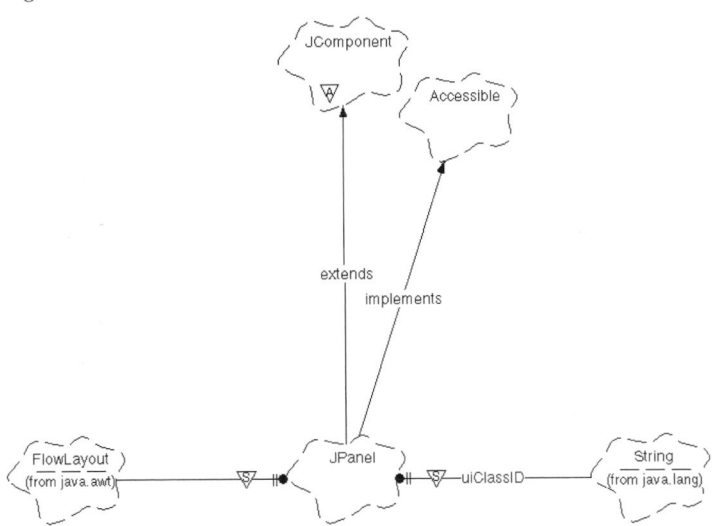

Figure 12-2 JPanel Class Diagram

JPanel is a simple extension of JComponent that does not have a model.
JPanel does little more than set defaults for its layout manager, double
buffering, and opaque properties, in addition to implementing the Accessible
interface. By default, the layout manager for instances of JPanel is set to a shared
instance of FlowLayout, and the inherited double buffering and opaque
properties are set to true.

Note that JPanel itself does not implement any functionality for containing
components. Because JComponent extends the java.awt.Container class, all
lightweight Swing components are fully functional AWT containers.

JPanel Defaults

JPanel is one of Swing's simplest components, and as a result, it is very easy to use. The main thing to remember about instances of JPanel are the default values for the layout manager, double buffering, and opaque properties, which are summarized below:

Layout Manager: A shared instance of FlowLayout

Double Buffering: True

Opaque: True

JPanel Properties

The JPanel class does not define any properties of its own; all properties are inherited from the JComponent class.

JPanel Events

The JPanel class also does not fire any events of its own accord; all event firing is inherited from the JComponent class.

JPanel Class Summaries

The public and protected variables and methods for JPanel are listed in Class Summary 12-1.

Class Summary 12-1   JPanel

Extends: JComponent
Implements: javax.accessibility.Accessible

Constructors

public <u>JPanel</u>()
public <u>JPanel</u>(boolean isDoubleBuffered)
public <u>JPanel</u>(LayoutManager)
public <u>JPanel</u>(LayoutManager, boolean isDoubleBuffered)

JPanel provides the four constructors listed above. The no-argument constructor fits the panel with a shared instance of FlowLayout and sets the double buffering and opaque properties to true. The other three constructors can be used for specifying the double buffering property (the boolean value) and the layout manager for the panel.

Methods

public AccessibleContext <u>getAccessibleContext</u>()
public String <u>getUIClassID</u>()
public String <u>paramString</u>()
public void <u>updateUI</u>()

JPanel methods are simple overrides of inherited methods that collectively identify instances of JPanel.

AWT Compatibility

JPanel is fully source code compatible with java.awt.Panel, but that is not as impressive as it sounds because java.awt.Panel does not define any public methods of its own.[1]

Instances of JPanel and java.awt.Panel both share a single instance of FlowLayout by default, and both provide constructors that allow the layout manager to be set at the time of construction if the default FlowLayout is not sufficient.

JPanel, by way of JComponent, provides double buffering and opaque properties that have no parallel in the AWT's Panel class.

JRootPane

Nearly every Swing component ultimately resides in an instance of JRootPane because all of Swing's top-level containers contain an instance of JRootPane. Root panes provide a convenient containment hierarchy.

The topmost component in a root pane is the glass pane. When the glass pane is visible, it floats above all other components in the root pane and intercepts all mouse events.

Underneath the glass pane is an instance of JLayeredPane, which as its name suggests, allows components to be placed on separate layers. The layered pane, in turn, contains an optional menu bar and a content pane. The content pane is where applets and applications set up shop.

Swing defines an interface for containers that contain an instance of JRootPane. The RootPaneContainer interface is discussed in "The RootPaneContainer Interface" below.

---

1. Other than the overridden addNotify method.

The components contained in instances of JRootPane are listed in Table 12-1.

Table 12-1   JRootPane Components

Component	Class	Description
contentPane	JPanel	Contains applet/application's components and resides in layeredPane.
glassPane	JPanel	Floats above all other components, traps mouse events, and can be transparent.
layeredPane	JLayeredPane	Contains contentPane and menuBar.
menuBar	JMenuBar	Resides in layeredPane above the contentPane.

The RootPaneContainer Interface

The RootPaneContainer interface is summarized in Interface Summary 12-1.

Interface Summary 12-1   RootPaneContainer

---

public abstract Container getContentPane()
public abstract Component getGlassPane()
public abstract JLayeredPane getLayeredPane()
public abstract JRootPane getRootPane()

public abstract void setContentPane(Container)
public abstract void setGlassPane(Component)
public abstract void setLayeredPane(JLayeredPane)

The RootPaneContainer interface defines accessors for the root pane itself, the glass pane, layered pane, and content pane contained within the root pane. The RootPaneContainer interface is defined by the following Swing containers:

- JApplet
- JDialog
- JFrame

- `JInternalFrame`
- `JRootPane`
- `JWindow`

Figure 12-3 shows a class diagram that depicts the relationship between the `RootPaneContainer` interface and Swing containers.

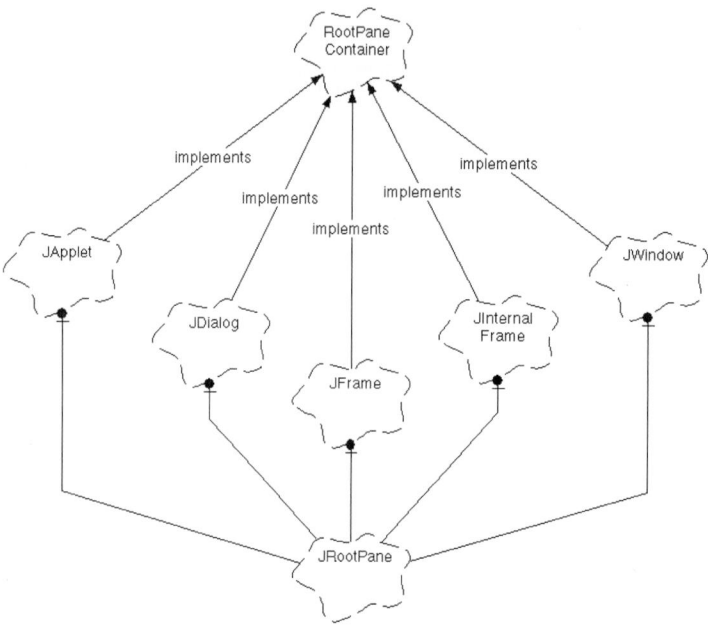

Figure 12-3 The `RootPaneContainer` Interface

Every Swing component that implements the `RootPaneContainer` interface maintains a reference to an instance of `JRootPane`. The methods defined by `RootPaneContainer` interface are implemented by simply delegating to the enclosed root pane.

Glass Panes

The glass pane has the highest fun quotient of any of the root pane's components because glass panes float on top of other components, trap mouse events in the root pane, and can be transparent.

These unique abilities qualify the glass pane for a wide range of special effects. Everything from animations for drag-and-drop to a cockroach "utility"—where little roaches scurry about as windows are opened and closed—are good candidates for dusting off the glass pane.

Glass panes float over all other components in a root pane because the glass pane is the first component added to a root pane.

The zorder—or depth—for Swing components is determined by the order in which they are added to their respective containers. The first component added to a container is displayed on top of all the other components in the same container, whereas the last component added to a container is displayed underneath the other components. See "Zorder" on page 43 for more on the manner in which zorder is determined for both lightweight and heavyweight components.

Glass panes, when they are visible, are also capable of trapping mouse events. When a mouse event occurs inside an AWT container, the event is routed to the topmost lightweight component that is interested in receiving mouse events. A component is interested in receiving mouse events if it has installed a mouse listener or has specifically enabled mouse events.

The applet shown in Figure 12-4 contains two buttons: an instance of JButton and an instance of JRadioButton. The radio button is fitted with a rollover image so that when the mouse enters the button, the rollover image is displayed— see "JButton" on page 387 for more information concerning buttons and rollover images. When the button is activated, the glass pane associated with the applet's root pane is made visible. A subsequent mouse click anywhere in the applet while the glass pane is visible hides the glass pane, and the applet is essentially reset to the state it was in when it was started.

Figure 12-4 shows the applet in three states. The top two images show the applet when its glass pane is not visible; the right-hand image shows the radio button displaying its rollover image after the cursor has entered the button. The bottom image shows the applet after the "show glass pane" button has been activated and the glass pane is made visible.

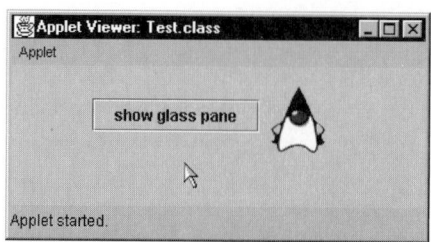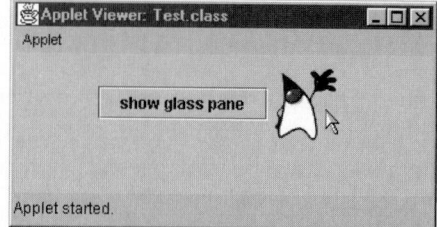

Figure 12-4 The Glass Pane

Notice that the rollover image for the radio button is not displayed when the glass pane is visible, even when cursor has entered the radio button. This is because the glass pane has a mouse listener, which signifies that is interested in handling mouse events. Because the AWT's delegation event model does not automatically propagate events from containers to the components they contain, mouse events are sent to the glass pane, but not to the components underneath the glass pane.

The applet swaps out its original glass pane for a custom version—an instance of CustomGlassPane.

```
public class GlassPaneTest extends JApplet {
    private Component glassPane = new CustomGlassPane();

    public void init() {
        ...
        setGlassPane(glassPane);
        ...
    }
    ...
}
```

CustomGlassPane extends JPanel and overrides the paintComponent
method. When the glass pane is visible, the string "glass pane ..." is tiled
over its background. Notice that the CustomGlassPane.paintComponent
method does not invoke super.paintComponent because it is transparent.

```
class CustomGlassPane extends JPanel {
   ...
   private String displayString = "glass pane ...   ";

   public void paintComponent(Graphics g) {
      Dimension size = getSize();
      FontMetrics fm = g.getFontMetrics();
      int sw = fm.stringWidth(displayString);
      int fh = fm.getHeight();

      g.setColor(Color.blue);

      for(int row=fh; row < size.height; row += fh)
         for(int col=0; col < size.width; col += sw)
            g.drawString(displayString, col, row);
   }
   ...
}
```

CustomGlassPane reacts to mouse pressed events by making itself invisible,
allowing events to be handled by the button in the content pane.

```
class CustomGlassPane extends JPanel {
   private JButton button;
   private String displayString = "glass pane ...   ";

   public CustomGlassPane() {
      setOpaque(false);

      addMouseListener(new MouseAdapter() {
         public void mousePressed(MouseEvent e) {
            setVisible(false);
         }
      });
   }
   ...
}
```

The applet shown in Figure 12-4 is listed in its entirety in Example 12-2.

Example 12-2 GlassPaneTest Applet

```java
import java.awt.*;
import java.awt.event.*;
import javax.swing.*;

public class GlassPaneTest extends JApplet {
    private Component glassPane = new CustomGlassPane();

    public void init() {
        Container contentPane = getContentPane();
        JButton button = new JButton("show glass pane");

        contentPane.setLayout(new FlowLayout());
        contentPane.add(button);

        setGlassPane(glassPane);

        button.addActionListener(new ActionListener() {
            public void actionPerformed(ActionEvent e) {
                glassPane.setVisible(true);
            }
        });
    }
}
class CustomGlassPane extends JPanel {
    private JButton button;
    private String displayString = "glass pane ...   ";

    public CustomGlassPane() {
        setOpaque(false);

        addMouseListener(new MouseAdapter() {
            public void mousePressed(MouseEvent e) {
                setVisible(false);
            }
        });
    }
    public void paintComponent(Graphics g) {
        Dimension size = getSize();
        FontMetrics fm = g.getFontMetrics();
        int sw = fm.stringWidth(displayString);
        int fh = fm.getHeight();

        g.setColor(Color.blue);

        for(int row=fh; row < size.height; row += fh)
            for(int col=0; col < size.width; col += sw)
                g.drawString(displayString, col, row);
    }
}
```

Swing Tip ...

Glass Panes and Mouse Events

Whenever a mouse event occurs in a lightweight container, the event is routed to the container's topmost lightweight component that is interested in handling mouse events. As a result, if the root pane's glass pane is visible and the glass pane has expressed interest in handling mouse events, mouse events will be routed to the glass pane.

Components can express interest in handling mouse events in one of two ways, either by adding a mouse listener or by enabling mouse events. Enabling mouse events is accomplished by invoking the enableEvents methods with an appropriate AWTEvent constant, like this:

```
aComponent.enableEvents(AWTEvent.MOUSE_EVENT_MASK);
```

If a glass pane has not expressed interest in handling mouse events, mouse events will be sent to the components below the glass pane even when the glass pane is visible.

Content Panes

The content pane is the container where applets and applications place their components. By default, the content pane is an instance of JPanel that is fitted with a border layout by the protected JRootPane.createContentPane method.

The applet shown in Figure 12-5 implements a custom content pane that tiles its background with an image.

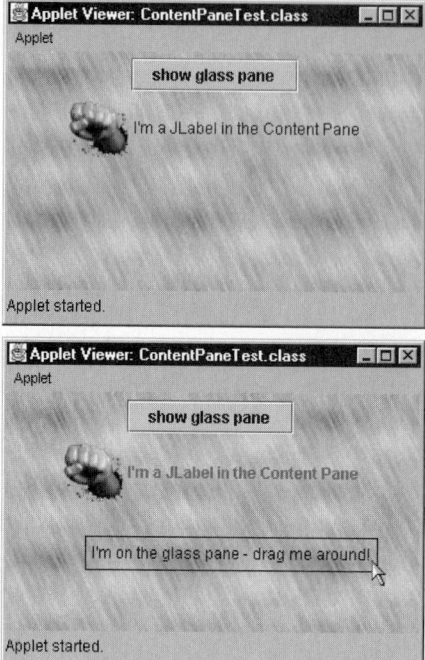

Figure 12-5 The Content Pane

The applet replaces its glass pane and its content pane with custom versions that are extensions of the JPanel class.

```
public class ContentPaneTest extends JApplet {
    private JButton button = new JButton("show glass pane");

    public void init() {
        setGlassPane(new CustomGlassPane(button));
        setContentPane(new CustomContentPane(button));
        ...
    }
    ...
}
```

The upper-left picture in Figure 12-5 shows the applet in its initial state. The applet's content pane tiles the rain.gif image over its background and adds a label and a button.

```
class CustomContentPane extends JPanel {
    private ImageIcon rain = new ImageIcon("rain.gif");
    private ImageIcon punch = new ImageIcon("punch.gif");
    private int rainw = rain.getIconWidth();
    private int rainh = rain.getIconHeight();

    public CustomContentPane(JButton button) {
        add(button);
        add(new JLabel("I'm a JLabel in the Content Pane",
                       punch, SwingConstants.RIGHT));
    }
    public void paintComponent(Graphics g) {
        Dimension size = getSize();

        // tile rain image over backgroundTo
        for(int row=0; row < size.height; row += rainh)
            for(int col=0; col < size.width; col += rainw)
                rain.paintIcon(this,g,col,row);
    }
}
```

When the show glass pane button is activated, the applet's glass pane is made visible. The glass pane contains a draggable object—a string surrounded by a black rectangle. After the string has been dragged, it disappears. If the button is subsequently activated, the string will appear at its last drag location.

The upper-right picture in Figure 12-5 shows the applet after the button has been activated and the glass pane made visible. The bottom picture in Figure 12-5 shows the applet after the string has been dragged on the glass pane.

The key to dragging the string on the glass pane lies with the CustomGlassPane class. A mouse listener and a mouse motion listener control the dragging by updating the position of the string and repainting it every time a mouse dragged event occurs within the glass pane. It should be noted that the manner in which the string is dragged is not very efficient, but it will do for illustrating the use of the content pane.

```
class CustomGlassPane extends JPanel {
    ...
    private Point ulhc = new Point(20,20), last;
    private String displayString =
                "I'm on the glass pane - drag me around!";

    public CustomGlassPane(JButton b) {
        ...
        addMouseListener(new MouseAdapter() {
            public void mousePressed(MouseEvent e) {
```

```
                              last = e.getPoint();
                          }
                          public void mouseReleased(MouseEvent e) {
                              setVisible(false);
                          }
                      });
                      addMouseMotionListener(new MouseMotionAdapter() {
                          public void mouseDragged(MouseEvent e) {
                              Point drag = e.getPoint();
                              ulhc.x += drag.x - last.x;
                              ulhc.y += drag.y - last.y;

                              repaint();

                              last.x = drag.x;
                              last.y = drag.y;
                          }
                      });
                      ...
              }
              ...
      }
```

The applet shown in Figure 12-5 is listed in its entirety in Example 12-3.

Example 12-3   A Custom Content Pane

```
import java.awt.*;
import java.awt.event.*;
import javax.swing.*;

public class ContentPaneTest extends JApplet {
    private JButton button = new JButton("show glass pane");

    public void init() {
        setGlassPane(new CustomGlassPane(button));
        setContentPane(new CustomContentPane(button));

        button.addActionListener(new ActionListener() {
            public void actionPerformed(ActionEvent e) {
                getGlassPane().setVisible(true);
            }
        });
    }
}
class CustomContentPane extends JPanel {
    private ImageIcon rain = new ImageIcon("rain.gif");
    private ImageIcon punch = new ImageIcon("punch.gif");
    private int rainw = rain.getIconWidth();
    private int rainh = rain.getIconHeight();
```

```
    public CustomContentPane(JButton button) {
        add(button);
        add(new JLabel("I'm a JLabel in the Content Pane",
                      punch, SwingConstants.RIGHT));
    }
    public void paintComponent(Graphics g) {
        Dimension size = getSize();

        for(int row=0; row < size.height; row += rainh)
            for(int col=0; col < size.width; col += rainw)
                rain.paintIcon(this,g,col,row);
    }
}
class CustomGlassPane extends JPanel {
    private JButton button;
    private Point ulhc = new Point(20,20), last;
    private String displayString =
                  "I'm on the glass pane - drag me around!";

    public CustomGlassPane(JButton b) {
        button = b;

        setOpaque(false);

        addMouseListener(new MouseAdapter() {
            public void mousePressed(MouseEvent e) {
                last = e.getPoint();
            }
            public void mouseReleased(MouseEvent e) {
                setVisible(false);
            }
        });
        addMouseMotionListener(new MouseMotionAdapter() {
            public void mouseDragged(MouseEvent e) {
                Point drag = e.getPoint();
                ulhc.x += drag.x - last.x;
                ulhc.y += drag.y - last.y;

                repaint();

                last.x = drag.x;
                last.y = drag.y;
            }
        });
    }
    public void paintComponent(Graphics g) {
        FontMetrics fm = g.getFontMetrics();
        int sw = fm.stringWidth(displayString);
        int sh = fm.getHeight();
        int ascent = fm.getAscent();
```

```
        g.drawRect(ulhc.x, ulhc.y, sw + 10, sh + 10);
        g.drawString(displayString,
                    ulhc.x + 5, ulhc.y + ascent + 5);
    }
}
```

Swing Tip ...

Layout Managers for Content Panes and Glass Panes

By default, content panes and glass panes are panels—instances of JPanel—that are created by the protected createContentPane and createGlassPane methods from the JRootPane class.

The glass pane created by JRootPane.createGlassPane retains the default layout manager for instances of JPanel—an instance of FlowLayout. On the other hand, the content pane created by JRootPane.createContentPane is fitted with an instance of BorderLayout.

The `JRootPane` class is summarized in Component Summary 12-2.

Component Summary 12-2   JRootPane

Model(s)	——
UI Delegate(s)	——
Renderer(s)	——
Editor(s)	——
Events Fired	——
Replacement For	——

Class Diagrams

Figure 12-6 JRootPane Class Diagram

JRootPane extends JComponent and implements the Accessible interface. JRootPane, like JPanel, does not have a model or a UI delegate. JRootPane maintains protected references to instances of JLayeredPane and JMenuBar. JRootPane also maintains a protected reference to an instance of JButton that is the default button for the root pane.

Notice that a root pane's glass pane and content pane are represented by instances of java.awt.Component and java.awt.Container, respectively. Swing does not provide specific classes for glass panes and content panes.

JRootPane Properties

The properties maintained by the JRootPane class are listed in Table 12-2.

Table 12-2 JRootPane Properties

Property Name	Data Type	Property Type[1]	Access[2]	Default[3]
contentPane	Container	S	SG	JPanel[4]
defaultButton	JButton	B	SG	null
glassPane	Component	S	SG	JPanel
jMenuBar	JMenuBar	S	G	true
layeredPane	JLayeredPane	S	SG	null
validateRoot	JRootPane	S	G	JPanel

1. B = bound (fires PropertyChangeEvent) / C = constrained/ I = indexed /
   S = simple / Ch = fires ChangeEvent
2. C = settable at construction time / G = getter method / S = setter method
3. L&F = look-and-feel dependent
4. By default, the layout manager for a content pane is a BorderLayout

contentPane — A container into which applets and applications place their components.

defaultButton — A button that can be activated with a key stroke whenever any component in the root pane has focus.

glassPane — A component that floats above all other components contained in a root pane.

jmenuBar — A menu bar that is located above the content pane.

layeredPane — An instance of JLayeredPane that contains the content pane and the menu bar.

validateRoot — If a Swing container returns true from isValidateRoot, the container will validate all of its components whenever revalidate() is invoked for one of the components contained in the container. JRootPane and JScrollPane are the only Swing containers that return true from

`isValidateRoot()`. In practice, this means that invoking `revalidate()` for any component contained in a root pane or scrollpane will result in `validate()` being called for the root pane or scrollpane. The effect is that all of the components contained in either a root pane or scrollpane will be laid out whenever `revalidate()` is invoked for one of the components contained in the root pane.

JRootPane Events

Other than property change events that are fired in response to the modification of its bound properties, the `JRootPane` class does not fire events of its own accord.

Because `JRootPane` is a simple container, it is more interesting to discuss event handling from the perspective of the components `JRootPane` contains rather than the events fired by the root pane itself.

Recall that the glass pane contained within a root pane will consume mouse events if the glass pane has indicated that is interested in handling mouse events. The applet shown in Figure 12-4 on page 640 and discussed in Example 12-2 on page 642 illustrates the fact that mouse events handled by the glass pane are not automatically forwarded to components underneath the glass pane. Sometimes however, is convenient to have a glass pane that lets events pass through to components underneath.

Figure 12-7 shows an applet that uses the glass pane to display annotations made to a document—in this case the document is the source code for the applet itself. The applet contains a check box that toggles the visibility of the glass pane and, therefore, the visibility of the annotations. If the glass pane consumed mouse events, there would be no way to get rid of the annotations after they were displayed for the first time because mouse clicks over the check box would be consumed by the glass pane. For this reason, the glass pane does not express interest in mouse events.

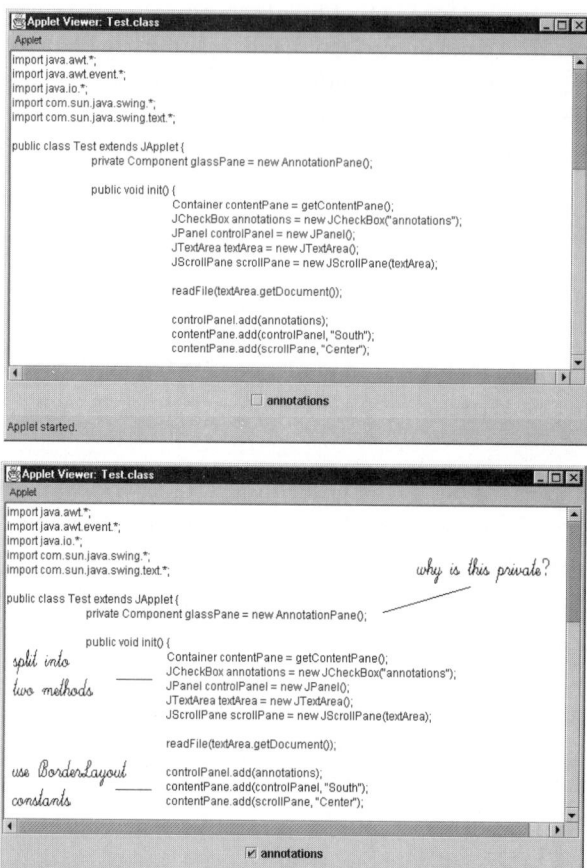

Figure 12-7 Using the Glass Pane for Annotations

The applet creates an instance of `AnnotationPane`, that is used as the root pane's glass pane. The applet also creates an instance of `JCheckBox` that is used to toggle the visibility of the glass pane. The top picture in Figure 12-7 shows the applet as it appears initially, and the bottom picture shows the applet after the glass pane has been made visible.

Two `private` methods that are invoked in the applet's `init` method create the applet's container hierarchy and set up the glass pane.

```
public class Test extends JApplet {
    Component glassPane = new AnnotationPane();
    JCheckBox annotations = new JCheckBox("annotations");

    public void init() {
        createContainerHierarchy();
        setupGlassPane();
    }
    ...
```

The createContainerHierarchy method creates an instance of JPanel to house the check box. An instance of JTextArea is instantiated to display the document, and the text area is embedded in an instance of JScrollPane. The check box is added to the panel, and the scrollpane and panel are added to the applet's content pane. The readFile method reads the text from the source file and adds it to the text area.

```
        ...
    private void createContainerHierarchy() {
        Container contentPane = getContentPane();

        JPanel controlPanel = new JPanel();
        JTextArea textArea = new JTextArea();
        JScrollPane scrollPane = new JScrollPane(textArea);

        readFile(textArea.getDocument());

        controlPanel.add(annotations);

        contentPane.add(scrollPane, "Center"); // scrollpane
        contentPane.add(controlPanel, "South"); // panel

        textArea.addMouseListener(new MouseAdapter() {
            public void mouseEntered(MouseEvent e) {
                System.out.println("enter");
            }
        });
    }
    ...
```

The setupGlassPane method invokes the JApplet.setGlassPane method, which in turn invokes setGlassPane() for the applet's root pane, as discussed in "The RootPaneContainer Interface" on page 638. An item listener added to the check box sets of visibility of the glass pane whenever the check box is selected or deselected.

```
   ...
   private void setupGlassPane() {
      setGlassPane(glassPane);

      annotations.addItemListener(new ItemListener() {
         public void itemStateChanged(ItemEvent e) {
            if(e.getStateChange() == ItemEvent.SELECTED)
               glassPane.setVisible(true);
            else
               glassPane.setVisible(false);
         }
      });
   }
   ...
```

The applet shown in Figure 12-7 is listed in its entirety in Example 12-4.

Example 12-4 A Glass Pane That Lets Events Pass Through

```
import java.awt.*;
import java.awt.event.*;
import java.io.*;
import javax.swing.*;
import javax.swing.text.*;

public class Test extends JApplet {
   Component glassPane = new AnnotationPane();
   JCheckBox annotations = new JCheckBox("annotations");

   public void init() {
      createContainerHierarchy();
      setupGlassPane();
   }
   private void createContainerHierarchy() {
      Container contentPane = getContentPane();

      JPanel controlPanel = new JPanel();
      JTextArea textArea = new JTextArea();
      JScrollPane scrollPane = new JScrollPane(textArea);

      readFile(textArea.getDocument());

      controlPanel.add(annotations);

      contentPane.add(scrollPane, "Center"); // scrollpane
      contentPane.add(controlPanel, "South"); // panel

      textArea.addMouseListener(new MouseAdapter() {
         public void mouseEntered(MouseEvent e) {
            System.out.println("enter");
         }
```

```
        });
    }
    private void setupGlassPane() {
        setGlassPane(glassPane);

        annotations.addItemListener(new ItemListener() {
            public void itemStateChanged(ItemEvent e) {
                if(e.getStateChange() == ItemEvent.SELECTED)
                    glassPane.setVisible(true);
                else
                    glassPane.setVisible(false);
            }
        });
    }
    private void readFile(Document doc) {
        try {
            Reader in = new FileReader("Test.java");
            char[] buff = new char[4096];
            int next;

            while ((next = in.read(buff, 0, buff.length)) != -1)
             doc.insertString(
                doc.getLength(), new String(buff, 0, next), null);
        }
        catch(Exception e) {
            System.out.println("interruption");
        }
    }
}
class AnnotationPane extends JPanel {
    private Icon annotations[] = {
        new ImageIcon("annotation.gif"),
        new ImageIcon("annotation_1.gif"),
        new ImageIcon("annotation_2.gif")
    };
    public void paintComponent(Graphics g) {
        annotations[0].paintIcon(this, g, 400, 50);
        annotations[1].paintIcon(this, g, 10, 150);
        annotations[2].paintIcon(this, g, 10, 265);
    }
}
```

JRootPane Class Summaries

The public and protected variables and methods for JRootPane are listed in
Class Summary 12-2.

Class Summary 12-2   JRootPane

Extends: JComponent
Implements: Javax.accessibility.Accessible

Constructors

---

public JRootPane()

JRootPane provides a single no-argument constructor. The constructor instantiates the root pane's content pane, glass pane, layered pane, and layout manager. The constructor also sets double buffering to `true` and sets the background color of the root pane to the value returned by `UIManager.getColor("control")`.

Methods

Initialization

---

public void addNotify()
public void removeNotify()

protected Container createContentPane()
protected Component createGlassPane()
protected JLayeredPane createLayeredPane()
protected LayoutManager createRootLayout()

JRootPane overrides the `protected addImpl` method to ensure that the glass pane is always the topmost component in the root pane.

The protected `create...` methods create the root pane's content pane, glass pane, layered, pane and layout manager. The methods are all invoked from the `JRootPane` no-argument constructor and can be overridden by extensions if the defaults are not appropriate. Note that it is not necessary to extend `JRootPane` to set a root pane's glass pane, content pane, layered pane, or layout manager because `JRootPane` provides setter methods for them.

ContentPane/GlassPane/LayeredPane/MenuBar/DefaultButton Accessors

public Container <u>getContentPane</u>()
public JButton <u>getDefaultButton</u>()
public Component <u>getGlassPane</u>()
public JLayeredPane <u>getLayeredPane</u>()
public JMenuBar <u>getJMenuBar</u>()

public void <u>setContentPane</u>(Container)
public void <u>setDefaultButton</u>(JButton)
public void <u>setGlassPane</u>(Component)
public void <u>setLayeredPane</u>(JLayeredPane)
public void <u>setJMenuBar</u>(JMenuBar)

The methods listed above are accessors for `JRootPane`'s properties. Setter and getter methods are provided for a root pane's content pane, default buttons, glass pane, layered pane, and menu bar.

Focus Cycle and Validate Roots

public boolean <u>isFocusCycleRoot</u>()
public boolean <u>isValidateRoot</u>()

`JRootPane` overrides `isFocusCycleRoot` to return `true`, meaning a TAB key press in a root pane does not move focus out of the root pane.

The isValidateRoot method is also overridden to return true, meaning that components contained in a root pane will always be laid out if revalidate is invoked for one of the components. See "Validate, Invalidate, and Revalidate Methods" on page 144 for more information on revalidate() and isValidateRoot().

Miscellaneous Methods

---

protected void <u>addImpl</u>(Component, Object, int)
public AccessibleContext <u>getAccessibleContext</u>()
protected String <u>paramString</u>()

JRootPane implements the Accessible interface, and therefore provides a getAccessibleContext method.

AWT Compatibility

The AWT does not have a component that is analogous to JRootPane.

JLayeredPane

JLayeredPane is a container that allows components to be placed on specific layers. Layers allow the depth of components to be controlled more precisely than with the default zorder mechanism provided by the AWT. See "Zorder" on page 43 for more information on how zorder is defined by AWT containers. The six layers defined by the JLayeredPane class are summarized in Table 12-3.

Table 12-3 JLayeredPane Layers

Layer	Value	Description
FRAME_CONTENT_LAYER	-3000	The bottom-most layer, where a root pane's menu bar and content pane reside.
DEFAULT_LAYER	0	The layer above the frame content layer. This is where components are placed by default.
PALETTE_LAYER	100	The layer above the default layer. Useful for palettes and floating toolbars.
MODAL_LAYER	200	The layer above the palette layer. Used by modal dialogs to ensure that dialogs appear on top of components, palettes, and floating toolbars.
POPUP_LAYER	300	The layer above the modal layer. Used for popup menus to ensure that popups appear above components, palettes, floating toolbars, and dialogs that the popups reside within.
DRAG_LAYER	400	The topmost layer. Useful for dragging components, or in other situations where a component must appear above all other components.

Each layer is specified with a numerical value; layers with higher values are displayed above layers with lower values. Layers other than those listed in Table 12-3 can be specified with numerical values. For example, setting the layer of a component to a value between 1 and 99 will place the component between the default and palette layers.

The layers maintained by instances of JLayeredPane are a logical construct; there is no Layer class defined by Swing. Layers are implemented by means of the zorder mechanism provided by the AWT. In addition to layers, the depth for components on the same layer can be controlled by specifying the position of a component relative to other components on the same layer.

In all, three logical properties are assigned to every component contained in an instance of `JLayeredPane`. The properties are summarized Table 12-4.

Table 12-4 Logical Properties for Layered Pane Components

Property	Description
Index	The index into an array of components maintained by a layered pane. The index of a component has a direct correlation to its zorder; components with *lower indexes are displayed above* components with *higher indexes.*
Layer	The layer upon which a component resides. Components that reside in *lower-numbered layers are displayed below* components that reside in *higher-numbered layers.*
Position	The position of a component relative to other components in the same layer. Components with *lower positions are displayed above* components with *higher positions.*

Components with lower indexes are displayed above components with higher indexes. For example, a component with an index of 0 is displayed above a component with an index of 1.

Likewise, components with lower positions are displayed above components with higher positions, provided that the components reside on the same layer. For example, if two components reside on the same layer and one component has a position of 0, and the other component has a position of 1, the former will be displayed above the latter.

Layers behave in a manner opposite that of indexes and positions. For example, components that reside on layer 0 are displayed below components that reside on layer 1.

Because layers are implemented with the zorder mechanism provided by the AWT, it is useful to review how zorder works for lightweight Swing components.

Swing Tip ...

JLayeredPane Is for Lightweight Components Only

Recall from "Mixing Swing and AWT Components" on page 43 that heavyweight components are always displayed on top of lightweight components. As a result, it does not make sense to add heavyweight components to layered panes. For example, if an instance of java.awt.Button is added to a layered pane, it will be displayed above any lightweight components that reside in the layered pane, regardless of the layer it is assigned.

Objects that are extensions of java.awt.Component can be added to layered panes, and layers can be assigned to them. However, this does not mean that it makes sense to add any type of object that extends java.awt.Component to a layered pane. Only objects that are lightweight extensions of java.awt.Component should be added to a layered pane.

Zorder for Lightweight Components Revisited

The applet shown in Figure 12-8 contains six instances of JButton whose position and size are explicitly set. The zorder, meaning the depth of each component, is controlled by the order in which the buttons are added to the applet's content pane. The first button added to the content pane is displayed above the other buttons, whereas the last button added to the content pane is displayed underneath the other buttons.

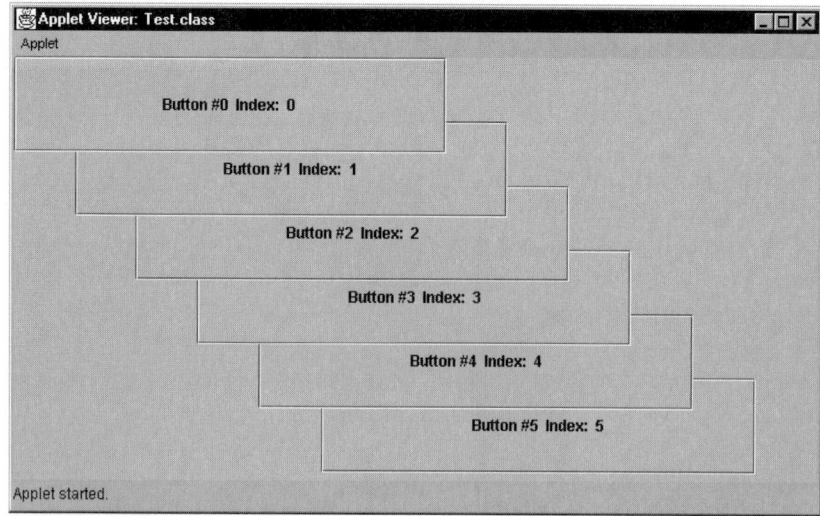

Figure 12-8 Illustrating Zorder for Lightweight Swing Components

The applet shown in Figure 12-8 is listed in Example 12-5.

Example 12-5 Zorder for Buttons Added to a Content Pane

```
import java.awt.*;
import java.awt.event.*;
import javax.swing.*;

public class Test extends JApplet {
    Container cp = getContentPane();

    private final Component[] comps = {
        new JButton(), new JButton(),
        new JButton(), new JButton(),
        new JButton(), new JButton(),
    };
    public void init() {
        cp.setLayout(null);

        for(int i=0; i < comps.length; ++i) {
            AbstractButton button = (AbstractButton)comps[i];
            cp.add(button);

            String t = "Button #";

            t += i + "  Index:  " + getIndexOf(button);
```

```
                button.setText(t);
                button.setBounds(i*50, i*50, 350, 75);
                System.out.println("Adding: " + button.getText());
            }
        }
        private int getIndexOf(Component button) {
            int ncomponents = cp.getComponentCount();

            for(int i=0; i < ncomponents; ++i) {
                Component c = cp.getComponent(i);
                if(button == c)
                    return i;
            }
            return -1;
        }
    }
```

The applet sets the layout manager for its content pane to null to position the buttons so they overlap one another. The text of each button indicates the order in which the buttons are added to the content pane. The JPanel class does not provide a method that returns the index of a component, so a getIndexOf method is implemented by the applet to do so.

The applet also prints information regarding the buttons as they are added to the content pane. The output of the applet is shown below.

```
Adding: Button #0  Index:  0
Adding: Button #1  Index:  1
Adding: Button #2  Index:  2
Adding: Button #3  Index:  3
Adding: Button #4  Index:  4
Adding: Button #5  Index:  5
```

Assigning Layers to Components

The applet shown in Figure 12-9 is similar to the one shown in Figure 12-8, except that the applet's content pane to set to an instance of JLayeredPane. Each button is assigned to a specific layer by the JLayeredPane.setLayer method.

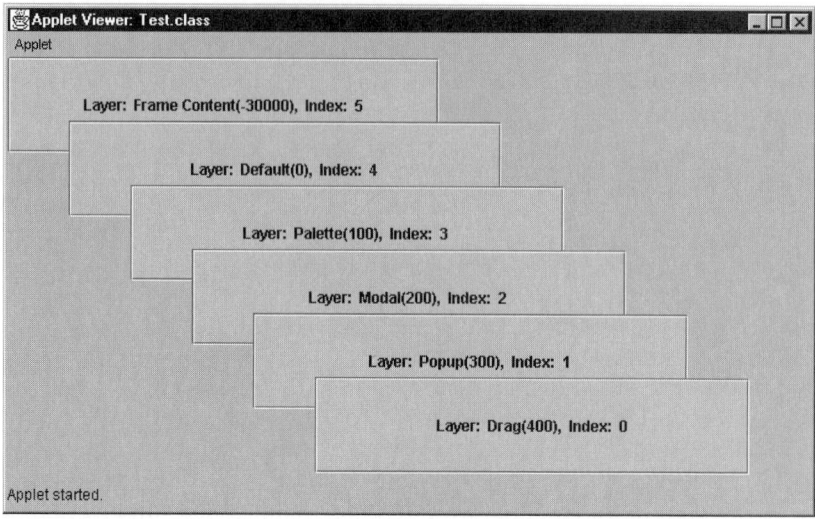

Figure 12-9 Assigning Layers to Components in a Layered Pane

The applet defines an array of `Integer` values corresponding to the `JLayeredPane` constants listed in Table 12-3. The `Integer` values are used to set each button's layer just before the buttons are added to the layered pane.

```
public class Test extends JApplet {
    private JLayeredPane lp = new JLayeredPane();

    private Integer[] layers = {
        JLayeredPane.FRAME_CONTENT_LAYER,
        JLayeredPane.DEFAULT_LAYER,
        JLayeredPane.PALETTE_LAYER,
        JLayeredPane.MODAL_LAYER,
        JLayeredPane.POPUP_LAYER,
        JLayeredPane.DRAG_LAYER,
    };
    private final Component[] comps = {
        new JButton("Frame Content"), new JButton("Default"),
        new JButton("Palette"), new JButton("Modal"),
        new JButton("Popup"), new JButton("Drag"),
    };
    public void init() {
        ...
        for(int i=0; i < comps.length; ++i) {
            AbstractButton button = (AbstractButton)comps[i];
            ...
            lp.setLayer(button, layers[i].intValue());
```

```
        lp.add(button);
    }
    . . .
```

After the buttons have been added to the layered pane, the text for each button is set to reflect the layer upon which the button resides and the button's index. Notice that JLayeredPane constants representing layers are Integer values; however, JLayeredPane.setLayer() is passed an int value. Because of this behavior, Integer.intValue() is used to convert the Integer values into ints.

```
        . . .
        for(int i=0; i < comps.length; ++i) {
            AbstractButton button = (AbstractButton)comps[i];
            String t = button.getText();
            String replacement = new String("Layer:   ");

            replacement += t + "(" + lp.getLayer(button) + "),";
            replacement += "  Index:   " + lp.getIndexOf(button);

            button.setText(replacement);
            button.setBounds(i*50, i*50, 350, 75);
        }
    }
```

Like the applet shown in Figure 12-8, the applet shown in Figure 12-9 prints information about the buttons as they are added to the layered pane. Notice that the JLayeredPane class provides a getIndexOf method that returns the index for a specific component. The output from the applet is shown below.

```
Adding: Frame Content
Adding: Default
Adding: Palette
Adding: Modal
Adding: Popup
Adding: Drag
```

There are two important points concerning this applet versus the applet shown in Figure 12-8.

First, for the applet that uses an instance of JLayeredPane, the order in which the buttons are added to the layered pane is immaterial as far as the zorder for each button. The first button added to the layered pane is not displayed on top of the other buttons as was the case for the applet shown in Figure 12-8. In fact, the first button added to the layered pane is assigned to the FRAME_CONTENT_LAYER, which by definition is the bottom-most layer.

Second, the text for each button is not set in the `for` loop where the buttons are added to the layered pane because the index for each button does not settle until all of the buttons are added to the layered pane. Instances of `JLayeredPane` continually adjust the indexes of the components they contain as other components are added to the layered pane, depending upon each component's layer and position. For example, after the first button is added to the layered pane, the button's index is 0, but as can be seen in Figure 12-9, after all of the buttons have been added to the layered pane, the index for the first button is 5.

The applet shown in Figure 12-9 is listed in Example 12-6.

Example 12-6 Assigning Layers to Components Contained in a Layered Pane

```java
import java.awt.*;
import java.awt.event.*;
import javax.swing.*;

public class Test extends JApplet {
    private JLayeredPane lp = new JLayeredPane();

    private Integer[] layers = {
        JLayeredPane.FRAME_CONTENT_LAYER,
        JLayeredPane.DEFAULT_LAYER,
        JLayeredPane.PALETTE_LAYER,
        JLayeredPane.MODAL_LAYER,
        JLayeredPane.POPUP_LAYER,
        JLayeredPane.DRAG_LAYER,
    };
    private final Component[] comps = {
        new JButton("Frame Content"), new JButton("Default"),
        new JButton("Palette"), new JButton("Modal"),
        new JButton("Popup"), new JButton("Drag"),
    };
    public void init() {
        setContentPane(lp);
        lp.setLayout(null);

        for(int i=0; i < comps.length; ++i) {
            AbstractButton button = (AbstractButton)comps[i];

            System.out.println("Adding: " + button.getText());

            lp.setLayer(button, layers[i].intValue());
            lp.add(button);
        }
```

```
    for(int i=0; i < comps.length; ++i) {
        AbstractButton button = (AbstractButton)comps[i];
        String t = button.getText();
        String replacement = new String("Layer:   ");

        replacement += t + "(" + lp.getLayer(button) + "),";
        replacement += "  Index:  " + lp.getIndexOf(button);

        button.setText(replacement);
        button.setBounds(i*50, i*50, 350, 75);
    }
  }
}
```

Positioning Components on the Same Layer

The depth of a component relative to other components on the same layer can be controlled by specifying the component's position. JLayeredPane provides a setPosition method for that very purpose.

The applet shown in Figure 12-10 illustrates the manner in which components on the same layer are positioned by default.

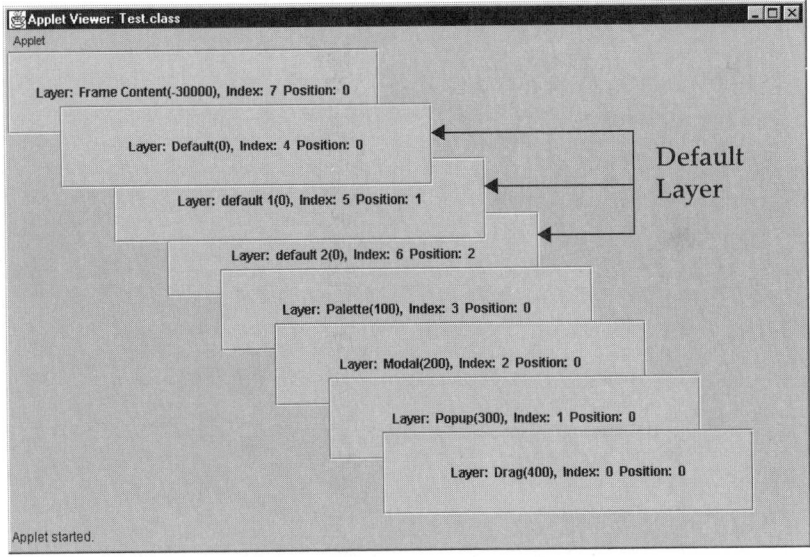

Figure 12-10 Default Positioning for Components on the Same Layer

The applet contains three buttons that reside on the default layer. By default, the position of components residing on the same layer is determined by the order in which they are added to a layered pane. The buttons residing on the default layer in the applet shown in Figure 12-10 are added to the layered pane in the following order: "Default", "default 1", "default 2", and therefore the "Default" button is displayed above the "default 1" button, which is displayed above the "default 2" button.

The applet shown in Figure 12-10 is listed in Example 12-7.

Example 12-7 Default Positioning for Components on the Same Layer

```
import java.awt.*;
import java.awt.event.*;
import javax.swing.*;

public class Test extends JApplet {
    private JLayeredPane lp = new JLayeredPane();

    private Integer[] layers = {
        JLayeredPane.FRAME_CONTENT_LAYER,
        JLayeredPane.DEFAULT_LAYER,
        JLayeredPane.DEFAULT_LAYER,
        JLayeredPane.DEFAULT_LAYER,
        JLayeredPane.PALETTE_LAYER,
        JLayeredPane.MODAL_LAYER,
        JLayeredPane.POPUP_LAYER,
        JLayeredPane.DRAG_LAYER,
    };
    private final Component[] comps = {
        new JButton("Frame Content"), new JButton("Default"),
        new JButton("default 1"), new JButton("default 2"),
        new JButton("Palette"), new JButton("Modal"),
        new JButton("Popup"), new JButton("Drag"),
    };
    public void init() {
        setContentPane(lp);
        lp.setLayout(null);

        for(int i=0; i < comps.length; ++i) {
            AbstractButton button = (AbstractButton)comps[i];

            lp.setLayer(button, layers[i].intValue());
            lp.add(button);
        }
        for(int i=0; i < comps.length; ++i) {
            AbstractButton button = (AbstractButton)comps[i];
            String t = button.getText();
            String replacement = new String("Layer:   ");
```

```
        replacement += t + "(" + lp.getLayer(button) + "),";
        replacement += "  Index:  " + lp.getIndexOf(button);
        replacement += "  Position:  " +
                       lp.getPosition(button);

        button.setText(replacement);
        button.setBounds(i*50, i*50, 350, 75);
      }
    }
}
```

The applet shown in Figure 12-11 is nearly identical to the applet shown in Figure 12-10, except that positions are explicitly set for the three buttons on the default layer.

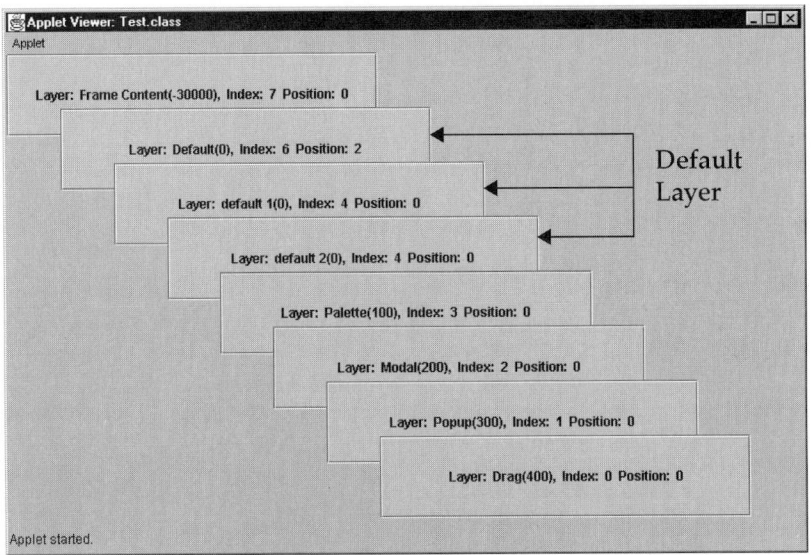

Figure 12-11 Explicitly Positioning Components on the Same Layer

The applet shown in Figure 12-11 is listed in Example 12-8.

Example 12-8 Explicitly Positioning Components on the Same Layer

```
import java.awt.*;
import java.awt.event.*;
import javax.swing.*;
```

```java
public class Test extends JApplet {
    private JLayeredPane lp = new JLayeredPane();

    private Integer[] layers = {
        JLayeredPane.FRAME_CONTENT_LAYER,
        JLayeredPane.DEFAULT_LAYER,
        JLayeredPane.DEFAULT_LAYER,
        JLayeredPane.DEFAULT_LAYER,
        JLayeredPane.PALETTE_LAYER,
        JLayeredPane.MODAL_LAYER,
        JLayeredPane.POPUP_LAYER,
        JLayeredPane.DRAG_LAYER,
    };
    private final Component[] comps = {
        new JButton("Frame Content"), new JButton("Default"),
        new JButton("default 1"), new JButton("default 2"),
        new JButton("Palette"), new JButton("Modal"),
        new JButton("Popup"), new JButton("Drag"),
    };
    public void init() {
        setContentPane(lp);
        lp.setLayout(null);

        for(int i=0; i < comps.length; ++i) {
            AbstractButton button = (AbstractButton)comps[i];
            String t = button.getText();

            lp.setLayer(button, layers[i].intValue());
            lp.add(button);
        }
        for(int i=0; i < comps.length; ++i) {
            AbstractButton button = (AbstractButton)comps[i];
            String t = button.getText();
            String replacement = new String("Layer:  ");

            if(t.equals("Default"))
                lp.setPosition(button, 2);
            else if(t.equals("default 2"))
                lp.setPosition(button, 0);

            replacement += t + "(" + lp.getLayer(button) + "),";
            replacement += "  Index:  " + lp.getIndexOf(button);
            replacement += "  Position:  " +
                            lp.getPosition(button);

            button.setText(replacement);
            button.setBounds(i*50, i*50, 350, 75);
        }
    }
}
```

The applet listed in Example 12-8 switches the depth of the "Default" and "default 2" buttons by explicitly setting their positions. Notice that positions are not specified until all of the buttons have been added to the layered pane, because positions, like indexes, are continually adjusted as components are added to a layered pane.

Swing Tip ...

Layers Are Specified as int Values

JLayeredPane.setLayer() is passed a component and an int value. The int value specifies the layer upon which the component will be placed. On the other hand, JLayeredPane constants for commonly used layers, such as JLayered-Pane.DEFAULT_LAYER and JLayeredPane.POPUP_LAYER are defined as Integer values. If a component is to be placed on a layer defined by one of the JLayeredPane constants listed in Table 12-3 on page 659, the Integer value must be converted to an int. This can be accomplished by invocation of the Integer.intValue method, like this:

```
aLayeredPane.setLayer(aComponent,
              JLayeredPane.POPUP_LAYER.intValue());
```

Using the Drag Layer

Because the drag layer sits above all other layers, it can be used to drag components over the top of all other components contained within a layered pane.

The applet shown in Figure 12-12 shows the drag layer in action, by dragging an instance of JLabel. The applet contains two labels and a check box. The label that contains a picture of a skeleton smoking a cigarette can be dragged, whereas the label containing the picture of a fist is stationary. The check box controls whether or not the draggable label resides on the drag layer. If the check box is checked, the layer for the label is set to the drag layer; if the check box is not checked, the layer for the label is set to the default layer.

The top-left picture in Figure 12-12 shows the applet in its initial state. Both labels are added to the layered pane without a layer being specified, and as a result, both are placed on the default layer.

Figure 12-12 Using the Drag Layer in a Layered Pane

The applet sets its content pane to an instance of CustomContentPane, which
extends JLayeredPane. The CustomContentPane instantiates the icons,
labels, and check box and adds them without specifying layers. Notice that
CustomContentPane sets its layout manager to an instance of FlowLayout
because, by default, JLayeredPane has a null layout manager.

```
public class Test extends JApplet {
    public void init() {
        setContentPane(new CustomContentPane());
    }
}
class CustomContentPane extends JLayeredPane {
    private ImageIcon rain = new ImageIcon("rain.gif");
    private ImageIcon punch = new ImageIcon("punch.gif");
    private ImageIcon skelly = new ImageIcon("skelly.gif");
    private int rainw = rain.getIconWidth();
    private int rainh = rain.getIconHeight();

    private JLabel[] labels = {
```

```
        new JLabel("I stay put", punch, SwingConstants.RIGHT),
        new JLabel("Drag me around!",
                   skelly, SwingConstants.RIGHT),
    };

    public CustomContentPane() {
        Dragger listener = new Dragger();
        JCheckBox onDragLayer = new JCheckBox("Drag Layer");

        // JLayeredPane has a null layout by default
        setLayout(new FlowLayout());

        add(onDragLayer);
        add(labels[0]);
        add(labels[1]);
        . . .
```

The top-right picture in Figure 12-12 shows the applet after the draggable label has been dragged. Because the fist label is the first label added to the layered pane, it is displayed above the draggable label, and therefore the draggable label is dragged underneath the fist label.

The bottom-left picture in Figure 12-12 shows the applet after the check box has been checked. An item listener that sets the appropriate layer for the draggable label is added to the check box. After the layer is set, the text associated with the label is updated and the CustomContentPane is validated, meaning that all of the components contained within the layered pane are laid out. Notice that the draggable label is now the first component displayed in the layered pane. This happens because changing the layer for the label also modifies its index, and instances of FlowLayout position the component with an index of 0 in the upper-left corner of the container by default.

```
        . . .
        onDragLayer.addItemListener(new ItemListener() {
            public void itemStateChanged(ItemEvent e) {
                if(e.getStateChange() == ItemEvent.SELECTED) {
                    setLayer(labels[1],
                        JLayeredPane.DRAG_LAYER.intValue());
                }
                else {
                    setLayer(labels[1],
                        JLayeredPane.DEFAULT_LAYER.intValue());
                }
                setLabelText();
                validate();
            }
        });
    }
    private void setLabelText() {
```

```
        for(int i=0; i < labels.length; ++i) {
            JLabel label = labels[i];
            String t = new String("Layer:   ");

            t += "(" + getLayer(label) + "),";
            t += "  Index:   " + getIndexOf(label);

            label.setText(t);
        }
    }
    ...
}
```

The bottom-right picture shown in Figure 12-12 was taken after the draggable label was placed on the drag layer and dragged. Because the draggable label is on the drag layer, it is displayed above the stationary label.

The applet shown in Figure 12-12 is listed in its entirety in Example 12-9.

Example 12-9 Using the Drag Layer

```
import java.awt.*;
import java.awt.event.*;
import javax.swing.*;

public class Test extends JApplet {
    public void init() {
        setContentPane(new CustomContentPane());
    }
}
class CustomContentPane extends JLayeredPane {
    private ImageIcon rain = new ImageIcon("rain.gif");
    private ImageIcon punch = new ImageIcon("punch.gif");
    private ImageIcon skelly = new ImageIcon("skelly.gif");
    private int rainw = rain.getIconWidth();
    private int rainh = rain.getIconHeight();

    private JLabel[] labels = {
        new JLabel("I stay put", punch, SwingConstants.RIGHT),
        new JLabel("Drag me around!",
                    skelly, SwingConstants.RIGHT),
    };

    public CustomContentPane() {
        Dragger listener = new Dragger();
        JCheckBox onDragLayer = new JCheckBox("Drag Layer");

        // JLayeredPane has a null layout by default
        setLayout(new FlowLayout());
```

```
        add(onDragLayer);
        add(labels[0]);
        add(labels[1]);

        labels[1].addMouseMotionListener(listener);
        labels[1].addMouseListener(listener);

        setLabelText();

        onDragLayer.addItemListener(new ItemListener() {
            public void itemStateChanged(ItemEvent e) {
                if(e.getStateChange() == ItemEvent.SELECTED) {
                    setLayer(labels[1],
                        JLayeredPane.DRAG_LAYER.intValue());
                }
                else {
                    setLayer(labels[1],
                        JLayeredPane.DEFAULT_LAYER.intValue());

                }
                setLabelText();
                validate();
            }
        });
    }
    public void paintComponent(Graphics g) {
        Dimension size = getSize();

        for(int row=0; row < size.height; row += rainh)
            for(int col=0; col < size.width; col += rainw)
                rain.paintIcon(this,g,col,row);
    }
    private void setLabelText() {
        for(int i=0; i < labels.length; ++i) {
            JLabel label = labels[i];
            String t = new String("Layer:  ");

            t += "(" + getLayer(label) + "),";
            t += "  Index:  " + getIndexOf(label);

            label.setText(t);
        }
    }
}
class Dragger extends MouseAdapter
                        implements MouseMotionListener {
    Pointpress = new Point();
    boolean dragging = false;

    public void mousePressed(MouseEvent event) {
        press.x = event.getX();
        press.y = event.getY();
```

```
            dragging = true;
        }
        public boolean isDragging() {
            return dragging;
        }
        public void mouseReleased(MouseEvent event) {
            dragging = false;
        }
        public void mouseClicked(MouseEvent event) {
            dragging = false;
        }
        public void mouseMoved(MouseEvent event) {
            // don't care
        }
        public void mouseDragged(MouseEvent event) {
            Component c = (Component)event.getSource();

            if(dragging) {
                Point loc = c.getLocation();
                Point pt  = new Point();
                pt.x = event.getX() + loc.x - press.x;
                pt.y = event.getY() + loc.y - press.y;
                c.setLocation(pt.x, pt.y);
                c.getParent().repaint();
            }
        }
    }
```

The JLayeredPane class is summarized in Component Summary 12-3.

Component Summary 12-3   JLayeredPane

Model(s)	——
UI Delegate(s)	——
Renderer(s)	——
Editor(s)	——
Events Fired	——
Replacement For	——

Class Diagrams

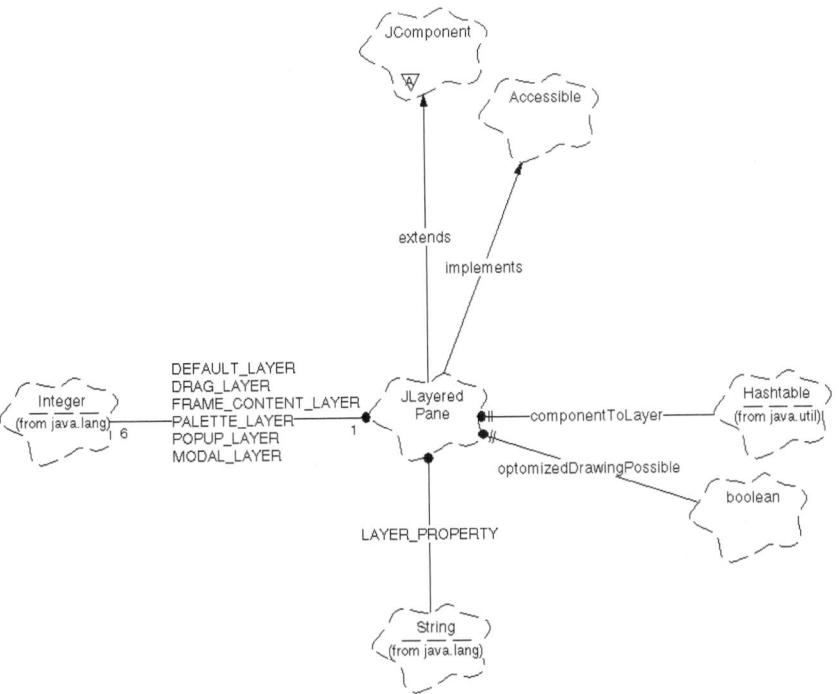

Figure 12-13 JLayeredPane Class Diagram

Like `JRootPane`, `JLayeredPane` is a simple extension of `JComponent` that does not have a model or a UI delegate. `JLayeredPane` defines constants, in the form of `Integers`, that define a set of commonly used layers. Additionally, `JLayeredPane` defines a `String` constant for the name of its `layer` property.

`JLayeredPane` also maintains `private` references to a `Hashtable` and a `boolean` value. The `Hashtable` keeps track of each instance of `java.awt.Component` contained in the layered pane and its corresponding layer. Layers for instances of `JComponent` are stored as a client property—see "Client Properties" on page 186 for more on `JComponents` and client properties.

The `boolean` value tracks whether optimized drawing is possible for the layered pane. If none of the components can overlap the other components contained in a layered pane, then optimized drawing is possible, and `JLayeredPane` draws its components in a more efficient manner.

JLayeredPane Properties

The properties maintained by the `JLayeredPane` class are listed in Table 12-5.

Table 12-5 JLayeredPane Properties

Property Name	Data Type	Property Type[1]	Access[2]	Default[3]
componentCountInLayer	int	I	G	—
componentsInLayer	int	I	G	
indexOf	int	S	G	—
optimizedDrawingEnabled	boolean	S	G	—
layer	int	S	SG	—
position	JRootPane	S	SG	—

1. B = bound (fires PropertyChangeEvent) / C = constrained/ I = indexed / S = simple / Ch = fires ChangeEvent
2. C = settable at construction time / G = getter method / S = setter method
3. L&F = look-and-feel dependent

componentCountInLayer — The number of components contained in a specific layer.

componentsInLayer — An array of components contained in a specific layer.

indexOf — The index for a specific component.

optimizedDrawingEnabled — If no components in the layered pane overlap, optimized drawing is possible.

layer — The layer for a specific component.

position — The position for a specific component.

Properties for `JLayeredPane` are somewhat unique among Swing components because the properties mostly apply to the components contained in a layered pane, and not the layered pane itself. Only the `optimizedDrawingEnabled` property applies to the layered pane itself; the rest of the properties apply to components contained in a layered pane.

Notice that the `indexOf` property is read-only, whereas the `layer` and `position` properties can be set. This is because the `indexOf` property corresponds to the index into the array of components maintained by the layered pane and is controlled by the layered pane as components are added and their positions and layers are set.

JLayeredPane Class Summaries

The `public` and `protected` variables and methods for `JLayeredPane` are listed in Class Summary 12-3.

Class Summary 12-3   JLayeredPane

Constructors

---

public <u>JLayeredPane</u>()

`JLayeredPane` provides a single, no-argument constructor. The constructor sets the layout manager for the layered pane to `null`.

Methods

Static Methods

---

public static int <u>getLayer</u>(JComponent)
public static void <u>putLayer</u>(JComponent, int)

public static JLayeredPane <u>getLayeredPaneAbove</u>(Component)

The first two methods have instance method (non-`static`) equivalents:
`setLayer(Component, int)` and `getLayer(Component)`. The differences
between the two sets of methods are these: the `static` methods are passed
instances of `JComponent`, whereas the instance methods are passed instances of
`Component`; the `static` methods do not result in any side effects. For example,
the `JLayeredPane.setLayer(Component, int)` instance method results in a
repaint of the region occupied by the component whose layer is set, whereas the
`static JLayeredPane.putLayer(JComponent, int)` method does not
result in a repaint.

The `getLayeredPaneAbove(Component)` returns the layered pane that
contains the component that the method is passed. If the component passed to
`getLayeredPaneAbove()` does not reside in a layered pane, the method
returns `null`.

Adding Components / Components and Layers

---

protected void <u>addImpl</u>(Component, Object constraints, int index)
protected int <u>insertIndexForLayer</u>(int, int)
protected Hashtable <u>getComponentToLayer</u>()

The protected `addImpl` method is overridden to adjust the index of the
component being added, depending upon the component's layer and position.
The `Object` argument can be an `Integer` value that specifies the component's
layer. If extensions of `JLayeredPane` are to perform some action at the point in
time when components are added to the layered pane, `addImpl()` can be
overridden. In practice, the method will rarely be overridden.

The `insertIndexForLayer` method calculates the index for a component,
given the component's layer and position. The method is invoked by the
`addImpl` method.

The `getComponentToLayer` method returns the `Hashtable` that instances of
`JLayeredPane` use to keep track of the layers associated with instances of
`java.awt.Component`. Note that the `Hashtable` does not necessarily contain
all of the components contained in the layered pane, because layers for instances
of `JComponent` are stored as a client property of the component. Because
instances of `java.awt.Component` do not have client properties, an alternative
mechanism, namely the `Hashtable`, is used to track layers.

Painting / Layer Access

public void <u>paint</u>(Graphics)
public int <u>getComponentCountInLayer</u>(int layer)
public Component[] <u>getComponentsInLayer</u>(int layer)
public int <u>highestLayer</u>()
public int <u>lowestLayer</u>()
protected Integer <u>getObjectForLayer</u>(int layer)
public boolean <u>isOptimizedDrawingEnabled</u>()

The `paint` method is overridden by `JLayeredPane` for the same purpose that it is overridden in `JPanel`. Because `JLayeredPane` and `JPanel` do not have a UI delegate, both components override the `paint` method to fill the background for opaque components with the background color. If a background color has not been explicitly set for a layered pane, light gray is used as the background color.

The rest of the methods listed above provide information about the layered pane. A count of the components contained in a specific layer is returned by the `getComponentCountInLayer` method, and the `getComponentsInLayer` method returns an array of components that reside in a specific layer. The `highestLayer` and `lowestLayer` methods return the numerical values associated with the highest and lowest layers, respectively. The `getObjectForLayer` method returns an `Integer` value given an `int` value representing the layer. Finally, the `isOptimizedDrawingEnabled` method returns a `boolean` value indicating whether any of the components contained in the layered pane can possibly overlap. If no two components can overlap, instances of `JLayeredPane` are able to draw their components in a more efficient manner, and the method returns `true`.

Index / Layer / Position

public int <u>getIndexOf</u>(Component)
public int <u>getLayer</u>(Component)
public int <u>getPosition</u>(Component)

The methods listed above return information about a specific component contained within a layered pane. If the component passed to the methods is not contained by the layered pane, getIndexOf() and getPosition() return –1, and getLayer() returns 0.

Setting Layers and Positions / Moving/Removing Components

```
public void setLayer(Component, int layer)
public void setLayer(Component, int layer, int position)
public void setPosition(Component, int position)

public void moveToBack(Component)
public void moveToFront(Component)
public void remove(int)
```

The methods listed above operate on a specific component contained in the layered pane. The two ints passed to the second setLayer method listed above specify the layer and position of the component, respectively.

The moveToFront and moveToBack methods adjust the position of the component within its layer. The remove method is overridden from the JComponent class to determine if optimized drawing can be enabled when a component is removed from a layered pane.

AccessibleContext / Param String

```
public AccessibleContext getAccessibleContext()
protected String paramString()
```

JLayeredPane implements the getAccessibleContext method that is defined in the Accessible interface. The paramString method returns a string representation of the layered pane.

AWT Compatibility

The AWT does not have a component that is analogous to `JLayeredPane`.

Instances of JLayeredPane Have a null Layout Manager by Default

If components are added to an instance of JLayeredPane and the components do not appear in the layered pane, it is probably because layout manager has not been explicitly set for the layered pane. By default, instances of JLayered-Pane have a null layout manager, and therefore components added to a layered pane will not be laid out unless the layout manager is explicitly set for the lay-ered pane.

JTabbedPane

Tabbed panes are a common user interface component that provide convenient access to more than one panel. For example, Figure 12-14 shows the SwingSet application, which uses a tabbed pane to show different aspects of Swing.

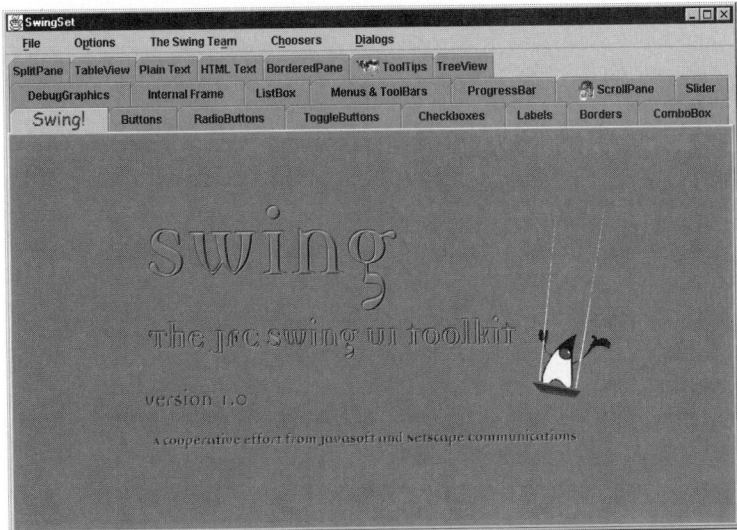

Figure 12-14 The SwingSet Example Uses a Tabbed Pane

Swing's tabbed pane is implemented by `JTabbedPane`. The tabs contained in an instance of `JTabbedPane` have a single component associated with them that is displayed below the tab. Tabs can display both an icon and text and can have their background color set. Additionally, tooltips can be associated with the tabs contained in a tabbed pane.

The tabs contained in an instance of `JTabbedPane` are similar to the layers in an instance of `JLayeredPane` in that both tabs and layers are logical constructs. In other words, tabs contained in instance of `JTabbedPane` are not Swing components. In practice, this means that tabs are limited to displaying icons and text; for example, arbitrary components cannot be added to a tab.

Figure 12-15 shows an applet with a tabbed pane. The tabbed pane contains two tabs, each of which has a panel associated with it that contains a single button. The second tab displays both an icon and text, and has a tooltip associated with it.

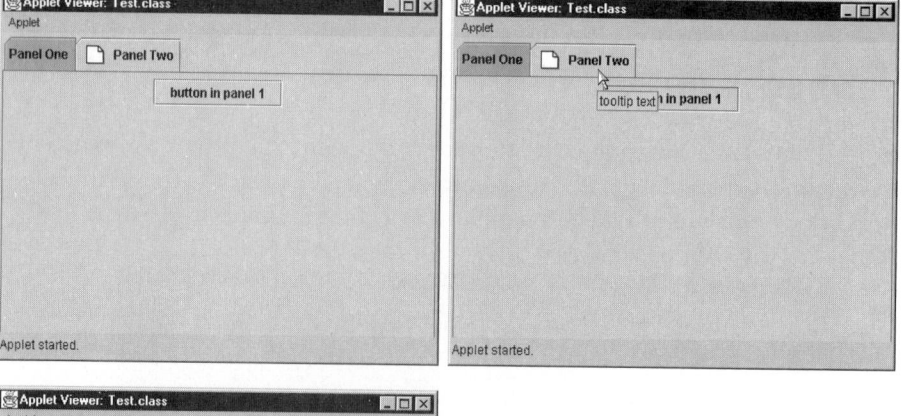

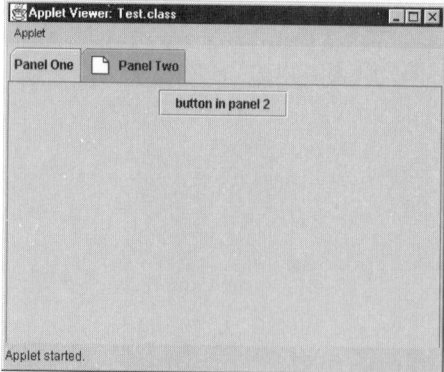

Figure 12-15 Tabbed Panes

685

The upper-left picture in Figure 12-15 shows the applet with the "Panel One" tab selected. The upper-right picture also shows the applet with the "Panel One" tab selected but with the cursor resting over the "Panel Two" tab. The bottom picture shows the "Panel Two" tab selected.

The applet shown in Figure 12-15 is listed in Example 12-10.

Example 12-10 A Simple Illustration of JTabbedPane

```java
import java.awt.*;
import java.awt.event.*;
import javax.swing.*;

public class Test extends JApplet {
    public Test() {
        Container contentPane = getContentPane();
        JTabbedPane tp = new JTabbedPane();
        JPanel panelOne = new JPanel();
        JPanel panelTwo = new JPanel();

        panelOne.add(new JButton("button in panel 1"));
        panelTwo.add(new JButton("button in panel 2"));

        tp.add(panelOne, "Panel One");
        tp.addTab("Panel Two",
                new ImageIcon("document.gif"),
                panelTwo,
                "tooltip text");

        contentPane.add(tp, BorderLayout.CENTER);
    }
}
```

The applet constructs an instance of JTabbedPane with the no-argument constructor. The panels associated with the tabs are added with the JTabbedPane.add and JTabbedPane.addTab methods. The addTab method allows the text, icon, and tooltip text to be set for the tab.

Tab Placement

JTabbedPane allows its tabs to be placed along the left, right, top, and bottom of the tabbed pane. Tab placement can be specified when instances of JTabbedPane are constructed or after construction with the JTabbedPane.setTabPlacement method. The following constants are used to specify tab placement:

- `SwingConstants.TOP`
- `SwingConstants.BOTTOM`
- `SwingConstants.LEFT`
- `SwingConstants.RIGHT`

Because `JTabbedPane` implements the `SwingConstants` interface, the constants listed above can be specified with either a `JTabbedPane.` or `SwingConstants.` prefix.

Figure 12-16 shows an applet that allows tab placement to be set.

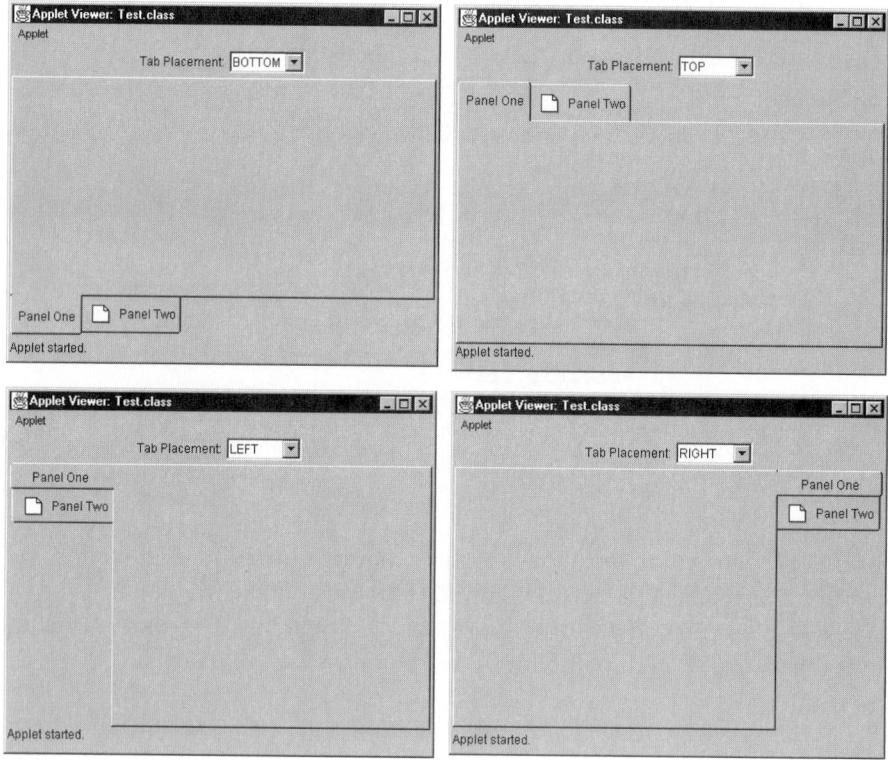

Figure 12-16 Tab Placement for Tabbed Panes

The applet creates an instance of JTabbedPane and specifies
SwingConstants.BOTTOM as the initial tab placement. The applet also
instantiates an instance of JComboBox and populates it with appropriate strings.

```
public class Test extends JApplet {
    private JTabbedPane tp =
                new JTabbedPane(SwingConstants.BOTTOM);
    private JComboBox combo = new JComboBox();

    public Test() {
        Container contentPane = getContentPane();
        JPanel comboPanel = new JPanel();
        JPanel panelOne = new JPanel();
        JPanel panelTwo = new JPanel();

        tp.add(panelOne, "Panel One");
        tp.addTab("Panel Two",
                new ImageIcon("document.gif"),
                panelTwo,
                "tooltip text");

        combo.addItem("TOP");
        combo.addItem("LEFT");
        combo.addItem("RIGHT");
        combo.addItem("BOTTOM");
        . . .
```

The combo box and a label are added to a panel that is then added to the applet's
content pane as the NORTH component. The layered pane is added to the
applet's content pane as the CENTER component. A private method—
setComboValue—implemented by the applet is then invoked to select the
appropriate item in the combo box.

setComboValue obtains the initial tab placement from the
JTabbedPane.getTabPlacement method and selects the corresponding item
in the combo box.

```
        . . .
        comboPanel.add(new JLabel("Tab Placement:"));
        comboPanel.add(combo);

        contentPane.add(comboPanel, BorderLayout.NORTH);
        contentPane.add(tp, BorderLayout.CENTER);

        setComboValue();
```

```
    ...
    }
    private void setComboValue() {
        int placement = tp.getTabPlacement();
        String selectedItem = null;

        switch(placement) {
            case JTabbedPane.TOP:
                    selectedItem = "TOP";
                    break;
            case JTabbedPane.LEFT:
                    selectedItem = "LEFT";
                    break;
            case JTabbedPane.RIGHT:
                    selectedItem = "RIGHT";
                    break;
            case JTabbedPane.BOTTOM:
                    selectedItem = "BOTTOM";
                    break;
        }
        combo.setSelectedItem(selectedItem);
    }
}
```

The combo box is fitted with an item listener that sets the tab placement for the tabbed pane, depending upon the currently selected item in the combo box. The tab placement is set by the JTabbedPane.setTabPlacement method. As Table 12-6 on page 692 shows, when the tab placement property is set, the tabbed pane is invalidated. This means that a subsequent call to validate the tabbed pane will result in the tabbed pane being laid out. As a result, after the tab placement has been set, validate() is invoked for the tabbed pane.

```
    ...
    combo.addItemListener(new ItemListener() {
        public void itemStateChanged(ItemEvent e) {
            JComboBox cb = (JComboBox)e.getSource();
            int state = e.getStateChange();

            if(state == ItemEvent.SELECTED) {
                String s = (String)cb.getSelectedItem();

                if(s.equals("TOP"))
                    tp.setTabPlacement(JTabbedPane.TOP);
                else if(s.equals("LEFT"))
                    tp.setTabPlacement(JTabbedPane.LEFT);
                else if(s.equals("RIGHT"))
                    tp.setTabPlacement(JTabbedPane.RIGHT);
                else if(s.equals("BOTTOM"))
```

```
            tp.setTabPlacement(JTabbedPane.BOTTOM);

        tp.validate();
      }
    }
  });
  ...
```

Notice that the item listener for the combo box uses the JTabbedPane. prefix to specify the tab placement, whereas the SwingConstants. prefix was passed to the JTabbedPane constructor. Again, since JTabbedPane implements the SwingConstants interface, either prefix can be used to specify tab placement constants.

The applet shown in Figure 12-16 is listed in its entirety in Example 12-11.

Example 12-11 Setting Tab Placement for Instances of JTabbedPane

```java
import java.awt.*;
import java.awt.event.*;
import javax.swing.*;

public class Test extends JApplet {
    private JTabbedPane tp =
                new JTabbedPane(SwingConstants.BOTTOM);
    private JComboBox combo = new JComboBox();

    public Test() {
        Container contentPane = getContentPane();
        JPanel comboPanel = new JPanel();
        JPanel panelOne = new JPanel();
        JPanel panelTwo = new JPanel();

        tp.add(panelOne, "Panel One");
        tp.addTab("Panel Two",
                new ImageIcon("document.gif"),
                panelTwo,
                "tooltip text");

        combo.addItem("TOP");
        combo.addItem("LEFT");
        combo.addItem("RIGHT");
        combo.addItem("BOTTOM");

        comboPanel.add(new JLabel("Tab Placement:"));
        comboPanel.add(combo);

        contentPane.add(comboPanel, BorderLayout.NORTH);
        contentPane.add(tp, BorderLayout.CENTER);
```

```
            setComboValue();


            combo.addItemListener(new ItemListener() {
                public void itemStateChanged(ItemEvent e) {
                    JComboBox cb = (JComboBox)e.getSource();
                    int state = e.getStateChange();

                    if(state == ItemEvent.SELECTED) {
                        String s = (String)cb.getSelectedItem();

                        if(s.equals("TOP"))
                            tp.setTabPlacement(JTabbedPane.TOP);
                        else if(s.equals("LEFT"))
                            tp.setTabPlacement(JTabbedPane.LEFT);
                        else if(s.equals("RIGHT"))
                            tp.setTabPlacement(JTabbedPane.RIGHT);
                        else if(s.equals("BOTTOM"))
                            tp.setTabPlacement(JTabbedPane.BOTTOM);

                        tp.validate();
                    }
                }
            });
        }
        private void setComboValue() {
            int placement = tp.getTabPlacement();
            String selectedItem = null;

            switch(placement) {
                case JTabbedPane.TOP:
                        selectedItem = "TOP";
                        break;
                case JTabbedPane.LEFT:
                        selectedItem = "LEFT";
                        break;
                case JTabbedPane.RIGHT:
                        selectedItem = "RIGHT";
                        break;
                case JTabbedPane.BOTTOM:
                        selectedItem = "BOTTOM";
                        break;
            }
            combo.setSelectedItem(selectedItem);
        }
    }
```

The JTabbedPane class is summarized in Component Summary 12-4.

Component Summary 12-4   JTabbedPane

Model(s)	DefaultSingleSelectionModel
UI Delegate(s)	javax.swing.plaf.basic.BasicTabbedPaneUI
Renderer(s)	——
Editor(s)	——
Events Fired	PropertyChangeEvent, ChangeEvent
Replacement For	——

Class Diagrams

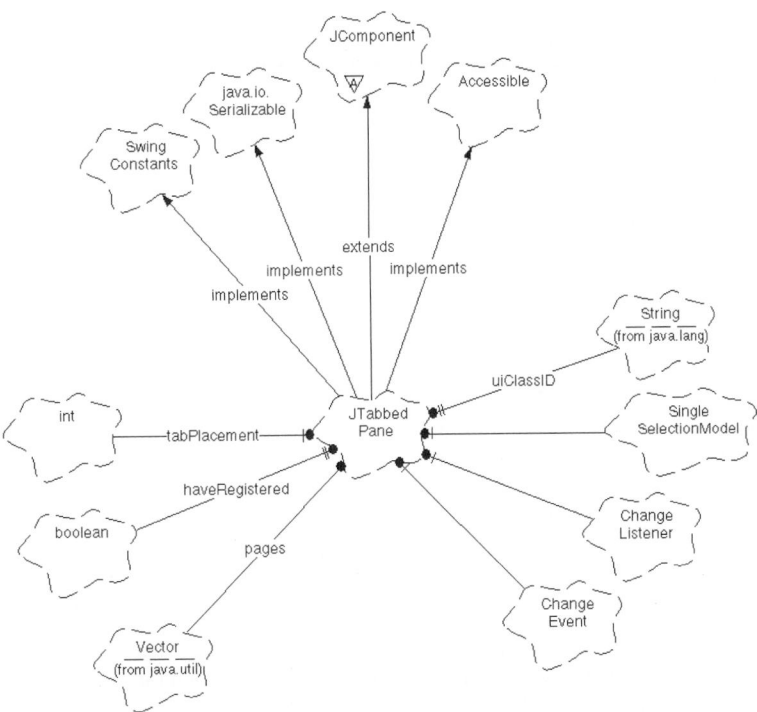

Figure 12-17 JTabbedPane Class Diagram

JTabbedPane extends JComponent and implements the SwingConstants, Serializable, and Accessible interfaces. As is typically the case for Swing components that have a model and fire change events, an instance of ChangeListener is used to respond to model changes, and a single instance of ChangeEvent is passed to change listeners associated with the JTabbedPane.

JTabbedPane maintains a protected int that tracks tab placement. JTabbedPane also maintains a private boolean value that keeps track of whether the tabbed pane has registered with the tooltip manager. A vector with package scope access is maintained by JTabbedPane to keep track of a set of Pages. Page is a class that is private to the JTabbedPane class that encapsulates the properties associated with tabs.

JTabbedPane Properties

The properties maintained by the JTabbedPane class are listed in Table 12-6.

Table 12-6 JTabbedPane Properties

Property Name	Data Type	Access[1]	Type[2]	Default[3]
backgroundAt	Color	SG	I	L&F
boundsAt	Rectangle	G	I	L&F
componentAt	Component	SG	I	null
disabledIconAt	Icon	SG	I	Grayed-out icon
enabledAt	boolean	SG	I	——
foregroundAt	Color	SG	I	L&F
iconAt	Icon	SG	I	——
model	SingleSelection Model	SG	B	DefaultSingleSelection Model
selectedComponent	Component	SG	S	——
selectedIndex	int	SG	S	——
tabCount	int	G	S	——
tabPlacement	int	CSG	B	TOP
tabRunCount	int	G	S	——
titleAt	String	SG	S	——

1. C = settable at construction time / G = getter method / S = setter method
2. b = boolean / B = bound / C = constrained/ I = indexed / S = simple / RO = read only
3. L&F = look-and-feel dependent

backgroundAt — Specifies the background color for a tab identified by an index. If the `backgroundAt` property for a tab is set to `null`, the tab's background color will default to the background color of the tabbed pane in which the tab resides. When the property is changed, the region of the tabbed pane representing the bounds of the associated tab is repainted.

boundsAt — A rectangle representing the bounds of a tab identified by an index. The property is read-only, and if the specified tab is not visible, the `JTabbedPane.getBoundsAt` method returns `null`.

componentAt — Represents a tab's component, where the tab is identified by an index. If `JTabbedPane.getComponentAt()` is passed an invalid index, an `ArrayIndexOutOfBoundsException` is thrown.

disabledIconAt — Represents an icon that is displayed in a tab when the tab is disabled. If the `disabledIconAt` property is set for a tab that is disabled, the entire tabbed pane will be laid out and repainted.

enabledAt — A `boolean` property that represents the enabled state for individual tabs. If the specified tab index is invalid, an `ArrayIndexOutOfBoundsException` is thrown. When the property is changed, the region of the tabbed pane representing the bounds of the associated tab is repainted.

foregroundAt — Specifies the foreground color for a tab identified by an index. If the `foregroundAt` property for a tab is set to `null`, the tab's foreground color will default to the foreground color of the tabbed pane in which the tab resides. When the property is changed, the region of the tabbed pane representing the bounds of the associated tab is repainted.

iconAt — Represents the icon displayed in an enabled tab; the tab is identified by an index. Tab icons can be set to `null`, in which case no icon is displayed in the tab. Changing a tab's icon results in the tabbed pane being laid out and repainted.

model — The model for tabbed panes is an implementation of the `SingleSelectionModel` interface. By default, tabbed pane models are instances of `DefaultSingleSelectionModel`. If the model is explicitly set after construction, a property change event is fired and the tabbed pane is repainted.

selectedComponent — Tabbed panes always have a selected tab, and the `selectedComponent` property represents the component associated with the selected tab. The selected tab can be set programmatically with the `JTabbedPane.setSelectedComponent` method, which throws an IllegalArgumentException if passed a null reference.

selectedIndex — Tabs can be selected by an index in addition to their associated component (see the selectedComponent property). The selectedIndex property is maintained by a tabbed pane's model, and setting the property with the JTabbedPane.setSelectedIndex method results in the model firing a change event, which is handled by the tabbed pane's UI delegate by laying out and repainting the tabbed pane.

tabCount — Represents the number of tabs contained in a tabbed pane and is read-only.

tabPlacement — Determines where a tabbed pane's tabs are displayed. Valid values are:

- JTabbedPane.TOP
- JTabbedPane.LEFT
- JTabbedPane.BOTTOM
- JTabbedPane.RIGHT

tabRunCount — Represents the number of rows or columns of tabs, for tabbed panes with tabPlacement properties of JTabbedPane.TOP/JTabbedPane.BOTTOM and JTabbedPane.LEFT/JTabbedPane.RIGHT, respectively. The tabRunCount property is read-only.

titleAt — Represents the string displayed by a tab. Setting the titleAt property results in a layout and subsequent repaint of the tabbed pane.

JTabbedPane Events

In addition to firing property change events when its bound properties are modified, an instance of JTabbedPane fires change events whenever a tab is selected. Because the only state maintained by instances of ChangeEvent is the source of the event, each instance of JTabbedPane uses a single instance of ChangeEvent to send to its change listeners whenever one of its tabs is selected.

The applet shown in Figure 12-18 handles change events fired by an instance of JTabbedPane.

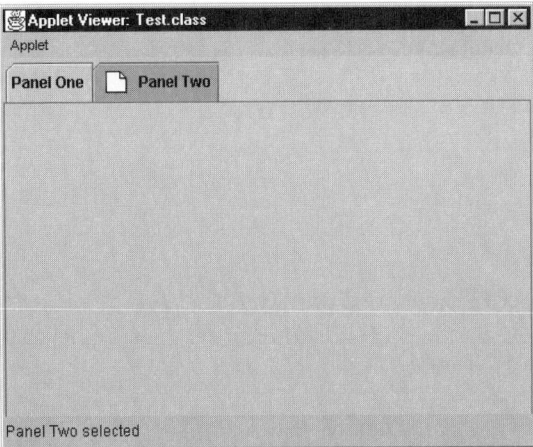

Figure 12-18 Handling JTabbedPane Change Events

The applet shown in Figure 12-18 is listed in Example 12-12.

Example 12-12 Reacting to JTabbedPane Change Events

```java
import java.awt.*;
import java.awt.event.*;
import javax.swing.*;
import javax.swing.event.*;

public class Test extends JApplet {

    public Test() {
        Container contentPane = getContentPane();
        JTabbedPane tp = new JTabbedPane();
        JPanel panelOne = new JPanel();
        JPanel panelTwo = new JPanel();

        tp.add(panelOne, "Panel One");
        tp.addTab("Panel Two",
                  new ImageIcon("document.gif"),
                  panelTwo,
                  "tooltip text");

        contentPane.add(tp, BorderLayout.CENTER);

        tp.addChangeListener(new ChangeListener() {
            public void stateChanged(ChangeEvent e) {
                JTabbedPane tabbedPane =
                                (JTabbedPane)e.getSource();
```

```
                    int index = tabbedPane.getSelectedIndex();
                    String s = tabbedPane.getTitleAt(index);

                    showStatus(s + " selected");
                }
            });
        }
    }
```

The applet adds a change listener to the tabbed pane and uses the `JTabbedPane`
`getSelectedIndex` and `getTitleAt` methods to print which tab was selected
in the applet's status area.

JTabbedPane Class Summaries

The `public` and `protected` variables and methods for `JTabbedPane` are listed
in Class Summary 12-4.

Class Summary 12-4   JTabbedPane

Extends: JComponent

Implements: SwingConstants, javax.accessibility.Accessible,
               java.io.Serializable

Constructors

---

public JTabbedPane()
public JTabbedPane(int tabPlacement)

`JTabbedPane` provides two constructors—a no-argument constructor and a constructor that is passed an `int` value that specifies the tab placement to be used. By default, the tab placement is set to TOP when the no-argument constructor is used.

Methods

Adding / Removing Tabs and Components

---

public Component <u>add</u>(Component)
public Component <u>add</u>(Component, int index)
public void <u>add</u>(Component, Object constraints)
public void <u>add</u>(Component, Object, int index)
public Component <u>add</u>(String, Component)

public void <u>addTab</u>(String title, Icon, Component)
public void <u>addTab</u>(String title, Icon, Component, String title)
public void <u>addTab</u>(String title, Component)

public void <u>insertTab</u>(String title, Icon, Component, String tip, int index)

public void <u>remove</u>(Component)
public void <u>removeAll</u>()
public void <u>removeTabAt</u>(int index)

The methods listed above are for adding, inserting, and removing tabs and their associated components. The `Object` arguments passed to the `add` methods can be either a string representing the title of the tab or an icon that is displayed in the tab. The component argument passed to the `add` methods represents the component that is displayed beneath a tab when the tab is selected. The `int` argument passed to the `add` methods specifies the index, and therefore the position, of the tab. If a title is not specified for a tab, the name of the component associated with the tab is used as the tab's title.

The `insertTab` method is passed two strings. The first string specifies the title of the tab, and the second string specifies the tooltip text associated with the tab.

The `remove` methods remove tabs and their associated components from the tabbed pane. The `remove(Component)` method removes the component and its associated tab by invoking `removeTabAt()`.

Property Accessors

---

public Color getBackgroundAt(int index)
public Rectangle getBoundsAt(int index)
public Component getComponentAt(int index)
public Icon getDisabledIconAt(int index)
public Color getForegroundAt(int index)
public Icon getIconAt(int index)
public SingleSelectionModel getModel()
public Component getSelectedComponent()
public int getSelectedIndex()
public int getTabCount()
public int getTabPlacement()
public int getTabRunCount()
public String getTitleAt(int index)
public String getToolTipText(MouseEvent)

public void setBackgroundAt(int index, Color)
public void setComponentAt(int index, Component)
public void setDisabledIconAt(int index, Icon)
public void setEnabledAt(int index, boolean)
public void setForegroundAt(int index, Color)
public void setIconAt(int index, Icon)
public void setModel(SingleSelectionModel)
public void setSelectedComponent(Component)
public void setSelectedIndex(int index)
public void setTabPlacement(int)
public void setTitleAt(int index, String)

public boolean isEnabledAt(int)

public int indexOfComponent(Component)
public int indexOfTab(Icon)
public int indexOfTab(String)

The methods listed above are accessors for JTabbedPane properties. The int values passed to most of the methods represent the index of a specific tab. For example, invoking aTabbedPane.getBackgroundAt(3) returns the background color for the tab at index 3, which is the fourth tab from the upper-left corner of the tabbed pane (indexes start at 0). The index of a tab can be obtained by invoking one of the indexOf... methods.

The getTabRunCount method returns the number of tab columns (for tabs placed at the top or bottom of the tabbed pane) or the number of tab rows (for tabs placed at the left or right of the tabbed pane).

The getToolTipText(MouseEvent) method is overridden from JComponent to return the tooltip text associated with the tab that resides at the position specified by the mouse event. See "Tooltips Based on Mouse Position" on page 173 or more information on overriding JComponent.getToolTipText(MouseEvent).

Change Listeners

---

public void addChangeListener(ChangeListener)
public void removeChangeListener(ChangeListener)

protected ChangeListener createChangeListener()
protected void fireStateChanged()

When a change occurs to a tabbed pane's selection model, meaning a tab has been selected, the tabbed pane fires a change event with the tabbed pane as the source of the event. Change listeners can be added and removed from instances of JTabbedPane with the first two methods listed above.

The protected createChangeListener method creates a change listener that is attached to the tabbed pane's model. The listener invokes the fireStateChanged method whenever the tabbed pane's model changes. Extensions of JTabbedPane can insert their own listener by overriding the createChangeListener method and can modify the manner in which change events are fired by overriding the fireStateChanged method.

Accessibility / Pluggable Look And Feel

---

public AccessibleContext getAccessibleContext()
public TabbedPaneUI getUI()
public String getUIClassID()
public void setUI(TabbedPaneUI)
public void updateUI()

The methods listed above can be found in most extensions of `JComponent`. Swing lightweight components can return an accessibility context that contains accessibility information for the component and the class name of their UI delegate. The `updateUI` method is invoked when the component is fitted with a UI delegate.

JSplitPane

Swing provides a split pane component, in the form of `JSplitPane`, that displays two components. The components are separated by a divider that can be dragged to adjust the sizes of the components. The components contained in a split pane can be oriented either vertically or horizontally.

The applet shown in Figure 12-19 contains an instance of `JSplitPane` that contains two buttons. The applet also contains a control panel that allows some of the properties associated with the split pane to be adjusted.

The top picture shown in Figure 12-19 shows the applet as it appears initially. The bottom picture shows that applet after the *one-touch expandable* and *continuous layout* properties have been set to `true`, the size of the divider has been set to 20 pixels, and the orientation of the components has been set to vertical.

The *continuous layout* property controls whether or not the components contained in a split pane are continuously updated as the divider is dragged. If the property is `true`, the components are continuously updated; if the property is `false`, the components are not updated until the divider has been dragged to its new location.

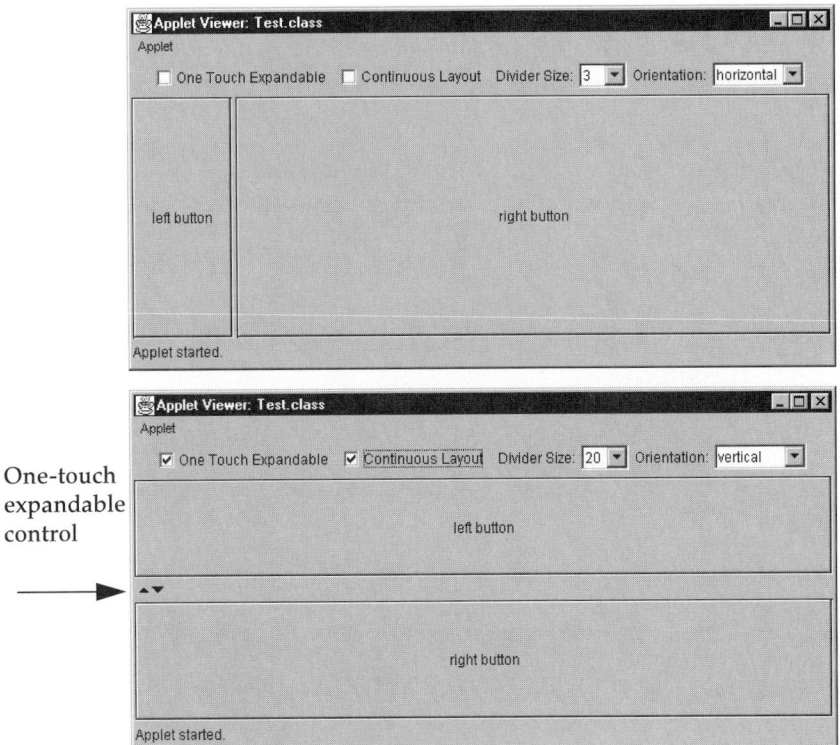

Figure 12-19 JSplitPane in Action

The *one-touch expandable* property determines whether a control is painted in the divider. The control allows the components to be expanded and contracted when the control is clicked. If the *one-touch expandable* property is `true`, the control is painted; if the property is `false`, the control is not available.

The applet creates the split pane and control panel and adds the split pane to its content pane as the `CENTER` component. The control panel is added to the applet's content pane as the `NORTH` component.

The split pane is constructed with the `JSplitPane` no-argument constructor, which adds two buttons to the split pane. References to the buttons are obtained from the split pane by invocation of `JSplitPane.getTopComponent()` and `JSplitPane.getBottomComponent()`. Even though the buttons are originally oriented horizontally, the left button can be obtained with `getTopComponent()`, and the right button can be obtained with `getBottomComponent()`.

It should be noted that `JSplitPane` also provides `getRightComponent` and `getLeftComponent` methods, but the applet illustrates that the right and left components in a split pane can be accessed through the `getBottomComponent` and `getTopComponent` methods, respectively.

After obtaining references to the two components contained in the split pane, the minimum sizes for the components are printed. The output of the applet looks like this:

```
left button minimum size: java.awt.Dimension[width=85,height=23]
right button minimum size: java.awt.Dimension[width=93,height=23]
```

The minimum sizes are printed because `JSplitPane` will not allow its divider to be dragged to a location that causes one of its components to be smaller than the component's minimum size.

```
public class Test extends JApplet {
    public Test() {
        Container contentPane = getContentPane();
        JButton left, right;
        JSplitPane sp = new JSplitPane();
        ControlPanel cp = new ControlPanel(sp);

        contentPane.add(sp, BorderLayout.CENTER);
        contentPane.add(cp, BorderLayout.NORTH);

        left  = (JButton)sp.getTopComponent();
        right = (JButton)sp.getBottomComponent();

        System.out.println("left button minimum size: " +
                left.getMinimumSize());
        System.out.println("right button minimum size: " +
                right.getMinimumSize());

    }
}
```

The control panel is an instance of `ControlPanel`, which is an extension of `JPanel`. The interesting aspect of the `ControlPanel` class from the perspective of split panes is the event handling for each of the controls in the control panel.

Each of the check boxes and combo boxes has an item listener added to it. The "One Touch Expandable" check box invokes the JSplitPane setOneTouchExpandable method with either a true or false value, depending upon whether the check box is selected.

The item listener for the "Continuous Layout" check box invokes JSplitPane.setContinuousLayout() with a true value if the check box is selected, and a false value if the check box is not selected.

The item listener for the "Divider Size" check box invokes JSplitPane.setDividerSize() and passes the integer value corresponding to the string selected in check box.

The ItemListener for the "Orientation" check box invokes JSplitPane.setOrientation() and passes either JSplitPane.HORIZONTAL_SPLIT or JSplitPane.VERTICAL_SPLIT, depending upon the selection made in the check box.

```java
class ControlPanel extends JPanel {
    private JSplitPane sp;
    ...

    oneTouch.addItemListener(new ItemListener() {
        public void itemStateChanged(ItemEvent e) {
            if(e.getStateChange() == ItemEvent.SELECTED)
                sp.setOneTouchExpandable(true);
            else
                sp.setOneTouchExpandable(false);
        }
    });
    continuous.addItemListener(new ItemListener() {
        public void itemStateChanged(ItemEvent e) {
            if(e.getStateChange() == ItemEvent.SELECTED)
                sp.setContinuousLayout(true);
            else
                sp.setContinuousLayout(false);
        }
    });
    dividerSize.addItemListener(new ItemListener() {
        public void itemStateChanged(ItemEvent e) {
            JComboBox combo = (JComboBox)e.getSource();
            String s = (String)combo.getSelectedItem();

            sp.setDividerSize(Integer.parseInt(s));
        }
    });
    orientation.addItemListener(new ItemListener() {
        public void itemStateChanged(ItemEvent e) {
```

```
                              JComboBox combo = (JComboBox)e.getSource();
                              String s = (String)combo.getSelectedItem();

                              if(s.equals("horizontal"))
                                 sp.setOrientation(
                                        JSplitPane.HORIZONTAL_SPLIT);
                              else
                                 sp.setOrientation(JSplitPane.VERTICAL_SPLIT);
                           }
                        });
                        ...
                  }
```

The applet shown in Figure 12-19 is listed in its entirety in Example 12-13.

Example 12-13 JSplitPane in Action

```
      import java.awt.*;
      import java.awt.event.*;
      import javax.swing.*;

      public class Test extends JApplet {
         public Test() {
            Container contentPane = getContentPane();
            JButton left, right;
            JSplitPane sp = new JSplitPane();
            ControlPanel cp = new ControlPanel(sp);

            contentPane.add(sp, BorderLayout.CENTER);
            contentPane.add(cp, BorderLayout.NORTH);

            left = (JButton)sp.getTopComponent();
            right = (JButton)sp.getBottomComponent();

            System.out.println("left button minimum size: " +
                    left.getMinimumSize());
            System.out.println("right button minimum size: " +
                    right.getMinimumSize());

         }
      }
      class ControlPanel extends JPanel {
         private JSplitPane sp;

         public ControlPanel(JSplitPane splitPane) {
            sp = splitPane;

            JComboBox dividerSize = new JComboBox();
            JComboBox orientation = new JComboBox();
```

```java
JCheckBox continuous = new JCheckBox(
                        "Continuous Layout");
JCheckBox oneTouch = new JCheckBox(
                        "One Touch Expandable");

Integer initialSize = new Integer(sp.getDividerSize());
dividerSize.addItem(initialSize.toString());
dividerSize.addItem("10");
dividerSize.addItem("20");
dividerSize.addItem("30");
dividerSize.addItem("40");

orientation.addItem("horizontal");
orientation.addItem("vertical");

int initialOrientation = sp.getOrientation();
if(initialOrientation == JSplitPane.HORIZONTAL_SPLIT)
   orientation.setSelectedItem("horizontal");
else
   orientation.setSelectedItem("vertical");

boolean initialContinuousLayout = sp.isContinuousLayout();
if(initialContinuousLayout)
   continuous.setSelected(true);

add(oneTouch);
add(continuous);
add(new JLabel("Divider Size:"));
add(dividerSize);
add(new JLabel("Orientation:"));
add(orientation);

oneTouch.addItemListener(new ItemListener() {
   public void itemStateChanged(ItemEvent e) {
      if(e.getStateChange() == ItemEvent.SELECTED)
         sp.setOneTouchExpandable(true);
      else
         sp.setOneTouchExpandable(false);
   }
});
continuous.addItemListener(new ItemListener() {
   public void itemStateChanged(ItemEvent e) {
      if(e.getStateChange() == ItemEvent.SELECTED)
         sp.setContinuousLayout(true);
      else
         sp.setContinuousLayout(false);
   }
});
dividerSize.addItemListener(new ItemListener() {
   public void itemStateChanged(ItemEvent e) {
      JComboBox combo = (JComboBox)e.getSource();
      String s = (String)combo.getSelectedItem();
```

```
                sp.setDividerSize(Integer.parseInt(s));
          }
      });
      orientation.addItemListener(new ItemListener() {
          public void itemStateChanged(ItemEvent e) {
              JComboBox combo = (JComboBox)e.getSource();
              String s = (String)combo.getSelectedItem();

              if(s.equals("horizontal"))
                  sp.setOrientation(
                        JSplitPane.HORIZONTAL_SPLIT);
              else
                  sp.setOrientation(JSplitPane.VERTICAL_SPLIT);
          }
      });
    }
  }
```

The JSplitPane component is summarized in Component Summary 12-5.

Component Summary 12-5   JSplitPane

Model(s)	——
UI Delegate(s)	javax.swing.plaf.basic.BasicSplitPaneUI
Renderer(s)	——
Editor(s)	——
Events Fired	PropertyChangeEvent
Replacement For	——

Class Diagrams

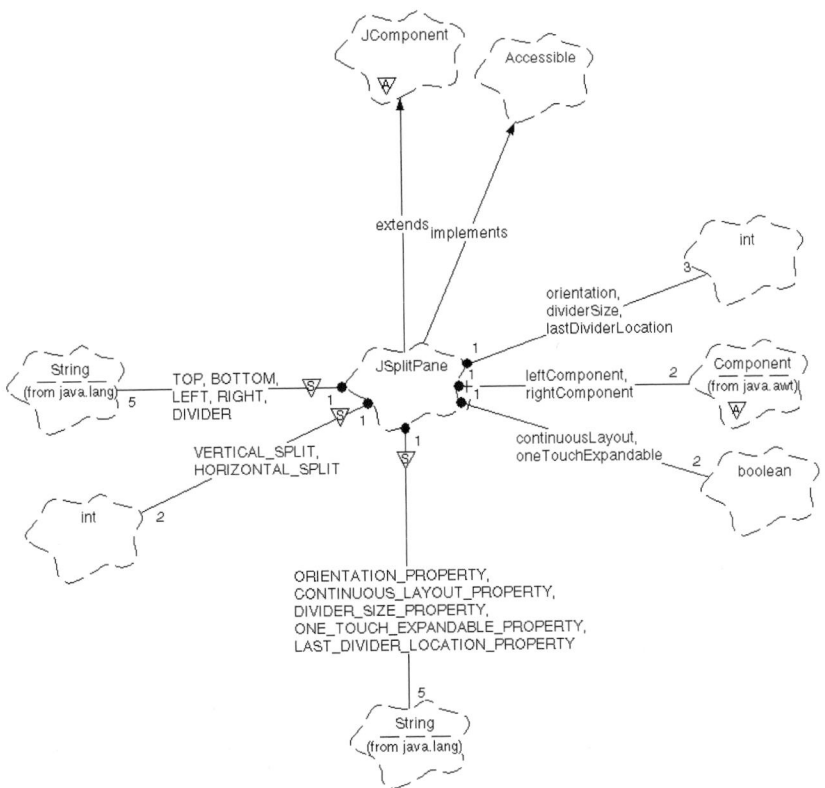

Figure 12-20 JSplitPane Class Diagram

JSplitPane extends JComponent and implements the Accessible interface.
JSplitPane defines a number of string constants for the types of components
that can be added to a split pane, and the orientations and various properties
supported by the JSplitPane class.

JSplitPane Properties

The properties maintained by the JSplitPane class are listed in Table 12-7.

Table 12-7 JSplitPane Properties

Property Name	Data Type	Access[1]	Type[2]	Default[3]
bottomComponent	Component	CSG	S	null
continuousLayout	boolean	CSG	B	false
dividerLocation (proportional)	double	S	S	L&F
dividerLocation (pixel location)	int	SG	S	L&F
dividerSize	int	SG	B	L&F
lastDividerLocation	int	SG	B	L&F
leftComponent	Component	CSG	S	null
minimumDividerLocation	int	G	S	L&F / -1
oneTouchExpandable	boolean	S	B	L&F
orientation	int	CSG	B	horizontal
rightComponent	Component	CSG	S	null
topComponent	Component	CSG	S	null

1. C = settable at construction time / G = getter method / S = setter method
2. b = boolean / B = bound / C = constrained/ I = indexed / S = simple / RO = read only
3. L&F = look-and-feel dependent

bottomComponent — The component displayed on the bottom/right side of the split pane.

continuousLayout — If true, the two components are continuously resized and repainted as the divider moves.

dividerLocation (proportional) — A number between 0.0 and 1.0 that sets divider location.

dividerLocation (pixel location) — Pixel value for divider location from the top/left of the split pane.

dividerSize — Represents the size of a split pane's divider in pixels.

lastDividerLocation — The last location, in pixels from the left/top of the split pane, for the divider.

leftComponent — The component displayed at the top/left of the split pane.

minimumDividerLocation — Minimum pixel value for divider location.

oneTouchExpandable — If true, a control is displayed to expand/contract the size of the components.

orientation — Specifies the orientation of the components contained in the split pane, not the orientation of the split pane's divider. A split pane with a horizontal orientation orients the components horizontally with a vertical divider. Likewise, a split pane with a vertical orientation orients the components vertically with a horizontal divider.

rightComponent — The component displayed on the right/bottom side of the split pane.

topComponent — The component displayed at the top/left of the split pane.

JSplitPane Events

The JSplitPane class does not fire events other than property change events when its bound properties are modified.

The applet shown in Figure 12-21 monitors a split pane's divider location and displays the divider location and sizes of the two buttons contained in the split pane whenever the divider is moved.

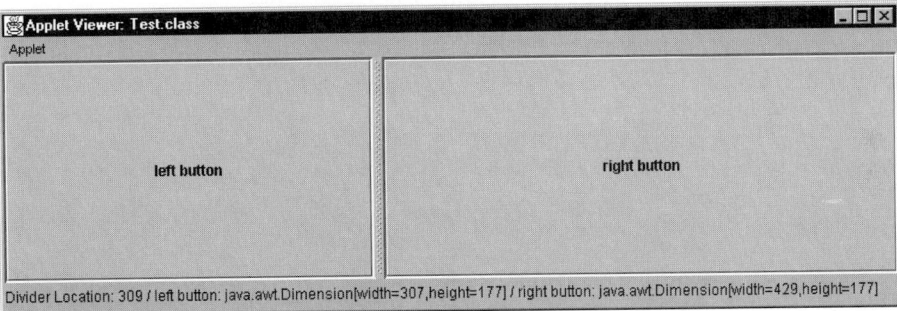

Figure 12-21 Monitoring Divider Location

The applet shown in Figure 12-21 is listed in Example 12-14.

Example 12-14   Monitoring a Split Pane's Divider Location

```
import java.awt.*;
import java.awt.event.*;
import java.beans.*;
import javax.swing.*;

public class Test extends JApplet {
    public Test() {
        Container contentPane = getContentPane();
        JSplitPane sp = new JSplitPane();

        contentPane.add(sp, BorderLayout.CENTER);

        sp.addPropertyChangeListener(
                            new PropertyChangeListener() {
            public void propertyChange(PropertyChangeEvent e) {
                if(e.getPropertyName().equals(
                    JSplitPane.LAST_DIVIDER_LOCATION_PROPERTY)) {
                    JSplitPane jsp = (JSplitPane)e.getSource();

                    int dl = jsp.getDividerLocation();

                    JButton lb = (JButton)jsp.getLeftComponent();
                    JButton rb = (JButton)jsp.getRightComponent();

                    showStatus("Divider Location: " + dl + " / " +
                        lb.getText() + ": " + lb.getSize() + " / " +
                        rb.getText() + ": " + rb.getSize());
                }
            }
        });
    }
}
```

The applet adds a property change listener to the split pane. The listener reacts only to changes to the last divider location by comparing the property name to `JSplitPane.LAST_DIVIDER_LOCATION`. The divider location is obtained by invocation of `JSplitPane.getDividerLocation()`, and references to the buttons contained in the split pane are obtained by invocation of the `JSplitPane` methods `getLeftComponent()` and `getRightComponent()`.

JSplitPane Class Summaries

The `public` and `protected` variables and methods for `JSplitPane` are listed in Class Summary 12-5.

Class Summary 12-5   JSplitPane

Extends: JComponent
Implements: Javax.accessibility.Accessible

Constructors

public JSplitPane()
public JSplitPane(int orientation)
public JSplitPane(int orientation, boolean continuousLayout)
public JSplitPane(int orientation, boolean continuousLayout, Component top/left,
                 Component bottom/right)
public JSplitPane(int orientation, Component top/left, Component bottom/right)

The no-argument constructor adds two buttons to the split pane and is provided primarily for JavaBeans builder tools to show something interesting. The no-argument constructor sets the continuous layout property to `false` and sets the orientation of the components to horizontal, as can be seen from Table 12-7.

The two components passed to the constructors listed above represent the top/left and bottom/right components, respectively.

The `integer` value specifies the orientation of the split pane: `JSplitPane.HORIZONTAL_SPLIT` and `JSplitPane.VERTICAL_SPLIT` are valid orientation values. If the value specified for orientation is something other than `HORIZONTAL_SPLIT` or `VERTICAL_SPLIT`, an `IllegalArgumentException` is thrown.

The `boolean` value specifies the continuous layout property for the split pane. If continuous layout is `true`, the two components contained within the split pane will resize as the divider is moved. If continuous layout is `false`, the two components will not update their sizes until the divider has reset to a new location.

Methods

Adding Components / Painting Children

---

protected void <u>addImpl</u>(Component, Object constraints, int index)
protected void <u>paintChildren</u>(Graphics)

The `protected` methods listed above are overridden to ensure that components are added to the split pane in the correct order and that the UI delegate is notified when the split pane has finished painting its children. The methods listed above should rarely, if ever, be overridden by extensions of `JSplitPane`.

Removing Components

---

public void <u>remove</u>(int index)
public void <u>remove</u>(Component)
public void <u>removeAll</u>()

public void <u>resetToPreferredSizes</u>()

The remove methods are overridden from `java.awt.Container` so that `JSplitPane` can set its `leftComponent` and `rightComponent` instance variables accordingly. The `resetToPreferredSizes` method forces the split pane to be laid out on the basis of the preferred sizes of the components contained in the split pane.

Property Accessors

---

public Component <u>getBottomComponent</u>()
public int <u>getDividerLocation</u>()
public int <u>getDividerSize</u>()
public int <u>getLastDividerLocation</u>()
public Component <u>getLeftComponent</u>()
public int <u>getMaximumDividerLocation</u>()

public int getMinimumDividerLocation()
public int getOrientation()
public Component getRightComponent()
public Component getTopComponent()

public void setBottomComponent(Component)
public void setContinuousLayout(boolean)
public void setDividerLocation(double)
public void setDividerLocation(int)
public void setDividerSize(int)
public void setLastDividerLocation(int)
public void setLeftComponent(Component)
public void setOneTouchExpandable(boolean)
public void setOrientation(int)
public void setRightComponent(Component)
public void setTopComponent(Component)

public boolean isContinuousLayout()
public boolean isOneTouchExpandable()

The methods listed above are accessors for JSplitPane properties.

Accessibility / Pluggable Look And Feel

public AccessibleContext getAccessibleContext()
public void setUI(SplitPaneUI)
public void updateUI()
public SplitPaneUI getUI()
public String getUIClassID()

The methods listed above can be found in most extensions of JComponent.
Swing lightweight components can return an accessibility context that contains
accessibility information for the component and the class name of their UI
delegate. The updateUI method is invoked when the component is fitted with a
UI delegate.

AWT Compatibility

The AWT does not have a component that is analogous to `JSplitPane`.

Parting Shots

Swing provides a wealth of basic containers from the simple `JPanel` component to the more complex `JLayeredPane`, `JTabbedPane` and `JSplitPane` containers. This chapter covers the basic Swing containers; however, Swing also provides other containers such as the `JViewport` and `JScrollPane` classes, which are discussed in "Scrolling" on page 717.

CHAPTER 13

Scrolling

This chapter discusses the Swing scrolling architecture, which includes two lightweight Swing containers—JViewport and JScrollPane—a Scrollable interface designed to support components with special scrolling needs and a JScrollBar class.

Instances of JViewport are rarely instantiated and used directly; however, a considerable portion of this chapter is dedicated to the JViewport class because it is the fundamental component in the Swing scrolling architecture.

The JScrollPane component is designed to replace the AWT's heavyweight ScrollPane component. JScrollPane offers many improvements over the AWT's ScrollPane, including the ability to attach row and column headers and to specify components that reside in the corners of the scrollpane.

The Scrollable interface is designed for scrollable components that contain rows or columns of data such as tables, trees, text components, and lists.

The JScrollBar component is a scrollbar that can be used to implement manual scrolling. Although Swing's JScrollPane component is sufficient for most scrolling situations, there are times when scrolling must be implemented manually for performance or resource considerations. In such cases, the JScrollBar component can be used to scroll the contents of a container.

JViewport

The JViewport class is the cornerstone of the Swing scrolling architecture. As its name suggests, instances of JViewport provide a *porthole* through which a particular region of a *view* is displayed. The position of the view displayed by a viewport can be manipulated so that different regions of the view appear in the viewport at any given time.

The applet shown in Figure 13-1 contains an instance of JViewport whose view is an instance of JLabel. The label is fitted with an image that is larger than the viewport in which the image is displayed. The applet provides four buttons that can be used to adjust the position of the viewport's view.

Figure 13-1 Using JViewport to Scroll an Image

The left-hand picture in Figure 13-1 shows the applet as it appears initially. The right-hand picture shows the applet after the up and left buttons are repeatedly activated. It should be emphasized that repeatedly activating buttons is not the most ideal manner in which to scroll a view in a viewport (to say the least), but it serves to illustrate how a viewport adjusts the position of its view.

The applet creates an instance of JViewport and an instance of JLabel. The label is specified as the viewport's view by invoking JViewport.setView(). The applet also creates an instance of ControlPanel—an extension of JPanel—that contains the buttons used to scroll the label.

```
public class Test extends JApplet {
    public void init() {
        Container contentPane = getContentPane();
        JViewport viewport = new JViewport();
        JPanel view = new JPanel();

        view.add(new JLabel(
                new ImageIcon("anjinAndMariko.gif")));

        viewport.setView(view);

        contentPane.add(new ControlPanel(viewport),
                    BorderLayout.NORTH);
        contentPane.add(viewport, BorderLayout.CENTER);
    }
    ...
```

The ControlPanel class creates four buttons and adds a single instance of ActionListener to each. The listener invokes a private scroll method, passing the action command string associated with the button that was activated. The scroll method invokes JViewport.getViewPosition() to obtain the current view position and subsequently adjusts the view's position by invoking JViewport.setViewPosition(). The JViewport.setViewPosition method is passed a point that represents the view coordinate displayed in the upper-left corner of the viewport.

```
class ControlPanel extends JPanel {
    private JViewport viewport;
    ...

    private void scroll(String actionCmd) {
        Point vp = viewport.getViewPosition();

        if(actionCmd.equals("up")) vp.y += 5;
        else if(actionCmd.equals("down")) vp.y -= 5;
        else if(actionCmd.equals("left")) vp.x += 5;
        else if(actionCmd.equals("right")) vp.x -= 5;

        viewport.setViewPosition(vp);
    }
}
```

The coordinate system for Swing (and AWT) components defines the origin—(0,0)—at the upper-left corner of a component with X and Y values increasing from left to right and top to bottom, respectively. As a result, to move the label displayed in the viewport up, the Y value of the current view position is increased. Correspondingly, to move the viewport's view down, the Y value of the current view position is decreased. The X value of the view's position is increased to move the view to the left and decreased to move the view to the right.

The applet shown in Figure 13-1 is listed in its entirety in Example 13-1.

Example 13-1 Scrolling an Image with an Instance of JViewport

```java
import java.awt.*;
import java.awt.event.*;
import javax.swing.*;

public class Test extends JApplet {
    public void init() {
        Container contentPane = getContentPane();
        JViewport viewport = new JViewport();
        JPanel view = new JPanel();

        view.add(new JLabel(
                new ImageIcon("anjinAndMariko.gif")));

        viewport.setView(view);

        contentPane.add(new ControlPanel(viewport),
                    BorderLayout.NORTH);
        contentPane.add(viewport, BorderLayout.CENTER);
    }
}
class ControlPanel extends JPanel {
    private JViewport viewport;

    private JButton[] buttons = {
        new JButton("up"), new JButton("down"),
        new JButton("left"), new JButton("right")
    };

    public ControlPanel(JViewport vp) {
        viewport = vp;

        for(int i=0; i < buttons.length; ++i) {
            add(buttons[i]);
```

```
            buttons[i].addActionListener(new ActionListener() {
                public void actionPerformed(ActionEvent e) {
                    scroll(e.getActionCommand());
                }
            });
        }
    }
    private void scroll(String actionCmd) {
        Point vp = viewport.getViewPosition();

        if(actionCmd.equals("up")) vp.y += 5;
        else if(actionCmd.equals("down")) vp.y -= 5;
        else if(actionCmd.equals("left")) vp.x += 5;
        else if(actionCmd.equals("right")) vp.x -= 5;

        viewport.setViewPosition(vp);
    }
}
```

Swing Tip ...

Viewports and Their Views

Swing viewports display a portion of a component, known as the viewport's view. The JViewport class maintains a view position property that represents the view's coordinate displayed in the upper-left corner of the viewport. Setter and getter methods are provided for the view position property.

The coordinate system for Swing and AWT components defines the coordinate (0,0) at the upper-left corner of the component, with X and Y coordinates increasing to the right and down, respectively. Because of this, use the following as a guide for moving a viewport's view:

- Move the view up: Increase the view's Y coordinate.
- Move the view down: Decrease the view's Y coordinate.
- Move the view left: Increase the view's X coordinate.
- Move the view right: Decrease the view's X coordinate.

Dragging a Viewport's View

Using the `JViewport` methods `setViewPosition` and `getViewPosition`, it is a simple matter to implement a listener that can be attached to a viewport that allows the viewport's view to be dragged. The applet shown in Figure 13-2 implements such a listener.

Figure 13-2 Dragging an Image in a Viewport

The left-hand picture shown in Figure 13-2 shows the applet as it appears initially. The right-hand picture shows the applet after the viewport's view has been dragged.

The applet implements a listener that extends the `java.awt.event.MouseAdapter` class and implements the `java.awt.event.MouseMotionListener` interface. The `mousePressed` method of the listener records the location of the mouse pressed event, and the `mouseDragged` method calculates an offset between the location of the mouse dragged event and the position of the previous mouse event. The offset is subtracted from the current view position, and the result is used to reset the position of the viewport's view.

```
class ViewportDragListener extends MouseAdapter
                           implements MouseMotionListener {
    private JViewport viewport;
    private Point last = new Point(), scrollTo = new Point();

    public ViewportDragListener(JViewport viewport) {
        this.viewport = viewport;
    }
    public void mousePressed(MouseEvent e) {
        last.x = e.getPoint().x;
        last.y = e.getPoint().y;
    }
    public void mouseMoved(MouseEvent e) {
        // must be implemented for ViewportDragListener
        // to implement the MouseMotionListener interface
    }
    public void mouseDragged(MouseEvent e) {
        Point drag = e.getPoint();
        Point viewPos = viewport.getViewPosition();
        Point offset = new Point(drag.x-last.x, drag.y-last.y);
        last.x = drag.x;
        last.y = drag.y;

        if(viewport.contains(drag)) {
            scrollTo.x = viewPos.x - offset.x;
            scrollTo.y = viewPos.y - offset.y;
            viewport.setViewPosition(scrollTo);
        }
    }
}
```

The applet shown in Figure 13-2 is listed in its entirety in Example 13-2.

Example 13-2 Dragging a Viewport's View

```
import java.awt.*;
import java.awt.event.*;
import javax.swing.*;

public class Test extends JApplet {
    public void init() {
        Container contentPane = getContentPane();
        JLabel label = new JLabel(new ImageIcon("pic.gif"));
        JViewport vp = new JViewport();
        ViewportDragListener listener =
                    new ViewportDragListener(vp);

        vp.setView(label);
        vp.addMouseListener(listener);
        vp.addMouseMotionListener(listener);
```

```
            contentPane.add(vp, BorderLayout.CENTER);
        }
    }
    class ViewportDragListener extends MouseAdapter
                            implements MouseMotionListener {
        private JViewport viewport;
        private Point last = new Point(), scrollTo = new Point();

        public ViewportDragListener(JViewport viewport) {
            this.viewport = viewport;
        }
        public void mousePressed(MouseEvent e) {
            last.x = e.getPoint().x;
            last.y = e.getPoint().y;
        }
        public void mouseMoved(MouseEvent e) {
            // must be implemented for ViewportDragListener
            // to implement the MouseMotionListener interface
        }
        public void mouseDragged(MouseEvent e) {
            Point drag = e.getPoint();
            Point viewPos = viewport.getViewPosition();
            Point offset = new Point(drag.x-last.x, drag.y-last.y);
            last.x = drag.x;
            last.y = drag.y;

            if(viewport.contains(drag)) {
                scrollTo.x = viewPos.x - offset.x;
                scrollTo.y = viewPos.y - offset.y;
                viewport.setViewPosition(scrollTo);
            }
        }
    }
}
```

Using the scrollRectToVisible Method

The JViewport class overrides the scrollRectToVisible method from the JComponent class to scroll the view so that the rectangle passed to the method is made visible. However, JViewport.scrollRectToVisible is rarely invoked directly; instead, scrollRectToVisible is typically invoked for a viewport's view.

The applet shown in Figure 13-3 creates an array of 18 buttons that are contained in a panel specified as the center component in the applet's content pane. A panel containing a combo box is specified as the north component in the content pane. Selecting a button from the combo box results in the selected button being

scrolled into view. The left-hand picture in Figure 13-3 shows the applet as it appears initially. The right-hand picture shows the applet after button number 15 has been selected from the combo box.

The buttons are laid out by an instance of GridLayout in three columns, and the size of the applet is purposely set so that only two of the columns are visible at any given time.

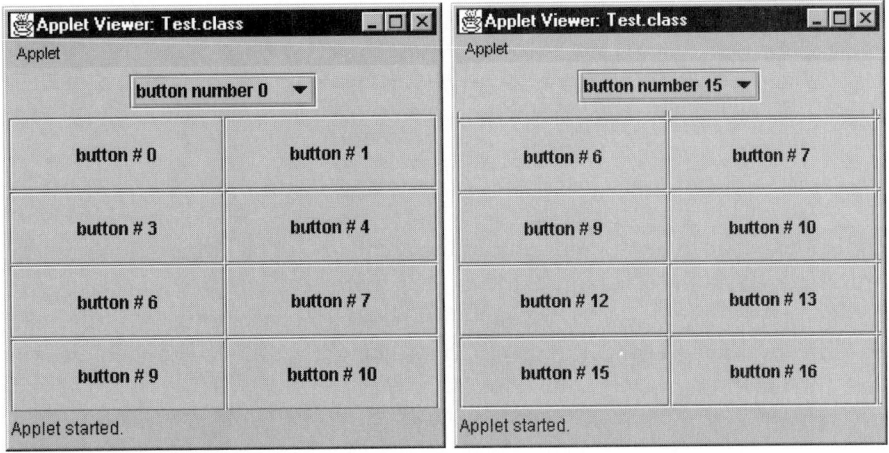

Figure 13-3 Invoking scrollRectToVisible for a Viewport's View

The applet creates an instance of JViewport and the viewport's view, which is an instance of JPanel. The layout manager for the view is set to an instance of GridLayout that is constructed so that it lays out the buttons in three columns. The buttons are initialized and added to the view, and the view is specified as the viewport's view by invocation of JViewport.setView(). The applet also creates an instance of ControlPanel—an extension of JPanel—that contains the combo box. Finally, the control panel and viewport are added to the applet's content pane.

```
public class Test extends JApplet {
    private JButton buttons[] = {
        . . .
    };
    public void init() {
        Container contentPane = getContentPane();
        JViewport viewport = new JViewport();
```

```
JPanel view = new JPanel();
JPanel controlPanel = new ControlPanel(buttons);

view.setLayout(new GridLayout(0,3));

for(int i=0; i < buttons.length; ++i) {
    buttons[i].setText("button # " + i);
    buttons[i].setPreferredSize(new Dimension(150,50));
    view.add(buttons[i]);
}

viewport.setView(view);

contentPane.add(controlPanel, BorderLayout.NORTH);
contentPane.add(viewport, BorderLayout.CENTER);
    }
}
```

The control panel adds an item listener to the combo box that obtains a reference
to a button based on the selection made in the combo box.
scrollRectToVisible is then invoked for the button, specifying the upper-left
corner of the button and the button's width and height for the rectangle to be
scrolled into view.

```
class ControlPanel extends JPanel {
    private JComboBox combo = new JComboBox();

    public ControlPanel(final JButton[] buttons) {
        add(combo);

        for(int i=0; i < buttons.length; ++i) {
            combo.addItem("button number " + i);
        }
        combo.addItemListener(new ItemListener() {
            public void itemStateChanged(ItemEvent e) {
                int index = combo.getSelectedIndex();
                JButton button = buttons[index];
                Dimension size = button.getSize();

                buttons[index].scrollRectToVisible(
                    new Rectangle(0,0,size.width,size.height));
            }
        });
    }
}
```

When `scrollRectToVisible` is called for a button,
`JComponent.scrollRectToVisible` is invoked because the `JButton` class
does not override `scrollRectToVisible`. The `JComponent` implementation
of `scrollRectToVisible` traverses the containers contained in a component's
containment hierarchy and invokes `scrollRectToVisible` for each container.
If the containers have not overridden `scrollRectToVisible`, the coordinate of
the upper-left corner is translated into the container's coordinate system, and the
request is then forwarded to the next container.

`JViewport.scrollRectToVisible` is overridden to scroll the rectangle it is
passed into view. As a result, when `scrollRectToVisible` is invoked for one
of the buttons in the applet shown in Figure 13-3, `scrollRectToVisible` is
invoked for each container in the button's containment hierarchy until the
instance of `JViewport` is found, and the viewport scrolls the button into view.

The applet shown in Figure 13-3 is listed in its entirety in Figure 13-3.

Example 13-3 Using scrollRectToVisible()

```
import java.awt.*;
import java.awt.event.*;
import javax.swing.*;
import javax.swing.event.*;

public class Test extends JApplet {
    private JButton buttons[] = {
        new JButton(), new JButton(), new JButton(),
        new JButton(), new JButton(), new JButton(),
        new JButton(), new JButton(), new JButton(),
        new JButton(), new JButton(), new JButton(),
        new JButton(), new JButton(), new JButton(),
        new JButton(), new JButton(), new JButton(),
    };
    public void init() {
        Container contentPane = getContentPane();
        JViewport viewport = new JViewport();
        JPanel view = new JPanel();
        JPanel controlPanel = new ControlPanel(buttons);

        view.setLayout(new GridLayout(0,3));

        for(int i=0; i < buttons.length; ++i) {
            buttons[i].setText("button # " + i);
            buttons[i].setPreferredSize(new Dimension(150,50));
            view.add(buttons[i]);
        }

        viewport.setView(view);
```

```
            contentPane.add(controlPanel, BorderLayout.NORTH);
            contentPane.add(viewport, BorderLayout.CENTER);
        }
    }
    class ControlPanel extends JPanel {
        private JComboBox combo = new JComboBox();

        public ControlPanel(final JButton[] buttons) {
            add(combo);

            for(int i=0; i < buttons.length; ++i) {
                combo.addItem("button number " + i);
            }
            combo.addItemListener(new ItemListener() {
                public void itemStateChanged(ItemEvent e) {
                    int index = combo.getSelectedIndex();
                    JButton button = buttons[index];
                    Dimension size = button.getSize();

                    buttons[index].scrollRectToVisible(
                        new Rectangle(0,0, size.width,size.height));
                }
            });
        }
    }
```

Swing Tip ...

Swing Components and the scrollRectToVisible Method

The scrollRectToVisible method is defined in the JComponent class and therefore can be invoked for any Swing lightweight component. When scrollRectToVisible() is invoked for a lightweight Swing component contained in a viewport or text field, the specified rectangle relative to the component is scrolled into view.

It is important to remember that the rectangle passed to scrollRectToVisible() is relative to the component, and not the component's container. For example, to scroll the entire bounds of a component into view, scrollRectToVisible() would be invoked as follows:

```
Dimension size = aComponent.getSize();
aComponent.scrollRectToVisible(0, 0, size.width, size.height);
```

The JViewport component is summarized in Component Summary 13-1.

Component Summary 13-1   JViewport

Model(s) ——

UI Delegate(s) ——

Renderer(s) ——

Editor(s) ——

Events Fired   ChangeEvents

Replacement For ——

Class Diagrams

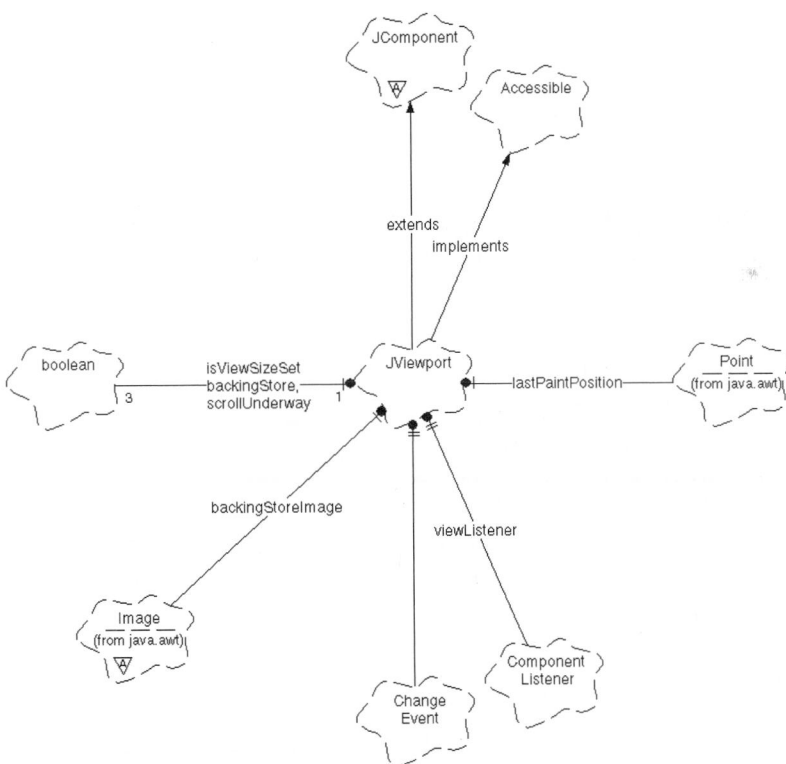

Figure 13-4 JViewport Class Diagram

The `JViewport` class extends `JComponent` and implements the `Accessible` interface. `JViewport`, like most lightweight Swing containers, does not have a model or a UI delegate.

Instances of `JViewport` maintain a `protected` reference to a point representing the position of the view the last time the viewport was painted.

A `protected` reference is also maintained to an instance of `java.awt.Image` which is used as an offscreen buffer for the view, in addition to a `boolean` reference that tracks whether the offscreen buffer is actually used to paint the view.

The `protected isViewSizeSet boolean` reference tracks whether the view's size has been set. `JViewport.getViewSize` returns the actual size of its view if the view's size has been set; otherwise, it returns the preferred size of the view. If the viewport's view has not been set, `JViewport.getViewSize` returns a dimension of (0,0).

The `scrollUnderway boolean` member is used to ensure that autoscrolling—see "Autoscrolling" on page 165—works properly for instances of `JViewport`.

A `private` reference to an instance of `ComponentListener` is used to fire change events when the size of the viewport's view changes. A single instance of `ChangeEvent` is used to broadcast change events to listeners.

JViewport Properties

The properties maintained by the `JViewport` class are listed in Table 13-1.

Table 13-1   JViewport Properties

Property Name	Data Type	Property Type[1]	Access[2]	Default[3]
backingStoreEnabled	boolean	S	SG	false
extentSize	Dimension	Ch	SG	——
view	Component	S	SG	——
viewPosition	Point	Ch	SG	——
viewRect	Rectangle	——	G	——
viewSize	Dimension	Ch	SG	——

1. B = bound (fires PropertyChangeEvent) / C = constrained/ I = indexed / S = simple / Ch = fires ChangeEvent
2. C = settable at construction time / G = getter method / S = setter method
3. L&F = look-and-feel dependent

backingStoreEnabled — If true, an offscreen buffer is used to paint the view when its position relative to the viewport is changed in small increments in one direction.

extentSize — An instance of Dimension representing the visible part of the view.

view — The component displayed in the viewport.

viewPosition — A point representing the view coordinates that appear in the upper-left corner of the viewport.

viewRect — An instance of Rectangle representing the size and position of the visible portion of the view. The width and height of the rectangle is the same as the extent size.

viewSize — An instance of Dimension representing the size of the view. If the view's size has not been explicitly set, the viewSize defaults to the view's preferred size. If there is no view, the view size is (0,0).

JViewport Events

Instances of JViewport fire change events when their view's position, size, and extent size properties are modified. The applet shown in Figure 13-5 is nearly identical to the one shown in Figure 13-1 on page 718, except that it displays the extent, size, and position of the viewport's view.

The applet specifies an instance of StatusPanel as the south component for its content pane. The StatusPanel class is an extension of JPanel containing three labels that are laid out by an instance of BoxLayout along the Y axis. The labels are centered because their X alignments are set to 0.5—see "BoxLayout" on page 273 for more on the alignments of components laid out by instances of BoxLayout.

Figure 13-5 Responding to JViewport Change Events

The applet adds an instance of `ChangeListener` to the viewport to update the labels contained in the `StatusPanel`; then, because the labels may change size when the properties they represent are modified, the applet invokes `revalidate()` to ensure that the labels are laid out and repainted. See "Validate, Invalidate, and Revalidate Methods" on page 144 for more information about the `revalidate` method.

```
class StatusPanel extends JPanel {
    private JLabel extentLabel = new JLabel(),
                   viewPositionLabel = new JLabel(),
                   viewSizeLabel = new JLabel();
    private JViewport viewport;

    public StatusPanel(JViewport vp) {
        viewport = vp;

        setBorder(BorderFactory.createEtchedBorder());
        setLayout(new BoxLayout(this, BoxLayout.Y_AXIS));

        extentLabel.setAlignmentX(0.5f);
        viewPositionLabel.setAlignmentX(0.5f);
        viewSizeLabel.setAlignmentX(0.5f);

        add(extentLabel);
        add(viewPositionLabel);
```

```
        add(viewSizeLabel);

        viewport.addChangeListener(new ChangeListener() {
            public void stateChanged(ChangeEvent e) {
                Dimension extent = viewport.getExtentSize();
                Point viewPosition = viewport.getViewPosition();
                Rectangle viewSize = viewport.getViewRect();

                extentLabel.setText("View Extent: " +
                                    extent.toString());
                viewPositionLabel.setText("View Position: " +
                                    viewPosition.toString());
                viewSizeLabel.setText("View Size: " +
                                    viewSize.toString());
                revalidate();
            }
        });
    }
}
```

The applet shown in Figure 13-5 is listed in its entirety in Example 13-4.

Example 13-4 Responding to JViewport Change Events

```
import java.awt.*;
import java.awt.event.*;
import javax.swing.*;
import javax.swing.event.*;

public class Test extends JApplet {
    public void init() {
        Container contentPane = getContentPane();
        JViewport viewport = new JViewport();
        JPanel view = new JPanel();

        view.add(new JLabel(
                new ImageIcon("anjinAndMariko.gif")));

        viewport.setView(view);

        contentPane.add(new ControlPanel(viewport),
                    BorderLayout.NORTH);
        contentPane.add(viewport, BorderLayout.CENTER);
        contentPane.add(new StatusPanel(viewport),
                    BorderLayout.SOUTH);
    }
}
class StatusPanel extends JPanel {
    private JLabel extentLabel = new JLabel(),
                viewPositionLabel = new JLabel(),
                viewSizeLabel = new JLabel();
```

```
        private JViewport viewport;

        public StatusPanel(JViewport vp) {
            viewport = vp;

            setBorder(BorderFactory.createEtchedBorder());
            setLayout(new BoxLayout(this, BoxLayout.Y_AXIS));

            extentLabel.setAlignmentX(0.5f);
            viewPositionLabel.setAlignmentX(0.5f);
            viewSizeLabel.setAlignmentX(0.5f);

            add(extentLabel);
            add(viewPositionLabel);
            add(viewSizeLabel);

            viewport.addChangeListener(new ChangeListener() {
                public void stateChanged(ChangeEvent e) {
                    Dimension extent = viewport.getExtentSize();
                    Point viewPosition = viewport.getViewPosition();
                    Rectangle viewSize = viewport.getViewRect();

                    extentLabel.setText("View Extent: " +
                                        extent.toString());
                    viewPositionLabel.setText("View Position: " +
                                        viewPosition.toString());
                    viewSizeLabel.setText("View Size: " +
                                        viewSize.toString());
                    invalidate();
                    validate();
                }
            });
        }
    }
    class ControlPanel extends JPanel {
        private JViewport viewport;

        private JButton[] buttons = {
            new JButton("up"), new JButton("down"),
            new JButton("left"), new JButton("right"),
        };

        public ControlPanel(JViewport vp) {
            viewport = vp;

            for(int i=0; i < buttons.length; ++i) {
                add(buttons[i]);

                buttons[i].addActionListener(new ActionListener() {
                    public void actionPerformed(ActionEvent e) {
                        scroll(e.getActionCommand());
                    }
```

```
        });
    }
}
private void scroll(String actionCmd) {
    Point vp = viewport.getViewPosition();

    if(actionCmd.equals("up")) vp.y += 5;
    else if(actionCmd.equals("down")) vp.y -= 5;
    else if(actionCmd.equals("left")) vp.x += 5;
    else if(actionCmd.equals("right")) vp.x -= 5;

    viewport.setViewPosition(vp);
}
}
```

JViewport Class Summaries

The `public` and `protected` variables and methods for `JViewport` are listed in Class Summary 13-1.

Class Summary 13-1   JViewport

Extends: JComponent
Implements: Javax.accessibility.Accessible

Constructors

---

public <u>JViewport</u>()

`JViewport` provides a single no-argument constructor, which means that a viewport's view can be specified only after the viewport is constructed.

Methods

Change Events

---

public void <u>addChangeListener</u>(ChangeListener)
protected void <u>fireStateChanged</u>()
public void <u>removeChangeListener</u>(ChangeListener)

JViewport fires change events when its bound properties are modified. Change listeners are added to instances of JViewport with the addChangeListener method and removed with the removeChangeListener method. The protected fireStateChanged method is used to fire change events to registered change listeners. Extensions of JViewport can override the fireStateChanged method to modify the manner in which change listeners are notified of property changes, but in practice the method will rarely be overridden.

Protected Utility Methods

---

protected void <u>addImpl</u>(Component, Object, int)
protected boolean <u>computeBlit</u>(int dx, int dy, Point blitFrom,
                          Point blitTo, Dimension blitSize, Rectangle blitPaint)
protected LayoutManager <u>createLayoutManager</u>()
protected JViewport.ViewListener <u>createViewListener</u>()

JViewport is a lightweight Swing component that always contains a single component, namely, its view. As a result, the JViewport class overrides the addImpl method (from the java.awt.Container class), which removes the current view and replaces it with the specified component. Because JViewport overrides addImpl(), a viewport's view can be specified by invocation of JViewport.setView or JViewport.add(aComponent).

computeBlit() computes the parameters required for copying (a.k.a. blitting) the image of the view from the offscreen buffer to its onscreen representation. Extensions of JViewport should rarely, if ever, have reason to override or invoke this method.

The createLayoutManager method creates an instance of
swing.ViewportLayout that is used as the default layout manager for
instances of JViewport. ViewportLayout takes into account whether the
viewport's view implements the Scrollable interface and sizes the view
accordingly. See Interface Summary 13-2 on page 764 for more information about
the Scrollable interface.

The createViewListener method creates an instance of
JViewport.ViewListener that is added to the viewport's view. The
ViewListener class extends the java.awt.event.ComponentAdapter class
and fires a state change event when the viewport's view is resized. Extensions of
JViewport can override the createViewListener method to modify this
simple behavior, if desired.

When a component is added to an instance of JViewport—meaning its view is
set—a component listener, in the form of an instance of
JViewport.ViewListener, is added to the view in order to fire state change
events when the view is resized. As a result, the remove method is overridden to
remove the listener from the view.

Property Accessors

public Dimension getExtentSize()
public final Insets getInsets()
public Component getView()
public Point getViewPosition()
public Rectangle getViewRect()
public Dimension getViewSize()

public void setBackingStoreEnabled(boolean)
public final void setBorder(Border)
public void setExtentSize(Dimension)
public void setView(Component)
public void setViewPosition(Point)
public void setViewSize(Dimension)

public boolean isBackingStoreEnabled()
public boolean isOptimizedDrawingEnabled()

The methods listed above are accessors for the JViewport properties listed in
Table 13-1 on page 730.

JViewport is the only Swing component that disallows the setting of a border. It is thought that allowing a border to be set for instances of JViewport would make the geometry of the viewport too complex and, as a result, would make subclassing JViewport difficult. To ensure that borders cannot be set for viewports, the JViewport class overrides two methods from the JComponent class as final[1]—setBorder() and getInsets(). The setBorder method throws an exception indicating that borders cannot be set for viewports, and the getInsets method is overridden to return an insets of (0,0,0,0). If a border is desired for an instance of JViewport, the viewport can be placed in a panel and the panel equipped with a border.

The setBackingStore method controls whether instances of JViewport use an offscreen buffer to paint their views. Use of an offscreen buffer can significantly improve performance when the view is scrolled in one direction in small increments. The isBackingStoreEnabled method returns a boolean value indicating whether the backing store is currently enabled.

Painting / Removing / Reshaping

---

public void <u>paint</u>(Graphics)
public void <u>repaint</u>(long time, int x, int y, int w, int h)
public void <u>reshape</u>(int x, int y, int w, int h)

Because JViewport uses an offscreen buffer when its backingStoreEnabled property is set to true, JViewport overrides the paint method to use an offscreen buffer when appropriate. JViewport also overrides repaint() to repaint in a more efficient manner. The reshape method is overridden to fire a state change event if the width or height is changed.

View Coordinates / Scrolling

---

public void <u>scrollRectToVisible</u>(Rectangle)
public Dimension <u>toViewCoordinates</u>(Dimension)
public Point <u>toViewCoordinates</u>(Point)

---

1.   Final methods cannot be overridden by subclasses.

The scrollRectToVisible method scrolls the specified rectangle within the viewport's view so that the rectangle is contained within the viewport. See "Using the scrollRectToVisible Method" on page 724 for an example of using scrollRectToVisible().

The toViewCoordinate methods can be used to return a point or dimension for extensions of JViewport that support logical (as opposed to pixel) scrolling. The JViewport implementation of the methods simply returns a point or dimension that is identical to the point or dimension they were passed.

Accessibility and Pluggable Look and Feel

---

public AccessibleContext getAccessibleContext()
public String paramString()

The getAccessibleContext method is defined in the Accessible interface and returns an instance of AccessibleContext. Instances of AccessibleContext provide accessibility information about a component.

The paramString method returns a string representation of the component.

AWT Compatibility

The AWT does not provide a component analogous to JViewport.

JScrollPane

The JScrollPane class is a lightweight Swing container that contains a viewport with optional scrollbars and row/column headers. Scrollpane components are illustrated in Figure 13-6.

The scrollbars are used to scroll the viewport's view and the row/column headers. Scrollbar display policy can be set individually for each scrollbar—see "JScrollPane Properties" on page 754 for a list of JScrollPane properties.

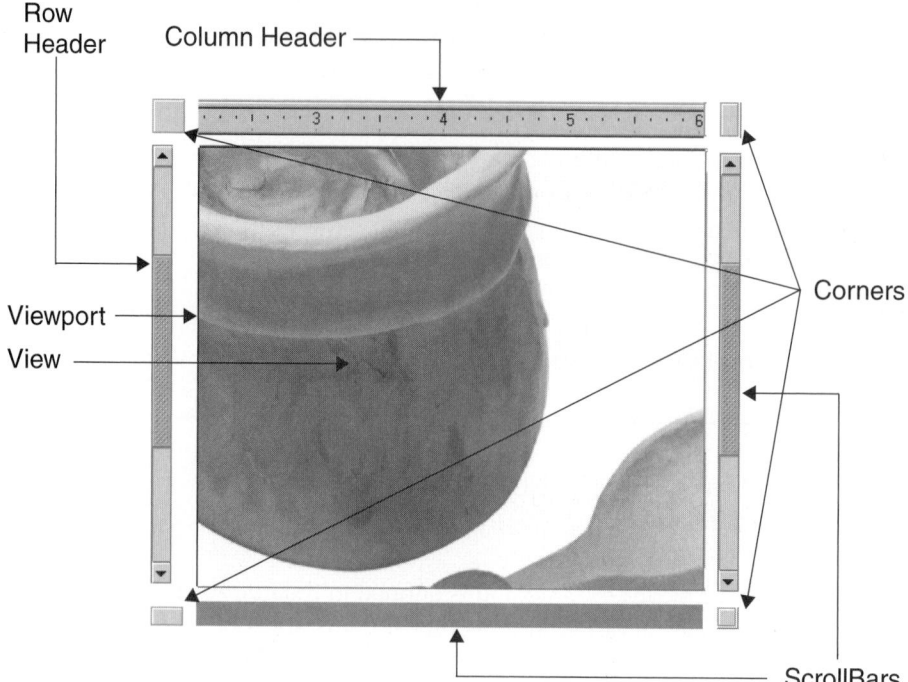

Figure 13-6 JScrollPane Components

The row header scrolls vertically to track the scrolling of the viewport in the vertical direction. Likewise, the column header scrolls horizontally to track the scrolling of the viewport in the horizontal direction. Headers are useful in a number of situations, from cell indicators for spreadsheets to rulers for text editors.

By default, the corners—meaning the empty space between headers and scrollbars—contain an instance of JPanel whose background color is the same as the background color of the scrollpane. Components can be specified to replace the default corner panels.

The viewport displayed in a scrollpane can be specified at construction time or with the JScrollPane.setViewport method, and a border can be placed around the scrollpane's viewport with the JScrollPane.setViewportBorder method.

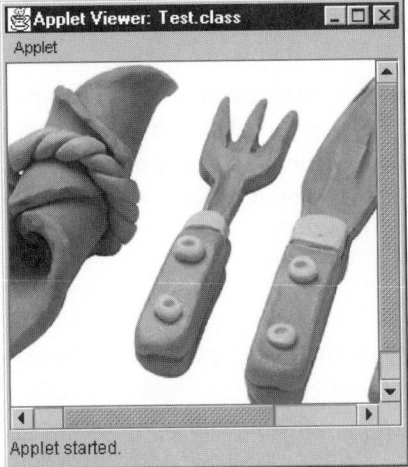

Figure 13-7 Using JScrollPane

The scrollpane in the applet shown in Figure 13-7 contains a label with an icon that is larger than the extent of the scrollpane's viewport.

The applet shown in Figure 13-7 is listed in Example 13-5.

Example 13-5 Using JScrollPane

```java
import java.awt.*;
import java.awt.event.*;
import javax.swing.*;
import javax.swing.event.*;

public class Test extends JApplet {
    public Test() {
        Container contentPane = getContentPane();
        JLabel view = new JLabel(new ImageIcon("cutlery.jpg",
                                 "A picture of cutlery"));
        JScrollPane sp = new JScrollPane(view);

        contentPane.add(sp);
    }
}
```

The applet creates instances of JLabel and JScrollPane. The label is passed to the JScrollPane constructor, signifying that it will be used as the view for the scrollpane's viewport. The scrollpane is then added to the applet's content pane.

Scrollpane Headers

A scrollpane's optional row and column header components are both instances of JViewport, and the default header viewports provided by the JScrollPane class can be replaced with custom versions. Additionally, the components (a.k.a. views) displayed in the row and column header viewports are settable.

Header Views

The views displayed in the row and column headers are specified by the JScrollPane methods setRowHeaderView() and setColumnHeaderView(), respectively. Any type of component can be specified as a view for a scrollpane's row or column header, but the most common are instances of JLabel that are fitted with an image icon.

The applet shown in Figure 13-8 demonstrates setting a scrollpane's row and column header views. The applet's scrollpane has header views that are labels containing icons with images of a ruler.

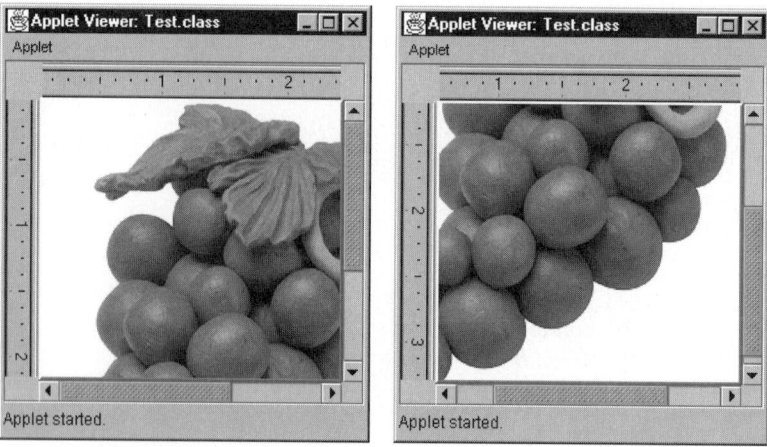

Figure 13-8 JScrollPane Header Views

The applet shown in Figure 13-8 is listed in Example 13-6.

Example 13-6 Specifying Views for JScrollPane Headers

```java
import java.awt.*;
import javax.swing.*;

public class Test extends JApplet {
    public Test() {
        Container contentPane = getContentPane();
        JLabel columnHeaderView = new JLabel(
                      new ImageIcon("horizontalRuler.jpg",
                                    "horizontal ruler"));
        JLabel rowHeaderView = new JLabel(
                      new ImageIcon("verticalRuler.jpg",
                                    "vertical ruler"));
        JLabel view = new JLabel(
                      new ImageIcon("grapes.jpg",
                                    "grapes"));

        JScrollPane sp = new JScrollPane(view);

        sp.setColumnHeaderView(columnHeaderView);
        sp.setRowHeaderView(rowHeaderView);

        sp.setViewportBorder(
                  BorderFactory.createRaisedBevelBorder());

        contentPane.add(sp);
    }
}
```

The applet creates two instances of JLabel, with images representing horizontal and vertical rulers. The labels are specified as row and column header views by invocation of JScrollPane.setRowHeaderView() and JScrollPane.setColumnHeaderView(), respectively.

The applet also specifies a raised bevel border as the viewport's border. Recall from Class Summary 13-1 on page 735 that borders cannot be specified directly for Swing viewports, but the JScrollPane class provides a setViewportBorder method that wraps a border around the viewport.

Notice that row and column header viewports are not visible unless views are specified for them. This is evident from the difference between the applet shown in Figure 13-7 on page 741 and the applet shown in Figure 13-8.

Header Viewports

In addition to providing accessor methods for the row and column header views, the JScrollPane class also provides accessors for the viewports themselves. The viewports can be set by the JScrollPane.setRowHeader and JScrollPane.setColumnHeader methods, and references to the viewports can be obtained by invoking the JScrollPane.getRowHeader and JScrollPane.getColumnHeader methods.

The applet shown in Figure 13-9 contains a scrollpane that users can scroll by dragging its headers. The left-hand picture shows the applet in its initial state with the cursor in position to drag the column header. The right-hand picture shows the applet after the column header—and the viewport's view—have been dragged from left to right. The applet implements dragging of the headers by creating custom row and column header viewports and adding a custom listener to them.

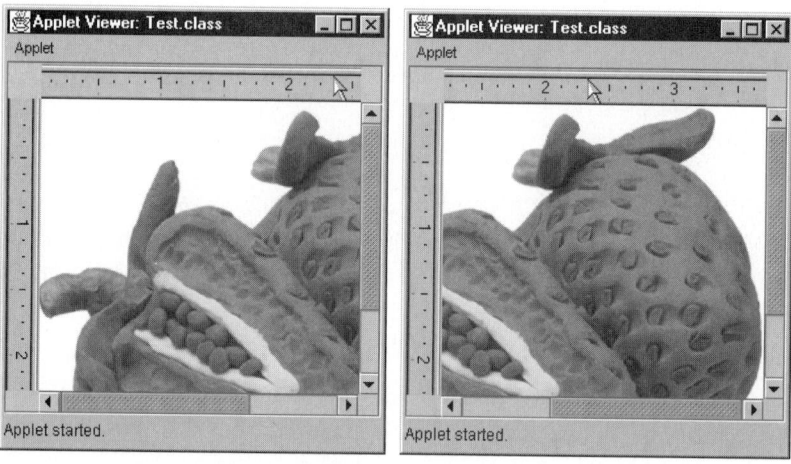

Figure 13-9 JScrollPane Header Viewports

The applet creates an instance of JScrollPane, two instances of JLabel, and two instances of JViewport. The viewports are specified as the scrollpane's row and column headers, and the labels are designated as the viewport's views.

```
public class Test extends JApplet {
    public void init() {
        Container contentPane = getContentPane();
        JViewport columnHeaderViewport = new JViewport();
        JViewport rowHeaderViewport = new JViewport();

        JLabel columnHeaderView = new JLabel(
                        new ImageIcon("horizontalRuler.jpg"));
        JLabel rowHeaderView = new JLabel(
                        new ImageIcon("verticalRuler.jpg"));

        ...


        // headers must be set before header views

        sp.setColumnHeader(columnHeaderViewport);
        sp.setRowHeader(rowHeaderViewport);

        sp.setColumnHeaderView(columnHeaderView);
        sp.setRowHeaderView(rowHeaderView);
        ...
```

Notice that the header viewports must be specified before their views. If the views are specified before the viewports, the views will be attached to the default viewports created by the scrollpane. Subsequently, when the custom viewports replace the scrollpane's default viewports, they will not be associated with the views.

The applet also creates two instances of HeaderViewDragListener that are added to the viewports as mouse and mouse motion listeners.

```
        ...
        HeaderViewDragListener verticalHeaderListener =
                new HeaderViewDragListener(sp,
                        SwingConstants.VERTICAL);

        HeaderViewDragListener horizontalHeaderListener =
                new HeaderViewDragListener(sp,
                        SwingConstants.HORIZONTAL);

        columnHeaderViewport.addMouseListener(
                                horizontalHeaderListener);
        columnHeaderViewport.addMouseMotionListener(
                                horizontalHeaderListener);

        rowHeaderViewport.addMouseListener(
                                verticalHeaderListener);
        rowHeaderViewport.addMouseMotionListener(
                                verticalHeaderListener);
        ...
```

The HeaderViewDragListener class extends the
java.awt.event.MouseAdapter class and implements the
java.awt.event.MouseMotionListener and SwingConstants interfaces.

Instances of HeaderViewDragListener are constructed with a reference to a
scrollpane and the orientation of the header viewport with which the instances
are associated. When a mouse pressed event occurs in the header viewport, the
location of the mouse press is recorded.

```
class HeaderViewDragListener extends MouseAdapter
                         implements MouseMotionListener,
                                  SwingConstants {
    private Point last = new Point();
    private JScrollPane scrollpane;
    private int orientation;

    public HeaderViewDragListener(JScrollPane sp, int orient) {
        scrollpane = sp;
        orientation = orient;
    }
    public void mousePressed(MouseEvent e) {
        last.x = e.getPoint().x;
        last.y = e.getPoint().y;
    }
    public void mouseMoved(MouseEvent e) {
    }
    ...
```

When the mouse is dragged in a header viewport, a reference to the header
viewport in which the event occurred is obtained by invocation of
java.Util.EventObject.getSource(). The main viewport associated with
the scrollpane is obtained by invocation of JScrollPane.getViewport().
Subsequently, the size and extent of the main viewport are obtained by invocation
of the JViewport getViewSize and getExtentSize methods.

The location of the drag event is obtained by invocation of
MouseEvent.getPoint(), and an offset from the current drag location and the
location of the last mouse event is calculated. The current position of the main
viewport's view is then obtained by invocation of
JViewport.getViewPosition().

```
    ...
    public void mouseDragged(MouseEvent e) {
        JViewport headerViewport = (JViewport)e.getSource();
        JViewport scrollpaneViewport = scrollpane.getViewport();
```

```
      Dimension viewSize = scrollpaneViewport.getViewSize(),
               extent = scrollpaneViewport.getExtentSize();

      Point drag = e.getPoint();
      Point offset = new Point(drag.x-last.x, drag.y-last.y);
      Point headerPosition = new Point(), viewportPosition;

      viewportPosition = scrollpaneViewport.getViewPosition();
      ...
```

The next drag location is calculated by subtracting the offset between the current drag location and the last mouse event from the current position of the main viewport. If the next drag location lies within the bounds of the main viewport, positions for both the header viewport and the main viewport are updated.

```
      ...
      if(orientation == HORIZONTAL) {
          int nextX = viewportPosition.x - offset.x;
          int rightEdge = extent.width + nextX;

          if(nextX > 0 && rightEdge < viewSize.width) {
              headerPosition.x = nextX;
              viewportPosition.x = nextX;
          }
      }
      if(orientation == VERTICAL)  {
          int nextY = viewportPosition.y - offset.y;
          int bottomEdge = extent.height + nextY;

          if(nextY > 0 && bottomEdge < viewSize.height) {
              headerPosition.y = nextY;
              viewportPosition.y = nextY;
          }
      }
      headerViewport.setViewPosition(headerPosition);
      scrollpaneViewport.setViewPosition(viewportPosition);

      last.x = drag.x;
      last.y = drag.y;
   }
}
```

The applet shown in Figure 13-9 is listed in its entirety in Figure 13-7.

Example 13-7   Setting Header Viewports

```java
import java.awt.*;
import java.awt.event.*;
import javax.swing.*;

public class Test extends JApplet {
    public void init() {
        Container contentPane = getContentPane();
        JViewport columnHeaderViewport = new JViewport();
        JViewport rowHeaderViewport = new JViewport();

        JLabel columnHeaderView = new JLabel(
                    new ImageIcon("horizontalRuler.jpg"));
        JLabel rowHeaderView = new JLabel(
                    new ImageIcon("verticalRuler.jpg"));
        JLabel view = new JLabel(
                    new ImageIcon("strawberry.jpg"));

        JScrollPane sp = new JScrollPane(view);

        sp.setToolTipText(
                "Drag the headers to drag the picture!");

        HeaderViewDragListener verticalHeaderListener =
                new HeaderViewDragListener(sp,
                        SwingConstants.VERTICAL);

        HeaderViewDragListener horizontalHeaderListener =
                new HeaderViewDragListener(sp,
                        SwingConstants.HORIZONTAL);

        columnHeaderViewport.addMouseListener(
                                horizontalHeaderListener);
        columnHeaderViewport.addMouseMotionListener(
                                horizontalHeaderListener);

        rowHeaderViewport.addMouseListener(
                                verticalHeaderListener);
        rowHeaderViewport.addMouseMotionListener(
                                verticalHeaderListener);

        // headers must be set before header views
        sp.setColumnHeader(columnHeaderViewport);
        sp.setRowHeader(rowHeaderViewport);

        sp.setColumnHeaderView(columnHeaderView);
        sp.setRowHeaderView(rowHeaderView);

        contentPane.add(sp);
    }
}
```

```
class HeaderViewDragListener extends MouseAdapter
                            implements MouseMotionListener,
                                       SwingConstants {
    private Point last = new Point();
    private JScrollPane scrollpane;
    private int orientation;

    public HeaderViewDragListener(JScrollPane sp, int orient) {
        scrollpane = sp;
        orientation = orient;
    }
    public void mousePressed(MouseEvent e) {
        last.x = e.getPoint().x;
        last.y = e.getPoint().y;
    }
    public void mouseMoved(MouseEvent e) {
    }
    public void mouseDragged(MouseEvent e) {
        JViewport headerViewport = (JViewport)e.getSource();
        JViewport scrollpaneViewport = scrollpane.getViewport();
        Dimension viewSize = scrollpaneViewport.getViewSize(),
                  extent = scrollpaneViewport.getExtentSize();

        Point drag = e.getPoint();
        Point offset = new Point(drag.x-last.x, drag.y-last.y);
        Point headerPosition = new Point(), viewportPosition;

        viewportPosition = scrollpaneViewport.getViewPosition();

        if(orientation == HORIZONTAL) {
            int nextX = viewportPosition.x - offset.x;
            int rightEdge = extent.width + nextX;

            if(nextX > 0 && rightEdge < viewSize.width) {
                headerPosition.x = nextX;
                viewportPosition.x = nextX;
            }
        }
        if(orientation == VERTICAL)  {
            int nextY = viewportPosition.y - offset.y;
            int bottomEdge = extent.height + nextY;

            if(nextY > 0 && bottomEdge < viewSize.height) {
                headerPosition.y = nextY;
                viewportPosition.y = nextY;
            }
        }
        headerViewport.setViewPosition(headerPosition);
        scrollpaneViewport.setViewPosition(viewportPosition);

        last.x = drag.x;
        last.y = drag.y;
    }
}
```

Scrollpane Corners

Each instance of `JScrollPane` has four corners representing the spaces between the scrollpane's scrollbars and headers. `JScrollPane` provides a `setCorner` method to insert a component in any of the four corners. The method is passed a string representing the corner and an instance of `java.awt.Component`. The string is one of four constants defined by the `ScrollPaneConstants` interface. See "ScrollPaneConstants" on page 756 for a discussion of the `ScrollPaneConstants` interface.

By default, a scrollpane's corners are occupied by opaque instances of `JPanel` that paint their backgrounds with the color returned from `UIManager.getColor("control")`. See "UI Manager" on page 334 for more information on using `UIManager` to access default values.

The applet shown in Figure 13-10 inserts components into each corner of the scrollpane it contains.

Figure 13-10 Specifying Components for Scrollpane Corners

The applet shown in Figure 13-10 is listed in Example 13-8.

Example 13-8 Specifying Components for JScrollPane Corners

```java
import java.awt.*;
import javax.swing.*;
import javax.swing.border.*;

public class Test extends JApplet {
    public Test() {
        Container contentPane = getContentPane();
        JLabel columnHeaderView = new JLabel(
                       new ImageIcon("horizontalRuler.jpg"));
        JLabel rowHeaderView = new JLabel(
                       new ImageIcon("verticalRuler.jpg"));
        JLabel view = new JLabel(
                       new ImageIcon("anjinAndMariko.gif"));

        JScrollPane sp = new JScrollPane(view);

        JPanel corners[] = {
                new JPanel(), new JPanel(),
                new JPanel(), new JPanel()
        };
        String cornerConstants[] = {
            ScrollPaneConstants.UPPER_LEFT_CORNER,
            ScrollPaneConstants.LOWER_LEFT_CORNER,
            ScrollPaneConstants.UPPER_RIGHT_CORNER,
            ScrollPaneConstants.LOWER_RIGHT_CORNER,
        };
        Border border = BorderFactory.createEtchedBorder();

        for(int i=0; i < corners.length; ++i) {
            corners[i].setBorder(border);
            sp.setCorner(cornerConstants[i], corners[i]);
        }

        sp.setColumnHeaderView(columnHeaderView);
        sp.setRowHeaderView(rowHeaderView);
        contentPane.add(sp);
    }
}
```

The applet creates four instances of JPanel that are used as corner components. Each panel is fitted with an etched border obtained from the Swing border factory. The JScrollPane.setCorner method inserts each panel into a corner of the scrollpane contained by the applet.

Swing Tip ...

Default Components for Scrollpane Corners

It should be noted that the applet listed in Example 13-8 does not have to create instances of JPanel for the corner components because, by default, the corners are already occupied by instances of JPanel. The for loop in the applet listed in Example 13-8 could have been written like this ...

```
for(int i=0; i < corners.length; ++i) {
   JComponent panel =
              (JComponent) sp.getCorner(cornerConstants[i]);
   panel.setBorder(border);
}
```

... and the applet could dispense with creating panels altogether. However, since the JScrollPane.getCorner method returns an instance of java.awt.Component, the for loop listed above relies upon an implementation detail—namely, that the default corner components are instances of JPanel—instead of relying upon the public methods provided by the JScrollPane class. Relying upon implementation details of a class is risky business because implementation details are subject to change, whereas the API of a class is much more stable.

The JScrollPane component is summarized in Component Summary 13-2.

Component Summary 13-2   JScrollPane

Model(s)	——
UI Delegate(s)	javax.swing.plaf.basic.BasicScrollPaneUI
Renderer(s)	——
Editor(s)	——
Events Fired	PropertyChangeEvent
Replacement For	java.awt.ScrollPane

Class Diagrams

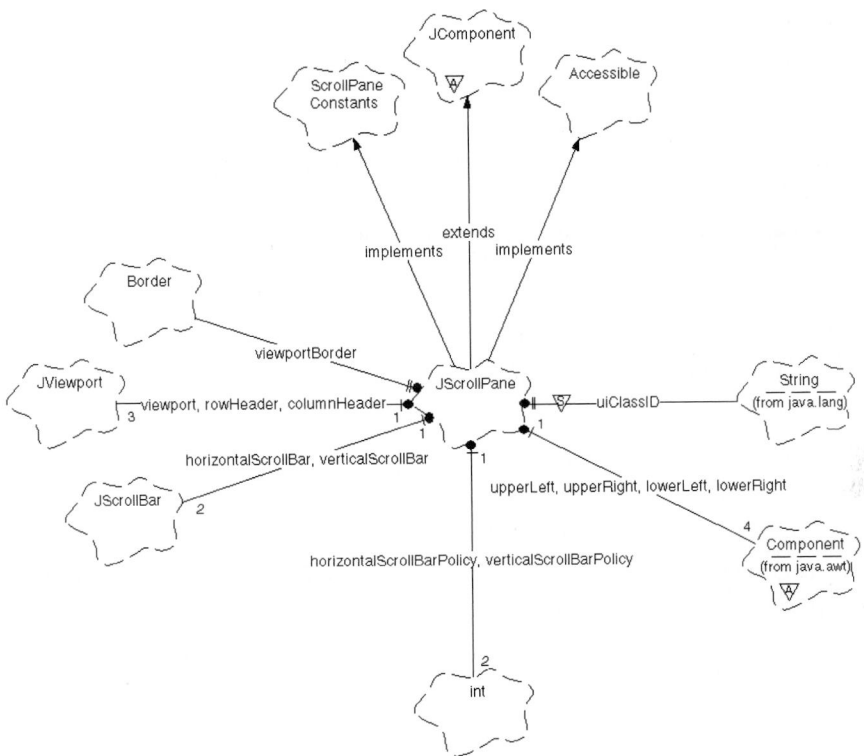

Figure 13-11 JScrollPane Class Diagram

JScrollPane extends JComponent and implements the
ScrollPaneConstants and Accessible interfaces.

Instances of JScrollPane maintain protected references to the scrollpane's
main viewport, row header viewport, and column header viewport. The
JScrollPane class also maintains protected references to the scrollpane's
horizontal and vertical scrollbars and the policies that govern their display, in
addition to the components that occupy the scrollpane's corners.

JScrollPane Properties

The properties maintained by the JScrollPane class are listed in Table 13-2.

Table 13-2   JScrollPane Properties

Property Name	Data Type	Property Type[1]	Access[2]	Default[5]
columnHeader	JViewport	B	SG	null
columnHeaderView	Component	B	S[3]	null
corner	Component	IB	SG	null
horizontalScrollbar	JScrollBar	B	SG	——
horizontalScrollbarPolicy	int	B	CSG	As needed[6]
rowHeader	JViewport	B	SG	null
rowHeaderView	Component	B	S[4]	null
verticalScrollbar	JScrollBar	B	SG	——
verticalScrollbarPolicy	int	B	CSG	As needed[7]
viewport	JViewport	B	SG	JViewport
viewportBorder	Border	B	SG	null
viewportView	Component	B	CSG	null

1. b = boolean / B = bound (fires PropertyChangeEvent) / C = constrained/ I = indexed /
   S = simple / Ch = fires ChangeEvent
2. C = settable at construction time / G = getter method / S = setter method
3. getColumnHeader.getView() returns the column header view
4. getRowHeader.getView() returns the row header view
5. L&F = look and feel dependent
6. JScrollPane.HORIZONTAL_SCROLLBAR_AS_NEEDED
7. JScrollPane.VERTICAL_SCROLLBAR_AS_NEEDED

columnHeader — An instance of JViewport for the column header.

columnHeaderView — An instance of Component used as the column header viewport's view.

corner — A component that is displayed in one of the scrollpane's corners. The corner is specified by one of the following strings:

- ScrollPaneConstants.UPPER_LEFT_CORNER
- ScrollPaneConstants.LOWER_LEFT_CORNER

- `ScrollPaneConstants.UPPER_RIGHT_CORNER`
- `ScrollPaneConstants.LOWER_RIGHT_CORNER`

horizontalScrollbar — The horizontal scrollbar used by the scrollpane. The scrollbar is an instance of `JScrollPane.ScrollBar`, an extension of `JScrollBar` that takes into account whether the view contained in the scrollpane implements the `Scrollable` interface.

horizontalScrollbarPolicy — The policy used for determining circumstances under which the horizontal scrollbar is displayed. The policy is specified as one of the following `integer` values:

- `ScrollPaneConstants.HORIZONTAL_SCROLLBAR_AS_NEEDED`
- `ScrollPaneConstants.HORIZONTAL_SCROLLBAR_NEVER`
- `ScrollPaneConstants.HORIZONTAL_SCROLLBAR_ALWAYS`

rowHeader — An instance of `JViewport` for the row header.

rowHeaderView — An instance of `Component` used as the row header viewport's view.

verticalScrollbar — The vertical scrollbar used by the scrollpane. The scrollbar is an instance of `JScrollPane.ScrollBar`, an extension of `JScrollBar` that takes into account whether the view contained in the scrollpane implements the `Scrollable` interface.

verticalScrollbarPolicy — The policy used for determining circumstances under which the vertical scrollbar is displayed. The policy is specified as one of the following `integer` values:

- `ScrollPaneConstants.VERTICAL_SCROLLBAR_AS_NEEDED`
- `ScrollPaneConstants.VERTICAL_SCROLLBAR_NEVER`
- `ScrollPaneConstants.VERTICAL_SCROLLBAR_ALWAYS`

viewport — An instance of `JViewport` for displaying the component scrolled by the scrollpane.

viewportBorder — A border for the viewport.

viewportView — The component displayed in the scrollpane's viewport.

JScrollPane Events

The JScrollPane class fires property change events when its bound properties are modified. See Table 13-2 on page 754 for a list of JScrollPane's bound properties.

JScrollPane Class Summaries

JScrollPane implements the ScrollPaneConstants interface, which defines the string and integer constants listed in Interface Summary 13-1.

Interface Summary   13-1   ScrollPaneConstants

Constants

---

public static final String <u>COLUMN_HEADER</u>
public static final String <u>HORIZONTAL_SCROLLBAR</u>
public static final int <u>HORIZONTAL_SCROLLBAR_ALWAYS</u>
public static final int <u>HORIZONTAL_SCROLLBAR_AS_NEEDED</u>
public static final int <u>HORIZONTAL_SCROLLBAR_NEVER</u>
public static final String <u>HORIZONTAL_SCROLLBAR_POLICY</u>
public static final String <u>LOWER_LEFT_CORNER</u>
public static final String <u>LOWER_RIGHT_CORNER</u>
public static final String <u>ROW_HEADER</u>
public static final String <u>UPPER_LEFT_CORNER</u>
public static final String <u>UPPER_RIGHT_CORNER</u>
public static final String <u>VERTICAL_SCROLLBAR</u>
public static final int <u>VERTICAL_SCROLLBAR_ALWAYS</u>
public static final int <u>VERTICAL_SCROLLBAR_AS_NEEDED</u>
public static final int <u>VERTICAL_SCROLLBAR_NEVER</u>
public static final String <u>VERTICAL_SCROLLBAR_POLICY</u>
public static final String <u>VIEWPORT</u>

The `ScrollPaneConstants` class defines the constants listed above for representing scrollbar display policies and the components contained in a scrollpane. Most of the constants defined by the `ScrollPaneConstants` interface are used internally by `JScrollPane`, `ScrollPaneLayout`, and the scrollpane's UI delegate. However, the constants listed below are used by developers to specify corner components in addition to horizontal and vertical scrollbar display policies.

ScrollBar Display Policies

public static final int <u>HORIZONTAL_SCROLLBAR_ALWAYS</u>
public static final int <u>HORIZONTAL_SCROLLBAR_AS_NEEDED</u>
public static final int <u>HORIZONTAL_SCROLLBAR_NEVER</u>

public static final int <u>VERTICAL_SCROLLBAR_ALWAYS</u>
public static final int <u>VERTICAL_SCROLLBAR_AS_NEEDED</u>
public static final int <u>VERTICAL_SCROLLBAR_NEVER</u>

The `integer` constants listed above specify a scrollpane's scrollbar display policy; their meaning should be self-evident. Scrollbar display policy can be specified when instances of `JScrollPane` are constructed or after construction by invocation of the `JScrollPane` methods `setHorizontalScrollBarPolicy` and `setVerticalScrollBarPolicy`, both of which must be passed one of the constants listed above.

If a scrollbar policy is not explicitly set, the defaults are `HORIZONTAL_SCROLLBAR_AS_NEEDED` for the horizontal scrollbar and `VERTICAL_SCROLLBAR_AS_NEEDED` for the vertical scrollbar.

Corner Constants

public static final String <u>LOWER_LEFT_CORNER</u>
public static final String <u>LOWER_RIGHT_CORNER</u>
public static final String <u>UPPER_LEFT_CORNER</u>
public static final String <u>UPPER_RIGHT_CORNER</u>

The string constants listed above are passed to the `JScrollPane` methods `setCorner` and `getCorner` to specify a particular corner.

The public and protected variables and methods for JScrollPane are listed in Class Summary 13-2.

Class Summary 13-2   JScrollPane

Extends: JComponent

Implements: ScrollPaneConstants, javax.accessibility.Accessible

Constructors

---

public JScrollPane()
public JScrollPane(int vsbPolicy, int hsbPolicy)
public JScrollPane(Component view)
public JScrollPane(Component view, int vsbPolicy, int hsbPolicy)

JScrollPane provides four constructors. The integer values passed to JScrollPane constructors represent the vertical and horizontal scrollbar display policies, in that order. The component passed to the constructors is used as the viewport's view, meaning it is the component that is scrolled by the scrollpane.

The no-argument constructor constructs a scrollpane with a null component for the viewport's view, and scrollbar display policies that display both the horizontal and vertical scrollbars as needed.

Methods

Creation Methods

---

public JScrollBar createHorizontalScrollBar()
public JScrollBar createVerticalScrollBar()
protected JViewport createViewport()

Like most Swing components, JScrollPane provides create... methods that create its subcomponents. Unlike most Swing components however, JScrollPane implements the methods that create its scrollbars as public instead of protected because the methods are invoked from the scrollpane's UI delegate.

The createHorizontalScrollBar and createVerticalScrollBar methods both return instances of JScrollPane.ScrollBar, which is an extension of JScrollBar that takes into account whether the scrollpane's view implements the Scrollable interface. See Interface Summary 13-2 on page 764 for more information on the Scrollable interface.

The createViewport method returns an instance of JViewport that is used as the scrollpane's default viewport.

As with all Swing components that implement create... methods, the methods can be overridden in extension classes to replace the default subcomponents with custom versions.

Property Accessors

---

public JViewport getColumnHeader()
public Component getCorner(String)
public JScrollBar getHorizontalScrollBar()
public void setHorizontalScrollBar(JScrollBar)
public int getHorizontalScrollBarPolicy()
public JViewport getRowHeader()
public JScrollBar getVerticalScrollBar()
public int getVerticalScrollBarPolicy()
public JViewport getViewport()
public Border getViewportBorder()
public void getViewportBorderBounds(Border)

public void setColumnHeader(JViewport)
public void setColumnHeaderView(Component)
public void setCorner(String, Component)
public void setHorizontalScrollBarPolicy(int)
public void setRowHeader(JViewport)
public void setRowHeaderView(Component)
public void setVerticalScrollBar(JScrollBar)
public void setVerticalScrollBarPolicy(int)

public void <u>setViewport</u>(JViewport)
public void <u>setViewportBorder</u>(Border)
public void <u>setViewportView</u>(Component)

public boolean <u>isOpaque</u>()
public boolean <u>isValidateRoot</u>()

The methods listed above are accessors for JScrollPane properties. Nearly all of the methods listed above have been used in the applets earlier in this chapter.

JScrollPane, like JRootPane and JTextField, overrides isValidateRoot to return true. If a Swing container returns true from isValidateRoot, invoking revalidate() on one of the contained components causes the container to validate all of the components it contains. Validating all of the components in a Swing (or AWT) container results in the components being laid out and repainted. See "The Scrollable Interface" on page 764 and "JScrollPane Events" on page 756 for examples of how the revalidate method is used.

JScrollPane overrides isOpaque to return true if its viewport is smaller than the view the viewport contains. If the viewport is larger than its view, the scrollpane is transparent, meaning that the background of whatever is underneath the scrollpane will show through between the viewport's view and the scrollpane.

Accessibility / Pluggable Look And Feel

---

public AccessibleContext <u>getAccessibleContext</u>()
public ScrollPaneUI <u>getUI</u>()
public String <u>getUIClassID</u>()
public void <u>setUI</u>(ScrollPaneUI)
public void <u>updateUI</u>()

The methods listed above can be found in most extensions of JComponent. Swing lightweight components can return the class name of their UI delegate and an accessibility context that contains accessibility information for the component. The updateUI method is invoked when the component is fitted with a UI delegate.

Opaque vs. Transparent Scrollpanes

The applet shown in Figure 13-12 illustrates an opaque scrollpane versus a transparent one. The applet contains two scrollpanes; the scrollpane on the left has a transparent background, whereas the scrollpane on the right is opaque. The scrollpane on the left is transparent because its view does not completely fill the scrollpane's viewport. On the other hand, the scrollpane on the right is opaque because its view is larger than the scrollpane's viewport, and therefore there is no empty space for the background to show through.

Figure 13-12 Transparent and Opaque Scrollpanes

The applet sets its content pane to an instance of `CustomContentPane`, which tiles its background with an image. Two instances of `JLabel` and two instances of `JScrollPane` are instantiated, and the labels are specified as the views for the scrollpane's viewports. The scrollpanes are then added to the custom content pane.

```java
public class Test extends JApplet {
    public void init() {
        Container contentPane = new CustomContentPane();
        JLabel view1 = new JLabel(
                        new ImageIcon("gjMedium.gif"));
        JLabel view2 = new JLabel(
                        new ImageIcon("anjinAndMariko.gif"));

        JScrollPane sp1 = new JScrollPane(view1);
        JScrollPane sp2 = new JScrollPane(view2);
```

```
            setContentPane(contentPane);
            sp1.setPreferredSize(new Dimension(250,250));
            sp2.setPreferredSize(new Dimension(250,250));

            contentPane.add(sp1);
            contentPane.add(sp2);
        }
    }
```

The applet shown in Figure 13-12 is listed in its entirety in Example 13-9.

Example 13-9 Transparent and Opaque Scrollpanes

```
    import java.awt.*;
    import java.awt.event.*;
    import javax.swing.*;

    public class Test extends JApplet {
        public void init() {
            Container contentPane = new CustomContentPane();
            JLabel view1 = new JLabel(
                            new ImageIcon("gjMedium.gif"));
            JLabel view2 = new JLabel(
                            new ImageIcon("anjinAndMariko.gif"));

            JScrollPane sp1 = new JScrollPane(view1);
            JScrollPane sp2 = new JScrollPane(view2);

            setContentPane(contentPane);
            sp1.setPreferredSize(new Dimension(250,250));
            sp2.setPreferredSize(new Dimension(250,250));

            contentPane.add(sp1);
            contentPane.add(sp2);
        }
    }
    class CustomContentPane extends JPanel {
        private ImageIcon rain = new ImageIcon("rain.gif");

        public CustomContentPane() {
            setLayout(new FlowLayout());
        }
        public void paintComponent(Graphics g) {
            int rainw = rain.getIconWidth();
            int rainh = rain.getIconHeight();

            Dimension size = getSize();

            for(int row=0; row < size.height; row += rainh)
```

```
        for(int col=0; col < size.width; col += rainw)
            rain.paintIcon(this,g,col,row);
    }
}
```

AWT Compatibility

The scrolling architecture for Swing components differs a great deal from the
AWT's scrolling architecture. AWT viewports are a logical construct, meaning that
a viewport class is not included in the AWT. As a result, some of the methods
implemented in `java.awt.ScrollPane` have a corresponding method in
Swing's `JViewport` class, but not in `JScrollPane`. For example, the AWT
`ScrollPane` class provides a `getViewportSize` method, but Swing's
`JScrollPane` does not provide an analogous method. To obtain the size of a
Swing scrollpane's viewport, the viewport is first obtained from the scrollpane
with `JScrollPane.getViewport()`, and the size of the viewport is
subsequently obtained with `JViewport.getSize()`.

The `java.awt.ScrollPane` methods and the corresponding `JScrollPane`
equivalents are listed in Table 13-3.

Table 13-3   java.awt.ScrollPane Methods and JScrollPane Equivalents

java.awt.ScrollPane Method	JScrollPane Equivalent
Adjustable getHAdjustable()	JScrollBar getHorizontalScrollBar()
int getHScrollbarHeight()	——
int getScrollbarDisplayPolicy()	int getHorizontalScrollBarPolicy() / int getVerticalScrollBarPolicy()
Point getScrollPosition()	aScrollPane.getViewport().getViewPosition()
Adjustable getVAdjustable()	JScrollBar getVerticalScrollBar()
Dimension getViewportSize()	aScrollPane.getViewport().getSize()
int getVScrollbarWidth()	——
void setScrollPosition(int, int)	aScrollPane.getViewport().setViewPosition(Point)
void setScrollPosition(Point)	——

The scrollbars associated with instances of `java.awt.ScrollPane` are accessed
as instances of `java.awt.Adjustable`, whereas `JScrollPane` scrollbars are
accessed as instances of `JScrollBar`.

Another difference between `java.awt.ScrollPane` and `JScrollPane` is that `JScrollPane` allows its scrollbars to have different display policies, whereas the AWT's `ScrollPane` forces both of its scrollbars to have the same display policy.

The Scrollable Interface

The `Scrollable` interface is somewhat of a misnomer because any Swing or AWT component can be scrolled in an instance of `JScrollPane`. In actuality, components that implement the `Scrollable` interface have special scrolling needs. The following Swing components implement the `Scrollable` interface:

- `JList`
- `JTable`
- `JTextComponent`
- `Tree`

The `Scrollable` interface defines the five methods discussed in Interface Summary 13-2.

Interface Summary 13-2   Scrollable

---

public abstract Dimension <u>getPreferredScrollableViewportSize</u>()

For a scrollable component contained in a viewport, the `getPreferredScrollableViewportSize` method returns *the size that the component would like its viewport to be.*

For example, a list's preferred height is set to accommodate the number of rows that are visible when a list is placed in a scrolling container. Although the preferred height for an instance of `JList` is the height required to display all of its rows, the preferred height for a list's viewport is the height required to display the list's visible rows.

public abstract int <u>getScrollableBlockIncrement</u>(Rectangle visibleRect,
                                 int orientation, int direction)
public abstract int <u>getScrollableUnitIncrement</u>(Rectangle visibleRect,
                                 int orientation, int direction)

The `getScrollableBlockIncrement` should return the number of pixels required to completely expose one block of rows or columns. A block is typically defined as the number of rows or columns currently visible in the viewport. The `getScrollableUnitIncrement` should return the number of pixels required to completely expose the next row or column contained in the viewport's view.

Both `getScrollableUnitIncrement` and `getScrollableBlockIncrement` are passed a rectangle representing the currently visible portion of the view and an `integer` value representing the scroll orientation, either `SwingConstants.VERTICAL` or `SwingConstants.HORIZONTAL`. Additionally, an `integer` value representing the direction of the scroll is also passed to the methods. A direction less than 0 represents a direction of up/down, whereas a direction greater than 0 represents a direction of left/right.

The applet shown in Figure 13-13 illustrates unit and block increments for scrollable components.

The top-left picture shows the applet as it appears initially, with the mouse cursor in position to click on the scrollbar's down arrow, which will cause the table to scroll by a unit increment. The result of the unit increment scroll is depicted in the top-right picture.

The bottom-left picture also shows the applet as it appears initially, with the mouse cursor in position to click in the scrollbar's trough, which will cause the table to scroll by a block increment. The result of the block scroll is depicted in the lower right picture.

The applet shown in Figure 13-13 is not listed in this chapter; see "Tables" on page 1133 for more information on `JTable`.

public abstract boolean <u>getScrollableTracksViewportHeight</u>()
public abstract boolean <u>getScrollableTracksViewportWidth</u>()

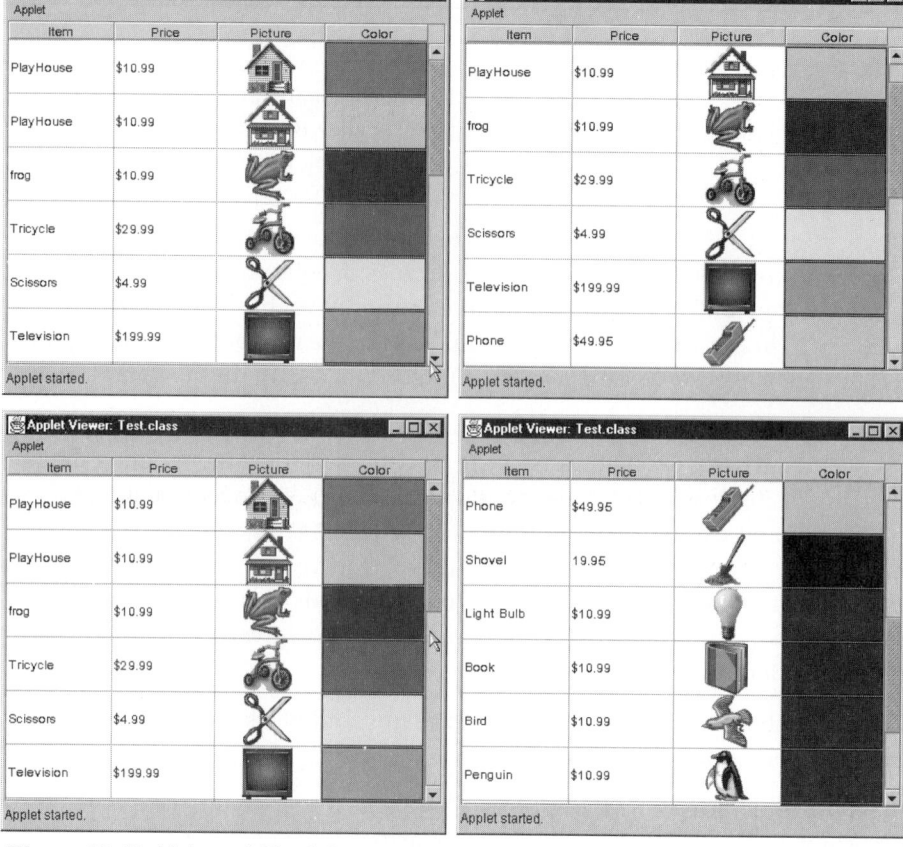

Figure 13-13 Unit and Block Increments

The two methods listed above return `boolean` values indicating whether a viewport should force the width or height of its view to match that of the viewport.

The `JTextArea` component implements `getScrollableTracksViewportWidth` to return `true` if line wrapping is enabled for the text area. This ensures that the text displayed in the text area will be wrapped and will not extend beyond the right edge of the viewport.

The applet shown in Figure 13-14 contains a text area contained in a scrollpane and a check box to set line wrapping for the text area. When line wrapping is set to `false`, as is the case for the left-hand picture in Figure 13-14, the width of the text area exceeds the width of the scrollpane, as evidenced by the horizontal

scrollbar. When line wrapping is set to `true`, as is the case for the right-hand picture in Figure 13-14, the width of the text area is forced to be the same as the width of the scrollpane, and therefore no horizontal scrollbar is displayed.

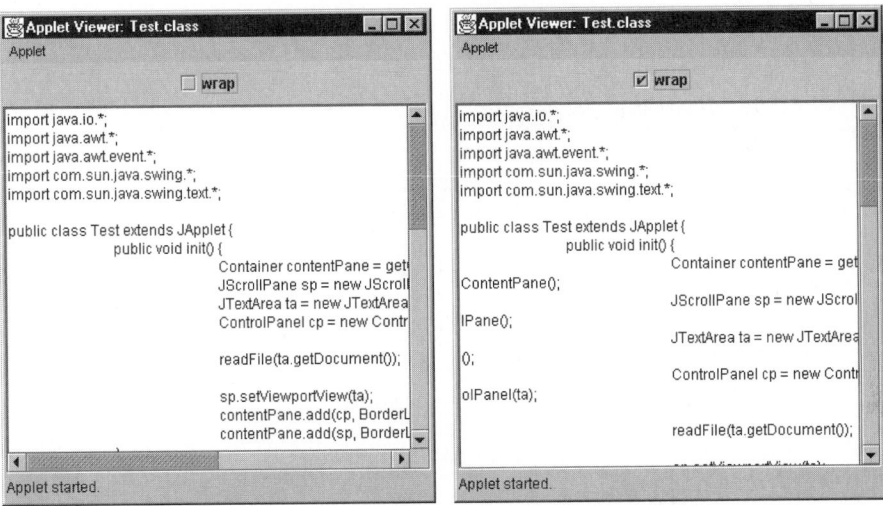

Figure 13-14 Tracking Viewport Size for Scrollable Components

The check box is contained in an instance of `ControlPanel` which is an extension of the `JPanel` class. When the check box is selected, line wrapping is enabled for the text area. When the check box is deselected, line wrapping is disabled.

```
class ControlPanel extends JPanel {
    public ControlPanel(final JTextArea ta) {
        final JCheckBox cb = new JCheckBox("wrap");

        add(cb);

        cb.addItemListener(new ItemListener() {
            public void itemStateChanged(ItemEvent e) {
                if(cb.isSelected())
                    textArea.setLineWrap(true);
                else
                    textArea.setLineWrap(false);
            }
        });
    }
}
```

The applet shown in Figure 13-14 is listed in its entirety in Example 13-10. See "JTextArea" on page 1490 for more information about text areas.

Example 13-10 Tracking Viewport Width

```
import java.io.*;
import java.awt.*;
import java.awt.event.*;
import javax.swing.*;
import javax.swing.text.*;

public class Test extends JApplet {
    private JTextArea textArea = new JTextArea();

    public void init() {
        Container contentPane = getContentPane();

        readFile();

        contentPane.add(new ControlPanel(), BorderLayout.NORTH);
        contentPane.add(new JScrollPane(textArea),
                    BorderLayout.CENTER);
    }
    private void readFile() {
        DefaultEditorKit kit = new DefaultEditorKit();

        try {
            kit.read(new FileReader("Test.java"),
                    textArea.getDocument(), 0);
        }
        catch(Exception ex) { ex.printStackTrace(); }
    }
    class ControlPanel extends JPanel {
        public ControlPanel() {
            final JCheckBox cb = new JCheckBox("wrap");

            add(cb);

            cb.addItemListener(new ItemListener() {
                public void itemStateChanged(ItemEvent e) {
                    if(cb.isSelected())
                        textArea.setLineWrap(true);
                    else
                        textArea.setLineWrap(false);
                }
            });
        }
    }
}
```

JScrollBar

The Swing scrolling architecture, consisting of the JViewport and JScrollPane classes, is sufficient for most scrolling situations. As illustrated previously in this chapter, Swing's scrolling architecture is predicated upon a fixed-size viewport that displays a portion of a component that is typically larger—at least in one dimension—than its associated viewport.

However, there are times when the viewport/view scrolling model does not suffice. For example, if the view associated with a viewport contains an enormous amount of data, constructing the view and scrolling by adjusting the position of the view within the viewport can be impractical due to performance and resource considerations. Fortunately, Swing provides a scrollbar class that can be used to circumvent the Swing scrolling architecture by implementing manual scrolling.

Manual Scrolling with Swing's JScrollBar Class

Sometimes it can be impractical to construct a view (a.k.a. component) that is scrolled in a viewport. For example, consider an applet that implements a scrollable view of a list of names and social security numbers for every United States citizen. The start-up time for creating a view containing approximately 250 million entries would be prohibitive, not to mention the resources involved. Instead of creating an enormous view containing all of the names and social security numbers, a better approach would be to read data from a storage device as the list is scrolled. Such an approach requires an inversion of the Swing scrolling architecture; instead of a *fixed-size viewport* that scrolls a large view, a *fixed-size view* is repainted as an associated scrollbar is manipulated.

The applet shown in Figure 13-15 implements a scrolling list of names and social security numbers. The applet consists of a panel and a vertical scrollbar and serves to illustrate two things: the use of instances of JScrollBar and the inversion of the Swing scrolling architecture as described above. The applet contains only one scrollbar by design for simplicity's sake; the techniques presented for manipulation of the vertical scrollbar can be applied to horizontal scrollbars as well. Also in the interest of simplicity, the applet shown in Figure 13-15 does not read data from a disk or implement a data caching algorithm. However, the applet does illustrate inversion of the Swing scrolling model by manually scrolling a fixed-size view.

JScrollBar is a fairly simple component that displays arrow buttons and a knob (a.k.a. thumb or slider). The model for instances of JScrollBar is an implementation of the BoundedRangeModel interface that encapsulates the manipulation of an integer value with associated maximum, minimum, and extent values such that minimum <= value <= value + extent <= maximum.

The applet shown in Figure 13-15 implements an extension of the JPanel class for displaying names and social security numbers. The panel defines (an admittedly contrived) array of strings representing a fixed set of names and social security numbers. The panel also keeps track of the index of the string displayed at the top of the panel in addition to the height of the font used to display the strings.

Figure 13-15 Manual Scrolling with Scrollbars

The SSPanel class overrides paintComponent() to paint the strings. First, super.paintComponent() is invoked to clear the background of the panel. The foreground color of the panel is saved and subsequently restored after the call to super.paintComponent() because JPanel.paintComponent() sets the color of the graphics it is passed to the panel's background color—see "JPanel" on page 630 for more information on the JPanel class and its opaque property.

```
class SSPanel extends JPanel {
    private int topIndex = 0;
    private int fh;

    private String[] data = {
        "Brown, Ted:  000-00-0001", "Brown, Ted:  000-00-0002",
        "Brown, Ted:  000-00-0003", "Brown, Ted:  000-00-0004",
```

```
         "Brown, Ted:   000-00-0005", "Brown, Ted:   000-00-0006",
         "Brown, Ted:   000-00-0007", "Brown, Ted:   000-00-0008",
         "Brown, Ted:   000-00-0009", "Brown, Ted:   000-00-00010",
         "Brown, Ted:   000-00-00011", "Brown, Ted:   000-00-00012",
         "Brown, Ted:   000-00-00013", "Brown, Ted:   000-00-00014",
         "Brown, Ted:   000-00-00015", "Brown, Ted:   000-00-00016",
         "Brown, Ted:   000-00-00017", "Brown, Ted:   000-00-00018",
         "Brown, Ted:   000-00-00019", "Brown, Ted:   000-00-00020",
         "Brown, Ted:   000-00-00021", "Brown, Ted:   000-00-00022",
         "Brown, Ted:   000-00-00023", "Brown, Ted:   000-00-00024",
         "Brown, Ted:   000-00-00025", "Brown, Ted:   000-00-00026",
         "Brown, Ted:   000-00-00027", "Brown, Ted:   000-00-00028",
         "Brown, Ted:   000-00-00029", "Brown, Ted:   000-00-00030",
      };
      . . .
```

The `paintComponent` method paints the strings in the panel starting with the string `data[topIndex]` and ending with either the last string in the array or the last visible string in the panel.

```
   . . .
   public void paintComponent(Graphics g) {
       Color color = g.getColor();
       super.paintComponent(g);
       g.setColor(color);

       Dimension size = getSize();
       Insets insets = getInsets();
       int y = insets.top;

       for(int i = topIndex; i < data.length; ++i, y += fh) {
           g.drawString(data[i], 0, y);

           if(y + fh > size.height - insets.bottom)
               break;
       }
   }
   . . .
```

The `SSPanel` class implements a method to set its `topIndex`, given a pixel offset from the top of the panel. The `getPreferredSize` method is overridden to return a dimension representing the width of the widest string displayed in the panel and a height representing the total height required to display all of its strings.

```
   . . .
   public void setTopIndexByPixelValue(int pixelValue) {
       topIndex = pixelValue / fh;
```

```
      }
   public Dimension getPreferredSize() {
      Dimension dim = new Dimension();
      Graphics g = getGraphics();

      try {
         FontMetrics fm = g.getFontMetrics();
         dim.width = fm.stringWidth(data[data.length-1]);
         dim.height = fm.getHeight() * (data.length + 1);
      }
      finally {
         g.dispose();
      }
      return dim;
   }
}
```

Two things should be noted about the getPreferredSize method.

First, the graphics obtained by a call to getGraphics() is disposed of. This is a necessity for graphics obtained via calls to getGraphics()—see the first volume of *Graphic Java* for a discussion of graphics and their use.

Second, the preferred height of the panel is actually the height required to display one more string than the panel displays. The panel will not display a string at the bottom of the panel that is partially cut off, so the preferred height is given a little extra breathing room.

The applet creates the vertical scrollbar and instance of the SSPanel class. The panel is specified as the center component for the applet's content pane, and the scrollbar as the east component.

Instances of JScrollBar fire adjustment events when a scrollbar's value is modified. As the result, an adjustment listener that is added to the applet's scrollbar invokes SSPanel.setTopIndexByPixelValue() with the current scrollbar value and subsequently repaints the panel. The listener also invokes the applet's showScrollBarValues method, which displays the scrollbar's values in the applet's status area.

```
public class Test extends JApplet {
   private JScrollBar vsb = new JScrollBar(JScrollBar.VERTICAL);
   private SSPanel panel = new SSPanel();

   public Test() {
      Container contentPane = getContentPane();

      contentPane.add(panel, BorderLayout.CENTER);
```

```
    contentPane.add(vsb, BorderLayout.EAST);

    vsb.addAdjustmentListener(new AdjustmentListener() {
        public void adjustmentValueChanged(
                                    AdjustmentEvent e) {
            JScrollBar sb = (JScrollBar)e.getSource();
            showScrollBarValues();

            panel.setTopIndexByPixelValue(e.getValue());
            panel.repaint();
        }
    });
}
...
```

Finally, the applet's `paint` method is overridden to ensure that the scrollbar is updated when the applet is resized.

The visible amount, or extent, of the panel is its current height, and the maximum height is the panel's preferred height. The value for the scrollbar is set to 0 if the panel's visible amount is greater than the panel's maximum height—meaning that all of the strings in the panel are visible and no scrollbar is needed—in which case the visibility of the scrollbar is set to `false`.

If the panel's visible amount is less than its maximum height—meaning that not all of the strings can be displayed, and therefore the scrollbar is needed—the value for the scrollbar is set to the minimum between the scrollbar's current value and the maximum value minus the visible amount, and the scrollbar is made visible. This results in the scrollbar's value remaining constant until the applet is sized tall enough to result in a change to the string displayed at the top of the panel.

```
    ...
    public void paint(Graphics g) {
        Dimension pref = panel.getPreferredSize();
        Dimension size = panel.getSize();
        int extent = size.height, max = pref.height;
        int value = Math.max(0,
                    Math.min(vsb.getValue(), max - extent));

        vsb.setVisible(extent < max);
        vsb.setValues(value, extent, 0, max);

        showScrollBarValues();
        super.paint(g);
    }
}
```

A slightly modified version of the applet shown in Figure 13-15 is listed in Example 13-11 on page 777, so the applet is not listed here.

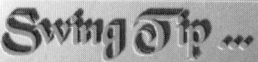

Invert the Scrolling Model for Maximum Performance

Swing's scrolling model is based on a *fixed-size viewport* that displays a portion of a typically much larger view.

Although the Swing scrolling model is sufficient for most scrolling needs, for views that display large amounts of data, performance and resource considerations may make the viewport/view model unworkable. In such cases, it is better to invert the scrolling model by providing a *fixed-size view* that is repainted as an associated scrollbar is manipulated.

A number of strategies can be applied to an inverted scrolling model to further boost performance, such as caching the next and previous blocks of information and copying graphics from an offscreen buffer to the view's onscreen representation.

Block and Unit Increments

Instances of JScrollBar define unit and block increments that typically define the pixel amount needed to scroll one item (a.k.a. unit) and the number of items that can be displayed in the currently visible area, respectively. For example, in a text editor the unit increment would represent one line of text, whereas the block increment would represent one page of text. The initial values for unit and block increments for instances of JScrollBar are look-and-feel dependent.

The applet shown in Figure 13-16 is identical to the applet shown in Figure 13-15 on page 770, except that unit and block increments are defined by the scrollbar to scroll one line and one page, respectively.

The top-left picture in the applet shown in Figure 13-16 shows the applet as it appears initially. The top-right picture shows the applet after the scrollbar's down arrow has been activated once. Activating a scrollbar's arrow button results in the scrollbar scrolling by a unit increment.

The bottom-left picture shows the applet after the scrollbar's up arrow is subsequently activated, causing the panel to scroll up one unit. The bottom-right picture shows the applet after a mouse pressed event has occurred in the scrollbar's trough, which results in a block scroll.

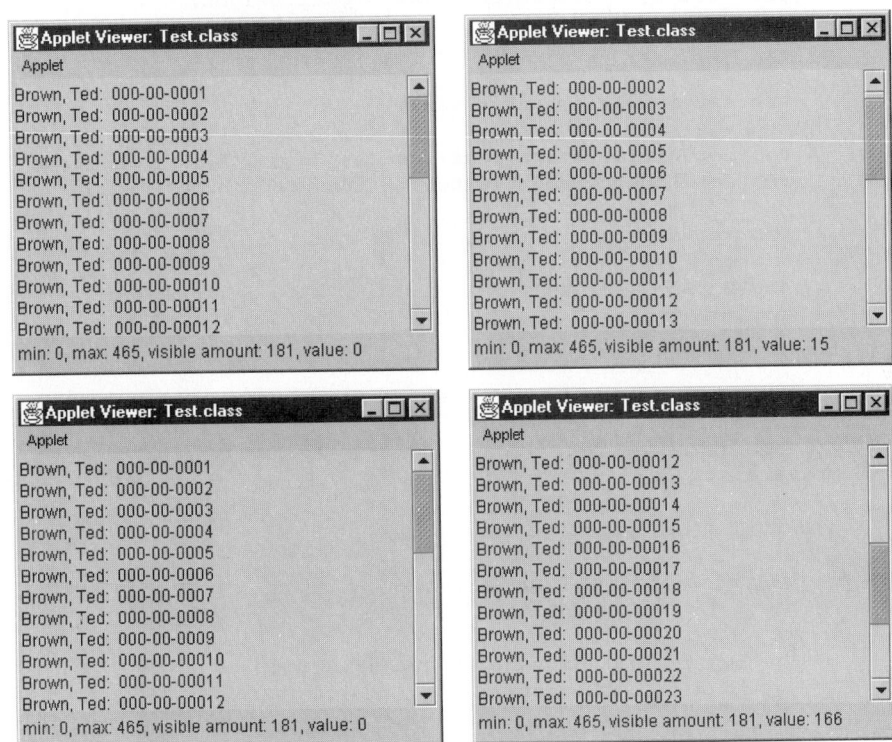

Figure 13-16 Specifying Block and Unit Increments with JScrollBar

The unit increment for the scrollbar contained in the applet is defined to be the same as the font height of the pane; thus, the panel scrolls by one line when the scrollbar's arrow buttons are activated.

The block increment for the scrollbar is set to the panel's visible amount minus the scrollbar's unit increment. This setting results in the panel scrolling by the number of visible lines minus one, meaning that the line at the bottom of the panel is scrolled to the top. The applet shown in Figure 13-16 invokes the JScrollBar setUnitIncrement and setBlockIncrement methods as follows.

```
public class Test extends JApplet {
    ...
    public void paint(Graphics g) {
        Dimension pref = panel.getPreferredSize();
        Dimension size = panel.getSize();

        int extent = size.height, max = pref.height;
        int value = Math.max(0,
                        Math.min(vsb.getValue(), max - extent));

        vsb.setVisible(extent < max);

        vsb.setUnitIncrement(panel.getUnitHeight());
        vsb.setBlockIncrement(extent - vsb.getUnitIncrement());

        vsb.setValues(value, extent, 0, max);

        showScrollBarValues();
        super.paint(g);
    }
    ...
}
class SSPanel extends JPanel {
    private int topIndex = 0;
    private int fh;
    ...
    public Dimension getPreferredSize() {
        ...
        Graphics g = getGraphics();
        ...
        try {
            FontMetrics fm = g.getFontMetrics();
            fh = fm.getHeight();
            ...
        }
        finally {
            g.dispose();
        }
        ...
    }
    public int getUnitHeight() {
        return fh;
    }
    ...
}
```

Because the applet shown in Figure 13-16 is identical to the applet shown in Figure 13-15 with the exception that unit and block increments are set for the scrollbar, the rest of the applet is not discussed here. See "Manual Scrolling with Swing's JScrollBar Class" on page 769 for a discussion of the rest of the applet.

The applet shown in Figure 13-16 is listed in its entirety in Example 13-11.

Example 13-11 Specifying Unit and Block Increments for Instances of JScrollBar

```
import java.awt.*;
import java.awt.event.*;
import javax.swing.*;
import javax.swing.event.*;

public class Test extends JApplet {
    private JScrollBar vsb = new JScrollBar(JScrollBar.VERTICAL);
    private SSPanel panel = new SSPanel();

    public Test() {
        Container contentPane = getContentPane();

        contentPane.add(panel, BorderLayout.CENTER);
        contentPane.add(vsb, BorderLayout.EAST);

        vsb.addAdjustmentListener(new AdjustmentListener() {
            public void adjustmentValueChanged(
                                        AdjustmentEvent e) {
                JScrollBar sb = (JScrollBar)e.getSource();
                showScrollBarValues();
                panel.setTopIndexByPixelValue(e.getValue());
                repaint();
            }
        });
    }
    public void paint(Graphics g) {
        Dimension pref = panel.getPreferredSize();
        Dimension size = panel.getSize();

        int extent = size.height, max = pref.height;
        int value = Math.max(0,
                    Math.min(vsb.getValue(), max - extent));

        vsb.setVisible(extent < max);
        vsb.setUnitIncrement(panel.getUnitHeight());
        vsb.setBlockIncrement(extent - vsb.getUnitIncrement());
        vsb.setValues(value, extent, 0, max);
```

```
            showScrollBarValues();
            super.paint(g);
        }

        private void showScrollBarValues() {
            showStatus("min: " + vsb.getMinimum() +
                       ", max: " + vsb.getMaximum() +
                       ", visible amount: " +
                       vsb.getVisibleAmount() +
                       ", value: " + vsb.getValue());
        }
    }
    class SSPanel extends JPanel {
        private int topIndex = 0;
        private int fh;

        private String[] data = {
            "Brown, Ted:   000-00-0001", "Brown, Ted:   000-00-0002",
            "Brown, Ted:   000-00-0003", "Brown, Ted:   000-00-0004",
            "Brown, Ted:   000-00-0005", "Brown, Ted:   000-00-0006",
            "Brown, Ted:   000-00-0007", "Brown, Ted:   000-00-0008",
            "Brown, Ted:   000-00-0009", "Brown, Ted:   000-00-00010",
            "Brown, Ted:   000-00-00011", "Brown, Ted:   000-00-00012",
            "Brown, Ted:   000-00-00013", "Brown, Ted:   000-00-00014",
            "Brown, Ted:   000-00-00015", "Brown, Ted:   000-00-00016",
            "Brown, Ted:   000-00-00017", "Brown, Ted:   000-00-00018",
            "Brown, Ted:   000-00-00019", "Brown, Ted:   000-00-00020",
            "Brown, Ted:   000-00-00021", "Brown, Ted:   000-00-00022",
            "Brown, Ted:   000-00-00023", "Brown, Ted:   000-00-00024",
            "Brown, Ted:   000-00-00025", "Brown, Ted:   000-00-00026",
            "Brown, Ted:   000-00-00027", "Brown, Ted:   000-00-00028",
            "Brown, Ted:   000-00-00029", "Brown, Ted:   000-00-00030",
        };
        public void paintComponent(Graphics g) {
            Color color = g.getColor();
            super.paintComponent(g);
            g.setColor(color);

            Dimension size = getSize();
            Insets insets = getInsets();
            int y = insets.top;

            for(int i = topIndex; i < data.length; ++i, y += fh) {
                g.drawString(data[i], 0, y);
```

```
                if(y + fh > size.height - insets.bottom)
                    break;
            }
        }
        public void setTopIndexByPixelValue(int pixelValue) {
            topIndex = pixelValue / fh;
        }
        public int To() {
            return fh;
        }
        public Dimension getPreferredSize() {
            Dimension dim = new Dimension();
            Graphics g = getGraphics();

            try {
                FontMetrics fm = g.getFontMetrics();
                fh = fm.getHeight();

                dim.width = fm.stringWidth(data[data.length-1]);
                dim.height = fm.getHeight() * (data.length + 1);
            }
            finally {
                g.dispose();
            }
            return dim;
        }
    }
}
```

JScrollBar is summarized in Component Summary 13-3.

Component Summary 13-3   JScrollBar

Model(s)	BoundedRangeModel
UI Delegate(s)	javax.swing.plaf.basic.BasicScrollBarUI
Renderer(s)	——
Editor(s)	——
Events Fired	java.awt.event.AdjustmentEvent
Replacement For	java.awt.ScrollBar

Class Diagrams

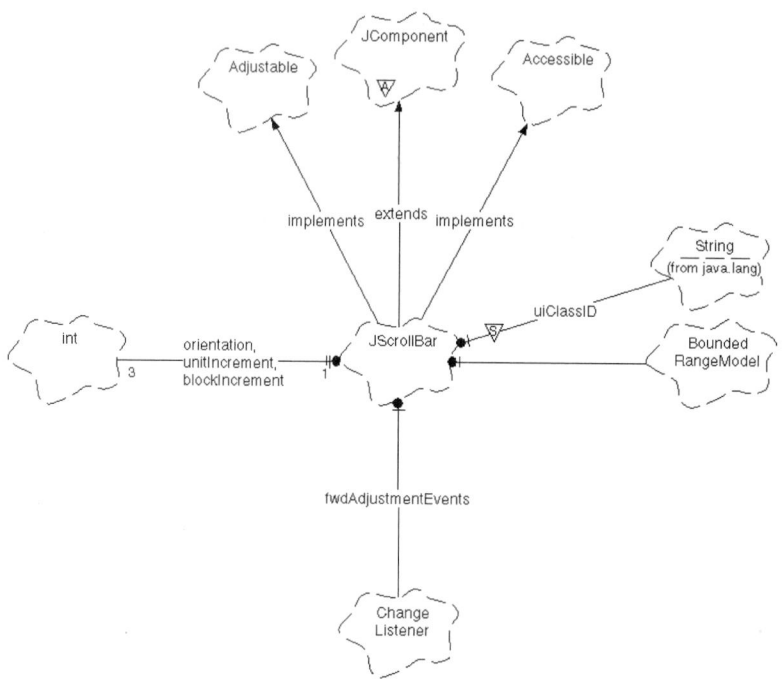

Figure 13-17 JScrollBar Class Diagram

JScrollBar extends JComponent and implements the Adjustable and Accessible interfaces. The Adjustable interface is implemented to retain compatibility with the AWT's Scrollbar class. See page 788 for more information on JScrollBar's compatibility with the java.awt.Scrollbar class.

JScrollBar maintains private integer values for its orientation and unit/block increments. JScrollBar also maintains protected references to its model and an instance of ChangeListener. The change listener listens for change events fired by the scrollbar's model which are transformed into adjustment events and forwarded to adjustment listeners registered with the scrollbar.

JScrollBar Properties

The properties maintained by the JScrollBar class are listed in Table 13-4.

Table 13-4 JScrollBar Properties

Property Name	Data Type	Property Type[2]	Access[3]	Default[4]
blockIncrement	int	B	SG	L&F
maximum	int	A	CSG	100
minimum	int	A	CSG	0
model	BoundedRangeModel	B	SG	Default-Bounded-RangeModel
orientation	int	B	CSG	VERTICAL
unitIncrement	int	B	SG	L&F
value	int	A	CSG	0
valueIsAdjusting	boolean	——	SG	false
visibleAmount[1]	int	A	CSG	0

1. The model property for visible amount is known as extent
2. b = boolean / B = bound (fires PropertyChangeEvent) / C = constrained/ I = indexed / S = simple / Ch = fires ChangeEvent / A = fires AdjustmentEvent
3. C = settable at construction time / G = getter method / S = setter method
4. L&F = look-and-feel dependent

blockIncrement — The amount the scrollbar's value changes for a block request, which typically represents one page of data.

maximum — The maximum value represented by the scrollbar.

minimum — The minimum value represented by the scrollbar.

model — The scrollbar's model, which is an implementation of the BoundedRangeModel interface.

orientation — The orientation of the scrollbar, either JScrollBar.HORIZONTAL or JScrollBar.VERTICAL.

unitIncrement — The amount the scrollbar's value changes for a unit request, which typically represents one line of data.

value — The current value represented by the left/top edge of the scrollbar's knob.

valueIsAdjusting — If true, the scrollbar's knob is being dragged.

visibleAmount — The amount of the view that is currently visible. The size of the scrollbar's knob is proportional to the visible amount.

Notice that model properties fire adjustment events. This is in contrast to most other Swing components, which fire change events when model properties are modified. JScrollBar fires adjustment events in response to modifications made to model properties in order to maintain compatibility with the AWT's Scrollbar class.

JScrollBar Events

As noted previously, instances of JScrollBar fire adjustment events when their model properties—maximum, minimum, value, and visible amount—are modified. All of the other properties associated with instances of JScrollBar, with the exception of the valueIsAdjusting property, are bound properties, meaning that modifications to the properties result in the firing of property change events.

Although instances of JScrollBar fire an adjustment event when their knob is dragged, it is not always desirable to scroll the contents of the scrollbar's associated container while the knob is being dragged. As a result, the valueIsAdjusting property can be examined to determine whether the knob is being dragged.

The applet shown in Figure 13-18 adds an adjustment listener to its scrollbar. If the scrollbar's valueIsAdjusting property is true, the applet prints the string "adjusting ..." in its status area, as can be seen from the left-hand picture. If the scrollbar's valueIsAdjusting property is false, the applet prints the value associated with the scrollbar, as can be seen from the right-hand picture.

The applet shown in Figure 13-18 is listed in Example 13-12.

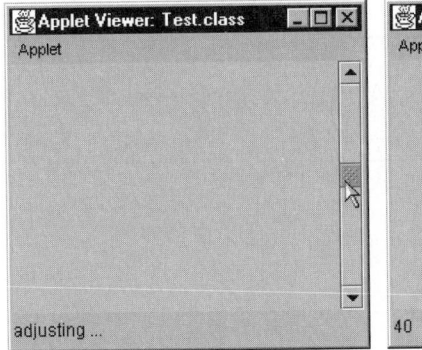
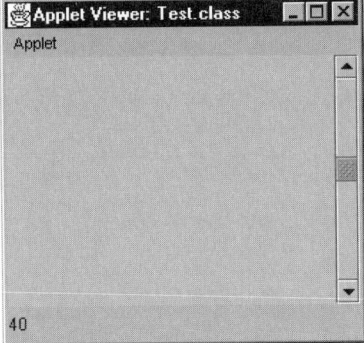

Figure 13-18 JScrollBar's ValueIsAdjusting Property

Example 13-12 Using JScrollBar's ValueIsAdjusting Property

```
import java.awt.*;
import java.awt.event.*;
import javax.swing.*;

public class Test extends JApplet {
    public Test() {
        Container contentPane = getContentPane();
        JScrollBar sb = new JScrollBar();

        contentPane.add(sb, BorderLayout.EAST);

        sb.addAdjustmentListener(new AdjustmentListener() {
            public void adjustmentValueChanged(
                                        AdjustmentEvent e) {
                JScrollBar jsb = (JScrollBar)e.getAdjustable();

                if(jsb.getValueIsAdjusting())
                    showStatus("adjusting ...");
                else
                    showStatus(Integer.toString(e.getValue()));
            }
        });
    }
}
```

Instances of `AdjustmentEvent` are passed to the `adjustmentValueChanged` method, which is the only method defined by the `AdjustmentListener` interface. The `AdjustmentEvent` class is summarized in Class Summary 13-3.

Class Summary 13-3   java.awt.AdjustmentEvent

Extends: java.awt.AWTEvent

Constants

---

public static final int <u>ADJUSTMENT FIRST</u>
public static final int <u>ADJUSTMENT LAST</u>
public static final int <u>ADJUSTMENT VALUE CHANGED</u>

public static final int <u>BLOCK DECREMENT</u>
public static final int <u>BLOCK INCREMENT</u>
public static final int <u>TRACK</u>
public static final int <u>UNIT DECREMENT</u>
public static final int <u>UNIT INCREMENT</u>

The first three constants listed above define the ID of the event. All adjustment events have an ID of ADJUSTMENT_VALUE_CHANGED. The ADJUSTMENT_FIRST and ADJUSTMENT_LAST define the range of IDs used by the AdjustmentEvent class and are not used directly by developers.

The last five constants listed above represent the type of adjustment event that occurred. Unfortunately, all adjustment events fired by instances of JScrollBar have a type of TRACK, regardless of whether the event represents a unit or block increment/decrement. This is because instances of JScrollBar create adjustment events as a result of change event notifications from the scrollbar's model. Because change events are stateless, is not possible for instances of JScrollBar to determine the exact type of event.

Constructors

---

public <u>AdjustmentEvent</u>(Adjustable source, int id, int type, int value)

`AdjustmentEvents` are constructed with the source of the event, the ID of the event, the event type, and the value of the event source. The `JScrollBar` class is in the business of creating `AdjustmentEvents`, but users of `JScrollBar` typically are not.

Methods

public Adjustable <u>getAdjustable</u>()
public int <u>getAdjustmentType</u>()
public int <u>getValue</u>()
public String <u>paramString</u>()

The `getAdjustable` method returns a reference to the `JScrollBar` that fired the event. As discussed above, `getAdjustmentType` always returns a value of `AdjustmentEvent.TRACK`. The `getValue` method returns the current value of the scrollbar. The `paramString` method translates the type of event into a string, but the method will always return `"TRACK"` because that is the only type of adjustment event fired by instances of `JScrollBar`.

Swing Tip ...

Adjustment Events Fired by Instances of JScrollBar

Instead of firing change events like most other Swing components, the JScrollBar class fires adjustment events to maintain maximum compatibility with the AWT's scrollbar component.

Instances of JScrollBar are notified when their model properties are modified with a change event that is fired from the scrollbar's model. When an instance of JScrollBar receives a change event from its model, it creates an adjustment event that it fires to its adjustment listeners.

Because the only information available from change events fired by a scrollbar's model is the source of the event, the adjustment event does not contain any state information. As a result, all adjustment events fired by instances of JScrollBar have an event ID of AdjustmentEvent.TRACK.

JScrollBar Class Summaries

The public and protected variables and methods for JScrollBar are listed in Class Summary 13-4.

Class Summary 13-4   JScrollBar

Constructors

---

public JScrollBar()
public JScrollBar(int)
public JScrollBar(int orientation, int value, int extent, int minimum, int maximum)

The no-argument constructor creates an instance of JScrollBar with a minimum value of 0, a maximum value of 100, and a value and extent (visible amount) of 0.

The second constructor listed above is passed an integer value specifying the orientation of the scrollbar. Valid values are either SwingConstants.HORIZONTAL or SwingConstants.VERTICAL.

The third constructor listed above is passed integer values for orientation, value, extent, and minimum and maximum values, in that order.

Methods

Adjustment Events

---

public void addAdjustmentListener(AdjustmentListener)
protected void fireAdjustmentValueChanged(int id, int type, int value)
public void removeAdjustmentListener(AdjustmentListener)

The methods listed above add and remove adjustment listeners to and from instances of JScrollBar. The fireAdjustmentValueChanged method is used to fire adjustment events to adjustment listeners. The method is always passed the same event ID—ADJUSTMENT_VALUE_CHANGED—and the same event type—TRACK. Only the value parameter changes from one call to the next. Extensions of JScrollBar can override the method to fire events in a different manner, if so desired.

Property Accessors

---

public int getBlockIncrement()
public int getBlockIncrement(int)
public int getMaximum()
public Dimension getMaximumSize()
public int getMinimum()
public Dimension getMinimumSize()
public BoundedRangeModel getModel()
public int getOrientation()
public int getUnitIncrement()
public int getUnitIncrement(int)
public int getValue()
public boolean getValueIsAdjusting()
public int getVisibleAmount()

public void setBlockIncrement(int)
public void setEnabled(boolean)
public void setMaximum(int)
public void setMinimum(int)
public void setModel(BoundedRangeModel)
public void setOrientation(int)
public void setUnitIncrement(int)
public void setValue(int)
public void setValueIsAdjusting(boolean)
public void setValues(int value, int extent, int min, int max)
public void setVisibleAmount(int)

The methods listed above are accessors for `JScrollBar` properties. The `getBlockIncrement(int)` and `getUnitIncrement(int)` methods are passed an `integer` value specifying the direction of the scroll. The `integer` value is ignored by the `JScrollBar` methods, and the block increment or unit increment is returned. Extensions of `JScrollBar` can override the methods to return different increments depending upon the direction of the scroll.

Accessibility and Pluggable Look And Feel

---

public AccessibleContext <u>getAccessibleContext</u>()
public ScrollBarUI <u>getUI</u>()
public String <u>getUIClassID</u>()
public void <u>updateUI</u>()

The methods listed above can be found in most extensions of `JComponent`. Swing lightweight components can return the class name of their UI delegate and an accessibility context that contains accessibility information for the component. The `updateUI` method is invoked when the component is fitted with a UI delegate.

AWT Compatibility

`JScrollBar` is 100 percent compatible with `java.awt.Scrollbar`, as is clear from Table 13-5. Not only does `JScrollBar` implement the exact same methods as `java.awt.Scrollbar`, but it provides identical constructors.

The only API difference between `JScrollBar` and `java.awt.Scrollbar` are two deprecated methods implemented by `java.awt.Scrollbar` that are not implemented by `JScrollBar`. The `java.awt.Scrollbar` `getLineIncrement` and `getPageIncrement` methods have been deprecated in favor of `getUnitIncrement()` and `getBlockIncrement()`, respectively.

Table 13-5 java.awt.Scrollbar Methods and JScrollBar Equivalents

java.awt.Scrollbar Method	JScrollBar Equivalent
void addAdjustmentListener(AdjustmentListener)	void addAdjustmentListener(Adjustment-Listener)
int getBlockIncrement()	int getBlockIncrement()
int getMaximum()	int getMaximum()
int getMinimum()	int getMinimum()
int getOrientation()	int getOrientation()
int getUnitIncrement()	int getUnitIncrement()
int getValue()	int getValue()
int getVisibleAmount()	int getVisibleAmount()
void removeAdjustmentListener(Adjustment-Listener)	void removeAdjustmentListener(Adjustment-Listener)
void setBlockIncrement(int)	void setBlockIncrement(int)
void setMaximum(int)	void setMaximum(int)
void setMinimum(int)	void setMinimum(int)
void setOrientation(int)	void setOrientation(int)
void setUnitIncrement(int)	void setUnitIncrement(int)
void setValue(int)	void setValue(int)
void setValues(int,int,int,int)	void setValues(int,int,int,int)
void setVisibleAmount(int)	void setVisibleAmount(int)

Parting Shots

Swing's scrolling architecture is a good indicator of just how far Java's user interface components have come since the original AWT. Originally, the AWT did not even provide a scrollpane component. In the early days of the AWT, scrolling a component meant manually fitting a container with scrollbars and handling all of the low-level details of reacting to scrollbars events and scrolling the component.

With the advent of the 1.1 AWT, a scrollpane container was finally introduced. However, the AWT's scrollpane was not very robust. The AWT did not provide a separate viewport class; instead, the viewport contained within the AWT's scrollpane was a logical construct, which made it impossible to reuse the viewport

functionality embedded within the scrollpane class. Additionally, although the AWT's scrollpane supported scrollbar display policies identical to the policies supported by Swing's scrollpane class, different policies could not be applied to individual scrollbars. Finally, the AWT's scrollpane did not support headers, corners, or transparency, as does Swing's `JScrollPane`.

Swing's scrolling architecture is a welcome addition to the Java GUI developer's toolkit. With a separate viewport class, developers are able to reuse and extend viewport functionality. See "Autoscrolling" on page 165 for an example of extending `JViewport` to support dragging and autoscrolling of a viewport's view. Also, it is possible to add row and column headers to a viewport, allowing for features such as the draggable headers illustrated in the applet shown in Figure 13-9 on page 744.

Finally, Swing provides a scrollbar, in the form of the `JScrollBar` class, for times when it becomes necessary to take scrolling into one's own hands. The Swing scrolling architecture can be inverted for maximum performance and resource usage by implementing scrolling directly with instances of `JScrollBar`.

CHAPTER

14

Windows and Dialogs

Swing windows, frames, and dialogs are heavyweight components that extend the AWT `Window`, `Frame`, and `Dialog` classes, respectively. While all three components are windows, the differences between the three are not always readily apparent, and therefore it can sometimes be difficult to decide which component to use in a given situation. To clarify, some of the properties associated with the three components are listed in Table 14-1.

Table 14-1 Window, Frame, and Dialog Properties [1],[2]

Property	Window	Frame	Dialog
Modal	No	No	No/CSG
Resizable	No	Yes/SG	Yes/SG
Title Bar	No	Yes	Yes
Border	No	Yes	Yes
Title	No	Yes/CSG	Yes/CSG
Menu Bar	No	Yes/SG	No
Focus Manager	Yes	Yes	Yes
Warning String	Yes/G	Yes/G	Yes/G

Table 14-1 Window, Frame, and Dialog Properties (Continued)[1],[2]

Property	Window	Frame	Dialog
Icon Image[3]	No	Yes/SG	No
Anchored to a Frame	Yes	No	Yes

1. Yes/No refers to default status of the property.
2. C = settable at construction time, S = setter method available,
   G = getter method available (either `get...()` or `is...()`).
3. Not all platforms support iconizing of windows.

Windows are the most basic component of the three and, in fact, `java.awt.Window` is the superclass of both `Frame` and `Dialog`. Windows have no border, title bar, or menu bar and cannot be resized. Windows are best suited for displaying something in a borderless rectangular region that needs to appear on top of other components.

Frames are an extension of `Window` that comes with a border and a title bar and is resizable. Frames are the component of choice when a required application window needs to be iconified or fitted with a menu bar.

Dialogs are also an extension of `Window` that, like frames, come with a border and a title bar and are resizable. Dialogs can be modal, whereas frames and windows cannot. Dialogs are the window of choice when a temporary window is required to capture user input.

Swing windows, frames, and dialogs add a root pane to the respective AWT classes that they extend. As a result, components are added to Swing windows, frames, and dialogs by being added to the content pane that resides in the root pane. Also, layout managers are set by setting the layout manager for the content pane, not the container itself.

Root panes, represented by the `JRootPane` class, and frames, represented by the `JFrame` class, are not discussed in this chapter. Root panes and frames are discussed in "Swing Basics" on page 25. The AWT `Frame`, `Window`, and `Dialog` classes are discussed at length in the first volume of *Graphic Java*.

JWindow

`JWindow` is a heavyweight Swing component that extends `java.awt.Window` and installs an instance of `JRootPane` as the window's only component. Instances of `JWindow` do not have a border, title bar, or menu bar and do not

provide a control for resizing. Swing windows are typically used to display components or graphics in a borderless region of the screen that is displayed on top of all other components. For example, Swing's tooltips are implemented with instances of JWindow.

The application shown in Figure 14-1 illustrates another use of the JWindow class—a splash screen. The application creates a window that contains an instance of JLabel fitted with an image icon. The window is displayed until a mouse pressed event is detected within the window.

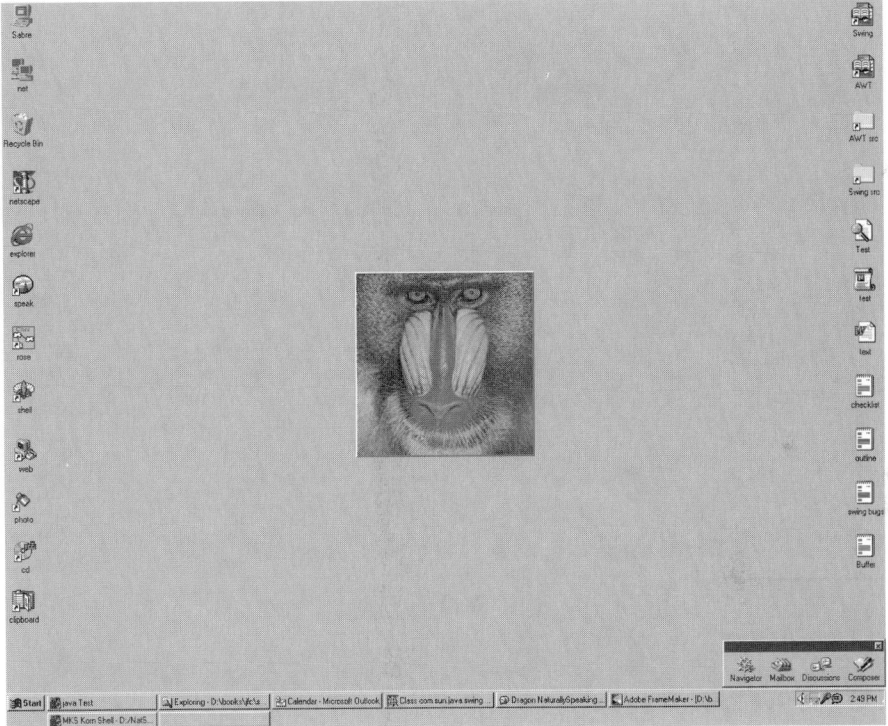

Figure 14-1 An Instance of JWindow Used as a Splash Screen

The applet shown in Figure 14-1 is listed in Example 14-1.

Example 14-1 Implementing a Splash Screen Using JWindow

```java
import java.awt.*;
import java.awt.event.*;
import javax.swing.*;

public class Test extends JFrame {
    Toolkit toolkit = Toolkit.getDefaultToolkit();
    JWindow window = new JWindow();
    JLabel label = new JLabel(new ImageIcon("mandrill.jpg"));

    static public void main(String[] args) {
        JFrame frame = new Test();
    }
    public Test() {
        label.setBorder(BorderFactory.createRaisedBevelBorder());
        window.getContentPane().add(label, BorderLayout.CENTER);
        centerWindow();
        window.show();

        window.addMouseListener(new MouseAdapter() {
            public void mousePressed(MouseEvent e) {
                window.dispose();
                System.exit(0);
            }
        });
    }
    private void centerWindow() {
        Dimension scrnSize  = toolkit.getScreenSize();
        Dimension labelSize = label.getPreferredSize();
        int       labelWidth  = labelSize.width,
                  labelHeight = labelSize.height;

        window.setLocation(scrnSize.width/2  - (labelWidth/2),
                           scrnSize.height/2 - (labelHeight/2));
        window.pack();
    }
}
```

The application creates an instance of JWindow with the JWindow no-argument
constructor and creates an instance of JLabel with an image icon. The label is
fitted with a raised bevel border obtained from the border factory and added to
the window's content pane as the center component. Subsequently, the location of
the window is calculated so that it is centered on the screen, using the AWT's
toolkit to obtain screen dimensions.

After the window has been configured, it is packed and displayed with the show method. Packing a window, frame, or dialog causes it to be resized so that it is just large enough for its content. A mouse listener added to the window disposes of the window and subsequently exits the application. The dispose method hides the window and disposes of the window's native resources.

It is important to keep in mind that instances of JWindow are heavyweight components and therefore do not inherit any of the capabilities implemented in the JComponent class. For example, it is not possible to fit instances of JWindow with a border because the JWindow class does not implement a setBorder method.

However, instances of JWindow contain a lightweight component in the form of an instance of JRootPane, and root panes can be manipulated like any lightweight component. For example, the applet shown in Figure 14-2 creates an instance of JWindow that has a raised bevel border set for its root pane. Because the root pane is specified as the window's center component, it completely fills the window, and therefore setting a border for the root pane in effect sets a border for the window. Additionally, a menu bar is attached to the window's root pane.

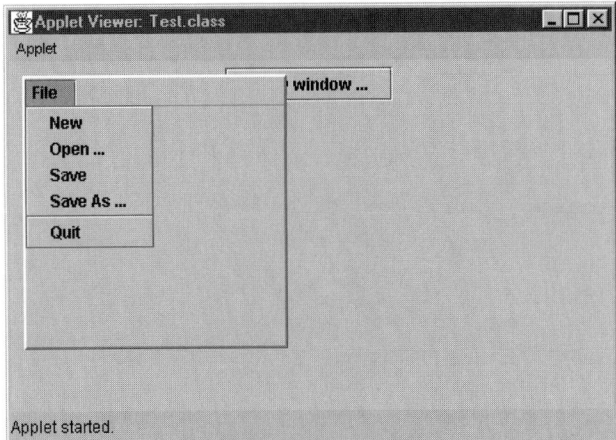

Figure 14-2 An Instance of JWindow Used as an Application Window

Windows such as one shown in Figure 14-2 should be used with care. Swing windows are not adorned with minimize, maximize, or close box controls as is the case for frames. Typically, if an application window is desired, it is better to use an instance of JFrame. The applet shown in Figure 14-2 and listed in Example 14-2 is primarily meant to illustrate the manipulation of a window's root pane.

Example 14-2 An Instance of JWindow Used as an Application Window

```java
import java.awt.*;
import java.awt.event.*;
import javax.swing.*;

public class Test extends JApplet {
    JWindow window = new JWindow();
    JMenuBar menuBar = new JMenuBar();
    JMenu fileMenu = new JMenu("File");
    JMenuItem quitItem;

    public Test() {
        final Container contentPane = getContentPane();
        JButton button = new JButton("show window ...");
        JRootPane windowRootPane = window.getRootPane();

        contentPane.setLayout(new FlowLayout());
        contentPane.add(button);

        fileMenu.add("New");
        fileMenu.add("Open ...");
        fileMenu.add("Save");
        fileMenu.add("Save As ...");
        fileMenu.addSeparator();
        fileMenu.add(quitItem = new JMenuItem("Quit"));

        menuBar.add(fileMenu);

        windowRootPane.setMenuBar(menuBar);
        windowRootPane.setBorder(
                    BorderFactory.createRaisedBevelBorder());

        button.addActionListener(new ActionListener() {
            public void actionPerformed(ActionEvent e) {
                Point pt = contentPane.getLocation();

                SwingUtilities.convertPointToScreen(
                                        pt, contentPane);

                // display 10 pixels below and to the right of the
                // upper-left corner of the content pane

                window.setBounds(pt.x + 10, pt.y + 10, 200, 200);
```

```
window.show();

quitItem.addActionListener(new ActionListener() {
    public void actionPerformed(ActionEvent e) {
        window.dispose();
    }
});
        }
    });
    }
}
```

The applet creates an instance of JWindow, using the JWindow no-argument constructor, and obtains a reference to the window's root pane.

The applet also creates a button that is used to show the window. A menu bar and menu are created, the menu is attached to the menu bar, and the menu bar is attached to the window's root pane. A border is obtained from the border factory and set as the border for the window's root pane.

When the button contained in the applet is activated, the bounds of the window are set so that the window is displayed near the upper-left corner of the applet and is 200 pixels wide and 200 pixels high.

Because instances of JWindow are not adorned with a close box, as is the case for instances of JFrame, a listener is added to the Quit menu item that disposes of the window.

The JWindow component is summarized in Component Summary 14-1.

Component Summary 14-1   JWindow

Model(s)	——
UI Delegate(s)	——
Renderer(s)	——
Editor(s)	——
Events Fired	——
Replacement For	java.awt.Window

Class Diagrams

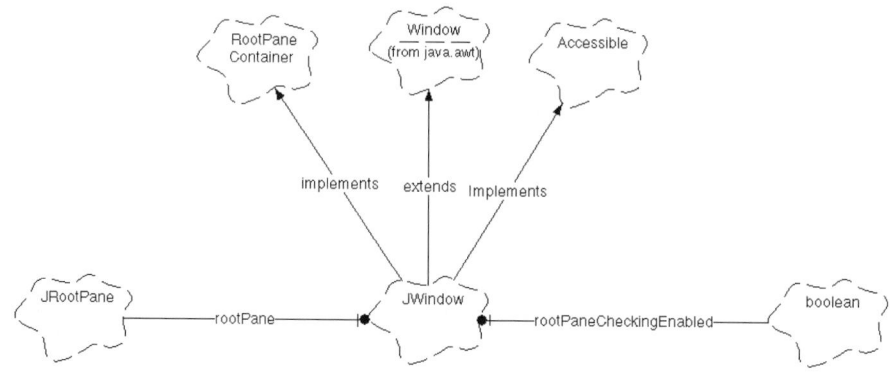

Figure 14-3 JWindow Class Diagram

JWindow is a heavyweight container and so does not have a model, UI delegate, renderer, or editor.

The JWindow class extends java.awt.Window and implements the Accessible and RootPaneContainer interfaces. JWindow maintains two protected references, one for its root pane and another for a boolean variable that tracks whether root pane checking is enabled. See "JRootPane" on page 636 or more information on root pane checking.

JWindow Properties

The properties maintained by the JWindow class are listed in Table 14-2.

Table 14-2   JWindow Properties

Property Name	Data Type	Property Type[1]	Access[2]	Default[3]
contentPane	Container	S	SG	JPanel instance
glassPane	Component	S	SG	Component instance
layeredPane	JLayeredPane	S	SG	JLayeredPane instance
rootPane	JRootPane	S	SG	JRootPane instance

1. B = bound (fires PropertyChangeEvent) / C = constrained/ I = indexed /
   S = simple / Ch = fires ChangeEvent
2. C = settable at construction time / G = getter method / S = setter method
3. L&F = look-and-feel dependent

contentPane — A container where the components that reside in an instance of JWindow are placed.

glassPane — A component that "floats" above all other components in a root pane.

layeredPane — Every root pane contains an instance of JLayeredPane that contains the root pane's menu bar and content pane.

rootPane — The only component that is contained directly within instances of JWindow.

Root panes and the components they contain—glass pane, layered pane, and content pane—are discussed at length in "Lightweight Containers" on page 629.

JWindow Class Summaries

The public and protected variables and methods for JWindow are listed in Class Summary 14-1.

Class Summary 14-1   JWindow

Constructors

---

public <u>JWindow</u>()
public <u>JWindow</u>(Frame)

All heavyweight windows must be anchored to a frame, which is known as the window's owner. For this reason, the JWindow class provides a constructor that takes a java.awt.Frame reference.

The JWindow class also provides a no-argument constructor that anchors the window to a shared, invisible frame that serves as the owner for all instances of JDialog and JWindow created with no-argument constructors. The shared frame is obtained from the SwingUtilities.getSharedOwnerFrame method.

Methods

Root Pane / Adding Components / Setting Layout Manager

---

protected void addImpl(Component, Object, int)
protected JRootPane createRootPane()
protected boolean isRootPaneCheckingEnabled()
protected void setRootPaneCheckingEnabled(boolean)
protected void setRootPane(JRootPane)

public void setLayout(LayoutManager)
protected void windowInit()

The first five methods listed above are used to set the window's root pane. JWindow, like other Swing components that implement the RootPaneContainer interface, disallows directly adding components to, or setting the layout manager for, the window. However, JWindow itself must add the root pane and set its layout manager. To accommodate this requirement, the setRootPaneCheckingEnabled and isRootPaneCheckingEnabled methods are used to enable instances of JWindow to add their root pane and set their layout manager, while at the same time disallowing these activities for outsiders.

The createRootPane method creates an instance of JRootPane. The method is protected so that extensions of JWindow can insert a specialized root pane, if desired.

The setLayout method throws an exception indicating that setting the layout manager by anyone other than the window itself is a forbidden activity.

The `windowInit` method is invoked by the `JWindow` constructors. Its only responsibility is to set the root pane and enable root pane checking after the root pane has been set. The method is `protected` so that `JWindow` extensions can perform some other tasks at construction time or override the default behavior, if desired.

RootPaneContainer Methods

---

public Container <u>getContentPane</u>()
public Component <u>getGlassPane</u>()
public JLayeredPane <u>getLayeredPane</u>()
public JRootPane <u>getLayeredPane</u>()

public void <u>setContentPane</u>(Container)
public void <u>setGlassPane</u>(Component)
public void <u>setLayeredPane</u>(JLayeredPane)

The methods listed above are defined by the `RootPaneContainer` interface. The `RootPaneContainer` interface and the `JRootPane` class are discussed in "Lightweight Containers" on page 629.

Accessible Context

---

public AccessibleContext <u>getAccessibleContext</u>()

`JWindow` implements the `Accessible` interface and therefore implements the method listed above. For more information on the `Accessible` interface and accessibility in general, see "Accessibility" on page 196.

AWT Compatibility

`JWindow` is an extension of `java.awt.Window` and therefore inherits all of the `public` methods implemented by the AWT's `Window` class.

The main difference between Swing windows and AWT windows is that Swing windows contain a root pane. As a result, components are added to Swing windows by accessing the window's content pane. Additionally, layout managers cannot be set for a Swing window directly; instead, layout managers must be set for the window's content pane.

JDialog

Like `JWindow`, `JDialog` is a heavyweight Swing container that contains an instance of `JRootPane` as its only component. Unlike Swing windows, Swing dialogs have a border and a title bar. Swing dialogs also typically have a close box in their title bar that dismisses the dialog. The exact nature of the components contained in a dialog's title bar is window-system dependent.

Swing dialogs can be *modal*, which means that access to other windows in the dialog's ancestry is denied while the dialog is being shown. Additionally, the thread that displays a modal dialog is blocked until the dialog is dismissed. By default, Swing dialogs are not modal.

Instances of `JDialog` are basic in nature; they are essentially native dialogs that are fitted with an instance of `JRootPane`. Creating dialogs by directly using the `JDialog` class involves laying out the components contained in the dialog, creating buttons for dismissing the dialog, and installing listeners that react to button activations. Swing provides a class that automates many of the activities involved in creating and displaying dialogs—the `JOptionPane` class, which is discussed in "JOptionPane" on page 815.

The applet shown in Figure 14-4 contains a button whose activation results in a dialog being displayed. The left-hand picture in Figure 14-4 shows the applet as it appears initially, and the right-hand picture shows the applet after the dialog has been displayed.

The applet creates an instance of `ConstraintsPanel` that contains all of the components in the dialog except for the OK, Apply, and Cancel buttons. The implementation of the `ConstraintsPanel` has no bearing on the concepts discussed here and so is not listed in the text. The implementation of the `ConstraintsPanel` is included on the CD in the back of this book.

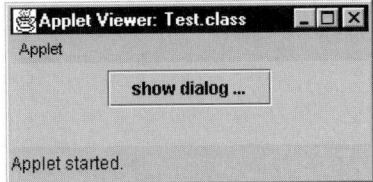

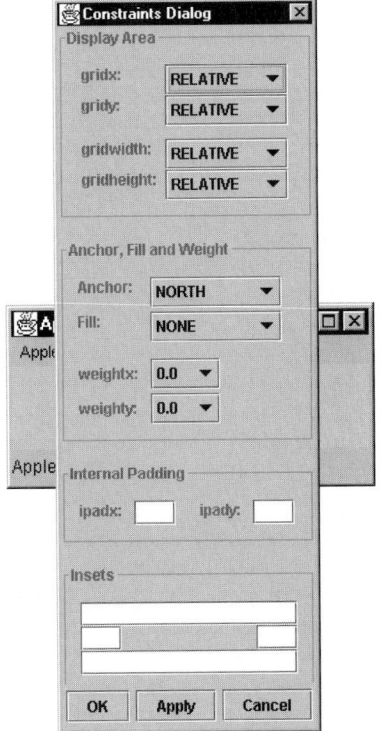

Figure 14-4 JDialog in Action

The applet creates an instance of `JPanel` that is used to contain the OK, Apply, and Cancel buttons. The applet also creates an instance of `JDialog`, specifying `null` as the frame for the dialog's owner, "Constraints Dialog" as the dialog's title, and `true` for the modal property.

A reference to the dialog's content pane is obtained by invocation of `getContentPane()` for the dialog, and the constraints and button panels are added to the content pane as the center and south components, respectively. The dialog is subsequently packed by invocation of the `pack` method, which sizes the dialog so that it is large enough to contain its components.

Note: A bug in the pack method sizes the dialog slightly shorter than it should be.

```
public class Test extends JApplet {
    private ConstraintsPanel cp = new ConstraintsPanel();
    private JPanel buttonsPanel = new JPanel();

    private JButton showButton = new JButton("show dialog ..."),
                    okButton = new JButton("OK"),
                    applyButton = new JButton("Apply"),
                    cancelButton = new JButton("Cancel");

    private JButton[] buttons = new  JButton[] {
        okButton, applyButton, cancelButton,
    };
    private JDialog dialog = new JDialog(null, // owner
                            "Constraints Dialog", // title
                            true); // modal

    public Test() {
        Container contentPane = getContentPane();
        Container dialogContentPane = dialog.getContentPane();

        contentPane.setLayout(new FlowLayout());
        contentPane.add(showButton);

        dialogContentPane.add(cp, BorderLayout.CENTER);
        dialogContentPane.add(buttonsPanel, BorderLayout.SOUTH);
        dialog.pack();

        // setLocationRelativeTo must be called after pack()
        // because dialog placement is based on dialog size.
        // Because the applet is not yet showing, calling
        // setLocationRelativeTo() here causes the dialog to be
        // shown centered on the screen.
        //
        // If setLocationRelativeTo() is not invoked, the dialog
        // will be located at (0,0) in screen coordinates.
        // dialog.setLocationRelativeTo(this);

        for(int i=0; i < buttons.length; ++i) {
            buttonsPanel.add(buttons[i]);
        }
        addButtonListeners();
    }
    ...
```

Listeners are added to the button displayed in the applet and the buttons displayed in the dialog. When the button contained in the applet is activated, it sets the location of the dialog relative to the applet itself and subsequently shows the dialog. The JDialog.setLocationRelativeTo method is discussed in Class Summary 14-2 on page 812.

Listeners are added to the OK, Apply, and Cancel buttons. Activating the OK and Cancel buttons disposes of the dialog by invoking the dispose method, which hides the dialog and disposes of the native resources associated with the dialog's window.

```
    . . .
    private void addButtonListeners() {
        showButton.addActionListener(new ActionListener() {
            public void actionPerformed(ActionEvent e) {
                // calling setLocationRelativeTo() here causes
                // the dialog to be centered over the applet.

                dialog.setLocationRelativeTo(Test.this);
                dialog.show();
            }
        });
        okButton.addActionListener(new ActionListener() {
            public void actionPerformed(ActionEvent e) {
                showStatus("OK button Activated");
                dialog.dispose();
            }
        });
        applyButton.addActionListener(new ActionListener() {
            public void actionPerformed(ActionEvent e) {
                showStatus("Apply button Activated");
            }
        });
        cancelButton.addActionListener(new ActionListener() {
            public void actionPerformed(ActionEvent e) {
                showStatus("Cancel button Activated");
                dialog.dispose();
            }
        });
    }
}
```

The applet shown in Figure 14-4 is listed in its entirety in Example 14-3.

Example 14-3   JDialog in Action

```
import java.awt.*;
import java.awt.event.*;
import javax.swing.*;

public class Test extends JApplet {
    private ConstraintsPanel cp = new ConstraintsPanel();
    private JPanel buttonsPanel = new JPanel();
```

```
private JButton showButton = new JButton("show dialog ..."),
            okButton = new JButton("OK"),
            applyButton = new JButton("Apply"),
            cancelButton = new JButton("Cancel");

private JButton[] buttons = new  JButton[] {
   okButton, applyButton, cancelButton,
};

private JDialog dialog = new JDialog(null, // owner
                           "Constraints Dialog", // title
                           true); // modal
public Test() {
   Container contentPane = getContentPane();
   Container dialogContentPane = dialog.getContentPane();

   contentPane.setLayout(new FlowLayout());
   contentPane.add(showButton);

   dialogContentPane.add(cp, BorderLayout.CENTER);
   dialogContentPane.add(buttonsPanel, BorderLayout.SOUTH);
   dialog.pack();

   // setLocationRelativeTo must be called after pack(),
   // because dialog placement is based on dialog size.
   // Because the applet is not yet showing, calling
   // setLocationRelativeTo() here causes the dialog to be
   // shown centered on the screen.
   //
   // If setLocationRelativeTo() is not invoked, the dialog
   // will be located at (0,0) in screen coordinates.
   // dialog.setLocationRelativeTo(this);

   for(int i=0; i < buttons.length; ++i) {
      buttonsPanel.add(buttons[i]);
   }
   addButtonListeners();
}
private void addButtonListeners() {
   showButton.addActionListener(new ActionListener() {
      public void actionPerformed(ActionEvent e) {
         // calling setLocationRelativeTo() here causes
         // the dialog to be centered over the applet.
         dialog.setLocationRelativeTo(Test.this);
         dialog.show();
      }
   });
```

```
        okButton.addActionListener(new ActionListener() {
            public void actionPerformed(ActionEvent e) {
                showStatus("OK button Activated");
                dialog.dispose();
            }
        });
        applyButton.addActionListener(new ActionListener() {
            public void actionPerformed(ActionEvent e) {
                showStatus("Apply button Activated");
            }
        });
        cancelButton.addActionListener(new ActionListener() {
            public void actionPerformed(ActionEvent e) {
                showStatus("Cancel button Activated");
                dialog.dispose();
            }
        });
    }
}
```

The JDialog component is summarized in Component Summary 14-2.

Component Summary 14-2   JDialog

Model(s)	——
UI Delegate(s)	——
Renderer(s)	——
Editor(s)	——
Events Fired	——
Replacement For	java.awt.Dialog

Class Diagrams

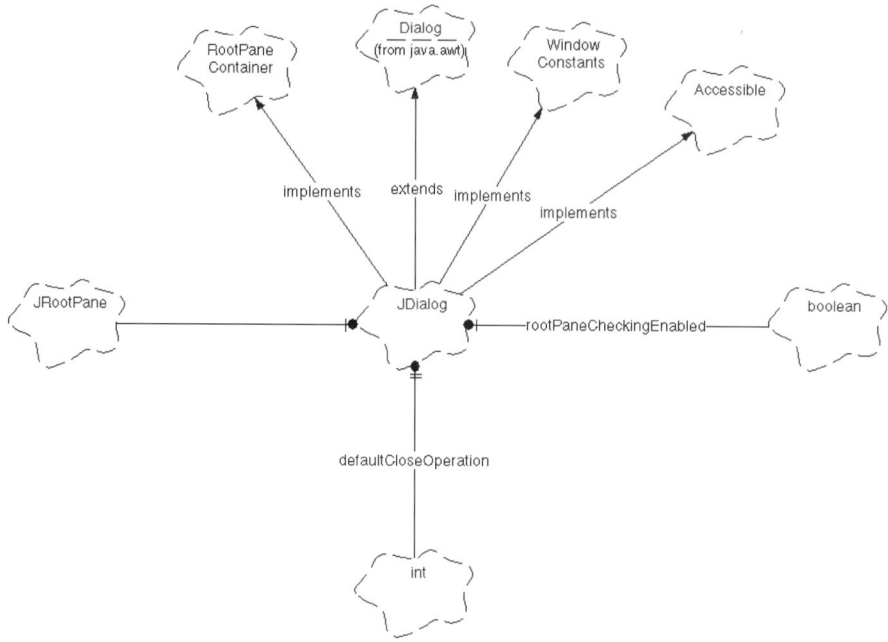

Figure 14-5 JDialog Class Diagram

The JDialog class extends java.awt.Dialog and implements the Accessible, WindowConstants and RootPaneContainer interfaces. Like JWindow, JDialog has no model, UI delegate, renderers, or editors.

The JDialog class maintains protected references to its root pane and a boolean value that tracks whether root pane checking is enabled. Each instance of JDialog also maintains a protected integer value that specifies the default close operation. See "JDialog Properties" for more information on the default close operation.

JDialog Properties

The properties maintained by the `JDialog` class are listed in Table 14-3.

Table 14-3   JDialog Properties

Property Name	Data Type	Property Type[1]	Access[2]	Default[3]
contentPane	Container	S	SG	JPanel instance
defaultCloseOperation	int	S	SG	HIDE_ON_CLOSE
glassPane	Component	S	SG	Component instance
jMenuBar	JMenuBar	S	SG	null
layeredPane	JLayeredPane	S	SG	JLayeredPane instance
locationRelativeTo	Component	S	G	
rootPane	JRootPane	S	SG	JRootPane instance

1. B = bound (fires PropertyChangeEvent) / C = constrained/ I = indexed / S = simple / Ch = fires ChangeEvent
2. C = settable at construction time / G = getter method / S = setter method
3. L&F = look-and-feel dependent

contentPane — A container where the components that reside in an instance of `JDialog` are placed.

defaultCloseOperation — An operation that will be performed when a dialog is closed. The `defaultCloseOperation` property must be specified as one of the following `integer` values:

- `WindowConstants.HIDE_ON_CLOSE`
- `WindowConstants.DISPOSE_ON_CLOSE`
- `WindowConstants.DO_NOTHING_ON_CLOSE`

glassPane — A component that "floats" above all other components in a root pane.

jMenuBar — The menu bar associated with a dialog.

layeredPane — Every root pane contains an instance of `JLayeredPane` that contains the root pane's menu bar and content pane.

locationRelativeTo — Specifies where the dialog will be shown. If the component passed to setLocationRelativeTo() is null, the dialog will be displayed at (0,0) in screen coordinates.

   If the component is non-null but is not visible when the call to setRelativeTo() is made, the dialog will be centered on the screen.

   If the component is non-null and is visible when the call to setLocationRelativeTo() is made, the dialog will be centered over the component that was specified.

rootPane — The only component that is contained directly within instances of JDialog.

JDialog Class Summaries

The public and protected variables and methods for JDialog are listed in Class Summary 14-3.

Class Summary 14-2   JDialog

Constructors

---

public JDialog()
public JDialog(Frame owner)
public JDialog(Frame owner, boolean modal)
public JDialog(Frame owner, String title)
public JDialog(Frame owner, String title, boolean modal)

The `JDialog` class provides the five constructors listed above. The no-argument constructor creates a non-modal dialog with no title and with a shared frame as its owner.

The last four constructors listed above are passed a frame that serves as the dialog's owner. The `boolean` argument specifies the modality of the dialog, and the string argument represents the title displayed in the dialog's title bar.

Methods

Root Pane / Adding Components / Window Events

---

protected void <u>addImpl</u>(Component, Object, int)
protected JRootPane <u>createRootPane</u>()
protected boolean <u>isRootPaneCheckingEnabled</u>()
protected void <u>setRootPaneCheckingEnabled</u>(boolean)
protected void <u>setRootPane</u>(JRootPane)

protected void <u>dialogInit</u>()
protected void <u>processWindowEvent</u>(WindowEvent)

The first group of `protected` methods listed above are used to set the dialog's root pane. The methods are identical to methods of the same name in the `JWindow` class.

The `dialogInit` method is invoked by `JDialog` constructors and sets the root pane for the dialog in addition to enabling window events.

The `processWindowEvent` method is overridden from the `java.awt.Component` class to account for the dialog's default close operation, which is discussed below.

Default Close Operation / Menu Bar / Layout Manager

---

public int <u>getDefaultCloseOperation</u>()
public void <u>setDefaultCloseOperation</u>(int)

public JMenuBar getJMenuBar()
public void setJMenuBar(JMenuBar)

public void setLayout(LayoutManager)

Like the JFrame class, JDialog maintains a default close operation that is defined by one of the constants defined by the WindowConstants interface.

Unlike AWT dialogs, Swing dialogs can support a menu bar, as evidenced by the menu bar accessors listed above.

JDialog, like JFrame, overrides setLayout to throw an exception if an attempt is made to set a dialog's layout manager when root pane checking is enabled.

RootPaneContainer Methods

public Container getContentPane()
public Component getGlassPane()
public JLayeredPane getLayeredPane()
public JRootPane getRootPane()

public void setContentPane(Container)
public void setGlassPane(Component)
public void setLayeredPane(JLayeredPane)

The methods listed above are defined by the RootPaneContainer interface. The RootPaneContainer interface and the JRootPane class are discussed in "JRootPane" on page 636.

Relative Location / Updating

public void setLocationRelativeTo(Component)
public void update(Graphics)

The setLocationRelativeTo method can be used to set the position of a dialog relative to a component. See "JDialog Properties" on page 811 for more information on the setLocationRelativeTo method.

JDialog, like most Swing components that do not have a UI delegate, overrides its update method to call paint() directly. Doing so eliminates clearing the background of the dialog because by default, update() clears the background and subsequently invokes paint().

Accessible Context

---

public AccessibleContext getAccessibleContext()

JDialog implements the Accessible interface and therefore implements the method listed above. For more information on the Accessible interface and accessibility in general, see "Accessibility" on page 196.

AWT Compatibility

JDialog is an extension of java.awt.Dialog and therefore inherits all of the public methods implemented by the AWT's Dialog class.

The main difference between Swing dialogs and AWT dialogs is that Swing dialogs contain a root pane. As a result, components are added to Swing dialogs via the dialog's content pane. Additionally, layout managers cannot be set for a Swing dialog directly; instead, layout managers must be set for the dialog's content pane.

JOptionPane

Option panes, represented by the JOptionPane class, are components that are meant to be placed in a dialog box. Option panes can display an icon, a message, one or more selectable values, and a row of buttons.

Option panes are quite flexible and can be used in almost any type of dialog. For example, the "message" displayed in an option pane is specified with a reference to an `Object`, meaning that any object can be used as the message displayed in an option pane. The manner in which message objects are displayed is dependent upon the actual type of the object; strings and components are displayed as is, whereas icons are wrapped in an instance of `JLabel`. Message objects that are not strings, components, or icons are represented by displaying the string returned from the object's `toString` method. The message object can also be an `Object` array where each item in the array is displayed as described above and stacked vertically, from top to bottom, in the order in which it is stored in the array. See Example 14-8 on page 836 for an option pane whose message is specified with an array of strings.

The icon and buttons displayed in an option pane can be automatically configured by an option pane's look and feel, or they can be explicitly specified. The `JOptionPane` class provides two properties—`icon` and `optionType`—that determine the icon and buttons, respectively, that are used in an option pane. Additionally, the `JOptionPane` class provides another property—`options`— that can be used to specify the buttons explicitly.

The `JOptionPane` class provides a convenience method that creates a dialog and installs an instance of `JOptionPane` in the dialog. Additionally, `JOptionPane` also provides numerous `static` convenience methods that create dialogs containing fully configured option panes.

The applet shown in Figure 14-6 contains two buttons that cause dialogs to be displayed when the buttons are activated. Activating the top button results in the creation of an instance of `JOptionPane` and the subsequent creation of a dialog containing the option pane. The activation of the bottom button results in the creation of a dialog by invoking the `static` `JOptionPane.createMessageDialog` method.

The top picture in Figure 14-6 shows the applet as it appears initially. The middle picture shows the dialog created when the top button is activated, and the bottom picture shows the dialog created when the bottom button is activated.

The applet adds action listeners to each of the buttons. The listener for the top button creates an instance of `JOptionPane` by specifying the message and a message type of `JOptionPane.INFORMATION_MESSAGE`. A dialog is subsequently created by invocation of `JOptionPane.createDialog()`, which is passed a *parent component* and a title for the dialog. The dialog is made visible by invocation of its `show` method.

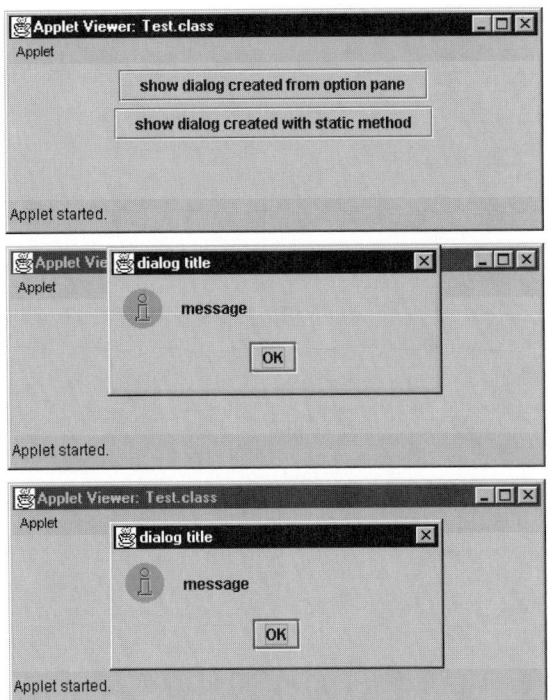

Figure 14-6 Creating Dialogs with JOptionPane

The parent component passed to JOptionPane.createDialog() positions the dialog, which is centered above the parent component. In this case, the parent component is specified as the button whose activation resulted in the dialog being created.

```
public class Test extends JApplet {
    ...
    private String title = "dialog title";
    private String message = "message";

    public Test() {
    ...
        topButton.addActionListener(new ActionListener() {
            public void actionPerformed(ActionEvent e) {
                JOptionPane optionPane = new JOptionPane(
                  message, // message
                  JOptionPane.INFORMATION_MESSAGE); // messageType
```

```
                    JDialog dialog = optionPane.createDialog(
                       topButton, // parentComponent
                       title); // title

                    dialog.show();
                 }
             });
             ...
```

The listener for the bottom button in the applet shown in Figure 14-6 creates a dialog by invoking the static JOptionPane.showMessageDialog method. Notice that the parent component for the dialog associated with the bottom button is also the button that shows the dialog. As the pictures in Figure 14-6 indicate, the dialogs shown by the applet are centered over the buttons that are specified as the dialog's parent components.

```
         bottomButton.addActionListener(new ActionListener() {
             public void actionPerformed(ActionEvent e) {
                 JOptionPane.showMessageDialog(
                    bottomButton, // parentComponent
                    message, // message
                    title, // title
                    JOptionPane.INFORMATION_MESSAGE); // messageType
             }
         });
         ...
      }
      ...
   }
```

Both of the dialogs shown by the applet are modal dialogs, which means that access to windows in the dialog's ancestry is denied when the dialogs are displayed. In addition, modal dialogs also block execution of the thread that displays the dialog. All dialogs created by the JOptionPane class are modal.

The applet shown in Figure 14-6 is listed in its entirety in Example 14-4.

Example 14-4 Creating Dialogs with JOptionPane

```
   import java.awt.*;
   import java.awt.event.*;
   import javax.swing.*;

   public class Test extends JApplet {
      private JButton topButton = new JButton(
                   "show dialog created from option pane");
```

```
    private JButton bottomButton = new JButton(
                "show dialog created with static method");

    private String title = "dialog title";
    private String message = "message";

    public Test() {
        Container contentPane = getContentPane();

        contentPane.setLayout(new FlowLayout());
        contentPane.add(topButton);
        contentPane.add(bottomButton);

        topButton.addActionListener(new ActionListener() {
            public void actionPerformed(ActionEvent e) {
                JOptionPane optionPane = new JOptionPane(
                  message, // message
                  JOptionPane.INFORMATION_MESSAGE); // messageType

                JDialog dialog = optionPane.createDialog(
                  topButton, // parentComponent
                  title); // title

                dialog.show();
            }
        });
        bottomButton.addActionListener(new ActionListener() {
            public void actionPerformed(ActionEvent e) {
                JOptionPane.showMessageDialog(
                  bottomButton, // parentComponent
                  message, // message
                  title, // title
                  JOptionPane.INFORMATION_MESSAGE); // messageType
            }
        });
    }
}
```

Internal Frames

In addition to `static` methods that create dialogs equipped with option panes, the `JOptionPane` class also provides a full complement of analogous methods that create internal frames.

The applet shown in Figure 14-7 contains a button whose activation results in the creation of an internal frame.

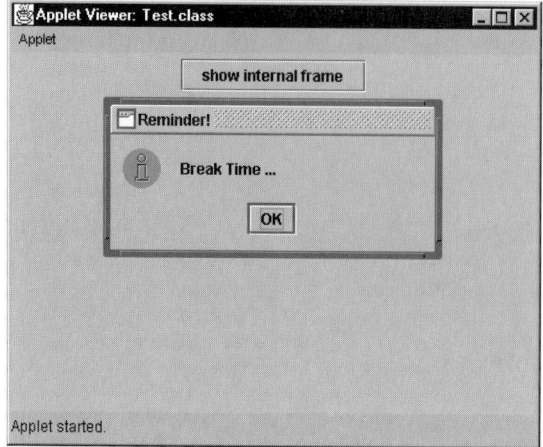

Figure 14-7 Creating Internal Frames with JOptionPane

The applet shown in Figure 14-7 is listed in Example 14-5.

Example 14-5 Creating Internal Frames with JOptionPane

```java
import java.awt.*;
import java.awt.event.*;
import javax.swing.*;

public class Test extends JApplet {
    private JButton button = new JButton("show internal frame");

    public Test() {
        Container contentPane = getContentPane();

        contentPane.setLayout(new FlowLayout());
        contentPane.add(button);

        button.addActionListener(new ActionListener() {
            public void actionPerformed(ActionEvent e) {
                JOptionPane.showInternalMessageDialog(
                    button, // parentComponent
                    "Break Time ...", // message
                    "Reminder!", // title
                    JOptionPane.INFORMATION_MESSAGE); // messageType
            }
        });
    }
}
```

The applet adds an action listener to its button that is nearly identical to the listener associated with the applet shown in Figure 14-6. The only difference between the two listeners is that the listener for the button in the applet shown in Figure 14-7 invokes the `showInternalMessageDialog` method instead of `showMessageDialog`.

Swing Tip ...

Dialogs Created by the JOptionPane Class Are Modal

Dialogs created by static JOptionPane methods or JOptionPane.createDialog() are modal. Modal dialogs disallow access to windows in the dialog's ancestry and block execution of the thread that displayed the dialog.

Because dialogs created by static JOptionPane methods are modal, the next line of code following calls to JOptionPane.showXXXDialog methods is not executed until the dialog is dismissed:

```
...
JOptionPane.showMessageDialog(parentComponent, "a message");

// the following line of code is not executed until the message
dialog is dismissed

someObject.someMethod();
...
```

Note: *As of Swing 1.1 FCS, internal frames created by* `JOptionPane` `static` *methods are not modal.*

Creating Dialogs with JOptionPane Static Methods

The `JOptionPane` class provides seven constructors that allow option panes to be created with an infinite variety of configurations. See Figure 14-18 on page 861 for an example of an applet that creates instances of `JOptionPane` of various configurations.

`JOptionPane` also provides a set of `static` methods that create dialogs containing option panes that represent common dialog configurations. The types of dialogs created by `JOptionPane` `static` methods are summarized in Table 14-4.

Table 14-4   Dialog Types Created by Static JOptionPane Methods

Dialog Type	Description	Value Returned	Configurable Items
Message	Displays a message and an OK button	——	title, message, message type, icon
Confirmation	Asks a question answered by button selection	An integer representing the selected button	title, message, message type, icon, option type (buttons)
Input	Prompts for input with a text field, combo box, or list[1]	A string representing the response	title, message, message type, icon, selection values, initial value
Option	Similar to confirmation dialog, except that objects in button row are fully configurable	An integer representing the selected button	title, message, message type, option type (buttons), icon, options, initial value

1. Actual components used are look-and-feel dependent

Message dialogs are the simplest types of dialogs that can be created with JOptionPane static methods. Message dialogs display a message and come equipped with a single button labeled OK.

Confirmation dialogs pose a question that is answered by the selection of a button displayed in the dialog. Static JOptionPane methods that create confirmation dialogs return an integer value indicating the button that was activated. The buttons displayed in confirmation dialogs can be configured from a predetermined set of buttons; see Table 14-5 for a list of button configurations that can be specified with the optionType parameter.

Input dialogs capture input by displaying a component such as a text field, combo box, or list. The actual component used is look-and-feel dependent and depends upon the selection values specified for the input dialog.

Option dialogs are the only type of dialog created by static JOptionPane methods that allows complete configuration of the components that reside in the dialog's button row.

The parameters passed to static JOptionPane methods that create the types of dialogs listed in Table 14-4 follow a consistent pattern, so it is worthwhile to present the different types of parameters listed in Table 14-5.

Table 14-5 Parameters Used In Constructing JOptionPane Dialogs

Parameter	Description	Applies to
parent Component (Component)	The dialog's parent is set to the frame that contains the component. The dialog is typically centered above the component; however, dialog placement is look-and-feel dependent.	All

message (Object)	The message displayed in the option pane. The data type of the object determines how the message is displayed:
	
	Object[]: Each object in the array is recursively interpreted as outlined below and arranged vertically from top to bottom, in order.
	
	    String: Strings are displayed as is.
	    Component: Components are displayed as is.
	    Icon: Icon is wrapped in a JLabel.
	    Object: The string returned from toString() is displayed.
		All

messageType (int)	Defines the style of the dialog including layout and the icon used. Dialog style is look-and-feel dependent. Allowable values are:
	
	`JOptionPane.ERROR_MESSAGE`
	`JOptionPane.INFORMATION_MESSAGE`
	`JOptionPane.WARNING_MESSAGE`
	`JOptionPane.QUESTION_MESSAGE`
	`JOptionPane.PLAIN_MESSAGE`
		All

icon (Icon)	A decorative icon. If not explicitly set, the icon used is determined by the messageType parameter.	All
title (String)	The dialog's title.	All

optionType (int)	Defines the buttons displayed in the option pane. Allowable values are:
	
	`JOptionPane.DEFAULT_OPTION`
	`JOptionPane.YES_NO_OPTION`
	`JOptionPane.YES_NO_CANCEL_OPTION`
	`JOptionPane.OK_CANCEL_OPTION`
		Confirm Option

selection Values (Object[])	An array of objects used as entries in combo boxes or lists for input dialogs. Strings are most commonly used, but any object can be used as a selection value. If an object in the array is not a string, the string returned from the toString method is used as an entry.	Input

Table 14-5   Parameters Used In Constructing JOptionPane Dialogs (Continued)

Parameter	Description	Applies to
initial SelectionValue (Object)	The initially selected object from the selectionValues parameter.	Input
options (Object[])	Defines the objects displayed in the button row (overrides optionType). Data type determines how the options are displayed: Object[]: Each object in the array is recursively interpreted as outlined below and arranged horizontally in the button row from left to right, in order. String[]: Each string in the array is interpreted as outlined below and arranged horizontally in the button row in order. String: Used as the label for a button. Icon: Icon is wrapped in a JButton. Component: Component is added to button row as is.	Option
initialValue (Object)	The component in the button row that is initially given focus when the dialog is displayed.	Option

Recall that messages displayed in dialogs containing option panes can be any type of object, with strings, components, and icons receiving special consideration. Likewise, the objects displayed in the button row—specified by the options property—can also be any type of object, including an array of objects that are displayed horizontally from left to right in the order in which they appear in the array.

The parent component, message, message type, and dialog title can be specified for all types of dialogs created by static JOptionPane methods.

The option type parameter, which determines the set of buttons displayed in the dialog's button row, can be specified for confirmation and option dialogs. Message dialogs always contain a single button labeled OK, and input dialogs always contain two buttons labeled OK and Cancel, so the option type parameter cannot be specified for message or input dialogs.

The selection values and initially selected value parameters apply only to input dialogs because input dialogs are the only type of dialog that supports selections made from a list of values.

The options parameter, which is used to customize the components contained in the dialog's button row, can only be specified for option dialogs because only option dialogs can customize their button row. Likewise, the initial value parameter, which determines the component in the button row that initially receives focus, can only be specified for option dialogs.

Message Dialogs

Message dialogs display an informational message and always have a single button labeled OK. The message, title, icon, and message type for the dialog can be set.

The `static JOptionPane` methods used to create message dialogs are listed below.

---

public static void <u>showMessageDialog</u>(Component parentComponent,
                          Object message)
public static void <u>showMessageDialog</u>(Component parentComponent,
                          Object message,
                          String title,
                          int messageType)
public static void <u>showMessageDialog</u>(Component parentComponent,
                          Object message,
                          String title,
                          int messageType,
                          Icon *icon*)

The parameters passed to `JOptionPane showMessageDialog` methods are summarized in Table 14-6. See Table 14-5 for more information concerning the parameters listed in Table 14-6.

Table 14-6   Parameters Used In Creating Message Dialogs

Property	Allowable Values	Default
parentComponent	Any visible component	Must be specified
message	An Object	Must be specified

Table 14-6   Parameters Used In Creating Message Dialogs (Continued)

Property	Allowable Values	Default
title	A string	"Message"
messageType	ERROR_MESSAGE INFORMATION_MESSAGE PLAIN_MESSAGE QUESTION_MESSAGE WARNING_MESSAGE	INFORMATION_MESSAGE
icon	An icon	Selected by look and feel, depending upon messageType

The dialogs shown in Figure 14-8 represent the five message types that can be specified for JOptionPane dialogs: information, warning, error, question, and plain. The dialogs shown in Figure 14-8 are configured with the Metal look and feel.

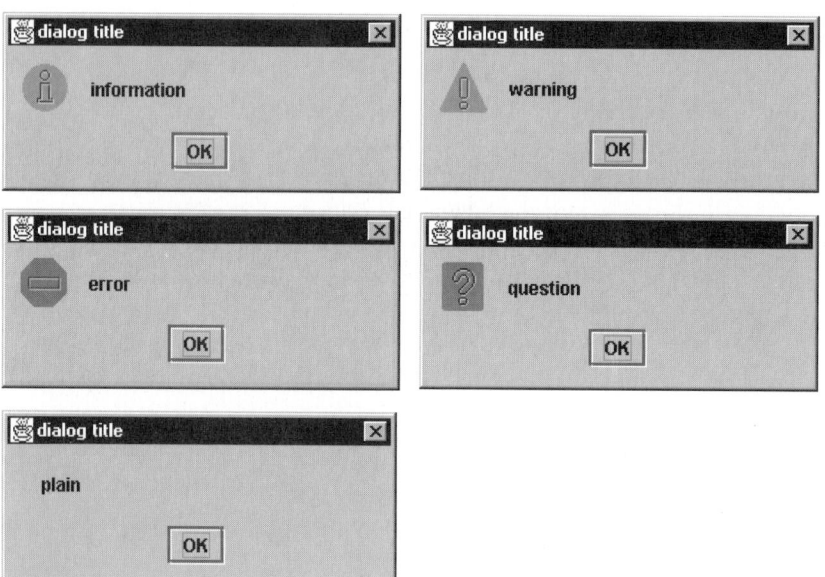

Figure 14-8 Message Types with Metal Look and Feel

The message type specified for a dialog determines the icon displayed in the dialog, provided that an icon has not been explicitly specified. The standard Swing look and feels modify only the icon displayed in the option pane, but other look and feels are free to modify other characteristics, such as the dialog's layout, as well.

The applet shown in Figure 14-9 is responsible for creating and displaying the dialogs shown in Figure 14-8.

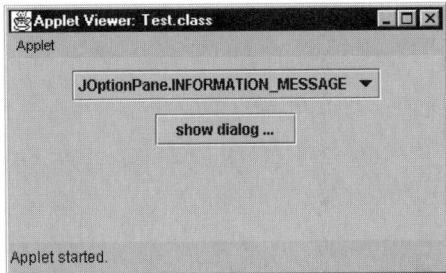

Figure 14-9 Displaying Message Dialogs with Different Message Types

The applet contains a combo box for selecting the message type and a button for creating and displaying a message dialog with the selected message type.

The combo box is contained in an instance of ControlPanel, which is an extension of the JPanel class. An item listener added to the combo box sets the message type for the next dialog to be created, depending upon the selection made in combo box.

```
class ControlPanel extends JPanel {
    private JComboBox messageTypes = new JComboBox();
    private int[] typeValues = {
        JOptionPane.INFORMATION_MESSAGE,
        JOptionPane.ERROR_MESSAGE,
        JOptionPane.WARNING_MESSAGE,
        JOptionPane.QUESTION_MESSAGE,
        JOptionPane.PLAIN_MESSAGE,
    };
    private String[] typeNames = {
        "JOptionPane.INFORMATION_MESSAGE",
        "JOptionPane.ERROR_MESSAGE",
        "JOptionPane.WARNING_MESSAGE",
        "JOptionPane.QUESTION_MESSAGE",
```

```
            "JOptionPane.PLAIN_MESSAGE",
      };

      public ControlPanel(final Test applet) {
          add(messageTypes);

          for(int i=0; i < typeNames.length; ++i) {
              messageTypes.addItem(typeNames[i]);
          }
          messageTypes.addItemListener(new ItemListener() {
              public void itemStateChanged(ItemEvent e) {
                  String s = (String)messageTypes.getSelectedItem();
                  int type;

                  for(int i=0; i < typeNames.length; ++i) {
                      if(s.equals(typeNames[i]))
                          applet.setMessageType(typeValues[i]);
                  }
              }
          });
      }
      ...
  }
```

The applet implements a `setMessageType` method that is invoked by the item listener associated with the combo box. The `setMessageType` method is passed an integer constant representing the message type and selects an appropriate message to be displayed in the dialog.

```
      ...
      public void setMessageType(int messageType) {
          this.messageType = messageType;

          switch(messageType) {
              case JOptionPane.INFORMATION_MESSAGE:
                  message = messages[0];
                  break;
              case JOptionPane.ERROR_MESSAGE:
                  message = messages[1];
                  break;
              case JOptionPane.WARNING_MESSAGE:
                  message = messages[2];
                  break;
              case JOptionPane.QUESTION_MESSAGE:
                  message = messages[3];
                  break;
              case JOptionPane.PLAIN_MESSAGE:
                  message = messages[4];
                  break;
```

```
        }
    }
}
```

The applet adds an action listener to the button that invokes
JOptionPane.showMessageDialog(), which is passed the button and
message type. The button is used as a parent component for the dialog.

```
public class Test extends JApplet {
    private JButton button = new JButton("show dialog ...");

    private String title = "dialog title";
    private String message = "information";
    private int messageType = JOptionPane.INFORMATION_MESSAGE;
    private String messages[] = {
        "information", "error", "warning", "question", "plain"
    };

    public Test() {
        Container contentPane = getContentPane();
        JPanel controlPanel = new ControlPanel(this);

        contentPane.setLayout(new FlowLayout());
        contentPane.add(controlPanel);
        contentPane.add(button);

        button.addActionListener(new ActionListener() {
            public void actionPerformed(ActionEvent e) {
                JOptionPane.showMessageDialog(
                  button, // parentComponent
                  message, // message
                  title, // title
                  messageType);
            }
        });
    }
    ...
```

The applet shown in Figure 14-9 is listed in its entirety in Example 14-6.

Example 14-6 Displaying Message Dialogs with Different Message Types

```
import java.awt.*;
import java.awt.event.*;
import javax.swing.*;

public class Test extends JApplet {
```

```java
    private JButton button = new JButton("show dialog ...");

    private String title = "dialog title";
    private String message = "information";
    private int messageType = JOptionPane.INFORMATION_MESSAGE;
    private String messages[] = {
        "information", "error", "warning", "question", "plain"
    };

    public Test() {
        Container contentPane = getContentPane();
        JPanel controlPanel = new ControlPanel(this);

        contentPane.setLayout(new FlowLayout());
        contentPane.add(controlPanel);
        contentPane.add(button);

        button.addActionListener(new ActionListener() {
            public void actionPerformed(ActionEvent e) {
                JOptionPane.showMessageDialog(
                    button, // parentComponent
                    message, // message
                    title, // title
                    messageType);
            }
        });
    }
    public void setMessageType(int messageType) {
        this.messageType = messageType;

        switch(messageType) {
            case JOptionPane.INFORMATION_MESSAGE:
                    message = messages[0];
                    break;
            case JOptionPane.ERROR_MESSAGE:
                    message = messages[1];
                    break;
            case JOptionPane.WARNING_MESSAGE:
                    message = messages[2];
                    break;
            case JOptionPane.QUESTION_MESSAGE:
                    message = messages[3];
                    break;
            case JOptionPane.PLAIN_MESSAGE:
                    message = messages[4];
                    break;
        }
    }
}
class ControlPanel extends JPanel {
    private JComboBox messageTypes = new JComboBox();
    private int[] typeValues = {
```

```
            JOptionPane.INFORMATION_MESSAGE,
            JOptionPane.ERROR_MESSAGE,
            JOptionPane.WARNING_MESSAGE,
            JOptionPane.QUESTION_MESSAGE,
            JOptionPane.PLAIN_MESSAGE,
        };
        private String[] typeNames = {
            "JOptionPane.INFORMATION_MESSAGE",
            "JOptionPane.ERROR_MESSAGE",
            "JOptionPane.WARNING_MESSAGE",
            "JOptionPane.QUESTION_MESSAGE",
            "JOptionPane.PLAIN_MESSAGE",
        };

        public ControlPanel(final Test applet) {
            add(messageTypes);

            for(int i=0; i < typeNames.length; ++i) {
                messageTypes.addItem(typeNames[i]);
            }
            messageTypes.addItemListener(new ItemListener() {
                public void itemStateChanged(ItemEvent e) {
                    String s = (String)messageTypes.getSelectedItem();
                    int type;

                    for(int i=0; i < typeNames.length; ++i) {
                        if(s.equals(typeNames[i]))
                            applet.setMessageType(typeValues[i]);
                    }
                }
            });
        }
    }
```

The dialog shown in Figure 14-10 is also a message dialog that has been fitted with an explicit icon. The icon specified replaces the icon that would normally be displayed by the option pane's look and feel, depending upon the message type associated with the option pane.

Figure 14-10 Replacing the Default Icon In a Message Dialog

The dialog shown in Figure 14-10 is created and displayed by the applet listed in Example 14-7.

Example 14-7   Replacing the Default Icon in a Message Dialog

```java
import java.awt.*;
import java.awt.event.*;
import javax.swing.*;

public class Test extends JApplet {
    private JButton button = new JButton("show dialog ...");

    private String title = "Reminder!";
    private String message = "Dinner time";

    public Test() {
        Container contentPane = getContentPane();

        contentPane.setLayout(new FlowLayout());
        contentPane.add(button);

        button.addActionListener(new ActionListener() {
            public void actionPerformed(ActionEvent e) {
                JOptionPane.showMessageDialog(
                    button, // parentComponent
                    message, // message
                    title, // title
                    JOptionPane.INFORMATION_MESSAGE,// messageType
                    new ImageIcon("dining.gif")); // icon
            }
        });
    }
}
```

The applet invokes the version of `JOptionPane.showMessageDialog()`, which is passed a reference to an icon to use in the dialog.

Swing Tip ...

Interpretation of Message Type Is Look-and-Feel Dependent

All option panes have a message type property that specifies a particular look and feel for the option pane. The standard Swing look and feels determine the icon displayed in an option pane, based on the message type property. However, other look and feels are free to modify other characteristics of an option pane, depending upon the option pane's message type property. For example, a custom look and feel can modify an option pane's layout, depending upon the option pane's message type.

Confirmation Dialogs

Whereas message dialogs display an informational message that requires no response, confirmation dialogs ask a question that is answered by a user selecting a button. As a result, there are two major differences between message dialogs and confirmation dialogs.

First, the static JOptionPane methods that show confirmation dialogs return an integer value indicating the button that was activated, whereas the methods that show message dialogs do not return a value. The integer value returned from the static showConfirmDialog methods is one of the following constants:

- JOptionPane.YES_OPTION
- JOptionPane.NO_OPTION
- JOptionPane.CANCEL_OPTION
- JOptionPane.OK_OPTION
- JOptionPane.CLOSED_OPTION

The constants listed above correspond to the button that was activated, with the exception of JOptionPane.CLOSED_OPTION. If the dialog is closed without one of the buttons in the button row being activated, for instance, by a user clicking the close box, JOptionPane.CLOSED_OPTION is returned.

Second, the `option type` property can be specified when a confirmation dialog is created and shown. The `option type` property determines which buttons are displayed in the dialog, as outlined in Table 14-5 on page 823. Notice that there is no provision with confirmation dialogs for specifying custom buttons (or other components) to be placed in the button row for a confirmation dialog. Confirmation dialogs are limited to Yes, No, and Cancel buttons.

The `static JOptionPane` methods used to create confirmation dialogs are listed below.

---

public static int <u>showConfirmDialog</u>(Component parentComponent,
                                  Object message)
public static int <u>showConfirmDialog</u>(Component parentComponent,
                                  Object message,
                                  String title,
                                  int optionType)
public static int <u>showConfirmDialog</u>(Component parentComponent,
                                  Object message,
                                  String title,
                                  int optionType,
                                  int messageType)
public static int <u>showConfirmDialog</u>(Component parentComponent,
                                  Object message,
                                  String title,
                                  int optionType,
                                  int messageType,
                                  Icon icon)

The parameters passed to `JOptionPane showConfirmDialog` methods are summarized in Figure 14-7. See Table 14-5 on page 823 for more information concerning the parameters listed in Figure 14-7.

Table 14-7   Parameters Used In Creating Confirmation Dialogs

Property	Allowable Values	Default
parentComponent	Any visible component	Must be specified
message	An Object	Must be specified
title	A string	"Select an Option"

Table 14-7 Parameters Used In Creating Confirmation Dialogs (Continued)

Property	Allowable Values	Default
messageType	ERROR_MESSAGE INFORMATION_MESSAGE PLAIN_MESSAGE QUESTION_MESSAGE WARNING_MESSAGE	QUESTION_MESSAGE
icon	An icon	Selected by look and feel, depending upon messageType
optionType	YES_NO_OPTION YES_NO_CANCEL_OPTION OK_CANCEL_OPTION	YES_NO_CANCEL_OPTION

The applet shown in Figure 14-11 contains a button whose activation results in the creation and display of a confirmation dialog. After the dialog is dismissed by activation of one of its buttons, the label associated with the activated button is displayed in the applet's status area.

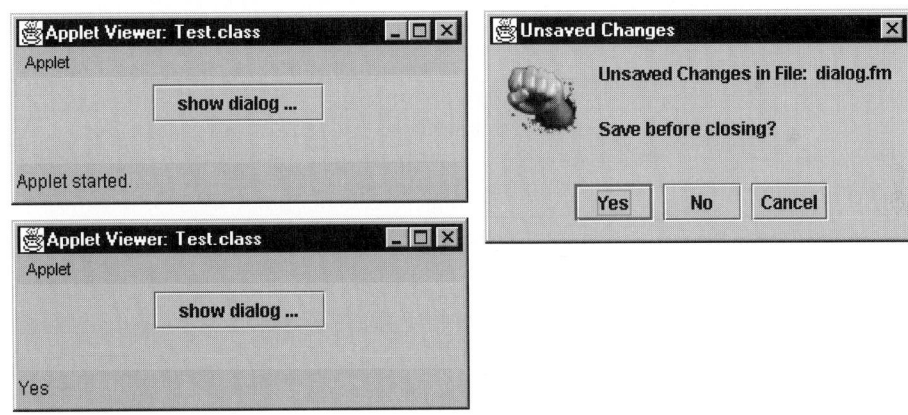

Figure 14-11 Using Confirmation Dialogs

The applet shown in Figure 14-11 is listed in Figure 14-8.

Example 14-8   Using Confirmation Dialogs

```java
import java.awt.*;
import java.awt.event.*;
import javax.swing.*;

public class Test extends JApplet {
    private JButton button = new JButton("show dialog ...");

    private String title = "Unsaved Changes";
    private String message[] = {
                "Unsaved Changes in File:  dialog.fm",
                " ",
                "Save before closing?",
                " ",
    };

    public Test() {
        Container contentPane = getContentPane();

        contentPane.setLayout(new FlowLayout());
        contentPane.add(button);

        button.addActionListener(new ActionListener() {
            public void actionPerformed(ActionEvent e) {
                int result = JOptionPane.showConfirmDialog(
                    button, // parentComponent
                    message, // message
                    title, // title
                    JOptionPane.YES_NO_CANCEL_OPTION, // optionType
                    JOptionPane.WARNING_MESSAGE, // messageType
                    new ImageIcon("punch.gif")); // icon

                switch(result) {
                    case JOptionPane.JOptionPane.CLOSED_OPTION:
                        showStatus("Dialog Closed");
                        break;
                    case JOptionPane.YES_OPTION:
                        showStatus("Yes");
                        break;
                    case JOptionPane.NO_OPTION:
                        showStatus("No");
                        break;
                    case JOptionPane.CANCEL_OPTION:
                        showStatus("Cancel");
                        break;
                }
            }
        });
    }
}
```

The message displayed in the dialog is specified as an array of strings. Each string is displayed in the dialog's message area in the order in which the strings appear in the array.

The message type for the dialog is specified as `JOptionPane.WARNING_MESSAGE`, but in effect the message type does not affect the appearance of the dialog because an icon is explicitly specified. Even though setting the `WARNING_MESSAGE` message type in this case has no effect with the Metal look and feel, it is still specified because the applet could be used with a look and feel that modifies other characteristics of the dialog based upon the message type.

The applet displays an appropriate string based upon the button that was activated in the dialog.

Input Dialogs

Input dialogs, as their name suggests, allow data to be input to a dialog. An array of objects can be specified as values that can be selected, and a particular object can be specified as the initially selected value.

Selection values are displayed by invocation of the `toString` method on each object. This means, for example, that instances of `JLabel` specified as selection values will not be displayed in the combo box or list contained in input dialog. Instead, the string returned from `JLabel.toString()` will be displayed in the list or combo box.

The component used to capture input is look-and-feel dependent. The Swing standard look and feels provide a Swing component for displaying selection values and capturing input, as listed in Table 14-8.

Table 14-8   Swing Components Used in Input Dialogs

Component ...	Is Used When ...
JTextField	No selection values are specified.
JComboBox	Fewer than 20 selection values are specified.
JList	Twenty or more selection values are specified.

If no selection values are specified, a text field is used. If fewer than 20 selection values are specified, a combo box is used, and if more than 20 selection values are specified, a list is used. It is important to reiterate that custom look and feels are free to substitute other components (or take an entirely different approach for capturing input) if they wish.

The `static JOptionPane` methods used to create input dialogs are listed below.

---

public static String <u>showInputDialog</u>(Object message)
public static String <u>showInputDialog</u>(Component parentComponent,
                   Object message)
public static String <u>showInputDialog</u>(Component parentComponent,
                   Object message
                   String title,
                   int messageType)
public static Object <u>showInputDialog</u>(Component parentComponent,
                   Object message
                   String title,
                   int messageType,
                   Icon icon,
                   Object[] selectionValues,
                   Object *initialSelectionValue*)

The first three `static JOptionPane` methods listed above return a string representing the text typed into a text field. The last method listed above allows an array of objects to be specified as selection values in addition to an object that is specified as the initially selected value. The method returns an `Object` reference that refers to the value selected.

The buttons displayed for input dialogs are not configurable; input dialogs always have OK and Cancel buttons. If a `null` value is returned from one of the `static showInputDialog` methods, the Cancel button was activated; otherwise, the OK button was activated.

The parameters passed to `JOptionPane showInputDialog` methods are summarized in Table 14-9. See Table 14-5 on page 823 for more information concerning the parameters listed in Table 14-9.

Table 14-9   Parameters Used in Creating Input Dialogs

Property	Allowable Values	Default
parentComponent	Any visible component	null
message	An Object	Must be specified
title	A string	"Input"
messageType	ERROR_MESSAGE INFORMATION_MESSAGE PLAIN_MESSAGE QUESTION_MESSAGE WARNING_MESSAGE	QUESTION_MESSAGE
icon	An icon	Selected by look and feel, depending upon messageType
selectionValues	An array of objects	null
initialSelectionValue	An Object reference	null

Notice that the optionType property cannot be specified when input dialogs are created. This means that buttons for input dialogs are not configurable; input dialogs are always fitted an OK button and a Cancel button.

The applet shown in Figure 14-12 contains a button whose activation results in the display of an input dialog. No selection values are specified, and therefore a text field is used to capture input. After the dialog is dismissed by activation of either the OK or Cancel buttons, the text typed into the text field is displayed in the applet's status area.

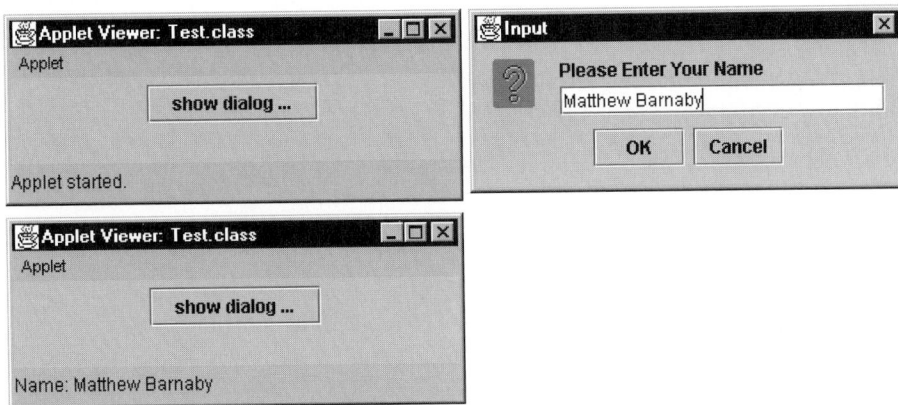

Figure 14-12 An Input Dialog with a Text Field

The applet shown in Figure 14-12 is listed in Example 14-9.

Example 14-9   An Input Dialog with a Text Field

```
import java.awt.*;
import java.awt.event.*;
import javax.swing.*;

public class Test extends JApplet {
    private JButton button = new JButton("show dialog ...");
    private String message = "Please Enter Your Name";

    public Test() {
        Container contentPane = getContentPane();

        contentPane.setLayout(new FlowLayout());
        contentPane.add(button);

        button.addActionListener(new ActionListener() {
            public void actionPerformed(ActionEvent e) {
                String s = JOptionPane.showInputDialog(message);

                if(s == null)
                    showStatus("cancel button activated");
                else
                    showStatus("Name: " + s);
            }
        });
    }
}
```

The applet creates an input dialog with a simple message. A string is returned from the `showInputDialog` method and is displayed in the applet's status area.

The applet shown in Figure 14-13 also displays an input dialog. The input dialog uses a combo box to display selection values because fewer than 20 selection values are specified.

The applet shown in Figure 14-13 is listed in Example 14-10.

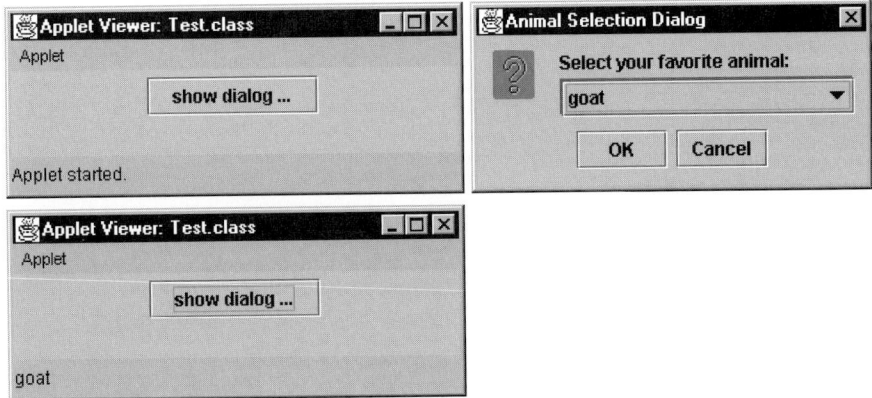

Figure 14-13 An Input Dialog with a Combo Box

Example 14-10 An Input Dialog with a Combo Box

```java
import java.awt.*;
import java.awt.event.*;
import javax.swing.*;

public class Test extends JApplet {
    private JButton button = new JButton("show dialog ...");

    private String title = "Animal Selection Dialog";
    private String message = "Select your favorite animal:";
    private String[] selectionValues = {
        "dog", "cat", "mouse", "goat", "koala", "rabbit",
    };

    public Test() {
        Container contentPane = getContentPane();

        contentPane.setLayout(new FlowLayout());
        contentPane.add(button);

        button.addActionListener(new ActionListener() {
            public void actionPerformed(ActionEvent e) {
                String s = (String)JOptionPane.showInputDialog(
                    Test.this, // parentComponent
                    message, // message
                    title, // title
                    JOptionPane.QUESTION_MESSAGE, // messageType
                    null, // icon
                    selectionValues, // selectionValues
                    selectionValues[3]); // initialSelectionValue
```

```
            if(s == null)
                showStatus("cancel button activated");
            else
                showStatus(s);
        }
    });
}
}
```

In addition to specifying selection values, the applet specifies a value corresponding to the fourth item in the `selectionValues` array as the initially selected value.

The applet displays the value selected from the combo box in its status area.

The applet shown in Figure 14-14 is nearly identical to that applet shown in Figure 14-13, except that more than 20 selection values are specified. As a result, a list is used to present the selection values.

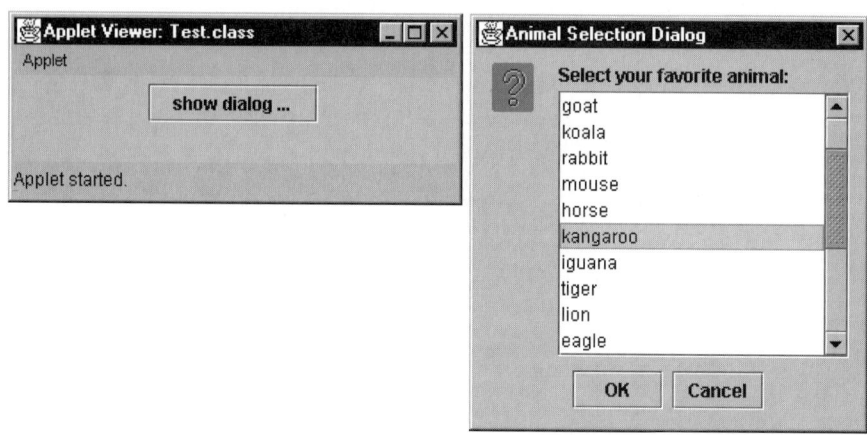

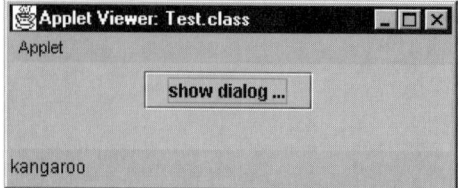

Figure 14-14 An Input Dialog with a List

The applet shown in Figure 14-14 is listed in Example 14-11.

Example 14-11 An Input Dialog with a List

```java
import java.awt.*;
import java.awt.event.*;
import javax.swing.*;

public class Test extends JApplet {
    private JButton button = new JButton("show dialog ...");

    private String title = "Animal Selection Dialog";
    private String message = "Select your favorite animal:";
    private Object[] selectionValues = {
        "dog", "cat", "mouse", "goat", "koala", "rabbit",
        "mouse", "horse", "kangaroo", "iguana", "tiger", "lion",
        "eagle", "vulture", "wolf", "coyote", "owl", "snake",
        "shrew", "zebra", "wildebeast"
    };

    public Test() {
        Container contentPane = getContentPane();

        contentPane.setLayout(new FlowLayout());
        contentPane.add(button);

        button.addActionListener(new ActionListener() {
            public void actionPerformed(ActionEvent e) {
                String s = (String)JOptionPane.showInputDialog(
                    Test.this, // parentComponent
                    message, // message
                    title, // title
                    JOptionPane.QUESTION_MESSAGE, // messageType
                    null, // icon
                    selectionValues, // selectionValues
                    selectionValues[3]); // initialSelectionValue

                if(s == null)
                    showStatus("cancel button activated");
                else
                    showStatus(s);
            }
        });
    }
}
```

Selection Values Are Displayed as Strings

Selection values for input dialogs are specified as objects and are displayed by displaying the string returned from the object's toString method. As can be seen from Table 14-5 on page 823, this is in contrast to messages and option types that are displayed as labels if their actual types are Icon or JLabel, or displayed as is if the message is a component. The reason for this inconsistent handling of object types between messages/option types and selection values stems from the fact that combo boxes and lists must be fitted with custom renderers in order to display labels.

If objects other than strings are to be used as selection values for input dialogs, the objects should have a toString method that returns a string suitable for display.

Option Dialogs

Option dialogs are the only dialogs created by `static JOptionPane` methods that provide the option of fully customizing the dialog's button row. Option dialogs also allow a component in the button row to receive initial focus when the dialog is displayed.

The button row for an option dialog is customized with the `options` parameter, and the component that initially receives focus is specified with the `initialValue` parameter. See Table 14-5 on page 823 for more information on the `options` and `initialValue` parameters.

The `JOptionPane` class provides a single method for showing an option dialog.

```
public static int showOptionDialog(Component parentComponent,
                        Object message,
                        String title,
                        int optionType,
                        int messageType,
                        Icon icon,
                        Object[] options,
                        Object initialValue)
```

The parameters passed to JOptionPane showInputDialog methods are summarized in Table 14-10. See Table 14-5 on page 823 for more information concerning the parameters listed in Figure 14-10. Like the showConfirmDialog methods, showOptionDialog() returns an integer value indicating the button that was activated.

Table 14-10 Parameters Used in Creating Option Dialogs

Property	Allowable Values	Default
parentComponent	Any visible component	Must be specified
message	An Object	Must be specified
title	A string	Must be specified
messageType	ERROR_MESSAGE INFORMATION_MESSAGE PLAIN_MESSAGE QUESTION_MESSAGE WARNING_MESSAGE	Must be specified
icon	An icon	Must be specified
options	An array of objects	Must be specified
initialValue	An Object reference	Must be specified

The applet shown in Figure 14-15 creates an option dialog equipped with a panel for its message and Ok, Apply, and Cancel buttons. After the dialog is dismissed, the applet shows the angle selected from the dialog in its status area.

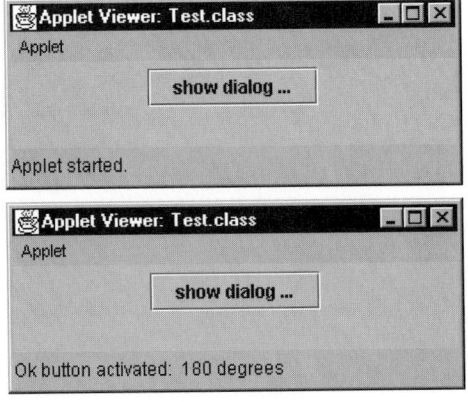

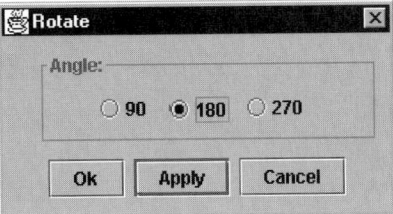

Figure 14-15 Using an Option Dialog

The applet creates an instance of `RotatePanel`, which is an extension of `JPanel`, that contains the radio buttons used to select an angle. The rotate panel is specified as the dialog's message. Since messages that are specified as components are displayed as is, the rotate panel is displayed in the dialog's message area.

The buttons in the dialog's button row are specified with an `Object` array containing two strings and an instance of `JButton`. The strings are used by the `showOptionDialog` method to create buttons whose labels correspond to the strings. Only buttons that are created by the `showOptionDialog` method—in this case, the Ok and Cancel buttons—cause the dialog to be dismissed when the buttons are activated. In other words, for the applet shown in Figure 14-15, activation of the Ok and Cancel buttons will dismiss the dialog, but activating the Apply button will not.

The `rotatePanel` and the `buttonRowObjects` array are passed to the `showOptionDialog` method as the dialog's message and options parameters, respectively. The Apply button is also specified as the `initialValue` parameter, which means that it will receive focus when the dialog is displayed.

```
public class Test extends JApplet {
    private JButton button = new JButton("show dialog ...");
    private JButton applyButton = new JButton("Apply");
    private RotatePanel rotatePanel = new RotatePanel();
    private String title = "Rotate";
    private Object[] buttonRowObjects = new Object[] {
        "Ok",
        applyButton,
        "Cancel",
    };
    public Test() {
        ...
        button.addActionListener(new ActionListener() {
            public void actionPerformed(ActionEvent e) {
                int value = JOptionPane.showOptionDialog(
                    button, // parentComponent
                    rotatePanel, // message
                    title, // title
                    JOptionPane.DEFAULT_OPTION, // optionType
                    JOptionPane.PLAIN_MESSAGE, // messageType
                    null, // icon
                    buttonRowObjects, // options
                    applyButton); // initialValue
        ...
```

An action listener added to the Apply button updates the applet's status area. The JOptionPane.showOptionDialog method adds listeners to instances of JButton that are created by the method; the listeners dismiss the dialog when the buttons are activated. However, no listeners are added to buttons that are specified with existing instances of JButton, as is the case for the Apply button.

```
...
applyButton.addActionListener(new ActionListener(){
    public void actionPerformed(ActionEvent e) {
        showStatus(rotatePanel.getSelectedAngle() +
                " degrees");
    }
});
...
```

After the dialog is dismissed, the applet's status area is updated, depending upon the button that was activated.

```
...
switch(value) {
    case JOptionPane.CLOSED_OPTION:
        showStatus(
                "Dialog closed with close box");
        break;
    case JOptionPane.OK_OPTION:
        showStatus("Ok button activated:   " +
                rotatePanel.getSelectedAngle() +
                " degrees");
        break;
    case JOptionPane.CANCEL_OPTION:
        showStatus("Cancel button activated");
        break;
    }
}
});
}
}
...
```

The applet shown in Figure 14-15 is listed in its entirety in Example 14-12.

Example 14-12   Using an Option Dialog

```java
import java.awt.*;
import java.awt.event.*;
import javax.swing.*;

public class Test extends JApplet {
    private JButton button = new JButton("show dialog ...");
    private JButton applyButton = new JButton("Apply");
    private RotatePanel rotatePanel = new RotatePanel();
    private String title = "Rotate";
    private Object[] buttonRowObjects = new Object[] {
        "Ok",
        applyButton,
        "Cancel",
    };

    public Test() {
        Container contentPane = getContentPane();

        contentPane.setLayout(new FlowLayout());
        contentPane.add(button);

        applyButton.addActionListener(new ActionListener() {
            public void actionPerformed(ActionEvent e) {
                showStatus(rotatePanel.getSelectedAngle() +
                        " degrees");
            }
        });
        button.addActionListener(new ActionListener() {
            public void actionPerformed(ActionEvent e) {
                int value = JOptionPane.showOptionDialog(
                        button, // parentComponent
                        rotatePanel, // message
                        title, // title
                        JOptionPane.DEFAULT_OPTION, // optionType
                        JOptionPane.PLAIN_MESSAGE, // messageType
                        null, // icon
                        buttonRowObjects, // options
                        applyButton); // initialValue

                switch(value) {
                    case JOptionPane.CLOSED_OPTION:
                        showStatus(
                                "Dialog closed with close box");
                        break;
                    case JOptionPane.OK_OPTION:
                        showStatus("Ok button activated:  " +
                                rotatePanel.getSelectedAngle() +
                                " degrees");
                        break;
                    case JOptionPane.CANCEL_OPTION:
```

```
                    showStatus("Cancel button activated");
                    break;
            }
        }
    });
  }
}
class RotatePanel extends JPanel {
    private ButtonGroup group = new ButtonGroup();

    private JRadioButton[] buttons = {
        new JRadioButton("0"),
        new JRadioButton("90"),
        new JRadioButton("180"),
        new JRadioButton("270"),
    };
    public RotatePanel() {
        setBorder(BorderFactory.createTitledBorder("Angle:"));

        for(int i=0; i < buttons.length; ++i) {
            if(i ==0)
                buttons[i].setSelected(true);

            add(buttons[i]);
            group.add(buttons[i]);
        }
    }
    public String getSelectedAngle() {
        String rv = null;   // rv = return value

        for(int i=0; i < buttons.length; ++i) {
            if(buttons[i].isSelected())
                rv = buttons[i].getText();
        }
        return rv;
    }
}
```

The JOptionPane component is summarized in Component Summary 14-3.

Component Summary 14-3   JOptionPane

Model(s)   ——

UI Delegate(s)   javax.swing.plaf.basic.BasicOptionPaneUI

Renderer(s)	——
Editor(s)	——
Events Fired	PropertyChangeEvents
Replacement For	——

Class Diagrams

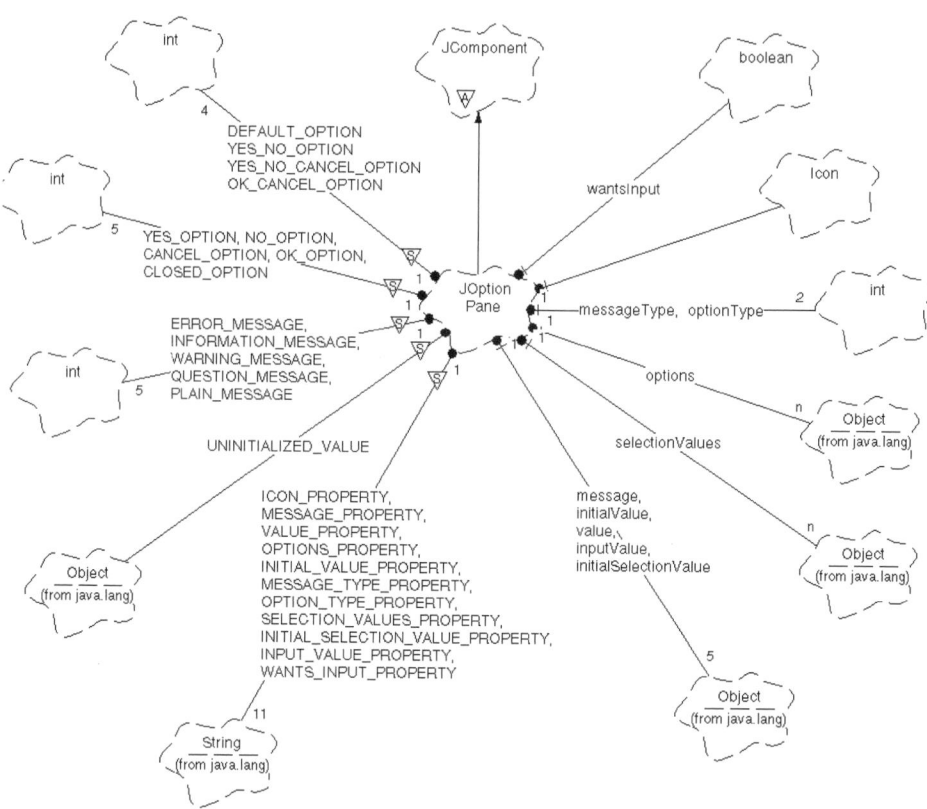

Figure 14-16 JOptionPane Class Diagram

JOptionPane extends JComponent and does not implement any interfaces.

JOptionPane defines a great deal of `public static` constants used for setting properties in addition to constants used to access properties when property change events are fired.

JOptionPane also maintains a number of `protected` references for tracking its properties, such as `Object` references for message, initial value, input value, and initial selection value. References to object arrays are also maintained for the options and selection values properties.

JOptionPane Properties

The properties maintained by the JOptionPane class are listed in Table 14-11.

Table 14-11 JOptionPane Properties

Property Name	Data Type	Property Type[1]	Access[2]	Default[3]
icon	Icon	B	SG	L&F
initialSelectionValue	Object	B	SG	null
initialValue	Object	B	SG	null
inputValue	Object	B	SG	UNINITIALIZED_VALUE
maxCharacters PerLineCount	int	S	G	Integer.MAX_VALUE
message	Object	B	SG	"JOptionPane message"
messageType	int	B	SG	PLAIN_ MESSAGE
options	Object[]	B	SG	null
optionType	int	B	SG	DEFAULT_ OPTION
selectionValues	Object[]	B	SG	null
value	Object	B	SG	UNINITIALIZED_VALUE
wantsInput	boolean	B	SG	false[4]

1. B = bound (fires PropertyChangeEvent) / C = constrained/ I = indexed / S = simple / Ch = fires ChangeEvent
2. C = settable at construction time / G = getter method / S = setter method
3. L&F = look-and-feel dependent
4. true when selection values are explicitly set

icon — The icon displayed in the option pane. Icons are typically displayed on the left-hand side of the option pane, but icon placement is ultimately left up to the option pane's look and feel. If the icon displayed in an option pane is not explicitly specified, the look and feel determines the icon from the option pane's messageType property.

initialSelectionValue — Used with input dialogs only to select an initial value. If the input dialog uses a text field to capture input, the initial value is displayed in the text field when the dialog is shown. If the input dialog uses a combo box or list, the initial selection value represents the value initially selected in the combo box or list.

initialValue — An object that is assigned keyboard focus when the option pane is initially displayed. If the initialValue object is an instance of JButton, it is made the default button for the option pane.

inputValue — The object representing the value that was input for an input dialog. For example, setting this property for an input dialog with a text field will cause the text field to display the input value initially. Also, the getInputValue method can be used to obtain a reference to the object that was selected from the selection values.

maxCharactersPerLineCount — A read-only property that represents the maximum number of characters that can be placed on one line in a message. The JOptionPane class returns Integer.MAX_VALUE from getMaxCharactersPerLineCount(), but extensions of JOptionPane can override the method if they wish to restrict the number of characters displayed on a line.

message — An instance of Object that is quite flexible. See Table 14-5 on page 823 for a description of how this property is interpreted for different data types.

messageType — Used by an option pane's look and feel to determine the icon, and potentially the layout, used in the option pane. Although the standard look and feels lay out option panes without regard to the messageType property, custom look and feels may alter their layouts depending upon the messageType of the option pane. See Table 14-5 on page 823 for a list of valid messageType constants defined by the JOptionPane class.

options — Overrides the optionType property and allows a set of custom components to be placed in the button row of an option pane. The data type for the options property is an array of objects. Each object in the array is interpreted as outlined in Table 14-5 on page 823.

optionType — Determines the buttons that are displayed in the option pane. Valid values for this property are defined as constants by the JOptionPane class and are listed in Table 14-5 on page 823. Each value corresponds to a standard set of buttons; for example, setting the optionType property to JOptionPane.YES_NO_CANCEL fits the option pane with three buttons labeled Yes, No, and Cancel.

To allow custom buttons, the optionType property can be overridden by the options property, as discussed above.

selectionValues — An array of objects displayed in an option pane from which a selection can be made. Each object in the array is interpreted and displayed as outlined in Table 14-5 on page 823.

value — Represents one of the options, meaning the components (usually buttons) contained in the dialog's button row.

If none of the options has yet been selected, the getValue method returns JOptionPane.UNINITIALIZED_VALUE.

If the dialog was closed by some other means other than activation of a button from the dialog's button row, getValue() returns null. Usually this means that the dialog was dismissed by a user clicking on its close box.

wantsInput — An internal flag used by the JOptionPane class that will rarely, if ever, be directly manipulated by developers. The flag is set to true whenever the selectionValues property has been set.

JOptionPane Events

All of the properties maintained by instances of JOptionPane are bound properties, meaning that a property change event is fired when any of the properties are modified.

The applet shown in Figure 14-17 creates and shows a dialog containing an option pane. The message object for the option pane is a JPanel containing a set of check boxes. A property change listener added to the option pane listens for changes to the value property. When the value property is modified, meaning either the OK or Cancel button has been activated, the value is printed. The applet is executed with the Windows look and feel for the sake of variety.

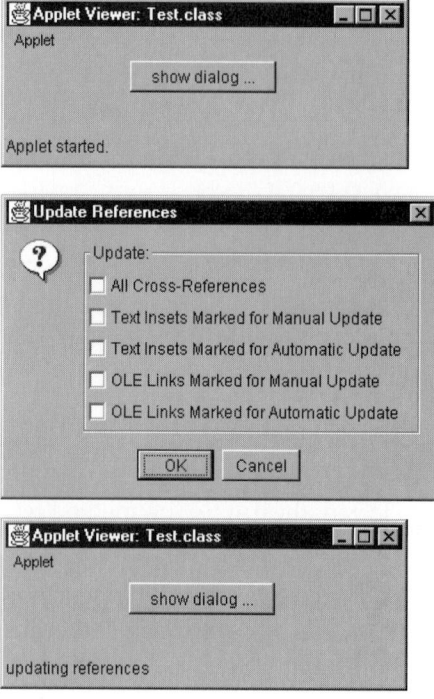

Figure 14-17 Listening for PropertyChangeEvents

The applet creates an instance of `JPanel` that is specified as the message object for the option pane. The option pane is constructed with a message type of `QUESTION_MESSAGE` and an option type of `OK_CANCEL_OPTION`.

An action listener added to the applet's button creates a dialog with the `JOptionPane.createDialog` method. After the dialog is shown and subsequently dismissed, the value of the option pane is obtained by invocation of `JOptionPane.getValue()`. If the `Integer` value returned from `JOptionPane.getValue()` equates to `JOptionPane.OK_OPTION`, the applet's `updateReferences` method, which merely prints a message to the applet's status area, is called. If the option pane's value does not equate to `JOptionPane.OK_OPTION`, the Cancel button was activated and an appropriate message is displayed in the applet's status area.

```
public class Test extends JApplet {
    ...
    private JPanel messagePanel = new JPanel();
    ...
    public void init() {
        ...
        final JOptionPane pane = new JOptionPane(
                    messagePanel, // message
                    JOptionPane.QUESTION_MESSAGE, // messageType
                    JOptionPane.OK_CANCEL_OPTION); // optionType
        ...
        button.addActionListener(new ActionListener() {
            public void actionPerformed(ActionEvent e) {
                JDialog dialog = pane.createDialog(
                                    Test.this, // parentComponent
                                    title); // title

                dialog.show();  // blocks

                Integer value = (Integer)pane.getValue();

                if(value.intValue() == JOptionPane.OK_OPTION)
                    updateReferences();
                else
                    showStatus("dialog canceled");
            }
        });
        ...
```

A property change listener that checks the property name against
JOptionPane.VALUE_PROPERTY is added to the option pane. If the property
name equates to VALUE_PROPERTY, the property name and value are printed.

```
        ...
        pane.addPropertyChangeListener(
                            new PropertyChangeListener() {
            public void propertyChange(PropertyChangeEvent e) {
                String name = e.getPropertyName();

                if(name.equals(JOptionPane.VALUE_PROPERTY))
                    System.out.println(name + ": " +
                                            e.getNewValue());
            }
        });
        ...
    }
}
```

The applet shown in Figure 14-17 is listed in its entirety in Example 14-13.

Example 14-13 Listening for PropertyChangeEvents Fired from an Option Pane

```java
import java.awt.*;
import java.awt.event.*;
import java.beans.*;
import javax.swing.*;

public class Test extends JApplet {
    private JButton button = new JButton("show dialog ...");

    private String title = "Update References";

    private JPanel messagePanel = new JPanel();

    private JCheckBox[] checkBoxes = {
        new JCheckBox("All Cross-References"),
        new JCheckBox("Text Insets Marked for Manual Update"),
        new JCheckBox("Text Insets Marked for Automatic Update"),
        new JCheckBox("OLE Links Marked for Manual Update"),
        new JCheckBox("OLE Links Marked for Automatic Update"),
    };

    public void init() {
        Container contentPane = getContentPane();

        messagePanel.setBorder(
            BorderFactory.createTitledBorder("Update:"));

        messagePanel.setLayout(new BoxLayout(messagePanel,
                        BoxLayout.Y_AXIS));

        for(int i=0; i < checkBoxes.length; ++i)
            messagePanel.add(checkBoxes[i]);

        final JOptionPane pane = new JOptionPane(
                messagePanel, // message
                JOptionPane.QUESTION_MESSAGE, // messageType
                JOptionPane.OK_CANCEL_OPTION); // optionType

        contentPane.setLayout(new FlowLayout());
        contentPane.add(button);

        button.addActionListener(new ActionListener() {
            public void actionPerformed(ActionEvent e) {
                JDialog dialog = pane.createDialog(
                    Test.this, // parentComponent
                    title); // title

                dialog.show();  // blocks

                Integer value = (Integer)pane.getValue();
```

```
            if(value.intValue() == JOptionPane.OK_OPTION)
                updateReferences();
            else
                showStatus("dialog canceled");
        }
    });
    pane.addPropertyChangeListener(
                        new PropertyChangeListener() {
        public void propertyChange(PropertyChangeEvent e) {
            String name = e.getPropertyName();

            if(name.equals(JOptionPane.VALUE_PROPERTY))
                System.out.println(name + ":" +
                                          e.getNewValue());
        }
    });
}
private void updateReferences() {
    showStatus("updating references");
}
}
```

JOptionPane Class Summaries

The public and protected variables and methods for JOptionPane are listed in Class Summary 14-3.

Class Summary 14-3   JOptionPane

Constants

Option Types

---

public static final int <u>DEFAULT OPTION</u>
public static final int <u>OK CANCEL OPTION</u>
public static final int <u>YES NO CANCEL OPTION</u>
public static final int <u>YES NO OPTION</u>

The constants listed above specify the `optionType` property that determines the buttons that populate an option pane's button row. Specifying `DEFAULT_OPTION` results in a lone OK button.

Button Configuration Options

---

public static final int <u>CANCEL_OPTION</u>
public static final int <u>CLOSED_OPTION</u>
public static final int <u>NO_OPTION</u>
public static final int <u>OK_OPTION</u>
public static final int <u>YES_OPTION</u>

The constants listed above determine which button was activated in an option pane. Static `JOptionPane` methods that create confirmation dialogs return one of the constants listed above after the dialog is dismissed. The button activated in option panes that reside in dialogs other than confirmation dialogs can be determined by a call to the `getValue` method, which also returns one of the constants listed above.

Message Types

---

public static final int <u>ERROR_MESSAGE</u>
public static final int <u>INFORMATION_MESSAGE</u>
public static final int <u>PLAIN_MESSAGE</u>
public static final int <u>QUESTION_MESSAGE</u>
public static final int <u>WARNING_MESSAGE</u>

The constants listed above specify an option pane's `messageType` property, which determines the icon displayed in the option pane.

Properties

---

public static final String <u>ICON_PROPERTY</u>
public static final String <u>INITIAL_SELECTION_VALUE_PROPERTY</u>

```
public static final String INITIAL_VALUE_PROPERTY
public static final String INPUT_VALUE_PROPERTY
public static final String MESSAGE_PROPERTY
public static final String MESSAGE_TYPE_PROPERTY
public static final String OPTIONS_PROPERTY
public static final String OPTION_TYPE_PROPERTY
public static final String SELECTION_VALUES_PROPERTY
public static final Object UNINITIALIZED_VALUE
public static final String VALUE_PROPERTY
public static final String WANTS_INPUT_PROPERTY
```

All of the properties associated with instances of `JOptionPane` are bound properties (with the exception of `maxCharactersPerLineCount`), meaning that modification of the properties results in the firing of a `PropertyChangeEvent`. The constants listed above can be used to differentiate the property that was modified when a `PropertyChangeEvent` is fired by an instance of `JOptionPane`. For example, the following code fragment determines whether a `PropertyChangeEvent` represents the modification of an option pane's message property.

```
// code fragment ...

anOptionPane.addPropertyChangeListener(
                            new PropertyChangeListener() {
    public void propertyChange(PropertyChangeEvent e) {
        String name = e.getPropertyName();

        if(name.equals(JOptionPane.MESSAGE_PROPERTY)) {
            // property modified is message property
        }
    }
});
```

Constructors

```
public JOptionPane()
public JOptionPane(Object message)
public JOptionPane(Object message, int messageType)
public JOptionPane(Object message, int messageType, int optionType)
public JOptionPane(Object message, int messageType, int optionType, Icon icon)
```

public <u>JOptionPane</u>(Object message, int messageType, int optionType, Icon icon, Object[]
    options)
public <u>JOptionPane</u>(Object message, int messageType, int optionType, Icon icon, Object[]
    options, Object initialValue)

The constructors listed above create instances of JOptionPane of various
configurations. The arguments that can be passed to JOptionPane constructors
represent the message, messageType, optionType, icon, options, and
initialValue properties. See "JOptionPane Properties" on page 851 for an
explanation of each of the properties that can be specified when instances of
JOptionPane are constructed, and see Table 14-11 on page 851 for a listing of
default values.

The applet shown in Figure 14-18 uses most of the constructors listed above to
create the option panes it displays. The applet also illustrates that instances of
JOptionPane are components that do not necessarily have to reside in a dialog.

The top option pane in the applet shown in Figure 14-18 is constructed with the
JOptionPane no-argument constructor, which creates an option pane with a
default message and a single OK button.

```
. . .
JOptionPane defaultPane = new JOptionPane();
. . .
```

The next option pane is constructed with the JOptionPane constructor that is
passed an object representing the message displayed in the option pane. In this
case, the message is a string, but messages can be any type of object, as outlined in
Table 14-5 on page 823.

```
. . .
JOptionPane messagePane = new JOptionPane(
    "JOptionPane(Object message)");
. . .
```

The third option pane constructed by the applet shown in Figure 14-18 specifies
an array of objects for the option pane's message. The Object array contains
three objects: an instance of JLabel, an instance of JCheckBox, and an instance
of VerboseObject. The VerboseObject class is a simple extension of
java.lang.Object that overrides the toString method.

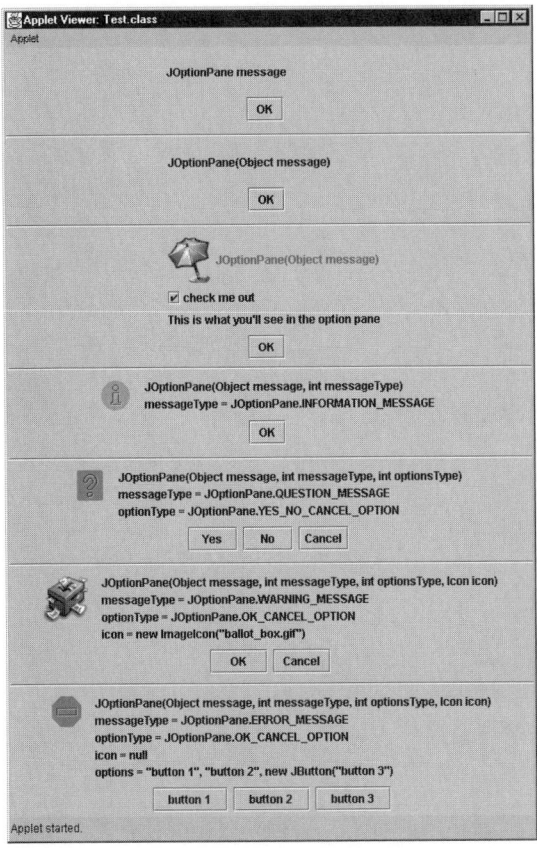

Figure 14-18 Constructing Option Panes of Various Configurations

Each object in the array of objects is displayed as outlined in Table 14-5 on page 823. The label and check box are components and therefore are displayed as is. Because the VerboseObject class is not a component, the string returned from its toString method is displayed in the option pane's message area.

```
...
Object[] objects = new Object[] {
        new JLabel("JOptionPane(Object message)",
                new ImageIcon("beach_umbrella.gif"),
                JLabel.LEFT),
        new JCheckBox("check me out"),
        new VerboseObject(),
};
...
```

```
                JOptionPane objectPane = new JOptionPane(objects);
                ...
        }
        class VerboseObject extends Object {
            public String toString() {
                return "This is what you'll see in the option pane";
            }
        }
```

The fourth option pane constructed by the applet specifies a message that is a string corresponding to the JOptionPane constructor used and the parameters it is passed, and a message type of JOptionPane.INFORMATION_MESSAGE. Notice that the three previous option panes constructed by the applet do not display an icon in the option pane's icon area.

If a message type is not explicitly specified for an option pane, an icon is not displayed. This is in contrast to the static JOptionPane methods that create dialogs, which display an icon regardless of whether a message type is explicitly specified.

```
        ...
        Object[] objects2 = new Object[] {
                "JOptionPane(Object message, int messageType)",
                "messageType = JOptionPane.INFORMATION_MESSAGE",
        };
        ...
        JOptionPane messageTypePane = new JOptionPane(
                objects2, JOptionPane.INFORMATION_MESSAGE);
        ...
```

The next option pane constructed by the applet specifies a message, message type, and option type. The option type is specified as YES_NO_CANCEL_OPTION, which populates the button row with Yes, No, and Cancel buttons.

```
        ...
        Object[] objects3 = new Object[] {
                "JOptionPane(Object message, " +
                "int messageType, int optionsType)",
                "messageType = JOptionPane.QUESTION_MESSAGE",
                "optionType = JOptionPane.YES_NO_CANCEL_OPTION",
        };
        ...
        JOptionPane messageAndOptionTypePane = new JOptionPane(
                objects3, JOptionPane.QUESTION_MESSAGE,
                JOptionPane.YES_NO_CANCEL_OPTION);
        ...
```

The next option pane constructed by the applet specifies a message, message type of WARNING_MESSAGE, option type of OK_CANCEL_OPTION, and an explicit icon. Notice that the message type has no visible effect on the option pane because an icon is explicitly specified.

```
...
Object[] objects4 = new Object[] {
        "JOptionPane(Object message, " +
        "int messageType, int optionsType, Icon icon)",
        "messageType = JOptionPane.WARNING_MESSAGE",
        "optionType = JOptionPane.OK_CANCEL_OPTION",
        "icon = new ImageIcon(\"ballot_box.gif\")",
};
...
JOptionPane messageOptionAndIconPane = new JOptionPane(
        objects4, JOptionPane.WARNING_MESSAGE,
        JOptionPane.OK_CANCEL_OPTION,
        new ImageIcon("ballot_box.gif"));
...
```

The last option pane constructed by the applet specifies a message type of ERROR_MESSAGE, an option type of OK_CANCEL_OPTION, a null icon, and an options property that is an Object array containing two strings and an instance of JButton.

Notice that the option type is overridden by the options property. Although the option type specifies that the option pane should be fitted with OK and Cancel buttons, it is overridden by the options property, which explicitly specifies buttons to be placed in the button row.

```
...
Object[] objects5 = new Object[] {
        "JOptionPane(Object message, " +
        "int messageType, int optionsType, Icon icon)",
        "messageType = JOptionPane.ERROR_MESSAGE",
        "optionType = JOptionPane.OK_CANCEL_OPTION",
        "icon = null",
        "options = \"button 1\", \"button 2\", " +
                "new JButton(\"button 3\")",
};
...
Object[] options = {
    "button 1", "button 2", new JButton("button 3"),
};
JOptionPane messageOptionIconAndOptionsPane =
                                    new JOptionPane(
        objects5, JOptionPane.ERROR_MESSAGE,
```

```
                    JOptionPane.OK_CANCEL_OPTION,
                    null,
                    options,
                    options[2]);
        ...
```

The applet shown in Figure 14-18 is listed in its entirety in Example 14-14.

Example 14-14 Constructing Option Panes of Various Configurations

```
import java.awt.*;
import java.awt.event.*;
import javax.swing.*;

public class Test extends JApplet {
    public Test() {
        Container contentPane = getContentPane();
        Object[] objects = new Object[] {
                new JLabel("JOptionPane(Object message)",
                            new ImageIcon("beach_umbrella.gif"),
                            JLabel.LEFT),
                new JCheckBox("check me out"),
                new VerboseObject(),
        };
        Object[] objects2 = new Object[] {
                "JOptionPane(Object message, int messageType)",
                "messageType = JOptionPane.INFORMATION_MESSAGE",
        };
        Object[] objects3 = new Object[] {
                "JOptionPane(Object message, " +
                "int messageType, int optionsType)",
                "messageType = JOptionPane.QUESTION_MESSAGE",
                "optionType = JOptionPane.YES_NO_CANCEL_OPTION",
        };
        Object[] objects4 = new Object[] {
                "JOptionPane(Object message, " +
                "int messageType, int optionsType, Icon icon)",
                "messageType = JOptionPane.WARNING_MESSAGE",
                "optionType = JOptionPane.OK_CANCEL_OPTION",
                "icon = new ImageIcon(\"ballot_box.gif\")",
        };
        Object[] objects5 = new Object[] {
                "JOptionPane(Object message, " +
                "int messageType, int optionsType, Icon icon)",
                "messageType = JOptionPane.ERROR_MESSAGE",
                "optionType = JOptionPane.OK_CANCEL_OPTION",
                "icon = null",
                "options = \"button 1\", \"button 2\", " +
                        "new JButton(\"button 3\")",
        };
```

```java
        JOptionPane defaultPane = new JOptionPane();

        JOptionPane messagePane = new JOptionPane(
                "JOptionPane(Object message)");

        JOptionPane objectPane = new JOptionPane(objects);

        JOptionPane messageTypePane = new JOptionPane(
                objects2, JOptionPane.INFORMATION_MESSAGE);

        JOptionPane messageAndOptionTypePane = new JOptionPane(
                objects3, JOptionPane.QUESTION_MESSAGE,
                JOptionPane.YES_NO_CANCEL_OPTION);

        JOptionPane messageOptionAndIconPane = new JOptionPane(
                objects4, JOptionPane.WARNING_MESSAGE,
                JOptionPane.OK_CANCEL_OPTION,
                new ImageIcon("ballot_box.gif"));

        Object[] options = {
            "button 1", "button 2", new JButton("button 3"),
        };
        JOptionPane messageOptionIconAndOptionsPane =
                                          new JOptionPane(
                objects5, JOptionPane.ERROR_MESSAGE,
                JOptionPane.OK_CANCEL_OPTION,
                null,
                options,
                options[2]);

        contentPane.setLayout(new BoxLayout(contentPane,
                                  BoxLayout.Y_AXIS));
        contentPane.add(defaultPane);
        contentPane.add(new JSeparator());
        contentPane.add(messagePane);
        contentPane.add(new JSeparator());
        contentPane.add(objectPane);
        contentPane.add(new JSeparator());
        contentPane.add(messageTypePane);
        contentPane.add(new JSeparator());
        contentPane.add(messageAndOptionTypePane);
        contentPane.add(new JSeparator());
        contentPane.add(messageOptionAndIconPane);
        contentPane.add(new JSeparator());
        contentPane.add(messageOptionIconAndOptionsPane);
    }
}
class VerboseObject extends Object {
    public String toString() {
        return "This is what you'll see in the option pane";
    }
}
```

Static Convenience Methods

---

public static JDesktopPane getDesktopPaneForComponent(Component)
public static Frame getFrameForComponent(Component)
public static Frame getRootFrame()
public static void setRootFrame(Frame)

The methods listed above are convenience methods used by the JOptionPane class, which are made available for use in other contexts. The get... methods recursively traverse the containment hierarchy of the component they are passed until an appropriate type of container is found.

Confirmation Dialog

---

public static int showConfirmDialog(Component, Object)
public static int showConfirmDialog(Component, Object, String, int)
public static int showConfirmDialog(Component, Object, String, int, int)
public static int showConfirmDialog(Component, Object, String, int, int, Icon)

public static int showInternalConfirmDialog(Component, Object)
public static int showInternalConfirmDialog(Component, Object, String, int)
public static int showInternalConfirmDialog(Component, Object, String, int, int)
public static int showInternalConfirmDialog(Component, Object, String, int, int, Icon)

The methods listed above create confirmation dialogs and internal frames. The names of the arguments passed to the methods are not listed here for the sake of clarity; see "Confirmation Dialogs" on page 833 for the argument names passed to the methods.

As is the case for all types of dialogs created by static JOptionPane methods, a full complement of analogous methods that create internal frames is provided by the JOptionPane class.

Input Dialog

---

public static String showInputDialog(Component, Object)
public static String showInputDialog(Component, Object, String, int)
public static Object showInputDialog(Component, Object, String, int,
                                    Icon, Object[], Object)
public static String showInputDialog(Object)

public static String showInternalInputDialog(Component, Object)
public static String showInternalInputDialog(Component, Object, String, int)
public static Object showInternalInputDialog(Component, Object, String, int,
                                    Icon, Object[], Object)

The methods listed above create input dialogs and internal frames. See "Input Dialogs" on page 837 for more information on the manner in which input dialogs are created and used.

Message Dialog

---

public static void showMessageDialog(Component, Object)
public static void showMessageDialog(Component, Object, String, int)
public static void showMessageDialog(Component, Object, String, int, Icon)

public static void showInternalMessageDialog(Component, Object)
public static void showInternalMessageDialog(Component, Object, String, int)
public static void showInternalMessageDialog(Component, Object, String, int, Icon)

The methods listed above create message dialogs and internal frames. See "Message Dialogs" on page 825 for more information on the manner in which message dialogs are created and used.

Option Dialog

---

public static int <u>showOptionDialog</u>(Component, Object, String, int, int,
Icon, Object[], Object)

public static int <u>showInternalOptionDialog</u>(Component, Object, String, int, int,
Icon, Object[], Object)

The methods listed above create option dialogs and internal frames. See "Option Dialogs" on page 844 for more information on the manner in which option dialogs are created and used.

Creating Dialog and Internal Frames / Icon

---

public JDialog <u>createDialog</u>(Component parentComponent, String title)
public JInternalFrame <u>createInternalFrame</u>(Component parentComponent, String title)
public Icon <u>getIcon</u>()

The methods listed above create dialogs and internal frames from an option pane instance.

The `createDialog` method creates an instance of `JDialog`, using the frame associated with the `parentComponent` as the dialog's owner. The option pane is added to the dialog's content pane as its center component, and the dialog's location is set so that the dialog is centered over the `parentComponent`. A listener is added to the dialog to ensure that the component specified as the option pane's initial value receives keyboard focus when the dialog is displayed.

If the `parentComponent` passed to `createInternalFrame` resides in an instance of `JDesktopPane`, an instance of `JInternalFrame` is created, the option pane is placed inside the internal frame, and the internal frame is added to the desktop pane. If the `parentComponent` does not reside in an instance of `JDesktopPane`, the method throws a runtime exception.

The `getIcon` method returns the icon associated with an instance of `JOptionPane`.

Property Accessors

---

public Object <u>getInitialSelectionValue</u>()
public Object <u>getInitialValue</u>()
public Object <u>getInputValue</u>()
public int <u>getMaxCharactersPerLineCount</u>()
public Object <u>getMessage</u>()
public int <u>getMessageType</u>()
public int <u>getOptionType</u>()
public Object[] <u>getOptions</u>()
public Object[] <u>getSelectionValues</u>()
public OptionPaneUI <u>getUI</u>()
public String <u>getUIClassID</u>()
public Object <u>getValue</u>()
public boolean <u>getWantsInput</u>()

public void <u>setIcon</u>(Icon)
public void <u>setInitialSelectionValue</u>(Object)
public void <u>setInitialValue</u>(Object)
public void <u>setInputValue</u>(Object)
public void <u>setMessage</u>(Object)
public void <u>setMessageType</u>(int)
public void <u>setOptionType</u>(int)
public void <u>setOptions</u>(Object[])
public void <u>setSelectionValues</u>(Object[])
public void <u>setValue</u>(Object)
public void <u>setWantsInput</u>(boolean)

The methods listed above are accessors for JOptionPane properties. See
"JOptionPane" on page 849 for more information on the properties and how they
are used.

Initial Value

---

public void <u>selectInitialValue</u>()

The `selectInitialValue` method selects the component designated as the option pane's initial value. `JOptionPane` delegates this responsibility to its UI delegate.

Update/Set UI

---

public void <u>updateUI</u>()
public void <u>setUI</u>(OptionPaneUI)

The methods listed above can be found in most extensions of `JComponent` that have a UI delegate.

AWT Compatibility

The AWT does not provide a component analogous to `JOptionPane`.

Parting Shots

Both `JWindow` and `JDialog` are simple extensions of the AWT's `Window` and `Dialog` classes, respectively. As a result, Swing windows and dialogs are heavyweight containers that contain root panes.

The most interesting component discussed in this chapter has to be `JOptionPane`, which significantly simplifies the process of creating a dialog and retrieving any information supplied by the user. `JOptionPane` supports message, confirmation, option, and input dialogs that can be created and displayed by `static JOptionPane` methods. Alternatively an option pane can be created that is subsequently displayed in a dialog created by `JOptionPane.createDialog`.

CHAPTER

15

Internal Frames and Desktop Panes

Swing provides a set of components for implementing Multiple Document Interface (MDI) applications. MDI applications, such as Microsoft Word and Adobe FrameMaker, are implemented with a window that acts as a desktop for documents created in the application.

Swing offers MDI functionality with a desktop—represented by the JDesktopPane class—and internal frames, represented by the JInternalFrame class. Internal frames reside on a desktop and can be opened, closed, maximized, and iconified within a desktop. Swing also provides a DesktopManager class that is used to implement look-and-feel-specific behavior for internal frames that reside on a desktop.

JInternalFrame

Internal frames are frames because they are facsimiles of external frames; they are internal because they are contained within another Swing container, usually a desktop pane.

The controls that are contained in an internal frame's border are look-and-feel dependent. The standard Swing look and feels all provide close, maximize, and minimize buttons, which can be seen for the Metal look and feel in Figure 15-1. Additionally, the Metal look and feel provides both a grip and an icon in its title bar, as can be seen from the bottom picture in Figure 15-1.

Clicking the button in the applet shown in Figure 15-1 churns out internal frames. The top frame in Figure 15-1 is selected, highlighting the frame's border.

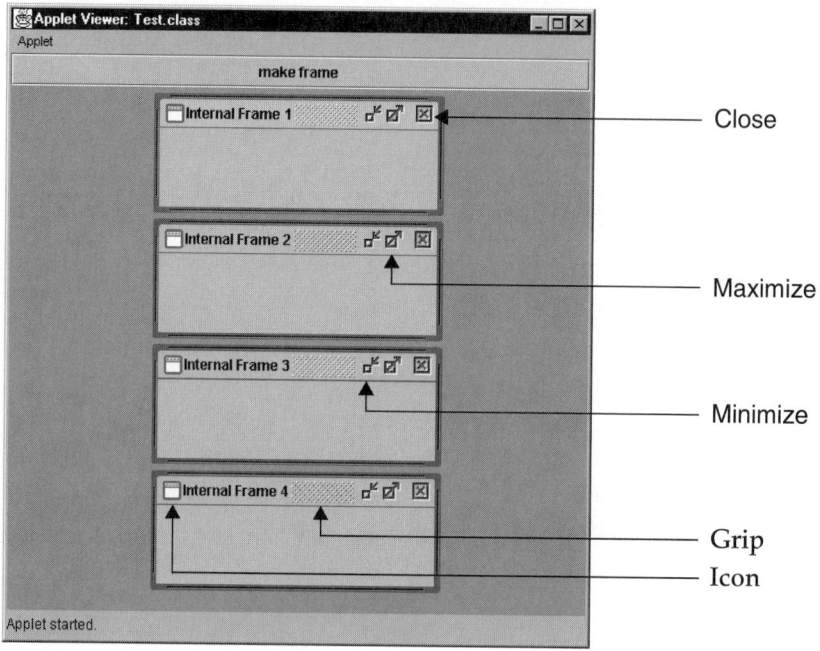

Figure 15-1 JInternalFrame in Action

The applet shown in Figure 15-1 is listed in Example 15-1.

Example 15-1 JInternalFrame in Action

```
import java.awt.*;
import java.awt.event.*;
import javax.swing.*;

public class Test extends JApplet {
```

```
JButton b = new JButton("make frame");
JDesktopPane desktopPane = new JDesktopPane();
int windowCount = 1;

public void init() {
    Container contentPane = getContentPane();

    contentPane.add(b, BorderLayout.NORTH);
    contentPane.add(desktopPane, BorderLayout.CENTER);

    // JDesktopPane has a null layout manager by default
    desktopPane.setLayout(new FlowLayout());

    b.addActionListener(new ActionListener() {
        public void actionPerformed(ActionEvent event) {
            JInternalFrame jif = new JInternalFrame(
                "Internal Frame " + windowCount++, // title
                true,   // resizable
                true,   // closable
                true,   // maximizable
                true);  // iconifiable

            jif.setPreferredSize(new Dimension(250, 100));
            desktopPane.add(jif);
            desktopPane.revalidate();
        }
    });
}
}
```

The applet creates an instance of JDesktopPane and adds it as the center component for the applet's content pane. The layout manager for the desktop pane is set to an instance of FlowLayout because desktop panes have a null layout manager by default.

When the make frame button is activated, an internal frame is constructed that is resizable, closable, maximizable, and iconifiable. Instances of JInternalFrame constructed with the JInternalFrame no-argument constructor are none of the above.

Since the layout manager for the desktop pane is an instance of FlowLayout, the preferred size for the internal frames is set. FlowLayout sizes components according to their preferred sizes.[1]

---

1. See the first volume of *Graphic Java* for more information on layout managers.

After the internal frame is added to the desktop pane, `revalidate()` is invoked on behalf of the desktop pane.

Internal Frames Belong in Desktop Panes

Internal frames are lightweight components that can be contained in any Swing or AWT container. However, internal frames expect to be contained by an instance of JDesktopPane; for example, JInternalFrame.setMaximum() throws a NullPointerException if it does not have an instance of JDesktopPane in its container ancestry.

The `JInternalFrame` component is summarized in Component Summary 15-1.

Component Summary 15-1   JInternalFrame

Model(s)	——
UI Delegate(s)	javax.swing.plaf.basic.BasicInternalFrameUI
Renderer(s)	——
Editor(s)	——
Events Fired	PropertyChangeEvents
Replacement For	——

Class Diagrams

`JInternalFrame` extends `JComponent` and implements three interfaces: `Accessible`, `WindowConstants`, and `RootPaneContainer`.

`JInternalFrame` maintains a number of `boolean` references for tracking its state, such as whether a frame is iconified or maximized. `JInternalFrame` also keeps track of its title, frame icon, and default close operation.

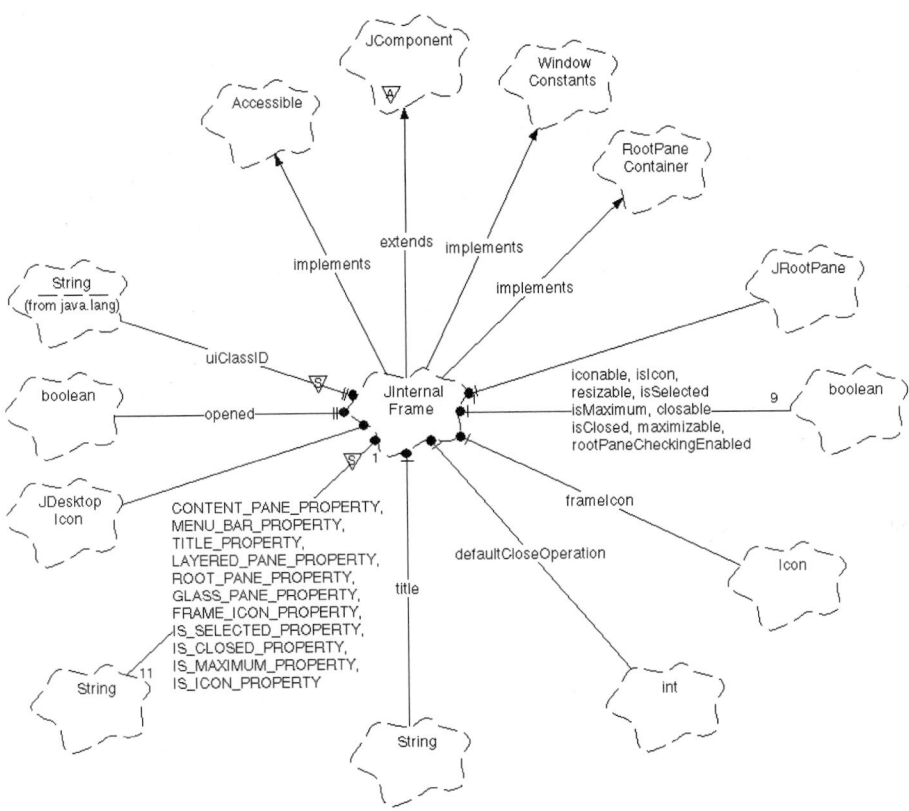

Figure 15-2 JInternalFrame Class Diagram

JInternalFrame Properties

The properties maintained by the `JInternalFrame` class are listed in Table 15-1.

Table 15-1 JInternalFrame Properties

Property Name	Data Type	Property Type[1]	Access[2]	Default[3]
closable	boolean	S	CSG	false
closed	boolean	CF	SG	false
contentPane	Container	B	SG	JPanel instance
defaultCloseOperation	int	S	SG	HIDE_ON_CLOSE

Table 15-1   JInternalFrame Properties (Continued)

Property Name	Data Type	Property Type[1]	Access[2]	Default[3]
desktopIcon	JDesktopIcon	S	SG	L&F
desktopPane	JDesktopPane	——	G	——
frameIcon	Icon	B	SG	L&F
glassPane	Component	B	SG	JPanel instance
icon	boolean	CBF	SG	false
iconifiable	boolean	S	CSG	false
layer	Integer	S	SG	DEFAULT_LAYER
layeredPane	JLayeredPane	B	SG	JLayeredPane
maximizable	boolean	S	CSG	false
maximum	boolean	CB	SG	false
jMenuBar	JMenuBar	B	SG	null
resizable	boolean	S	CSG	false
rootPane	JRootPane	B	SG	JRootPane
selected	boolean	CBF	SG	false
title	String	B	CSG	null
warningString	String	——	G	null

1. B = bound (fires PropertyChangeEvent) / C = constrained / I = indexed /
   S = simple / Ch = fires ChangeEvent / <u>F = fires InternalFrameEvent</u>
2. C = settable at construction time / G = getter method / S = setter method
3. L&F = look-and-feel dependent

closable — Indicates whether a frame can be closed by a user action such as clicking on a close button in the title bar. The `closable` property does not affect whether a frame can be closed programmatically.

closed — Indicates whether a frame is currently closed. The `closed` property is constrained, which means that closing and restoring an internal frame can be vetoed by a vetoable change listener.

contentPane — The content pane associated with a frame's root pane. The content pane is the container that contains the components that reside in the frame. Components should be added to a frame's content pane, not directly to the frame itself.

defaultCloseOperation — An operation that takes place when a frame is closed. The default value for internal frames is WindowConstants.HIDE_ON_CLOSE, as is the case for instances of JFrame and JDialog. See "JDialog Properties" on page 811 for more information on the defaultCloseOperation property.

desktopIcon — An icon that is displayed when an internal frame is iconified. The look and feel associated with an internal frame is responsible for specifying the desktop icon.

desktopPane — An instance of JDesktopPane that contains one or more internal frames. The desktopPane property is read-only.

frameIcon — The icon displayed in an internal frame's title bar. If the icon is not explicitly specified, the look and feel specifies the icon.

glassPane — The glass pane associated with an internal frame's root pane. See "Glass Panes" on page 639 for more information on root panes and their glass panes.

icon — Determines whether an internal frame is iconified. Invoking setIcon(true) iconifies an internal frame, and invoking setIcon(false) restores the frame to its previous location and size. The icon property is constrained, which means that iconifying and deiconifying an internal frame can be vetoed by a vetoable change listener.

iconifiable — Determines whether an internal frame can be iconified and deiconified by calls to setIcon(). See the icon property for more information on iconifying and deiconifying internal frames.

layer — The layer upon which an internal frame resides. By default, internal frames are assigned to the DEFAULT_LAYER. See "JLayeredPane" on page 658 for more information concerning the JLayeredPane class and the use of layers.

layeredPane — The layered pane associated with an internal frame's root pane. See "JRootPane" on page 636 for more information concerning root panes and their layered panes.

maximizable — Indicates whether an internal frame can be maximized by the user action of clicking an icon displayed in the frame's title bar. This property does not affect whether an internal frame can be maximized programmatically.

maximum — Determines whether an internal frame is maximized. Invoking `setMaximum(true)` maximizes an internal frame, and invoking `setMaximum(false)` restores the frame to its previous location and size. The `maximum` property is constrained, which means that maximizing and restoring an internal frame can be vetoed by a vetoable change listener.

jMenuBar — The menu bar associated with an internal frame's root pane. See "JRootPane" on page 636 for more information concerning root panes and their menu bars.

resizable — Determines whether an internal frame can be resized. Internal frames cannot be resized when they are maximized.

rootPane — The root pane associated with an internal frame.

selected — Selects or deselects an internal frame. Internal frames that are selected are typically drawn so that they are highlighted in some fashion. The Swing standard look and feels draw a selected frame's title bar with a color that communicates the frame's selected status. The `selected` property is constrained, which means that selecting and deselecting an internal frame can be vetoed by a vetoable change listener.

title — The title displayed in an internal frame's title bar. A title must be explicitly specified, either at construction time or afterward by `setTitle(String)`; by default, internal frames are constructed with a `null` string for a title.

warningString — Provided to maintain compatibility with heavyweight frames (instances of `java.awt.Window`), which display a warning string at the bottom of the window when displayed in a browser. The warning string associated with instances of `JInternalFrame` is a `null` string because internal frames are always contained within a heavyweight window, and therefore they do not need a warning string.

JInternalFrame Events

Instances of `JInternalFrame` fire instances of `InternalFrameEvent` when the following properties are modified: `closed`, `icon`, and `selected`, as can be seen from Table 15-1 on page 877. Additionally, `JInternalFrame` maintains the following constrained properties: `closed`, `icon`, `maximizable`, and `selected`.

Internal Frame Events

Whenever an internal frame is closed, iconified, or selected, an
`InternalFrameEvent` is fired to all registered `InternalFrameListeners`.
The `InternalFrameListener` interface is summarized in Interface Summary
15-1.

Interface Summary 15-1   Internal FrameListener

---

public abstract void <u>internalFrameActivated</u>(InternalFrameEvent)
public abstract void <u>internalFrameClosed</u>(InternalFrameEvent)
public abstract void <u>internalFrameClosing</u>(InternalFrameEvent)
public abstract void <u>internalFrameDeactivated</u>(InternalFrameEvent)
public abstract void <u>internalFrameDeiconified</u>(InternalFrameEvent)
public abstract void <u>internalFrameIconified</u>(InternalFrameEvent)
public abstract void <u>internalFrameOpened</u>(InternalFrameEvent)

The methods defined by the `InternalFrameListener` interface are invoked
just prior to the events the methods represent. For example,
`internalFrameActivated()` is invoked immediately after input (such as a
mouse click in the frame) is detected, but before the frame is actually made active.

Some methods defined by the `InternalFrameListener` interface are invoked
sequentially as the result of a single user gesture. For example, clicking an internal
frame's iconify icon will result in `internalFrameDeactivated()` followed by
`internalFrameIconified()`. Likewise, deiconifying an internal frame results
in calls to `internalFrameActivated()` followed by
`internalFrameDeiconified()`.

The `InternalFrameEvent` class is summarized in Class Summary 15-1.

Class Summary 15-1   InternalFrameEvent

Extends: java.awt.AWTEvent

Constants

---

public static final int <u>INTERNAL_FRAME_FIRST</u>
public static final int <u>INTERNAL_FRAME_LAST</u>

The constants listed above represent the first and last `integer` values used for `InternalFrameEvent` constants.

---

public static final int <u>INTERNAL_FRAME_ACTIVATED</u>
public static final int <u>INTERNAL_FRAME_CLOSED</u>
public static final int <u>INTERNAL_FRAME_CLOSING</u>
public static final int <u>INTERNAL_FRAME_DEACTIVATED</u>
public static final int <u>INTERNAL_FRAME_DEICONIFIED</u>
public static final int <u>INTERNAL_FRAME_ICONIFIED</u>
public static final int <u>INTERNAL_FRAME_OPENED</u>

The constants listed above represent the different types of events that the `InternalFrameEvent` class encompasses. The constants are used as the ID of an event and can be retrieved with the `getID` method.

Constructors

---

public <u>InternalFrameEvent</u>(JInternalFrame, int id)

As is typically the case for Swing (and AWT) events, the `InternalFrameEvent` class provides a single constructor that is passed the source of the event and an `integer` value corresponding to one of the constants listed above.

Methods

---

public String <u>paramString</u>()

The `paramString` method returns a string that identifies the event. The `paramString` method is useful for debugging and logging events.

The applet shown in Figure 15-3 contains a single instance of `JInternalFrame`. An instance of `InternalFrameListener` is added to the internal frame that updates the applet's status area whenever one of the methods defined by the `InternalFrameListener` interface is invoked.

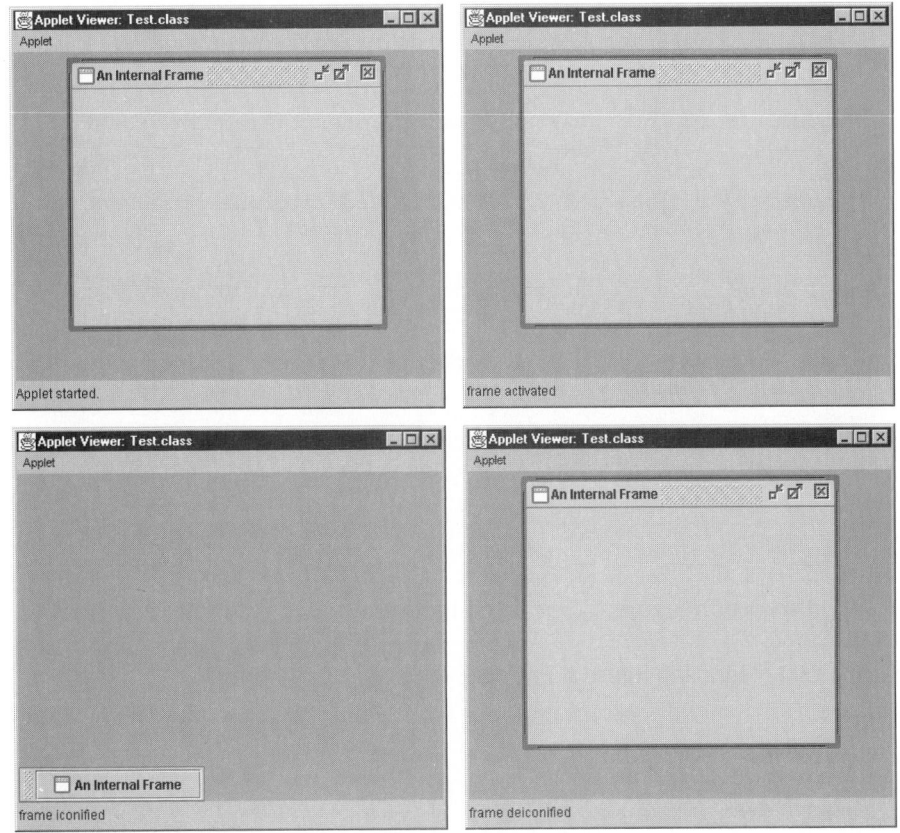

Figure 15-3 Handling InternalFrameEvents

The upper-left picture shows the applet as it appears initially. The upper-right picture shows the applet after the internal frame has been activated. The lower-left picture shows the internal frame after it has been iconified. The lower-right picture shows the internal frame after it has subsequently been deiconified.

The listener associated with the internal frame is listed below. The listener simply updates the applet's status area whenever one of its methods is invoked.

```
class Listener implements InternalFrameListener {
    private JApplet applet;

    public Listener(JApplet applet) {
        this.applet = applet;
    }
    public void internalFrameActivated(InternalFrameEvent e) {
        applet.showStatus("frame activated");
    }
    public void internalFrameClosed(InternalFrameEvent e) {
        applet.showStatus("frame closed");
    }
    public void internalFrameClosing(InternalFrameEvent e) {
        applet.showStatus("frame closing");
    }
    public void internalFrameDeactivated(InternalFrameEvent e) {
        applet.showStatus("frame deactivated");
    }
    public void internalFrameDeiconified(InternalFrameEvent e) {
        applet.showStatus("frame deiconified");
    }
    public void internalFrameIconified(InternalFrameEvent e) {
        applet.showStatus("frame iconified");
    }
    public void internalFrameOpened(InternalFrameEvent e) {
        applet.showStatus("frame opened");
    }
}
```

The applet shown in Figure 15-3 is listed in its entirety in Example 15-2.

Example 15-2 Handling Internal Frame Events

```
import java.awt.*;
import java.awt.event.*;
import java.beans.*;
import javax.swing.*;
import javax.swing.event.*;

public class Test extends JApplet {
    JDesktopPane desktopPane = new JDesktopPane();

    public void init() {
        Container contentPane = getContentPane();

        contentPane.add(desktopPane, BorderLayout.CENTER);
        desktopPane.setLayout(new FlowLayout());

        JInternalFrame jif = new JInternalFrame(
                            "An Internal Frame", // title
```

```
                        false, // resizable
                        true,  // closable
                        true,  // maximizable
                        true); // iconifiable

        jif.setPreferredSize(new Dimension(300, 250));
        jif.addInternalFrameListener(new Listener(this));

        desktopPane.add(jif);
    }
}
class Listener implements InternalFrameListener {
    private JApplet applet;

    public Listener(JApplet applet) {
        this.applet = applet;
    }
    public void internalFrameActivated(InternalFrameEvent e) {
        applet.showStatus("frame activated");
    }
    public void internalFrameClosed(InternalFrameEvent e) {
        applet.showStatus("frame closed");
    }
    public void internalFrameClosing(InternalFrameEvent e) {
        applet.showStatus("frame closing");
    }
    public void internalFrameDeactivated(InternalFrameEvent e) {
        applet.showStatus("frame deactivated");
    }
    public void internalFrameDeiconified(InternalFrameEvent e) {
        applet.showStatus("frame deiconified");
    }
    public void internalFrameIconified(InternalFrameEvent e) {
        applet.showStatus("frame iconified");
    }
    public void internalFrameOpened(InternalFrameEvent e) {
        applet.showStatus("frame opened");
    }
}
```

JInternalFrame Constrained Properties

JInternalFrame has the distinction of being the only Swing component that
maintains constrained properties.

Constrained properties, like bound properties, fire property change events when modifications are made to a property. Unlike the case with bound properties, changes to constrained properties can be vetoed—and therefore constrained—by any vetoable change listener. JInternalFrame implements the following properties as constrained properties:

- closed
- icon
- maximum
- selected

The application shown in Figure 15-4 contains a closable internal frame equipped with a VetoableChangeListener that intervenes when the frame is closed. When the frame fires a PropertyChangeEvent, the listener responds with a confirmation dialog asking whether changes should be saved. If the Cancel button is activated, the change is vetoed by a PropertyVetoException thrown by the listener.

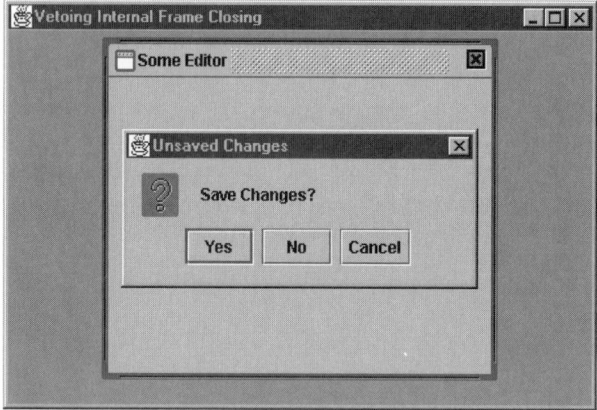

Figure 15-4 Vetoing the Closing of an Internal Frame

The application shown in Figure 15-4 is listed in Example 15-3.

Example 15-3   Vetoing the Closing of an Internal Frame

```java
import java.awt.*;
import java.awt.event.*;
import java.beans.*;
import javax.swing.*;
import java.util.*;

public class Test extends JFrame {
    JDesktopPane desktopPane = new JDesktopPane();

    public Test() {
        Container contentPane = getContentPane();

        contentPane.add(desktopPane, BorderLayout.CENTER);
        desktopPane.setLayout(new FlowLayout());

        JInternalFrame jif = new JInternalFrame(
                            "Some Editor", // title
                            false,  // resizable
                            true);  // closable

        jif.setPreferredSize(new Dimension(300, 250));
        jif.addVetoableChangeListener(new CloseListener());

        desktopPane.add(jif);
    }
    public static void main(String args[]) {
        GJApp.launch(new Test(),
                "Vetoing Internal Frame Closing",
                300,300,450,300);
    }
}
class CloseListener implements VetoableChangeListener {
    public void vetoableChange(PropertyChangeEvent e)
                            throws PropertyVetoException {
        String name = e.getPropertyName();

        if(name.equals(JInternalFrame.IS_CLOSED_PROPERTY)) {
            Component internalFrame = (Component)e.getSource();
            Boolean oldValue = (Boolean)e.getOldValue(),
                newValue = (Boolean)e.getNewValue();

            if(oldValue == Boolean.FALSE &&
                            newValue == Boolean.TRUE) {
                int answer = JOptionPane.showConfirmDialog(
                        internalFrame,// parentComponent
                        "Save Changes?", // message
                        "Unsaved Changes", // title
                        JOptionPane.YES_NO_CANCEL_OPTION);

                if(answer == JOptionPane.CANCEL_OPTION) {
```

```
                         throw new PropertyVetoException(
                                             "close cancelled", e);
                  }
               }
            }
         }
      }
```

The application creates an instance of `JDesktopPane`, which is specified as the center component for the application's content pane. A closable instance of `JInternalFrame` is subsequently instantiated and added to the desktop pane.

A vetoable change listener, in the form of an instance of `CloseListener`, is added to the internal frame.

The `CloseListener` class implements `VetoableChangeListener` and is responsible for displaying the confirmation dialog.

The `VetoableChangeListener` interface defines a single method—`vetoableChange(PropertyChangeEvent)`, that is implemented by the `CloseListener` class. The `vetoableChange` method obtains the name of the property from the property change event and checks to see if the property being modified is the `closed` property. If so, a reference is obtained to the internal frame from whence the event was fired.

The old and new values for the property are extracted from the property change event. The dialog is shown only if the old value is `false`—meaning that the frame has not yet been closed—and the new value is `true`, meaning that an attempt is being made to close the frame by setting the `closed` property, which is currently `false`, to `true`.

If the `closed` property is being modified and the frame is closing, a confirmation dialog is shown by invoking the `static JOptionPane.showConfirmDialog` method. If the response is `Cancel`, a `PropertyVetoException` is thrown.

An interesting characteristic of the application listed in Example 15-3 is the fact that the `CloseListener.vetoableChange` method is called twice if the closing of the internal frame is vetoed. The reasoning is as follows:

There may be other listeners listening for the closing of an internal frame, and they may have already been notified of the change before it is vetoed by the `CloseListener`. Those listeners may have already acted upon the proposed change before it was vetoed, and therefore a second property change event is needed to reverse the change. The second property change event has the new and old values reversed from the original change.

Swing Tip ...

Vetoable Listeners Are Notified Twice When a Property Is Vetoed

Classes that maintain constrained properties also maintain a list of vetoable listeners. When a call it is made to modify a constrained property's value, each vetoable listener is notified of the proposed change via the listener's vetoableChange method which is passed a PropertyChangeEvent.

If one of vetoable listeners vetoes the proposed change by throwing a PropertyVetoException, a second PropertyChangeEvent is fired with the old and new values for the properties reversed from those specified in the original PropertyChangeEvent. Since the original PropertyChangeEvent may have been acted upon by listenesr that found that change acceptable prior to it being vetoed, those listeners must be given the chance to undo any changes they may have made in light of the proposed property change.

The `JInternalFrame` class is summarized in Class Summary 15-2.

Class Summary 15-2   JInternalFrame

Constructors

---

public <u>JInternalFrame</u>()
public <u>JInternalFrame</u>(String title)
public <u>JInternalFrame</u>(String title, boolean resizable)
public <u>JInternalFrame</u>(String title, boolean resizable, boolean closable)
public <u>JInternalFrame</u>(String title, boolean resizable, boolean closable,
                    boolean maximizable)
public <u>JInternalFrame</u>(String title, boolean resizable, boolean closable,
                    boolean maximizable, boolean iconifiable)

The list of properties that can be specified at construction time can be seen by examining the argument list of the last constructor listed above.

The no-argument constructor constructs an internal frame that cannot be resized, closed, maximized or iconified.

Methods

Layout Manager / Root Pane / Adding Components

---

protected void <u>addImpl</u>(Component, Object, int)
protected JRootPane <u>createRootPane</u>()
protected boolean <u>isRootPaneCheckingEnabled</u>()
protected void <u>setRootPaneCheckingEnabled</u>(boolean)
protected void <u>setRootPane</u>(JRootPane)

public void <u>setLayout</u>(LayoutManager)

The first five methods listed above are used to set the frame's root pane. `JInternalFrame`, like other Swing components that implement the `RootPaneContainer` interface, disallows directly adding components to, or setting the layout manager for, the frame. However, `JInternalFrame` itself must add the root pane and set its layout manager. As a result, the `setRootPaneCheckingEnabled` and `isRootPaneCheckingEnabled` methods enable instances of `JInternalFrame` to add their root pane and set their layout manager, while at the same time disallowing these activities for outsiders.

The `createRootPane` method creates an instance of `JRootPane`. The method is `protected` so that extensions of `JInternalFrame` can insert a specialized root pane, if desired.

The `setLayout` method throws an exception indicating that setting the layout manager by anyone other than the window itself is a forbidden activity.

Internal Frame Events

---

public synchronized void <u>addInternalFrameListener</u>(InternalFrameListener)
public synchronized void <u>removeInternalFrameListener</u>(InternalFrameListener)
protected void <u>fireInternalFrameEvent</u>()

The methods listed above manage internal frame listeners for an instance of
`JInternalFrame`. The protected `fireInternalFrameEvent` method is
used by instances of `JInternalFrame` to fire internal frame events to internal
frame listeners.

Foreground and Background Colors

---

public Color getBackground()
public void setBackground(Color)
public Color getForeground()
public void setForeground(Color)

Methods for getting and setting the background color for instances of
`JInternalFrame` are overridden to delegate to an internal frame's content pane.

Vetoable Property Accessors

---

public boolean isClosed()
public boolean isIcon()
public boolean isMaximum()
public boolean isSelected()

public void setClosed(boolean) throws PropertyVetoException
public void setIcon(boolean) throws PropertyVetoException
public void setMaximum(boolean) throws PropertyVetoException
public void setSelected(boolean) throws PropertyVetoException

The methods listed above are accessors for `JInternalFrame` constrained
properties. Notice that each `set...()` method may throw a
`PropertyVetoException` if the proposed change is vetoed by a listener.

Properties

---

public Container getContentPane()
public int getDefaultCloseOperation()
public JInternalFrame.JDesktopIcon getDesktopIcon()
public JDesktopPane getDesktopPane()
public Icon getFrameIcon()
public Component getGlassPane()
public int getLayer()
public JLayeredPane getLayeredPane()
public JMenuBar getJMenuBar()
public String getTitle()
public final String getWarningString()

public boolean isClosable()
public boolean isIconifiable()
public boolean isMaximizable()
public boolean isResizable()

public void setClosable(boolean)
public void setContentPane(Container)
public void setDefaultCloseOperation(int)
public void setDesktopIcon(JInternalFrame.JDesktopIcon)
public void setFrameIcon(Icon)
public void setGlassPane(Component)
public void setIconifiable(boolean)
public void setLayer(Integer)
public void setLayeredPane(JLayeredPane)
public void setMaximizable(boolean)
public void setJMenuBar(JMenuBar)
public void setResizable(boolean)
public void setTitle(String)
public void setVisible(boolean)

The methods listed above are accessors for most of the properties defined by the
`JInternalFrame` class. `JInternalFrame` properties are discussed in
"JInternalFrame Properties" on page 877.

The applet shown in Figure 15-5 displays an internal frame whose icon has been
explicitly set with the `JInternalFrame.setFrameIcon()`.

The applet shown in Figure 15-5 is listed in Example 15-4.

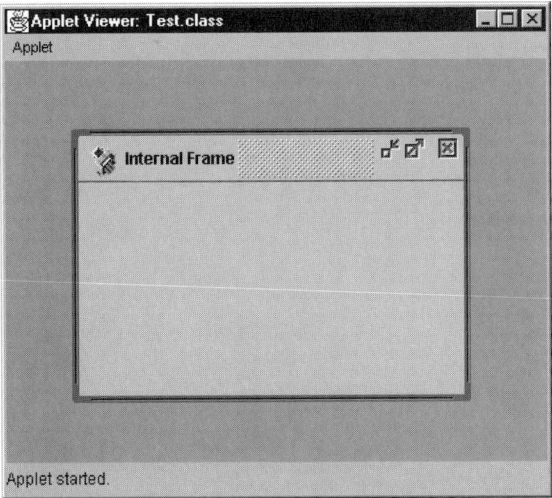

Figure 15-5 Replacing an Internal Frame's Icon

Example 15-4 Replacing an Internal Frame's Icon

```java
import java.awt.*;
import java.awt.event.*;
import javax.swing.*;

public class Test extends JApplet {
    JDesktopPane desktopPane = new JDesktopPane();
    JInternalFrame jif = new JInternalFrame(
                "Internal Frame", // title
                true,   // resizable
                true,   // closable
                true,   // maximizable
                true);  // iconifiable

    public void init() {
        Container contentPane = getContentPane();

        contentPane.add(desktopPane, BorderLayout.CENTER);

        jif.setSize(new Dimension(250, 100));
        jif.setFrameIcon(new ImageIcon("print.gif"));
        desktopPane.add(jif);
    }
}
```

The applet creates a desktop pane and an internal frame. The desktop pane is added to the applet's content pane, and the internal frame is an added to the desktop pane.

The icon displayed in the frame's title bar is specified with the `JInternalFrame.setFrameIcon()`, which should not be confused with `JInternalFrame.setIcon()`, which iconifies and deiconifies an internal frame.

Show / Move Front-Back / Reshape / Dispose

---

public void <u>show</u>()
public void <u>toBack</u>()
public void <u>toFront</u>()
public void <u>moveToBack</u>()
public void <u>moveToFront</u>()
public void <u>pack</u>()
public void <u>reshape</u>(int x, int y, int w, int h)
public void <u>dispose</u>()

The methods listed above manipulate an internal frame by modifying its visibility, bounds, or location.

The `pack` method, like the `java.awt.Window` method of the same name, resizes a frame so that it is just large enough to display all of the components it contains.

The `show` method packs the frame and invokes `super.show()`. If the frame is already visible, invoking `show()` causes the frame to be placed in front of all other internal frames in the same desktop pane.

The `toFront` and `toBack` methods are implemented to be compatible with `java.awt.Window`. The `toFront` method simply invokes `moveToFront()` and the `toBack` method invokes `moveToBack()`. `moveToBack()` alters the index of the internal frame so that it is displayed behind all other internal frames in the same desktop pane. `moveToFront()` moves the internal frame so that it is displayed in front of all other internal frames in the same desktop pane.

`reshape()` is overridden from the `JComponent` class and validates and repaints the frame after invoking `super.reshape()`.

Accessibility / Pluggable Look And Feel

---

public AccessibleContext <u>getAccessibleContext</u>()
public InternalFrameUI <u>getUI</u>()

public String <u>getUIClassID</u>()
public void <u>setUI</u>(InternalFrameUI)
public void <u>updateUI</u>()

The methods listed above can be found in most extensions of `JComponent`. Swing lightweight components can return the class name of their UI delegate and an accessibility context that contains accessibility information for the component. The `updateUI` method is invoked when the component is fitted with a UI delegate.

AWT Compatibility

The AWT does not provide a component analogous to an internal frame. Nonetheless, the `JInternalFrame` class strives to maintain a degree of compatibility with `java.awt.Window`. Table 15-2 lists the `public` methods implemented by `java.awt.Window`, and their `JInternalFrame` equivalents.

Table 15-2   java.awt.Window Methods and JInternalFrame Equivalents[1]

java.awt.Window Method	JInternalFrame Equivalent
void addWindowListener(WindowListener)	**void addInternalFrameListener(InternalFrameListener)**
void applyResourceBundle(String)	——
void applyResourceBundle(ResourceBundle)	——
void dispose()	void dispose()
Component getFocusOwner()	——
InputContext getInputContext()	——
Locale getLocale()	——
Window[] getOwnedWindows()	——
Toolkit getToolkit	——
String getWarningString()	String getWarningString()
boolean isShowing()	**boolean isVisible()**
void pack()	void pack()
void show()	void show()
void toBack()	void toBack()
void toFront()	void toFront()

1. Differing signatures are highlighted in bold.

In addition to providing a level of compatibility between `java.awt.Window` and `JInternalFrame`, the AWT's `WindowListener` is functionally equivalent to Swing's `InternalFrameListener`. Table 15-3 lists the methods defined via the `java.awt.WindowListener` interface and the corresponding methods defined by the `InternalFrameListener` class.

Table 15-3 java.awt.WindowListener Methods and InternalFrameListener Equivalents

java.awt.WindowListener Method	JInternalFrame Equivalent
windowActivated()	internalFrameActivated()
windowClosed()	internalFrameClosed()
windowClosing()	internalFrameClosing()
windowDeactivated()	internalFrameDeactivated()
windowDeiconified()	internalFrameDeiconified()
windowIconified()	internalFrameIconified()

JDesktopPane

Desktop panes, represented by the `JDesktopPane` class, are containers designed to contain internal frames. `JDesktopPane` is an extension of the `JLayeredPane` class and maintains an association with a desktop manager. `JDesktopPane` uses its layering capabilities to manage the zorder of the internal frames it contains. Each instance of `JDesktopPane` has a desktop manager that is responsible for implementing look-and-feel behavior and is discussed further in "DesktopManager" on page 906.

The manner in which instances of `JDesktopPane` are typically used has already been illustrated in the code examples that have been discussed in this chapter. Instances of `JDesktopPane` are constructed with the `JDesktopPane` no-argument constructor, which is the only constructor `JDesktopPane` provides. Instances of `JInternalFrame` are subsequently added to the desktop pane.

`JDesktopPane` can also be extended to provide customized behavior. For example, a common feature of Multiple Document Interface (MDI) applications is the ability to cascade the frames contained in the desktop pane. The applet shown in Figure 15-6 does exactly that—it provides an extension of `JDesktopPane` that can cascade its frames on demand.

The left picture shown in Figure 15-6 shows the applet as it appears initially. The internal frames are initially randomly placed in the desktop pane contained in the applet. A `Window` menu is provided that contains three menu items: `open all`, `close all`, and `cascade`. The middle picture shown in Figure 15-6 shows the applet after the Cascade menu item has been selected and the internal frames contained in the desktop pane have been resized and repositioned. The right picture shows the applet after the close all menu item has been selected and the frames have been closed.

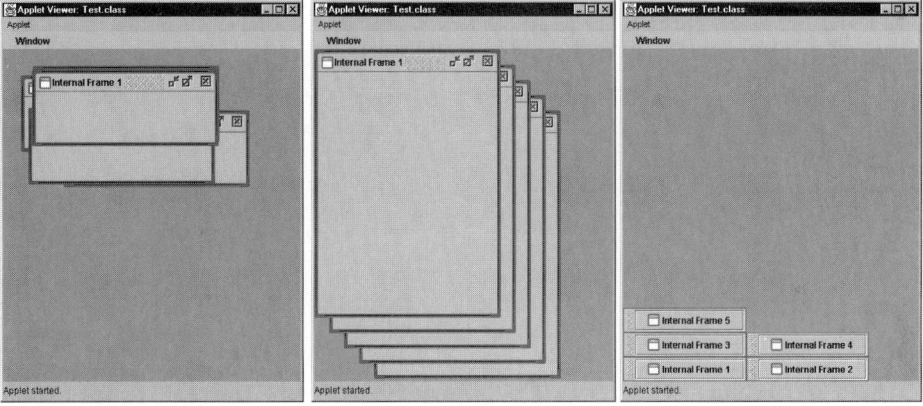

Figure 15-6 A Custom Desktop Pane

The applet creates an instance of `CustomDesktopPane` and populates it with five internal frames placed at random locations.

```
public class Test extends JApplet {
    CustomDesktopPane desktopPane = new CustomDesktopPane();
    int frameCount = 1, numFrames = 5, x, y;

    public void init() {
        Container contentPane = getContentPane();
```

```
    setJMenuBar(createMenuBar());
    contentPane.add(desktopPane, BorderLayout.CENTER);

    for(int i=0; i < numFrames; ++i) {
        JInternalFrame jif = new JInternalFrame(
            "Internal Frame " + frameCount++, // title
            true,   // resizable
            true,   // closable
            true,   // maximizable
            true); // iconifiable

        x = (int)(Math.random() * 100);
        y = (int)(Math.random() * 100);

        jif.setBounds(x, y, 250, 100);
        desktopPane.add(jif);
    }
}
```

The `CustomDesktopPane` class extends `JDesktopPane` and implements three methods: `closeAll()`, `openAll()`, and `cascade()`.

```
class CustomDesktopPane extends JDesktopPane {
    private int xoffset = 20, yoffset = 20, w = 250, h = 350;

    public void closeAll() {
        JInternalFrame[] frames = getAllFrames();

        for(int i=0; i < frames.length; ++i) {
            if( ! frames[i].isIcon()) {
                try {
                    frames[i].setIcon(true);
                }
                catch(java.beans.PropertyVetoException ex) {
                    System.out.println("iconification vetoed!");
                }
            }
        }
    }
    public void openAll() {
        JInternalFrame[] frames = getAllFrames();

        for(int i=0; i < frames.length; ++i) {
            if(frames[i].isIcon()) {
                try {
                    frames[i].setIcon(false);
                }
                catch(java.beans.PropertyVetoException ex) {
                    System.out.println("restoration vetoed!");
                }
```

```
                }
            }
        }
        public void cascade() {
            JInternalFrame[] frames = getAllFrames();
            int x = 0, y = 0;

            for(int i=0; i < frames.length; ++i) {
                if( ! frames[i].isIcon()) {
                    frames[i].setBounds(x,y,w,h);
                    x += xoffset;
                    y += yoffset;
                }
            }
        }
    }
```

Each method invokes the `JInternalFrame.getAllFrames` method to obtain an array of the internal frames contained in the `CustomDesktopPane`. The `closeAll` and `openAll` methods invoke `JInternalFrame.setIcon()`, which is passed a `boolean` argument that specifies whether the frame should be iconified (`true`) or deiconified (`false`). The `closeAll` method iconifies all of the frames that are currently not open, and the `openAll` method deiconifies any frames that are iconified. Because iconifying and deiconifying internal frames can be vetoed by listeners—see "JInternalFrame Constrained Properties" on page 885—both methods must be prepared to catch a `PropertyVetoException`.

The `cascade` method sets the size and location for all of the internal frames that are not iconified. The size is arbitrarily chosen, and the location of the first frame is set to (`0,0`) with each subsequent frame being located 10 pixels down and to the right of the previous frame.

The applet shown in Figure 15-6 is listed in its entirety in Example 15-5.

Example 15-5 A Custom Desktop Pane

```
import java.awt.*;
import java.awt.event.*;
import javax.swing.*;

public class Test extends JApplet {
    CustomDesktopPane desktopPane = new CustomDesktopPane();
    int frameCount = 1, numFrames = 5, x, y;

    public void init() {
        Container contentPane = getContentPane();
```

```java
        setJMenuBar(createMenuBar());
        contentPane.add(desktopPane, BorderLayout.CENTER);

        for(int i=0; i < numFrames; ++i) {
            JInternalFrame jif = new JInternalFrame(
                    "Internal Frame " + frameCount++, // title
                    true,   // resizable
                    true,   // closable
                    true,   // maximizable
                    true);  // iconifiable

            x = (int)(Math.random() * 100);
            y = (int)(Math.random() * 100);

            jif.setBounds(x, y, 250, 100);
            desktopPane.add(jif);
        }
    }
    private JMenuBar createMenuBar() {
        JMenuBar menubar = new JMenuBar();
        JMenu windowMenu = new JMenu("Window");

        windowMenu.add(new OpenAllAction());
        windowMenu.add(new CloseAllAction());
        windowMenu.add(new CascadeAction());

        menubar.add(windowMenu);
        return menubar;
    }
    class OpenAllAction extends AbstractAction {
        public OpenAllAction() {
            super("open all");
        }
        public void actionPerformed(ActionEvent e) {
            desktopPane.openAll();
        }
    }
    class CloseAllAction extends AbstractAction {
        public CloseAllAction() {
            super("close all");
        }
        public void actionPerformed(ActionEvent e) {
            desktopPane.closeAll();
        }
    }
    class CascadeAction extends AbstractAction {
        public CascadeAction() {
            super("cascade");
        }
```

```java
        public void actionPerformed(ActionEvent e) {
            desktopPane.cascade();
        }
    }
}
class CustomDesktopPane extends JDesktopPane {
    private int xoffset = 20, yoffset = 20, w = 250, h = 350;

    public void closeAll() {
        JInternalFrame[] frames = getAllFrames();

        for(int i=0; i < frames.length; ++i) {
            if( ! frames[i].isIcon()) {
                try {
                    frames[i].setIcon(true);
                }
                catch(java.beans.PropertyVetoException ex) {
                    System.out.println("iconification vetoed!");
                }
            }
        }
    }
    public void openAll() {
        JInternalFrame[] frames = getAllFrames();

        for(int i=0; i < frames.length; ++i) {
            if(frames[i].isIcon()) {
                try {
                    frames[i].setIcon(false);
                }
                catch(java.beans.PropertyVetoException ex) {
                    System.out.println("restoration vetoed!");
                }
            }
        }
    }
    public void cascade() {
        JInternalFrame[] frames = getAllFrames();
        int x = 0, y = 0;

        for(int i=0; i < frames.length; ++i) {
            if( ! frames[i].isIcon()) {
                frames[i].setBounds(x,y,w,h);
                x += xoffset;
                y += yoffset;
            }
        }
    }
}
```

Desktop Panes Have Null Layout Managers

By default, instances of JDesktopPane have a null layout manager. As a result, internal frames contained in a desktop pane must have their bounds explicitly specified or they will not appear in the desktop pane.

If a layout manager is explicitly set for a desktop pane, explicitly setting the size and location for internal frames contained in the desktop pane will likely have no effect because the layout manager will override the size and location of the frames.

The applet listed in Example 15-3 on page 887 sets the preferred size for the internal frame contained in the applet's desktop pane because a layout manager (that sizes components according to their preferred sizes) is explicitly set for the desktop pane. On the other hand, because the desktop pane has a null layout manager, the applet listed in Figure 15-5 sets the actual bounds for the internal frames contained in the applet's desktop pane.

The JDesktopPane component is summarized in Component Summary 15-2.

Component Summary 15-2   JDesktopPane

Model(s)	——
UI Delegate(s)	javax.swing.plaf.basic.BasicDesktopPaneUI
Renderer(s)	——
Editor(s)	——
Events Fired	——
Replacement For	——

Class Diagrams

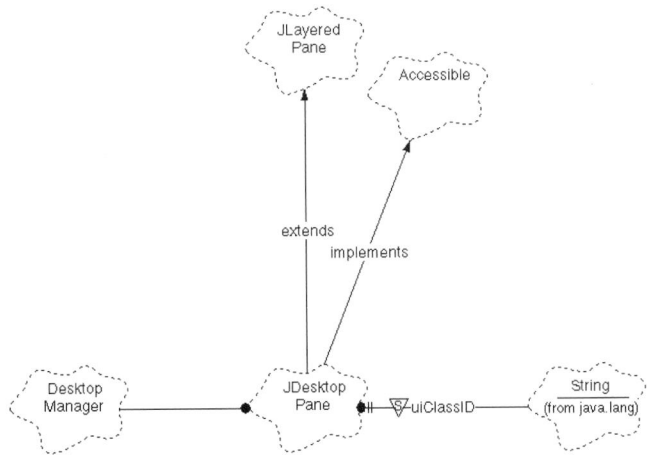

Figure 15-7 JDesktopPane Class Diagram

JDesktopPane is a simple extension of JLayeredPane, which implements the Accessible interface. Each instance of JDesktopPane has its own desktop manager that implements look-and-feel-specific behavior for the internal frames contained in the desktop pane.

JDesktopPane Properties

The properties maintained by the JDesktopPane class are listed in Table 15-4.

Table 15-4 JDesktopPane Properties

Property Name	Data Type	Property Type[1]	Access[2]	Default[3]
desktopManager	DesktopManager	S	SG	DesktopManager
allFrames	JInternalFrame[]	—	G	——
allFramesInLayer	JInternalFrame[]	I	G	

1. B = bound (fires PropertyChangeEvent) / C = constrained/ I = indexed /
   S = simple / Ch = fires ChangeEvent
2. C = settable at construction time / G = getter method / S = setter method
3. L&F = look-and-feel dependent

desktopManager — Implements look-and-feel-specific behavior for the desktop panes with which it is associated. Desktop managers are discussed in "DesktopManager" on page 906.

allFrames — All of the internal frames contained in an instance of JDesktopPane.

allFramesInLayer — All of the internal frames contained in an instance of JDesktopPane that reside in a specific layer.

JDesktopPane Events

JDesktopPane does not fire any events of its own accord. See "JLayeredPane" on page 658 for a discussion of events fired by JLayeredPane, which is JDesktopPane's superclass.

JDesktopPane Class Summaries

The public and protected variables and methods for JDesktopPane are listed in Class Summary 15-3.

Class Summary 15-3   JDesktopPane

Extends: JLayeredPane
Implements: javax.accessibility.Accessible

Constructors

---

public <u>JDesktopPane</u>()

`JDesktopPane` provides a lone no-argument constructor. The desktop pane is constructed with a desktop manager that is appropriate for the look and feel associated with the desktop pane.

Methods

Property Accessors

---

public JInternalFrame[] <u>getAllFrames</u>()
public JInternalFrame[] <u>getAllFramesInLayer</u>(int)
public DesktopManager <u>getDesktopManager</u>()

public boolean <u>isOpaque</u>()

public void <u>setDesktopManager</u>(DesktopManager)

The methods listed above are accessors for `JDesktopPane` properties. Arrays of instances of `JInternalFrame` can be obtained by invocation of the `getAllFrames` or `getAllFramesInLayer` methods.

The desktop manager can be set, and a reference to the current desktop manager can be obtained by the `setDesktopManager` and `getDesktopManager` methods, respectively.

`JDesktopPane` overrides the `isOpaque` method from the `JComponent` class to return `true`, meaning that all desktop panes paint every pixel they contain and therefore do not have transparent backgrounds.

Accessibility / Pluggable Look and Feel

---

public AccessibleContext <u>getAccessibleContext</u>()
public DesktopPaneUI <u>getUI</u>()
public String <u>getUIClassID</u>()
public void <u>setUI</u>(DesktopPaneUI)
public void <u>updateUI</u>()

The methods listed above can be found in most extensions of `JComponent`. Swing lightweight components can return the class name of their UI delegate and an accessibility context that contains accessibility information for the component. The `updateUI` method is invoked when the component is fitted with a UI delegate.

AWT Compatibility

The AWT does not provide a component analogous to `JDesktopPane`.

DesktopManager

Desktop managers implement look-and-feel-specific behavior for desktop panes. For example, the manner in which internal frames are dragged and resized in a desktop pane is the responsibility of the desktop pane's desktop manager. When an internal frame is manipulated, for example, by closing the frame by invoking `JInternalFrame.setClosed()`, the frame delegates to its UI delegate, which in turn delegates to a desktop manager.

Desktop managers are responsible for implementing the following behavior:

- frame activation/deactivation
- frame dragging/resizing
- frame opening/closing
- frame iconifying/deiconifying
- frame maximizing/minimizing

The scenario diagram shown in Figure 15-8 illustrates the sequence of the events that occurs when `JInternalFrame.setClosed()` is invoked.

Calls to `JInternalFrame.setClosed()` that are not vetoed result in the firing of a property change event. The property change event is delivered to the internal frame's UI delegate,[2] which delegates to its desktop manager. The default desktop manager responds to the closing of an internal frame by obtaining a reference to the desktop pane associated with the internal frame and invoking

---

2. UI delegates typically listen to their components for property change events.

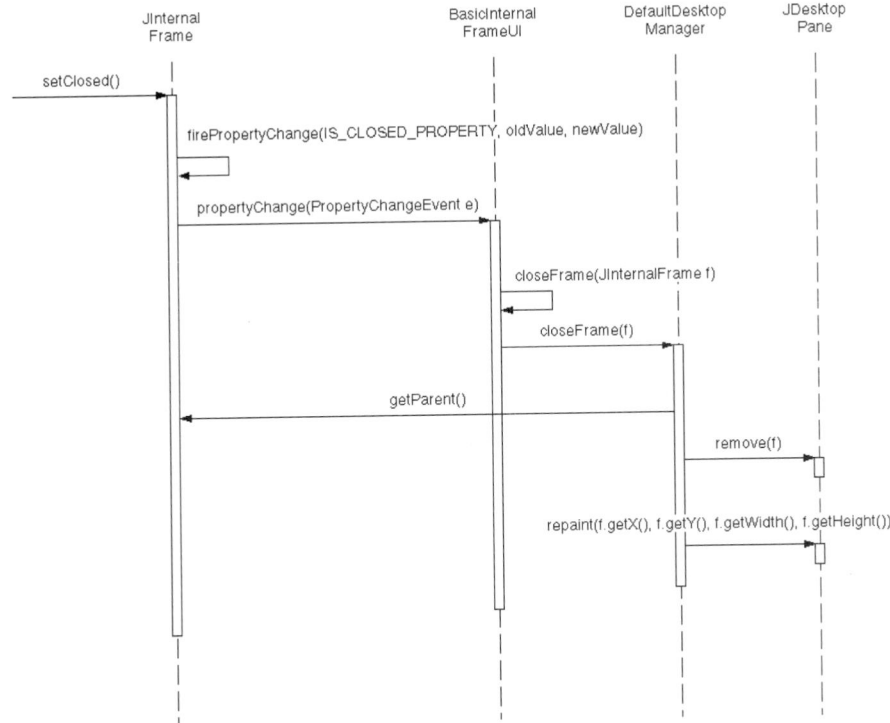

Figure 15-8 Closing Internal Frames

`JDesktopPane.remove()`, passing a reference to the internal frame that is to be removed. Subsequently, the default desktop manager repaints the affected area of the desktop pane.

Scenario diagrams for other types of actions that can be performed on an internal frame would be similar to the one shown in Figure 15-8. A `JInternalFrame` method is invoked, and the internal frame delegates to its UI delegate, which in turn delegates to a desktop manager. In this way, look-and-feel-specific behavior is encapsulated in a pluggable desktop manager.

The applet shown in Figure 15-9 contains a single internal frame that is contained in an instance of `JDesktopPane`. The desktop pane is fitted with a custom desktop manager that drags and resizes frames by drawing the outline of the frame instead of the contents of the frame.[3] The three pictures on the left (from top to bottom) illustrate dragging the frame, and the three pictures on the right illustrate resizing the frame.

3. The `DefaultDesktopManager` class drags the contents of the frame.

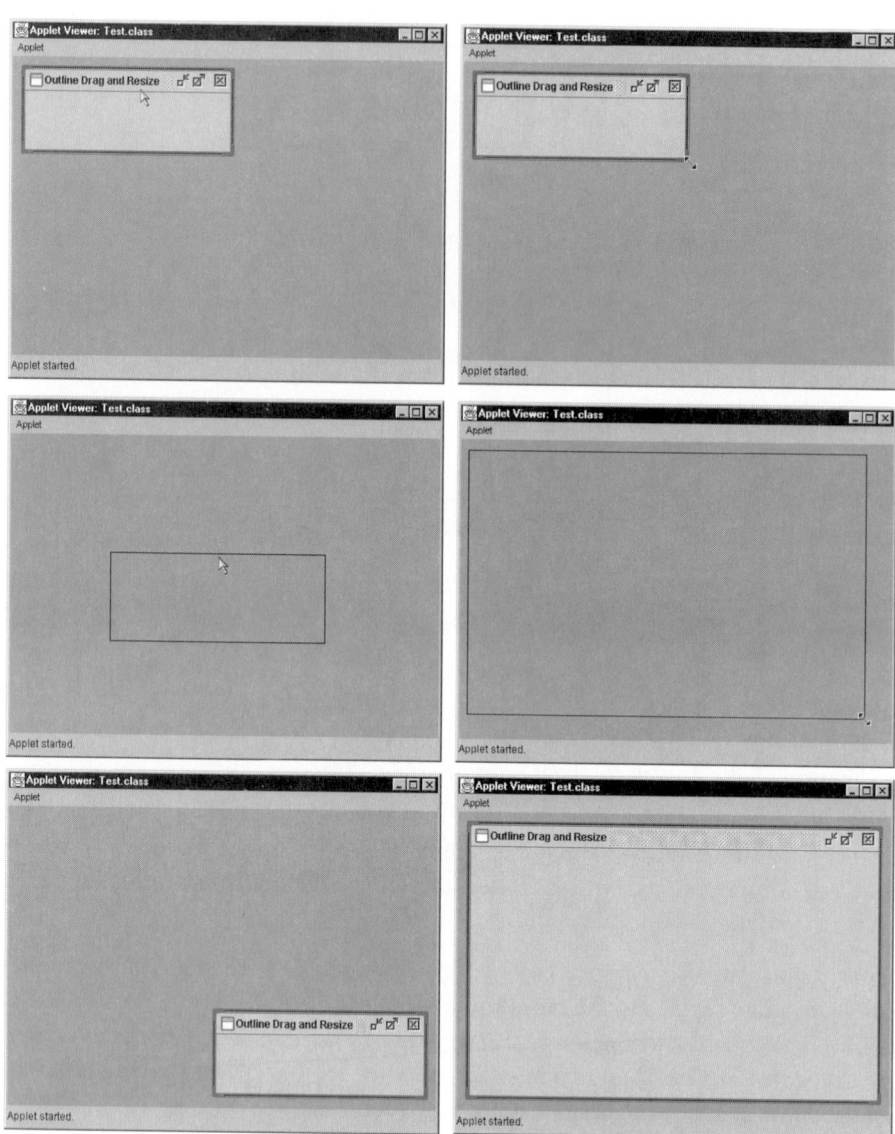

Figure 15-9 A Custom DesktopManager

Note: *Desktop panes under Swing 1.1 FCS with a client property of "JDesktopPane.dragMode" can set their drag mode to outline mode by setting the property to "outline". If the property's value is set to null, or a desktop pane does not have a "JDesktopPane.dragMode" property, the default dragging behavior is used.*

The applet creates an instance of `JDesktopPane` and sets the desktop manager for the desktop pane to an instance of `OutlineManager`. An internal frame is subsequently instantiated and added to the desktop pane.

```
public class Test extends JApplet {
    JDesktopPane desktopPane = new JDesktopPane();

    public void init() {
        Container contentPane = getContentPane();

        contentPane.add(desktopPane, BorderLayout.CENTER);
        desktopPane.setDesktopManager(new OutlineManager());

        JInternalFrame jif = new JInternalFrame(
                "Drag and Resize Me", // title
                true,   // resizable
                true,   // closable
                true,   // maximizable
                true);  // iconifiable

        jif.setBounds(10, 10, 250, 100);
        desktopPane.add(jif);
    }
}
```

`OutlineManager` is an extension of `DefaultDesktopManager` that overrides the methods involved in dragging and resizing an internal frame. Dragging and resizing internal frames result in calls to three `DesktopManager` methods: one method is invoked when the operation begins, another is called repeatedly during the operation, and a third is called when the operation is completed.

```
class OutlineManager extends DefaultDesktopManager {
    private Rectangle start, last;
    private boolean first = true;

    // dragging methods ...

    public void beginDraggingFrame(JComponent frame) {
        initializeOutline(frame);
```

```
    }
    public void dragFrame(JComponent frame, int x, int y) {
        updateOutline(frame, x, y, start.width, start.height);
    }
    public void endDraggingFrame(JComponent frame) {
        endOutline(frame);
    }

    // resizing methods ...

    public void beginResizingFrame(JComponent frame, int dir) {
        initializeOutline(frame);
    }
    public void resizeFrame(JComponent frame,
                               int x, int y, int w, int h) {
        updateOutline(frame, x, y, w, h);
    }
    public void endResizingFrame(JComponent frame) {
        endOutline(frame);
    }
    ...
```

From the perspective of the `OutlineManager`, dragging and resizing frames involves initializing and updating an outline of the frame. As a result, dragging and resizing is handled in a similar fashion. When a drag or resize is initiated, `initalizeOutline()` is invoked, and while the operation is being performed, `updateOutline()` is invoked. Finally, when the operation is completed, `endOutline()` is called.

```
    ...
    private void initializeOutline(final JComponent frame) {
        frame.setVisible(false);
        start = frame.getBounds();
        last = new Rectangle(start);
        first = true;
    }
    ...
```

The `initializeOutline` method hides the internal frame by setting its visibility to `false`. A rectangle representing the initial bounds of the frame is obtained by invoking the frame's `getBounds` method. Another rectangle is instantiated with the same values as the initial bounds of the frame, and the boolean variable `first` is set to `true`.

The `OutlineManager.updateOutline` method is invoked repeatedly during a drag or resize operation.

```
. . .
private void updateOutline(JComponent frame,
                           int x, int y, int w, int h) {
    Container container = frame.getParent();
    Graphics g = container.getGraphics();

    try {
        g.setXORMode(container.getBackground());

        if( ! first) {
            g.drawRect(last.x, last.y,
                             last.width-1, last.height-1);
        }
        g.drawRect(x, y, w-1, h-1);
        first = false;
    }
    finally {
        g.dispose();
        last.setBounds(x,y,w,h);
    }
}
. . .
```

The `updateOutline` method is passed a reference to the internal frame and the bounds of the current outline rectangle. References to the internal frame's container and the container's graphics are obtained.

The drawing mode for the graphics is set to XOR mode, which allows graphics to be drawn and subsequently erased without disturbing whatever is underneath. For more information on graphics in general and XOR mode, see the first volume of *Graphic Java*.

If it is not the first update after the drag or resize operation has begun, a rectangle is drawn at the last update location, erasing the last rectangle that was drawn in the internal frame's container. Subsequently, another rectangle is drawn at the new location.

After the graphics in the internal frame's container is updated, the graphics obtained by the call to `getGraphics()` is disposed of and the last update location is set to the current location.

The `OutlineManager.endOutline` method is invoked when a drag or resize operation is completed.

```
...
private void endOutline(JComponent frame) {
    frame.setVisible(true);
    setBoundsForFrame(
            frame, last.x, last.y, last.width, last.height);
}
...
```

The endOutline method sets the visibility of the frame to true and invokes the DefaultDesktopManager.setBoundsForFrame method.

One drawback to the implementation of OutlineManager discussed above is that the frame outline is not drawn until the cursor is dragged. In practice, this is usually not a problem because the cursor is normally dragged immediately after the mouse button is pressed. However, if the mouse button is pressed when the cursor is in the frame's title bar and the mouse is not immediately dragged, the frame will be hidden and no outline will be visible.

It might seem that an easy fix would be to call updateOutline() from the initializeOutline method, like this:

```
...
private void initializeOutline(final JComponent frame) {
    frame.setVisible(false);
    start = frame.getBounds();
    last = new Rectangle(start);
    first = true;

    updateOutline(frame, start.x, start.y,
                  start.width, start.height);
}
...
```

However, the implementation of initializeOutline() as listed above will not achieve the desired effect; that is, the outline still will not be visible until the mouse is dragged. The outline will not be visible because the call to setVisible() results in a call to repaint(), which places a paint event on the event queue. As a result, the frame is not erased until the call to a initializeOutline() returns and the paint event is handled. The call to updateOutline() draws the outline of the frame before the frame is erased, and therefore the outline is not visible.

The solution is to use the SwingUtilities.invokeLater method:

```
      ...
    private void initializeOutline(final JComponent frame) {
        // the call to setVisible() calls repaint, which
        // places a paint event on the event queue.
        // therefore, the effect of the setVisible() call is
        // not apparent until after this method returns

        frame.setVisible(false);
        start = frame.getBounds();
        last = new Rectangle(start);
        first = true;

        // the Runnable below paints the initial outline
        // after the repaint event spawned by setVisible() is
        // handled

        SwingUtilities.invokeLater(new Runnable() {
            public void run() {
                updateOutline(frame,start.x,start.y,
                                     start.width,start.height);
            }
        });
    }
      ...
```

SwingUtilities.invokeLater places the Runnable object on the event queue after the paint event has also been placed on the event queue. After the paint event is handled and the internal frame is erased, the run method of Runnable is invoked and the outline of the frame is drawn. See "Swing Utilities" on page 262 for more information concerning the SwingUtilities.invokeLater method.

The applet shown in Figure 15-9 is listed in its entirety in Example 15-6.

Example 15-6 A Custom DesktopManager

```
import java.awt.*;
import java.awt.event.*;
import javax.swing.*;

public class Test extends JApplet {
    JDesktopPane desktopPane = new JDesktopPane();

    public void init() {
        Container contentPane = getContentPane();

        contentPane.add(desktopPane, BorderLayout.CENTER);
        desktopPane.setDesktopManager(new OutlineManager());
```

```
        JInternalFrame jif = new JInternalFrame(
                "Drag and Resize Me", // title
                true,  // resizable
                true,  // closable
                true,  // maximizable
                true); // iconifiable

        jif.setBounds(10, 10, 250, 100);
        desktopPane.add(jif);
    }
}
class OutlineManager extends DefaultDesktopManager {
    private Rectangle start, last;
    private boolean first = true;

    // dragging ...

    public void beginDraggingFrame(JComponent frame) {
        initializeOutline(frame);
    }
    public void dragFrame(JComponent frame, int x, int y) {
        updateOutline(frame, x, y, start.width, start.height);
    }
    public void endDraggingFrame(JComponent frame) {
        endOutline(frame);
    }

    // resizing ...

    public void beginResizingFrame(JComponent frame, int dir) {
        initializeOutline(frame);
    }
    public void resizeFrame(JComponent frame,
                            int x, int y, int w, int h) {
        updateOutline(frame, x, y, w, h);
    }
    public void endResizingFrame(JComponent frame) {
        endOutline(frame);
    }

    // outline ...

    private void initializeOutline(final JComponent frame) {
        // the call to setVisible() calls repaint, which
        // places a paint event on the event queue.
        // therefore, the effect of the setVisible() call is
        // not apparent until after this method returns

        frame.setVisible(false);
        start = frame.getBounds();
        last = new Rectangle(start);
        first = true;
```

```
            // the Runnable below paints the initial outline
            // after the repaint event spawned by setVisible() is
            // handled

            SwingUtilities.invokeLater(new Runnable() {
                public void run() {
                    updateOutline(frame,start.x,start.y,
                                       start.width,start.height);
                }
            });
        }
        private void updateOutline(JComponent frame,
                                   int x, int y, int w, int h) {
            Container container = frame.getParent();
            Graphics g = container.getGraphics();

            try {
                g.setXORMode(container.getBackground());

                if( ! first) {
                    g.drawRect(last.x, last.y,
                                   last.width-1, last.height-1);
                }
                g.drawRect(x, y, w-1, h-1);
                first = false;
            }
            finally {
                g.dispose();
                last.setBounds(x,y,w,h);
            }
        }
        private void endOutline(JComponent frame) {
            frame.setVisible(true);
            setBoundsForFrame(
                    frame, last.x, last.y, last.width, last.height);
        }
    }
}
```

DesktopManager Class Summaries

The public and protected variables and methods for
DefaultDesktopManager class are listed in Class Summary 15-4.

Class Summary 15-4   DefaultDesktopManager

Extends: java.lang.Object
Implements: DesktopManager, java.io.Serializable

Constructors

public <u>DefaultDesktopManager</u>()

The no-argument constructor is compiler generated.

Methods

DesktopManager Methods

public void <u>activateFrame</u>(JInternalFrame)
public void <u>beginDraggingFrame</u>(JComponent)
public void <u>beginResizingFrame</u>(JComponent, int direction)
public void <u>closeFrame</u>(JInternalFrame)
public void <u>deactivateFrame</u>(JInternalFrame)
public void <u>deiconifyFrame</u>(JInternalFrame)
public void <u>dragFrame</u>(JComponent, int x, int y)
public void <u>endDraggingFrame</u>(JComponent)
public void <u>endResizingFrame</u>(JComponent)
public void <u>iconifyFrame</u>(JInternalFrame)
public void <u>maximizeFrame</u>(JInternalFrame)
public void <u>minimizeFrame</u>(JInternalFrame)
public void <u>openFrame</u>(JInternalFrame)
protected void <u>removeIconFor</u>(JInternalFrame)
public void <u>resizeFrame</u>(JComponent, int x, int y, int w, int h)
public void <u>setBoundsForFrame</u>(JComponent, int x, int y, int w, int h)

The methods listed above are all defined in the `DesktopManager` interface. When custom desktop managers are implemented, the methods listed above are the most likely candidates to be overridden.

Protected Utility Methods

---

protected Rectangle <u>getBoundsForIconOf</u>(JInternalFrame)
protected Rectangle <u>getPreviousBounds</u>(JInternalFrame)

protected void <u>setPreviousBounds</u>(JInternalFrame, Rectangle)
protected void <u>setWasIcon</u>(JInternalFrame, Boolean)
protected boolean <u>wasIcon</u>(JInternalFrame)

The `protected` methods listed above are utility methods used by the `DefaultDesktopManager` class.

The `getBoundsForIconOf` method is invoked by the `DefaultDesktopManager.iconifyFrame` method to determine the bounds for an internal frame's desktop icon.

The bounds of an internal frame are stored when an internal frame is maximized, minimized, or closed. The `setPreviousBounds` and `getPreviousBounds` methods track the bounds of an internal frame.

The `wasIcon` and `setWasIcon` methods track whether an internal frame has been iconifed.

Parting Shots

Swing provides the basic classes necessary for implementing multiple document interfaces with the `JInternalFrame`, `JDesktopPane` and `DesktopManager` classes and interfaces. Additionally, desktop management can be customized for incorporating features such as cascading and tiling internal frames.

CHAPTER
16

Choosers

This chapter discusses two Swing chooser components—JFileChooser and JColorChooser—that are used to select files and colors, respectively.

JFileChooser

File choosers, like option panes—see "JOptionPane" on page 815—are lightweight components that are meant to be placed in a dialog. Once an instance of JFileChooser has been instantiated, it can be added to a dialog. Additionally, the JFileChooser class provides methods that add an existing file chooser to a modal dialog and display the dialog. The methods return an integer value indicating whether the chooser's approve button was activated or the dialog was dismissed.

File choosers support three display modes: files only, directories only, and files and directories. Additionally file choosers support both single and multiple selection.[1]

---

1. Multiple selection is not fully supported in Swing 1.1 FCS

File choosers can be customized in a number of different ways, as Figure 16-1 illustrates. The top picture in Figure 16-1 shows the standard dialog displayed as a result of invoking `JFileChooser.showSaveDialog()`. The bottom picture in Figure 16-1 shows a file chooser with customized text for the dialog title, approve button and its tooltip, custom filters, custom icons, and an accessory component.

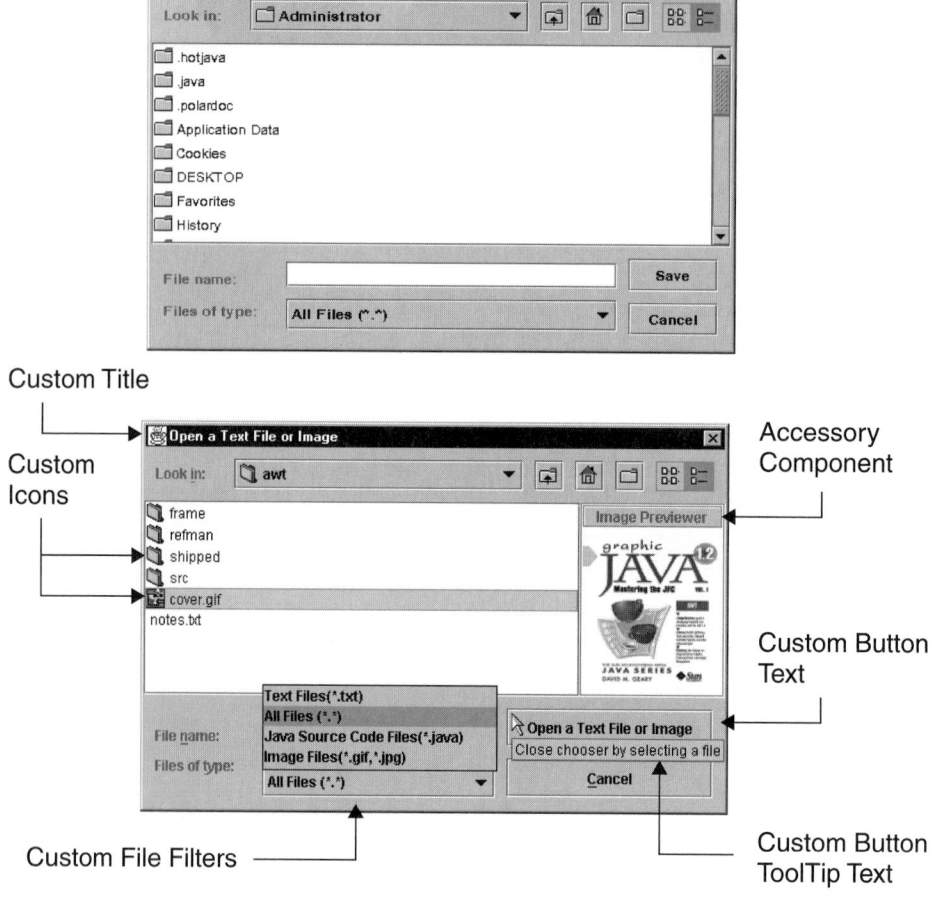

Figure 16-1 Customizing File Choosers

File chooser features are summarized in Feature Summary 16-1.

Feature Summary 16-1   JFileChooser

Open/Save/Custom Dialogs

JFileChooser provides three methods that display a *modal* dialog containing choosers: showOpenDialog(), showSaveDialog(), and showDialog().[2] Each of the methods sets the dialog title and the string displayed in the file chooser's approve button and returns an integer value indicating whether the approve button was activated or the dialog was canceled.

Display Modes

JFileChooser supports three display modes: files only, directories only, and files and directories.

Multiple Selection

File choosers come with both single and multiple selection; however, multiple selection is not fully supported in Swing 1.1.

Approve Button

Three facets of a file chooser's approve button can be customized: the button's text, its tooltip text, and mnemonic.

File Filters

Specific files or types of files can be filtered from a file chooser. File choosers can have multiple filters, but only one is active at any given time.

File Views

Given a file, the icons and file names displayed in a file chooser are obtained from a file view—an object that extends the FileView class. File choosers can be fitted with custom file views.

---

2.   The methods do not return until the dialogs are dismissed.

Accessory Component

A component can be installed in a file chooser for any number of purposes. Previewers for specific types of files—such as image previewers—represent one use for accessory components.

Figure 16-2 shows an application that displays a file dialog. After the dialog is dismissed, a message dialog communicates the selected file (or lack thereof). The top picture in Figure 16-2 shows the application as it appears initially, and the middle picture shows the file chooser displayed as a result of activation of the application's button. The bottom picture shows the message dialog displayed after a file has been selected.

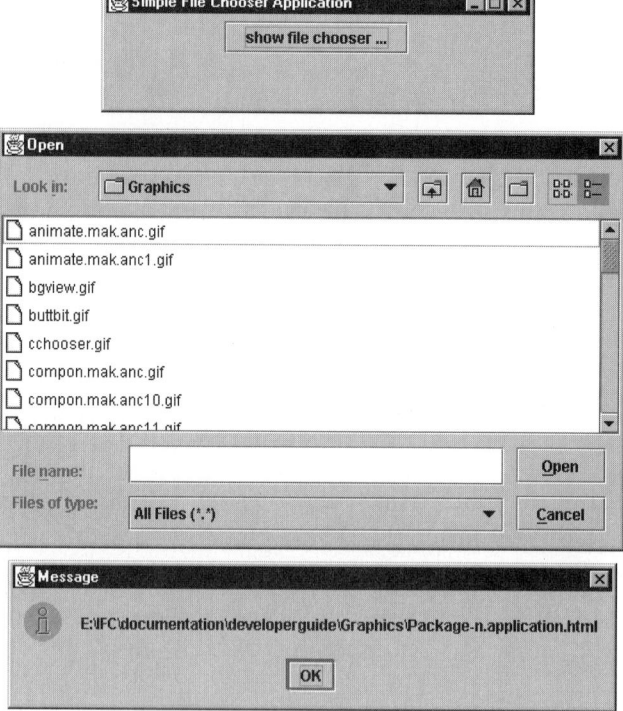

Figure 16-2 A Simple File Chooser Example

The application creates a button that is added to the application frame's content pane. The application also creates a file chooser with the JFileChooser no-argument constructor.

When the button contained in the application is activated, JFileChooser.showOpenDialog() is invoked to display the file chooser in a modal dialog. Because the dialog is modal, the call to showOpenDialog() does not return until the dialog is dismissed.

After the dialog is dismissed, JFileChooser.getSelectedFile() obtains a reference to the file that was selected in the file chooser. Subsequently, a message dialog is displayed that indicates whether the chooser's approve button was activated or the dialog was canceled, depending upon the value returned from JFileChooser.showOpenDialog().

```
public class Test extends JFrame {
    JFileChooser chooser = new JFileChooser();
    JButton button = new JButton("show file chooser ...");

    public Test() {
        super("Simple File Chooser Application");
        Container contentPane = getContentPane();

        contentPane.setLayout(new FlowLayout());
        contentPane.add(button);

        button.addActionListener(new ActionListener() {
            public void actionPerformed(ActionEvent e) {
                int state = chooser.showOpenDialog(null);
                File file = chooser.getSelectedFile();

                if(file != null &&
                    state == JFileChooser.APPROVE_OPTION) {
                    JOptionPane.showMessageDialog(
                                    null, file.getPath());
                }
                else if(state == JFileChooser.CANCEL_OPTION) {
                    JOptionPane.showMessageDialog(
                                    null, "Canceled");
                }
            }
        });
    }
```

The application shown in Figure 16-2 is listed in its entirety in Example 16-1.

Example 16-1 A Simple File Chooser Example

```
import java.awt.*;
import java.awt.event.*;
import java.io.File;
import javax.swing.*;

public class Test extends JFrame {
    JFileChooser chooser = new JFileChooser();
    JButton button = new JButton("show file chooser ...");

    public Test() {
        super("Simple File Chooser Application");
        Container contentPane = getContentPane();

        contentPane.setLayout(new FlowLayout());
        contentPane.add(button);

        button.addActionListener(new ActionListener() {
            public void actionPerformed(ActionEvent e) {
                int state = chooser.showOpenDialog(null);
                File file = chooser.getSelectedFile();

                if(file != null &&
                    state == JFileChooser.APPROVE_OPTION) {
                    JOptionPane.showMessageDialog(
                                      null, file.getPath());
                }
                else if(state == JFileChooser.CANCEL_OPTION) {
                    JOptionPane.showMessageDialog(
                                      null, "Canceled");
                }
            }
        });
    }
    public static void main(String args[]) {
        JFrame f = new Test();
        f.setBounds(300,300,350,100);
        f.setVisible(true);

        f.setDefaultCloseOperation(
            WindowConstants.DISPOSE_ON_CLOSE);

        f.addWindowListener(new WindowAdapter() {
            public void windowClosed(WindowEvent e) {
                System.exit(0);
            }
        });
    }
}
```

Swing Tip ...

Check for null Selected Files

If a file chooser's approve button is activated without a file being selected, the file returned from JFileChooser.getSelectedFile() will be null. As a result, before a file returned from JFileChooser.getSelectedFile() is used, a check should be made to ensure that a file has actually been selected.

For example, the application listed in Example 16-1 makes the following check:

```
button.addActionListener(new ActionListener() {
    public void actionPerformed(ActionEvent e) {
        int state = chooser.showOpenDialog(null);
        File file = chooser.getSelectedFile();

        if(file != null && state == JFileChooser.APPROVE_OPTION)
            JOptionPane.showMessageDialog(null, file.getPath());
        . . .
    }
    . . .
}
```

In other words, just because a JFileChooser.show...() method returns JFile-Chooser.APPROVE_OPTION does not necessarily mean that a file was selected.

File Chooser Types

The JFileChooser class supports three types of preconfigured file choosers and associated dialogs—custom, open, and save—that are differentiated by the dialog title and the text used for the file chooser's approve button.

JFileChooser dialog types are listed in Table 16-1, along with the JFileChooser instance methods used to show the dialogs.

Table 16-1 JFileChooser Dialog Types

Dialog Type	Method Used to Show Dialog	Dialog Title / Approve Button Text
Custom	int showDialog(Component parent, String approveButtonText)	Specified by second argument
Open	int showOpenDialog(Component parent)	Open
Save	int showSaveDialog(Component parent)	Save

The methods listed in Table 16-1 display a modal dialog containing a file chooser and return an `integer` value after the dialog has been dismissed, signifying whether the chooser's approve button was activated or the dialog was canceled. The dialog is centered over the parent component that is passed to the methods. If the methods are passed a `null` value for the parent component, the dialog is centered on the screen.

The following constants are returned from the methods listed in Table 16-1.

- `JFileChooser.APPROVE_OPTION`
- `JFileChooser.CANCEL_OPTION`

The first method listed in Table 16-1 is passed a string that is used as the text for the file chooser's approve button and the dialog's title. The last two methods listed in Table 16-1 set the dialog title and the file chooser's approve button text to "Open" and "Save", respectively.

Figure 16-3 shows an application that uses the methods listed above to display a file chooser in a modal dialog. The application contains a combo box that allows the type of file chooser to be displayed and a button that displays the dialog. The top pictures in Figure 16-3 show a "Save" file chooser, and the middle pictures show an "Open" file chooser. The bottom pictures show a custom file chooser whose approve button text and dialog title are specified with an input dialog.

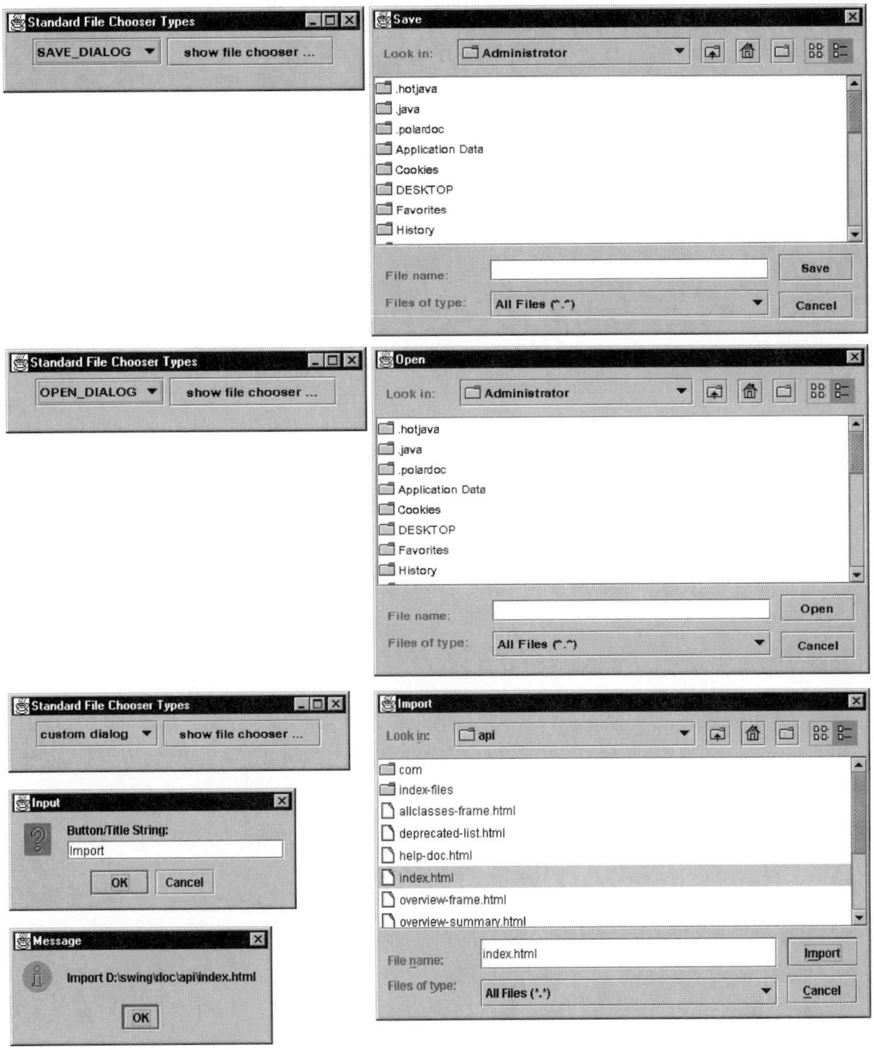

Figure 16-3 Default File Chooser Types

The application creates a file chooser, a combo box, and a button; the combo box and button are subsequently added to the application frame's content pane. When the button is activated, the file chooser is displayed in either an open, save, or custom dialog, depending upon the value selected from the combo box. After the dialog has been dismissed, a message dialog is displayed that indicates whether a file was selected or the dialog was canceled.

```
public class Test extends JFrame {
    JFileChooser chooser = new JFileChooser();
    JComboBox comboBox = new JComboBox();
    JButton button = new JButton("show file chooser ...");

    public Test() {
        super("Standard File Chooser Types");
        Container contentPane = getContentPane();

        contentPane.setLayout(new FlowLayout());
        contentPane.add(comboBox);
        contentPane.add(button);

        comboBox.addItem("OPEN_DIALOG");
        comboBox.addItem("SAVE_DIALOG");
        comboBox.addItem("custom dialog");

        button.addActionListener(new ActionListener() {
            public void actionPerformed(ActionEvent e) {
                String message = "CANCELED";
                int state = showChooser(
                        (String)comboBox.getSelectedItem());
                File file = chooser.getSelectedFile();

                if(file != null &&
                    state == JFileChooser.APPROVE_OPTION) {
                    message = chooser.getApproveButtonText() +
                            " " + file.getPath();
                }
                JOptionPane.showMessageDialog(null, message);
            }
        });
    }
```

The application's showChooser method is passed the string selected in the combo box and displays an appropriate file chooser dialog. If custom dialog was selected from the combo box, an input dialog is displayed to obtain the string used for the file chooser's approve button text and the dialog's title.

```
    private int showChooser(String s) {
        int state;

        if(s.equals("OPEN_DIALOG")) {
            state = chooser.showOpenDialog(null);
        }
        else if(s.equals("SAVE_DIALOG")) {
            state = chooser.showSaveDialog(null);
        }
        else { // custom dialog
```

```
        String string = JOptionPane.showInputDialog(
                            null,
                            "Button/Title String:");

        chooser.setApproveButtonMnemonic(string.charAt(1));
        state = chooser.showDialog(Test.this, string);
    }
    return state;
}
```

The application shown in Figure 16-3 is listed in its entirety in Example 16-2.

Example 16-2 Default File Chooser Types

```
import java.awt.*;
import java.awt.event.*;
import java.io.File;
import javax.swing.*;

public class Test extends JFrame {
    JFileChooser chooser = new JFileChooser();
    JComboBox comboBox = new JComboBox();
    JButton button = new JButton("show file chooser ...");

    public Test() {
        super("Standard File Chooser Types");
        Container contentPane = getContentPane();

        contentPane.setLayout(new FlowLayout());
        contentPane.add(comboBox);
        contentPane.add(button);

        comboBox.addItem("OPEN_DIALOG");
        comboBox.addItem("SAVE_DIALOG");
        comboBox.addItem("custom dialog");

        button.addActionListener(new ActionListener() {
            public void actionPerformed(ActionEvent e) {
                String message = "CANCELED";
                int state = showChooser(
                            (String)comboBox.getSelectedItem());
                File file = chooser.getSelectedFile();

                if(file != null &&
                    state == JFileChooser.APPROVE_OPTION) {
                    message = chooser.getApproveButtonText() +
                            " " + file.getPath();
                }
                JOptionPane.showMessageDialog(null, message);
            }
        });
```

```
        }
    private int showChooser(String s) {
        int state;

        if(s.equals("OPEN_DIALOG")) {
            state = chooser.showOpenDialog(null);
        }
        else if(s.equals("SAVE_DIALOG")) {
            state = chooser.showSaveDialog(null);
        }
        else { // custom dialog
            String string = JOptionPane.showInputDialog(
                                    null,
                                    "Button/Title String:");

            chooser.setApproveButtonMnemonic(string.charAt(1));
            state = chooser.showDialog(Test.this, string);
        }
        return state;
    }
    public static void main(String args[]) {
        JFrame f = new Test();
        f.setBounds(300,300,350,100);
        f.setVisible(true);

        f.setDefaultCloseOperation(
            WindowConstants.DISPOSE_ON_CLOSE);

        f.addWindowListener(new WindowAdapter() {
            public void windowClosed(WindowEvent e) {
                System.exit(0);
            }
        });
    }
}
```

Accessory Components

File choosers can accommodate an accessory component, as illustrated in Figure 16-4. The accessory component is placed to the right of the file listing area[3] and is sized as tall as the file listing area and as wide as the accessory component's preferred width. Accessory components can be used for any purpose, the most common of which is a previewer that allows the content of files to be displayed as files are selected in the file chooser.

3. Actual placement is look-and-feel dependent.

Figure 16-4 shows a file chooser equipped with an image previewer accessory component. When a GIF or JPEG file is selected, the image previewer displays a scaled version of the image.

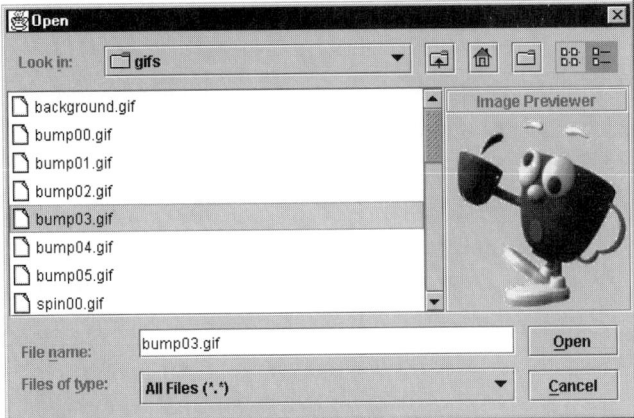

Figure 16-4 An Image Previewer Accessory

The application shown in Figure 16-4 implements an `ImagePreviewer` class that extends `JLabel`. When a file is selected in the file chooser, `ImagePreviewer.configure()` is passed a reference to the selected file. The image displayed in the previewer is an image icon created with the selected file's path.

After the image icon is created, its image is reset to a scaled version of the image by invocation of `Image.getScaledInstance()`. The scaled version of the image is used to create another image icon that is used as the label's icon.

```
class ImagePreviewer extends JLabel {
    public void configure(File f) {
        Dimension size = getSize();
        Insets insets = getInsets();

        // used to create full-size image
        ImageIcon icon = new ImageIcon(f.getPath());

        // set label's icon to new image icon
        // with scaled image
        setIcon(
          new ImageIcon(icon.getImage().getScaledInstance(
                 size.width - insets.left - insets.right,
```

```
                              size.height - insets.top - insets.bottom,
                              Image.SCALE_SMOOTH)));
                    . . .
              }
                . . .
        }
```

Note: The `configure` method could create the original image by hand, thereby eliminating the need for a second image icon, but the implementation presented here is more readable.

The image previewer is placed in an instance of `PreviewPanel`, which is an extension of `JPanel`. The `PreviewPanel` class sets its preferred size to a dimension of `(150,0)` because the preferred height of accessory components is ignored.[4]

The `PreviewPanel` class also sets its border to an etched border and adds the previewer as its center component. A label that identifies the previewer is specified as the preview panel's north component.

```
        class PreviewPanel extends JPanel {
            public PreviewPanel() {
                JLabel label = new JLabel("Image Previewer",
                                        SwingConstants.CENTER);
                setPreferredSize(new Dimension(150,0));
                setBorder(BorderFactory.createEtchedBorder());

                setLayout(new BorderLayout());

                label.setBorder(BorderFactory.createEtchedBorder());
                add(label, BorderLayout.NORTH);
                add(previewer, BorderLayout.CENTER);
            }
            . . .
        }
```

The application creates a button, file chooser, image previewer, and preview panel. The button is added to the application frame's content pane, and the preview panel is specified as the file chooser's accessory component by invocation of `JFileChooser.setAccessory()`.

```
        public class Test extends JFrame {
```

4.   Results may vary with nonstandard look and feels.

```
JFileChooser    chooser = new JFileChooser();
ImagePreviewer previewer = new ImagePreviewer();
PreviewPanel    previewPanel = new PreviewPanel();
...

public Test() {
    super("Image Previewer Accessory");

    Container contentPane = getContentPane();
    JButton button = new JButton("Select A File");

    contentPane.setLayout(new FlowLayout());
    contentPane.add(button);

    chooser.setAccessory(previewPanel);
    ...
```

An action listener that invokes `JFileChooser.showOpenDialog()` is added
to the button. Subsequently, a message dialog is displayed indicating whether a
file was selected or the dialog was canceled.

```
    ...
    button.addActionListener(new ActionListener() {
        public void actionPerformed(ActionEvent e) {
            int state = chooser.showOpenDialog(null);
            File file = chooser.getSelectedFile();
            String s = "CANCELED";

            if(file != null &&
                state == JFileChooser.APPROVE_OPTION) {
                s = "File Selected: " + file.getPath();
            }
            JOptionPane.showMessageDialog(null, s);
        }
    });
    ...
```

A property change listener that reacts to file selections is added to the file chooser.
If the selected file has a suffix of ".gif" or ".jpg", the previewer is configured by
invocation of `ImagePreviewer.configure()`.

```
    ...
    chooser.addPropertyChangeListener(
                        new PropertyChangeListener() {
        public void propertyChange(PropertyChangeEvent e) {
            if(e.getPropertyName().equals(
```

```
                          JFileChooser.SELECTED_FILE_CHANGED_PROPERTY)) {
                          File f = (File)e.getNewValue();
                          String s = f.getPath(), suffix = null;
                          int i = s.lastIndexOf('.');

                          if(i > 0 &&  i < s.length() - 1)
                              suffix = s.substring(i+1).toLowerCase();

                          if(suffix.equals("gif") ||
                              suffix.equals("jpg"))
                              previewer.configure(f);
                      }
                  }
              });
          }
          ...
      }
```

The application shown in Figure 16-4 is listed in its entirety in Example 16-3.

Example 16-3 An Image Previewer Accessory

```
      import javax.swing.*;
      import java.awt.*;
      import java.awt.event.*;
      import java.beans.*;
      import java.io.*;

      public class Test extends JFrame {
          JFileChooser   chooser = new JFileChooser();
          ImagePreviewer previewer = new ImagePreviewer();
          PreviewPanel   previewPanel = new PreviewPanel();

          class PreviewPanel extends JPanel {
              public PreviewPanel() {
                  JLabel label = new JLabel("Image Previewer",
                                         SwingConstants.CENTER);
                  setPreferredSize(new Dimension(150,0));
                  setBorder(BorderFactory.createEtchedBorder());

                  setLayout(new BorderLayout());

                  label.setBorder(BorderFactory.createEtchedBorder());
                  add(label, BorderLayout.NORTH);
                  add(previewer, BorderLayout.CENTER);
              }
          }
          public Test() {
              super("Image Previewer Accessory");
```

```
      Container contentPane = getContentPane();
      JButtonbutton = new JButton("Select A File");

      contentPane.setLayout(new FlowLayout());
      contentPane.add(button);

      chooser.setAccessory(previewPanel);


      button.addActionListener(new ActionListener() {
         public void actionPerformed(ActionEvent e) {
            int state = chooser.showOpenDialog(null);
            File file = chooser.getSelectedFile();
            String s = "CANCELED";

            if(file != null &&
               state == JFileChooser.APPROVE_OPTION) {
               s = "File Selected: " + file.getPath();
            }
            JOptionPane.showMessageDialog(null, s);
         }
      });

      chooser.addPropertyChangeListener(
                      new PropertyChangeListener() {
         public void propertyChange(PropertyChangeEvent e) {
            if(e.getPropertyName().equals(
               JFileChooser.SELECTED_FILE_CHANGED_PROPERTY)) {
               File f = (File)e.getNewValue();
               String s = f.getPath(), suffix = null;
               int i = s.lastIndexOf('.');

            if(i > 0 &&  i < s.length() - 1)
               suffix = s.substring(i+1).toLowerCase();

               if(suffix.equals("gif") ||
                  suffix.equals("jpg"))
                  previewer.configure(f);
            }
         }
      });
   }
   public static void main(String a[]) {
      JFrame f = new Test();
      f.setBounds(300, 300, 300, 75);
      f.setVisible(true);

      f.setDefaultCloseOperation(
                      WindowConstants.DISPOSE_ON_CLOSE);

      f.addWindowListener(new WindowAdapter() {
         public void windowClosed(WindowEvent e) {
```

```
                            System.exit(0);
                    }
            });
        }
    }
    class ImagePreviewer extends JLabel {
        public void configure(File f) {
            Dimension size = getSize();
            Insets insets = getInsets();
            ImageIcon icon = new ImageIcon(f.getPath());

            setIcon(new ImageIcon(icon.getImage().getScaledInstance(
                        size.width - insets.left - insets.right,
                        size.height - insets.top - insets.bottom,
                        Image.SCALE_SMOOTH)));
        }
    }
```

Filtering File Types

Files that fit a certain criteria, such as files that end with ".gif", can be filtered out of a file chooser with a file filter. Any number of filters can be associated with a single file chooser, but only one of the filters can be active at any given time.

By default, file choosers are fitted with a single "accept all" filter, that, as its name suggests, accepts all files. The default filter can be replaced with a custom filter by invocation of JFileChooser.setFileFilter(), which replaces the current filter.

File filters are implemented by extension of the abstract swing.filechooser.FileFilter class, which is summarized in Class Summary 15-5.

Class Summary 15-5   fileFilter

Extends: java.lang.Object

Constructors

---

public <u>FileFilter</u>()

The no-argument constructor is compiler generated.

Methods

---

public abstract boolean <u>accept</u>(File)
public abstract String <u>getDescription</u>()

The `accept` method returns a `boolean` value indicating whether a particular file is accepted by a filter. The `getDescription` method returns a short description of the types of files that a filter accepts. The description is displayed in the file filter combo box.[5]

The file chooser shown in Figure 16-5 has a text file filter that accepts only files ending in ".txt". The file chooser is also fitted with a text previewer, which is listed in Example 16-4 but not discussed.

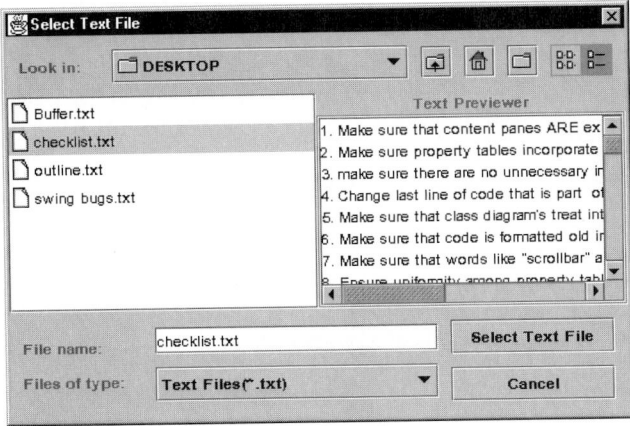

Figure 16-5 A Text File Filter and Previewer

---

5.   How descriptions are displayed is look-and-feel dependent.

The file chooser shown in Figure 16-5 is created by the application listed below, which sets the file filter for the chooser with the `JFileChooser.setFileFilter` method.

```java
public class Test extends JFrame {
    JFileChooser    chooser = new JFileChooser();
    TextPreviewer   previewer = new TextPreviewer();
    PreviewPanel    previewPanel = new PreviewPanel();

    . . .
    public Test() {
        super("Filtering Files");

        Container contentPane = getContentPane();
        JButtonbutton = new JButton("Select A File");

        contentPane.setLayout(new FlowLayout());
        contentPane.add(button);

        chooser.setAccessory(previewPanel);
        chooser.setFileFilter(new TextFilter());

    . . .
    }
}
```

The `TextFilter` class extends `FileFilter` and accepts only files that end in ".txt". The description is used in the file chooser's file filter combo box, as can be seen from Figure 16-5.

```java
class TextFilter
            extends javax.swing.filechooser.FileFilter {
    public boolean accept(File f) {
        boolean accept = f.isDirectory();

        if( ! accept) {
            String suffix = getSuffix(f);

            if(suffix != null)
                accept = suffix.equals("txt");
        }
        return accept;
    }
    public String getDescription() {
        return "Text Files(*.txt)";
    }
    private String getSuffix(File f) {
        String s = f.getPath(), suffix = null;
```

```
        int i = s.lastIndexOf('.');

        if(i > 0 &&  i < s.length() - 1)
        suffix = s.substring(i+1).toLowerCase();

        return suffix;
    }
}
```

The application shown in Figure 16-5 is listed in its entirety in Example 16-4.

Example 16-4   A Text File Filter and Previewer

```java
import javax.swing.*;
import java.awt.*;
import java.awt.event.*;
import java.beans.*;
import java.io.*;
import java.net.URL;

public class Test extends JFrame {
    JFileChooser    chooser = new JFileChooser();
    TextPreviewer   previewer = new TextPreviewer();
    PreviewPanel    previewPanel = new PreviewPanel();

    class PreviewPanel extends JPanel {
        public PreviewPanel() {
            JLabel label = new JLabel("Text Previewer",
                              SwingConstants.CENTER);
            setPreferredSize(new Dimension(350,0));
            setBorder(BorderFactory.createEtchedBorder());

            setLayout(new BorderLayout());

            label.setBorder(BorderFactory.createEtchedBorder());
            add(label, BorderLayout.NORTH);
            add(previewer, BorderLayout.CENTER);
        }
    }
    public Test() {
        super("Filtering Files");

        Container contentPane = getContentPane();
        JButtonbutton = new JButton("Select A File");

        contentPane.setLayout(new FlowLayout());
        contentPane.add(button);

        button.addActionListener(new ActionListener() {
            public void actionPerformed(ActionEvent e) {
```

```
                int state = chooser.showOpenDialog(null);
                File file = chooser.getSelectedFile();
                String s = "CANCELED";

                if(file != null &&
                    state == JFileChooser.APPROVE_OPTION) {
                    s = "File Selected: " + file.getPath();
                }
                JOptionPane.showMessageDialog(null, s);
            }

        });

        chooser.setAccessory(previewPanel);
        chooser.setFileFilter(new TextFilter());

        chooser.addPropertyChangeListener(
                            new PropertyChangeListener() {
            public void propertyChange(PropertyChangeEvent e) {
                if(e.getPropertyName().equals(
                    JFileChooser.SELECTED_FILE_CHANGED_PROPERTY)) {
                    previewer.configure((File)e.getNewValue());
                }
            }
        });
    }
    public static void main(String a[]) {
        JFrame f = new Test();
        f.setBounds(300, 300, 300, 75);
        f.setVisible(true);

        f.setDefaultCloseOperation(
                        WindowConstants.DISPOSE_ON_CLOSE);

        f.addWindowListener(new WindowAdapter() {
            public void windowClosed(WindowEvent e) {
                System.exit(0);
            }
        });
    }
}
class TextFilter
            extends javax.swing.filechooser.FileFilter {
    public boolean accept(File f) {
        boolean accept = f.isDirectory();

        if( ! accept) {
            String suffix = getSuffix(f);

            if(suffix != null)
                accept = suffix.equals("txt");
        }
```

```
            return accept;
    }
    public String getDescription() {
        return "Text Files(*.txt)";
    }
    private String getSuffix(File f) {
        String s = f.getPath(), suffix = null;
        int i = s.lastIndexOf('.');

        if(i > 0 &&  i < s.length() - 1)
        suffix = s.substring(i+1).toLowerCase();

        return suffix;
    }
}
class TextPreviewer extends JComponent {
    private JTextArea textArea = new JTextArea();
    private JScrollPane scrollPane = new JScrollPane(textArea);

    public TextPreviewer() {
        textArea.setEditable(false);

        setBorder(BorderFactory.createEtchedBorder());
        setLayout(new BorderLayout());
        add(scrollPane, BorderLayout.CENTER);
    }
    public void configure(File file) {
        textArea.setText(contentsOfFile(file));

        SwingUtilities.invokeLater(new Runnable() {
            public void run() {
                JViewport vp = scrollPane.getViewport();

                vp.setViewPosition(new Point(0,0));
            }
        });
    }
    public static String contentsOfFile(File file) {
        String s = new String();
        char[] buff = new char[50000];
        InputStream is;
        InputStreamReader reader;
        URL url;

        try {
            reader = new FileReader(file);

            int nch;

            while ((
                nch = reader.read(buff, 0, buff.length)) != -1) {
                s = s + new String(buff, 0, nch);
```

```
            }
        }
        catch (java.io.IOException ex) {
            s = "Could not load file";
        }
        return s;
    }
}
```

Choosable Filters

As illustrated in "Filtering File Types" on page 936,
`JFileChooser.setFileFilter()` replaces the default file filter with the filter
that is passed to the method. If it is desirable to equip a file chooser with multiple
filters, the `JFileChooser.addChoosableFilter` method can be used to add a
filter to the current list of filters. The current list of filters can be accessed, and
filters can be removed with the `JFileChooser` methods
`getChoosableFilters()` and `removeChoosableFilter()`, respectively.

Figure 16-6 shows a file chooser with three filters, one for text files, another for
Java source code files, and the default filter that accepts all files. The file chooser is
also equipped with a text previewer, which is listed in Example 16-5 but not
discussed.[6]

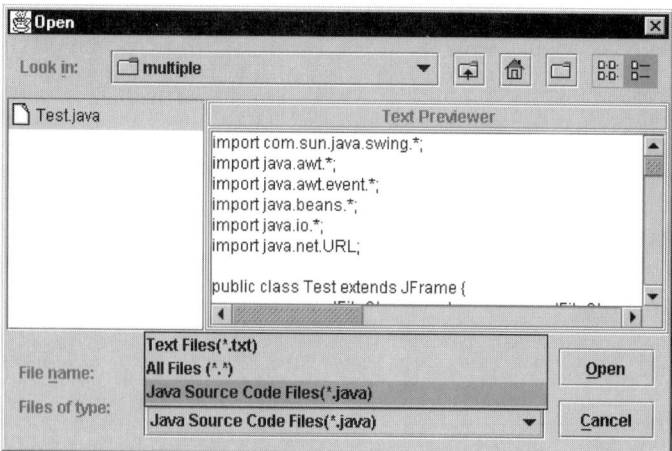

Figure 16-6 Multiple File Filters

---

6.   See "Accessory Components" on page 930 for a discussion of accessory compo-
     nents.

The application that shows the file chooser in Figure 16-6 creates an instance of
JFileChooser and invokes JFileChooser.addChoosableFileFilter to
add the text and Java code filters.

```
public Test() {
    JFileChooser    chooser = new JFileChooser();
    TextPreviewer   previewer = new TextPreviewer();
    PreviewPanel    previewPanel = new PreviewPanel();

    super("Filtering Files");

    Container contentPane = getContentPane();
    JButtonbutton = new JButton("Select A File");

    contentPane.setLayout(new FlowLayout());
    contentPane.add(button);

    chooser.setAccessory(previewPanel);
    chooser.addChoosableFileFilter(new TextFilter());
    chooser.addChoosableFileFilter(new JavaCodeFilter());
    ...
}
```

Because both filters determine the acceptability of files according to file name
suffix, the filters extend a filter that is suffix aware. The SuffixAwareFilter is
an abstract filter that accepts all directories and provides a method that returns a
file name suffix, given a file. The SuffixAwareFilter is abstract because it
leaves the getDescription method for subclasses to implement.

```
...
abstract class SuffixAwareFilter
          extends javax.swing.filechooser.FileFilter {
public String getSuffix(File f) {
    String s = f.getPath(), suffix = null;
    int i = s.lastIndexOf('.');

    if(i > 0 &&  i < s.length() - 1)
    suffix = s.substring(i+1).toLowerCase();

    return suffix;
}
public boolean accept(File f) {
    return f.isDirectory();
}
}
...
```

Both `TextFilter` and `JavaCodeFilter` will accept a file if it is accepted by the `SuffixAwareFilter` superclass (which means the file is a directory) or the file's suffix matches ".txt" or ".java", respectively.

```
  . . .
  class JavaCodeFilter extends SuffixAwareFilter {
      public boolean accept(File f) {
          boolean accept = super.accept(f);

          if( ! accept) {
              String suffix = getSuffix(f);

              if(suffix != null)
                  accept = super.accept(f) || suffix.equals("java");
          }
          return accept;
      }
      public String getDescription() {
          return "Java Source Code Files(*.java)";
      }
  }
  class TextFilter extends SuffixAwareFilter {
      public boolean accept(File f) {
          String suffix = getSuffix(f);

          if(suffix != null)
              return super.accept(f) || suffix.equals("txt");

          return false;
      }
      public String getDescription() {
          return "Text Files(*.txt)";
      }
  }
```

The application shown in Figure 16-6 is listed in its entirety in Example 16-5.

Example 16-5 Multiple File Filters

```
  import javax.swing.*;
  import java.awt.*;
  import java.awt.event.*;
  import java.beans.*;
  import java.io.*;
  import java.net.URL;

  public class Test extends JFrame {
      JFileChooser   chooser = new JFileChooser();
      TextPreviewer  previewer = new TextPreviewer();
```

```
PreviewPanel    previewPanel = new PreviewPanel();

class PreviewPanel extends JPanel {
    public PreviewPanel() {
        JLabel label = new JLabel("Text Previewer",
                            SwingConstants.CENTER);
        setPreferredSize(new Dimension(350,0));
        setBorder(BorderFactory.createEtchedBorder());

        setLayout(new BorderLayout());

        label.setBorder(BorderFactory.createEtchedBorder());
        add(label, BorderLayout.NORTH);
        add(previewer, BorderLayout.CENTER);
    }
}
public Test() {
    super("Filtering Files");

    Container contentPane = getContentPane();
    JButtonbutton = new JButton("Select A File");

    contentPane.setLayout(new FlowLayout());
    contentPane.add(button);

    chooser.setAccessory(previewPanel);
    chooser.addChoosableFileFilter(new TextFilter());
    chooser.addChoosableFileFilter(new JavaCodeFilter());

    button.addActionListener(new ActionListener() {
        public void actionPerformed(ActionEvent e) {
            int state = chooser.showOpenDialog(null);
            String s = "CANCELED";

            if(state == JFileChooser.APPROVE_OPTION) {
                s = "File Selected: " +
                    chooser.getSelectedFile().getPath();
            }
            JOptionPane.showMessageDialog(null, s);
        }
    });

    chooser.addPropertyChangeListener(
                        new PropertyChangeListener() {
        public void propertyChange(PropertyChangeEvent e) {
            if(e.getPropertyName().equals(
                JFileChooser.SELECTED_FILE_CHANGED_PROPERTY)) {
                previewer.configure((File)e.getNewValue());
            }
        }
    });
}
public static void main(String a[]) {
```

```
        JFrame f = new Test();
        f.setBounds(300, 300, 300, 75);
        f.setVisible(true);

        f.setDefaultCloseOperation(
                            WindowConstants.DISPOSE_ON_CLOSE);

        f.addWindowListener(new WindowAdapter() {
           public void windowClosed(WindowEvent e) {
              System.exit(0);
           }
        });
    }
}
abstract class SuffixAwareFilter
            extends javax.swing.filechooser.FileFilter {
    public String getSuffix(File f) {
        String s = f.getPath(), suffix = null;
        int i = s.lastIndexOf('.');

        if(i > 0 &&  i < s.length() - 1)
        suffix = s.substring(i+1).toLowerCase();

        return suffix;
    }
    public boolean accept(File f) {
        return f.isDirectory();
    }
}
class JavaCodeFilter extends SuffixAwareFilter {
    public boolean accept(File f) {
        boolean accept = super.accept(f);

        if( ! accept) {
           String suffix = getSuffix(f);

           if(suffix != null)
               accept = super.accept(f) || suffix.equals("java");
        }
        return accept;
    }
    public String getDescription() {
        return "Java Source Code Files(*.java)";
    }
}
class TextFilter extends SuffixAwareFilter {
    public boolean accept(File f) {
        String suffix = getSuffix(f);

        if(suffix != null)
            return super.accept(f) || suffix.equals("txt");
```

```java
            return false;
        }
    public String getDescription() {
        return "Text Files(*.txt)";
    }
}
class TextPreviewer extends JComponent {
    private JTextArea textArea = new JTextArea();
    private JScrollPane scrollPane = new JScrollPane(textArea);

    public TextPreviewer() {
        textArea.setEditable(false);

        setBorder(BorderFactory.createEtchedBorder());
        setLayout(new BorderLayout());
        add(scrollPane, BorderLayout.CENTER);
    }
    public void configure(File file) {
        textArea.setText(contentsOfFile(file));

        SwingUtilities.invokeLater(new Runnable() {
            public void run() {
                JViewport vp = scrollPane.getViewport();

                vp.setViewPosition(new Point(0,0));
            }
        });
    }
    static String contentsOfFile(File file) {
        String s = new String();
        char[] buff = new char[50000];
        InputStream is;
        InputStreamReader reader;
        URL url;

        try {
            reader = new FileReader(file);

            int nch;

            while ((
                nch = reader.read(buff, 0, buff.length)) != -1) {
                s = s + new String(buff, 0, nch);
            }
        }
        catch (java.io.IOException ex) {
            s = "Could not load file";
        }
        return s;
    }
}
```

File Filters

File chooser filters can be accessed by the following JFileChooser methods:

- void setFileFilter(swing.filechooser.FileFilter)
- void addChoosableFileFilter(swing.filechooser.FileFilter)
- void removeChoosableFileFilter(swing.filechooser.FileFilter)
- swing.filechooser.FileFilter getChoosableFileFilters()

setFileFilter() sets the currently displayed filter, whereas the rest of the methods listed above operate on the list of choosable filters displayed by the filter combo box.[1]

1. Actual components used are look and feel dependent.

File Views

File choosers obtain the icons and file names they display from an object that is an extension of the abstract `swing.filechooser.FileView` class. The default file view is implemented by the `BasicFileChooserUI.BasicFileView` class, but it can be wholly or partially replaced if a file view is explicitly set with the `JFileChooser.setFileView` method.

If a file chooser is explicitly fitted with a file view that returns `null` from any of its methods, the default file view is queried for the information. For example, if a file chooser has a file view that returns `null` from the `getName` method, the name is obtained from an instance of `BasicFileView`. Therefore, default file view behavior can be partially overridden.

The `swing.filechooser.FileView` class is summarized in Class Summary 15-6.

Class Summary 15-6   FileView

Extends: java.lang.Object

Constructors

---

public <u>FileView</u>()

The FileView constructor is compiler generated, because no constructors are implemented by the FileView class.

Methods

Icon / Name / Is Traversable

---

public abstract Icon <u>getIcon</u>(File)
public abstract String <u>getName</u>(File)
public abstract Boolean <u>isTraversable</u>(File)

The first two methods listed above return an icon and a string respectively, given a file. The icon and string represent files in a file chooser.

The isTraversable method indicates whether a file (typically a directory) can be opened. For example, implementing an extension of FileView that returns new Boolean(false) from isTraversable will not allow a directory to be opened; instead, double-clicking on a directory will select the directory instead of opening it.

It should be pointed out that isTraversable returns a Boolean object and not a boolean value because returning null from FileView methods causes the associated file chooser to get the corresponding value from the default file view.[7]

File Type and Description

---

public abstract String getDescription(File)
public abstract String getTypeDescription(File)

The getDescription and getTypeDescription methods return a description of a specific file and a description of a file type, respectively. For example, for a file named FileChooserExample.java, the getDescription method might return "an example of using file choosers" and the getTypeDescription might return "a Java source code file."

As of Swing1.1 FCS, the getDescription and getTypeDescription methods are not used within Swing. The methods are meant for look and feels that wish to provide additional information about files in a file chooser.

The file chooser shown in Figure 16-7 is fitted with a custom extension of the FileView class that provides alternative icons for files and directories. Files ending in ".gif", ".bmp," and ".jpg" are represented by a different icon than the one used for other types of files.

Figure 16-7 A Custom File View

7. boolean is an intrinsic type and therefore not an object.

The application that shows the file chooser shown in Figure 16-7 creates an instance of `CustomFileView` that is subsequently specified as the file chooser's file view.

```
public class Test extends JFrame {
    JFileChooser chooser = new JFileChooser();
    JButton button = new JButton("show file chooser ...");

    public Test() {
        super("Custom File View Example");
        Container contentPane = getContentPane();

        contentPane.setLayout(new FlowLayout());
        contentPane.add(button);

        chooser.setFileView(new CustomFileView());
        ...
    }
    ...
}
```

The `CustomFileView` class implements the `getName`, `getDescription`, and `getTypeDescription` to return `null`, which causes the values to be obtained from the file chooser's look and feel.

The `CustomFileView` method implements the `getIcon` and `isTraversable` methods. `CustomFileView.getIcon()` returns an icon that is appropriate for the type of file, and `isTraversable` method returns `true` except for a file—`D:\file.txt`—and a directory, `D:\books`.

```
class CustomFileView extends FileView {
    private Icon fileIcon = new ImageIcon("file.gif"),
                 directoryIcon = new ImageIcon("folder.gif"),
                 imageIcon = new ImageIcon("photo.jpg");

    public String getName(File f) { return null; }
    public String getDescription(File f) { return null; }
    public String getTypeDescription(File f) { return null; }

    public Icon getIcon(File f) {
        Icon icon = null;

        if(isImage(f))    icon = imageIcon;
        else if(f.isDirectory()) icon = directoryIcon;
        else              icon = fileIcon;

        return icon;
```

```
   }
   public Boolean isTraversable(File f) {
      Boolean b;

      if(f.getPath().equals("D:\\file.txt")) {
         b = new Boolean(false);
      }
      else if(f.getPath().equals("D:\\books")) {
         b = new Boolean(false);
      }
      return b == null ? new Boolean(true) : b;
   }
   private boolean isImage(File f) {
      String suffix = getSuffix(f);
      boolean isImage = false;

      if(suffix != null) {
         isImage = suffix.equals("gif") ||
                   suffix.equals("bmp") ||
                   suffix.equals("jpg");
      }
      return isImage;
   }
   private String getSuffix(File file) {
      String filestr = file.getPath(), suffix = null;
      int i = filestr.lastIndexOf('.');

      if(i > 0 && i < filestr.length()) {
         suffix = filestr.substring(i+1).toLowerCase();
      }
      return suffix;
   }
}
```

The application shown in Figure 16-7 is listed in its entirety in Example 16-6.

Example 16-6   A Custom File View

```
import javax.swing.*;
import javax.swing.filechooser.FileView;
import java.awt.*;
import java.awt.event.*;
import java.io.*;

public class Test extends JFrame {
   JFileChooser chooser = new JFileChooser();
   JButton button = new JButton("show file chooser ...");

   public Test() {
      super("Custom File View Example");
```

```
        Container contentPane = getContentPane();

        contentPane.setLayout(new FlowLayout());
        contentPane.add(button);

        chooser.setFileView(new CustomFileView());

        button.addActionListener(new ActionListener() {
            public void actionPerformed(ActionEvent e) {
                int state = chooser.showSaveDialog(null);
                File file = chooser.getSelectedFile();
                String s = "CANCELED";

                if(state == JFileChooser.APPROVE_OPTION)
                    s = "File: " + file.getPath();

                JOptionPane.showMessageDialog(null, s);
            }
        });
    }
    public static void main(String args[]) {
        JFrame f = new Test();
        f.setBounds(300,300,350,100);
        f.setVisible(true);

        f.setDefaultCloseOperation(
                        WindowConstants.DISPOSE_ON_CLOSE);

        f.addWindowListener(new WindowAdapter() {
            public void windowClosed(WindowEvent e) {
                System.exit(0);
            }
        });
    }
}
class CustomFileView extends FileView {
    private Icon fileIcon = new ImageIcon("file.gif"),
                directoryIcon = new ImageIcon("folder.gif"),
                imageIcon = new ImageIcon("photo.jpg");

    public String getName(File f) { return null; }
    public String getDescription(File f) { return null; }
    public String getTypeDescription(File f) { return null; }

    public Icon getIcon(File f) {
        Icon icon = null;

        if(isImage(f))   icon = imageIcon;
        else if(f.isDirectory()) icon = directoryIcon;
        else             icon = fileIcon;

        return icon;
```

```
        }
        public Boolean isTraversable(File f) {
            Boolean b;

            if(f.getPath().equals("D:\\file.txt")) {
                b = new Boolean(false);
            }
            else if(f.getPath().equals("D:\\books")) {
                b = new Boolean(false);
            }
            return b == null ? new Boolean(true) : b;
        }
        private boolean isImage(File f) {
            String suffix = getSuffix(f);
            boolean isImage = false;

            if(suffix != null) {
                isImage = suffix.equals("gif") ||
                        suffix.equals("bmp") ||
                        suffix.equals("jpg");
            }
            return isImage;
        }
        private String getSuffix(File file) {
            String filestr = file.getPath(), suffix = null;
            int i = filestr.lastIndexOf('.');

            if(i > 0 && i < filestr.length()) {
                suffix = filestr.substring(i+1).toLowerCase();
            }
            return suffix;
        }
    }
```

Multiple Selection

Instances of `JFileChooser` allow multiple files to be selected; however, for Swing 1.1 FCS, although multiple files can be selected in a file chooser, the files selected cannot be accessed.

The file chooser shown in Figure 16-8 allows multiple selection.

The file chooser shown in Figure 16-8 has multiple selection enabled by a call to `JFileChooser.setMultiSelectionEnabled(true)`. After the file chooser has been dismissed, the selected files are retrieved with `JFileChooser.getSelectedFiles()`, which under Swing 1.1 FCS always returns `null`.

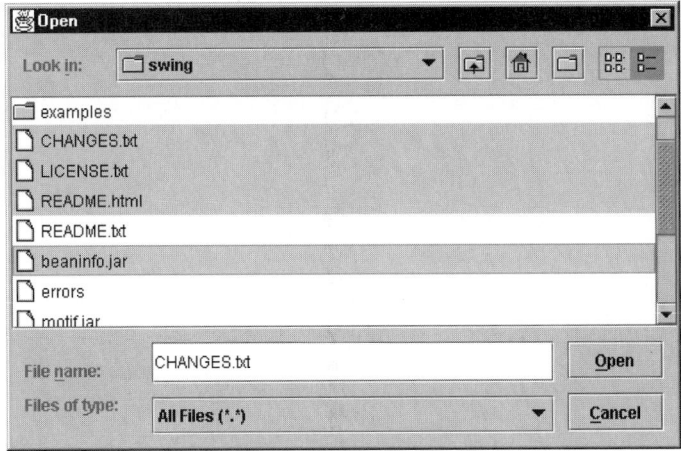

Figure 16-8 Selecting Multiple Files

The applet shown in Figure 16-8 is listed in its entirety in Example 16-7.

Example 16-7 Multiple Selection for File Chooser

```java
import java.awt.*;
import java.awt.event.*;
import java.io.File;
import javax.swing.*;
import java.beans.*;

public class Test extends JFrame {
    JFileChooser chooser = new JFileChooser();
    JButton button = new JButton("show file chooser ...");

    public Test() {
        super("Simple File Chooser Application");
        Container contentPane = getContentPane();

        contentPane.setLayout(new FlowLayout());
        contentPane.add(button);

        chooser.setMultiSelectionEnabled(true);

        button.addActionListener(new ActionListener() {
            public void actionPerformed(ActionEvent e) {
                int state = chooser.showOpenDialog(null);
                File[] files = chooser.getSelectedFiles();
                String[] filenames = getFilenames(files);
```

```
                    if(filenames != null &&
                       state == JFileChooser.APPROVE_OPTION) {
                       JOptionPane.showMessageDialog(null,filenames);
                    }
                    else if(state == JFileChooser.CANCEL_OPTION) {
                       JOptionPane.showMessageDialog(
                                         null, "Canceled");
                    }
                    else if(state == JFileChooser.ERROR_OPTION) {
                       JOptionPane.showMessageDialog(
                                         null, "Error!");
                    }
                }
            });
        }
        private String[] getFilenames(File[] files) {
            String[] filenames = null;
            int numFiles = files.length;

            if(files.length > 0) {
                filenames = new String[numFiles];

                for(int i=0; i < numFiles; ++i) {
                    filenames[i] = files[i].getPath();
                    System.out.println(filenames[i]);
                }
            }
            return filenames;
        }
        public static void main(String args[]) {
            JFrame f = new Test();
            f.setBounds(300,300,350,100);
            f.setVisible(true);

            f.setDefaultCloseOperation(
                WindowConstants.DISPOSE_ON_CLOSE);

            f.addWindowListener(new WindowAdapter() {
                public void windowClosed(WindowEvent e) {
                    System.exit(0);
                }
            });
        }
    }
```

The JFileChooser class is summarized in Component Summary 16-1.

Component Summary 16-1   JFileChooser

Model(s)	——
UI Delegate(s)	javax.swing.plaf.basic.BasicFileChooserUI
Renderer(s)	——
Editor(s)	——
Events Fired	PropertyChangeEvents, ActionEvents
Replacement For	java.awt.FileDialog
Class Diagrams	

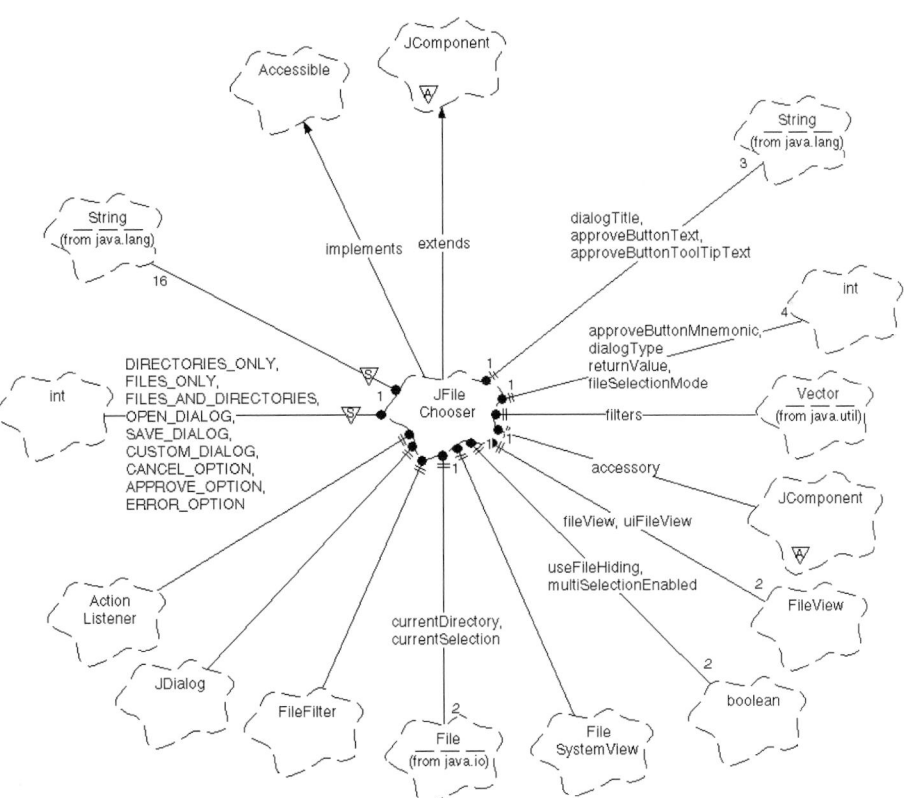

Figure 16-9   JFileChooser Class Diagram

JFileChooser extends JComponent and implements the Accessible interface. JFileChooser maintains private references to its accessory component, file filters, and file views. JFileChooser maintains private references to objects that represent JFileChooser properties, which are discussed in "JFileChooser Properties" on page 958.

JFileChooser also maintains public static integer values representing the three file chooser modes: DIRECTORIES_ONLY, FILES_ONLY, and FILES_AND_DIRECTORIES, in addition to dialog types and selection options. Additionally, JFileChooser maintains public static strings representing property names, open and save dialogs, etc. See "JFileChooser Class Summaries" on page 968 for more information concerning the public string constants defined by the JFileChooser class.

JFileChooser Properties

The properties maintained by the JFileChooser class are listed in Table 16-2.

Table 16-2   JFileChooser Properties

Property Name	Data Type	Property Type[1]	Access[2]	Default[3]
acceptAllFileFilter	FileFilter	S	G	L&F
accessory	JComponent	B	SG	null
approveButton-Mnemonic	int	B	SG	0
approveButton-Text	String	B	SG	——
approveButton-ToolTipText	String	B	SG	null
choosableFile-Filters	FileFilter[]	B	G	see discussion below
currentDirectory	File	B	CSG	——
description	String	S	G	——
dialogTitle	String	B	SG	L&F
dialogType	int	B	SG	OPEN_DIALOG
fileFilter		B	SG	L&F
fileHidingEnabled	boolean	B	SG	true
fileSelectionMode	int	B	SG	FILES_ONLY
fileSystemView	FileSystemView	B	CSG	null

Table 16-2 JFileChooser Properties (Continued)

Property Name	Data Type	Property Type[1]	Access[2]	Default[3]
fileView	FileView	B	SG	null
icon	Icon	S	G	L&F
multiSelection-Enabled	boolean	B	SG	false
name	String	S	G	——
selectedFile	File	B	SG	null
selectedFiles	File[]	B	SG	null
traversable	boolean	S	G	——
typeDescription	String	S	G	——

1. B = bound (fires PropertyChangeEvent) / C = constrained Of/ I = indexed / S = simple / Ch = fires ChangeEvent
2. C = settable at construction time / G = getter method / S = setter method
3. L&F = look-and-feel dependent

acceptAllFileFilter — Represents the default file filter that accepts all files. The property is maintained by the file chooser's UI delegate, making it look-and-feel dependent. It also is read-only and is accessible with the `JFileChooser.getAcceptAllFilter` method.

See "Filtering File Types" on page 936 for more information concerning the `acceptAllFileFilter` property and file filters in general.

accessory — An instance of `JComponent` that can be used for multiple purposes, the most common of which are previewers for different file types. See "Accessory Components" on page 930 for more information concerning file chooser accessory components.

approveButtonMnemonic — Represents the mnemonic associated with a file chooser's approve button. The mnemonic is set with the `JFileChooser.setApproveButtonMnemonic` method. See "Button Mnemonics" on page 415 for more information concerning button mnemonics in general.

approveButtonText — File choosers are equipped with two buttons, one for approving the selected file and another for canceling the file chooser dialog. The text associated with the approve button can be explicitly set.

Setting the approve button text sets the `dialogType` property to `CUSTOM_DIALOG`. Calling `JFileChooser.showOpenDialog()` or

`JFileChooser.showSaveDialog()` sets the approve button text to a look-and-feel-specific string.

approveButtonToolTipText — A file chooser's approve button can have a tooltip associated with it. The default tooltip is look-and-feel dependent and can be overridden with the `JFileChooser.setApproveButtonText` method.

choosableFileFilters — A file chooser can have any number of choosable file filters associated with it. Choosable file filters can be added to and removed from a file chooser with the `JFileChooser addChoosableFileFilter` and `removeChoosableFileFilter` methods, respectively.

The set of choosable file filters always includes the "accept all" file filter. See the `acceptAllFilter` property for more information concerning the "accept all" file filter.

currentDirectory — An instance of `java.io.File` that represents the directory currently displayed in a file chooser. The `currentDirectory` property can be set at construction time or any time thereafter.

If the `currentDirectory` property is specified as a file instead of a directory, the current directory is set to the first traversable parent directory of the file specified.

dialogTitle — Is look-and-feel dependent and represents the title of the dialog in which a file chooser is displayed when the following `JFileChooser` methods are used: `showOpenDialog()`, `showSaveDialog()`, and `showDialog()`.

The `dialogTitle` property has no effect if a file chooser is manually placed in a dialog. See Example 16-8 on page 967 for an example of manually placing a file chooser in a dialog.

dialogType — The `dialogType` property can be assigned one of the following `JFileChooser` constants:

- `JFileChooser.OPEN_DIALOG`
- `JFileChooser.SAVE_DIALOG`
- `JFileChooser.CUSTOM_DIALOG`

The `dialogType` property sets a file chooser's approve button text if the property is set to either `OPEN_DIALOG` or `CLOSE_DIALOG`. See the `dialogType` property for more information concerning the constants listed above.

fileFilter — File filters for a file chooser can be set in one of two ways: with `JFileChooser.addChoosableFileFilter()` or with `JFileChooser.setFileFilter()`, both of which are passed an extension of the abstract `swing.filechooser.FileFilter` class.

`JFileChooser.setFileFilter()` replaces the current file filter(s), whereas `addChoosableFileFilter` adds a filter to the current list of file filters.

fileHidingEnabled — A `boolean` value that determines whether or not hidden files are displayed in `JFileChooser`.

fileSelectionMode — The `fileSelectionMode` property can be set to one of the following values:

- `JFileChooser.FILES_ONLY`
- `JFileChooser.FILES_AND_DIRECTORIES`
- `JFileChooser.DIRECTORIES_ONLY`

The `fileSelectionMode` property determines whether files and/or directories are displayed in a file chooser.

fileSystemView — An instance of the `swing.filechooser.FileSystemView` class, which is summarized in Class Summary 15-7.

Class Summary 15-7   FileSystemView

Extends: java.lang.Object

Constructors

---

public FileSystemView()

The constructor is compiler generated.

Methods

---

public static FileSystemView getFileSystemView()
public File createFileObject(File, String)

public File <u>createFileObject</u>(String)
public abstract File <u>createNewFolder</u>(File) throws IOException
public File[] <u>getFiles</u>(File, boolean)
public File <u>getHomeDirectory</u>()
public File <u>getParentDirectory</u>(File)
public abstract File[] <u>getRoots</u>()
public abstract boolean <u>isHiddenFile</u>(File)
public abstract boolean <u>isRoot</u>(File)

`FileSystemView` provides platform-specific file information, such as root partitions and file type information, that is not available from the JDK1.1 `java.io.File` API.

The `JFileChooser` `fileSystemView` property will rarely be explicitly set by developers.

`fileView` — An object whose class is an extension of the `abstract` `swing.filechooser.FileView` class. File views provide information pertaining to the manner in which files are represented in a file chooser. By default, the information provided by a file view is obtained from a file chooser's look and feel; however, a file chooser's file view can be explicitly set.

See "FileView" on page 949 for more information concerning file views.

`multiSelectionEnabled` — File choosers support multiple selection, and the `multiSelectionEnabled` property controls whether a file chooser allows single or multiple selection. By default, file choosers allow single selection.

If a file chooser supports only single selection, the selected file is obtained by invocation of `JFileChooser.getSelectedFile()`—see the `selectedFile` property. If a file chooser supports multiple selection, the selected files are obtained by invocation of `JFileChooser.getSelectedFiles()`—see the `selectedFiles` property.

`selectedFile` — Represents the currently selected file in a file chooser. The selected file can be set either by user manipulation of a file chooser or programmatically with the `JFileChooser.setSelectedFile` method.

`selectedFiles` — If a file chooser has multiple selection enabled—see the `multiSelectionEnabled` property—the selected files are obtained by invocation of `JFileChooser.getSelectedFiles()`.

The selected files in a file chooser can be set programmatically with the `JFileChooser.setSelectedFiles` method, which is passed an array of `java.io.File` instances.

description
name
icon
typeDescription — The properties listed above are actually maintained by a file chooser's file view. All of the properties listed above are read-only, and the values are obtained from the file chooser's file view.

JFileChooser Events

The JFileChooser class fires two types of events: action events and property change events. Action events are fired by file choosers whenever their Approve or Cancel buttons are activated.

Property change events are fired whenever a file chooser's bound properties are modified—see "JFileChooser Properties" on page 958 for a list of bound JFileChooser properties.

Action Events

By default, the dialogs displayed as a result of invoking showOpenDialog(), showSaveDialog(), or showDialog() are modal, and therefore references to the selected file(s) can be obtained with a line of code after the call to one of the methods listed above, as the code fragment below illustrates.

```
// code fragment

int state = chooser.showOpenDialog();  // shows modal dialog
file = chooser.getSelectedFile();   // invoked after dialog
                                    // dialog is dismissed
```

In the code fragment listed above, the second line of code is not executed until the dialog is dismissed, and therefore the file returned from getSelectedFile() represents the file selected from the file chooser.

On the other hand, non-modal dialogs do not suspend execution of the thread that displays the dialog. As a result, a reference to selected file(s) for a file chooser displayed in a non-modal dialog cannot be obtained in the same fashion as illustrated in the code fragments above. For example, consider the following code fragment:

```
// code fragment

JDialog dialog = new JDialog(null, title, false);

// add chooser to dialog, set dialog title, etc.

dialog.setVisible(true);             // show non-modal dialog
file = chooser.getSelectedFile();    // dialog has not
                                     // been dismissed
```

In the code fragment listed above, the dialog is non-modal, which means the line of code that invokes `JFileChooser.getSelectedFile()` is executed before the dialog is dismissed. As a result, the file returned from `getSelectedFile()` in the code fragment above will return the last file selected from the file chooser or `null` if it is the first time the chooser has been displayed.

An alternative method for reacting to the dismissal of a file chooser dialog is to register an action listener with the file chooser. When the Approve or Cancel buttons in a file chooser are activated, the file chooser fires an action event. As a result, action listeners can be used to react to selections from—or cancellations of—a file chooser.

The file chooser shown in Figure 16-10 is contained in a non-modal dialog. The application that displays the dialog illustrates reacting to selections made from a file chooser.

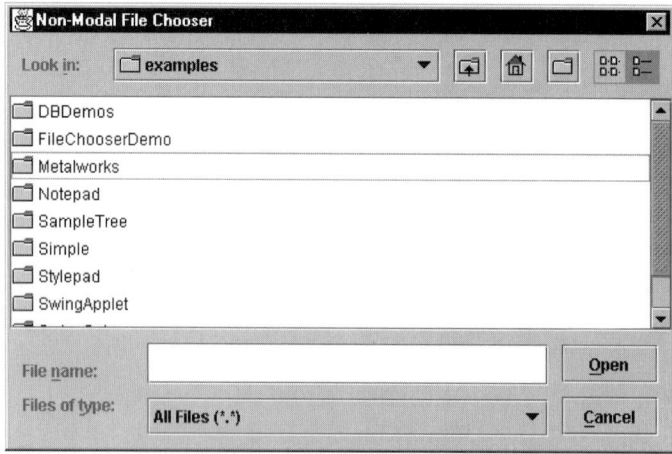

Figure 16-10 JFileChooser Action Events

The application contains a button whose activation results in the display of the dialog shown in Figure 16-10. The application creates a file chooser and a button. The button is added to the applet's content pane, and an action listener is added to the button that creates a non-modal dialog, adds the file chooser to the dialog, and displays the dialog.

The dialog's title is obtained by first invoking `JFileChooser.getDialogTitle()`. If the dialog title has been explicitly set, the call to `JFileChooser.getDialogTitle()` will return the title; otherwise, the method will return `null`. If the dialog title has not been explicitly set, the title is obtained from the chooser's UI delegate.

The dialog is created with a `null` frame, which results in the dialog being centered on the screen when it is displayed. The third argument to the `JDialog` constructor determines the modality of the dialog; in this case, a `false` value results in a non-modal dialog.

```
public class Test extends JFrame {
    JFileChooser chooser = new JFileChooser();
    JDialog dialog;
    JButton button = new JButton("show file chooser ...");

    public Test() {
        super("Simple File Chooser Application");
        Container contentPane = getContentPane();

        contentPane.setLayout(new FlowLayout());
        contentPane.add(button);

        button.addActionListener(new ActionListener() {
            public void actionPerformed(ActionEvent e) {
                String title = chooser.getDialogTitle();

                if(title == null)
                    chooser.getUI().getDialogTitle(chooser);

                dialog = new JDialog((Frame)null, title, false);

                Container dialogContentPane =
                            dialog.getContentPane();

                dialogContentPane.setLayout(new BorderLayout());
                dialogContentPane.add(chooser,
                            BorderLayout.CENTER);

                dialog.setTitle("Non-Modal File Chooser");

                dialog.pack();
```

```
                    dialog.setLocationRelativeTo(Test.this);

                    dialog.setVisible(true);
                }
            });
            ...
```

An action listener is also added to the chooser itself. The listener uses the action command associated with the action event to determine if a selection was made from the file chooser or if the dialog containing the chooser was canceled. If a selection was made from the file chooser, the selected file is obtained by invocation of JFileChooser.getSelectedFile. Subsequently, a message dialog is displayed, and the visibility of the dialog containing the chooser dialog is set to false.

```
            ...
        chooser.addActionListener(new ActionListener() {
            public void actionPerformed(ActionEvent e) {
                String state = (String)e.getActionCommand();
                File file = chooser.getSelectedFile();

                if(file != null &&
                    state.equals(JFileChooser.APPROVE_SELECTION)) {
                    JOptionPane.showMessageDialog(
                                    null, file.getPath());
                }
                else if(
                    state.equals(JFileChooser.CANCEL_SELECTION)) {
                    JOptionPane.showMessageDialog(
                                    null, "Canceled");
                }
                // JFileChooser action listeners are notified
                // when either the approve button or
                // cancel button is activated
                dialog.setVisible(false);
            }
        });
    }
```

The applet shown in Figure 16-10 is listed in its entirety in Example 16-8.

Example 16-8 JFileChooser Action Events

```java
import java.awt.*;
import java.awt.event.*;
import java.io.File;
import javax.swing.*;

public class Test extends JFrame {
    JFileChooser chooser = new JFileChooser();
    JDialog dialog;
    JButton button = new JButton("show file chooser ...");

    public Test() {
        super("Simple File Chooser Application");
        Container contentPane = getContentPane();

        contentPane.setLayout(new FlowLayout());
        contentPane.add(button);

        button.addActionListener(new ActionListener() {
            public void actionPerformed(ActionEvent e) {
                String title = chooser.getDialogTitle();

                if(title == null)
                    chooser.getUI().getDialogTitle(chooser);

                dialog = new JDialog(null, title, false);

                Container dialogContentPane =
                            dialog.getContentPane();

                dialogContentPane.setLayout(new BorderLayout());
                    dialogContentPane.add(chooser,
                            BorderLayout.CENTER);

                dialog.setTitle("Non-Modal File Chooser");

                dialog.pack();
                dialog.setLocationRelativeTo(Test.this);

                dialog.setVisible(true);
            }
        });
        chooser.addActionListener(new ActionListener() {
            public void actionPerformed(ActionEvent e) {
                String state = (String)e.getActionCommand();
                File file = chooser.getSelectedFile();
```

```
                    if(file != null &&
                        state.equals(JFileChooser.APPROVE_SELECTION)) {
                        JOptionPane.showMessageDialog(
                                        null, file.getPath());
                    }
                    else if(
                        state.equals(JFileChooser.CANCEL_SELECTION)) {
                        JOptionPane.showMessageDialog(
                                        null, "Canceled");
                    }
                    // JFileChooser action listeners are notified
                    // when either the approve button or
                    // cancel button is activated
                    dialog.setVisible(false);
                }
            });
        }
        public static void main(String args[]) {
            JFrame f = new Test();
            f.setBounds(300,300,350,100);
            f.setVisible(true);

            f.setDefaultCloseOperation(
                WindowConstants.DISPOSE_ON_CLOSE);

            f.addWindowListener(new WindowAdapter() {
                public void windowClosed(WindowEvent e) {
                    System.exit(0);
                }
            });
        }
    }
```

JFileChooser Class Summaries

The public and protected variables and methods for JFileChooser are listed in Class Summary 15-8.

Class Summary 15-8   JFileChooser

Extends: JComponent

Implements: javax.accessibility.Accessible

Constants

---

public static final String <u>ACCESSORY CHANGED PROPERTY</u>

public static final String
<u>APPROVE BUTTON MNEMONIC CHANGED PROPERTY</u>

public static final String <u>APPROVE BUTTON TEXT CHANGED PROPERTY</u>
public static final String
<u>APPROVE BUTTON TOOL TIP TEXT CHANGED PROPERTY</u>

public static final String <u>CHOOSABLE FILE FILTER CHANGED PROPERTY</u>
public static final String <u>DIALOG TYPE CHANGED PROPERTY</u>
public static final String <u>DIRECTORY CHANGED PROPERTY</u>
public static final String <u>FILE FILTER CHANGED PROPERTY</u>
public static final String <u>FILE HIDING CHANGED PROPERTY</u>
public static final String <u>FILE SELECTION MODE CHANGED PROPERTY</u>
public static final String <u>FILE SYSTEM VIEW CHANGED PROPERTY</u>
public static final String <u>FILE VIEW CHANGED PROPERTY</u>
public static final String <u>MULTI SELECTION ENABLED CHANGED PROPERTY</u>
public static final String <u>SELECTED FILE CHANGED PROPERTY</u>

The constants listed above identify the properties maintained by the
JFileChooser class, as in the code fragment listed below:

```
// code fragment

chooser.addPropertyChangeListener(new PropertyChangeListener() {
    public void propertyChange(PropertyChangeEvent e) {
        if(e.getPropertyName().equals(
                        JFileChooser.ACCESSORY_CHANGED_PROPERTY)
        // react to accessory change
    }
});
```

Dialog Types

---

public static final int <u>CUSTOM DIALOG</u>
public static final int <u>OPEN DIALOG</u>
public static final int <u>SAVE DIALOG</u>

The constants listed above are mostly used internally by `JFileChooser` but are also passed to the `JFileChooser.setDialogType` method. If file choosers are displayed with the `JFileChooser` methods `showOpenDialog()`, `showSaveDialog()`, or `showDialog()`, dialog type is automatically set to `OPEN_DIALOG`, `SAVE_DIALOG`, and `CUSTOM_DIALOG`, respectively. If a file chooser is displayed in a dialog without the use of `JFileChooser.show...` methods, the dialog type will default to `OPEN_DIALOG`.

Because dialog type corresponds to a file chooser's approve button text, it may be desirable to explicitly set dialog type with either `OPEN_DIALOG` or `SAVE_DIALOG` when file choosers are displayed by means other than the `JFileChooser.show...` methods. (Setting dialog type to `CUSTOM_DIALOG` does not affect a file chooser's approve button text.)

Modes

---

public static final int <u>DIRECTORIES ONLY</u>
public static final int <u>FILES AND DIRECTORIES</u>
public static final int <u>FILES ONLY</u>

The constants listed above represent the three modes supported by the `JFileChooser` class. The constants are passed to the `JFileChooser.setFileSelectionMode` method.

Options / Approve-Cancel

---

public static final int <u>APPROVE OPTION</u>
public static final int <u>CANCEL OPTION</u>
public static final int <u>ERROR OPTION</u>

public static final String <u>APPROVE SELECTION</u>
public static final String <u>CANCEL SELECTION</u>

The first group of constants listed above are returned from
`JFileChooser.showDialog()`, `JFileChooser.showOpenDialog()`, and
`JFileChooser.showSaveDialog()`. If the file chooser's approve button is
activated, the methods return `APPROVE_OPTION`, whereas `CANCEL_OPTION` is
returned in response to an activation of the Cancel button. The `ERROR_OPTION` is
reserved for use when an error occurs while a file chooser dialog is displayed. As
of Swing1.1, `JFileChooser.ERROR_OPTION` is not used within Swing.

The second group of constants are used as action command strings for action
events fired by file choosers as a result of either Approve or Cancel button
activation.

Constructors

---

public JFileChooser()
public JFileChooser(FileSystemView)
public JFileChooser(File currentDirectory)
public JFileChooser(File currentDirectory, FileSystemView)
public JFileChooser(String currentDirectoryPath)
public JFileChooser(String currentDirectoryPath, FileSystemView)

protected void setup(FileSystemView)

The no-argument constructor creates a file chooser with the user's home directory
as the initially displayed directory.

Files passed to `JFileChooser` constructors determine the initially displayed
directory. If the file is not a directory, the initially displayed directory is set to the
file's first ancestor directory that is traversable.

`FileSystemView` objects passed to `JFileChooser` constructors are used to
obtain file information. See "JFileChooser Properties" on page 958 for a
discussion of the `JFileChooser fileSystemView` property.

The `protected setup` method sets the file system view, updates the UI
delegate, and updates the file chooser's UI delegate.

Methods

Accessory Component

---

public JComponent getAccessory()
public void setAccessory(JComponent)

The methods listed above are accessors for a file chooser's accessory component. The setAccessory method fires a property change event if the new accessory component is different from the old.

Approve Button

---

public int getApproveButtonMnemonic()
public String getApproveButtonText()
public String getApproveButtonToolTipText()

public void setApproveButtonMnemonic(char)
public void setApproveButtonMnemonic(int)
public void setApproveButtonText(String)
public void setApproveButtonToolTipText(String)

A file chooser's approve button can be customized in three ways: the button's text, its tooltip, and its mnemonic. The methods listed above are accessors for the button's properties.

All of the setter methods listed above fire property change events if the value they are passed is different from the file chooser's current value. The approve button mnemonic can be set with either an `integer` or a `character`.

The `setApproveButtonToolTipText` method sets the dialog type to `JFileChooser.CUSTOM_DIALOG`.

Boolean Properties

---

public void setFileHidingEnabled(boolean)
public boolean isFileHidingEnabled()

public boolean isDirectorySelectionEnabled()
public boolean isFileSelectionEnabled()

File hiding corresponds to whether hidden files (such as files that begin with '.' under UNIX) are displayed in a file chooser.

The last two methods listed above can be used to determine whether directory or file selection is enabled.

Dialogs

---

public int showDialog(Component parent, String approveButtonText)
public int showOpenDialog(Component parent)
public int showSaveDialog(Component parent)

public String getDialogTitle()
public int getDialogType()

public void setDialogTitle(String)
public void setDialogType(int)

The first group of methods listed above display a modal dialog containing a file chooser on whose behalf the method is invoked. The integer value returned by the methods is one of the following constants:

- JFileChooser.CANCEL_OPTION
- JFileChooser.APPROVE_OPTION

Dialog title and type are accessed by the last four methods listed above. The setDialog... methods take effect only if a file chooser is displayed by one of the JFileChooser.show... methods.

Files and Directories

---

public void <u>changeToParentDirectory</u>()
public void <u>rescanCurrentDirectory</u>()

public File <u>getCurrentDirectory</u>()
public void <u>setCurrentDirectory</u>(File)

The `changeToParentDirectory` method delegates to the file chooser's file system view, and the `rescanCurrentDirectory` delegates to the UI delegate.

The last two methods listed above are accessors for a file chooser's current directory. If a file is passed to `setCurrentDirectory` that is not a directory, the current directory is set to the first traversable parent directory of the specified file.

File Filters

---

public FileFilter <u>getAcceptAllFileFilter</u>()
public FileFilter <u>getFileFilter</u>()
public void <u>setFileFilter</u>(FileFilter)

public void <u>addChoosableFileFilter</u>(FileFilter)
public boolean <u>removeChoosableFileFilter</u>(FileFilter)

public FileFilter[] <u>getChoosableFileFilters</u>()
public void <u>resetChoosableFileFilters</u>()

By default, file choosers are equipped with a single "accept all" filter that accepts all files. The "accept all" filter can be accessed by the `getAcceptAllFileFilter` method. The `getFileFilter` and `setFileFilter` methods can be used to get and set the currently selected filter.

File choosers can have more than one filter, although only one can be active at any given time. Filters can be added to and removed from a file chooser with the `addChoosableFileFilter` and `removeChoosableFileFilter` methods.

The getChoosableFileFilters method returns all of the filters associated with a file chooser, and the resetChoosableFileFilters method resets the list of filters to the "accept all" filter.

FileViews

public FileView getFileView()
public void setFileView(FileView)

public boolean accept(File)
public String getDescription(File)
public Icon getIcon(File)
public String getName(File)
public String getTypeDescription(File)
public boolean isTraversable(File)

File choosers have a file view object that extends the abstract swing.filechooser.FileView class, and JFileChooser provides accessors for the file view.

The second group of methods delegate directly to a file chooser's file view.

FileSystemView

public FileSystemView getFileSystemView()
public void setFileSystemView(FileSystemView)

File choosers delegate operating-system-dependent functionality to an object that extends the abstract swing.filechooser.FileSystemView class. The methods listed above are accessors for a file chooser's file system view.

Listeners

public void addActionListener(ActionListener)
public void removeActionListener(ActionListener)

protected void fireActionPerformed(String)

File choosers fire action events when their buttons are activated. As a result, JFileChooser provides methods for adding and removing action listeners. The protected fireActionPerformed method fires an action event to all registered action listeners.

Programmatic Manipulation

public void <u>approveSelection</u>()
public void <u>cancelSelection</u>()
public void <u>ensureFileIsVisible</u>(File)

File choosers can be manipulated programmatically by the methods listed above. Invoking approveSelection() mimics the activation of a file chooser's approve button, and the cancelSelection method mimics the activation of a file chooser's cancel button. There is no way to distinguish whether a selection or cancellation was initiated programmatically or by a user gesture.

The ensureFileIsVisible method scrolls the specified file into view.

Note: ensureFileIsVisible() *does not work for all look and feels as of Swing 1.1 FCS.*

File Selection Mode

public void <u>setFileSelectionMode</u>(int)
public int <u>getFileSelectionMode</u>()

File choosers support three selection modes, as defined by the integer constants listed below:

- DIRECTORIES_ONLY
- FILES_AND_DIRECTORIES
- FILES_ONLY

The constants are passed to the `setFileSelectionMode` method. The current selection mode can be obtained by `getFileSelectionMode()`.

Multiple Selection and Selected Files

---

public void <u>setMultiSelectionEnabled</u>(boolean)
public boolean <u>isMultiSelectionEnabled</u>()

public File <u>getSelectedFile</u>()
public void <u>setSelectedFile</u>(File)

public File[] <u>getSelectedFiles</u>()
public void <u>setSelectedFiles</u>(File[])

File choosers support both single and multiple selection. The first two methods listed above are accessors for the `boolean multiSelectionEnabled` property.

The last four methods listed above are accessors for the selected file(s); the first two methods are used for file choosers with single selection, and the last two methods are used for file choosers with multiple selection.

Note: *Multiple selection is not fully supported in Swing 1.1 FCS.*

Accessibility / Pluggable Look and Feel

---

public AccessibleContext <u>getAccessibleContext</u>()
public FileChooserUI <u>getUI</u>()
public String <u>getUIClassID</u>()
public void <u>updateUI</u>()

The methods listed above can be found in most extensions of `JComponent`. Swing lightweight components can return the class name of their UI delegate and an accessibility context that contains accessibility information for the component. The `updateUI` method is invoked when the component is fitted with a UI delegate.

AWT Compatibility

The main difference between the AWT's `FileDialog` and Swing's
`JFileChooser`—other than the fact that Swing file choosers are much more
capable—is the fact that the AWT's file dialogs deal in strings, whereas
`JFileChooser` deals with files.

Table 16-3 lists the `public` methods implemented by the
`java.awt.FileDialog` class and their `JFileChooser` equivalents.

Table 16-3 java.awt.FileDialog Methods & JFileChooser Equivalents

java.awt.FileDialog Methods	JFileChooser Equivalent
String getDirectory()	File getCurrentDirectory()
String getFile()	File getSelectedFile()
FilenameFilter getFilenameFilter()	FileFilter getFileFilter()
int getMode()	int getFileSelectionMode()
void setDirectory(String)	void setCurrentDirectory(File)
void setFile(String)	void setSelectedFile(File)
void setFilenameFilter(FilenameFilter)	void setFileFilter(FileFilter)
void setMode(int)	void setFileSelectionMode(int)

JColorChooser

Color choosers, represented by the `JColorChooser` class, are components that
allow a color to be selected. A color chooser is composed of two separate areas: a
set of color chooser panels displayed in a tabbed pane[8] and a preview panel that
visually communicates the selected color. Both areas can be customized by
replacing the default panels.

Like file choosers and option panes, color choosers are typically displayed in a
dialog, but since color choosers are components, they can be contained in any
AWT or Swing container.

---

8. there is more than one chooser panel.

`JColorChooser` features are listed in Feature Summary 16-1.

Feature Summary 16-1   JColorChooser

Color Chooser Panels

By default, color choosers come with three panels that allow a color chooser to be selected: `Swatches`, `HSB`, and `RGB`. Any of the default panels can be removed, and custom panels can be added.

Preview Panel

A color chooser's selected color is communicated through a preview panel. The default preview panel can be replaced with a custom version.

Prefabricated Dialogs

`JColorChooser` provides two `static` methods: `createDialog()` and `showDialog()` that create dialogs containing color choosers. The former creates and returns a dialog containing the color chooser it is passed; the latter creates both color chooser and dialog and shows the dialog. Both dialogs are modal.

The applet shown in Figure 16-11 contains a color chooser. By default, color choosers are equipped with three chooser panels contained in a tabbed pane, each of which is shown in Figure 16-11.

The applet shown in Figure 16-11 creates a color chooser with the `JColorChooser` no-argument constructor, and the chooser is added to the applet's content pane.

Color choosers have a selection model that is an implementation of the `swing.colorchooser.ColorSelectionModel` interface. The applet shown in Figure 16-11 adds a change listener to the color chooser's selection model to determine when a color has been selected. The listener responds to selections by updating the applet's status area.

The applet shown in Figure 16-11 is listed in Example 16-9.

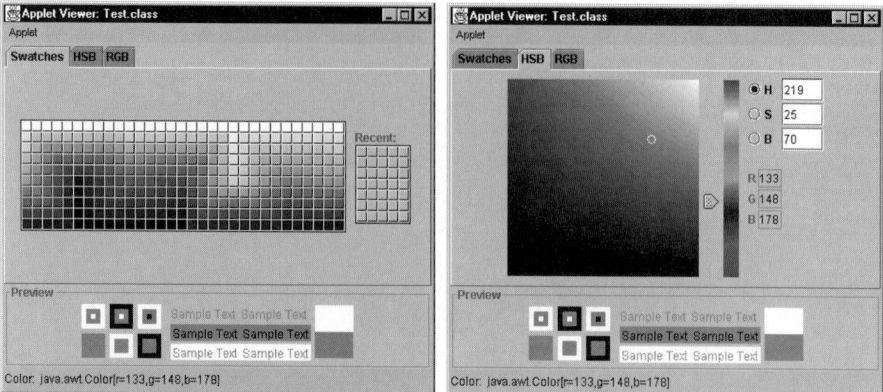

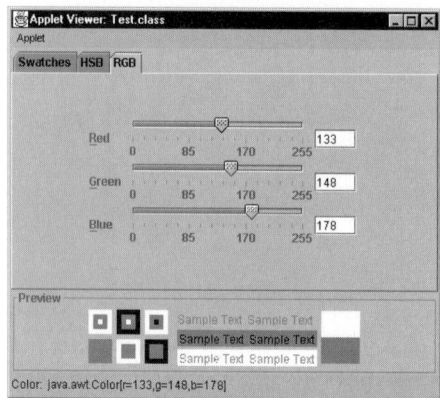

Figure 16-11 A Color Chooser Displayed in an Applet

Example 16-9 A Color Chooser Displayed in an Applet

```
import javax.swing.*;
import javax.swing.colorchooser.*;
import javax.swing.event.*;
import java.awt.*;

public class Test extends JApplet {
    JColorChooser chooser = new JColorChooser();
    ColorSelectionModel model = chooser.getSelectionModel();
```

```
public void init() {
    getContentPane().add(chooser, BorderLayout.CENTER);

    model.addChangeListener(new ChangeListener() {
        public void stateChanged(ChangeEvent e) {
            showStatus("Color:  " + chooser.getColor());
        }
    });
}
}
```

Displaying Color Choosers In Dialogs

Color choosers can be displayed in a dialog in one of two ways. The static `JColorChooser.showDialog` method creates a color chooser that is placed in a newly created dialog every time the method is invoked.

The `JColorChooser.createDialog` method is passed an existing color chooser that is also placed in a newly created dialog every time the method is invoked.

The following sections illustrate the use of the methods described above.

Showing Color Chooser Dialogs

The applet shown in Figure 16-12 contains a grid of `ColorPatch` objects that are contained in a `Palette`; both the `ColorPatch` and `Palette` classes are implemented by the applet. The upper-left picture in Figure 16-12 shows the applet as it appears initially. The upper-right picture shows the color chooser displayed as a result of clicking on the upper-left color patch. The lower-left picture shows a message dialog that the applet displays after the color chooser has been dismissed. The lower-right picture shows the applet after white has been selected from the color chooser. The selected color is set as the background color for the color patch in which the mouse pressed event occurred.

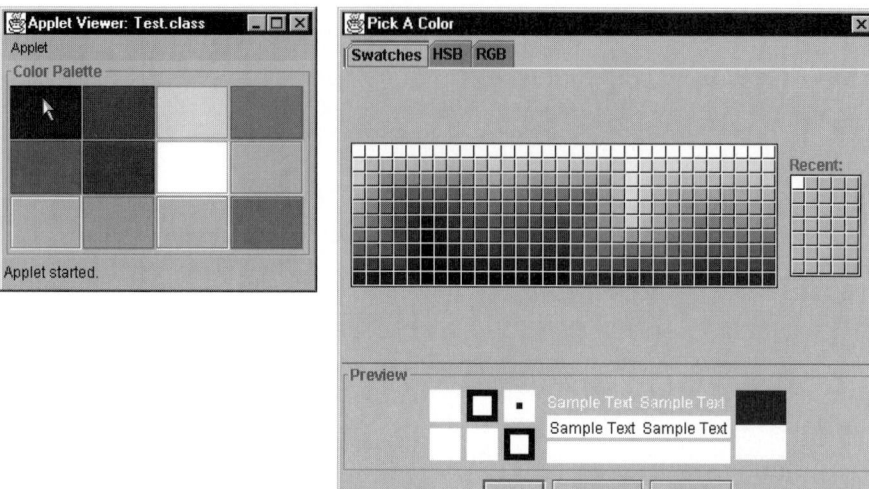

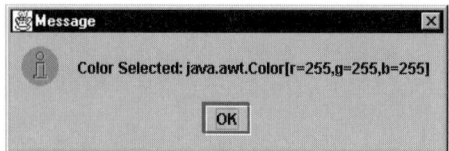

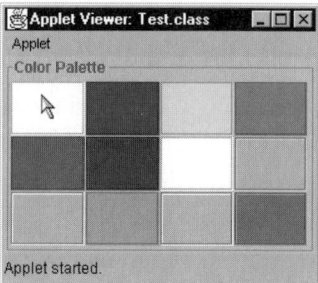

Figure 16-12 Using JFileChooser.showDialog()

The applet creates an instance of `Palette`, which is subsequently added to the applet's content pane.

```
public class Test extends JApplet {
    public void init() {
        getContentPane().add(new Palette(), BorderLayout.CENTER);
    }
}
```

The `Palette` class is a simple extension of `JPanel` that contains a grid of `ColorPatch` objects representing a set of default colors.

```
class Palette extends JPanel {
    private Color[] defaultColors = new Color[] {
        Color.blue, Color.red, Color.yellow, Color.green,
        Color.magenta, Color.darkGray, Color.white, Color.orange,
        Color.pink, Color.cyan, Color.lightGray, Color.gray,
    };

    public Palette() {
        int columns = 3;

        setBorder(
            BorderFactory.createTitledBorder("Color Palette"));

        setLayout(new GridLayout(columns,0,1,1));

        for(int i=0; i < defaultColors.length; ++i)
            add(new ColorPatch(defaultColors[i]));
    }
}
```

`ColorPatch` class is the most interesting class the applet implements.
`ColorPatch` is also an extension of `JPanel` with a mouse listener that invokes
`JColorChooser.showDialog` when a mouse pressed event is detected.

`JColorChooser.showDialog` creates a color chooser and a modal dialog, adds
the chooser to the dialog, displays the dialog, and returns a reference to the color
selected from the chooser. If the dialog is canceled—by activating the color
chooser's Cancel button, pressing the `Esc` key, or clicking the dialog's close
button—the `showDialog` method returns a `null` reference.

The mouse listener for the `ColorPatch` class displays a message dialog with a
message corresponding to whether a color was selected or the dialog was
dismissed. If a color is selected, the listener sets the background color for the color
patch that launched the dialog to the selected color and repaints the color patch.

```
class ColorPatch extends JPanel {
    JApplet applet;
    Color selectedColor;

    public ColorPatch(Color color) {
        // add border and set background color ...

        addMouseListener(new MouseAdapter() {
            public void mousePressed(MouseEvent e) {
                selectedColor = JColorChooser.showDialog(
                        ColorPatch.this,  // parent comp
                        "Pick A Color",   // dialog title
                        getBackground()); // initial color
```

```
                    if(selectedColor == null) {
                        JOptionPane.showMessageDialog(ColorPatch.this,
                            "ColorChooser Canceled");
                    }
                    else {
                        setBackground(selectedColor);
                        repaint();

                        JOptionPane.showMessageDialog(ColorPatch.this,
                            "Color Selected: " + selectedColor);
                    }
                }
            });
        }
    }
```

`JColorChooser.showDialog()` takes three arguments: a component over which the dialog is centered, a title for the dialog, and the color chooser's initial color.

The applet shown in Figure 16-12 is listed in its entirety in Example 16-10.

Example 16-10 A Color Chooser Displayed in a Dialog

```
import javax.swing.*;
import java.awt.*;
import java.awt.event.*;

public class Test extends JApplet {
    public void init() {
        getContentPane().add(new Palette(), BorderLayout.CENTER);
    }
}
class Palette extends JPanel {
    private Color[] defaultColors = new Color[] {
        Color.blue, Color.red, Color.yellow, Color.green,
        Color.magenta, Color.darkGray, Color.white, Color.orange,
        Color.pink, Color.cyan, Color.lightGray, Color.gray,
    };

    public Palette() {
        int columns = 3;

        setBorder(
            BorderFactory.createTitledBorder("Color Palette"));

        setLayout(new GridLayout(columns,0,1,1));

        for(int i=0; i < defaultColors.length; ++i)
```

```
                add(new ColorPatch(defaultColors[i]));
    }
}
class ColorPatch extends JPanel {
    JApplet applet;
    Color selectedColor;

    public ColorPatch(Color color) {
        setBorder(BorderFactory.createEtchedBorder());
        setBackground(color);

        addMouseListener(new MouseAdapter() {
            public void mousePressed(MouseEvent e) {
                selectedColor = JColorChooser.showDialog(
                            ColorPatch.this,  // parent comp
                            "Pick A Color",   // dialog title
                            getBackground()); // initial color

                if(selectedColor == null) {
                    JOptionPane.showMessageDialog(ColorPatch.this,
                        "ColorChooser Canceled");
                }
                else {
                    setBackground(selectedColor);
                    repaint();

                    JOptionPane.showMessageDialog(ColorPatch.this,
                        "Color Selected: " + selectedColor);
                }
            }
        });
    }
}
```

Creating Color Chooser Dialogs

As an alternative to JColorChooser.showDialog(), the JColorChooser
class provides a static createDialog method that creates a dialog, given a
color chooser. The JColorChooser.createDialog method is passed six
arguments:

- A component over which the dialog will be centered
- A string representing dialog's title
- A boolean value representing the modality of the dialog
- A color chooser that is placed in the dialog
- Two action listeners that are notified when the color chooser's buttons are activated

The `ColorPatch` class listed below is similar to the one listed in Example 16-10 on page 984, except that `JFileChooser.createDialog()` is used instead of `JFileChooser.showDialog()`. The `ColorPatch` class listed below contains a `static` color chooser that is shared by all instances of the `ColorPatch` class. Color choosers are somewhat expensive to create; as a result, creating a color chooser for each color patch in the palette would result in a perceptible performance penalty.

```java
class ColorPatch extends JPanel {
    JApplet applet;
    static JColorChooser chooser = new JColorChooser();
    JDialog dialog;

    public ColorPatch(Color color) {
        setBorder(BorderFactory.createEtchedBorder());
        setBackground(color);

        addMouseListener(new MouseAdapter() {
            public void mousePressed(MouseEvent e) {
                if(dialog == null)
                    dialog = JColorChooser.createDialog(
                                ColorPatch.this,  // parent comp
                                "Pick A Color",   // dialog title
                                false,         // modality
                                chooser,
                                new OkListener(),
                                new CancelListener());

                chooser.setColor(getBackground());
                dialog.setVisible(true);
            }
        });
    }
    class OkListener implements ActionListener {
        public void actionPerformed(ActionEvent e) {
            Color color = chooser.getColor();
            setBackground(color);
            repaint();

            JOptionPane.showMessageDialog(chooser,
                "Color Selected: " + chooser.getColor());
        }
    }
    class CancelListener implements ActionListener {
        public void actionPerformed(ActionEvent e) {
            JOptionPane.showMessageDialog(null,
                "ColorChooser Canceled");

        }
    }
}
```

After the mouse listener associated with the `ColorPatch` class creates the dialog, the chooser's color is set to the background color of the patch and the dialog is made visible.

The action listeners passed to the `JFileChooser.createDialog` method show a message dialog in a similar fashion to the mouse listener associated with the `ColorPatch` class listed in Example 16-10. If the color chooser's button is activated, the selected color is obtained with the `JColorChooser.getColor` method, the background of the color patch is set, and the color patch is repainted.

The applet that uses the `ColorPatch` class listed above is identical to the applet listed in Example 16-10, with the exception of the `ColorPatch` class itself. The applet is not listed; however, the listing is contained on the CD in the back of the book.

Speed vs. Convenience

The easiest way to display a color chooser in a dialog is to use the JColor-Chooser.showDialog method; however, there is a fairly steep price to pay for the convenience. Every time showDialog() is invoked, a newly created color chooser is displayed in a newly created dialog.

Although it requires a little more effort, manually constructing a color chooser and a dialog can result in a significant performance boost. If the applications discussed in "Showing Color Chooser Dialogs" on page 981 and "Creating Color Chooser Dialogs" on page 985 are run simultaneously, a perceptible performance difference can be seen from the time a mouse click occurs in a color patch and the color chooser dialog is displayed.

Customizing Color Choosers

By default, color choosers are fitted with three color chooser panels contained in a tabbed pane and a preview panel, as illustrated in Figure 16-1 on page 920. Although the default color chooser panels and preview panel are likely to be sufficient for most color choosers, both the color choosers panels and preview panel can be replaced with custom versions, as the following sections illustrate.

Preview Panels

When a color is selected in a color chooser, the default preview panel's foreground color is set to the selected color and the default preview panel is repainted.

A color chooser's preview component can be customized by specifying the preview component `JColorChooser.setPreviewPanel(JComponent)`. However, although the component specified by the `setPreviewPanel` method is substituted for the default preview panel, custom preview panels are not updated when a color is selected due to a bug in `JColorChooser` in Swing 1.1 FCS.

Note: *The following application does not work properly under Swing 1.1 FCS because of the bug cited in the previous paragraph. It should work when a subsequent release of Swing fixes the bug.*

The color chooser shown in Figure 16-13 contains a custom preview panel.

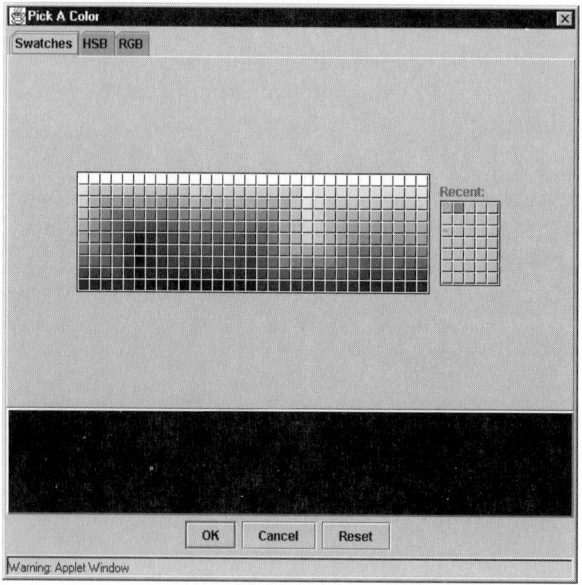

Figure 16-13 A Custom Preview in a Color Chooser

The application that shows the color chooser shown in Figure 16-13 is listed in Example 16-11.

Example 16-11 A Custom Preview in a Color Chooser

```
import javax.swing.*;
import javax.swing.colorchooser.*;
import java.awt.*;
import java.awt.event.*;

public class Test extends JApplet {
    private JColorChooser chooser = new JColorChooser();
    private JButton button = new JButton("Show Color Chooser");
    private JDialog dialog;

    public void init() {
        Container contentPane = getContentPane();

        contentPane.setLayout(new FlowLayout());
        contentPane.add(button, BorderLayout.CENTER);

        chooser.setPreviewPanel(new PreviewPanel());

        button.addActionListener(new ActionListener() {
            public void actionPerformed(ActionEvent e) {

                if(dialog == null)
                    dialog= JColorChooser.createDialog(
                            Test.this,  // parent comp
                            "Pick A Color",   // dialog title
                            false,        // modality
                            chooser,
                            null, null);

                dialog.setVisible(true);
            }
        });
    }
    class PreviewPanel extends JPanel {
        public PreviewPanel() {
            setPreferredSize(new Dimension(0,100));
            setBorder(BorderFactory.createRaisedBevelBorder());
        }
        public void paintComponent(Graphics g) {
            Dimension size = getSize();

            g.setColor(getForeground());
            g.fillRect(0,0,size.width,size.height);
        }
    }
}
```

The application sets the preview panel for its color chooser by invoking `JColorChooser.setPreviewPanel()`, which is passed an instance of `PreviewPanel`.

The `PreviewPanel` class extends `JPanel` and specifies a preferred height of 100 pixels. The preferred width for color chooser preview panels is ignored, so it is set to 0. The preview panel is fitted with a raised bevel border obtained from the Swing border factory.

When a color is selected in a color chooser, the foreground color of the preview panel is set to the selected color and the preview panel is repainted. The `PreviewPanel` class overrides `paintComponent` to fill the panel with the foreground color. Unfortunately, only the default preview panel is updated when a color is selected; as a result, the application listed in Figure 16-13 does not work as advertised.

Color Chooser Panels

The set of color chooser panels contained in a color chooser can be modified with `JColorChooser.setChooserPanels()` or individual panels can be added or removed with the `addChooserPanel` and `removeChooserPanel` methods. This section discusses the former.

The color chooser panels displayed in a color chooser are objects that extend the `swing.colorchooser.AbstractColorChooserPanel` class, which is summarized in Class Summary 15-9.

Class Summary 15-9   AbstractColorChooserPanel

Extends: JPanel

Constructors

---

public <u>AbstractColorChooserPanel</u>()

The AbstractColorChooserPanel class does not implement any constructors, and therefore the no-argument constructor is compiler generated.

Methods

Color/Color Selection Model / Installing Chooser Panel / Painting

---

public ColorSelectionModel getColorSelectionModel()
protected Color getColorFromModel()

public void installChooserPanel(JColorChooser)
public void uninstallChooserPanel(JColorChooser)

public void paint(Graphics)

The first two methods listed above are convenience methods that return the selection model associated with the panel's color chooser, and the color maintained by the selection model, respectively.

The installChooserPanel method is invoked when a color chooser is instantiated. The method invokes buildChooser() and updateChooser() and adds a change listener to the color chooser's selection model. The listener works in concert with the paint method so that updateChooser() is invoked when the panel is painted if changes have been made to the chooser's selection model before the chooser is displayed.

The uninstallChooserPanel method removes the listener that was added to the chooser's selection model by the installChooserPanel method.

Building and Updating Chooser

---

protected abstract void buildChooser()
public abstract void updateChooser()

The `buildChooser` method is invoked when a color chooser's chooser panels are set with the `JColorChooser.setChooserPanels` method. The `buildChooser` method is expected to create the components contained in the panel and to add the components to the panel.

The `updateChooser` method is also invoked when color chooser panels are set with the `JColorChooser.setChooserPanels` method. Additionally, `updateChooser()` is invoked when a change is made to the chooser's color selection model.

The `buildChooser` and `updateChooser` methods are abstract and therefore must be implemented by concrete extensions of `AbstractColorChooserPanel`.

Display Names and Icons

---

public abstract String <u>getDisplayName</u>()
public abstract Icon <u>getLargeDisplayIcon</u>()
public abstract Icon <u>getSmallDisplayIcon</u>()

The three methods listed above return information about a color chooser panel. As of Swing 1.1 FCS / 1.2 JDK, only the `getDisplayName` method is used for the string displayed in the tab associated with a panel. For example, the default display names for the default chooser panels are "Swatches", "HSB", and "RBG", as can be seen from Figure 16-11 on page 980. The icons returned from `getLargeDisplayIcon()` and `getSmallDisplayIcon()` are not currently used within Swing.

The applet shown in Figure 16-14 contains a button whose activation results in a color chooser being displayed in a dialog. The default chooser panels in the color chooser are replaced by an extension of the `AbstractColorChooserPanel` class. It should be noted that the chooser panel contained in the color chooser shown in Figure 16-14 is short on usability and long on simplicity for the sake of illustration.

The applet creates a color chooser and an array of objects that implement the `AbstractColorChooserPanel` class. The array contains a single instance of `ListPanel`, which is implemented by the applet. Notice that the `ListPanel` instance is not contained in a tabbed pane because only one chooser panel is contained in the array.

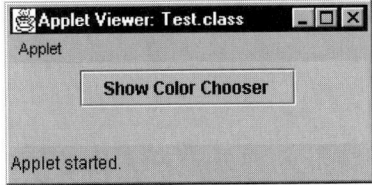

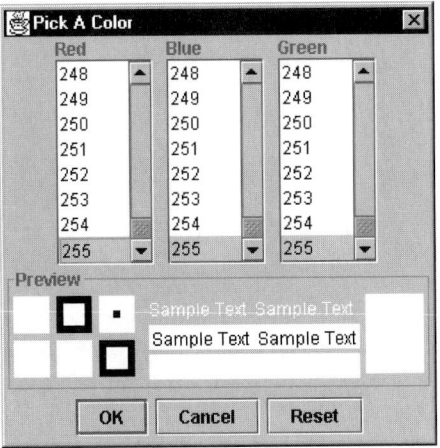

Figure 16-14 Replacing Chooser Panels

The applet's `init` method invokes `JColorChooser.setChooserPanels()`, passing the array of color chooser panels.

```
public class Test extends JApplet {
    private JColorChooser chooser = new JColorChooser();
    private AbstractColorChooserPanel colorPanels[] =
        new AbstractColorChooserPanel[] {
            new ListPanel(),
        };
    private JButton button = new JButton("Show Color Chooser");
    private JDialog dialog;

    public void init() {
        Container contentPane = getContentPane();

        contentPane.setLayout(new FlowLayout());
        contentPane.add(button, BorderLayout.CENTER);

        chooser.setChooserPanels(colorPanels);

        button.addActionListener(new ActionListener() {
            public void actionPerformed(ActionEvent e) {
                if(dialog == null)
                    dialog= JColorChooser.createDialog(
                            Test.this,  // parent comp
                            "Pick A Color",   // dialog title
                            false,       // modality
                            chooser,
```

```
                            null, null);
                dialog.setVisible(true);
            }
        });
    }
    ...
}
```

The `ListPanel` class extends abstract `ColorChooserPanel` class and implements the `ListSelectionListener` interface. Two panels are created, one for the "Red", "Green", and "Blue" labels and another for their associated lists. Additionally, three default list models are created for each of the lists, and a boolean `isAdjustingValue` is set to `false`.

```
    ...
    class ListPanel extends AbstractColorChooserPanel
                              implements ListSelectionListener {
        private JPanel labelPanel = new JPanel(),
                       listPanel = new JPanel();

        private JList redList = new JList(), blueList = new JList(),
                      greenList = new JList();

        private DefaultListModel redModel = new DefaultListModel(),
                                 blueModel = new DefaultListModel(),
                                 greenModel = new DefaultListModel();

        private boolean isAdjusting = false;
        ...
```

The `buildChooser` method populates each of the lists with strings representing values from 0 to 256. The lists are added to the list panel, the labels are added to the label panel, and the list and label panels are added to the chooser panel.

Each of the lists has the chooser panel specified as a list selection listener. When a value changes in a list, the chooser panel's `valueChanged` method retrieves the values from the lists and updates the chooser's selection model accordingly.

```
        ...
        protected void buildChooser() {
            redList.setFixedCellWidth(50);
            greenList.setFixedCellWidth(50);
            blueList.setFixedCellWidth(50);
```

```
        for(int i=0; i < 256; ++i) {
            redModel.addElement(Integer.toString(i));
            greenModel.addElement(Integer.toString(i));
            blueModel.addElement(Integer.toString(i));
        }

        redList.setModel(redModel);
        greenList.setModel(greenModel);
        blueList.setModel(blueModel);

        listPanel.setLayout(new GridLayout(0,3,10,0));

        listPanel.add(new JScrollPane(redList));
        listPanel.add(new JScrollPane(blueList));
        listPanel.add(new JScrollPane(greenList));

        labelPanel.setLayout(new GridLayout(0,3,10,0));

        labelPanel.add(new JLabel("Red"));
        labelPanel.add(new JLabel("Blue"));
        labelPanel.add(new JLabel("Green"));

        setLayout(new BorderLayout());
        add(labelPanel, BorderLayout.NORTH);
        add(listPanel, BorderLayout.CENTER);

        redList.addListSelectionListener(this);
        greenList.addListSelectionListener(this);
        blueList.addListSelectionListener(this);
    }
    public void valueChanged(ListSelectionEvent e) {
        int r = redList.getSelectedIndex(),
            b = blueList.getSelectedIndex(),
            g = greenList.getSelectedIndex();

        if(r != -1 && g != -1 && b != -1)
            getColorSelectionModel().setSelectedColor(
                                    new Color(r,g,b));
    }
    ...
```

The updateChooser method updates the selected values in the lists, depending upon the current color from the chooser's selection model.

The isAdjusting boolean variable is used in order to avoid an infinite loop when JList.setSelectedIndex() is called. The gory details are enumerated below.

A call to JList.setSelectedIndex() causes the list to fire a list selection event, resulting in a call to ListPanel.valueChanged()—recall that ListPanel adds itself as a listener for each list. valueChanged() updates the

chooser's selection model, causing `ListPanel.updateChooser()` to be
invoked, and `updateChooser` invokes `JList.setSelectedIndex()`.

```
    . . .
    public void updateChooser() {
        if( ! isAdjusting) {
            isAdjusting = true;

            Color color = getColorFromModel();
            int r = color.getRed(), g = color.getGreen(),
                b = color.getBlue();

            redList.setSelectedIndex(r);
            redList.ensureIndexIsVisible(r);

            blueList.setSelectedIndex(b);
            blueList.ensureIndexIsVisible(b);

            greenList.setSelectedIndex(g);
            greenList.ensureIndexIsVisible(g);

            isAdjusting = false;
        }
    }
    . . .
```

The `getDisplayName`, `getSmallDisplayIcon`, and `getLargeDisplayIcon`
methods must be implemented by the `ListPanel` class because they are defined
as abstract in `AbstractColorChooserPanel`. The `get...Icon` methods
return `null` references because the icons are currently not used within Swing.
The `getDisplayName` method returns a non-`null` string that would normally
be used as the string displayed in the tab associated with the chooser panel.
However, because the `ListPanel` instance is the only chooser panel displayed in
the color chooser, the string returned from `getDisplayName` is not used.

```
    . . .
    public String getDisplayName() {
        return "lists";
    }
    public Icon getSmallDisplayIcon() {
        return null;
    }
    public Icon getLargeDisplayIcon() {
        return null;
    }
}
```

The applet shown in Figure 16-14 is listed in its entirety in Example 16-12.

Example 16-12 Implementing a Custom Color Chooser Panel

```java
import javax.swing.*;
import javax.swing.event.*;
import javax.swing.colorchooser.*;
import java.awt.*;
import java.awt.event.*;

public class Test extends JApplet {
    private JColorChooser chooser = new JColorChooser();
    private AbstractColorChooserPanel colorPanels[] =
            new AbstractColorChooserPanel[] {
                new ListPanel(),
            };
    private JButton button = new JButton("Show Color Chooser");
    private JDialog dialog;

    public void init() {
        Container contentPane = getContentPane();

        contentPane.setLayout(new FlowLayout());
        contentPane.add(button, BorderLayout.CENTER);

        chooser.setChooserPanels(colorPanels);

        button.addActionListener(new ActionListener() {
            public void actionPerformed(ActionEvent e) {
                if(dialog == null)
                    dialog= JColorChooser.createDialog(
                            Test.this,  // parent comp
                            "Pick A Color",   // dialog title
                            false,       // modality
                            chooser,
                            null, null);

                dialog.setVisible(true);
            }
        });
    }
}
class ListPanel extends AbstractColorChooserPanel
            implements ListSelectionListener {
    private JPanel labelPanel = new JPanel(),
                listPanel = new JPanel();

    private JList redList = new JList(), blueList = new JList(),
                greenList = new JList();

    private DefaultListModel redModel = new DefaultListModel(),
                    blueModel = new DefaultListModel(),
```

```java
                            greenModel = new DefaultListModel();

      private boolean isAdjusting = false;

      public void updateChooser() {
          if( ! isAdjusting) {
              isAdjusting = true;

              Color color = getColorFromModel();
              int r = color.getRed(), g = color.getGreen(),
                  b = color.getBlue();

              redList.setSelectedIndex(r);
              redList.ensureIndexIsVisible(r);

              blueList.setSelectedIndex(b);
              blueList.ensureIndexIsVisible(b);

              greenList.setSelectedIndex(g);
              greenList.ensureIndexIsVisible(g);

              isAdjusting = false;
          }
      }
      protected void buildChooser() {
         redList.setFixedCellWidth(50);
         greenList.setFixedCellWidth(50);
         blueList.setFixedCellWidth(50);

         for(int i=0; i < 256; ++i) {
             redModel.addElement(Integer.toString(i));
             greenModel.addElement(Integer.toString(i));
             blueModel.addElement(Integer.toString(i));
         }

         redList.setModel(redModel);
         greenList.setModel(greenModel);
         blueList.setModel(blueModel);

         listPanel.setLayout(new GridLayout(0,3,10,0));

         listPanel.add(new JScrollPane(redList));
         listPanel.add(new JScrollPane(blueList));
         listPanel.add(new JScrollPane(greenList));

         labelPanel.setLayout(new GridLayout(0,3,10,0));

         labelPanel.add(new JLabel("Red"));
         labelPanel.add(new JLabel("Blue"));
         labelPanel.add(new JLabel("Green"));
```

```
        setLayout(new BorderLayout());
        add(labelPanel, BorderLayout.NORTH);
        add(listPanel, BorderLayout.CENTER);

        redList.addListSelectionListener(this);
        greenList.addListSelectionListener(this);
        blueList.addListSelectionListener(this);
    }
    public void valueChanged(ListSelectionEvent e) {
        int r = redList.getSelectedIndex(),
            b = blueList.getSelectedIndex(),
            g = greenList.getSelectedIndex();

        if(r != -1 && g != -1 && b != -1)
            getColorSelectionModel().setSelectedColor(
                                    new Color(r,g,b));
    }
    public String getDisplayName() {
        return "display name";
    }
    public Icon getSmallDisplayIcon() {
        return null;
    }
    public Icon getLargeDisplayIcon() {
        return null;
    }
}
```

The JColorChooser class is summarized in Component Summary 16-2.

Component Summary 16-2   JColorChooser

Model(s)	javax.swing.colorchooser.ColorSelectionModel
UI Delegate(s)	javax.swing.plaf.basic.BasicColorChooserUI
Renderer(s)	——
Editor(s)	——
Events Fired	ActionEvents / ChangeEvents / PropertyChangeEvents
Replacement For	——

Class Diagrams

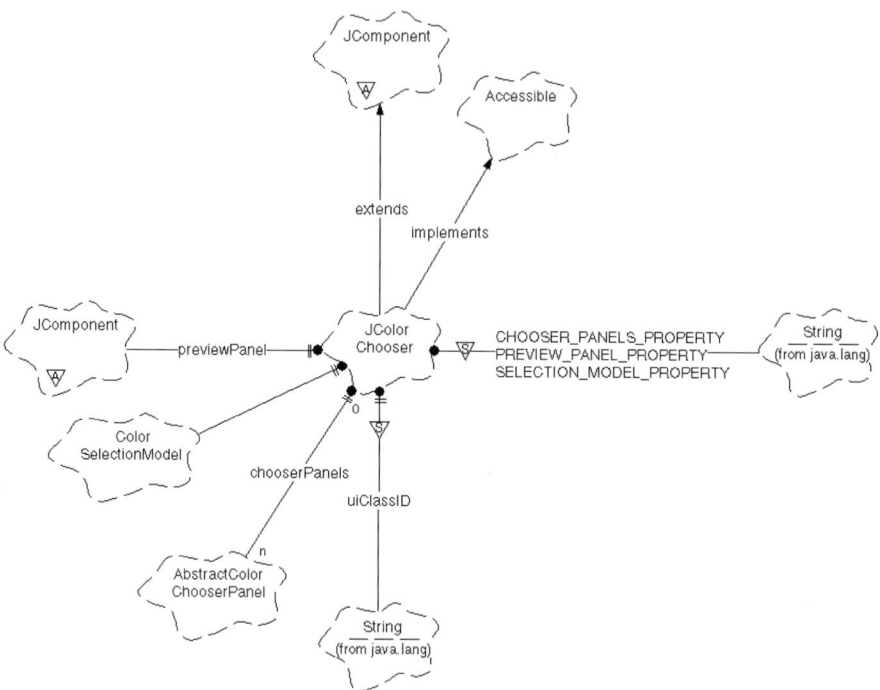

Figure 16-15 JColorChooser Class Diagram

JColorChooser extends JComponent and implements the Accessible interface. JColorChooser maintains protected references to its preview panel—an instance of JComponent and an array of color chooser panels—objects that implement the AbstractColorChooserPanel class. Additionally, the JColorChooser class defines a set of public static strings used to represent the properties associated with instances of JColorChooser.

JColorChooser Properties

The properties maintained by the JColorChooser class are listed in Table 16-4.

Table 16-4 JColorChooser Properties

Property Name	Data Type	Property Type[1]	Access[3]	Default[4]
chooserPanels	AbstractColorChooserPanel[]	B	SG	L&F
color	Color	S[2]	CSG	L&F
previewPanel	JComponent	B	SG	L&F
selectionModel	ColorSelectionModel	B	CSG	L&F

1. B = bound (fires PropertyChangeEvent) / C = constrained/ I = indexed /
   S = simple / Ch = fires ChangeEvent / LD = fires ListDataEvent
2. selection model fires a change event when color is changed
3. C = settable at construction time / G = getter method / S = setter method
4. L&F = look-and-feel dependent

chooserPanels — The panels displayed in a color chooser that are used to select a color.

color — The currently selected color in a color chooser.

previewPanel — A panel that visually communicates the currently selected color. The default preview panel can be replaced with the JColorChooser.setPreviewPanel method. See "Preview Panels" on page 988 for more information concerning replacing the default preview panel.

selectionModel — A selection model that implements the swing.colorchooser.ColorSelectionModel interface. Color chooser selection models fire change events when the currently selected color is modified.

JColorChooser Events

The most commonly handled events for color choosers are action events fired when the non-modal color chooser dialog created by JColorChooser.createDialog() is dismissed. Listeners cannot be specified for the buttons contained in the modal color chooser dialogs created with JColorChooser.showDialog().

Significant events fired by the classes that comprise color choosers are listed in Table 16-5.

Table 16-5 Color Chooser Events

Event	Fired by	Triggers/Handling
Action	JColorChooser	*trigger:* OK/Cancel buttons
Change	DefaultColor SelectionModel	*trigger:* color selection, *handling:* UI delegate sets preview panel's foreground color
Property Change	JColorChooser	*handling:* UI delegate reacts to preview panel and chooser panel changes

The default color selection model for color choosers fires change events when the selected color is modified. The file chooser's UI delegate reacts to change events from the selection model by setting the preview panel's foreground color to the selected color and repainting the panel.

Color choosers fire property change events when their bound properties are modified. To react to changes in a color chooser's `color` property, a change listener must be registered with the chooser's selection model, as illustrated in Example 16-9 on page 980.

JColorChooser Class Summaries

The `public` and `protected` variables and methods for `JColorChooser` are listed in Class Summary 15-10.

Class Summary 15-10   JColorChooser

Constants

public static final String CHOOSER_PANELS_PROPERTY
public static final String PREVIEW_PANEL_PROPERTY
public static final String SELECTION_MODEL_PROPERTY

The constants defined by the JColorChooser class identify color chooser properties.

Constructors

---

public JColorChooser()

public JColorChooser(Color)
public JColorChooser(ColorSelectionModel)

The JColorChooser class provides the three constructors listed above. The no-argument constructor creates a color chooser with an initial color of white. The initial color can also be specified explicitly with the last two constructors listed above by a color or color selection model, respectively.

Methods

Creating and Showing Color Chooser Dialogs

---

public static JDialog createDialog(Component, String, boolean, JColorChooser,
                                    ActionListener, ActionListener)
public static Color showDialog(Component, String, Color)

The static methods listed above can be used to create or show a dialog containing an instance of JColorChooser. The methods are discussed in "Displaying Color Choosers In Dialogs" on page 981.

Chooser Panels

---

public void addChooserPanel(AbstractColorChooserPanel)
public AbstractColorChooserPanel removeChooserPanel(AbstractColorChooserPanel)

public AbstractColorChooserPanel[] getChooserPanels()
public void setChooserPanels(AbstractColorChooserPanel[])

Color choosers allow total control over the color chooser panels that they display. The first two methods listed above can be used to add and remove panels from the array of color chooser panels maintained by instances of JColorChooser.

The last two methods listed above can be used to access the entire array of color chooser panels and to set the array, respectively. See "Color Chooser Panels" on page 990 for an example of replacing the color chooser panels that reside in a color chooser.

Color and Color Selection Model

---

public Color <u>getColor</u>()
public void <u>setColor</u>(int colorBits)
public void <u>setColor</u>(int red, int green, int blue)
public void <u>setColor</u>(Color)

public ColorSelectionModel <u>getSelectionModel</u>()
public void <u>setSelectionModel</u>(ColorSelectionModel)

The selected color in a color chooser can be explicitly controlled by the setColor methods listed above. A color can be specified by an integer value whose low-order byte specifies the blue component, followed by the green component in the next byte, and the red component in the high-order byte.

Setting a color chooser's color causes its selection model to fire a change event. See Example 16-9 on page 980 for an example of to a change in a color chooser's color.

JColorChoosers have a color selection model that implements the swing.colorchooser.ColorSelectionModel interface. A color chooser's selection model can be obtained or set after construction with the last two methods listed above.

Preview Panels

---

public JComponent <u>getPreviewPanel</u>()
public void <u>setPreviewPanel</u>(JComponent)

Color choosers display a preview panel that visually communicates the currently selected color. The standard preview panel can be replaced with the last method listed above.

Accessibility / Pluggable Look and Feel

public AccessibleContext getAccessibleContext()
public ColorChooserUI getUI()
public String getUIClassID()
public void setUI(ColorChooserUI)
public void updateUI()

The methods listed above can be found in most extensions of `JComponent`. Swing lightweight components can return the class name of their UI delegate and an accessible context that contains accessibility information for the component. The `updateUI` method is invoked when the component is fitted with a UI delegate.

AWT Compatibility

The AWT does not provide a component analogous to `JColorChooser`.

Parting Shots

Swing's file and color choosers are highly configurable components that are vital to modern graphical user interfaces. The file chooser can be customized in a number of different ways including accessory components and file filters. Both choosers are easily displayed in dialogs.

As of Swing 1.1 FCS, multiple selection for file choosers is not yet implemented and preview panels cannot be set for color choosers due to bugs.

CHAPTER

17

Lists

Swing lists, represented by the `JList` class, display a list of selectable objects and support three selection modes: single selection, single interval selection, and multiple interval selection.

The `JList` class delegates the responsibilities of maintaining and rendering a list of objects; a list's model maintains a list of objects that are rendered in list cells by a list cell renderer.

By default, list cell renderers are instances of `DefaultListCellRenderer`, which renders objects as listed in Table 17-1. Icons and strings are displayed as is, whereas all other object types are rendered by displaying the string returned from the object's `toString` method.

Table 17-1 DefaultListCellRenderer Rendering

Object type ...	... is rendered
Icon	as is
Object	with the string returned from toString()
String	as is

Unlike buttons and labels, list cells by default can display a string or an icon, but not both because `DefaultListCellRenderer` displays a single object as outlined in Table 17-1. Fortunately, it is a simple matter to implement a custom renderer that can render any type of object as desired.

`JList` itself does not provide support for scrolling the objects it displays, but instances of `JList` can be placed inside of a scrollpane. See "JScrollPane" on page 739 for more information concerning Swing scrollpanes.

The `JList` component delegates three major responsibilities to other objects: data handling, item selection, and cell rendering, which are handled by classes that implement the `ListModel`, `ListSelectionModel`, and `ListCellRenderer` interfaces, respectively.

The applet shown in Figure 17-1 contains an instance of `JList` that contains ten strings.

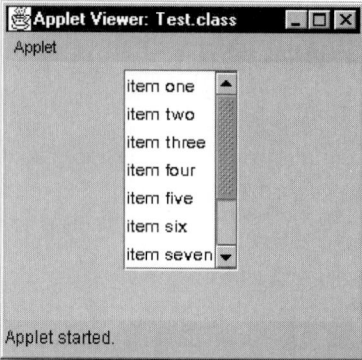

Figure 17-1 A Simple List Example

The applet shown in Figure 17-1 is listed in Example 17-1.

Example 17-1 A Simple List Example

```
import java.awt.*;
import javax.swing.*;

public class Test extends JApplet {
    public void init() {
        Container contentPane = getContentPane();
        Object[] items = { "item one", "item two", "item three",
                        "item four", "item five", "item six",
                        "item seven", "item eight",
                        "item nine", "item ten" };
```

```
        JList list = new JList(items);
        JScrollPane sp = new JScrollPane(list);

        list.setVisibleRowCount(7);

        contentPane.setLayout(new FlowLayout());
        contentPane.add(sp);
    }
}
```

The list is constructed with an array of strings and is placed in a scrollpane. The number of visible rows displayed in the scrollpane is set to seven by invocation of the `JList.setVisibleRowCount` method, and the scrollpane is subsequently added to the applet's content pane.

The strings displayed in the list are specified as an array of objects to emphasize the fact that instances of `JList` can display any type of object. By default, lists display either icons or strings as is; all other types of objects are represented by the string returned from the object's `toString` method.

By default, when a list is placed in a scrollpane, eight of the list's rows are visible in the scrollpane. The number of visible rows when a list is contained in a scrollpane can be set with the `JList.setVisibleRowCount` method. The `setVisibleRowCount` method takes effect only when a list is displayed in a scrollpane.

Swing Tip ...

Place Instances of JList in a Scrollpane

The JList component does not provide a means to scroll the objects it displays. Additionally, it is not uncommon for instances of JList to be sized so that all of the items contained in the list are not visible. As a result, lists are almost always placed in a scrollpane.

By default, when a list is placed in a scrollpane, eight of the lists rows are visible. The number of visible rows can be explicitly set with the JList.setVisibleRow-Count method. The setVisibleRowCount method only takes effect if a list is contained in a scrollpane.

List Models

The `JList` class does not maintain references to the objects it displays. All instances of `JList` delegate the management of their data to an object that implements the `ListModel` interface.

The objects displayed in a list can be specified when an instance of `JList` is constructed with the following `JList` constructors:

- `public JList(ListModel)`
- `public JList(Object[])`
- `public JList(Vector)`

The objects displayed in a list can also be specified after construction with the following `JList` methods:

- `public void setModel(ListModel)`
- `public void setListData(Object[])`
- `public void setListData(Vector)`

Other than the constructors and methods listed above, the `JList` class itself does not provide methods for manipulating its data. For example, there are no `JList` methods for inserting or removing objects. Inserting or removing list data, other than replacing all of the data in a list, must be performed by direct manipulation of a list's model.

All list models implement the `ListModel` interface, which is summarized in Interface Summary 17-1.

Interface Summary 17-1 ListModel

ListDataListener Registration

---

public abstract void <u>addListDataListener</u>(ListDataListener)
public abstract void <u>removeListDataListener</u>(ListDataListener)

The `ListModel` interface defines methods for adding and removing instances of `ListDataListener`, which are notified when the data maintained by the list model is modified. See Interface Summary 17-5 on page 1053 for more information on the `ListDataListener` interface and its use.

List Size and Element Accessors

public abstract int <u>getSize</u>()
public abstract Object <u>getElementAt</u>(int)

The `ListModel` interface also defines methods for obtaining the number of objects displayed in the list—`getSize()`—and for obtaining a reference to a specific object in the list, `getElementAt()`.

Swing provides two classes that implement the `ListModel` interface: `AbstractListModel` and `DefaultListModel`, as illustrated in Figure 17-2.

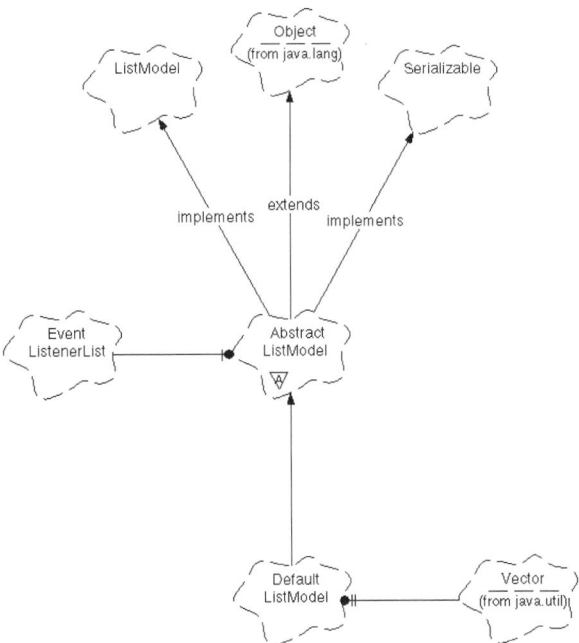

Figure 17-2 List Models

AbstractListModel extends Object and implements the ListModel and Serializable interfaces. AbstractListModel implements methods defined in the model interface for registering ListDataListeners by maintaining an EventListenerList. AbstractListModel does not implement the methods defined by the ListModel interface that are concerned with the model's data.

DefaultListModel extends AbstractListModel and implements the ListModel methods that its superclass leaves unimplemented. DefaultListModel stores its data in a vector.

AbstractListModel

AbstractListModel does not concern itself with storing data and therefore does not implement the getSize and getElementAt methods defined by the ListModel interface. Because AbstractListModel does not implement all of the methods defined by the ListModel interface, it is an abstract class.

The AbstractListModel class extends Object and implements the ListModel and Serializable interfaces. The DefaultListModel class is an extension of AbstractListModel.

The AbstractListModel class is summarized in Class Summary 17-1.

Class Summary 17-1   AbstractListModel

Extends: java.lang.Object
Implements: ListModel, java.io.Serializable

Constructors

---

public <u>AbstractListModel</u>()

The no-argument constructor is provided by the compiler— AbstractListModel does not implement any constructors.

Methods

public void <u>addListDataListener</u>(ListDataListener)
protected void <u>fireContentsChanged</u>(Object source, int index0, int index1)
protected void <u>fireIntervalAdded</u>(Object source, int index0, int index1)
protected void <u>fireIntervalRemoved</u>(Object source, int index0, int index1)
public void <u>removeListDataListener</u>(ListDataListener)

`AbstractListModel` is only concerned about firing list data events to listeners; it implements the `addListDataListener` and `removeListDataListener` methods defined in the `ListModel` interface. `AbstractListModel` also provides three `protected` methods for firing events to listeners when the contents of the list are modified or when intervals are added or removed from the list data.

When objects displayed in a list are specified as an array of objects or a vector, an inner class extension of the `AbstractListModel` is instantiated and associated with the list. For example, `JList.setListData(Object[])` and `JList.setListData(Vector)` are implemented as follows:

```
// From the JList class ...

public void setListData(final Object[] listData) {
    setModel(new AbstractListModel() {
        public int getSize() {
            return listData.length;
        }
        public Object getElementAt(int i) {
            return listData[i];
        }
    });
}
public void setListData(final Vector listData) {
    setModel(new AbstractListModel() {
        public int getSize() {
            return listData.size();
        }
        public Object getElementAt(int i) {
            return listData.elementAt(i);
        }
    });
}
```

When list data is specified as an array of objects or a vector, the manner in which the data is stored is known, and therefore the getSize and getElementAt methods from the ListModel interface can be implemented.

Specifying list data as an array of objects or a vector does not provide the ability to insert and remove objects. As mentioned previously, the JList class does not provide methods for inserting or removing objects, and as can be seen from Class Summary 17-1, neither does the AbstractListModel class. If objects must be inserted or removed from a list model, instances of JList must be explicitly fitted with an instance of DefaultListModel or an extension thereof.

DefaultListModel

The DefaultListModel class is a concrete (nonabstract) extension of AbstractListModel that implements the java.util.Vector API and delegates data storage and retrieval to an instance of Vector. The DefaultListModel class is summarized in Class Summary 17-2.

Class Summary 17-2   DefaultListModel

Extends: AbstractListModel

Constructors

---

public <u>DefaultListModel</u>()

The DefaultListModel no-argument constructor is compiler generated.

Methods

---

public void <u>add</u>(int, Object)
public void <u>addElement</u>(Object)
public int <u>capacity</u>()
public void <u>clear</u>()
public boolean <u>contains</u>(Object)
public void <u>copyInto</u>(Object[])
public Object <u>elementAt</u>(int)
public Enumeration <u>elements</u>()
public void <u>ensureCapacity</u>(int minCapacity)
public Object <u>firstElement</u>()
public Object <u>get</u>(int)
public Object <u>getElementAt</u>(int index)
public int <u>getSize</u>()
public int <u>indexOf</u>(Object)
public int <u>indexOf</u>(Object element, int)
public void <u>insertElementAt</u>(Object element, int index)
public boolean <u>isEmpty</u>()
public Object <u>lastElement</u>()
public int <u>lastIndexOf</u>(Object element)
public int <u>lastIndexOf</u>(Object element, int index)
public Object <u>remove</u>(int index)
public void <u>removeAllElements</u>()
public boolean <u>removeElement</u>(Object element)
public void <u>removeElementAt</u>(int index)
public void <u>removeRange</u>(int index0, int index1)
public Object <u>set</u>(int index, Object element)
public void <u>setElementAt</u>(Object element, int index)
public void <u>setSize</u>(int size)
public int <u>size</u>()
public Object[] <u>toArray</u>()
public String <u>toString</u>()
public void <u>trimToSize</u>()

DefaultListModel implements the getSize and getElementAt methods
from the ListModel interface and therefore is not an abstract class. The rest of
the methods implemented by DefaultListModel duplicate the
java.util.Vector API and delegate to a vector. Note from Figure 17-2 on page
1011 that the vector is a private member of the DefaultListModel class
because the vector may be changed to a collection in a future Swing release.

The most important aspect of the `DefaultListModel` class is the fact that insertion and removal methods are provided. If objects must be inserted or removed from a list, the list should be fitted with an instance of `DefaultListModel` or a custom extension of `AbstractListModel` that also provides insertion and removal methods.

The applet shown in Figure 17-3 contains a list that is fitted with an instance of `DefaultListModel`. The applet provides buttons for removing the currently selected items in the list and for adding an item to the list.

The upper-left picture in Figure 17-3 shows the applet with two items from the list selected. The upper-right picture shows the applet after the "remove selected items" button has subsequently been activated. The lower-left picture was taken after the "add item" button was activated and the input dialog displayed. The lower-right picture shows the applet after an item has been added to the list.

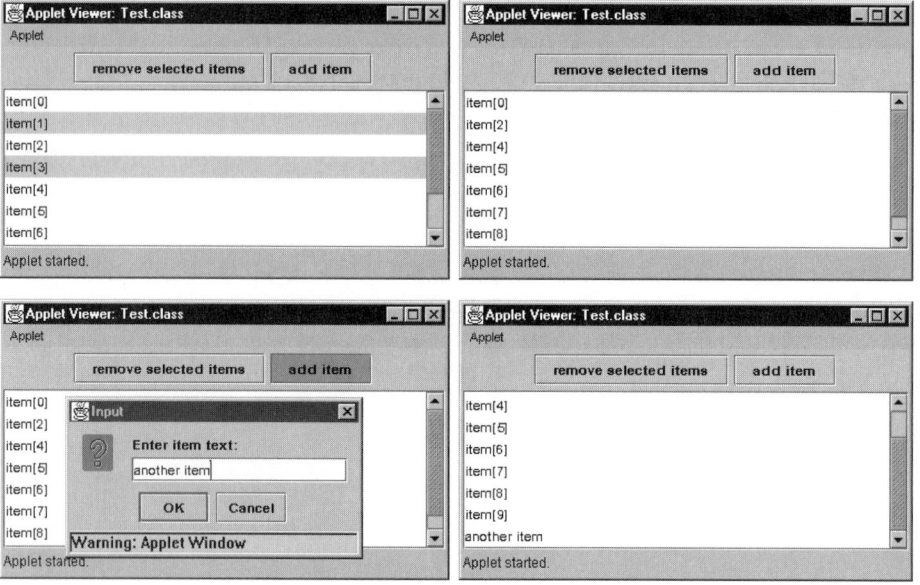

Figure 17-3 A List with a Default List Model

The applet creates a list with the `JList` no-argument constructor that is placed in a scrollpane. An instance of `ControlPanel`—an extension of `JPanel` that contains the applet's buttons—is instantiated, and the control panel and scrollpane are added to the applet's content pane.

An instance of `DefaultListModel` is instantiated, and each string from the array is added to the model. Subsequently, the model is specified as the list's model with the `JList.setModel` method.

```
public class Test extends JApplet {
    private JList list = new JList();

    String[] items = { "item[0]", "item[1]", "item[2]",
                       "item[3]", "item[4]", "item[5]",
                       "item[6]", "item[7]",
                       "item[8]", "item[9]" };

    public void init() {
        // create ControlPanel and add list and control panel
        // to applet's content pane ...

        populateList();
    }
    public void populateList() {
        DefaultListModel model = new DefaultListModel();

        for(int i=0; i < items.length; ++i)
            model.addElement(items[i]);

        list.setModel(model);
    }
}
```

When the remove selected items button is activated, the selected indices in the list are obtained by invocation of the `JList.getSelectedIndices` method, and a reference to the list's model is obtained by invocation of `JList.getModel()`. For each selected index in the list, `DefaultListModel.removeElementAt` is invoked to remove the corresponding string from the list.

```
class ControlPanel extends JPanel {
    JButton remove = new JButton("remove selected items");
    JButton add = new JButton("add item");

    public ControlPanel(final JList list) {
        add(remove);
        add(add);
```

```
remove.addActionListener(new ActionListener() {
    public void actionPerformed(ActionEvent e) {
        int[] selected = list.getSelectedIndices();

        DefaultListModel model =
                    (DefaultListModel)list.getModel();

        for(int i=0; i < selected.length; ++i) {
            model.removeElementAt(selected[i] - i);
        }
    }
});
...
```

When the add item button is activated, JOptionPane.showInputDialog() is invoked to obtain the string that is added to the list. See "JOptionPane" on page 815 for more information concerning JOptionPane and input dialogs.

```
    ...
add.addActionListener(new ActionListener() {
    public void actionPerformed(ActionEvent e) {
        final DefaultListModel model =
                    (DefaultListModel)list.getModel();

        String s = JOptionPane.showInputDialog(
                    list, "Enter item text:");

        model.addElement(s);

        SwingUtilities.invokeLater(new Runnable() {
            public void run() {
                list.ensureIndexIsVisible(
                            model.getSize()-1);
            }
        });
    }
});
    }
}
```

After the dialog is dismissed, the string from the dialog's text field is added to the list's model. After the string is added to the model, JList.ensureIndexIsVisible is invoked to ensure that the new item is visible. The call to ensureIndexIsVisible is wrapped in a Runnable object and executed via SwingUtilities.invokeLater()—see "Swing and

Threads" on page 57 for more information concerning
`SwingUtilities.invokeLater()`. The reason for using `invokeLater()` is
as follows:

Adding data to a list model results in a call to `revalidate()` for the list. The
`revalidate` method places an event on the event queue that causes the list to be
resized to accommodate the new data—see "Validate, Invalidate, and Revalidate
Methods" on page 144 for more information concerning the `revalidate` method.

As a result, the list shown in Figure 17-3 will not be resized until the call to
`addActionListener` returns. If `JList.ensureIndexIsVisible()` is
invoked directly in the `addActionListener` method, the second-last item in the
list will be made visible because the list has not been resized to accommodate the
item added to the list. Wrapping the call to `ensureIndexIsVisible()` in a
`Runnable` that is passed to `SwingUtilities.invokeLater()` ensures that the
call to `ensureIndexIsVisible` is made after the list resize event is handled.

The applet shown in Figure 17-3 is listed in its entirety in Example 17-2.

Example 17-2 • A List with a Default List Model

```
import java.awt.*;
import java.awt.event.*;
import javax.swing.*;
import javax.swing.event.*;

public class Test extends JApplet {
    private JList list = new JList();

    String[] items = { "item[0]", "item[1]", "item[2]",
                       "item[3]", "item[4]", "item[5]",
                       "item[6]", "item[7]",
                       "item[8]", "item[9]" };

    public void init() {
        Container contentPane = getContentPane();
        JPanel controlPanel = new ControlPanel(list);

        contentPane.add(controlPanel, BorderLayout.NORTH);
        contentPane.add(new JScrollPane(list),
                                    BorderLayout.CENTER);
        populateList();
    }
    public void populateList() {
        DefaultListModel model = new DefaultListModel();
```

```
                for(int i=0; i < items.length; ++i)
                    model.addElement(items[i]);

                list.setModel(model);
            }
        }
        class ControlPanel extends JPanel {
            JButton remove = new JButton("remove selected items");
            JButton add = new JButton("add item");

            public ControlPanel(final JList list) {
                add(remove);
                add(add);

                remove.addActionListener(new ActionListener() {
                    public void actionPerformed(ActionEvent e) {
                        int[] selected = list.getSelectedIndices();
                        DefaultListModel model =
                                    (DefaultListModel)list.getModel();

                        for(int i=0; i < selected.length; ++i) {
                            model.removeElementAt(selected[i] - i);
                        }
                    }
                });
                add.addActionListener(new ActionListener() {
                    public void actionPerformed(ActionEvent e) {
                        final DefaultListModel model =
                                    (DefaultListModel)list.getModel();

                        String s = JOptionPane.showInputDialog(
                                    list,
                                    "Enter item text:");

                        model.addElement(s);

                        SwingUtilities.invokeLater(new Runnable() {
                            public void run() {
                                list.ensureIndexIsVisible(
                                            model.getSize()-1);
                            }
                        });
                    }
                });
            }
        }
```

Swing Tip ...

Specifying an Explicit List Model

Data can be associated with instances of JList by specifying an array of objects, a vector, or a list model, either at construction time or any time thereafter. Specifying an array of objects or a vector results in the creation of a simple extension of AbstractListModel that is subsequently associated with the list in question.

Specifying a list model entails instantiating an instance of DefaultListModel—or a custom extension of either AbstractListModel or DefaultListModel—and subsequently passing the model to JList.setModel() or the appropriate JList constructor. Typically, list models are explicitly specified for one of the following reasons:

1. Insertion and/or removal of items from the list is necessary.

2. The data must be represented by a data structure other than a vector or an Object array.

List Selections

In addition to delegating data management to a list model, the JList class also delegates tracking of selected items to a list selection model. The JList class delegates selection management to an object that implements the ListSelectionModel interface. List selection models support three selection modes, as illustrated in Figure 17-4: single, single interval, and multiple interval, from left to right.

item[0]	item[0]	item[0]
item[1]	item[1]	item[1]
item[2]	item[2]	item[2]
item[3]	item[3]	item[3]
item[4]	item[4]	item[4]
item[5]	item[5]	item[5]
item[6]	item[6]	item[6]
item[7]	item[7]	item[7]

Figure 17-4 ListSelectionModel Selection Modes

Single selection mode allows only one item in the list to be selected at any given time. Single interval selection mode allows multiple selections, but the selections must be contiguous. Multiple interval selection mode allows multiple contiguous intervals of selected items. The default selection mode for instances of JList is multiple interval selection.The ListSelectionModel interface is summarized in Interface Summary 17-2.

Interface Summary 17-2   ListSelectionModel

Constants

---

public static final int <u>MULTIPLE INTERVAL SELECTION</u>
public static final int <u>SINGLE INTERVAL SELECTION</u>
public static final int <u>SINGLE SELECTION</u>

The ListSelectionModel interface defines constants for its selection modes. ListSelectionModel also defines methods for adding and removing selection intervals, clearing selection, and setter and getter methods for the following selection properties: anchor, lead, max, min and valueIsAdjusting. JList selection properties are discussed in "JList Properties" on page 1035.

Methods[1]

---

public abstract void <u>addListSelectionListener</u>(ListSelectionListener)

---

1.   Italicized methods are implemented by the JList class.

public abstract void <u>addSelectionInterval</u>(int, int)
public abstract void <u>clearSelection</u>()
public abstract int <u>getAnchorSelectionIndex</u>()
public abstract int <u>getLeadSelectionIndex</u>()
public abstract int <u>getMaxSelectionIndex</u>()
public abstract int <u>getMinSelectionIndex</u>()
public abstract int <u>getSelectionMode</u>()
public abstract boolean <u>getValueIsAdjusting</u>()
public abstract void <u>insertIndexInterval</u>(int, int, boolean)
public abstract boolean <u>isSelectedIndex</u>(int)
public abstract boolean <u>isSelectionEmpty</u>()
public abstract void <u>removeIndexInterval</u>(int, int)
public abstract void <u>removeListSelectionListener</u>(ListSelectionListener)
public abstract void <u>removeSelectionInterval</u>(int index0, int index1)
public abstract void <u>setAnchorSelectionIndex</u>(int)
public abstract void <u>setLeadSelectionIndex</u>(int)
public abstract void <u>setSelectionInterval</u>(int index0, int index1)
public abstract void <u>setSelectionMode</u>(int)
public abstract void <u>setValueIsAdjusting</u>(boolean)

By default, instances of `JList` are fitted with an instance of `DefaultListSelectionModel`, which is the only implementation of the `ListSelectionModel` interface provided by Swing. A class diagram for the `DefaultListSelectionModel` class is shown in Figure 17-5.

The `DefaultListSelectionModel` class extends `Object` and implements the `Cloneable`, `Serializable`, and `ListSelectionModel` interfaces. `DefaultListSelectionModel` maintains a number of `private` references for tracking selection state and an `EventListenerList` that tracks list selection listeners.

Unlike list models, list selection models will rarely be implemented or directly manipulated by developers. The reasons for this are twofold.

First, the three selection modes provided by the default list selection model are sufficient for nearly all uses of the `JList` class. As a result, developers will rarely need to implement their own list selection models to provide alternative selection modes. This is in contrast to custom list models that are frequently implemented to allow insertion and removal of items in a list.

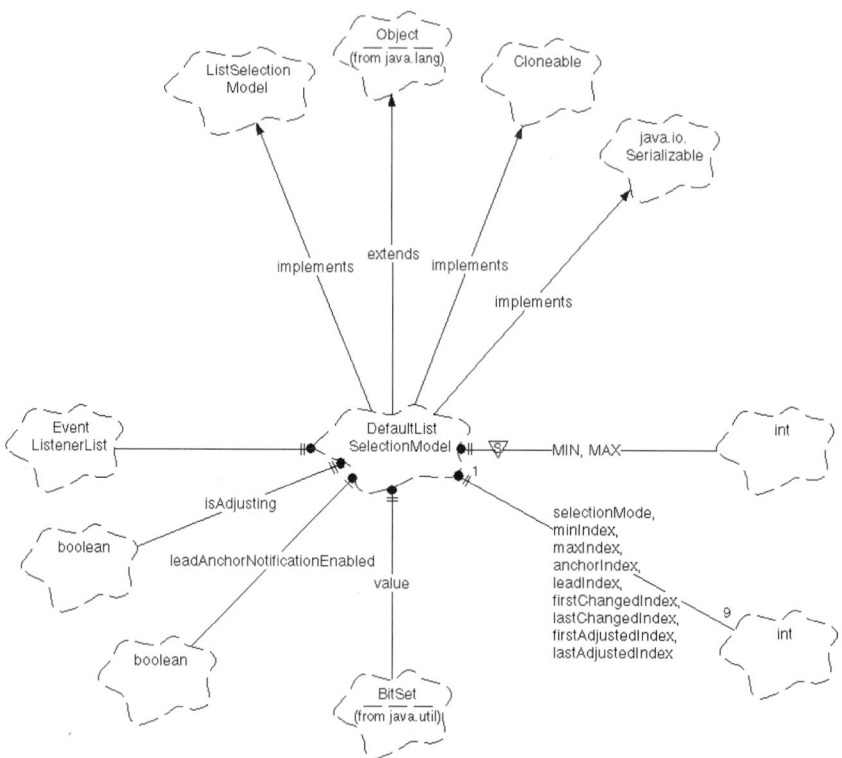

Figure 17-5 DefaultListSelectionModel Class Diagram

Second, nearly all of the methods defined by the `ListSelectionModel` interface are implemented by the `JList` class itself by delegating to the list's selection model. As a result, unlike the case with list models, it is not necessary to access the list selection model directly to modify the selection state for a list. The methods defined by the `ListModel` interface are not implemented by the `JList` class.

See "List Selection Events" on page 1040 for a discussion of handling list selection events.

List Models vs. List Selection Models

Unlike most Swing components, the JList class has two models: a list model and a list selection model defined by the ListModel and ListSelectionModel interfaces, respectively. Both models are accessible with the JList.getModel and JList.getSelectionModel methods.

The JList class implements all of the methods defined by the ListSelectionModel interface by delegating to its selection model. As a result, a selection model can be manipulated without being directly accessed by JList methods. On the other hand, the JList class does not implement the methods defined by the ListModel interface, and therefore list data can only be directly manipulated by accessing a lists model.

Another difference between list models and list selection models is that the default list selection model (ListSelectionModel) is used much more frequently than the default list model (AbstractListModel). Because AbstractListModel does not provide methods for inserting and removing items, list models are frequently explicitly specified. On the other hand, DefaultListSelectionModel provides nearly everything that most lists will desire; as a result, custom list selection models are rarely implemented.

List Cell Renderers

In addition to delegating data management and selection, the JList class delegates the rendering of its cells to another object. Each instance of JList maintains a reference to an object that implements that ListCellRenderer interface, which is summarized in Interface Summary 17-3.

Interface Summary 17-3   ListCellRenderer

The ListCellRenderer interface defines a single method that returns a component:

public abstract Component <u>getListCellRendererComponent</u>(JList list,
Object value,
int index,
boolean isSelected,
boolean cellHasFocus)

The component returned by `getListCellRendererComponent` acts like a rubber stamp by painting the component into the region occupied by items in a list. Notice that the component is not *contained* in list cells but instead is *painted into* them. The distinction is important because the component cannot be manipulated; only the visual representation of the component is used to paint list cells.

The `getListCellRendererComponent` method is passed a list, the value associated with a cell, the index of the cell, and information as to whether the cell is selected or has focus.

By default, instances of `JList` are fitted with a renderer that is a simple implementation of the `ListCellRenderer` interface—the `DefaultListCellRenderer` class. `DefaultListCellRenderer` extends `JLabel` and can display either a string or an icon (but not both in the same cell). Objects other than strings or icons are handled by displaying the string returned from the object's `toString` method. If the need arises to render list cells in a different fashion, a custom list cell renderer must be implemented and an instance of the renderer must be associated with the list in question.

The `DefaultListCellRenderer` class is summarized in Class Summary 17-3.

Class Summary 17-3   DefaultListCellRenderer

Extends: JLabel
Implements: ListCellRenderer, java.io.Serializable

Constructors

---

public <u>DefaultListCellRenderer</u>()

`DefaultListCellRenderer` provides a single no-argument constructor and implements the `getListCellRendererComponent` method to return the renderer itself—recall that `DefaultListCellRenderer` extends `JLabel`.

Methods

---

public Component <u>getListCellRendererComponent</u>(JList list,
                                        Object value,
                                        int index,
                                        boolean isSelected,
                                        boolean cellHasFocus)

`DefaultListCellRenderer` maintains a `static noFocusBorder` that is an empty border—an instance of `swing.border.EmptyBorder`—that takes up one pixel around the edge of the renderer. The border is `static` because one border can be shared among any number of components, and therefore all instances of `DefaultListCellRenderer` use the same border. See "The Border Factory—Sharing Borders" on page 216 for more information on sharing borders.

Perhaps it does not need to be stated, but the `noFocusBorder` is used when the renderer does not have focus. When the renderer does have focus, a border is obtained from the `UIManager` class:

```
// from DefaultListCellRenderer.getDefaultListCellRendererCom-
   ponent()

setBorder((cellHasFocus) ?
   UIManager.getBorder("List.focusCellHighlightBorder") :
   noFocusBorder);
```

See "UI Manager" on page 334 for more information concerning the `UIManager` class and the installation of default borders and colors.

The applet shown in Figure 17-6 contains a list that is fitted with a custom list cell renderer that can display an icon and a string in the same cell. As is often the case, the applet implements a custom list model that works in concert with the custom renderer.

The applet creates two string arrays, one representing the strings displayed in the cells and another representing file names of images for the icons.

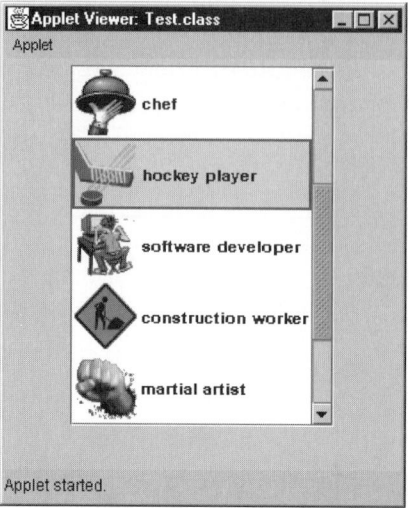

Figure 17-6 Implementing Custom List Cell Renderers

The applet also creates instances of NameAndPictureListModel and
NameAndPictureListCellRenderer, which are specified as the list's model
and renderer respectively.

```
public class Test extends JApplet {
    private String[] names = new String[] {
        ...
    };
    private String[] pics = new String[] {
        ...
    };

    public void init() {
        Container contentPane = getContentPane();

        ListModel model =
                    new NameAndPictureListModel(names, pics);

        ListCellRenderer renderer =
                    new NameAndPictureListCellRenderer();

        JList list = new JList(model);
```

```
        list.setCellRenderer(renderer);
        list.setVisibleRowCount(5);

        contentPane.setLayout(new FlowLayout());
        contentPane.add(new JScrollPane(list));
    }
}
```

The NameAndPictureListModel class extends DefaultListModel and is constructed with an array of names and an array of image file names. Each of the file names is used to construct icons, and the name/icon pairs are stored in the model as an Object array with two elements.

The NameAndPictureListModel class also provides accessors for the names and icons, given an Object representing an item stored in the model. The accessors are provided so that the renderer does not need to know how the names and icons are stored in the model.

```
class NameAndPictureListModel extends DefaultListModel {
    public NameAndPictureListModel(String[] names,
                                             String[] pics) {

        for(int i=0; i < names.length; ++i) {
            addElement(new Object[] {
                        names[i], new ImageIcon(pics[i]) } );
        }
    }
    public String getName(Object object) {
        Object[] array = (Object[])object;
        return (String)array[0];
    }
    public Icon getIcon(Object object) {
        Object[] array = (Object[])object;
        return (Icon)array[1];
    }
}
```

The NameAndPictureListCellRenderer class extends JLabel and implements the ListCellRenderer interface. Two borders are constructed; their use depends upon whether a list cell has focus.

The NameAndPictureListCellRenderer constructor sets the opaque property to true because, by default, instances of JLabel are not opaque.

```
class NameAndPictureListCellRenderer extends JLabel
                             implements ListCellRenderer {
   private Border
      lineBorder = BorderFactory.createLineBorder(Color.red, 2),
      emptyBorder = BorderFactory.createEmptyBorder(2,2,2,2);

   public NameAndPictureListCellRenderer() {
      setOpaque(true);
   }
   ...
```

The getListCellRendererComponent method obtains a reference to the list's model and obtains the name and icon associated with the value of the cell. The name and icon are passed to the JLabel.setText and JLabel.setIcon methods—recall that the NameAndPictureListCellRenderer class extends JLabel.

```
   public Component getListCellRendererComponent(
                         JList list,
                         Object value,
                         int index,
                         boolean isSelected,
                         boolean cellHasFocus) {
      NameAndPictureListModel model =
                (NameAndPictureListModel)list.getModel();

      setText(model.getName(value));
      setIcon(model.getIcon(value));
      ...
```

If the cell is selected, the background and foreground colors are set to the selection background and foreground colors, which are obtained by invocation of JList.getSelectionBackground() and JList.getSelectionForeground(), respectively.

If the cell has focus, the label's border is set to the line border; if not, the border is set to the empty border.

The getListCellRendererComponent method returns a reference to the renderer itself, which extends the JLabel class.

```
      ...
      if(isSelected) {
         setForeground(list.getSelectionForeground());
         setBackground(list.getSelectionBackground());
      }
```

```
        else {
            setForeground(list.getForeground());
            setBackground(list.getBackground());
        }

        if(cellHasFocus)  setBorder(lineBorder);
        else              setBorder(emptyBorder);

        return this;
    }
}
```

It should be noted that implementing custom renderers that extend a component class, such as JLabel, is an idiom implemented by default Swing renderers. However, custom renderers need not be components themselves. For example, the custom renderer implemented in the previous example could have extended Object and contained an instance of JLabel, which would be returned from the getListCellRendererComponent method.

The applet shown in Figure 17-6 is listed in its entirety in Example 17-3.

Example 17-3 Implementing a Custom List Cell Renderer

```
import java.awt.*;
import java.awt.event.*;
import javax.swing.*;
import javax.swing.border.*;

public class Test extends JApplet {
    private String[] names = new String[] {
        "baseball player", "basketball player",
        "beach player", "chef",
        "hockey player","software developer",
        "construction worker", "martial artist",
        "soccer", "movie star"
    };
    private String[] pics = new String[] {
        "baseball.gif", "basketball.gif",
        "beach_umbrella.gif", "dining.gif",
        "hockey.gif", "mad_hacker.gif",
        "men_at_work.gif", "punch.gif",
        "soccer.gif", "filmstrip.gif"
    };

    public void init() {
        Container contentPane = getContentPane();
        ListModel model =
                    new NameAndPictureListModel(names, pics);

        ListCellRenderer renderer =
```

```
                                new NameAndPictureListCellRenderer();

        JList list = new JList(model);

        list.setCellRenderer(renderer);
        list.setVisibleRowCount(5);

        contentPane.setLayout(new FlowLayout());
        contentPane.add(new JScrollPane(list));
    }
}
class NameAndPictureListModel extends DefaultListModel {
    public NameAndPictureListModel(String[] names,
                                            String[] pics) {
        for(int i=0; i < names.length; ++i) {
            addElement(new Object[] {
                    names[i], new ImageIcon(pics[i]) } );
        }
    }
    public String getName(Object object) {
        Object[] array = (Object[])object;
        return (String)array[0];
    }
    public Icon getIcon(Object object) {
        Object[] array = (Object[])object;
        return (Icon)array[1];
    }
}
class NameAndPictureListCellRenderer extends JLabel
                            implements ListCellRenderer {
    private Border
        lineBorder = BorderFactory.createLineBorder(Color.red, 2),
        emptyBorder = BorderFactory.createEmptyBorder(2,2,2,2);

    public NameAndPictureListCellRenderer() {
        setOpaque(true);
    }
    public Component getListCellRendererComponent(
                            JList list,
                            Object value,
                            int index,
                            boolean isSelected,
                            boolean cellHasFocus) {
        NameAndPictureListModel model =
                    (NameAndPictureListModel)list.getModel();

        setText(model.getName(value));
        setIcon(model.getIcon(value));

        if(isSelected) {
            setForeground(list.getSelectionForeground());
            setBackground(list.getSelectionBackground());
        }
```

```
    else {
        setForeground(list.getForeground());
        setBackground(list.getBackground());
    }

    if(cellHasFocus) setBorder(lineBorder);
    else             setBorder(emptyBorder);

    return this;
    }
}
```

Swing Tip ...

Cell Renderer Components Are for Looks Only

All Swing cell renderers return a component that is painted into a cell. It's important to realize that renderer components cannot be manipulated; they are simply used to paint a cell.

The JList component is summarized in Component Summary 17-1.

Component Summary 17-1 JList

Model(s)	AbstractListModel
UI Delegate(s)	javax.swing.plaf.basic.BasicListUI
Renderer(s)	DefaultListCellRenderer
Editor(s)	——
Events Fired	PropertyChangeEvents, ListSelectionEvents, ListDataEvents[2]
Replacement For	java.awt.List

2. Fired by list models

Class Diagrams

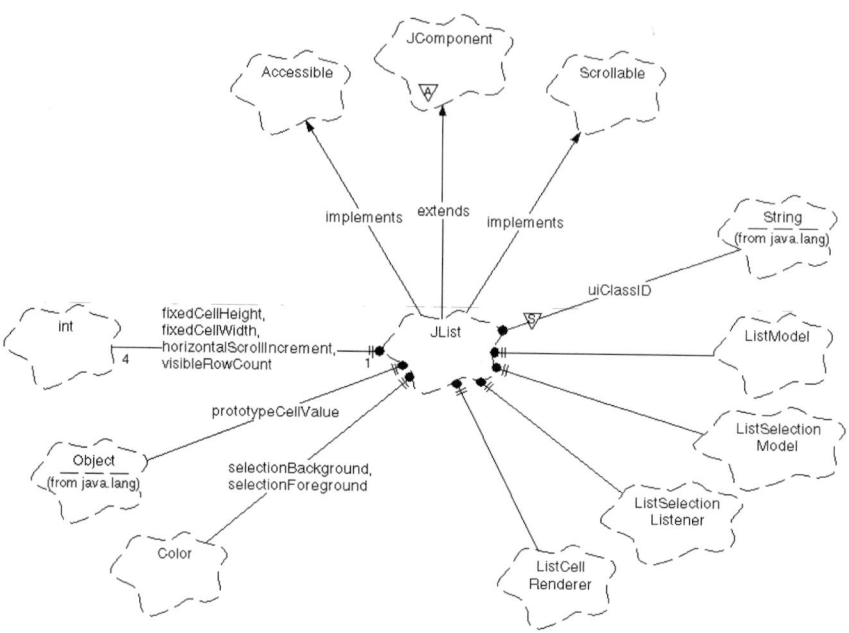

Figure 17-7 JList Class Diagram

The JList class extends JComponent, implements the Accessible and Scrollable interfaces, and maintains references to its model, selection model, and renderer.

The JList class maintains a reference to a ListSelectionListener that is added to the selection model so that lists can react to selections by forwarding events to list selection listeners that have registered with the list itself.

The JList class also keeps track of its selection background and foreground colors. The colors are actually set by the list's UI delegate, but the list maintains the values. References are also maintained to the prototypeCellValue—see "Handling List Selection Events" on page 1050—and a set of four integer values that track the fixed cell width and height, the visible row count, and the pixel increment for scrolling in the horizontal direction.

JList Properties

The properties maintained by the JList class are listed in Table 17-2.

Table 17-2 JList Properties

Property Name	Data Type	Property Type[1]	Access[2]	Default[3]
anchorSelectionIndex	int	S	G	−1
cellBounds	Rectangle	S	G	——
cellRenderer	ListCell-Renderer	B	SG	DefaultListCell-Renderer
firstVisibleIndex	int	S	G	——
fixedCellHeight	int	B	SG	−1
fixedCellWidth	int	B	SG	−1
lastVisibleIndex	int	S	G	——
leadSelectionIndex	int	S	G	−1
listData	Object[]/Vector	B	S	null
maxSelectionIndex	int	S	G	Integer.MAX_VALUE
minSelectionIndex	int	S	G	−1
model	ListModel	B	CSG	AbstractListModel
preferredScrollable-ViewportSize	Dimension	S	G	see discussion below
prototypeCellValue	Object	B	SG	null
scrollableBlockIncrement	int	S	G	see discussion below
scrollableTracks-ViewportHeight	boolean	S	G	see discussion below
scrollableTracks-ViewportWidth	boolean	S	G	see discussion below
scrollableUnitIncrement	int	S	G	see discussion below
selectedIndex	int	B	SG	−1
selectedIndicies	int[]	B	SG	int[0]
selectedValue	Object	B	SG	null
selectedValues	Object[]	S	G	Object[0]
selectionBackground	Color	B	SG	see discussion below

Table 17-2 JList Properties (Continued)

Property Name	Data Type	Property Type[1]	Access[2]	Default[3]
selectionEmpty	boolean	S	G	true
selectionForeground	Color	B	SG	see discussion below
selectedIndex	boolean	S	SG	−1
selectionInterval	int,int	B	S	——
selectionMode	int	S	SG	MULTIPLE_ INTERVAL_ SELECTION
selectionModel	List- Selection- Model	B	SG	DefaultListSelection- Model
valueIsAdjusting	boolean	B	SG	false
visibleRowCount	int	B	SG	8

1. B = bound (fires PropertyChangeEvent) / C = constrained/ I = indexed /
   S = simple / Ch = fires ChangeEvent
2. C = settable at construction time / G = getter method / S = setter method
3. L&F = look-and-feel dependent

anchorSelectionIndex — The index that anchored the most recent interval selection or deselection. If a single item is selected, the anchorSelectionIndex will be the same as the leadSelectionIndex. If an interval of items is selected by a user selecting a single item and subsequently Shift-clicking on another item, the anchorSelectionIndex will be equal to the index of first item selected.

cellBounds — A rectangle representing the bounds occupied by an interval of list cells. The getCellBounds method is passed two indexes representing individual cells within a list. The method can be passed the same value for both indexes to ascertain the bounds occupied by a single list cell.

cellRenderer — An object that renders the cells contained in a list. By a default, instances of JList are fitted with an instance of DefaultListCellRenderer, which can display any type of object, although objects other than strings and icons are represented by the string returned from their toString method.

firstVisibleIndex — The index of the first visible—wholly or partially—cell at the top of the list. Returns −1 if the list is empty.

fixedCellHeight — By default, the height of a list cell is as tall as its tallest item. A list's height can be set to a fixed pixel value by setFixedCellHeight() or by a prototype component provided by invocation of setPrototypeCellValue().

See the prototypeCellValue and fixedCellWidth properties.

fixedCellWidth — By default, the width of a list is as wide as its widest item. A list's width can be set to a fixed pixel value by setFixedCellWidth() or by a prototype component provided by invocation of invoking setPrototypeCellValue().

See the prototypeCellValue and fixedCellHeight properties.

lastVisibleIndex — The index of the last visible—wholly or partially—cell at the bottom of the list. Returns −1 if the list is empty.

See the firstVisibleIndex property.

listData — A write-only property representing the data displayed in the list that can be specified as either an Object array or a vector.

maxSelectionIndex — The index of the bottom-most selected cell. For example, if indexes 2, 6, 9 were selected in a list, the max selection index would be 9.

minSelectionIndex — The index of the topmost selected cell. For example, if indexes 2, 6, 9 were selected in a list, the max selection index would be 2.

model — An implementation of the ListModel interface, which maintains the data displayed in a list's cells.

preferredScrollableViewportSize — The preferred size of a list that is placed in a viewport, which typically resides in an instance of JScrollPane. The preferred height specified is the height required to display the number of rows specified by the visibleRowCount property (settable by the JList.setVisibleRowCount method). By default, the visibleRowCount property is set to 8.

See the visibleRowCount, scrollableBlockIncrement, scrollableTracksViewportWidth, and scrollableTracksViewportHeight properties.

prototypeCellValue — Instead of allowing a list to be sized so that its width will accommodate its widest item, an object can be specified as a prototype cell value. When the prototypeCellValue property—which is null by default—is specified, the list's fixedCellWidth and fixedCellHeight properties are set to the preferred width and preferred height respectively, of the prototypeCellValue object. Additionally, the list's font is set to the font used by the prototypeCellValue object.

See the fixedCellWidth and fixedCellHeight properties.

scrollableBlockIncrement — When a list resides in a scrollpane and is scrolled by a block increment, the list is scrolled by the number of pixels returned from JList.getScrollbleBlockIncrement(). By default, the block increment is set so that the list is scrolled by the number of visible items.

The getScrollableBlockIncrement method is defined by the Scrollable interface. See "The Scrollable Interface" on page 764 for more information concerning the Scrollable interface.

See the visibleRowCount, preferredScrollableViewportSize, scrollableTracksViewportWidth, and scrollableTracksViewportHeight properties.

scrollableTracksViewportHeight — The height of a scrollable component can be forced to match the height of the viewport in which the component resides by returning true from the getScrollableTracksViewportHeight method. See "The Scrollable Interface" on page 764 for more information concerning the Scrollable interface.

The JList class sets its scrollableTracksViewportHeight property to false to ensure that its contents can be scrolled vertically.

scrollableTracksViewportWidth — The width of a scrollable component can be forced to match the width of the viewport in which the component resides by returning true from the getScrollableTracksViewportWidth method.

The JList class sets its scrollableTracksViewportWidth property to false to ensure that its contents can be scrolled horizontally.

scrollableUnitIncrement — The scrollableUnitIncrement property specifies how many pixels a list will be scrolled by when it is scrolled by a unit increment.

By default, for vertical scrolling, the unit increment is the number of pixels required to scroll the next cell into view.

For horizontal scrolling, that unit increment is set to the size of the list's font or 1 if the list has a `null` font. For lists that display text with a fixed width font, scrolling in the horizontal direction will expose the next character.

selectedIndex — The `selectedIndex` property is the same as the `minIndex` property.

selectedIndices — An array of `integer` values representing indices of the selected cells in the list.

selectedValue — The first selected value in a list.

selectedValues — An array of `Object` references representing the selected items in a list.

selectionBackground — The background color used for the background of selected cells. The color is set by the list's UI delegate, but it is maintained by the list.

selectionEmpty — A read-only `boolean` property that signifies whether a list has any selected items.

selectionForeground — The foreground color used for the foreground of selected cells. The color is set by the list's UI delegate, but it is maintained by the list.

selectedIndex — The index of the first selected item in a list.

selectionInterval — A selection interval specified by `setSelectionInterval(int anchor, int lead)` or `addSelectionInterval(int anchor, int lead)`.

See "JList Class Summaries" on page 1062 for a discussion of the `setSelectionInterval` and `addSelectionInterval` methods.

selectionMode — The selection mode for a list. Selection modes are discussed in "List Selections" on page 1021.

selectionModel — The selection model for a list. By default, lists are fitted with an instance of `AbstractListModel` and not `DefaultListModel`. The `setSelectionModel` method may be invoked anytime after a list is constructed to set the selection model.

valueIsAdjusting — A `boolean` property that indicates whether the current selection event was fired when the mouse was being dragged over items in the list. If the mouse is being dragged, the `valueIsAdjusting` property is `true`; otherwise, it is `false`.

Note: *A bug in Swing1.1 FCS erroneously reports mouse clicks that are qualified with either the Shift or Ctrl keys as adjusting.*

`visibleRowCount` — The number of visible rows displayed when a list is contained in a viewport. Setting the `visibleRowCount` property has no effect if a list is not contained in a viewport.

JList Events

The `JList` class fires two types of events: `PropertyChangeEvents` and `ListSelectionEvents`. In addition, `ListDataEvents` are fired by the list's model when list data is modified.

List Selection Events

List selection events are handled by objects that implement the `ListSelectionListener` interface, which is summarized in Interface Summary 17-4.

Interface Summary 17-4   ListSelectionListener

---

public abstract void <u>valueChanged</u>(ListSelectionEvent)

The `valueChanged` method is invoked for list selection listeners when a list's selection changes. The method is passed a reference to a `ListSelectionEvent`.

The `ListSelectionEvent` class is summarized in Class Summary 17-4.

Class Summary 17-4   ListSelectionEvent

Extends: java.util.EventObject

Constructors

---

public <u>ListSelectionEvent</u>(Object source, int firstIndex, int lastIndex,
                        boolean valueIsAdjusting)

`ListSelectionEvents` are constructed with a reference to the source of the
event, the first index and last indexes that changed, and a `boolean` variable
indicating whether the event is one of a rapid series of events. The
`valueIsAdjusting` parameter is `true` when the mouse is being dragged over
list items, and `false` when the mouse button is released.

Methods

---

public int <u>getFirstIndex</u>()
public int <u>getLastIndex</u>()
public boolean <u>getValueIsAdjusting</u>()
public String <u>toString</u>()

The methods implemented by the `ListSelectionEvent` class are accessors for
the values passed to the `ListSelectionEvent` constructor. The `toString`
method returns a string representing the event and is useful for event logging and
debugging.

The applet shown in Figure 17-8 illustrates selection events that have adjusting
values. As the cursor is dragged over the first three items, list selection events are
fired whose values are adjusting. The lower-right picture was taken after the
mouse button was released, resulting in a selection event whose value was not
adjusting.

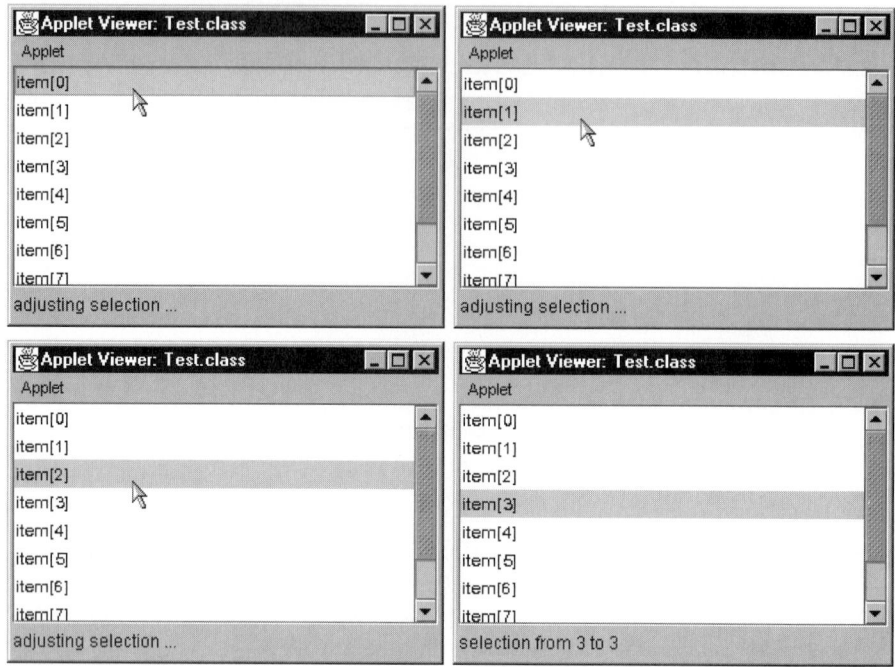

Figure 17-8 Adjusting Values for List Selections

The applet shown in Figure 17-8 is listed in Example 17-4.

Example 17-4 Detecting Adjusting Values for List Selections

```
import java.awt.*;
import javax.swing.*;
import javax.swing.event.*;

public class Test extends JApplet {
    public void init() {
        Container contentPane = getContentPane();

        String[] items = { "item[0]", "item[1]", "item[2]",
                    "item[3]", "item[4]", "item[5]",
                    "item[6]", "item[7]",
                    "item[8]", "item[9]" };

        JList list = new JList(items);

        contentPane.add(new JScrollPane(list),
                    BorderLayout.CENTER);

        list.addListSelectionListener(
                            new ListSelectionListener() {
            public void valueChanged(ListSelectionEvent e) {
                String s;

                if(e.getValueIsAdjusting()) {
                    s = "adjusting selection ...";
                }
                else {
                    s = "selection from " + e.getFirstIndex() +
                    " to " + e.getLastIndex();
                }
                showStatus(s);
            }
        });
    }
}
```

The applet creates a list wrapped in a scrollpane and adds a list selection listener to the list. The listener displays an appropriate string in the applet's content pane, depending upon whether the value associated with the event is adjusting.

Reacting to List Selections

There are two ways to register as a listener for list selection events: register directly with a list by invoking the addListSelectionListener method from the JList class, or register with a list's selection listener by invoking the method of the same name from the ListSelectionModel class. The fact that list selection models are accessible via the JList.getSelectionModel method affords the latter approach.

The only difference between registering with a list vs. the list's model is the source of the ListSelectionEvent passed to the ListSelectionListener.valueChanged method—the source of the event is the object with which the listener registered.

The applet shown in Figure 17-9 contains a list and a panel. The panel contains a combo box for selecting the list's selection mode and labels that show the current selection properties for the list.

Selection properties and their meanings are recapped in Table 17-3.

Table 17-3   JList Selection Properties

Property	Meaning
anchor	the index that most recently anchored an interval selection
lead	the last index of the most recently specified selection interval
maximum	the highest index from the selected items
minimum	the lowest index from the selected items

The four pictures shown in Figure 17-9 were taken when the selection mode for the list was set to multiple interval selection. Each picture shows different sets of selected items and the corresponding values of the selection properties. The pictures were created by the following sequence of mouse clicks, in the order that they are listed.

> Top-Left Picture:
> > Click on item[1]

> Top-Right Picture:
> > Shift-Click on item[3]

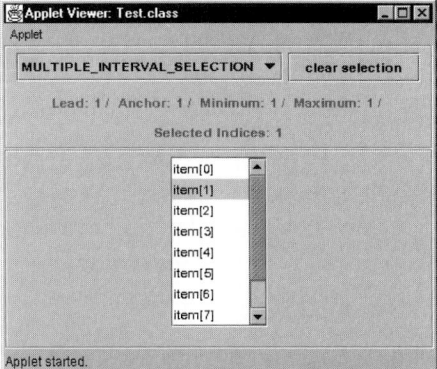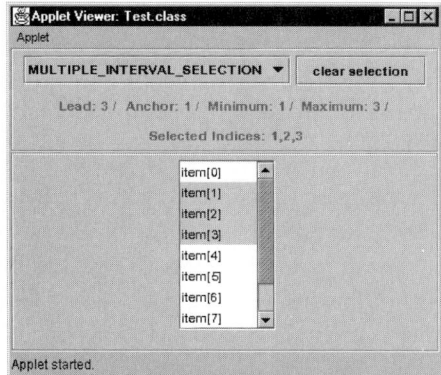
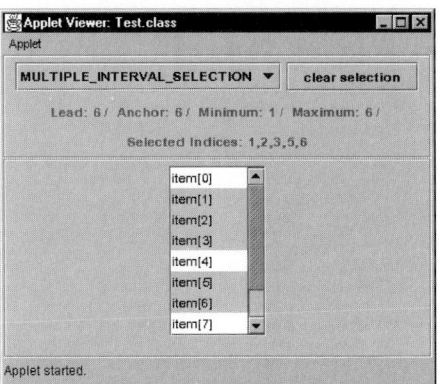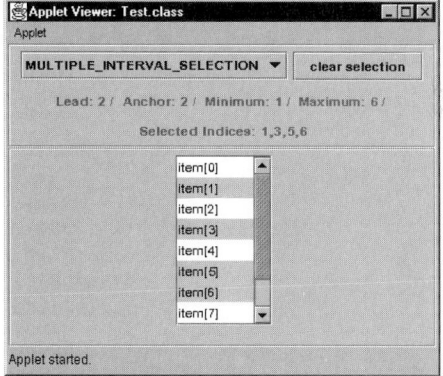

Figure 17-9 List Selections

Bottom-Left Picture:
    Ctrl-Click on item[5]
    Ctrl-Click on item[6]

Bottom-Right Picture:
    Ctrl-Click on item[2]

Unadorned mouse clicks clear the current selection (if any) and select the item that was clicked on. Shift-clicks set the lead index to the item that was clicked on, and Ctrl-clicks add (if the item was not selected) or remove (if the item was selected) the item to the list's set of selected items.

The applet creates a list and a control panel containing the combo box, button, and labels. The list is wrapped in a scrollpane, and the control panel and scrollpane are added to the applet's content pane. A list selection listener is added to the list to update the control panel whenever the selection state of the list is modified.

The applet also invokes JList.setPrototypeCellValue(Object), which sets the width of the list to the width of the specified object. By default, instances of JList are sized horizontally so that the list is as wide as its widest item. By means of the setPrototypeCellValue method, the width of a list can be explicitly controlled, and a performance increase in rendering lists of significant lengths can be realized.

```
public class Test extends JApplet {
    private ControlPanel controlPanel;

    public void init() {
        Container contentPane = getContentPane();
        JPanel listPanel = new JPanel();

        String[] items = { "item[0]", "item[1]", "item[2]",
                     "item[3]", "item[4]", "item[5]",
                     "item[6]", "item[7]",
                     "item[8]", "item[9]" };

        JList list = new JList(items);

        list.setPrototypeCellValue("MMMMMMM");

        controlPanel = new ControlPanel(list);
        controlPanel.update();

        listPanel.setBorder(BorderFactory.createEtchedBorder());
        listPanel.add(new JScrollPane(list));

        contentPane.add(controlPanel, BorderLayout.NORTH);
        contentPane.add(listPanel, BorderLayout.CENTER);

        list.addListSelectionListener(
                            new ListSelectionListener() {
            public void valueChanged(ListSelectionEvent e) {
                controlPanel.update();
            }
        });
    }
}
```

The `ControlPanel` class extends `JPanel` and creates the combo box, button, and labels, which are added to three panels contained in the control panel.

The combo box is initialized with the `initializeSelectionMode` method (listed below), and an item listener that is added to the combo box sets the selection mode when an item is selected.

An action listener that is added to the clear button invokes `JList.clearSelection()` when the button is activated.

```
class ControlPanel extends JPanel {
    private JComboBox mode = new JComboBox();
    private JButton clear = new JButton("clear selection");

    private String single = "SINGLE_SELECTION",
             singleInterval = "SINGLE_INTERVAL_SELECTION",
             multipleInterval = "MULTIPLE_INTERVAL_SELECTION";

    private JLabel  leadLabel = new JLabel(),
              anchorLabel = new JLabel(),
              minLabel = new JLabel(),
              maxLabel = new JLabel(),
              selIndicesLabel = new JLabel();

    private JList list;

    public ControlPanel(JList l) {
        // create three panels ...

        this.list = l;

        // add combo box, button, and labels to the panels
        // created above ...

        mode.addItem(single);
        mode.addItem(singleInterval);
        mode.addItem(multipleInterval);

        initializeSelectionMode();
        ...
        mode.addItemListener(new ItemListener() {
            public void itemStateChanged(ItemEvent e) {
                if(e.getStateChange() == ItemEvent.SELECTED)
                    setSelectionMode((String)e.getItem());
            }
        });
        clear.addActionListener(new ActionListener() {
            public void actionPerformed(ActionEvent e) {
                list.clearSelection();
            }
        });
    }
```

The `initializeSelectionMode` method is invoked from the `ControlPanel` constructor and sets the selected item in the combo box, depending upon the initial selection mode of the list.

```
...
private void initializeSelectionMode() {
    int m = list.getSelectionMode();

    switch(m) {
        case ListSelectionModel.SINGLE_SELECTION:
            mode.setSelectedItem(single);
            break;
        case ListSelectionModel.SINGLE_INTERVAL_SELECTION:
            mode.setSelectedItem(singleInterval);
            break;
        case ListSelectionModel.MULTIPLE_INTERVAL_SELECTION:
            mode.setSelectedItem(multipleInterval);
            break;
    }
}
...
```

Note that the `initializeSelectionMode` goes above and beyond the call of duty to initialize the combo box because the default selection mode for instances of `JList` is known (`MULTIPLE_SELECTION_MODE`), and therefore the combo box could be initialized without querying the list for its selection mode. However, that would be relying upon an implementation detail of the `JList` class rather than upon the `JList` API.[3] As it stands, the `initializeSelectionMode` method will continue to work correctly if the default selection mode for instances of `JList` is modified in the future.

The `setSelectionMode` method is invoked when a selection is made from the combo box and is passed the string that was selected. The method sets the selection mode for the list, depending upon the string it is passed.

```
...
private void setSelectionMode(String s) {
    if(s.equals("SINGLE_SELECTION")) {
        list.setSelectionMode(
            ListSelectionModel.SINGLE_SELECTION);
    }
    else if(s.equals("SINGLE_INTERVAL_SELECTION")) {
        list.setSelectionMode(
```

3. Good object-oriented design does not rely upon implementation details of a class.

```
                ListSelectionModel.SINGLE_INTERVAL_SELECTION);
        }
        else if(s.equals("MULTIPLE_INTERVAL_SELECTION")) {
            list.setSelectionMode(
                ListSelectionModel.MULTIPLE_INTERVAL_SELECTION);
        }
    }
    . . .
```

The `update` method is invoked when the selection state of the list is modified. The `lead`, `min`, `max`, and `anchor` selection properties are obtained from the list, and the labels contained in the control panel are updated. After the labels are updated, `validate()` is invoked for the control panel, causing the panel to be laid out. The call to `validate()` is necessary in the event that the length of the strings displayed by the labels is modified.

```
    . . .
    public void update() {
        int lead = list.getLeadSelectionIndex(),
            min = list.getMinSelectionIndex(),
            max = list.getMaxSelectionIndex(),
            anchor = list.getAnchorSelectionIndex();

        leadLabel.setText(Integer.toString(lead) + " / ");
        anchorLabel.setText(Integer.toString(anchor) + " / ");
        minLabel.setText(Integer.toString(min) + " / ");
        maxLabel.setText(Integer.toString(max) + " / ");

        int[] selected = list.getSelectedIndices();
        String s = new String();

        for(int i = 0; i < selected.length; ++i) {
            s += Integer.toString(selected[i]);

            if(i < selected.length-1)
                s += ",";
        }
        selIndicesLabel.setText(s);
        validate();
    }
    . . .
```

The applet shown in Figure 17-9 is listed in its entirety in Example 17-5.

Example 17-5 Handling List Selection Events

```java
import java.awt.*;
import java.awt.event.*;
import javax.swing.*;
import javax.swing.event.*;

public class Test extends JApplet {
    private ControlPanel controlPanel;

    public void init() {
        Container contentPane = getContentPane();
        JPanel listPanel = new JPanel();

        String[] items = { "item[0]", "item[1]", "item[2]",
                    "item[3]", "item[4]", "item[5]",
                    "item[6]", "item[7]",
                    "item[8]", "item[9]" };

        JList list = new JList(items);

        list.setPrototypeCellValue("MMMMMMM");

        controlPanel = new ControlPanel(list);
        controlPanel.update();

        listPanel.setBorder(BorderFactory.createEtchedBorder());
        listPanel.add(new JScrollPane(list));

        contentPane.add(controlPanel, BorderLayout.NORTH);
        contentPane.add(listPanel, BorderLayout.CENTER);

        list.addListSelectionListener(
                            new ListSelectionListener() {
            public void valueChanged(ListSelectionEvent e) {
                controlPanel.update();
            }
        });
    }
}
class ControlPanel extends JPanel {
    private JComboBox mode = new JComboBox();
    private JButton clear = new JButton("clear selection");

    private String single = "SINGLE_SELECTION",
            singleInterval = "SINGLE_INTERVAL_SELECTION",
            multipleInterval = "MULTIPLE_INTERVAL_SELECTION";

    private JLabel  leadLabel = new JLabel(),
                anchorLabel = new JLabel(),
                minLabel = new JLabel(),
                maxLabel = new JLabel(),
```

```
            selIndicesLabel = new JLabel();

private JList list;

public ControlPanel(JList l) {
    JPanel top = new JPanel(),
           mid = new JPanel(),
           bottom = new JPanel();

    this.list = l;

    setLayout(new BoxLayout(this, BoxLayout.Y_AXIS));
    setBorder(BorderFactory.createEtchedBorder());

    top.add(mode);
    top.add(clear);

    mid.add(new JLabel("Lead:")); mid.add(leadLabel);
    mid.add(new JLabel("Anchor:")); mid.add(anchorLabel);
    mid.add(new JLabel("Minimum:")); mid.add(minLabel);
    mid.add(new JLabel("Maximum:")); mid.add(maxLabel);

    add(top);
    add(mid);
    add(bottom);

    mode.addItem(single);
    mode.addItem(singleInterval);
    mode.addItem(multipleInterval);
    initializeSelectionMode();

    bottom.add(new JLabel("Selected Indices:"));
    bottom.add(selIndicesLabel);

    mode.addItemListener(new ItemListener() {
        public void itemStateChanged(ItemEvent e) {
            if(e.getStateChange() == ItemEvent.SELECTED)
                setSelectionMode((String)e.getItem());
        }
    });
    clear.addActionListener(new ActionListener() {
        public void actionPerformed(ActionEvent e) {
            list.clearSelection();
        }
    });
}
public void update() {
    int lead = list.getLeadSelectionIndex(),
        min = list.getMinSelectionIndex(),
        max = list.getMaxSelectionIndex(),
        anchor = list.getAnchorSelectionIndex();
```

```
        leadLabel.setText(Integer.toString(lead) + " / ");
        anchorLabel.setText(Integer.toString(anchor) + " / ");
        minLabel.setText(Integer.toString(min) + " / ");
        maxLabel.setText(Integer.toString(max) + " / ");

        int[] selected = list.getSelectedIndices();
        String s = new String();

        for(int i = 0; i < selected.length; ++i) {
            s += Integer.toString(selected[i]);

            if(i < selected.length-1)
                s += ",";
        }
        selIndicesLabel.setText(s);
        validate();
    }
    private void initializeSelectionMode() {
        int m = list.getSelectionMode();

        switch(m) {
            case ListSelectionModel.SINGLE_SELECTION:
                mode.setSelectedItem(single);
                break;
            case ListSelectionModel.SINGLE_INTERVAL_SELECTION:
                mode.setSelectedItem(singleInterval);
                break;
            case ListSelectionModel.MULTIPLE_INTERVAL_SELECTION:
                mode.setSelectedItem(multipleInterval);
                break;
        }
    }
    private void setSelectionMode(String s) {
        if(s.equals("SINGLE_SELECTION")) {
            list.setSelectionMode(
                ListSelectionModel.SINGLE_SELECTION);
        }
        else if(s.equals("SINGLE_INTERVAL_SELECTION")) {
            list.setSelectionMode(
                ListSelectionModel.SINGLE_INTERVAL_SELECTION);
        }
        else if(s.equals("MULTIPLE_INTERVAL_SELECTION")) {
            list.setSelectionMode(
                ListSelectionModel.MULTIPLE_INTERVAL_SELECTION);
        }
    }
}
```

List Data Events

When data associated with a list is modified, list data events are fired by the list's model. Unlike most Swing components, the JList class does not listen to its model for the purpose of forwarding events to listeners registered with the list. If notification of list data events is desired, a listener must be directly registered with a list model.

The ListDataListener interface is summarized in Interface Summary 17-5.

Interface Summary 17-5   ListDataListener

---

public abstract void contentsChanged(ListDataEvent)
public abstract void intervalAdded(ListDataEvent)
public abstract void intervalRemoved(ListDataEvent)

One of the three methods defined by the ListDataListener class is invoked whenever the data associated with a list is modified. When intervals of items are added or removed from a list's model, the intervalAdded and intervalRemoved methods are invoked, respectively.

If a change that is more complex than simply adding or removing an interval is made to list data, the contentsChanged method is invoked.

The most interesting aspect of being a list data listener is tracking the event that is passed to the methods defined by the ListDataListener interface. The ListDataEvent class is summarized in Class Summary 17-5.

Class Summary 17-5   ListDataEvent

Extends: java.util.EventObject

Constants

---

public static final int <u>CONTENTS CHANGED</u>
public static final int <u>INTERVAL ADDED</u>
public static final int <u>INTERVAL REMOVED</u>

The constants listed above define the types of list data events.

Constructors

---

public <u>ListDataEvent</u>(Object <u>source</u>, int <u>type</u>, int <u>index0</u>, int <u>index1</u>)

`ListDataEvents` are constructed with the source of the event, the type of event—defined by one of the `static final` constants listed above—and the beginning and ending indexes for the range of items that were modified.

Methods

---

public int <u>getIndex0</u>()
public int <u>getIndex1</u>()
public int <u>getType</u>()

The applet shown in Figure 17-10 contains a list and two buttons for removing selected items from the list and repopulating the list. The applet adds a list data listener to the list that displays a dialog whenever an interval of items is removed from the list.

The top-left picture shown in Figure 17-10 shows the applet as it appears initially. The third item in the list—at index 2—is selected in the top-right picture. The remove selected items button is activated, and the result is shown in the lower-left picture. A dialog is shown that indicates the item that was removed and the number of remaining items. The lower-right picture shows the list after the item has been removed.

The applet creates a list wrapped in a scrollpane, and the scrollpane is added to the applet's content pane. The list is subsequently populated with creatively named strings.

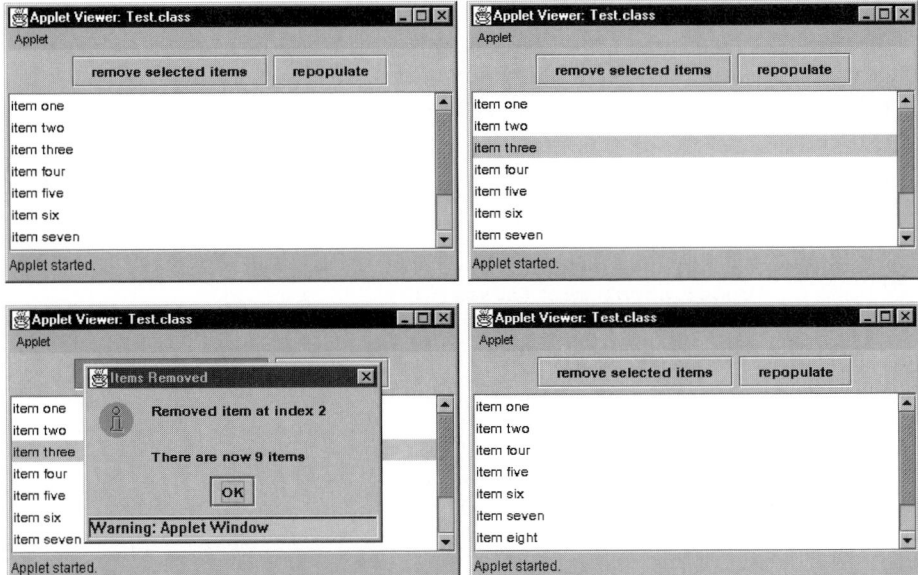

Figure 17-10 Handling List Data Events

```
public class Test extends JApplet {
    private JList list = new JList();

    private String[] items = {
                    "item one", "item two", "item three",
                    "item four", "item five", "item six",
                    "item seven", "item eight",
                    "item nine", "item ten"
    };

    public void init() {
        Container contentPane = getContentPane();

        JPanel controlPanel = new ControlPanel(this, list);

        contentPane.add(controlPanel, BorderLayout.NORTH);
        contentPane.add(new JScrollPane(list),
                                    BorderLayout.CENTER);

        populateList();
    }
```

The `populateList` method creates an instance of `DefaultListModel` and adds strings from the items array, and the model is subsequently specified as the list's model. The model is fitted with an instance of `ListDataListener` that reacts to intervals removed by showing a message dialog.

```java
public void populateList() {
    final DefaultListModel model = new DefaultListModel();

    for(int i=0; i < items.length; ++i)
        model.addElement(items[i]);

    list.setModel(model);

    if(list.isShowing())
        list.revalidate();

    model.addListDataListener(new ListDataListener() {
        public void contentsChanged(ListDataEvent e) {
            showStatus("contents changed");
        }
        public void intervalRemoved(ListDataEvent e) {
            Object[] message = new Object[] {
                "Removed item at index " + e.getIndex0(),
                " ",
                "There are now " + model.getSize() + " items"
            };
            JOptionPane.showMessageDialog(Test.this,
                message,
                "Items Removed", // title
                JOptionPane.INFORMATION_MESSAGE); // type
        }
        public void intervalAdded(ListDataEvent e) {
            showStatus("interval added");
        }
    });
}
```

The `ControlPanel` extends `JPanel` and contains the applet's remove selected items and repopulate buttons. The buttons are fitted with action listeners that remove elements from the model and repopulate the list.

```java
class ControlPanel extends JPanel {
    JButton remove = new JButton("remove selected items");
    JButton repopulate = new JButton("repopulate");

    public ControlPanel(final Test applet, final JList list) {
```

```
        add(remove);
        add(repopulate);

        remove.addActionListener(new ActionListener() {
            public void actionPerformed(ActionEvent e) {
                int[] selected = list.getSelectedIndices();
                DefaultListModel model =
                        (DefaultListModel)list.getModel();

                for(int i=0; i < selected.length; ++i) {
                    model.removeElementAt(selected[i] - i);
                }
            }
        });
        repopulate.addActionListener(new ActionListener() {
            public void actionPerformed(ActionEvent e) {
                applet.populateList();
            }
        });
    }
}
```

The applet shown in Figure 17-10 is listed in its entirety in Example 17-6.

Example 17-6 Handling List Data Events

```
import java.awt.*;
import java.awt.event.*;
import javax.swing.*;
import javax.swing.event.*;

public class Test extends JApplet {
    private JList list = new JList();

    private String[] items = {
                    "item one", "item two", "item three",
                    "item four", "item five", "item six",
                    "item seven", "item eight",
                    "item nine", "item ten"
    };

    public void init() {
        Container contentPane = getContentPane();

        JPanel controlPanel = new ControlPanel(this, list);

        contentPane.add(controlPanel, BorderLayout.NORTH);
        contentPane.add(new JScrollPane(list),
                                    BorderLayout.CENTER);
        populateList();
```

```
    }
    public void populateList() {
        final DefaultListModel model = new DefaultListModel();

        for(int i=0; i < items.length; ++i)
            model.addElement(items[i]);

        list.setModel(model);

        if(list.isShowing())
            list.revalidate();

        model.addListDataListener(new ListDataListener() {
            public void contentsChanged(ListDataEvent e) {
                showStatus("contents changed");
            }
            public void intervalRemoved(ListDataEvent e) {
                Object[] message = new Object[] {
                    "Removed item at index " + e.getIndex0(),
                    " ",
                    "There are now " + model.getSize() + " items"
                };
                JOptionPane.showMessageDialog(Test.this,
                    message,
                    "Items Removed", // title
                    JOptionPane.INFORMATION_MESSAGE); // type
            }
            public void intervalAdded(ListDataEvent e) {
                showStatus("interval added");
            }
        });
    }
}
class ControlPanel extends JPanel {
    JButton remove = new JButton("remove selected items");
    JButton repopulate = new JButton("repopulate");

    public ControlPanel(final Test applet, final JList list) {
        add(remove);
        add(repopulate);

        remove.addActionListener(new ActionListener() {
            public void actionPerformed(ActionEvent e) {
                int[] selected = list.getSelectedIndices();
                DefaultListModel model =
                        (DefaultListModel)list.getModel();

                for(int i=0; i < selected.length; ++i) {
                    model.removeElementAt(selected[i] - i);
                }
            }
        });
```

```
        repopulate.addActionListener(new ActionListener() {
            public void actionPerformed(ActionEvent e) {
                applet.populateList();
            }
        });
    }
}
```

Handling Double and Triple Mouse Clicks

This section discusses the manner in which double and triple mouse clicks are handled in a list. This discussion affords us the opportunity to illustrate how to translate into an index the point at which a mouse click occurred and how to detect whether a mouse click is a double or triple click.

The applet shown in Figure 17-11 contains a list wrapped in a scrollpane. When a double or triple click is inflicted upon the list, the applet's status bar is updated accordingly.

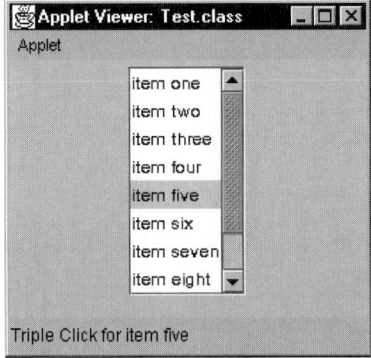

Figure 17-11 Detecting Double and Triple Clicking in a List

The applet creates an instance of JList with an array of strings and places the list in a scrollpane. The scrollpane is then added to the list's content pane.

```
public class Test extends JApplet {
    public void init() {
        Container contentPane = getContentPane();

        Object[] items = { "item one", "item two", "item three",
```

```
                        "item four", "item five", "item six",
                        "item seven", "item eight",
                        "item nine", "item ten" };

    JList list = new JList(items);

    contentPane.setLayout(new FlowLayout());
    contentPane.add(new JScrollPane(list));
    ...
```

A mouse listener is added to the list to update the applet's status bar. The list is the source of the event, so a reference to it is obtained by invocation of `EventObject.getSource()`. From the list, the list's model is accessed, and the index of the item that was clicked on is obtained by invocation of `JList.locationToIndex()`.

Once the model is in hand and the index is known, the string associated with the item is obtained by invocation of `AbstractListModel.getElementAt()`. A string is constructed with the item string and the type of click. The `getClickCount` method detects whether the click was single, double, or triple.

```
        ...
    list.addMouseListener(new MouseAdapter() {
        public void mouseClicked(MouseEvent e) {
            JList theList = (JList)e.getSource();
            ListModel model = theList.getModel();

            int index = theList.locationToIndex(e.getPoint());
            String itemString =
                        (String)model.getElementAt(index);

            String s = new String(" for " +
                        model.getElementAt(index));

            switch(e.getClickCount()) {
                case 1:
                    showStatus("Single Click" + s);
                    break;
                case 2:
                    showStatus("Double Click" + s);
                    break;
                case 3:
                    showStatus("Triple Click" + s);
                    break;
            }
        }
    });
}
}
```

The applet shown in Figure 17-11 is listed in its entirety in Example 17-7.

Example 17-7 Handling Double and Triple Mouse Clicks

```
import java.awt.*;
import java.awt.event.*;
import javax.swing.*;
import javax.swing.event.*;

public class Test extends JApplet {
    public void init() {
        Container contentPane = getContentPane();

        Object[] items = { "item one", "item two", "item three",
                    "item four", "item five", "item six",
                    "item seven", "item eight",
                    "item nine", "item ten" };

        JList list = new JList(items);

        contentPane.setLayout(new FlowLayout());
        contentPane.add(new JScrollPane(list));

        list.addMouseListener(new MouseAdapter() {
            public void mouseClicked(MouseEvent e) {
                JList theList = (JList)e.getSource();
                ListModel model = theList.getModel();

                int index = theList.locationToIndex(e.getPoint());
                String itemString =
                            (String)model.getElementAt(index);

                String s = new String(" for " +
                        model.getElementAt(index));

                switch(e.getClickCount()) {
                    case 1:
                        showStatus("Single Click" + s);
                        break;
                    case 2:
                        showStatus("Double Click" + s);
                        break;
                    case 3:
                        showStatus("Triple Click" + s);
                        break;
                }
            }
        });
    }
}
```

JList Class Summaries

The `public` and `protected` variables and methods for `JList` are listed in Class Summary 17-6.

Class Summary 17-6   JList

Extends: JComponent

Implements: Scrollable, javax.accessibility.Accessible

Constructors

---

public <u>JList</u>()

public <u>JList</u>(ListModel)
public <u>JList</u>(Object[])
public <u>JList</u>(Vector)

The `JList` class can be constructed with no data or with data specified as an `Object` array, vector, or list model. A good percentage of the time, the second constructor listed above is passed instances of `DefaultListModel`, which provides methods for inserting and removing items.

Instances of `JList` constructed with either an `Object` array or a vector are fitted with a simple list model that extends `AbstractListModel`.

List Selection Events

---

public void <u>addListSelectionListener</u>(ListSelectionListener)
public void <u>removeListSelectionListener</u>(ListSelectionListener)

protected void <u>fireSelectionValueChanged</u>(int firstIndex, int lastIndex, boolean isAdjusting)

The first two methods listed above register list selection listeners with an instance of `JList`. The first time `addListSelectionListener` is called for a list, a selection listener is instantiated and registered with the list's selection model. The `addListSelectionListener` method also registers the specified listener with the list's selection listener.

When the list's selection model fires a list selection event, the list's selection listener forwards the events to the list's own selection listeners. The result of all this is that listeners passed to `addListSelectionListener` are notified of selection changes with the list specified as the source of the event. Listeners that register with a list's selection model will be notified of the same events, but the event source will be the selection model and not the list.

The `protected fireSelectionValueChanged` method fires selection events to list selection listeners registered with the list. The method can be overridden if the manner in which listeners are notified needs to be changed or augmented.

List Selection

---

protected ListSelectionModel createSelectionModel()

public void addSelectionInterval(int, int)
public void removeSelectionInterval(int, int)
public void clearSelection()

public int getAnchorSelectionIndex()
public int getLeadSelectionIndex()
public int getMaxSelectionIndex()
public int getMinSelectionIndex()
public int getSelectedIndex()
public int[] getSelectedIndices()
public Object getSelectedValue()
public Object[] getSelectedValues()
public ListSelectionModel getSelectionModel()
public int getSelectionMode()

public boolean isSelectedIndex(int)
public boolean isSelectionEmpty()

public void setSelectedIndex(int)
public void setSelectedIndices(int[])

public void <u>setSelectedValue</u>(Object, boolean)
public void <u>setSelectionInterval</u>(int, int)
public void <u>setSelectionMode</u>(int)
public void <u>setSelectionModel</u>(ListSelectionModel)

All of methods listed above concern list selection. Many of the methods simply delegate directly to the list's selection model. For example, the `getAnchorSelectionIndex` method is implemented as follows:

```
// From JList.java

public int getAnchorSelectionIndex() {
        return getSelectionModel().getAnchorSelectionIndex();
}
```

`createSelectionModel()` creates a selection model. The method exists so that extensions of `JList` can override it to install a custom selection model. It should be noted that a custom selection model can be installed for a list simply by invocation of `JList.setSelectionModel()`. Extending `JList` and overriding `createSelectionModel` is typically reserved for custom list components that are tightly coupled with their selection models.

List selection mode can be set with the `setSelectionMode` method, which is passed one of the following `integer` constants:

- `ListSelectionModel.MULTIPLE_INTERVAL_SELECTION`
- `ListSelectionModel.SINGLE_INTERVAL_SELECTION`
- `ListSelectionModel.SINGLE_SELECTION`

The `setSelectionInterval` method clears the current selection and selects the specified interval if the selection mode is `SINGLE_INTERVAL_SELECTION` or `MULTIPLE_INTERVAL_SELECTION`. If the selection mode is `SINGLE_SELECTION`, the method has no effect.

The `addSelectionInterval` method adds the specified interval to the currently selected items if the selection mode is `MULTIPLE_INTERVAL_SELECTION`. If the selection mode is `SINGLE_INTERVAL_SELECTION`, the method clears the current selection and selects the specified interval. If the selection mode is `SINGLE_SELECTION`, the method has no effect.

Scrollable Methods

---

public Dimension <u>getPreferredScrollableViewportSize</u>()
public int <u>getScrollableBlockIncrement</u>(Rectangle, int, int)
public boolean <u>getScrollableTracksViewportHeight</u>()
public boolean <u>getScrollableTracksViewportWidth</u>()
public int <u>getScrollableUnitIncrement</u>(Rectangle, int, int)

The methods listed above are defined by the Scrollable interface.

The `getPreferredScrollableViewportSize` method returns the preferred viewport size for lists that are contained in a viewport. Lists prefer their viewports to be as wide as their widest item and as tall as the number of visible rows, specified by `JList.setVisibleRowCount()`.

`getScrollableBlockIncrement` returns either the height of the currently visible portion of the list for vertical scrolling or the width of the currently visible portion of the list for horizontally scrolling. This algorithm results in block scrolls that scroll the visible portion of the list.

For vertical scrolling, `getScrollableUnitIncrement()` returns the number of pixels necessary to scroll the next cell into view. For horizontal scrolling, the value returned represents the size of the list's font or 1 if the font is `null`.

The `getScrollableTracksViewportWidth` and `getScrollableTracksViewportHeight` methods return `boolean` values indicating whether the list prefers to keep its width and height the same as its viewport's size, otherwise known as tracking the viewport's size. Lists that are larger than their viewports do not track the viewport's size, so the methods return `false`. Lists that are smaller than their viewports track the viewport's size, meaning the methods return `true`.

Prototype Cell and Fixed Width and Height

---

public int <u>getFixedCellHeight</u>()
public int <u>getFixedCellWidth</u>()
public Object <u>getPrototypeCellValue</u>()

public void <u>setFixedCellHeight</u>(int)
public void <u>setFixedCellWidth</u>(int)

public void <u>setPrototypeCellValue</u>(Object)

By default, lists size their cells as wide as the list's widest item and as tall as the sum of each cell's renderer component. The width of the widest item in the list is stored as an `integer`, and an array of `integers` is used to represent cell heights. Both values must be recomputed whenever list data is modified.

As an alternative to having list cells sized as outlined above, a fixed cell width and height can be specified with the `setFixedCell...()` methods. If fixed cell width or height is explicitly specified, then the values are not computed as outlined above.

In addition to fixed cell width and height being set by methods, the values can be specified indirectly by passing `setPrototypeCellValue()` an object. The preferred size of the object specified as the prototype cell's value sets fixed cell width and height for a list.

Property Accessors

---

public Rectangle <u>getCellBounds</u>(int index1, int index2)
public ListCellRenderer <u>getCellRenderer</u>()
public int <u>getFirstVisibleIndex</u>()
public int <u>getLastVisibleIndex</u>()
public ListModel <u>getModel</u>()
public Color <u>getSelectionBackground</u>()
public Color <u>getSelectionForeground</u>()
public boolean <u>getValueIsAdjusting</u>()
public int <u>getVisibleRowCount</u>()

public void <u>setCellRenderer</u>(ListCellRenderer)
public void <u>setListData</u>(Object[])
public void <u>setListData</u>(Vector)
public void <u>setModel</u>(ListModel)
public void <u>setSelectionBackground</u>(Color)
public void <u>setSelectionForeground</u>(Color)
public void <u>setValueIsAdjusting</u>(boolean)
public void <u>setVisibleRowCount</u>(int)

The methods listed above are accessors for `JList` properties, which are discussed in "JList Properties" on page 1035.

Item Indexes and Locations

---

public void <u>ensureIndexIsVisible</u>(int)

public Point <u>indexToLocation</u>(int)
public int <u>locationToIndex</u>(Point)

The `ensureIndexIsVisible` method takes effect only if the list is contained in a viewport. `ensureIndexIsVisible()` calls `scrollRectToVisible()` to scroll the cell associated with the specified index into view. See "Using the scrollRectToVisible Method" on page 724 for more information concerning viewports and the `scrollRectToVisible` method.

If `ensureIndexIsVisible` is called for an item that has just been added to a list, the item will not be made visible if the list has not been resized to accommodate the new item(s). Because of this behavior, it is common to wrap calls to `ensureIndexIsVisible()` in a `Runnable` that is passed to `SwingUtilities.invokeLater()`.

The `indexToLocation` and `locationToIndex` methods are convenience methods for translating indexes to locations, and vice versa. See "Handling Double and Triple Mouse Clicks" on page 1059 for an illustration of the use of the `JList.locationToIndex` method.

Accessibility / Pluggable Look and Feel

---

public AccessibleContext <u>getAccessibleContext</u>()
public ListUI <u>getUI</u>()
public String <u>getUIClassID</u>()
public void <u>setUI</u>(ListUI)
public void <u>updateUI</u>()

The methods listed above can be found in most extensions of `JComponent`. Swing lightweight components can return the class name of their UI delegate and an accessibility context that contains accessibility information for the component. The `updateUI` method is invoked when the component is fitted with a UI delegate.

JList.setPrototypeCellValue() Controls List Width and Font

By default, lists are sized wide enough to accommodate the widest item displayed in the list. For lists with a large number of items, calculating the width of the list can incur a performance penalty.

The JList.setPrototypeCellValue(Object) method can be used to explicitly set cell width and height to the preferred width and height respectively, of the object that is passed to the method. For lists with a large number of items, using the setPrototypeCellValue method can result in a performance increase when items are added to or removed from the list. Additionally, the list's font is set to the font used by the prototype cell value object.

The JList class also provides setFixedCellWidth(int) and setFixedCellHeight(int) methods that set the pixel width and height to the values passed to the methods.

AWT Compatibility

Swing and AWT lists are about as different as two fundamentally similar components can be. Although both components display items in a list, JList is much more robust than the AWT's List. AWT lists are limited to displaying strings, but Swing lists can render anything in a custom cell renderer. AWT lists are limited to selections of a contiguous range of strings, whereas Swing lists support multiple intervals.

Table 17-4 lists the public methods implemented by the java.awt.List and their JList equivalents where applicable.

Table 17-4 Public java.awt.List Methods and JList Equivalents

java.awt.List Method	JList Equivalent
void add(String)	void DefaultListModel.addElement(Object)
void add(String, int)	void DefaultListModel.add(int, Object)
void addActionListener(ActionListener)	——
void addItemListener(ItemListener)	void addListSelectionListener(ListSelectionListener)
String getItem(int)	list.getModel().getItemAt(int)
int getItemCount()	list.getModel().getSize()
String[] getItems()	Object[] DefaultListModel.toArray()
Dimension getMinimumSize(int)	——
Dimension getPreferredSize(int)	——
int getRows	int getVisibleRowCount()
int getSelectedIndex()	int getSelectedIndex()
int[] getSelectedIndexes()	int getSelectedIndices()
String getSelectedItem()	Object getSelectedValue()
String[] getSelectedItems()	Object[] getSelectedValues()
Object[] getSelectedObjects()	Object[] getSelectedValues()
int getVisibleIndex()	——
boolean isIndexSelected(int)	boolean isSelectedIndex()
boolean isMultipleMode()	int getSelectionMode()
void makeVisible(int)	void ensureIndexIsVisible(int)
void remove(int)	void DefaultListModel.removeElementAt(int)
void remove(String)	void DefaultListModel.removeElement(Object)
void removeActionListener(ActionListener)	——
void removeAll()	void setListData(null)
void removeItemListener(ItemListener)	——
void replaceItem(String, int)	void DefaultListModel.removeElementAt(int) / void DefaultListModel.addElement(Object)
void select(int)	void setSelectedIndex()
void setMultipleMode(boolean)	void setSelectionMode(int)

AWT lists fire item events when items are selected or deselected and fire action events when an item is double-clicked. Swing lists fire list selection events when items are selected or deselected, and list data events when list data is modified.

`JList` does not provide methods for adding or removing items; therefore, the `JList` equivalents to the `List.add` and `List.remove` methods involve `DefaultListModel` methods.

Parting Shots

This chapter marks a right of passage of sorts into the realm of Swing's more complex components. The `JList` component is the first component presented in this book that has a renderer. The three chapters that follow discuss combo boxes, tables and trees, all of which have renderers and editors.

CHAPTER

18

Combo Boxes

Combo boxes, implemented by the JComboBox class, are a combination of an editable area (by default, a text field) and a drop-down list of selectable items. As a result, it is instructive to introduce JComboBox by comparing it with JList.

JComboBox vs. JList

JList and JComboBox are similar because both components display a list of items. As a result, they both have models that extend the ListModel interface. Additionally, both components have renderers that render list cells by implementing the ListCellRenderer interface.

Lists and combo boxes differ in a number of areas. List cells are not editable, but combo boxes can be fitted with an editor. The JComboBox component delegates editing to an object that implements the ComboBoxEditor interface.

Lists support three selection modes and delegate selection responsibilities to an object that implements the ListSelectionModel interface. Combo boxes can have only one item selected at a time, and selection is handled by combo box models. On the other hand, combo boxes support key selection, where a key press can select an item, but lists do not.

Data types for list and combo box delegates are listed in Table 18-1.

Table 18-1   Delegate Data Types for Lists and Combo Boxes

Delegate	JList	JComboBox
Editor	——	ComboBoxEditor
Model	ListModel	ComboBoxModel[1]
Renderer	ListCellRenderer	ListCellRenderer
Selection Model	DefaultListSelectionModel	——
Key Selection Manager	——	JComboBox. DefaultKeySelectionManager

1. The ComboBoxModel interface extends the ListModel interface.

The JList class does not provide any methods for adding, inserting, or removing items. The only way to modify list data after a list is constructed is with the JList.setListData method, which allows all of the items to be specified at once. The JComboBox class is the inverse; items can be added to and removed from combo boxes, but the only way to reset all of the data for a combo box is to set its model with JComboBox.setModel(ComboBoxModel).

The JComboBox Component

Instances of JComboBox are not editable by default, but a simple call to JComboBox.setEditable(true) is all that's required to enable editing.

The applet shown in Figure 18-1 contains a combo box and a check box that controls the editable state of the combo box.

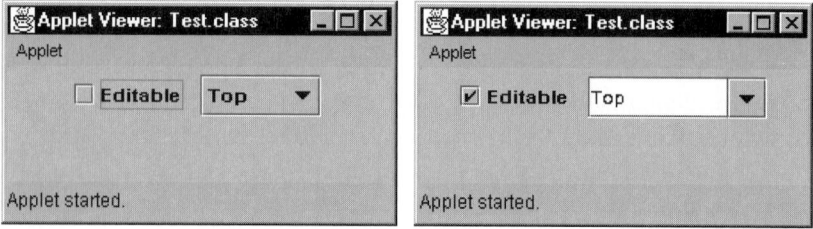

Figure 18-1 Editable and Noneditable Combo Boxes

The applet shown in Figure 18-1 is listed in Example 18-1.

Example 18-1 Editable and Noneditable Combo Boxes

```java
import java.applet.Applet;
import java.awt.*;
import java.awt.event.*;
import javax.swing.*;

public class Test extends JApplet {
    private JCheckBox checkBox = new JCheckBox("Editable");
    private JComboBox comboBox = new JComboBox();

    public void init() {
        Container contentPane = getContentPane();

        comboBox.addItem("Top");
        comboBox.addItem("Center");
        comboBox.addItem("Bottom");

        checkBox.setSelected(comboBox.isEditable());

        contentPane.setLayout(new FlowLayout());
        contentPane.add(checkBox);
        contentPane.add(comboBox);

        checkBox.addActionListener(new ActionListener() {
            public void actionPerformed(ActionEvent e) {
                comboBox.setEditable(checkBox.isSelected());
            }
        });
    }
}
```

The applet creates a combo box with the `JComboBox` no-argument constructor. Three items are added to the combo box, and the check box and combo box are added to the applet's content pane.

The initial state of the check box is set with the `boolean` value returned from `JComboBox.isEditable()`. An action listener that is added to the check box sets the editable state of combo box with the `boolean` value returned from `JCheckBox.isSelected()`.

Combo Box Models

Like the `JList` class, `JComboBox` does not maintain references to the objects it contains. All instances of `JComboBox` delegate the management of their data to an object that implements the `ComboBoxModel` interface.

The objects displayed in a combo box can be specified with the following `JComboBox` constructors:

- `public JComboBox(ComboBoxModel)`
- `public JComboBox(Object[])`
- `public JComboBox(Vector)`

The objects displayed in a combo box can also be specified after construction with the following `JComboBox` method:

- `public void setModel(ComboBoxModel)`

A class diagram for combo box models is shown in Figure 18-2.

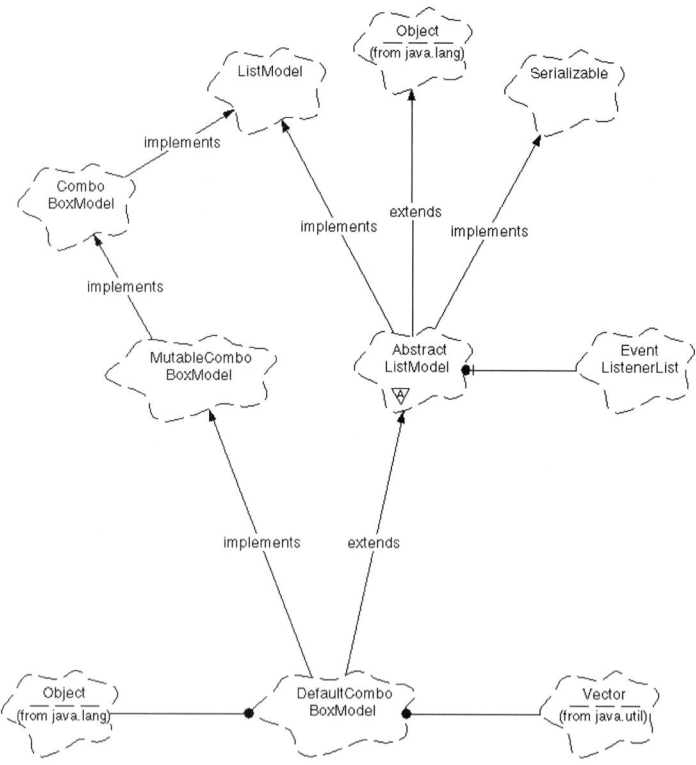

Figure 18-2 Combo Box Models

When instances of JComboBox are instantiated without an explicit model being specified, they are fitted with a model that is an instance of DefaultComboBoxModel. The DefaultComboBoxModel class extends AbstractListModel and implements the MutableComboBoxModel interface.

ListModel, which is extended by both AbstractListModel and MutableComboBoxModel, defines four methods, two for adding and removing list data listeners and two for obtaining the number of elements in the list and obtaining a reference to an element given its index. See "List Models" on page 1010 for more information concerning the ListModel interface.

The ComboBoxModel interface extends ListModel and defines two methods for getting and setting the currently selected item. Because combo boxes always display a single selected item, combo box models must provide methods for accessing it.

MutableComboBoxModel is an interface that extends the ComboBoxModel interface. MutableComboBoxModel defines methods for adding, inserting, and removing items.

DefaultComboBoxModel has much in common with DefaultListModel. Both classes extend AbstractListModel, and both provide data storage methods that are delegated to a vector. DefaultComboBoxModel is the default model for combo boxes that do not explicitly specify a model.

Table 18-2 outlines the responsibilities of the classes and interfaces discussed above and suggests when it is appropriate to use, implement, or extend them.

Table 18-2 JComboBox Models

Model	Class/ Interface	Responsibilities	Used/Implemented/ Extended When …
ComboBoxModel	interface	accessors for selected item; extends ListModel	data is static or MutableComboBoxModel methods will not suffice
MutableCombo BoxModel	interface	adding, inserting, and removing objects	DefaultComboBoxModel is undesirable
DefaultCombo BoxModel	class	implements MutableComboBox-Model and stores data in a vector	when data is likely to be modified (also by default)

If combo box data is mutable and can be stored in an object array or a vector, then the default combo box model—an instance of `DefaultComboBoxModel`—can be used.

If the data is mutable but cannot be stored in an object array or a vector, a custom model that extends `MutableComboBoxModel` should be used.

Custom combo box models that extend `ComboBoxModel` directly are warranted if the data is static, or if mutable data cannot be served by the methods defined by the `MutableComboBoxModel` interface.

ComboBoxModel

The `ComboBoxModel` interface is summarized in Interface Summary 18-1.

Interface Summary 18-1   ComboBoxModel

Extends: ListModel

public abstract Object <u>getSelectedItem</u>()
public abstract void <u>setSelectedItem</u>(Object)

Combo boxes, unlike lists, always display a single selected item. As a result, the `ListModel` interface is extended to include methods for getting and setting the currently selected item.

MutableComboBoxModel

The `MutableComboBoxModel` interface is summarized in Interface Summary 18-2.

Interface Summary 18-2   MutableComboBoxModel

---

public abstract void <u>addElement</u>(Object)
public abstract void <u>insertElementAt</u>(Object element, int index)
public abstract void <u>removeElement</u>(Object)
public abstract void <u>removeElementAt</u>(int index)

By default, neither the `ListModel` nor `ComboBoxModel` interfaces define methods for adding, inserting, or removing list elements. A basic set of such methods is defined by the `MutableComboBoxModel` interface.

Custom combo box models will implement the `MutableComboBoxModel` interface when the elements displayed in a combo box can change dynamically and the methods defined by `MutableComboBoxModel` are sufficient to manipulate the data. The `DefaultComboBoxModel` class is one such model.

DefaultComboBoxModel

The `DefaultComboBoxModel` class is summarized in Class Summary 18-1.

Class Summary 18-1   DefaultComboBoxModel

Extends: AbstractListModel
Implements: MutableComboBoxModel, java.io.Serializable

Constructors

---

public <u>DefaultComboBoxModel</u>()
public <u>DefaultComboBoxModel</u>(Object[])
public <u>DefaultComboBoxModel</u>(Vector)

If an object array is used to construct an instance of `DefaultComboBoxModel`, a vector is allocated and references to each object are copied to the vector.

If instances of `DefaultComboBoxModel` are constructed with the no-argument constructor, data should be added to the model after construction with the `addElement` or `insertElementAt` methods discussed below.

Methods

Elements / Size

---

public Object <u>getElementAt</u>(int)
public int <u>getSize</u>()

public void <u>addElement</u>(Object)
public void <u>insertElementAt</u>(Object element, int index)
public void <u>removeElement</u>(Object)
public void <u>removeElementAt</u>(int index)
public void <u>removeAllElements</u>()

The first group of methods listed above are defined by the `ListModel` interface, which is extended by the `ComboBoxModel` interface. `DefaultComboBoxModel` implements the methods by delegating to an enclosed instance of `java.util.Vector`.

The second group of methods listed above are defined by the `MutableComboBoxModel` interface. Like the `getSize` and `getElementAt` methods, the methods are implemented by delegation to an enclosed vector.

Selected Item / Indexes

---

public Object <u>getSelectedItem</u>()
public void <u>setSelectedItem</u>(Object)

public int <u>getIndexOf</u>(Object)

The methods listed above are defined by the `ComboBoxModel` interface. The methods provided access to a combo box's selected item.

The `getIndexOf` and `removeAllElements` (listed above) are convenience methods that are not defined by any of the interfaces implemented by `DefaultComboBoxModel`. Both methods delegate to the model's enclosed vector.

Combo Box Cell Renderers

Combo boxes, like lists, render cells with a list cell renderer. In fact, the drop-down lists displayed by combo boxes are instances of `JList` displayed in a popup menu. When a list cell renderer is specified for an instance of `JComboBox`, the combo box forwards the renderer to the list in the popup menu with `JList.setCellRenderer()`

The applet shown in Figure 18-3 contains a combo box with a custom cell renderer that paints a text/icon pair representing a color.

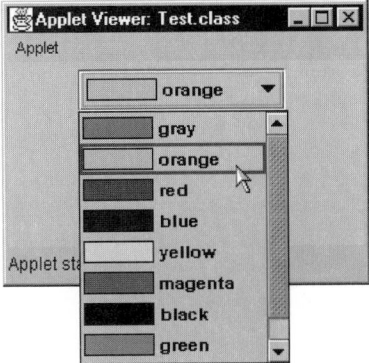

Figure 18-3 A Combo Box with a Custom List Cell Renderer

By default, combo box renderers are instances of `BasicComboBoxRenderer`, from the `swing.plaf.basic` package. `BasicComboBoxRenderer` extends `JLabel` and treats model values in one of two ways: icons are set for the renderer—which is a label—with the `setIcon` method, and all other types of objects become the text displayed in the label with the `toString()` method. Default renderers for lists and combo boxes treat data in an identical fashion—see "List Cell Renderers" on page 1025.

Even though `JLabel` is capable of displaying both text and an icon, `BasicComboBoxRenderer` can only display one or the other because a renderer's `getListCellRendererComponent` method is only passed a single value. Values that are strings or icons are rendered as is, and all other types of objects (including for example, an `Object` array with a string and an icon) are rendered with the string returned from the object's `toString` method. As a result, a custom renderer must be implemented to render both text and an image.

See "List Cell Renderers" on page 1025 for more information concerning list cell renderers and the `ListCellRenderer` interface and the `DefaultListCellRenderer` class.

The applet shown in Figure 18-3 creates a combo box with the `JComboBox(Object[])` constructor. Each item in the array is an `Object` array containing a color and a string.

```
public class Test extends JApplet {
    public void init() {
        Container contentPane = getContentPane();
        JComboBox combo = new JComboBox(new Object[] {
            new Object[] { Color.gray, "gray" },
            new Object[] { Color.orange, "orange" },
            new Object[] { Color.red, "red" },
            new Object[] { Color.blue, "blue" },
            new Object[] { Color.yellow, "yellow" },
            new Object[] { Color.magenta, "magenta" },
            new Object[] { Color.black, "black" },
            new Object[] { Color.green, "green" },
            new Object[] { Color.lightGray, "lightGray"} });

        combo.setRenderer(new ColorRenderer());

        contentPane.setLayout(new FlowLayout());
        contentPane.add(combo);
    }
}
```

The combo box's renderer is set to an instance of `ColorRenderer`, which renders the text and icon.

```
class ColorRenderer extends JLabel implements ListCellRenderer {
    private static ColorIcon icon = new ColorIcon();
    ...
```

The `ColorRenderer` class extends `JLabel` and implements the `ListCellRenderer` interface. `ColorRenderer` contains a `static` instance of `ColorIcon` that is used to paint the colored rectangles in the list cells. `ColorIcon` is a simple implementation of the `Icon` interface. Because icons can be shared among components, a single icon can be used to paint the colored rectangles in the list cells. See "Sharing Icons Among Components" on page 225 for more information concerning sharing icons among components.

```
    ...
    private Border
        redBorder = BorderFactory.createLineBorder(Color.red,2),
        emptyBorder = BorderFactory.createEmptyBorder(2,2,2,2);

    public Component getListCellRendererComponent(
                            JList list,
                            Object value,
                            int index,
                            boolean isSelected,
                            boolean cellHasFocus) {
        Object[] array = (Object[])value;

        icon.setColor((Color)array[0]);

        setIcon(icon);
        setText((String)array[1]);

        if(isSelected) setBorder(redBorder);
        else        setBorder(emptyBorder);

        return this;
    }
}
```

The renderer creates two borders that indicate whether a cell is selected. If the cell being rendered is selected, the red border is used to indicate selection; otherwise, the empty border is used.

The value passed to `getListCellRendererComponent()` is a value stored in the combo box's model. In this case, the value is one of the `Object` arrays specified when the combo box was created. The renderer extracts the color from the array and uses it to set the color of the icon. The icon is then specified as the icon for the label—recall that `ColorRenderer` extends `JLabel`. Subsequently, the text of the label is set to the string stored in the array.

The applet shown in Figure 18-3 is listed in its entirety in Example 18-2.

Example 18-2 A Custom List Cell Renderer

```
import java.awt.*;
import java.awt.event.*;
import javax.swing.*;
import javax.swing.border.*;

public class Test extends JApplet {
   public void init() {
      Container contentPane = getContentPane();
      JComboBox combo = new JComboBox(new Object[] {
         new Object[] { Color.gray, "gray" },
         new Object[] { Color.orange, "orange" },
         new Object[] { Color.red, "red" },
         new Object[] { Color.blue, "blue" },
         new Object[] { Color.yellow, "yellow" },
         new Object[] { Color.magenta, "magenta" },
         new Object[] { Color.black, "black" },
         new Object[] { Color.green, "green" },
         new Object[] { Color.lightGray, "lightGray"} });

      combo.setRenderer(new ColorRenderer());

      contentPane.setLayout(new FlowLayout());
      contentPane.add(combo);
   }
}
class ColorRenderer extends JLabel implements ListCellRenderer {
   private static ColorIcon icon = new ColorIcon();

   private Border
      redBorder = BorderFactory.createLineBorder(Color.red,2),
      emptyBorder = BorderFactory.createEmptyBorder(2,2,2,2);

   public Component getListCellRendererComponent(
                        JList list,
                        Object value,
                        int index,
                        boolean isSelected,
                        boolean cellHasFocus) {
      Object[] array = (Object[])value;
```

```
        icon.setColor((Color)array[0]);

        setIcon(icon);
        setText((String)array[1]);

        if(isSelected) setBorder(redBorder);
        else       setBorder(emptyBorder);

        return this;
    }
}
class ColorIcon implements Icon {
    private Color color;
    private int w, h;

    public ColorIcon() {
        this(Color.gray, 50, 15);
    }
    public ColorIcon(Color color, int w, int h) {
        this.color = color;
        this.w = w;
        this.h = h;
    }
    public void paintIcon(Component c, Graphics g, int x, int y) {
        g.setColor(Color.black);
        g.drawRect(x, y, w-1, h-1);
        g.setColor(color);
        g.fillRect(x+1, y+1, w-2, h-2);
    }
    public Color getColor() {
        return color;
    }
    public void setColor(Color color) {
        this.color = color;
    }
    public int getIconWidth() {
        return w;
    }
    public int getIconHeight() {
        return h;
    }
}
```

Combo Box Key Selection Managers

Combo boxes allow items to be selected with a key press. If a key is pressed when a combo box has focus, a search is initiated for a match between the key and an item in the combo box's list; if a match is found, the item is selected. JComboBox

delegates searching and matching to an object that implements the
JComboBox.KeySelectionManager interface, which is listed in Interface
Summary 18-3.

Interface Summary 18-3   JComboBox.KeySelectionManager

---

public abstract int <u>selectionForKey</u>(char key, ComboBoxModel model)

Each instance of JComboBox maintains a reference to an object that implements
the KeySelectionManager interface. When a key is pressed, the key selection
manager's selectionForKey method is called to obtain the index of the item to
select. If selectionForKey returns an index greater than −1, the corresponding
item is selected.

By default, a combo box's key selection manager is an instance of
JComboBox.DefaultKeySelectionManager. The search for an item is
performed by JComboBox.DefaultKeySelectionManager in two passes, as
illustrated in Figure 18-4. The first pass is from the item below the currently
selected item to the last item in the list.[1] If the first pass does not produce a match
between the key pressed and an item, a second search is made from the first item
in the list to the item above the selected item.

For example, for the combo box list shown in Figure 18-4, a 'b' key press when
"yellow" is selected will result in "black" being selected. A subsequent ' b' key
press will select "blue." The "blue" selection is the most noteworthy because it
requires two passes.

A match is defined by the JComboBox.DefaultKeySelectionManager class
as a match between a key and the first character of the string returned from an
item's toString method.

The KeySelectionManager interface and DefaultKeySelectionManager
class are nested in the JComboBox class because they have meaning only within
the context of a combo box (although one could certainly make an argument in
favor of the same functionality for lists, which do not provide key selection).

---

1.   If the selected item is the last item in the list, the search begins with the first item.

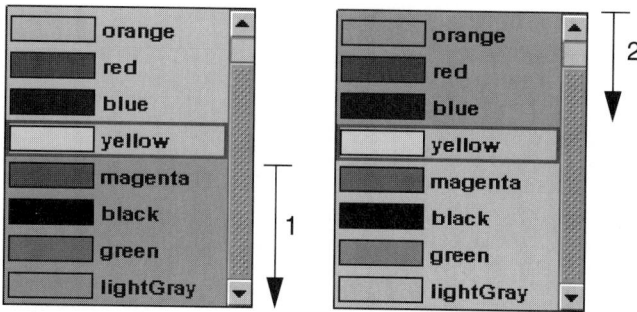

Figure 18-4 Default Key Selection Manager Search Algorithm

The JComboBox.DefaultKeySelectionManager class has package scope, meaning that it can only be accessed by other classes in the swing package. The JComboBox.KeySelectionManager interface is public so that it can be implemented outside of the swing package.

Using the Default Key Selection Manager

Figure 18-4 shows the combo box list for the applet shown in Figure 18-3. However, the combo box shown in Figure 18-3 does not react to key presses because the items contained in the combo box's model are Object arrays.

Recall that the default key selection manager matches a key to the first character of the string returned from an item's toString method. The string returned from an Object array's toString method is an identifier that looks something like this: [Ljava.lang.Object;@f5f0e605. Because the identifiers have no correlation to the colors represented by the items, key selection does not work for the applet shown in Figure 18-3.[2]

At first glance, it may seem that a custom key selection manager that matches a key to the first character of the string contained in the item's array might be in order. However, a simpler solution is to wrap the Object array in a class that implements a toString method. Such a class is listed below.

---

2. In fact, since all identifiers begin with the same character, pressing keys does not move selection at all.

```
class Item {
    private Color color;
    private String string;

    public Item(Object[] array) {
        color = (Color)array[0];
        string = (String)array[1];
    }
    public Color getColor() { return color; }
    public String toString() { return string; }
}
```

Instances of Item are constructed with an Object array containing a color and a string representing the color. The color and string are extracted from the Object array and are available through the getColor and toString methods, respectively.

The most important aspect of the Item class is its toString method. Although the default key selection manager for combo boxes does not work well with Object arrays for the reasons cited above, it does work for classes that implement an appropriate toString method, such as that implemented by the Item class.

The applet shown in Figure 18-5 contains a combo box whose items are instances of the Item class. When a key is pressed while the combo box has focus, the key and the string associated with the corresponding item is shown in the applet's status area.

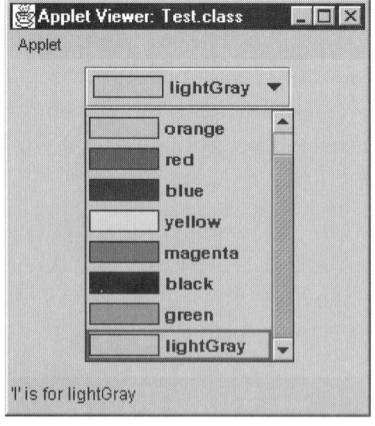 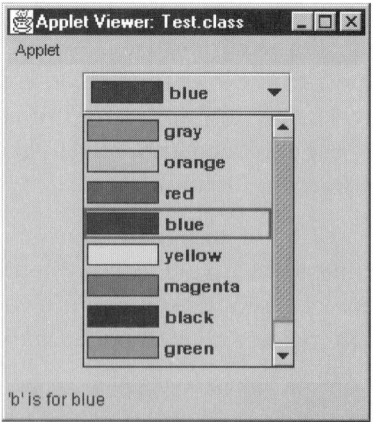

Figure 18-5 Using a Combo Box's Default Key Selection Manager

The applet creates a combo box with an array of Item instances, and adds to the combo box an action listener that updates the applet's status area.

```
public class Test extends JApplet {
    private JComboBox colorCombo = new JComboBox(new Object[] {
        new Item(new Object[] { Color.gray, "gray" }),
        new Item(new Object[] { Color.orange, "orange" }),
        new Item(new Object[] { Color.red, "red" }),
        new Item(new Object[] { Color.blue, "blue" }),
        new Item(new Object[] { Color.yellow, "yellow" }),
        new Item(new Object[] { Color.magenta, "magenta" }),
        new Item(new Object[] { Color.black, "black" }),
        new Item(new Object[] { Color.green, "green" }),
        new Item(new Object[] { Color.lightGray, "lightGray"})
    });

    public void init() {
        final Container contentPane = getContentPane();

        colorCombo.setRenderer(new ColorRenderer());

        contentPane.setLayout(new FlowLayout());
        contentPane.add(colorCombo);

        colorCombo.addActionListener(new ActionListener(){
            public void actionPerformed(ActionEvent e) {
                Item item = (Item)colorCombo.getSelectedItem();
                String first = item.toString().substring(0,1);

                showStatus("'" + first + "'" + " is for " + item);
            }
        });
    }
}
```

The listener obtains a reference to the selected item by invoking
JComboBox.getSelectedItem(), and the first character of the item's string is
obtained by invocation of Item.toString() followed by a subsequent call to
String.substring(0,1).

The applet shown in Figure 18-5 is listed in its entirety in Example 18-3.

Example 18-3 Using the Default Key Selection Manager

```java
import java.awt.*;
import java.awt.event.*;
import javax.swing.*;
import javax.swing.border.*;

public class Test extends JApplet {
    private JComboBox colorCombo = new JComboBox(new Object[] {
            new Item(new Object[] { Color.gray, "gray" }),
            new Item(new Object[] { Color.orange, "orange" }),
            new Item(new Object[] { Color.red, "red" }),
            new Item(new Object[] { Color.blue, "blue" }),
            new Item(new Object[] { Color.yellow, "yellow" }),
            new Item(new Object[] { Color.magenta, "magenta" }),
            new Item(new Object[] { Color.black, "black" }),
            new Item(new Object[] { Color.green, "green" }),
            new Item(new Object[] { Color.lightGray, "lightGray"})
    });

    public void init() {
        final Container contentPane = getContentPane();

        colorCombo.setRenderer(new ColorRenderer());

        contentPane.setLayout(new FlowLayout());
        contentPane.add(colorCombo);

        colorCombo.addActionListener(new ActionListener(){
            public void actionPerformed(ActionEvent e) {
                Item item = (Item)colorCombo.getSelectedItem();
                String first = item.toString().substring(0,1);

                showStatus("'" + first + "'" + " is for " + item);
            }
        });
    }
}
class Item {
    private Color color;
    private String string;

    public Item(Object[] array) {
        color = (Color)array[0];
        string = (String)array[1];
    }
    public Color getColor() { return color; }
    public String toString() { return string; }
}
```

ColorRenderer and ColorIcon listings omitted;
see Example 18-6 on page 1112 for the class listings

Custom Key Selection Managers

When the key/item matching algorithm implemented by the
JComboBox.DefaultKeySelectionManager class is not sufficient, the
JComboBox.KeySelectionManager interface can be implemented to provide
a custom key selection manager.

Recall that the default algorithm for matching keys and items compares each key
with the first character of the string returned from the item's toString method.
For example, if the top item is selected in the combo box shown in Figure 18-6,
typing "blu" results in the following selections: 'b' selects blue, 'l' selects light
gray, and 'u' selects nothing because none of the colors begin with 'u'.

The applet shown in Figure 18-6 contains a combo box with a custom key
selection manager that stores consecutive keystrokes typed within half-second
intervals in a string that is used instead of a single keystroke for comparison. For
example, typing "blu" without pausing for more than half a second between
keystrokes will select blue, not light gray, as is the case for the default key
selection manager (JComboBox.DefaultKeySelectionManager).

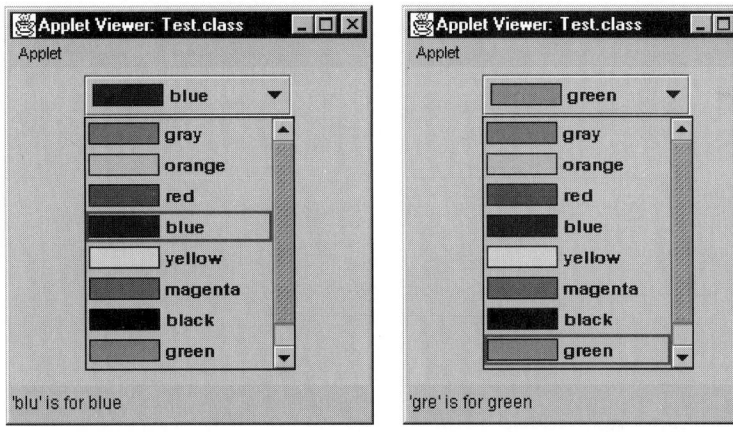

Figure 18-6 Implementing a Custom Key Selection Manager

The applet creates a combo box with an array of Item instances. The Item listing
is repeated below for convenience.

```
class Item {
    private Color color;
    private String string;

    public Item(Object[] array) {
        color = (Color)array[0];
        string = (String)array[1];
    }
    public Color getColor() { return color; }
    public String toString() { return string; }
}
```

The applet sets the key selection manager for the combo box to an instance of
ColorKeySelectionManager (listed below) and adds an action listener to the
combo box. The listener updates the applet's status bar whenever an item is
selected in the combo box.

```
public class Test extends JApplet {
    private ColorKeySelectionManager ksm =
                            new ColorKeySelectionManager();

    private JComboBox colorCombo = new JComboBox(new Object[] {
            new Item(new Object[] { Color.gray, "gray" }),
            new Item(new Object[] { Color.orange, "orange" }),
            new Item(new Object[] { Color.red, "red" }),
            new Item(new Object[] { Color.blue, "blue" }),
            new Item(new Object[] { Color.yellow, "yellow" }),
            new Item(new Object[] { Color.magenta, "magenta" }),
            new Item(new Object[] { Color.black, "black" }),
            new Item(new Object[] { Color.green, "green" }),
            new Item(new Object[] { Color.lightGray, "lightGray"})
    });
    public void init() {
        final Container contentPane = getContentPane();

        colorCombo.setRenderer(new ColorRenderer());
        colorCombo.setKeySelectionManager(ksm);

        contentPane.setLayout(new FlowLayout());
        contentPane.add(colorCombo);

        colorCombo.addActionListener(new ActionListener(){
            public void actionPerformed(ActionEvent e) {
                Item item = (Item)colorCombo.getSelectedItem();
                String itemString = item.toString();

                showStatus("'" + ksm.getSearchString() +
                        "'" + " is for " + itemString);
            }
        });
    }
}
```

The `ColorKeySelectionManager` class implements the
`JComboBox.KeySelectionManager` interface and maintains a search string
and a time stamp. The `selectionForKey` method, which is defined in
`JComboBox.KeySelectionManager()`, updates the search string and
performs a search from the item after the selected item to the last item in the list. If
the search did not prove fruitful and did not start at the top of the list, another
search is performed from the top of the list.[3]

```
class ColorKeySelectionManager
            implements JComboBox.KeySelectionManager {
    private String searchString = new String();
    private long lastTime;

    public int selectionForKey(char key,ComboBoxModel model) {
        updateSearchString(model, key);

        int start = findIndex(model, getSelectedString(model));
        int selection = search(model, start);

        if(selection == -1 && start != 0)
            selection = search(model, 0);

        return selection;
    }
    public String getSearchString() {
        return searchString;
    }
}
```

The `getSearchString` method is provided so that the action listener that
updates the applet's status bar has easy access to the search string.

The rest of the methods implemented by the `ColorKeySelectionManager`
class are support methods for the `selectionForKey` method and are listed
below, but not discussed.

```
private int search(ComboBoxModel model, int start) {
    for(int i=start; i < model.getSize(); ++i) {
        String s = getString(model, i);
        int searchLength = searchString.length();

        if(s.regionMatches(0,searchString,0,searchLength))
            return i;
```

3. The second search searches the entire list for the sake of simplicity. The search
    should end with the item above the selected item.

```
            }
            return -1;
        }
        private int findIndex(ComboBoxModel model, String find) {
            int size = model.getSize();

            if(find != null) {
                for(int i=0; i < size; ++i) {
                    String s = getString(model, i);

                    if(s.compareToIgnoreCase(find) == 0) {
                        return (i == size-1) ? 0 : i + 1;
                    }
                }
            }
            return 0;
        }
        private String getString(ComboBoxModel model, int index) {
            Item item = (Item)model.getElementAt(index);
            return item.toString();
        }
        private String getSelectedString(ComboBoxModel model) {
            Item item = (Item)model.getSelectedItem();
            return item.toString();
        }
        private void updateSearchString(
                            ComboBoxModel model, char key) {
            long time = System.currentTimeMillis();

            if(time - lastTime < 500)  searchString += key;
            else                       searchString = "" + key;

            lastTime = time;
        }
    }
```

The applet shown in Figure 18-6 is listed in its entirety in Example 18-4.

Example 18-4 Implementing a Custom Key Selection Manager

```
        import java.awt.*;
        import java.awt.event.*;
        import javax.swing.*;
        import javax.swing.border.*;

        public class Test extends JApplet {
            private ColorKeySelectionManager ksm =
                                new ColorKeySelectionManager();

            private JComboBox colorCombo = new JComboBox(new Object[] {
                new Item(new Object[] { Color.gray, "gray" }),
```

```
                new Item(new Object[] { Color.orange, "orange" }),
                new Item(new Object[] { Color.red, "red" }),
                new Item(new Object[] { Color.blue, "blue" }),
                new Item(new Object[] { Color.yellow, "yellow" }),
                new Item(new Object[] { Color.magenta, "magenta" }),
                new Item(new Object[] { Color.black, "black" }),
                new Item(new Object[] { Color.green, "green" }),
                new Item(new Object[] { Color.lightGray, "lightGray"})
        });
        public void init() {
            final Container contentPane = getContentPane();

            colorCombo.setRenderer(new ColorRenderer());
            colorCombo.setKeySelectionManager(ksm);

            contentPane.setLayout(new FlowLayout());
            contentPane.add(colorCombo);

            colorCombo.addActionListener(new ActionListener(){
                public void actionPerformed(ActionEvent e) {
                    Item item = (Item)colorCombo.getSelectedItem();
                    String itemString = item.toString();

                    showStatus("'" + ksm.getSearchString() +
                            "'" + " is for " + itemString);
                }
            });
        }
}
class Item {
    private Color color;
    private String string;

    public Item(Object[] array) {
        color = (Color)array[0];
        string = (String)array[1];
    }
    public Color getColor() { return color; }
    public String toString() { return string; }
}
class ColorKeySelectionManager
            implements JComboBox.KeySelectionManager {
    private String searchString = new String();
    private long lastTime;

    public int selectionForKey(char key,ComboBoxModel model) {
        updateSearchString(model, key);

        int start = findIndex(model, getSelectedString(model));
        int selection = search(model, start);

        if(selection == -1 && start != 0)
```

```
            selection = search(model, 0);

        return selection;
    }
    public String getSearchString() {
        return searchString;
    }
    private int search(ComboBoxModel model, int start) {
        for(int i=start; i < model.getSize(); ++i) {
            String s = getString(model, i);
            int searchLength = searchString.length();

            if(s.regionMatches(0,searchString,0,searchLength))
                return i;
        }
        return -1;
    }
    private int findIndex(ComboBoxModel model, String find) {
        int size = model.getSize();

        if(find != null) {
            for(int i=0; i < size; ++i) {
                String s = getString(model, i);

                if(s.compareToIgnoreCase(find) == 0) {
                    return (i == size-1) ? 0 : i + 1;
                }
            }
        }
        return 0;
    }
    private String getString(ComboBoxModel model, int index) {
        Item item = (Item)model.getElementAt(index);
        return item.toString();
    }
    private String getSelectedString(ComboBoxModel model) {
        Item item = (Item)model.getSelectedItem();
        return item.toString();
    }
    private void updateSearchString(
                        ComboBoxModel model, char key) {
        long time = System.currentTimeMillis();

        if(time - lastTime < 500) searchString += key;
        else                      searchString = "" + key;

        lastTime = time;
    }
}
```

ColorRenderer and ColorIcon listings omitted;
see Example 18-6 on page 1112 for the class listings

Programmatic Key Selection

Pressing a key while a combo box has focus can be accomplished programmatically with the JComboBox.selectWithKeyChar(char) method. The selectWithKeyChar method is passed a character that represents a key, and uses the combo box's key selection manager to select a corresponding item.

The applet shown in Figure 18-7 contains two combo boxes. Characters selected from the left-hand combo box select items in the right-hand combo box by passing the selected character to JComboBox.selectWithChar(). When an item is selected in the right-hand combo box, a message dialog is displayed and indicates the item that was selected and the character used to select it.

The left-hand picture shown in Figure 18-7 shows the applet as it appears initially. The right-hand picture was taken after "1" was selected from the left-hand combo box and the message dialog was displayed. The bottom picture was taken after the message dialog was dismissed.

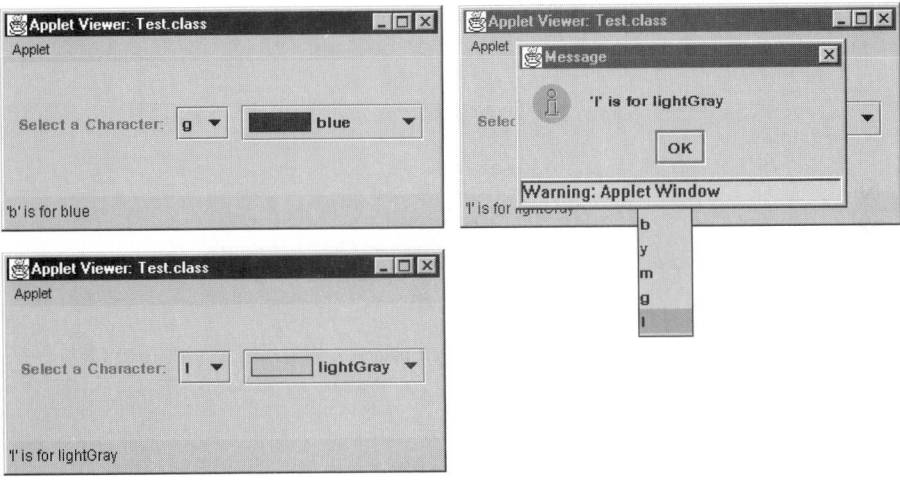

Figure 18-7 Using a Key to Select an Item in a Combo Box

The applet creates two combo boxes. The left-hand combo box is populated by instances of java.lang.Character, and the right-hand combo box contains instances of Item.

```
public class Test extends JApplet {
    private JComboBox charsCombo = new JComboBox(new Object[] {
            new Character('g'), new Character('o'),
            new Character('r'), new Character('b'),
            new Character('y'), new Character('m'),
            new Character('g'), new Character('l'),
    });
    private JComboBox colorCombo = new JComboBox(new Object[] {
            new Item(new Object[] { Color.gray, "gray" }),
            new Item(new Object[] { Color.orange, "orange" }),
            new Item(new Object[] { Color.red, "red" }),
            new Item(new Object[] { Color.blue, "blue" }),
            new Item(new Object[] { Color.yellow, "yellow" }),
            new Item(new Object[] { Color.magenta, "magenta" }),
            new Item(new Object[] { Color.black, "black" }),
            new Item(new Object[] { Color.green, "green" }),
            new Item(new Object[] { Color.lightGray, "lightGray"})
    });
```

Action listeners are added to both combo boxes. The character combo box reacts to selections by invoking `selectWithKeyChar` for the color combo box and subsequently showing the message dialog. The color combo box reacts to selections by updating the applet's status area.

```
public void init() {
    final Container contentPane = getContentPane();

    colorCombo.setRenderer(new ColorRenderer());

    charsCombo.addActionListener(new ActionListener() {
        public void actionPerformed(ActionEvent e) {
            final Character c = (Character)
                            charsCombo.getSelectedItem();

            colorCombo.selectWithKeyChar(c.charValue());

            Item item = (Item)colorCombo.getSelectedItem();

            JOptionPane.showMessageDialog(contentPane,
                    "'" + c.toString() + "'" +
                    " is for " + item.toString());
        }
    });
    colorCombo.addActionListener(new ActionListener() {
        public void actionPerformed(ActionEvent e) {
            Item item = (Item)colorCombo.getSelectedItem();
            Character first = new Character(
                            item.toString().charAt(0));
```

```
            showStatus("'" + first.toString() + "'" +
                    " is for " + item);
        }
    });

    contentPane.setLayout(
            new FlowLayout(FlowLayout.CENTER, 10, 35));

    contentPane.add(new JLabel("Select a Character:"));
    contentPane.add(charsCombo);
    contentPane.add(colorCombo);
    }
}
```

It is rather obvious from looking at Figure 18-7 that something is amiss in the right-hand picture because the drop-down list for the character combo box is visible beneath the dialog. The unsightly drop-down list can be erased, as shown in Figure 18-8, before the dialog is displayed by wrapping the call to `JOptionPane.showMessageDialog()` in a `Runnable` that is passed to `SwingUtilites.invokeLater()`.

```
charsCombo.addActionListener(new ActionListener() {
    public void actionPerformed(ActionEvent e) {
        final Character c = (Character)
                            charsCombo.getSelectedItem();

        colorCombo.selectWithKeyChar(c.charValue());

        SwingUtilities.invokeLater(new Runnable() {
            public void run() {
                Item item = (Item)colorCombo.getSelectedItem();

                JOptionPane.showMessageDialog(contentPane,
                        "'" + c.toString() + "'" +
                        " is for " + item.toString());
            }
        });
    }
});
```

When the dialog is displayed from a `Runnable` passed to `SwingUtilities.invokeLater()` as listed above, the result is as shown in Figure 18-8.

The applet shown in Figure 18-8 is listed in its entirety in Example 18-5.

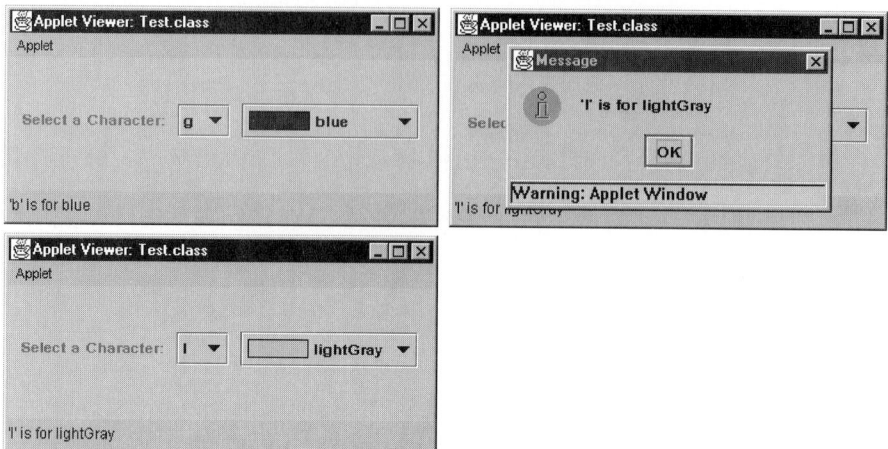

Figure 18-8 Using SwingUtilities.invokeLater()

Example 18-5 Using SwingUtilities.invokeLater()

```java
import java.awt.*;
import java.awt.event.*;
import javax.swing.*;
import javax.swing.border.*;

public class Test extends JApplet {
    private JComboBox charsCombo = new JComboBox(new Object[] {
            new Character('g'), new Character('o'),
            new Character('r'), new Character('b'),
            new Character('y'), new Character('m'),
            new Character('g'), new Character('l'),
    });
    private JComboBox colorCombo = new JComboBox(new Object[] {
            new Item(new Object[] { Color.gray, "gray" }),
            new Item(new Object[] { Color.orange, "orange" }),
            new Item(new Object[] { Color.red, "red" }),
            new Item(new Object[] { Color.blue, "blue" }),
            new Item(new Object[] { Color.yellow, "yellow" }),
            new Item(new Object[] { Color.magenta, "magenta" }),
            new Item(new Object[] { Color.black, "black" }),
            new Item(new Object[] { Color.green, "green" }),
            new Item(new Object[] { Color.lightGray, "lightGray"})
    });

    public void init() {
        final Container contentPane = getContentPane();
```

```
        colorCombo.setRenderer(new ColorRenderer());

        colorCombo.addActionListener(new ActionListener(){
            public void actionPerformed(ActionEvent e) {
                Item item = (Item)colorCombo.getSelectedItem();
                Character first = new Character(
                                    item.toString().charAt(0));

                showStatus("'" + first.toString() + "'" +
                        " is for " + item);
            }
        });
        charsCombo.addActionListener(new ActionListener() {
            public void actionPerformed(ActionEvent e) {
                final Character c = (Character)
                                    charsCombo.getSelectedItem();

                colorCombo.selectWithKeyChar(c.charValue());

                Item item = (Item) colorCombo.getSelectedItem();

                JOptionPane.showMessageDialog(contentPane,
                        "'" + c.toString() + "'" +
                        " is for " + item.toString());
            }
        });
        contentPane.setLayout(
                new FlowLayout(FlowLayout.CENTER, 10, 35));

        contentPane.add(new JLabel("Select a Character:"));
        contentPane.add(charsCombo);
        contentPane.add(colorCombo);
    }
}
class Item {
    private Color color;
    private String string;

    public Item(Object[] array) {
        color = (Color)array[0];
        string = (String)array[1];
    }
    public Color getColor() { return color; }
    public String toString() { return string; }
}
```

ColorRenderer and ColorIcon listings omitted;
see Example 18-6 on page 1112 for the class listings

Combo Box Editors

Unlike lists, combo boxes can be edited. Whether a combo box is editable is controlled by the JComboBox.setEditable method. By default, instances of JComboBox are not editable, and setEditable(true) must be called for editable combo boxes after they are constructed. JComboBox.isEditable() returns a boolean value indicating a combo box's editability.

Combo boxes provide a visual cue indicating that they are editable, as can be seen from Figure 18-9, which shows combo boxes for standard Swing look and feels; editable on the right and noneditable on the left.

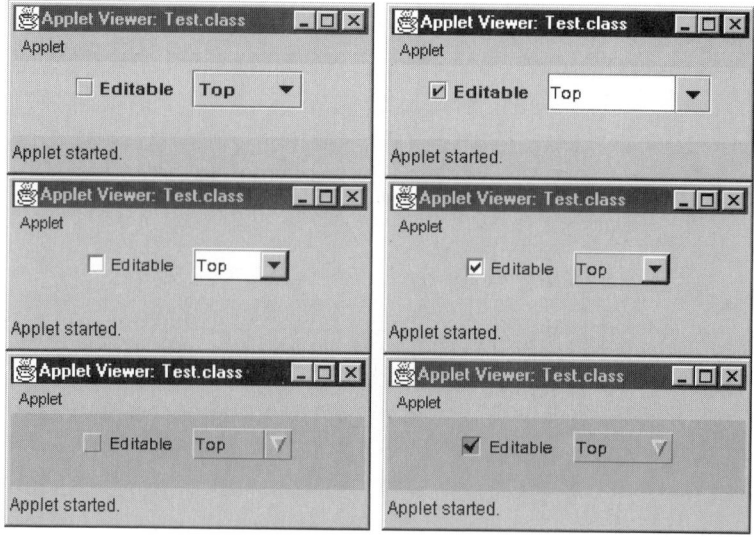

Figure 18-9 Editable and Noneditable Check Boxes

Enabling editing with a call to JComboBox.setEditable(true) causes a component provided by the editor to be added to the combo box. By default, a text field is provided by an instance of BasicComboBoxEditor.

Figure 18-10 shows the sequence of events that occurs when
`JComboBox.setEditable(true)` is invoked. The editable property for
`JComboBox` is a bound property, and therefore instances of `JComboBox` fire
property change events when their editable state is modified. The property
change is ultimately handled by the combo box's UI delegate, which adds the
editor's component to the combo box.

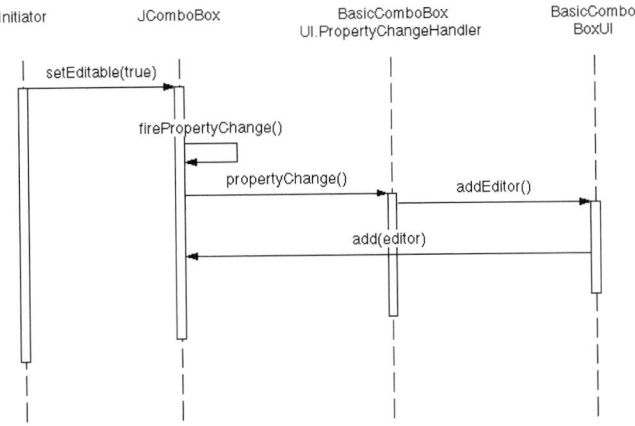

Figure 18-10 Adding an Editor Component to a Combo Box

Exactly what it means to be edited is not precisely defined for combo boxes. The
default combo box editor—an instance of `BasicComboBoxEditor`—edits the
selected item, and the items displayed in the combo box's list remain unchanged.

For example, Figure 18-11 illustrates a combo box being edited. The upper-left
picture shows the combo box in its initial state. In the upper-right picture, the
selected item has been edited, but the edit has not been committed by the user
pressing the Enter key. The lower-left picture was taken after the Enter key was
pressed, and the lower-right picture was taken after a subsequent selection was
made in the combo box.

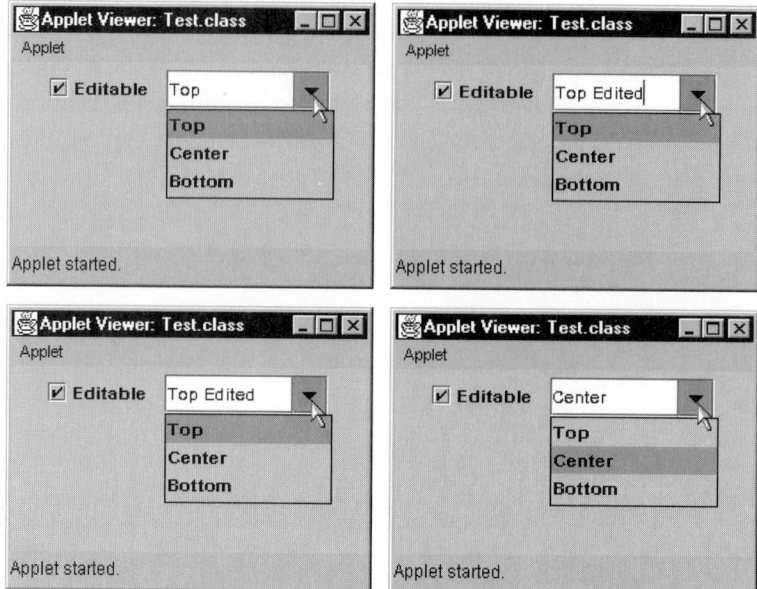

Figure 18-11 Editing an Item with BasicComboBoxEditor

Notice that editing does not affect the items displayed in a combo box's drop-down list. Editing is only applied to the selected item, and editing changes are lost after a subsequent selection is made from the list. However, custom combo box editors do not have to abide by the same rules; for example, an editor may add an edited item to the combo box's list.

If an editor is not explicitly specified, instances of JComboBox are fitted with an instance of BasicComboBoxEditor from the swing.plaf.basic package. BasicComboBoxEditor implements the ComboBoxEditor interface and provides a text field for editing. Swing does not provide an implementation of the ComboBoxEditor interface in the swing package.

Figure 18-12 shows a class diagram for combo box editors.

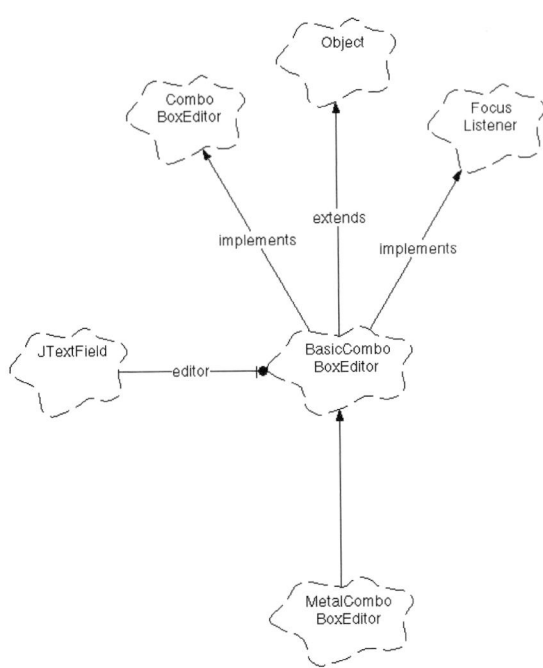

Figure 18-12 Class Diagram for Combo Box Editors

The responsibilities of a combo box editor are defined by the `ComboBoxEditor` interface. The `BasicComboBoxEditor` class implements the `ComboBoxEditor` and `java.awt.event.FocusListener` interfaces. `BasicComboBoxEditor` maintains a `protected` reference to its text field and is extended by the `MetalComboBoxEditor` class from the `swing.plaf.metal` package.

Swing Tip ...

Combo Box Editors vs. Renderers

Combo box renderers and editors both implement methods that return a component. The components are used—not surprisingly—to render and edit cells, respectively.

Components returned from a renderer's getListCellRendererComponent method are used like a rubber stamp to render cells in a combo box's drop-down list. A renderer's component can never be manipulated or respond to events because only the visual representation of the component is used.

On the other hand, components returned from an editor's getEditorComponent, are inserted into the area used to display a combo box's selected item. An editor's component is present on-screen and therefore can be manipulated.

The ComboBoxEditor interface is summarized in Interface Summary 18-4.

Interface Summary 18-4   ComboBoxEditor

Action Listener Registration

---

public abstract void <u>addActionListener</u>(ActionListener)
public abstract void <u>removeActionListener</u>(ActionListener)

Combo box editors should fire an action event after an item has been added and therefore must provide methods for adding and removing action listeners. BasicComboBoxEditor adds and removes listeners from its text field. Text fields fire action events when the Enter key is pressed and the text field has focus.

Editor Component

---

public abstract Component <u>getEditorComponent</u>()
public abstract void <u>selectAll</u>()

A call to JComboBox.setEditable(true) ultimately results in a call to the editor's getEditorComponent() method. The component returned is inserted into the area occupied by the selected item.

The selectAll method should select all of the items being edited. BasicComboBoxEditor implements the method by invoking JTextField.selectAll() for its editor component. However, ComboBoxEditor.selectAll() is not called from anywhere within Swing.

Items

---

public abstract Object <u>getItem</u>()
public abstract void <u>setItem</u>(Object)

The setItem and getItem methods deal with objects stored in a combo box's model. For example, if an editable combo box stores strings that represent colors in its model and has a renderer that renders the colors with icons in a label, the editor's setItem method will be passed a string from the model, not an icon or a label. Likewise, the editor's getItem method would be bound to return a string.

The applet shown in Figure 18-13 contains a combo box representing a list of colors. The combo box is fitted with a custom editor that allows the selected color to be edited. A mouse click on the selected item causes the editor to display a color chooser, from which a color can be selected.

The top picture shows the applet as it appears initially. The middle picture shows a color being selected from the color chooser, and the bottom picture shows the applet after the selected item has been edited.

The applet creates a combo box with an array of Object arrays, each containing a color and a string identifying the color. The combo box's renderer is set to an instance of ColorRenderer; the ColorRenderer class extends JLabel and displays a color icon and a string.

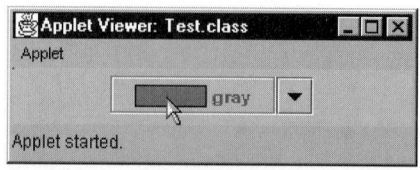

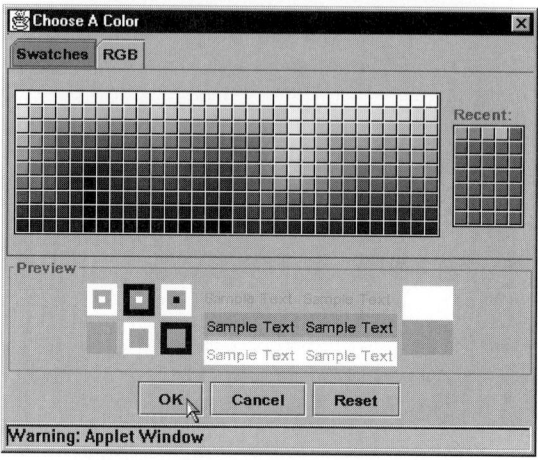

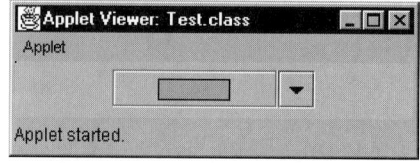

Figure 18-13 A Custom Combo Box Editor

The applet also creates an instance of `ColorComboBoxEditor` and specifies it as the editor for the combo box. Because combo boxes are not editable by default, `JComboBox.setEditable(true)` is invoked by the applet's `init` method.

```
public class Test extends JApplet {
    private JComboBox comboBox =
        new JComboBox(new Object[] {
            new Object[] { Color.gray, "gray" },
            new Object[] { Color.orange, "orange" },
            new Object[] { Color.red, "red" },
            new Object[] { Color.blue, "blue" },
            new Object[] { Color.yellow, "yellow" },
            new Object[] { Color.magenta, "magenta" },
            new Object[] { Color.black, "black" },
```

```
            new Object[] { Color.green, "green" },
            new Object[] { Color.lightGray, "lightGray" },
            new Object[] { Color.white, "white" },
        });

    public void init() {
        Container contentPane = getContentPane();

        comboBox.setRenderer(new ColorRendererer());
        comboBox.setEditor(new ColorComboBoxEditor());
        comboBox.setEditable(true);

        contentPane.setLayout(new FlowLayout());
        contentPane.add(comboBox);
    }
}
```

A design idiom commonly used throughout Swing is to layer objects with an
interface that is implemented by an abstract class, which in turn is extended by a
default class. The interface defines basic behavior, the abstract class typically
implements functionality that is not subject to change, making it attractive for
subclassing, and the default class implements default behaviors for functionality
that are likely to be customized. For example, the ListModel interface is
implemented by the AbstractListModel class, which in turn is extended by
the DefaultListModel class. See "List Models" on page 1011 for more
information concerning list models.

However, the *interface* —> *abstract class* —> *default class* idiom is not used for
combo box editors. As a result, implementing custom editors involves
implementing the ComboBoxEditor interface directly, which includes managing
a list of action listeners and firing action events to the listeners. Because
management of action listeners and firing action events represent highly reusable
functionality, they should be implemented in an AbstractComboBoxEditor
class, like the one listed below.

```
abstract class AbstractComboBoxEditor implements ComboBoxEditor {
    EventListenerList listenerList = new EventListenerList();

    public void addActionListener(ActionListener listener) {
        listenerList.add(ActionListener.class, listener);
    }
    public void removeActionListener(ActionListener listener) {
        listenerList.remove(ActionListener.class, listener);
    }
    protected void fireActionPerformed(ActionEvent e) {
        // Guaranteed to return a non-null array
```

```
            Object[] listeners = listenerList.getListenerList();

            // Process the listeners last to first, notifying
            // those that are interested in this event
            for (int i = listeners.length-2; i>=0; i-=2) {
                if (listeners[i]==ActionListener.class) {
                    ((ActionListener)
                        listeners[i+1]).actionPerformed(e);
                }
            }
        }
    }
}
```

The `ColorComboBoxEditor` class extends the `AbstractComboBoxEditor` class listed above. `ColorComboBoxEditor` uses a label to display a color icon and text. The color icon is an instance of the `ColorIcon` class which implements the `Icon` interface and paints a filled rectangle with a black border. The `ColorIcon` class is listed in Example 18-6 on page 1112.

A color chooser is instantiated and wrapped in a dialog with a call to `JColorChooser.createDialog()`. See "JColorChooser" on page 978 for more information on the `JColorChooser` class.

```
    class ColorComboBoxEditor extends AbstractComboBoxEditor {
        ColorIcon editorIcon = new ColorIcon();
        JLabel editorLabel = new JLabel(editorIcon);

        Object[] comboBoxItem;

        JColorChooser colorChooser = new JColorChooser();
        ActionListener okListener = new OKListener();
        Dialog dialog = JColorChooser.createDialog(
                        null,   // parentComponent
                        "Choose A Color",// title
                        true,       // modal
                        colorChooser,
                        okListener,
                        null);      // cancel listener
        ...
```

When the `ColorComboBoxEditor` is constructed, a mouse listener is added to the editor's label to show the dialog when the mouse is pressed. The label is also the component returned from the editor's `getEditorComponent` method.

```
...
public ColorComboBoxEditor() {
    editorLabel.setBorder(BorderFactory.createEtchedBorder());

    editorLabel.addMouseListener(new MouseAdapter() {
        public void mousePressed(MouseEvent e) {
            dialog.setVisible(true);
        }
    });
}
public Component getEditorComponent() {
    return editorLabel;
}
...
```

When the color chooser is constructed, an instance of OKListener is specified as the listener to be notified when the OK button in the color chooser is activated.

Recall that the items contained in the combo box were specified as Object arrays containing a color and a string. The OK listener uses the color selected from the color chooser and a null string to construct an Object array. The array is returned from the getItem method. The listener also fires an action event to all registered action listeners, as is required whenever an item is edited.

```
...
class OKListener implements ActionListener {
    public void actionPerformed(ActionEvent e) {
        comboBoxItem =
            new Object[] { colorChooser.getColor(), null };

        fireActionPerformed(e);
    }
}
...
```

The editor implements the setItem, getItem, and selectAll methods defined by the interface.

The setItem method stores the item in the editor's ComboBoxEditor member variable and sets the icon's color and the label's text. The getItem method simply returns the item. Because the editor does not display a selectable item, the selectAll method is implemented as a no-op.

```
public Object getItem() {
    return comboBoxItem;
}
public void setItem(Object item) {
    comboBoxItem = (Object[])itemToSet;

    editorIcon.setColor((Color)comboBoxItem[0]);
    editorLabel.setText((String)comboBoxItem[1]);
}
public void selectAll() {
    // from ComboBoxModel interface:  nothing to select
}
}
```

The applet shown in Figure 18-13 is listed in its entirety in Example 18-6.

Example 18-6 Implementing a Custom Combo Box Editor

```
import java.awt.*;
import java.awt.event.*;
import javax.swing.*;
import javax.swing.event.*;
import javax.swing.border.*;

public class Test extends JApplet {
    private JComboBox comboBox =
        new JComboBox(new Object[] {
            new Object[] { Color.gray, "gray" },
            new Object[] { Color.orange, "orange" },
            new Object[] { Color.red, "red" },
            new Object[] { Color.blue, "blue" },
            new Object[] { Color.yellow, "yellow" },
            new Object[] { Color.magenta, "magenta" },
            new Object[] { Color.black, "black" },
            new Object[] { Color.green, "green" },
            new Object[] { Color.lightGray, "lightGray" },
            new Object[] { Color.white, "white" },
        });

    public void init() {
        Container contentPane = getContentPane();

        comboBox.setRenderer(new ColorRendererer());
        comboBox.setEditor(new ColorComboBoxEditor());
        comboBox.setEditable(true);

        contentPane.setLayout(new FlowLayout());
        contentPane.add(comboBox);
    }
}
```

```
class ColorComboBoxEditor extends AbstractComboBoxEditor {
    ColorIcon editorIcon = new ColorIcon();
    JLabel editorLabel = new JLabel(editorIcon);

    Object[] comboBoxItem;

    JColorChooser colorChooser = new JColorChooser();
    ActionListener okListener = new OKListener();
    Dialog dialog = JColorChooser.createDialog(
                    null,   // parentComponent
                    "Choose A Color",// title
                    true,        // modal
                    colorChooser,
                    okListener,
                    null);       // cancel listener

    public ColorComboBoxEditor() {
        editorLabel.setBorder(BorderFactory.createEtchedBorder());

        editorLabel.addMouseListener(new MouseAdapter() {
            public void mousePressed(MouseEvent e) {
                dialog.setVisible(true);
            }
        });
    }
    class OKListener implements ActionListener {
        public void actionPerformed(ActionEvent e) {
            comboBoxItem =
                new Object[] { colorChooser.getColor(), null };

            fireActionPerformed(e);
        }
    }
    public Component getEditorComponent() {
        return editorLabel;
    }
    public Object getItem() {
        return comboBoxItem;
    }
    public void selectAll() {
        // from ComboBoxModel interface:  nothing to select
    }
    public void setItem(Object item) {
        comboBoxItem = (Object[])itemToSet;

        editorIcon.setColor((Color)comboBoxItem[0]);
        editorLabel.setText((String)comboBoxItem[1]);
    }
}
abstract class AbstractComboBoxEditor implements ComboBoxEditor {
    EventListenerList listenerList = new EventListenerList();

    public void addActionListener(ActionListener listener) {
```

```
                    listenerList.add(ActionListener.class, listener);
            }
            public void removeActionListener(ActionListener listener) {
                listenerList.remove(ActionListener.class, listener);
            }
            protected void fireActionPerformed(ActionEvent e) {
                // Guaranteed to return a non-null array
                Object[] listeners = listenerList.getListenerList();

                // Process the listeners last to first, notifying
                // those that are interested in this event
                for (int i = listeners.length-2; i>=0; i-=2) {
                    if (listeners[i]==ActionListener.class) {
                        ((ActionListener)
                            listeners[i+1]).actionPerformed(e);
                    }
                }
            }
        }
}
class ColorRendererer extends JLabel
                                implements ListCellRenderer {
    private ColorIcon icon = new ColorIcon();

    public ColorRendererer() {
        setOpaque(true);
        setIcon(icon);
    }
    public Component getListCellRendererComponent(
                            JList list,
                            Object value,
                            int index,
                            boolean isSelected,
                            boolean cellHasFocus) {
        Object[] array = (Object[])value;

        icon.setColor((Color)array[0]);
        setText((String)array[1]);

        if(isSelected) {
            setForeground(list.getSelectionForeground());
            setBackground(list.getSelectionBackground());
        }
        else {
            setForeground(list.getForeground());
            setBackground(list.getBackground());
        }
        return this;
    }
}
class ColorIcon implements Icon {
    private Color color;
    private int w, h;
```

```
   public ColorIcon() {
      this(Color.gray, 50, 15);
   }
   public ColorIcon(Color color, int w, int h) {
      this.color = color;
      this.w = w;
      this.h = h;
   }
   public void paintIcon(Component c, Graphics g, int x, int y) {
      g.setColor(Color.black);
      g.drawRect(x, y, w-1, h-1);
      g.setColor(color);
      g.fillRect(x+1, y+1, w-2, h-2);
   }
   public Color getColor() {
      return color;
   }
   public void setColor(Color color) {
      this.color = color;
   }
   public int getIconWidth() {
      return w;
   }
   public int getIconHeight() {
      return h;
   }
}
```

The JComboBox class is summarized in Component Summary 18-1.

Component Summary 18-1   JComboBox

Model(s)	ComboBoxModel
UI Delegate(s)	javax.swing.plaf.basic.BasicComboBoxUI
Renderer(s)	javax.swing.plaf.basic.BasicComboBoxRenderer
Editor(s)	ComboBoxEditor
Events Fired	ActionEvents,
	ItemEvents,

PropertyChangeEvents

Replacement For   java.awt.Choice

Class Diagrams

Figure 18-14 JComboBox Class Diagram

Like all lightweight Swing components, JComboBox extends JComponent and implements the Accessible interface.

JComboBox implements the java.awt.ItemSelectable interface to maintain compatibility with java.awt.Choice, which fires item events when items are selected or deselected.

Combo box editors fire action events to registered action listeners whenever an item is edited. One of those listeners is the combo box itself, which reacts to editing by updating the model's selected item and hiding the list popup. As a result, JComboBox implements the ActionListener interface.

Combo box models fire list data events when a combo box's data is modified. JComboBox implements the ListDataListener interface and listens to its model for the purpose of possibly resetting the selected item when combo box data changes.

The objects maintained by JComboBox illustrate the responsibilities that combo boxes delegate to other objects. JComboBox maintains references to its model, list cell renderer, editor, and key selection manager.

When a combo box's selected item is modified, two item events are fired, one for deselecting the previously selected item and another for selecting the currently selected item. The Object reference to selectedItemReminder keeps track of the last selected item so that it can be designated as the source of the deselection event.

Action events come with a string, known as the action command, that identifies the action. JComboBox maintains an actionCommand string that by default is "comboBoxChanged".

Finally, JComboBox maintains a string, an integer, and two boolean references, all of which represent combo box properties.

JComboBox Properties

The properties maintained by the JComboBox class are listed in Table 18-3.

Table 18-3 JComboBox Properties

Property Name	Data Type	Property Type[1]	Access[2]	Default[3]
actionCommand	String	S	SG	"comboBox Changed"
editable	boolean	B	S	false
editor	ComboBox-Editor	B	SG	null
itemAt	Object	I	G	null
itemCount	int	S	G	-1

Table 18-3   JComboBox Properties (Continued)

Property Name	Data Type	Property Type[1]	Access[2]	Default[3]
keySelectionManager	KeySelection-Manager	S	SG	null
lightWeightPopupEnabled	boolean	S	SG	true
maximumRowCount	int	B	SG	8
model	ComboBox-Model	B	SG	ComboBoxModel
popupVisible	boolean		S	false
renderer	ListCell-Renderer	B	SG	See discussion below
selectedIndex	int	S	SG	-1
selectedItem	Object	S	SG	null

1. B = bound (fires PropertyChangeEvent) / C = constrained/ I = indexed /
   S = simple / Ch = fires ChangeEvent
2. C = settable at construction time / G = getter method / S = setter method
3. L&F = look-and-feel dependent

actionCommand — Instances of JComboBox fire action events when combo box items are selected. Action events have an associated action command, which is a string that identifies a type of action. JComboBox specifies its actionCommand property as the action command for all the action events it fires.

editable — A boolean variable that keeps track of whether instances of JComboBox are editable. See "Combo Box Editors" on page 1102 for more information concerning combo box editing.

itemAt — A read-only model property for an object, given its index.

itemCount — A read-only model property that represents the number of items contained in a combo box drop-down list.

keySelectionManager — An object that implements the JComboBox.KeySelectionManager interface. See "Combo Box Key Selection Managers" on page 1085 for information concerning combo boxes and key selection management.

lightWeightPopupEnabled — Combo boxes display their lists in a popup menu. By default, the popup menu is a lightweight menu, but there are circumstances that require the use of a heavyweight menu. As a result, the lightWeightPopupEnabled property can be set to false in order to force the use of a heavyweight popup menu.

maximumRowCount — There is no limit as to the number of items that can be displayed in a combo box drop-down list. However, the number of visible rows in the list can be controlled with the maximumRowCount property, which by default is defined to be 8.

model — An implementation of the ComboBoxModel interface which extends ListModel.

popupVisible — A boolean property that controls the visibility of the popup menu that contains a combo box's list.

renderer — Renderers render list cells by implementing the ListCellRenderer interface.

selectedIndex — Represents the index of the selected item in a combo box list.

selectedItem — The object that is currently selected in the combo box.

JComboBox Events

Instances of JComboBox fire two item events when their selected item changes—either by selection or editing—one for deselecting the previously selected item and another for selecting the currently selected item. After the item events are fired, an action event is also fired.

Figure 18-15 illustrates the sequence of events when a combo box's selected index is modified.

Combo box editors fire action events immediately after an item has been edited. Action listeners can be added directly to a combo box editor for handling editing events.

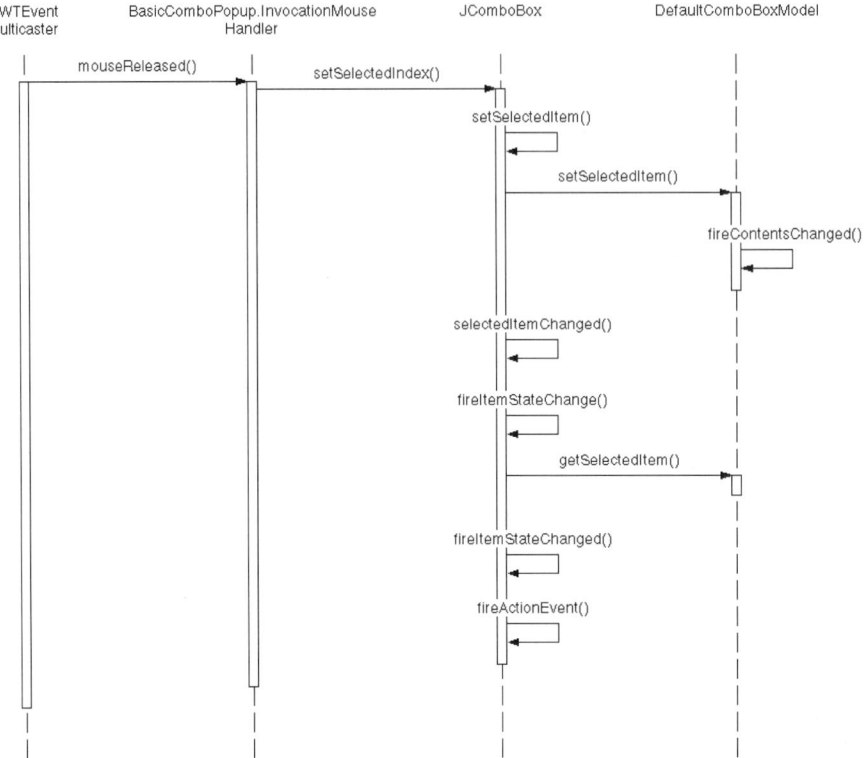

Figure 18-15 JComboBox Events

Selection Events

The applet shown in Figure 18-16 adds an item listener to the combo box it contains. The listener shows a message dialog that displays information about the selection or deselection.

The top picture shows the applet as it appears initially. The middle pictures were taken after the Center item was selected; the pictures show the successive dialogs displayed for each of the item events fired when the selection changes. The bottom picture shows the combo box with the Center item selected.

The applet shown in Figure 18-16 is listed in Example 18-7.

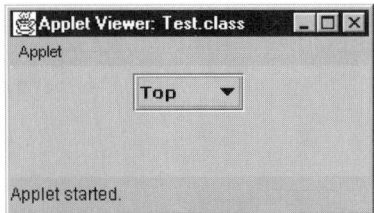

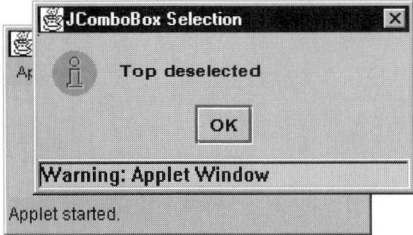 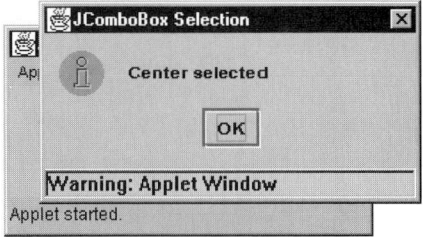

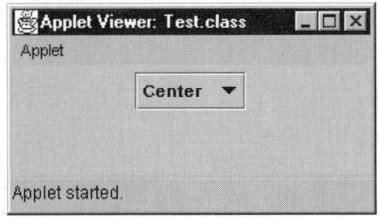

Figure 18-16 Handling Selection Events

Example 18-7 Handling Selection Events

```java
import java.applet.Applet;
import java.awt.*;
import java.awt.event.*;
import javax.swing.*;

public class Test extends JApplet {
    private JComboBox comboBox = new JComboBox();

    public void init() {
        Container contentPane = getContentPane();

        comboBox.addItem("Top");
        comboBox.addItem("Center");
        comboBox.addItem("Bottom");

        contentPane.setLayout(new FlowLayout());
        contentPane.add(comboBox);
```

```
comboBox.addItemListener(new ItemListener() {
    public void itemStateChanged(ItemEvent event) {
        int state = event.getStateChange();
        String item = (String)event.getItem(), s;

        if(event.getStateChange() == ItemEvent.SELECTED)
            s = " selected";
        else
            s = " deselected";

        JOptionPane.showMessageDialog(
            comboBox, // parent component
            item + s, // message
            "JComboBox Selection", // title
            JOptionPane.INFORMATION_MESSAGE); // type
    }
});
    }
}
```

The applet creates the combo box, adds three items to the combo box, and adds the combo box to its content pane.

An item listener that shows a message dialog conveying the item that was selected or deselected is added to the combo box. The listener obtains the state of the event—either `ItemEvent.SELECTED` or `ItemEvent.DESELECTED`—by invoking `getStateChange` on the event. The item itself is obtained by invoking `getItem` on the event, and the state and item string are used in the message dialog.

Editing Events

Combo box editors fire action events whenever the currently displayed value is edited. The applet shown in Figure 18-17 contains a combo box and adds an action listener to the combo box's editor. The listener updates the applet's status area whenever the value displayed in the check box is edited.

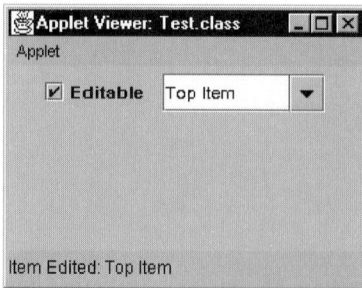

Figure 18-17 Handling Editing Events

The applet shown in Figure 18-17 is listed in Example 18-8.

Example 18-8 Handling Editing Events

```java
import java.awt.*;
import java.awt.event.*;
import javax.swing.*;

public class Test extends JApplet {
    private JComboBox comboBox = new JComboBox();
    private ComboBoxEditor editor = comboBox.getEditor();

    public void init() {
        Container contentPane = getContentPane();

        comboBox.setEditable(true);

        comboBox.addItem("Top");
        comboBox.addItem("Center");
        comboBox.addItem("Bottom");

        contentPane.setLayout(new FlowLayout());
        contentPane.add(comboBox);

        editor.addActionListener(new ActionListener() {
            public void actionPerformed(ActionEvent e) {
                String s = (String)editor.getItem();
                showStatus("Item Edited: " + s);
            }
        });
    }
}
```

The listener obtains the current value displayed by the check box by invoking
`ComboBoxEditor.getItem()` for the combo box's editor.

JComboBox Class Summaries

The `public` and `protected` variables and methods for `JComboBox` are listed in
Class Summary 18-2.

Class Summary 18-2   JComboBox

Extends: JComponent

Implements: javax.accessibility.Accessible, java.awt.ItemSelectable,
                      java.awt.event.ActionListener,
                      javax.swing.event.ListDataListener

Constructors

---

public <u>JComboBox</u>()
public <u>JComboBox</u>(Object[])
public <u>JComboBox</u>(Vector)
public <u>JComboBox</u>(ComboBoxModel)

JComboBox provides four constructors that are nearly identical to the
constructors provided by the JList class—see "JList Class Summaries" on
page 1062 for a discussion of JList constructors.

Each of the first three constructors listed above fits combo boxes with models that
are instances of DefaultComboBoxModel. References to objects contained in the
Object array passed to the second constructor listed above are copied into a
vector maintained by the DefaultComboBoxModel.

A particular combo box model can be explicitly specified at construction with the
last constructor listed above.

Methods

Methods Defined by ActionListener/ItemListener/ListDataListener

---

public void <u>actionPerformed</u>(ActionEvent)

public void <u>addItemListener</u>(ItemListener)

```
public void removeItemListener(ItemListener)
public Object[] getSelectedObjects()

public void contentsChanged(ListDataEvent)
public void intervalAdded(ListDataEvent)
public void intervalRemoved(ListDataEvent)
```

Instances of `JComboBox` register themselves as action listeners for their editors. When a value is edited in a combo box, the combo box editor fires an action event to the combo box by way of its `actionPerformed` method. `JComboBox.actionPerformed()` sets the selected item of the combo box to the edited value and hides the popup menu associated with the combo box.

`JComboBox` implements the `java.awt.event.ItemListener` interface to maintain compatibility with `java.awt.Choice`. The `getSelectedObjects` method returns an `Object` array that always has one item—a reference to the combo box's selected item.

Instances of `JComboBox` register themselves with their models as list data listeners. When the data stored in a combo box model is modified, the associated combo box is notified with one of the last three methods listed above. All data modifications are handled by `JComboBox` in the same manner, by updating the selected item if necessary.

Combo Box Delegates: Editor/Key Selection Manager/Model/Renderer

```
public ComboBoxEditor getEditor()
public JComboBox.KeySelectionManager getKeySelectionManager()
public ComboBoxModel getModel()
public ListCellRenderer getRenderer()

public void setEditor(ComboBoxEditor)
public void setKeySelectionManager(JComboBox.KeySelectionManager)
public void setModel(ComboBoxModel)
public void setRenderer(ListCellRenderer)

protected JComboBox.KeySelectionManager createDefaultKeySelectionManager()
public void configureEditor(ComboBoxEditor editor, Object item)
public boolean selectWithKeyChar(char)
```

The first eight methods listed above are accessors for the four combo box delegates. Editing, key selection, data storage/retrieval, and cell rendering are all pluggable behaviors for combo boxes.

Default key selection managers are created by the aptly named `createDefaultKeySelectionManager` method, which is `protected` so that the default can be overridden for an extension of `JComboBox`.

The `configureEditor` method is called whenever the contents of a combo box are modified. The method sets the item for the editor.

The `selectWithKeyChar` method programmatically simulates key selection.

Item Methods

---

public void <u>addItem</u>(Object)
public void <u>insertItemAt</u>(Object item, int index)
public void <u>removeAllItems</u>()
public void <u>removeItem</u>(Object)
public void <u>removeItemAt</u>(int index)

public Object <u>getItemAt</u>(int index)
public int <u>getItemCount</u>()

public Object <u>getSelectedItem</u>()
public void <u>setSelectedItem</u>(Object)
protected void <u>selectedItemChanged</u>()

The methods listed above all deal with combo box items. The first group of methods listed above is somewhat of an object-oriented abnormality because the methods do not work properly with all combo boxes; an exception will be thrown if the methods are invoked for combo boxes that have immutable models. The `getItemAt` and `getItemCount` methods do not modify data and therefore will work for both mutable and immutable combo boxes.

The last of methods listed above are concerned with the selected item. The `getSelectedItem` and `setSelectedItem` methods have the same signatures as the methods defined in `ComboBoxModel`. In fact, `JComboBox` delegates directly to its model for both methods.

The `selectedItemChanged` methods fires two item events—one for deselection of the previously selected item (if any) and another for the currently selected item. After the item events are fired, an action event is also fired.

Event/Listener Methods

---

public void <u>addActionListener</u>(ActionListener)
public void <u>removeActionListener</u>(ActionListener)

public String <u>getActionCommand</u>()
public void <u>setActionCommand</u>(String)

protected void <u>fireActionEvent</u>()
protected void <u>fireItemStateChanged</u>(ItemEvent)
protected void <u>installAncestorListener</u>()

public void <u>processKeyEvent</u>(KeyEvent)

The methods listed above deal with events. Combo boxes fire action events when their selected item is modified. As a result, methods are provided for adding and removing action listeners.

Every action event (`java.awt.event.ActionEvent`) has a string, known as an *action command*, that is typically used to identify the type of action. By default, the action command associated with action events fired by instances of `JComboBox` is `"comboBoxChanged"`. The action command is settable.

`JComboBox` provides two `protected` methods for firing item and action events to all registered item and action listeners, respectively. The methods can be overridden by extensions of `JComboBox`.

All Swing components fire ancestor events when a component or one of its ancestors is moved or made visible or invisible. The `installAncestorListener` method adds to the combo box an ancestor listener that hides the combo box's popup menu whenever an ancestor event occurs.

The `processKeyEvent` method is overridden from the `JComponent` class to hide the combo box's popup if the TAB key is pressed.

Popup Menu Methods

---

public void <u>hidePopup</u>()
public void <u>showPopup</u>()

public void <u>setPopupVisible</u>(boolean)
public boolean <u>isPopupVisible</u>()

public boolean <u>isLightWeightPopupEnabled</u>()
public void <u>setLightWeightPopupEnabled</u>(boolean)

Invoking `setLightWeightPopupEnabled(false)` forces a combo box to use medium weight or heavyweight popup menus. By default, combo boxes use a lightweight popup menu, unless it is determined that a heavyweight must be used. For example, if a combo box's popup menu exceeds the boundaries of its parent window, a lightweight popup will be clipped to the boundaries of its window. In such case, a heavyweight popup will be used by default.

However, there are times when a heavyweight popup should be used but a lightweight is used by default. For example, if a popup overlaps a heavyweight component, the popup will be displayed underneath the heavyweight component. In such a case, is necessary to force a combo box to use a heavyweight popup menu.

That applet shown in Figure 18-18 contains a button and a combo box. An action listener is added to the button to invoke `showPopup()` for the combo box.

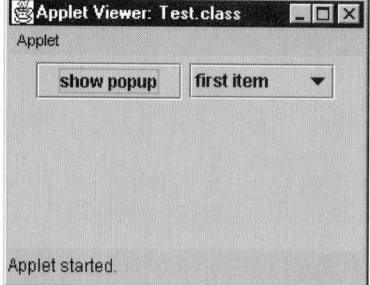 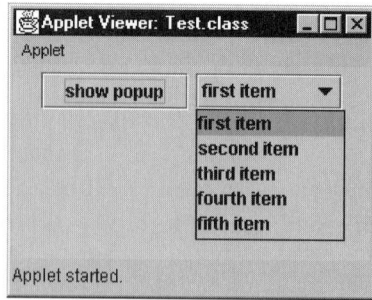

Figure 18-18 Programmatically Showing a Combo Box Popup

The applet shown in Figure 18-18 is listed in Example 18-9.

Example 18-9   Manually Showing a Combo Box Popup

```
import javax.swing.*;
import java.awt.*;
import java.awt.event.*;

public class Test extends JApplet {
    public void init() {
        Container contentPane = getContentPane();
        JButton button = new JButton("show popup");
        final JComboBox combo = new JComboBox();

        combo.addItem("first item");
        combo.addItem("second item");
        combo.addItem("third item");
        combo.addItem("fourth item");
        combo.addItem("fifth item");

        button.addActionListener(new ActionListener() {
            public void actionPerformed(ActionEvent e) {
                combo.showPopup();
            }
        });
        contentPane.setLayout(new FlowLayout());
        contentPane.add(button);
        contentPane.add(combo);
    }
}
```

Property Accessors

public int getMaximumRowCount()
public int getSelectedIndex()

public boolean isEditable()
public boolean isFocusTraversable()

public void setEditable(boolean)
public void setEnabled(boolean)
public void setMaximumRowCount(int)
public void setSelectedIndex(int)

The methods listed above are straightforward accessors for the combo box properties discussed in "JComboBox Class Summaries" on page 1123.

Accessibility / Pluggable Look and Feel

---

public AccessibleContext getAccessibleContext()
public ComboBoxUI getUI()
public String getUIClassID()
public void setUI(ComboBoxUI)
public void updateUI()

The methods listed above can be found in most extensions of JComponent. Swing lightweight components can return the class name of their UI delegate and an accessibility context that contains accessibility information for the component. The updateUI method is invoked when the component is fitted with a UI delegate.

AWT Compatibility

JComboBox offers the same basic functionality as java.awt.Choice, and then some. AWT Choice components are not editable and can only display strings, whereas instances of JComboBox can be edited and have cell renderers and key selection managers.

Both java.awt.Choice and JComboBox implement the java.awt.ItemSelectable interface, which defines the following methods:

- void addItemListener(ItemListener)
- Object[] getSelectedObjects()
- void removeItemListener(ItemListener)

Table 18-4 lists the `public` methods provided by `java.awt.Choice` and the corresponding methods from the `JComboBox` class.

Table 18-4 Public java.awt.Choice Methods and JComboBox Equivalents[1]

java.awt.Choice Method	JComboBox Equivalent
synchronized void add(String)	void addItem(Object)
synchronized void addItem(String)	void addItem(Object)
synchronized void addItemListener(ItemListener)	void addItemListener(ItemListener)
String getItem(int)	Object getItemAt(int)
int getItemCount()	*int getItemCount()*
int getSelectedIndex()	*int getSelectedIndex()*
synchronized String getSelectedItem()	Object getSelectedItem()
synchronized Object[] getSelectedObjects()	Object[] getSelectedObjects()
synchronized void insert(String, int)	void insertItemAt(Object, int)
synchronized void remove(int)	void removeItemAt(Object, int)
synchronized void remove(String)	void removeItem(Object)
synchronized void removeAll()	void removeAllItems()
synchronized void removeItemListener(ItemListener)	void removeItemListener()
synchronized void select(int)	void setSelectedIndex(int)
synchronized void select(String)	void setSelectedItem(Object)

1. Italics indicate matching signatures

Parting Shots

`JComboBox` is a highly functional and configurable component. Custom renderers and editors and can be written for combo boxes to accommodate the wildest of combo box scenarios. Additionally, combo boxes provide key selection management that can be customized by implementing custom key selection managers. Unfortunately, the `JList` component does not share the key selection management functionality implemented by `JComboBox`.

CHAPTER

19

Tables

Swing tables display rows and columns of data and are Swing's most complex component. In fact, Swing provides a separate package—swing.table—that contains table support interfaces and classes.

Swing tables are composed of a table header that displays column headings, table columns, and cell values. Tables also contain rows and table cells, although rows and cells are not objects as are headers and columns. The anatomy of a Swing table is shown in Figure 19-1.

Tables are capable of supporting a number of selection modes including row, column, and cell selection. Table cell values are rendered by an object that implements the TableCellRenderer interface and are edited by objects that implement the CellEditor interface.

Table Header

Row

Cells

Column

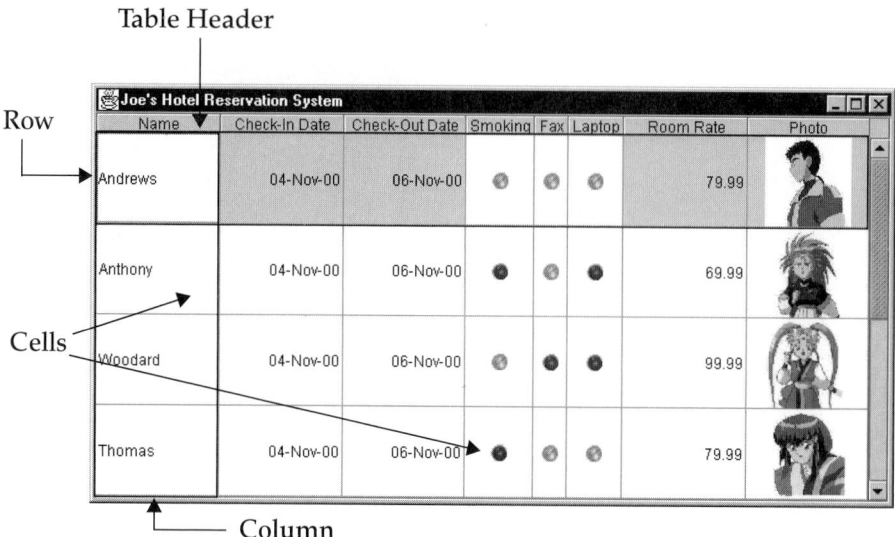

Figure 19-1 Swing Table Anatomy

Tables and Scrolling

Two issues concerning tables and scrolling need to be addressed: the effects of placing a table in a scrollpane and JTable's implementation of the Scrollable interface.

The application shown in Figure 19-2 contains two identical tables; the bottom table is contained in a scrollpane, whereas the top table is added directly to the application's content pane.

From Figure 19-2, two differences are obvious between tables that reside in a scrollpane versus those that do not: the visibility of column headers and the manner in which the tables are sized. Column headers are implemented as the header view for the scrollpane in which a table is contained, and therefore only tables that reside in scrollpanes display column headers. Therefore, if a table is not contained in a scrollpane, its column headers will not be visible. See "Scrollpane Headers" on page 742 for more information concerning scrollpane headers and header views.

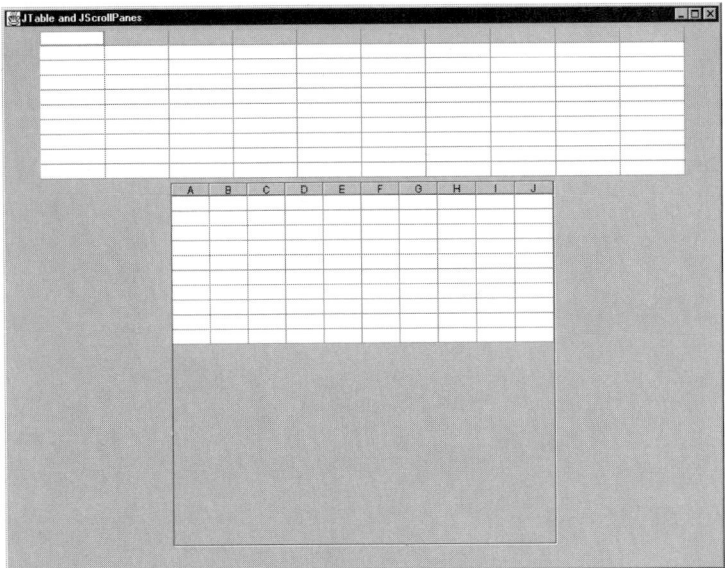

Figure 19-2 Tables and Scrollpanes

Tables contained in a scrollpane can also be sized differently than tables that are not contained in a scrollpane. Here's why:

`JTable` implements the `Scrollable` interface—see "The Scrollable Interface" on page 764 for a discussion of the `Scrollable` interface. One of the methods defined by the `Scrollable` interface—`getPreferredScrollableViewportSize()`—is implemented by `JTable` to return a default dimension of (450, 400),[1] which represents the table's preferred size for its viewport. The content pane for the application shown in Figure 19-2 has a `FlowLayout` layout manager, which sizes components according to their preferred size. As a result, the viewport is 450 pixels wide and 400 pixels high.

Another method defined by the `Scrollable` interface—`getScrollableTracksViewportWidth()`—is implemented by `JTable` so that by default, tables contained in viewports have the same width as their viewport. Thus, the table contained in a scrollpane in Figure 19-2 is the same width as its viewport.

---

1. The default may change in a subsequent Swing release.

The application shown in Figure 19-2 has a simple implementation and is listed in Example 19-1.

Example 19-1 Tables and Scrollpanes

```
import javax.swing.*;
import java.awt.*;
import java.awt.event.*;

public class Test extends JFrame {
    public Test() {
        Container contentPane = getContentPane();

        contentPane.setLayout(new FlowLayout());
        contentPane.add(new JTable(10,10));
        contentPane.add(new JScrollPane(new JTable(10,10)));
    }
    public static void main(String args[]) {
        GJApp.launch(new Test(),
                    "Tables and Scrollpanes",100,100,850,700);
    }
}
```

𝔖𝔴𝔦𝔫𝔤 𝔗𝔦𝔭 ...

Place Instances of JTable in a Scrollpane

Swing tables should almost always be contained in a scrollpane. The most compelling reason to embed a table in a scrollpane is that only tables contained in scrollpanes automatically display column headers. Table column headers are components that are specified as the header view for a table's scrollpane. As a result, if a table is not contained in a scrollpane, the column headers will not be visible.

Note: With Swing 1.02 and before, the (now deprecated) JScrollPane.create-ScrollPaneForTable() static method must be used to create a scrollpane for a table.

Block and Unit Increments

The block and unit scrolling increments for tables are defined by JTable's implementation of two methods defined by the Scrollable interface: getScrollableBlockIncrement() and

`getScrollableUnitIncrement()`, respectively. See "Block and Unit Increments" on page 774 for more information concerning block and unit scrolling increments.

For vertical scrolling, the unit increment is equal to the table's row height, and the block increment is equal to the number of visible rows – 1, as illustrated by Figure 19-3. The top picture in Figure 19-3 shows a table with cell (0, 0) displayed in the upper-left corner. The middle and bottom pictures shows the table after it has scrolled down from the top by unit and block increments, respectively.

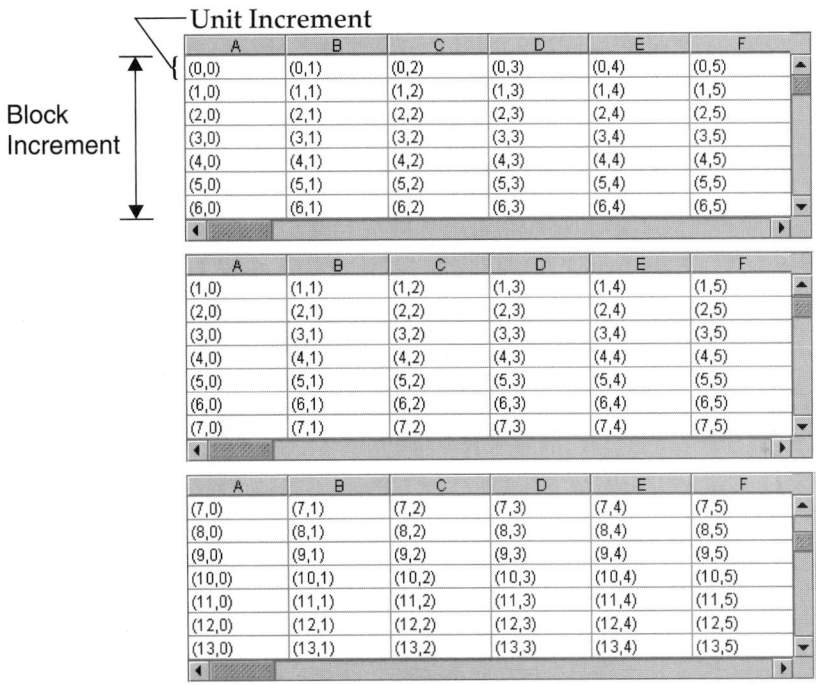

Figure 19-3 Unit and Block Increments for Vertical Scrolling

Block and unit increments for horizontal scrolling are depicted in Figure 19-4. The block increment for horizontal scrolling is equal to the visible width of the table. The unit increment, as of Swing 1.1 FCS, is equal to 100 pixels.

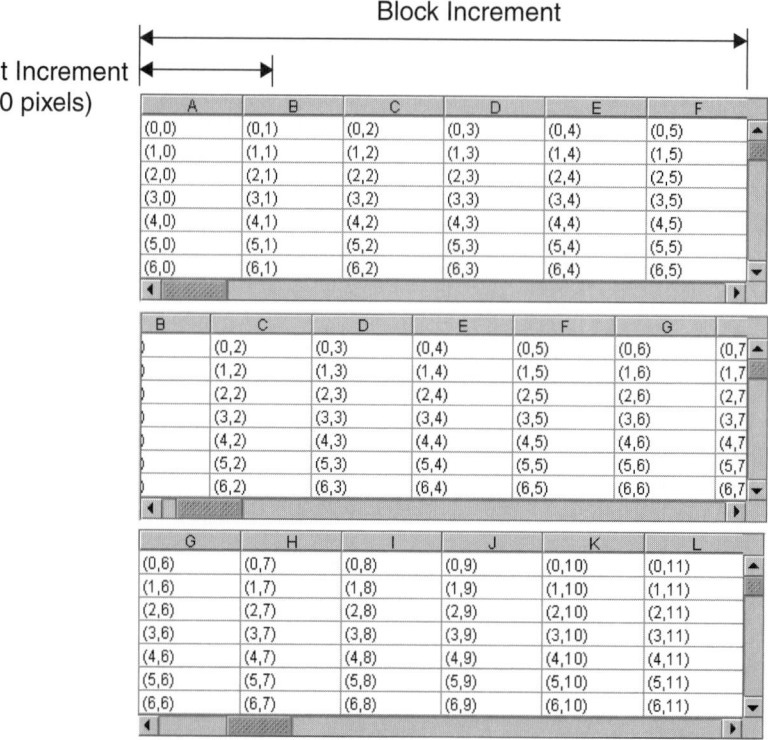

Figure 19-4 Unit and Block Increments for Horizontal Scrolling

Table Models

Tables maintain three different types of models: a table model, a table column model, and a list selection model, as shown in Figure 19-5.

Table models implement the `TableModel` interface and are responsible for maintaining table cell values.

A table's list selection model is responsible for table row selection, whereas column selection is the responsibility of a table's column model, which has its own list selection model. Table column models also maintain references to a table's columns and provide the ability to add, move, and remove columns.

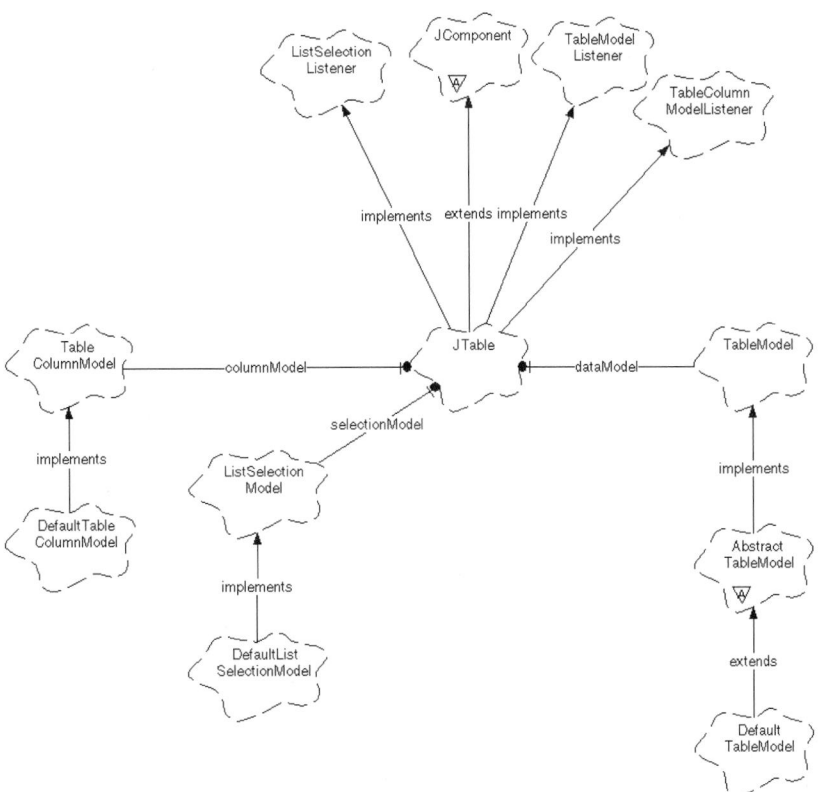

Figure 19-5 Table Models Class Diagram

The `JTable` class implements the `ListSelectionListener`, `TableModelListener`, and `TableColumnModelListener` interfaces for the purpose of listening to its models. Changes to the table's model or the table's column model are handled by firing events to the table's listeners. Changes to selection are handled by repainting the appropriate region of the table.

The responsibilities of each model and the events they fire are summarized in Table 19-1.

Table 19-1   Table Models

Model	Responsibilities	Events Fired
ListSelection Model	Maintains row selection mode, selection intervals, and whether a selection is adjusting	ListSelectionEvent
TableColumn Model	Stores table columns; adds, moves and removes columns; tracks the following column properties: selection, margins, indexes, total width, and count	TableColumnModel Event / ChangeEvent[1]
TableModel	Accessor methods for: cell data and data types, row count, column count, and whether a given cell is editable	TableModelEvent

1. Fired by `DefaultTableColumnModel` when the column margin is set.

Table Data Models

`JTable` does not store its cell data. All instances of `JTable` delegate the management of their cell values to an object that implements the `TableModel` interface.

Table cell values can be specified when an instance of `JTable` is constructed with the following `JTable` constructors:

- `public JTable(Object[][] rowData,`
  `               Object[] columnNames)`
- `public JTable(Vector rowData, Vector columnNames)`
- `public JTable(TableModel, TableColumnModel)`
- `public JTable(TableModel)`

Cell values can be specified at construction time as data—in the form of either `Object` arrays or vectors—or as table and/or table column models.

The objects displayed in a table can also be specified after construction with the following `JTable` methods:

- `public void setModel(TableModel)`
- `public void setValueAt(Object value, int row, int col)`[2]

---

2.   The `setValueAt` method only takes effect if a table's model is editable.

Table data models are defined by the `TableModel` interface, which is implemented by the `AbstractTableModel` class, which in turn is extended by `DefaultTableModel`, as shown in Figure 19-6.

`AbstractTableModel` provides default model behavior and takes care of registering table model listeners, as evidenced by the `EventListenerList` it contains. `DefaultTableModel` stores two vectors, one containing references to column identifiers and another for the table's row data.

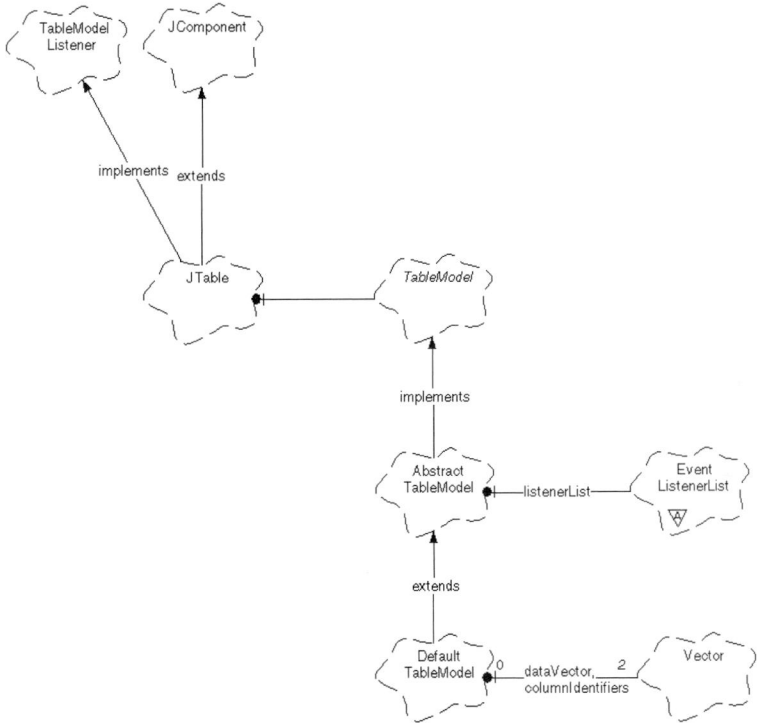

Figure 19-6 Table Data Models Class Diagram

The `TableModel` interface will rarely be directly implemented by developers because `AbstractTableModel` provides sane default behavior that can be selectively overridden and a handy set of methods that fire events to table model listeners. As a result, most custom table models are likely to extend `AbstractTableModel` instead of directly implementing the `TableModel` interface.

The `DefaultTableModel` class provides two features in addition to the functionality implemented by `AbstractTableModel`: mutability and a storage mechanism. `DefaultTableModel` stores cell values in a vector of vectors and provides a number of methods for modifying both rows and columns. `DefaultTableModel` also overrides `AbstractTableModel`'s empty implementation of `setValueAt()`.

`JTable` data model classes are summarized in Table 19-2.

Table 19-2   Table Data Models

Model	Class/ Interface	Responsibilities/ Intentions	Used/Implemented/ Extended
TableModel	interface	listener registration; cell value accessors; column names; class accessors	rarely directly implemented
AbstractTableModel	class	event firing methods	extended by most custom table models
DefaultTableModel	class	stores cell values in a vector of vectors	used for small to medium models for mutable data that is a good fit for a vector of vectors

The TableModel Interface

The `TableModel` interface defines the manner in which table data is manipulated. Table models are in the business of maintaining cell values and firing `TableModelEvents` to `TableModelListeners` when the values are modified.

The `TableModel` interface is summarized in Interface Summary 19-1.

Interface Summary 19-1   TableModel

TableModelListener Registration

---

public abstract void <u>addTableModelListener</u>(TableModelListener)
public abstract void <u>removeTableModelListener</u>(TableModelListener)

Table models fire `TableModelEvents` to `TableModelListeners` and so must keep track of registered listeners.

Cell Values and Editability

---

public abstract Object <u>getValueAt</u>(int row, int column)
public abstract void <u>setValueAt</u>(Object value, int row, int column)

public abstract boolean <u>isCellEditable</u>(int row, int column)

Table cell values are accessed as `Object` references, which means that any type of object can be stored in a table cell. Table cells are editable if a table's model returns `true` from the `isCellEditable` method.

Columns and Rows

---

public abstract int <u>getColumnCount</u>()
public abstract int <u>getRowCount</u>()

public abstract Class <u>getColumnClass</u>(int index)
public abstract String <u>getColumnName</u>(int index)

Table models keep track of the number of rows and columns, which are accessed with the first two methods listed above.

Table models also maintain column names and the class of the objects stored in a particular column.

AbstractTableModel

`AbstractTableModel` implements the methods defined by the `TableModel` interface, except for methods that return data-specific information:

- `public Object getValueAt(int row, int col)`
- `public int getRowCount()`
- `public int getColumnCount()`

`AbstractTableModel` also provides seven methods that fire `TableModelEvents`. The methods exist mainly for subclasses; they are not called anywhere within `AbstractTableModel`. See Table 19-3 on page 1147 for guidelines as to when the methods should be invoked.

The table model for the table shown in Figure 19-7 is an extension of `AbstractTableModel` that represents 100 rows of data, each of which contains 10 immutable `Integer` values.

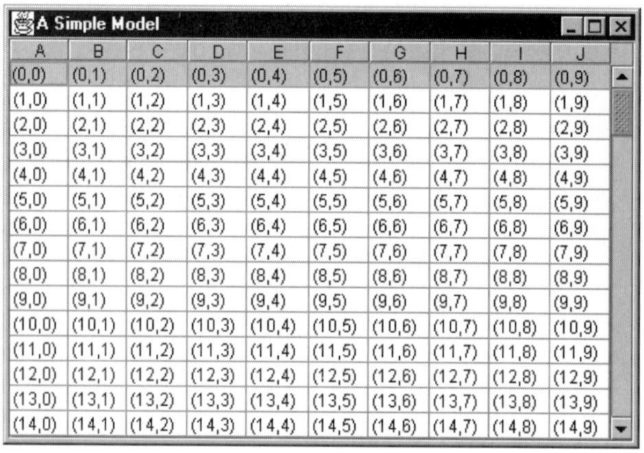

A	B	C	D	E	F	G	H	I	J
(0,0)	(0,1)	(0,2)	(0,3)	(0,4)	(0,5)	(0,6)	(0,7)	(0,8)	(0,9)
(1,0)	(1,1)	(1,2)	(1,3)	(1,4)	(1,5)	(1,6)	(1,7)	(1,8)	(1,9)
(2,0)	(2,1)	(2,2)	(2,3)	(2,4)	(2,5)	(2,6)	(2,7)	(2,8)	(2,9)
(3,0)	(3,1)	(3,2)	(3,3)	(3,4)	(3,5)	(3,6)	(3,7)	(3,8)	(3,9)
(4,0)	(4,1)	(4,2)	(4,3)	(4,4)	(4,5)	(4,6)	(4,7)	(4,8)	(4,9)
(5,0)	(5,1)	(5,2)	(5,3)	(5,4)	(5,5)	(5,6)	(5,7)	(5,8)	(5,9)
(6,0)	(6,1)	(6,2)	(6,3)	(6,4)	(6,5)	(6,6)	(6,7)	(6,8)	(6,9)
(7,0)	(7,1)	(7,2)	(7,3)	(7,4)	(7,5)	(7,6)	(7,7)	(7,8)	(7,9)
(8,0)	(8,1)	(8,2)	(8,3)	(8,4)	(8,5)	(8,6)	(8,7)	(8,8)	(8,9)
(9,0)	(9,1)	(9,2)	(9,3)	(9,4)	(9,5)	(9,6)	(9,7)	(9,8)	(9,9)
(10,0)	(10,1)	(10,2)	(10,3)	(10,4)	(10,5)	(10,6)	(10,7)	(10,8)	(10,9)
(11,0)	(11,1)	(11,2)	(11,3)	(11,4)	(11,5)	(11,6)	(11,7)	(11,8)	(11,9)
(12,0)	(12,1)	(12,2)	(12,3)	(12,4)	(12,5)	(12,6)	(12,7)	(12,8)	(12,9)
(13,0)	(13,1)	(13,2)	(13,3)	(13,4)	(13,5)	(13,6)	(13,7)	(13,8)	(13,9)
(14,0)	(14,1)	(14,2)	(14,3)	(14,4)	(14,5)	(14,6)	(14,7)	(14,8)	(14,9)

Figure 19-7 A Simple Table Model

The applet shown in Figure 19-7 is listed in Example 19-2.

Example 19-2 A Simple Extension of AbstractTableModel

```
import java.awt.*;
import java.awt.event.*;
import javax.swing.*;
import javax.swing.table.*;
import java.util.*;

public class Test extends JFrame {
    JTable table = new JTable(
        new AbstractTableModel() {
            int rows = 100, cols = 10;

            public int getRowCount() { return rows; }
            public int getColumnCount() { return cols; }

            public Object getValueAt(int row, int col) {
                return "(" + row + "," + col + ")";
            }
        });

    public Test() {
        getContentPane().add(new JScrollPane(table),
                        BorderLayout.CENTER);
    }
    public static void main(String args[]) {
        GJApp.launch(
            new Test(), "A Simple Model",300,300,450,300);
    }
}
```

The application creates an instance of JTable with an inner class extension of AbstractTableModel. The model manufactures values on-the-fly instead of storing data. Because the model's storage requirements are not compatible with the vector of vectors approach taken by DefaultTableModel, AbstractTableModel is extended instead of DefaultTableModel.

The AbstractTableModel class is summarized in Class Summary 19-1.

Class Summary 19-1   AbstractTableModel

Extends: java.lang.Object

Implements: TableModel, java.io.Serializable

Methods

Table Model Listeners

---

public void <u>addTableModelListener</u>(TableModelListener)
public void <u>removeTableModelListener</u>(TableModelListener)

An event listener list is used to maintain a list of `TableModelListeners`. See "Event Listener Lists" on page 258 for more information concerning the `EventListenerList` class.

Columns

---

public int <u>findColumn</u>(String)
public Class <u>getColumnClass</u>(int)
public String <u>getColumnName</u>(int)

`AbstractTableModel` defines column names that conform to the pattern `A, B, C, … AA, AB, AC …`. The `findColumn` method returns the index of a column with the specified name, or −1 if the name does not match any columns.

Nearly every `AbstractTableModel` extension overrides `getColumnName()` for more meaningful column names.

`AbstractTableModel` defines the class of its columns as the universal `Object` class. `AbstractTableModel` extensions almost always override `getColumnClass()` to return a more specific class to increase the likelihood of being matched up with more appropriate renderers and editors.

Cells and Values

---

public boolean <u>isCellEditable</u>(int row, int col)
public void <u>setValueAt</u>(Object value, int row, int col)

`AbstractTableModel` disallows editing for all of its cells by returning `false` from `isCellEditable()`.

Table models—even models with immutable data—must implement setValueAt() from the TableModel interface.[3] AbstractListModel offers an empty implementation of setValueAt(), which absolves immutable extensions of AbstractListModel of the responsibility.

Event Firing

public void <u>fireTableCellUpdated</u>(int row, int col)
public void <u>fireTableChanged</u>(TableModelEvent)
public void <u>fireTableDataChanged</u>()
public void <u>fireTableRowsDeleted</u>(int firstRow, int lastRow)
public void <u>fireTableRowsInserted</u>(int firstRow, int lastRow)
public void <u>fireTableRowsUpdated</u>(int firstRow, int lastRow)
public void <u>fireTableStructureChanged</u>()

AbstractTableModel bends over backwards to make sure that extensions have a full complement of methods that fire events to TableModelListeners in response to various modifications of the model's data.

Table models that extend AbstractTableModel must be careful to call appropriate fire...() methods when their data is modified. Table 19-3 indicates when each of the methods should be invoked.

Table 19-3 AbstractTableModel Event Firing Methods

Method	Fired when …
fireTableCellUpdated(int row, int column)	cell value has been updated
fireTableDataChanged()	any or all cell values have changed
fireTableRowsDeleted(int first, int last)	first through last (inclusive) rows have been deleted
fireTableRowsInserted(int first, int last)	first through last (inclusive) rows have been inserted
fireTableRowsUpdated(int first, int last)	first through last (inclusive) rows have been updated
fireTableStructureChanged()	Any aspect of table structure may have changed; equivalent to setting a table's model

3. They must do so in order to be concrete (nonabstract) classes.

AbstractTableModel Extensions Must Fire Appropriate Events

AbstractTableModel provides seven methods that can be used to fire TableModelEvents under various data modification scenarios. For example, if rows 3 through 7 are deleted, an extension of AbstractTableModel should invoke AbstractTableModel.fireTableRowsDeleted(3,7) after the rows have been deleted. Likewise, if an individual cell value is modified, AbstractTable-Model.fireTableCellUpdated() should be invoked.

Table models that represent mutable data must implement setValueAt(). Because setValueAt() modifies a table cell's value, the method must fire a table cell updated event; this can be accomplished with AbstractTableModel.fire-CellUpdated().

DefaultTableModel

`DefaultTableModel` extends `AbstractTableModel` and implements the data manipulation methods that its superclass leaves unimplemented.

`DefaultTableModel` stores cell values in a vector representing rows, where each object in the vector is also a vector of objects representing cell values. For example, a cell value at row 1 column 2 could be accessed in the following manner:

```
DefaultTableModel defaultTableModel = ...
Vector dataVector = defaultTableModel.getDataVector();
Vector rowVector = (Vector)dataVector.elementAt(1);
Object cellValue = (Vector)rowVector.elementAt(2);
```

In addition to providing a storage mechanism, `DefaultTableModel` also provides methods for adding columns and adding, inserting, and removing rows. Individual cell values can be modified with `DefaultTableModel`'s implementation of `setValueAt()`, which stores the specified value and fires a `TableModelEvent`.

The primary motivation for using `DefaultTableModel` is its ability to add and remove data after a model has been constructed.

`DefaultTableModel`'s storage mechanism is of lesser importance because most of the time data must be reformatted into the model's vector of vectors. The reformatting can be costly for some (admittedly huge) tables, and the inconvenience of extending `AbstractTableModel` and implementing the three data accessor methods is usually a small price to pay for leaving the data in its native format. On the other hand, implementing methods that add, insert, or remove rows or columns can be a more ambitious undertaking worthy of enlisting `DefaultTableModel`'s help via inheritance.

The application shown in Figure 19-8 contains a table equipped with an instance of `DefaultTableModel`. The application provides buttons for adding rows and columns, showcasing `DefaultTableModel`'s ability to modify its data.

Column 0	Column 1	Column 2	Column 3	Column 4
(0,0)	(0,1)	(0,2)	(0,3)	(0,4)
(1,0)	(1,1)	(1,2)	(1,3)	(1,4)
(2,0)	(2,1)	(2,2)	(2,3)	(2,4)

Using DefaultTableModel — Add Row — Add Column

Column 0	Column 1	Column 2	Column 3	Column 4	Column 5	Column 6	Column 7
(0,0)	(0,1)	(0,2)	(0,3)	(0,4)			
(1,0)	(1,1)	(1,2)	(1,3)	(1,4)			
(2,0)	(2,1)	(2,2)	(2,3)	(2,4)			
(3,0)	(3,1)	(3,2)	(3,3)	(3,4)			
(4,0)	(4,1)	(4,2)	(4,3)	(4,4)			
(5,0)	(5,1)	(5,2)	(5,3)	(5,4)			
(6,0)	(6,1)	(6,2)	(6,3)	(6,4)	(6,5)	(6,6)	(6,7)
(7,0)	(7,1)	(7,2)	(7,3)	(7,4)	(7,5)	(7,6)	(7,7)
(8,0)	(8,1)	(8,2)	(8,3)	(8,4)	(8,5)	(8,6)	(8,7)

Figure 19-8 Using DefaultTableModel

The top picture in Figure 19-8 shows the application as it appears initially. The bottom picture was taken after three columns were added, followed by the addition of three rows.

The table's model is initialized with five columns and three rows. The columns are added to the model with `DefaultTableModel.addColumn()`, followed by the addition of each row with `DefaultTableModel.addRow()`.

```java
public class Test extends JFrame {
    private int rows=3, cols=5;
    private Object[] rowData = new Object[cols];

    private DefaultTableModel model = new DefaultTableModel();
    private JTable table = new JTable(model);

    public Test() {
        for(int c=0; c < cols; ++c)
            model.addColumn("Column " + Integer.toString(c));

        for(int r=0; r < rows; ++r) {
            for(int c=0; c < cols; ++c) {
                rowData[c] = "(" + r + "," + c + ")";
            }
            model.addRow(rowData);
        }
        getContentPane().add(new JScrollPane(table),
                             BorderLayout.CENTER);
        getContentPane().add(new ControlPanel(),
                             BorderLayout.NORTH);
    }
    ...
```

The application's buttons have action listeners that add data to the model. The Add Row button allocates the `rowData` array if columns have been added and inserts cleverly named strings into the array. The data is subsequently added to the model.

```java
    ...
class ControlPanel extends JPanel {
    private JButton rowButton = new JButton("Add Row"),
            colButton = new JButton("Add Column");

    public ControlPanel() {
        add(rowButton);
        add(colButton);

        rowButton.addActionListener(new ActionListener() {
            public void actionPerformed(ActionEvent e) {
                int rowCount = model.getRowCount();
                int colCount = model.getColumnCount();

                if(colCount > rowData.length)
                    rowData = new Object[colCount];
```

```
                for(int c=0; c < colCount; ++c) {
                    rowData[c] = "(" + rowCount + "," +
                                        c + ")";
                }
                model.addRow(rowData);
            }
        });
        ...
```

The Add Column button adds an appropriately named column to the model. The call to JTable.sizeColumnsToFit() is necessary because of a JTable bug that does not correctly update the table after columns have been added or removed.

```
        ...
        colButton.addActionListener(new ActionListener() {
            public void actionPerformed(ActionEvent e) {
                int colCount = model.getColumnCount();
                model.addColumn("Column " + colCount);

                // Bug: the call to sizeColumnsToFit()
                // should not be necessary
                table.sizeColumnsToFit(-1);
            }
        });
    }
}
```

The application shown in Figure 19-8 is listed in its entirety in Example 19-3.

Example 19-3 Using DefaultTableModel

```
import java.awt.*;
import java.awt.event.*;
import javax.swing.*;
import javax.swing.table.*;
import java.util.*;

public class Test extends JFrame {
    private int rows=3, cols=5;
    private Object[] rowData = new Object[cols];

    private DefaultTableModel model = new DefaultTableModel();
    private JTable table = new JTable(model);

    public Test() {
        for(int c=0; c < cols; ++c)
            model.addColumn("Column " + Integer.toString(c));
```

```
        for(int r=0; r < rows; ++r) {
            for(int c=0; c < cols; ++c) {
                rowData[c] = "(" + r + "," + c + ")";
            }
            model.addRow(rowData);
        }
        getContentPane().add(new JScrollPane(table),
                        BorderLayout.CENTER);
        getContentPane().add(new ControlPanel(),
                        BorderLayout.NORTH);
    }
    public static void main(String args[]) {
        GJApp.launch(new Test(),
            "Using DefaultTableModel",150,150,600,350);
    }
    class ControlPanel extends JPanel {
        private JButton rowButton = new JButton("Add Row"),
                    colButton = new JButton("Add Column");120

        public ControlPanel() {
            add(rowButton);
            add(colButton);

            rowButton.addActionListener(new ActionListener() {
                public void actionPerformed(ActionEvent e) {
                    int rowCount = model.getRowCount();
                    int colCount = model.getColumnCount();

                    if(colCount > rowData.length)
                        rowData = new Object[colCount];

                    for(int c=0; c < colCount; ++c) {
                        rowData[c] = "(" + rowCount + "," +
                                        c + ")";
                    }
                    model.addRow(rowData);
                }
            });
            colButton.addActionListener(new ActionListener() {
                public void actionPerformed(ActionEvent e) {
                    int colCount = model.getColumnCount();
                    model.addColumn("Column " + colCount);

                    // Bug: the call to sizeColumnsToFit()
                    // should not be necessary
                    table.sizeColumnsToFit(-1);
                }
            });
        }
    }
}
```

The `DefaultTableModel` class is summarized in Class Summary 19-2.

Class Summary 19-2   DefaultTableModel

Extends: AbstractTableModel
Implements: java.io.Serializable

Constructors

---

public <u>DefaultTableModel</u>()
public <u>DefaultTableModel</u>(int numRows, int numColumns)
public <u>DefaultTableModel</u>(Object[] columnNames, int numRows)
public <u>DefaultTableModel</u>(Object[][] data, Object[] columnNames)
public <u>DefaultTableModel</u>(Vector columnNames, int numRows)
public <u>DefaultTableModel</u>(Vector data, Vector columnNames)

`DefaultTableModel` provides constructors that specify one or more of the following: the number of rows or columns, the column names, and the table data. A no-argument constructor is also provided.

Methods

---

protected static Vector <u>convertToVector</u>(Object[])
protected static Vector <u>convertToVector</u>(Object[][])

The convenience methods listed above are used to convert column names and table data into vectors. The methods are `protected` and therefore available to extensions of `DefaultTableModel`.

Data

---

public Vector getDataVector()
public void setDataVector(Object[][] data, Object[] columnNames)
public void setDataVector(Vector data, Vector columnNames)

public void newDataAvailable(TableModelEvent)

public Object getValueAt(int row, int column)
public void setValueAt(Object value, int row, int column)

public boolean isCellEditable(int row, int column)

`DefaultTableModel` provides setter and getter accessors for its data vector. The `newDataAvailable()` method is a synonym for `AbstractTableModel.fireTableChanged()`—`newDataAvailable()` is not called from within `DefaultTableModel` or anywhere within Swing.[4]

The last three methods listed above are defined by the `TableModel` interface. `DefaultTableModel` defines all of its cells to be editable, in contrast to its superclass—`AbstractTableModel`—which defines all cells to be noneditable. `DefaultTableModel.setValueAt()` fires a `TableModelEvent` indicating that a cell's value was updated.

Columns

---

public void addColumn(Object columnIdentifier)
public void addColumn(Object columnIdentifier, Object[] columnData)
public void addColumn(Object columnIdentifier, Vector columnData)

public void setColumnIdentifiers(Object[] columnIdentifiers)
public void setColumnIdentifiers(Vector columnIdentifiers)

public int getColumnCount()
public String getColumnName(int index)

---

4. The `newDataAvailable` method will probably be deprecated in a future Swing release.

`DefaultTableModel` provides methods for adding columns purely as a convenience; table columns can also be added to a table's column model. If it is necessary to move or remove columns, a table column model must be used.

The identifiers passed to the first five methods listed above are displayed in the column's header; typically, identifiers are strings.

The `getColumnName` method returns `columnIdentifier.toString()`, where `columnIdentifier` is an appropriate identifier for the column in question.

Rows

---

public void <u>addRow</u>(Object[] rowData)
public void <u>addRow</u>(Vector rowData)
public int <u>getRowCount</u>()

public void <u>insertRow</u>(int index, Object[] rowData)
public void <u>insertRow</u>(int index, Vector rowData)
public void <u>moveRow</u>(int startIndex, int endIndex, int toIndex)
public void <u>newRowsAdded</u>(TableModelEvent)
public void <u>removeRow</u>(int index)
public void <u>rowsRemoved</u>(TableModelEvent)

public void <u>setNumRows</u>(int numRows)

Although columns are objects, rows are a logical construct perpetuated by table models. Columns are typically manipulated with the `TableColumnModel` and `TableColumn` classes, not through instances of `DefaultTableModel`. On the other hand, because rows are not objects—there are no `TableRowModel` or `TableRow` classes, for example—`DefaultTableModel` must provide enough row-oriented methods to facilitate developers needs.

The Pros and Cons of DefaultTableModel

DefaultTableModel provides two main features over and above the basic functionality offered by its superclass (AbstractTableModel): data storage and mutability.

Data storage is implemented in the form of a vector of vectors; if data is specified in a different format at construction time, references to the data are copied into the model's vector of vectors. Having such a default storage mechanism is convenient; however, performance and design considerations often make it worth the effort to implement a custom storage mechanism.

The ability to modify table data at runtime is not always a necessity, but it's nice to have it available. Unfortunately, modifying data cannot be separated from the manner in which the data is stored, so the mutability provided by DefaultTableModel is tied to the vector of vectors storage mechanism.

Table Models and Default Renderers and Editors

With minimal effort, table models can drastically affect the manner in which their data is rendered and edited on a per-column basis.

The `JTable` class maintains sets of default renderers and editors that are used in conjunction with the class returned from the `getColumnClass` method defined in the `TableModel` interface. For example, if a renderer has not been explicitly specified for a table column and the table model's `getColumnClass` method returns the `Boolean` class, a check box will be used to render the values in the column. Likewise, if an editor has not been explicitly specified for the column, a check box will also be used to edit the `Boolean` values.

Table 19-4 lists classes that have default table renderers and editors[5] and lists the components that are used to render or edit table cell values.

---

5.   As of Swing 1.1 FCS

Table 19-4 Default Renderers and Editors by Class

Class	Renderer Component	Editor Component
Object	JLabel	JTextField
Date	JLabel (right aligned)[1]	JTextField
Number	JLabel (right aligned)[2]	JTextField (right aligned)
ImageIcon	JLabel (center aligned)	—
Boolean	JCheckBox (center aligned)	JCheckBox (center aligned)

1. Renderer uses `java.text.NumberFormat` to format numbers.
2. Renderer uses `java.text.DateFormat` to format dates.

The rather unattractive table in Figure 19-9 is a mockup that could be used in a hotel reservation application. The row data for the table is specified with an array of objects: `Strings` for the name, `java.util.Dates` for the check-in and check-out dates, `booleans` for smoking, fax, and laptop, `Doubles` for the room rate, and an `ImageIcon` for the photo.

Name	Check-In Date	Check-Out D...	Smoking	Fax	Laptop	Room Rate	Photo
Andrews	Sun Nov 05 ...	Tue Nov 07 ...	true	true	true	79.99	com.sun.ja...
Anthony	Sun Nov 05 ...	Tue Nov 07 ...	false	false	false	69.99	com.sun.ja...
Woodard	Sun Nov 05 ...	Tue Nov 07 ...	true	false	false	99.99	com.sun.ja...
Thomas	Sun Nov 05 ...	Tue Nov 07 ...	false	true	true	79.99	com.sun.ja...
Reed	Sun Nov 05 ...	Tue Nov 07 ...	true	true	true	79.99	com.sun.ja...
Crenshaw	Sun Nov 05 ...	Tue Nov 07 ...	false	false	false	69.99	com.sun.ja...
Royal	Sun Nov 05 ...	Tue Nov 07 ...	true	false	false	99.99	com.sun.ja...
Moore	Sun Nov 05 ...	Tue Nov 07 ...	false	true	true	79.99	com.sun.ja...

Figure 19-9 Using DefaultTableModel

The application creates an array of strings representing column names and a two-dimensional `Object` array for cell values. The arrays are passed to a `DefaultTableModel` constructor.

```
public class Test extends JFrame {
    String[] columnNames = {
        "Name", "Check-In Date", "Check-Out Date", "Smoking",
        "Fax", "Laptop", "Room Rate", "Photo",
    };

    Date dayOne = (new GregorianCalendar(2000, 10, 5)).getTime();
    Date dayTwo = (new GregorianCalendar(2000, 10, 7)).getTime();
```

```
Object[][] data = {
       { "Andrews", dayOne, dayTwo,
          new Boolean(true), new Boolean(true),
          new Boolean(true), new Double(79.99),
          new ImageIcon("tenchi.jpg")},

       { "Anthony", dayOne, dayTwo,
          new Boolean(false), new Boolean(false),
          new Boolean(false), new Double(69.99),
          new ImageIcon("washu.jpg")},
       ...
};

JTable table = new JTable(data, columnNames);

public Test() {
    getContentPane().add(new JScrollPane(table),
                         BorderLayout.CENTER);
}
...
```

Obviously, the table shown in Figure 19-9 is in need of a face lift. Figure 19-10 shows the same table, this time using default renderers for `Date`, `Boolean`, and `Double` values. The default renderers made a marked improvement over the table shown in Figure 19-9; however, there are still a number of rendering and editing improvements that could be made; those issues are addressed later in this chapter.

Name	Check-In Date	Check-Out D...	Smoking	Fax	Laptop	Room Rate	Photo
Andrews	04-Nov-00	06-Nov-00	✔	✔	✔	79.99	
Anthony	04-Nov-00	06-Nov-00	☐	☐	☐	69.99	
Woodard	04-Nov-00	06-Nov-00	✔	☐	☐	99.99	
Thomas	04-Nov-00	06-Nov-00	☐	✔	✔	79.99	
Reed	04-Nov-00	06-Nov-00	✔	✔	✔	79.99	
Crenshaw	04-Nov-00	06-Nov-00	☐	☐	☐	69.99	
Royal	04-Nov-00	06-Nov-00	✔	☐	☐	99.99	
Moore	04-Nov-00	06-Nov-00	☐	✔	✔	79.99	

Figure 19-10 Default Renderers and Editors

The table's model is an extension of `DefaultTableModel` that implements `getColumnClass()` to return the class of the value in the first row of the corresponding column.

```
class CustomModel extends DefaultTableModel {
```

```
public CustomModel(Object[][] data, Object[] columnNames) {
    super(data, columnNames);
}
public Class getColumnClass(int col) {
    // dataVector is a protected member of DefaultTableModel

    Vector v = (Vector)dataVector.elementAt(0);
    return v.elementAt(col).getClass();
}
...
```

Although it is not apparent from Figure 19-10, the Boolean and Double values in the table are editable with default editors. Editing was enabled by overriding isCellEditable() in the table's model. If a column's class is anything besides ImageIcon or java.util.Date, the cell is identified as editable.

```
public boolean isCellEditable(int row, int col) {
    Class columnClass = getColumnClass(col);
    return columnClass != ImageIcon.class &&
                       columnClass != Date.class;
}
}
```

The application shown in Figure 19-10 is listed in its entirety in Example 19-4.

Example 19-4 Using Default Renderers and Editors

```
import java.awt.*;
import java.awt.event.*;
import java.util.*;
import javax.swing.*;
import javax.swing.table.DefaultTableModel;

public class Test extends JFrame {
    String[] columnNames = {
            "Name", "Check-In Date", "Check-Out Date", "Smoking",
            "Fax", "Laptop", "Room Rate", "Photo",
    };

    Date dayOne = (new GregorianCalendar(2000, 10, 5)).getTime();
    Date dayTwo = (new GregorianCalendar(2000, 10, 7)).getTime();

    Object[][] data = {
            // lengthy listing omitted for brevity

    JTable table = new JTable(new CustomModel(data, columnNames));

    public Test() {
```

```
            getContentPane().add(new JScrollPane(table),
                            BorderLayout.CENTER);
        }
    public static void main(String args[]) {
        GJApp.launch(
            new Test(),
            "A Custom Table Model That Specifies Column Classes",
            300,300,650,182);
        }
    }
class CustomModel extends DefaultTableModel {
    public CustomModel(Object[][] data, Object[] columnNames) {
        super(data, columnNames);
    }
    public Class getColumnClass(int col) {
        // dataVector is a protected member of DefaultTableModel

        Vector v = (Vector)dataVector.elementAt(0);
        return v.elementAt(col).getClass();
    }
    public boolean isCellEditable(int row, int col) {
        Class columnClass = getColumnClass(col);
        return columnClass != ImageIcon.class &&
                        columnClass != Date.class;
    }
}
```

Swing Tip ...

Two TableModel Methods Affect Rendering and Editing

The following TableModel methods are used to fit table columns with default renderers and editors:

```
public Class getColumnClass()
public boolean isCellEditable()
```

If the class returned from TableModel.getColumnClass() is one of a predetermined set of classes defined by a JTable class—see "Table Models and Default Renderers and Editors" on page 1156—the values in the specified column are fitted with default renderers and/or editors.

Whether or not an editor is actually used depends upon the value returned from a table model's isCellEditable method. If the method returns false, the cell value cannot be edited.

Table Columns

Swing tables are column oriented; for example, table data is rendered and edited on a per-column basis. Further evidence of column bias is found in the fact that the table package provides classes for table columns but not for table rows. As a result, table columns, represented by the TableColumn class, are the backbone of Swing tables.

Table columns are represented by the TableColumn class. Table columns are not components; the TableColumn class simply maintains properties that pertain to table columns.

The only events fired by the TableColumn class are property change events that are fired when its bound properties are modified.

A class diagram for the TableColumn class is shown in Figure 19-11.

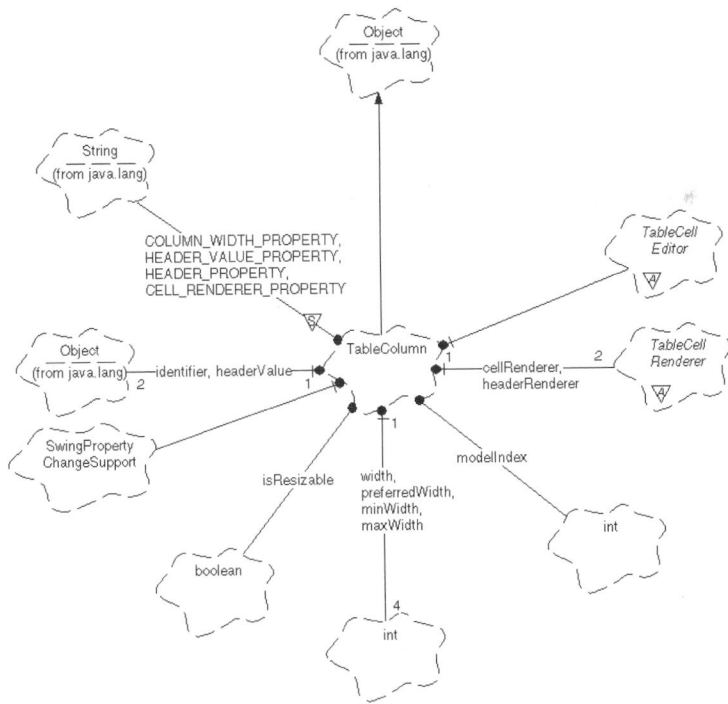

Figure 19-11 TableColumn Class Diagram

Instances of `TableColumn` have two renderers—one for the column's header and another for its cells. Table columns also have a single editor for editing cell values.

Table column headers display an object referred to as the column's header value. The header value is a property of the `TableColumn` class and is painted into column headers with the column's header renderer.

Table columns do not control their height, which is determined by the number of rows in a table and the table's row height. However, table columns do control their width; in fact, instances of `TableColumn` keep track of their actual, preferred, minimum, and maximum widths. Table columns are resizable by default, but their widths can be fixed after they are constructed.

Table columns retain a remnant from the early design of Swing tables. At one point in time, columns were identified by `Object` identifiers. Later on, `JTable` was streamlined for exclusively integer-based column access, and Swing classes no longer use column identifiers. However, the `TableColumn` class retained its identifier property and the corresponding accessor methods for developers to use as they see fit. Column identifiers, if not explicitly set, default to the column's header value.

Columns can be reordered in a table, but the data displayed in the column stays put in the model. In other words, even though columns are reordered onscreen, the data stored in the table's model does not move in response to reordering. Maintaining two column orderings—one onscreen and another in the model—is accomplished by storing the model index for each column in the column itself.

`TableColumn` fires property change events when its bound properties are modified with the help of a `SwingPropertyChangeSupport` object. `TableColumn` also provides `public static` strings that can be used by property change listeners to identify which property has been modified.

Column Resize Modes

When a column is resized, the space that the column gains or loses must come from—or be distributed to—the other columns in the table. The `JTable` class provides five column resize modes that distribute space in the manner described in Table 19-5.

Table 19-5   JTable Column Resize Modes

Mode	Space Comes From / Is Distributed to …
AUTO_RESIZE_OFF	column being sized
AUTO_RESIZE_LAST_COLUMN	rightmost column
AUTO_RESIZE_SUBSEQUENT_COLUMNS	columns to the right of column being sized
AUTO_RESIZE_NEXT_COLUMN	column to the right of column being sized
AUTO_RESIZE_ALL_COLUMNS	all columns uniformly

Figure 19-12 shows an application that allows a table's resize mode to be set. The application illustrates the manner in which a table's resize mode is set, and it also provides a visual description of the JTable resize modes.

The application shown in Figure 19-12 creates two arrays, one containing strings representing table resize modes and another containing the corresponding integer constants. The application also creates an instance of JTable with six rows and five columns. The table is placed in a scrollpane and added to the application's content pane as the center component.

The combo box is contained in an inner class extension of JPanel that is added to the application's content pane as the north component.

```
public class Test extends JFrame {
    Object[] resizeModes = new Object[] {
            "JTable.AUTO_RESIZE_OFF",
            "JTable.AUTO_RESIZE_NEXT_COLUMN",
            "JTable.AUTO_RESIZE_SUBSEQUENT_COLUMNS",
            "JTable.AUTO_RESIZE_LAST_COLUMN",
            "JTable.AUTO_RESIZE_ALL_COLUMNS",
    };
    int[] resizeConstants = {
            JTable.AUTO_RESIZE_OFF,
            JTable.AUTO_RESIZE_NEXT_COLUMN,
            JTable.AUTO_RESIZE_SUBSEQUENT_COLUMNS,
            JTable.AUTO_RESIZE_LAST_COLUMN,
            JTable.AUTO_RESIZE_ALL_COLUMNS,
    };
    JTable table = new JTable(6,5);

    public Test() {
        Container contentPane = getContentPane();

        contentPane.add(new ControlPanel(), BorderLayout.NORTH);
        contentPane.add(new JScrollPane(table),
                    BorderLayout.CENTER);

    }
    ...
```

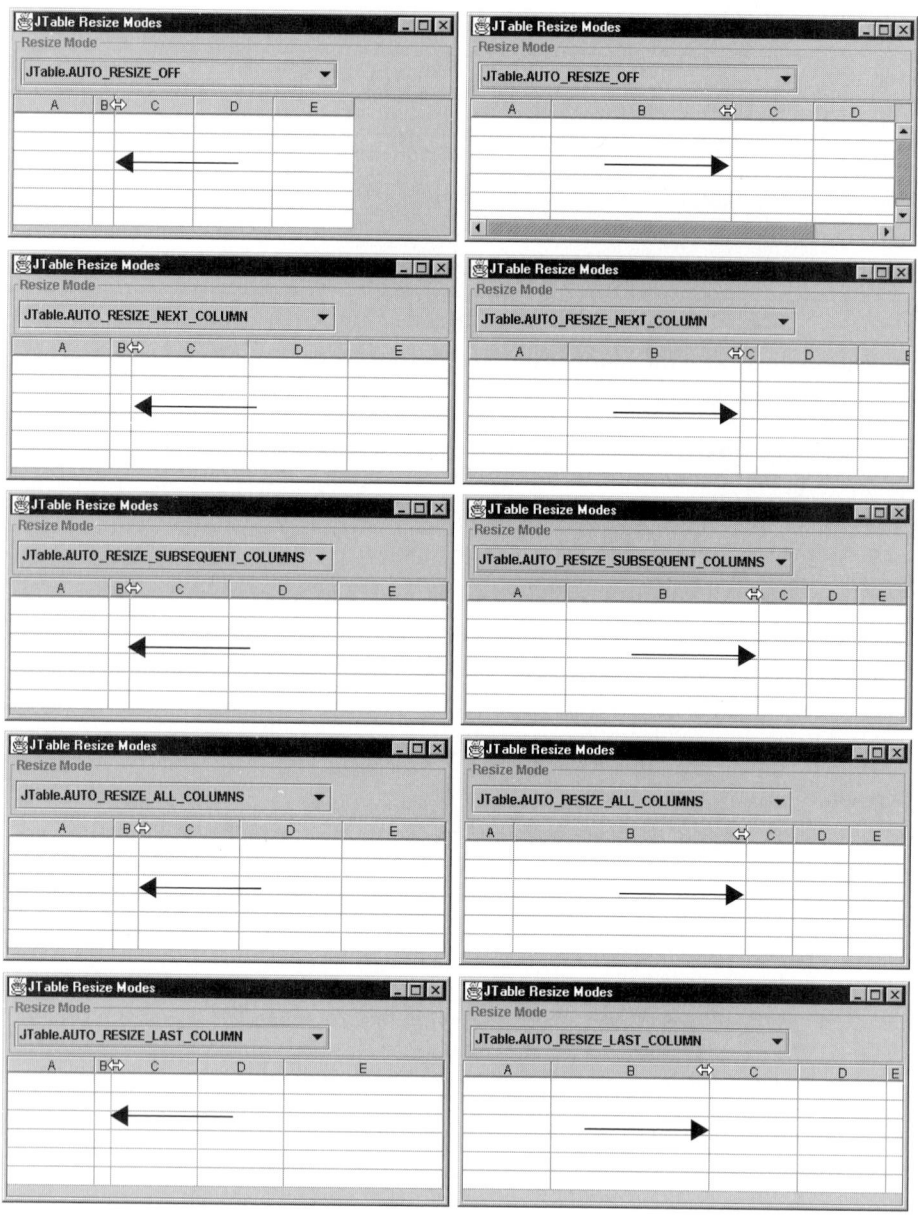

Figure 19-12 JTable Resize Modes

The combo box is constructed with the array of strings and is initialized by obtaining the table's initial resize mode.

A listener added to the combo box sets the table's resize mode depending upon the item selected from the combo box.

```
...
class ControlPanel extends JPanel {
    JComboBox resizeModeCombo = new JComboBox(resizeModes);

    public ControlPanel() {
        initializeCombo();
        ...
        resizeModeCombo.addActionListener(
                             new ActionListener() {
            public void actionPerformed(ActionEvent e) {
                int index =
                    resizeModeCombo.getSelectedIndex();

                table.setAutoResizeMode(
                             resizeConstants[index]);
            }
        });
    }
    private void initializeCombo() {
        int resizeMode = table.getAutoResizeMode();

        if(resizeMode == JTable.AUTO_RESIZE_OFF)
            resizeModeCombo.setSelectedIndex(0);
        else if(resizeMode == JTable.AUTO_RESIZE_NEXT_COLUMN)
            resizeModeCombo.setSelectedIndex(1);
        ...
    }
}
```

The application shown in Figure 19-12 is listed in its entirety in Example 19-5.

Example 19-5   JTable Resize Modes

```
import javax.swing.*;
import javax.swing.event.*;
import javax.swing.table.*;
import java.awt.*;
import java.awt.event.*;

public class Test extends JFrame {
    Object[] resizeModes = new Object[] {
            "JTable.AUTO_RESIZE_OFF",
            "JTable.AUTO_RESIZE_NEXT_COLUMN",
```

```
                "JTable.AUTO_RESIZE_SUBSEQUENT_COLUMNS",
                "JTable.AUTO_RESIZE_LAST_COLUMN",
                "JTable.AUTO_RESIZE_ALL_COLUMNS",
   };
   int[] resizeConstants = {
           JTable.AUTO_RESIZE_OFF,
           JTable.AUTO_RESIZE_NEXT_COLUMN,
           JTable.AUTO_RESIZE_SUBSEQUENT_COLUMNS,
           JTable.AUTO_RESIZE_LAST_COLUMN,
           JTable.AUTO_RESIZE_ALL_COLUMNS,
   };
   JTable table = new JTable(6,5);

   public Test() {
       Container contentPane = getContentPane();

       contentPane.add(new ControlPanel(), BorderLayout.NORTH);
       contentPane.add(new JScrollPane(table),
                    BorderLayout.CENTER);

   }
   class ControlPanel extends JPanel {
       JComboBox resizeModeCombo = new JComboBox(resizeModes);

       public ControlPanel() {
           initializeCombo();

           setBorder(BorderFactory.createTitledBorder(
                        "Resize Mode"));

           setLayout(new FlowLayout(FlowLayout.LEFT,2,2));
           add(resizeModeCombo);

           resizeModeCombo.addActionListener(
                                new ActionListener() {
               public void actionPerformed(ActionEvent e) {
                   int index =
                        resizeModeCombo.getSelectedIndex();

                   table.setAutoResizeMode(
                                resizeConstants[index]);
               }
           });
       }
       private void initializeCombo() {
           int resizeMode = table.getAutoResizeMode();

           if(resizeMode == JTable.AUTO_RESIZE_OFF)
              resizeModeCombo.setSelectedIndex(0);
           else if(resizeMode == JTable.AUTO_RESIZE_NEXT_COLUMN)
              resizeModeCombo.setSelectedIndex(1);
           else if(resizeMode == JTable.AUTO_RESIZE_LAST_COLUMN)
              resizeModeCombo.setSelectedIndex(2);
```

```
            else if(resizeMode == JTable.AUTO_RESIZE_ALL_COLUMNS)
               resizeModeCombo.setSelectedIndex(3);
            else if(
               resizeMode == JTable.AUTO_RESIZE_SUBSEQUENT_COLUMNS)
               resizeModeCombo.setSelectedIndex(4);
      }
   }
   public static void main(String args[]) {
      GJApp.launch(
         new Test(), "JTable Resize Modes", 300,300,425,210);
   }
}
```

Column Widths

More often than not, table columns are not set to desirable widths by default. For example, the top application shown in Figure 19-13 contains a table that by default has allotted equal space to its three columns. The MI (middle initial) column is much wider than it needs to be, and the Last Name column is not wide enough to accommodate its widest item.

The bottom application shown in Figure 19-13 modifies column widths so that the MI column takes up just the space that it needs, and the Last Name column is wide enough to accommodate its widest item.

First Name	MI	Last Name
Lynn	M.	Seckinger
Carol	R.	Seckinger
Roy	D.	Martin
Bill	O.	Veryveryveryver...
Richard	A.	Tattersall
Philip	D.	Edwards

First Name	MI	Last Name
Lynn	M.	Seckinger
Carol	R.	Seckinger
Roy	D.	Martin
Bill	O.	Veryveryveryverylonglastname
Richard	A.	Tattersall
Philip	D.	Edwards

Figure 19-13 Specifying Column Widths

All that is required to resize columns as shown in Figure 19-13 is a method that calculates a column's *actual* preferred width. Although columns maintain a `preferredWidth` property that is accessible with `TableColumn.getPreferredWidth()`, columns by default have a preferred width of 75 pixels; in other words, a column's preferred width is not a calculated value by default.

The *actual* preferred width for a column is just wide enough to accommodate the width of its header and the widths of the components that are rendered in its cells. The application shown in the bottom picture in Figure 19-13 implements a method that calculates a column's actual preferred width.

The bottom application shown in Figure 19-13 creates a table with an array of column names and a two-dimensional array of strings representing first names, last names, and middle initials.

```
public class Test extends JFrame {
    Object[] columnNames =
            {"First Name", "MI", "Last Name"};

    Object[][] names = {
        { "Lynn", "M.", "Seckinger" },
        { "Carol", "R.", "Seckinger" },
        { "Roy", "D.", "Martin" },
        { "Bill", "O.", "Veryveryveryverylonglastname" },
        { "Richard", "A.", "Tattersall" },
        { "Philip", "B.", "Edwards" },
        { "Moore", "T.", "Moore" },
    };

    JTable table = new JTable(names, columnNames);
    ...
```

The application's constructor invokes the `getPreferredWidthForColumn` method (listed below), which returns a column's actual preferred width, taking into account the manner in which the column's header and cell values are rendered.

The `MI` column has its minimum and maximum widths set to its preferred width, meaning the column's width will be fixed at its preferred width. The minimum width for the `Last Name` column is set to the column's preferred width, and therefore the column will not be sized smaller than its preferred width.

```
    . . .
    public Test() {
        TableColumn mid = table.getColumn(columnNames[1]);
        TableColumn last = table.getColumn(columnNames[2]);

        int midWidth = getPreferredWidthForColumn(mid),
            lastWidth = getPreferredWidthForColumn(last);

        mid.setMinWidth(midWidth);
        mid.setMaxWidth(midWidth);

        last.setMinWidth(lastWidth);

        // sizeColumnsToFit() must be called due to a JTable
        // bug ...
        table.sizeColumnsToFit(0);

        . . .
    }
    . . .
```

Note: `JTable.sizeColumnsToFit()` *must be invoked above because of a JTable bug.*

The `getPreferredWidthForColumn()` method listed below calculates the actual preferred width for a column. Actual preferred widths for a column's header and cells are obtained by invoking two of the application's `private` methods. The wider of the two values is returned from the method.

```
    . . .
    public int getPreferredWidthForColumn(TableColumn col) {
        int hw = columnHeaderWidth(col),    // hw = header width
            cw = widestCellInColumn(col);   // cw = column width

        return hw > cw ? hw : cw;
    }
    . . .
```

The `columnHeaderWidth` method calculates the actual preferred width for a column's header. First, a reference to the column's header renderer is obtained with the `TableColumn.getHeaderRenderer` method. The renderer is then used to obtain a reference to the renderer's component. Subsequently, the preferred size of the component is returned. See "Table Headers" on page 1251 for more information concerning table header and cell renderers.

A column's header renderer implements the `TableCellRenderer` interface that defines the `getTableCellRendererComponent` method, which among other things is passed the row and column for the value that is rendered. For header renderers (unlike cell renderers), the row and column values passed to `getTableCellRendererComponent` are ignored, and therefore the `columnHeaderWidth` method passes 0 for both the row and column to the `getTableCellRendererComponent` method.

```
. . .
private int columnHeaderWidth(TableColumn col) {
   TableCellRenderer renderer = col.getHeaderRenderer();

   Component comp = renderer.getTableCellRendererComponent(
                       table, col.getHeaderValue(),
                       false, false, 0, 0);

   return comp.getPreferredSize().width;
}
. . .
```

The `widestCellInColumn` method obtains a reference to the column's cell renderer and the renderer's component. The maximum of the component's preferred sizes is returned by the method.

```
. . .
private int widestCellInColumn(TableColumn col) {
   int c = col.getModelIndex(), width=0, maxw=0;

   for(int r=0; r < table.getRowCount(); ++r) {
      TableCellRenderer renderer =
                   table.getCellRenderer(r,c);

      Component comp =
         renderer.getTableCellRendererComponent(
                       table, table.getValueAt(r,c),
                       false, false, r, c);

      width = comp.getPreferredSize().width;
      maxw = width > maxw ? width : maxw;
   }
   return maxw;
}
. . .
```

It should be noted that the `TableColumn` class provides a `getCellRenderer()` method that could be used by the method listed above instead of `JTable.getCellRenderer(int row, int col)`. The advantage to using the `JTable` method is that `JTable.getCellRenderer()` will return the default renderer for the class of data represented by the column if the column's renderer has not been explicitly set.

The bottom application shown in Figure 19-13 on page 1167 is listed in its entirety in Example 19-6.

Example 19-6 Specifying Column Widths

```
import java.awt.*;
import java.awt.event.*;
import javax.swing.*;
import javax.swing.table.*;
import java.util.*;

public class Test extends JFrame {
    Object[] columnNames =
            {"First Name", "MI", "Last Name"};

    Object[][] names = {
        { "Lynn", "M.", "Seckinger" },
        { "Carol", "R.", "Seckinger" },
        { "Roy", "D.", "Martin" },
        { "Bill", "O.", "Veryveryveryverylonglastname" },
        { "Richard", "A.", "Tattersall" },
        { "Philip", "B.", "Edwards" },
        { "Moore", "T.", "Moore" },

        // shorten scrollbar grip with these ...
        { "Lynn", "M.", "Seckinger" },
        { "Carol", "R.", "Seckinger" },
        { "Roy", "D.", "Martin" },
        { "Bill", "O.", "Veryveryveryverylonglastname" },
        { "Richard", "A.", "Tattersall" },
        { "Philip", "B.", "Edwards" },
        { "Moore", "T.", "Moore" },
    };
    JTable table = new JTable(names, columnNames);

    public Test() {
        TableColumn mid = table.getColumn(columnNames[1]);
        TableColumn last = table.getColumn(columnNames[2]);

        int midWidth = getPreferredWidthForColumn(mid),
            lastWidth = getPreferredWidthForColumn(last);

        mid.setMinWidth(midWidth);
```

```java
        mid.setMaxWidth(midWidth);

        last.setMinWidth(lastWidth);

        getContentPane().add(new JScrollPane(table),
                        BorderLayout.CENTER);
    }
    public int getPreferredWidthForColumn(TableColumn col) {
        int hw = columnHeaderWidth(col),    // hw = header width
            cw = widestCellInColumn(col);   // cw = column width

        return hw > cw ? hw : cw;
    }
    private int columnHeaderWidth(TableColumn col) {
        TableCellRenderer renderer = col.getHeaderRenderer();

        Component comp = renderer.getTableCellRendererComponent(
                            table, col.getHeaderValue(),
                            false, false, 0, 0);

        return comp.getPreferredSize().width;
    }
    private int widestCellInColumn(TableColumn col) {
        int c = col.getModelIndex(), width=0, maxw=0;

        for(int r=0; r < table.getRowCount(); ++r) {
            TableCellRenderer renderer =
                        table.getCellRenderer(r,c);

            Component comp =
                renderer.getTableCellRendererComponent(
                            table, table.getValueAt(r,c),
                            false, false, r, c);

            width = comp.getPreferredSize().width;
            maxw = width > maxw ? width : maxw;
        }
        return maxw;
    }
    public static void main(String args[]) {
        GJApp.launch(
            new Test(),"Setting Column Widths",300,300,320,140);
    }
```

Swing Tip ...

Use JTable.getCellRenderer() and JTable.getCellEditor()

The JTable methods getCellRenderer(int row, int col) and getCellEditor(int row, int col) should be used to obtain references to renderers and editors for a particular table cell.

References to table renderers and editor can be obtained from a table's columns with the TableColumn methods getCellRenderer() and getCellEditor(), but it is preferable to use the JTable methods because the JTable methods will return default renderers and editors if a column's renderer or editor has not been explicitly set.

Notice that JTable methods for accessing renderers and editors are passed both a row and a column. By default, the JTable methods will return the same renderer or editor for every row in a particular column, but they could be overridden by JTable subclasses to return a renderer specific to a table cell.

The TableColumn class is summarized in Class Summary 19-3.

Class Summary 19-3   TableColumn

Extends: java.lang.Object
Implements: java.io.Serializable

Constructors

public TableColumn()
public TableColumn(int modelIndex)
public TableColumn(int modelIndex, int width)
public TableColumn(int modelIndex, int width, TableCellRenderer, TableCellEditor)

If not specified, `modelIndex` defaults to 0, `width` defaults to 75, and the `renderer` and `editor` are null. `JTable` provides default renderers and editors for columns that have not had them explicitly set.

Methods

Cell Editors

---

public TableCellEditor <u>getCellEditor</u>()
public void <u>setCellEditor</u>(TableCellEditor)

A table column's cell editor can be set anytime after a column is constructed. The `cellEditor` property is a simple property, which means that a property change event is not fired when the cell editor is set. Notice that this is in contrast to the `cellRenderer` property, which is a bound property.[6]

Cell Renderers

---

public TableCellRenderer <u>getCellRenderer</u>()
public void <u>setCellRenderer</u>(TableCellRenderer)

A table column's cell renderer can also be set anytime after a column is constructed. The `cellRenderer` property is a bound property, which means that a property change event is fired when the cell editor is set. Notice that this is in contrast to the `cellEditor` property, which is not a bound property.

Header Renderer

---

public TableCellRenderer <u>getHeaderRenderer</u>()
public void <u>setHeaderRenderer</u>(TableCellRenderer)

protected TableCellRenderer <u>createDefaultHeaderRenderer</u>()

---

6.   The `cellEditor` property will probably be bound in a future Swing release.

Unlike column cells, the JTable class does not provide default renderers for column headers. As a result, TableColumn.setHeaderRenderer() throws an exception if passed a null renderer. The headerRenderer property is a bound property.

The createDefaultHeaderRenderer method creates a header renderer that table columns are fitted with by default. The renderer extends DefaultTableCellRenderer (which extends JLabel) and renders the value returned from the header value's toString method.

Header Value

public Object getHeaderValue()
public void setHeaderValue(Object)

A table column's header value is the object displayed by the column's header renderer. By default, column header values are initialized with table column names. The headerValue property is a bound property.

Property Change Listeners

public synchronized void addPropertyChangeListener(PropertyChangeListener)
public synchronized void removePropertyChangeListener(PropertyChangeListener)

TableColumn fires property change events when its bound properties are modified. The methods listed above allow listeners to be added and removed from the table column.

Preferred/Minimum/Maximum Widths

public int getWidth()
public int getMaxWidth()
public int getMinWidth()
public int getPreferredWidth()

```
public void setMaxWidth(int)
public void setMinWidth(int)
public void setPreferredWidth(int)
public void setWidth(int)
```

The methods above are accessors for a table column's actual, minimum, maximum, and preferred widths.

Like components, columns are sized by another object (JTable). Unlike components, whose minimum, maximum, and preferred sizes can be ignored by layout managers, the JTable class always takes column widths into account when sizing columns—a table column will never be sized smaller than its minimum width or wider than its maximum width.

Because table columns are sized by the JTable class, setting the actual width of a column with the setWidth method is typically a temporary change.

Identifier / Model Index / Resizable

```
public Object getIdentifier()
public int getModelIndex()
public boolean getResizable()

public void setIdentifier(Object)
public void setModelIndex(int)
public void setResizable(boolean)
```

The methods listed above are accessors for a table column's identifier, model index, and resizability (or lack thereof).

Note: As of Swing1.1 FCS, the setResizable *method has no effect; table columns are always resizable.*

Utility Methods

```
public void disableResizedPosting()
public void enableResizedPosting()

public void sizeWidthToFit()
```

Invoking the first two methods listed above has no effect on table columns, and the methods are not invoked from anywhere within Swing.

The `sizeWidthToFit` method sizes a column so that the column's width matches the preferred width of the column header.

Note: As of Swing1.1 FCS, the `enable/disableResizedPosting` *methods are essentially empty implementations of methods that are never called within Swing.*

Table Column Models

A table's columns are maintained by an object that implements the `TableColumnModel` interface. Table column models can be accessed through the `JTable` class and are responsible for selecting, adding, moving, and removing table columns.

Table column models also maintain a handful of properties that pertain to table columns as a whole; for example, `TableColumnModel.setColumnMargin()` sets a margin between columns that is uniform among all columns in a given table.

The `TableColumnModel` interface is summarized in Interface Summary 19-2.

Interface Summary 19-2   TableColumnModel

Listener Registration

---

public abstract void <u>addColumnModelListener</u>(TableColumnModelListener)
public abstract void <u>removeColumnModelListener</u>(TableColumnModelListener)

Table column model listeners are notified of column property and selection changes. The methods listed above add and remove listeners.

Adding/Removing/Moving Columns

---

public abstract void <u>addColumn</u>(TableColumn)
public abstract void <u>removeColumn</u>(TableColumn)

public abstract void <u>moveColumn</u>(int fromIndex, int toIndex)

Columns can be added and removed from a table column model. Adding and removing columns does not affect a table's data; it only affects which columns are displayed in a table.

Columns can be moved from one index to another with the last method listed above.

Column Selection

---

public abstract void <u>setColumnSelectionAllowed</u>(boolean)
public abstract boolean <u>getColumnSelectionAllowed</u>()

public abstract int <u>getSelectedColumnCount</u>()
public abstract int[] <u>getSelectedColumns</u>()

public abstract ListSelectionModel <u>getSelectionModel</u>()
public abstract void <u>setSelectionModel</u>(ListSelectionModel)

Column selection can be enabled or disabled with the first method listed above. The `getColumnSelectionAllowed` method returns `true` if column selection is allowed, and `false` otherwise.

A count of the currently selected columns and an array of their indexes can be obtained with the `getSelectedColumnCount` and `getSelectedColumns` methods.

The list selection model used by the table column model can be accessed by the last two methods listed above.

Miscellaneous Column Properties

---

public abstract TableColumn getColumn(int)
public abstract int getColumnCount()
public abstract int getColumnIndex(Object)
public abstract int getColumnIndexAtX(int x)
public abstract int getColumnMargin()
public abstract Enumeration getColumns()
public abstract int getTotalColumnWidth()

public abstract void setColumnMargin(int)

The table column model provides a number of getter methods for various properties, such as a column at a given index, the number of columns in the model, and the total width occupied by all of the columns.

It is interesting to note the high degree of read-only properties for table column models. Only the columnMargin, selectionModel, and columnSelectionAllowed properties are settable. In addition, of the three settable properties, columnMargin is the only property whose modification results in an event (ChangeEvent) being fired.[7]

The DefaultTableColumnModel Class

Swing provides a single implementation of the TableColumnModel interface: the DefaultTableColumnModel class. A class diagram of the DefaultTableColumnModel class is shown in Figure 19-14.

DefaultTableColumnModel extends Object and implements the TableColumnModel interface.

DefaultTableColumnModel stores its columns in a Vector and contains an instance of ListSelectionModel. The selection model is used to implement column selections—see "Table Selection" on page 1193 for more information on tables and column selection.

---

7. All of the properties should be bound and probably will be bound in a future Swing release.

Figure 19-14 DefaultTableColumnModel Class Diagram

DefaultTableColumnModel also implements the PropertyChangeListener interface in order to react to property changes in its columns, and the ListSelectionListener interface to detect column selection events. Column property change events and column selection events are forwarded to registered TableColumnModelListeners.

DefaultTableColumnModel maintains a boolean variable indicating whether column selection is allowed and maintains an integer value representing the column margin.

Column Margins

A table column's column margin represents margins between adjacent cells in a row. `DefaultTableColumnModel` fires a `ChangeEvent` to registered `TableColumnModelListeners` when its column margin is modified.

The application shown in Figure 19-15 contains a table and a slider that controls the column margin.

The top picture in Figure 19-15 shows the application as it appears initially. By default, column margins are 1 pixel. The space taken up by margins is used to draw vertical lines of the grid. When the margin is 0, grid lines are invisible.

The middle picture shows a column margin of 0 pixels, which causes the vertical grid lines to disappear because there is no room between margins.

The bottom picture in Figure 19-15 shows a column margin of 20 pixels, which makes the margins apparent because only the backgrounds of cells—and not margins—are highlighted.

The application creates a table with a simple table model and adds the table, wrapped in a scrollpane, to the application's content pane as the center component. An instance of `ControlPanel` is created and added to the content pane as the north component.

```
public class Test extends JFrame {
    JTable table = new JTable(
        new AbstractTableModel() {
            public int getRowCount() { return 10; }
            public int getColumnCount() { return 10; }

            public Object getValueAt(int row, int col) {
                return "(" + Integer.toString(row) + "," +
                        Integer.toString(col) + ")";
            }
        });

    public Test() {
        Container cp = getContentPane();
        cp.add(new JScrollPane(table), BorderLayout.CENTER);
        cp.add(new ControlPanel(), BorderLayout.NORTH);
    }
    ...
```

Column Margins _ □ ×

Column Margin: 1

A	B	C	D	E	F	G	H	I	J	
(0,0)	(0,1)	(0,2)	(0,3)	(0,4)	(0,5)	(0,6)	(0,7)	(0,8)	(0,9)	▲
(1,0)	(1,1)	(1,2)	(1,3)	(1,4)	(1,5)	(1,6)	(1,7)	(1,8)	(1,9)	
(2,0)	(2,1)	(2,2)	(2,3)	(2,4)	(2,5)	(2,6)	(2,7)	(2,8)	(2,9)	
(3,0)	(3,1)	(3,2)	(3,3)	(3,4)	(3,5)	(3,6)	(3,7)	(3,8)	(3,9)	
(4,0)	(4,1)	(4,2)	(4,3)	(4,4)	(4,5)	(4,6)	(4,7)	(4,8)	(4,9)	
(5,0)	(5,1)	(5,2)	(5,3)	(5,4)	(5,5)	(5,6)	(5,7)	(5,8)	(5,9)	
(6,0)	(6,1)	(6,2)	(6,3)	(6,4)	(6,5)	(6,6)	(6,7)	(6,8)	(6,9)	
(7,0)	(7,1)	(7,2)	(7,3)	(7,4)	(7,5)	(7,6)	(7,7)	(7,8)	(7,9)	▼

Column Margins _ □ ×

Column Margin: 0

A	B	C	D	E	F	G	H	I	J	
(0,0)	(0,1)	(0,2)	(0,3)	(0,4)	(0,5)	(0,6)	(0,7)	(0,8)	(0,9)	▲
(1,0)	(1,1)	(1,2)	(1,3)	(1,4)	(1,5)	(1,6)	(1,7)	(1,8)	(1,9)	
(2,0)	(2,1)	(2,2)	(2,3)	(2,4)	(2,5)	(2,6)	(2,7)	(2,8)	(2,9)	
(3,0)	(3,1)	(3,2)	(3,3)	(3,4)	(3,5)	(3,6)	(3,7)	(3,8)	(3,9)	
(4,0)	(4,1)	(4,2)	(4,3)	(4,4)	(4,5)	(4,6)	(4,7)	(4,8)	(4,9)	
(5,0)	(5,1)	(5,2)	(5,3)	(5,4)	(5,5)	(5,6)	(5,7)	(5,8)	(5,9)	
(6,0)	(6,1)	(6,2)	(6,3)	(6,4)	(6,5)	(6,6)	(6,7)	(6,8)	(6,9)	
(7,0)	(7,1)	(7,2)	(7,3)	(7,4)	(7,5)	(7,6)	(7,7)	(7,8)	(7,9)	▼

Column Margins _ □ ×

Column Margin: 20

A	B	C	D	E	F	G	
(0,0)	(0,1)	(0,2)	(0,3)	(0,4)	(0,5)	(0,6)	▲
(1,0)	(1,1)	(1,2)	(1,3)	(1,4)	(1,5)	(1,6)	
(2,0)	(2,1)	(2,2)	(2,3)	(2,4)	(2,5)	(2,6)	
(3,0)	(3,1)	(3,2)	(3,3)	(3,4)	(3,5)	(3,6)	
(4,0)	(4,1)	(4,2)	(4,3)	(4,4)	(4,5)	(4,6)	
(5,0)	(5,1)	(5,2)	(5,3)	(5,4)	(5,5)	(5,6)	
(6,0)	(6,1)	(6,2)	(6,3)	(6,4)	(6,5)	(6,6)	
(7,0)	(7,1)	(7,2)	(7,3)	(7,4)	(7,5)	(7,6)	▼

Figure 19-15 Setting Column Margins

The control panel contains the slider, which is initialized with the default column margin. In addition to the slider, the panel also contains two labels: one that identifies the slider and another that shows the slider's value.

```
....
class ControlPanel extends JPanel {
    private JSlider slider = new JSlider(
            JSlider.HORIZONTAL,0,100,
            table.getColumnModel().getColumnMargin());

    private JLabel label = new JLabel();

    public ControlPanel() {
        add(new JLabel("Column Margin:"));
        add(slider);
        add(label);
```

```
label.setText(
    Integer.toString(
        table.getColumnModel().getColumnMargin()));
...
```

Listeners are added to the slider and the table's column model. When the slider's value changes, the column margin is set to the slider's value. The call to `TableColumnModel.setColumnMargin()` results in a change event being fired by the table column model, handled by updating the label's text.

```
        ...
        slider.addChangeListener(new ChangeListener() {
            public void stateChanged(ChangeEvent e) {
                table.getColumnModel().setColumnMargin(
                                slider.getValue());
            }
        });
        table.getColumnModel().addColumnModelListener(
                        new TableColumnModelListener() {
            public void columnMarginChanged(ChangeEvent e) {
                TableColumnModel m = table.getColumnModel();
                label.setText(
                    Integer.toString(m.getColumnMargin()));
            }

            // unfortunately, Swing does not have many
            // event adapter classes ...
            public void columnAdded(TableColumnModelEvent e) {
            }
            public void columnMoved(TableColumnModelEvent e) {
            }
            public void columnRemoved(
                            TableColumnModelEvent e) {
            }
            public void columnSelectionChanged(
                            ListSelectionEvent e) {
            }
        });
    }
}
```

The application shown in Figure 19-15 is listed in its entirety in Example 19-7.

Example 19-7 Setting Column Margins

```
import java.awt.*;
import java.awt.event.*;
import javax.swing.*;
import javax.swing.event.*;
```

```
import javax.swing.table.*;
import java.util.*;

public class Test extends JFrame {
    JTable table = new JTable(
        new AbstractTableModel() {
            public int getRowCount() { return 10; }
            public int getColumnCount() { return 10; }

            public Object getValueAt(int row, int col) {
                return "(" + Integer.toString(row) + "," +
                            Integer.toString(col) + ")";
            }
        });

    public Test() {
        Container cp = getContentPane();
        cp.add(new JScrollPane(table), BorderLayout.CENTER);
        cp.add(new ControlPanel(), BorderLayout.NORTH);
    }
    class ControlPanel extends JPanel {
        private JSlider slider = new JSlider(
                    JSlider.HORIZONTAL,0,100,
                    table.getColumnModel().getColumnMargin());

        private JLabel label = new JLabel();

        public ControlPanel() {
            add(new JLabel("Column Margin:"));
            add(slider);
            add(label);

            label.setText(
                Integer.toString(
                    table.getColumnModel().getColumnMargin()));

            slider.addChangeListener(new ChangeListener() {
                public void stateChanged(ChangeEvent e) {
                    table.getColumnModel().setColumnMargin(
                                    slider.getValue());
                }
            });
            table.getColumnModel().addColumnModelListener(
                        new TableColumnModelListener() {
                public void columnMarginChanged(ChangeEvent e) {
                    TableColumnModel m = table.getColumnModel();
                    label.setText(
                        Integer.toString(m.getColumnMargin()));
                }

                // unfortunately, Swing does not have many
                // event adapter classes ...
```

```
        public void columnAdded(TableColumnModelEvent e) {
        }
        public void columnMoved(TableColumnModelEvent e) {
        }
        public void columnRemoved(
                        TableColumnModelEvent e) {
        }
        public void columnSelectionChanged(
                        ListSelectionEvent e) {
        }
      });
    }
  }
  public static void main(String args[]) {
    GJApp.launch(new Test(),
            "Column Margins",150,150,500,200);
  }
}
```

Hiding Columns

Table column models provide methods for adding, moving, and removing columns, all of which are put to use in the application shown in Figure 19-16. The application contains a simple table and a check box that toggles the visibility of the First Name column.

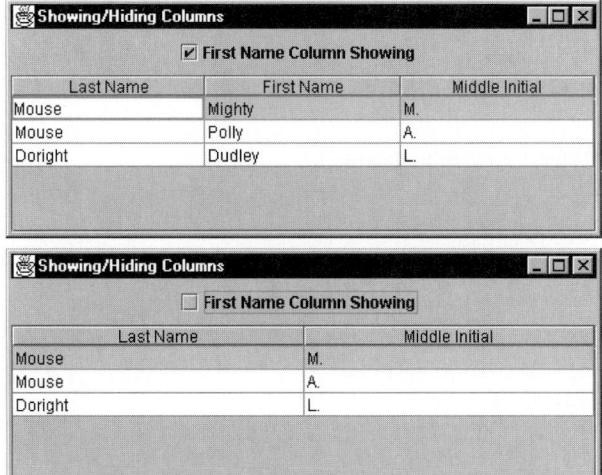

Figure 19-16 Adding and Removing Columns

The application creates an instance of `JTable` and a control panel, both of which are added to the application's content pane.

```
public class Test extends JFrame {
    JTable table = new JTable(
        new Object[][] {
            {"Mouse", "Mighty", "M." },
            {"Mouse", "Polly", "A." },
            {"Doright", "Dudley", "L." }
        },
        new Object[] {
            "Last Name", "First Name", "Middle Initial"
        }
    );
    public Test() {
        Container cp = getContentPane();

        cp.add(new JScrollPane(table), BorderLayout.CENTER);
        cp.add(new ControlPanel(), BorderLayout.NORTH);
    }
    ...
```

The control panel contains the check box. An action listener is added to the check box that removes the `First Name` column from the table's column model when the check box is deselected. When the check box is selected, the listener adds the column to the table's column model; however, the `TableColumnModel.addColumn` method adds the specified column as the rightmost column. Therefore, after the column is added to the column model, it is moved from the third column (index 2) to the second column (index 1).

```
    ...
class ControlPanel extends JPanel {
    private JCheckBox checkBox = new JCheckBox(
                        "First Name Column Showing");
    public ControlPanel() {
        final TableColumnModel tcm = table.getColumnModel();
        final TableColumn firstNameColumn =
                        table.getColumn("First Name");

        checkBox.setSelected(true);
        add(checkBox);

        checkBox.addActionListener(new ActionListener() {
            public void actionPerformed(ActionEvent event) {
                if(checkBox.isSelected()) {
                    tcm.addColumn(firstNameColumn);
                    tcm.moveColumn(2,1);
```

```
            }
            else {
                tcm.removeColumn(firstNameColumn);
            }

            // Bug: the call to sizeColumnsToFit()
            // should not be necessary
            table.sizeColumnsToFit(-1);
        }
    });
    }
}
```

The application shown in Figure 19-16 is listed in its entirety in Example 19-8.

Example 19-8 Adding and Removing Columns

```
import javax.swing.*;
import javax.swing.table.*;
import java.awt.*;
import java.awt.event.*;
import java.util.*;

public class Test extends JFrame {
    JTable table = new JTable(
        new Object[][] {
            {"Mouse", "Mighty", "M." },
            {"Mouse", "Polly", "A." },
            {"Doright", "Dudley", "L." }
        },
        new Object[] {
            "Last Name", "First Name", "Middle Initial"
        }
    );
    public Test() {
        Container cp = getContentPane();

        cp.add(new JScrollPane(table), BorderLayout.CENTER);
        cp.add(new ControlPanel(), BorderLayout.NORTH);
    }
    class ControlPanel extends JPanel {
        private JCheckBox checkBox = new JCheckBox(
                            "First Name Column Showing");
        public ControlPanel() {
            final TableColumnModel tcm = table.getColumnModel();
            final TableColumn firstNameColumn =
                            table.getColumn("First Name");

            checkBox.setSelected(true);
            add(checkBox);
```

```
        checkBox.addActionListener(new ActionListener() {
            public void actionPerformed(ActionEvent event) {
                if(checkBox.isSelected()) {
                    tcm.addColumn(firstNameColumn);
                    tcm.moveColumn(2,1);
                }
                else {
                    tcm.removeColumn(firstNameColumn);
                }
                table.sizeColumnsToFit(-1);
            }
        });
    }
}
public static void main(String args[]) {
    GJApp.launch(
        new Test(), "Showing/Hiding Columns",300,300,450,175);
}
}
```

Locking the Left-Hand Column

Occasionally it is desirable to lock the left-hand column of a table in the horizontal direction. For example, consider the application shown in Figure 19-17, which displays television listings. The left-hand column can be locked so that it is still apparent what channel the shows are on when the listings are scrolled horizontally.

Tables do not support locking their columns, so to provide the illusion that a table's left-hand column is locked horizontally, a second table—hereafter referred to as the header table—is placed in the scrollpane's row header, and the column's header is placed in the scrollpane's upper-left corner. The width of the header table is constrained to the width of the left-hand column, and reordering for the header table's columns is disallowed. Finally, the left-hand column is removed from the original table's column model.

The application shown in Figure 19-17 contains a table and a check box. Selecting the check box locks the left-hand column, and deselecting the check box unlocks it. The top picture in Figure 19-17 shows the table before the column is locked, and the bottom picture shows that table after the column is locked. Both tables are scrolled to the far right.

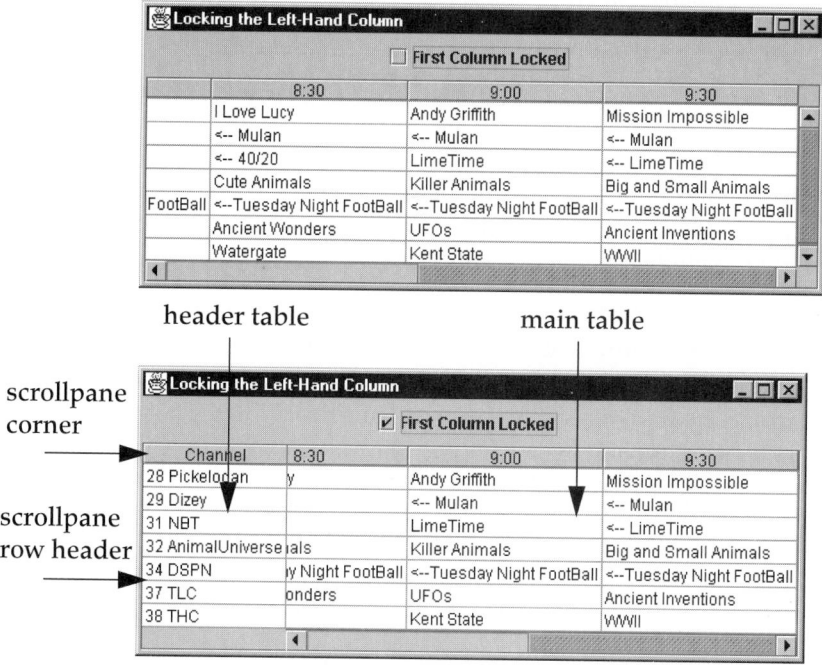

Figure 19-17 Locking the Left-Hand Column Horizontally

The application creates a simple table model that is shared between the main table and the header table. Realize that this means the header table, like the main table, has 10 columns, although only the first column will ever be visible.

The main table's column model is used to obtain a reference to the left-hand column.

```
public class Test extends JFrame {
    class SharedModel extends AbstractTableModel {
        public int getRowCount() { return 10; }
        public int getColumnCount() { return 10; }

        public Object getValueAt(int row, int col) {
            return "(" + Integer.toString(row) + "," +
                        Integer.toString(col) + ")";
        }
    }
    TableModel sharedModel = new SharedModel();

    JTable table = new JTable(sharedModel),
```

```
    headerTable = new JTable(sharedModel);

TableColumnModel tcm = table.getColumnModel();
TableColumn firstColumn = tcm.getColumn(0);
...
```

Auto-resize modes for both tables are set to JTable.AUTO_RESIZE_OFF so that columns will be sized according to their preferred widths and the main table will be fitted with a scrollbar when the table is larger than its scrollpane.

As mentioned above, the header table has 10 columns because it shares the main table's model. If reordering were allowed for the header table, the "locked" column could be dragged to the right and the header table's second column would become the first column. To preclude this behavior, the header table is not allowed to reorder its columns.

The preferred scrollable viewport size[8] for the header table is set to the preferred width of the first column plus the column's margin. If the margin is not accounted for, the right grid line will not be drawn for the column—see "Column Margins" on page 1181 for more information on column margins.

```
...
public Test() {
    Container cp = getContentPane();

    table.setAutoResizeMode(JTable.AUTO_RESIZE_OFF);
    headerTable.setAutoResizeMode(JTable.AUTO_RESIZE_OFF);

    headerTable.getTableHeader().setReorderingAllowed(false);

    headerTable.setPreferredScrollableViewportSize(
        new Dimension(
            firstColumn.getPreferredWidth() +
            headerTable.getColumnModel().getColumnMargin(),
            0));

    cp.add(new ControlPanel(), BorderLayout.NORTH);
    cp.add(new JScrollPane(table), BorderLayout.CENTER);
}
...
```

8. The preferred scrollable viewport size is the table's preferred size for its scroll-pane.

An action listener added to the application's check box obtains a reference to the main table's scrollpane with the `SwingUtilities getAncestorOfClass` method. See "Swing Utilities" on page 262 for more information concerning the `SwingUtilities` class.

If the check box is selected, the first column is removed from the main table's column model and the header table is installed as the scrollpane's row header view. The table header for the header table is installed as the scrollpane's upper-left corner.

If the check box is deselected, the first column is inserted back into the main table's column model. Because columns are appended onto the list of columns maintained by the column model, the first column is added on to the right end of the table. As a result, the column is moved from one end of the table to another. Finally, the scrollpane's row header view is set to `null`.

```
...
class ControlPanel extends JPanel {
    JCheckBox checkBox = new JCheckBox("First Column Locked");

    public ControlPanel() {
        add(checkBox);

        checkBox.addActionListener(new ActionListener() {
            public void actionPerformed(ActionEvent e) {
                JScrollPane scrollPane = (JScrollPane)
                    SwingUtilities.getAncestorOfClass(
                        JScrollPane.class, table);

                if(checkBox.isSelected()) {
                    tcm.removeColumn(firstColumn);

                    scrollPane.setRowHeaderView(headerTable);
                    scrollPane.setCorner(
                        JScrollPane.UPPER_LEFT_CORNER,
                        headerTable.getTableHeader());
                }
                else {
                    int numCols = tcm.getColumnCount();

                    tcm.addColumn(firstColumn);
                    tcm.moveColumn(numCols-1, 0);

                    scrollPane.setRowHeaderView(null);
                }
            }
        });
    }
}
```

The application shown in Figure 19-17 is listed in its entirety in Example 19-9.

Example 19-9 Locking a Table's Left-Hand Column in the Horizontal Direction

```java
import java.awt.*;
import java.awt.event.*;
import javax.swing.*;
import javax.swing.event.*;
import javax.swing.table.*;

public class Test extends JFrame {
    class SharedModel extends AbstractTableModel {
        public int getRowCount() { return 10; }
        public int getColumnCount() { return 10; }

        public Object getValueAt(int row, int col) {
            return "(" + Integer.toString(row) + "," +
                          Integer.toString(col) + ")";
        }
    }
    TableModel sharedModel = new SharedModel();

    JTable table = new JTable(sharedModel),
           headerTable = new JTable(sharedModel);

    TableColumnModel tcm = table.getColumnModel();
    TableColumn firstColumn = tcm.getColumn(0);

    public Test() {
        Container cp = getContentPane();

        table.setAutoResizeMode(JTable.AUTO_RESIZE_OFF);
        headerTable.setAutoResizeMode(JTable.AUTO_RESIZE_OFF);

        headerTable.getTableHeader().setReorderingAllowed(false);

        headerTable.setPreferredScrollableViewportSize(
            new Dimension(
                firstColumn.getPreferredWidth() +
                headerTable.getColumnModel().getColumnMargin(),
                0));

        cp.add(new ControlPanel(), BorderLayout.NORTH);
        cp.add(new JScrollPane(table), BorderLayout.CENTER);
    }
    class ControlPanel extends JPanel {
        JCheckBox checkBox = new JCheckBox("First Column Locked");

        public ControlPanel() {
            add(checkBox);
```

```
            checkBox.addActionListener(new ActionListener() {
                public void actionPerformed(ActionEvent e) {
                    JScrollPane scrollPane = (JScrollPane)
                        SwingUtilities.getAncestorOfClass(
                            JScrollPane.class, table);

                    if(checkBox.isSelected()) {
                        tcm.removeColumn(firstColumn);
                        scrollPane.setRowHeaderView(headerTable);
                        scrollPane.setCorner(
                            JScrollPane.UPPER_LEFT_CORNER,
                            headerTable.getTableHeader());
                    }
                    else {
                        tcm.addColumn(firstColumn);

                        int numCols = tcm.getColumnCount();
                        tcm.moveColumn(numCols-1, 0);
                        scrollPane.setRowHeaderView(null);
                    }
                    table.revalidate();
                }
            });
        }
    }
    public static void main(String args[]) {
        GJApp.launch(
            new Test(),"Locking the Left-Hand Column",
                300,300,425,210);
    }
}
```

Table Selection

Table rows, columns, and individual cells can all be selected with one of the
selection modes supported by the `ListSelectionModel` class:

- `ListSelectionModel.SINGLE_SELECTION`
- `ListSelectionModel.SINGLE_INTERVAL_SELECTION`
- `ListSelectionModel.MULTIPLE_INTERVAL_SELECTION`

Both `JTable` and `TableColumnModel` have list selection models that track
selection state for rows/cells and columns, respectively. See "List Models" on
page 1010 for more information concerning the `ListSelectionModel` class.

Which objects—either rows, columns, or cells—are selectable in a table is controlled by the following `JTable` methods:

- `JTable.setColumnSelectionAllowed(boolean)`
- `JTable.setRowSelectionAllowed(boolean)`
- `JTable.setCellSelectionEnabled(boolean)`

The application shown in Figure 19-18 allows the selection mode and the selectable objects (either rows, columns, or cells) in a table to be set. All of the pictures shown in Figure 19-18 were taken with selection enabled for columns and rows, but not for cells.

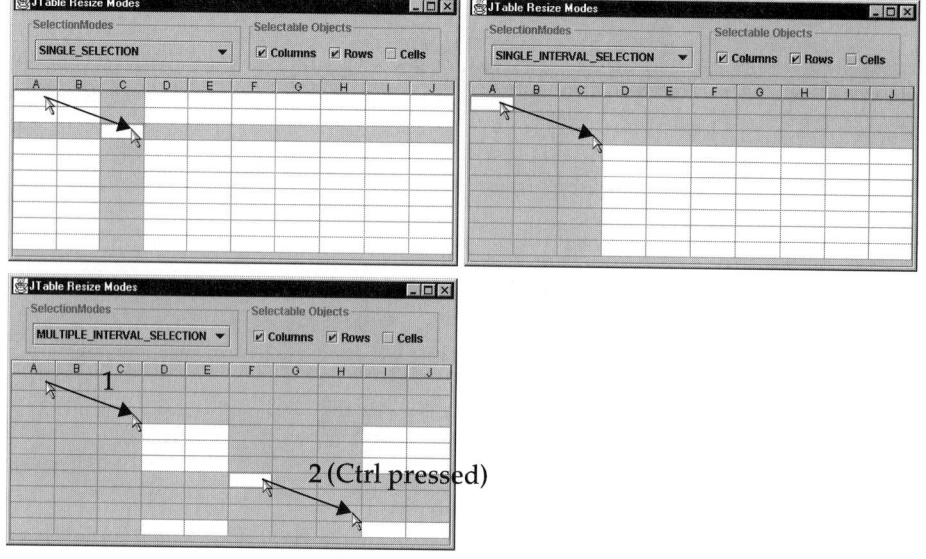

Figure 19-18 Table Selection

The upper-left picture in Figure 19-18 shows the results of dragging the mouse in the direction of the arrow when the selection mode is set to single selection. The upper-right picture shows the rows and columns that are selected when the mouse is dragged in single interval selection mode. The lower-right picture shows the results of two mouse drags (the second of which was performed with the CTRL key pressed) under multiple interval selection mode.

The application creates a simple table and an instance of `ControlPanel`—an extension of `JPanel` listed below. Both the table and the control panel are added to the content pane: the control panel as the north component and the table as the center component.

```
public class Test extends JFrame {
    JTable table = new JTable(10,10);

    public Test() {
        Container cp = getContentPane();

        cp.add(new ControlPanel(), BorderLayout.NORTH);
        cp.add(new JScrollPane(table), BorderLayout.CENTER);
    }
    ...
```

The `ControlPanel` class contains two panels, one containing a combo box and another containing three check boxes. Two arrays are instantiated, one containing strings that are displayed in the combo box and another representing the corresponding selection constants from the `ListSelectionModel` class.

```
class ControlPanel extends JPanel
                    implements ActionListener, ItemListener {
    Object[] selectionModes = new Object[] {
        "SINGLE_SELECTION",
        "SINGLE_INTERVAL_SELECTION",
        "MULTIPLE_INTERVAL_SELECTION",
    };
    int[] selectionConstants = {
        ListSelectionModel.SINGLE_SELECTION,
        ListSelectionModel.SINGLE_INTERVAL_SELECTION,
        ListSelectionModel.MULTIPLE_INTERVAL_SELECTION,
    };

    JPanel selectionPanel = new JPanel(),
           selectablesPanel = new JPanel();

    JCheckBox[] selectables = new JCheckBox[] {
        new JCheckBox("Columns"),
        new JCheckBox("Rows"),
        new JCheckBox("Cells"),
    };

    JComboBox modeCombo = new JComboBox(selectionModes);
    ...
```

The `ControlPanel` constructor sets borders for the two panels and adds the combo box and check boxes to their respective panels. The panels are subsequently added to the control panel, and a `private initializeControls` method is invoked.

The `ControlPanel` class implements the `ActionListener` and `ItemListener` interfaces to listen for selections from its check boxes and combo box, respectively. As a result, the control panel is added to the combo box as an item listener and to the check boxes as an action listener.

```
    ...
    public ControlPanel() {
        selectionPanel.setBorder(
                    BorderFactory.createTitledBorder(
                        "SelectionModes"));
        selectablesPanel.setBorder(
                    BorderFactory.createTitledBorder(
                        "Selectable Objects"));

        selectionPanel.add(modeCombo);

        for(int i=0; i < selectables.length; ++i) {
            selectablesPanel.add(selectables[i]);
            selectables[i].addItemListener(this);
        }

        initializeControls();

        add(selectionPanel);
        add(selectablesPanel);

        modeCombo.addActionListener(this);
    }
    ...
```

The `initializeControls` method initializes the combo box by selecting the appropriate item for the table's current selection mode. The check boxes are initialized according to the type of selections that are allowed or enabled.

```
    ...
    private void initializeControls() {
        int mode =
            table.getSelectionModel().getSelectionMode();

        if(mode == ListSelectionModel.SINGLE_SELECTION)
            modeCombo.setSelectedIndex(0);
```

```
            else if(mode ==
                ListSelectionModel.SINGLE_INTERVAL_SELECTION)
                modeCombo.setSelectedIndex(1);
            else if(mode ==
                ListSelectionModel.MULTIPLE_INTERVAL_SELECTION)
                modeCombo.setSelectedIndex(2);

            selectables[0].setSelected(
                        table.getColumnSelectionAllowed());

            selectables[1].setSelected(
                        table.getRowSelectionAllowed());

            selectables[2].setSelected(
                        table.getCellSelectionEnabled());
        }
        ...
```

`ControlPanel.actionPerformed()` is invoked when an item is fired from the combo box and reacts by setting the table's selection mode with `JTable.setSelectionMode()`.

`ControlPanel.itemStateChanged()` is invoked when a check box is selected or deselected. The appropriate `JTable` method is invoked to allow/enable the type of selection signified by the check box.

```
        ...
        public void actionPerformed(ActionEvent e) {
            int index = modeCombo.getSelectedIndex();
            table.setSelectionMode(selectionConstants[index]);
        }
        public void itemStateChanged(ItemEvent e) {
            JCheckBox checkBox = (JCheckBox)e.getSource();
            boolean b = checkBox.isSelected();

            if(checkBox == selectables[0])
                table.setColumnSelectionAllowed(b);
            else if(checkBox == selectables[1])
                table.setRowSelectionAllowed(b);
            else if(checkBox == selectables[2])
                table.setCellSelectionEnabled(b);
        }
    }
```

The application shown in Figure 19-18 is listed in its entirety in Example 19-10.

Example 19-10 Table Selection

```
import javax.swing.*;
import javax.swing.event.*;
import javax.swing.table.*;
import java.awt.*;
import java.awt.event.*;
import java.util.*;

public class Test extends JFrame {
    JTable table = new JTable(10,10);

    public Test() {
        Container cp = getContentPane();

        cp.add(new ControlPanel(), BorderLayout.NORTH);
        cp.add(new JScrollPane(table), BorderLayout.CENTER);
    }
    class ControlPanel extends JPanel
                    implements ActionListener, ItemListener {
        Object[] selectionModes = new Object[] {
            "SINGLE_SELECTION",
            "SINGLE_INTERVAL_SELECTION",
            "MULTIPLE_INTERVAL_SELECTION",
        };
        int[] selectionConstants = {
            ListSelectionModel.SINGLE_SELECTION,
            ListSelectionModel.SINGLE_INTERVAL_SELECTION,
            ListSelectionModel.MULTIPLE_INTERVAL_SELECTION,
        };

        JPanel selectionPanel = new JPanel(),
               selectablesPanel = new JPanel();

        JCheckBox[] selectables = new JCheckBox[] {
            new JCheckBox("Columns"),
            new JCheckBox("Rows"),
            new JCheckBox("Cells"),
        };

        JComboBox modeCombo = new JComboBox(selectionModes);

        public ControlPanel() {
            selectionPanel.setBorder(
                        BorderFactory.createTitledBorder(
                            "SelectionModes"));
            selectablesPanel.setBorder(
                        BorderFactory.createTitledBorder(
                            "Selectable Objects"));

            selectionPanel.add(modeCombo);

            for(int i=0; i < selectables.length; ++i) {
```

```
            selectablesPanel.add(selectables[i]);
            selectables[i].addItemListener(this);
        }

        initializeControls();

        add(selectionPanel);
        add(selectablesPanel);

        modeCombo.addActionListener(this);
    }
    private void initializeControls() {
        int mode =
            table.getSelectionModel().getSelectionMode();

        if(mode == ListSelectionModel.SINGLE_SELECTION)
            modeCombo.setSelectedIndex(0);
        else if(mode ==
            ListSelectionModel.SINGLE_INTERVAL_SELECTION)
            modeCombo.setSelectedIndex(1);
        else if(mode ==
            ListSelectionModel.MULTIPLE_INTERVAL_SELECTION)
            modeCombo.setSelectedIndex(2);

        selectables[0].setSelected(
                    table.getColumnSelectionAllowed());

        selectables[1].setSelected(
                    table.getRowSelectionAllowed());

        selectables[2].setSelected(
                    table.getCellSelectionEnabled());
    }
    public void actionPerformed(ActionEvent e) {
        int index = modeCombo.getSelectedIndex();
        table.setSelectionMode(selectionConstants[index]);
    }
    public void itemStateChanged(ItemEvent e) {
        JCheckBox checkBox = (JCheckBox)e.getSource();
        boolean b = checkBox.isSelected();

        if(checkBox == selectables[0])
            table.setColumnSelectionAllowed(b);
        else if(checkBox == selectables[1])
            table.setRowSelectionAllowed(b);
        else if(checkBox == selectables[2])
            table.setCellSelectionEnabled(b);
    }
}
public static void main(String args[]) {
    GJApp.launch(
        new Test(), "JTable Resize Modes",300,300,500,290);
}
}
```

Rendering and Editing

As with other Swing components that have cells, Swing tables have renderers and, optionally, editors for cell values.

The following sections diverge somewhat from the beaten path of this book by discussing a single application that covers many aspects of table cell rendering and editing. Renderers and editors are almost always related and are best presented together. The application is discussed before the renderers and editors used by the application are introduced. As a result, the application's listing in Figure 19-19 will refer to renderers and editors that will subsequently be discussed.

Using Table Cell Renderers and Editors

Even as we approach the year 2000, most car stereo stores allow stereos to be previewed with a particle board control panel where a button is pushed to select a stereo. Some imagination is required, but the table shown in Figure 19-19 is meant to simulate such a control panel.

In Use	Manufacturer	Model	Price	Dolby	Bass	Volume
●	Sony	1501A	$129.99	☑	☑	50
●	Phillips	86A4	$159.99	☑	☐	35
●	Kenwood	33-801-A	$199.99	☐	☑	77
●	Blaupunkt	7622A	$229.99	☑	☐	19
●	Akai	9733	$259.99	☑	☐	68
●	Sony	1520B	$349.99	☐	☐	94
●	Kenwood	2289B	$499.99	☐	☐	44

Figure 19-19 A Car Stereo Deck with Custom Renderers and Editors

Stereos are selected from the table shown in Figure 19-19—hereafter referred to as the stereo deck table—by clicking on an associated In Use bulb. The bulbs are mutually exclusive; selecting one of the bulbs deselects the others. Also, selecting a row selects the row's In Use bulb, and vice versa. The In Use column has a custom renderer that extends DefaultTableCellRenderer and an editor that implements the CellEditor interface.

The Manufacturer and Model columns are unremarkable—they display text, are not editable, and have default renderers.

Only store employees can change the Price column, so the column is editable, but password protected. The column's editor displays a password dialog when the editor is activated—see Figure 19-27 on page 1229—and if the correct password is entered, access is granted in the form of a combo box.

The Dolby column represents whether the stereo has Dolby sound. The column is noneditable because the feature cannot be changed. Bass, on the other hand, can be switched on and off. Both the Dolby and Bass columns are rendered with the default renderer for Boolean values—a check box. The Bass column is also fitted with a default editor.

Cells in the Volume column contain a slider and a label that tracks the slider's value. The label and slider are only enabled when the row in which they reside is selected, and double-clicking the label resets the volume to its last setting. Volume cells are only enabled if their row is selected.

The stereo deck table is fitted with an instance of StereoDeckModel, which extends AbstractTableModel and is listed in Example 19-11.

Example 19-11 StereoDeckModel Class

```
class StereoDeckModel extends AbstractTableModel {
    String[] columnNames = {
        "In Use", "Manufacturer", "Model", "Price", "Dolby",
        "Bass", "Volume"
    };
    Object[][] data = {
            { Boolean.FALSE, "Sony", "1501A",
              new Double(129.99), Boolean.TRUE,
              Boolean.TRUE, new Integer(50) },

            // rest of data omitted
    };
    public Object getValueAt(int row, int col) {
        return data[row][col];
    }
    public int getRowCount() {
```

```
            return data.length;
        }
        public int getColumnCount() {
            return columnNames.length;
        }
        public String getColumnName(int col) {
            return columnNames[col];
        }
        public Class getColumnClass(int col) {
            return data[0][col].getClass();
        }
        public void setValueAt(Object value, int row, int col) {
            data[row][col] = value;
            fireTableCellUpdated(row, col);
        }
        public boolean isCellEditable(int row, int col) {
            Class cls = getColumnClass(col);
            String name = getColumnName(col);

            return (cls == Boolean.class && !name.equals("Dolby")) ||
                    cls == Integer.class || cls == Double.class;
        }
        public void updateBulbs(int selectedRow) {
            for(int r=0; r < getRowCount(); ++r) {
                data[r][0] = new Boolean(r == selectedRow);
            }
        }
    }
}
```

The model's data consists of arrays of objects, most of which have been omitted from the listing in Example 19-11. The model defines editable cells to be cells in the In Use, Price, Bass, and Volume columns.

Notice that the overridden setValueAt method fires a table cell updated event when it is invoked. As pointed out in "AbstractTableModel Extensions Must Fire Appropriate Events" on page 1148, extensions of AbstractTableModel must fire appropriate events when their data is modified.

The model also provides an updateBulbs method that implements mutually exclusive selection behavior among the bulbs in the first column. The method sets all of the values representing the bulbs to false except for the bulb in the selected row.

The application shown in Figure 19-19 creates a table with an instance of StereoDeckModel. The application's constructor initializes columns that have custom renderers and editors. The table's columns are sized, and the list's selection mode is set to single selection.

A selection listener added to the table's selection model updates the bulbs in the left column and repaints the table as long as the selection is not adjusting.

```
public class Test extends JFrame {
    JTable table = new JTable(new StereoDeckModel());

    public Test() {
        initializeInUseColumn();
        initializePriceColumn();
        initializeVolumeColumn();
        sizeColumns();

        table.setSelectionMode(
                    ListSelectionModel.SINGLE_SELECTION);

        table.getSelectionModel().addListSelectionListener(
                                new ListSelectionListener() {
            public void valueChanged(ListSelectionEvent e) {
                StereoDeckModel model =
                            (StereoDeckModel)table.getModel();

                if(!e.getValueIsAdjusting()) {
                    model.updateBulbs(table.getSelectedRow());
                    table.repaint();
                }
            }
        });
        getContentPane().add(new JScrollPane(table),
                    BorderLayout.CENTER);
    }
    ...
```

The methods that initialize columns with custom renderers and editors are listed below. The `initializeInUseColumn` method fits the In Use column with a bulb renderer and bulb editor. The renderers and editors used by the application are discussed in the sections that follow.

The Price column is initialized by setting the column's renderer and editor to instances of `TableCellCurrencyRenderer` and `PriceEditor`, respectively. Additionally, the `PriceEditor`'s combo box is instantiated and initialized with `Double` values. The combo box's renderer is set to an instance of `ListCellCurrencyRenderer`.

```
    ...
    private void initializeInUseColumn() {
        TableColumn inUseColumn = table.getColumn("In Use");
```

```
            inUseColumn.setCellRenderer(new BulbRenderer());
            inUseColumn.setCellEditor(new BulbEditor());
        }
        private void initializePriceColumn() {
            TableColumn priceColumn = table.getColumn("Price");
            JComboBox combo = new JComboBox();

            combo.addItem(new Double(159.99));
            combo.addItem(new Double(169.99));
            combo.addItem(new Double(229.99));
            combo.addItem(new Double(449.99));
            combo.addItem(new Double(699.99));

            combo.setRenderer(new ListCellCurrencyRenderer());

            priceColumn.setCellRenderer(
                            new TableCellCurrencyRenderer());

            priceColumn.setCellEditor(new PriceEditor(combo));
        }
        ...
```

The Volume column has its renderer and editor set to instances of
VolumeRenderer and VolumeEditor, respectively. The table's row height is set
to the height of the Volume column's renderer.

```
        ...
        private void initializeVolumeColumn() {
            TableColumn volumeColumn = table.getColumn("Volume");
            TableCellRenderer renderer = new VolumeRenderer();
            TableCellEditor editor = new VolumeEditor();

            volumeColumn.setCellRenderer(renderer);
            volumeColumn.setCellEditor(editor);

            Dimension ps = ((JPanel)renderer).getPreferredSize();
            table.setRowHeight(ps.height);
        }
        private void sizeColumns() {
            ...

        }
        ...
    }
```

The application shown in Figure 19-19 is listed in its entirety in Example 19-12.[9]

---

9.   Renderer and editor classes are not listed in Example 19-12.

Example 19-12 Using Renderers and Editors

```java
import java.awt.*;
import java.awt.event.*;
import java.text.*;
import java.util.*;
import javax.swing.*;
import javax.swing.event.*;
import javax.swing.table.*;

public class Test extends JFrame {
    JTable table = new JTable(new StereoDeckModel());

    public Test() {
        initializeInUseColumn();
        initializePriceColumn();
        initializeVolumeColumn();
        sizeColumns();

        TableColumnModel tcm = table.getColumnModel();
        TableCellEditor ce;

        table.setSelectionMode(
                ListSelectionModel.SINGLE_SELECTION);

        table.getSelectionModel().addListSelectionListener(
                        new ListSelectionListener() {
            public void valueChanged(ListSelectionEvent e) {
                StereoDeckModel model =
                        (StereoDeckModel)table.getModel();

                if(!e.getValueIsAdjusting()) {
                    model.updateBulbs(table.getSelectedRow());
                }
            }
        });
        getContentPane().add(new JScrollPane(table),
                        BorderLayout.CENTER);
    }
    private void initializeInUseColumn() {
        TableColumn inUseColumn = table.getColumn("In Use");

        inUseColumn.setCellRenderer(new BulbRenderer());
        inUseColumn.setCellEditor(new BulbEditor());
    }
    private void initializePriceColumn() {
        TableColumn priceColumn = table.getColumn("Price");
        JComboBox combo = new JComboBox();

        combo.addItem(new Double(159.99));
        combo.addItem(new Double(169.99));
        combo.addItem(new Double(229.99));
        combo.addItem(new Double(449.99));
```

```
            combo.addItem(new Double(699.99));

            combo.setRenderer(new ListCellCurrencyRenderer());

            priceColumn.setCellRenderer(
                            new TableCellCurrencyRenderer());

            priceColumn.setCellEditor(new PriceEditor(combo));
        }
        private void initializeVolumeColumn() {
            TableColumn volumeColumn = table.getColumn("Volume");
            TableCellRenderer renderer = new VolumeRenderer();
            TableCellEditor editor = new VolumeEditor();

            volumeColumn.setCellRenderer(renderer);
            volumeColumn.setCellEditor(editor);

            Dimension ps = ((JPanel)renderer).getPreferredSize();
            table.setRowHeight(ps.height);
        }
        private void sizeColumns() {
            // listing omitted for brevity's sake.
        }
        public static void main(String args[]) {
            GJApp.launch(
                new Test(), "Car Stereo Deck", 300,300,559,368);
        }
    }
    class ListCellCurrencyRenderer extends DefaultListCellRenderer {
        public Component getListCellRendererComponent(
                            JList list,
                            Object value,
                            int index,
                            boolean isSelected,
                            boolean hasFocus) {
            JLabel c = (JLabel)
                    super.getListCellRendererComponent(
                            list, value, index,
                            isSelected, hasFocus);

            Format format = NumberFormat.getCurrencyInstance();
            c.setText(value == null ? "" : format.format(value));
            return c;
        }
    }
    class TableCellCurrencyRenderer extends DefaultTableCellRenderer
    {
        public void setValue(Object value) {
            Format format = NumberFormat.getCurrencyInstance();
            setText(value == null ? "" : format.format(value));
        }
    }
```

Table Cell Rendering

Like other Swing renderers, table cell renderers are defined by an interface that defines a single method that returns a component. The `TableCellRenderer` interface is summarized in Interface Summary 19-3.

Interface Summary 19-3   TableCellRenderer

The `TableCellRenderer` interface defines a single method that returns a component:

public abstract Component <u>getTableCellRendererComponent</u>(JTable table,
                                       Object value,
                                       boolean isSelected,
                                       boolean cellHasFocus,
                                       int row, int col)

The component returned by `getTableCellRendererComponent` is used like a rubber stamp to paint the component into table cells. The method is passed the table and the value to be rendered, in addition to the row and column in which the value resides and whether the cell is selected or has focus.

The `swing.table` package provides a default renderer in the form of the `DefaultTableCellRenderer` class, which extends `JLabel` and implements the `TableCellRenderer` interface.

If a label is a good fit for a renderer's component, it is usually preferable to extend `DefaultTableCellRenderer` instead of implementing the `TableCellRenderer` interface directly, as specified in Table 19-6.

Table 19-6   Table Cell Renderers

Renderer	Class/ Interface	Responsibilities	Used, Implemented, or Extended when ...
TableCellRenderer	interface	provide access to renderer component	renderer component is not a label
DefaultTableCell-Renderer	class	provide access to renderer component, fg/bg color, and set value	renderer component is a label

A volume renderer from the application shown in Figure 19-19 on page 1200 is shown in Figure 19-20. The `VolumeRenderer` class extends `JPanel` and contains a label and a slider representing the volume level.

Figure 19-20 A Volume Renderer

Because the `VolumeRenderer` class is a panel and not a label, the `TableCellRenderer` interface is implemented directly instead of by extension of `DefaultTableCellRenderer`. The `VolumeRenderer` class is listed in Example 19-13.

The `VolumeRenderer` class initializes the slider's orientation and preferred size, in addition to specifying the `JSlider.isFilled` client property, which causes Metal look and feel sliders to fill their troughs to the left of the grip. See "Filled Sliders" on page 596 for more information on the `JSlider.isFilled` client property.

The label's horizontal alignment and horizontal text position are set to `JLabel.CENTER`, so that the label's text is centered. The label is added as the panel's north component, and the slider is specified as the panel's center component.

Finally, a change listener is added to the slider to keep the label's text in synch with the slider.

Example 19-13 VolumeRenderer

```
import java.awt.*;
import javax.swing.*;
import javax.swing.event.*;
import javax.swing.table.*;

class VolumeRenderer extends JPanel
                     implements TableCellRenderer {
    private JSlider slider = new JSlider();
    private JLabel label = new JLabel("value");

    public VolumeRenderer() {
        slider.setOrientation(SwingConstants.HORIZONTAL);
        slider.setPreferredSize(new Dimension(200,30));
```

```
    slider.putClientProperty("JSlider.isFilled",Boolean.TRUE);

    label.setHorizontalAlignment(JLabel.CENTER);
    label.setHorizontalTextPosition(JLabel.CENTER);

    setLayout(new BorderLayout());
    add(label, BorderLayout.NORTH);
    add(slider, BorderLayout.CENTER);

    slider.addChangeListener(new ChangeListener() {
        public void stateChanged(ChangeEvent e) {
            label.setText(
                    Integer.toString(slider.getValue()));
        }
    });
}
...
```

The component returned from the getTableCellRendererComponent method is the renderer—which is a panel—itself. Both the slider and label values are set, and their enabled states are set according to whether the cell is selected. If a volume cell is not selected, the label and slider are not enabled, as can be seen from Figure 19-19 on page 1200.

The VolumeRenderer class provides accessors for its label and slider. The accessors are used by the volume editor—see "Extending AbstractCellEditor" on page 1223.

```
    ...
    public Component getTableCellRendererComponent(
                            JTable table, Object value,
                            boolean isSelected,
                            boolean hasFocus,
                            int row, int col) {
        Integer v = (Integer)value;

        slider.setValue(v.intValue());
        label.setText(v.toString());

        slider.setEnabled(isSelected);
        label.setEnabled(isSelected);

        return this;
    }
    public JSlider getSlider() {
        return slider;
    }
    public JLabel getLabel() {
        return label;
    }
}
```

DefaultTableCellRenderer

A class diagram for the `DefaultTableCellRenderer` class, which is the lone table cell renderer that Swing provides, is shown in Figure 19-21.

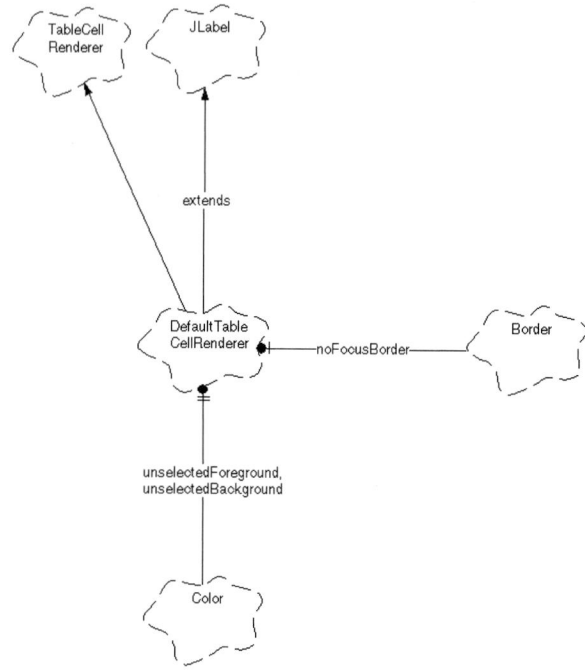

Figure 19-21 DefaultTableCellRenderer Class Diagram

`DefaultTableCellRenderer` extends `JLabel` and maintains references to a border and unselected foreground and background colors. The colors are used to reset the renderer's colors after they have been set to the selected foreground and background colors.

Figure 19-22 shows two rows from the table shown in Figure 19-19 on page 1200. The bulbs in the left column are rendered by an instance of `BulbRenderer`, which is listed in Example 19-14. If a row is selected, the `boolean` value representing the bulb is set to `true` and the bulb is rendered with a brighter icon. Conversely, if a row is not selected, the value is set to `false`, and the bulb is rendered with a darker icon.

⬤	Kenwood	33-801-A	$199.99	☐	☑	77 ━━━━━━━━━━━━◣
⬤	Blaupunkt	7622A	$229.99	☑	☐	19 ━◣━━━━━━━━━━━━

Figure 19-22 Bulb Renderers

The `BulbRenderer` class has a simpler implementation than the `VolumeRenderer` class—see Example 19-13 on page 1208—mostly because `BulbRenderer` extends `DefaultTableCellRenderer`. Instances of `BulbRenderer` are labels because `DefaultTableCellRenderer` implements the `JLabel` class. The `BulbRenderer` constructor sets the horizontal alignment so that the label's content (meaning the bulb) is centered.

The `getTableCellRendererComponent` method sets the label's icon depending upon whether the cell's value is `true` or `false`. As with the volume renderer (and most other renderers, for that matter), the `getTableCellRendererComponent` returns the renderer itself.

Example 19-14 BulbRenderer

```
import java.awt.*;
import javax.swing.*;
import javax.swing.table.*;

class BulbRenderer extends DefaultTableCellRenderer {
    private ImageIcon darkBulb = new ImageIcon("button.jpg"),
                      brightBulb = new ImageIcon("button_lit.jpg");

    public BulbRenderer() {
        setHorizontalAlignment(JLabel.CENTER);
    }
    public Component getTableCellRendererComponent(
                        JTable table, Object value,
                        boolean isSelected,
                        boolean hasFocus,
                        int row, int col) {
        Boolean b = (Boolean)value;
        setIcon(b.booleanValue() ? brightBulb : darkBulb);
        return this;
    }
}
```

Table Formatting Renderers

The DefaultTableCellRenderer class implements a public setValue method that sets the renderer's value.

DefaultTableCellRenderer.setValue() is invoked from the renderer's getTableCellRendererComponent method after the renderer's border, colors, and fonts have been configured according to whether the cell is selected or has focus.

DefaultTableCellRenderer.setValue() offers a convenient hook that can be used to format the data displayed in a table cell. By extending DefaultTableCellRenderer and overriding setValue(), a renderer's value can be modified in any number of ways. For example, the Price column in the table shown in Figure 19-19 on page 1200 is fitted with a renderer that overrides setValue() to format a Double value as currency. The renderer is listed below.

```
class TableCellCurrencyRenderer
                        extends DefaultTableCellRenderer {
    public void setValue(Object value) {
        Format format = NumberFormat.getCurrencyInstance();
        super.setValue(value == null ? "" : format.format(value));
    }
}
```

TableCellCurrencyRenderer formats its value with an instance of java.text.NumberFormat. The formatted value is then passed on to DefaultTableCellRenderer.setValue().

Swing Tip ...

Formatting Renderers Can Override DefaultTableCellRenderer.setValue()

DefaultTableCellRenderer extends JLabel and therefore returns a reference to itself from getTableCellRendererComponent(). Before the reference is returned, the renderer's border, colors, and font are set according to whether the table cell is selected and/or has focus, followed by a call to DefaultTableCellRenderer.set-Value().

The DefaultTableCellRenderer.setValue method sets the renderer's text to the string returned from the cell value's toString method, like so:

```
// from DefaultTableCellRenderer.java

protected void setValue(Object value) {
    setText((value == null) ? "" : value.toString());
}
```

The setValue method provides a convenient hook that allows DefaultTableCell-Renderer extensions to override the manner in which values are displayed. For example, formatting renderers like the one discussed in "Table Formatting Renderers" on page 1212, can override setValue() to format values without having to concern themselves with the renderer's border, color, or font.

The `DefaultTableCellRenderer` class is summarized in Class Summary 19-4.

Class Summary 19-4   DefaultTableCellRenderer

Extends: JLabel

Implements: TableCellRenderer

Constructors

---

public <u>DefaultTableCellRenderer</u>()

The only constructor provided by the `DefaultTableCellRenderer` class creates an empty border with insets: `(1,2,1,2)`. The border is installed as the renderer's border, and the renderer is made opaque with a call to `setOpaque(true)`.

Methods

---

public Component getTableCellRendererComponent(JTable,
                                    Object value,
                                    boolean isSelected,
                                    boolean hasFocus,
                                    int row, int column)

protected void setValue(Object)
public void setBackground(Color)
public void setForeground(Color)

public void updateUI()

The `getTableCellRendererComponent` sets the renderer's colors, font, and border, depending upon whether the component is selected and/or has focus, and subsequently invokes `setValue()`.

`DefaultTableCellRenderer.setValue()` simply sets the string returned from the value's `toString` method to the text displayed by the renderer, but extensions of `DefaultTableCellRenderer` may wish to override `setValue()` to perform additional operations such as formatting.

The `setBackground` and `setForeground` methods are overridden from the `JLabel` class to store the colors so that they can be restored after the renderer's colors have been set to selection colors.

The `updateUI` method is overridden from `JLabel` to set foreground and background colors.

Cell Editors

Cell editors have the following responsibilities:

- Provide a component for editing a cell's value
- Notify `CellEditorListeners` when editing is canceled or stopped
- Determine whether cells are editable and/or selectable
- Return an edited value

Like renderers, editors are asked for a component. Unlike renderer components, which are used as a sort of virtual rubber stamp to paint cells, editor components are actually installed in a cell and used to edit a value.

Editors for both tables and trees implement the `CellEditor` interface, which defines the methods listed in Interface Summary 19-4.

Interface Summary 19-4 CellEditor

Cell Editor Listeners

---

public abstract void <u>addCellEditorListener</u>(CellEditorListener)
public abstract void <u>removeCellEditorListener</u>(CellEditorListener)

`CellEditorListeners` are notified when editing is stopped or canceled. The methods listed above allow listeners to be registered with cell editors.

Editing State

---

public abstract void <u>cancelCellEditing</u>()
public abstract boolean <u>stopCellEditing</u>()

The `cancelCellEditing` method should *unconditionally stop editing* and restore the edited value.

The `stopCellEditing` method, on the other hand, is a *request* for the editor to stop editing; only if `true` is returned from `stopCellEditing()` is it assumed that editing has been stopped.

Cell Editable/Selectable

---

public abstract boolean <u>isCellEditable</u>(EventObject)
public abstract boolean <u>shouldSelectCell</u>(EventObject)

The `isCellEditable` method is used, along with `TableModel.isCellEditable()`, by the `JTable` class to determine whether a cell is editable. If both the model and the cell's editor return `true` from their respective `isCellEditable` methods, the cell is deemed editable.

The `shouldSelectCell` method determines whether an event should select the cell with which an editor is associated. Unfortunately, placing the responsibility for determining which cells are selectable with editors makes it impossible for cells without editors to be unselectable. See "Table Selection" on page 1193 for more information concerning editors and cell selectability.

Cell Value

---

public abstract Object <u>getCellEditorValue</u>()

The `getCellEditorValue` method, not surprisingly, returns the editor's value. Typically, the `getCellEditorValue` method is not invoked directly by developers but instead is called at the appropriate time by `JTable.editingStopped()`.

Table Cell Editors

Notice that `CellEditor` defines methods matching the cell editor responsibilities listed in "Cell Editors" except for providing a component. That responsibility is left to extensions of the `CellEditor` interface, namely, `TableCellEditor` and `TreeCellEditor`. See "Tree Cell Editing" on page 1344 for more information concerning tree editing in general and the `TreeCellEditor` class.

The `TableCellEditor` interface is summarized in Interface Summary 19-5.

Interface Summary 19-5 TableCellEditor

---

public abstract Component <u>getTableCellEditorComponent</u>(JTable table,
                                      Object value,
                                      boolean isSelected,
                                      int row, int col)

Table cell editors must provide a component for editing in addition to implementing the methods defined by the `CellEditor` interface. As with renderers, it is often the case that the component returned from `TableCellEditor.getTableCellEditorComponent()` is the editor itself.

Installing Editor Components

For proficiency at implementing table editors, it is important to understand the sequence of events that take place when editors are installed in a table and when an editor's value is retrieved. The former is illustrated by Figure 19-23.

Theoretically, any type of event can initiate editing, but by default `BasicTableUI` starts the ball rolling when a mouse pressed event is detected by invocation of `JTable.editCellAt()`.

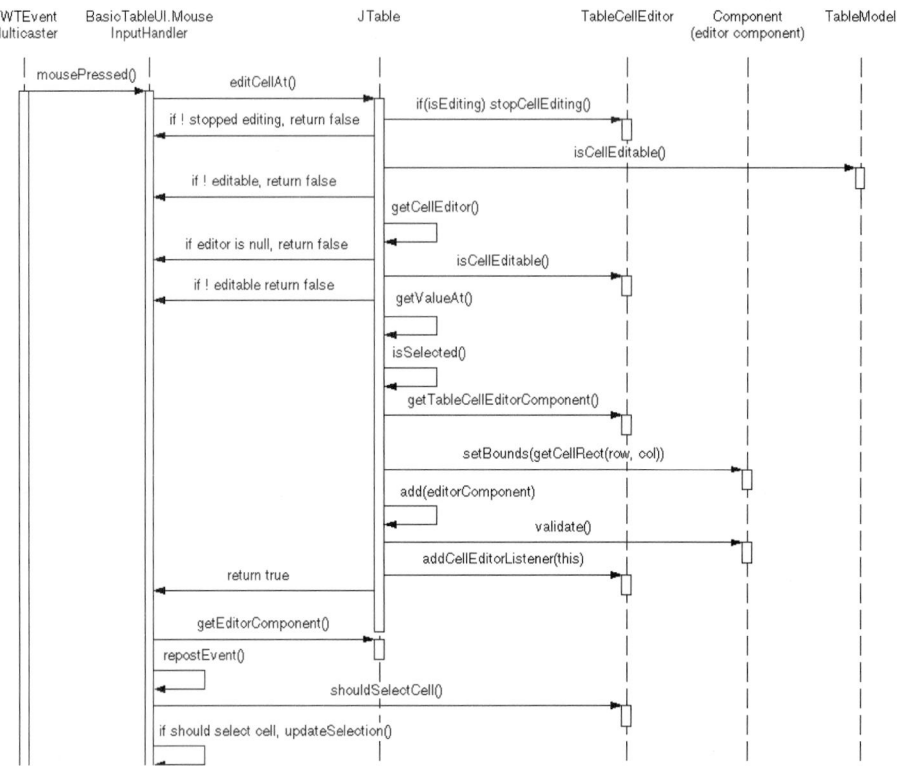

Figure 19-23 Installing Editor Components

If a cell in the table is currently being edited, the editor is asked, via the `CellEditor.stopCellEditing` method, to stop editing. If the editor's `stopCellEditing` method returns `false`, indicating that the editor has not stopped editing, the table returns from the `editCellAt` method. Otherwise, the table asks both its model and editor if the cell in question is editable.

If the table's model and editor agree that the cell can be edited, the table obtains the cell's value and whether the cell is selected, both of which are passed to the editor's `getTableCellEditorComponent` method.

Once the table has the editor's component, it sets the bounds of the component to the rectangle occupied by the cell and adds the component to the table. The subsequent validation of the component results in the component being resized and repositioned to fit in the cell. Finally, the table registers itself with the editor as a cell editor listener and returns `true` from the `editCellAt` method.

After the table has installed the editor's component in the appropriate cell, the table's UI delegate reposts the mouse pressed event to the editor's component. This means that *the same mouse pressed event that causes an editor to be installed is passed on to the editor's component*.

After reposting the mouse event to the newly installed editor, the table's UI delegate invokes the editor's `shouldSelectCell` method to find out whether the row in which the cell resides should be selected. If `shouldSelectCell()` returns `true`, the row in which the cell resides is selected with the UI delegate's method.

Setting Edited Values

Figure 19-23 shows the sequence of method calls that occur when editing is initiated, and Figure 19-24 shows the sequence of calls that occur when editing is stopped.

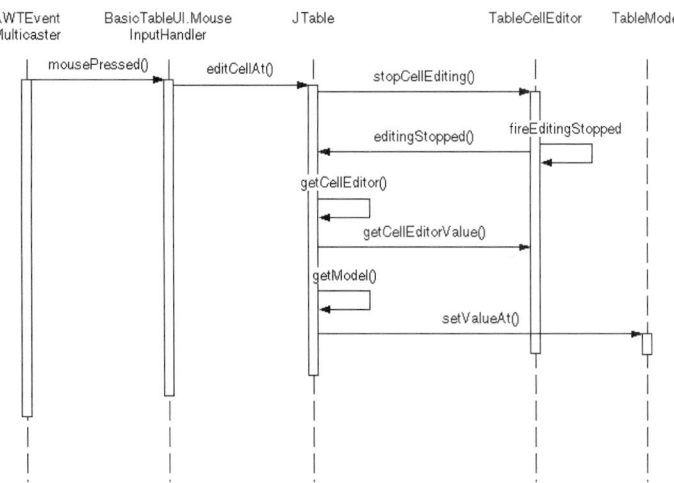

Figure 19-24 Setting Edited Values

As discussed in "Installing Editor Components" on page 1217, a mouse pressed event results in a call to `JTable.editCellAt()`, which asks the currently active editor to stop editing. If the editor stops, a change event is fired to all of the editor's registered `CellEditorListeners`.

Recall from Figure 19-23 that when an editor is installed in a table the table registers with the editor as a `CellEditorListener`. As a result, when the editor fires a change event signifying that it has stopped editing, the table reacts by obtaining the editor's value which is passed to the table model's `setValueAt` method.

Implementing the TableCellEditor Interface

Unfortunately, implementing the `TableCellEditor` interface is more difficult than it should be because Swing does not provide an abstract editor class that encapsulates the mundane housekeeping chores that `TableCellEditor` requires.[10] For example, methods defined in `CellEditor` for registering cell editor listeners and firing events are essentially boilerplate code that must be implemented for table cell editors that implement the `TableCellEditor` interface directly.

The `DefaultCellEditor` class implements such functionality, but `DefaultCellEditor` is limited as far as its ability to be effectively extended.

See "DefaultCellEditor" on page 1226 for more information concerning the `DefaultCellEditor` class.

Because Swing does not provide an abstract cell editor class, an `AbstractCellEditor` implementation is provided in the next section.

AbstractCellEditor

The `AbstractCellEditor` class implements the `TableCellEditor` and `TreeCellEditor` interface. `AbstractCellEditor` is listed in Example 19-15.

Example 19-15 AbstractCellEditor

```
import java.awt.*;
import javax.swing.*;
import javax.swing.event.*;
import javax.swing.table.*;
import javax.swing.tree.*;
import java.awt.event.MouseEvent;
import java.util.EventObject;
```

10. The interface—>abstract class—>default class idiom is widely used within Swing, but not in this case.

```
abstract public class AbstractCellEditor
              implements TableCellEditor {
    protected EventListenerList listenerList =
                              new EventListenerList();
    protected Object value;
    protected ChangeEvent changeEvent = null;
    protected int clickCountToStart = 1;
    ...
```

AbstractCellEditor uses an EventListenerList to maintain a list of
CellEditorListeners and provides two protected methods for firing
editing-stopped and editing-canceled events to listeners.

```
    ...
    public void addCellEditorListener(CellEditorListener l) {
        listenerList.add(CellEditorListener.class, l);
    }
    public void removeCellEditorListener(CellEditorListener l) {
        listenerList.remove(CellEditorListener.class, l);
    }
    protected void fireEditingStopped() {
        Object[] listeners = listenerList.getListenerList();
        for (int i = listeners.length-2; i>=0; i-=2) {
            if (listeners[i] == CellEditorListener.class) {
                if (changeEvent == null)
                    changeEvent = new ChangeEvent(this);
                ((CellEditorListener)
                listeners[i+1]).editingStopped(changeEvent);
            }
        }
    }
    protected void fireEditingCanceled() {
        Object[] listeners = listenerList.getListenerList();
        for (int i = listeners.length-2; i>=0; i-=2) {
            if (listeners[i]==CellEditorListener.class) {
                if (changeEvent == null)
                    changeEvent = new ChangeEvent(this);
                ((CellEditorListener)
                listeners[i+1]).editingCanceled(changeEvent);
            }
        }
    }
    ...
```

AbstractCellEditor maintains an Object reference that represents the
editor's value. For convenience, in addition to implementing the
TableCellEditor.getCellEditorValue method, AbstractCellEditor
also provides a setter method for the value.

```
  . . .
  public Object getCellEditorValue() {
     return value;
  }
  public void setCellEditorValue(Object value) {
     this.value = value;
  }
  . . .
```

AbstractCellEditor, like DefaultCellEditor, provides a clickCountToStart property that specifies the number of mouse clicks required to initiate editing.

```
  . . .
  public void setClickCountToStart(int count) {
     clickCountToStart = count;
  }
  public int getClickCountToStart() {
     return clickCountToStart;
  }
  . . .
```

AbstractCellEditor defines a cell to be editable if the event passed to isCellEditable() is a mouse event and the click count is equal to (or greater than) the clickCountToStart. AbstractCellEditor also defines all cells to be selectable.

```
  . . .
  public boolean isCellEditable(EventObject anEvent) {
     if (anEvent instanceof MouseEvent) {
        if (((MouseEvent)anEvent).getClickCount() <
                                 clickCountToStart)
           return false;
     }
     return true;
  }
  public boolean shouldSelectCell(EventObject anEvent) {
     return true;
  }
  . . .
```

The stopCellEditing and cancelCellEditing methods fire appropriate events, and stopCellEditing() returns true, indicating that editing was stopped.

```
    ...
    public boolean stopCellEditing() {
        fireEditingStopped();
        return true;
    }
    public void cancelCellEditing() {
        fireEditingCanceled();
    }
    ...
}
```

The AbstractCellEditor class leaves the getTableCellEditorComponent method defined by TableCellEditor unimplemented. Extensions of AbstractCellEditor must implement getTableCellEditorComponent().

Extending AbstractCellEditor

The AbstractCellEditor class illustrated in Figure 19-25 can be used to substantially simplify implementing custom cell editors. For example, editors for the bulb and volume columns in the table shown in Figure 19-19 on page 1200 extend AbstractCellEditor.[11]

A single volume editor is shown in Figure 19-25. The top picture shows the editor component immediately after it is activated, and the middle picture shows the editor after the slider's grip has been dragged to a new location. The bottom picture depicts a double click in the editor's label, which cancels editing and resets the editor's value.

Figure 19-25 Double-Clicking on the Editor's Label Cancels the Edit

---

11. The AbstractCellEditor class is not a Swing component— see "Abstract-CellEditor" on page 1220.

The VolumeEditor class is listed in Example 19-16.

Example 19-16 VolumeEditor

```java
import java.awt.*;
import java.awt.event.*;
import javax.swing.*;
import javax.swing.table.*;

class VolumeEditor extends AbstractCellEditor {
    VolumeRenderer renderer = new VolumeRenderer();

    public VolumeEditor() {
        renderer.getLabel().addMouseListener(new MouseAdapter() {
            public void mousePressed(MouseEvent e) {
                if(e.getClickCount() == 2)
                    cancelCellEditing();
            }
        });
    }
    public Component getTableCellEditorComponent(
                        JTable table, Object value,
                        boolean isSelected,
                        int row, int column) {
        JSlider slider = renderer.getSlider();
        slider.setValue(((Integer)value).intValue());
        return renderer;
    }
    public boolean stopCellEditing() {
        JSlider slider = renderer.getSlider();

        setCellEditorValue(new Integer(slider.getValue()));

        return super.stopCellEditing();
    }
}
```

It is often the case that cell editor components are exact duplicates of a cell's renderer component.[12] For example, the volume editor displays a slider and a label, which are also the components displayed by the volume renderer. In such cases, it is not uncommon for editors to use a renderer for editing. This is the case for the VolumeEditor class, which returns an instance of VolumeRenderer from its getTableCellEditorComponent method.

---

12. This is not always the case, of course; cells with combo box editors for example, usually do not render combo boxes.

The `VolumeEditor` constructor adds a `MouseListener` to the renderer's label to react to double clicks by canceling editing. The call to `cancelCellEditing()` is fielded by the `AbstractCellEditor` class, which fires an appropriate event to all registered `CellEditorListeners`.

The `VolumeEditor` class also overrides `stopCellEditing()` to save the edited value. Editors must keep track of the value they represent, either by continuously updating the value as the editor's component is manipulated or by overriding `stopCellEditing()`. Notice that the `VolumeEditor` class would have to override `cancelCellEditing()` to restore the original value if it updated its value in response to changes to the slider.

The table shown in Figure 19-19 on page 1200 has another editor that extends the `AbstractCellEditor` class. Dark bulbs in the left column are switched to bright bulbs when the mouse is pressed in a cell. The switching is performed by an instance of `BulbEditor`, which is listed below.

```
class BulbEditor extends AbstractCellEditor {
    BulbRenderer renderer = new BulbRenderer();

    public BulbEditor() {
        renderer.addMouseListener(new MouseAdapter() {
            public void mousePressed(MouseEvent e) {
                SwingUtilities.invokeLater(new Runnable() {
                    public void run() {
                        setCellEditorValue(Boolean.TRUE);
                        fireEditingStopped();
                    }
                });
            }
        });
    }
    public Component getTableCellEditorComponent(
                        JTable table, Object value,
                        boolean isSelected,
                        int row, int col) {
        return renderer.getTableCellRendererComponent(
                        table, value, true, true,
                        row, col);
    }
}
```

Bulb editors always return a renderer that displays a bright version of the bulb by indicating to the renderer's `getTableCellRendererComponent` method that the cell is selected. As a result, anytime a bulb editor is activated, it immediately displays a bright bulb regardless of the previous state of the bulb.

Because `BulbEditor`'s superclass—`AbstractCellEditor`—returns `true` from `shouldSelectCell()`, the row in which the bulb resides will be selected immediately after the editor is activated.[13] When the editor is uninstalled, the bulb's row will be selected and the renderer will display a bright bulb. Therefore, the editor's only responsibility is to display a bright bulb while it is briefly installed.

Recall that the mouse pressed event that causes an editor to be installed is reposted to the editor immediately after the editor is installed. Bulb editors add a mouse listener to the renderer that reacts to the mouse pressed event by stopping editing, because, as noted above, the editor's job is done as soon as it displays a renderer with a bright bulb.

Unfortunately, due to a table bug, stopping an editor immediately after it is installed results in an exception being thrown by the table's UI delegate. If the call to `fireEditingStopped()` is placed in a `Runnable` and passed to `SwingUtilities.invokeLater()`, the exception is avoided because the code is executed the next time around the event dispatch loop. See "Swing and Threads" on page 57 for more information concerning the `SwingUtilities.invokeLater` method.

DefaultCellEditor

Swing provides one implementation of the `TableCellEditor` interface, the `DefaultCellEditor` class, that provides a convenient way to construct editors that have a text field, check box, or combo box as their editor component. The `DefaultCellEditor` class provides (exactly) three constructors, each of which is passed a text field, check box, or combo box.

The `DefaultCellEditor` class implements a `protected` nested class called `EditorDelegate`, and every `DefaultCellEditor` maintains a reference to an `EditorDelegate`. Instances of `DefaultCellEditor` delegate most of their responsibilities to an instance of `EditorDelegate`. For example, `DefaultCellEditor.getCellEditorValue()` is implemented like this:

```
// From DefaultCellEditor.java ...

public Object getCellEditorValue() {
   return delegate.getCellEditorValue();
}
```

---

13. See "Installing Editor Components" on page 1217 for more information concerning the sequence of events that takes place when an editor is installed.

When an instance of `DefaultCellEditor` is asked for its value, it returns the value supplied by its delegate. Other `DefaultCellEditor` methods follow suit.

Each `DefaultCellEditor` constructor instantiates an inner class extension of `EditorDelegate` that is tailored to the type of component passed to the constructor. For example, `DefaultCellEditor(JTextField)` creates a delegate that overrides `EditorDelegate.getCellEditorValue()` to return the text contained in the text field. As a result, for default cell editors constructed with a text field, `DefaultCellEditor.getCellEditorValue()` returns the text field's text. Likewise, the delegate created by `DefaultCellEditor(JCheckBox)` returns a `boolean` value that represents whether the check box is selected. For default cell editors constructed with a check box, the editor will return a `boolean` value from `DefaultCellEditor.getCellEditorValue()`.

A class diagram for the `DefaultCellEditor` class is shown in Figure 19-26.

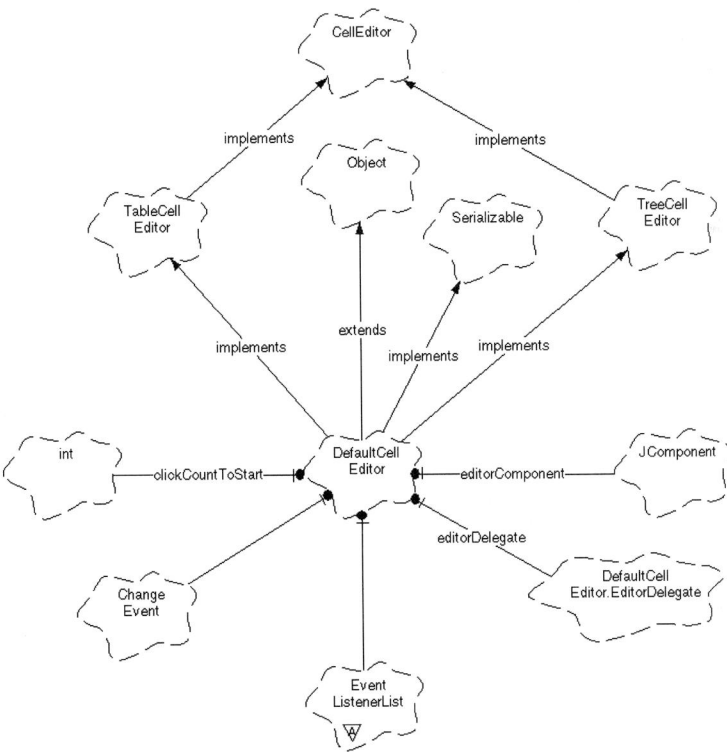

Figure 19-26 DefaultCellEditor Class Diagram

DefaultCellEditor extends Object and implements the TableCellEditor and TreeCellEditor interfaces, so default cell editors can be used for both tables and trees.

The DefaultCellEditor class maintains references to its component and editor delegate. DefaultCellEditor also maintains an integer value representing the number of mouse clicks required to start editing. An EventListenerList notifies cell editor listeners when editing has stopped or been canceled.

The Price column in the table shown in Figure 19-19 on page 1200 is fitted with an instance of PriceEditor, an extension of DefaultCellEditor. The PriceEditor constructor is passed a combo box that is passed on to the DefaultCellEditor constructor.

Whether or not a cell in the Price column is editable depends upon whether the user can provide a password. Figure 19-27 shows, from top to bottom, the editing of a cell in the Price column. When the mouse is clicked in the cell, a password dialog is presented. If the password is correct, a combo box appears for editing; if the password is incorrect, the editing session is over before it starts.

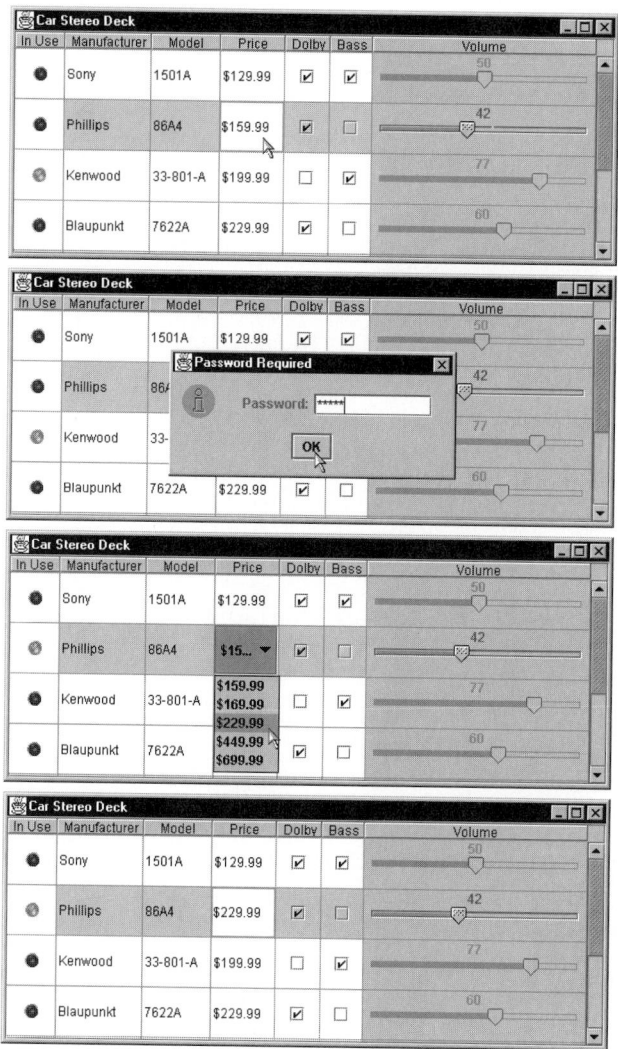

Figure 19-27 A Password-Protected Editable Cell

Note: *A table bug causes the password dialog to be displayed twice in succession.*

The `PriceEditor` class is listed in Example 19-17.

Example 19-17 PriceEditor

```java
import javax.swing.*;
import java.util.EventObject;

class PriceEditor extends DefaultCellEditor {
    public PriceEditor(JComboBox combo) {
        super(combo);
    }
    public boolean isCellEditable(EventObject e) {
        JPanel messagePanel = new JPanel();
        JPasswordField pwf = new JPasswordField(10);

        messagePanel.add(new JLabel("Password:"));
        messagePanel.add(pwf);

        JOptionPane.showMessageDialog(null,
                  messagePanel, "Password Required",
                  JOptionPane.INFORMATION_MESSAGE);

        if(pwf.getText().equals("dolby")) {
            return true;
        }
        else {
            JOptionPane.showMessageDialog(null,
                "Wrong Password!", "Access Failed",
                JOptionPane.INFORMATION_MESSAGE);
            return false;
        }
    }
}
```

The PriceEditor class overrides isCellEditable() to show a message dialog that contains a password field. If the correct password is given, the method returns true and the cell will be edited. If the password is incorrect, isCellEditable() returns false.

The DefaultCellEditor class is summarized in Class Summary 19-5.

Class Summary 19-5 DefaultCellEditor

Extends: Object

Implements: TableCellEditor

Constructors

---

public <u>DefaultCellEditor</u>(JCheckBox)
public <u>DefaultCellEditor</u>(JComboBox)
public <u>DefaultCellEditor</u>(JTextField)

`DefaultCellEditor` provides three constructors, each of which is passed a delegate component, as discussed in"DefaultCellEditor" on page 1226.

The `DefaultCellEditor` class would be much more reusable if it provided a no-argument constructor, because it could be extended along with `DefaultCellEditor.EditorDelegate` and used with any component. In fact, a simple no-argument constructor for `DefaultCellEditor` would mostly obviate the need for the `AbstractCellEditor` class discussed in "AbstractCellEditor" on page 1220, as it would make basic functionality available to extensions.

Methods

CellEditor Methods

---

public void <u>addCellEditorListener</u>(CellEditorListener)
public void <u>removeCellEditorListener</u>(CellEditorListener)

public boolean <u>isCellEditable</u>(EventObject)
public boolean <u>shouldSelectCell</u>(EventObject)

public boolean <u>cancelCellEditing</u>()
public boolean <u>stopCellEditing</u>()

public Object <u>getCellEditorValue</u>()

All of the methods defined by the `CellEditor` interface are implemented by `DefaultCellEditor` by delegating to the editor's delegate, except for the first two methods listed above.

DefaultCellEditors consider cells to be editable if the number of mouse clicks is equal to the clickCountToStart property and if the editor's delegate also considers the cell to be editable.

DefaultCellEditors are selected by the mouse pressed event that installed the editor if the click count has been satisfied. In addition, DefaultCellEditor.shouldSelectCell() invokes the delegate's startCellEditing method.

Both stopCellEditing() and cancelCellEditing() fire change events to registered CellEditorListeners. The stopCellEditing method invokes the delegate's stopCellEditing method.

Tree/Table Editor Components

---

public Component <u>getTableCellEditorComponent</u>(JTable, Object, boolean, int, int)
public Component <u>getTreeCellEditorComponent</u>(JTree, Object, boolean, boolean, boolean, int)

The methods defined by the TableCellEditor and TreeCellEditor interfaces return the component that the DefaultCellEditor constructor was passed. The components are configured by the two methods listed above for use in tables and trees, respectively.

Click Count

---

public int <u>getClickCountToStart</u>()
public void <u>setClickCountToStart</u>(int)

The clickCountToStart property determines how many successive mouse clicks are needed to install an editor.

Component

---

public Component <u>getComponent</u>()

When a look and feel is installed, JTable.updateUI() invokes DefaultCellEditor.getComponent() to invoke updateUI() for the component.

Notice that the getComponent method is not defined in the CellEditor interface, and therefore JTable.updateUI() checks to see if the editor is in fact an instance of DefaultCellEditor; if so, DefaultCellEditor.getComponent() is invoked. All of this would be irrelevant except that it makes it more difficult than ever to extend DefaultCellEditor in a manner that works for all look and feels.

Event Firing

---

protected void <u>fireEditingCanceled</u>()
protected void <u>fireEditingStopped</u>()

DefaultCellEditor provides two protected methods that fire events to registered CellEditorListeners when editing is stopped or canceled.

Table Rows

Table rows are second-class citizens because, unlike the case with table columns, Swing does not provide a class for table rows. As a result, a number of methods that manipulate rows are distributed among the JTable class and the table model classes.

Row Height

The row height for a table is set with the JTable.setRowHeight method. It is frequently desirable to set a table's row height to the height of the tallest cell, which is the case for the table shown in Figure 19-28.

The application shown in Figure 19-28 creates a table and populates it with strings and icons. The application also implements a getMaxRowHeight method that returns the maximum row height for the cells contained in the application's table.

Figure 19-28 Setting Row Height

For every column contained in the table, the getMaxRowHeight method invokes getMaxRowHeightForColumn(), which returns the maximum row height for cells in a single column.

```
public class Test extends JFrame {
    ...
    public Test() {
        table.setRowHeight(getMaxRowHeight());
        ...
    }
    ...
    public int getMaxRowHeight() {
        int columnCount = table.getColumnCount(), h=0, maxh=0;

        for(int i=0; i < columnCount; ++i) {
            TableColumn column =
                    table.getColumnModel().getColumn(i);

            h = getMaxRowHeightForColumn(column);
            maxh = Math.min(h,maxh);
        }
        return maxh;
    }
}
    ...
```

The getMaxRowHeightForColumn method obtains a reference to the column's renderer, which is used to obtain a reference to the renderer's component. For every cell in the column, the maximum height for the renderer's component is calculated, and the method returns the height of the tallest component.

```
    ...
    public int getMaxRowHeightForColumn(TableColumn column) {
        int height = 0, maxh = 0, c = column.getModelIndex();

        for(int r=0; r < table.getRowCount(); ++r) {
            TableCellRenderer renderer =
                        table.getCellRenderer(r,c);
            Component
              comp = renderer.getTableCellRendererComponent(
                        table, table.getValueAt(r,c),
                        false, false, r, c);

            height = comp.getMaximumSize().height;
            maxh = height > maxh ? height : maxh;
        }
        return maxh;
    }
    ...
}
```

The application shown in Figure 19-28 is listed in its entirety in Example 19-18.

Example 19-18 Calculating and Setting Row Height

```
import java.awt.*;
import java.awt.event.*;
import javax.swing.*;
import javax.swing.event.*;
import javax.swing.table.*;

public class Test extends JFrame {
    Object[] columnNames = {"Name", "Cost/Lb.", "Picture"};

    Object[][] rowData = {
        { "cake", "$1.29", new ImageIcon("cake.gif") },
        { "pear", "$1.29", new ImageIcon("pear.gif") },
        { "pineapple", "$1.29", new ImageIcon("pineapple.gif") },
        { "apple", "$1.29", new ImageIcon("apple.gif") },
        { "bread", "$1.29", new ImageIcon("bread.gif") },
    };
    class RowSizingModel extends DefaultTableModel {
        public RowSizingModel(Object[][] data,
                            Object[] colNames) {
            super(data, colNames);
        }
        public Class getColumnClass(int c) {
            if(c == 2) return ImageIcon.class;
            else    return super.getColumnClass(c);
        }
    }
    JTable table = new JTable(new RowSizingModel(rowData,
```

```
                                           columnNames));

      public Test() {
          table.setRowHeight(getMaxRowHeight());
          getContentPane().add(new JScrollPane(table),
                               BorderLayout.CENTER);
      }
      public int getMaxRowHeight() {
          int columnCount = table.getColumnCount(), h=0, maxh=0;

          for(int i=0; i < columnCount; ++i) {
              TableColumn column =
                      table.getColumnModel().getColumn(i);

              h = getMaxRowHeightForColumn(column);
              maxh = h > maxh ? h : maxh;
          }
          return maxh;
      }
      public int getMaxRowHeightForColumn(TableColumn column) {
          int height = 0, maxh = 0, c = column.getModelIndex();

          for(int r=0; r < table.getRowCount(); ++r) {
              TableCellRenderer renderer =
                      table.getCellRenderer(r,c);
              Component
                comp = renderer.getTableCellRendererComponent(
                        table, table.getValueAt(r,c),
                        false, false, r, c);

              height = comp.getMaximumSize().height;
              maxh = height > maxh ? height : maxh;
          }
          return maxh;
      }
      public static void main(String args[]) {
          GJApp.launch(
              new Test(), "Sizing Rows", 300,300,450,300);
      }
  }
```

Rendering By Rows

Renderers and editors for Swing tables are assigned on a column basis; however, sometimes it is necessary to render—or edit—on a row or cell basis. The application shown in Figure 19-29 implements a renderer that renders on a cell basis. The same logic can easily be extended for editing.

Every other column in the table shown in Figure 19-29 is fitted with a renderer that renders in blue the cells that reside in even-numbered rows; cells that reside in odd-numbered rows are rendered in orange.

A	B	C	D	E	F	G	H	I	J
(0,0)	(0,1)	(0,2)	(0,3)	(0,4)	(0,5)	(0,6)	(0,7)	(0,8)	(0,9)
(1,0)	(1,1)	(1,2)	(1,3)	(1,4)	(1,5)	(1,6)	(1,7)	(1,8)	(1,9)
(2,0)	(2,1)	(2,2)	(2,3)	(2,4)	(2,5)	(2,6)	(2,7)	(2,8)	(2,9)
(3,0)	(3,1)	(3,2)	(3,3)	(3,4)	(3,5)	(3,6)	(3,7)	(3,8)	(3,9)
(4,0)	(4,1)	(4,2)	(4,3)	(4,4)	(4,5)	(4,6)	(4,7)	(4,8)	(4,9)
(5,0)	(5,1)	(5,2)	(5,3)	(5,4)	(5,5)	(5,6)	(5,7)	(5,8)	(5,9)
(6,0)	(6,1)	(6,2)	(6,3)	(6,4)	(6,5)	(6,6)	(6,7)	(6,8)	(6,9)
(7,0)	(7,1)	(7,2)	(7,3)	(7,4)	(7,5)	(7,6)	(7,7)	(7,8)	(7,9)
(8,0)	(8,1)	(8,2)	(8,3)	(8,4)	(8,5)	(8,6)	(8,7)	(8,8)	(8,9)
(9,0)	(9,1)	(9,2)	(9,3)	(9,4)	(9,5)	(9,6)	(9,7)	(9,8)	(9,9)
(10,0)	(10,1)	(10,2)	(10,3)	(10,4)	(10,5)	(10,6)	(10,7)	(10,8)	(10,9)
(11,0)	(11,1)	(11,2)	(11,3)	(11,4)	(11,5)	(11,6)	(11,7)	(11,8)	(11,9)
(12,0)	(12,1)	(12,2)	(12,3)	(12,4)	(12,5)	(12,6)	(12,7)	(12,8)	(12,9)
(13,0)	(13,1)	(13,2)	(13,3)	(13,4)	(13,5)	(13,6)	(13,7)	(13,8)	(13,9)
(14,0)	(14,1)	(14,2)	(14,3)	(14,4)	(14,5)	(14,6)	(14,7)	(14,8)	(14,9)

Figure 19-29 Rendering by Rows

The application instantiates a table with a simple extension of `AbstractTableModel`, and the application's constructor sets the cell renderer for odd-numbered columns to an instance of `RowRenderer`.

```
public class Test extends JFrame {

    // instantiate table with simple model ...

    public Test() {
        TableColumn column;
        int columnCount = table.getColumnCount();

        for(int i=0; i < columnCount; ++i) {
            column = table.getColumn(table.getColumnName(i));

            if(i % 2 == 0)
                column.setCellRenderer(new RowRenderer());
        }
        getContentPane().add(new JScrollPane(table),
                        BorderLayout.CENTER);
    }
    ...
}
```

The RowRenderer class overrides getTableCellRendererComponent() to set the foreground color depending upon the row. The renderer component is subsequently obtained from the DefaultTableCellRenderer.getTableCellRendererComponent method.

```
class RowRenderer extends DefaultTableCellRenderer {
    public Component getTableCellRendererComponent(JTable table,
                            Object value, boolean isSelected,
                            boolean hasFocus,
                            int row, int column) {
        if(row % 2 == 0) setForeground(Color.blue);
        else             setForeground(Color.orange);

        return super.getTableCellRendererComponent(table,
                            value, isSelected, hasFocus,
                            row, column);
    }
}
```

The application shown in Figure 19-29 is listed in its entirety in Example 19-19.

Example 19-19 Rendering by Rows and Columns

```
import java.awt.*;
import java.awt.event.*;
import javax.swing.*;
import javax.swing.table.*;

public class Test extends JFrame {
    JTable table = new JTable(
        new AbstractTableModel() {
            int rows = 100, cols = 10;

            public int getRowCount() { return rows; }
            public int getColumnCount() { return cols; }

            public Object getValueAt(int row, int col) {
                return "(" + Integer.toString(row) + "," +
                        Integer.toString(col) + ")";
            }
        });

    public Test() {
        TableColumn column;
        int columnCount = table.getColumnCount();

        for(int i=0; i < columnCount; ++i) {
            column = table.getColumn(table.getColumnName(i));
```

```
            if(i % 2 == 0)
                column.setCellRenderer(new RowRenderer());
        }
        getContentPane().add(new JScrollPane(table),
                        BorderLayout.CENTER);
    }
    public static void main(String args[]) {
        GJApp.launch(
            new Test(), "Rendering By Columns and Rows",
                    300,300,450,300);
    }
}
class RowRenderer extends DefaultTableCellRenderer {
    public Component getTableCellRendererComponent(JTable table,
                            Object value, boolean isSelected,
                            boolean hasFocus,
                            int row, int column) {
        if(row % 2 == 0) setForeground(Color.blue);
        else             setForeground(Color.orange);

        return super.getTableCellRendererComponent(table,
                            value, isSelected, hasFocus,
                            row, column);
    }
}
```

Table Decorators

In Java, functionality is often added to objects through the use of inheritance. For example, adding an icon to a table column header could be accomplished with a custom renderer that extends TableCellRenderer and displays an icon in addition to the header's value.

One drawback to inheritance is that it does not allow functionality to be added to *individual objects at runtime*. For example, with the custom renderer described above, icons cannot be added to *any* column header; only columns fitted with the custom renderer could display the icon.

Adding functionality to objects at runtime can be implemented with the use of the decorator design pattern. Decorators are wrappers that delegate their responsibilities to an enclosed object. Decorators implement the interface of their enclosed object, so they can substitute for it. Decorators forward requests to their enclosed object and typically perform additional operations.[14]

Decorators are best illustrated with an example. The Price/Lb. column in the table shown in Figure 19-30 is fitted with a renderer decorator that adds an icon to the column's header.

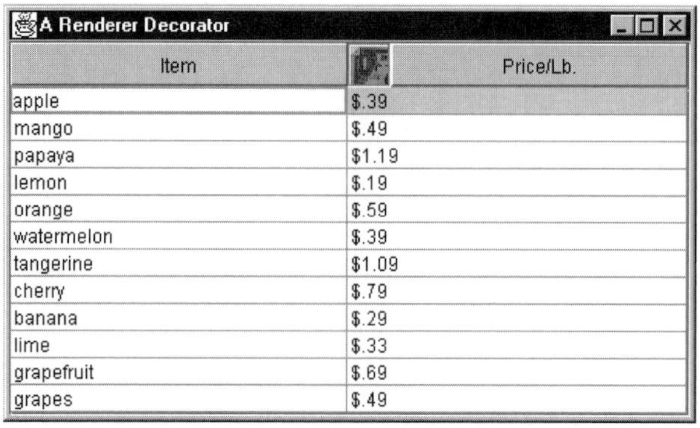

Figure 19-30 A Renderer Decorator

The application shown in Figure 19-30 creates a table with a simple model. The application's constructor obtains a reference to the Price/Lb. column, and subsequently a reference to the column's header renderer is obtained.

The column's header is then set to an instance of RendererDecorator, which is constructed with the column's original header renderer.

```
public class Test extends JFrame {
    // create table with simple model

    public Test() {
        TableColumn column = table.getColumn("Price/Lb.");
        TableCellRenderer renderer = column.getHeaderRenderer();

        column.setHeaderRenderer(new RendererDecorator(renderer));

        getContentPane().add(new JScrollPane(table),
                                  BorderLayout.CENTER);
    }
    ...
}
...
```

14. `java.io.FilterInputStream` is an example of the decorator pattern.

The `RendererDecorator` class implements the `TableCellRenderer`
interface, so it can pass as a renderer and therefore be passed to
`TableColumn.setHeaderRenderer()`. The `RendererDecorator` class also
maintains a reference to the table cell renderer that is passed to the
`RendererDecorator` constructor.

```
...
class RendererDecorator implements TableCellRenderer {
    TableCellRenderer realRenderer;
    JPanel panel;
    JLabel iconLabel = new JLabel(new ImageIcon("money.gif"));

    public RendererDecorator(TableCellRenderer r) {
        realRenderer = r;
        iconLabel.setBorder(BorderFactory.createEtchedBorder());
    }
    ...
```

When a component is obtained from the header renderer for the Price/Lb.
column, the decorator's `getTableCellRendererComponent` method is
invoked. The decorator obtains the real renderer's component and then
embellishes it by placing the component in a panel along with a label that
displays an icon. The panel is then returned as the renderer component.

```
...
public Component getTableCellRendererComponent(
                    JTable table, Object value,
                    boolean isSelected, boolean hasFocus,
                    int row, int col) {
    Component c = realRenderer.getTableCellRendererComponent(
                    table, value, isSelected,
                    hasFocus, row, col);
    embellishComponent(c);
    return panel;
}
private void embellishComponent(Component c) {
    if(panel == null) {
        panel = new JPanel();

        panel.setLayout(new BorderLayout());
        panel.add(c, BorderLayout.CENTER);
        panel.add(iconLabel, BorderLayout.WEST);
    }
}
}
```

The advantage to using a renderer decorator is that any table cell renderer can be decorated with an icon by an instance of `RendererDecorator`.

The application shown in Figure 19-30 is listed in its entirety in Example 19-20.

Example 19-20 A Renderer Decorator

```java
import java.awt.*;
import java.awt.event.*;
import javax.swing.*;
import javax.swing.event.*;
import javax.swing.table.*;

public class Test extends JFrame {
    JTable table = new JTable(new Object[][] {
                {"apple", "$.39"}, {"mango", "$.49"},
                {"papaya", "$1.19"}, {"lemon", "$.19"},
                {"orange", "$.59"}, {"watermelon", "$.39"},
                {"tangerine", "$1.09"}, {"cherry", "$.79"},
                {"banana", "$.29"}, {"lime", "$.33"},
                {"grapefruit", "$.69"}, {"grapes", "$.49"},
            },
            new Object[] { "Item", "Price/Lb." });

    public Test() {
        TableColumn column = table.getColumn("Price/Lb.");
        TableCellRenderer renderer = column.getHeaderRenderer();

        column.setHeaderRenderer(new RendererDecorator(renderer));

        getContentPane().add(new JScrollPane(table),
                                BorderLayout.CENTER);
    }
    public static void main(String args[]) {
        GJApp.launch(
            new Test(), "A Renderer Decorator", 300,300,450,182);
    }
}
class RendererDecorator implements TableCellRenderer {
    TableCellRenderer realRenderer;
    JPanel panel;
    JLabel iconLabel = new JLabel(new ImageIcon("money.gif"));

    public RendererDecorator(TableCellRenderer r) {
        realRenderer = r;
        iconLabel.setBorder(BorderFactory.createEtchedBorder());
```

```
    }
    public Component getTableCellRendererComponent(
                        JTable table, Object value,
                        boolean isSelected, boolean hasFocus,
                        int row, int col) {
        Component c = realRenderer.getTableCellRendererComponent(
                        table, value, isSelected,
                        hasFocus, row, col);
        embellishComponent(c);
        return panel;
    }
    private void embellishComponent(Component c) {
        if(panel == null) {
            panel = new JPanel();

            panel.setLayout(new BorderLayout());
            panel.add(c, BorderLayout.CENTER);
            panel.add(iconLabel, BorderLayout.WEST);
        }
    }
}
```

Sorting Decorators

The decorator pattern can be put to good use when it comes to sorting table columns. Using the decorator pattern for sorting allows any table column to be sorted without modifications to the table's model. The application shown in Figure 19-31 contains a table that is fitted with an instance of SortDecorator.

The top picture shown in Figure 19-31 shows the application as it appears initially. The middle picture shows the table after the Item column has been sorted, and the bottom picture shows the table after the Price/Lb. column has been sorted. Sorting is initiated by clicking on a column's header and is performed by an instance of SortDecorator.

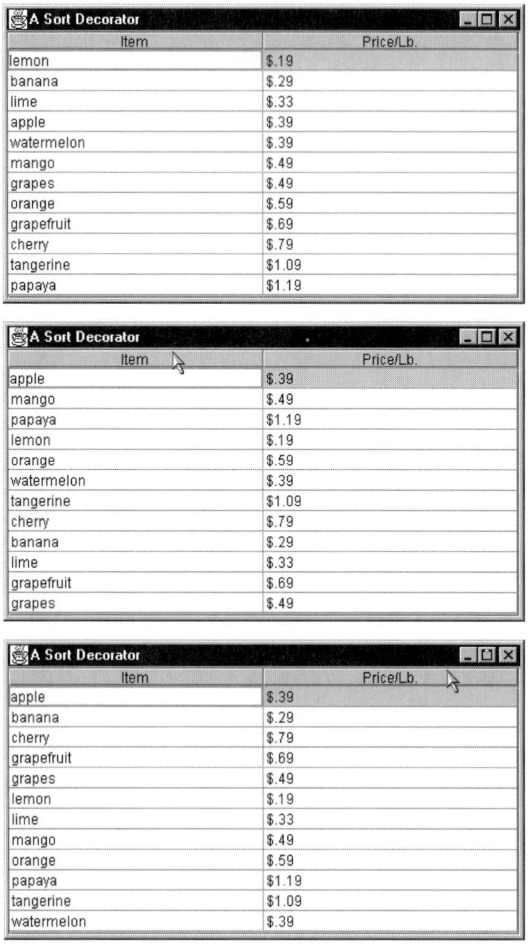

A Sort Decorator	
Item	Price/Lb.
lemon	$.19
banana	$.29
lime	$.33
apple	$.39
watermelon	$.39
mango	$.49
grapes	$.49
orange	$.59
grapefruit	$.69
cherry	$.79
tangerine	$1.09
papaya	$1.19

A Sort Decorator	
Item	Price/Lb.
apple	$.39
mango	$.49
papaya	$1.19
lemon	$.19
orange	$.59
watermelon	$.39
tangerine	$1.09
cherry	$.79
banana	$.29
lime	$.33
grapefruit	$.69
grapes	$.49

A Sort Decorator	
Item	Price/Lb.
apple	$.39
banana	$.29
cherry	$.79
grapefruit	$.69
grapes	$.49
lemon	$.19
lime	$.33
mango	$.49
orange	$.59
papaya	$1.19
tangerine	$1.09
watermelon	$.39

Figure 19-31 Table Sorting with a Decorator

A class diagram for the SortDecorator class is shown in Figure 19-32.

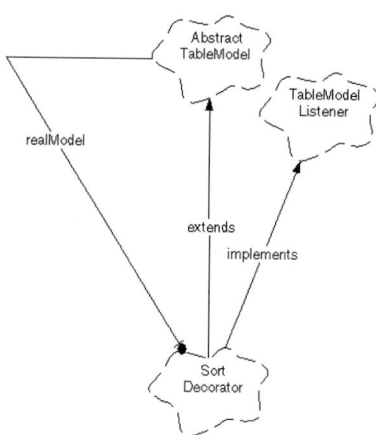

Figure 19-32 SortDecorator Class Diagram

The `SortDecorator` class extends the `AbstractTableModel` class and delegates to an enclosed table model. The `SortDecorator` class also implements the `TableModelListener` interface by listening to its enclosed table model.

The application shown in Figure 19-31 creates an instance of `JTable` with a custom model. The application's constructor creates an instance of `SortDecorator` that is created with a reference to the table's original model. Subsequently, the table's model is set to the sort decorator.

```
public class Test extends JFrame {
    // create table with model

    public Test() {
        final SortDecorator decorator =
                            new SortDecorator(table.getModel());

        table.setModel(decorator);
        ...
```

A mouse listener added to the table's header reacts to mouse clicks by sorting the column in which the mouse click occurred.

```
    . . .
JTableHeader hdr = (JTableHeader)table.getTableHeader();

hdr.addMouseListener(new MouseAdapter() {
    public void mouseClicked(MouseEvent e) {
        TableColumnModel tcm = table.getColumnModel();
        int vc = tcm.getColumnIndexAtX(e.getX());
        int mc = table.convertColumnIndexToModel(vc);

        decorator.sort(mc);
    }
});
getContentPane().add(new JScrollPane(table),
                            BorderLayout.CENTER);
    }
    . . .
}
```

Sort decorators maintain a reference to the table's real model and to an array of `integer` values representing sorted row indexes.

The `SortDecorator` constructor stores the reference to the real model and adds itself to the real model as a table model listener. The constructor then invokes a `private allocate` method that allocates the `indexes` array.

Changes to the real model are handled by the `SortDecorator.tableChanged` method, which reallocates the `indexes` array and initializes the integers in the array from 0 to `indexes.length-1`.

```
class SortDecorator extends AbstractTableModel,
                    implements TableModelListener {
    private  TableModel realModel;
    private int indexes[];

    public SortDecorator(TableModel model) {
        if(model == null)
            throw new IllegalArgumentException(
                        "null models are not allowed");
        this.realModel = model;

        realModel.addTableModelListener(this);
        allocate();
    }
    public void tableChanged(TableModelEvent e) {
```

```
    allocate();
}
private void allocate() {
    indexes = new int[getRowCount()];

    for(int i=0; i < indexes.length; ++i) {
        indexes[i] = i;
    }
}
...
```

Sorting is implemented by the SortDecorator.sort method, which rearranges the indexes stored in the indexes array. A simple sorting algorithm compares the strings returned from each of the cell value's toString method and sorts accordingly. Notice that the sort method fires a table structure changed event; see "AbstractTableModel Extensions Must Fire Appropriate Events" on page 1148.

```
...
public void sort(int column) {
    int rowCount = getRowCount();

    for(int i=0; i < rowCount; i++) {
        for(int j = i+1; j < rowCount; j++) {
            if(compare(indexes[i], indexes[j], column) < 0) {
                swap(i,j);
            }
        }
    }
    fireTableStructureChanged();
}
public void swap(int i, int j) {
    int tmp = indexes[i];
    indexes[i] = indexes[j];
    indexes[j] = tmp;
}
public int compare(int i, int j, int column) {
    Object io = realModel.getValueAt(i,column);
    Object jo = realModel.getValueAt(j,column);

    int c = jo.toString().compareTo(io.toString());
    return (c < 0) ? -1 : ((c > 0) ? 1 : 0);
}

...
```

The SortDecorator's getValueAt and setValueAt methods are overridden to store and retrieve values, using the sorted index array.

```
    . . .
    public Object getValueAt(int row, int column) {
        return realModel.getValueAt(indexes[row], column);
    }
    public void setValueAt(Object aValue, int row, int column) {
        realModel.setValueAt(aValue, indexes[row], column);
    }

    . . .
```

Finally, the SortDecorator implements the rest of the methods defined by the TableModel interface by delegating to the real model.

```
    . . .

    // TableModel pass-through methods follow ...

    public int getRowCount() {
        return realModel.getRowCount();
    }
    public int getColumnCount() {
        return realModel.getColumnCount();
    }
    public String getColumnName(int columnIndex) {
        return realModel.getColumnName(columnIndex);
    }
    public Class getColumnClass(int columnIndex) {
        return realModel.getColumnClass(columnIndex);
    }
    public boolean isCellEditable(int rowIndex, int columnIndex) {
        return realModel.isCellEditable(rowIndex, columnIndex);
    }
    public void addTableModelListener(TableModelListener l) {
        realModel.addTableModelListener(l);
    }
    public void removeTableModelListener(TableModelListener l) {
        realModel.removeTableModelListener(l);
    }
}
```

The application shown in Figure 19-31 is listed in its entirety in Example 19-21.

Example 19-21 Sorting with a Decorator

```java
import java.awt.*;
import java.awt.event.*;
import java.util.*;
import javax.swing.*;
import javax.swing.event.*;
import javax.swing.table.*;

public class Test extends JFrame {
    JTable table = new JTable(new Object[][] {
                {"apple", "$.39"}, {"mango", "$.49"},
                {"papaya", "$1.19"}, {"lemon", "$.19"},
                {"orange", "$.59"}, {"watermelon", "$.39"},
                {"tangerine", "$1.09"}, {"cherry", "$.79"},
                {"banana", "$.29"}, {"lime", "$.33"},
                {"grapefruit", "$.69"}, {"grapes", "$.49"},
            },
            new Object[] { "Item", "Price/Lb." });

    public Test() {
        final SortDecorator decorator =
                            new SortDecorator(table.getModel());

        table.setModel(decorator);

        JTableHeader hdr = (JTableHeader)table.getTableHeader();

        hdr.addMouseListener(new MouseAdapter() {
            public void mouseClicked(MouseEvent e) {
                TableColumnModel tcm = table.getColumnModel();
                int vc = tcm.getColumnIndexAtX(e.getX());
                int mc = table.convertColumnIndexToModel(vc);

                decorator.sort(mc);
            }
        });
        getContentPane().add(new JScrollPane(table),
                                BorderLayout.CENTER);
    }
    public static void main(String args[]) {
        GJApp.launch(
            new Test(),"A Sort Decorator",300,300,450,250);
    }
}
class SortDecorator implements TableModel, TableModelListener {
    private  TableModel realModel;
    private int indexes[];

    public SortDecorator(TableModel model) {
        if(model == null)
            throw new IllegalArgumentException(
```

```
                                        "null models are not allowed");
        this.realModel = model;

        realModel.addTableModelListener(this);
        allocate();
    }
    public Object getValueAt(int row, int column) {
        return realModel.getValueAt(indexes[row], column);
    }
    public void setValueAt(Object aValue, int row, int column) {
        realModel.setValueAt(aValue, indexes[row], column);
    }
    public void tableChanged(TableModelEvent e) {
        allocate();
    }
    public void sort(int column) {
        int rowCount = getRowCount();

        for(int i=0; i < rowCount; i++) {
            for(int j = i+1; j < rowCount; j++) {
                if(compare(indexes[i], indexes[j], column) < 0) {
                    swap(i,j);
                }
            }
        }
    }
    public void swap(int i, int j) {
        int tmp = indexes[i];
        indexes[i] = indexes[j];
        indexes[j] = tmp;
    }
    public int compare(int i, int j, int column) {
        Object io = realModel.getValueAt(i,column);
        Object jo = realModel.getValueAt(j,column);

        int c = jo.toString().compareTo(io.toString());
        return (c < 0) ? -1 : ((c > 0) ? 1 : 0);
    }
    private void allocate() {
        indexes = new int[getRowCount()];

        for(int i=0; i < indexes.length; ++i) {
            indexes[i] = i;
        }
    }

    // TableModel pass-through methods follow ...

    public int getRowCount() {
        return realModel.getRowCount();
    }
    public int getColumnCount() {
```

```
            return realModel.getColumnCount();
      }
      public String getColumnName(int columnIndex) {
            return realModel.getColumnName(columnIndex);
      }
      public Class getColumnClass(int columnIndex) {
            return realModel.getColumnClass(columnIndex);
      }
      public boolean isCellEditable(int rowIndex, int columnIndex) {
            return realModel.isCellEditable(rowIndex, columnIndex);
      }
      public void addTableModelListener(TableModelListener l) {
            realModel.addTableModelListener(l);
      }
      public void removeTableModelListener(TableModelListener l) {
            realModel.removeTableModelListener(l);
      }
}
```

Table Headers

Table headers are components that are displayed in the header viewport of a table's scrollpane. If a table is not contained in a scrollpane, the table's header will not be visible, as illustrated in Figure 19-2 on page 1135.

Table headers, although they are components, do not paint themselves. Table headers are painted by renderers maintained by table columns. See "Table Columns" on page 1161 for more information concerning table column renderers.

JTableHeader

Table headers are implemented by the JTableHeader component. JTableHeader is one of only two Swing components that do not reside in the swing package.[15] JTableHeader can be found in the swing.table package because it is more of an implementation detail of Swing tables than a general-purpose component that developers will use directly.

A class diagram for the JTableHeader class is shown in Figure 19-33.

---

15. The other component is JTextComponent from the swing.text package.

Figure 19-33 JTableHeader Class Diagram

JTableHeader extends JComponent and implements the Accessible and TableColumnModelListener interfaces. Instances of JTableHeader listen to their column models mostly to repaint and/or resize when column properties are modified.

JTableHeader maintains a reference to its table and the table's column model. JTableHeader also maintains TableColumn references for keeping track of columns that are being resized or dragged. JTableHeader also keeps track of the distance a column has been dragged as an integer value.

JTableHeader is responsible for maintaining properties that pertain to whether columns can be reordered or resized. JTableHeader also tracks whether dragged columns are updated in real time.

Column Header Renderers and Header ToolTips

Two of the most frequently asked questions concerning table headers have to do with implementing multiline headers and fitting headers with tooltips. Both concerns are addressed in the application shown in Figure 19-34, which implements a multiline header and sets tooltips for the header as a whole as well as for the middle initial column.

The pictures shown in Figure 19-34 show the multiline header as it responds to changes in the table's width by updating the number of lines of text that it displays.

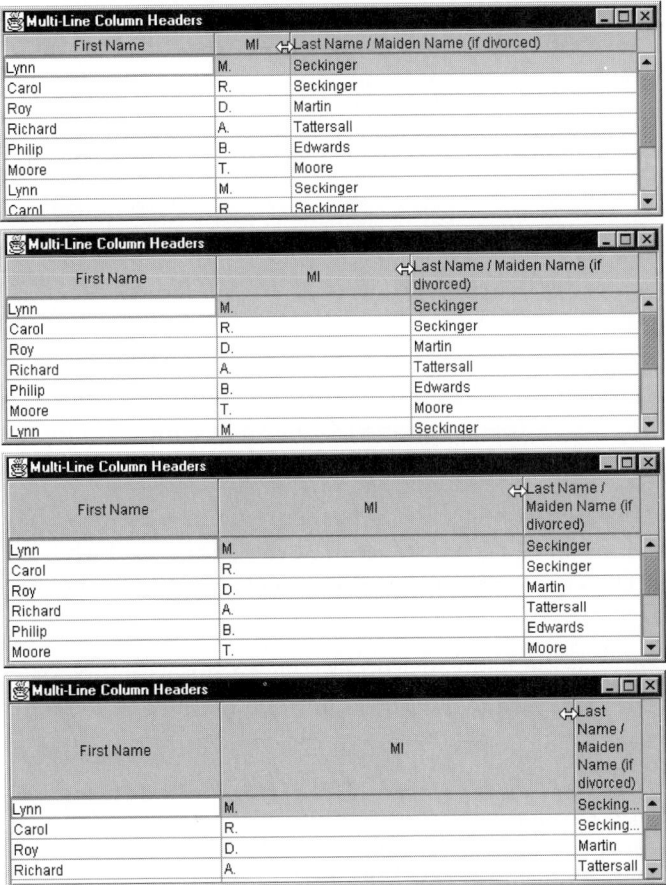

Figure 19-34 A Multiline Table Column Header

Note: *Due to a* JTextArea *bug, the multiline header shown in Figure 19-34 does not display correctly when the application's window is resized. Resizing the window a second time by a small amount fixes the problem. If the columns are sized as shown in Figure 19-34, the header works as advertised.*

Figure 19-35 shows the tooltip for the table's header in the First Name column, and the tooltip for the column's header renderer.

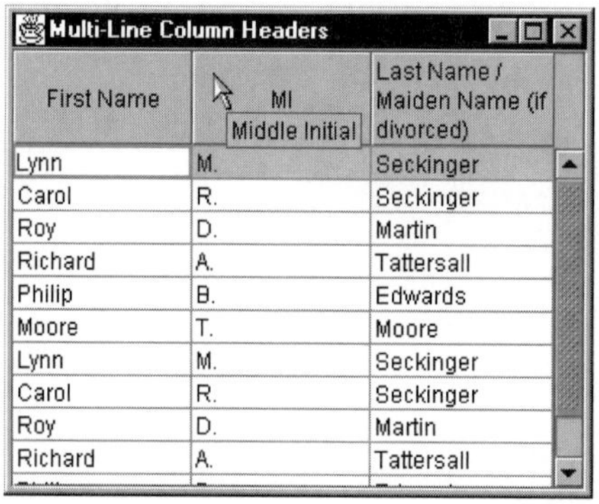

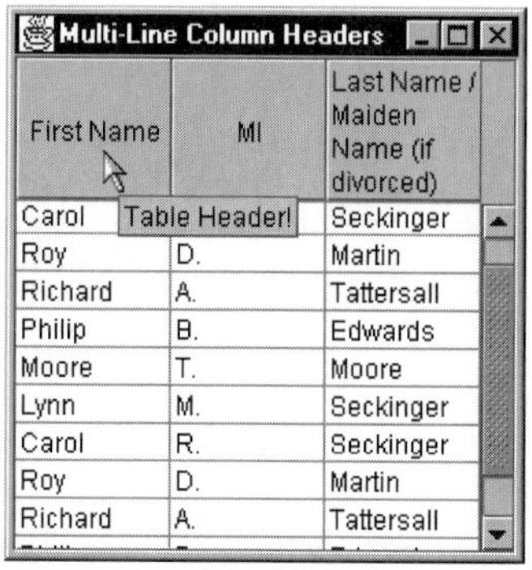

Figure 19-35 Table Column Header Tooltips

The application's constructor creates an instance of MultilineHeaderRenderer that is specified as the Last Name column's header renderer. The MultilineHeaderRenderer class is discussed below.

The constructor also obtains a reference to the header renderer's component for the MI column. If the component is an instance of JComponent—which it is by default—its tooltip text is set. Additionally, tooltip text is set for the table's header as a whole.

Tooltips specified for header renderers override a table header's tooltip; for example, the tooltip text displayed in the MI column is the text specified for the header renderer's tooltip.

```
public class Test extends JFrame {
    String longTitle = "Last Name / Maiden Name (if divorced)";
    MultilineHeaderRenderer multilineRenderer =
                new MultilineHeaderRenderer(longTitle);

    JTable table = new JTable(
```

```
    new Object[][] {
        { "Lynn", "M.", "Seckinger" },
        // other row data omitted
    },
    new Object[] {"First Name", "MI", longTitle});

public Test() {
    TableColumn middleColumn = table.getColumn("MI"),
            lastColumn = table.getColumn(longTitle);

    lastColumn.setHeaderRenderer(multilineRenderer);

    TableCellRenderer hdrRenderer =
                        middleColumn.getHeaderRenderer();

    Component hdrComponent =
        hdrRenderer.getTableCellRendererComponent(table,
                "MI", false, false, 0, 0);

    if(hdrComponent instanceof JComponent) {
        JComponent c = (JComponent)hdrComponent;
        c.setToolTipText("Middle Initial");
    }

    table.getTableHeader().setToolTipText("Table Header!");

    getContentPane().add(
                new JScrollPane(table), BorderLayout.CENTER);
    }
    ...
}
...
```

The `MultilineHeaderRenderer` implements the `TableCellRenderer`
interface and returns a scrollpane that contains an instance of
`MultilineHeader`, which is discussed below.

The rationale for wrapping the multiline header in a scrollpane is discussed
below.

```
    ...
class MultilineHeaderRenderer implements TableCellRenderer {
    MultilineHeader mlh;
    JScrollPane scrollPane;

    public MultilineHeaderRenderer(String title) {
        mlh = new MultilineHeader(title);
        scrollPane = new JScrollPane(mlh);
```

```
                scrollPane.setHorizontalScrollBarPolicy(
                    JScrollPane.HORIZONTAL_SCROLLBAR_NEVER);

                scrollPane.setVerticalScrollBarPolicy(
                    JScrollPane.VERTICAL_SCROLLBAR_NEVER);

                scrollPane.setBorder(null);
            }
            public Component getTableCellRendererComponent(JTable table,
                                     Object value,
                                     boolean isSelected,
                                     boolean hasFocus,
                                     int row, int col) {
                mlh.setText((String)value);
                return scrollPane;
            }
        }
        ...
```

The `MultilineHeader` class extends `JTextArea` because text areas provide the ability to wrap their text on word boundaries. The `MultilineHeader` enables lines to wrap, sets the wrap style to break on word boundaries, sets the text area's highlighter to `null`, and disables editing.

`MultilineHeader` overrides `updateUI()` to make the text area look and behave like a table header. The `updateUI` method is invoked whenever a look and feel is installed, and `MultilineHeader`'s overridden version of the method installs colors, fonts, and a border that are used by the look and feel for table headers.

```
        ...
    class MultilineHeader extends JTextArea {
        public MultilineHeader(String s) {
            super(s);
        }
        public void updateUI() {
            super.updateUI();

            // turn on wrapping and disable editing and highlighting

            setLineWrap(true);
            setWrapStyleWord(true);
            setHighlighter(null);
            setEditable(false);

            // make the text area look like a table header

            LookAndFeel.installColorsAndFont(this,
                                    "TableHeader.background",
```

```
                          "TableHeader.foreground",
                          "TableHeader.font");

        LookAndFeel.installBorder(this, "TableHeader.cellBorder");
    }
}
```

The multiline header returned by the `MultilineHeaderRenderer` listed above is wrapped in a scrollpane because the width of a text area when placed in a scrollpane tracks the width of the scrollpane. As a result, the multiline header's width is always the same as that of the column's header, resulting in changes to the number of lines of text displayed when the column is resized. See "The Scrollable Interface" on page 764 for more information concerning the `Scrollable` interface and how it is implemented by the `JTextArea` class.

The application shown in Figure 19-35 is listed in its entirety in Example 19-22.

Example 19-22 A Multiline Table Column Header and Header Tooltips

```
import javax.swing.*;
import javax.swing.border.*;
import javax.swing.table.*;
import java.awt.*;
import java.awt.event.*;

public class Test extends JFrame {
    String longTitle = "Last Name / Maiden Name (if divorced)";
    MultilineHeaderRenderer multilineRenderer =
                    new MultilineHeaderRenderer(longTitle);

    JTable table = new JTable(
        new Object[][] {
            { "Lynn", "M.", "Seckinger" },
            { "Carol", "R.", "Seckinger" },
            { "Roy", "D.", "Martin" },
            { "Richard", "A.", "Tattersall" },
            { "Philip", "B.", "Edwards" },
            { "Moore", "T.", "Moore" },

            // shorten scrollbar grip with these ...

            { "Lynn", "M.", "Seckinger" },
            { "Carol", "R.", "Seckinger" },
            { "Roy", "D.", "Martin" },
            { "Richard", "A.", "Tattersall" },
            { "Philip", "B.", "Edwards" },
            { "Moore", "T.", "Moore" },
        },
        new Object[] {"First Name", "MI", longTitle});
```

```java
    public Test() {
        TableColumn middleColumn = table.getColumn("MI"),
                    lastColumn = table.getColumn(longTitle);

        lastColumn.setHeaderRenderer(multilineRenderer);

        TableCellRenderer hdrRenderer =
                            middleColumn.getHeaderRenderer();

        Component hdrComponent =
            hdrRenderer.getTableCellRendererComponent(table,
                    "MI", false, false, 0, 0);

        if(hdrComponent instanceof JComponent) {
            JComponent c = (JComponent)hdrComponent;
            c.setToolTipText("Middle Initial");
        }

        table.getTableHeader().setToolTipText("Table Header!");

        getContentPane().add(
                    new JScrollPane(table), BorderLayout.CENTER);
    }
    public static void main(String args[]) {
        GJApp.launch(new Test(),
            "Multi-Line Column Headers",300,300,300,250);
    }
}
class MultilineHeaderRenderer implements TableCellRenderer {
    MultilineHeader mlh;
    JScrollPane scrollPane;

    public MultilineHeaderRenderer(String title) {
        mlh = new MultilineHeader(title);
        scrollPane = new JScrollPane(mlh);

        scrollPane.setHorizontalScrollBarPolicy(
            JScrollPane.HORIZONTAL_SCROLLBAR_NEVER);

        scrollPane.setVerticalScrollBarPolicy(
            JScrollPane.VERTICAL_SCROLLBAR_NEVER);

        scrollPane.setBorder(null);
    }
    public Component getTableCellRendererComponent(JTable table,
                        Object value,
                        boolean isSelected,
                        boolean hasFocus,
                        int row, int col) {
        mlh.setText((String)value);
        return scrollPane;
```

```
        }
    }
    class MultilineHeader extends JTextArea {
        public MultilineHeader(String s) {
            super(s);
        }
        public void updateUI() {
            super.updateUI();

            // turn on wrapping and disable editing and highlighting

            setLineWrap(true);
            setWrapStyleWord(true);
            setHighlighter(null);
            setEditable(false);

            // make the text area look like a table header

            LookAndFeel.installColorsAndFont(this,
                                "TableHeader.background",
                                "TableHeader.foreground",
                                "TableHeader.font");

            LookAndFeel.installBorder(this, "TableHeader.cellBorder");
        }
    }
```

Component Summary 19-1   JTable

Model(s)	TableModel
UI Delegate(s)	javax.swing.basic.BasicTableUI
Renderer(s)	TableCellRenderer
Editor(s)	TableCellEditor
Events Fired	PropertyChangeEvents, TableModelEvents
	TableColumnModelEvents, ListSelectionEvents
Replacement For	——

Class Diagrams

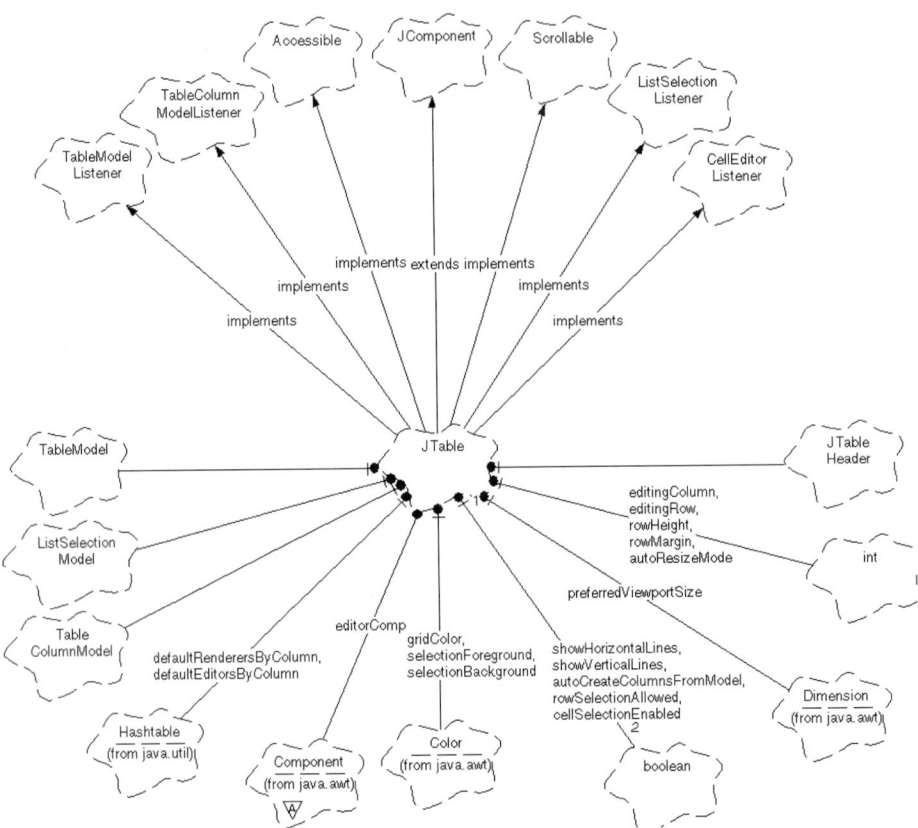

Figure 19-36 JTable Class Diagram

The JTable class extends JComponent and implements a number of interfaces. JTable, like other Swing components, implements the Accessible interface and also implements the Scrollable interface. The listener interfaces implemented by the JTable class are implemented so that the table can listen for, and react to, events fired by its models and editors.

JTable maintains protected references to all three of its models, in addition to an instance of JTableHeader and an editor component. Hash tables are also maintained for default renderers and editors. Additionally, JTable maintains a number of boolean and integer values for tracking its properties. See "JTable Properties" on page 1261 for more information concerning JTable properties.

JTable Properties

The properties maintained by the `JTable` class are listed in Table 19-7.

Table 19-7   JTable Properties

Property Name	Data Type	Property Type[1]	Access[2]	Default[3]
autoCreateColumns-FromModel	boolean	S	SG	true
autoResizeMode	int	S	SG	see discussion below
cellEditable	boolean	S	G	——
cellSelectionEnabled	boolean	S	SG	false
columnModel	TableColumn-Model	B	SG	Default-TableColumn-Model
columnSelectionAllowed	boolean	S	SG	false
defaultEditor	TableCellEditor	S	SG	——
defaultRenderer	TableCell-Renderer	S	SG	see discussion below
editing	boolean	S	G	false
editingColumn	int	S	SG	−1
editingRow	int	S	SG	−1
editorComponent	Component	S	G	——
gridColor	Color	S	SG	see discussion below
intercellSpacing	Dimension	TCM	SG	1
model	TableModel	B	SG	DefaultTable-Model
rowHeight	int	S	SG	16
rowMargin	int	S	SG	1
rowCount	int	——	G	——
rowSelectionAllowed	boolean	S	SG	true
selectionBackground	Color	B	SG	UIM
selectionForeground	Color	B	SG	UIM

Table 19-7   JTable Properties (Continued)

Property Name	Data Type	Property Type[1]	Access[2]	Default[3]
selectionMode	int	S	S	MULTIPLE_ SELECTION_ INTERVAL
selectionModel	ListSelection-Model	S	SG	DefaultList-Selection-Model
showGrid	boolean	S	SG	true
showHorizontalLines	boolean	S	SG	true
showVerticalLines	boolean	S	SG	true
tableHeader	JTableHeader	S	SG	JTableHeader

1. B = bound (fires PropertyChangeEvent) / C = constrained/ I = indexed / S = simple / Ch = fires ChangeEvent / TCM = table column model fires Table-ColumnModelEvent / LS = selection model fires ListSelectionEvent / TM = table model fires TableModelEvent
2. C = settable at construction time / G = getter method / S = setter method
3. L&F = look-and-feel dependent / UIM = UIManager sets default

autoCreateColumnsFromModel — Determines whether tables create default columns from their model. If the property is `true`, setting a table's model with the `setModel` method will remove existing columns and create new ones. By default, the property is `true`.

autoResizeMode — One of five resize modes; can be set with the `setAutoResizeMode` method. See "Column Resize Modes" on page 1162 for more information concerning table resize modes.

cellEditable — Determines whether a cell's value is editable. `JTable.isCellEditable()` defers to its model to determine whether a cell is editable. Notice that the property represents whether the cell's value is editable, not necessarily the cell itself. Cell editors can specify a cell to be noneditable even though the cell's value may be editable.

cellSelectionEnabled — Specifies whether row and column selection can exist simultaneously. If cell selection is enabled, it overrides the row and column selection modes.

columnModel — A table's model that implements the `TableModel` interface.

columnSelectionAllowed — A column model property that determines whether columns can be selected.

defaultEditor — The default editor for a specific class of objects. JTable maintains a set of default editors for specific data types that can be overridden, if desired.

defaultRenderer — The default renderer for a specific class of objects. JTable maintains a set of default renderers for specific data types that can be overridden, if desired.

editing — A read-only property that specifies whether a table cell is currently being edited.

editingColumn — If a table cell is being edited, the editingColumn property represents the column of the cell being edited.

editingRow — If a table cell is being edited, the editingRow property represents the row of the cell being edited.

editorComponent — If a table cell is being edited, the editorComponent property represents the component being used to edit the cell.

gridColor — The color used to draw grid lines. By default, table grid color is obtained from the UI manager with a call to UIManager.getColor("Table.gridColor").

intercellSpacing — A dimension that represents horizontal and vertical margins between cells. The vertical margin is maintained by a table's column model, whereas the horizontal margin is maintained as the table's rowMargin property.

model — A table's model, which is an object that implements the TableModel interface.

rowHeight — Table rows are all the same height for a given table; the rowHeight property determines, in pixels, the height of a table's rows.

Row height must be greater than 0—JTable.setRowHeight() throws an IllegalArgumentException if the value it is passed is less than or equal to 0.

rowMargin — The vertical margin between rows.

rowCount — The number of rows displayed in a table.

rowSelectionAllowed — Determines whether table rows can be selected. The property is true by default.

selectionBackground — The background color for selected cells.

selectionForeground — The foreground color for selected cells.

selectionMode — One of five selection modes supported by the JTable class. See "Table Selection" on page 1193 for more information concerning table selection modes.

selectionModel — A table's selection model, which by default is an instance of DefaultListSelectionModel.

showGrid — Determines whether horizontal and vertical lines are displayed. Setting this property sets the showHorizontalLines and showVerticalLines properties. The property is true by default.

showHorizontalLines — Determines whether horizontal grid lines are displayed. The property is true by default.

showVerticalLines — Determines whether vertical grid lines are displayed. The property is true by default.

tableHeader — The table's header, which is an instance of the JTableHeader class. See "JTableHeader" on page 1251 for more information concerning JTableHeader.

Table Events

Tables fire events when changes are made to any of its three models, as listed in Table 19-8.

Table 19-8   Table Events

Event	Fired by	Fired when …
TableModel-Event	table model	cell values changed; table structure changed; rows inserted/deleted/updated; cell updated
TableColumn-ModelEvent	table column model	columns added/removed/moved; column margin changed; column selection changed
ListSelection-Event	table selection model	row selection changed
ChangeEvent	DefaultCellEditor	editing stopped/canceled

The JTable class does not provide any methods for adding listeners. Listeners must be added directly to one of a table's three models or to a cell editor. See "Table Models" on page 1138 for a discussion of table models.[16]

Table Model Events

Table model events are fired when changes are made to a table's model. Table model events are handled by `TableModelListeners`, which is defined in Interface Summary 19-6.

Interface Summary 19-6   TableModelListener

---

public abstract void <u>tableChanged</u>(TableModelEvent)

The `TableModelListener.tableChanged` method is passed an instance of `TableModelEvent`, which is summarized in Class Summary 19-6.

Class Summary 19-6   TableModelEvent

Constants

---

public static final int <u>DELETE</u>
public static final int <u>INSERT</u>
public static final int <u>UPDATE</u>

public static final int <u>ALL_COLUMNS</u>
public static final int <u>HEADER_ROW</u>

.

16. Listener registration methods will likely be added to `JTable` in a future Swing release.

The constants listed above all specify the type of the event that has occurred. One of the first three constants is returned from the `TableModelEvent.getType()` method.

The `ALL_COLUMNS` and `HEADER_ROW` constants specify the column and first row that changed, respectively. `ALL_COLUMNS` specifies that every column in the table may have changed. Likewise, the `HEADER_ROW` signifies that the header row has changed, indicating that the names, types and order of columns may all have changed.

Constructors

---

public <u>TableModelEvent</u>(TableModel)
public <u>TableModelEvent</u>(TableModel, int row)
public <u>TableModelEvent</u>(TableModel, int firstRow, int lastRow)
public <u>TableModelEvent</u>(TableModel, int firstRow, int lastRow, int column)
public <u>TableModelEvent</u>(TableModel, int firstRow, int lastRow, int column, int type)

The `TableModelEvent` class provides a number of constructors for specifying different types of events. In general, developers will not typically instantiate table model events, because the event firing convenience methods are implemented by `AbstractTableModel`.

Methods

---

public int <u>getColumn</u>()
public int <u>getFirstRow</u>()
public int <u>getLastRow</u>()
public int <u>getType</u>()

The `TableModelEvent` class provides the methods listed above for obtaining information about the event.

The application shown in Figure 19-37 contains a table whose model has been fitted with an instance of `TableModelListener`. The top picture in Figure 19-37 shows a table cell in the process of being edited. After the cell has been edited, a `TableModelEvent` is fired that is handled by showing a message dialog.

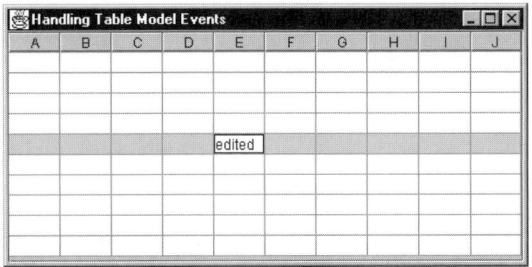

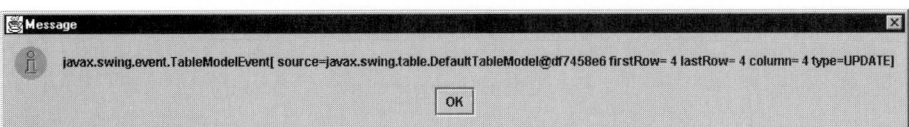

Figure 19-37 Handling Table Model Events

The application creates a table with a simple model and adds a
`TableModelListener` to the table's model.

```
public class Test extends JFrame {
JTable table = new JTable(10,10);

public Test() {
      Container contentPane = getContentPane();

      table.getModel().addTableModelListener(
                        new TableModelListener() {
          public void tableChanged(TableModelEvent e) {
             int firstRow = e.getFirstRow(),
                 column = e.getColumn();

             String properties = " source=" + e.getSource() +
             " firstRow= " +
                     (firstRow == TableModelEvent.HEADER_ROW ?
                            "HEADER_ROW" :
                            Integer.toString(firstRow)) +

             " lastRow= " + e.getLastRow() +

             " column= " +
                     (firstRow == TableModelEvent.ALL_COLUMNS ?
                            "ALL_COLUMNS" :
                            Integer.toString(column));

             String typeString = new String();
```

```
            int type = e.getType();

            switch(type) {
                case TableModelEvent.DELETE:
                    typeString = "DELETE"; break;
                case TableModelEvent.INSERT:
                    typeString = "INSERT"; break;
                case TableModelEvent.UPDATE:
                    typeString = "UPDATE"; break;
            }
            properties += " type=" + typeString;

            JOptionPane.showMessageDialog(Test.this,
                    e.getClass().getName() +
                    "[" + properties + "]");
        }
    });
}
```

The listener obtains information about the event by invoking `TableModelEvent` methods.

The application shown in Figure 19-37 is listed in its entirety and Example 19-23.

Example 19-23 Handling Table Model Events

```
import javax.swing.*;
import javax.swing.event.*;
import javax.swing.table.*;
import java.awt.*;
import java.awt.event.*;

public class Test extends JFrame {
    JTable table = new JTable(10,10);

    public Test() {
        Container contentPane = getContentPane();

        contentPane.add(new JScrollPane(table),
                BorderLayout.CENTER);

        table.getModel().addTableModelListener(
                        new TableModelListener() {
            public void tableChanged(TableModelEvent e) {
                int firstRow = e.getFirstRow(),
                    column = e.getColumn();

                String properties = " source=" + e.getSource() +
                " firstRow= " +
                        (firstRow == TableModelEvent.HEADER_ROW ?
```

```
                              "HEADER_ROW" :
                              Integer.toString(firstRow)) +

              " lastRow= " + e.getLastRow() +

              " column= " +
                    (firstRow == TableModelEvent.ALL_COLUMNS ?
                           "ALL_COLUMNS" :
                           Integer.toString(column));

              String typeString = new String();
              int type = e.getType();

              switch(type) {
                  case TableModelEvent.DELETE:
                      typeString = "DELETE"; break;
                  case TableModelEvent.INSERT:
                      typeString = "INSERT"; break;
                  case TableModelEvent.UPDATE:
                      typeString = "UPDATE"; break;
              }
              properties += " type=" + typeString;

              JOptionPane.showMessageDialog(Test.this,
                      e.getClass().getName() +
                      "[" + properties + "]");
          }
      });
  }
  public static void main(String args[]) {
      GJApp.launch(new Test(),
            "Handling Table Model Events",300,300,450,220);
  }
}
```

TableColumnModel Events

Under normal circumstances, the TableColumnModel and its associated events can be regarded as an implementation detail of the JTable class. Although you can register to receive TableColumnModel events, it is rarely necessary to do so.

TableColumnModel events are handled by instances of TableColumnModelListener, which are registered with column models with the TableColumnModel.addTableColumnModelListener method.

The TableColumnModelListener interface is summarized in Interface Summary 19-7.

Interface Summary 19-7   TableColumnModelListener

public abstract void <u>columnAdded</u>(TableColumnModelEvent)
public abstract void <u>columnMarginChanged</u>(ChangeEvent)
public abstract void <u>columnMoved</u>(TableColumnModelEvent)
public abstract void <u>columnRemoved</u>(TableColumnModelEvent)
public abstract void <u>columnSelectionChanged</u>(ListSelectionEvent)

`TableColumnModelListeners` can detect when columns have been added, moved, or removed from a table column model in addition to column margin and selection changes.

All of the methods defined by the `TableColumnModelListener` interface, with the exception of `columnMarginChanged()` and `columnSelectionChanged()`, are passed a `TableColumnModelEvent`. The `TableColumnModelEvent` class is summarized in Class Summary 19-7.

Class Summary 19-7   TableColumnModelEvent

Constructors

public <u>TableColumnModelEvent</u>(TableColumnModel model, int from, int to)

The `TableColumnModelEvent` class provides a single constructor that is passed a reference to a `TableColumnModel` and the indexes of the columns that were affected by the event.

Methods

public int <u>getFromIndex</u>()
public int <u>getToIndex</u>()

The methods listed above return indexes to the columns that were affected by the event. For example, the applet shown in Figure 19-38 adds a `TableColumnModelListener` to the table's column model. When a column is moved, the listener shows in the applet's status area the column indexes that were affected by the move.

B	A	C	D	E	F	G	H	I	J
(0,1)	(0,0)	(0,2)	(0,3)	(0,4)	(0,...	(0,6)	(0,...	(0,8)	(0,...
(1,1)	(1,0)	(1,2)	(1,3)	(1,4)	(1,...	(1,6)	(1,...	(1,8)	(1,...
(2,1)	(2,0)	(2,2)	(2,3)	(2,4)	(2,...	(2,6)	(2,...	(2,8)	(2,...
(3,1)	(3,0)	(3,2)	(3,3)	(3,4)	(3,...	(3,6)	(3,...	(3,8)	(3,...
(4,1)	(4,0)	(4,2)	(4,3)	(4,4)	(4,...	(4,6)	(4,...	(4,8)	(4,...
(5,1)	(5,0)	(5,2)	(5,3)	(5,4)	(5,...	(5,6)	(5,...	(5,8)	(5,...
(6,1)	(6,0)	(6,2)	(6,3)	(6,4)	(6,...	(6,6)	(6,...	(6,8)	(6,...
(7,1)	(7,0)	(7,2)	(7,3)	(7,4)	(7,...	(7,6)	(7,...	(7,8)	(7,...
(8,1)	(8,0)	(8,2)	(8,3)	(8,4)	(8,...	(8,6)	(8,...	(8,8)	(8,...
(9,1)	(9,0)	(9,2)	(9,3)	(9,4)	(9,...	(9,6)	(9,...	(9,8)	(9,...

Column Moved From 0 To 1

Figure 19-38 Handling Column Model Events

The applet shown in Figure 19-38 is listed in Example 19-24.

Example 19-24 Handling Column Model Events

```
import javax.swing.*;
import javax.swing.event.*;
import javax.swing.table.*;
import java.awt.*;
import java.awt.event.*;

public class Test extends JApplet {
    JTable table = new JTable(
        new AbstractTableModel() {
            int rows = 10, cols = 10;

            public int getRowCount() { return rows; }
```

```
                    public int getColumnCount() { return cols; }

                    public Object getValueAt(int row, int col) {
                        return "(" + Integer.toString(row) + "," +
                                        Integer.toString(col) + ")";
                    }
                }
            );

        public void init() {
            Container contentPane = getContentPane();

            contentPane.add(new JScrollPane(table),
                        BorderLayout.CENTER);

            table.getColumnModel().addColumnModelListener(
                            new TableColumnModelListener() {
                public void columnAdded(TableColumnModelEvent e) { }
                public void columnMarginChanged(ChangeEvent e) { }
                public void columnRemoved(TableColumnModelEvent e) { }
                public void columnSelectionChanged(
                                    ListSelectionEvent e) { }

                public void columnMoved(TableColumnModelEvent e) {
                    String s = "Column Moved From " +
                            e.getFromIndex() + " To " +
                            e.getToIndex();

                    showStatus(s);
                }
            });
        }
    }
```

Classes that implement the `TableColumnModelListener` interface must provide empty implementations of methods representing uninteresting events because Swing does not provide an adapter class for table column model listeners.

The listener listed above reacts to column moved events by obtaining the From and To indexes from the event. The listener subsequently updates the applet's status area.

List Selection Events

List selection events are handled by objects that implement the
`ListSelectionListener` interface, which is summarized in
"ListSelectionListener" on page 1040.

The application shown in Figure 19-39 contains a table whose selection model is
fitted with a list selection listener. The listener prints information about selection
event as they occur.

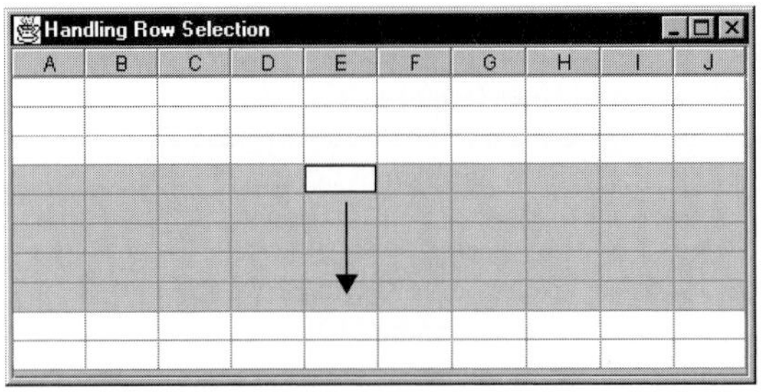

Figure 19-39 Handling Row Selection Events

Figure 19-39 depicts a mouse dragged from cell (3,4) to cell (7,4). Adjusting events
are fired as the cursor is dragged over cells. When the mouse button is released, a
nonadjusting event is fired.

```
Selection Model:javax.swing.event.ListSelectionEvent[
source=javax.swing.DefaultListSelectionModel 2048245 ={0}
firstIndex= 0 lastIndex= 0 isAdjusting= false ]]

Selection Model adjusting ...
Selection Model adjusting ...
Selection Model adjusting ...
Selection Model adjusting ...
Selection Model adjusting ...

Selection Model:javax.swing.event.ListSelectionEvent[
source=javax.swing.DefaultListSelectionModel 2048245 ={3, 4, 5,
6, 7} firstIndex= 0 lastIndex= 7 isAdjusting= false ]
```

The application creates a table with a simple model and adds a listener to the table's selection model. If the value associated with the event is adjusting, the listener prints the string "adjusting...". Events that are not adjusting are handled by the event's `toString` method.

```
public class Test extends JFrame {
    JTable table = new JTable(10,10);

    public Test() {
        // add table, wrapped in scrollpane, to content pane ...

        table.getSelectionModel().addListSelectionListener(
                                new ListSelectionListener() {
            public void valueChanged(ListSelectionEvent e) {
                if(e.getValueIsAdjusting()) {
                    System.out.println("Selection Model " +
                                    "adjusting ...");
                }
                else {
                    System.out.println("Selection Model:" +
                                    e.toString());
                }
            }
        });
    }
```

The application shown in Figure 19-39 is listed in its entirety in Example 19-25.

Example 19-25 Handling Row Selection Events

```
import javax.swing.*;
import javax.swing.event.*;
import javax.swing.table.*;
import java.awt.*;
import java.awt.event.*;

public class Test extends JFrame {
    JTable table = new JTable(10,10);

    public Test() {
        Container contentPane = getContentPane();

        contentPane.add(new JScrollPane(table),
                    BorderLayout.CENTER);

        table.getSelectionModel().addListSelectionListener(
                                new ListSelectionListener() {
            public void valueChanged(ListSelectionEvent e) {
                if(e.getValueIsAdjusting()) {
```

```
                System.out.println("Selection Model " +
                                "adjusting ...");
            }
            else {
                System.out.println("Selection Model:" +
                                e.toString());
            }
        }
    });
    }
    public static void main(String args[]) {
        GJApp.launch(new Test(),
                "Handling Row Selection",300,300,450,220);
    }
}
```

JTable Class Summaries

The `public` and `protected` methods for `JTable` are listed in Class Summary 19-8.

Class Summary 19-8   JTable

Constructors

---

public JTable()

public JTable(int numRows, int numColumns)

public JTable(Object[][], Object[])
public JTable(Vector, Vector)

public JTable(TableModel)
public JTable(TableModel, TableColumnModel)
public JTable(TableModel, TableColumnModel, ListSelectionModel)

The JTable class provides a number of constructors for constructing tables with either data or models.

The no-argument constructor creates a JTable instance with default values for its table model, table column model, and list selection model. Tables can also be constructed with a JTable constructor that is passed the number of rows and columns contained in the table.

The last five JTable constructors listed above are all passed data in some format; the first two constructors are passed Object arrays and vectors and are fitted with simple extensions of AbstractTableModel. The last three constructors are passed models that are assigned as the table's table model, table column model, and list selection model. If any of the models are null, models are created with the protected JTable methods listed below.

Methods

Initialization

---

protected TableColumnModel createDefaultColumnModel()
protected TableModel createDefaultDataModel()
protected ListSelectionModel createDefaultSelectionModel()

protected void createDefaultEditors()
protected void createDefaultRenderers()

protected JTableHeader createDefaultTableHeader()

protected void initializeLocalVars()

The methods listed above create default models, editors, renderers, and a table header. The default models created are instances of DefaultTableModel, DefaultTableColumnModel, and DefaultListSelectionModel. The default table header is an instance of JTableHeader.

The renderers and editors created by the methods listed above are defaults for certain object types; the defaults are listed in Table 19-4 on page 1157.

The initializeLocalVars method initializes JTable properties to their defaults. See Table 19-7 on page 1261 for JTable properties defaults.

Tables and Scrollpanes

---

public static JScrollPane createScrollPaneForTable(JTable)
public void addNotify()
protected void configureEnclosingScrollPane()

In Swing's early days, tables had to be added to a specially configured scrollpane that was returned from the `static createScrollPaneForTable` method, which is now deprecated.

Subsequently, an alternative approach of overriding `addNotify()`—which is called when a table is added to a container—obviated the need for the `createScrollPaneForTable` method. `JTable.addNotify()` invokes `super.addNotify()` and then calls `configureEnclosingScrollPane()`.

The `configureEnclosingScrollPane` method checks to see if the table is contained in a scrollpane; if so, the table's header is set as the scrollpane's header view, backing store is enabled for the scrollpane, and the scrollpane is fitted with a look-and-feel-specific border.

TableModelListener Method

---

public void tableChanged(TableModelEvent)

Instances of `JTable` react to model changes with the `tableChanged` method. Depending upon the type of change, an appropriate action is taken, and the table is resized and repainted.

TableColumnModelListener Methods

---

public void columnAdded(TableColumnModelEvent)
public void columnMarginChanged(ChangeEvent)
public void columnMoved(TableColumnModelEvent)
public void columnRemoved(TableColumnModelEvent)
public void columnSelectionChanged(ListSelectionEvent)

The methods listed above are defined by the `TableColumnModelListener` interface. Instances of `JTable` register themselves as listeners with their column models, and the methods listed above react to events fired by the table's column model.

The first four methods listed above check to see if editing is currently in progress; if so, editing is stopped and the editor is removed from the table. The methods subsequently either repaint or resize/repaint the table, depending upon the type of change. The last method listed above reacts to changes to column selections by repainting the affected columns.

ListSelectionListener Method

---

public void <u>valueChanged</u>(ListSelectionEvent)

Instances of `JTable` also listen to their selection models by implementing the `ListSelectionListener` method. `JTable.valueChanged()` repaints the rows affected by the selection change.

Scrollable Methods

---

public int <u>getScrollableBlockIncrement</u>(Rectangle visibleRect, int orientation,
                                        int direction)
public boolean <u>getScrollableTracksViewportHeight</u>()
public boolean <u>getScrollableTracksViewportWidth</u>()
public int <u>getScrollableUnitIncrement</u>(Rectangle, int, int)
public Dimension <u>getPreferredScrollableViewportSize</u>()

The methods listed above are defined by the `Scrollable` interface, which is implemented by the `JTable` class. The block and unit scrolling increments are set as discussed in "Block and Unit Increments" on page 1136.

Instances of `JTable` track their viewport's width if the `autoResizeMode` property is set to anything other than `JTable.AUTO_RESIZE_OFF`. Tables do not track their viewport's height by default. See on page 764 for more information concerning the `Scrollable` interface.

CellEditorListener Methods

---

public void <u>editingCanceled</u>(ChangeEvent)
public void <u>editingStopped</u>(ChangeEvent)

JTable listens to cell editors by implementing the CellEditorListener interface. Both editingStopped() and editingCanceled() remove the editor from the table, and editingStopped() uses the editor's value to set the value of the cell being edited. See "Rendering and Editing" on page 1200 for more information concerning table editing.

Selection

---

public void <u>addColumnSelectionInterval</u>(int, int)
public int <u>getSelectedColumn</u>()
public int <u>getSelectedColumnCount</u>()
public int[] <u>getSelectedColumns</u>()

public int <u>getSelectedRow</u>()
public int <u>getSelectedRowCount</u>()
public int[] <u>getSelectedRows</u>()

public void <u>addRowSelectionInterval</u>(int, int)
public void <u>clearSelection</u>()

public void <u>removeColumnSelectionInterval</u>(int, int)
public void <u>removeRowSelectionInterval</u>(int, int)

public void <u>setSelectionBackground</u>(Color)
public void <u>setSelectionForeground</u>(Color)

public void <u>setSelectionMode</u>(int)
public void <u>setSelectionModel</u>(ListSelectionModel)

public void <u>setCellSelectionEnabled</u>(boolean)
public void <u>setColumnSelectionAllowed</u>(boolean)
public void <u>setColumnSelectionInterval</u>(int, int)

public boolean <u>getCellSelectionEnabled</u>()
public boolean <u>getColumnSelectionAllowed</u>()

public void <u>selectAll</u>()

Tables support selecting rows, columns, and cells. The methods listed above can set selection modes, add or remove row and column intervals, and set the table's selection model. Additionally, instances of `JTable` maintain selection foreground and background colors that can be accessed with the accessor methods listed above. The `selectAll` method selects all of the rows and columns in a table.

Table Cell Editing

---

public TableCellEditor <u>getCellEditor</u>()
public TableCellEditor <u>getCellEditor</u>(int row, int column)
public TableCellEditor <u>getDefaultEditor</u>(Class)
public void <u>setDefaultEditor</u>(Class, TableCellEditor)

public int <u>getEditingColumn</u>()
public int <u>getEditingRow</u>()

public boolean <u>editCellAt</u>(int row, int column)
public boolean <u>editCellAt</u>(int row, int column, EventObject)
public Component <u>getEditorComponent</u>()
public boolean <u>isEditing</u>()
public Component <u>prepareEditor</u>(TableCellEditor, int row, int column)

public void <u>removeEditor</u>()
public void <u>setEditingColumn</u>(int)
public void <u>setEditingRow</u>(int)
public void <u>setCellEditor</u>(TableCellEditor)

The methods listed above support table editing by providing access to the current editor. The methods that set the editing row and column should not be directly invoked by developers.

Table Cell Rendering

public TableCellRenderer getCellRenderer(int row, int column)
public TableCellRenderer getDefaultRenderer(Class)
public void setDefaultRenderer(Class, TableCellRenderer)
public Component prepareRenderer(TableCellRenderer, int row, int column)

The methods listed above support table cell rendering by providing access to default renderers and the renderer for a particular table cell. During painting, tables funnel all of their rendering requirements through the methods listed above. As a result, the methods can be overridden to provide renderers in ways other than the column-centric default implementation.

Utility Methods

public void sizeColumnsToFit(int)
public int convertColumnIndexToModel(int)
public int convertColumnIndexToView(int)
public void createDefaultColumnsFromModel()
public int columnAtPoint(Point)
public int rowAtPoint(Point)
public void addColumn(TableColumn)
protected void resizeAndRepaint()
public void moveColumn(int, int)
protected String paramString()
public void removeColumn(TableColumn)
public void reshape(int x, int y, int w, int h)

The methods listed above are miscellaneous utility methods that perform a number of functions, including returning the row or column at a coordinate location and moving and removing table columns.

Miscellaneous Properties

---

public TableColumn <u>getColumn</u>(Object)
public Class <u>getColumnClass</u>(int)
public int <u>getColumnCount</u>()
public TableColumnModel <u>getColumnModel</u>()
public String <u>getColumnName</u>(int)
public boolean <u>getAutoCreateColumnsFromModel</u>()
public int <u>getAutoResizeMode</u>()
public Rectangle <u>getCellRect</u>(int, int, boolean)
public Color <u>getGridColor</u>()
public Dimension <u>getIntercellSpacing</u>()
public TableModel <u>getModel</u>()
public int <u>getRowCount</u>()
public int <u>getRowHeight</u>()
public int <u>getRowMargin</u>()
public boolean <u>getRowSelectionAllowed</u>()
public Color <u>getSelectionBackground</u>()
public Color <u>getSelectionForeground</u>()
public ListSelectionModel <u>getSelectionModel</u>()
public boolean <u>getShowHorizontalLines</u>()
public boolean <u>getShowVerticalLines</u>()
public JTableHeader <u>getTableHeader</u>()
public String <u>getToolTipText</u>(MouseEvent)
public Object <u>getValueAt</u>(int, int)

public boolean <u>isCellSelected</u>(int, int)
public boolean <u>isColumnSelected</u>(int)
public boolean <u>isManagingFocus</u>()
public boolean <u>isRowSelected</u>(int)

public void <u>setAutoCreateColumnsFromModel</u>(boolean)
public void <u>setAutoResizeMode</u>(int)
public void <u>setColumnModel</u>(TableColumnModel)
public void <u>setGridColor</u>(Color)
public void <u>setIntercellSpacing</u>(Dimension)
public void <u>setModel</u>(TableModel)
public void <u>setRowHeight</u>(int)
public void <u>setRowMargin</u>(int)
public void <u>setRowSelectionAllowed</u>(boolean)
public void <u>setRowSelectionInterval</u>(int, int)
public void <u>setShowGrid</u>(boolean)

```
public void setShowHorizontalLines(boolean)
public void setShowVerticalLines(boolean)
public void setTableHeader(JTableHeader)
public void setValueAt(Object, int, int)
```

The methods listed above are accessors for miscellaneous JTable properties. See "JTable Properties" on page 1261 for more information concerning JTable properties.

Accessibility / Pluggable Look and Feel

```
public AccessibleContext getAccessibleContext()
public TableUI getUI()
public String getUIClassID()
public void setUI(TableUI)
public void updateUI()
```

The methods listed above can be found in most extensions of JComponent. Swing lightweight components can return the class name of their UI delegate and an accessibility context that contains accessibility information for the component. The updateUI method is invoked when the component is fitted with a UI delegate.

AWT Compatibility

The AWT does not provide a component analogous to Swing's JTable.

Parting Shots

With three models, a header component and a cell renderer and editor, JTable is arguably Swing's most complex component; thus, the size of this chapter. Tables are not difficult to use; however the many different aspects of tables (table columns, headers, renderer, editor, etc.) pose a formidable learning curve. As a result, this chapter has presented a number of techniques for frequently performed table tasks such as hiding columns ("Hiding Columns" on page 1185) and rendering by rows instead of columns ("Rendering By Rows" on page 1236).

CHAPTER
20

Trees

Swing trees display hierarchical data by using a well-known paradigm of folders and leaf items. The most widely used tree component[1] is undoubtedly Windows Explorer, which contains a tree component for navigating directories.

Like tables, trees are made up of a number of classes and interfaces defined in their own package—the `swing.tree` package. The tree component is represented by the `JTree` class, which resides in the `swing` package.

Trees are composed of nodes, which can be either folders or leaves. Folders can have child nodes, and all nodes but a tree's root node have a single parent node. Empty folders can be differentiated from leaves by whether they allow children.

Figure 20-1 shows a `JTree` extension that can be used to navigate directories and files. Folders and leaves are represented by different icons that are look-and-feel dependent. Folders can be expanded and collapsed, either by double-clicking on the folder or by clicking on the folder's handle. The visibility of the root node's handle can be set; for example, the root node for the tree shown in Figure 20-1 does not display a handle.

---

1. Tree components are also known as outline controls.

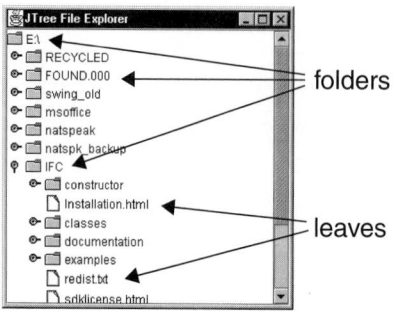

Figure 20-1 JTree Anatomy

In addition to parent and child nodes, tree nodes also have a user object.[2] User objects are of type `Object` and therefore provide a way to associate any object with a node.

Trees have a simple model, and each `JTree` instance maintains references to a renderer and an editor that are used for all nodes in the tree. The key classes from the `swing.tree` package are listed in Table 20-1.

Table 20-1   swing.tree Package Key Classes

Name	Implementation
DefaultMutableTreeNode	A mutable node with one parent, (possibly) many children, and one user object. Accessors are provided for related nodes. Nodes are leaves if they have no children.
DefaultTreeModel	A simple, mutable model that fires TreeModelEvents. Provides children (but not parent) accessor methods.
DefaultTreeCellEditor	Wrapper for renderer and editor that places a "real" editor component next to the node's icon.
DefaultTreeCellRenderer	A JLabel extension with accessors for font, colors, and icons. Provides defaults for icons.
TreePath	A path from one node to another. Nodes in the path are stored in an array. Paths are used to communicate selections.

2.   The user object is present when `DefaultTreeModel` is used.

Creating Trees

The applet shown in Figure 20-2 contains a table created with the JTree no-argument constructor.

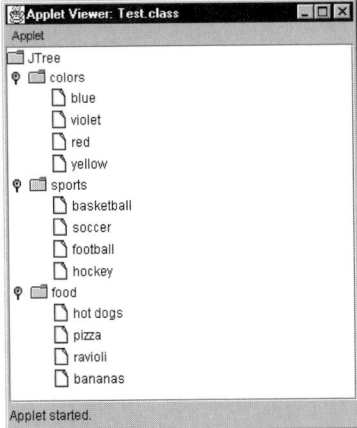

Figure 20-2 Default Tree Nodes

The applet shown in Figure 20-2 adds a tree, wrapped in a scrollpane, to the applet's content pane. The applet is listed in Example 20-1. By default, folders are initially collapsed when a tree is displayed. The tree shown in Figure 20-2 had its folders expanded after the applet was started.

Example 20-1 A Simple Tree Example

```
import javax.swing.*;

public class Test extends JApplet {
    public void init() {
        getContentPane().add(new JScrollPane(new JTree()));
    }
}
```

If a model or nodes are not explicitly specified at construction time, instances of JTree are constructed with the nodes shown in Figure 20-2.

Almost all trees are constructed by creating a root node and subsequently building a hierarchy, or by creating a tree model. For example, `JTree.getDefaultTreeModel()` is invoked by the `JTree` default constructor to create the default hierarchy of nodes shown in Figure 20-2.

```
// From JTree.java:

protected static TreeModel getDefaultTreeModel() {
    DefaultMutableTreeNode root =
                      new DefaultMutableTreeNode("JTree");

    DefaultMutableTreeNode parent;

    parent = new DefaultMutableTreeNode("colors");
    root.add(parent);

    parent.add(new DefaultMutableTreeNode("blue"));
    parent.add(new DefaultMutableTreeNode("violet"));
    parent.add(new DefaultMutableTreeNode("red"));
    parent.add(new DefaultMutableTreeNode("yellow"));

    parent = new DefaultMutableTreeNode("sports");
    root.add(parent);

    parent.add(new DefaultMutableTreeNode("basketball"));
    parent.add(new DefaultMutableTreeNode("soccer"));
    parent.add(new DefaultMutableTreeNode("football"));
    parent.add(new DefaultMutableTreeNode("hockey"));

    ...

    return new DefaultTreeModel(root);
}
```

A node with the string "`JTree`" for a user object is instantiated and ultimately specified as the root node for the tree's model. The "`colors`" node has four child nodes added to it and is specified as the only child of the root node. The "`sports`" node also has four nodes and is also added to the root node.

The `JTree` class also provides constructors for creating trees with `Object` arrays, hash tables, and vectors, as illustrated by the applet shown in Figure 20-3.

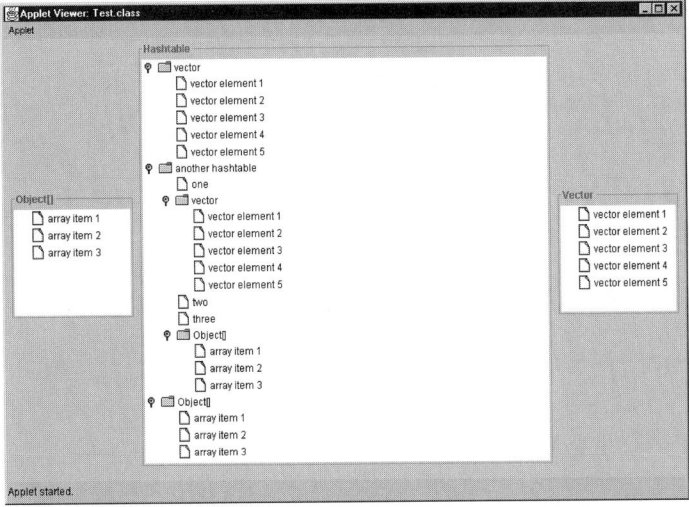

Figure 20-3 Creating Trees with Objects, Vectors, and Hash Tables

Two things should be noted about constructing trees with data, as opposed to building a hierarchy of nodes.

First, trees are almost never constructed with data; trees are typically populated with nodes, as is the case for the applet shown in Figure 20-2.

Second, because the order in which objects are added to a hash table has no correlation to the manner in which the objects are stored, trees created with hash tables exhibit an unpredictable node order.

The applet shown in Figure 20-3 is listed in Example 20-2.

Example 20-2 Creating Trees with Objects, Vectors, and Hash Tables

```
import javax.swing.*;
import javax.swing.tree.TreePath;
import java.awt.*;
import java.awt.event.*;
import java.util.*;

public class Test extends JApplet {
    Hashtable ht = new Hashtable(), ht2 = new Hashtable();
    Vector vector = new Vector();
    Object[] objs = new Object[] {
            "array item 1", "array item 2", "array item 3"
    };
```

```
public void init() {
    Container contentPane = getContentPane();

    vector.addElement("vector element 1");
    vector.addElement("vector element 2");
    vector.addElement("vector element 3");
    vector.addElement("vector element 4");
    vector.addElement("vector element 5");

    ht.put("another hashtable", ht2);
    ht.put("vector", vector);
    ht.put("Object[]", objs);

    ht2.put("Object[]", objs);
    ht2.put("vector", vector);
    ht2.put("one", new Integer(1));
    ht2.put("two", new Integer(2));
    ht2.put("three", new Integer(3));

    // trees must be created after data is populated

    JTree hashTree = new JTree(ht);
    JTree vectorTree = new JTree(vector);
    JTree objectTree = new JTree(objs);

    JScrollPane objPane = new JScrollPane(objectTree);
    JScrollPane hashPane = new JScrollPane(hashTree);
    JScrollPane vectorPane = new JScrollPane(vectorTree);

    objPane.setPreferredSize(new Dimension(150,150));
    hashPane.setPreferredSize(new Dimension(500,500));
    vectorPane.setPreferredSize(new Dimension(150,150));

    objPane.setBorder(
        BorderFactory.createTitledBorder("Object[]"));

    hashPane.setBorder(
        BorderFactory.createTitledBorder("Hashtable"));

    vectorPane.setBorder(
        BorderFactory.createTitledBorder("Vector"));

    hashTree.expandPath(new TreePath(
                    hashTree.getModel().getRoot()));

    contentPane.setLayout(new FlowLayout());
    contentPane.add(objPane);
    contentPane.add(hashPane);
    contentPane.add(vectorPane);
    }
}
```

Tree Nodes

Just as columns are the backbone of Swing tables, tree nodes are the key ingredients to Swing trees. Tree nodes are defined by the `TreeNode` interface, which is extended by the `MutableTreeNode` interface, which in turn is implemented by the `DefaultMutableTreeNode` class.

The TreeNode Interface

The `TreeNode` interface defines the essence of what it means to be a (immutable) tree node, and is summarized in Interface Summary 20-1.

Interface Summary 20-1   TreeNode

---

public abstract Enumeration <u>children</u>()
public abstract TreeNode <u>getParent</u>()

public abstract TreeNode <u>getChildAt</u>(int)
public abstract int <u>getChildCount</u>()
public abstract int <u>getIndex</u>(TreeNode)

public abstract boolean <u>getAllowsChildren</u>()
public abstract boolean <u>isLeaf</u>()

The first two groups of methods listed above are accessors for a node's parent and children. A node's children can be accessed by obtaining an enumeration from the children's parent, or children can be accessed by an index. Additionally, methods are defined for obtaining a node's index and a count of the number of children a node contains.

The last two methods listed above determine whether a node is a folder or a leaf. See "DefaultTreeModel" on page 1310 for more information concerning the `getAllowsChildren` method.

The TreeNode interface will rarely be directly implemented by developers because Swing provides a generally useful default implementation of the TreeNode interface in the DefaultMutableTreeNode class. The vast majority of tree nodes extend DefaultMutableTreeNode.

The MutableTreeNode Interface

The MutableTreeNode interface extends TreeNode and defines methods for modifying a node's parent and children in addition to specifying a user object. The MutableTreeNode interface is summarized in Interface Summary 20-2.

Interface Summary 20-2   MutableTreeNode

Extends: TreeNode

public abstract void <u>insert</u>(MutableTreeNode child, int index)
public abstract void <u>remove</u>(int index)
public abstract void <u>remove</u>(MutableTreeNode child)

public abstract void <u>removeFromParent</u>()

public abstract void <u>setParent</u>(MutableTreeNode)
public abstract void <u>setUserObject</u>(Object)

The first group of methods listed above insert and remove child nodes. Children can be removed by index or reference.

The removeFromParent method removes a node from its parent node and updates the parent's child count.

The last two methods listed above set a node's parent and user object. Note that MutableTreeNode inherits a getParent method but not a getUserObject method. The absence of a getUserObject method is an oversight that will be corrected in a subsequent Swing release. In practice, the omission of a getUserObject method is of little consequence because the method is implemented in the DefaultMutableTreeNode class.

The DefaultMutableTreeNode class

The `TreeNode` and `MutableTreeNode` interfaces are rarely implemented directly in practice because Swing provides a reasonable and robust implementation of the `MutableTreeNode` interface in the form of the `DefaultMutableTreeNode` class.

A class diagram for the `DefaultMutableTreeNode` class shown in Figure 20-4.

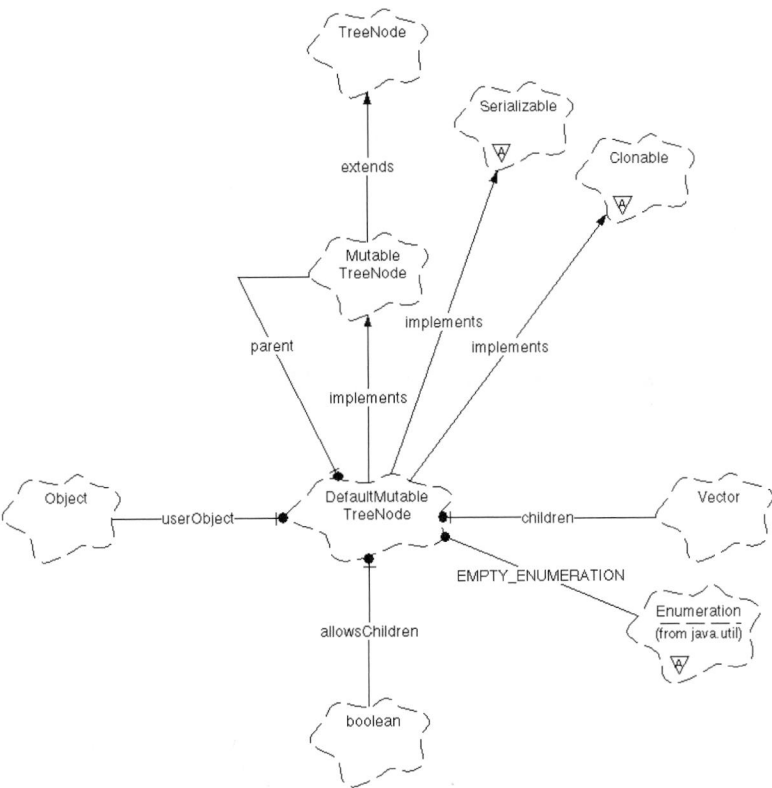

Figure 20-4 DefaultMutableTreeNode Class Diagram

`DefaultMutableTreeNode` implements the `MutableTreeNode` interface and maintains references to its parent, user object, and children. By maintaining a reference to its parent and children, the `DefaultMutableTreeNode` class

implements the Composite design pattern,[3] which allows folders and leaf nodes to be nested. The AWT's `Component` and `Container` classes are also an example of the Composite design pattern.[4]

Using DefaultMutableTreeNode

Tree nodes are almost always instances of `DefaultMutableTreeNode` or extensions thereof; the default nodes created by a tree, for example, are instances of `DefaultMutableTreeNode`.

The `DefaultMutableTreeNode` class provides many methods over and above those defined in the `TreeNode` and `MutableTreeNode` interfaces for accessing related nodes. For example, `DefaultMutableTreeNode` provides `getFirstLeaf` and `getNextLeaf` methods that return the first child node that is a leaf and the next sibling node that is a leaf for a given node, respectively.

The `DefaultMutableTreeNode` class also provides methods that return an enumeration of a node's descendants in a depth-first or breadth-first traversal. The difference between depth-first vs. breadth-first traversal for a tree's root node is illustrated in Figure 20-5.

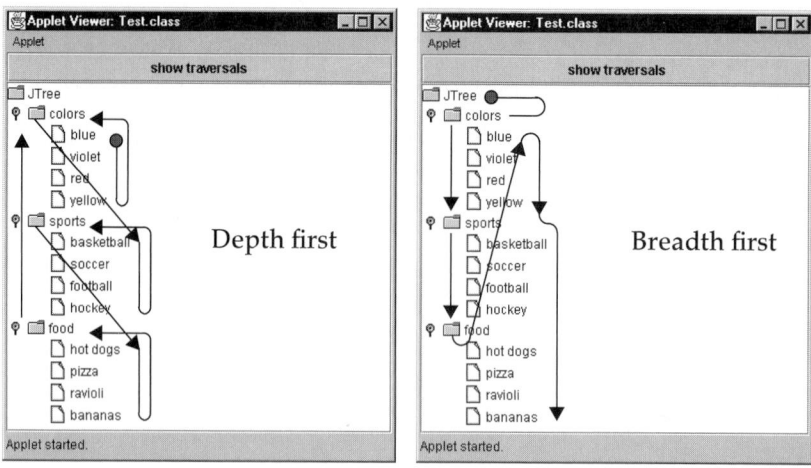

● = start of traversal

Figure 20-5 Tree Traversal Orders

3. See Gamma, Helm, Johnson, Vlissides. *Design Patterns*, p. 163. Addison-Wesley, 1995.
4. See Geary, David, *Graphic Java Mastering the JFC*, Volume I: AWT, p. 385. Sun Microsystems Press, Prentice Hall, 1998.

The applet listed in Example 20-3 prints the nodes obtained from invoking
`DefaultMutableTreeNode.depthFirstEnumeration()` and
`DefaultMutableTreeNode.breadthFirstEnumeration()` for a tree's root
node.

Example 20-3   Depth-First Vs. Breadth-First Traversal

```java
import java.awt.*;
import java.awt.event.*;
import javax.swing.*;
import javax.swing.tree.*;
import java.util.*;

public class Test extends JApplet {
    private JTree tree = new JTree();
    private JButton button = new JButton("show traversals");

    private DefaultMutableTreeNode root =
            (DefaultMutableTreeNode)tree.getModel().getRoot();

    public void init() {
        getContentPane().add(new JScrollPane(tree),
                        BorderLayout.CENTER);
        getContentPane().add(button, BorderLayout.NORTH);

        button.addActionListener(new ActionListener() {
            public void actionPerformed(ActionEvent e) {
                Enumeration df = root.depthFirstEnumeration();
                Enumeration bf = root.breadthFirstEnumeration();

                while(df.hasMoreElements()) {
                    System.out.println(
                                df.nextElement().toString());
                }

                System.out.println("");
                System.out.println("");

                while(bf.hasMoreElements()) {
                    System.out.println(
                                bf.nextElement().toString());
                }
            }
        });
    }
}
```

Extending DefaultMutableTreeNode

Perhaps the most natural application for a tree component is a file explorer that provides navigation of directories and files. The application shown in Figure 20-6 contains an instance of JTree that can be used as a file explorer.

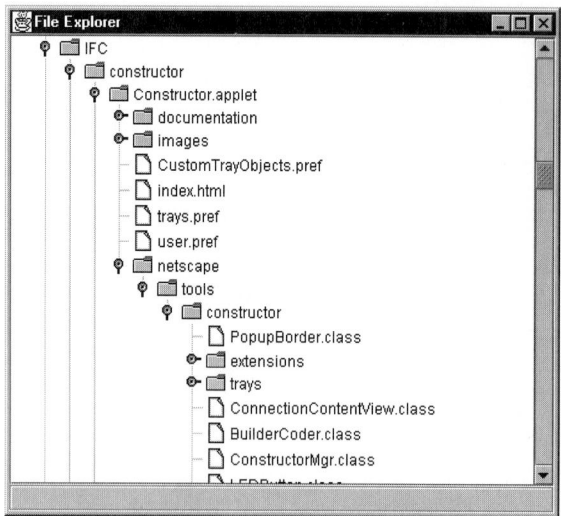

Figure 20-6 A JTree File Explorer

As a testament to the fundamentally sound design of Swing trees, the application shown in Figure 20-6 has a simple implementation. The tree contains custom nodes that are instances of a FileNode class that maintains a File instance as its user object.

The FileNode class is a simple extension of DefaultMutableTreeNode whose instances are constructed with a reference to a File. A file is specified as the node's user object by the FileNode constructor.

The `FileNode` class overrides `getAllowsChildren()` and `isLeaf()` from `DefaultMutableTreeNode`. A `FileNode` allows children if it represents a directory; likewise, a `FileNode` is a leaf if it does not represent a directory.

The `FileNode` class also provides convenience methods for obtaining a reference to the file the node represents, determining whether a node represents a directory, and for exploring a node's children. Notice that a directory is explored only once; a more industrial-strength implementation might include an option to force a directory to explore its contents even after it has been explored for the first time.

The `FileNode` class also overrides `toString()` to return the last component of the path represented by the node's file; see "Tree Paths" on page 1303 or more information on tree paths.

```java
class FileNode extends DefaultMutableTreeNode {
    private boolean explored = false;

    public FileNode(File file) {
        setUserObject(file);
    }
    public boolean getAllowsChildren() { return isDirectory(); }
    public boolean isLeaf() { return !isDirectory(); }
    public File getFile(){ return (File)getUserObject(); }

    public boolean isExplored() { return explored; }

    public boolean isDirectory() {
        File file = (File)getUserObject();
        return file.isDirectory();
    }
    public String toString() {
        File file = getFile();
        String filename = file.toString();
        int index = filename.lastIndexOf("\\");

        return (index != -1 && index != filename.length()-1) ?
                        filename.substring(index+1) :
                        filename;
    }
    public void explore() {
        if(!isDirectory())
            return;
```

```
        if(!isExplored) {
            File file = getFile();
            File[] children = file.listFiles();

            for(int i=0; i < children.length; ++i)
                add(new FileNode(children[i]));

            explored = true;
        }
    }
}
```

Once the `FileNode` class has been implemented, all that is left is to create an initial root node representing the drive to explore. The node is subsequently specified as the tree's root node by instantiating an instance of `DefaultTreeModel` that is specified as the tree's model.

A tree expansion listener—see "Tree Expansion Events" on page 1381 for more information concerning `TreeExpansionListener`—is added to the tree so that unexplored nodes are explored when they are expanded.

```
    . . .
    public class Test extends JFrame {
        public Test() {
            final JTree tree = new JTree(createTreeModel());
            JScrollPane scrollPane = new JScrollPane(tree);

            getContentPane().add(scrollPane, BorderLayout.CENTER);
            . . .

            tree.addTreeExpansionListener(new TreeExpansionListener(){
                public void treeCollapsed(TreeExpansionEvent e) {
                    // must implement because Swing does not provide
                    // event adapters like the AWT
                }
                public void treeExpanded(TreeExpansionEvent e) {
                    TreePath path = e.getPath();
                    FileNode node = (FileNode)
                                    path.getLastPathComponent();
```

```
            if( ! node.isExplored()) {
                DefaultTreeModel model =
                        (DefaultTreeModel)tree.getModel();
                ...
                node.explore();
                model.nodeStructureChanged(node);
                ...
            }
        }
        ...
    });
}
private DefaultTreeModel createTreeModel() {
    File root = new File("E:/");
    FileNode rootNode = new FileNode(root), node;

    rootNode.explore();
    return new DefaultTreeModel(rootNode);
}
}
```

The expansion listener obtains the node being expanded by obtaining the tree path associated with the expansion event. The `FileNode` instance is subsequently extracted from the tree path with the `TreePath.getLastPathComponent` method.

After a node has been explored, a call is made to the tree model's `nodeStructureChanged` method, which fires an event indicating that child nodes have been added or removed from the node. See "Tree Events" on page 1369 or more information concerning tree events.

An Aside

The file explorer shown in Figure 20-6 has a feature that was not discussed in the previous section. While a directory is being explored, the application's status area is updated with the string "exploring …", as shown in Figure 20-7.

Typically, the exploration happens so fast that the string will not be seen if it is only displayed for the duration of the exploration. As a result, a separate thread is created by the tree's expansion listener to clear the status area after a delay of 450 milliseconds.

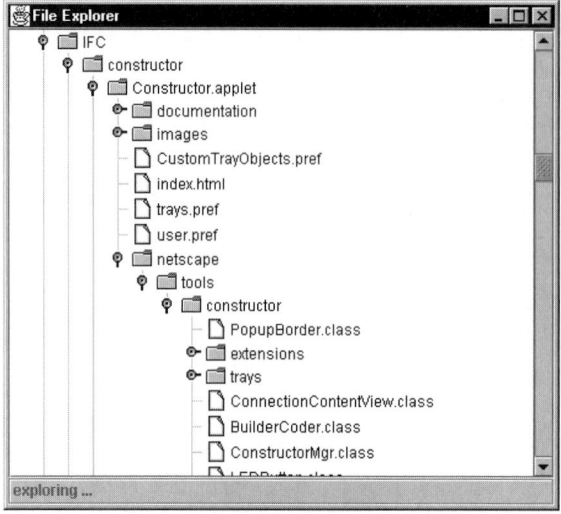

Figure 20-7 A JTree File Explorer

```
...
tree.addTreeExpansionListener(new TreeExpansionListener(){
    public void treeCollapsed(TreeExpansionEvent e) {
    }
    public void treeExpanded(TreeExpansionEvent e) {
        UpdateStatus updateThread;
        TreePath path = e.getPath();
        FileNode node = (FileNode)
                        path.getLastPathComponent();

        if( ! node.isExplored()) {
            ...
            GJApp.updateStatus("exploring ...");

            UpdateStatus us = new UpdateStatus();
            us.start();

            node.explore();
            ...
        }
    }
    ...
```

Before a node is explored, the application's status area is updated with the "exploring ..." string, and an UpdateStatus thread is created and started.

.

```
...
class UpdateStatus extends Thread {
    public void run() {
        try { Thread.currentThread().sleep(450); }
        catch(InterruptedException e) { }

        SwingUtilities.invokeLater(new Runnable() {
            public void run() {
                GJApp.updateStatus(" ");
            }
        });
    }
}
});
}
...
```

The run method of the UpdateStatus thread sleeps for 450 milliseconds and then calls SwingUtilities.invokeLater() to place a Runnable on the event dispatch thread that clears the application's status area.[5] See "Swing and Threads" on page 57 for a discussion of Swing multithreading and the SwingUtilities.invokeLater method.

As a result of using an instance of UpdateStatus to clear the application's status area, the "exploring..." string is displayed for approximately 1/2 second every time a node is explored.

The application shown in Figure 20-6 and Figure 20-7 is listed in its entirety in Example 20-4.

Example 20-4 A JTree File Explorer

```
import javax.swing.*;
import javax.swing.event.*;
import javax.swing.tree.*;
import java.awt.*;
import java.awt.event.*;
import java.io.File;
import java.util.EventObject;

public class Test extends JFrame {
    public Test() {
        final JTree tree = new JTree(createTreeModel());
        JScrollPane scrollPane = new JScrollPane(tree);

        getContentPane().add(scrollPane, BorderLayout.CENTER);
```

5. The UpdateStatus thread is not the event dispatch thread and therefore cannot safely update Swing components directly.

```
            getContentPane().add(GJApp.getStatusArea(),
                                      BorderLayout.SOUTH);

        tree.addTreeExpansionListener(new TreeExpansionListener(){
            public void treeCollapsed(TreeExpansionEvent e) {
            }
            public void treeExpanded(TreeExpansionEvent e) {
                UpdateStatus updateThread;
                TreePath path = e.getPath();
                FileNode node = (FileNode)
                                path.getLastPathComponent();

                if( ! node.isExplored()) {
                    DefaultTreeModel model =
                            (DefaultTreeModel)tree.getModel();

                    GJApp.updateStatus("exploring ...");

                    UpdateStatus us = new UpdateStatus();
                    us.start();

                    node.explore();
                    model.nodeStructureChanged(node);

                }
            }
            class UpdateStatus extends Thread {
                public void run() {
                    try { Thread.currentThread().sleep(450); }
                    catch(InterruptedException e) { }

                    SwingUtilities.invokeLater(new Runnable() {
                        public void run() {
                            GJApp.updateStatus(" ");
                        }
                    });
                }
            }
        });
    }
    private DefaultTreeModel createTreeModel() {
        File root = new File("E:/");
        FileNode rootNode = new FileNode(root), node;

        rootNode.explore();
        return new DefaultTreeModel(rootNode);
    }
    public static void main(String args[]) {
        GJApp.launch(new Test(),"JTree File Explorer",
                            300,300,450,400);
    }
}
class FileNode extends DefaultMutableTreeNode {
```

```
    private boolean explored = false;

    public FileNode(File file) {
        setUserObject(file);
    }
    public boolean getAllowsChildren() { return isDirectory(); }
    public boolean isLeaf() { return !isDirectory(); }
    public File getFile(){ return (File)getUserObject(); }

    public boolean isExplored() { return explored; }

    public boolean isDirectory() {
        File file = getFile();
        return file.isDirectory();
    }
    public String toString() {
        File file = (File)getUserObject();
        String filename = file.toString();
        int index = filename.lastIndexOf("\\");

        return (index != -1 && index != filename.length()-1) ?
                         filename.substring(index+1) :
                         filename;
    }
    public void explore() {
        if(!isExplored()) {
            File file = getFile();
            File[] children = file.listFiles();

            for(int i=0; i < children.length; ++i)
                add(new FileNode(children[i]));

            explored = true;
        }
    }
}
```

Tree Paths

Tree nodes are often quantified by tree paths; for example, when a tree node is selected, the selection is identified by an instance of `TreePath`. The `TreePath` class identifies a set of nodes that form a path from one node to another.

Figure 20-8 shows an application with a tree equipped with a selection listener that displays the path of the most recently selected node in the application's status area.

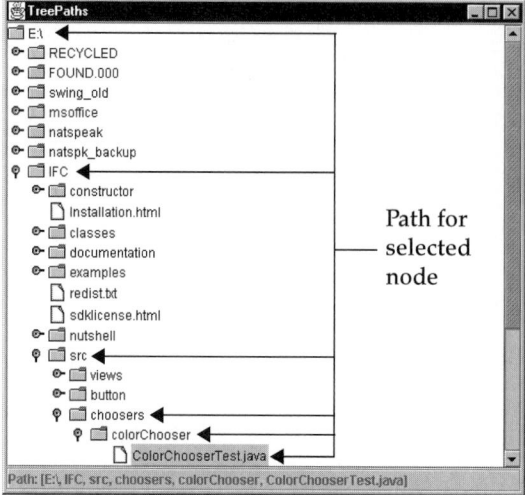

Figure 20-8 Tree Paths

A selection listener that obtains the path associated with the last selected node is added to the tree. The tree path is subsequently used to update the application's status area.

```
...
tree.addTreeSelectionListener(new TreeSelectionListener() {
    public void valueChanged(TreeSelectionEvent e) {
        TreePath path = e.getNewLeadSelectionPath();

        if(path != null)
            GJApp.showStatus("Path: " + path.toString());
    }
});
...
```

The application shown in Figure 20-8 is not listed because, with the addition of the tree selection listener discussed above, the application is identical to the application listed in Example 20-4 on page 1301. The application shown in Figure 20-8 is contained on the CD in the back of the book.

The `TreePath` class is a simple extension of `Object` that maintains an array of objects representing a path. The `TreePath` class is summarized in Class Summary 20-1.

Class Summary 20-1   TreePath

Extends: java.lang.Object

Implements: java.io.Serializable

Constructors

---

protected <u>TreePath</u>()
public <u>TreePath</u>(Object singlePath)
public <u>TreePath</u>(Object[] pathObjects)
protected <u>TreePath</u>(Object[] pathObjects, int length)
protected <u>TreePath</u>(TreePath parentPath, Object lastPathObject)

Most tree paths are instantiated by the Swing classes, and therefore developers will rarely construct instances of `TreePath`. The `TreePath` class provides five constructors that specify a path in one form or another.

The no-argument constructor is provided primarily for `TreePath` extensions that wish to store path objects differently than they are stored in the `TreePath` class.

All of the `TreePath` constructors will throw exceptions if they are passed `null` references or empty arrays.

Methods

---

public Object <u>getLastPathComponent</u>()
public TreePath <u>getParentPath</u>()
public Object[] <u>getPath</u>()
public Object <u>getPathComponent</u>(int index)
public int <u>getPathCount</u>()
public TreePath <u>pathByAddingChild</u>(Object child)

public boolean <u>equals</u>(Object)

public boolean <u>isDescendant</u>(TreePath)

public int <u>hashCode</u>()
public String <u>toString</u>()

The first group of methods listed above all return information about a tree path. The most frequently used method is undoubtedly the `getLastPathComponent` method, which returns a reference to the last object in the path. The `getLastPathComponent` method was used in the application shown in Figure 20-8 on page 1304.

The second group of methods listed above are convenience methods for determining whether a tree path is equal to an object (presumably another tree path), and whether a given tree path is a descendant of another tree path. If each object in a path is equal to every corresponding object in another path, the paths are equal.

The last two methods listed above are overridden from `Object`. The hash code for a `TreePath` is equal to the hash code of the last object in the path.

The applet shown in Figure 20-9 contains a tree equipped with a selection listener that prints information obtained with a number of `TreePath` methods.

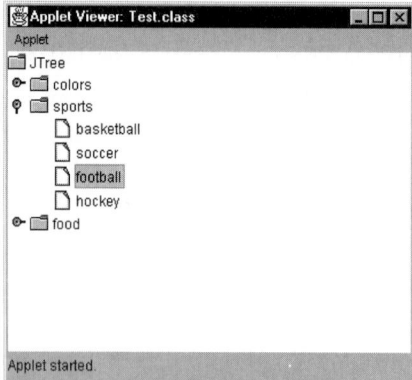

Figure 20-9 Using Tree Paths

The applet shown in Figure 20-9 is listed in Example 20-5.

Example 20-5 Using Tree Paths

```java
import javax.swing.*;
import javax.swing.event.*;
import javax.swing.tree.*;
import java.awt.*;

public class Test extends JApplet {
    JTree tree = new JTree();
    DefaultTreeModel model = (DefaultTreeModel)tree.getModel();
    TreeSelectionModel selectionModel = tree.getSelectionModel();

    public void init() {
        getContentPane().add(tree, BorderLayout.CENTER);

        tree.addTreeSelectionListener(
                            new TreeSelectionListener() {
            public void valueChanged(TreeSelectionEvent e) {
                TreePath path = e.getNewLeadSelectionPath();

                if(path == null)
                    System.out.println("Selection Cleared");
                else {
                    TreePath parentPath = path.getParentPath();
                    Object
                        lastNode = path.getLastPathComponent(),
                        firstNode= path.getPathComponent(0);

                    System.out.println("Path: " + path +
                                " has " +
                                path.getPathCount() +
                                " nodes");
                    System.out.println("Last Path Component: " +
                                lastNode.toString());
                    System.out.println("First Path Component: " +
                                firstNode.toString());
                    System.out.println("Parent Path: " +
                                parentPath);

                    // the following if statement is always true

                    if(parentPath.isDescendant(path)) {
                        System.out.println(parentPath +
                                " is a descendant of " + path);
                    }
                    DefaultMutableTreeNode last =
                            (DefaultMutableTreeNode)lastNode;
                    DefaultMutableTreeNode first =
                            (DefaultMutableTreeNode)lastNode;

                    if(first.isNodeDescendant(last)) {
                        System.out.println(
```

```
                              "last is descendant of first");
                    }
                    System.out.println("");
              }


           }
       });
     }
   }
```

The selection listener obtains a reference to the path associated with the selection by invocation of `TreeSelectionEvent.getNewLeadSelectionPath()`. The path is subsequently used to obtain references to the parent path, last path component, and path count. The parent path determines whether the new lead selection path is a descendant of the parent path (which it always is).

For the selection shown in Figure 20-9, the following information is printed:

```
Path: [JTree, sports, football] has 3 nodes
Last Path Component: football
First Path Component: JTree
Parent Path: [JTree, sports]
[JTree, sports] is a descendant of [JTree, sports, football]
last is descendant of first
```

Tree Models

Compared to models for other Swing components, tree models have a somewhat diminished role because they do not implement the manner in which tree data is stored. Because tree nodes have a parent and child nodes, they are linked together in much the same manner as nodes in a linked list.[6] As a result, tree models only keep track of a tree's root node.

Tree models are defined by the `TreeModel` interface, which is implemented by the `DefaultTreeModel` class. The `TreeModel` interface is summarized in Interface Summary 20-3.

---

6.   When `DefaultTreeModel` is used.

Interface Summary 20-3   TreeModel

TreeModelListener Registration

---

public abstract void <u>addTreeModelListener</u>(TreeModelListener)
public abstract void <u>removeTreeModelListener</u>(TreeModelListener)

Tree models fire tree model events when nodes are inserted, removed, or changed. The methods listed above register tree model listeners.

Root Node Accessor / Child Accessors

---

public abstract Object <u>getRoot</u>()

public abstract Object <u>getChild</u>(Object parent, int index)
public abstract int <u>getChildCount</u>(Object parent)
public abstract int <u>getIndexOfChild</u>(Object parent, Object child)

The `TreeModel` interface defines an accessor for a tree's root node. The second group of methods listed above are accessors for child nodes, node count, and an index of a particular child node. It should be noted that the same information can be obtained directly from the nodes themselves; in fact, `DefaultTreeModel` simply delegates to the parent node passed to the methods.

Leaf Identification / Node Value Changed

---

public abstract boolean <u>isLeaf</u>(Object node)
public abstract void <u>valueForPathChanged</u>(TreePath, Object node)

The `TreeModel` interface defines an `isLeaf` method for determining whether a particular node is a leaf. Tree nodes also provide an `isLeaf` method; however, default tree models may determine whether a node is a leaf depending upon whether the node allows children.

The `valueForPathChanged` method sets the user object for the last node in the path and fires a tree model event indicating that the node has changed.

DefaultTreeModel

The `DefaultTreeModel` class is Swing's lone implementation of the `TreeModel` interface. `DefaultTreeModel` implements the methods defined by the `TreeModel` interface, in addition to providing a number of additional methods.

A class diagram for the `DefaultTreeModel` class is shown in Figure 20-10.

Figure 20-10 DefaultTreeModel Class Diagram

DefaultTreeModel extends Object and implements the TreeModel and Serializable interfaces. An instance of EventListenerList maintains a list of tree model listeners, and a TreeNode reference representing the root of the tree is also maintained by the listener list.

Recall that the TreeModel interface defines an isLeaf method that is used to determine if a node is a leaf or a folder. DefaultTreeModel implements the isLeaf method as shown below.

```
// from DefaultTreeModel.java ...

public boolean isLeaf(Object node) {
    if(asksAllowsChildren)
        return !((TreeNode)node).getAllowsChildren();
    return ((TreeNode)node).isLeaf();
}
```

If the model's asksAllowsChildren property is true, a node's leaf status is determined depending upon whether the node allows children. Otherwise, a node is a leaf if its isLeaf method returns true. If asksAllowsChildren is false, a node is qualified as a folder if it returns true from its isLeaf method.

The DefaultTreeModel class is summarized in Class Summary 20-2.

Class Summary 20-2   DefaultTreeModel

Extends: Object

Implements: TreeModel, Serializable

Constructors

---

public <u>DefaultTreeModel</u>(TreeNode root)
public <u>DefaultTreeModel</u>(TreeNode root, boolean asksAllowsChildren)

The `DefaultTreeModel` class provides two constructors, both of which are passed the tree's root node. Whether or not the model determines node leaf status by asking whether the node allows children is controlled by the `asksAllowsChildren` `boolean` variable.

Notice that `DefaultTreeModel` does not provided a no-argument constructor, which means that a root node must be specified at the time of construction.

Methods

TreeModel Methods

---

public void <u>addTreeModelListener</u>(TreeModelListener)
public void <u>removeTreeModelListener</u>(TreeModelListener)

public Object <u>getChild</u>(Object parent, int index)
public int <u>getChildCount</u>(Object parent)
public int <u>getIndexOfChild</u>(Object parent, Object child)

public void <u>getRoot</u>(TreeNode)
public void <u>valueForPathChanged</u>(TreePath, Object)

The methods listed above are defined by the `TreeModel` interface. The second group of methods delegate directly to the parent node passed to the methods.

Event Firing

---

protected void <u>fireTreeNodesChanged</u>(Object, Object[], int[], Object[])
protected void <u>fireTreeNodesInserted</u>(Object, Object[], int[], Object[])
protected void <u>fireTreeNodesRemoved</u>(Object, Object[], int[], Object[])
protected void <u>fireTreeStructureChanged</u>(Object, Object[], int[], Object[])

Like many Swing models, `DefaultTreeModel` provides a set of methods for firing events. `DefaultTreeModel` extensions must fire appropriate events when nodes are changed, inserted, or removed or when the structure of the tree is modified.

The methods listed above can be used by `DefaultTreeModel` extensions to fire events to registered tree model listeners. The methods are also used internally by `DefaultTreeModel`.

Setting Root / Paths to Root / Inserting and Removing Nodes

---

public Object <u>setRoot</u>()

public TreeNode[] <u>getPathToRoot</u>(TreeNode)
protected TreeNode[] <u>getPathToRoot</u>(TreeNode, int depth)

public void <u>insertNodeInto</u>(MutableTreeNode, MutableTreeNode, int index)
public void <u>removeNodeFromParent</u>(MutableTreeNode)

`DefaultTreeModel` provides an accessor for the root node, in addition to accessors for arrays of `TreeNodes` representing a path from the root node to a given node. The `getPathToRoot` method that is passed an `integer` value is called recursively and is not meant to be called outside of the `DefaultTreeModel` class (or its extensions).

The last two methods listed above can be used to insert a child node into a parent or to remove a child node from a parent. The methods fire tree model events and therefore are preferable to using similar `DefaultMutableTreeNode` methods.

Notification Methods

---

public void <u>nodeChanged</u>(TreeNode)
public void <u>nodeStructureChanged</u>(TreeNode)
public void <u>nodesChanged</u>(TreeNode, int[])
public void <u>nodesWereInserted</u>(TreeNode, int[])
public void <u>nodesWereRemoved</u>(TreeNode, int[], Object[])

The methods listed above create appropriate events and fire them to registered tree model listeners. `DefaultTreeModel` uses the methods internally to fire events; for example, `DefaultTreeModel.insertNodeInto()` invokes `nodesWereInserted()` after the nodes have been inserted.

Reloading / Asks Allows Children / Is Leaf

---

public void <u>reload</u>()
public void <u>reload</u>(TreeNode)

public void <u>setAsksAllowsChildren</u>(boolean)
public boolean <u>asksAllowsChildren</u>()

public boolean <u>isLeaf</u>(Object)

The `reload` methods fire events indicating that descendants of a given node have been modified. The no-argument reload method invokes `reload(TreeNode)` with the root node, indicating that all of the nodes in the tree may have been modified.

Invoking `reload()` will cause all expanded folders to be collapsed, and the entire tree will be redrawn.

The second group of methods listed above are accessors for the `asksAllowsChildren` property maintained by `DefaultTreeModel`. If `setAsksAllowsChildren(true)` is invoked, `DefaultTreeModel.isLeaf()` will determine whether a node is a leaf according to whether the node allows children. If the `asksAllowsChildren` property is `false`, which is the default, `DefaultTreeModel.isLeaf()` simply returns the value returned from the node's `isLeaf` method.

The application shown in Figure 20-11 illustrates adding and removing nodes to/from a tree model. Two buttons are provided for adding and removing nodes.

An action listener for the "Add node" button displays a dialog that prompts for a node name, as can be seen from the upper-left picture in Figure 20-11. The newly created node is added below the currently selected node.

A tree model listener added to the tree's model displays a dialog that communicates which node was added or removed, as illustrated by the upper-right and lower-left pictures in Figure 20-11.

A tree selection listener is added to the tree to set the enabled state of the buttons. The buttons are enabled only when a node in the tree is selected. If no nodes are selected, the buttons are disabled, as can be seen from the lower-right picture in Figure 20-11.

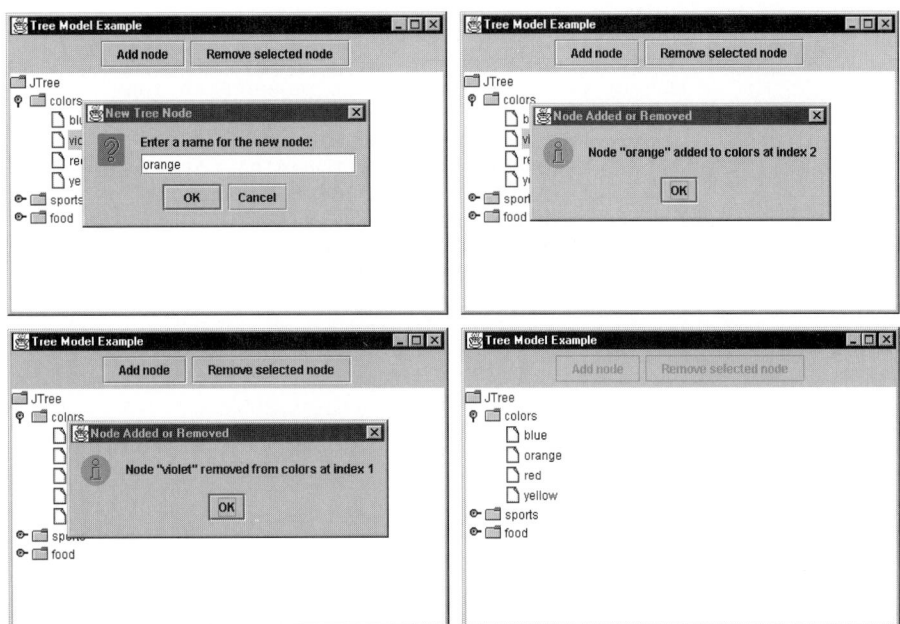

Figure 20-11 Inserting and Removing Tree Nodes

The application creates an instance of `JTree` and obtains a reference to the tree's model. Notice that the tree model listener must implement all of the methods defined by the `TreeModelListener` interface because the 1.1 FCS version of Swing does not provide event adapter classes as does the AWT.

```
public class Test extends JFrame {
    JTree tree = new JTree();
    DefaultTreeModel model = (DefaultTreeModel)tree.getModel();

    ...

    public Test() {
        ...
        model.addTreeModelListener(new TreeModelListener() {
            public void treeNodesInserted(TreeModelEvent e) {
                showInsertionOrRemoval(e, " added to ");
            }
            public void treeNodesRemoved(TreeModelEvent e) {
                showInsertionOrRemoval(e, " removed from ");
            }
            private void showInsertionOrRemoval(TreeModelEvent e,
                                        String s) {
```

```
                      Object[] parentPath = e.getPath();
                      int[] indexes = e.getChildIndices();
                      Object[] children = e.getChildren();
                      Object parent = parentPath[parentPath.length-1];

                      JOptionPane.showMessageDialog(Test.this,
                              "Node \"" + children[0].toString() +
                              "\"" + s + parent.toString() +
                              " at index " + indexes[0],
                              "Node Added or Removed",
                              JOptionPane.INFORMATION_MESSAGE);
                  }
                  public void treeNodesChanged(TreeModelEvent e) {}
                  public void treeStructureChanged(TreeModelEvent e) {}
              });
          }
      }
      ...
```

The application's buttons are contained in an instance of `ControlPanel`, which extends the `JPanel` class. An action listener added to the "Add node" button obtains a reference to the selected node's parent and calculates the index after the selected node. An input dialog that prompts for a node name is subsequently displayed. The node name is then used to create an instance of `DefaultMutableTreeNode`, which is added to the selected node's parent at the calculated index.

```
      class ControlPanel extends JPanel {
          public ControlPanel() {
              ...
              addButton.addActionListener(new ActionListener() {
                  public void actionPerformed(ActionEvent e) {
                      TreePath path =
                              selectionModel.getSelectionPath();

                      MutableTreeNode parent, node =
                      (MutableTreeNode)path.getLastPathComponent();

                      if(path.getPathCount() > 1)
                          parent = (MutableTreeNode)node.getParent();
                      else
                          parent = (MutableTreeNode)node; // root node

                      int index = parent.getIndex(node) + 1;

                      String s = JOptionPane.showInputDialog(
                              Test.this,
                              "Enter a name for the new node:",
```

```
                    "New Tree Node",
                    JOptionPane.QUESTION_MESSAGE);

            MutableTreeNode newNode =
                    new DefaultMutableTreeNode(s);

            model.insertNodeInto(newNode, parent, index);
          }
        });
        ...
```

An action listener is also added to the Remove selected node button; the
listener obtains a reference to the selected node and invokes the model's
removeNodeFromParent() method.

```
        ...
        removeButton.addActionListener(new ActionListener() {
          public void actionPerformed(ActionEvent e) {
            TreePath path =
                    selectionModel.getSelectionPath();

            if(path.getPathCount() == 1) { // root node
                JOptionPane.showMessageDialog(
                        ControlPanel.this,
                        "Can't remove root node!");
                return;
            }

            MutableTreeNode node =
              (MutableTreeNode)path.getLastPathComponent();

            model.removeNodeFromParent(node);
          }
        });
      }
    }
```

The application shown in Figure 20-11 is listed in its entirety in Example 20-6.

Example 20-6 Adding and Removing Nodes

```
import javax.swing.*;
import javax.swing.event.*;
import javax.swing.tree.*;
import java.awt.*;
import java.awt.event.*;

public class Test extends JFrame {
    JTree tree = new JTree();
    DefaultTreeModel model = (DefaultTreeModel)tree.getModel();
```

```
TreeSelectionModel selectionModel = tree.getSelectionModel();

JButton removeButton = new JButton("Remove selected node");
JButton addButton = new JButton("Add node");

public Test() {
    Container contentPane = getContentPane();

    selectionModel.setSelectionMode(
                TreeSelectionModel.SINGLE_TREE_SELECTION);

    contentPane.add(new ControlPanel(), BorderLayout.NORTH);
    contentPane.add(tree, BorderLayout.CENTER);

    tree.addTreeSelectionListener(
                            new TreeSelectionListener() {
        public void valueChanged(TreeSelectionEvent e) {
            TreePath path = e.getNewLeadSelectionPath();
            boolean nodesAreSelected = (path != null);

            addButton.setEnabled(nodesAreSelected);
            removeButton.setEnabled(nodesAreSelected);
        }
    });
    model.addTreeModelListener(new TreeModelListener() {
        public void treeNodesInserted(TreeModelEvent e) {
            showInsertionOrRemoval(e, " added to ");
        }
        public void treeNodesRemoved(TreeModelEvent e) {
            showInsertionOrRemoval(e, " removed from ");
        }
        private void showInsertionOrRemoval(TreeModelEvent e,
                                            String s) {
            Object[] parentPath = e.getPath();
            int[] indexes = e.getChildIndices();
            Object[] children = e.getChildren();
            Object parent = parentPath[parentPath.length-1];

            JOptionPane.showMessageDialog(Test.this,
                    "Node \"" + children[0].toString() +
                    "\"" + s + parent.toString() +
                    " at index " + indexes[0],
                    "Node Added or Removed",
                    JOptionPane.INFORMATION_MESSAGE);
        }
        public void treeNodesChanged(TreeModelEvent e) {}
        public void treeStructureChanged(TreeModelEvent e) {}
    });
}
class ControlPanel extends JPanel {
    public ControlPanel() {
        addButton.setEnabled(false);
        removeButton.setEnabled(false);
```

```
        add(addButton);
        add(removeButton);

        addButton.addActionListener(new ActionListener() {
            public void actionPerformed(ActionEvent e) {
                TreePath path =
                        selectionModel.getSelectionPath();

                MutableTreeNode parent, node =
                (MutableTreeNode)path.getLastPathComponent();

                if(path.getPathCount() > 1)
                    parent = (MutableTreeNode)node.getParent();
                else
                    parent = (MutableTreeNode)node;

                int index = parent.getIndex(node) + 1;

                String s = JOptionPane.showInputDialog(
                        Test.this,
                        "Enter a name for the new node:",
                        "New Tree Node",
                        JOptionPane.QUESTION_MESSAGE);

                MutableTreeNode newNode =
                        new DefaultMutableTreeNode(s);

                model.insertNodeInto(newNode, parent, index);
            }
        });
        removeButton.addActionListener(new ActionListener() {
            public void actionPerformed(ActionEvent e) {
                TreePath path =
                        selectionModel.getSelectionPath();

                if(path.getPathCount() == 1) {
                    JOptionPane.showMessageDialog(
                            ControlPanel.this,
                            "Can't remove root node!");
                    return;
                }

                MutableTreeNode node =
                  (MutableTreeNode)path.getLastPathComponent();

                model.removeNodeFromParent(node);
            }
        });
    }
}
public static void main(String args[]) {
    GraphicJavaApplication.launch(new Test(),
```

```
                          "Tree Model Example",300,300,450,300);
      }
   }
   class GraphicJavaApplication extends WindowAdapter {
      public static void launch(final JFrame f, String title,
                                final int x, final int y,
                                final int w, int h) {
         f.setTitle(title);
         f.setBounds(x,y,w,h);
         f.setVisible(true);

         f.setDefaultCloseOperation(
                     WindowConstants.DISPOSE_ON_CLOSE);

         f.addWindowListener(new WindowAdapter() {
            public void windowClosed(WindowEvent e) {
               System.exit(0);
            }
         });
      }
   }
```

Swing Tip ...

Leaf or Folder?

Two properties come into play when a node's leaf status is determined: the node's allowsChildren property and the tree model's asksAllowsChildren property.

If a tree model's asksAllowsChildren property is true, the model determines whether a node is a leaf by the node's allowsChildren property; if a node allows children, it is a folder, whereas a node that does not allow children is a leaf. If a tree model's asksAllowsChildren property is false, the model uses a node's isLeaf property to determine if a node is a leaf.

Notice that the mechanism for determining a node's leaf status provides two degrees of freedom; in other words, whether an individual node is a leaf or a folder can vary depending upon the tree model with which it is associated.

Tree Selection

Tree selection is defined by the `TreeSelectionModel` interface, which is summarized in Interface Summary 20-4.

Interface Summary 20-4   TreeSelectionModel

Constants

---

public static final int <u>CONTIGUOUS TREE SELECTION</u>
public static final int <u>DISCONTIGUOUS TREE SELECTION</u>
public static final int <u>SINGLE TREE SELECTION</u>

The constants listed above represent tree selection modes. Contiguous selection allows a single set of contiguous nodes to be selected at any given time. Discontinuous selection allows more than one contiguous set of nodes to be selected, and single selection restricts selection to a single node.

The default tree selection mode is `DISCONTIGUOUS_TREE_SELECTION`.

Methods

Selection Mode

---

public abstract int <u>getSelectionMode</u>()
public abstract void <u>setSelectionMode</u>(int)

The methods listed above are accessors for tree selection modes. The `setSelectionMode` method must be passed one of constants listed above.

Listeners

---

public abstract void <u>addPropertyChangeListener</u>(PropertyChangeListener)
public abstract void <u>addTreeSelectionListener</u>(TreeSelectionListener)

public abstract void <u>removePropertyChangeListener</u>(PropertyChangeListener)
public abstract void <u>removeTreeSelectionListener</u>(TreeSelectionListener)

Tree selection models fire property change and tree selection events. The methods listed above allow listeners to be registered with the selection model.

Tree selection events are discussed in "Tree Selection Events" on page 1374.

Selection Paths

---

public abstract void <u>addSelectionPath</u>(TreePath)
public abstract void <u>addSelectionPaths</u>(TreePath[])

public abstract void <u>setSelectionPath</u>(TreePath)
public abstract void <u>setSelectionPaths</u>(TreePath[])

public abstract void <u>removeSelectionPath</u>(TreePath)
public abstract void <u>removeSelectionPaths</u>(TreePath[])

public abstract TreePath <u>getSelectionMode</u>()
public abstract TreePath[] <u>getSelectionPaths</u>()

public abstract TreePath <u>getLeadSelectionPath</u>()
public abstract boolean <u>isPathSelected</u>(TreePath)

Tree selections are specified in terms of an array of selection paths. The first three groups of methods listed above add, set, and remove selection paths. The methods are used internally by Swing to set tree selections and can also be used by developers to programmatically set selection.

The last two groups of methods obtain information about the current selection. The getSelectionPaths method returns an array of all of the current selection paths, whereas getSelectionPath() returns the first selection path. The

getLeadSelectionPath method returns the last path that was added to the selection, and isPathSelected() can determine whether a path is selected.

Selection Rows

---

public abstract int[] getSelectionRows()
public abstract int getLeadSelectionRow()
public abstract int getMaxSelectionRow()
public abstract int getMinSelectionRow()
public abstract boolean isRowSelected(int)

public abstract void setRowMapper(RowMapper)
public abstract RowMapper getRowMapper()

The first group of methods listed above returns information about selected rows. The getSelectionRows method returns an integer array representing all of the currently selected rows, whereas getLeadSelectionRow() returns the last row that was added to the selection. The getMaxSelectionRow and getMinSelectionRow methods return the maximum and minimum selected row indexes, respectively. The isRowSelected method can determine whether or not a row is selected.

Each tree selection model maintains a row mapper that translates paths into an array of integer values representing rows. The TreeSelectionModel interface provides accessors for its row mapper. In practice, the methods will rarely, if ever, be used or extended by developers.

Utility Methods

---

public abstract int getSelectionCount()
public abstract void clearSelection()
public abstract boolean isSelectionEmpty()
public abstract void resetRowSelection()

The TreeSelectionModel interface defines a handful of utility methods for obtaining the number of selected nodes, clearing selection, and determining whether any nodes are selected.

Because the selected rows can change when folders are expanded or collapsed, the `resetRowSelection` method calculates which rows are selected with the aid of the selection model's row mapper. The `resetRowSelection` method is called internally by Swing and should never need to be invoked directly by developers.

DefaultTreeSelectionModel

Swing provides a single implementation of the `TreeSelectionModel` interface in the form of the `DefaultTreeSelectionModel` class. A class diagram for `DefaultTreeSelectionModel` is shown in Figure 20-12.

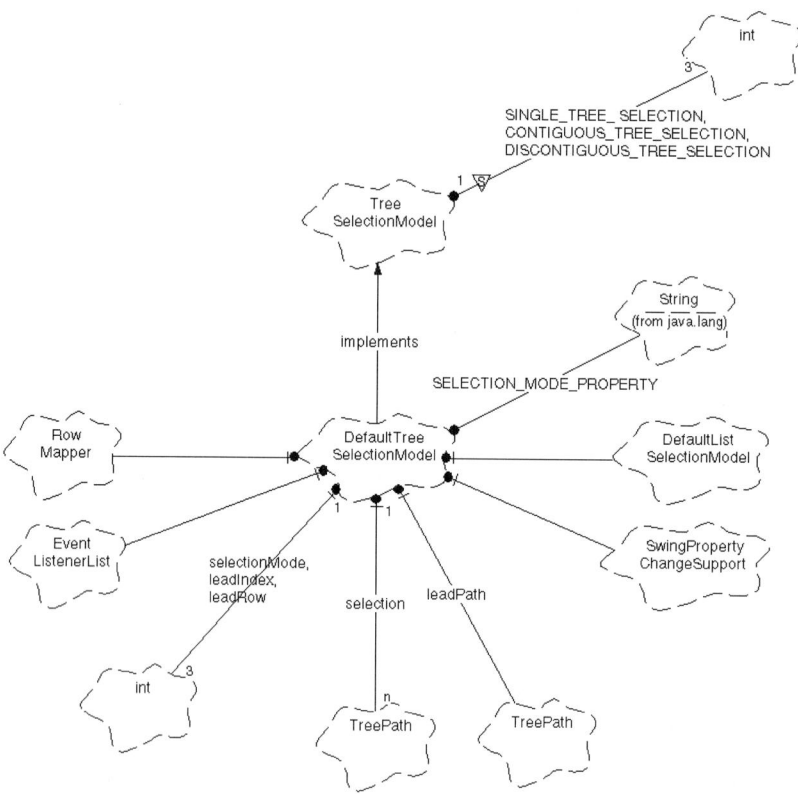

Figure 20-12 DefaultTreeSelectionModel Class Diagram

`DefaultTreeSelectionModel` implements the `TreeSelectionModel`
interface and maintains references to a list selection model, row mapper, and
event listener list. The `DefaultTreeSelectionModel` class also maintains an
array of `TreePaths` representing the current selection, and a `TreePath`
representing the lead path (meaning the last path added to the selection). Integer
values are also maintained for the selection mode and lead index and row.

The applet shown in Figure 20-13 illustrates tree selection modes and the use of a
tree selection model. The applet provides a combo box for selecting the tree
selection mode and a button for clearing the selection.

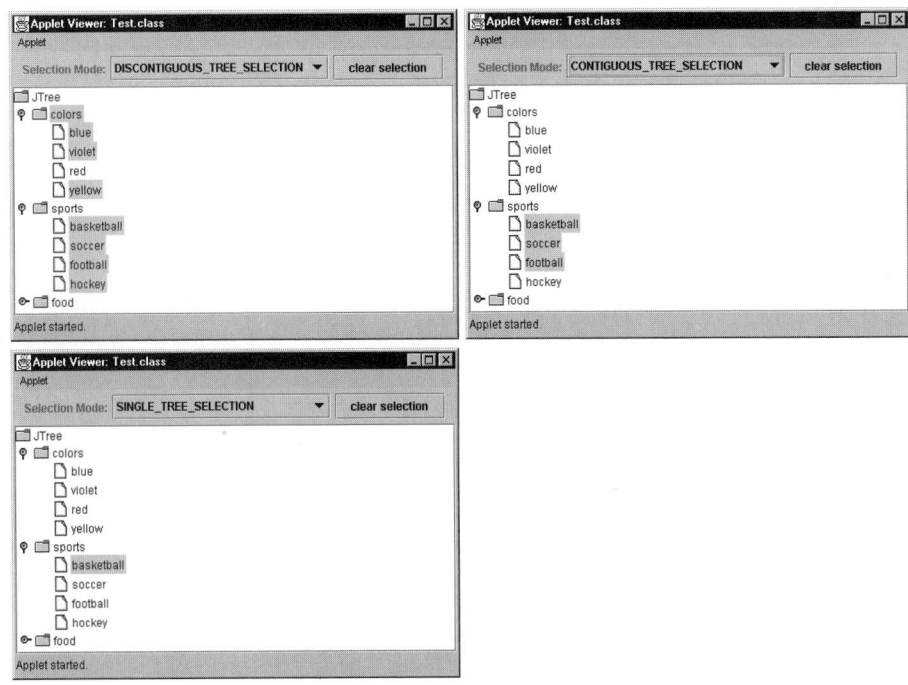

Figure 20-13 Tree Selection Modes

The applet shown in Figure 20-13 creates a tree with the `JTree` no-argument
constructor and obtains a reference to the tree's selection model. The applet also
defines arrays of strings and integers representing selection modes.

```
public class Test extends JApplet {
    JTree tree = new JTree();

    TreeSelectionModel selectionModel = tree.getSelectionModel();

    String modes[] = {
        "CONTIGUOUS_TREE_SELECTION",
        "DISCONTIGUOUS_TREE_SELECTION",
        "SINGLE_TREE_SELECTION"
    };
    int modeIds[] = {
        TreeSelectionModel.CONTIGUOUS_TREE_SELECTION,
        TreeSelectionModel.DISCONTIGUOUS_TREE_SELECTION,
        TreeSelectionModel.SINGLE_TREE_SELECTION,
    };
    ...
}
...
```

The combo box in the applet shown in Figure 20-13 is contained in an instance of ControlPanel, which extends JPanel. The ControlPanel constructor initializes the combo box depending upon the initial selection mode and adds an action listener to the combo box that updates the tree's selection mode.

```
...
class ControlPanel extends JPanel {
    JComboBox combo = new JComboBox();

    public ControlPanel() {
        for(int i=0; i < modes.length; ++i) {
            combo.addItem(modes[i]);
        }
        add(new JLabel("Selection Mode:"));
        add(combo);

        int initialMode = selectionModel.getSelectionMode();

        if(initialMode == modeIds[0])
            combo.setSelectedIndex(0);
        else if(initialMode == modeIds[1])
            combo.setSelectedIndex(1);
        else if(initialMode == modeIds[2])
            combo.setSelectedIndex(2);

        combo.addActionListener(new ActionListener() {
            public void actionPerformed(ActionEvent e) {
                int index = combo.getSelectedIndex();
                selectionModel.setSelectionMode(
                                    modeIds[index]);
            }
        });
        ...
```

An action listener is added to the clear selection button that invokes the
`clearSelection` method of the tree's selection model.

```
    ...
    button.addActionListener(new ActionListener() {
        public void actionPerformed(ActionEvent e) {
            selectionModel.clearSelection();
        }

    });

}
}
```

The applet shown in Figure 20-13 is listed in its entirety in Example 20-7.

Example 20-7 Tree Selection Modes

```
import javax.swing.*;
import javax.swing.tree.*;
import java.awt.*;
import java.awt.event.*;

public class Test extends JApplet {
    JTree tree = new JTree();

    TreeSelectionModel selectionModel = tree.getSelectionModel();

    String modes[] = {
        "CONTIGUOUS_TREE_SELECTION",
        "DISCONTIGUOUS_TREE_SELECTION",
        "SINGLE_TREE_SELECTION"
    };
    int modeIds[] = {
        TreeSelectionModel.CONTIGUOUS_TREE_SELECTION,
        TreeSelectionModel.DISCONTIGUOUS_TREE_SELECTION,
        TreeSelectionModel.SINGLE_TREE_SELECTION,
    };

    public void init() {
        Container contentPane = getContentPane();

        contentPane.add(new ControlPanel(), BorderLayout.NORTH);
        contentPane.add(new JScrollPane(tree),
                    BorderLayout.CENTER);
    }
    class ControlPanel extends JPanel {
        JComboBox combo = new JComboBox();
        JButton button = new JButton("clear selection");
```

```
public ControlPanel() {
    for(int i=0; i < modes.length; ++i) {
        combo.addItem(modes[i]);
    }
    add(new JLabel("Selection Mode:"));
    add(combo);
    add(button);

    int initialMode = selectionModel.getSelectionMode();

    if(initialMode == modeIds[0])
        combo.setSelectedIndex(0);
    else if(initialMode == modeIds[1])
        combo.setSelectedIndex(1);
    else if(initialMode == modeIds[2])
        combo.setSelectedIndex(2);

    combo.addActionListener(new ActionListener() {
        public void actionPerformed(ActionEvent e) {
            int index = combo.getSelectedIndex();
            selectionModel.setSelectionMode(
                                    modeIds[index]);
        }
    });
    button.addActionListener(new ActionListener() {
        public void actionPerformed(ActionEvent e) {
            selectionModel.clearSelection();
        }
    });
}
    }
}
```

Tree Cell Rendering

Like other Swing renderers, tree cell renderers are defined by an interface that defines a single method that returns a component. The `TreeCellRenderer` interface is summarized in Interface Summary 20-5.

Interface Summary 20-5   TreeCellRenderer

---

public abstract Component getTreeCellRendererComponent(JTree tree,
                                                        Object value,
                                                        boolean selected,
                                                        boolean expanded,
                                                        boolean leaf,
                                                        int row,
                                                        boolean hasFocus)

The component returned by getTreeCellRendererComponent is used like a rubber stamp to paint the component into tree nodes. The method is passed the tree and the value to be rendered, in addition to whether the cell is selected, expanded, is a leaf, and has focus. The node's row is also provided.

DefaultTreeCellRenderer

The swing.tree package provides a default renderer in the form of the DefaultTreeCellRenderer class. A class diagram for the DefaultTreeCellRenderer class is shown in Figure 20-14.

DefaultTreeCellRenderer extends JLabel and implements the TreeCellRenderer interface. DefaultTreeCellRenderer maintains three Icon references for leaf nodes and open/closed folder nodes. Colors for text, background, and the renderer's border are also maintained.

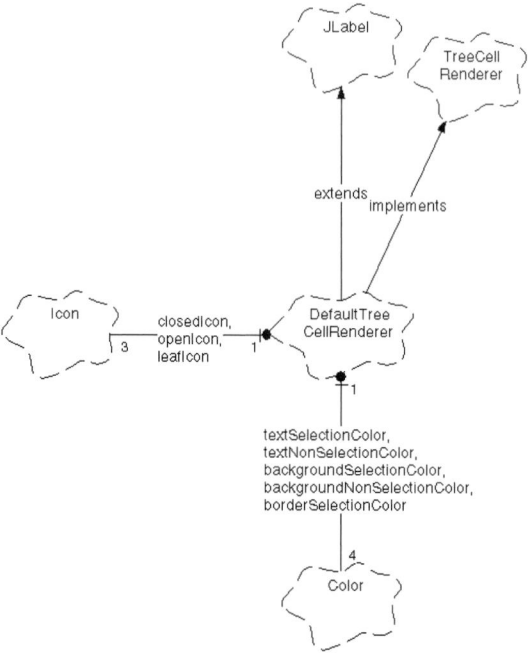

Figure 20-14   DefaultTreeCellRenderer Class Diagram

The `DefaultTreeCellRenderer` class is summarized in Class Summary 20-3.

Class Summary 20-3   DefaultTreeCellRenderer

Constructors

---

public <u>DefaultTreeCellRenderer</u>()

The only constructor provided by a `DefaultTreeCellRenderer` class is a no-argument constructor that sets the renderer's horizontal alignment to `JLabel.LEFT` and obtains icons and colors from the `UIManager` class.

Methods

Icons

---

public Icon getClosedIcon()
public Icon getLeafIcon()
public Icon getOpenIcon()

public void setClosedIcon(Icon)
public void setLeafIcon(Icon)
public void setOpenIcon(Icon)

public Icon getDefaultClosedIcon()
public Icon getDefaultLeafIcon()
public Icon getDefaultOpenIcon()

The methods listed above are accessors for a renderer's leaf and open and closed icons.

Due to a bug in Swing 1.1 FCS, the last three methods listed above return the renderer's current icons instead of defaults.

Colors and Font

---

public void setBackground(Color)
public void setBackgroundNonSelectionColor(Color)
public void setBackgroundSelectionColor(Color)
public void setBorderSelectionColor(Color)

public Color getBackgroundNonSelectionColor()
public Color getBackgroundSelectionColor()
public Color getBorderSelectionColor()

public void setTextNonSelectionColor(Color)
public void setTextSelectionColor(Color)

public Color getTextNonSelectionColor()
public Color getTextSelectionColor()

public void <u>setFont</u>(Font)

The methods listed above are simple accessors for a renderer's colors and fonts. The `setBackground` and `setFont` methods are overridden from the `JLabel` class to accept only the color or font, respectively, if the color or font is not a UI resource. See "UI Resources" on page 342 for more information concerning UI resources.

Painting/Preferred Size / Renderer Component

---

public Component <u>getTreeCellRendererComponent</u>(JTree, Object node,
                                 boolean selected, boolean expanded,
                                 boolean leaf, int row, boolean hasFocus)
public Dimension <u>getPreferredSize</u>()
public void <u>paint</u>(Graphics)

The `getTreeCellRendererComponent` method converts the value it is passed to a string, using the `JTree.convertValueToText` method, which simply returns `value.toString()`. If the value is an instance of `DefaultMutableTreeNode`, which is almost always the case, the `DefaultMutableTreeNode.toString` method returns the string representation of the node's user object. The string value is used to set a renderer's text (by invoking `JLabel.setText()`), and the renderer's foreground color and icon are set.

`DefaultTreeCellRenderer` overrides its `paint` method from `JLabel` to fill the background, based on selection, and to draw a focus border if the node being rendered has focus. The `paint` method subsequently calls `super.paint()`.

`DefaultTreeCellRenderer` also overrides `getPreferredSize()` to return a preferred size that is slightly wider than the preferred size of its superclass (`JLabel`).

Note: *The javadoc documentation for* `DefaultTreeCellRenderer.java` *incorrectly states that the preferred size for instances of* `DefaultTreeCellRenderer` *is slightly taller than the preferred size of the renderer's superclass.*

Using DefaultTreeCellRenderer

`DefaultTreeCellRenderer` can be used to customize the colors, icons, and font associated with tree nodes. For example, the applet shown in Figure 20-15 uses an instance of `DefaultTreeCellRenderer` to modify leaf, open and closed icons, and font.

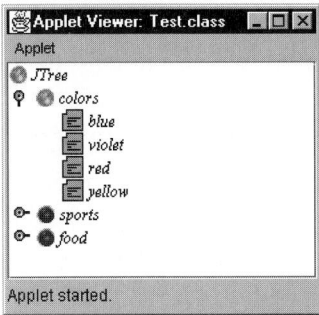

Figure 20-15 Using DefaultTreeCellRenderer

The applet shown in Figure 20-15 has a simple implementation and is listed in Example 20-8.

Example 20-8 Using DefaultTreeCellRenderer

```
import javax.swing.*;
import javax.swing.tree.*;
import java.awt.*;
import java.awt.event.*;

public class Test extends JApplet {
    static private Icon
                openFolder = new ImageIcon("button_lit.jpg"),
                closedFolder = new ImageIcon("button.jpg"),
                leafIcon = new ImageIcon("leaf.gif");

    public void init() {
        JTree tree = new JTree();
        JScrollPane scrollPane = new JScrollPane(tree);
        DefaultTreeCellRenderer renderer =
                        new DefaultTreeCellRenderer();

        renderer.setClosedIcon(closedFolder);
        renderer.setOpenIcon(openFolder);
```

```
renderer.setLeafIcon(leafIcon);
renderer.setFont(new Font("Serif", Font.ITALIC, 12));

tree.setCellRenderer(renderer);
tree.setEditable(true);
getContentPane().add(scrollPane);
    }
}
```

The applet creates an instance of `DefaultTreeCellRenderer` and sets icons and font, using `DefaultTreeCellRenderer` methods. Subsequently, the tree's renderer is set to the newly created renderer.

Icons and colors for all tree renderers can be set by means of the `UIManager` class. The applet listed in Example 20-9 is similar to the applet listed in Example 20-8, except that the leaf and open and closed icons for all trees are set by the `UIManager` class. See "UI Manager" on page 334 for more information concerning the `UIManager` class.

Example 20-9 Using the UIManager Class to Set Tree Icon Defaults

```
import javax.swing.*;
import javax.swing.tree.*;
import java.awt.*;
import java.awt.event.*;

public class Test extends JApplet {
    static private Icon
                    openFolder = new ImageIcon("button_lit.jpg"),
                    closedFolder = new ImageIcon("button.jpg"),
                    leafIcon = new ImageIcon("leaf.gif");

    public void init() {
        UIManager.put("Tree.closedIcon", closedFolder);
        UIManager.put("Tree.openIcon", openFolder);
        UIManager.put("Tree.leafIcon", leafIcon);

        JTree tree = new JTree();
        JScrollPane scrollPane = new JScrollPane(tree);

        getContentPane().add(scrollPane);
    }
}
```

Notice that the applet listed in Example 20-9 specifies default icons with the `UIManager.put` method before the applet's tree is created. Only trees created after the defaults are set will take on the new default values.

Extending DefaultTreeCellRenderer

Sometimes it is necessary to modify the manner in which tree nodes are rendered beyond changing icons, colors, or fonts. For example, the application shown in Figure 20-16 contains a `JTree` file explorer that simulates backup software by equipping folders with a check box. The check box is rendered by an extension of `DefaultTreeCellRenderer`.

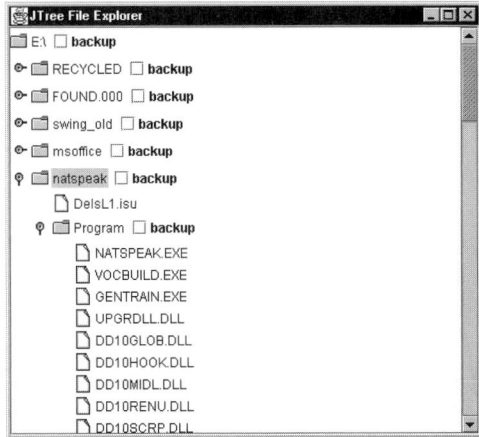

Figure 20-16 Extending DefaultTreeCellRenderer

The renderer extends `DefaultTreeCellRenderer` and instantiates a check box, horizontal strut, and a panel. The strut is used to insert some space between the label and the check box. The panel is returned from the renderer's `getTreeCellRendererComponent` method.

The renderer's constructor sets the background color for the panel to the default text background color for the current look and feel, and sets the opaque property for the renderer, check box, and panel to `false`. The panel is fitted with an instance of `FlowLayout`, with horizontal and vertical gaps between components of 0 pixels.

The renderer, which is a label because `DefaultTreeCellRenderer` extends `JLabel`, is added to the panel, followed by the horizontal strut and check box.

```
class FileNodeRenderer extends DefaultTreeCellRenderer {
    protected JCheckBox checkBox = new JCheckBox("backup");
    private Component strut = Box.createHorizontalStrut(5);
    private JPanel panel = new JPanel();

    public FileNodeRenderer() {
        panel.setBackground(
                    UIManager.getColor("Tree.textBackground"));

        setOpaque(false);
        checkBox.setOpaque(false);
        panel.setOpaque(false);

        panel.setLayout(new FlowLayout(FlowLayout.CENTER,0,0));
        panel.add(this);
        panel.add(strut);
        panel.add(checkBox);

    }
    ...
```

The renderer's `getTreeCellRendererComponent` method obtains a reference to the node being rendered by casting the value it is passed. The method subsequently invokes `super.getTreeCellRendererComponent`, which configures the renderer's foreground color and icon as described in Class Summary 20-3 on page 1330. The check box's visibility and selected property are then set according to whether the node is a directory and is selected. The simplistic backup software simulated by the applet provides backup check boxes for directories but not for files.

The panel, which contains a label (the renderer), horizontal strut, and check box is returned from the `getTreeCellRendererComponent` method.

```
            ...
    public Component getTreeCellRendererComponent(
                    JTree tree, Object value,
                    boolean selected, boolean expanded,
                    boolean leaf, int row,
                    boolean hasFocus) {
        FileNode node = (FileNode)value;

        super.getTreeCellRendererComponent(
                        tree, value, selected, expanded,
                        leaf, row, hasFocus);

        checkBox.setVisible(node.isDirectory());
        checkBox.setSelected(node.isSelected());

        return panel;
    }
}
```

The application shown in Figure 20-16 is listed in Example 20-10. Note that the application listed in Example 20-10 is nearly identical to the application listed in Example 20-4 on page 1301, except that the tree is fitted with a custom renderer. Thus, in the interest of brevity, Example 20-10 omits the FileNode class listing that overlaps between the two applications.

Example 20-10 Extending DefaultTreeCellRenderer

```java
import javax.swing.*;
import javax.swing.event.*;
import javax.swing.tree.*;
import java.awt.*;
import java.awt.event.*;
import java.io.File;

public class Test extends JFrame {
    public Test() {
        final JTree tree = new JTree(createTreeModel());
        JScrollPane scrollPane = new JScrollPane(tree);
        FileNodeRenderer renderer = new FileNodeRenderer();

        tree.setEditable(true);
        tree.setCellRenderer(renderer);

        getContentPane().add(scrollPane, BorderLayout.CENTER);

        tree.addTreeExpansionListener(new TreeExpansionListener(){
            public void treeCollapsed(TreeExpansionEvent e) {
            }
            public void treeExpanded(TreeExpansionEvent e) {
                TreePath path = e.getPath();
                FileNode node = (FileNode)
                                    path.getLastPathComponent();

                if( ! node.isExplored()) {
                    DefaultTreeModel model =
                            (DefaultTreeModel)tree.getModel();

                    node.explore();
                    model.nodeStructureChanged(node);
                }
            }
        });
    }
    private DefaultTreeModel createTreeModel() {
        File root = new File("E:/");
        FileNode rootNode = new FileNode(root), node;

        rootNode.explore();
        return new DefaultTreeModel(rootNode);
    }
    public static void main(String args[]) {
```

```
                GJApp.launch(new Test(),"JTree File Explorer",
                                300,300,450,400);
        }
}
class FileNode extends DefaultMutableTreeNode {
    // Listing omitted: see Example 20-4 on page 1301
}
class FileNodeRenderer extends DefaultTreeCellRenderer {
    protected JCheckBox checkBox = new JCheckBox("backup");
    private Component strut = Box.createHorizontalStrut(5);
    private JPanel panel = new JPanel();

    public FileNodeRenderer() {
        panel.setBackground(
                UIManager.getColor("Tree.textBackground"));

        setOpaque(false);
        checkBox.setOpaque(false);
        panel.setOpaque(false);

        panel.setLayout(new FlowLayout(FlowLayout.CENTER,0,0));
        panel.add(this);
        panel.add(strut);
        panel.add(checkBox);

    }
    public Component getTreeCellRendererComponent(
                    JTree tree, Object value,
                    boolean selected, boolean expanded,
                    boolean leaf, int row,
                    boolean hasFocus) {
        FileNode node = (FileNode)value;

        super.getTreeCellRendererComponent(
                        tree, value, selected, expanded,
                        leaf, row, hasFocus);

        checkBox.setVisible(node.isDirectory());
        checkBox.setSelected(node.isSelected());

        return panel;
    }
}
```

It should be noted that the check box rendered by the custom renderer cannot be manipulated because renderers use components as a stamp to render cells. In other words, the check box is not actually added to the tree and therefore cannot be selected or deselected. If the check box is to be manipulated, the tree must be fitted with a custom editor, as illustrated in "Rendering and Editing: A Case Study" on page 1354.

Tree Formatting Renderers

Sometimes it is necessary to format cell values according to some criteria. For example, the tree shown in Figure 20-17 formats certain nodes as currency.

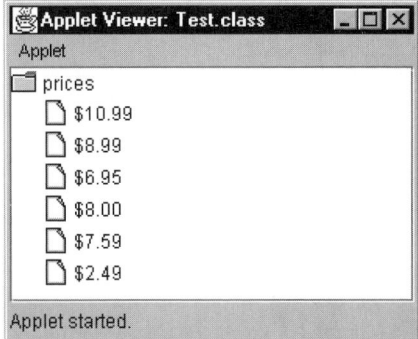

Figure 20-17 A Formatting Renderer

Swing *table* cell renderers provide a convenient hook for formatting renderers with the `DefaultTableCellRenderer.setValue` method as described in "Table Formatting Renderers" on page 1212. Unfortunately, tree cell renderers are not implemented in a similar fashion and, as a result, implementing formatting renderers for trees requires more work on the developer's part than for tables.

The applet shown in Figure 20-17 is listed in Example 20-11. The applet creates an instance of `JTree` and populates it with default mutable tree nodes. The tree's renderer is set to an instance of `FormattingRenderer`, which formats nodes representing prices.

Example 20-11 Formatting User Objects as Currency

```
import java.awt.*;
import java.awt.event.*;
import javax.swing.*;
import javax.swing.tree.*;
import java.text.*;

public class Test extends JApplet {
    public void init() {
        JTree tree = new JTree();
```

```
        JScrollPane scrollPane = new JScrollPane(tree);

        DefaultMutableTreeNode root =
                    new DefaultMutableTreeNode("prices");

        root.add(new DefaultMutableTreeNode(new Double(10.99)));
        root.add(new DefaultMutableTreeNode(new Double(8.99)));
        root.add(new DefaultMutableTreeNode(new Double(6.95)));
        root.add(new DefaultMutableTreeNode(new Double(8.00)));
        root.add(new DefaultMutableTreeNode(new Double(7.59)));
        root.add(new DefaultMutableTreeNode(new Double(2.49)));

        DefaultTreeModel model =
                    (DefaultTreeModel)tree.getModel();

        model.setRoot(root);

        tree.setCellRenderer(new FormattingRenderer());
        getContentPane().add(scrollPane);
    }
  }
  ...
```

The formatting renderer extends `DefaultTreeCellRenderer` and, like the renderer discussed in "Extending DefaultTreeCellRenderer" on page 1335, invokes `super.TreeCellRendererComponent()` to initialize the renderer's foreground color and icon. A reference to the user object associated with the node being rendered is obtained, and user objects of type `Double` are formatted with an instance of `NumberFormat` from the `java.text` package. The formatted string is then set as the text for the renderer. Finally, the renderer returns itself from the `getTreeCellRendererComponent` method.

```
    ...
  class FormattingRenderer extends DefaultTreeCellRenderer {
     public Component getTreeCellRendererComponent(
                    JTree tree, Object value,
                    boolean selected, boolean expanded,
                    boolean leaf, int row,
                    boolean hasFocus) {
        // initialize renderer component (this) ...

        super.getTreeCellRendererComponent(
                    tree, value, selected, expanded,
                    leaf, row, hasFocus);

        // now format label text ...

        DefaultMutableTreeNode n = (DefaultMutableTreeNode)value;
        Object userObject = n.getUserObject();
```

```
    if(userObject instanceof Double) {
        Double d = (Double)userObject;
        Format format = NumberFormat.getCurrencyInstance();

        setText(value == null ? "" : format.format(d));
    }
    return this;
  }
}
```

Swing Tip ...

Formatting Renderers: Trees Vs. Tables

Both the DefaultTableCellRenderer and DefaultTreeCellRenderer classes extend JLabel and are useful for displaying text and/or an icon. DefaultTable-CellRenderer implements a protected setValue method that is invoked after the renderer's border, colors, and font have been updated. Extensions of DefaultTableCellRenderer can override the setValue method to easily implement formatting renderers. See "Table Formatting Renderers" on page 1212 or more information concerning table formatting renderers.

The DefaultTreeCellRenderer class does not implement a setValue method as does its table counterpart. As a result, tree formatting renderers typically override getTreeCellRendererComponent and invoke super.getTreeCellRendererComponent() to update the renderer's border, colors, and fonts. See "Tree Formatting Renderers" on page 1339 for an example of a tree formatting renderer.

Metal Look and Feel

If a client property with a key of "JTree.lineStyle" is specified for a tree, the manner in which connecting lines are drawn between nodes can be affected for Metal look-and-feel trees. The three values supported for the "JTree.lineStyle" client property are:

- "None"
- "Horizontal"
- "Angled"

Figure 20-18 shows an application that exhibits the connecting lines corresponding to the strings listed above.

Figure 20-18 JTree.lineStyle Client Property for Metal Look and Feel

The "`JTree.lineStyle`" client property is set like this:

```
tree.setClientProperty("JTree.lineStyle", "Angled");
```

Root Nodes and Root Handles

Instances of `JTree` can set the visibility of their root node and their root node's handle. Handles are the small controls to the left of folders that expands and collapses the node.

The applet shown in Figure 20-19 contains a tree and two check boxes for controlling the visibility of the tree's root node and root node handle.

Action listeners are added to the applet's check boxes to invoke the appropriate `JTree` accessors for root node and root node handle visibility. The applet shown in Figure 20-19 is listed in Example 20-12.

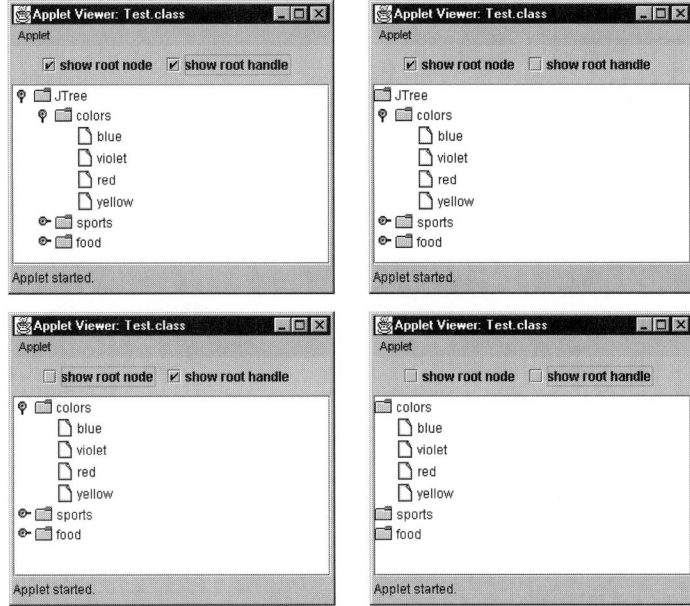

Figure 20-19 Showing Root Node and Root Handles

Example 20-12 Showing Root Node and Root Handles

```java
import javax.swing.*;
import java.awt.*;
import java.awt.event.*;
import java.util.*;

public class Test extends JApplet {
    JTree tree = new JTree();

    public void init() {
        Container contentPane = getContentPane();
        JScrollPane scrollPane = new JScrollPane(tree);

        contentPane.add(new ControlPanel(), BorderLayout.NORTH);
        contentPane.add(scrollPane, BorderLayout.CENTER);
    }
    class ControlPanel extends JPanel {
        JCheckBox showRoot = new JCheckBox("show root node");
        JCheckBox showRootHandles = new JCheckBox(
                                    "show root handle");
        public ControlPanel() {
            initializeCheckBoxes();
```

```
        setLayout(new FlowLayout());
        add(showRoot);
        add(showRootHandles);

        showRoot.addActionListener(new ActionListener() {
            public void actionPerformed(ActionEvent e) {
                tree.setRootVisible(showRoot.isSelected());
            }
        });
        showRootHandles.addActionListener(
                                    new ActionListener() {
            public void actionPerformed(ActionEvent e) {
                tree.setShowsRootHandles(
                            showRootHandles.isSelected());
            }
        });
    }
    private void initializeCheckBoxes() {
        showRoot.setSelected(tree.isRootVisible());
        showRootHandles.setSelected(
                            tree.getShowsRootHandles());
    }
  }
}
```

Tree Cell Editing

Tree cell editors are defined by the TreeCellEditor interface, which extends the CellEditor interface. The discussion that follows concerning tree cell editing assumes an understanding of the CellEditor interface, which is discussed in "Cell Editors" on page 1215.

The TreeCellEditor interface is summarized in Interface Summary 20-6.

Interface Summary 20-6   TreeCellEditor

Extends: CellEditor

---

public abstract Component <u>getTreeCellEditorComponent</u>(JTree tree,
Object value,
boolean isSelected,
boolean expanded,
boolean leaf,
int row)

In addition to the methods defined by the `CellEditor` interface, the `TreeCellEditor` interface defines a `getTreeCellEditorComponent` method that returns a component.

Tree cell editors must provide a component for editing in addition to implementing the methods defined by the `CellEditor` interface. As with renderers, it is often the case that the component returned from `TreeCellEditor.getTreeCellEditorComponent()` is the editor itself.

Swing provides two implementations of the `TreeCellEditor` interface: the `DefaultCellEditor` and `DefaultTreeCellEditor` classes. Instances of `DefaultCellEditor` can be used for both tables and trees because `DefaultCellEditor` also implements the `TableCellEditor` interface; see "DefaultCellEditor" on page 1226 for a discussion of the `DefaultCellEditor` class.

The `DefaultTreeCellEditor` class is a tree cell editor that does not obliterate a node's icon when editing. The `DefaultTreeCellEditor` class is discussed in "Using DefaultTreeCellEditor" on page 1352.

Extending DefaultCellEditor

Figure 20-20 shows a tree equipped with an editor that extends the `DefaultCellEditor` class. The editor provides a combo box with a list of colors, and the editor is activated only for nodes whose parent node is the "colors" node. From left to right, Figure 20-20 shows a node that is changed from blue to yellow.

The applet shown in Figure 20-20 is listed in Example 20-13. The applet creates an instance of `ColorEditor`, which is specified as the editor for the applet's tree. `JTree.setEditable(true)` is invoked by the applet because by default instances of `JTree` are not editable.

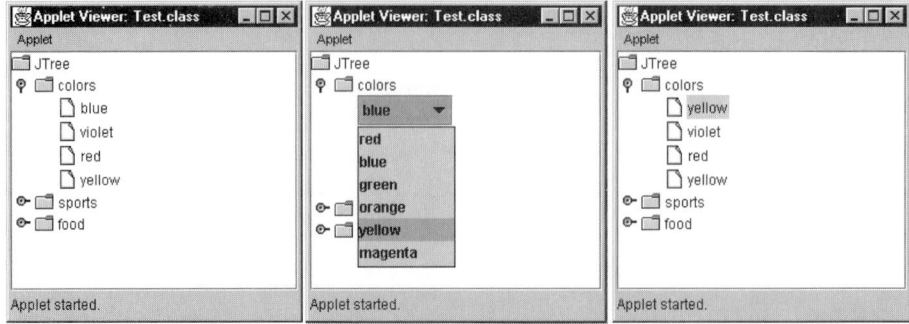

Figure 20-20 Extending DefaultCellEditor

Example 20-13 An Editor That Extends DefaultCellEditor

```java
import javax.swing.*;
import javax.swing.tree.*;
import java.awt.*;
import java.awt.event.*;
import java.util.*;

public class Test extends JApplet {
    public void init() {
        JTree tree = new JTree();
        JScrollPane scrollPane = new JScrollPane(tree);
        JComboBox combo = new JComboBox();

        combo.addItem("red");
        combo.addItem("blue");
        combo.addItem("green");
        combo.addItem("orange");
        combo.addItem("yellow");
        combo.addItem("magenta");

        tree.setCellEditor(new ColorEditor(tree, combo));
        tree.setEditable(true);

        getContentPane().add(scrollPane);
    }
}
class ColorEditor extends DefaultCellEditor {
    private JTree tree;

    public ColorEditor(JTree tree, JComboBox comboBox) {
        super(comboBox);
        this.tree = tree;
    }
```

```
public boolean isCellEditable(EventObject e) {
    boolean rv = false;  // return value

    if(e instanceof MouseEvent) {
        MouseEvent me = (MouseEvent)e;

        if(me.getClickCount() == 3) {
            TreePath path =
                tree.getPathForLocation(me.getX(), me.getY());

            if(path.getPathCount() == 1) // root node
                return false;

            DefaultMutableTreeNode node =
                (DefaultMutableTreeNode)
                            path.getLastPathComponent();

            rv = node.getParent().toString().equals("colors");
        }
    }
    return rv;
}
```

The `ColorEditor` class extends `DefaultCellEditor`, and the `ColorEditor` constructor passes along the combo box it is passed to the `DefaultCellEditor` constructor. The `DefaultCellEditor` class takes care of displaying the combo box and returning the edited value.

Because the color editor is used only for nodes representing colors, the `ColorEditor` class overrides `isCellEditable()` from the `CellEditor` interface to return `true` for nodes whose parent is the "colors" folder, and `false` for all other nodes. The color editor is activated by a triple click.

DefaultTreeCellEditor

The `DefaultTreeCellEditor` class was a late addition to Swing 1.1 that was necessitated because instances of `DefaultCellEditor` tend to obliterate a node's icon, as can be seen from Figure 20-20.

Instances of `DefaultTreeCellEditor` are wrappers for a "real" editor. The real editor is placed in a container that is added to the tree when the editor is activated. The `DefaultTreeCellEditor` class also maintains a reference to an instance of `DefaultTreeCellRenderer`, which the editor uses to obtain an icon that is rendered next to the real editor.

Default tree cell editors are activated by either a triple click or by two single clicks followed by a delay of 1200 milliseconds.

A class diagram for the `DefaultTreeCellEditor` class shown in Figure 20-21.

Figure 20-21   DefaultTreeCellEditor Class Diagram

`DefaultTreeCellEditor` extends `Object` and implements the `TreeCellEditor` interface. The `DefaultTreeCellEditor` class maintains references to its real editor and a default tree cell renderer that is used for obtaining a node's icons.

`DefaultTreeCellEditor` also maintains a number of references to other objects, such as the editing container in which the real editor is placed, the editing component obtained from the real editor, and the editing icon obtained from the renderer.

`DefaultTreeCellEditor` also maintains a number of properties, including the offset from a node's left edge for placing the editing container and a timer for tracking the 1200 millisecond delay.

`DefaultTreeCellEditor` maintains a reference to its tree and the last row that was passed the `getTreeCellEditorComponent` method. A reference to the font used by the editor is maintained by instances of `DefaultTreeCellEditor`.

The `DefaultTreeCellEditor` class is summarized in Class Summary 20-4.

Class Summary 20-4   DefaultTreeCellEditor

Extends: Object
Implements: TreeCellEditor

Constructors

---

public DefaultTreeCellEditor(JTree, DefaultTreeCellRenderer)
public DefaultTreeCellEditor(JTree, DefaultTreeCellRenderer, TreeCellEditor)

`DefaultTreeCellEditor` provides two constructors. Both constructors are passed the tree that the editor is used with and an instance of `DefaultTreeCellRenderer` that is used to obtain the editing icon. The second constructor listed above is also passed a tree cell editor.

If a tree cell editor is not specified at the time of construction, a default editor containing a text field will be used.

Methods

CellEditor Methods

---

public void <u>addCellEditorListener</u>(CellEditorListener)
public void <u>removeCellEditorListener</u>(CellEditorListener)

public void <u>cancelCellEditing</u>()
public boolean <u>stopCellEditing</u>()

public boolean <u>isCellEditable</u>(EventObject)
public boolean <u>shouldSelectCell</u>(EventObject)
public Object <u>getCellEditorValue</u>()

The methods listed above are defined by the `CellEditor` interface. All of the methods delegate to the real editor, with the exception of `isCellEditable()`. If the event passed to `isCellEditable()` represents a triple click or if a 1200 millisecond delay has occurred since a second mouse click, `isCellEditable()` returns `true`.

TreeCellEditor Method

---

public abstract Component <u>getTreeCellEditorComponent</u>(JTree tree,
                                       Object value,
                                       boolean isSelected,
                                       boolean expanded,
                                       boolean leaf,
                                       int row)

The `getTreeCellEditorComponent` method obtains the editor component from the real editor and configures the editing container's font. The editing container is returned from the `getTreeCellEditorComponent` method.

Start Editing

---

protected boolean shouldStartEditingTimer(EventObject)
protected void startEditingTimer()
protected boolean canEditImmediately(EventObject)
public void actionPerformed(ActionEvent)

The methods listed above conspire to activate the editor after a click, pause, click, and delay of 1200 milliseconds. The `actionPerformed` method is called by the editor's timer after the 1200 millisecond delay has elapsed.

Border Selection Color / Font / Tree Properties

---

public Color getBorderSelectionColor()
public Font getFont()

public void setBorderSelectionColor(Color)
public void setFont(Font)
protected void setTree(JTree)

`DefaultTreeCellEditor` provides accessors for its font, tree, and border selection color.

Utility Methods

---

protected Container createContainer()
protected TreeCellEditor createTreeCellEditor()

protected void determineOffset(JTree tree,
                              Object value,
                              boolean isSelected,
                              boolean expanded,
                              boolean leaf,
                              int row)

protected boolean inHitRegion(int, int)

protected void prepareForEditing()

The methods listed above are utility methods used internally by the `DefaultTreeCellEditor` class. The methods are `protected` so that they are available to extensions of `DefaultTreeCellEditor`.

TreeSelectionListener Method

---

public void <u>valueChanged</u>(TreeSelectionEvent)

Instances of `DefaultTreeCellEditor` register themselves as tree selection listeners with their tree in order to detect selections during the 1200 millisecond delay. If a selection is made during the delay, editing will not occur.

Using DefaultTreeCellEditor

The applet shown in Figure 20-22 is similar to the applet shown in Figure 20-20 on page 1346, except that the tree is fitted with an instance of `DefaultTreeCellEditor`. Because the tree is fitted with an instance of `DefaultTreeCellEditor` instead of `DefaultCellEditor`, the editor is placed to the right of a node's icon.

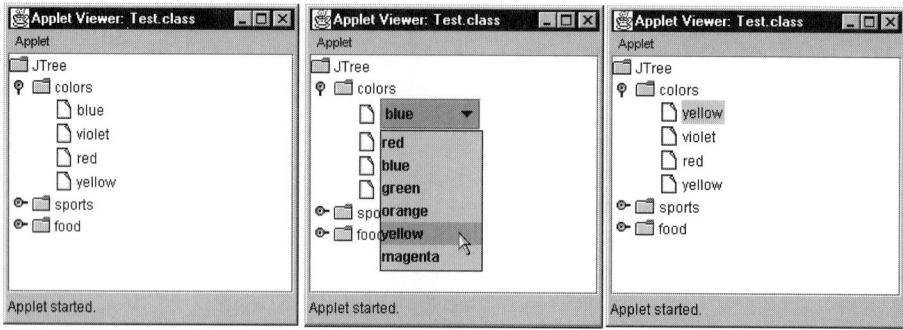

Figure 20-22 Using DefaultTreeCellEditor

The applet shown in Figure 20-22 is listed in Example 20-14.

Example 20-14   Using DefaultTreeCellEditor

```java
import javax.swing.*;
import javax.swing.tree.*;
import java.awt.*;
import java.awt.event.*;
import java.util.*;

public class Test extends JApplet {
    public void init() {
        JTree tree = new JTree();
        JScrollPane scrollPane = new JScrollPane(tree);
        JComboBox combo = new JComboBox();

        combo.addItem("red");
        combo.addItem("blue");
        combo.addItem("green");
        combo.addItem("orange");
        combo.addItem("yellow");
        combo.addItem("magenta");

        tree.setCellEditor(new DefaultTreeCellEditor(
            tree, new DefaultTreeCellRenderer(),
            new ColorEditor(tree, combo)));

        tree.setEditable(true);

        getContentPane().add(scrollPane);
    }
}
class ColorEditor extends DefaultCellEditor {
    private JTree tree;

    public ColorEditor(JTree tree, JComboBox comboBox) {
        super(comboBox);
        this.tree = tree;
    }
    public boolean isCellEditable(EventObject e) {
        boolean rv = false;  // return value

        if(e instanceof MouseEvent) {
            MouseEvent me = (MouseEvent)e;

            if(me.getClickCount() == 3) {
                TreePath path =
                    tree.getPathForLocation(me.getX(), me.getY());

                DefaultMutableTreeNode node =
                    (DefaultMutableTreeNode)
                                path.getLastPathComponent();

                rv = node.getParent().toString().equals("colors");
```

```
            }
        }
        return rv;
    }
}
```

Notice that the applet listed in Example 20-14 is identical to the applet listed in Example 20-13, except that the `ColorEditor` is wrapped in an instance of `DefaultTreeCellEditor`.

Rendering and Editing: A Case Study

The previous examples of tree cell rendering and editing are rather simplistic; this section discusses a more complicated example of rendering and editing.

The application shown in Figure 20-23 simulates backup software that backs up directories that have their backup check box selected. For the sake of illustration, only folders have backup check boxes.

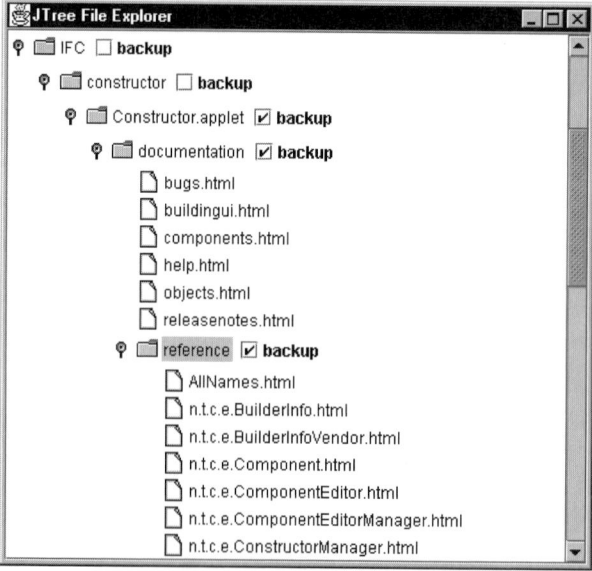

Figure 20-23 Advanced Rendering and Editing

The application shown in Figure 20-23 is an extrapolation of the applications discussed in "Extending DefaultMutableTreeNode" on page 1296 and "Extending DefaultTreeCellRenderer" on page 1335. Like the former, the tree shown in Figure 20-23 contains instances of a `FileNode` class that allow the directory hierarchy to be explored. Also, like the latter, the tree is fitted with a custom renderer that renders check boxes.

Unlike either of the applications cited above, the tree shown in Figure 20-23 is equipped with a custom editor that allows the check boxes to be selected and deselected.

The application shown in Figure 20-23 implements a number of classes that are discussed in the following sections. Before the classes are individually discussed, an introduction to the classes and their responsibilities may be helpful. The classes are listed below in the order of presentation.

Test — Extends `JFrame` and creates the tree and its associated renderer and editor. The `Test` class also adds expansion and editor listeners to the tree.

SelectableFile — A simple wrapper for an instance of `File`. Instances of `SelectableFile` can be selected and deselected; their selection state is kept in sync with the check box associated with a folder.

FileNode — An extension of `DefaultMutableTreeNode` that maintains an instance of `SelectableFile` as its user object.

FileNodeRenderer — An extension of `DefaultTreeCellRenderer` that renders a `FileNode`'s file name and, optionally, a check box if the file node represents a folder.

FileNodeEditorRenderer — An extension of `FileNodeRenderer` that is used by the tree's editor.

FileNodeEditor — A simple editor that uses an instance of `FileNodeRenderer` to produce the editor's component.

ImmediateEditor — An extension of `DefaultTreeCellEditor` that enables editing for a single mouse click when the mouse is clicked in the renderer's check box. The editor also determines whether an event should select a node.

Some of the classes listed above are a necessary rehash of topics that have been discussed previously. The more advanced aspects of tree cell editing are illustrated by the `ImmediateEditor` and `FileNodeEditor` classes.

Recall from "DefaultTreeCellEditor" on page 1347 that instances of `DefaultTreeCellEditor` act as a wrapper for a "real" editor. The `ImmediateEditor` class extends `DefaultTreeCellEditor`, and the real editor for `ImmediateEditor` is a `FileNodeEditor`.

`ImmediateEditor` overrides `DefaultTreeCellEditor.canEditImmediately()` and `DefaultTreeCellEditor.shouldSelectCell()`. The former is overridden to enable editing on a single mouse click, instead of the default behavior provided by `DefaultTreeCellEditor` of a triple click or click/pause/click/1200 ms delay. The `shouldSelectCell` method is overridden to inhibit selection if a mouse click occurs in a folder's check box.

Note: *An AWT event handling bug in JDK 1.2 results in two mouse clicks required to edit a node's check box.*

The Test Class

The application creates an instance of `JTree` with a tree model whose root node is an instance of `FileNode` representing the `E:\` drive.

The application creates instances of `FileNodeRenderer` and `FileNodeEditor`. The `FileNodeEditor` instance is specified as the tree's real editor by being passed to the `ImmediateEditor` constructor, where it is passed along to the `DefaultTreeCellEditor` constructor. `JTree.setEditable(true)` is invoked by the `Test` constructor to enable editing for the tree.

Two listeners are added to the tree to handle expansion and editing events. Expansion events are handled by exploring unexplored nodes, and editing events are handled by printing information about the event.

Example 20-15 Rendering and Editing: A Case Study

```
import javax.swing.*;
import javax.swing.event.*;
import javax.swing.tree.*;
import java.awt.*;
import java.awt.event.*;
import java.io.File;
import java.util.EventObject;
```

```
public class Test extends JFrame {
    public Test() {
        final JTree tree = new JTree(createTreeModel());
        JScrollPane scrollPane = new JScrollPane(tree);

        FileNodeRenderer renderer = new FileNodeRenderer();
        FileNodeEditor editor = new FileNodeEditor();

        tree.setEditable(true);
        tree.setCellRenderer(renderer);
        tree.setCellEditor(new ImmediateEditor(tree,
                                    renderer, editor));

        getContentPane().add(scrollPane, BorderLayout.CENTER);

        tree.addTreeExpansionListener(new TreeExpansionListener(){
            public void treeCollapsed(TreeExpansionEvent e) {
            }
            public void treeExpanded(TreeExpansionEvent e) {
                TreePath path = e.getPath();
                FileNode node = (FileNode)
                                path.getLastPathComponent();

                if( ! node.isExplored()) {
                    DefaultTreeModel model =
                            (DefaultTreeModel)tree.getModel();

                    node.explore();
                    model.nodeStructureChanged(node);
                }
            }
        });
        tree.getCellEditor().addCellEditorListener(
                    new CellEditorListener() {
            public void editingCanceled(ChangeEvent e) {
                CellEditor cellEditor = (CellEditor)e.getSource();
                SelectableFile sf =
                        (SelectableFile)
                        cellEditor.getCellEditorValue();

                System.out.println("editing canceled: " +
                                sf.toString());
            }
            public void editingStopped(ChangeEvent e) {
                CellEditor cellEditor = (CellEditor)e.getSource();
                SelectableFile sf =
                        (SelectableFile)
                        cellEditor.getCellEditorValue();

                System.out.println("editing stopped: " +
                                sf.toString());
            }
        });
```

```
    }
    private DefaultTreeModel createTreeModel() {
        File root = new File("E:/");
        FileNode rootNode = new FileNode(root);

        rootNode.explore();
        return new DefaultTreeModel(rootNode);
    }
    public static void main(String args[]) {
        GJApp.launch(new Test(),"JTree File Explorer",
                            300,300,450,400);
    }
} // End of Test class
...
```

The SelectableFile and FileNode Classes

The tree shown in Figure 20-23 contains nodes of type `FileNode` that have
instances of `SelectableFile` as their user objects. The `SelectableFile` class
essentially adds a `boolean selected` property to a file.

```
...
class SelectableFile {
    private File file;
    private boolean selected = false;

    public SelectableFile(File file) {
        this.file = file;
    }
    public String toString() {
        return file.toString() + " selected: " + selected;
    }
    public void setSelected(boolean s) { selected = s; }
    public boolean isSelected()   { return selected; }
    public File getFile()    { return file; }
}
...
```

The `FileNode` class extends `DefaultMutableTreeNode` and sets its user
object to an instance of `SelectableFile`. `FileNodes` that represent directories
are folders, whereas files are leaves. A `FileNode` provides accessors to its user
object's selected state, allowing `FileNode` instances to be manipulated as
selectable objects. The `FileNode` class can explore child files and folders and also
keeps track of whether the node has been explored.

```
...
class FileNode extends DefaultMutableTreeNode {
    private boolean explored = false;

    public FileNode(File file) {
        setUserObject(new SelectableFile(file));
    }
    public boolean getAllowsChildren() { return isDirectory(); }
    public boolean isLeaf() { return !isDirectory(); }

    public File getFile() {
        SelectableFile sf = (SelectableFile)getUserObject();
        return sf.getFile();
    }
    public boolean isSelected() {
        SelectableFile sf = (SelectableFile)getUserObject();
        return sf.isSelected();
    }
    public void setSelected(boolean b) {
        SelectableFile sf = (SelectableFile)getUserObject();
        sf.setSelected(b);
    }
    public boolean isDirectory() {
        File file = getFile();
        return file.isDirectory();
    }
    public String toString() {
        File file = getFile();
        String filename = file.toString();
        int index = filename.lastIndexOf("\\");

        return (index != -1 && index != filename.length()-1) ?
                            filename.substring(index+1) :
                            filename;
    }
    public void explore() { explore(); }
    public boolean isExplored() { return explored; }

    public void explore() {
        if(!isExplored()) {
            File file = getFile();
            File[] children = file.listFiles();

            for(int i=0; i < children.length; ++i)
                add(new FileNode(children[i]));

            explored = true;
        }
    }
}
...
```

The Renderers

The application shown in Figure 20-23 uses two renderers: one to render the nodes in the tree and another for the editor. Because the components used to render and edit are identical, the editor's renderer (`FileNodeEditorRenderer`) is an extension of the tree's renderer (`FileNodeRenderer`).

FileNodeRenderer

The `FileNodeRenderer` class is similar to the class of the same name discussed in "Extending DefaultMutableTreeNode" on page 1296, except for the addition of a method that calculates the offset of the check box from the left edge of the renderer's panel. The method—`getCheckBoxOffset()`—is used by the `ImmediateEditor` class, which uses the offset to determine whether a mouse click in a folder should select the folder or invoke the editor.

Notice that all nodes rendered by `FileNodeRenderer` have a check box, but check box visibility is enabled only for folders.

```
...
class FileNodeRenderer extends DefaultTreeCellRenderer {
    protected JCheckBox checkBox = new JCheckBox("backup");
    private Component strut = Box.createHorizontalStrut(5);
    private JPanel panel = new JPanel();

    public FileNodeRenderer() {
        panel.setBackground(
                    UIManager.getColor("Tree.textBackground"));

        setOpaque(false);
        checkBox.setOpaque(false);
        panel.setOpaque(false);

        panel.setLayout(new FlowLayout(FlowLayout.CENTER,0,0));
        panel.add(this);
        panel.add(strut);
        panel.add(checkBox);
    }
    public Component getTreeCellRendererComponent(
                    JTree tree, Object value,
                    boolean selected, boolean expanded,
                    boolean leaf, int row,
                    boolean hasFocus) {
        FileNode node = (FileNode)value;
```

```
            super.getTreeCellRendererComponent(
                            tree, value, selected, expanded,
                            leaf, row, hasFocus);

            checkBox.setVisible(node.isDirectory());
            checkBox.setSelected(node.isSelected());
            return panel;
        }
        public Dimension getCheckBoxOffset() {
            Graphics g = panel.getGraphics();
            int xoffset = 0;

            if(g != null) {
                try {
                    FontMetrics fm = g.getFontMetrics();
                    xoffset = fm.stringWidth(getText()) +
                            strut.getPreferredSize().width;
                }
                finally  {
                    g.dispose();
                }
            }
            return new Dimension(xoffset, 0);
        }
    }
}
...
```

The getCheckBoxOffset method will be used by the editor to determine whether a mouse click in a node should select the node.

FileNodeEditorRenderer

Instances of FileNodeEditorRenderer are used by a FileNodeEditor to provide the editing component. The FileNodeEditorRenderer class extends FileNodeRenderer, meaning that the same component is used to render and edit nodes. However, recall that ImmediateEditor, which is an extension of DefaultTreeCellEditor, places the real editor—in this case, an instance of FileNode editor—to the right of the folder's icon. As result, the FileNodeEditorRenderer sets its icon to null, to avoid two icons being drawn next to each other when the editor component is installed.

```
  ...
  class FileNodeEditorRenderer extends FileNodeRenderer {
      public Component getTreeCellRendererComponent(
                      JTree tree, Object value,
                      boolean selected, boolean expanded,
```

```
                            boolean leaf, int row,
                            boolean hasFocus) {
        Component c = super.getTreeCellRendererComponent(tree,
                            value, selected, expanded,
                            leaf, row, hasFocus);
        setIcon(null);
        return c;
    }
    public JCheckBox getCheckBox() {
        return checkBox;
    }
}
...
```

The Editors

The application shown in Figure 20-23 on page 1354 implements two editors: the `ImmediateEditor` class and the `FileNodeEditor` class.

The `ImmediateEditor` class is an extension of `DefaultTreeCellEditor` that is specified as the tree's editor.

The `FileNodeEditor` class represents the real editor passed to the `ImmediateEditor` constructor.

FileNodeEditor

The `FileNodeEditor` class is a simple extension of `AbstractCellEditor` that uses an instance of `FileNodeEditorRenderer` to return the editor's component. Note that the `AbstractCellEditor` class is not a Swing class but is a useful implementation of the `CellEditor` interface, discussed in "AbstractCellEditor" on page 1220.

The `FileNodeEditor` class creates an instance of `FileNodeEditorRenderer` and `JCheckBox` in its constructor.

An action listener is added to the check box to set the selected state of the node being edited and to invoke `stopCellEditing()`, which ends the editing session. As a result, a single mouse click is responsible for starting and stopping editing.

`FileNode` overrides `getCellEditorValue()` to return the edited node's user object, which is an instance of `SelectableFile`.

```
class FileNodeEditor extends AbstractCellEditor {
    FileNodeEditorRenderer renderer;
    FileNode nodeBeingEdited;
    JCheckBox checkBox;

    public FileNodeEditor() {
        renderer = new FileNodeEditorRenderer();
        checkBox = renderer.getCheckBox();

        checkBox.addActionListener(new ActionListener() {
            public void actionPerformed(ActionEvent e) {
                nodeBeingEdited.setSelected(checkBox.isSelected());
                stopCellEditing();
            }
        });
    }
    public Component getTreeCellEditorComponent(
                    JTree tree, Object value,
                    boolean selected, boolean expanded,
                    boolean leaf, int row) {
        nodeBeingEdited = (FileNode)value;

        return renderer.getTreeCellRendererComponent(tree,
                        value, selected, expanded,
                        leaf, row, true); // hasFocus ignored
    }
    public Object getCellEditorValue() {
        return nodeBeingEdited.getUserObject();
    }
}
```

ImmediateEditor

The ImmediateEditor class is an extension of DefaultTreeCellEditor that exists for two purposes: to start editing immediately when a mouse click is detected in a node and to inhibit selection when a check box is checked.

Recall that by default, DefaultTreeCellEditor starts editing for a triple click or a click/pause/click followed by a 1200 millisecond delay. For the application shown in Figure 20-23 on page 1354, it is much more desirable to start editing immediately when a mouse click is detected in a node. Because the ImmediateEditor class starts editing immediately, it appears to the user that the check box rendered by the tree renderer has actually been added to the tree.

The ImmediateEditor constructor is passed a tree, a renderer, and an editor, which are passed on to the DefaultTreeCellEditor constructor. A reference to the renderer is retained to make use of the renderer's getCheckBoxOffset method.

```
class ImmediateEditor extends DefaultTreeCellEditor {
    private FileNodeRenderer renderer;

    public ImmediateEditor(JTree tree,
                           FileNodeRenderer renderer,
                           FileNodeEditor editor) {
        super(tree, renderer, editor);
        this.renderer = renderer;
    }
    ...
```

`DefaultTreeCellEditor` implements a `protected` method that determines
if editing should start immediately—the `canEditImmediately` method.

The `ImmediateEditor` class overrides `canEditImmediately` to return `true`
if the event it is passed is a mouse click that occurred in the checkbox region of the
renderer.

```
    ...
    protected boolean canEditImmediately(EventObject e) {
        boolean rv = false;   // rv = return value

        if(e instanceof MouseEvent) {
            MouseEvent me = (MouseEvent)e;
            rv = inCheckBoxHitRegion(me);
        }
        return rv;
    }
    public boolean inCheckBoxHitRegion(MouseEvent e) {
        TreePath path = tree.getPathForLocation(e.getX(),
                                                e.getY());
        FileNode node = (FileNode)path.getLastPathComponent();
        boolean rv = false;

        if(node.isDirectory()) {
            // offset and lastRow DefaultTreeCellEditor
            // protected members

            Rectangle bounds = tree.getRowBounds(lastRow);
            Dimension checkBoxOffset =
                                 renderer.getCheckBoxOffset();

            bounds.translate(offset + checkBoxOffset.width,
                      checkBoxOffset.height);

            rv = bounds.contains(e.getPoint());
        }
        return rv;
    }
    ...
```

Tree editors are also responsible for determining whether an event should select a node. `ImmediateEditor` overrides the `shouldSelectCell` method to return `true` if the node in question is a leaf or if a mouse click has occurred in a folder node outside the check box region.

```
public boolean shouldSelectCell(EventObject e) {
    boolean rv = false;  // only mouse events

    if(e instanceof MouseEvent) {
        MouseEvent me = (MouseEvent)e;
        TreePath path = tree.getPathForLocation(me.getX(),
                                                me.getY());
        FileNode node = (FileNode)
                            path.getLastPathComponent();

        rv = node.isLeaf() || !inCheckBoxHitRegion(me);
    }
    return rv;
}
```

The `JTree` component is summarized in Component Summary 20-1.

Component Summary 20-1   JTree

Model(s)	javax.swing.tree.TreeModel
UI Delegate(s)	javax.swing.plaf.basic.BasicTreeUI
Renderer(s)	TreeCellRenderer
Editor(s)	CellEditor
Events Fired	PropertyChangeEvents / TreeModelEvents / TreeSelectionEvents / TreeExpansionEvents / ChangeEvents
Replacement For	——

Class Diagrams

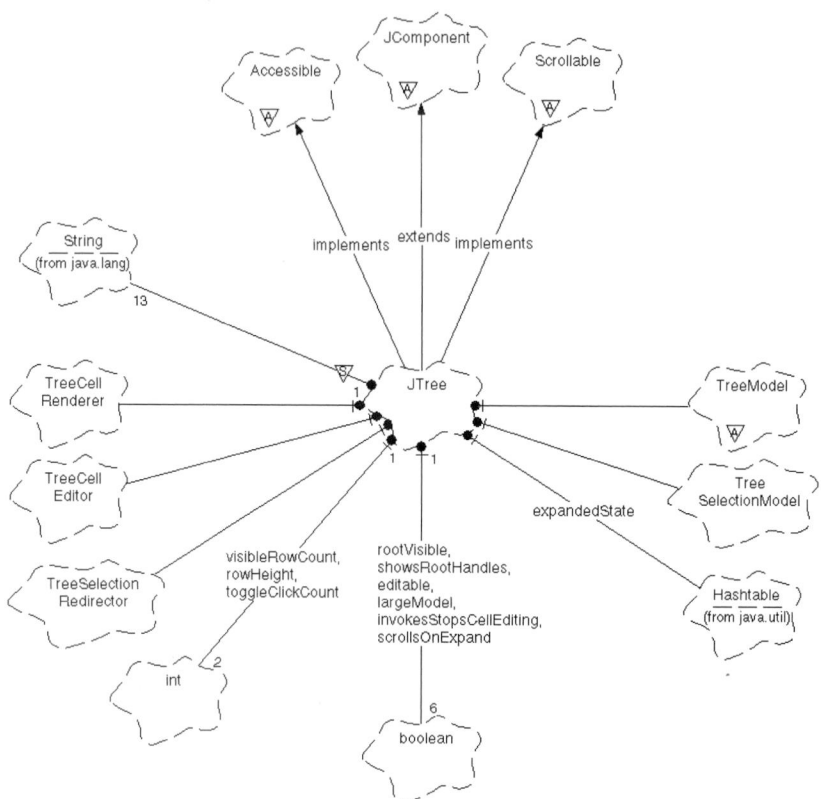

Figure 20-24 JTree Class Diagram

JTree extends JComponent, implements the Accessible and Scrollable interfaces, and has two models—a tree model and a tree selection model—in addition to a tree cell renderer and editor.

The JTree class also maintains a hash table and a number of integer and boolean values representing tree properties. The TreeSelectionRedirector is a protected JTree inner class that reacts to selection events fired by a tree's selection model by forwarding the event to the tree's selection listeners.

JTree Properties

Properties maintained by the `JTree` class are listed in Table 20-2.

Table 20-2   JTree Properties

Property Name	Data Type	Property Type[2]	Access[3]	Default[4]
cellEditor	TreeCellEditor	B	SG	null
cellRenderer	TreeCellRenderer	B	SG	DefaultTreeCell-Renderer
editable	boolean	B	SG	false
fixedRowHeight	boolean	B	SG	true if rowHeight>0
invokesStopCellEditing	boolean	B	SG	false
largeModel	boolean	B	SG	false
model	TreeModel	B	SG	DefaultTreeModel
rootVisible	boolean		SG	true
rowHeight	int	B	SG	16
scrollsOnExpand	boolean	B	SG	true
selectionModel	TreeSelectionModel	B	SG	DefaultTree-SelectionModel
showsRootHandles	boolean	B	SG	true
toggleClickCount[1]	int	B	SG	2
visibleRowCount	int	B	SG	20

1. toggleClickCount property is not available as of Swing 1.1 FCS.
2. B = bound (fires PropertyChangeEvent) / C = constrained/ I = indexed / S = simple / Ch = fires ChangeEvent / RO = read-only / TCM = table column model fires TableColumnModelEvent / LS = selection model fires ListSelection-Event / TM = table model fires TableModelEvent
3. C = settable at construction time / G = getter method / S = setter method
4. L&F = look-and-feel dependent / UIM = UIManager used to set default

cellEditor — By default, trees are not editable and therefore have a `null` cell editor. If editing is enabled for a tree with the `JTree.setEditable` method, the tree will be fitted with an instance of `DefaultTreeCellEditor`.

cellRenderer — By default, all trees are fitted with an instance of DefaultTreeCellRenderer. The DefaultTreeCellRenderer class extends JLabel, and therefore tree cell renderers are labels by default.

editable — Tree editing must be explicitly enabled after a tree is selected by invocation of JTree.setEditable(true).

invokesStopCellEditing — Normally, tree cell editing can be canceled—by a call to cancelCellEditing()—by the user clicking outside of the node being edited. By default, when editing is canceled, any editing changes are lost. However, if the invokesStopCellEditing property is set to true, editing changes will presumably be saved—by a call to stopCellEditing()—when editing is canceled.

largeModel — Used by a tree's look and feel to determine if the tree's display should be optimized. For trees with large amounts of data, setting the largeModel property to true may result in a rendering performance increase and a decrease in the amount of memory used.

Look and feels are not obligated to accommodate a tree's largeModel property, and the manner in which node display is optimized is look-and-feel dependent. By default, all Swing supplied look and feels use a fixed height layout cache if a tree's largeModel property is true and the tree has a fixed row height. Otherwise, a variable height layout cache is used. Note that specifying the large model only makes sense if the tree nodes have fixed heights.

model — A tree's model is an instance of DefaultTreeModel by default.

rootVisible — Determines whether a tree's root node is displayed. If the rootVisible property is false, the root node's children are displayed along the left side of the tree, as illustrated in "Showing Root Node and Root Handles" on page 1343.

rowHeight — Because a great majority of trees have a fixed row height, the JTree class allows row height to be explicitly set. If the rowHeight is less than or equal to 0, the tree's cell renderer calculates the height for each row in the tree. If the rowHeight has been set to a value greater than 0, the row height is not calculated.

scrollsOnExpand — By default, when a folder is expanded, the tree is scrolled to make as many of the folder's children as visible as possible. Setting the scrollsOnExpand property to false defeats the feature.

selectionModel — A tree's selection model implements the TreeSelectionModel interface and, by default, is an instance of DefaultTreeSelectionModel. If a tree's selection model is set to null with JTree.setSelectionModel(null), the tree is fitted with a shared selection model that does not allow selections.

showsRootHandles — All tree folders have a control that toggles the expansion state of the folder. The root node is the only folder that can hide its handle by invoking JTree.showsRootHandles().

toggleClickCount — By default, folders expand and collapse in response to a double click. The toggleClickCount property allows the number of mouse clicks to be explicitly set.

As of Swing 1.1 FCS, the toggleClickCount property is pending, meaning it will be implemented in a future release.

visibleRowCount — The number of visible rows when a tree is contained in a scrollpane, by default is 20 rows.

Tree Events

Tree models fire events in response to changes to nodes and removal and insertion of nodes. The JTree class fires events in response to event selections and node expansion/collapse. Tree cell editors fire events when editing is stopped or canceled. Table 20-3 lists the more interesting tree events.

Table 20-3 Tree Events

Event	Fired by	Fired when …
TreeModel-Event	tree model	nodes changed; nodes inserted; nodes removed; tree structure changed
TreeSelection-Event	JTree	selection cleared; selection paths changed
TreeExpansion Event	JTree	folder expanded; folder will expand; folder collapsed; / folder will collapse
ChangeEvent	DefaultCellEditor	editing stopped or canceled

Tree Mouse Events

In addition to the events listed in Table 20-3, trees fire mouse events. The applet shown in Figure 20-25 contains a tree fitted with a mouse listener that updates the applet's status area when a mouse pressed event occurs in the tree.

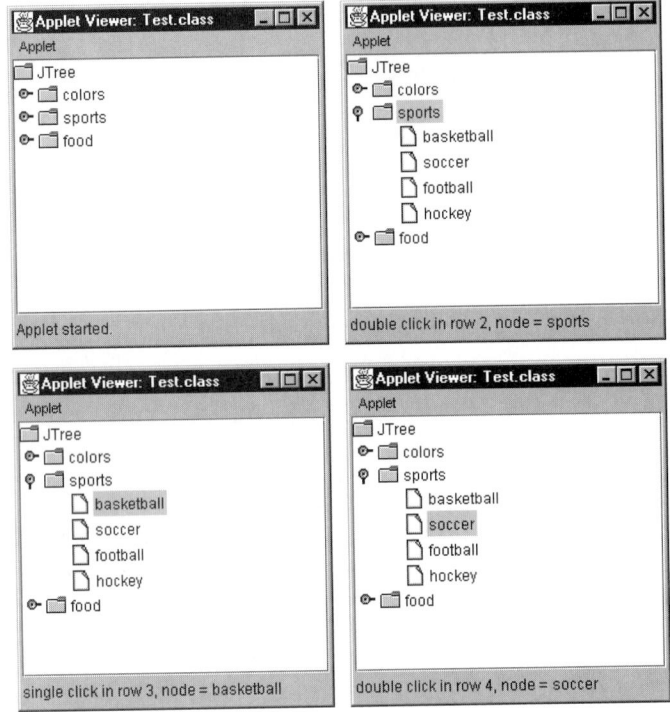

Figure 20-25 Handling Tree Mouse Events

The applet shown in Figure 20-25 is listed in Example 20-16.

Example 20-16 Handling Tree Mouse Events

```java
import javax.swing.*;
import javax.swing.tree.*;
import java.awt.*;
import java.awt.event.*;

public class Test extends JApplet {
```

```
public Test() {
    JTree tree = new JTree();

    getContentPane().add(new JScrollPane(tree));

    tree.addMouseListener(new MouseAdapter() {
        public void mousePressed(MouseEvent e) {
            String s = null;
            JTree t = (JTree)e.getSource();
            int row = t.getRowForLocation(e.getX(), e.getY());

            if(e.getClickCount() == 2)
                s = "double click in row " + row;
            else
                s = "single click in row " + row;

            if(row != -1) {
                TreePath path = t.getPathForRow(row);
                TreeNode node = (TreeNode)
                                path.getLastPathComponent();

                s += ", node = " + node.toString();
            }
            showStatus(s);
        }
    });
}
```

The mouse listener obtains a reference to the source of the event, which is the tree itself, and subsequently obtains the row in which the mouse pressed event occurred.

If the mouse was not pressed over a node, the row returned from JTree.getRowForLocation() will return −1. As a result, the listener displays information about the node only if the row is something other than −1.

If the mouse was pressed over a node, a path for the row is obtained with the JTree.getPathForRow method, and the node is subsequently obtained with the TreePath.getLastPathComponent method. See "Tree Paths" on page 1303 for more information concerning tree paths.

Tree Editing Events

Change events are fired by tree cell editors when editing is stopped or canceled. The events are handled by cell editor listeners, which are defined by the CellEditorListener interface that is summarized in Interface Summary 20-7.

Interface Summary 20-7   CellEditorListener

---

public abstract void <u>editingStopped</u>(ChangeEvent)
public abstract void <u>editingCanceled</u>(ChangeEvent)

The `editingStopped` method is invoked after an edit has been committed, whereas `editingCanceled` is invoked if editing is canceled. By default, editing for trees is canceled when a node is selected while an editor is active. Committing an edit is dependent upon the editor in use; for example, editors equipped with a text field typically commit edits when the Enter key is pressed.

The applet shown in Figure 20-26 adds a cell editor listener to the tree's cell editor and updates the applet's status area when editing is stopped or canceled.

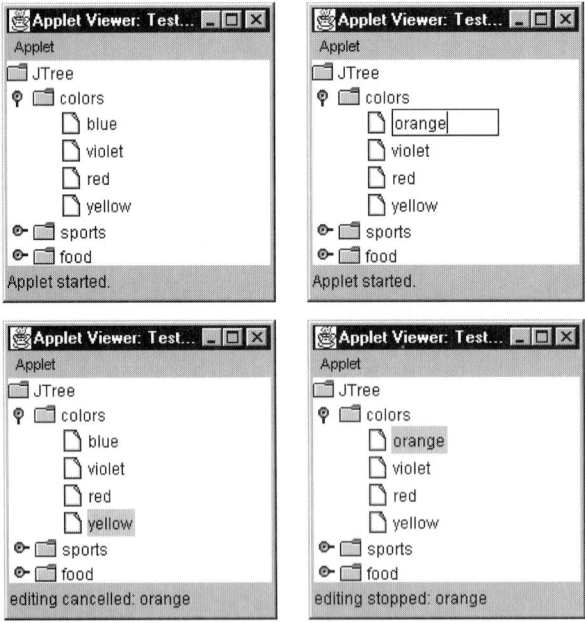

Figure 20-26 Handling Tree Editing Events

The applet shown in Figure 20-26 is listed and Example 20-17.

Example 20-17 Handling Tree Editing Events

```java
import javax.swing.*;
import javax.swing.event.*;
import javax.swing.tree.*;
import java.awt.*;
import java.awt.event.*;
import java.util.*;

public class Test extends JApplet {
    public void init() {
        JTree tree = new JTree();

        contentPane.add(tree, BorderLayout.CENTER);

        // must invoke setEditable, or the call below to
        // getCellEditor() will return null.

        tree.setEditable(true);

        tree.getCellEditor().addCellEditorListener(
                    new CellEditorListener() {
            public void editingCanceled(ChangeEvent e) {
                CellEditor editor = (CellEditor)e.getSource();
                String s = (String)editor.getCellEditorValue();

                showStatus("editing cancelled: " + s);
            }
            public void editingStopped(ChangeEvent e) {
                CellEditor editor = (CellEditor)e.getSource();
                String s = (String)editor.getCellEditorValue();

                showStatus("editing stopped: " + s);
            }
        });
    }
}
```

The applet implements two inner class listeners that obtain the edited value from the editor, which is the source of the event. The CellEditor.getCellEditorValue method returns the edited node's user object, which in this case is a string.

Tree Selection Events

Tree selection events are handled by objects that implement the
`TreeSelectionListener` interface, which is summarized in Interface
Summary 20-8.

Interface Summary 20-8 TreeSelectionListener

---

public abstract void <u>valueChanged</u>(TreeSelectionEvent e)

The `TreeSelectionListener` interface defines a single method that is passed
an instance of `TreeSelectionEvent`. The `TreeSelectionEvent` class offers a
good deal of information concerning the selection event, and therefore only one
method is necessary for tree selection listeners.

The `TreeSelectionEvent` class is summarized in Class Summary 20-5.

Class Summary 20-5 TreeSelectionEvent

Extends: java.util.EventObject

Constructors

---

public <u>TreeSelectionEvent</u>(Object source, TreePath path, boolean isNew,
                    TreePath oldLeadSelectionPath,
                    TreePath newLeadSelectionPath)

public <u>TreeSelectionEvent</u>(Object source, TreePath[] paths, boolean[] areNew,
                    TreePath oldLeadSelectionPath,
                    TreePath newLeadSelectionPath)

`TreeSelectionEvent` provides two constructors for constructing events with either a single path or an array of paths. `TreeSelectionEvents` are created by tree selection models; developers will rarely instantiate `TreeSelectionEvents`.

Methods

---

public TreePath getNewLeadSelectionPath()
public TreePath getOldLeadSelectionPath()

public TreePath getPath()
public TreePath[] getPaths()

public boolean isAddedPath()
public boolean isAddedPath(TreePath)

public Object cloneWithSource(Object source)

The first two methods listed above return references to tree paths representing the new and old lead selection paths. The lead selection path is defined as the last path that was added to the selection.

Note: *Because of a bug in Swing 1.1 FCS, the lead selection path is incorrectly set when the newly selected node is in a row that is numerically higher than the row for the previous lead selection path.*

The `getPath` and `getPaths` methods return the first selection path and an array of selection paths. The `isAddedPath` method determines whether the last selection resulted in a path being added or removed from the selection. The `isAddedPath(TreePath)` method determines whether a particular selection path was added or removed from the selection.

The `cloneWithSource` method returns a copy of the event with the specified object as the source of the event.

The applet shown in Figure 20-27 contains a split pane that contains a tree and a text area. When a selection is made in the tree, information about the selection event is appended to the text area.

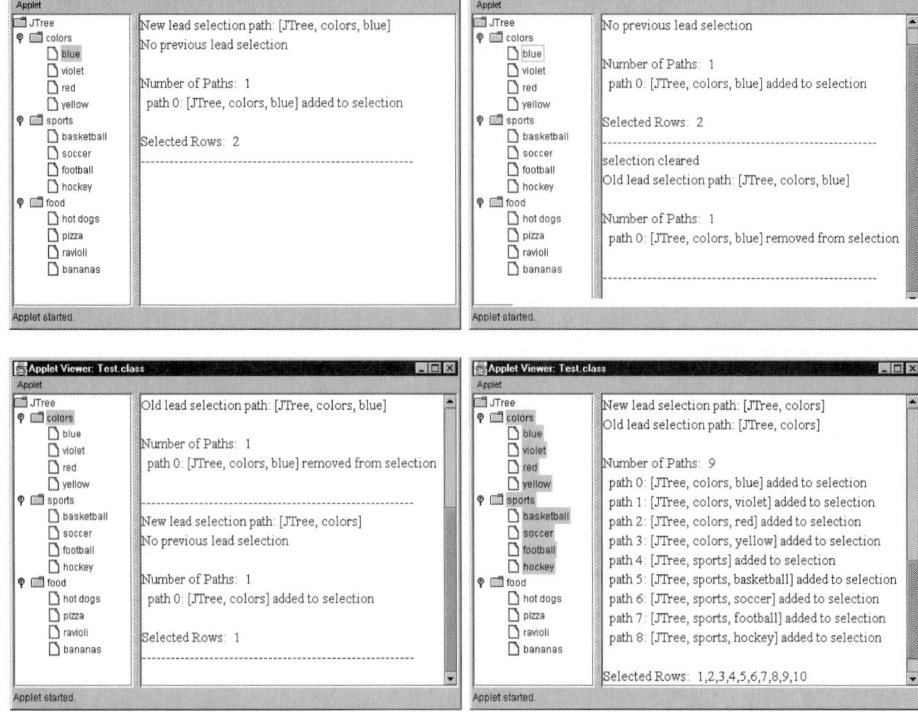

Figure 20-27 Tree Selection Events

The upper-left picture in Figure 20-27 shows the applet after the `blue` node is selected. The new lead selection path is a path from the root node to the `blue` node, and the old lead selection path is `null` because there was no previous selection. The event contains one path—the new lead selection path that was added to the selection.

The upper-right picture in Figure 20-27 shows the applet after the `blue` node has been deselected (by CTRL-clicking on the `blue` node). The new lead selection path is now `null`, indicating that selection has been cleared. The event contains one path—the old lead selection path that was removed from the selection.

The lower-left picture shows the applet after a subsequent selection of the `colors` node. The new lead selection path is now a path from the root node to the `colors` node, and the event contains a single path representing the new lead selection path.

The lower-right picture shows the applet after the nodes from the `colors` node to the `hockey` node have been selected (by SHIFT-clicking on the `hockey` node). The new lead selection path is the same as the old selection path because of a Swing 1.1 FCS bug. The new lead selection path should be updated to represent the newly selected node. The number of selection paths is 9, one for each of the nodes that were selected by the selection event.

The applet adds a tree selection listener to the tree to obtain references to the new and old lead selection paths. If the new lead selection path is `null`, selection has been cleared. Information about the new and old lead selection paths is subsequently added to the applet's text area. A call is then made to the listener's `printSelectionInformation()`, which prints additional information about the tree selection.

```
public class Test extends JApplet {
    ...
    public void init() {
        ...
        tree.addTreeSelectionListener(
                            new TreeSelectionListener() {
            public void valueChanged(TreeSelectionEvent e) {
                TreePath path = e.getNewLeadSelectionPath();
                String s = new String();

                if(path != null) {
                    s += "New lead selection path: " +
                                    path.toString() + "\n";
                }
                else
                    s += "selection cleared\n";

                path = e.getOldLeadSelectionPath();

                if(path != null) {
                    s += "Old lead selection node: " +
                                    path.toString() + "\n";
                }
                else
                    s += "No previous lead selection\n";

                textArea.append(s + "\n");
                printSelectionInformation(e);
            }
        ...
```

The `printSelectionInformation` method obtains the tree paths from the event and appends information about each path to the text area. The

`TreeSelectionEvent.isAddedPath` method is used to determine whether a path was added or removed from the selection.

```
    . . .
    void printSelectionInformation(TreeSelectionEvent e) {
        showPaths(e);
        showRows();

        textArea.append("\n----------------------------");
        textArea.append("----------------------------");
        textArea.append("--------------------------\n");
    }
    private void showPaths(TreeSelectionEvent e) {
        TreePath[] paths = e.getPaths();

        textArea.append("Number of Paths:   " +
                        paths.length + "\n");

        for(int i=0; i < paths.length; ++i) {
            TreePath path = paths[i];
            boolean wasAdded = e.isAddedPath(path);

            textArea.append("   path " + i + ": ");
            textArea.append(path +
                (wasAdded ? " added to selection" :
                 " removed from selection") + "\n");
        }

    }
    . . .
```

The listener's `showRows` method appends information to the text area concerning the tree's currently selected rows. An `integer` array representing selected rows is obtained from the tree with the `JTree.getSelectionRows` method.

```
    . . .
    private void showRows() {
        int[] rows = tree.getSelectionRows();

        if(rows != null && rows.length > 0) {
            textArea.append("\nSelected Rows:   ");

            for(int i=0; i < rows.length; ++i) {
                textArea.append(
                            Integer.toString(rows[i]));

                if(i != rows.length-1)
                    textArea.append(",");
```

```
            }
        }

    }
    });
    }
}
```

The applet shown in Figure 20-27 is listed in its entirety in Example 20-18.

Example 20-18 Handling Tree Selection Events

```java
import javax.swing.*;
import javax.swing.tree.*;
import javax.swing.event.*;
import java.awt.*;
import java.awt.event.*;

public class Test extends JApplet {
    JTree tree = new JTree();
    JTextArea textArea = new JTextArea();
    JSplitPane splitPane = new JSplitPane(
                        JSplitPane.HORIZONTAL_SPLIT,
                        new JScrollPane(tree),
                        new JScrollPane(textArea));
    public void init() {
        splitPane.setDividerLocation(150);

        getContentPane().add(splitPane, BorderLayout.CENTER);

        tree.addTreeSelectionListener(
                        new TreeSelectionListener() {
            public void valueChanged(TreeSelectionEvent e) {
                TreePath path = e.getNewLeadSelectionPath();
                String s = new String();

                if(path != null) {
                    s += "New lead selection path: " +
                                path.toString() + "\n";
                }
                else
                    s += "selection cleared\n";

                path = e.getOldLeadSelectionPath();

                if(path != null) {
                    s += "Old lead selection node: " +
                                path.toString() + "\n";
                }
                else
                    s += "No previous lead selection\n";
```

```
            textArea.append(s + "\n");
            printSelectionInformation(e);
        }
        void printSelectionInformation(TreeSelectionEvent e) {
            showPaths(e);
            showRows();

            textArea.append("\n----------------------------");
            textArea.append("----------------------------");
            textArea.append("---------------------------\n");
        }
        private void showPaths(TreeSelectionEvent e) {
            TreePath[] paths = e.getPaths();

            textArea.append("Number of Paths:  " +
                        paths.length + "\n");

            for(int i=0; i < paths.length; ++i) {
                TreePath path = paths[i];
                boolean wasAdded = e.isAddedPath(path);

                textArea.append("  path " + i + ": ");
                textArea.append(path +
                        (wasAdded ? " added to selection" :
                        " removed from selection") + "\n");
            }

        }
        private void showRows() {
            int[] rows = tree.getSelectionRows();

            if(rows != null && rows.length > 0) {
                textArea.append("\nSelected Rows:  ");

                for(int i=0; i < rows.length; ++i) {
                    textArea.append(
                                Integer.toString(rows[i]));

                    if(i != rows.length-1)
                        textArea.append(",");
                }
            }
        }
    });
    }
}
```

Tree Expansion Events

After a folder is expanded or collapsed, the JTree class fires a tree expansion event to all registered listeners that implement the TreeExpansionListener interface. The TreeExpansionListener interface is summarized in Interface Summary 20-9.

Interface Summary 20-9   TreeExpansionListener

---

public abstract void <u>treeCollapsed</u>(TreeExpansionEvent)
public abstract void <u>treeExpanded</u>(TreeExpansionEvent)

The TreeExpansionListener interface defines the two methods listed above. It is left as an exercise to the reader to discern which methods are called when a folder expansion or collapse has occurred.

Both methods defined by the TreeExpansionListener interface are passed an instance of TreeExpansionEvent. The TreeExpansionEvent class is summarized in Class Summary 20-6.

Class Summary 20-6   TreeExpansionEvent

Constructors

---

public <u>TreeExpansionEvent</u>(Object source, TreePath path)

`TreeExpansionEvents` are instantiated with the source of the event, which is always an instance of `JTree` in which the expansion or collapse occurred. The lone `TreeExpansionEvent` constructor is also passed an instance of `TreePath` representing the node that was expanded or collapsed.

Methods

---

public TreePath getPath()

The only information available from a tree expansion event is the path to the folder that was expanded or collapsed.

The applet shown in Figure 20-28 reacts to folder expansion and collapse by updating the applet's status area.

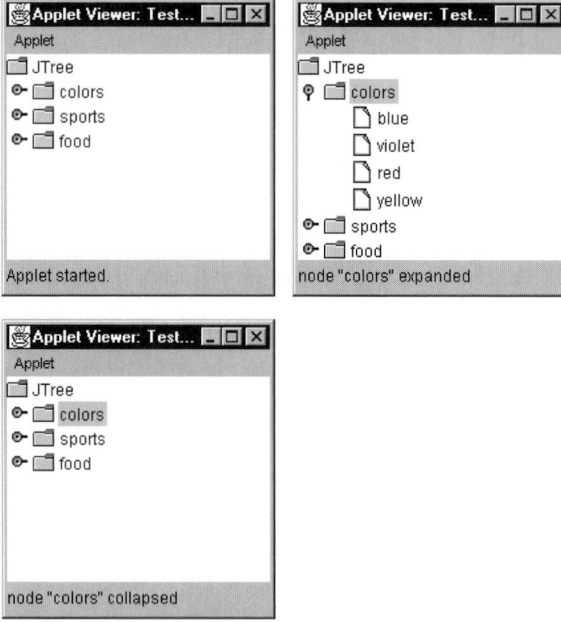

Figure 20-28 Handling Tree Expansion Events

The applet shown in Figure 20-28 is listed in Example 20-19.

Example 20-19   Handling Tree Expansion Events

```java
import javax.swing.*;
import javax.swing.event.*;
import javax.swing.tree.*;
import java.awt.*;
import java.awt.event.*;

public class Test extends JApplet {
    public void init() {
        Container contentPane = getContentPane();
        JTree tree = new JTree();

        contentPane.add(tree);

        tree.addTreeExpansionListener(
                        new TreeExpansionListener() {
            public void treeCollapsed(TreeExpansionEvent e) {
                TreePath path = e.getPath();
                TreeNode node = (TreeNode)
                        path.getLastPathComponent();

                showStatus("node " + "\"" + node.toString() +
                        "\"" + " collapsed");
            }
            public void treeExpanded(TreeExpansionEvent e) {
                TreePath path = e.getPath();
                TreeNode node = (TreeNode)
                        path.getLastPathComponent();

                showStatus("node " + "\"" + node.toString() +
                        "\"" + " expanded");
            }
        });
    }
}
```

The applet adds a tree expansion listener to the tree that obtains the folder that was expanded or collapsed. The listener obtains the tree path from the event and subsequently obtains the node from the path. The node is then used to update that applet's status area.

Vetoing Node Expansion and Collapse

The JTree class actually fires two events every time a tree folder is expanded or collapsed. Prior to expanding or collapsing a folder, a tree expansion event is fired to registered listeners that implement the TreeWillExpandListener interface.

If the expansion or collapse is not vetoed by any of the listeners, the expansion or collapse is performed and another tree expansion event is fired to registered listeners that implement the `TreeExpansionListener` interface.

The `TreeWillExpandListener` interface is summarized in Interface Summary 20-10.

Interface Summary 20-10   TreeWillExpandListener

---

public abstract void <u>treeWillCollapse</u>(TreeExpansionEvent) throwExpandVetoException
public abstract void <u>treeWillExpand</u>(TreeExpansionEvent) throws ExpandVetoException

The `TreeWillExpandListener` interface defines the two methods listed above that are invoked just prior to folder collapse or expansion. Both methods are passed a `TreeExpansionEvent`, and both methods may throw with an expand veto exception.

The `ExpandVetoException` class is summarized in Class Summary 20-7.

Class Summary 20-7   ExpandVetoException

Constructors

---

public <u>ExpandVetoException</u>(TreeExpansionEvent)
public <u>ExpandVetoException</u>(TreeExpansionEvent, String)

Like most exception classes, ExpandVetoException provides constructors but no methods. ExpandVetoExceptions are constructed with a TreeExpansionEvent and an optional string representing a message. It should be noted that the message, if supplied, is not used by the Swing classes.

The applet shown in Figure 20-29 contains a tree that is fitted with a TreeWillExpandListener that vetoes expansion of the tree's colors folder and collapsing of the food folder.

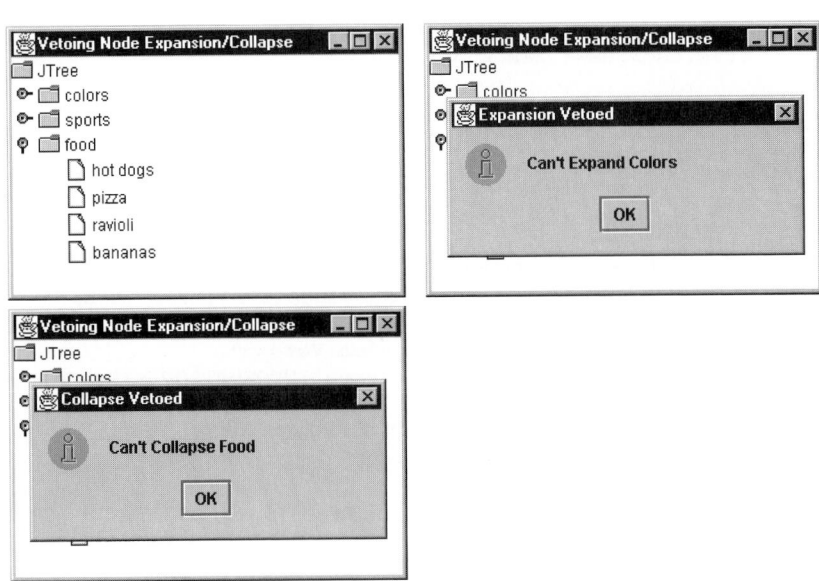

Figure 20-29 Vetoing Node Expansion and Collapse

The applet shown in Figure 20-29 is listed in Example 20-20.

Example 20-20 Vetoing Node Expansion and Collapse

```java
import javax.swing.*;
import javax.swing.event.*;
import javax.swing.tree.*;
import java.awt.*;
import java.awt.event.*;

public class Test extends JFrame {
    public Test() {
        JTree tree = new JTree();
        getContentPane().add(tree);

        tree.addTreeWillExpandListener(
                            new TreeWillExpandListener() {
            public void treeWillExpand(TreeExpansionEvent e)
                            throws ExpandVetoException {
                TreePath path = e.getPath();
                TreeNode node = (TreeNode)
                        path.getLastPathComponent();

                if(node.toString().equals("colors")) {
                    JOptionPane.showMessageDialog(Test.this,
                            "Can't Expand Colors",
                            "Expansion Vetoed",
                            JOptionPane.INFORMATION_MESSAGE);

                    throw new ExpandVetoException(e);
                }
            }
            public void treeWillCollapse(TreeExpansionEvent e)
                            throws ExpandVetoException {
                TreePath path = e.getPath();
                TreeNode node = (TreeNode)
                        path.getLastPathComponent();

                if(node.toString().equals("food")) {
                    JOptionPane.showMessageDialog(Test.this,
                            "Can't Collapse Food",
                            "Collapse Vetoed",
                            JOptionPane.INFORMATION_MESSAGE);

                    throw new ExpandVetoException(e);
                }
            }
        });
    }
    public static void main(String args[]) {
        GraphicJavaApplication.launch(new Test(),
            "Vetoing Node Expansion/Collapse",300,300,300,200);
    }
}
```

The `treeWillExpand` and `treeWillCollapse` methods of the listener obtain the node that will be expanded or collapsed, respectively, and veto the expansion or a collapse by throwing an expand veto exception.

JTree Class Summaries

The `public` and `protected` variables and methods for `JTree` are listed in Class Summary 20-8.

Class Summary 20-8   JTree

Constants

---

public static final String <u>CELL EDITOR PROPERTY</u>
public static final String <u>CELL RENDERER PROPERTY</u>
public static final String <u>EDITABLE PROPERTY</u>
public static final String <u>INVOKES STOP CELL EDITING PROPERTY</u>
public static final String <u>LARGE MODEL PROPERTY</u>
public static final String <u>ROOT VISIBLE PROPERTY</u>
public static final String <u>ROW HEIGHT PROPERTY</u>
public static final String <u>SCROLLS ON EXPAND PROPERTY</u>
public static final String <u>SELECTION MODEL PROPERTY</u>
public static final String <u>SHOWS ROOT HANDLES PROPERTY</u>
public static final String <u>TREE MODEL PROPERTY</u>
public static final String <u>VISIBLE ROW COUNT PROPERTY</u>

The constants listed above represent `JTree` bound properties. The constants can be used to determine which property was modified in a property change listener's `propertyChange` method.

Constructors

---

public <u>JTree</u>()

public <u>JTree</u>(Object[])
public <u>JTree</u>(Hashtable)
public <u>JTree</u>(Vector)

public <u>JTree</u>(TreeModel)

public <u>JTree</u>(TreeNode)
public <u>JTree</u>(TreeNode, boolean asksAllowsChildren)

The `JTree` class provides constructors for creating trees with or without data. Trees created with the no-argument constructor are fitted a default set of nodes. The no-argument constructor is provided mainly for JavaBeans builder tools and is of little practical use otherwise.

Constructors are provided for creating trees with arrays of objects, a hash table, or a vector, but in practice the constructors will rarely be used. Most trees will be created with one of the last three constructors listed above.

Methods

Scrollable Interface Methods

---

public Dimension <u>getPreferredScrollableViewportSize</u>()
public int <u>getScrollableBlockIncrement</u>(Rectangle, int orientation, int direction)
public boolean <u>getScrollableTracksViewportHeight</u>()
public boolean <u>getScrollableTracksViewportWidth</u>()
public int <u>getScrollableUnitIncrement</u>(Rectangle, int orientation, int direction)

The `JTree` class implements the `Scrollable` interface; see "The Scrollable Interface" on page 764 for more information concerning the `Scrollable` interface.

The `getPreferredScrollableViewportSize` method defines a tree's preferred size for its viewport when a tree is contained in a scrollpane. The

preferred viewport height is calculated from the tree's visible row count and row height. The preferred width is equal to a tree's preferred width.

The `getScrollableBlockIncrement` method returns the pixel amount a tree is scrolled when it is scrolled by a block increment. The block increment is equal to the width or height (depending on the orientation parameter) of the tree's visible rectangle.

The `getScrollableUnitIncrement` method returns the pixel amount a tree is scrolled when it is scrolled by a unit increment. The unit increment height is the number of pixels necessary to scroll the next node into view. The unit increment width is equal to 4 pixels.

The `getScrollableTracksViewportHeight` and `getScrollableTracksViewportWidth` methods determine whether a tree's height or width, respectively, are kept the same as the tree's viewport. If a tree is smaller than in its viewport, the methods return `true`; otherwise, they return `false`. The methods ensure that a tree is never smaller than its viewport.

Tree Model

---

protected static TreeModel <u>getDefaultTreeModel</u>()
protected static TreeModel <u>createTreeModel</u>(Object)

protected TreeModelListener <u>createTreeModelListener</u>()

public void <u>setModel</u>(TreeModel)
public TreeModel <u>getModel</u>()

public void <u>setLargeModel</u>(boolean)
public boolean <u>isLargeModel</u>()

The `getDefaultTreeModel` method creates the default model used when trees are constructed with the `JTree` no argument constructor. The `createTreeModel` method creates a tree model when trees are created with `JTree` constructors that are passed `Object` arrays, hash tables, or vectors.

The `createTreeModelListener` creates an instance of `JTree.TreeModelHandler` that reacts to insertion or removal of nodes by updating the expanded state of the nodes in a tree.

The JTree class provides setter and getter methods for its model with the setModel and getModel methods, respectively.

If a tree contains an enormous amount of data, setLargeModel(true) can be invoked to speed up the tree's display. The speedup is implemented by a tree's look and feel; not all look and feels will support a large model.

Tree Selection

---

public void addTreeSelectionListener(TreeSelectionListener)
public void removeTreeSelectionListener(TreeSelectionListener)

public void addSelectionInterval(int, int)
public void addSelectionPath(TreePath)
public void addSelectionPaths(TreePath[])
public void addSelectionRow(int)
public void addSelectionRows(int[])

public void clearSelection()

public Object getLastSelectedPathComponent()
public TreePath getLeadSelectionPath()
public int getLeadSelectionRow()
public int getMaxSelectionRow()
public int getMinSelectionRow()
public int getSelectionCount()
public TreePath getSelectionPath()
public TreePath[] getSelectionPaths()
public int[] getSelectionRows()

public boolean isSelectionEmpty()

public void removeSelectionInterval(int, int)
public void removeSelectionPath(TreePath)
public void removeSelectionPaths(TreePath[])
public void removeSelectionRow(int)
public void removeSelectionRows(int[])

public void setSelectionInterval(int, int)

public void setSelectionModel()
public void setSelectionModel(TreeSelectionModel)

public void setSelectionPath(TreePath)
public void setSelectionPaths(TreePath[])
public void setSelectionRow(int)
public void setSelectionRows(int[])

protected void fireValueChanged(TreeSelectionEvent)

The JTree class provides a wealth of methods related to tree selection. Many of the methods listed above delegate directly to a tree's selection model. Selection intervals, paths, and rows can be set, added, and removed from the current selection. Selection can be cleared with the clearSelection method.

Tree Expansion

public void addTreeExpansionListener(TreeExpansionListener)
public void addTreeWillExpandListener(TreeWillExpandListener)

public void removeTreeExpansionListener(TreeExpansionListener)
public void removeTreeWillExpandListener(TreeWillExpandListener)

public void fireTreeCollapsed(TreePath)
public void fireTreeExpanded(TreePath)
public void fireTreeWillCollapse(TreePath) throws ExpandVetoException;
public void fireTreeWillExpand(TreePath) throws ExpandVetoException;

public void collapsePath(TreePath)
public void collapseRow(int row)
public void expandPath(TreePath)
public void expandRow(int row)

public boolean hasBeenExpanded(TreePath)
public boolean isCollapsed(int row)
public boolean isCollapsed(TreePath)
public boolean isExpanded(int row)
public boolean isExpanded(TreePath)
protected void clearToggledPaths()
protected void setExpandedState(TreePath, boolean)

public boolean getScrollsOnExpand()
public void setScrollsOnExpand(boolean)

The JTree class provides methods for adding and removing TreeExpansionListeners and TreeWillExpandListeners; see "Tree Expansion Events" on page 1381 for more information on handling tree expansion events. Methods are also provided for firing tree expansion events to listeners. Because TreeWillExpandListeners can veto folder expansion and collapse, the fireTreeWillCollapse and fireTreeWillExpand methods may throw exceptions.

Trees can also have their folders expanded or collapsed programmatically. The JTree class also provides a number of methods for determining whether a row or path is expanded or collapsed.

By default, when a tree is contained in a scrollpane and a folder is expanded, the tree is scrolled to show as many of the folder's descendants as possible. The feature can be turned off by invocation of setScrollsOnExpand(false).

Tree Cell Editing and Rendering

---

public TreeCellEditor getCellEditor()
public TreeCellRenderer getCellRenderer()
public void setCellEditor(TreeCellEditor)
public void setCellRenderer(TreeCellRenderer)

public boolean isEditable()
public void setEditable(boolean)

public boolean getInvokesStopCellEditing()
public void setInvokesStopCellEditing(boolean)

public void startEditingAtPath(TreePath)
public boolean isEditing()

public boolean stopEditing()
public void cancelEditing()

Trees have a single renderer and a single editor, and the JTree class provides accessors for both. By default, trees are not editable, so setEditable(true) must be invoked to enable editing for an instance of JTree.

By default, when a tree editor is active and another node is selected, editing is canceled. setInvokesStopCellEditing(true) can be invoked to force a tree to save editing changes when an editor is active and another node is selected.

The startEditingAtPath method starts editing for a given node. Editing will only be started if the tree's editor deems the node identified by the path to be editable. The startEditingAtPath will rarely be invoked by developers.

The isEditing method determines whether a tree is currently editing a node. The stopEditing and cancelEditing methods stop or cancel editing, respectively.

Tree Paths

protected TreePath[] getPathBetweenRows(int index0, int index1)
public Rectangle getPathBounds(TreePath)
public TreePath getClosestPathForLocation(int x, int y)
public TreePath getPathForLocation(int x, int y)
public TreePath getPathForRow(int)
protected Enumeration getDescendantToggledPaths(TreePath)
public TreePath getEditingPath()
public Enumeration getExpandedDescendants(TreePath)
public boolean isPathEditable(TreePath)
public boolean isPathSelected(TreePath)
public boolean isVisible(TreePath)

public void makeVisible(TreePath)
public void scrollPathToVisible(TreePath)
protected void removeDescendantToggledPaths(Enumeration)

The methods listed above obtain paths for rows and locations and determine characteristics of a path, such as whether the path is visible or selected. For example, the getPathForLocation method is passed a location, and if the location coincides with a node, the method returns a path to the node; otherwise, it returns null. The getClosestPathForLocation returns the closest path for a given location, regardless of whether the location coincides with a node.

The makeVisible method expands a folder identified by the path it is passed and ensures that the node is viewable; the scrollPathToVisible scrolls a node into view if the tree is contained in a scrollpane.

Tree Rows

___

```
public Rectangle getRowBounds(int row)
public int getRowCount()
public int getRowForLocation(int x, int y)
public int getClosestRowForLocation(int x, int y)
public int getRowForPath(TreePath)

public boolean isFixedRowHeight()
public boolean isRowSelected(int row)

public int getRowHeight()
public void setRowHeight(int row)

public int getVisibleRowCount()
public void setVisibleRowCount(int row)

public void scrollRowToVisible(int row)
```

The `JTree` class provides a number of methods that deal with rows. For example, a row's bounds can be obtained in addition to the row corresponding to a given location. The number of rows that are visible when a tree is contained in a scrollpane can be set, and a row can be scrolled into view.

Utility Methods

___

```
public String convertValueToText((JTree tree, Object value, boolean isSelected,
                                  boolean expanded, boolean leaf, int row)
public boolean getShowsRootHandles()
public void setShowsRootHandles(boolean)

public void setRootVisible(boolean)
public boolean isRootVisible()

public String getToolTipText(MouseEvent)

protected String paramString()
public void treeDidChange()
```

A number of utility methods are provided by the JTree class. For renderers, the convertValueToText converts the value passed to a renderer to text. Accessors are provided for the visibility of the root node and root node handles; see "Root Nodes and Root Handles" on page 1342 for more information concerning root node visibility and root node handles.

The getToolTipText method is overridden from JComponent to allow renderer tooltips to be displayed. See "Tooltips" on page 171 for more information concerning the getToolTipText method.

The paramString method is overridden from the Object class to return a textual description of a tree. The treeDidChange method is provided for a tree's UI delegate and should never be invoked directly by developers.

Accessibility / Pluggable Look and Feel

---

public AccessibleContext getAccessibleContext()
public TreeUI getUI()
public String getUIClassID()
public void setUI(TreeUI)
public void updateUI()

The methods listed above can be found in most extensions of JComponent. Swing lightweight components can return the class name of their UI delegate and an accessibility context that contains accessibility information for the component. The updateUI method is invoked when the component is fitted with a UI delegate.

AWT Compatibility

The AWT does not provide a component analogous to JTree.

Parting Shots

Like JTable, JTree is one of Swing's most complex components. JTree is a very well-designed component that despite its complexity is relatively easy to use. JTree also provides excellent performance when expanding/collapsing nodes and scrolling.

CHAPTER
21

Text Fundamentals

Swing text components are relatively simple components built upon a complex infrastructure provided by the classes and interfaces from the `javax.swing.text` package. Swing text is covered in three chapters: this chapter discusses the fundamental capabilities that all text components inherit from the `JTextComponent` class. "Text Components" on page 1457 discusses the text components themselves, and "Customizing Text Components" on page 1531 discusses more advanced aspects of Swing text, such as views, elements, attribute sets, and styles.

Swing Text Components

Swing provides five text components, which are listed in Table 21-1. All of the Swing text components ultimately extend the `JComponent` class, which provides a great deal of fundamental capabilities for its extensions. The `JComponent` class is summarized in "JTextComponent" on page 1442.

Table 21-1   Swing Text Components

Component	Multiple Lines	Plain/Styled Text	Use ...
JTextArea	•	Plain	for short editable documents with optional word wrapping and one font
JTextField		Plain	for one-line text entry
JPasswordField		Plain	for entering one-line passwords
JEditorPane	•	Plain/Styled	for viewing different content types
JTextPane	•	Styled	for documents with multiple fonts, embedded images, or components

Although all Swing text components extend the JTextComponent class and use functionality from the swing.text package, Swing text components come in two distinct flavors: simple text components, and styled components.

The first three components listed in Table 21-1—JTextArea, JTextField, and JPasswordField—are simple text components that can display only one font and color at a time. JTextField and JTextArea are implemented to retain compatibility with the AWT's TextField and TextArea components.

The last two components listed in Table 21-1—JEditorPane and JTextPane— are styled components that can display text in more than one font and color. The JEditorPane component can display different types of content, such as HTML and RTF, and the JTextPane component can embed images and components.

Figure 21-1 is a class diagram that provides an overview of the Swing text components. Swing text components do not implement scrolling directly; instead, the JTextComponent class implements the Scrollable interface so that text components can be placed in a scrollpane.

Figure 21-1 Swing Text Component Overview

The JTextField, JTextArea and JEditorPane classes extend the
JComponent class directly. One extension of JTextField is provided for
entering passwords.

The JTextArea class, unlike JTextField and its extensions, can display
multiple lines of text and can wrap text on word or character boundaries.

The JEditorPane class maintains a hash table for associating content types with
an editor kit, which enables it to display different types of content. The
JTextPane class is an extension of JEditorPane.

The Swing Text Package

The Swing text package provides many classes and interfaces that support the text components. Table 21-2 lists the main classes and interfaces defined in the Swing text package.

Table 21-2   Fundamental Swing Text Classes and Interfaces

Name	Class/Interface	Description
AttributeSet	Interface	A set of key/value attributes for an element.
EditorKit	Class	Provides a set of actions used to manipulate a text component. Creates document and views for styled text components.
View	Class	Paints a portion (or all) of a text component's content.
Document	Interface	Stores a text component's content and attributes that are applied to the content.
Element	Interface	Represents a span of content in a document with attributes.
Keymap	Interface	A set of keystroke/action bindings.
Caret	Interface	The text cursor.
Highlighter	Interface	Paints highlights in a text component.
Position	Interface	Represents a position in a document.
Style	Interface	A named, mutable attribute set.
StyleContext	Class[1]	A set of styles that can be shared across text components.
ViewFactory	Interface	A factory that creates views, given an element.

1. StyleContext implements the AbstractDocument.AttributeContext interface.

The classes and interfaces listed in Table 21-2 are discussed in detail in this chapter and the two chapters that follow. The following classes and interfaces can be accessed through the `JTextComponent` class and are introduced in this chapter:

- `Document`
- `Keymap`
- `Caret`
- `Highlighter`
- `Position`

Actions

Much of a text component's functionality is encapsulated in a set of actions that are maintained by the component's editor kit. A text component's actions are accessible through the JTextComponent.getActions method, which returns an Action array.

There are a couple of major advantages to encapsulating text component functionality in actions. First, actions can be shared among multiple components, and indeed, all text components share a set of default actions; see "Actions" on page 235 for more information on sharing actions. Second, actions are easily associated with keystrokes, toolbar buttons, and menu items.

Text Actions

By default, a text component's actions are instances of the TextAction class, which extends AbstractAction. Recall from "Actions as a Central Point of Control" on page 238 that actions are not associated with a single component, thus allowing actions to be shared among multiple components. Therefore, when a text action is fired—meaning its actionPerformed method is invoked—the action must locate a text object upon which to operate.

The TextAction class provides a protected getTextComponenent method that is passed an action event. If the source of the event is a text component, the component is returned from getTextComponent(). If the source of the event is not a text component, getTextComponent() returns the text component that last had focus.

The code fragment from the DefaultEditorKit class listed below illustrates how extensions of TextAction use the TextAction.getTextComponent method.

```
// From DefaultEditorKit ...

public static class CutAction extends TextAction {
    public CutAction() {
        super(cutAction);
    }
    public void actionPerformed(ActionEvent e) {
        JTextComponent target = getTextComponent(e);
```

```
        if (target != null) {
            target.cut();
        }
    }
}
```

The `CutAction` class is one of several extensions of `TextAction` implemented by the `DefaultEditorKit` class; see Table 21-3 on page 1409 for a list of such classes. The `cutAction` variable passed to the superclass (`TextAction`) constructor is a string defined in `DefaultEditorKit` that identifies the cut action.

The `CutAction.actionPerformed` method obtains the text component upon which to operate with the `TextAction.getTextComponent` method and invokes the component's `cut` method.

The `TextAction` class is summarized in Class Summary 21-1.

Class Summary 21-1   TextAction

Extends: AbstractAction

Constructors

---

public <u>TextAction</u>(String name)

The `TextAction` class provides a single constructor that is passed a name for the action. The action's name is passed along to the `AbstractAction` constructor.

Methods

---

public static final Action[] <u>augmentList</u>(Action[], Action[])

protected final JTextComponent <u>getFocusedComponent</u>()
protected final JTextComponent <u>getTextComponent</u>(ActionEvent)

The `TextAction` class implements a `static` convenience method for augmenting an array of actions with another array of actions. The `augmentList` method comes in handy when a text component adds a set of actions to the default set that comes with every text component. See Example 23-4 on page 1553 for an example that uses the `TextAction.augmentList` method.

The `getFocusedComponent` method returns the text component that last had focus. The last focused text component is actually maintained by the `JTextComponent` class; see "JTextComponent" on page 1442 for a discussion of `JTextComponent` methods.

The `getTextComponent` method returns either the source of the event if the source is a text component, or the last focused text component.

The application shown in Figure 21-2 contains a split pane with a text area on the left and a list of the text area's actions on the right. Selecting an action from the list causes the action to be performed on the text area. The left picture in Figure 21-2 shows the application after a selection has been made in the text area. The right picture shows the application after the cut-to-clipboard action has been fired on behalf of the text area.

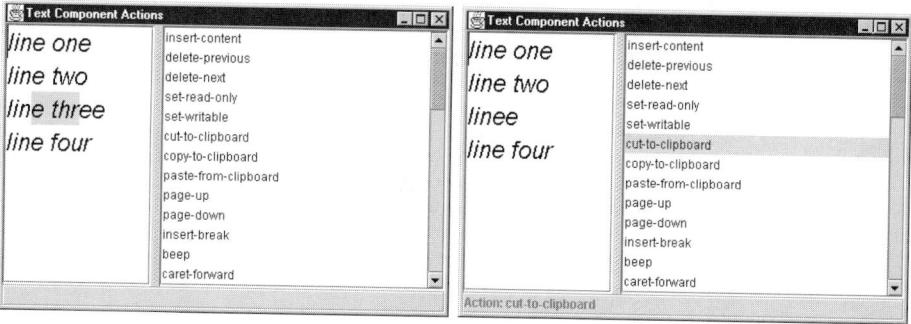

Figure 21-2 Text Component Actions

The application creates the text area and the list and adds them to a split pane. The split pane is subsequently added to the application's content pane as the center component. The application also installs the `GJApp` status area as the content pane's south component. See "GJApp" on page 40 or more information on the `GJApp` class. The status area is updated when an action is performed with the action 's name.

The text area's actions are obtained by invoking `getActions()` for the text area. The actions are passed to the applet's `createActionList` method, which adds each of the actions to the applet's list.

```
public class Test extends JFrame {
    private JTextArea textArea = createTextArea();
    private Action[] actions = textArea.getActions();

    private JList actionList = createActionList(actions);
    private JSplitPane splitPane = new JSplitPane(
                        JSplitPane.HORIZONTAL_SPLIT,
                        new JScrollPane(textArea),
                        new JScrollPane(actionList));
    public Test() {
        Container contentPane = getContentPane();
        ...
        contentPane.add(splitPane, BorderLayout.CENTER);
        contentPane.add(GJApp.getStatusArea(),
                    BorderLayout.SOUTH);
    }
    private JList createActionList(Action[] actions) {
        DefaultListModel model = new DefaultListModel();
        final JList list = new JList(model);


        ...
        for(int i=0; i < actions.length; ++i) {
            model.addElement(actions[i]);
        }
        ...
        list.addListSelectionListener(new ListSelectionListener(){
            public void valueChanged(ListSelectionEvent e) {
                if(!e.getValueIsAdjusting()) {
                    Action source =
                        (Action)actionList.getSelectedValue();

                    source.actionPerformed(null);

                    GJApp.showStatus("Action: " +
                            (String)source.getValue(Action.NAME));
                }
            }
        });
        return list;
    }
}
```

The actions are fired by a list selection listener that is added to the application's list. The listener obtains a reference to the selected action and invokes `actionPerformed` with a `null` action event, causing the action to be performed on the last focused text component.

After the action is performed, the application's status area is updated to reflect the action that was performed.

The application shown in Figure 21-2 is listed in its entirety in Example 21-1.

Example 21-1 Using Text Component Actions

```java
import java.awt.*;
import java.awt.event.*;
import javax.swing.*;
import javax.swing.event.*;
import javax.swing.text.*;
import java.util.*;

public class Test extends JFrame {
    private JTextArea textArea = createTextArea();
    private Action[] actions = textArea.getActions();

    private JList actionList = createActionList(actions);
    private JSplitPane splitPane = new JSplitPane(
                        JSplitPane.HORIZONTAL_SPLIT,
                        new JScrollPane(textArea),
                        new JScrollPane(actionList));
    public Test() {
        Container contentPane = getContentPane();

        splitPane.setDividerLocation(150);

        contentPane.add(splitPane, BorderLayout.CENTER);
        contentPane.add(GJApp.getStatusArea(),
                    BorderLayout.SOUTH);

    }
    private JList createActionList(Action[] actions) {
        DefaultListModel model = new DefaultListModel();
        final JList list = new JList(model);

        list.setSelectionMode(
                    ListSelectionModel.SINGLE_SELECTION);

        for(int i=0; i < actions.length; ++i) {
            model.addElement(actions[i]);
        }

        list.setCellRenderer(new DefaultListCellRenderer() {
```

```
            public Component getListCellRendererComponent(
                            JList list, Object value,
                            int index, boolean isSelected,
                            boolean cellHasFocus) {
                super.getListCellRendererComponent(list, value,
                    index, isSelected, cellHasFocus);

                Action action = (Action)value;
                setText((String)action.getValue(Action.NAME));

                return this;
            }
        });
        list.addListSelectionListener(new ListSelectionListener(){
            public void valueChanged(ListSelectionEvent e) {
                if(!e.getValueIsAdjusting()) {
                    Action source =
                        (Action)actionList.getSelectedValue();

                    textArea.requestFocus();
                    source.actionPerformed(null);

                    GJApp.showStatus("Action: " +
                            (String)source.getValue(Action.NAME));
                }
            }
        });

        return list;
    }
    private JTextArea createTextArea() {
        JTextArea textArea = new JTextArea(
            "line one\nline two\nline three\nline four");

        textArea.setFont(new Font("Dialog", Font.ITALIC, 24));
        textArea.getCaret().setBlinkRate(0);
        return textArea;
    }
    public static void main(String args[]) {
        GJApp.launch(new Test(),
                "Text Component Actions",300,300,450,300);
    }
}
```

Actions and Editor Kits

As mentioned in "Actions" on page 1401, a text component's actions are maintained by the component's editor kit. The `DefaultEditorKit` class provides a default set of actions that are shared by all text components, and a corresponding set of names that identifies each of the actions.

The applet shown in Figure 21-3 illustrates how to use an editor kit to access specific actions associated with a text component. The applet creates a hash table of actions and their names, and it accesses cut, copy, and paste actions with string constants defined by the `DefaultEditorKit` class.

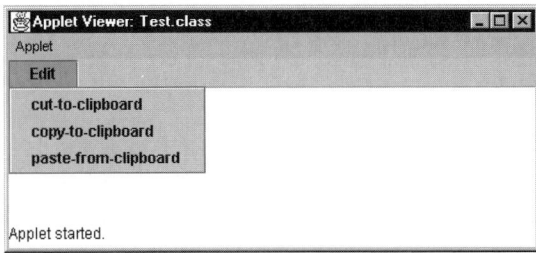

Figure 21-3 Text Component Actions

The applet shown in Figure 21-3 is listed in Example 21-2.

Example 21-2 Accessing Actions with Default Editor Kit Constants

```
import java.awt.*;
import javax.swing.*;
import javax.swing.text.*;
import java.util.*;

public class Test extends JApplet {
    private JTextArea textArea = new JTextArea("some content");
    private Hashtable actionTable = new Hashtable();

    public void init() {
        Container contentPane = getContentPane();

        textArea.setFont(new Font("Dialog", Font.PLAIN, 24));

        loadActionTable();

        setJMenuBar(createMenu());
```

```
            contentPane.add(textArea, BorderLayout.CENTER);
        }
        private void loadActionTable() {
            Action[] actions = textArea.getActions();

            for(int i=0; i < actions.length; ++i) {
                actionTable.put(actions[i].getValue(Action.NAME),
                          actions[i]);
            }
        }
        private Action getAction(String name) {
            return (Action)actionTable.get(name);
        }
        private JMenuBar createMenu() {
            JMenuBar menuBar = new JMenuBar();
            JMenu editMenu = new JMenu("Edit");

            editMenu.add(getAction(DefaultEditorKit.cutAction));
            editMenu.add(getAction(DefaultEditorKit.copyAction));
            editMenu.add(getAction(DefaultEditorKit.pasteAction));

            menuBar.add(editMenu);
            return menuBar;
        }
    }
```

The applet contains a text area and maintains a hash table of the text area's actions and their names. The applet also implements a getAction method that is passed an action name and returns the associated action.

The actions are added to the Edit menu by invoking the applet's getAction method, which is passed DefaultEditorKit string constants for the cut, copy, and paste actions.

The DefaultEditorKit class also provides a number of classes for certain actions. Alternatively, the applet listed in Example 21-2 could create new actions that are added to the Edit menu, like this:

```
    editMenu.add(new DefaultEditorKit.CutAction());
    editMenu.add(new DefaultEditorKit.CopyAction());
    editMenu.add(new DefaultEditorKit.PasteAction());
```

The string constants and classes defined by the DefaultEditorKit class are listed in Table 21-3.

Table 21-3 DefaultEditorKit Actions

Class[1]	String
	backwardAction
BeepAction	beepAction
	beginAction
	beginLineAction
	beginParagraphAction
	beginWordAction
CopyAction	copyAction
CutAction	cutAction
DefaultKeyTypedAction	defaultKeyTypedAction
	deleteNextCharAction
	deletePrevCharAction
	downAction
	endAction
	endLineAction
	endParagraphAction
	endWordAction
	forwardAction
InsertBreakAction	insertBreakAction
InsertContentAction	insertContentAction
InsertTabAction	insertTabAction
	nextWordAction
	pageDownAction
	pageUpAction
	pasteAction
	previousWordAction
	readOnlyAction
	selectAllAction
	selectLineAction
	selectParagraphAction
	selectWordAction
	selectionBackwardAction
	selectionBeginAction
	selectionBeginLineAction

1. All classes are DefaultEditorKit nested classes.

Table 21-3   DefaultEditorKit Actions (Continued)

Class[1]	String
	selectionBeginParagraphAction
	selectionBeginWordAction
	selectionDownAction
	selectionEndAction
	selectionEndLineAction
	selectionEndParagraphAction
	selectionEndWordAction
	selectionForwardAction
	selectionNextWordAction
	selectionPreviousWordAction
	selectionUpAction
	upAction
	writableAction

Text Actions and Editor Kits

One of the most significant aspects of the Swing text components is that much of a text component's functionality is encapsulated in a set of actions.

Because actions can be shared by multiple components and because text actions are performed on the last focused text component, sets of actions can be shared among different types of text components. For example, the DefaultEditorKit provides the set of actions listed in Table 21-3 that are shared among all Swing text components.

Keymaps

Perhaps the most fundamental undertaking by a text component is to translate keystrokes into specific actions. Every text component maintains a mapping of keystrokes to actions in the form of a keymap, that is defined by the `Keymap` interface. A text component's keymap is accessible through the `JTextComponent` methods `getKeymap()` and `setKeymap()`.

In addition to providing a `setKeymap` method for setting a text component's keymap outright, a keymap can be added to a text component by specifying a keymap and a parent keymap. Keymaps resolve hierarchically, meaning that keystrokes not defined in a child keymap are searched for in the parent keymap. The `JTextComponent` class provides a number of methods for manipulating a text component's keymap. See "JTextComponent" on page 1442 for more information concerning the `JTextComponent` class.

The `Keymap` interface is summarized in Interface Summary 21-1.

Interface Summary 21-1   Keymap

Actions

---

public abstract void <u>addActionForKeyStroke</u>(KeyStroke, Action)
public abstract Action <u>getAction</u>(KeyStroke)
public abstract Action[] <u>getBoundActions</u>()
public abstract Action <u>getDefaultAction</u>()
public abstract void <u>setDefaultAction</u>(Action)

The `addActionForKeyStroke` method adds a keystroke/action pair to a keymap, and the `getAction` method returns the action associated with the specified keystroke. The `getBoundActions` method returns an array of actions contained in the keymap that are bound to a keystroke.

Every text component has a default action that typically inserts keystrokes into the component. The default action can be accessed with the last two methods listed above.

Keystrokes

---

public abstract KeyStroke[] getBoundKeyStrokes()
public abstract KeyStroke[] getKeyStrokesForAction(Action)
public abstract boolean isLocallyDefined(KeyStroke)
public abstract void removeKeyStrokeBinding(KeyStroke)

The methods listed above all deal with a keymap's keystrokes. The `getBoundKeyStrokes` method returns an array of keystrokes that are bound to an action. An action can have multiple keystrokes associated with it, and the `getKeyStrokesForAction` method returns an array of keystrokes for a specific action.

The `isLocallyDefined` method returns a `boolean` value indicating whether a keystroke is defined in the keymap, as opposed to being contained in a parent keymap. The `removeKeyStrokeBinding` method removes a keystroke binding from a keymap.

Resolve Parent / Name

---

public abstract String getName()
public abstract Keymap getResolveParent()
public abstract void setResolveParent(Keymap)

public abstract void removeBindings()

Every keymap has a name and a parent keymap, known as the resolve parent. The first three methods listed above are accessors for the `name` and `resolveParent` properties. The `removeBindings` method effectively guts a keymap by removing all of its keystroke/action bindings.

The applet shown in Figure 21-4 contains a text area and a check box for setting the text area's keymap. The keymap is set for the text area when the check box is selected and is removed from the text area when the check box is deselected.

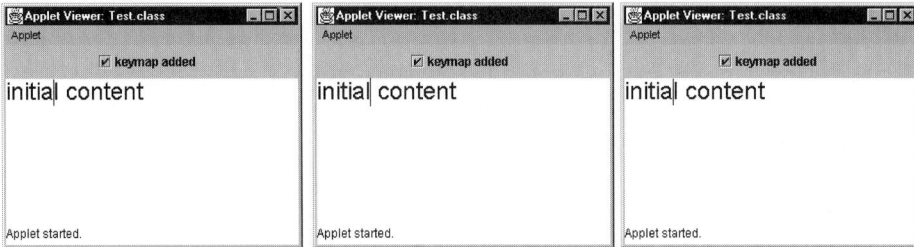

Figure 21-4 Adding and Removing Keymaps

Note: *An AWT bug in the 1.2 JDK causes the 'f' and 'b' keys to be sent to the text area when CTRL-f and CTRL-b are pressed, respectively. The applet works under Swing 1.1 FCS / 1.1.7 JDK.*

The keymap that is set for the text area when the check box is selected defines two pairs of keystroke/action bindings—one for ALT-F that moves the caret forward, and one for ALT-B that moves the caret backward. The keymap is created by the applet's `createKeymap` method.

```
...
private Keymap createKeymap() {
    Keymap map = JTextComponent.addKeymap("applet keymap",
                        textArea.getKeymap());

    KeyStroke forwardKeyStroke =
            KeyStroke.getKeyStroke(KeyEvent.VK_F,
                            InputEvent.ALT_MASK),
            backwardKeyStroke =
            KeyStroke.getKeyStroke(KeyEvent.VK_B,
                            InputEvent.ALT_MASK);
    Action forwardAction =
            getAction(DefaultEditorKit.forwardAction),
            backwardAction =
            getAction(DefaultEditorKit.backwardAction);

    map.addActionForKeyStroke(forwardKeyStroke,
                        forwardAction);
```

```
map.addActionForKeyStroke(backwardKeyStroke,
                           backwardAction);
    return map;
}
...
```

The keymap is created by the `JTextComponent.addKeymap` method, which is passed the name of the keymap and a parent keymap. The parent keymap is specified as the text area's original keymap.

After the keymap is created, keystrokes and actions are obtained and added to the keymap with the `Keymap.addActionForKeyStroke` method.

The text area's keymap is set by an action listener associated with the applet's check box. The listener sets the text area's keymap depending upon whether the check box is selected or deselected.

```
...
cbox.addActionListener(new ActionListener() {
    public void actionPerformed(ActionEvent e) {
        textArea.setKeymap(cbox.isSelected() ?
                           newKeymap : originalKeymap);

        textArea.requestFocus();
    }
});
...
```

The applet shown in Figure 21-4 is listed in its entirety in Example 21-3.

Example 21-3 Setting Keymaps

```
import javax.swing.*;
import javax.swing.text.*;
import java.awt.*;
import java.awt.event.*;
import java.util.*;

public class Test extends JApplet {
    private JTextArea textArea = new JTextArea("initial content");
    private JCheckBox cbox = new JCheckBox("keymap added");
    private Hashtable actionTable = new Hashtable();
    private Keymap originalKeymap, newKeymap;

    public void init() {
        Container contentPane = getContentPane();

        loadActionTable();
```

```
            originalKeymap = textArea.getKeymap();
            newKeymap = createKeymap();

            textArea.setFont(new Font("Dialog", Font.PLAIN, 24));

            contentPane.add(new ControlPanel(), BorderLayout.NORTH);
            contentPane.add(textArea, BorderLayout.CENTER);
        }
        private Keymap createKeymap() {
            Keymap map = JTextComponent.addKeymap("applet keymap",
                                    textArea.getKeymap());

            KeyStroke forwardKeyStroke =
                        KeyStroke.getKeyStroke(KeyEvent.VK_F,
                                            InputEvent.ALT_MASK),
                    backwardKeyStroke =
                        KeyStroke.getKeyStroke(KeyEvent.VK_B,
                                            InputEvent.ALT_MASK);
            Action forwardAction =
                        getAction(DefaultEditorKit.forwardAction),
                    backwardAction =
                        getAction(DefaultEditorKit.backwardAction);

            map.addActionForKeyStroke(forwardKeyStroke,
                                forwardAction);
            map.addActionForKeyStroke(backwardKeyStroke,
                                backwardAction);
            return map;
        }
        private void loadActionTable() {
            Action[] actions = textArea.getActions();

            for(int i=0; i < actions.length; ++i) {
                actionTable.put(actions[i].getValue(Action.NAME),
                            actions[i]);
            }
        }
        private Action getAction(String name) {
            return (Action)actionTable.get(name);
        }
        class ControlPanel extends JPanel {
            public ControlPanel() {
                add(cbox);

                cbox.addActionListener(new ActionListener() {
                    public void actionPerformed(ActionEvent e) {
                        textArea.setKeymap(cbox.isSelected() ?
                                    newKeymap : originalKeymap);

                        textArea.requestFocus();
                    }
                });
            }
        }
    }
```

Documents

Like other Swing components, text components are implemented by means of a modified Model-View-Controller architecture. Text component models are implementations of the Document interface. Documents maintain the content of a text component and any attributes, such as bold, italic, etc., that are associated with the content. Documents also fire document and undoable edit events when their content is modified.

The class hierarchy for documents is shown in Figure 21-5.

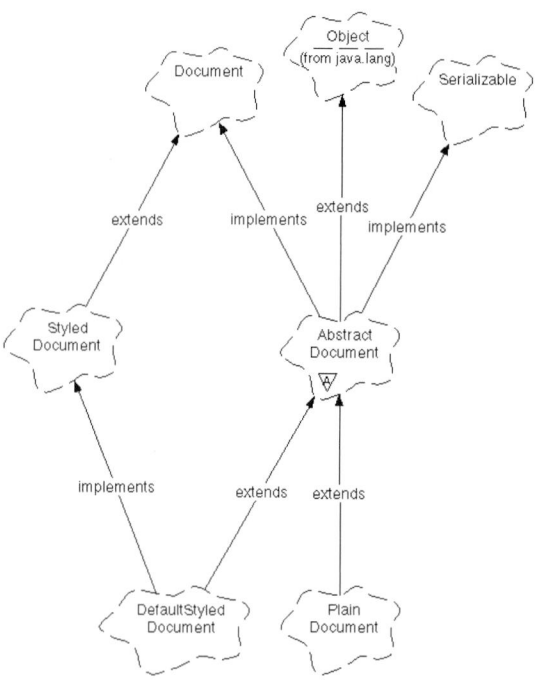

Figure 21-5 Swing Document Classes and Interfaces

The Document interface is implemented by the AbstractDocument class and extended by the StyledDocument interface. The PlainDocument class is an extension of AbstractDocument, as is the DefaultStyledDocument class, which also implements the StyledDocument interface.

The structure of a document is maintained by a hierarchy of *elements* that implement the `Element` interface. Each element has an associated set of attributes. Elements and attribute sets are discussed in more detail in "Customizing Text Components" on page 1531.

Documents also maintain positions. Positions are placed between characters in a document's content and retain their location when a document is modified. Figure 21-6 shows an application that contains a text component fitted with a custom view. The view graphically displays elements with a rectangle drawn at the position's location.

Notice that the positions maintain their location even when text is inserted into the document that changes the position's location in the view.

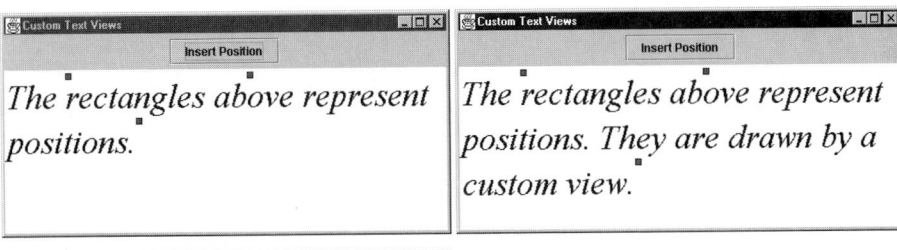

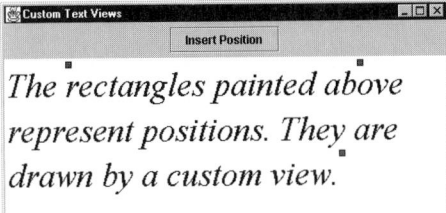

Figure 21-6 Positions

The application shown in Figure 21-6 is not listed in this chapter; see "Views" on page 1542 for a discussion of the application and its listing.

The `Document` interface is summarized in Interface Summary 21-2.

Interface Summary 21-2   Document

Constants

---

public static final String <u>StreamDescriptionProperty</u>
public static final String <u>TitleProperty</u>

The string constants listed above identify a stream from which a document is read and a document's title. The `StreamDescriptionProperty` constant is set by `JTextComponent.read()`; however, the `TitleProperty` is not used within Swing as of Swing 1.1 FCS.

The constants are meant to be used with the `Document.getProperty` and `Document.putProperty` methods.

Methods

Content

---

public abstract String <u>getText</u>(int offset, int length) throws BadLocationException
public abstract void <u>getText</u>(int offset, int length, Segment) throws BadLocationException
public abstract void <u>insertString</u>(int offset, String, AttributeSet)
                                                 throws BadLocationException
public abstract void <u>remove</u>(int offset, int length) throws BadLocationException

The first two methods listed above provide access to text stored in a document. Both methods are passed an offset from the beginning of the document and the length of the text to retrieve. The first method listed above returns a string, whereas the second method is passed an instance of the `Segment` class. Segments provide access to an array of characters without copying the text.

The `insertString` method inserts a specified string at a given offset with a specified set of attributes. The method will throw a `BadLocationException` if the offset is not valid.

The `remove` method removes a portion of a document's content, starting at the specified offset with the specified length.

Positions

```
public abstract Position createPosition(int offset) throws BadLocationException
public abstract Position getStartPosition()
public abstract Position getEndPosition()
```

The first method listed above creates a position within a document at the specified offset. If the offset is not valid, the method throws a `BadLocationException`.

The last two methods listed above provide access to the start and end positions for a document.

Root Elements

```
public abstract Element getDefaultRootElement()
public abstract Element[] getRootElements()
```

The methods listed above provide access to a document's default root element and the array of root elements maintained by a document. See "Elements" on page 1556 for more information concerning documents and elements.

Document and Undoable Edit Listeners

```
public abstract void addDocumentListener(DocumentListener)
public abstract void addUndoableEditListener(UndoableEditListener)
public abstract void removeDocumentListener(DocumentListener)
public abstract void removeUndoableEditListener(UndoableEditListener)
```

The methods listed above allow document and undoable edit listeners to be added to and removed from a document. See "Document Listeners" on page 1422 for more information concerning document listeners, and see "Undo / Redo" on page 1437 for more information on implementing undo/redo for text components.

Properties / Rendering

---

public abstract Object <u>getProperty</u>(Object key)
public abstract void <u>putProperty</u>(Object key, Object value)
public abstract void <u>render</u>(Runnable)

All documents maintain a set of properties that can be accessed with the first two methods listed above. The `render` method is passed a `Runnable` that is executed so that it can safely read a document in the face of concurrency. The `Runnable` passed to the `render` method should not modify the document.

Custom Documents

Documents are commonly extended to provide custom behavior such as text fields that limit the number of characters they can contain or text fields that allow only certain types of data.

The applet shown in Figure 21-7 contains a text field fitted with a custom document that allows only integer values to be inserted into the field.

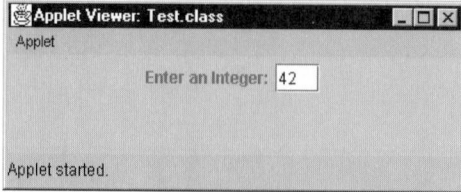

Figure 21-7 A Simple Custom Document

The applet shown in Figure 21-7 is listed in Example 21-4.

Example 21-4 A Document That Allows Only Integer Values

```
import javax.swing.*;
import javax.swing.text.*;
import java.awt.*;
import java.awt.event.*;

public class Test extends JApplet {
    JTextField tf = new JTextField(3);

    public Test() {
        Container contentPane = getContentPane();
        JLabel label = new JLabel("Enter an Integer:");

        tf.setDocument(new IntegerDocument());

        contentPane.setLayout(new FlowLayout());
        contentPane.add(label);
        contentPane.add(tf);
    }
}
class IntegerDocument extends PlainDocument {
    public void insertString(int offset, String s,
                        AttributeSet attributeSet)
                        throws BadLocationException {
        try {
            Integer.parseInt(s);
        }
        catch(Exception ex) { // only allow integer values
            Toolkit.getDefaultToolkit().beep();
            return;
        }
        super.insertString(offset, s, attributeSet);
    }
}
```

The applet creates a text field and sets the field's document to an instance of
IntegerDocument.

The IntegerDocument class extends PlainDocument—which is the default
document for text fields—and overrides the insertString method. The
IntegerDocument.insertString method attempts to parse the string to be
inserted. If the Integer.parseInt method throws an exception, the method
beeps and returns without inserting the string. If the string represents a valid
integer, the method invokes super.insertString().

Document Listeners

Changes to a document can be tracked by a document listener. The
`DocumentListener` interface, which resides in the `javax.swing.event`
package, is summarized in Interface Summary 21-3.

Interface Summary 21-3   DocumentListener

---

public abstract void <u>changedUpdate</u>(DocumentEvent)
public abstract void <u>insertUpdate</u>(DocumentEvent)
public abstract void <u>removeUpdate</u>(DocumentEvent)

Document listeners are notified when document attributes are changed, an
insertion is made to the document, or content is removed from a document.

Each of the methods defined by the `DocumentListener` interface is passed a
document event, which is represented by the `DocumentEvent` interface. The
`DocumentEvent` interface is summarized in Interface Summary 21-4.

Interface Summary 21-4   DocumentEvent

---

public abstract DocumentEvent.ElementChange <u>getChange</u>(Element)
public abstract Document <u>getDocument</u>()
public abstract int <u>getLength</u>()
public abstract int <u>getOffset</u>()
public abstract DocumentEvent.EventType <u>getType</u>()

The first method listed above returns an instance of
`DocumentEvent.ElementChange`, which describes the changes made to one of
a document's elements. The `getChange` method is used when a document
listener's `changedUpdate` method is invoked.

The next three methods listed above return the document associated with the
event, and the offset and length of the modified content.

The last method listed above returns the type of the event, represented by an instance of DocumentEvent.EventType, which is summarized in Class Summary 21-2.

Class Summary 21-2   DocumentEvent.EventType

Extends: java.lang.Object

Constants

---

public static final DocumentEvent.EventType <u>CHANGE</u>
public static final DocumentEvent.EventType <u>INSERT</u>
public static final DocumentEvent.EventType <u>REMOVE</u>

The DocumentEvent.EventType class defines the three constants listed above that represent a document event type.

Methods

---

public String <u>toString</u>()

The DocumentEvent.EventType class also implements a toString method that returns a string representing the type of event.

The application shown in Figure 21-8 contains two text areas. The top text area contains a document that contains the text of the application, and the bottom text area displays changes to the top text area's document. The application also contains a menu that allows text to be cut, copied, and pasted. The Edit menu contains a Save menu item that allows the document to be saved after the first modification to the document.

Figure 21-8 Using Document Listeners

The top-left picture shows selected text being cut to the clipboard, resulting in the bottom text area being updated as shown in the top-right picture. Notice that the Save menu item is originally disabled but is enabled after the first modification to the top text area's document.

The bottom-left picture shows the same text pasted from the clipboard, resulting in the bottom text area being updated as shown in the bottom-right picture.

The application's constructor adds a document listener to the top text area that reacts to document modifications by enabling the Save menu item and updating the bottom text area.

```
public Test() {
    ...
    textArea.getDocument().addDocumentListener(
                        new DocumentListener() {
        public void insertUpdate(DocumentEvent e) {
            saveAction.setEnabled(true);
            updateStatus(e);
        }
        public void removeUpdate(DocumentEvent e) {
            saveAction.setEnabled(true);
            updateStatus(e);
        }
        public void changedUpdate(DocumentEvent e) {
            saveAction.setEnabled(true);
            updateStatus(e);
        }
        private void updateStatus(DocumentEvent e) {
            status.append(e.getType().toString());
            status.append(" Offset: " + e.getOffset());
            status.append(" Length: " + e.getLength() + "\n");
        }
    });
```

The application shown in Figure 21-8 is listed in its entirety in Example 21-5.

Example 21-5 Using Document Listeners

```
import java.awt.*;
import java.awt.event.*;
import javax.swing.*;
import javax.swing.event.*;
import javax.swing.text.*;
import java.util.*;
import java.io.*;

public class Test extends JFrame {
    private JTextArea textArea = new JTextArea();
    private Document document = textArea.getDocument();
    private DefaultEditorKit kit = new DefaultEditorKit();
    private Action saveAction = new AbstractAction() {
        public void actionPerformed(ActionEvent e) {
                String s = JOptionPane.showInputDialog(
                                Test.this,
                                "Enter Filename:");
            if(s != null) {
                    try {
                        kit.write(new FileWriter(s),
                                document, 0,
                                document.getLength());
                }
```

```
                catch(Exception ex) {
                    ex.printStackTrace();
                }
            }
        }
    };

    public Test() {
        Container contentPane = getContentPane();

        try {
            kit.read(new FileReader("Test.java"), document, 0);
        }
        catch(Exception ex) {
            ex.printStackTrace();
        }

        final JTextArea status = new JTextArea();
        JPanel p = new JPanel();
        JSplitPane sp = new JSplitPane(JSplitPane.VERTICAL_SPLIT,
                                p, status);
        sp.setDividerLocation(200);

        saveAction.putValue(Action.NAME, "Save ...");
        saveAction.setEnabled(false);

        p.setLayout(new BorderLayout());
        p.add(new JScrollPane(textArea), BorderLayout.CENTER);

        contentPane.add(sp, BorderLayout.CENTER);

        textArea.getDocument().addDocumentListener(
                                new DocumentListener() {
            public void insertUpdate(DocumentEvent e) {
                saveAction.setEnabled(true);
                updateStatus(e);
            }
            public void removeUpdate(DocumentEvent e) {
                saveAction.setEnabled(true);
                updateStatus(e);
            }
            public void changedUpdate(DocumentEvent e) {
                saveAction.setEnabled(true);
                updateStatus(e);
```

```
            }
            private void updateStatus(DocumentEvent e) {
                status.append(e.getType().toString());
                status.append(" Offset: " + e.getOffset());
                status.append(" Length: " + e.getLength() + "\n");
            }
        });

        setJMenuBar(createMenuBar());
    }
    private JMenuBar createMenuBar() {
        JMenuBar menuBar = new JMenuBar();
        JMenu editMenu = new JMenu("Edit");

        editMenu.add(new DefaultEditorKit.CutAction());
        editMenu.add(new DefaultEditorKit.CopyAction());
        editMenu.add(new DefaultEditorKit.PasteAction());
        editMenu.addSeparator();
        editMenu.add(saveAction);

        menuBar.add(editMenu);
        return menuBar;
    }
    public static void main(String args[]) {
        GJApp.launch(new Test(),
                "Using Document Listeners",
                300,300,650,500);
    }
}
```

Carets and Highlighters

All text components have a caret and a highlighter, discussed in the following sections.

Carets

A caret represents a location within a text component's view where content can be inserted. Text component carets are represented by the Caret interface, which is summarized in Interface Summary 21-5.

Interface Summary 21-5   Caret

Change Listener

---

public abstract void <u>addChangeListener</u>(ChangeListener)
public abstract void <u>removeChangeListener</u>(ChangeListener)

Carets support change listeners that are notified whenever the caret's position is changed. The methods listed above are used to add and remove change listeners to and from a caret, respectively.

Installation

---

public abstract void <u>install</u>(JTextComponent)
public abstract void <u>deinstall</u>(JTextComponent)

The `install` and `deinstall` methods are invoked when a text component's UI delegate is installed and uninstalled. The `install` method is typically used to obtain a reference to the text component's document for the purpose of adding listeners to the document. The `deinstall` method undoes whatever was done in the `install` method so that the text component is left in its original state when the text component's UI delegate is uninstalled.

Marks, Dots, and Blink Rate

---

public abstract int <u>getBlinkRate</u>()
public abstract int <u>getDot</u>()
public abstract int <u>getMark</u>()

```
public abstract void moveDot(int position)
public abstract void setBlinkRate(int)
public abstract void setDot(int)
```

Carets maintain a *dot* and *mark*, where the dot represents the current position of the caret. The mark is the same as the dot, unless a selection has been made. When text is selected in a text, the caret's mark represents the beginning of the selection and the dot represents the end of the selection.

Carets also have a blink rate, which can be accessed through the `getBlinkRate` and `setBlinkRate` methods.

Painting / Visibility / Selection

```
public abstract boolean isVisible()
public abstract void setVisible(boolean)
public abstract void setSelectionVisible(boolean)
public abstract boolean isSelectionVisible()
public abstract void paint(Graphics)
```

Carets provide the methods listed above for setting their visibility and the visibility of selections made with a caret. The `paint` method renders the caret.

Magic Caret Position

```
public abstract Point getMagicCaretPosition()
public abstract void setMagicCaretPosition(Point)
```

The magic caret position maintains the end position for uneven lines of text. For example, if the caret is at the end of a long line in the document, and the up arrow key is pressed and moves the caret to a shorter line above, the caret will be placed at the end of the short line.

Caret Listeners

As discussed in Interface Summary 21-5, carets support listeners that are notified whenever a caret's position is changed. Caret listeners implement the `CaretListener` interface, summarized in Interface Summary 21-6, from the `javax.swing.event` package.

Interface Summary 21-6   CaretListener

---

public abstract void <u>caretUpdate</u>(CaretEvent)

The `CaretListener` interface defines a single method that is passed an instance of `CaretEvent`. The `CaretEvent` class resides in the `javax.swing.event` package and is summarized in Class Summary 21-3.

Class Summary 21-3   CaretEvent

Extends: java.util.EventObject

Constructors

---

public <u>CaretEvent</u>(Object source)

Caret events are constructed with the source of the event, which is the text component that contains the caret.

Methods

public abstract int <u>getDot</u>()
public abstract int <u>getMark</u>()

Caret events provide methods that return the dot and mark associated with the caret whose position was modified.

The applet shown in Figure 21-9 contains a text area with a caret listener that updates the applet's status area when a caret event is fired.

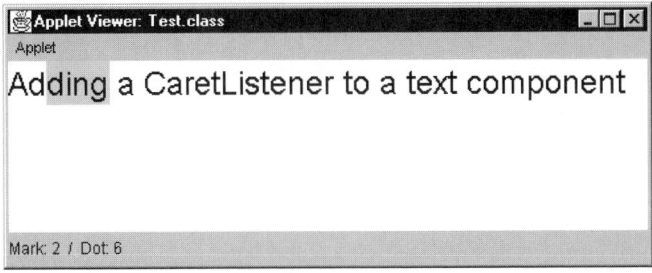

Figure 21-9 Caret Listeners

The applet shown in Figure 21-9 is listed in Example 21-6.

Example 21-6 Implementing a Caret Listener

```
import java.awt.*;
import javax.swing.*;
import javax.swing.event.*;
import javax.swing.text.*;

public class Test extends JApplet {
    public Test() {
        Container contentPane = getContentPane();
        JTextArea textArea = new JTextArea();

        contentPane.add(textArea, BorderLayout.CENTER);

        textArea.setFont(new Font("Dialog", Font.PLAIN, 24));

        textArea.addCaretListener(new CaretListener() {
            public void caretUpdate(CaretEvent e) {
```

```
            showStatus("Mark: " + e.getMark() +
                    "   /   Dot: " + e.getDot());
      }
    });
  }
}
```

The applet invokes the text area's `addCaretListener` method to add a caret
listener that invokes the applet's `showStatus` method.

Custom Carets

The `JTextComponent` class provides a `setCaret` method that allows a caret to
be set for any Swing text component. Swing also provides a `DefaultCaret` class
that extends `java.awt.Rectangle` and implements the `Caret` interface. The
`DefaultCaret` class can be extended for implementing custom carets.

The applet shown in Figure 21-10 contains a text area that is fitted with a custom
caret. The custom caret is rendered as a triangle at the text's baseline.

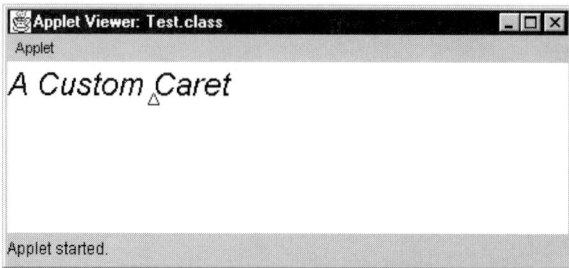

Figure 21-10 Custom Carets

The applet shown in Figure 21-10 is listed in Example 21-7.

Example 21-7 Implementing a Custom Caret

```
import javax.swing.*;
import javax.swing.plaf.*;
import javax.swing.text.*;
import java.awt.*;
import java.awt.event.*;
import java.util.*;

public class Test extends JApplet {
```

```java
    public Test() {
        Container contentPane = getContentPane();
        JTextArea textArea = new JTextArea();

        textArea.setCaret(new TriangleCaret(8));
        textArea.setFont(new Font("Dialog", Font.ITALIC, 24));
        contentPane.add(textArea, BorderLayout.CENTER);
    }
}
class TriangleCaret extends DefaultCaret {
    private int triangleWidth, left, right, top, bottom, middle;

    public TriangleCaret(int triangleWidth) {
        this.triangleWidth = triangleWidth;
    }
    public void paint(Graphics g) {
        if(isVisible()) {
            try {
                JTextComponent comp = getComponent();
                Rectangle r = comp.modelToView(getDot());

                setLocations(r);
                g.setColor(comp.getCaretColor());

                g.drawLine(left, bottom, middle, top);
                g.drawLine(middle, top, right, bottom);
                g.drawLine(right, bottom, left, bottom);
            }
            catch(BadLocationException ex) {
                ex.printStackTrace();
            }
        }
    }
    protected synchronized void damage(Rectangle r) {
        if(r != null) {
            setLocations(r);
            x = left;
            y = top;
            width = right - left + 1;
            height = bottom - top + 1;
        }
    }
    private void setLocations(Rectangle r) {
        left = r.x - triangleWidth/2;
        right = r.x + triangleWidth/2;
        bottom = r.y + r.height - 1;
        top = bottom - triangleWidth;
        middle = r.x;

        repaint();
    }
}
```

The `TriangleCaret` class extends `DefaultCaret` and overrides the `paint` and `damage` methods. The `paint` method uses the `DefaultCaret.getComponent` method to obtain a reference to the text component in which the caret resides. The component is subsequently used to translate the caret's dot to a corresponding rectangle in the component's view, and the caret's color is set to the caret color for the component. Finally, the `paint` method draws a triangle at the location calculated by the `setLocations` method.

The `damage` method is responsible for setting the location and bounds of the caret. Custom carets that override `paint` must be sure to also override the `damage` method, or the caret will not be painted correctly when it is moved.

Highlighters

A highlighter allows a region of text to be highlighted in a text component. Highlighting is used to indicate selection but can also be used for other purposes, such as highlighting misspelled words in a document.

Highlighters are defined by the `Highlighter` interface, which is summarized in Interface Summary 21-7.

Interface Summary 21-7   Highlighter

Installation

---

public abstract void <u>install</u>(JTextComponent)
public abstract void <u>deinstall</u>(JTextComponent)

Like carets, highlighters are installed and uninstalled when a text component's UI delegate is installed and uninstalled, respectively. By default, highlighters retain a reference to the text component passed to the `install` method for accessing the component's document and UI delegate.

Painting

---

public abstract void <u>paint</u>(Graphics)

Highlighters also must implement a `paint` method that paints any highlights added to the highlighter.

Highlights

---

public abstract Object <u>addHighlight</u>(int startPosition, int endPosition,
        Highlighter.HighlightPainter) throws BadLocationException
public abstract Highlighter.Highlight[] <u>getHighlights</u>()
public abstract void <u>changeHighlight</u>(Object tag, int startPosition, int endPosition) throws
        BadLocationException

public abstract void <u>removeAllHighlights</u>()
public abstract void <u>removeHighlight</u>(Object)

The `Highlighter` interface defines methods for adding, changing, and removing highlights. All of a highlighter's highlights can be removed in one shot with the `changeHighlight` method.

The `DefaultCaret` class uses a highlighter to highlight selection; a default caret's highlighter can be accessed with the `DefaultCaret.getSelectionPainter` method. The applet shown in Figure 21-11 contains a text area fitted with a custom caret that implements a custom highlight painter.

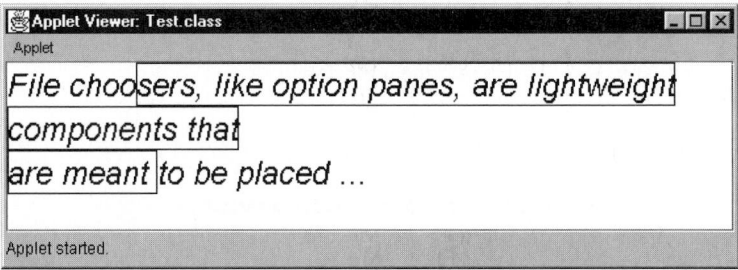

Figure 21-11 A Custom Highlighter

The applet shown in Figure 21-11 is listed in Example 21-8.

Example 21-8 A Custom Highlighter

```
import java.awt.*;
import java.awt.event.*;
import javax.swing.*;
import javax.swing.text.*;

public class Test extends JApplet {
    public Test() {
        Container contentPane = getContentPane();
        JTextArea textArea = new JTextArea(
          "File choosers, like option panes, are lightweight\n" +
          "components that\n" +
          "are meant to be placed ...");

        textArea.setCaret(new BoxHighlightingCaret());
        textArea.setFont(new Font("Dialog", Font.ITALIC, 24));

        contentPane.add(new JScrollPane(textArea),
                    BorderLayout.CENTER);
    }
}
class BoxHighlightingCaret extends DefaultCaret {
    private static BoxHighlighterPainter painter =
                        new BoxHighlighterPainter(null);

    public Highlighter.HighlightPainter getSelectionPainter(){
        return painter;
    }
    static class BoxHighlighterPainter
        extends DefaultHighlighter.DefaultHighlightPainter {
        private Color color;

        public BoxHighlighterPainter(Color color) {
            super(color);
            this.color = color;
        }
        public Shape paintLayer(Graphics g, int p0, int p1,
                            Shape shape, JTextComponent comp,
                            View view) {
            Rectangle b = shape.getBounds();

            try {
                g.setColor(getColor(comp));

                Rectangle r1 = comp.modelToView(p0);
                Rectangle r2 = comp.modelToView(p1);

                g.drawRect(r1.x, r1.y,        // x,y
```

```
                    r2.x - r1.x - 1, // width
                    r1.height - 1);  // height
        }
        catch(BadLocationException ex) {
            ex.printStackTrace();
        }
        return b;
    }
    private Color getColor(JTextComponent comp) {
        return color != null ? color :
                comp.getSelectionColor();
    }
  }
}
```

The applet sets the caret for its text area to an instance of
BoxHighlightingCaret, which extends DefaultCaret and overrides the
getSelectionPainter method to return a custom highlight painter.

The BoxHighlighterPainter extends
DefaultHighlighter.DefaultHighlightPainter and overrides the
paintLayer method, which is called for every line of text in the highlight
painter's associated text component. The paintLayer method is passed a
graphics in which to draw and is passed positions within the text component's
document representing the region to paint.

The BoxHighlighterPainter.paintLayer method converts the positions
into rectangles in the text component's view and simply draws a rectangle with
the component's selection color.

Undo / Redo

In addition to firing document events as discussed in "Document Listeners" on
page 1422, Swing text components also fire undoable edit events. Swing's undo
facilities are discussed in "Undo/Redo" on page 292.

The applet shown in Figure 21-12 contains a text area that is fitted with an
undoable edit listener that allows the last undoable edit to the document to be
undone and redone.

The top-left picture in Figure 21-12 shows the applet as it appears initially, and the top-right picture shows the applet after some of the original content of the text area has been cut to the clipboard. The middle pictures shown in Figure 21-12 show the deletion being undone, and the bottom pictures show the deletion being redone.

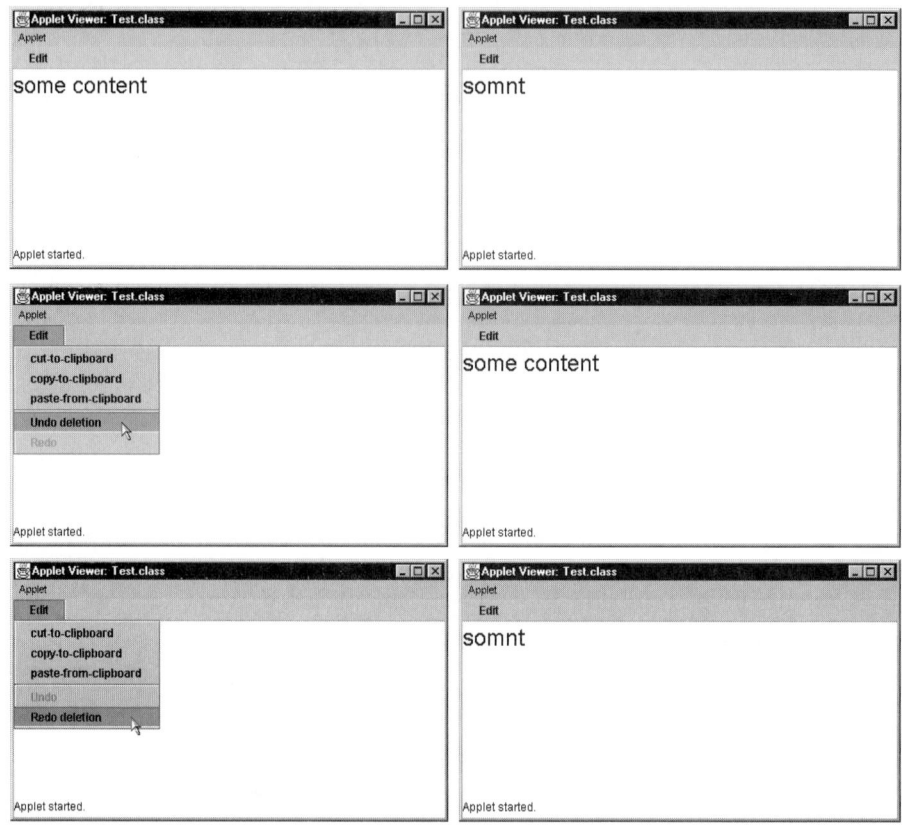

Figure 21-12 Implementing Undo/Redo

The applet creates a text area and adds an undoable edit listener to the text area's document.The applet also creates an instance of UndoManager and two actions that are used to undo and redo the last undoable edit applied to the text area's document.

The undoable edit listener added to the text area adds the undoable edit to the undo manager and updates the undo and redo actions.

```
public class Test extends JApplet {
    private JTextArea textArea = new JTextArea("some content");
    private Document document = textArea.getDocument();
    private UndoManager undoManager = new UndoManager();
    private UndoLastAction undoAction = new UndoLastAction();
    private RedoAction redoAction = new RedoAction();

    ...
    public Test() {
        document.addUndoableEditListener(
                            new UndoableEditListener() {
            public void undoableEditHappened(UndoableEditEvent e){
                undoManager.addEdit(e.getEdit());
                undoAction.update();
                redoAction.update();
            }
        });
    }
    ...
```

The UndoLastAction and RedoLastAction classes extend AbstractAction
and invoke UndoManager.undo() and UndoManager.redo(), respectively.
After undoing or redoing the last undoable edit applied to the text area's
document, each action updates the other action, which sets the action's enabled
state and name.

```
    ...
    class RedoAction extends AbstractAction {
        public RedoAction() {
            super("Redo");
            update();
        }
        public void actionPerformed(ActionEvent e) {
            undoManager.redo();
            undoAction.update();
            update();
        }
        public void update() {
            boolean canRedo = undoManager.canRedo();

            if(canRedo) {
                setEnabled(true);
                putValue(Action.NAME,
                        undoManager.getRedoPresentationName());
            }
            else {
                setEnabled(false);
                putValue(Action.NAME, "Redo");
            }
```

```
        }
    }
    class UndoLastAction extends AbstractAction {
        public UndoLastAction() {
            super("Undo");
            update();
        }
        public void actionPerformed(ActionEvent e) {
            undoManager.undo();
            redoAction.update();
            update();
        }
        public void update() {
            boolean canUndo = undoManager.canUndo();

            if(canUndo) {
                setEnabled(true);
                putValue(Action.NAME,
                        undoManager.getUndoPresentationName());
            }
            else {
                setEnabled(false);
                putValue(Action.NAME, "Undo");
            }
        }
    }
}
```

The applet shown in Figure 21-12 is listed in its entirety in Example 21-9.

Example 21-9 An Undo/Redo Implementation

```
import java.awt.*;
import java.awt.event.*;
import javax.swing.*;
import javax.swing.event.*;
import javax.swing.text.*;
import javax.swing.undo.*;

public class Test extends JApplet {
    private JTextArea textArea = new JTextArea("some content");
    private Document document = textArea.getDocument();
    private UndoManager undoManager = new UndoManager();
    private UndoLastAction undoAction = new UndoLastAction();
    private RedoAction redoAction = new RedoAction();

    public Test() {
        Container contentPane = getContentPane();

        createMenu();
```

```
        contentPane.add(textArea, BorderLayout.CENTER);

        textArea.setFont(new Font("Dialog", Font.PLAIN, 24));
        document.addUndoableEditListener(
                            new UndoableEditListener() {
            public void undoableEditHappened(UndoableEditEvent e){
                undoManager.addEdit(e.getEdit());
                undoAction.update();
                redoAction.update();
            }
        });
    }
    private void createMenu() {
        JMenuBar menuBar = new JMenuBar();
        JMenu editMenu = new JMenu("Edit");

        editMenu.add(new DefaultEditorKit.CutAction());
        editMenu.add(new DefaultEditorKit.CopyAction());
        editMenu.add(new DefaultEditorKit.PasteAction());

        editMenu.addSeparator();

        editMenu.add(undoAction);
        editMenu.add(redoAction);

        menuBar.add(editMenu);
        setJMenuBar(menuBar);
    }
    class RedoAction extends AbstractAction {
        public RedoAction() {
            super("Redo");
            update();
        }
        public void actionPerformed(ActionEvent e) {
            undoManager.redo();
            undoAction.update();
            update();
        }
        public void update() {
            boolean canRedo = undoManager.canRedo();

            if(canRedo) {
                setEnabled(true);
                putValue(Action.NAME,
                        undoManager.getRedoPresentationName());
            }
            else {
                setEnabled(false);
                putValue(Action.NAME, "Redo");
            }
        }
    }
```

```
class UndoLastAction extends AbstractAction {
    public UndoLastAction() {
        super("Undo");
        update();
    }
    public void actionPerformed(ActionEvent e) {
        undoManager.undo();
        redoAction.update();
        update();
    }
    public void update() {
        boolean canUndo = undoManager.canUndo();

        if(canUndo) {
            setEnabled(true);
            putValue(Action.NAME,
                     undoManager.getUndoPresentationName());
        }
        else {
            setEnabled(false);
            putValue(Action.NAME, "Undo");
        }
    }
}
```

JTextComponent

The JTextComponent class is the ultimate superclass of all Swing text components and is summarized in Component Summary 21-1.

Component Summary 21-1   JTextComponent

Model(s)	javax.swing.text.Document
UI Delegate(s)	javax.swing.plaf.basic.BasicTextUI
Renderer(s)	——
Editor(s)	——
Events Fired	——

Replacement For   java.awt.TextComponent

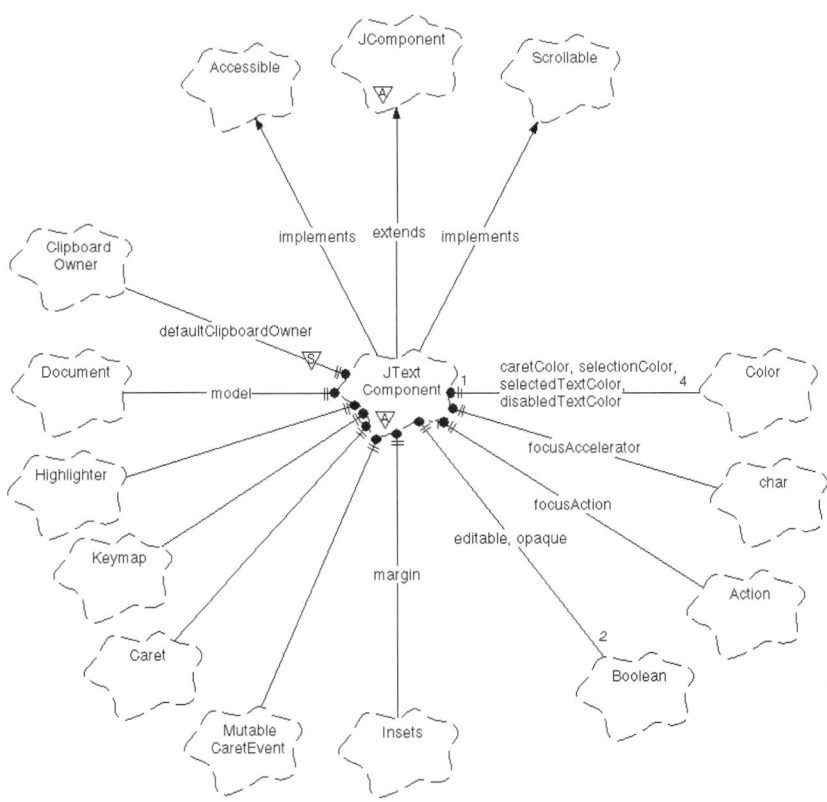

Figure 21-13 JTextComponent Class Diagram

The JTextComponent class extends JComponent and implements the Accessible and Scrollable interfaces. JTextComponent maintains private references to its document, keymap, caret, and highlighter. Instances of JTextComponent also keep track of colors used for painting selected text, and the text component's caret color.

Instances of JComponent also maintain private references to a character used to transfer focus to the text component and an action that is performed when the character is typed.

The mutable caret event is an instance of the
`JTextComponent.MutableCaretEvent` class, which implements the
`MouseListener` and `FocusListener` interfaces. When a text component
receives focus, the mutable caret event stores a reference to the component. When
a mouse pressed event occurs in the component, the mutable caret event updates
the component's caret and fires a caret update event specifying itself as the event.

JTextComponent Properties

The properties maintained by the `JTextComponent` class are listed in Table 21-4.

Table 21-4   JTextComponent Properties

Property Name	Data Type	Property Type[1]	Access[2]	Default[3]
actions	Action[]	S	G	L&F
caret	Caret	B	SG	BasicCaret
caretColor	Color	B	SG	L&F
caretPosition	int	S	SG	0
disabledTextColor	Color	B	SG	L&F
document	Document	B	SG	L&F
focusAccelerator	char	B	SG	—
highlighter	Highlighter	B	SG	L&F
keymap	Keymap	B	SG	L&F
margin	Insets	B	SG	L&F
selectedText	String	S	G	—
selectedTextColor	Color	B	SG	L&F
selectionColor	Color	B	SG	L&F
selectionEnd	int	S	SG	—
selectionStart	int	S	SG	—
text	String	S	SG	—

1. B = bound (fires PropertyChangeEvent) / C = constrained/ I = indexed /
   S = simple / Ch = fires ChangeEvent
2. C = settable at construction time / G = getter method / S = setter method
3. L&F = look-and-feel dependent

actions — A set of actions a text component can perform. The actions are specified by a text component's editor kit. Actions can be bound to keys and used in menu bars and toolbars.

caret — A text component's cursor. Carets are instantiated by a text component's UI delegate, but custom carets can be specified. See "Custom Carets" on page 1432 for an example of a custom caret.

caretColor — The color of a text component's caret. The `caretColor` property is a pass-through to a text component's caret.

caretPosition — The position of the caret in the document. The `caretPosition` property is a pass-through to a text component's caret.

disabledTextColor — The color used to paint disabled text.

document — The document used by a text component. Documents store content and can maintain attributes for the content. Documents are defined by the `Document` interface. See "Documents" on page 1416 for more information concerning documents.

focusAccelerator — A key that, when pressed, causes focus to jump to a text component. The key must be pressed when another component in the same window as the text component has focus.

highlighter — All text components support multiple highlights, which are painted by the component's highlighter. By default, a text component's UI delegate creates the component's highlighter, but custom highlighters can be specified. See "Highlighters" on page 1434 for more information concerning highlighters.

keymap — Every text component maintains a single keymap that maps keystrokes to actions. The `JTextComponent` class provides a number of ways to manipulate its keymap; see "Keymaps" on page 1411 for more information concerning keymaps.

margin — An insets that specifies space between a text component's border and the component's content.

selectedText — A read-only property that returns a text component's selected text. The string is obtained from the component's document, using the caret's dot and mark. See "Carets" on page 1427 for more information on carets.

selectedTextColor — The color used to paint selected text. If `JTextComponent.setSelectedTextColor()` is passed a `null` color, the color defaults to black.

selectionColor — The selection background color, which defaults to white if `JTextComponent.setSelectionColor()` is passed a `null` value.

selectionEnd — The end of the current selection, specified as a document position. The `selectionEnd` property can be set programmatically with the `setSelectionEnd` method, which adjusts the component's caret.

selectionStart — The start of the current selection, specified as a document position. The `selectionStart` property can be set programmatically with the `setSelectionStart` method, which adjusts the component's caret.

The `JTextComponent` class is summarized in Class Summary 21-4.

Class Summary 21-4   JTextComponent

Extends: JComponent
Implements: javax.accessibility.Accessible, Scrollable

Constants

---

public static final String <u>DEFAULT KEYMAP</u>
public static final String <u>FOCUS ACCELERATOR KEY</u>

The `DEFAULT_KEYMAP` string represents a default keymap that is accessed with the `static JTextComponent.getKeymap(String)` method.

The `FOCUS_ACCELERATOR_KEY` string represents the name of the bound `focusAccelerator` property. See "JTextComponent Properties" on page 1444 for more information concerning the `focusAccelerator` property. Note that the use of the term `KEY` is equivalent to `PROPERTY`, which is what most Swing components use to represent bound property names; for example, a `JTree`'s selection model is represented by the `JTree.SELECTION_MODEL_PROPERTY`.

Constructors

---

public <u>JTextComponent</u>()

The no-argument constructor is the only constructor provided by the
JTextComponent class. The constructor sets the component's layout manager to
null and sets the editable property (inherited from JComponent) to true.
Layout of a text component's content is the responsibility of the component's
view. See "Customizing Text Components" on page 1531 or more information
concerning text component views. The constructor also adds mouse and focus
listeners to the component that fire caret events.

Methods

Document / Text

---

public Document <u>getDocument</u>()
public void <u>setDocument</u>(Document)
public String <u>getText</u>()
public String <u>getText</u>(int offset, int length) throws BadLocationException
public void <u>setText</u>(String)
public Color <u>getDisabledTextColor</u>()
public void <u>setDisabledTextColor</u>(Color)

The methods listed above are accessors for a text component's document, text,
and disabled text color. The setDocument method fires a property change event
that is handled by creating and installing a view for the document.

A text component's text can be obtained with the getText method, or a region of
text can be accessed by specifying an offset in the document and the length of the
text to retrieve. The getText method can throw a BadLocationException if
the offset and length specified are not valid.

Actions

---

public Action[] <u>getActions</u>()

The `getActions` method returns an array of actions that can be performed by a text component. Actions are the primary mechanism by which text components implement fundamental functionality. Actions are useful in menus and toolbars and are also used in keymaps.

Keymaps

---

public static Keymap <u>addKeymap</u>(String name, Keymap)
public static Keymap <u>getKeymap</u>(String name)
public static Keymap <u>removeKeymap</u>(String name)
public static void <u>loadKeymap</u>(Keymap, JTextComponent.KeyBinding[], Action[])
public void <u>setKeymap</u>(Keymap)
public Keymap <u>getKeymap</u>()

Keymaps are a set of keystroke/action bindings, and every text component maintains a single keymap, as evidenced by the last two methods listed above. If `JTextComponent.setKeymap()` is passed a `null` reference, keyboard input will be disabled for the text component.

Keymaps can be set outright with the `JTextComponent.setKeymap` method; however, because keymaps can contain other keymaps and because keymaps resolve hierarchically, the `static` methods listed above are typically used to modify a text's keymap. See "Keymaps" on page 1411 for more information concerning keymaps and the use of the `static` methods listed above.

Carets / Caret Listener Registration

---

public void <u>addCaretListener</u>(CaretListener)
public void <u>removeCaretListener</u>(CaretListener)
protected void <u>fireCaretUpdate</u>(CaretEvent)
public Caret <u>getCaret</u>()

public Color getCaretColor()
public int getCaretPosition()
public void setCaret(Caret)
public void setCaretColor(Color)
public void setCaretPosition(int position)
public void moveCaretPosition(int position)

The methods listed above can be used to manipulate a text component's caret and to register caret listeners. See "Carets and Highlighters" on page 1427 for more information concerning carets and caret listeners.

The setCaretPosition and moveCaretPosition methods invoke Caret.setDot and Caret.moveDot, respectively. The former simply modifies the position of the caret, whereas the latter moves the position of the caret to form a selection from the previous caret location.

Highlighter

public Highlighter getHighlighter()
public void setHighlighter(Highlighter)

The methods listed above are accessors for a text component's highlighter. See "Carets and Highlighters" on page 1427 for more information concerning highlighters.

Cut / Copy / Paste

public void copy()
public void cut()
public void paste()

The methods listed above are convenience methods for cutting, copying, and pasting text to/from the system clipboard.

The copy method copies the currently selected text to the clipboard from a text component. The copy method does not remove the currently selected text from the text component. If there is no selection when the copy method is invoked, the method does nothing.

The cut method removes the currently selected text from a text component and copies it to the clipboard. If there is no selection when the cut method is invoked, the method does nothing.

The paste method copies the current selection from the system clipboard and inserts it ahead of the current caret position. If the system clipboard is empty, the paste method does nothing.

Selection

```
public String getSelectedText()
public Color getSelectedTextColor()
public Color getSelectionColor()
public int getSelectionEnd()
public int getSelectionStart()
public void setSelectionColor(Color)
public void setSelectionEnd(int)
public void setSelectionStart(int)
public void replaceSelection(String)
public void select(int start, int end)
public void selectAll()
```

The methods listed above are provided by JTextComponent for controlling selection. The first two methods listed above return the currently selected text and the color used to paint selected text, respectively. If there is no text selected when the getSelectedText method is invoked, a null reference is returned.

The getSelectionColor method returns the color used to paint the background of selected text. The getSelectionStart and getSelectionEnd methods return the start and end positions of the current selection. If there is no current selection, the caret dot position is returned. If there is no text in the document, 0 is returned.

The `replaceSelection` method replaces the current selection with the specified text. If there is no selection when the `replaceSelection` method is called, the text is inserted ahead of the current caret dot position. If the text passed to the method is `null`, the current selection is removed.

The `select` method is provided to retain compatibility with the AWT's text component. The method does nothing if the specified start and end positions are invalid. If the start and end positions are valid, the method calls `setCaretPosition()` followed by `moveCaretPosition()`.

Reading / Writing

---

public void <u>read</u>(Reader, Object) throws IOException
public void <u>write</u>(Writer) throws IOException

The `read` and `write` methods use the text component's editor kit to create and store, respectively, a document.

The `read` method creates a model that is appropriate for the component's editor kit and initializes the model with data from the stream. The `write` method stores the text contained in the document as plain text.

View/Model Transformations

---

public Rectangle <u>modelToView</u>(int position) throws BadLocationException
public int <u>viewToModel</u>(Point)

The methods listed above translate model positions to view coordinates, and vice versa. The methods delegate to the text component's UI delegate.

Scrollable Interface Implementation

---

public Dimension <u>getPreferredScrollableViewportSize</u>()
public int <u>getScrollableBlockIncrement</u>(Rectangle, int, int)

public boolean <u>getScrollableTracksViewportHeight</u>()
public boolean <u>getScrollableTracksViewportWidth</u>()
public int <u>getScrollableUnitIncrement</u>(Rectangle, int, int)

The methods listed above are defined by the `Scrollable` interface. See "The Scrollable Interface" on page 764 for more information concerning the `Scrollable` interface.

The `getPreferredScrollableViewportSize` method returns the preferred size of the component. The `getScrollableUnitIncrement` method returns 10 percent of the component's width or height, depending upon the orientation passed to the method.

The `getScrollableBlockIncrement` method returns the width or height of the component's visible area, depending upon the orientation passed to the method.

The `getScrollableTracksViewportWidth` and `getScrollableTracksViewportHeight` methods determine whether the width or height, respectively, of a text component tracks the width or height of the component's viewport (when the text component is contained in a viewport). Both methods return `true` if the width or height of the viewport is greater than the width or height of the component, `false` otherwise. In other words, by default, a text component's width and height are the same as the component's viewport only if the viewport is larger than the component or the viewport and component are the same size.

Miscellaneous Properties

---

public char <u>getFocusAccelerator</u>()
public Insets <u>getMargin</u>()

public boolean <u>isEditable</u>()
public boolean <u>isFocusTraversable</u>()
public boolean <u>isOpaque</u>()
public void <u>setEditable</u>(boolean)
public void <u>setEnabled</u>(boolean)
public void <u>setFocusAccelerator</u>(char)
public void <u>setMargin</u>(Insets)
public void <u>setOpaque</u>(boolean)

The methods listed above are accessors for a text component's properties. See "JTextComponent Properties" on page 1444 for more information concerning JTextComponent properties.

Miscellaneous Methods

---

protected String <u>paramString</u>()
protected void <u>processComponentKeyEvent</u>(KeyEvent)
public void <u>removeNotify</u>()

The `paramString` method returns a textual description of a text component. The method is typically used for debugging purposes only and is guaranteed to return a non-null string.

The `processComponentKeyEvent` method is invoked after a key event has been passed to the focus manager and key listeners registered with the component. If the event has not been consumed by the focus manager or a key listener, the `processComponentKeyEvent` method fires the default action and consumes the event.

The `removeNotify` method is called when a component is removed from its container. The method removes the reference to the component as the `focusedComponent`.

Accessibility / Pluggable Look And Feel

---

public AccessibleContext <u>getAccessibleContext</u>()
public TextUI <u>getUI</u>()
public void <u>setUI</u>(TextUI)
public void <u>updateUI</u>()

The methods listed above can be found in most extensions of `JComponent`. Swing lightweight components can return an accessibility context that contains accessibility information for the component and the class name of their UI delegate. The `updateUI` method is invoked when the component is fitted with a UI delegate.

Parting Shots

Swing text is undoubtedly the single most complex area of Swing. This chapter has introduced the fundamental capabilities that all Swing text components share, including actions, keymaps, documents, carets, highlighters, and undo/redo capabilities. This chapter has also covered the `JTextComponent` class, which is the ultimate superclass of all Swing text components. The more advanced aspects of Swing text, such as views, elements, attribute sets, styles, styles contexts, etc. have purposely been glossed over in this chapter.

The next chapter examines each of the Swing text components, and the following chapter explores advanced subject matter.

CHAPTER

22

Text Components

Swing provides two distinct types of text components: *simple* text controls that can only display one font and one color at a time and *styled* text components that can display multiple fonts and colors. The former are text fields (JTextField), password fields (JPasswordField), and text areas (JTextArea); the latter are editor panes (JEditorPane) and text panes (JTextPane).

Text fields and text areas are useful for editing plain text. JTextField and JTextArea are nearly source compatible with their AWT counterparts: java.awt.TextField and java.awt.TextArea, respectively.

Editor panes and text panes are useful for editing styled text and for displaying different types of content. The JTextPane class provides methods for setting character and paragraph attributes for the content displayed in a text pane. Text panes are also capable of embedding components and icons. JEditorPane and JTextPane have no AWT counterparts.

JTextField

The JTextField component displays a single line of editable text, using a single font and a single color. Horizontal alignment—either LEFT, CENTER, or RIGHT[1]— can be specified for a text field's text.

By default, pressing the Enter key (KeyEvent.VK_ENTER) while a text field has focus causes the field to fire an action event. This behavior is compatible with AWT text fields but is at odds with Swing default buttons, which are also activated with the Enter key. "JTextField Events" on page 1477 discusses a solution to the dilemma.

A text field's preferred width can be set by specifying the number of columns the text field would prefer to display. The actual width of a text field is typically set by a layout manager, so setting the number of columns for a text field does not guarantee anything about the field's actual width.

The applet shown in Figure 22-1 illustrates text field columns and horizontal alignment.

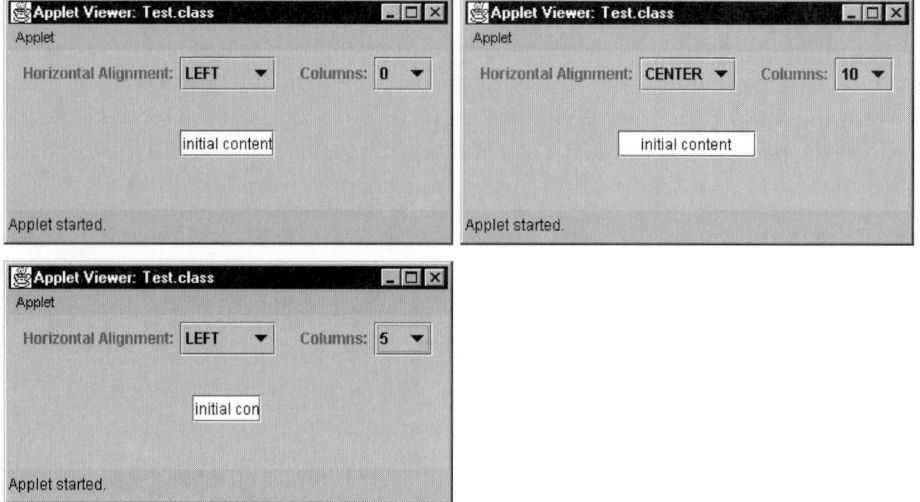

Figure 22-1 Explicitly Setting a Text Field's Columns

The top-left picture in Figure 22-1 shows the applet as it appears initially; the horizontal alignment and number of columns default to JTextField.LEFT and 0, respectively. The top-right picture shows the applet after the field's horizontal alignment has been set to JTextField.CENTER and the number of columns has been set to 10.

---

1.   The constants listed are JTextField public constants.

The bottom left picture in Figure 22-1 shows the text field with 5 columns and an alignment of LEFT. Notice that the text field can accommodate more characters than the number of columns because *column width is set to the width of the 'm' character*, which is the widest character for most fonts.

The applet creates a text field with a JTextField constructor that is passed a string representing the initial content of the text field. The text field is placed in a panel, and the panel is specified as the center component for the applet's content pane. The text field is wrapped in a panel because panels have a FlowLayout layout manager that lays out components according to their preferred sizes. Because the text field will be laid out according to its preferred size, setting the number of columns for the field will determine the actual width of the field.

```
public class Test extends JApplet {
    private JPanel textFieldPanel = new JPanel();
    private JTextField textField =
                new JTextField("initial content");

    public void init() {
        Container contentPane = getContentPane();

        textFieldPanel.add(textField);

        contentPane.setLayout(new BorderLayout(0,20));
        contentPane.add(new ControlPanel(), BorderLayout.NORTH);
        contentPane.add(textFieldPanel, BorderLayout.CENTER);
    }
    ...
```

The columns combo box has an action listener that sets the text field's columns and revalidates the field. Anytime a property that affects the appearance of a Swing component is modified, the component is responsible for updating its display. Therefore, the call to revalidate() after setting the text field's columns should not be necessary.

The alignments combo box has an action listener that sets the text field's horizontal alignment based on the combo box's current selection.

```
    ...
    class ControlPanel extends JPanel {
        private JComboBox alignments = new JComboBox();
        private JComboBox columns = new JComboBox();

        public ControlPanel() {
            ...
```

```
        columns.addActionListener(new ActionListener() {
            public void actionPerformed(ActionEvent e) {
                Integer c =
                    (Integer)columns.getSelectedItem();

                textField.setColumns(c.intValue());

                // the following call to revalidate()
                // should not be necessary
                revalidate();

                textField.setScrollOffset(0);
            }
        });
        alignments.addActionListener(new ActionListener() {
            public void actionPerformed(ActionEvent e) {
                int index = alignments.getSelectedIndex();

                if(index == 0)
                    textField.setHorizontalAlignment(
                                    JTextField.LEFT);
                else if(index == 1)
                    textField.setHorizontalAlignment(
                                    JTextField.CENTER);
                else if(index == 2)
                    textField.setHorizontalAlignment(
                                    JTextField.RIGHT);
            }
        });
    }
  }
}
```

The applet shown in Figure 22-1 is listed in its entirety in Example 22-1.

Example 22-1   Text Field Alignment and Number of Columns

```
import javax.swing.*;
import java.awt.*;
import java.awt.event.*;
import java.util.*;

public class Test extends JApplet {
    private JPanel textFieldPanel = new JPanel();
    private JTextField textField =
                new JTextField("initial content");

    public void init() {
        Container contentPane = getContentPane();

        textFieldPanel.add(textField);
```

```
        contentPane.setLayout(new BorderLayout(0,20));
        contentPane.add(new ControlPanel(), BorderLayout.NORTH);
        contentPane.add(textFieldPanel, BorderLayout.CENTER);
    }
    class ControlPanel extends JPanel {
        private JComboBox alignments = new JComboBox();
        private JComboBox columns = new JComboBox();

        public ControlPanel() {
            columns.addItem(new Integer(0));
            columns.addItem(new Integer(5));
            columns.addItem(new Integer(10));
            columns.addItem(new Integer(15));

            alignments.addItem("LEFT");
            alignments.addItem("CENTER");
            alignments.addItem("RIGHT");

            add(new JLabel("Horizontal Alignment:"));
            add(alignments);
            add(Box.createHorizontalStrut(10));
            add(new JLabel("Columns:"));
            add(columns);

            columns.addActionListener(new ActionListener() {
                public void actionPerformed(ActionEvent e) {
                    Integer c =
                        (Integer)columns.getSelectedItem();

                    textField.setColumns(c.intValue());

                    // the following call to revalidate()
                    // should not be necessary
                    revalidate();

                    textField.setScrollOffset(0);
                }
            });
            alignments.addActionListener(new ActionListener() {
                public void actionPerformed(ActionEvent e) {
                    int index = alignments.getSelectedIndex();

                    if(index == 0)
                        textField.setHorizontalAlignment(
                                        JTextField.LEFT);
                    else if(index == 1)
                        textField.setHorizontalAlignment(
                                        JTextField.CENTER);
                    else if(index == 2)
                        textField.setHorizontalAlignment(
                                        JTextField.RIGHT);
                }
            });
        }
    }
}
```

Text Field Columns

Specifying the number of columns for a text field can often produce unexpected results because two aspects of text field columns are misunderstood:

First, the width of a text field column is the width of the "m" character in the field's current font. Because most fonts are variable width and because "m" is typically the widest character, text fields are often slightly wider than they need to be.

Second, setting the number of columns for a text field merely sets the field's preferred size. Whether the actual size of the field corresponds to the number of columns depends upon whether the field is laid out according to its preferred size.

Horizontal Visibility and Scroll Offset

`JTextField` maintains a bounded range model that represents a text field's *horizontal visibility*. Recall that bounded range models maintain the following properties: `value`, `minimum`, `maximum`, and `extent`. For a text field, the `value` of the field's visibility represents the scroll offset of the text displayed in the field.

The applet shown in Figure 22-2 illustrates text field horizontal visibility and scroll offset. The top picture in Figure 22-2 shows the applet as it appears initially. The scroll offset defaults to 0, meaning that the x coordinate of the field's text is 0 at the field's upper-left corner.

The middle picture in Figure 22-2 shows the applet after the text field's scroll offset has been manipulated with the slider. The x coordinate of the text at the field's upper-left corner is 179.

The bottom picture in Figure 22-2 shows the applet after the text field's columns have been set to 0, in which case the text field is sized according to its preferred width. Notice that the extent—which defines the width of the visible portion—of the field's horizontal visibility changes in the bottom picture in accordance with the field's increased size.

Figure 22-2 Text Field Scroll Offset

The applet creates a text field with a `JTextField` constructor that is passed a string representing the initial content of the field and the number of columns the field would prefer to display.

The scroll offset slider and columns combo box both have listeners that set the text field's scroll offset and columns, respectively.

```
public class Test extends JApplet {
    private JTextField textField = new JTextField(
        "12345678901234567890123456789012345678901234567890", 10);

    ...
    class ControlPanel extends JPanel {
        ...
        public ControlPanel() {
            ...
            slider.addChangeListener(new ChangeListener() {
```

```
public void stateChanged(ChangeEvent e) {
    textField.setScrollOffset(slider.getValue());

    Integer i =
        new Integer(textField.getScrollOffset());
    BoundedRangeModel m =
            textField.getHorizontalVisibility();

    display.setText(i.toString());

    showStatus("Visibility -  min: " +
            m.getMinimum() +
            ", max: " + m.getMaximum() +
            ", extent: " + m.getExtent() +
            ", value: " + m.getValue() +
            ", isAdj: " +
            m.getValueIsAdjusting());
    }
});
columns.addActionListener(new ActionListener() {
    public void actionPerformed(ActionEvent e) {
        Integer c =
            (Integer)columns.getSelectedItem();

        textField.setColumns(c.intValue());

        // the following call to revalidate()
        // should not be necessary
        revalidate();

        textField.setScrollOffset(0);
    }
});
        }
    }
}
```

The applet shown in Figure 22-2 is listed in its entirety in Example 22-2.

Example 22-2 Text Field Scroll Offset

```
import java.awt.*;
import java.awt.event.*;
import javax.swing.*;
import javax.swing.event.*;

public class Test extends JApplet {
    private JTextField textField = new JTextField(
        "12345678901234567890123456789012345678901234567890", 10);

    public void init() {
```

```
    Container contentPane = getContentPane();
    JPanel textFieldPanel = new JPanel();

    textFieldPanel.add(textField);

    contentPane.add(new ControlPanel(), BorderLayout.NORTH);
    contentPane.add(textFieldPanel, BorderLayout.CENTER);
}
class ControlPanel extends JPanel {
    private JLabel display = new JLabel(" ");
    private JSlider slider = new JSlider(
                    textField.getHorizontalVisibility());
    private JComboBox columns = new JComboBox();

    public ControlPanel() {
        columns.addItem(new Integer(0));
        columns.addItem(new Integer(5));
        columns.addItem(new Integer(10));
        columns.addItem(new Integer(15));

        columns.setSelectedIndex(2);

        add(new JLabel("Scroll Offset:"));
        add(slider);
        add(display);
        add(Box.createHorizontalStrut(10));
        add(new JLabel("Columns:"));
        add(columns);

        slider.addChangeListener(new ChangeListener() {
            public void stateChanged(ChangeEvent e) {
                textField.setScrollOffset(slider.getValue());

                Integer i =
                    new Integer(textField.getScrollOffset());
                BoundedRangeModel m =
                    textField.getHorizontalVisibility();

                display.setText(i.toString());

                showStatus("Visibility -  min: " +
                        m.getMinimum() +
                        ", max: " + m.getMaximum() +
                        ", extent: " + m.getExtent() +
                        ", value: " + m.getValue() +
                        ", isAdj: " +
                        m.getValueIsAdjusting());
            }
        });
        columns.addActionListener(new ActionListener() {
            public void actionPerformed(ActionEvent e) {
                Integer c =
                    (Integer)columns.getSelectedItem();
```

```
                              textField.setColumns(c.intValue());

                              // the following call to revalidate()
                              // should not be necessary
                              revalidate();

                              textField.setScrollOffset(0);
                    }
                });
            }
        }
    }
```

Laying Out Text Fields

Swing text fields are relatively simple components that are easy to use, but they can be difficult to position and size correctly. This section provides a simple recipe for using the complex `GridBagLayout` layout manager. The recipe can be used to align label/text field pairs as depicted in Figure 22-3.

Applet Viewer: PurchaseApplet.class

Applet

Order Form

Name:	John Doe	
Address:	1243 Primrose Lane	
City:	New Castle	State: OR
Purchase Method:	Visa ▼	

[Purchase]   [Cancel]

Applet started.

Figure 22-3 Text Fields and GridBagLayout

The applet shown in Figure 22-3 lays out pairs of labels and text fields and aligns the labels and fields. The code shown below is from a panel that contains the labels and text fields. The panel's constructor instantiates instances of GridBagLayout and GridBagConstraints, and GridBagLayout is set as the container's layout manager.

```
    . . .
    GridBagLayout       gbl = new GridBagLayout();
    GridBagConstraints gbc = new GridBagConstraints();

    setLayout(gbl);
    . . .
```

Subsequently, constraints are set for the labels and text fields, and an interesting pattern emerges: Because the labels are positioned to the left of the text fields and because the fields fill the remainder of their grid, the gridwidth constraint alternates between 1 (for the labels) and GridBagConstraints.REMAINDER (for the text fields).

```
    . . .
    gbc.anchor      = GridBagConstraints.WEST;

    gbc.gridwidth = 1;
    gbc.insets      = new Insets(0,0,0,0);
    add(name, gbc);

    add(Box.createHorizontalStrut(10));

    gbc.gridwidth = GridBagConstraints.REMAINDER;
    add(nameField, gbc);

    gbc.gridwidth = 1;
    add(address, gbc);

    add(Box.createHorizontalStrut(10));

    gbc.gridwidth = GridBagConstraints.REMAINDER;
    add(addressField, gbc);

    gbc.gridwidth = 1;
    add(city, gbc);
    . . .
```

The applet shown in Figure 22-3 is listed in its entirety in Example 22-3.

Example 22-3 Using GridBagLayout to Lay Out Text Fields

```java
import java.applet.Applet;
import java.awt.*;
import javax.swing.*;

public class PurchaseApplet extends JApplet {
    public void init() {
        getContentPane().add(new ButtonPurchaseForm(),
                            BorderLayout.CENTER);
    }
}
class ButtonPurchaseForm extends JPanel {
    JSeparator sep = new JSeparator();
    JLabel title   = new JLabel("Order Form");
    JLabel name    = new JLabel("Name:");
    JLabel address = new JLabel("Address:");
    JLabel payment = new JLabel("Purchase Method:");
    JLabel phone   = new JLabel("Phone:");
    JLabel city    = new JLabel("City:");
    JLabel state   = new JLabel("State:");

    JTextField nameField    = new JTextField(25);
    JTextField addressField = new JTextField(25);
    JTextField cityField    = new JTextField(15);
    JTextField stateField   = new JTextField(2);

    JComboBox paymentChoice = new JComboBox();

    JButton paymentButton = new JButton("Purchase");
    JButton cancelButton  = new JButton("Cancel");

    public ButtonPurchaseForm() {
        GridBagLayout     gbl = new GridBagLayout();
        GridBagConstraints gbc = new GridBagConstraints();

        setLayout(gbl);

        paymentChoice.addItem("Visa");
        paymentChoice.addItem("MasterCard");
        paymentChoice.addItem("COD");

        title.setFont(new Font("Times-Roman",
                            Font.BOLD + Font.ITALIC,
                            16));

        gbc.anchor    = GridBagConstraints.NORTHWEST;
        gbc.gridwidth = GridBagConstraints.REMAINDER;
        add(title, gbc);

        gbc.anchor    = GridBagConstraints.NORTH;
```

```
      gbc.fill        = GridBagConstraints.HORIZONTAL;
      gbc.insets      = new Insets(0,0,10,0);
      add(sep, gbc);

      gbc.anchor      = GridBagConstraints.WEST;
      gbc.gridwidth = 1;
      gbc.insets      = new Insets(0,0,0,0);
      add(name, gbc);

      add(Box.createHorizontalStrut(10));
      gbc.gridwidth = GridBagConstraints.REMAINDER;
      add(nameField, gbc);

      gbc.gridwidth = 1;
      add(address, gbc);

      add(Box.createHorizontalStrut(10));
      gbc.gridwidth = GridBagConstraints.REMAINDER;
      add(addressField, gbc);

      gbc.gridwidth = 1;
      add(city, gbc);

      add(Box.createHorizontalStrut(10));
      add(cityField, gbc);
      add(Box.createHorizontalStrut(10));
      add(state, gbc);
      add(Box.createHorizontalStrut(5));

      gbc.gridwidth = GridBagConstraints.REMAINDER;
      gbc.fill = GridBagConstraints.NONE;
      add(stateField, gbc);

      gbc.gridwidth = 1;
      add(payment, gbc);

      gbc.insets = new Insets(5,0,5,0);

      add(Box.createHorizontalStrut(10));
      gbc.gridwidth = GridBagConstraints.REMAINDER;
      gbc.fill        = GridBagConstraints.NONE;
      add(paymentChoice, gbc);

      ButtonPanel buttonPanel = new ButtonPanel();
      buttonPanel.add(paymentButton);
      buttonPanel.add(cancelButton);

      gbc.anchor      = GridBagConstraints.SOUTH;
      gbc.insets      = new Insets(15,0,0,0);
      gbc.fill        = GridBagConstraints.HORIZONTAL;
      gbc.gridwidth = 7;
      add(buttonPanel, gbc);
   }
```

```
class ButtonPanel extends JPanel {
    JPanel  buttonPanel = new JPanel();
    JSeparator separator = new JSeparator();

    public ButtonPanel() {
        buttonPanel.setLayout(
                        new FlowLayout(FlowLayout.CENTER));

        setLayout(new BorderLayout(0,5));
        add(separator, "North");
        add(buttonPanel, "Center");
    }
    public void add(JButton button) {
        buttonPanel.add(button);
    }
}
```

Swing Tip ...

Consider GridBagLayout for Laying Out Label/Text Field Pairs

GridBagLayout is complicated enough that it is shunned by some developers; however, GridBagLayout is a powerful layout manager that is ideal for laying out pairs of labels and text fields. Label/text field pairs are often aligned as with the Name and Address fields in Figure 22-3. For such layouts, the gridwidth constraint is toggled between 1 (for the labels) and GridBagConstraints.REMAINDER (for the text fields).

Validating Text Fields

Text fields often need to validate input; for example, a simple text field that allows only integer values is discussed in "Custom Documents" on page 1420. This section discusses a more ambitious undertaking that implements a date field as shown in Figure 22-4.

The date field shown in Figure 22-4 is a JTextField instance that is fitted with a custom document. The document monitors text insertion and removal, as the pictures in Figure 22-4 illustrate. The upper-left picture shows the field after "0" and "2" have been typed. The upper-right picture shows the field after "1" is subsequently typed. Notice that the caret jumped over the separator after "1" was

typed. The bottom pictures show the effect of pressing the Backspace key when the caret is in front of the separator—the caret is moved back two spaces so the separator cannot be removed.

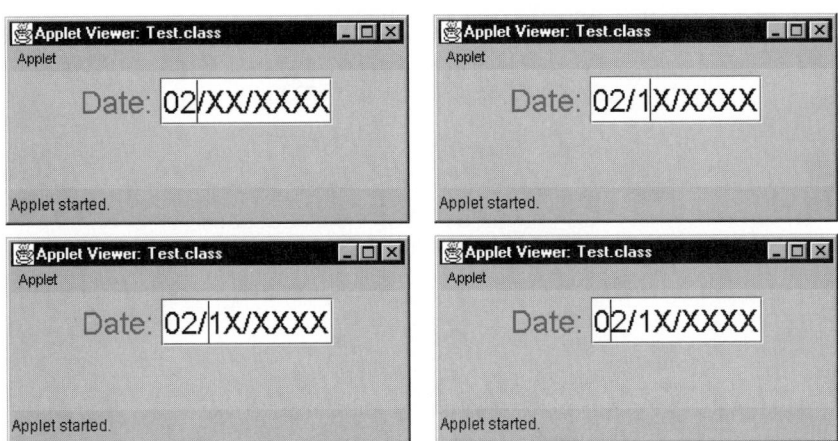

Figure 22-4 A Custom Document for a Date Field

The applet shown in Figure 22-4 instantiates a text field with a public constant string defined in `DateDocument` and sets the field's document to an instance of `DateDocument`.

```
public class Test extends JApplet {
    JTextField tf = new JTextField(DateDocument.initString);

    public Test() {
        ...
        tf.setDocument(new DateDocument(tf));
        ...
    }
    ...
}
```

The `DateDocument` class overrides `insertString()` and `remove()`. The `insertString` method checks to make sure that the string inserted is a valid `integer` and adjusts the text component's caret position as necessary. The `remove` method does not remove anything from the document; instead, the caret position is adjusted.

```
class DateDocument extends PlainDocument {
    public static String initString = "XX/XX/XXXX"; // Y10K!
    private static int sep1 = 2, sep2 = 5;
    private JTextComponent textComponent;
    private int newOffset;

    public DateDocument(JTextComponent tc) {
        textComponent = tc;
        try {
            insertString(0, initString, null);
        }
        catch(Exception ex) { }
    }
    public void insertString(int offset, String s,
                             AttributeSet attributeSet)
                             throws BadLocationException {
        if(s.equals(initString)) {
            super.insertString(offset, s, attributeSet);
        }
        else {
            try {
                Integer.parseInt(s);
            }
            catch(Exception ex) {
                return;   // only allow integer values
            }

            newOffset = offset;

            if(atSeparator(offset)) {
                newOffset++;
                textComponent.setCaretPosition(newOffset);
            }
            super.remove(newOffset, 1);
            super.insertString(newOffset, s, attributeSet);
        }
    }
    public void remove(int offset, int length)
                        throws BadLocationException {
        if(atSeparator(offset))
            textComponent.setCaretPosition(offset-1);
        else
            textComponent.setCaretPosition(offset);
    }
    private boolean atSeparator(int offset) {
        return offset == sep1 || offset == sep2;
    }
}
```

Note that a more robust DateDocument would also check for valid month, day, and year entries. The applet shown in Figure 22-4 is listed in its entirety in Example 22-4.

Example 22-4 Implementing a Custom Document

```java
import javax.swing.*;
import javax.swing.text.*;
import java.awt.*;
import java.awt.event.*;

public class Test extends JApplet {
    JTextField tf = new JTextField(DateDocument.initString);

    public Test() {
        Container contentPane = getContentPane();
        Font font = new Font("Dialog", Font.PLAIN, 24);
        JLabel label = new JLabel("Date:");

        tf.setDocument(new DateDocument(tf));

        label.setFont(font);
        tf.setFont(font);

        contentPane.setLayout(new FlowLayout());
        contentPane.add(label);
        contentPane.add(tf);
    }
}
class DateDocument extends PlainDocument {
    public static String initString = "XX/XX/XXXX"; // Y10K!
    private static int sep1 = 2, sep2 = 5;
    private JTextComponent textComponent;
    private int newOffset;

    public DateDocument(JTextComponent tc) {
        textComponent = tc;
        try {
            insertString(0, initString, null);
        }
        catch(Exception ex) { }
    }
    public void insertString(int offset, String s,
                        AttributeSet attributeSet)
                        throws BadLocationException {
        if(s.equals(initString)) {
            super.insertString(offset, s, attributeSet);
        }
        else {
            try {
                Integer.parseInt(s);
            }
            catch(Exception ex) {
                return;  // only allow integer values
            }

            newOffset = offset;
```

```
            if(atSeparator(offset)) {
                newOffset++;
                textComponent.setCaretPosition(newOffset);
            }
            super.remove(newOffset, 1);
            super.insertString(newOffset, s, attributeSet);
        }
    }
    public void remove(int offset, int length)
                        throws BadLocationException {
        if(atSeparator(offset))
            textComponent.setCaretPosition(offset-1);
        else
            textComponent.setCaretPosition(offset);
    }
    private boolean atSeparator(int offset) {
        return offset == sep1 || offset == sep2;
    }
}
```

JTextField Component Summary

The JTextField class is summarized in Component Summary 22-1.

Component Summary 22-1   JTextField

Model(s)	javax.swing.text.PlainDocument
UI Delegate(s)	javax.swing.plaf.basic.BasicTextFieldUI
Renderer(s)	——
Editor(s)	——
Events Fired	ActionEvents
Replacement For	java.awt.TextField

Class Diagrams

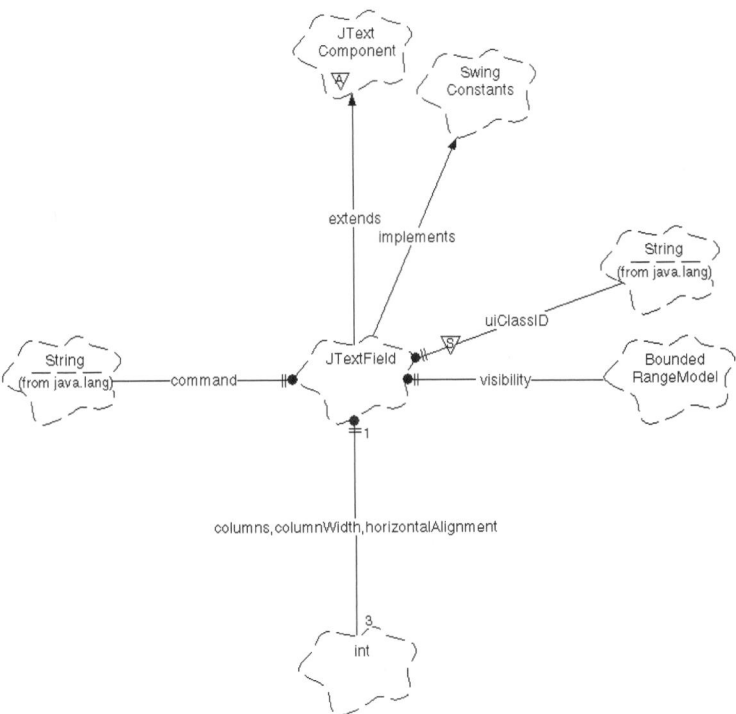

Figure 22-5 JTextField Class Diagram

JTextField extends JTextComponent and implements the SwingConstants interface. JTextField maintains private references to its action command string and visibility in the form of a BoundedRangeModel. Three integer values are maintained representing the number of columns, the column width, and the horizontal text alignment.

JTextField Properties

The properties maintained by the JTextField class are listed in Table 22-1.

Table 22-1 JTextField Properties

Property Name	Data Type	Property Type[1]	Access[2]	Default[3]
actionCommand	String	S	SG	text field text
columns	int	S	SG	0
horizontalAlignment	int	B	SG	LEFT
horizontalVisibility	Bounded RangeModel	S	G	BoundedRangeModel
scrollOffset	int	S	SG	0

1. B = bound (fires PropertyChangeEvent) / C = constrained/ I = indexed / S = simple / Ch = fires ChangeEvent
2. C = settable at construction time / G = getter method / S = setter method
3. L&F = look-and-feel dependent

actionCommand — When a text field fires an action event, the event's action command is set to the text field's `actionCommand`. If not explicitly set with the `JTextField.setActionCommand` method, the `actionCommand` defaults to the contents of the text field.

columns — A column's width is set to the width of the 'm' character for the text field's current font. As a result, setting the number of columns for a text field is an approximation.

horizontalAlignment — Determines the horizontal alignment of the text displayed in a text field. Valid values are:

- `JTextField.LEFT`
- `JTextField.CENTER`
- `JTextField.RIGHT`

Vertical text alignment is centered, and cannot be set.

horizontalVisibility — A bounded range model that tracks the visibility of the text display in a text field. Typically, the `horizontalVisibility` property is not accessed directly; see the `scrollOffset` property.

scrollOffset — Determines which portion of a field's text is visible. The scroll offset is maintained by the text field's horizontal visibility as the visibility's value. See the `horizontalVisibility` property.

JTextField Events

By default, text fields fire an action event when a field has focus and the Enter key is pressed. If a text field is in a window with a default button, pressing Enter in the text field will fire an action event from the text field instead of activating the button. Fortunately, it is a simple matter to modify the text field's keymap so that it does not fire the action event.

The application shown in Figure 22-6 provides a check box that adds or removes, depending upon the selected status of the check box, the keystroke binding for the Enter key. If the check box is selected, the Enter keystroke binding is in the text field's keymap and pressing Enter in the field will cause the text field to fire an action event. If the check box is not selected, an Enter keypress in the text field will be handled by the default button, which also fires an action event.

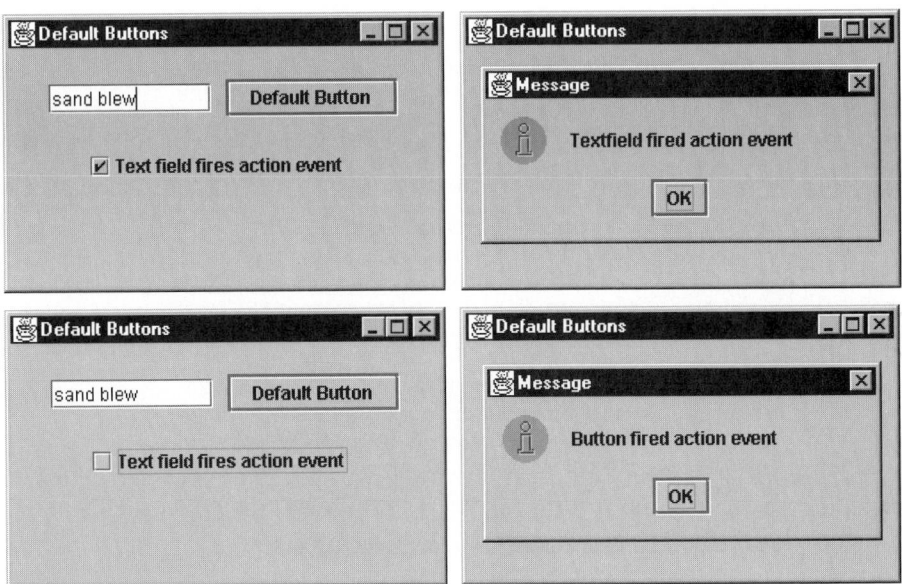

Figure 22-6 Text Fields and Default Buttons

The top pictures in Figure 22-6 show the text field firing an action event, and the lower pictures in Figure 22-6 show the default button firing the event.

The application shown in Figure 22-6 is listed in Example 22-5.

Example 22-5 Text Fields and Default Buttons

```
import javax.swing.*;
import javax.swing.text.*;
import java.awt.*;
import java.awt.event.*;
import java.util.*;

public class Test extends JFrame {
    private JTextField field = new JTextField(10);
    private JButton b = new JButton("Default Button");
    private JCheckBox cb = new JCheckBox(
                        "Text field fires action event");
    public Test() {
        Container contentPane = getContentPane();

        SwingUtilities.getRootPane(this).setDefaultButton(b);
        cb.setSelected(true);

        contentPane.setLayout(new FlowLayout(
                        FlowLayout.CENTER,10,20));
        contentPane.add(field);
        contentPane.add(b);
        contentPane.add(cb);

        b.addActionListener(new ActionListener() {
            public void actionPerformed(ActionEvent e) {
                JOptionPane.showMessageDialog(Test.this,
                    "Button fired action event");
            }
        });
        field.addActionListener(new ActionListener() {
            public void actionPerformed(ActionEvent e) {
                JOptionPane.showMessageDialog(Test.this,
                    "Textfield fired action event");
            }
        });
        cb.addActionListener(new ActionListener() {
            private Keymap km;
            private KeyStroke ks;
            private Action action;

            public void actionPerformed(ActionEvent e) {
                if(cb.isSelected()) {
                    km.addActionForKeyStroke(ks, action);
                }
                else {
                    if(ks == null) {
                        km = field.getKeymap();
```

```
                    ks = KeyStroke.getKeyStroke(
                                KeyEvent.VK_ENTER, 0);
                    action = km.getAction(ks);
                }
                km.removeKeyStrokeBinding(ks);
            }
        }
    });
}
public static void main(String args[]) {
    GJApp.launch(new Test(),
        "Default Buttons",300,300,350,200);
}
}
```

The application creates a text field, button and check box that are subsequently added to the application's content pane. The application specifies the button as the default button with the JRootPane.setDefaultButton method. The root pane is obtained with a call to SwingUtilities.getRootPane(). See "Swing Utilities" on page 262 for more information concerning the SwingUtilities class.

The button and text field are both fitted with action listeners that display a message dialog indicating the source of the action event. The check box has an action listener that removes the keystroke binding for the Enter key when the check box is deselected and restores the keystroke when the check box is selected.

JTextField Class Summaries

The JTextField class is summarized in Class Summary 22-1.

Class Summary 22-1   JTextField

Extends: JTextComponent
Implements: SwingConstants

Constants

---

public static final String <u>notifyAction</u>

The `notifyAction` string constant represents the name of the action that is fired when changes to a text field's text are committed.[2] The `notifyAction` string constant can be used to obtain a reference to the action.

Constructors

---

public <u>JTextField</u>()
public <u>JTextField</u>(int columns)
public <u>JTextField</u>(String initialString)
public <u>JTextField</u>(String initialString, int columns)
public <u>JTextField</u>(Document, String initialString, int columns)

A text field's initial string, number of columns, and document can all be specified when a text field is instantiated. The no-argument constructor constructs a text field that has a column width of 0, which means that only the text field's border is visible when laid out according to the field's preferred size.

Methods

Action Events

---

public synchronized void <u>addActionListener</u>(ActionListener)
public synchronized void <u>removeActionListener</u>(ActionListener)
protected void <u>fireActionPerformed</u>()

public void <u>postActionEvent</u>()

---

2.   By default, changes are committed by pressing the `KeyEvent.VK_ENTER` key.

Like other Swing components that fire action events, JTextField provides methods for registering action listeners and for firing action events to registers' listeners. The postActionEvent method is a public method that simply invokes the protected fireActionPerformed method; postActionEvent is called by a text field's UI delegate.

Default Model / Actions / Action Command

---

protected Document <u>createDefaultModel</u>()

public Action[] <u>getActions</u>()
public void <u>setActionCommand</u>(String)

The createDefaultModel method creates an instance of PlainDocument. Extensions of JTextField can override createDefaultModel to install custom models.

JTextField overrides getActions() from JTextComponent to add text field actions to the set of actions provided by JTextComponent. JTextField uses the TextAction.augmentList method as follows:

```
// From JTextField.java:

public Action[] getActions() {
    return TextAction.augmentList(
                    super.getActions(), defaultActions);
}
```

See "Actions" on page 1401 for more information concerning text actions and Example 23-4 on page 1553 for an example of using the TextAction.augmentList method in an editor kit.

A text field's action command is a string embedded in the action event fired when changes to the field's text are committed. The action command defaults to the text displayed in the text field when the action event is fired. The action command can be explicitly set with the setActionCommand method.

Columns / Font

---

public int <u>getColumns</u>()
public void <u>setColumns</u>(int width)

protected int <u>getColumnWidth</u>()

public void <u>setFont</u>(Font)

The number of columns for a text field can be explicitly set, either at construction time or at any time thereafter. A column is defined to be the width of the "m" character for a text field's font. For text fields with variable width fonts, explicitly setting the number of columns is an approximation.

The pixel width of a column can be obtained from the getColumnWidth method. The setFont method is overridden to reset the field's column width so that it will be recomputed the next time getColumnWidth is called.

Alignment / Visibility / Scroll Offset

---

public int <u>getHorizontalAlignment</u>()
public void <u>setHorizontalAlignment</u>(int alignment)

public BoundedRangeModel <u>getHorizontalVisibility</u>()

public int <u>getScrollOffset</u>()
public void <u>setScrollOffset</u>(int offset)

The horizontal alignment of a text field's text can be specified with one of the following constants:

- JTextField.LEFT
- JTextField.CENTER
- JTextField.RIGHT

Invoking setHorizontalAlignment() results in the text field being invalidated and repainted.

The horizontal visibility of a text field is modeled by an instance of BoundedRangeModel, which is accessible through the

`getHorizontalVisibility` method. The value of the model is the scroll offset, which is the location of the text displayed in a text field's upper-left corner. The scroll offset can be accessed with the last two methods listed above.

Accessibility / Pluggable Look And Feel

---

public AccessibleContext getAccessibleContext()
public String getUIClassID()

`JTextField`, like all other Swing components, provides access to its accessible context with the `getAccessibleContext` method. Like all other lightweight Swing components, `JTextField` implements `getUIClassID()`, which returns a string—`"TextField"`—identifying the class of a text field's UI delegate.

Miscellaneous Methods

---

public Dimension getPreferredSize()
public boolean isValidateRoot()
public void scrollRectToVisible(Rectangle)

protected String paramString()

`JTextField` overrides `getPreferredSize` to take into account whether the number of columns has been explicitly set. The preferred height is set to the height returned from `super.getPreferredSize()`. The preferred width is also obtained from the call to `super.getPreferredSize()` unless the number of columns has been explicitly set; if so, the preferred width is the number of columns multiplied by the column width.

`JTextField` overrides `isValidateRoot` to return `true`. This means that invoking `revalidate()` for a text field will revalidate the field and not all of the siblings and ancestors of the field that reside in the containing scrollpane or root pane. See "Validate, Invalidate, and Revalidate Methods" on page 144 for more information concerning the `revalidate` method.

The `scrollRectToVisible` method uses the `horizontalVisibility` bounded range property to scroll the text contained in a text field. The `paramString` method returns a string representation of a text field.

Text Fields and Default Buttons

In Swing, default buttons are activated by a user pressing the Enter key when a component in the same window as the default button has focus. Text fields, by default, fire action events when they have focus and the Enter key is pressed, and therefore the mouse pressed event does not activate the default button.

For a default button to be activated when a text field has focus and the Enter key is pressed, the keystroke binding for the Enter key can be removed from the field's keymap, like this:

```
Keymap km = textfield.getKeymap();
KeyStroke ks = km.getKeyStroke(KeyEvent.VK_ENTER, 0);
km.removeKeyStrokeBinding(ks);
```

AWT Compatibility

`JTextField` and `java.awt.TextField` are almost source compatible, as evidenced by Table 22-2. The only `TextField` methods that are not implemented by `JTextField` are concerned with the AWT text field's echo character. `JTextField` does not support disguising input; see "JPasswordField" for more information about password fields.

Table 22-2 java.awt.TextField Methods and JTextField Equivalents

java.awt.TextField Method	JTextField Equivalent
void addActionListener(ActionListener)	void addActionListener(ActionListener)
boolean echoCharIsSet()	see JPasswordField
int getColumns()	int getColumns()
char getEchoChar()	see JPasswordField
void removeActionListener(ActionListener)	void removeActionListener(ActionListener)
void setColumns(int)	void setColumns(int)
setEchoChar()	see JPasswordField
void setText(String)	void setText(String)

JPasswordField

Swing's password field conceals its text by displaying an '*' for every character entered in the field. The asterisk is referred to as an echo character and can be set after a password field is constructed.

The password field is simple to use, as the applet shown in Figure 22-7 illustrates. The applet contains a label and password field that has its echo character set to '?'. An action listener is added to the field; it updates the applet's status bar depending upon the password submitted.

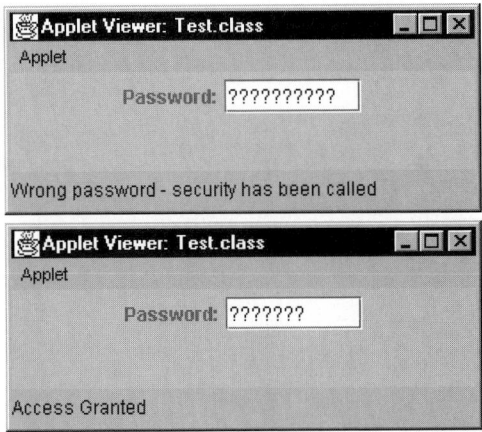

Figure 22-7 Using JPasswordField

The applet shown in Figure 22-7 is listed in Example 22-6.

Example 22-6 Using JPasswordField

```java
import javax.swing.*;
import java.awt.*;
import java.awt.event.*;
import java.util.*;

public class Test extends JApplet {
    private String pw = "dol42ce";
    private JPasswordField passwordField = new JPasswordField(8);

    public void init() {
```

```
    Container contentPane = getContentPane();
    JPanel panel = new JPanel();

    panel.add(new JLabel("Password:"));
    panel.add(passwordField);

    passwordField.setEchoChar('?');

    contentPane.add(panel, BorderLayout.CENTER);

    passwordField.addActionListener(new ActionListener() {
        public void actionPerformed(ActionEvent e) {
            String password = new String(
                            passwordField.getPassword());

            if(pw.equals(password))
                showStatus("Access Granted");
            else
                showStatus("Wrong password - security " +
                            "has been called");
        }
    });
  }
}
```

The applet creates an instance of JPasswordField with eight columns. An action listener retrieves the password from the field and checks to see if the password is valid.

JPasswordField Component Summary

The JPasswordField class is summarized in Component Summary 22-1.

Component Summary 22-2   JPasswordField

Model(s)	javax.swing.text.PlainDocument
UI Delegate(s)	javax.swing.plaf.basic.BasicPasswordFieldUI
Renderer(s)	——
Editor(s)	——
Events Fired	ActionEvents
Replacement For	——

Class Diagrams

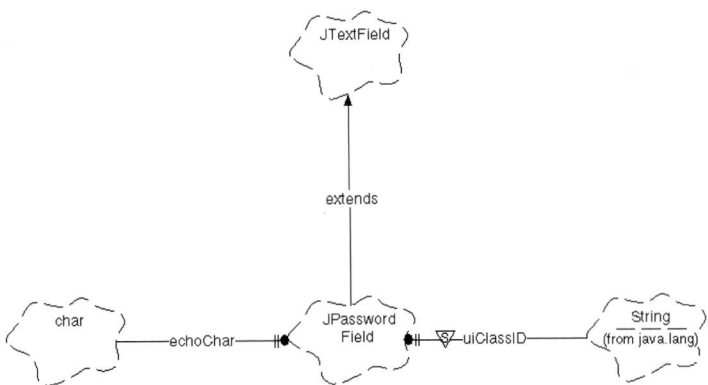

Figure 22-8 JPasswordField Class Diagram

JPasswordField is a simple extension of JTextField that maintains an echo character. Like its superclass, JPasswordField uses an instance of PlainDocument as its default document.

JPasswordField Properties

The properties maintained by the JPasswordField class are listed in Table 22-3.

Table 22-3 JPasswordField Properties

Property Name	Data Type	Property Type[1]	Access[2]	Default[3]
echoChar	char	S	SG	L&F
password	char[]	S	G	—

1. B = bound (fires PropertyChangeEvent) / C = constrained/ I = indexed / S = simple / Ch = fires ChangeEvent
2. C = settable at construction time / G = getter method / S = setter method
3. L&F = look-and-feel dependent

echoChar — The character that is displayed in a password field when a character is typed.

password — An array of characters containing the characters that were typed into the field.

JPasswordField Class Summary

The JPasswordField class is summarized in Class Summary 22-2.

Class Summary 22-2   JPasswordField

Extends: JTextField

Constructors

---

public JPasswordField()
public JPasswordField(int columns)
public JPasswordField(String initialString)
public JPasswordField(String initialString, int columns)
public JPasswordField(Document, String initialString, int columns)

JPasswordField provides the same set of constructors as its superclass, JTextField. The JPasswordField constructors invoke the superclass constructors and set the echo character to the '*'.

Password / Security

---

public char[] getPassword()

public void copy()
public void cut()

public String <u>getText</u>()
public String <u>getText</u>(int p0, int p1) throws BadLocationException

The `getPassword` method should be used to obtain the password instead of the `getText` methods inherited from `JTextField`, which are deprecated in `JPasswordField` to provide a compile-time warning.

The `copy` and `cut` methods are overridden to simply beep so that a password cannot be manipulated programmatically.

Echo Char

---

public char <u>getEchoChar</u>()
public void <u>setEchoChar</u>(char)

public boolean <u>echoCharIsSet</u>()

The three methods listed above are accessors for a password field's echo character. The methods have the same signatures as methods found in `java.awt.TextField` to maintain AWT compatibility.

Accessibility / Pluggable Look And Feel

---

public AccessibleContext <u>getAccessibleContext</u>()
public String <u>getUIClassID</u>()
protected String <u>paramString</u>()

`JPasswordField`, like all other Swing components, provides access to its accessible context with the `getAccessibleContext` method. Like all other lightweight Swing components, `JPasswordField` implements `getUIClassID()`, which returns a string—`"PasswordField"`—identifying the class of a password field's UI delegate.

The `paramString` method returns a textual description of a password field.

JTextArea

Swing text areas, represented by the `JTextArea` class, can display multiple lines of plain text, which is defined as text with one font and one color. Text areas can wrap lines, either on character or word boundaries. The `JTextArea` class is nearly source compatible with the `java.awt.TextArea` class.

`JTextArea` is a simple component that does not offer any of the sophistication found in Swing's other multiline text components: `JEditorPane` and `JTextPane`. Nonetheless, simple text areas are useful in countless situations, as the application shown in Figure 22-9 illustrates.

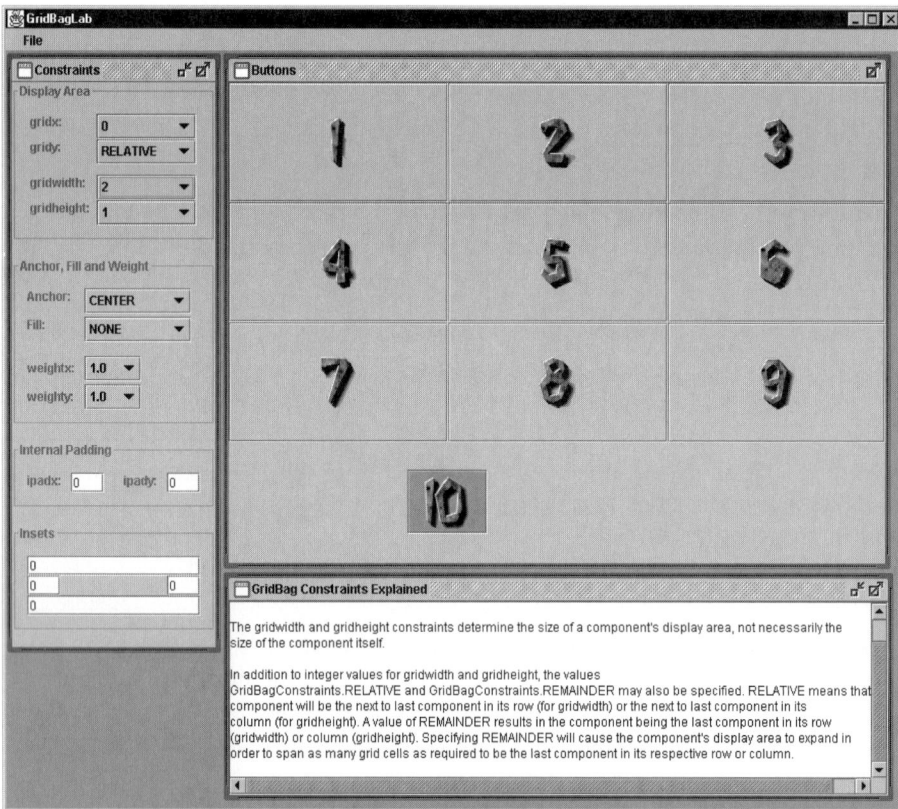

Figure 22-9 GridBagLab Uses a Text Area

The application shown in Figure 22-9 is a lab, of sorts, for exploring the GridBagLayout layout manager. The application uses a text area wrapped in a scrollpane, to display information about grid bag constraints as the cursor moves over items in the Constraints window.

The application creates an instance of JTextArea with the contents of a file. The text area wraps lines of text on word boundaries as a result of a call to JTextArea.setWrapStyleWord(true). The text area's font is set, and the text area's editability is set to false.

Like all other Swing text components, JTextArea does not implement scrolling on its own; instead, JTextArea implements the Scrollable interface and should be placed in a scrollpane if scrolling is desired.

```
public class GridBagLab extends JFrame {
    ...
    static JTextArea helpTextArea =
                new JTextArea(contentsOfFile("intro.txt"));
    ...
    helpTextArea.setWrapStyleWord(true);
    helpTextArea.setEditable(false);
    helpTextArea.setFont(
            new Font("Times-Roman", Font.PLAIN, 12));
    ...
    helpFrame.getContentPane().add(
            new JScrollPane(helpTextArea), "Center");
    }
    ...
}
```

Note: *For the sake of brevity, the application shown in Figure 22-9 is not listed; however, the application is on the CD in the back of the book.*

The applet shown in Figure 22-10 illustrates line wrapping for text areas. The applet contains a text area and provides three radio buttons for controlling the text area's wrapping behavior. The top-left picture in Figure 22-10 shows the applet as it appears initially, and the top-right and lower pictures show the text area wrapping characters and words, respectively.

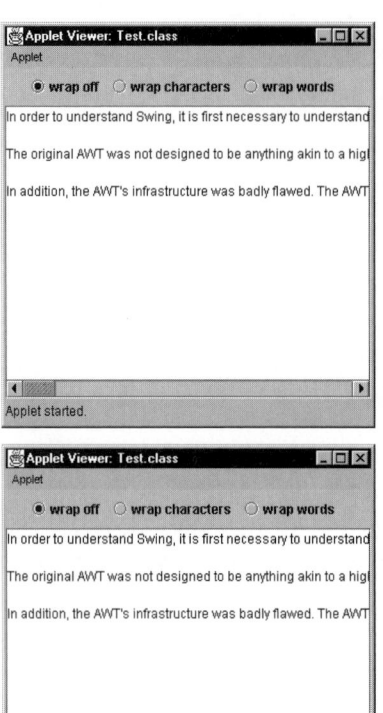

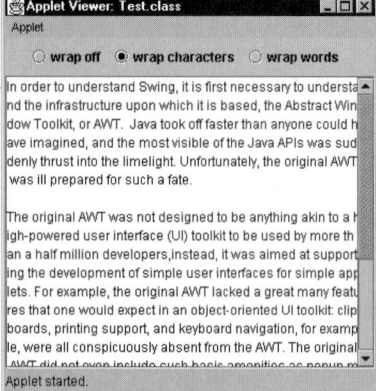

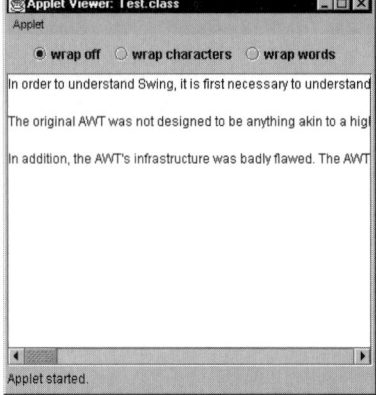

Figure 22-10 Text Field Wrapping

The applet shown in Figure 22-10 is listed in Example 22-7.

Example 22-7 Specifying JTextField Wrapping Behavior

```
import java.awt.*;
import java.awt.event.*;
import javax.swing.*;
import javax.swing.text.*;
import java.io.FileReader;

public class Test extends JApplet {
    private JTextArea textArea = new JTextArea();
    private Container contentPane = getContentPane();
```

```
public void init() {
    To(textArea, "text");
    contentPane.add(new ControlPanel(), BorderLayout.NORTH);

    contentPane.add(new JScrollPane(textArea),
                BorderLayout.CENTER);
}
private void readFile(JTextComponent textComponent,String s){
    try { (new DefaultEditorKit()).read(
            new FileReader(s), textComponent.getDocument(), 0);
    } catch(Exception ex) { ex.printStackTrace(); }
}
class ControlPanel extends JPanel {
    JRadioButton radioButtons[] = new JRadioButton[] {
        new JRadioButton("wrap off"),
        new JRadioButton("wrap characters"),
        new JRadioButton("wrap words"),
    };

    public ControlPanel() {
        ButtonGroup group = new ButtonGroup();
        Listener listener = new Listener();

        for(int i=0; i < radioButtons.length; ++i) {
            JRadioButton b = radioButtons[i];

            b.addActionListener(listener);
            group.add(b);
            add(b);

            if(i == 0)
                b.setSelected(true); // "wrap off"
        }
    }
    class Listener implements ActionListener {
        public void actionPerformed(ActionEvent e) {
            String action = e.getActionCommand();

            textArea.setLineWrap(!action.equals("wrap off"));
            textArea.setWrapStyleWord(
                        action.equals("wrap words"));
        }
    };
}
}
```

The applet adds an action listener to each of the radio buttons that enables or disables line wrapping and sets the wrap style depending upon the radio button that is selected.

JTextArea Component Summary

The JTextArea class is summarized in Component Summary 22-3.

Component Summary 22-3   JTextArea

Model(s)	javax.swing.text.PlainDocument
UI Delegate(s)	javax.swing.plaf.basic.BasicTextAreaUI
Renderer(s)	——
Editor(s)	——
Events Fired	——
Replacement For	java.awt.TextArea

Class Diagrams

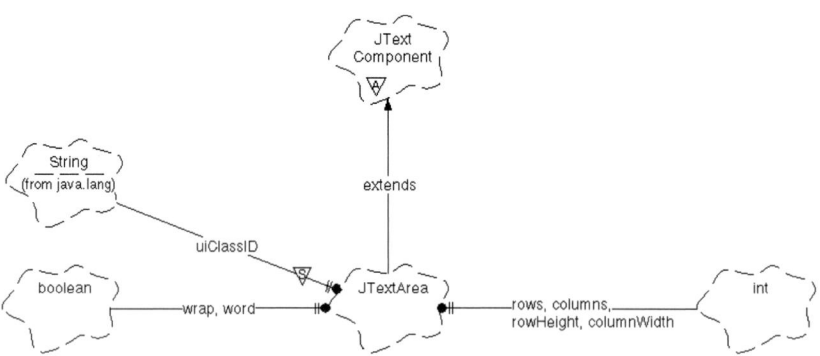

Figure 22-11 JTextArea Class Diagram

JTextArea extends JTextComponent and maintains private boolean values for maintaining a text area's wrapping state. JTextArea also maintains integer values for the number of rows and columns and the row height and column width.

JTextArea Properties

The properties maintained by the JTextArea class are listed in Table 22-4.

Table 22-4 JTextArea Properties

Property Name	Data Type	Property Type[1]	Access[2]	Default[3]
columns	int	S	CSG	0
lineCount	int	S	G	0
lineWrap	boolean	B	SG	false
rows	int	S	SG	0
tabSize	int	B	SG	from document
wrapStyleWord	boolean	B	SG	false

1. B = bound (fires PropertyChangeEvent) / C = constrained/ I = indexed /
   S = simple / Ch = fires ChangeEvent
2. C = settable at construction time / G = getter method / S = setter method
3. L&F = look-and-feel dependent

columns — The number of columns displayed in a text area. Like text fields, the width of a column is the width of the "m" character in the text area's current font.

lineCount — The number of lines of text contained in a text area.

lineWrap — Determines whether lines of text are wrapped at the right edge of a text area. The type of wrapping is determined by the wrapStyleWord property.

rows — The number of lines of text displayed in a text area.

tabSize — The number of characters inserted when the Tab key is pressed.

wrapStyleWord — A boolean property that, when set to true, causes lines to be wrapped on word boundaries. If the property is false, lines are wrapped on character boundaries.

JTextArea Class Summaries

The JTextArea class is summarized in Class Summary 22-3.

Class Summary 22-3   JTextArea

Extends: JTextComponent

Constructors

---

public <u>JTextArea</u>()
public <u>JTextArea</u>(int rows, int columns)
public <u>JTextArea</u>(String initialString)
public <u>JTextArea</u>(String initialString, int rows, int columns)
public <u>JTextArea</u>(Document)
public <u>JTextArea</u>(Document, String initialString, int rows, int columns)

Like JTextField, JTextArea offers a number of constructors for specifying the document, initial string, and number of columns. JTextArea also allows the number of rows to be set at construction time.

The JTextArea no-argument constructor constructs a text area with 0 rows and 0 columns and is therefore too small to be seen when sized according to the text area's preferred size.

Methods

Document / Text / Tab Size

---

protected Document <u>createDefaultModel</u>()

public void <u>append</u>(String)
public void <u>insert</u>(String, int start)
public void <u>replaceRange</u>(String, int start, int end)

public int <u>getTabSize</u>()
public void <u>setTabSize</u>(int)

Like text fields, the default model for text areas is an instance of
`PlainDocument`. The second group of methods listed above can be used to
append, insert, and replace text in a text area without directly accessing the text
area's document.

A text area's tab size represents the number of characters inserted when the Tab
key is pressed and can be accessed with the last group of methods listed above.

Columns and Rows

---

protected int <u>getColumnWidth</u>()
public int <u>getColumns</u>()
public void <u>setColumns</u>(int)

protected int <u>getRowHeight</u>()
public int <u>getRows</u>()
public void <u>setRows</u>(int)

The number of rows and columns and column width and row height in pixels can
be accessed with the methods listed above. If the number of columns or rows are
not explicitly set, `getColumns()` and `getRows()`, respectively, will return 0.
The row height is the font height specified by the text area's font metrics, and the
column width is the width of the 'm' character in the text area's current font.

Lines / Line Wrapping

---

public int <u>getLineCount</u>()

public int <u>getLineEndOffset</u>(int line) throws BadLocationException
public int <u>getLineStartOffset</u>(int line) throws BadLocationException
public int <u>getLineOfOffset</u>(int offset) throws BadLocationException

public boolean <u>getLineWrap</u>()
public void <u>setLineWrap</u>(boolean)

public boolean <u>getWrapStyleWord</u>()
public void <u>setWrapStyleWord</u>(boolean)

The number of lines returned from `getLineCount()` represents the number of lines in a text area's model.

The second group of methods listed above can be used to obtain a line number, given an offset and the start and end offsets for a given line. The offsets translate to positions in the model.

The last two groups of methods listed above access the `lineWrap` and `wrapStyleWord` properties, which are discussed in "JTextArea Properties" on page 1495.

Scrollable Interface

---

public Dimension <u>getPreferredScrollableViewportSize</u>()
public boolean <u>getScrollableTracksViewportWidth</u>()
public int <u>getScrollableUnitIncrement</u>(Rectangle visibleRect, int orientation, int direction)

The `getPreferredScrollableViewportSize` method returns the preferred size for a text area's viewport when a text area is contained in a scrollpane. If rows or columns have been explicitly set, the preferred row height or column width is the number of rows multiplied by the row height or the number of columns multiplied by the column width, respectively. If rows or columns have not been explicitly set, the preferred viewport size is obtained from the `JTextArea` superclass (`JTextComponent`).

The `getScrollableTracksViewportWidth` method is overridden from `JTextComponent` to take into account line wrapping. If line wrapping is enabled, the method returns `true`, indicating that the width of the text area should be kept the same as the width of the text area's viewport.

The `getScrollableUnitIncrement` method returns either the column width or the row height, depending upon the orientation passed to the method.

Miscellaneous Methods

---

public Dimension <u>getPreferredSize</u>()
public boolean <u>isManagingFocus</u>()
protected void <u>processComponentKeyEvent</u>(KeyEvent)
public void <u>setFont</u>(Font)
protected String <u>paramString</u>()

Like JTextField, JTextArea overrides getPreferredSize() to take into account whether the number of rows or columns has been explicitly set. If the number of rows has been explicitly set, the preferred height is calculated as the number of rows multiplied by the row height. If the number of columns has been explicitly set, the preferred width is the number of columns multiplied by the column width.

JTextArea overrides isManagingFocus() to return true, which means a Tab key press in a text area will not move focus to the next focus component. See "Focus Management" on page 191 for more information concerning focus management and the isManagingFocus method. The processComponentKeyEvent is overridden to ensure that Tab and Shift-Tab keys are consumed.

Like JTextField, JTextArea overrides setFont() to reset row height and column width to 0 when the font changes. The values are reset so that subsequent calls to getRowHeight() or getColumnWidth() will recalculate the values.

Accessibility / Pluggable Look And Feel

---

public AccessibleContext getAccessibleContext()
public String getUIClassID()

JTextArea, like all other Swing components, provides access to its accessible context with the getAccessibleContext method. Like all other lightweight Swing components, JTextArea implements getUIClassID(), which returns a string—"TextArea"—identifying the class of a text field's UI delegate.

AWT Compatibility

JTextArea is source compatible with java.awt.TextArea except for two TextArea methods that are not implemented by JTextArea, as shown in Table 22-5. Because Swing text areas do not implement scrolling directly, the java.awt.TextArea.getScrollbarVisibility() methods have no counterparts in the JTextArea class.

Table 22-5   java.awt.TextArea Methods and JTextArea Equivalents

java.awt.TextArea Method	JTextArea Equivalent
void append(String)	void append(String)
int getColumns()	int getColumns()
int getRows()	int getRows()
char getScrollbarVisibility()	—
int getScrollbarVisibility(int)	—
void insert(String, int)	void insert(String, int)
void replaceRange(String,int,int)	void replaceRange(String,int,int)
void setColumns(int)	void setColumns(int)
void setRows(int)	void setRows(int)

JEditorPane

Editor panes, like text areas, are capable of displaying multiple lines of editable text. Unlike text areas, editor panes are capable of displaying different types of content; by default, editor panes can display plain text, HTML and RTF. Editor panes are instances of the JEditorPane class, which is a direct extension of JTextComponent.

Two things should be understood about the JEditorPane class. First, JEditorPane does not do a top-notch job of displaying either HTML or RTF. Support for HTML and RTF will improve with future Swing releases, but for Swing 1.1 FCS, the implementation is immature. Second, JEditorPane is the superclass for JTextPane, and both JEditorPane and JTextPane are fundamentally different from JTextField and JTextArea. See "Editor Panes and Editor Kits" on page 1504 for information concerning fundamental differences between editor/text panes and text fields/areas.

The application shown in Figure 22-12 uses an editor pane to display an HTML file. Editor panes display HTML differently depending upon whether the editor pane itself is editable. The top picture in Figure 22-12 shows the HTML file when the editor pane is not editable and the lower picture shows the file when the editor is editable.

The application shown in Figure 22-12 is listed in Example 22-8.

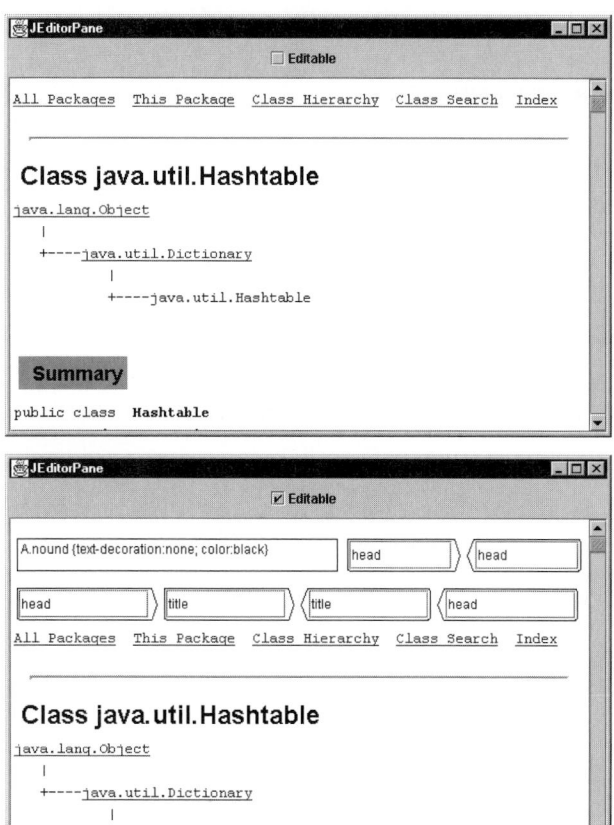

Figure 22-12 An Editor Pane with HTML Content

Example 22-8 Displaying HTML Files with an Editor Pane

```
import javax.swing.*;
import java.awt.*;
import java.awt.event.*;
import java.util.*;

public class Test extends JFrame {
    private JEditorPane editorPane = new JEditorPane();

    public Test() {
        Container contentPane = getContentPane();

        String url = "file:" + System.getProperty("user.dir") +
```

```
            System.getProperty("file.separator") +
            "java.util.Hashtable.html";

        editorPane.setEditable(false);

        try {
            editorPane.setPage(url);
        }
        catch(Exception ex) { ex.printStackTrace(); }

        contentPane.add(new ControlPanel(), BorderLayout.NORTH);
        contentPane.add(new JScrollPane(editorPane),
                    BorderLayout.CENTER);
    }
    class ControlPanel extends JPanel {
        private JCheckBox edit = new JCheckBox("Editable");

        public ControlPanel() {
            add(edit);

            edit.addActionListener(new ActionListener() {
                public void actionPerformed(ActionEvent e) {
                    editorPane.setEditable(edit.isSelected());
                }
            });
        }
    }
    public static void main(String args[]) {
        GJApp.launch(new Test(),
                "JEditorPane",300,300,650,450);
    }
}
```

The application creates an editor pane, a check box, and a URL for an HTML file on the local file system. The editability of the editor pane is set to false, and an action listener is added to the check box. The listener sets the editability of the editor pane when the check box is selected or deselected.

The JEditorPane component is summarized in Component Summary 22-4.

Component Summary 22-4   JEditorPane

Model(s)	javax.swing.text.PlainDocument
UI Delegate(s)	javax.swing.plaf.basic.BasicEditorPaneUI

Renderer(s)	——
Editor(s)	——
Events Fired	HyperlinkEvents
Replacement For	——

Class Diagrams

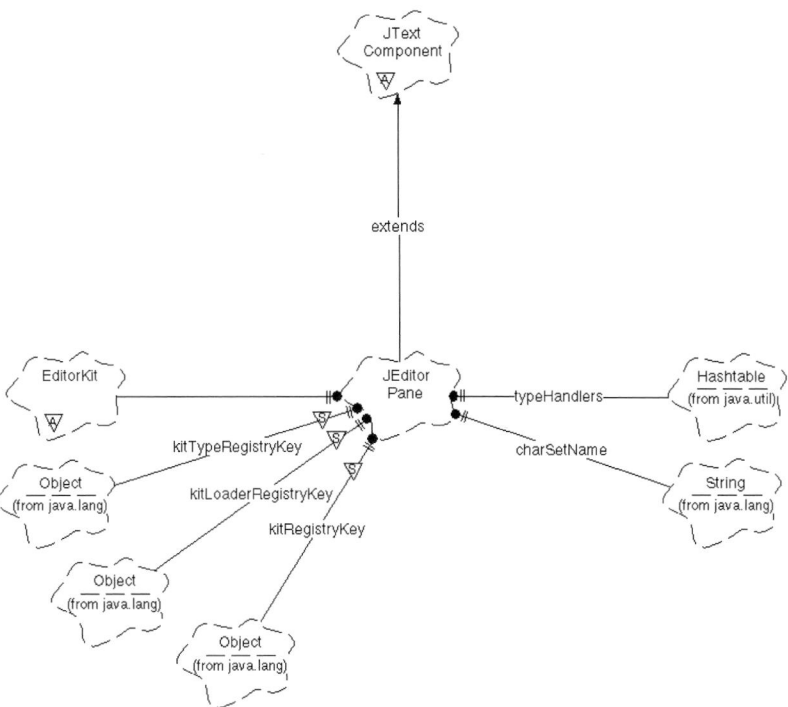

Figure 22-13   JEditorPane Class Diagram

The JEditorPane class extends JTextComponent and maintains a private reference to its editor kit. JEditorPane uses a hash table for equating editor kits with content type.

JEditorPane Properties

The properties maintained by the `JEditorPane` class are listed in Table 22-6.

Table 22-6   JEditorPane Properties

Property Name	Data Type	Property Type[1]	Access[2]	Default[3]
editorKit	EditorKit	B	SG	PlainEditorKit
editorKitForContentType	EditorKit	I	SG	—
page	String/URL	B	SG	—
text	String	S	SG	null

1. B = bound (fires PropertyChangeEvent) / C = constrained/ I = indexed /
   S = simple / Ch = fires ChangeEvent
2. C = settable at construction time / G = getter method / S = setter method
3. L&F = look-and-feel dependent

editorKit — The current editor kit for an editor pane. Editor panes can associate editor kits with different types of content; see the `editorKitForContentType` property.

editorKitForContentType — An editor kit associated with a particular type of content.

page — The URL of the currently displayed HTML file. The property is `null` if an editor pane is not currently displaying a URL.

text — The text displayed in an editor pane. When setting the text, the string passed to `setText()` must be in the format of the editor pane's current content type.

Editor Panes and Editor Kits

All Swing text components have an editor kit, but editor kits for editor and text panes have a bigger role than editor kits for text fields and text areas. For example, editor panes maintain a set of editor kits that are plugged into the editor pane for different types of content. Also, views for text fields and text areas are created by the component's look and feel, but views for editor and text panes are created by the component's editor kit.

JEditorPane Events

Hyperlink events are fired when a mouse pressed event occurs over a hyperlink in an editor pane that is displaying an HTML document. The `javax.swing.event` package defines a `HyperlinkListener` interface and a `HyperlinkEvent` class that allow hyperlink events to be handled. The `HyperlinkListener` interface is summarized in Interface Summary 22-1.

Interface Summary 22-1   HyperlinkListener

public abstract void <u>hyperlinkUpdate</u>(HyperlinkEvent)

The `HyperlinkListener` interface defines a single method that is called when an HTML hyperlink is activated. The `HyperlinkListener.hyperlink` method is passed an instance of `HyperlinkEvent`, which is summarized in Class Summary 22-4.

Class Summary 22-4   HyperlinkEvent

Extends: java.util.EventObject

Constructors

public <u>HyperlinkEvent</u>(Object source, HyperlinkEvent.EventType, URL)
public <u>HyperlinkEvent</u>(Object source, HyperlinkEvent.EventType, URL, String)

Hyperlink events are constructed with the source of the event, the event type, and a URL. Hyperlink events can also be constructed with a string describing the event.

Methods

public String <u>getDescription</u>()
public HyperlinkEvent.EventType <u>getEventType</u>()
public URL <u>getURL</u>()

`HyperlinkEvent` provides the accessors listed above for the URL corresponding to the hyperlink and the event type and description.

The application shown in Figure 22-14 illustrates the most common reaction to a hyperlink activation: the URL associated with the hyperlink is loaded into the editor pane. The top picture shows the All Packages hyperlink being activated, and the lower picture shows the associated HTML page.

Figure 22-14 Loading URLs with a Hyperlink Listener

The application shown in Figure 22-14 is listed in Example 22-9.

Example 22-9 Loading URLs with a Hyperlink Listener

```java
import javax.swing.*;
import javax.swing.event.*;
import java.awt.*;
import java.awt.event.*;
import java.util.*;
import java.io.IOException;

public class Test extends JFrame {
    private JEditorPane editorPane = new JEditorPane();

    public Test() {
        Container contentPane = getContentPane();
        String url = "file:" + System.getProperty("user.dir") +
            System.getProperty("file.separator") +
            "java.util.Hashtable.html";

        try {
            editorPane.setPage(url);
        }
        catch(IOException ex) { ex.printStackTrace(); }

        contentPane.add(new JScrollPane(editorPane),
                    BorderLayout.CENTER);

        editorPane.setEditable(false);

        editorPane.addHyperlinkListener(new HyperlinkListener() {
            public void hyperlinkUpdate(HyperlinkEvent e) {
                try {
                    editorPane.setPage(e.getURL());
                }
                catch(IOException ex) { ex.printStackTrace(); }
            }
        });
    }
    public static void main(String args[]) {
        GJApp.launch(new Test(),
                "JEditorPane",300,300,450,300);
    }
}
```

The application adds a hyperlink listener to the editor pane that invokes
JEditorPane.setPage() with the URL provided by the hyperlink event.

JEditorPane Class Summaries

The `JEditorPane` class is summarized in Class Summary 22-5.

Class Summary 22-5 JEditorPane

Extends: JTextComponent

Constructors

---

public <u>JEditorPane</u>()
public <u>JEditorPane</u>(String url) throws IOException
public <u>JEditorPane</u>(String contentType, String text)
public <u>JEditorPane</u>(URL) throws IOException

Editor panes can be constructed with a URL or a string representing a URL. Editor panes can also be constructed with a string representing the content type and the initial text displayed in the editor pane.

Methods

Text / Replace Selection

---

public String <u>getText</u>()
public void <u>setText</u>(String)
public void <u>replaceSelection</u>(String)

The methods listed above provide access to an editor pane's text and the ability to replace the current selection. The string passed to the setText method must be in the format corresponding to the editor pane's current content type.

The replaceSelection method replaces the current selection with the specified string. If there is no selection when replaceSelection() is called, the specified text will be inserted ahead of the caret. If the specified text is null, the current selection is removed.

Editor Kits / Content Type

---

public static void <u>registerEditorKitForContentType</u>(String type, String classname)
public static void <u>registerEditorKitForContentType</u>(String type, String classname,
                                        ClassLoader)

public static EditorKit <u>createEditorKitForContentType</u>(String type)

protected EditorKit <u>createDefaultEditorKit</u>()
public final EditorKit <u>getEditorKit</u>()
public EditorKit <u>getEditorKitForContentType</u>(String)

public void <u>setEditorKit</u>(EditorKit)
public void <u>setEditorKitForContentType</u>(String, EditorKit)

public final String <u>getContentType</u>()
public final void <u>setContentType</u>(String)

The first two methods listed above register a content type with a class name for a corresponding editor kit. The JEditorPane class maintains a hash table of content types stored as strings and editor kits. The createEditorKitForContentType method searches the hash table for an editor kit that corresponds to the specified content type.

The createDefaultEditorKit method creates an instance of PlainEditorKit, a JEditorPane inner class that extends DefaultEditorKit. JEditorPane.PlainEditorKit acts as a view factory for editor panes by creating views of type WrappedPlainView. The getEditorKit method creates the default editor kit if the editor kit is null and returns the editor pane's editor kit.

If an editor kit has previously been specified for the content type, it is returned from the `getEditorKitForContentType` method. If no editor kit is associated with the specified content type, the content pane's editor kit is returned.

The `getContentType` method returns the type of content for which an editor pane is configured. The `setContentType` sets the content type for an editor pane to the specified string, causing the editor pane to configure itself with an appropriate editor kit.

Page / Hyperlink Events

---

public URL <u>getPage</u>()

public void <u>setPage</u>(String) throws IOException
public void <u>setPage</u>(URL) throws IOException

public synchronized void <u>addHyperlinkListener</u>(HyperlinkListener)
public synchronized void <u>removeHyperlinkListener</u>(HyperlinkListener)
public void <u>fireHyperlinkUpdate</u>(HyperlinkEvent)

The `setPage` method loads the contents of the specified URL and sets the editor pane's content type to HTML if it is not already set. The `getPage` method returns the URL currently displayed in an editor pane. The `setPage` method throws an `IOException` if the specified URL is not valid, and the `getPage` method returns a `null` reference if a URL is not currently displayed in an editor pane.

The last group of methods listed above add and remove hyperlink listeners and fire hyperlink events to currently registered listeners. See "JEditorPane Events" on page 1505 for an example of handling hyperlink events.

Scrollable Interface

---

public boolean <u>getScrollableTracksViewportHeight</u>()
public boolean <u>getScrollableTracksViewportWidth</u>()

If the height of an editor pane's viewport falls between the minimum and maximum heights for the editor pane, the `getScrollableViewportHeight` method returns `true`, indicating that the height of the editor pane should be kept the same as the height of the editor pane's viewport.

If the width of an editor pane's viewport falls between the minimum and maximum widths for the editor pane, the `getScrollableViewportWidth` method returns `true`, indicating that the width of the editor pane should be kept the same as the width of the editor pane's viewport.

Accessibility / Pluggable Look and Feel

---

public AccessibleContext <u>getAccessibleContext</u>()
public String <u>getUIClassID</u>()

`JEditorPane`, like all other Swing components, provides access to its accessible context with the `getAccessibleContext` method. Like all other lightweight Swing components, `JEditorPane` implements `getUIClassID()`, which returns a string—`"EditorPane"`—identifying the class of a text field's UI delegate.

Miscellaneous Methods

---

protected InputStream <u>getStream</u>(URL) throws IOException
public Dimension <u>getPreferredSize</u>()
public boolean <u>isManagingFocus</u>()
protected String <u>paramString</u>()
protected void <u>processComponentKeyEvent</u>(KeyEvent)
public void <u>read</u>(InputStream, Object description) throws IOException
protected void <u>scrollToReference</u>(String)

The `getPreferredSize` method is overridden to account for the case where an editor pane's viewport is smaller than the editor pane's minimum size, in which case the minimum size of the editor pane is returned.

Like `JTextField` and `JTextArea`, `JEditorPane` overrides `isManagingFocus` so that pressing the Tab key in an editor pane will not move focus to the next component.

The `read` method fits an editor pane with an HTML editor kit and HTML document if the description is an instance of `HTMLDocument`.

JTextPane

Text panes, which are instances of the `JTextPane` class, are the Cadillac of Swing text components. `JTextPane` extends `JEditorPane`, and therefore text panes inherit the ability to display different types of content. The `JTextPane` class adds two significant capabilities: embedding icons and components and marking content with attributes.

Embedding Icons and Components

The `JTextPane` class provides two methods for inserting icons and components: `insertComponent(Component)` and `insertIcon(Icon)`. The application shown in Figure 22-15 uses the methods to insert a color chooser and an image icon into a text pane, as can be seen from the top picture. The bottom picture in Figure 22-15 shows the application after the color chooser has been manipulated to emphasize that components placed in a text pane are viable. The image icon displays an animated GIF of a bouncing ball, as the two pictures in Figure 22-15 illustrate. See "Animated Image Icons" on page 233 for more information concerning image icons and multiframe images.

The applet shown in Figure 22-15 is listed in Example 22-10.

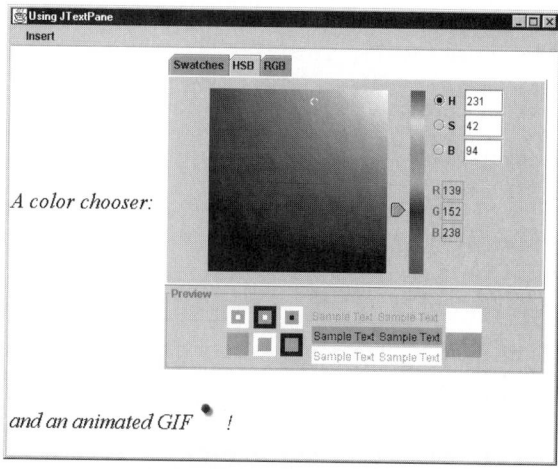

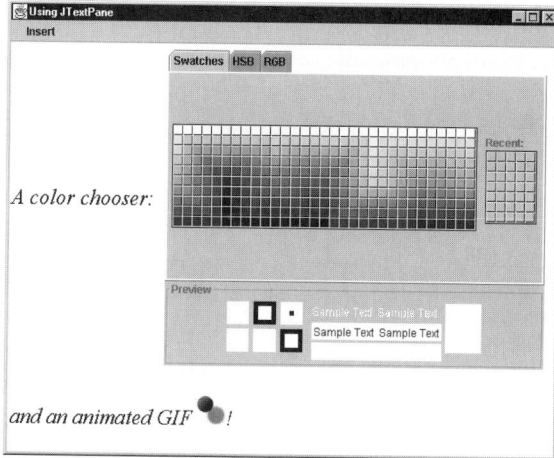

Figure 22-15 Inserting Components and Icons in a JTextPane

Example 22-10   Components and Icons in a Text Pane

```
import java.io.File;
import javax.swing.*;
import java.awt.*;
import java.awt.event.*;

public class Test extends JFrame {
    private JFileChooser chooser = new JFileChooser();
    private JTextPane textPane = new JTextPane();

    public Test() {
```

```
        Container contentPane = getContentPane();
        JMenuBar menuBar = new JMenuBar();
        JMenu insertMenu = new JMenu("Insert");
        JMenuItem imageItem = new JMenuItem("image"),
                chooserItem = new JMenuItem("color chooser");

        insertMenu.add(imageItem);
        insertMenu.add(chooserItem);

        menuBar.add(insertMenu);
        setJMenuBar(menuBar);

        textPane.setFont(new Font("Serif", Font.ITALIC, 24));

        contentPane.add(textPane, BorderLayout.CENTER);

        chooserItem.addActionListener(new ActionListener() {
            public void actionPerformed(ActionEvent e) {
                JColorChooser chooser = new JColorChooser();
                chooser.setMaximumSize(
                                chooser.getPreferredSize());
                textPane.insertComponent(chooser);
            }
        });
        imageItem.addActionListener(new ActionListener() {
            public void actionPerformed(ActionEvent e) {
                int option =
                    chooser.showDialog(Test.this,"Pick An Image");

                if(option == JFileChooser.APPROVE_OPTION) {
                    File file = chooser.getSelectedFile();

                    if(file != null) {
                        textPane.insertIcon(new ImageIcon(
                                        file.getPath()));
                    }

                }
            }
        });
    }
    public static void main(String args[]) {
        GJApp.launch(new Test(),
            "Using JTextPane",300,300,450,300);
    }
}
```

The application contains an Insert menu with menu items for inserting either an image or a color chooser. Both items have action listeners that insert the appropriate object. The chooser item's listener sets the maximum size for the color

chooser to the chooser's preferred size to limit the chooser's size. The listener subsequently adds the chooser to the text pane with the JTextPane.insertComponent method.

The image item's listener obtains a file name from a file chooser and creates an image icon that is added to the text pane with the JTextPane.insertIcon method. In the interest of simplicity, the image item listener does not check whether the file selected represents a valid image.

Marking Content with Attributes

Text panes have styled editor kits that provide a set of actions for setting well-known attributes such as bold, italic, underline, strikethrough, etc. The StyledEditorKit contains an array of default actions that are added to the actions from StyledEditorKit's superclass:

```
// From StyledEditorKit.java:

public Action[] getActions() {
    return TextAction.augmentList(
                    super.getActions(), this.defaultActions);
}
```

Text panes get their actions from their editor kit, so the actions from StyledEditorKit augmented with the actions from StyledEditorKit's superclass (DefaultEditorKit) are the actions returned from JTextPane.getActions().

The StyledEditorKit default actions are defined like this:

```
// From StyledEditorKit.java

private static final Action[] defaultActions = {
    new FontFamilyAction("font-family-SansSerif", "SansSerif"),
    new FontFamilyAction("font-family-Monospaced", "Monospaced"),
    new FontFamilyAction("font-family-Serif", "Serif"),
    new FontSizeAction("font-size-8", 8),
    new FontSizeAction("font-size-10", 10),
    new FontSizeAction("font-size-12", 12),
    new FontSizeAction("font-size-14", 14),
    new FontSizeAction("font-size-16", 16),
    new FontSizeAction("font-size-18", 18),
    new FontSizeAction("font-size-24", 24),
```

```
      new FontSizeAction("font-size-36", 36),
      new FontSizeAction("font-size-48", 48),
      new AlignmentAction("left-justify",
                          StyleConstants.ALIGN_LEFT),
      new AlignmentAction("center-justify",
                          StyleConstants.ALIGN_CENTER),
      new AlignmentAction("right-justify",
                          StyleConstants.ALIGN_RIGHT),
      new BoldAction(),
      new ItalicAction(),
      new UnderlineAction()
   };
```

All of the default `StyledEditorKit` actions operate on the current selection, so for example, selecting text and then firing the styled editor kit's bold action will set the bold attribute for the selected text, which will subsequently be repainted. If there is no selection when an action is fired, the action is applied to the text pane's input attributes, meaning that the attributes will be applied to text that is subsequently inserted.

The upshot of all this is that the array of actions returned from `JTextPane.getActions()` contains the actions from the array listed above (in addition to a considerable number of actions from the `DefaultEditorKit` class). The application shown in Figure 22-16 takes advantage of this feature to allow content contained within the text pane to be marked with attributes.

The application shown in Figure 22-16 provides a menu bar and a toolbar for cutting, copying, and pasting and for setting italic, bold, and underlining. The menu bar also allows the font's family and size to be set. The top picture in Figure 22-16 shows the menu structure, and the bottom picture shows the text pane after some of the text has been marked with attributes.

The application creates an instance of `JTextPane` and an array of strings representing cut, copy, and paste actions in addition to the name displayed in the menu and a GIF file name for the toolbar buttons.

```
public class Test extends JFrame {
    private JTextPane textPane = new JTextPane();
    ...
    private String[] cutCopyPasteActionNames = new String[] {
        DefaultEditorKit.cutAction, "Cut", "cut.gif",
        DefaultEditorKit.copyAction, "Copy", "copy.gif",
        DefaultEditorKit.pasteAction, "Paste", "paste.gif",
    };
    ...
```

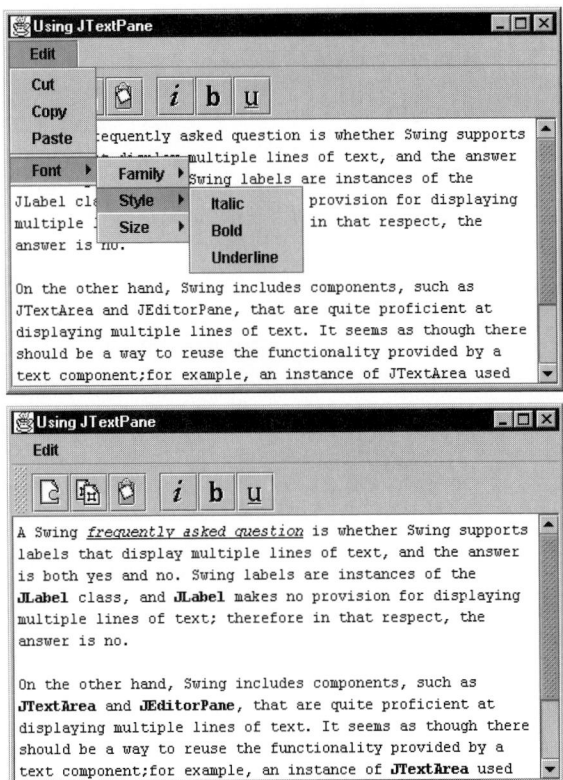

Figure 22-16 Setting Attributes in a Text Pane

Three string arrays are created for the rest of the actions in the application's menu bar and toolbar. The action names, such as `"font-family-SansSerif"`, are obtained from the `StyledEditorKit` default action array that was listed previously. It is interesting to note that `DefaultEditorKit` provides `public` constants for the names of its actions, but that is not the case for `StyledEditorKit`.

```
...
private String[] familyActionNames = new String[] {
    "font-family-SansSerif", "SanSerif",
    "font-family-Monospaced", "Monospaced",
    "font-family-Serif", "Serif",
};
private String[] styleActionNames = new String[] {
    "font-italic", "Italic", "italic.gif",
```

```
        "font-bold", "Bold", "bold.gif",
        "font-underline", "Underline", "underline.gif",
    };
    private String[] sizeActionNames = new String[] {
        "font-size-8",  "8",   "font-size-10", "10",
        "font-size-12", "12",  "font-size-14", "14",
        "font-size-16", "16",  "font-size-18", "18",
        "font-size-24", "24",  "font-size-36", "36",
        "font-size-48", "48",
    };
    ...
```

The application provides a `populate` method that populates the application's menu bar and toolbar from the string arrays discussed above. The application stores the text pane's actions and their names in a hash table and provides a `getAction` method that, given a name, returns an action. See "Actions and Editor Kits" on page 1407 for more information on accessing a text component's actions by name.

For each string array, the action associated with the name is obtained with the application's `getAction` method, and the action is added to the menu bar, toolbar, or both.

```
    ...
    private void populate() {
        JMenu editMenu = new JMenu("Edit"),
              fontMenu = new JMenu("Font"),
              styleMenu = new JMenu("Style"),
              sizeMenu = new JMenu("Size"),
              familyMenu = new JMenu("Family");

        for(int i=0; i < familyActionNames.length; ++i) {
            Action action = getAction(familyActionNames[i]);
            if(action != null) {
                JMenuItem item = familyMenu.add(action);
                item.setText(familyActionNames[++i]);
            }
        }
        for(int i=0; i < sizeActionNames.length; ++i) {
            Action action = getAction(sizeActionNames[i]);
            if(action != null) {
                JMenuItem item = sizeMenu.add(action);
                item.setText(sizeActionNames[++i]);
            }
        }
        for(int i=0; i < cutCopyPasteActionNames.length; ++i) {
            Action action = getAction(cutCopyPasteActionNames[i]);
```

```
        if(action != null) {
            JButton button = toolbar.add(action);
            JMenuItem item = editMenu.add(action);

            item.setText(cutCopyPasteActionNames[++i]);

            button.setText(null);
            button.setIcon(new ImageIcon(
                        cutCopyPasteActionNames[++i]));
        }
    }

    editMenu.addSeparator();
    toolbar.addSeparator();

    for(int i=0; i < styleActionNames.length; ++i) {
        Action action = getAction(styleActionNames[i]);

        if(action != null) {
            JButton button = toolbar.add(action);
            JMenuItem item = styleMenu.add(action);

            item.setText(styleActionNames[++i]);

            button.setText(null);
            button.setIcon(
                    new ImageIcon(styleActionNames[++i]));
        }
    }
    ...
}
...
}
```

The application shown in Figure 22-16 is listed in its entirety in Example 22-11.

Example 22-11 Setting Character Attributes in a Text Pane

```
import java.io.File;
import javax.swing.*;
import javax.swing.text.*;
import java.awt.*;
import java.awt.event.*;
import java.util.*;
import java.io.FileReader;

public class Test extends JFrame {
    private JTextPane textPane = new JTextPane();

    private JMenuBar menubar = new JMenuBar();
```

```java
    private JToolBar toolbar = new JToolBar();

    private Hashtable actionTable = new Hashtable();

    private String[] cutCopyPasteActionNames = new String[] {
        DefaultEditorKit.cutAction, "Cut", "cut.gif",
        DefaultEditorKit.copyAction, "Copy", "copy.gif",
        DefaultEditorKit.pasteAction, "Paste", "paste.gif",
    };

    private String[] familyActionNames = new String[] {
        "font-family-SansSerif", "SansSerif",
        "font-family-Monospaced", "Monospaced",
        "font-family-Serif", "Serif",
    };
    private String[] styleActionNames = new String[] {
        "font-italic", "Italic", "italic.gif",
        "font-bold", "Bold", "bold.gif",
        "font-underline", "Underline", "underline.gif",
    };
    private String[] sizeActionNames = new String[] {
        "font-size-8",  "8",  "font-size-10", "10",
        "font-size-12", "12", "font-size-14", "14",
        "font-size-16", "16", "font-size-18", "18",
        "font-size-24", "24", "font-size-36", "36",
        "font-size-48", "48",
    };

    public Test() {
        Container contentPane = getContentPane();
        JScrollPane scrollPane = new JScrollPane(textPane);

        loadActionTable();
        populate();
        readFile();
        setJMenuBar(menubar);

        contentPane.add(toolbar, BorderLayout.NORTH);
        contentPane.add(new JScrollPane(textPane),
                    BorderLayout.CENTER);
    }
    private void readFile() {
        try {
            textPane.getEditorKit().read(
                new FileReader("text"), textPane.getDocument(), 0);
        }
        catch(Exception ex) { ex.printStackTrace(); }
    }
    private void populate() {
        JMenu editMenu = new JMenu("Edit"),
               fontMenu = new JMenu("Font"),
               styleMenu = new JMenu("Style"),
```

```
          sizeMenu = new JMenu("Size"),
          familyMenu = new JMenu("Family");

   for(int i=0; i < familyActionNames.length; ++i) {
      Action action = getAction(familyActionNames[i]);
      if(action != null) {
         JMenuItem item = familyMenu.add(action);
         item.setText(familyActionNames[++i]);
      }
   }
   for(int i=0; i < sizeActionNames.length; ++i) {
      Action action = getAction(sizeActionNames[i]);
      if(action != null) {
         JMenuItem item = sizeMenu.add(action);
         item.setText(sizeActionNames[++i]);
      }
   }
   for(int i=0; i < cutCopyPasteActionNames.length; ++i) {
      Action action = getAction(cutCopyPasteActionNames[i]);

      if(action != null) {
         JButton button = toolbar.add(action);
         JMenuItem item = editMenu.add(action);

         item.setText(cutCopyPasteActionNames[++i]);

         button.setText(null);
         button.setIcon(new ImageIcon(
                     cutCopyPasteActionNames[++i]));
      }
   }

   editMenu.addSeparator();
   toolbar.addSeparator();

   for(int i=0; i < styleActionNames.length; ++i) {
      Action action = getAction(styleActionNames[i]);

      if(action != null) {
         JButton button = toolbar.add(action);
         JMenuItem item = styleMenu.add(action);

         item.setText(styleActionNames[++i]);

         button.setText(null);
         button.setIcon(
                  new ImageIcon(styleActionNames[++i]));
      }
   }
   fontMenu.add(familyMenu);
   fontMenu.add(styleMenu);
   fontMenu.add(sizeMenu);
```

```
        editMenu.add(fontMenu);
        menubar.add(editMenu);
    }
    private void loadActionTable() {
        Action[] actions = textPane.getActions();

        for(int i=0; i < actions.length; ++i) {
            actionTable.put(actions[i].getValue(Action.NAME),
                        actions[i]);
        }
    }
    private Action getAction(String name) {
        return (Action)actionTable.get(name);
    }
    public static void main(String args[]) {
        GJApp.launch(new Test(),
            "Using JTextPane",300,300,450,300);
    }
}
```

The JTextPane component is summarized in Component Summary 22-5.

Component Summary 22-5   JTextPane

Model(s)	javax.swing.text.StyledDocument
UI Delegate(s)	javax.swing.plaf.basic.BasicTextPaneUI
Renderer(s)	——
Editor(s)	——
Events Fired	——
Replacement For	——

Class Diagrams

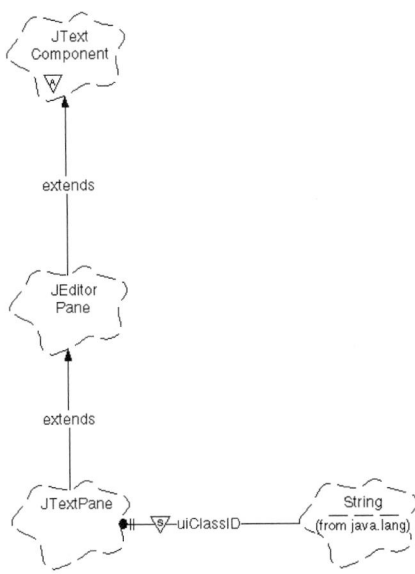

Figure 22-17 JTextPane Class Diagram

JTextPane is an extension of JEditorPane that contains no member variables except for a UI delegate class ID. The dearth of member variables in JTextPane is attributable to JTextPane's reliance upon its editor kit and document to provide functionality. For example, JTextPane delegates setting attributes to its document, which by default is an instance of DefaultStyledDocument.

JTextPane Properties

The properties maintained by the JTextPane class are listed in Table 22-7.

Table 22-7 JTextPane Properties

Property Name	Data Type	Property Type[1]	Access[2]	Default[3]
characterAttributes	AttributeSet	S	SG	—
inputAttributes	AttributeSet	S	G	—
logicalStyle	Style	I	SG	—
paragaphAttributes	AttributeSet	S	SG	—
style	Style	I	G	—

1. B = bound (fires PropertyChangeEvent) / C = constrained/ I = indexed /
   S = simple / Ch = fires ChangeEvent
2. C = settable at construction time / G = getter method / S = setter method
3. L&F = look-and-feel dependent

characterAttributes — An attribute set for the current selection. If no text is selected when the property is set, the attribute set is applied to text that is subsequently inserted.

inputAttributes — An attribute set that will be applied to the next insertion.

logicalStyle — A style that is used for a paragraph when character or paragraph attributes have not been explicitly specified.

paragraphAttributes — Attributes applied to the paragraph at the cursor location when the property is set.

style — A named style that was previously added to the text pane.

JTextPane Class Summaries

The JTextPane class is summarized in Class Summary 22-6.

Class Summary 22-6   JTextPane

Extends: JEditorPane

Constructors

---

public JTextPane()
public JTextPane(StyledDocument)

Text panes can be created with the no-argument constructor, which sets the text pane's editor kit to an instance of StyledEditorKit. By default, styled editor kits create documents that are instances of DefaultStyledDocument and also create a handful of different types of views.

Methods

Document / Editor Kit / Replacing Selection

---

public void setDocument(Document)
public final void setEditorKit(EditorKit)

public void replaceSelection(String)

Text panes must have an instance of StyledDocument as their document, so JTextPane overrides setDocument() to throw an illegal argument exception if the specified document is not an instance of StyledDocument. Text panes must also have an instance of StyledEditorKit as their editor kit, and therefore setEditorKit() is also overridden to throw an illegal argument exception if the editor kit specified is not an instance of StyledEditorKit.

The replaceSelection method replaces the current selection with the specified string if the text pane is editable. If no text is selected when the replaceSelection method is called, the text is inserted at the current caret location.

Styled Document / Styled Editor Kit

---

protected EditorKit <u>createDefaultEditorKit</u>()
protected final StyledEditorKit <u>getStyledEditorKit</u>()

public StyledDocument <u>getStyledDocument</u>()
public void <u>setStyledDocument</u>(StyledDocument)

The first two methods listed above are protected methods that create the JTextPane's default editor kit (an instance of StyledEditorKit) and provide access to the styled editor kit.

The getStyledDocument and setStyledDocument methods invoke super.getDocument() and super.setDocument(), respectively. The getStyledDocument method allows a text pane's document to be accessed as a StyledDocument without casting the document returned from getDocument().

Styles

---

public Style <u>addStyle</u>(String styleName, Style parent)
public Style <u>getStyle</u>(String styleName)
public void <u>removeStyle</u>(String styleName)

public Style <u>getLogicalStyle</u>()
public void <u>setLogicalStyle</u>(Style)

A text pane's document maintains a set of styles. The first three methods listed above provide access to those styles. The addStyle method creates and returns a named style that is added to the specified parent style.

The setLogicalStyle method sets the logical style—to be used when character or paragraph attributes have not been explicitly set—for the paragraph at the caret location when the method is called. The getLogicalStyle method returns the logical style for the paragraph at the current caret location.

Icons and Components

---

public void insertComponent(Component)
public void insertIcon(Icon)

The methods listed above insert a component and icon, respectively, as a replacement for the current selection. If there is no selection when the methods are called, the insertion takes place at the current caret location.

Attributes

---

public AttributeSet getCharacterAttributes()
public void setCharacterAttributes(AttributeSet, boolean replace)

public AttributeSet getParagraphAttributes()
public void setParagraphAttributes(AttributeSet, boolean replace)

public MutableAttributeSet getInputAttributes()

The setCharacterAttributes sets character attributes for the currently selected content. If there is no selection when the method is called, the attributes will be applied to content that it is subsequently inserted into the text pane. The getCharacterAttributes method returns the character attributes at the current caret location.

The setParagraphAttributes sets paragraph attributes for the currently selected content. If there is no selection when the method is called, the attributes will be applied to the paragraph at the current caret location. The getParagraphAttributes method returns the paragraph attributes for the paragraph at the current caret location.

The get InputAttributes method returns the attribute set that will be applied to content inserted at the current caret location.

Miscellaneous Methods

---

public boolean getScrollableTracksViewportWidth()
public String getUIClassID()
protected String paramString()

The getScrollableTracksViewportWidth method returns true, which means that the width of a text pane is always the same as the width of the viewport in which the text pane resides. The paramString method returns a string representation of a text pane, and getUIClassID returns a string— "TextPane"—identifying the UI delegate for instances of JTextPane.

AWT Compatibility

The AWT does not have a component analogous to JTextPane.

Parting Shots

The previous chapter—see "Text Fundamentals" on page 1397—discussed functionality that is fundamental to all Swing text components, including actions, keymaps, carets, highlighters, etc. This chapter has taken a close look at each of the Swing text components.

The material covered up to this point is sufficient to enable use of Swing text components but not to enable extension of the functionality provided to implement custom text components. The next chapter discusses the more advanced aspects of the Swing text package including views, styles, and style contexts.

CHAPTER
23

Customizing Text Components

Swing text is built upon a complex infrastructure of classes and interfaces from the `javax.swing.text` package. Everyday use of the Swing text components—discussed in the preceding two chapters—does not require an in-depth understanding of the Swing text package; however, customizing text components requires a basic grasp of the main classes and interfaces from `javax.swing.text` package. This chapter offers examples of common customization tasks, such as coloring text, setting character and paragraph attributes, and implementing custom views.

Overview

Like all Swing components, text components comprise a model (an implementation of the `Document` interface) and a UI delegate (an extension of the `javax.swing.plaf.basic.BasicTextUI` class). Text components also use an editor kit (an extension of the `EditorKit` class) and a view (an extension of the `View` class). Figure 23-1 shows a class diagram that illustrates the static relationships between a Swing text field and the field's model, UI delegate, editor kit and view.[1] Other Swing text components have similar class diagrams.

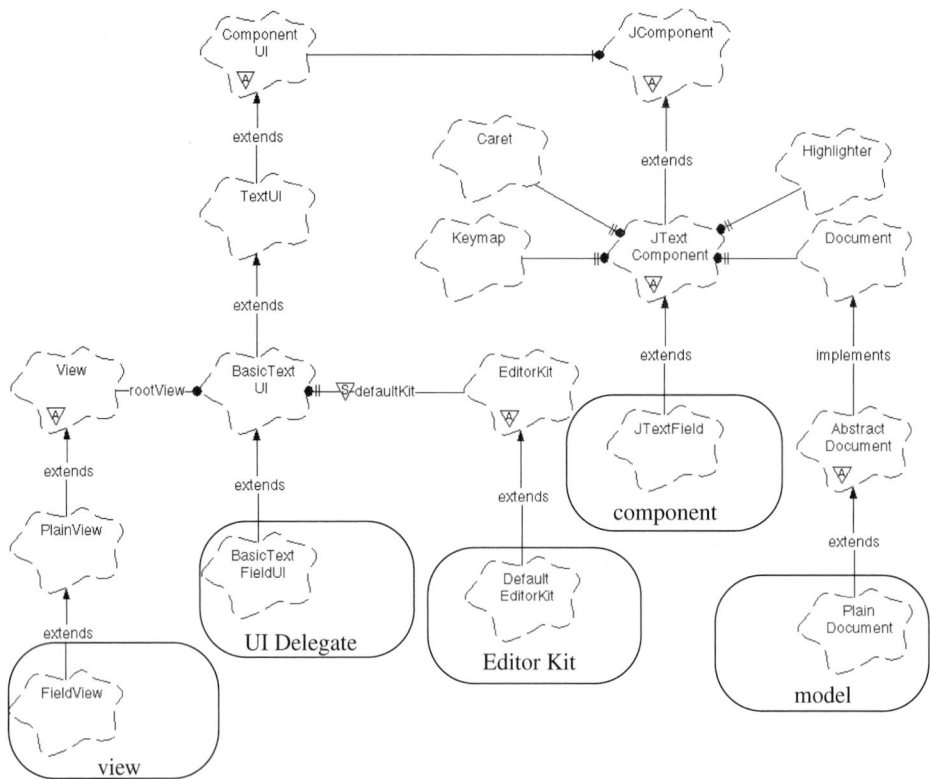

Figure 23-1 JTextField and Support Classes

All Swing text components extend the JTextComponent class from the javax.swing.text package. Instances of JTextComponent maintain a keymap, caret, highlighter, and document, as discussed in "Text Fundamentals" on page 1397.

The JTextComponent class, like all Swing lightweight components, extends JComponent, which in turn maintains a reference to the component's UI delegate (an extension of the javax.swing.plaf.ComponentUI class). All Swing text components have a UI delegate that extends the javax.swing.plaf.basic.BasicTextUI class. BasicTextUI maintains the editor kit and view for all text components.

1. Views are discussed in "Views" on page 1542; for now, it is enough to know that all text components have one or more views.

The JTextField class uses an editor kit that is an instance of the DefaultEditorKit class and a view that is an instance of the FieldView class. Table 23-1 lists the editor kit, document, and view used by each of the Swing text components.

Table 23-1 Default Editor Kits, Documents, and Views

Name	Editor Kit	Document	View
JTextArea	DefaultEditorKit	PlainDocument	PlainView / WrappedPlainView
JTextField	DefaultEditorKit	PlainDocument	FieldView
JPasswordField	DefaultEditorKit	PlainDocument	PasswordView
JEditorPane	JEditorPane.PlainEditorKit	PlainDocument	WrappedPlainView
JTextPane	StyledEditorKit	DefaultStyledDocument	LabelView

All text components have an editor kit, and all components use their editor kit for storing actions, creating default documents, and reading and writing documents. Text editors—JEditorPane and JTextPane—also use their editor kits to create views.

If documents are not explicitly specified, they are created when the component's UI delegate is installed. BasicTextUI overrides installUI() and creates the default document by delegating to the component's editor kit. Notice that it is the editor kit that is ultimately responsible for creating default documents.

```
// From javax.swing.plaf.basic.BasicTextUI:

public void installUI(JComponent c) {
    if (c instanceof JTextComponent) {
        editor = (JTextComponent) c;
        ...
        Document doc = editor.getDocument();

        if (doc == null) {
            editor.setDocument(
                getEditorKit(editor).createDefaultDocument());
        } else {
            ...
        }
    }
    ...
}
```

A text component's views are created by a view factory. View factories are defined by the ViewFactory interface, which defines a single method: View create(Element). Given an element,[2] a view factory creates a view.

`BasicTextUI` implements the `ViewFactory` interface and returns a `null` view:

```
// From javax.swing.plaf.basic.BasicTextUI:

public View create(Element element) {
    return null;
}
```

Some extensions of `BasicTextUI` override the `create` method; for example, `BasicTextFieldUI` and `BasicTextArea` implement the `create` method as listed below.

```
// From javax.swing.plaf.basic.BasicTextFieldUI:

public View create(Element element) {
    return new FieldView;
}

// From javax.swing.plaf.basic.BasicTextAreaUI:

public View create(Element elem) {
    JTextComponent c = getComponent();

    if (c instanceof JTextArea) {
        JTextArea area = (JTextArea) c;
        View v;

        if (area.getLineWrap()) {
            v =
            new WrappedPlainView(elem, area.getWrapStyleWord());
        } else {
            v = new PlainView(elem);
        }
        return v;
    }
    return null;
}
```

`BasicTextFieldUI.create()` always returns an instance of `FieldView` for the default view for a text field. `BasicTextAreaUI.create()` returns either a plain view or a wrapped plain view, depending upon whether the text area in question has line-wrap enabled.

`BasicTextPaneUI` and `BasicEditorPaneUI` do not override the `create` method. Views for editor panes and text panes are created by the component's editor kit.

2. See "Elements" on page 1556 for more information concerning elements.

Attribute Sets and Style Constants

Every text component has a document, and every document maintains a hierarchy of elements; see "Elements" on page 1556 for more information concerning documents and elements. Elements maintain start and end positions within a document and a set of attributes that are applied to the content between the start and end positions.

Attribute sets are defined by the `AttributeSet` interface. A class diagram for the `AttributeSet` interface is shown in Figure 23-2.

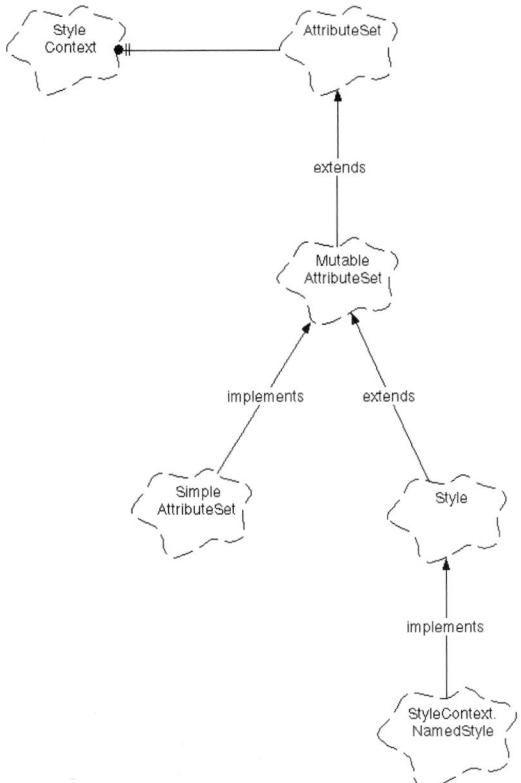

Figure 23-2 AttributeSet Class Diagram

The `AttributeSet` interface is extended by the `MutableAttributeSet` interface, which defines methods for modifying attributes contained in the set. The `MutableAttributeSet` is extended by the `Style` interface—styles are named mutable attribute sets that notify change listeners when their attributes are modified. The `MutableAttributeSet` interface is also implemented by the `SimpleAttribute` class, and the `Style` interface is implemented by the `StyleContext.NamedStyle` class.

The application shown in Figure 23-3 illustrates the use of attribute sets. The application contains a text pane, and attributes are set for the "component" and "container" strings contained in the text pane's model.

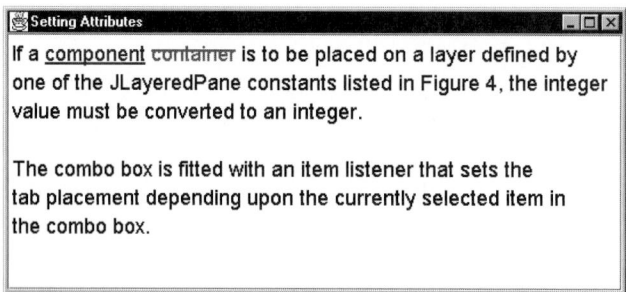

Figure 23-3 Setting Attributes

The application shown in Figure 23-3 is listed in Example 23-1.

Example 23-1 Using Attribute Sets

```java
import java.io.File;
import javax.swing.*;
import javax.swing.text.*;
import java.awt.*;
import java.awt.event.*;
import java.util.*;
import java.io.FileReader;

public class Test extends JFrame {
    private JTextPane textPane = new JTextPane();
    private StyledDocument document =
                    (StyledDocument)textPane.getDocument();

    public Test() {
        Container contentPane = getContentPane();
        readFile("text.txt");
        setAttributes();
```

```
        textPane.setFont(new Font("Dialog", Font.PLAIN, 18));
        contentPane.add(new JScrollPane(textPane),
                    BorderLayout.CENTER);
    }
    private void setAttributes() {
        SimpleAttributeSet attributes = new SimpleAttributeSet();

        StyleConstants.setForeground(attributes, Color.blue);
        StyleConstants.setUnderline(attributes, true);

        document.setCharacterAttributes(5,9,attributes,false);

        StyleConstants.setForeground(attributes, Color.red);
        StyleConstants.setStrikeThrough(attributes, true);

        document.setCharacterAttributes(15,9,attributes,false);
    }
    private void readFile(String filename) {
        EditorKit kit = textPane.getEditorKit();
        try {
            kit.read(new FileReader(filename), document, 0);
        }
        catch(Exception ex) {
            ex.printStackTrace();
        }
    }
    public static void main(String args[]) {
        GJApp.launch(new Test(),
                    "Setting Attributes",300,300,450,300);
    }
}
```

The document for text panes is an instance of `StyledDocument`, which provides a `setCharacterAttributes` method that applies a set of attributes to a specified range within the document. The foreground color attribute for "component" is set to blue and the underlined attribute set to `true`. The foreground color for "container" is set to red, and the strikethrough attribute is set to `true`.

The attributes are set with the help of the `StyleConstants` class, which provides more than 40 `static` methods for setting everything from bold and italic attributes to underlining and subscripting/superscripting for a specified attribute set.

Attribute sets, like keymaps, resolve hierarchically; that is, if an attribute is not found in an attribute set, the ancestors of the attribute set are searched for the attribute. The second argument to

`StyledDocument.setCharacterAttributes()` determines whether the specified attribute set should replace the document's attribute set, or whether it should be the added to the current attribute set. The example listed in Example 23-1 specifies `false` for the argument.

Style Constants

Attributes in an attribute set are specified with an attribute name and a value. The AttributeSet interface defines an addAttribute method: public void addAttribute(Object name, Object value), for adding an attribute to an attribute set.

The StyleConstants class provides static setter and getter methods for well-known attributes, such as: bold, italic, underline, strikeThrough, etc. Using the StyleConstants for setting attributes ensures that consistent names are used for well-known attributes.

Custom Actions

"Actions" on page 1401 introduced actions for text components and illustrated using default actions defined by editor kits. Custom actions are often implemented for custom text components, as illustrated in the application shown in Figure 23-4.

The application contains a text pane and provides a menu for modifying the background color of either the text pane's selected characters or the paragraph in which the caret resides. The top pictures in Figure 23-4 illustrate setting paragraph attributes, and the bottom pictures in Figure 23-4 illustrate setting character attributes.

The application implements a custom action as an inner class— `ForegroundFromChooserAction`—that sets foreground color with a color selected from a color chooser. See "JColorChooser" on page 978 for more information concerning color choosers. The `ForegroundFromChooserAction` class extends `StyledEditorKit.StyledAction` and is listed below.

The action maintains a mode, either `CharacterMode` or `ParagraphMode`, that is specified when the action is created. The mode determines whether the selected color is applied to the selection or the paragraph in which the caret resides.

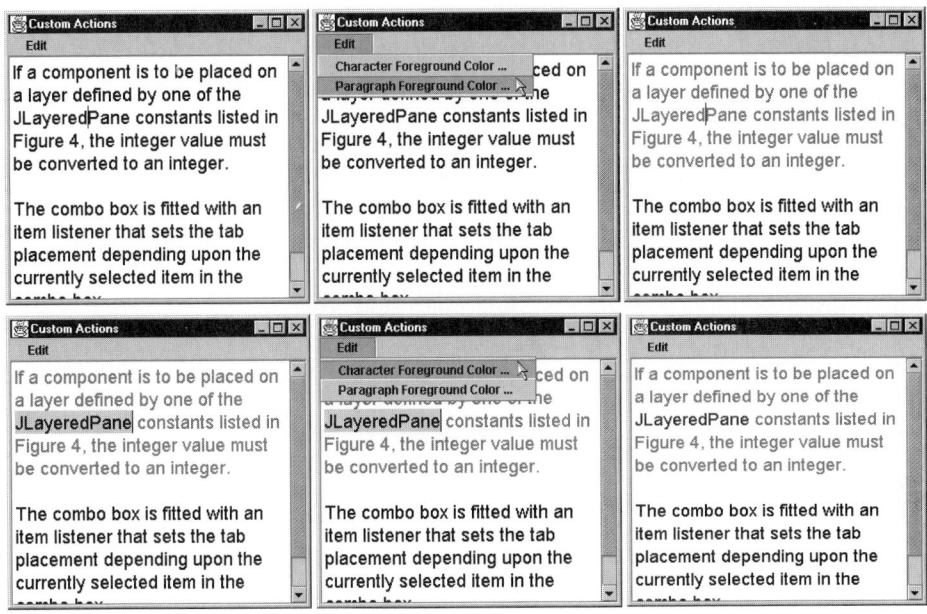

Figure 23-4 Custom Actions for Setting Character and Paragraph Attributes

```
   ...
   public class Test extends JFrame {
       ...
       private int CharacterMode = 0, ParagraphMode = 1;
       ...
       class ForegroundFromChooserAction
                   extends StyledEditorKit.StyledTextAction {

       protected Color fg;
       protected JColorChooser chooser = new JColorChooser();
       protected int mode;

       public ForegroundFromChooserAction(String nm, int mode) {
           super(nm);
           this.mode = mode;
       }
       ...
```

The `actionPerformed` method obtains a reference to the text pane by invoking the `getEditor` method inherited from `StyledEditorKit.StyledTextAction`. The character attributes associated with the text pane are obtained with `JTextPane.getCharacterAttributes()`, which returns the attributes associated with the current selection.[3] The foreground color for the text pane's character attributes is obtained by a call to the `StyleConstants.getForeground` method, and the foreground color is subsequently used to initialize the color chooser.

If a color was selected from the color chooser, an instance of `SimpleAttributeSet` is instantiated, and the foreground attribute is set with the `StyleConstants.setForeground` method. The simple attribute set is subsequently passed to either `setCharacterAttributes` or `setParagraphAttributes` to set the foreground color. If a color was not selected from the color chooser, the default toolkit is employed to issue a beep.

```
    . . .
public void actionPerformed(ActionEvent e) {
    JEditorPane editor = getEditor(e);

    if (editor != null) {
        AttributeSet attributes =
                    textPane.getCharacterAttributes();
        Color c =
                StyleConstants.getForeground(attributes);

        Color fg = chooser.showDialog(Test.this,
                        "Choose Color for Text",
                        c == null ? Color.black : c);

        if (fg != null) {
            MutableAttributeSet attr =
                        new SimpleAttributeSet();
            StyleConstants.setForeground(attr, fg);

            if(mode == CharacterMode)
               setCharacterAttributes(editor, attr, false);
            else
               setParagraphAttributes(editor, attr, false);
        }
        else {
            Toolkit.getDefaultToolkit().beep();
        }
    }
}
    . . .
}
```

The application shown in Figure 23-4 is listed in its entirety in Example 23-2.

---

3.   If there is no selection, the input attributes are returned.

Example 23-2 Implementing Custom Actions

```java
import java.io.File;
import javax.swing.*;
import javax.swing.text.*;
import java.awt.*;
import java.awt.event.*;
import java.util.*;
import java.io.FileReader;

public class Test extends JFrame {
    private JTextPane textPane = new JTextPane();
    private StyledDocument document =
                    (StyledDocument)textPane.getDocument();
    private StyledEditorKit kit =
                    (StyledEditorKit)textPane.getEditorKit();
    private JColorChooser chooser = new JColorChooser();
    private int CharacterMode = 0, ParagraphMode = 1;

    public Test() {
        Container contentPane = getContentPane();
        readFile("text.txt");

        textPane.setFont(new Font("Dialog", Font.PLAIN, 18));

        contentPane.add(new JScrollPane(textPane),
                    BorderLayout.CENTER);

        setJMenuBar(createMenuBar());
    }
    private JMenuBar createMenuBar() {
        JMenuBar menuBar = new JMenuBar();
        JMenu editMenu = new JMenu("Edit");

        editMenu.add(new ForegroundFromChooserAction(
                    "Character Foreground Color ... ",
                    CharacterMode));

        editMenu.add(new ForegroundFromChooserAction(
                    "Paragraph Foreground Color ... ",
                    ParagraphMode));

        menuBar.add(editMenu);
        return menuBar;
    }
    private void readFile(String filename) {
        try {
            kit.read(new FileReader(filename), document, 0);
        }
        catch(Exception ex) {
            ex.printStackTrace();
        }
    }
    public static void main(String args[]) {
        GJApp.launch(new Test(),
                    "Custom Actions",300,300,650,275);
```

```
        }
        class ForegroundFromChooserAction
                        extends StyledEditorKit.StyledTextAction {

            protected Color fg;
            protected JColorChooser chooser = new JColorChooser();
            protected int mode;

            public ForegroundFromChooserAction(String nm, int mode) {
                super(nm);
                this.mode = mode;
            }
            public void actionPerformed(ActionEvent e) {
                JEditorPane editor = getEditor(e);

                if (editor != null) {
                    AttributeSet attributes =
                            textPane.getCharacterAttributes();
                    Color c =
                        StyleConstants.getForeground(attributes);

                    Color fg = chooser.showDialog(Test.this,
                            "Choose Color for Text",
                            c == null ? Color.black : c);

                    if (fg != null) {
                        MutableAttributeSet attr =
                                new SimpleAttributeSet();
                        StyleConstants.setForeground(attr, fg);

                        if(mode == CharacterMode)
                            setCharacterAttributes(editor, attr, false);
                        else
                            setParagraphAttributes(editor, attr, false);

                        textPane.setCaretPosition(
                                textPane.getSelectionStart());
                    } else {
                        Toolkit.getDefaultToolkit().beep();
                    }
                }
            }
        }
    }
}
```

Views

Swing components are implemented with a Model-View-Controller architecture
that separates a component's visual representation, referred to as a UI delegate,
from its data (the model). Although it is possible to implement custom UI
delegates—see "Custom UI Delegates" on page 110 for an example of a custom UI

delegate—in practice, custom UI delegates are rarely implemented because the visual representation of a component is dictated by the current look and feel.

On the other hand, the manner in which a text component's content is displayed is unrelated to the component's look and feel. Furthermore, it is often desirable to modify the visual representation of a text's content without changing the component's look and feel; for example, a programmer's editor may have an option for coloring language keywords.

Because it is often necessary to modify a text component's visual representation, text components have a view in addition to a UI delegate. Text views allow the visual representation of a text component's content to be customized without replacing the component's UI delegate.

The Swing text package provides a fair number of views, as illustrated in Figure 23-5.

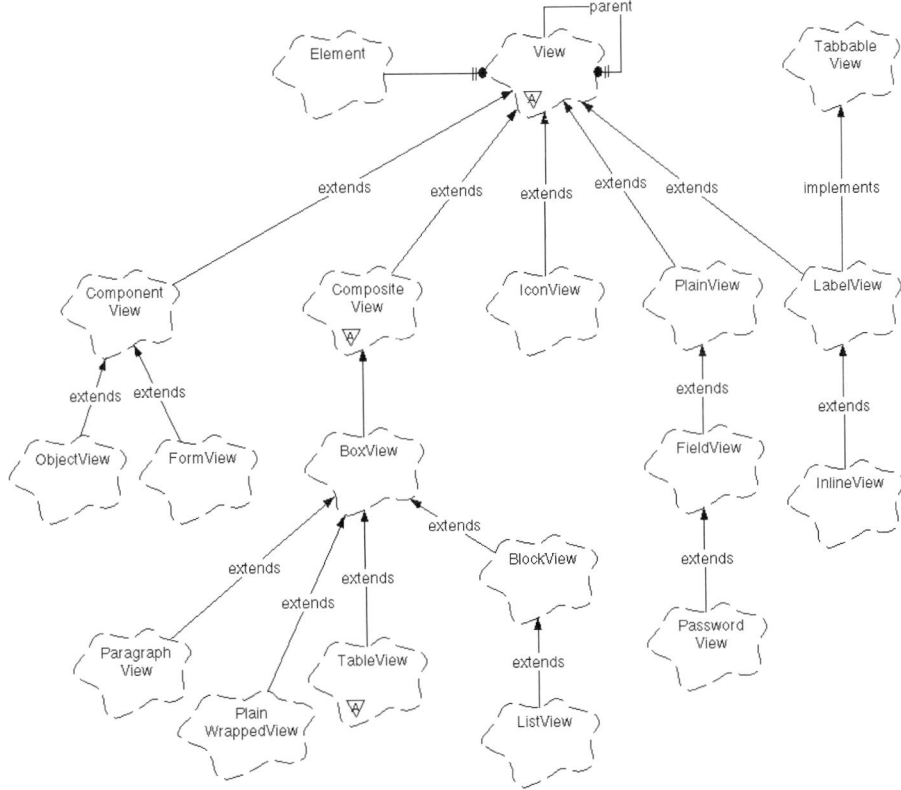

Figure 23-5 View Hierarchy Class Diagram

Views are defined by the abstract View class, which maintains a reference to an element. See Table 23-1 on page 1533 for a list of views used by the standard Swing text components.

Implementing Custom Views

As discussed in "Overview" on page 1531, views for text fields and text areas are created by the component's UI delegate. As a result, it is not possible to specify a custom view for a text field or text area without implementing a custom UI delegate.

Editor pane and text pane views, on the other hand, are created by the component's editor kit, and therefore views for editor panes and text panes can be customized—by fitting the editor with a custom editor kit—without modifying the component's UI delegate.

The application shown in Figure 23-6 contains an editor pane that is fitted with a custom view by way of a custom editor kit. The view provides graphical representations of positions contained within the editor pane's document. The application also provides a button for inserting a position at the caret location.

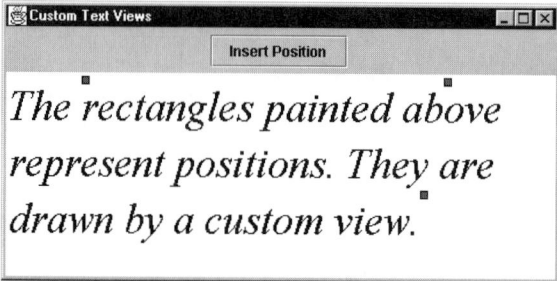

Figure 23-6 A Custom View That Paints Positions

The application creates an instance of JEditorPane and sets the editor pane's editor kit to an instance of CustomEditorKit. A custom editor kit is specified for the editor pane because views for editor panes and text panes are created by the component's editor kit.

```
public class Test extends JFrame {
    JEditorPane editorPane = new JEditorPane();
    Vector positions = new Vector();
    Position.Bias bias = Position.Bias.Forward;

    ...

    public Test() {
        JPanel panel = new JPanel();
        JButton button = new JButton("Insert Position");
        Container contentPane = getContentPane();

        panel.add(button);

        editorPane.setEditorKit(new CustomEditorKit());
        editorPane.setFont(new Font("Serif", Font.ITALIC, 36));
        ...
```

The `CustomEditorKit` class is an extension of `DefaultEditorKit` and
implements the `ViewFactory` interface. The editor kit's `getViewFactory`
method returns a reference to that editor kit itself, and the editor kit's `create`
method returns an instance of `CustomView`.

```
class CustomEditorKit extends DefaultEditorKit
                    implements ViewFactory {
    public ViewFactory getViewFactory() {
        return this;
    }
    public View create(Element elem) {
        return new CustomView(elem);
    }
};
```

The `CustomView` class extends `WrappedPlainView` and overrides the `paint`
method, which invokes `super.paint()` to draw the contents of the editor pane.
The `CustomView.paint` method then paints each of the positions that were
created by activating the application's button.

```
class CustomView extends WrappedPlainView {
    public CustomView(Element elem) {
        super(elem);
    }
    public void paint(Graphics g, Shape a) {
        super.paint(g,a);

        Enumeration e = positions.elements();
        Position p;

        while(e.hasMoreElements()) {
            try {
```

```
                    p = (Position)e.nextElement();
                    int offset = p.getOffset();

                    Shape shape = modelToView(offset,a,bias);
                    Rectangle r = shape.getBounds();

                    g.setColor(Color.black);
                    g.drawRect(r.x,r.y,6,6);

                    g.setColor(Color.red);
                    g.fillRect(r.x+1,r.y+1,5,5);
                }
                catch(BadLocationException ex) {
                    ex.printStackTrace();
                }
            }
        }
    };
```

The application shown in Figure 23-6 is listed in its entirety in Example 23-3.

Example 23-3 Implementing a Custom View

```
import javax.swing.*;
import javax.swing.event.*;
import javax.swing.text.*;
import java.awt.*;
import java.awt.event.*;
import java.util.*;

public class Test extends JFrame {
    JEditorPane editorPane = new JEditorPane();
    Vector positions = new Vector();
    Position.Bias bias = Position.Bias.Forward;

    class CustomView extends WrappedPlainView {
        public CustomView(Element elem) {
            super(elem);
        }
        public void paint(Graphics g, Shape a) {
            super.paint(g,a);

            Enumeration e = positions.elements();
            Position p;

            while(e.hasMoreElements()) {
                try {
                    p = (Position)e.nextElement();
                    int offset = p.getOffset();

                    Shape shape = modelToView(offset,a,bias);
                    Rectangle r = shape.getBounds();

                    g.setColor(Color.black);
```

```
                g.drawRect(r.x,r.y,6,6);

                g.setColor(Color.red);
                g.fillRect(r.x+1,r.y+1,5,5);
            }
            catch(BadLocationException ex) {
                ex.printStackTrace();
            }
        }
    }
};
class CustomEditorKit extends DefaultEditorKit
                implements ViewFactory {
    public ViewFactory getViewFactory() {
        return this;
    }
    public View create(Element elem) {
        return new CustomView(elem);
    }
};
public Test() {
    JPanel panel = new JPanel();
    JButton button = new JButton("Insert Position");
    Container contentPane = getContentPane();

    panel.add(button);

    editorPane.setEditorKit(new CustomEditorKit());
    editorPane.setFont(new Font("Serif", Font.ITALIC, 36));

    contentPane.add(panel, BorderLayout.NORTH);
    contentPane.add(editorPane, BorderLayout.CENTER);

    button.addActionListener(new ActionListener() {
        public void actionPerformed(ActionEvent e) {
            try {
                int p = editorPane.getCaretPosition();
                Document document =
                        editorPane.getDocument();

                positions.addElement(
                        document.createPosition(p));

                editorPane.repaint();
            }
            catch(BadLocationException ex) {
                ex.printStackTrace();
            }
        }
    });
}
public static void main(String args[]) {
    GJApp.launch(new Test(),
            "Custom Text Views",300,300,450,300);
}
```

Text Views

Swing lightweight components have UI delegates that provide a component's look and feel. Additionally, some Swing components such as lists, combo boxes, trees and tables, have cell renderers that are used to customize the appearance of objects that are displayed in a component's cells. Cell renderers are independent of a component's look and feel; for example, a custom cell renderer can be installed regardless of the current look and feel, and cell renderers will work with any look and feel.

Swing text components do not have cells, and therefore do not have cell renderers. However, Swing text components, like components that have cell renderers, do have content that often needs to be customized independent of the component's look and feel. To accommodate customization of a text component's content without changing the component's look and feel, components have views in addition to UI delegates.

Styles and Style Contexts

Simple attribute sets can easily be specified for ranges of content within a text component, as illustrated in "Attribute Sets and Style Constants" on page 1535. However, for more complex custom text components, it is usually preferable to use styles obtained from a style context for setting a document's attributes. This section discusses an application that uses styles to set paragraph attributes for a text pane.

Styles are simply named attribute sets that fire change events when they are modified. Styles are somewhat unique because they cannot be instantiated directly; instead, styles are created with the `StyleContext.addStyle` method.

The application shown in Figure 23-7 contains a text pane and a menu for setting paragraph attributes to either a "title" or "body" paragraph style. The application also displays the style associated with the paragraph containing the caret in the application's status area.

The upper-left picture shown in Figure 23-7 shows the application after it has been started and the caret has been placed in the first line of text. The middle- and bottom-left pictures show the effect of setting attributes for the first paragraph to the "title" style. The two right pictures in Figure 23-7 were taken after the second paragraph's style was set to "body". The top-right picture shows the application with the caret in the second paragraph, and the bottom-right picture shows the application with the caret in the third paragraph. Notice that the application's status area is updated to display the style of the selected paragraph; "title" for the second paragraph and "default" for the third.

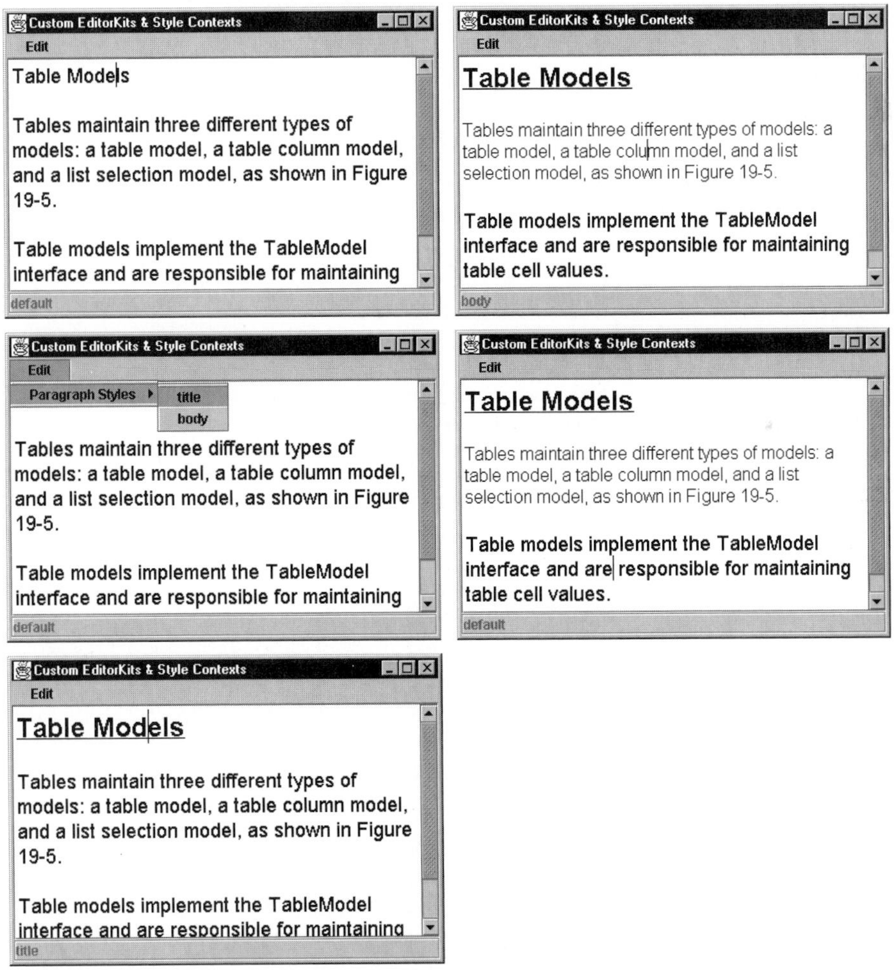

Figure 23-7 Using Styles and Style Contexts

The application creates an instance of `JTextPane` and sets the text pane's editor kit to an instance of `ChapterEditorKit`. Actions for the text pane are loaded into a hash table so that they can be retrieved by name. See "Actions and Editor Kits" on page 1407 for more information on actions and accessing them by name.

The application reads the contents of a text file named `"text.txt"`, and the text pane is wrapped in a scrollpane and specified as the center component for the application's content pane. The application's menu bar is subsequently created with a private `createMenuBar` method.

```
public class Test extends JFrame {
    private JTextPane textPane = new JTextPane();
    private Hashtable actionTable = new Hashtable();
    private JCheckBoxMenuItem titleItem, bodyItem;

    public Test() {
        Container contentPane = getContentPane();

        textPane.setEditorKit(new ChapterEditorKit());
        textPane.setFont(new Font("Dialog", Font.PLAIN, 18));

        // must load action table after setting editor kit ...
        loadActionTable();

        readFile("text.txt");

        contentPane.add(new JScrollPane(textPane),
                    BorderLayout.CENTER);
        contentPane.add(GJApp.getStatusArea(),BorderLayout.SOUTH);

        setJMenuBar(createMenuBar());
    }
}
...
```

The `ChapterEditorKit` creates an array of default actions that are added to the actions provided by the editor kit's superclass (`StyledEditorKit`). When `getActions()` is invoked for the application's text pane, the `Action` array returned is the array returned from the editor kit's `getActions` method.

```
class ChapterEditorKit extends StyledEditorKit {
    private CaretListener caretListener = new Listener();
    private static ChapterStyleContext context =
                            new ChapterStyleContext();

    private static Action[] defaultActions = new Action[] {
```

```
        new ParagraphStyleAction(
                ChapterStyleContext.titleStyle,
                context.getStyle(ChapterStyleContext.titleStyle)),
        new ParagraphStyleAction(
                ChapterStyleContext.bodyStyle,
                context.getStyle(ChapterStyleContext.bodyStyle)),
    };
    public Action[] getActions() {
        return TextAction.augmentList(super.getActions(),
                                      defaultActions);
    }
    ...
```

The actions specified by the `ChapterEditorKit` are obtained from an instance of `ChapterStyleContext`, which is an extension of the `StyleContext` class. The `ChapterStyleContext` class defines `public` constants for the styles it defines, and the `ChapterStyleContext` constructor creates title and body styles that are added to the default style (obtained by invoking `getStyle(DEFAULT_STYLE)`) that is shared by all editor kits.

```
    ...
    class ChapterStyleContext extends StyleContext {
        public static String titleStyle = "title",
                         bodyStyle = "body";

        private static String[] defaultStyleNames = new String[] {
                         new String(titleStyle),
                         new String(bodyStyle) };

        public ChapterStyleContext() {
            Style root = getStyle(DEFAULT_STYLE);

            for(int i=0; i < defaultStyleNames.length; ++i) {
                String name = defaultStyleNames[i];
                Style s = addStyle(name, root);

                if(name.equals(titleStyle)) {
                    StyleConstants.setFontFamily(s, "Dialog");
                    StyleConstants.setFontSize(s, 24);
                    StyleConstants.setBold(s, true);
                    StyleConstants.setUnderline(s, true);
                }
                else if(name.equals(bodyStyle)) {
                    StyleConstants.setFontFamily(s, "Times-Roman");
                    StyleConstants.setFontSize(s, 16);
                }
            }
        }
    }
    ...
```

Editor kits have `install` and `deinstall` methods that are invoked when an editor kit is installed and uninstalled, respectively, for a particular text component. The `ChapterStyleContext` class overrides the `install` method to add a caret listener to the kit's text component for the purpose of updating the application's status area. The `deinstall` method removes the listener so that the text component is in the same state as it was before the editor kit was installed.

The caret listener obtains the name of the style at the caret location and updates the application's status area accordingly.

```
   ...
   public void install(JEditorPane editorPane) {
      editorPane.addCaretListener(caretListener);
   }
   public void deinstall(JEditorPane editorPane) {
      editorPane.removeCaretListener(caretListener);
   }
   static class Listener implements CaretListener {
       public void caretUpdate(CaretEvent e) {
       int dot = e.getDot(), mark = e.getMark();

       if (dot == mark) {
           JTextComponent c = (JTextComponent) e.getSource();
           StyledDocument document =
                    (StyledDocument) c.getDocument();
           Element elem = document.getParagraphElement(dot);
           AttributeSet set = elem.getAttributes();
           String name = (String)set.getAttribute(
                       StyleConstants.NameAttribute);

           GJApp.showStatus(name);
        }
      }
   }
   ...
```

The `ParagraphStyleAction` used to set the style for a specified paragraph is an extension of `StyledEditorKit.StyledTextAction`. The action is constructed with a name and a style, and the `actionPerformed` method sets paragraph attributes for the paragraph with the caret and updates the application's status area with the name of the style.

```
   ...
   static class ParagraphStyleAction
              extends StyledEditorKit.StyledTextAction {
       private Style style;

       public ParagraphStyleAction(String nm, Style style) {
```

```
            super(nm);
            this.style = style;
        }
         public void actionPerformed(ActionEvent e) {
            setParagraphAttributes(getEditor(e), style, false);
            GJApp.showStatus(style.getName());
        }
    }
}
...
```

The application shown in Figure 23-7 is listed in its entirety in Example 23-4.

Example 23-4 Using Styles and Style Contexts

```
import java.io.File;
import javax.swing.*;
import javax.swing.text.*;
import javax.swing.event.*;
import java.awt.*;
import java.awt.event.*;
import java.util.*;
import java.io.FileReader;

public class Test extends JFrame {
    private JTextPane textPane = new JTextPane();
    private Hashtable actionTable = new Hashtable();
    private JCheckBoxMenuItem titleItem, bodyItem;

    public Test() {
        Container contentPane = getContentPane();

        textPane.setEditorKit(new ChapterEditorKit());
        textPane.setFont(new Font("Dialog", Font.PLAIN, 18));

        // must load action table after setting editor kit ...
        loadActionTable();

        readFile("text.txt");

        contentPane.add(new JScrollPane(textPane),
                    BorderLayout.CENTER);
        contentPane.add(GJApp.getStatusArea(),BorderLayout.SOUTH);

        setJMenuBar(createMenuBar());
    }
    private JMenuBar createMenuBar() {
        JMenuBar menuBar = new JMenuBar();
        JMenu editMenu = new JMenu("Edit"),
             styleMenu = new JMenu("Paragraph Styles");

        styleMenu.add(getAction(ChapterStyleContext.titleStyle));
        styleMenu.add(getAction(ChapterStyleContext.bodyStyle));
```

```
                    editMenu.add(styleMenu);
                    menuBar.add(editMenu);
                    return menuBar;
                }
                private void readFile(String filename) {
                    EditorKit kit = textPane.getEditorKit();
                    Document doc = textPane.getDocument();

                    try {
                        kit.read(new FileReader(filename), doc, 0);
                    }
                    catch(Exception ex) {
                        ex.printStackTrace();
                    }
                }
                private void loadActionTable() {
                    Action[] actions = textPane.getActions();

                    for(int i=0; i < actions.length; ++i) {
                        actionTable.put(actions[i].getValue(Action.NAME),
                                    actions[i]);
                    }
                }
                private Action getAction(String name) {
                    return (Action)actionTable.get(name);
                }
                public static void main(String args[]) {
                    GJApp.launch(new Test(),
                            "Custom EditorKits & Style Contexts",
                            300,300,650,275);
                }
            }
    class ChapterEditorKit extends StyledEditorKit {
                private CaretListener caretListener = new Listener();
                private static ChapterStyleContext context =
                                    new ChapterStyleContext();

                private static Action[] defaultActions = new Action[] {
                    new ParagraphStyleAction(
                            ChapterStyleContext.titleStyle,
                            context.getStyle(ChapterStyleContext.titleStyle)),
                    new ParagraphStyleAction(
                            ChapterStyleContext.bodyStyle,
                            context.getStyle(ChapterStyleContext.bodyStyle)),
                };
                public Action[] getActions() {
                    return TextAction.augmentList(super.getActions(),
                                        defaultActions);
                }
                public void install(JEditorPane editorPane) {
                    editorPane.addCaretListener(caretListener);
                }
                public void deinstall(JEditorPane editorPane) {
                    editorPane.removeCaretListener(caretListener);
                }
                static class Listener implements CaretListener {
                    public void caretUpdate(CaretEvent e) {
```

```
          int dot = e.getDot(), mark = e.getMark();

          if (dot == mark) {
              JTextComponent c = (JTextComponent) e.getSource();
              StyledDocument document =
                      (StyledDocument) c.getDocument();
              Element elem = document.getParagraphElement(dot);
              AttributeSet set = elem.getAttributes();
              String name = (String)set.getAttribute(
                              StyleConstants.NameAttribute);

              GJApp.showStatus(name);
          }
      }
    }
    static class ParagraphStyleAction
             extends StyledEditorKit.StyledTextAction {
      private Style style;

      public ParagraphStyleAction(String nm, Style style) {
       super(nm);
          this.style = style;
      }
       public void actionPerformed(ActionEvent e) {
          setParagraphAttributes(getEditor(e), style, false);
          GJApp.showStatus(style.getName());
      }
    }
}
class ChapterStyleContext extends StyleContext {
    public static String titleStyle = "title",
                  bodyStyle = "body";

    private static String[] defaultStyleNames = new String[] {
                      new String(titleStyle),
                      new String(bodyStyle) };

    public ChapterStyleContext() {
        Style root = getStyle(DEFAULT_STYLE);

        for(int i=0; i < defaultStyleNames.length; ++i) {
            String name = defaultStyleNames[i];
            Style s = addStyle(name, root);

            if(name.equals(titleStyle)) {
                StyleConstants.setFontFamily(s, "Dialog");
                StyleConstants.setFontSize(s, 24);
                StyleConstants.setBold(s, true);
                StyleConstants.setUnderline(s, true);
            }
            else if(name.equals(bodyStyle)) {
                StyleConstants.setFontFamily(s, "Times-Roman");
                StyleConstants.setFontSize(s, 16);
            }
        }
    }
}
```

Elements

In addition to maintaining a text component's content, documents also maintain a hierarchy of elements. Elements are objects that maintain start and end positions within a document and a set of attributes for the content between the start and end positions.

Figure 23-8 shows a class hierarchy of the element classes defined in the `javax.swing.text` package.

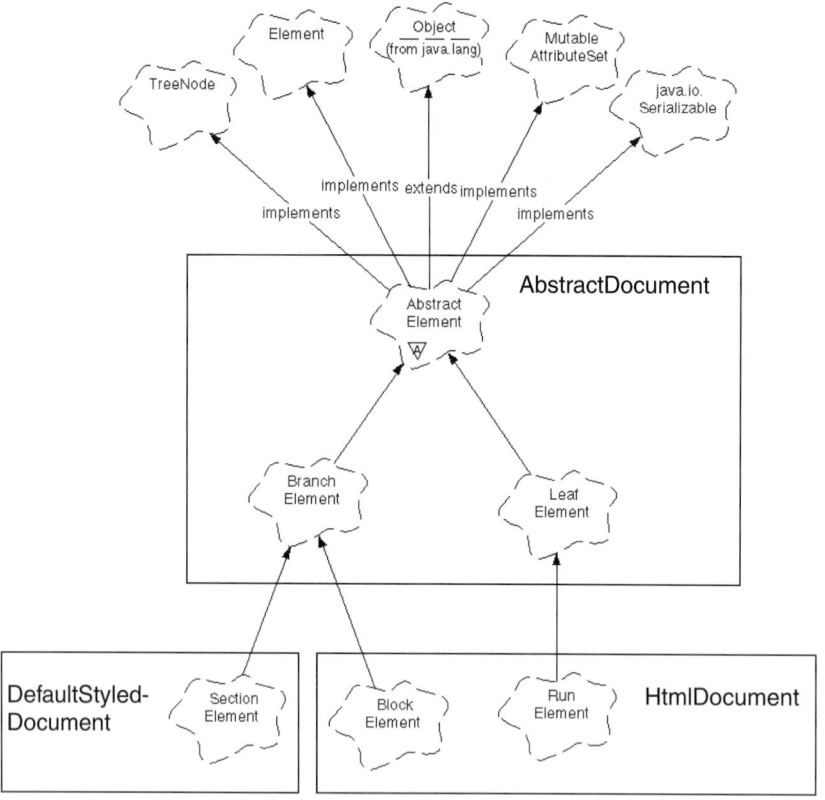

Figure 23-8 Document Class Diagram

The element interface is implemented by the `AbstractDocument.AbstractElement` class, which is extended by the `AbstractDocument.BranchElement` and `AbstractDocument.LeafElement` classes. Branch elements can have child

elements, whereas leaf elements do not have children. The `BranchElement` class is extended by `DefaultStyledDocument.SectionElement` and `HTMLDocument.BlockElement`. The `LeafElement` class is extended by `HTMLDocument.RunElement`.

The application shown in Figure 23-9 contains a split pane with a text field, text area, text pane, and editor pane in the left panel and an instance of `ElementTreePanel` as the right panel. The `ElementTreePanel` class uses a tree to show a document's element structure. The `ElementTreePanel` class is included in the Swing examples and therefore is not listed here.

Figure 23-9 Element Hierarchies

The four pictures shown in Figure 23-9 illustrate the element hierarchy for each of the Swing text components. Text fields have the simplest element hierarchy, which is a paragraph with content. The bottom picture in Figure 23-9 shows the element hierarchy for an editor pane that displays an HTML document and is by far the most complicated element hierarchy. The default element hierarchies will be sufficient for nearly all uses of text components.

The application shown in Figure 23-9 is listed in Example 23-5.

Example 23-5 Element Hierarchies

```java
import javax.swing.*;
import javax.swing.event.*;
import javax.swing.text.*;
import java.awt.*;
import java.awt.event.*;
import java.util.*;
import java.io.FileReader;

public class Test extends JFrame {
    private JTextComponent components[] = new JTextComponent[] {
        new JTextField("initial content"), new JTextArea(10,20),
        new JTextPane(), new JEditorPane(),
    };
    private String borderNames[] = new String[] {
        "JTextField", "JTextArea", "JTextPane", "JEditorPane"
    };
    private JPanel textComponentPanel = new JPanel();
    private ElementTreePanel treePanel =
                       new ElementTreePanel(components[0]);
    private JSplitPane sp = new JSplitPane(
                       JSplitPane.HORIZONTAL_SPLIT,
                       new JScrollPane(textComponentPanel),
                       new JScrollPane(treePanel));

    public Test() {
        Container contentPane = getContentPane();
        CaretListener listener = new Listener();

        textComponentPanel.setBorder(
            BorderFactory.createTitledBorder("Text Components"));

        for(int i=0; i < components.length; ++i) {
            JTextComponent c = (JTextComponent)components[i];

            c.addCaretListener(listener);
            c.setBorder(
                BorderFactory.createTitledBorder(borderNames[i]));

            if(i != 0) // ! JTextField
                readFile(c, "text.txt");
```

```
         if(i == 3) { // JEditorPane
             JEditorPane
                     editorPane = (JEditorPane)c;

             String url = "file:" +
                     System.getProperty("user.dir") +
                     System.getProperty("file.separator") +
                     "java.util.Hashtable.html";

             editorPane.setEditable(false);
             try {
                 editorPane.setPage(url);
             }
             catch(Exception ex) { ex.printStackTrace(); }

             JScrollPane sp = new JScrollPane(c);
             sp.setPreferredSize(new Dimension(450,450));
             panel.add(sp);
         }
         else
             panel.add(c);
     }
     sp.setDividerLocation(600);

     contentPane.add(sp, BorderLayout.CENTER);
}
class Listener implements CaretListener {
    public void caretUpdate(CaretEvent e) {
        JTextComponent c = (JTextComponent)e.getSource();

        if(c != treePanel.getEditor()) {
            sp.setRightComponent(treePanel =
                            new ElementTreePanel(c));
        }
    }
}
private void readFile(JTextComponent c, String filename) {
    try {
        c.read(new FileReader(filename), null);
    }
    catch(Exception ex) {
        ex.printStackTrace();
    }
}
public static void main(String args[]) {
    GJApp.launch(new Test(),
            "Element Hierarchies",300,300,800,300);
}
}
```

Parting Shots

The Swing text package contains many classes and interfaces, most of which are inner classes. The sheer number of classes and interfaces can be intimidating to developers moving along the Swing text learning curve. To aid in this process, this chapter has presented a handful of code examples that touch upon the most important classes and interfaces defined in the Swing text package.

APPENDIX

A

Class Diagrams

Class diagrams are to software development what blueprints are to the world of architecture. Class diagrams are essential for succinctly communicating one's design to others, and *Graphic Java* uses class diagrams extensively for documenting Java Foundation Classes.

The class diagrams throughout *Graphic Java* are of the *Booch* variety.[1] For those of you unfamiliar with Booch diagrams, a legend is shown and then a simple, yet fairly complete class diagram is discussed.

1.   See Booch, Grady. *Object-Oriented Analysis And Design*. Benjamin/Cummings.

Class Diagram Legend

The following is a legend of the elements used in class diagrams.

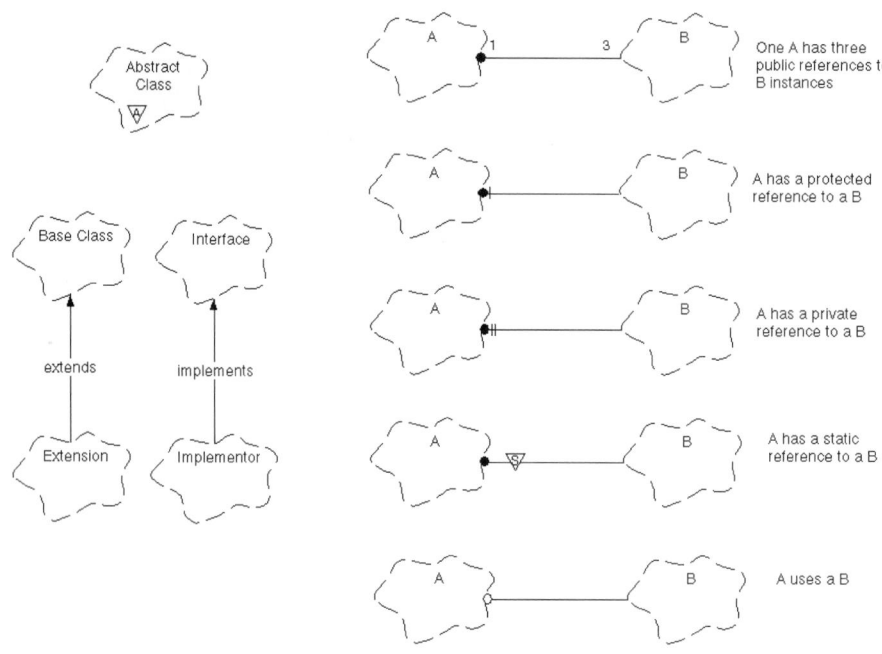

An Example Class Diagram

The class diagram below is for the JScrollBar class.

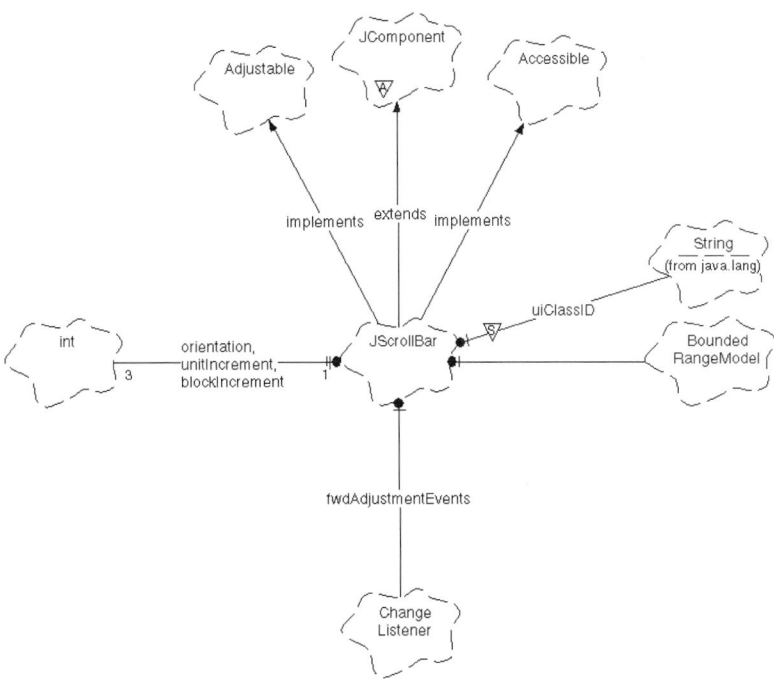

The JScrollBar class extends the abstract JComponent class and implements two interfaces: Adjustable and Accessible. Notice that the Accessible and Adjustable interfaces are identified as interfaces and not classes by virtue of the fact that JScrollBar implements the interfaces. In other words, there is nothing about the interfaces themselves that identifies them as interfaces.

The JScrollBar class maintains a static protected reference to a string. Because the role of the string is not apparent from the name of the class, the relationship between JScrollBar and the string is adorned with a name that clarifies the nature of the relationship (uiClassID).

JScrollBar also maintains 3 private integer values: orientation, unitIncrement and blockIncrement. Intrinsic types, such as integers, are depicted as classes in class diagrams.

JScrollBar also maintains protected references to instances of BoundedRangeModel and ChangeListener. The BoundedRangeModel is the scrollbar's model, and therefore the relationship does not include an identifier. The role of the ChangeListener is not apparent from the name of class, and therefore the relationship between JScrollBar and ChangeListener is identified as fwdAdjustmentEvents. Relationship identifiers are the same as the name of the references in the code; in this case, the scrollbar's change listener forwards adjustment events to its own listeners.

APPENDIX

B

Pluggable Look & Feel Constants

Table B-1 lists the constants defined by the
`javax.swing.plaf.basic.BasicLookAndFeel` class. The constants are
used as default values for many aspects of Swing component's look and feel. See
"Pluggable Look and Feel" on page 317 for more information concerning the use
of the constants listed in Table B-1.

Table B-1 UIManager Constants[1]

String Constant	Default Value
Button.font	dialogPlain12
Button.background	*control*
Button.foreground	*controlText*
Button.border	buttonBorder
Button.margin	new InsetsUIResource(2,14,2,14)
Button.textIconGap	new Integer(4)
Button.textShiftOffset	new Integer(0)
ToggleButton.font	dialogPlain12
ToggleButton.background	*control*
ToggleButton.foreground	*controlText*
ToggleButton.border	buttonToggleBorder

Table B-1   UIManager Constants[1]

String Constant	Default Value
ToggleButton.margin	new InsetsUIResource(2,14,2,14)
ToggleButton.textIconGap	new Integer(4)
ToggleButton.textShiftOffset	new Integer(0)
RadioButton.font	dialogPlain12
RadioButton.background	*control*
RadioButton.foreground	*controlText*
RadioButton.border	radioButtonBorder
RadioButton.margin	new InsetsUIResource(2,2,2,2)
RadioButton.textIconGap	new Integer(4)
RadioButton.textShiftOffset	new Integer(0)
RadioButton.icon	radioButtonIcon
CheckBox.font	dialogPlain12
CheckBox.background	*control*
CheckBox.foreground	*controlText*
CheckBox.border	radioButtonBorder
CheckBox.margin	new InsetsUIResource(2,2,2,2)
CheckBox.textIconGap	new Integer(4)
CheckBox.textShiftOffset	new Integer(0)
CheckBox.icon	checkBoxIcon
ColorChooser.font	dialogPlain12
ColorChooser.background	*control*
ColorChooser.foreground	*controlText*
ColorChooser.swatchesSwatchSize	new Dimension(10,10)
ColorChooser.swatchesRecentSwatchSize	new Dimension(10,10)
ColorChooser.swatchesDefaultRecentColor	*control*
ColorChooser.rgbRedMnemonic	new Integer(KeyEvent.VK_R)
ColorChooser.rgbGreenMnemonic	new Integer(KeyEvent.VK_G)
ColorChooser.rgbBlueMnemonic	new Integer(KeyEvent.VK_B)
ComboBox.font	dialogPlain12
ComboBox.background	white
ComboBox.foreground	black
ComboBox.selectionBackground	*textHighlight*
ComboBox.selectionForeground	*textHighlightText*

Table B-1 UIManager Constants[1]

String Constant	Default Value
ComboBox.disabledBackground	*control*
ComboBox.disabledForeground	*textInactiveText*
FileChooser.cancelButtonMnemonic	new Integer(KeyEvent.VK_C)
FileChooser.saveButtonMnemonic	new Integer(KeyEvent.VK_S)
FileChooser.openButtonMnemonic	new Integer(KeyEvent.VK_O)
FileChooser.updateButtonMnemonic	new Integer(KeyEvent.VK_U)
FileChooser.helpButtonMnemonic	new Integer(KeyEvent.VK_H)
FileChooser.newFolderIcon	newFolderIcon
FileChooser.upFolderIcon	upFolderIcon
FileChooser.homeFolderIcon	homeFolderIcon
FileChooser.detailsViewIcon	detailsViewIcon
FileChooser.listViewIcon	listViewIcon
FileView.directoryIcon	directoryIcon
FileView.fileIcon	fileIcon
FileView.computerIcon	computerIcon
FileView.hardDriveIcon	hardDriveIcon
FileView.floppyDriveIcon	floppyDriveIcon
InternalFrame.titleFont	dialogBold12
InternalFrame.border	internalFrameBorder
InternalFrame.icon	"icons/JavaCup.gif"
InternalFrame.maximizeIcon	BasicIconFactory.createEmptyFrameIcon()
InternalFrame.minimizeIcon	BasicIconFactory.createEmptyFrameIcon()
InternalFrame.iconifyIcon	BasicIconFactory.createEmptyFrameIcon()
InternalFrame.closeIcon	BasicIconFactory.createEmptyFrameIcon()
InternalFrame.activeTitleBackground	*activeCaption*
InternalFrame.activeTitleForeground	*activeCaptionText*
InternalFrame.inactiveTitleBackground	*inactiveCaption*
InternalFrame.inactiveTitleForeground	*inactiveCaptionText*
DesktopIcon.border	internalFrameBorder
Desktop.background	*desktop*
Label.font	dialogPlain12
Label.background	*control*
Label.foreground	*controlText*

Table B-1   UIManager Constants[1]

String Constant	Default Value
Label.disabledForeground	white
Label.disabledShadow	*controlShadow*
Label.border	null
List.font	dialogPlain12
List.background	*window*
List.foreground	*textText*
List.selectionBackground	*textHighlight*
List.selectionForeground	*textHighlightText*
List.focusCellHighlightBorder	focusCellHighlightBorder
List.border	null
List.cellRenderer	listCellRendererActiveValue
MenuBar.font	dialogPlain12
MenuBar.background	*menu*
MenuBar.foreground	*menuText*
MenuBar.border	menuBarBorder
MenuItem.font	dialogPlain12
MenuItem.acceleratorFont	dialogPlain12
MenuItem.background	*menu*
MenuItem.foreground	*menuText*
MenuItem.selectionForeground	*textHighlightText*
MenuItem.selectionBackground	*textHighlight*
MenuItem.disabledForeground	null
MenuItem.acceleratorForeground	*menuText*
MenuItem.acceleratorSelectionForeground	*textHighlightText*
MenuItem.border	marginBorder
MenuItem.borderPainted	Boolean.FALSE
MenuItem.margin	new InsetsUIResource(2,2,2,2)
MenuItem.checkIcon	menuItemCheckIcon
MenuItem.arrowIcon	menuItemArrowIcon
RadioButtonMenuItem.font	dialogPlain12
RadioButtonMenuItem.acceleratorFont	dialogPlain12
RadioButtonMenuItem.background	*menu*
RadioButtonMenuItem.foreground	*menuText*

Table B-1 UIManager Constants[1]

String Constant	Default Value
RadioButtonMenuItem.selectionForeground	*textHighlightText*
RadioButtonMenuItem.selectionBackground	*textHighlight*
RadioButtonMenuItem.disabledForeground	null
RadioButtonMenuItem.acceleratorForeground	*menuText*
RadioButtonMenuItem. acceleratorSelectionForeground	*textHighlightText*
RadioButtonMenuItem.border	marginBorder
RadioButtonMenuItem.borderPainted	Boolean.FALSE
RadioButtonMenuItem.margin	new InsetsUIResource(2,2,2,2)
RadioButtonMenuItem.checkIcon	radioButtonMenuItemIcon
RadioButtonMenuItem.arrowIcon	menuItemArrowIcon
CheckBoxMenuItem.font	dialogPlain12
CheckBoxMenuItem.acceleratorFont	dialogPlain12
CheckBoxMenuItem.background	*menu*
CheckBoxMenuItem.foreground	*menuText*
CheckBoxMenuItem.selectionForeground	*textHighlightText*
CheckBoxMenuItem.selectionBackground	*textHighlight*
CheckBoxMenuItem.disabledForeground	null
CheckBoxMenuItem.acceleratorForeground	*menuText*
CheckBoxMenuItem. acceleratorSelectionForeground	*textHighlightText*
CheckBoxMenuItem.border	marginBorder
CheckBoxMenuItem.borderPainted	Boolean.FALSE
CheckBoxMenuItem.margin	new InsetsUIResource(2,2,2,2)
CheckBoxMenuItem.checkIcon	checkBoxMenuItemIcon
CheckBoxMenuItem.arrowIcon	menuItemArrowIcon
Menu.font	dialogPlain12
Menu.acceleratorFont	dialogPlain12
Menu.background	*menu*
Menu.foreground	*menuText*
Menu.selectionForeground	*textHighlightText*
Menu.selectionBackground	*textHighlight*
Menu.disabledForeground	null

Table B-1   UIManager Constants[1]

String Constant	Default Value
Menu.acceleratorForeground	*menuText*
Menu.acceleratorSelectionForeground	*textHighlightText*
Menu.border	marginBorder
Menu.borderPainted	Boolean.FALSE
Menu.margin	new InsetsUIResource(2,2,2,2)
Menu.checkIcon	menuItemCheckIcon
Menu.arrowIcon	menuArrowIcon
Menu.consumesTabs	Boolean.TRUE
PopupMenu.font	dialogPlain12
PopupMenu.background	*menu*
PopupMenu.foreground	*menuText*
PopupMenu.border	raisedBevelBorder
OptionPane.font	dialogPlain12
OptionPane.background	*control*
OptionPane.foreground	*controlText*
OptionPane.messageForeground	*controlText*
OptionPane.border	optionPaneBorder
OptionPane.messageAreaBorder	zeroBorder
OptionPane.buttonAreaBorder	optionPaneButtonAreaBorder
OptionPane.minimumSize	optionPaneMinimumSize
OptionPane.errorIcon	"icons/Error.gif"
OptionPane.informationIcon	"icons/Inform.gif"
OptionPane.warningIcon	"icons/Warn.gif"
OptionPane.questionIcon	"icons/Question.gif"
Panel.font	dialogPlain12
Panel.background	*control*
Panel.foreground	*textText*
ProgressBar.font	dialogPlain12
ProgressBar.foreground	*textHighlight*
ProgressBar.background	*control*
ProgressBar.selectionForeground	*control*
ProgressBar.selectionBackground	*textHighlight*
ProgressBar.border	progressBarBorder

Table B-1 UIManager Constants[1]

String Constant	Default Value
ProgressBar.cellLength	new Integer(1)
ProgressBar.cellSpacing	new Integer(0)
Separator.shadow	*controlShadow*
Separator.highlight	*controlLtHighlight*
ScrollBar.background	*scrollBarTrack*
ScrollBar.foreground	*control*
ScrollBar.track	*scrollbar*
ScrollBar.trackHighlight	*controlDkShadow*
ScrollBar.thumb	*control*
ScrollBar.thumbHighlight	*controlLtHighlight*
ScrollBar.thumbDarkShadow	*controlDkShadow*
ScrollBar.thumbLightShadow	*controlShadow*
ScrollBar.border	null
ScrollBar.minimumThumbSize	minimumThumbSize
ScrollBar.maximumThumbSize	maximumThumbSize
ScrollPane.font	dialogPlain12
ScrollPane.background	*control*
ScrollPane.foreground	*controlText*
ScrollPane.border	etchedBorder
ScrollPane.viewportBorder	null
Viewport.font	dialogPlain12
Viewport.background	*control*
Viewport.foreground	*textText*
Slider.foreground	*control*
Slider.background	*control*
Slider.highlight	*controlLtHighlight*
Slider.shadow	*controlShadow*
Slider.focus	*controlDkShadow*
Slider.border	null
Slider.focusInsets	sliderFocusInsets
SplitPane.background	*control*
SplitPane.highlight	*controlLtHighlight*
SplitPane.shadow	*controlShadow*

Table B-1   UIManager Constants[1]

String Constant	Default Value
SplitPane.border	splitPaneBorder
SplitPane.dividerSize	new Integer(5)
TabbedPane.font	dialogPlain12
TabbedPane.background	*control*
TabbedPane.foreground	*controlText*
TabbedPane.lightHighlight	*controlLtHighlight*
TabbedPane.highlight	*controlHighlight*
TabbedPane.shadow	*controlShadow*
TabbedPane.darkShadow	*controlDkShadow*
TabbedPane.focus	*controlText*
TabbedPane.textIconGap	new Integer(4)
TabbedPane.tabInsets	tabbedPaneTabInsets
TabbedPane.selectedTabPadInsets	tabbedPaneTabPadInsets
TabbedPane.tabAreaInsets	tabbedPaneTabAreaInsets
TabbedPane.contentBorderInsets	tabbedPaneContentBorderInsets
TabbedPane.tabRunOverlay	new Integer(2)
Table.font	dialogPlain12
Table.foreground	*controlText*
Table.background	*window*
Table.selectionForeground	*textHighlightText*
Table.selectionBackground	*textHighlight*
Table.gridColor	gray
Table.focusCellBackground	*window*
Table.focusCellForeground	*controlText*
Table.focusCellHighlightBorder	focusCellHighlightBorder
Table.scrollPaneBorder	loweredBevelBorder
TableHeader.font	dialogPlain12
TableHeader.foreground	*controlText*
TableHeader.background	*control*
TableHeader.cellBorder	raisedBevelBorder
TextField.font	sansSerifPlain12
TextField.background	*window*
TextField.foreground	*textText*

Table B-1 UIManager Constants[1]

String Constant	Default Value
TextField.inactiveForeground	*textInactiveText*
TextField.selectionBackground	*textHighlight*
TextField.selectionForeground	*textHighlightText*
TextField.caretForeground	*textText*
TextField.caretBlinkRate	caretBlinkRate
TextField.border	textFieldBorder
TextField.margin	zeroInsets
TextField.keyBindings	fieldBindings
PasswordField.font	monospacedPlain12
PasswordField.background	*window*
PasswordField.foreground	*textText*
PasswordField.inactiveForeground	*textInactiveText*
PasswordField.selectionBackground	*textHighlight*
PasswordField.selectionForeground	*textHighlightText*
PasswordField.caretForeground	*textText*
PasswordField.caretBlinkRate	caretBlinkRate
PasswordField.border	textFieldBorder
PasswordField.margin	zeroInsets
PasswordField.keyBindings	fieldBindings
TextArea.font	monospacedPlain12
TextArea.background	*window*
TextArea.foreground	*textText*
TextArea.inactiveForeground	*textInactiveText*
TextArea.selectionBackground	*textHighlight*
TextArea.selectionForeground	*textHighlightText*
TextArea.caretForeground	*textText*
TextArea.caretBlinkRate	caretBlinkRate
TextArea.border	marginBorder
TextArea.margin	zeroInsets
TextArea.keyBindings	multilineBindings
TextPane.font	serifPlain12
TextPane.background	white
TextPane.foreground	*textText*

Table B-1 UIManager Constants[1]

String Constant	Default Value
TextPane.selectionBackground	lightGray
TextPane.selectionForeground	*textHighlightText*
TextPane.caretForeground	*textText*
TextPane.caretBlinkRate	caretBlinkRate
TextPane.inactiveForeground	*textInactiveText*
TextPane.border	marginBorder
TextPane.margin	editorMargin
TextPane.keyBindings	multilineBindings
EditorPane.font	serifPlain12
EditorPane.background	white
EditorPane.foreground	*textText*
EditorPane.selectionBackground	lightGray
EditorPane.selectionForeground	*textHighlightText*
EditorPane.caretForeground	red
EditorPane.caretBlinkRate	caretBlinkRate
EditorPane.inactiveForeground	*textInactiveText*
EditorPane.border	marginBorder
EditorPane.margin	editorMargin
EditorPane.keyBindings	multilineBindings
TitledBorder.font	dialogPlain12
TitledBorder.titleColor	*controlText*
TitledBorder.border	etchedBorder
ToolBar.font	dialogPlain12
ToolBar.background	*control*
ToolBar.foreground	*controlText*
ToolBar.dockingBackground	*control*
ToolBar.dockingForeground	red
ToolBar.floatingBackground	*control*
ToolBar.floatingForeground	darkGray
ToolBar.border	etchedBorder
ToolBar.separatorSize	toolBarSeparatorSize
ToolTip.font	sansSerifPlain12
ToolTip.background	*info*

Table B-1   UIManager Constants[1]

String Constant	Default Value
ToolTip.foreground	*infoText*
ToolTip.border	blackLineBorder
Tree.font	dialogPlain12
Tree.background	*window*
Tree.foreground	*textText*
Tree.hash	gray
Tree.textForeground	*textText*
Tree.textBackground	*text*
Tree.selectionForeground	*textHighlightText*
Tree.selectionBackground	*textHighlight*
Tree.selectionBorderColor	black
Tree.editorBorder	blackLineBorder
Tree.leftChildIndent	new Integer(7)
Tree.rightChildIndent	new Integer(13)
Tree.rowHeight	new Integer(16)
Tree.scrollsOnExpand	Boolean.TRUE
Tree.openIcon	"icons/TreeOpen.gif"
Tree.closedIcon	"icons/TreeClosed.gif"
Tree.leafIcon	"icons/TreeLeaf.gif"
Tree.expandedIcon	null
Tree.collapsedIcon	null
Tree.changeSelectionWithFocus	Boolean.TRUE
Tree.drawsFocusBorderAroundIcon	Boolean.FALSE

1. System color constants are italicized

Index

SUN MICROSYSTEMS, INC.
BINARY CODE LICENSE AGREEMENT

READ THE TERMS OF THIS AGREEMENT AND ANY PROVIDED SUPPLEMENTAL LICENSE TERMS (COLLECTIVELY "AGREEMENT") CAREFULLY BEFORE OPENING THE SOFTWARE MEDIA PACKAGE. BY OPENING THE SOFTWARE MEDIA PACKAGE, YOU AGREE TO THE TERMS OF THIS AGREEMENT. IF YOU ARE ACCESSING THE SOFTWARE ELECTRONICALLY INDICATE YOUR ACCEPTANCE OF THESE TERMS BY SELECTING THE "ACCEPT" BUTTON AT THE END OF THIS AGREEMENT. IF YOU DO NOT AGREE TO ALL OF THESE TERMS, PROMPTLY RETURN THE UNUSED SOFTWARE TO YOUR PLACE OF PURCHASE FOR A REFUND OR, IF THE SOFTWARE IS ACCESSED ELECTRONICALLY, SELECT THE "DECLINE" BUTTON AT THE END OF THIS AGREEMENT.

1. License to Use. Sun grants to you a non-exclusive and non-transferable license for the internal use only of the accompanying software and documentation and any error corrections provided by Sun (collectively "Software"), by the number of users and the class of computer hardware for which the corresponding fee has been paid.

2. Restrictions. Software is confidential and copyrighted. Title to Software and all associated intellectual property rights is retained by Sun and/or its licensors. Except as specifically authorized in any Supplemental License Terms, you may not make copies of Software, other than a single copy of Software for archival purposes. Unless enforcement is prohibited by applicable law, you may not modify, decompile, disassemble, or otherwise reverse engineer Software. Software is not designed or licensed for use in on-line control of aircraft, air traffic, aircraft or navigation or aircraft communications; or in the design, construction, operation or maintenance of any nuclear facility. You warrant that you will not use Software for these purposes. You may not publish or provide the results of any benchmark or comparison tests run on Software to any third party without the prior written consent of Sun. No right, title or interest in or to any trademark, service mark, logo, or trade name of Sun or its licensors is granted under this Agreement.

3. Limited Warranty. Sun warrants to you that for a period of ninety (90) days from the date of purchase, as evidenced by a copy of the receipt, the media on which Software is furnished (if any) will be free of defects in materials and workmanship under normal use. Except for the foregoing, Software is provided "AS IS". Your exclusive remedy and Sun's entire liability under this limited warranty will be at Sun's option to replace Software media or refund the fee paid for Software.

4. Disclaimer of Warranty. UNLESS SPECIFIED IN THIS AGREEMENT, ALL EXPRESS OR IMPLIED CONDITIONS, REPRESENTATIONS AND WARRANTIES, INCLUDING ANY IMPLIED WARRANTY OF MERCHANTABILITY, FITNESS FOR A PARTICULAR PURPOSE, OR NON-INFRINGEMENT, ARE DISCLAIMED, EXCEPT TO THE EXTENT THAT THESE DISCLAIMERS ARE HELD TO BE LEGALLY INVALID.

5. Limitation of Liability. TO THE EXTENT NOT PROHIBITED BY APPLICABLE LAW, IN NO EVENT WILL SUN OR ITS LICENSORS BE LIABLE FOR ANY LOST REVENUE, PROFIT OR DATA, OR FOR SPECIAL, INDIRECT, CONSEQUENTIAL, INCIDENTAL OR PUNITIVE DAMAGES, HOWEVER CAUSED AND REGARDLESS OF THE THEORY OF LIABILITY, ARISING OUT OF OR RELATED TO THE USE OF OR INABILITY TO USE SOFTWARE, EVEN IF SUN HAS BEEN ADVISED OF THE POSSIBILITY OF SUCH DAMAGES. In no event will Sun's liability to you, whether in contract, tort (including negligence), or otherwise, exceed the amount paid by you for Software under this Agreement. The foregoing limitations will apply even if the above stated warranty fails of its essential purpose.

6.   Termination. This Agreement is effective until terminated. You may terminate this Agreement at any time by destroying all copies of Software. This Agreement will terminate immediately without notice from Sun if you fail to comply with any provision of this Agreement. Upon termination, you must destroy all copies of Software.

7.   Export Regulations. All Software and technical data delivered under this Agreement are subject to U.S. export control laws and may be subject to export or import regulations in other countries. You agree to comply strictly with all such laws and regulations and acknowledge that you have the responsibility to obtain such licenses to export, re-export, or import as may be required after delivery to you.

8.   U.S. Government Restricted Rights. Use, duplication, or disclosure by the U.S. Government is subject to restrictions set forth in this Agreement and as provided in DFARS 227.7202-1(a) and 227.7202-3(a) (1995), DFARS 252.227-7013(c)(1)(ii) (Oct 1988), FAR 12.212(a)(1995), FAR 52.227-19 (June 1987), or FAR 52.227-14 (ALT III) (June 1987), as applicable.

9.   Governing Law. Any action related to this Agreement will be governed by California law and controlling U.S. federal law. No choice of law rules of any jurisdiction will apply.

10.   Severability. If any provision of this Agreement is held to be unenforceable, this Agreement will remain in effect with the provision omitted, unless omission of the provision would frustrate the intent of the parties, in which case this Agreement will immediately terminate.

11.   Integration. This Agreement is the entire agreement between you and Sun relating to its subject matter. It supersedes all prior or contemporaneous oral or written communications, proposals, representations and warranties and prevails over any conflicting or additional terms of any quote, order, acknowledgment, or other communication between the parties relating to its subject matter during the term of this Agreement. No modification of this Agreement will be binding, unless in writing and signed by an authorized representative of each party.

For inquiries please contact: Sun Microsystems, Inc., 901 San Antonio Road, Palo Alto, California 94303

JAVA™ DEVELOPMENT KIT VERSION 1.2
SUPPLEMENTAL LICENSE TERMS

These supplemental terms ("Supplement") add to the terms of the Binary Code License Agreement ("Agreement"). Capitalized terms not defined herein shall have the same meanings ascribed to them in the Agreement. The Supplement terms shall supersede any inconsistent or conflicting terms in the Agreement.

1. Limited License Grant. Sun grants to you a non-exclusive, non-transferable limited license to use the Software without fee for evaluation of the Software and for development of Java™ applets and applications provided that you: (i) may not re-distribute the Software in whole or in part, either separately or included with a product. (ii) may not create, or authorize your licensees to create additional classes, interfaces, or subpackages that are contained in the "java" or "sun" packages or similar as specified by Sun in any class file naming convention; and (iii) agree to the extent Programs are developed which utilize the Windows 95/98 style graphical user interface or components contained therein, such applets or applications may only be developed to run on a Windows 95/98 or Windows NT platform. Refer to the Java Runtime Environment Version 1.2 binary code license (http://java.sun.com/products/JDK/1.2/index.html) for the availability of runtime code which may be distributed with Java applets and applications.

2. Java Platform Interface. In the event that Licensee creates an additional API(s) which: (i) extends the functionality of a Java Environment; and, (ii) is exposed to third party software developers for the purpose of developing additional software which invokes such additional API, Licensee must promptly publish broadly an accurate specification for such API for free use by all developers.

3. Trademarks and Logos. This Agreement does not authorize Licensee to use any Sun name, trademark or logo. Licensee acknowledges as between it and Sun that Sun owns the Java trademark and all Java-related trademarks, logos and icons including the Coffee Cup and Duke ("Java Marks") and agrees to comply with the Java Trademark Guidelines at http://java.sun.com/trademarks.html.

4. High Risk Activities. Notwithstanding Section 2, with respect to high risk activities, the following language shall apply: the Software is not designed or intended for use in on-line control of aircraft, air traffic, aircraft navigation or aircraft communications; or in the design, construction, operation or maintenance of any nuclear facility. Sun disclaims any express or implied warranty of fitness for such uses.

5. Source Code. Software may contain source code that is provided solely for reference purposes pursuant to the terms of this Agreement.

LICENSE AGREEMENT AND LIMITED WARRANTY

READ THE FOLLOWING TERMS AND CONDITIONS CAREFULLY BEFORE OPENING THIS SOFTWARE MEDIA PACKAGE. THIS LEGAL DOCUMENT IS AN AGREEMENT BETWEEN YOU AND PRENTICE-HALL, INC. (THE "COMPANY"). BY OPENING THIS SEALED SOFTWARE MEDIA PACKAGE, YOU ARE AGREEING TO BE BOUND BY THESE TERMS AND CONDITIONS. IF YOU DO NOT AGREE WITH THESE TERMS AND CONDITIONS, DO NOT OPEN THE SOFTWARE MEDIA PACKAGE. PROMPTLY RETURN THE UNOPENED SOFTWARE MEDIA PACKAGE AND ALL ACCOMPANYING ITEMS TO THE PLACE YOU OBTAINED THEM FOR A FULL REFUND OF ANY SUMS YOU HAVE PAID.

1.   **GRANT OF LICENSE:** In consideration of your payment of the license fee, which is part of the price you paid for this product, and your agreement to abide by the terms and conditions of this Agreement, the Company grants to you a nonexclusive right to use and display the copy of the enclosed software program (hereinafter the "SOFTWARE") on a single computer (i.e., with a single CPU) at a single location so long as you comply with the terms of this Agreement. The Company reserves all rights not expressly granted to you under this Agreement.

2.   **OWNERSHIP OF SOFTWARE:** You own only the magnetic or physical media (the enclosed software media) on which the SOFTWARE is recorded or fixed, but the Company retains all the rights, title, and ownership to the SOFTWARE recorded on the original software media copy(ies) and all subsequent copies of the SOFTWARE, regardless of the form or media on which the original or other copies may exist. This license is not a sale of the original SOFTWARE or any copy to you.

3.   **COPY RESTRICTIONS:** This SOFTWARE and the accompanying printed materials and user manual (the "Documentation") are the subject of copyright. You may not copy the Documentation or the SOFTWARE, except that you may make a single copy of the SOFTWARE for backup or archival purposes only. You may be held legally responsible for any copying or copyright infringement which is caused or encouraged by your failure to abide by the terms of this restriction.

4.   **USE RESTRICTIONS:** You may not network the SOFTWARE or otherwise use it on more than one computer or computer terminal at the same time. You may physically transfer the SOFTWARE from one computer to another provided that the SOFTWARE is used on only one computer at a time. You may not distribute copies of the SOFTWARE or Documentation to others. You may not reverse engineer, disassemble, decompile, modify, adapt, translate, or create derivative works based on the SOFTWARE or the Documentation without the prior written consent of the Company.

5.   **TRANSFER RESTRICTIONS:** The enclosed SOFTWARE is licensed only to you and may not be transferred to any one else without the prior written consent of the Company. Any unauthorized transfer of the SOFTWARE shall result in the immediate termination of this Agreement.

6.   **TERMINATION:** This license is effective until terminated. This license will terminate automatically without notice from the Company and become null and void if you fail to comply with any provisions or limitations of this license. Upon termination, you shall destroy the Documentation and all copies of the SOFTWARE. All provisions of this Agreement as to warranties, limitation of liability, remedies or damages, and our ownership rights shall survive termination.

7.   **MISCELLANEOUS:** This Agreement shall be construed in accordance with the laws of the United States of America and the State of New York and shall benefit the Company, its affiliates, and assignees.

8.   **LIMITED WARRANTY AND DISCLAIMER OF WARRANTY:** The Company warrants that the SOFTWARE, when properly used in accordance with the Documentation, will

operate in substantial conformity with the description of the SOFTWARE set forth in the Documentation. The Company does not warrant that the SOFTWARE will meet your requirements or that the operation of the SOFTWARE will be uninterrupted or error-free. The Company warrants that the media on which the SOFTWARE is delivered shall be free from defects in materials and workmanship under normal use for a period of thirty (30) days from the date of your purchase. Your only remedy and the Company's only obligation under these limited warranties is, at the Company's option, return of the warranted item for a refund of any amounts paid by you or replacement of the item. Any replacement of SOFTWARE or media under the warranties shall not extend the original warranty period. The limited warranty set forth above shall not apply to any SOFTWARE which the Company determines in good faith has been subject to misuse, neglect, improper installation, repair, alteration, or damage by you. EXCEPT FOR THE EXPRESSED WARRANTIES SET FORTH ABOVE, THE COMPANY DISCLAIMS ALL WARRANTIES, EXPRESS OR IMPLIED, INCLUDING WITHOUT LIMITATION, THE IMPLIED WARRANTIES OF MERCHANTABILITY AND FITNESS FOR A PARTICULAR PURPOSE. EXCEPT FOR THE EXPRESS WARRANTY SET FORTH ABOVE, THE COMPANY DOES NOT WARRANT, GUARANTEE, OR MAKE ANY REPRESENTATION REGARDING THE USE OR THE RESULTS OF THE USE OF THE SOFTWARE IN TERMS OF ITS CORRECTNESS, ACCURACY, RELIABILITY, CURRENTNESS, OR OTHERWISE.

IN NO EVENT, SHALL THE COMPANY OR ITS EMPLOYEES, AGENTS, SUPPLIERS, OR CONTRACTORS BE LIABLE FOR ANY INCIDENTAL, INDIRECT, SPECIAL, OR CONSEQUENTIAL DAMAGES ARISING OUT OF OR IN CONNECTION WITH THE LICENSE GRANTED UNDER THIS AGREEMENT, OR FOR LOSS OF USE, LOSS OF DATA, LOSS OF INCOME OR PROFIT, OR OTHER LOSSES, SUSTAINED AS A RESULT OF INJURY TO ANY PERSON, OR LOSS OF OR DAMAGE TO PROPERTY, OR CLAIMS OF THIRD PARTIES, EVEN IF THE COMPANY OR AN AUTHORIZED REPRESENTATIVE OF THE COMPANY HAS BEEN ADVISED OF THE POSSIBILITY OF SUCH DAMAGES. IN NO EVENT SHALL LIABILITY OF THE COMPANY FOR DAMAGES WITH RESPECT TO THE SOFTWARE EXCEED THE AMOUNTS ACTUALLY PAID BY YOU, IF ANY, FOR THE SOFTWARE.

SOME JURISDICTIONS DO NOT ALLOW THE LIMITATION OF IMPLIED WARRANTIES OR LIABILITY FOR INCIDENTAL, INDIRECT, SPECIAL, OR CONSEQUENTIAL DAMAGES, SO THE ABOVE LIMITATIONS MAY NOT ALWAYS APPLY. THE WARRANTIES IN THIS AGREEMENT GIVE YOU SPECIFIC LEGAL RIGHTS AND YOU MAY ALSO HAVE OTHER RIGHTS WHICH VARY IN ACCORDANCE WITH LOCAL LAW.

ACKNOWLEDGMENT

YOU ACKNOWLEDGE THAT YOU HAVE READ THIS AGREEMENT, UNDERSTAND IT, AND AGREE TO BE BOUND BY ITS TERMS AND CONDITIONS. YOU ALSO AGREE THAT THIS AGREEMENT IS THE COMPLETE AND EXCLUSIVE STATEMENT OF THE AGREEMENT BETWEEN YOU AND THE COMPANY AND SUPERSEDES ALL PROPOSALS OR PRIOR AGREEMENTS, ORAL, OR WRITTEN, AND ANY OTHER COMMUNICATIONS BETWEEN YOU AND THE COMPANY OR ANY REPRESENTATIVE OF THE COMPANY RELATING TO THE SUBJECT MATTER OF THIS AGREEMENT.

Should you have any questions concerning this Agreement or if you wish to contact the Company for any reason, please contact in writing at the address below.

Robin Short
Prentice Hall PTR
One Lake Street
Upper Saddle River, New Jersey 07458

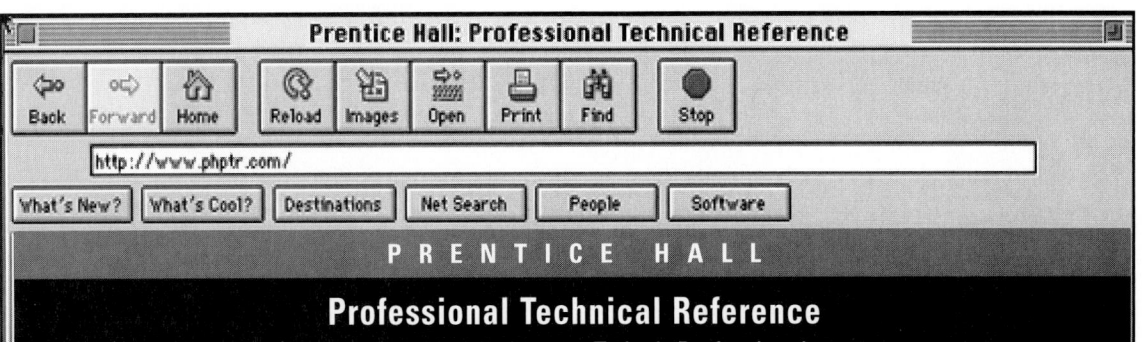

About the CD

Welcome to the *Graphic Java 2, Vol. II* CD. This CD is a standard ISO-9660 disc formatted with RockRidge and Joliet extensions. The software on this CD requires Solaris 2.x, Windows 95/98, or Windows NT. Windows 3.1 is not supported.

This CD contains the code examples referred to in the book. Every example is compiled and ready to run. The chapters directory contains a subdirectory for every chapter in the book, except Chapter 1. Subdirectories are included for each example.

In addition, the CD contains two versions of the GridBagLab application (one uses external windows and the other uses Swing internal frames).

The CD also contains JDK 1.2, which includes Swing 1.1 FCS and separate versions of JDK 1.1.7 and Swing 1.1.1 (See p. xxxii in the Preface for more details.)

Please note: Use of the JDK is subject to the Binary Code License terms and conditions on page 1618. To obtain the most current version of the JDK, go to http://java.sun.com and follow the instructions provided for downloading and installing the JDK. You should also note that what was formerly code-named JDK 1.2 is now being referred to as the Java 2 Platform.

Technical Support

Prentice Hall does not offer technical support for this software. If there is a problem with the media, however, you may obtain a replacement CD by emailing a description of the problem. Send your email to:

disc_exchange@prenhall.com